HOLLYWOOD FILM ARCHIVE
8344 Melrose Avenue
Hollywood, Calif. 90069
Phone: (213) 933-3345

VOLUME F1

THE AMERICAN FILM INSTITUTE CATALOG OF MOTION PICTURES PRODUCED IN THE UNITED STATES

★ FEATURE FILMS, 1911–1920

CREDIT AND SUBJECT INDEXES

THE AMERICAN FILM INSTITUTE CATALOG

OF MOTION PICTURES
PRODUCED IN THE
UNITED STATES

★ FEATURE FILMS, 1911–1920
CREDIT & SUBJECT INDEXES

Patricia King Hanson
Executive Editor

Alan Gevinson
Assistant Editor

University of California Press
Berkeley   Los Angeles   London

Published by: University of California Press

Printed and bound in the United States of America
3 4 5 6 7 8 9

Library of Congress Cataloging in Publication Data

American Film Institute
    The American Film Institute catalog of motion pictures
produced in the United States.

    Vol.   : Patricia King Hanson, executive editor;
Alan Gevinson, assistant editor.
    Vol.   has imprint: Berkeley : University of
California Press.
    Contents: v. F1. Feature films, 1911-1920, film
entries. Feature films, 1911-1920, credit & subject
indexes. 2 v. -- v. F2. Feature films, 1921-1930.
Feature films, 1921-1930, credit & subject indexes.
2 v.--   --v. F6. Feature films, 1961-1970. Feature
films, 1961-1970, indexes. 2 v.
    1. Motion pictures--United States--Catalogs.
I. Munden, Kenneth W. (Kenneth White), ed.
II. Hanson, Patricia King. III. Gevinson, Alan.
IV. Title.
PN1998.A57   016.79143'75'0973   88-040245
ISBN 0-520-06301-5

CONTENTS

INTRODUCTION TO THE INDEX VOLUME

★ The *AFI Catalog of Feature Films, 1911–1920* has seven separate indexes to assist the researcher. Unlike the previous two volumes of the *Catalog*, The Teens volume separates personal name and corporate entries into two indexes. In addition, we have provided a complete chronological list of film titles, a Genre Index, and a Geographic Index which were not in previous *Catalogs*. A Subject Index and a Literary and Dramatic Source Index are also provided.

We have indexed all elements of the catalog following the same basic arrangement: alphabetical heading followed by a chronological, then an alphabetical, list of film titles. An asterisk following a film title indicates that the credit is mentioned in the *note* rather than in the main body of the entry for that film.

A brief explanation is provided for the user at the beginning of each index. Following the Geographic Index we provide a bibliography of books for further research.

CHRONOLOGICAL INDEX OF FILM TITLES

★ In this index films are listed alphabetically under the year of release. Films whose release dates may have been in either of two years, for example 1914 or 1915, are listed between the entries for the two years. Films whose release dates cannot be determined are listed at the end under 19--.

CHRONOLOGICAL INDEX OF FILM TITLES

3

1914 Northern Lights
An Odyssey of the North
Officer 666
On the Belgian Battlefield
One of Millions
One of Our Girls
One Wonderful Night
The Only Son
The Opened Shutters
The Ordeal
The Outlaw Reforms
Over Niagara Falls
Pagan Rome
Paid in Full
Palestine, the Jewish Return from
Exile; Or, Life in the Holy
Land
The Patchwork Girl of Oz
The Path Forbidden
The Pawn of Fortune
The Phantom Violin
Pieces of Silver; A Story of
Hearts and Souls
Pierre of the Plains
The Pit
The Poison Needle
The Port of Missing Men
The Power of the Press
The Price He Paid
The Price of Treachery; Or, The
Lighthouse Keeper's Daughter
The Pride of Jennico
Prince Edward Island in Motion;
Home of the Silver Black Fox
Industry
A Prince of India
Protect Us
The Pursuit of the Phantom
The Quest of the Sacred Jewel
The Ragged Earl
Rainey's African Hunt
Ready Money
The Red Flame of Passion
The Redemption of David Corson
The Reign of Terror
The Rejuvenation of Aunt Mary
Rescue of the Stefansson Arctic
Expedition
Richelieu
The Ring and the Man
Rip Van Winkle
A Romance of the Mexican
Revolution
Rose of the Rancho
'Round the World in 80 Days
The Royal Box
St. Elmo
Salomy Jane
Samson
The Scales of Justice
The School for Scandal
The Seats of the Mighty
Shannon of the Sixth
Shore Acres
Shorty Escapes Marriage
Should a Woman Divorce?
The Sign of the Cross
Sins of the Parents
Sitting Bull—The Hostile Sioux
Indian Chief
Smashing the Vice Trust
Soldiers of Fortune
The Span of Life
The Spirit of the Conqueror
The Spirit of the Poppy
The Spitfire
The Spoilers
Sport and Travel in Central
Africa
Springtime
The Spy
The Squaw Man
The Straight Road
The Strange Story of Sylvia Gray
Such a Little Queen
A Suspicious Wife
The Taint
The Tangle
The Temptations of Satan
Tess of the Storm Country
Thais
The Thief
Thirty Leagues Under the Sea
Thou Shalt Not
Threads of Destiny
The Three Musketeers

1914 The Three of Us
Three Weeks
Through Dante's Flames
Through Fire to Fortune
The Tigress
Tillie's Punctured Romance
The Toll of Love
The Toll of Mammon
Too Late
The Trail of the Lonesome Pine
The Traitor
Trapped in the Great Metropolis
Il Trovatore
The Truth Wagon
The Typhoon
Uncle Tom's Cabin
Under the Black Robe
Under the Gaslight
The Unwelcome Mrs. Hatch
Uriel Acosta
The Valley of the Moon
The Virgin of the Rocks
The Virginian
The Voice at the Telephone
The Volunteer Parson
The Walls of Jericho
The War Extra
The War of the World
The War of Wars; Or, The
Franco-German Invasion
Washington at Valley Forge
What Is to Be Done?
What's His Name
When Broadway Was a Trail
When Fate Leads Trump
When Rome Ruled
Where the Trail Divides
Wildflower
The Will O' the Wisp
The Win(k)some Widow
Winning His First Case
The Wishing Ring; An Idyll of
Old England
With Serb and Austrian
Without Hope
The Wolf
Wolfe; Or, The Conquest of
Quebec
The Woman in Black
The Woman of Mystery
A Woman Who Did
A Woman's Triumph
The Wrath of the Gods
The Yellow Traffic
Your Girl and Mine: A Woman
Suffrage Play

1915 The Absentee
The Adventures of a Boy Scout
The Adventures of a Madcap
An Affair of Three Nations
After Dark
After Five
Alias Jimmy Valentine
Alice in Wonderland
The Alien
All for a Girl
Aloha Oe
The Alster Case
Always in the Way
American Game Trails
An American Gentleman
Anna Karenina
The Apaches of Paris
The Arab
Are They Born or Made?
Are You a Mason?
Armstrong's Wife
The Arrival of Perpetua
At Bay
Authentic European War
The Avalanche
The Bachelor's Romance
Barbara Frietchie
The Barnstormers
The Battle and Fall of Przemysl
The Battle Cry of Peace
The Battle of Ballots
The Battles of a Nation
The Beachcomber
Bella Donna
The Beloved Vagabond
The Better Woman
Betty in Search of a Thrill
Beulah
The Bigger Man
The Billionaire Lord

1915 The Birth of a Nation
The Birthmark
Black Fear
The Black Heart
A Black Sheep
Blackbirds
The Blindness of Devotion
The Blindness of Virtue
The Bludgeon
Blue Grass
Body and Soul
Bondwomen
The Boss
Bought
The Breath of Araby
Bred in the Bone
The Bridge of Sighs
The Brink
The Broken Law
Buckshot John
The Builder of Bridges
The Bulldogs of the Trail
A Bunch of Keys
Business Is Business
The Butterfly
A Butterfly on the Wheel
The Buzzard's Shadow
C.O.D.
The Call of the Dance
Camille
The Campbells Are Coming
Cap'n Eri
The Caprices of Kitty
Captain Courtesy
Captain Macklin
Captivating Mary Carstairs
The Captive
Carmen (Fox Film Corp.)
Carmen (Jesse L. Lasky Feature
Play Co.)
The Carpet from Bagdad
The Case of Becky
The Cave Man
The Celebrated Scandal
The Chalice of Courage
The Cheat
A Child of God
Children of Eve
Children of the Ghetto
Chimmie Fadden
Chimmie Fadden Out West
China
Chinatown Pictures
The Chocolate Soldier
The Chorus Lady
The Circular Staircase
The Clemenceau Case
The Climbers
The Closing Net
The Clue
Cohen's Luck
The College Orphan
The College Widow
Colonel Carter of Cartersville
Colorado
The Commanding Officer
The Commuters
Comrade John
The Concealed Truth
Conscience
A Continental Girl
The Coquette
Cora
Coral
The Cotton King
Count DeBesa's Mexican
Pictures, Parts I, II, III, IV, V
The Country Boy
Courtmartialed
The Coward
The Cowardly Way
The Cowboy and the Lady
The Cowpuncher
The Crimson Wing
Crooky
The Cub
The Cup of Life
The Curious Conduct of Judge
Legarde
The Dancing Girl
The Danger Signal
The Darkening Trail
A Daughter of the City
The Daughter of the People
The Daughter of the Sea
David Harum

1915 The Dawn of a Tomorrow
The Deathlock
The Deep Purple
The Despoiler
Destiny; Or, The Soul of a
Woman
The Destroying Angel
Destruction
The Devil
The Devil's Daughter
The Diamond Robbery
The Dictator
The Disciple
The District Attorney
Divorced
Divorçons
Dr. Rameau
Don Caesar de Bazan
Dora Thorne
Double Trouble
Du Barry
The Dust of Egypt
The Eagle's Nest
The Earl of Pawtucket
The Edge of the Abyss
Emmy of Stork's Nest
The End of the Road
An Enemy to Society
Enoch Arden
Environment
Esmeralda
The Eternal City
Eugene Aram
European War Pictures
The Evangelist
Evidence
Excuse Me
The Explorer
The Exposition's First Romance
An Eye for an Eye
The Face in the Moonlight
The Failure
The Fairy and the Waif
The Family Cupboard
The Family Stain
Fanchon the Cricket
The Fatal Card
Father and the Boys
Fatherhood
The Fifth Commandment
The Fight
Fighting Bob
The Fighting Hope
The Final Judgment
Fine Feathers
The Fixer
Flame of Passion
The Flaming Sword
The Flash of an Emerald
The Flying Twins
The Folly of a Life of Crime
The Fool and the Dancer
A Fool There Was
The Footsteps of Capt. Kidd
For $5,000 a Year
For the Honor of the Kingdom
The Forbidden Adventure
Forbidden Fruit
Four Feathers
The Fox Woman
The Frame-Up
Friends and Foes
From the Valley of the Missing
The Galley Slave
The Galloper
Gambier's Advocate
The Gambler of the West
Gambling Inside and Out
The Game of Three
The Garden of Lies
The Gentleman from Indiana
A Gentleman of Leisure
The German Side of the War
Ghosts
A Gilded Fool
The Girl from His Town
The Girl I Left Behind Me
The Girl of the Golden West
A Girl of Yesterday
Gladiola
The Glory of Youth
God's Witness
The Golden Claw
The Goose Girl
The Governor's Boss
The Governor's Lady

1915 The Grandee's Ring
Graustark
The Gray Mask
The Great Divide
The Great Ruby
Greater Love Hath No Man
The Greater Will
The Green Cloak
Gretna Green
Guarding Old Glory
Hear Ye, Israel
The Heart of a Painted Woman
The Heart of Jennifer
The Heart of Maryland
The Heart of the Blue Ridge
Heartaches
Hearts Aflame
Hearts and the Highway
Hearts in Exile
Hearts of Men
The Heights of Hazard
Heléne of the North
Help Wanted
Her Atonement
Her Great Match
Her Mother's Secret
Her Own Way
Her Reckoning
Her Shattered Idol
Her Triumph
Heritage
The High Hand
The High Road
His Turning Point
His Wife
History of the Great European
 War
The History of the World's
 Greatest War
The House of a Thousand
 Candles
The House of a Thousand
 Scandals
The House of Fear
The House of Tears
The House of the Lost Court
How Cissy Made Good
How Molly Malone Made Good
The Hungarian Nabob
The Hypocrites
I'm Glad My Boy Grew Up to Be
 a Soldier
The Immigrant
The Impostor
In the Amazon Jungles with the
 Captain Besley Expedition
In the Palace of the King
In the Shadow
The Incorrigible Dukane
Infatuation
Inspiration
The Iron Strain
The Island of Regeneration
The Italian
It's No Laughing Matter
The Ivory Snuff Box
Jack Chanty
Jane
Japan
Jewel
The Jewish Crown
Jim the Penman
John Glayde's Honor
Jordan Is a Hard Road
Judge Not; Or, The Woman of
 Mona Diggings
Judy Forgot
The Juggernaut
June Friday
Just Jim
Just Out of College
Keep Moving
Kilmeny
The Kindling
Kreutzer Sonata
The Labyrinth
Lady Audley's Secret
Lady Mackenzie's Big Game
 Pictures
The Lamb
The Last Concert
The Last of the Mafia
Life of American Indian *sic*
The Life of Sam Davis: A
 Confederate Hero of the Sixties
Life Without Soul

1915 The Lily and the Rose
The Lily of Poverty Flat
A Little Brother of the Rich
The Little Dutch Girl
The Little Girl That He Forgot
The Little Gypsy
The Little Mademoiselle
Little Miss Brown
Little Pal
Little Sunset
The Lone Star Rush
The Lonesome Heart
The Long Chance
Lord John in New York
The Lost House
The Love Route
The Lure of Alaska
The Lure of the Mask
The Lure of Woman
The Luring Lights
Lydia Gilmore
Maciste
Madame Butterfly
The Magic Skin
The Magic Toy Maker
The Majesty of the Law
The Making Over of Geoffrey
 Manning
A Man and His Mate
The Man Behind the Door
The Man from Oregon
The Man of Shame
The Man Trail
The Man Who Beat Dan Dolan
The Man Who Couldn't Beat
 God
The Man Who Found Himself
The Man Who Vanished
A Man's Making
A Man's Prerogative
The Marble Heart
The Marriage of Kitty
Marrying Money
Marse Covington
The Martyrs of the Alamo
Mary's Lamb
The Masqueraders
The Master Hand
The Master of the House
The Mating
Matrimony
May Blossom
The Melting Pot
The Menace of the Mute
Midnight at Maxim's
Mignon
Milestones of Life
The Mill on the Floss
The Millionaire Baby
The Miracle of Life
Mr. Grex of Monte Carlo
Mistress Nell
Mrs. Plum's Pudding
Mixed Up
M'liss
The Model
A Modern Magdalen
Money
The Money Master
Monsieur Lecoq
The Moonstone
The Morals of Marcus
Mortmain
The Moth and the Flame
A Mother's Confession
Mother's Roses
The Mummy and the Humming
 Bird
My Best Girl
My Madonna
My Valet
The Mystery of Room 13
The Nation's Peril
The Nature Man: Or, The
 Struggle for Existence
Nearly a Lady
Nedra
The Nigger
1915 World's Championship
 Series
Niobe
Not Guilty
Old Dutch
Old Heidelberg
The Old Homestead
On Dangerous Paths

1915 On Her Wedding Night
On the Firing Line with the
 Germans
On the Night Stage
On the Russian Frontier
On the Spanish Main
One Million Dollars
Out of the Darkness
The Outcast
The Outlaw's Revenge
Over Night
The Pageant of San Francisco
The Painted Soul
Passing of the Oklahoma Outlaw
The Patriot and the Spy
The Pearl of the Antilles
Pearls of Temptation
Peer Gynt
The Penitentes
Pennington's Choice
The Period of the Jew
A Phyllis of the Sierras
Pirate Haunts
The Pitfall
Playing Dead
The Ploughshare
The Plunderer
The Politicians
Poor Schmaltz
The Pretenders
Pretty Mrs. Smith
The Pretty Sister of Jose
The Price
A Price for Folly
The Price of Her Silence
The Primrose Path
The Prince and the Pauper
Princess Romanoff
Prohibition
The Puppet Crown
The Pursuing Shadow
Queen and Adventurer
The Quest
Rags
Ranson's Folly
The Raven
The Reform Candidate
Regeneration
The Reward
Richard Carvel
The Right of Way
Right off the Bat
The Rights of Man: A Story of
 War's Red Blotch
The Ring of the Borgias
The Ringtailed Rhinoceros
The Rosary
Rosemary
A Royal Family
The Rug Maker's Daughter
Rule G
Rumpelstiltskin
The Runaway Wife
The Running Fight
Russian Battlefields
The Sable Lorcha
Salvation Nell
Sam Davis, the Hero of
 Tennessee
Samson
Satan Sanderson
Saved from the Harem
Scandal
The Scarlet Sin
Sealed Lips
Sealed Valley
The Second in Command
The Secret Orchard
The Secret Sin
Secretary of Frivolous Affairs
Seeing America First
The Senator
The Sentimental Lady
Seven Sisters
The Seventh Noon
Shadows from the Past
The Shadows of a Great City
The Shame of a Nation
The Shooting of Dan McGrew
Should a Mother Tell?
Should a Wife Forgive?
The Silent Command
The Silent Voice
Silver Threads Among the Gold
Simon, the Jester
Sin

1915 The Sins of Society
The Sins of the Mothers
The Sioux City Round-Up
The Siren's Song
The Slim Princess
Snobs
Sold
A Soldier's Oath
Somewhere in France
The Song of Hate
The Song of the Wage Slave
The Soul of Broadway
The Spanish Jade
The Spender
The Spendthrift
The Sporting Duchess
Still Waters
Stolen Goods
The Stolen Voice
Stop Thief!
Strathmore
The Stubbornness of Geraldine
A Submarine Pirate
The Suburban
Sunday
Sunshine Molly
The Supreme Test
Sweet Alyssum
System, the Secret of Success
Tainted Money
The Tale of the Night Before
Temptation
A Texas Steer
Thou Shalt Not Kill
Through Turbulent Waters
Tillie's Tomato Surprise
Time Lock Number 776
To Cherish and Protect
The Toast of Death
A Trade Secret
Trilby
A Trip to the Argentine
The Truth About Helen
The Turn of the Road
'Twas Ever Thus
The Two Orphans
The Unafraid
The Unbroken Road
Under Southern Skies
The Unfaithful Wife
The Unknown
Unto the Darkness
The Unwelcome Wife
Up from the Depths
The Valley of Lost Hope
The Vampire
The Vanderhoff Affair
Vanity Fair
Vengeance of the Wilds
Via Wireless
The Victory of Virtue
Virtue
The Voice in the Fog
The Voice of Satan
The Vow
The Waif
War World Wide
The Warning
The Warrens of Virginia
The Warring Millions
Was She to Blame? Or, Souls
 That Meet in the Dark
The Way Back
What Happened to Father
What Happened to Jones
What Should a Woman Do to
 Promote Youth and Happiness?
Wheat and Tares; A Story of
 Two Boys Who Tackle Life on
 Diverging Lines
The Wheels of Justice
When a Woman Loves
When It Strikes Home
When We Were Twenty-One
Where Cowboy Is King
The Whirl of Life
The White Pearl
The White Scar
The White Sister
The White Terror
Who's Who in Society
The Wild Goose Chase
Wild Life of America in Films
The Wild Olive
Wildfire
The Winged Idol

1915 Winning the Futurity
The Wolf Man
The Wolf of Debt
The Woman
The Woman Next Door
The Woman Pays
The Woman Who Lied
A Woman's Past
A Woman's Resurrection
The Wonderful Adventure
Wormwood
A Yankee from the West
The Yankee Girl
A Yellow Streak
York State Folks
Young Romance
Zaza

1915-16
The Little Church Around the
  Corner
The Sins That Ye Sin

1916 The Abandonment
According to Law
According to the Code
Acquitted
The Adventures of Kathlyn
The Alibi
Alien Souls
All Man
The Almighty Dollar
Ambition
America Preparing
American Aristocracy
The American Beauty
And the Law Says
Anton the Terrible
The Apostle of Vengeance
April
The Argonauts of
  California—1849
Arms and the Woman
Around the World in Ninety
  Minutes
Artie, the Millionaire Kid
The Aryan
As a Woman Sows
As in a Looking Glass
Ashes of Embers
At Piney Ridge
At the Front with the Allies
Atta Boy's Last Race
Audrey
Autumn
The Awakening of Bess Morton
The Awakening of Helena Richie
The Bait
The Ballet Girl
Barriers of Society
The Battle of Hearts
The Battle of Life
Bawbs O' Blue Ridge
The Beast
The Beckoning Flame
The Beckoning Trail
The Beggar of Cawnpore
Behind Closed Doors
Behind the Lines
Ben Blair
Betrayed
Bettina Loved a Soldier
Betty of Graystone
Between Men
Big Jim Garrity
The Big Sister
Big Tremaine
A Bird of Prey
The Birth of a Man
The Birth of Character
The Bishop's Secret
The Black Butterfly
The Black Crook
Black Friday
The Black Sheep of the Family
The Blacklist
Blazing Love
The Blindness of Love
Blue Blood and Red
The Blue Envelope Mystery
Bluff
Bobbie of the Ballet
The Bondman
Boots and Saddles
Bought and Paid For
The Brand of Cowardice
The Breaker

1916 Britton of the Seventh
Broken Chains
Broken Fetters
The Bruiser
The Bugle Call
The Bugler of Algiers
Bullets and Brown Eyes
By Whose Hand?
The Call of the Cumberlands
The Call of the Soul
Caprice of the Mountains
Captain Jinks of the Horse
  Marines
The Captive God
Casey at the Bat
The Catspaw
The Chain Invisible
The Chalice of Sorrow
The Challenge
The Chaperon
Charity
Charlie Chaplin's Burlesque on
  "Carmen"
The Chattel
The Child of Destiny
A Child of Mystery
A Child of the Paris Streets
The Children in the House
Children of the Feud
The Children Pay
A Circus Romance
The City
The City of Failing Light
The City of Illusion
Civilization
Civilization's Child
The Clarion
The Closed Road
The Clown
The Code of Marcia Gray
The Colored American Winning
  His Suit
The Combat
The Come-Back
Common Ground
The Common Law
Common Sense Brackett
A Coney Island Princess
The Conflict
The Conqueror
The Conquest of Canaan
The Conscience of John David
The Corner
A Corner in Colleens
A Corner in Cotton
The Cossack Whip
The Country That God Forgot
The Courtesan
Cousin Jim
The Craving
The Criminal
The Crippled Hand
The Crisis
Cross Currents
The Crown Prince's Double
The Crucial Test
The Cycle of Fate
Daphne and the Pirate
Daredevil Kate
The Daring of Diana
The Dark Silence
D'Artagnan
The Daughter of MacGregor
The Daughter of the Don
A Daughter of the Gods
David Garrick
Davy Crockett
The Dawn Maker
The Dawn of Freedom
The Dawn of Love
The Dead Alive
The Decoy
Defense or Tribute?
The Deserter
Destiny's Toy
The Destroyers
The Devil at His Elbow
The Devil's Bondwoman
The Devil's Double
The Devil's Needle
The Devil's Prayer-Book
The Devil's Prize
The Devil's Toy
The Diamond Runners
Diane of the Follies
Dimples

1916 Diplomacy
The Discard
The Dividend
Divorce and the Daughter
Doctor Neighbor
The Dollar and the Law
Dollars and the Woman
Don Quixote
Dorian's Divorce
The Dragon
The Dream Girl
A Dream or Two Ago
The Drifter
Driftwood
Drugged Waters
Dulcie's Adventure
The Dumb Girl of Portici
The Dupe
Dust
Each Pearl a Tear
The Eagle's Wing
East Lynne
Elusive Isabel
Embers
The End of the Rainbow
The End of the Trail
The Enemy
An Enemy to the King
Energetic Eva
The Essanay-Chaplin Revue of
  1916
The Eternal Grind
The Eternal Question
The Eternal Sapho
The Evil Thereof
The Evil Women Do
Extravagance
The Eye of God
The Eye of the Night
The Faded Flower
Faith
The Fall of a Nation
Fate's Boomerang
Fate's Chessboard
Father and Son
Fathers of Men
The Fear of Poverty
The Feast of Life
Feathertop
The Female of the Species
The Feud Girl
Fifty-Fifty
Fighting Blood
The Fighting Chance
Fighting for Verdun
The Fighting Germans
The Final Curtain
The Fires of Conscience
The Five Faults of Flo
The Flames of Johannis
The Flight of the Duchess
The Flirt
Flirting with Fate
The Flower of Faith
The Flower of No Man's Land
The Flying Torpedo
Following the Flag in Mexico
The Folly of Revenge
The Foolish Virgin
A Fool's Paradise
The Fool's Revenge
The Footlights of Fate
For a Woman's Fair Name
For the Defense
The Fortunate Youth
The Foundling
The Fourth Estate
Friday the Thirteenth
From Broadway to a Throne
Fruits of Desire
The Fugitive
A Gamble in Souls
The Garden of Allah
The Gates of Eden
The Gay Lord Waring
The Gilded Cage
The Gilded Spider
The Girl O' Dreams
The Girl of the Lost Lake
The Girl Philippa
The Girl Who Doesn't Know
The Girl with the Green Eyes
Gloriana
God's Country and the Woman
God's Half Acre
The Gods of Fate

1916 Going Straight
Gold and the Woman
The Golden Chance
The Good Bad Man
The Grasp of Greed
The Great Problem
Greater New York by Day and
  by Night; The Wonder City of
  the World
The Green-Eyed Monster
Green Stockings
The Green Swamp
Gretchen, the Greenhorn
The Gringo
The Grip of Jealousy
A Gutter Magdalene
The Habit of Happiness
Half a Rogue
The Half-Breed
The Half Million Bribe
The Hand of Peril
The Haunted Manor
The Havoc
Hazel Kirke
He Fell in Love with His Wife
The Heart of a Hero
The Heart of New York
The Heart of Nora Flynn
The Heart of Paula
The Heart of Tara
The Heart of the Hills
The Heir to the Hoorah
The Heiress at Coffee Dan's
Hell-to-Pay Austin
Hell's Hinges
Her American Prince
Her Bitter Cup
Her Bleeding Heart
Her Debt of Honor
Her Double Life
Her Father's Gold
Her Father's Son
Her Great Hour
Her Great Price
Her Husband's Wife
Her Maternal Right
Her Redemption
Her Surrender
The Heritage of Hate
The Hero of Submarine D-2
Hesper of the Mountains
The Hidden Law
The Hidden Scar
Hidden Valley
The Highest Bid
His Brother's Wife
His Great Triumph
His Picture in the Papers
His Wife's Good Name
Home
The Honor of Mary Blake
Honor Thy Name
The Honorable Algy
The Honorable Friend
Honor's Altar
Hoodoo Ann
Hop, the Devil's Brew
A House Built upon Sand
The House of Lies
The House of Mirrors
The House with the Golden
  Windows
How Life Begins
Hulda from Holland
Human Driftwood
The Human Orchid
Humanizing Mr. Winsby
The Hunted Woman
A Huntress of Men
Husband and Wife
Hypocrisy
I Accuse
Idle Wives
The Idol of the Stage
Idols
If My Country Should Call
Ignorance
Immediate Lee
The Immortal Flame
The Impersonation
In the Diplomatic Service
In the Web of the Grafters
Indiana
Inherited Passions
The Inner Struggle
The Innocence of Lizette

1916 Thrown to the Lions
To Have and to Hold
The Toll of Justice
Tongues of Men
The Torch Bearer
A Tortured Heart
The Traffic Cop
The Trail of the Lonesome Pine
The Traveling Salesman
The Truant Soul
True Nobility
The Turmoil
20,000 Leagues Under the Sea
The Twin Triangle
The Twinkler
The Two Edged Sword
Two Men of Sandy Bar
The Unattainable
The Unborn
Under Cover
Under Two Flags
The Undertow
Undine
United States Marines Under
Fire in Haiti
The Unpardonable Sin
Unprotected
Unto Those Who Sin
The Unwelcome Mother
The Unwritten Law
The Upheaval
The Upstart
The Vagabond Prince
The Valiants of Virginia
The Valley of Decision
Vanity
The Velvet Paw
Vengeance Is Mine
The Victim
The Victoria Cross
The Victory of Conscience
La Vie de Boheme
The Vital Question
The Vixen
The Voice of Love
Vultures of Society
The Wager
The Waifs
The Wall Between
Wall Street Tragedy
Wanted—A Home
War As It Really Is
War Brides
The War Bride's Secret
War on Three Fronts
War-Torn Poland
Warning! The S.O.S. Call of
Humanity
The Wasted Years
The Way of the World
The Weakness of Man
The Weakness of Strength
The Whaling Industry
The Wharf Rat
What Happened at 22
What Love Can Do
What the World Should Know
What Will People Say?
The Wheel of the Law
When Love Is King
Where Are My Children?
Where D'Ye Get That Stuff?
Where Is My Father?
Where Love Leads
The Whirlpool of Destiny
Whispering Smith
The White Rosette
Who Killed Joe Merrion?
Whom the Gods Destroy
Whoso Findeth a Wife
A Wife's Sacrifice
The Wild Girl of the Sierras
Wild Oats
Willard-Johnson Boxing Match
Willard-Moran Fight
The Witch
Witchcraft
The Witching Hour
The Wolf Woman
The Woman in 47
The Woman in Politics
The Woman in the Case
The Woman Who Dared
A Woman's Daring
A Woman's Fight
A Woman's Honor

1916 The Woman's Law
A Woman's Power
A Woman's Way
The Wood Nymph
The World Against Him
The World and the Woman
World Series Games 1916, Boston
vs. Brooklyn
The World's Great Snare
The Writing on the Wall
The Wrong Door
The Yaqui
The Years of the Locust
The Yellow Passport
The Yellow Pawn
A Yoke of Gold
A Youth of Fortune
Youth's Endearing Charm
The Zeppelin Raids on London
and the Siege of Verdun

1917 The Accomplice
The Adopted Son
The Adventurer
The Adventures of Buffalo Bill
The Adventures of Carol
An Alabaster Box
Aladdin and the Wonderful Lamp
Aladdin from Broadway
Aladdin's Other Lamp
Alaska Wonders in Motion
Alias Mrs. Jessop
The Alien Blood
Alimony
All for a Husband
Alma, Where Do You Live?
An Amateur Orphan
The Amazons
America Is Ready
The American Consul
American Maid
American Methods
American—That's All
An American Widow
The Americano
The Angel Factory
Annie-for-Spite
The Antics of Ann
Anything Once
Apartment 29
The Apple-Tree Girl
The Argyle Case
Arms and the Girl
Arsene Lupin
As Man Made Her
As Men Love
Ashes of Hope
At First Sight
The Auction Block
The Auction of Virtue
The Avenging Trail
The Awakening
The Awakening of Ruth
Bab the Fixer
Babbling Tongues
The Babes in the Woods
Babette
Bab's Burglar
Bab's Diary
Bab's Matinee Idol
Baby Mine
Back of the Man
The Bad Boy
The Bar Sinister
Barbary Sheep
The Barker
The Barricade
The Barrier
The Baseball Revue of 1917
The Beautiful Adventure
The Beautiful Lie
Because of a Woman
Behind the Mask
The Beloved Adventuress
Beloved Jim
Beloved Rogues
The Best Man
Betrayed
Betsy Ross
Betsy's Burglar
Betty and the Buccaneers
Betty Be Good
Betty to the Rescue
Beware of Strangers
Big Timber
Billy and the Big Stick
Birth

1917 Birth Control
The Birth of Patriotism
A Bit O' Heaven
A Bit of Kindling
The Bitter Truth
Black Orchids
The Black Stork
The Black Wolf
The Blackmailers
Blind Man's Holiday
Blind Man's Luck
The Blood of His Fathers
Blood Will Tell
Blue Jeans
The Blue Streak
The Bond Between
The Bond of Fear
Bondage
The Bondage of Fear
The Book Agent
Borrowed Plumage
The Bottle Imp
The Bottom of the Well
The Boy Girl
The Brand of Satan
A Branded Soul
Brand's Daughter
The Bride of Hate
The Bride's Silence
Bridges Burned
Bringing Home Father
Broadway Arizona
Broadway Jones
The Broadway Sport
The Bronze Bride
Bucking Broadway
The Buffalo Bill Show
Builders of Castles
The Burglar
Burning the Candle
The Butterfly Girl
By Right of Possession
The Calendar Girl
The Call of Her People
The Call of the East
Camille
The Candy Girl
Captain Kiddo
The Captain of the Gray Horse
Troop
The Car of Chance
A Case at Law
Cassidy
Castles for Two
Charity Castle
The Charmer
The Checkmate
Cheerful Givers
Chicken Casey
A Child of the Wild
The Chosen Prince, or the
Friendship of David and
Jonathan
Chris and His Wonderful Lamp
The Cigarette Girl
Cinderella and the Magic Slipper
The Cinderella Man
The Circus of Life
The Clean Gun
The Clean-Up
Cleopatra
The Clever Mrs. Carfax
The Climber
The Clock
The Clodhopper
The Cloud
Clover's Rebellion
The Cold Deck
Come Through
The Conqueror
Conscience
The Cook of Canyon Camp
The Co-Respondent
The Corner Grocer
Corruption
The Cost of Hatred
The Countess Charming
The Courage of Silence
The Courage of the Common
Place
The Crab
The Cricket
Crime and Punishment
The Crimson Dove
A Crooked Romance
The Crystal Gazer

1917 The Curse of Eve
The Customary Two Weeks
Cy Whittaker's Ward
The Dancer's Peril
The Danger Trail
The Dark Road
Darkest Russia
The Darling of Paris
Daughter of Destiny
Daughter of Maryland
A Daughter of the Poor
The Dazzling Miss Davison
Dead Shot Baker
The Debt
The Deemster
The Defeat of the City
The Derelict
The Desert Man
The Desire of the Moth
The Devil Dodger
The Devil-Stone
The Devil's Assistant
The Devil's Bait
The Devil's Pay Day
Diamonds and Pearls
The Divorce Game
The Divorcee
A Doll's House
The Door Between
The Dormant Power
Double Crossed
Double Room Mystery
The Double Standard
Down to Earth
The Downfall of a Mayor
Draft 258
The Dream Doll
Du Barry
The Duchess of Doubt
The Dummy
The Duplicity of Hargraves
Durand of the Bad Lands
Each to His Kind
The Easiest Way
Easy Money
The Edge of the Law
Efficiency Edgar's Courtship
The Empress
The End of the Tour
Enlighten Thy Daughter
Environment
Envy
Eternal Love
The Eternal Mother
The Eternal Sin
The Eternal Temptress
Even As You and I
An Even Break
Every Girl's Dream
The Evil Eye
Exile
The Eye of Envy
The Eyes of the World
The Fair Barbarian
The False Friend
The Family Honor
Fanatics
Fear Not
Feet of Clay
The Fettered Woman
The Fibbers
The Field of Honor
Fighting Back
Fighting for Love
The Fighting Gringo
Fighting Mad
Fighting Odds
Filling His Own Shoes
The Final Payment
The Firefly of Tough Luck
Fires of Rebellion
The Fires of Youth
The Flame of the Yukon
The Flame of Youth
The Flaming Omen
The Flashlight
Flirting with Death
The Flower of Doom
Flying Colors
Follow the Girl
The Food Gamblers
Fools for Luck
For France
For Liberty
For the Freedom of the World
For Valour

1917 Pride and the Devil
Pride and the Man
The Pride of New York
The Pride of the Clan
The Primitive Call
The Primrose Ring
The Princess' Necklace
The Princess of Park Row
The Princess of Patches
Princess of the Dark
Princess Virtue
The Prison Without Walls
The Promise
The Public Be Damned
The Public Defender
The Pulse of Life
Putting the Bee in Herbert
Queen X
The Question
Raffles, the Amateur Cracksman
The Raggedy Queen
The Rainbow
The Rainbow Girl
The Range Boss
Rasputin, the Black Monk
Reaching for the Moon
Rebecca of Sunnybrook Farm
The Recoil
Red, White and Blue Blood
The Red Woman
Redemption
The Reed Case
The Regenerates
The Renaissance at Charleroi
Reputation
The Rescue
The Reward of the Faithless
A Rich Man's Plaything
Richard the Brazen
The Rise of Jennie Cushing
The Road Between
A Roadside Impresario
A Romance of the Redwoods
The Rose of Blood
Rosie O'Grady
The Royal Pauper
Royal Romance
The Runaway
Runaway Romany
S.O.S.
Sacrifice
Sadie Goes to Heaven
The Saintly Sinner
The Saint's Adventure
Sally in a Hurry
Salt of the Earth
Sands of Sacrifice
Sapho
Satan's Private Door
The Savage
The Sawdust Ring
Scandal
The Scarlet Car
The Scarlet Crystal
The Scarlet Letter
The Scarlet Pimpernel
A School for Husbands
The Sea Master
The Secret Game
The Secret Man
The Secret of Black Mountain
The Secret of Eve
The Secret of the Storm Country
A Self-Made Widow
The Serpent's Tooth
Seven Keys to Baldpate
The Seven Swans
The Seventh Sin
Shackles of Truth
Shall We Forgive Her?
Shame
She
The Ship of Doom
Shirley Kaye
Should She Obey?
The Show Down
The Silence Sellers
The Silent Lady
The Silent Lie
The Silent Man
The Silent Master
The Silent Partner
The Silent Witness
The Sin Woman
The Single Code
Sins of Ambition

1917 The Siren
Sirens of the Sea
Sister Against Sister
The Sixteenth Wife
Skinner's Baby
Skinner's Bubble
Skinner's Dress Suit
The Skylight Room
The Slacker (Metro Pictures
Corp.)
The Slacker (Peter P. Jones Film
Co.)
The Slacker's Heart
The Slave
The Slave Market
The Slave Mart
Sleeping Fires
A Sleeping Memory
Sloth
The Small Town Girl
The Small Town Guy
Snap Judgement
The Snarl
The Social Leper
Society's Driftwood
Sold at Auction
Soldiers of Chance
Some Boy!
Somewhere in America
The Son of His Father
A Son of the Hills
A Song of Sixpence
A Soul for Sale
The Soul Master
The Soul of a Magdalen
The Soul of Satan
Souls Adrift
Souls in Pawn
Souls Triumphant
Southern Justice
Southern Pride
Sowers and Reapers
The Spindle of Life
The Spirit of Romance
The Spirit of '76
The Spotted Lily
The Spreading Dawn
The Spy
A Square Deal
The Square Deal Man
The Square Deceiver
The Squaw Man's Son
Stagestruck
The Stainless Barrier
The Stolen Paradise
The Stolen Play
The Stolen Treaty
A Stormy Knight
Straight Shooting
Stranded in Arcady
A Strange Transgressor
The Streets of Illusion
Strife
The Strong Way
The Submarine Eye
The Sudden Gentleman
Sudden Jim
Sunlight's Last Raid
Sunny Jane
The Sunset Trail
Sunshine Alley
Sunshine and Gold
The Sunshine Maid
Susan's Gentleman
Sweetheart of the Doomed
Sylvia of the Secret Service
A Tale of Two Cities
Tangled Lives
The Tar Heel Warrior
Tears and Smiles
The Tell-Tale Step
Ten of Diamonds
The Tenderfoot
The Tenth Case
The Terror
The Test of Womanhood
Thais
Their Compact
They're Off
Think It Over
This Is the Life
Those Who Pay
Those Without Sin
Thou Shalt Not Steal
Threads of Fate
The Tides of Barnegat

1917 The Tides of Fate
The Tiger Woman
Tillie Wakes Up
Time Locks and Diamonds
To Honor and Obey
To the Death
To-Day
Told at Twilight
Tom Sawyer
The Trail of the Shadow
Transgression
Treason
A Trip Through China
A Trip Through Japan
Triumph
Trooper 44
The Trouble Buster
Troublemakers
The Trufflers
Truthful Tulliver
Twin Kiddies
Two-Bit Seats
Two Little Imps
Two Men and a Woman
Uncle Sam, Awake!
Unconquered
Under False Colors
Under Handicap
The Understudy
The Undying Flame
The Unforseen
Unknown 274
Until They Get Me
Unto the End
Up or Down?
The Upper Crust
The Valentine Girl
The Varmint
Vengeance Is Mine
Vengeance of the Dead
Vera, the Medium
The Vicar of Wakefield
The Voice of Conscience
The Volunteer
The Waiting Soul
War and the Woman
The War of the Tongs
The Warfare of the Flesh
The Wax Model
The Way to Happiness
The Weaker Sex
Weavers of Life
The Web of Desire
The Web of Life
Wee Lady Betty
What Money Can't Buy
When a Man Sees Red
When Baby Forgot
When Duty Calls
When False Tongues Speak
When Love Was Blind
When Men Are Tempted
When You and I Were Young
Where Love Is
The Whip
The White Raven
Whither Thou Goest
Who Goes There!
Who Knows?
Who Shall Take My Life?
Who Was the Other Man?
Who's Your Neighbor?
Whose Wife?
A Wife by Proxy
Wife Number Two
A Wife on Trial
The Wife Who Wouldn't Tell
Wild and Woolly
The Wild Girl
Wild Sumac
Wild Winship's Widow
The Wildcat
The Winged Mystery
The Winning of Sally Temple
Within the Law
Wolf Lowry
A Woman Alone
The Woman and the Beast
The Woman Beneath
The Woman God Forgot
The Woman in White
Womanhood, the Glory of the
Nation
A Woman's Awakening
Wooden Shoes
The World Apart

1917 Wrath
Wrath of Love
Yankee Pluck
The Yankee Way
The Yellow Bullet
Young Mother Hubbard
Youth
The Zeppelin's Last Raid
Zollenstein
1917-18
The Devil's Playground
Will You Marry Me?
1918 The Accidental Honeymoon
Ace High
After the War
Ali Baba and the Forty Thieves
Alias Mary Brown
An Alien Enemy
All Man
All Night
All the World to Nothing
All Woman
Amarilly of Clothes-Line Alley
American Buds
An American Live Wire
America's Answer; Following the
Fleet to France
Among the Cannibal Isles of the
South Pacific
And a Still Small Voice
And the Children Pay
Angel Child
Annexing Bill
Ann's Finish
The Answer
The Appearance of Evil
The Argument
Arizona
An Armenian Crucifixion
Arms in France
Ashes of Love
At the Mercy of Men
The Atom
A Bachelor's Children
Back to the Woods
Baree, Son of Kazan
Battling Jane
Beans
The Beautiful Mrs. Reynolds
Beauty and the Rogue
Beauty in Chains
The Belgian
Believe Me Xantippe
The Bells
The Beloved Blackmailer
The Beloved Impostor
The Beloved Traitor
Berlin Via America
The Better Half
Betty Takes a Hand
Beyond the Law
Beyond the Shadows
The Biggest Show on Earth
The Bird of Prey
The Birth of a Race
A Bit of Jade
The Blind Adventure
Blindfolded
The Blindness of Divorce
The Blot
The Blue Bird
Blue Blazes Rawden
Blue Blood
Blue-Eyed Mary
Bonnie Annie Laurie
The Border Legion
The Border Raiders
The Border Wireless
Borrowed Clothes
The Boss of the Lazy Y
Boston Blackie's Little Pal
Bound in Morocco
Brace Up
Branding Broadway
The Brass Check
Brave and Bold
The Bravest Way
The Brazen Beauty
Bread
Breakers Ahead
The Bride of Fear
The Bride's Awakening
Broadway Bill
Broadway Love
A Broadway Scandal

1918 The Menace
Merely Players
Mickey
The Midnight Burglar
Midnight Madness
The Midnight Patrol
The Midnight Trail
Milady O' the Beanstalk
Mile-a-Minute Kendall
The Million Dollar Dollies
The Million Dollar Mystery
Mirandy Smiles
Les Miserables
Miss Ambition
Miss Innocence
Miss Mischief Maker
Missing
Mr. Fix-It
Mr. Logan, U.S.A.
Mrs. Dane's Defense
Mrs. Leffingwell's Boots
Mrs. Slacker
M'liss
The Model's Confession
Modern Love
Molly, Go Get 'Em
Money Isn't Everything
Money Mad
The Moral Law
Moral Suicide
More Trouble
Morgan's Raiders
The Mortgaged Wife
A Mother's Secret
A Mother's Sin
Movie Marionettes
My Cousin
My Four Years in Germany
My Own United States
My Unmarried Wife
My Wife
The Mysterious Client
The Mysterious Mr. Browning
The Mystery Girl
Mystic Faces
Naked Hands
Nancy Comes Home
The Narrow Path
Naughty, Naughty!
The Naulahka
Neighbors
New Love for Old
A Nine O'Clock Town
Nine-Tenths of the Law
No Children Wanted
No Man's Land
Nobody's Wife
A Nymph of the Foothills
Oh, Johnny!
Old Hartwell's Cub
Old Love for New
Old Wives for New
The Oldest Law
On the Isonzo
On the Jump
On the Quiet
One Dollar Bid
One More American
One Thousand Dollars
The One Woman
The Only Road
Opportunity
The Ordeal of Rosetta
The Other Man
Other Men's Daughters
The Other Woman
Our Bridge of Ships
Our Little Wife
Our Mrs. McChesney
Our Navy
Out of a Clear Sky
Out of the Night
Over the Top
The Painted Lily
Painted Lips
A Pair of Cupids
A Pair of Silk Stockings
A Pair of Sixes
Pals First
The Panther Woman
Parentage
Patriotism
Pay Day
Paying His Debt
Peck's Bad Girl
Peg O' the Sea

1918 Peg of the Pirates
The Pen Vulture
A Perfect Lady
A Perfect 36
Pershing's Crusaders
A Petticoat Pilot
Petticoats and Politics
The Phantom Riders
Playing the Game
Playthings
The Poor Rich Man
The Power and the Glory
Powers That Prey
The Pretender
The Price of Applause
The Primitive Woman
The Prisoner of War
Prisoners of the Pines
Private Peat
The Prodigal Wife
Prunella
The Prussian Cur
The Purple Lily
The Queen of Hearts
Queen of the Sea
Quicksand
The Racing Strain
The Rainbow Trail
The Ranger
Real Folks
The Reason Why
The Reckoning Day
The Red-Haired Cupid
The Red, Red Heart
Restitution
Resurrection
The Return of Mary
Revelation
Revenge
Rich Man, Poor Man
A Rich Man's Darling
The Richest Girl
Riddle Gawne
Riders of the Night
Riders of the Purple Sage
Rimrock Jones
The Risky Road
The Road Through the Dark
The Road to France
The Romance of Tarzan
A Romance of the Air
A Romance of the Underworld
Rose O' Paradise
The Rose of the World
Rosemary Climbs the Heights
Rough and Ready
The Rough Lover
Ruggles of Red Gap
Ruler of the Road
Ruling Passions
The Safety Curtain
Salome
The Sand Rat
Sandy
Sauce for the Goose
The Savage Woman
Say, Young Fellow!
The Scarlet Drop
The Scarlet Road
The Scarlet Trail
The Sea Flower
The Sea Panther
The Sea Waif
The Seal of Silence
Secret Code
Secret Strings
The Secret Trap
Selfish Yates
The Service Star
Set Free
The Seventy-Five Mile Gun
Shackled
Shark Monroe
The She-Devil
She Hired a Husband
The Shell Game
Shifting Sands
The Shoes That Danced
The Shuttle
The Sign Invisible
The Silent Rider
The Silent Woman
The Sins of the Children
Sins of the Kaiser
Six Shooter Andy
Smashing Through

1918 The Snail
The Soap Girl
Social Ambition
Social Briars
Social Hypocrites
Social Quicksands
Society for Sale
A Society Sensation
A Son of Strife
The Song of Songs
The Song of the Soul
A Soul in Trust
The Soul of Buddha
A Soul Without Windows
The Source
The Spirit of '17
The Splendid Sinner
Sporting Life
The Spreading Evil
The Spurs of Sybil
The Square Deal
The Squaw Man
Staking His Life
The Star Prince
Station Content
Stella Maris
The Still Alarm
Stolen Honor
Stolen Hours
Stolen Orders
The Strange Woman
The Street of Seven Stars
String Beans
The Struggle Everlasting
The Studio Girl
A Successful Adventure
Such a Little Pirate
The Sunset Princess
Sunshine Nan
Suspicion
Swat the Spy
Sylvia on a Spree
The Talk of the Town
Tangled Lives
Tarzan of the Apes
Tell It to the Marines
Tempered Steel
The Temple of Dusk
The Test of Loyalty
The Testing of Mildred Vane
That Devil, Bateese
Thieves' Gold
The Thing We Love
Thirty a Week
Three Mounted Men
Three X Gordon
The Tidal Wave
The Tiger Man
Till I Come Back to You
Tinsel
To Hell with the Kaiser
To Him That Hath
To the Highest Bidder
Together
Tongues of Flame
Tony America
Too Fat to Fight
Too Many Millions
La Tosca
T'Other Dear Charmer
Toys of Fate
The Trail to Yesterday
The Transgressor
The Trap
Treason
Treasure Island
Treasure of the Sea
The Triumph of the Weak
The Triumph of Venus
True Blue
The Turn of a Card
The Turn of the Wheel
Twenty-One
Two-Gun Betty
The Two-Soul Woman
Tyrant Fear
The Unbeliever
The Unchastened Woman
Unclaimed Goods
Uncle Tom's Cabin
Under Four Flags
Under Suspicion
Under the Greenwood Tree
Under the Yoke
Uneasy Money
Unexpected Places

1918 Untamed
Up Romance Road
Up the Road with Sallie
The Uphill Path
The Vamp
The Vanity Pool
The Velvet Hand
Vengeance
The Venus Model
The Vigilantes
Virtuous Wives
Vive La France!
Viviette
The Voice of Destiny
The Vortex
Waifs
Wanted—A Brother
Wanted, a Mother
Wanted for Murder
The Wasp
The Way of a Man with a Maid
The Way Out
We Can't Have Everything
We Should Worry
A Weaver of Dreams
Wedlock
Western Blood
What Becomes of the Children?
What Does a Woman Need Most
Whatever the Cost
When a Woman Sins
When Destiny Wills
When Do We Eat?
When Men Betray
Which Woman?
Whims of Society
The Whip
The Whirlpool
The Whispered Word
The Whispering Chorus
The White Lie
The White Man's Law
Who Is to Blame?
Who Killed Walton?
Who Loved Him Best?
Why America Will Win
Why I Would Not Marry
The Widow's Might
The Wife He Bought
Wife or Country
Wild Honey
Wild Life
Wild Primrose
The Wild Strain
Wild Women
Wild Youth
The Wildcat of Paris
The Winding Trail
The Wine Girl
Winner Takes All
Winning Grandma
The Winning of Beatrice
The Witch Woman
With Hoops of Steel
With Neatness and Dispatch
Within the Cup
Without Honor
Wives and Other Wives
Wives of Men
The Wolf and His Mate
Wolves of the Border
Wolves of the Rail
Woman
Woman and the Law
Woman and Wife
The Woman Between Friends
A Woman of Impulse
A Woman of Redemption
The Woman the Germans Shot
The Woman Who Gave
A Woman's Fool
Women's Weapons
The Wooing of Princess Pat
The World for Sale
The Yanks Are Coming
The Yellow Dog
The Yellow Ticket
You Can't Believe Everything
Your Fighting Navy at Work and at Play
The Zero Hour
Zongar
1918-19
April Fool
The Candidates
The Kaiser's Bride

1919 The Lone Star Ranger
The Lone Wolf's Daughter
The Long Arm of Mannister
The Long Lane's Turning
Loot
Lord and Lady Algy
The Lord Loves the Irish
The Lost Battalion
Lost Money
The Lost Princess
The Lottery Man
Louisiana
Love and the Law
Love and the Woman
The Love Auction
The Love Burglar
The Love Call
The Love Cheat
The Love Defender
Love, Honor and—?
The Love Hunger
Love in a Hurry
Love Insurance
Love Is Love
The Love That Dares
The Loves of Letty
Love's Prisoner
Luck and Pluck
Luck in Pawn
Lure of Ambition
Maggie Pepper
Male and Female
A Man and His Money
The Man Beneath
The Man Hunter
The Man in the Moonlight
A Man in the Open
A Man of Honor
The Man Who Stayed at Home
The Man Who Turned White
The Man Who Won
Mandarin's Gold
A Man's Country
Man's Desire
A Man's Duty
A Man's Fight
Marie, Ltd.
Marked Men
The Market of Souls
Marriage for Convenience
The Marriage Price
Married in Haste
Mary Regan
The Master Man
The Mayor of Filbert
Me and Captain Kidd
Men, Women and Money
The Merry-Go-Round
The Microbe
A Midnight Romance
The Midnight Stage
The Millionaire Pirate
Mind the Paint Girl
The Mints of Hell
The Miracle Man
The Miracle of Love
A Misfit Earl
The Misleading Widow
Miss Adventure
Miss Arizona
Miss Crusoe
Miss Dulcie from Dixie
Mistaken Identity
Mrs. Wiggs of the Cabbage Patch
Modern Husbands
Molly of the Follies
The Money Corral
The Moonshine Trail
The Moral Deadline
More Deadly Than the Male
The Mother and the Law
Mother of Shadows
Muggsy
My Little Sister
The Mystery of the Yellow Room
The Nature Girl
Never Say Quit
The New Moon
Nobody Home
Nugget Nell
The Oakdale Affair
Oh, Boy!
Oh, You Women
The Old Maid's Baby
One Against Many
One of the Finest

1919 One-Thing-at-a-Time O'Day
One Week of Life
The Open Door
Open Your Eyes
The Other Half
The Other Man's Wife
Other Men's Wives
Our Better Selves
Out of the Fog
Out of the Shadow
Out Yonder
The Outcasts of Poker Flats
Over the Garden Wall
The Pagan God
Paid in Advance
Paid in Full
The Painted World
The Parisian Tigress
Partners Three
The Pawn of Fortune
The Peace of Roaring River
Peg O' My Heart
Peggy Does Her Darndest
Peppy Polly
The Perfect Lover
The Pest
The Petal on the Current
Pettigrew's Girl
The Phantom Honeymoon
Phil-for-Short
Pitfalls of a Big City
Playthings of Passion
Please Get Married
The Pointing Finger
The Poison Pen
The Poor Boob
Poor Relations
The Poppy Girl's Husband
The Praise Agent
Pretty Smooth
The Price of Innocence
The Price Woman Pays
The Prince and Betty
The Probation Wife
The Prodigal Liar
The Profiteer
The Profiteers
Prudence on Broadway
Puppy Love
Put Up Your Hands
Putting It Over
Putting One Over
The Quickening Flame
The Railroader
The Rebellious Bride
Reclaimed: The Struggle for a
    Soul Between Love and Hate
Red Blood and Yellow
Red Hot Dollars
The Red Lantern
The Red Peril
The Red Viper
Redhead
A Regular Fellow
A Regular Girl
The Rescuing Angel
Restless Souls
The Rider of the Law
Riders of Vengeance
The Right to Happiness
The Right to Lie
The Road Called Straight
The Roaring Road
A Rogue's Romance
Romance and Arabella
A Romance of Happy Valley
A Romance of Seattle
The Root of Evil
Roped
Rose O' the River
Rose of the West
Roses and Thorns
The Rough Neck
Rough Riding Romance
A Royal Democrat
Rustling a Bride
Sacred Silence
Sadie Love
A Sage Brush Hamlet
Sahara
Sandy Burke of the U-Bar-U
Satan Junior
The Sawdust Doll
The Scar
Scarlet Days
The Scarlet Shadow

1919 A Scream in the Night
The Sealed Envelope
Sealed Hearts
The Secret Garden
Secret Marriage
Secret Service
Shadows
Shadows of Suspicion
Shadows of the Past
The She Wolf
The Shepherd of the Hills
The Sheriff's Son
Should a Husband Forgive?
Should a Woman Tell?
Silent Strength
The Silk Lined Burglar
The Silver Girl
The Silver King
Sing-Sing and Great Meadows
    Prison
The Siren's Song
Sis Hopkins
Six Feet Four
The Sleeping Lion
Smiles
Snares of Paris
The Sneak
The Social Pirate
A Society Exile
Soldiers of Fortune
The Solitary Sin
Some Bride
Some Liar
Someone Must Pay
Something to Do
The Son-of-a-Gun!
The Spark Divine
The Speed Maniac
Speedy Meade
The Spender
The Spirit of Lafayette
The Spite Bride
The Spitfire of Seville
The Splendid Romance
The Splendid Sin
A Sporting Chance (American
    Film Co.)
A Sporting Chance (Famous
    Players-Lasky Corp.)
Spotlight Sadie
Square Deal Sanderson
The Steel King
Stepping Out
A Stitch in Time
The Stream of Life
Strictly Confidential
Stripped for a Million
The Stronger Vow
Sue of the South
The Sundown Trail
Suspense
Tangled Threads
A Taste of Life
Taxi
The Teeth of the Tiger
A Temperamental Wife
The Test of Honor
That's Good
Thieves
Thin Ice
The Third Degree
The Third Kiss
The Thirteenth Chair
This Hero Stuff
Thou Shalt Not
Three Black Eyes
Three Green Eyes
Three Men and a Girl
Through Hell and Back with the
    Men of Illinois
Through the Toils
Through the Wrong Door
The Thunderbolt
Thunderbolts of Fate
The Tiger Lily
Tiger of the Sea
Tin Pan Alley
Toby's Bow
Todd of the Times
Told in the Hills
The Tong Man
Too Many Crooks
Toton
The Trap
Treat 'Em Rough
The Trembling Hour

1919 A Trick of Fate
Trixie from Broadway
True Heart Susie
The Turn in the Road
Turning the Tables
23 1/2 Hours' Leave
Twilight
The Twin Pawns
The Two Brides
Two Women
The Unbroken Promise
Under Suspicion
Under the Top
The Undercurrent
The Unknown Love
The Unknown Quantity
The Unpainted Woman
The Unpardonable Sin
The Unveiling Hand
The Unwritten Code
The Uplifters
Upside Down
Upstairs
Upstairs and Down
The Usurper
Vagabond Luck
The Valley of the Giants
The Veiled Adventure
The Vengeance of Durand
Venus in the East
A Very Good Young Man
Victory
Virtuous Men
The Virtuous Model
Virtuous Sinners
The Virtuous Thief
A Virtuous Vamp
The Volcano
Wagon Tracks
Wanted—A Husband
Water Lily
The Way of a Woman
The Way of the Strong
The Weaker Vessel
The Web of Chance
The Westerners
What Am I Bid?
What Every Woman Learns
What Every Woman Wants
What Love Forgives
What Shall We Do with Him?
When a Girl Loves
When a Man Rides Alone
When Arizona Won
When Bearcat Went Dry
When Doctors Disagree
When Fate Decides
When Men Desire
When My Ship Comes In
When the Clouds Roll By
When the Desert Smiles
Where Bonds Are Loosed
Where the West Begins
Where's Mary?
The White Heather
A White Man's Chance
Whitewashed Walls
Who Cares?
Who Will Marry Me?
Whom the Gods Would Destroy
Who's Your Brother?
Why Smith Left Home
The Wicked Darling
Widow by Proxy
A Wild Goose Chase
Wild Oats
The Wilderness Trail
The Winchester Woman
Wings of the Morning
The Winning Girl
The Winning Stroke
The Wishing Ring Man
With Allenby in Palestine and
    Lawrence in Arabia
The Witness for the Defense
The Wolf
Wolves of the Night
The Woman Michael Married
The Woman Next Door
The Woman of Lies
A Woman of Pleasure
The Woman on the Index
A Woman There Was
The Woman Thou Gavest Me
The Woman Under Cover
The Woman Under Oath

1920 The Little Shepherd of Kingdom
    Come
The Little Wanderer
Live Sparks
The Living World
Locked Lips
The Lone Hand
Lone Hand Wilson
Love
Love and the Law
The Love Expert
The Love Flower
Love, Honor and Behave
Love, Honor and Obey
Love in the Wilderness
Love Madness
Love Without Question
Love's Battle
Love's Flame
Love's Harvest
Love's Protegé
Love's Triumph
The Luck of Geraldine Laird
The Luck of the Irish
The Lumber Jack
Luring Shadows
Madame Peacock
Madame X
Madonnas and Men
Man and His Woman
Man and Woman (A. H. Fischer
    Features, Inc.)
Man and Woman (Tyrad
    Pictures, Inc.)
The Man from Nowhere
The Man Who Dared
The Man Who Had Everything
The Man Who Lost Himself
A Manhattan Knight
Man's Plaything
The Mark of Zorro
Marooned Hearts
The Marriage Pit
Married Life
Mary Ellen Comes to Town
Mary's Ankle
The Master Mind
A Master Stroke
Merely Mary Ann
Mid-Channel
The Midlanders
The Midnight Bride
Milestones
The Miracle of Money
The Misfit Wife
The Misleading Lady
Miss Hobbs
Miss Nobody
Mrs. Temple's Telegram
A Modern Salome
Molly and I
The Mollycoddle
The Money-Changers
Moon Madness
The Mother of His Children
Mothers of Men
Mountain Madness
The Mutiny of the Elsinore
My Husband's Other Wife
My Lady's Garter
The Mysteries of Paris
Neptune's Bride
The New York Idea
The Night Riders
Nineteen and Phyllis
Nomads of the North
The North Wind's Malice
Nothing but Lies
Nothing but the Truth
The Notorious Miss Lisle
The Notorious Mrs. Sands
Number 99
Nurse Marjorie
Occasionally Yours
Officer 666
Oh, Lady, Lady
Oil
Old Dad
An Old Fashioned Boy
Old Lady 31
On the Trail of the
    Conquistadores
On with the Dance
Once a Plumber
Once to Every Woman
One Hour Before Dawn

1920 The One Way Trail
The Orphan
Other Men's Shoes
Our Christianity and Nobody's
    Child
Out of the Darkness
Out of the Dust
Out of the Snows
Out of the Storm
Outside the Law
Over the Hill to the Poorhouse
Overland Red
Pagan Love
The Palace of Darkened Windows
The Paliser Case
Paris Green
The Parish Priest
Parlor, Bedroom and Bath
Parted Curtains
Partners of the Night
Passers-By
Passion's Playground
The Path She Chose
Peaceful Valley
The Peddler of Lies
Pegeen
The Penalty
The Perfect Woman
The Phantom Melody
Pictorial History of the War
Pink Tights
Pinto
The Place of Honeymoons
Pleasure Seekers
The Plunger
The Point of View
Polly of the Storm Country
Polly with a Past
Pollyanna
The Poor Simp
Prairie Trails
The Prey
The Price of Redemption
The Price of Silence
The Prince Chap
The Prince of Avenue A
The Purple Cipher
Red Foam
The Red Lane
Reformation
Remodelling Her Husband
Respectable by Proxy
The Restless Sex
The Return of Tarzan
The Rich Slave
The Riddle: Woman
Riders of the Dawn
The Right of Way
The Right to Love
Rio Grande
Risky Business
The River's End
The Road of Ambition
The Road to Divorce
Rogues and Romance
Roman Candles
Romance
The Romance Promoters
A Romantic Adventuress
Rookie's Return
The Rose of Nome
Rouge and Riches
The Round-Up
The Sacred Flame
The Sacred Ruby
The Sagebrusher
Sand!
The Saphead
The Scarlet Dragon
The Scoffer
The Scrap of Paper
Scratch My Back
The Scuttlers
The Sea Rider
The Sea Wolf
The Secret Formula
The Secret Gift
Seeds of Vengeance
Seeing It Through
The Servant in the House
The Servant Question
Sex
The Shadow of Rosalie Byrnes
The Shark
She Couldn't Help It
She Loves and Lies

1920 Sherry
Shipwrecked Among Cannibals
Shod with Fire
Shore Acres
Should a Wife Work?
Sick Abed
The Silent Barrier
Silk Hosiery
Silk Husbands and Calico Wives
The Silver Horde
Simple Souls
The Sin That Was His
Sink or Swim
Sinners
The Sins of Rosanne
The Sins of St. Anthony
A Sister to Salome
The Six Best Cellars
Sky Eye
Skyfire
The Skywayman
A Slave of Vanity
Slaves of Pride
The Sleep of Cyma Roget
The Slim Princess
Smiling All the Way
Smoldering Embers
So Long Letty
Someone in the House
Something Different
Something New
Something to Think About
The Song of the Soul
Sooner or Later
Sophy of Kravonia; Or, The
    Virgin of Paris
The Soul of Youth
The Spenders
The Spirit of Good
A Splendid Hazard
The Sport of Kings
The Sporting Duchess
The Square Shooter
The Star Rover
Starvation
The Stealers
The Stolen Kiss
Stolen Moments
Stop Thief
The Strange Boarder
The Stranger
The Street Called Straight
Stronger Than Death
The Strongest
Suds
Sundown Slim
Sunset Sprague
Sweet Lavender
The Symbol of the Unconquered
Tarnished Reputations
The Tattlers
The Terror
Terror Island
The Testing Block
The Texan
That Something
Their Mutual Child
The Thief
The Third Generation
The Third Woman
The Thirteenth Commandment
The Thirtieth Piece of Silver
$30,000
Thirty Years Between
39 East
Thou Art the Man
Thoughtless Women
A Thousand to One
Three Gold Coins
Through Eyes of Men
The Tiger's Coat
The Tiger's Cub
To Please One Woman
A Tokio Siren
The Toll Gate
To-Morrow
Too Much Johnson
The Trail of the Arrow
The Trail of the Cigarette
Treasure Island
The Tree of Knowledge
The Triflers
A Trip Through Cairo
The Triple Clue
Trumpet Island
The Truth

1920 The Truth About Husbands
The Turning Point
Twin Beds
Twinkle Twinkle Little Star
Twins of Suffering Creek
Twisted Souls
Two Kinds of Love
Two Moons
Two Weeks
The U.P. Trail
The Ugly Duckling
Uncharted Channels
Uncle Sam of Freedom Ridge
Under Crimson Skies
Under Northern Lights
The Unfortunate Sex
The Unknown Ranger
Unseen Forces
The Unseen Witness
The Untamed
Up in Mary's Attic
The Valley of Doubt
The Valley of Night
The Valley of Tomorrow
The Veiled Marriage
Vengeance and the Girl
The Very Idea
The Vice of Fools
The Victim
The Village Sleuth
The Virgin of Stamboul
Voices
Wait for Me
The Walk-Offs
The Wall Street Mystery
Wanted at Headquarters
Water, Water Everywhere
Way Down East
The Way Women Love
The Web of Deceit
The Week-End
West Is West
What Happened to Jones
What Happened to Rosa
What Women Love
What Women Want
What Would You Do?
What's Your Hurry?
What's Your Husband Doing?
When Dawn Came
When Quackel Did Hide
While New York Sleeps
The Whisper Market
Whispering Devils
Whispers
The White Circle
The White Dove
White Lies
The White Moll
The White Rider
White Youth
Who's Your Servant?
Why Change Your Wife?
Why Leave Your Husband?
Why Pick on Me?
Why Tell?
Why Women Sin
The Willow Tree
Wings of Pride
Witch's Gold
Within Our Gates
Wits vs. Wits
Wolves of the Street
The Woman Above Reproach
The Woman and the Puppet
The Woman Game
The Woman Gives
The Woman God Sent
The Woman in His House
The Woman in Room 13
The Woman in the Suitcase
The Woman of Mystery
The Woman Untamed
A Woman Who Understood
A Woman's Business
Woman's Man
Women Men Forget
Women Men Love
The Wonder Man
The Wonderful Chance
The World and His Wife
A World of Folly
Would You Forgive?
The Wrong Woman
The Yellow Typhoon
Yes or No

PERSONAL NAME INDEX

★ Entries in the Personal Name Index are arranged alphabetically, with film credits listed below the names in chronological, then alphabetical, order. As mentioned in the Introduction, credits in the main volume are recorded exactly as found in contemporary sources. While this approach is invaluable for research on a particular film, it can lead to difficulties in an index. In answer to the problem, and in response to the many scholars who felt that the lack of an "authority list" for names in the *AFI Catalog of Feature Films, 1921–1930* was a hindrance to research, we attempted to list all filmographies under a "main entry."

To accomplish this, we established an authority file of personal names soon after we began work on the *Catalog*, then expanded and annotated it throughout the course of the project. When the credit indexes were made available by our computer system, we went through them, letter by letter, to ensure that each person would have his or her complete filmography listed under one name.

To arrive at a main entry, we ascertained what name a person used for the majority of his or her career or what name modern sources typically have used to identify the individual. Rudolph Valentino, for example, is always listed under that name in modern sources because in the twenties, at the height of his career, Rudolph Valentino was the name he used. In the teens, however, when the actor was not a major star, he was credited by a dozen variations of his name, as noted in the index.

A fairly simple determination in Valentino's case, however, became more difficult with lesser known individuals. We sometimes had to follow "hunches" with painstaking research into various editions of *The Motion Picture Studio Directory and Trade Annual*, biographical news items in trade papers, modern sources, and occasionally photographs to compare physical characteristics of persons with similar names. In some cases we were unable to confirm our "hunches." Thus a number of entries use the phrase *could be same as* to direct the user to the filmography of someone who could actually be the same person. For clarification we have also added the phrase *not the same as* when the names of two individuals were so similar that their filmographies might easily be confused. To further identify some similar names we have used terms like *actor* or *child actor*, and occasionally attached dates or birthplaces. When individuals seemed to be known by two or more name variations in equal measure, we simply selected one to be the main entry.

Once the main entry name was determined, we added all of the variations of the name to the entry as *same as* variations. For example, under the entry "Dwan, Allan," we list "*same as* Dwan, Alan; Dwan, Allen." Ample cross references are supplied from variations to the main entries. We have, however, refrained from including superfluous *see* references, such as "Dwan, Allen *see* Dwan, Allan," or "Morey, Harry *see* Morey, Harry T."

The reasons why there are so many *same as* names is threefold: first, filmmakers frequently changed their names; second, the proper recording of the name of every person who worked on a film was not as important in the teens as it is today; and third, mistakes or variations in trade reviews were very common. In addition, it was a common practice in the teens to abbreviate names, for example, "Edw." which could mean either "Edward" or "Edwin," or to use surnames only, that is, "Mr. Smith" or "Miss Browne."

We followed *Anglo-American Cataloging Rules II* for alphabetization. One exception to the rules, however, was the DeMille family, whose entries are all listed together in the D's, regardless of whether they were known as de Mille or DeMille.

PERSONAL NAME INDEX

Adams, Mae
1916　The Hidden Law
Adams, Marion
1917　The Rainbow
Adams, Mildred
1917　Their Compact
Adams, Peggy
1917　Chris and His Wonderful
　　　Lamp
　　　Salt of the Earth
19--　Barnaby Lee
Adams, Raymond A.
1920　Up in Mary's Attic
Adams, Rex
1917　The Penny Philanthropist
Adams, Robert
1920　Hidden Charms
Adams, Roy
1917　The Princess' Necklace
1919　The Indestructible Wife
Adams, William S.
1915　The Juggernaut*
1919　Dawn
　　　The Moonshine Trail
　　　The Painted World*
　　　Shadows of the Past
　　　The Wreck
1920　The Blood Barrier
　　　Forbidden Valley
　　　The House of the Tolling Bell
　　　Man and His Woman
　　　My Husband's Other Wife
　　　Passers-By
　　　Respectable by Proxy
Addams, Kate
1918　And the Children Pay
Ade, George
1915　Marse Covington
Adell, Marie
1917　God's Law and Man's
　　　Lady Barnacle
Adelman, Joseph
1915　A Continental Girl
　　　Virtue
1916　Where Is My Father?
Adler, B.
1914　Uriel Acosta
Adler, Jacob P.
1914　Michael Strogoff
Adler, Jane
1917　For the Freedom of the World
1919　The Road Called Straight
Adler, Sarah
1914　Sins of the Parents
Adler, William F. see **Alder, William F.**
Adolfi, John G. same as **Adolfi, Jack**
1915　A Child of God
　　　A Man and His Mate
1916　Caprice of the Mountains
　　　Little Miss Happiness
　　　The Man Inside
　　　Merely Mary Ann
　　　The Mischief Maker
　　　A Modern Thelma
　　　The Ragged Princess
　　　The Sphinx
1917　A Child of the Wild
　　　A Modern Cinderella
　　　Patsy
　　　The Small Town Girl
1918　The Burden of Proof
　　　The Heart of a Girl
　　　Queen of the Sea
　　　The Woman the Germans Shot
1919　Who's Your Brother?
1920　The Amazing Woman
　　　The Little 'Fraid Lady
　　　The Wonder Man
Adorée, Renée
1920　The Strongest
Adrizani, John see **Ardizoni, John**
Adrizoni, John see **Ardizoni, John**
Adrizonia, John see **Ardizoni, John**
Agnew, Robert
1920　The Frisky Mrs. Johnson
　　　The Sporting Duchess
　　　The Valley of Doubt
Agoust, Emile
1916　Vanity

Ah Toy
1919　Blackie's Redemption
Ahern, George same as **Ahearn, George**
1916　Bluff
　　　Overalls
　　　Powder
　　　The Strength of Donald
　　　　McKenzie
　　　The Undertow
1917　Charity Castle
　　　Peggy Leads the Way
　　　Periwinkle
　　　The Sea Master
　　　Shackles of Truth
Aide, Grace
1918　The Legion of Death
Aiken, Alma
1919　The Test of Honor
Aimee, Blanche
1915　The Green Cloak
Ainsley, James D.
1913　From the Manger to the Cross
Ainsworth, Charles Sydney see
　　Ainsworth, Sydney
Ainsworth, Leonora
1916　Drugged Waters
　　　The Madcap
Ainsworth, Phil
1918　The Man from Funeral Range
1920　The Chorus Girl's Romance
Ainsworth, Sydney same as **Ainsworth,
　　Charles Sydney; Ainsworth, Sidney**
1915　In the Palace of the King
　　　The White Sister
1916　According to the Code
　　　The Chaperon
　　　The Misleading Lady
　　　The Prince of Graustark
1917　On Trial
　　　The Trufflers
　　　Two-Bit Seats
1918　Brown of Harvard
1919　The Crimson Gardenia
　　　The Gay Lord Quex
　　　The Girl from Outside
　　　Heartsease
　　　The Little Rowdy
　　　The Loves of Letty
　　　A Man and His Money
　　　One Week of Life
1920　The Branding Iron
　　　The Cup of Fury
　　　A Double Dyed Deceiver
　　　Half a Chance
　　　Madame X
　　　Out of the Storm
　　　The Woman in Room 13
Ainsworth, Virginia
1915　A Black Sheep
1920　Passion's Playground
Aiston, Arthur C.
1914　At the Cross Roads
Aitken, Harry E.
1914　Home, Sweet Home
1915　The Birth of a Nation*
1916　Intolerance*
Aitken, Spottiswoode same as **Aitken,
　　Spottiswood; Aitkin, Spottiswood**
1914　The Avenging Conscience
　　　Home, Sweet Home
　　　Liberty Belles
1915　The Birth of a Nation
　　　Captain Macklin
　　　Her Shattered Idol
　　　The Outcast
　　　The Outlaw's Revenge
1916　Acquitted
　　　The Flying Torpedo
　　　An Innocent Magdalene
　　　Intolerance
　　　Macbeth
　　　The Old Folks at Home
　　　The Price of Power
　　　The Wharf Rat
1917　The Americano
　　　Charity Castle
　　　Cheerful Givers
　　　A Game of Wits
　　　Her Country's Call
　　　Melissa of the Hills
　　　Souls Triumphant
　　　Southern Pride
　　　Stagestruck

　　　A Woman's Awakening
1918　Beauty and the Rogue
　　　The Cruise of the
　　　　Make-Believes
　　　How Could You, Jean?
　　　In Judgment Of
　　　The Mating of Marcella
1919　Bonnie, Bonnie Lassie
　　　Broken Commandments
　　　Caleb Piper's Girl
　　　Captain Kidd, Jr.
　　　Evangeline
　　　Fighting Through
　　　Hay Foot, Straw Foot
　　　Her Kingdom of Dreams
　　　An Innocent Adventuress
　　　Jane Goes A-Wooing
　　　Rough Riding Romance
　　　The Secret Garden
　　　The Thunderbolt
　　　The White Heather
　　　Who Cares?
　　　The Wicked Darling
　　　A Woman of Pleasure
1920　Dangerous Love
　　　Nomads of the North
　　　The White Circle
　　　Witch's Gold
Alba, Orpha
1920　The Square Shooter
Alberni, Luis same as **Alberni, Louis**
1915　Children of the Ghetto
1920　39 East
Albert, Jack
1916　Unto Those Who Sin
Albert, Katherine
1920　The Saphead
Albertson, Arthur
1916　The Lotus Woman
1917　The Argyle Case
Albertson, E. Coit same as **Albertson,
　　C.; Albertson, Coit**
1918　For Freedom
1919　Who's Your Brother?
1920　Wits vs. Wits
Albion, Louis
1915　The Running Fight
Albro, Arthur
1915　The Closing Net
1919　A Damsel in Distress
Alcorn, Olive Ann same as **Acorn, Olive**
1919　For a Woman's Honor
　　　The Long Arm of Mannister
Alden, Hazel
1918　All Woman
　　　Marriage
Alden, Mabel
1916　One Day
Alden, Mary
1914　The Battle of the Sexes
　　　Home, Sweet Home
　　　Lord Chumley
1915　The Birth of a Nation
　　　Ghosts
　　　The Lily and the Rose
　　　A Man's Prerogative
　　　The Outcast
1916　Acquitted
　　　The Good Bad Man
　　　Hell-to-Pay Austin
　　　An Innocent Magdalene
　　　Intolerance
　　　Less Than the Dust
　　　Macbeth
　　　Pillars of Society
1917　The Argyle Case
　　　The Land of Promise
1918　The Narrow Path
　　　The Naulahka
1919　The Broken Butterfly
　　　Common Clay
　　　Erstwhile Susan
　　　The Mother and the Law
　　　The Unpardonable Sin
1920　Honest Hutch
　　　The Inferior Sex
　　　Milestones
　　　Miss Nobody
　　　Parted Curtains
　　　Silk Husbands and Calico
　　　　Wives

Aldenn, Byron
1918　A Pair of Sixes
Alder, William F. same as **Adler,
　　William F.; Alder, William**
1915　The Second in Command
　　　The Silent Voice
1920　Shipwrecked Among Cannibals
Alderson, Erville
1918　Her Man
1920　The Good-Bad Wife
Aldrich, Charles T.
1915　The Magic Toy Maker
Aldwyn, Irene same as **Aldwin, Irene**
1916　The Yellow Pawn
1917　The Double Standard
　　　A School for Husbands
1918　The Legion of Death
　　　The Narrow Path
1919　Chasing Rainbows
　　　The Solitary Sin
1920　The Confession
Alexander, Miss
1915　The Heights of Hazard
Alexander, A.
1918　Why America Will Win
Alexander, Alois see **Alexander, Lois**
Alexander, Ben same as **Alexander,
　　Bennie; Alexander, Benny**
1917　The Little American
1918　The Heart of Rachael
　　　Hearts of the World
　　　The Lady of the Dugout
　　　Little Orphant Annie
　　　The One Woman
1919　The Better Wife
　　　The Hushed Hour
　　　Josselyn's Wife
　　　The Mayor of Filbert
　　　Tangled Threads
　　　The Turn in the Road
　　　The White Heather
1920　The Family Honor
　　　The Notorious Mrs. Sands
　　　Through Eyes of Men
　　　The Triflers
Alexander, Claire
1915　A Girl of Yesterday
1919　Child of M'sieu
Alexander, Clifford same as **Alexander,
　　Cliff**
1918　An Alien Enemy
　　　Honor's Cross
　　　Maid O' the Storm
　　　One Dollar Bid
　　　Patriotism
　　　The Turn of a Card
　　　Wedlock
　　　With Hoops of Steel
1919　The Silver Girl
Alexander, Edward same as **Alexander,
　　Ed**
1914　The Spy
1916　The Bait
　　　The Heart of Tara
1917　The Chosen Prince, or the
　　　　Friendship of David and
　　　　Jonathan
　　　North of Fifty-Three
1918　By the World Forgot
　　　The Girl from Beyond
　　　In Judgment Of
　　　No Man's Land
　　　The Wild Strain
1919　The Heart of Youth
　　　The Island of Intrigue
　　　Love Insurance
　　　Putting It Over
　　　Secret Marriage
1920　The Saphead
Alexander, Frank
1917　Melting Millions
Alexander, Gerard same as **Alexander,
　　Girrard**
1916　Saving the Family Name
　　　A Son of the Immortals
1917　The Soul of Satan
1919　Who Cares?
　　　You Never Saw Such a Girl
Alexander, Miss Gerard
1920　The Little Grey Mouse

Amazar, Elivra could be same as
   Amazar, Elaine
   1919 The Volcano
Ames, Robert
   1920 What Women Want
Ames, Winthrop
   1916 Oliver Twist
        Snow White
Amick, Robert
   1920 Rogues and Romance
Anchell (full name unknown)
   1915 The Fairy and the Waif*
Anderson, Mrs.
   1919 Little Women
Anderson, Mother same as **Anderson,**
   Helen Relyea; Anderson, Relyea
   1919 Castles in the Air
        The Lion's Den
        Should a Woman Tell?
Anderson, Augusta
   1914 Classmates
   1916 The Rainbow Princess
   1917 The Seven Swans
   1918 Rich Man, Poor Man
        Uncle Tom's Cabin
   1919 The Career of Katherine Bush
        Come Out of the Kitchen
   1920 The Amateur Wife
        Guilty of Love
        A Romantic Adventuress
        Sinners
Anderson, Beatrice
   1917 Kitty MacKay
Anderson, "Broncho Billy" see
   Anderson, G. M.
Anderson, C. E. same as **Anderson, C.;**
   Anderson, Capt.
   1918 The Kaiser, the Beast of Berlin
   1920 Bullet Proof
        Hitchin' Posts
        Overland Red
Anderson, Claire
   1918 The Answer
        Crown Jewels
        The Fly God
        The Grey Parasol
        Mlle. Paulette
        The Mask
        The Painted Lily*
        The Price of Applause
   1919 The Blinding Trail
        The Rider of the Law
        The Spitfire of Seville
        Who Cares?
        You Never Saw Such a Girl
   1920 The Girl in Number 29
        The Palace of Darkened
          Windows
        The Path She Chose
        The Servant in the House
Anderson, David
   1920 The Blue Moon
Anderson, Florence
   1918 The Blue Bird
Anderson, Frank
   1917 For France
Anderson, G. M. same as **Anderson,**
   "Broncho Billy"; Anderson, Gilbert;
   Anderson, Gilbert M.
   1917 Humanity
        Vera, the Medium
   1918 Naked Hands
   1919 Red Blood and Yellow
        The Son-of-a-Gun!
Anderson, George same as **Anderson,**
   George M.
   1914 The Good-for-Nothing
   1915 Little Pal
   1916 The Almighty Dollar
        The Question
        The Shadow of a Doubt
   1917 The Co-Respondent
   1918 Her Man
Anderson, Gertrude H.
   1916 What Love Can Do
Anderson, Gilbert M. see **Anderson, G.**
   M.
Anderson, Helen Relyea see **Anderson,**
   Mother

Anderson, K. E.
   1919 A Woman of Pleasure
   1920 Help Wanted—Male
        The Parish Priest
Anderson, Mary
   1914 My Official Wife
   1915 C.O.D.
   1916 The Garden of Allah*
        The Last Man
   1917 By Right of Possession
        The Divorcee
        The Flaming Omen
        The Magnificent Meddler
        Sunlight's Last Raid
        When Men Are Tempted
   1918 His Birthright
        Playthings
   1919 The False Faces
        The Hushed Hour
        Johnny Get Your Gun
        The Spender
   1920 Bubbles
Anderson, Mignon
   1913 Robin Hood
   1914 Beating Back
   1915 Milestones of Life
        The Mill on the Floss
        The Price of Her Silence
   1916 The City of Illusion
        Her Husband's Wife
        Pamela's Past
        The Woman in Politics
   1917 The Circus of Life
        Even As You and I
        The Phantom's Secret
        A Wife on Trial
   1918 The Claim
   1919 Blind Man's Eyes
        The House of Intrigue
        The Midnight Stage
   1920 The Heart of a Woman
        King Spruce
        Mountain Madness
Anderson, Nellie
   1916 The Two Edged Sword
   1917 Her Secret
        Kitty MacKay
        The Little Duchess
   1918 Little Red Decides
        Over the Top
   1920 Forbidden Valley
Anderson, Mrs. R. S.
   1918 A Doll's House
Anderson, Relyea see **Anderson, Mother**
Anderson, Robert (actor)
   1916 Intolerance*
   1917 Draft 258
   1918 Hearts of the World
        The Hun Within
   1919 Common Property
        Fires of Faith
        The Heart of Humanity
        The Petal on the Current
        The Right to Happiness
   1920 Below the Deadline
        Once to Every Woman
Anderson, Robert Gordon (scen)
   1918 Over the Top
Anderson, Stephie
   1918 Sylvia on a Spree
Anderson, Warner
   1916 The Sunbeam
Anderson, William
   1917 The Bar Sinister
Andrada, David
   1914 Without Hope
Andrew, Maud
   1917 Outcast
Andrews, Ann
   1917 The Girl by the Roadside
Andrews, Frank same as **Andrews,**
   Frank B.
   1914 Captain Swift
        The Nightingale
   1915 Children of the Ghetto
        The Morals of Marcus
   1917 For France*
        The Poor Little Rich Girl
        The Road Between
        Strife
   1918 The Eyes of Mystery
        The Oldest Law

Andrews, Fred
   1920 Risky Business
Andrews, Gertrude
   1919 Brothers Divided
   1920 Dollar for Dollar*
Andrews, H. G.
   1917 Miss Nobody
Andriot, Lucien
   1914 The Marked Woman
   1915 A Butterfly on the Wheel
        Camille
        The Face in the Moonlight
        The Impostor
        M'liss
        The Price
   1916 The Almighty Dollar
        Broken Chains
        The Feast of Life
        La Vie de Boheme
   1917 The Mad Lover
        On Dangerous Ground
        The Poor Little Rich Girl
        The Pride of the Clan
        The Silent Master
        The Whip
   1918 Lest We Forget
   1919 Oh, Boy!
        The Right to Lie
        The Virtuous Model
   1920 A Connecticut Yankee at King
          Arthur's Court
        Half a Chance
        Help Wanted—Male
        The Man Who Lost Himself
Andruss, Albert
   1914 The Ring and the Man
   1915 The Woman Next Door
Angeles, Bert
   1915 The Politicians
Angelis, Jefferson de
   1918 Her Great Chance
Angelo, Charles
   1916 The Precious Packet
   1920 The Blue Pearl
Angelo, Jean
   1918 The Divine Sacrifice
Angus, Katherine
   1915 Salvation Nell
   1919 Just Squaw
   1920 The Flame of Hellgate
Anker, William
   1915 The Green Cloak
   1916 Wild Oats
   1920 The Sleep of Cyma Roget
Ankewich, Camille see **Manon, Marcia**
Annerly, Fred
   1914 The Man from Mexico
   1916 The Pursuing Vengeance
Anrooney, Alice
   1916 Purity
Anson, G. W.
   1915 The Builder of Bridges
Anthony, Clairette
   1919 The Marriage Price
Anthony, Joe
   1919 The Haunted Bedroom
Antiznat, Henri
   1914 The Nightingale
Aoki, Tsuru same as **Aoki, Tsura; Aoki,**
   Tsuri; Aoki, Tsuro; Hayakawa, Mrs.
   Sessue
   1914 The Typhoon*
        The Wrath of the Gods
   1916 Alien Souls
        The Beckoning Flame
        The Honorable Friend
        The Soul of Kura-San
   1917 The Call of the East
        Each to His Kind
   1918 The Bravest Way
        The Curse of Iku
        His Birthright
   1919 Bonds of Honor
        The Courageous Coward
        The Dragon Painter
        The Gray Horizon
        A Heart in Pawn
   1920 The Breath of the Gods
        Locked Lips
        A Tokio Siren

Aoyama, Yukio same as **Aoyana, U.;**
   Avyoma, Yukio
   1916 Pidgin Island
   1918 The Bravest Way
   1919 Thieves
   1920 Who's Your Servant?
Apfel, Oscar C. same as **Apfel, Oscar**
   1914 Brewster's Millions
        The Call of the North
        The Circus Man
        The Ghost Breaker
        The Last Volunteer
        The Man from Home*
        The Man on the Box
        The Master Mind
        The Only Son
        Ready Money
        The Squaw Man
   1915 After Five
        The Broken Law
        Kilmeny
        The Little Gypsy
        Peer Gynt
        The Rug Maker's Daughter
        Snobs
        A Soldier's Oath
        The Wild Olive
   1916 The Battle of Hearts
        The End of the Trail
        Fighting Blood
        The Fires of Conscience
        The Man from Bitter Roots
        A Man of Sorrow
   1917 The Hidden Children
        The Price of Her Soul
   1918 The Grouch
        The Interloper
        A Man's Man
        Merely Players
        Tinsel
        To Him That Hath
        The Turn of a Card
   1919 An Amateur Widow
        Auction of Souls
        Bringing Up Betty
        The Crook of Dreams
        The Little Intruder
        Mandarin's Gold
        Me and Captain Kidd
        The Oakdale Affair
        Phil-for-Short
        The Rough Neck
        The Steel King
Apling, Bert same as **Appling, Bert**
   1918 Beyond the Shadows
        Desert Law
        The Grand Passion
        The Light of Western Stars
   1919 The Best Man
        The Boomerang
        The End of the Game
        A Man's Fight
        A Regular Fellow
   1920 Just Pals
        Mary Ellen Comes to Town
Appel, Sam same as **Appel, Samuel**
   1916 Whispering Smith
   1918 The Light of Western Stars
        She Hired a Husband
   1919 The Silk Lined Burglar
        The Web of Chance
   1920 La La Lucille
Applegate, Baby
   1917 A Man's Law
Applegate, Ray could be same as
   Applegate, Roy
   1919 Upside Down
Applegate, Roy could be same as
   Applegate, Ray
   1914 Uncle Tom's Cabin
   1915 All for a Girl
        The Avalanche
        The Bludgeon
        The Curious Conduct of Judge
          Legarde
        The Daughter of the Sea
        The Game of Three
   1916 The Child of Destiny
        His Great Triumph
        The Kiss of Hate
   1917 A Man's Law
   1918 The Daredevil
   1918-19

1917 The Bondage of Fear
     The Divorce Game
     The Guardian
     The Iron Ring
     The Marriage Market
     Moral Courage
     The Page Mystery
     Rasputin, the Black Monk
     Shall We Forgive Her?
     The Social Leper
     A Woman Alone
1918 The Beautiful Mrs. Reynolds
     Broken Ties
1919 The American Way
     Forest Rivals
     The Praise Agent

Ashley, C. E. same as **Ashley, Charles E.**
1918 A Pair of Sixes

Ashley, Catherine
1919 The Mystery of the Yellow
     Room

Ashley, Charles E. see **Ashley, C. E.**

Ashley, Grace
1917 The Skylight Room

Ashley, Philip
1920 Sophy of Kravonia; Or, The
     Virgin of Paris

Ashton, Iris
1918 False Ambition
     You Can't Believe Everything

Ashton, Rosalie
1917 Who Knows?
1918 Humility

Ashton, Sylvia
1915 Beulah
     The Supreme Test
1916 Overalls
     Revelations
1918 Fuss and Feathers
     The Goat
     Old Wives for New
     A Pair of Silk Stockings
     We Can't Have Everything
1919 Don't Change Your Husband
     For Better, for Worse
     The Heart of Youth
     Johnny Get Your Gun
     The Lottery Man
     Men, Women and Money
     Peggy Does Her Darndest
     Rose O' the River
     Under the Top
     A Very Good Young Man
1920 A City Sparrow
     Conrad in Quest of His Youth
     The Fourteenth Man
     Jack Straw
     Jenny Be Good
     Mrs. Temple's Telegram
     The Soul of Youth
     Sweet Lavender
     Thou Art the Man
     Why Change Your Wife?

Ashton, Tom
1919 Destiny

Ashurst, Henry T.
1915 Prohibition*

Askins, Ida
1916 The Colored American
     Winning His Suit

Asquith, Elizabeth
1918 The Great Love*

Asquith, Mary
1914 Life's Shop Window
1915 Lady Audley's Secret
1916 The Awakening of Helena
     Richie
1917 The Power of Decision

Aster, Gertrude see **Astor, Gertrude**

Aster, Pauline
1916 Idle Wives

Astor, Camille
1915 Chimmie Fadden
     Chimmie Fadden Out West
1916 For the Defense
     The Garden of Allah
     The Thousand Dollar Husband
     To Have and to Hold

Astor, Gertrude same as **Aster, Gertrude**
1917 Bondage
     The Devil's Pay Day
     The Girl Who Won Out

     The Lash of Power
     The Little Orphan
     Polly Redhead
     The Price of a Good Time
     The Rescue
     The Scarlet Crystal
1918 After the War
     The Brazen Beauty
     The Girl Who Wouldn't Quit
1919 Destiny
     Loot
     Pretty Smooth
     The Trembling Hour
     What Am I Bid?
     The Wicked Darling
1920 The Branding Iron
     Burning Daylight
     Occasionally Yours

Astor, Grace
1916 Undine

Atchison, James W.
1918 The Flash of Fate

Atkins, H. L.
1920 Out of the Snows

Atkins, Thomas
1920 Out of the Snows

Atkinson, Florence
1918 The Marionettes

Atkinson, Frank
1919 Marked Men

Atwill, Lionel
1918 Eve's Daughter
1919 The Marriage Price
1920 The Eternal Mother

Aubert, Shirley
1918 Dodging a Million

Aubrey, Helen
1914 The County Chairman
     The Redemption of David
     Corson
     The Ring and the Man
     A Woman's Triumph

Aubrey, W. A.
1916 Vengeance Is Mine

Aüen, Signe see **Owen, Seena**

Auer, Florence
1916 Her Great Price
1917 A Modern Cinderella

Aug, Edna
1916 Where D'Ye Get That Stuff?

August, Edwin
1915 Bondwomen
     Evidence
     When It Strikes Home
1916 The Perils of Divorce
     The Social Highwayman
     The Summer Girl
     The Woman in 47*
     The Yellow Passport
1918 A Broadway Scandal
     The City of Tears
     The Mortgaged Wife
1919 The Poison Pen

August, Joe same as **August, Joseph;**
August, Joseph H.
1915 The Disciple
1916 The Apostle of Vengeance
     The Aryan
     Between Men
     Civilization
     The Dawn Maker
     The Devil's Double
     Hell's Hinges
     The Patriot
     The Primal Lure
     The Return of Draw Egan
1917 The Cold Deck
     The Desert Man
     The Gun Fighter
     The Narrow Trail
     The Silent Man
     The Square Deal Man
     Truthful Tulliver
     Wolf Lowry
1918 Blue Blazes Rawden
     The Border Wireless
     Branding Broadway
     He Comes Up Smiling*
     Riddle Gawne
     Selfish Yates
     Shark Monroe
     The Tiger Man
     Wolves of the Rail

1919 Breed of Men
     John Petticoats
     The Money Corral
     The Poppy Girl's Husband
     Square Deal Sanderson
     Wagon Tracks
1920 The Cradle of Courage
     Sand!
     The Testing Block
     The Toll Gate

Auker, William
1916 The Turmoil

Austen, Leslie same as **Austin, Leslie**
1915 Her Reckoning
1916 The City of Failing Light
1917 The Auction of Virtue
     The Courage of the Common
     Place
     The Final Payment
     A Man and the Woman
     Two Little Imps
1918 American Buds
     Caught in the Act
     Mrs. Dane's Defense
     A Woman of Impulse
1919 Marie, Ltd.
     My Little Sister
1920 Democracy
     Dr. Jekyll and Mr. Hyde
     (Pioneer Film Corp.)

Austin, Albert
1920 Suds

Austin, George
1917 The Secret of Black Mountain

Austin, J. W. could be same as **Austin,**
Jere or **Austin, William**
1915 The Morals of Marcus

Austin, Jere could be same as **Austin, J.**
W.
1914 The School for Scandal
     Wolfe; Or, The Conquest of
     Quebec
1915 Over Night
1917 The Seven Swans
1918 All Woman
     Fedora
     Hidden Fires
     Peg O' the Sea
     A Perfect Lady
     Resurrection
     Uncle Tom's Cabin
1919 Day Dreams
     Erstwhile Susan
     Someone Must Pay
     The Trap
     The Woman on the Index
1920 The Eternal Mother
     Why Leave Your Husband?
     The Woman Game

Austin, Leslie see **Austen, Leslie**

Austin, Ralph
1915 Destiny; Or, The Soul of a
     Woman

Austin, Rose
1914 Trapped in the Great
     Metropolis

Austin, William could be same as
     Austin, J. W.
1920 Common Sense

The Australian Wood Choppers
1914 America

Avery, Charles
1915 A Submarine Pirate
1916 A Modern Enoch Arden

Avyoma, Yukio see **Aoyama, Yukio**

Axel, Evelyn see **Axell, Evelyn**

Axzell, Carl
1917 The Adventures of Carol
1918 The Purple Lily

Axzell, Evelyn same as **Axzel, Evelyn**
1918 Daybreak
     The Gulf Between*
     The Hell Cat
1919 Forest Rivals

Axzell, Violet same as **Axzelle, Violet**
1916 The Flames of Johannis
     A Fool's Paradise
1917 Rasputin, the Black Monk
1918 The Gulf Between
     Her Boy
     A Soul Without Windows
1920 The Sacred Flame

Ayers, Clio see **Ayres, Clio**

Ayers, Dudley
1918 The Uphill Path

Ayers, Edward
1916 The American Beauty

Ayerton, Robert
1916 The Witching Hour
1919 A Regular Girl

Aylesworth, Arthur
1915 Over Night

Aylesworth, Grace
1915 The Deep Purple

Ayling, Herbert
1917 Outcast
1918 The Richest Girl

Ayling, James
1914 The $5,000,000 Counterfeiting
     Plot

Ayres, Agnes same as **Eyre, Agnes**
1917 The Bottom of the Well
     The Dazzling Miss Davison
     The Debt
     The Defeat of the City
     Mrs. Balfame
     Motherhood (Frank Powell
     Producing Corp.)
     The Renaissance at Charleroi
     Richard, the Brazen
1918 One Thousand Dollars
1919 The Gamblers
     The Girl Problem
     In Honor's Web
     Sacred Silence
     A Stitch in Time
1920 The Furnace
     Go and Get It
     Held by the Enemy
     The Inner Voice
     A Modern Salome

Ayres, Clio same as **Ayers, Clio; Ayres,**
Cleo
1916 The Devil's Prize
1917 The Courage of Silence
     Mary Jane's Pa
     The Price Mark
1918 To Him That Hath
     The Zero Hour

Ayres, Coral
1920 The Mysteries of Paris

Ayres, James F.
1915 The Unbroken Road

Ayres, Ruby Mildred
1918 Society for Sale

Ayrton, Robert
1919 The Silver King

B

Babcock, Theodore
1915 Destiny; Or, The Soul of a
     Woman
     The Master Hand

Babille, Edward
1914 One Wonderful Night

Baby Joan see **Joan, Baby**

Bach, Edward
1919 The Jungle Trail

Bach, William
1916 The Witch

Bachmann, Max
1918 Five Nights*

Backus, Bertha A.
1918 The Love Net

Backus, Frank
1914 The Fortune Hunter

Backus, George
1914 One of Our Girls
1915 The House of a Thousand
     Candles
     When We Were Twenty-One
1916 The Habit of Happiness
1917 National Red Cross Pageant*
     Shirley Kaye
1918 Rich Man, Poor Man
1919 Eyes of the Soul
     The Gamblers
     In Honor's Web
     The Indestructible Wife
     The Third Degree
1920 Marooned Hearts
     The Stolen Kiss

Bacon, Frank
1915 Rosemary
      The Silent Voice
1916 A Corner in Cotton
      Her Debt of Honor
Bacon, Gerald F.
1915 The Melting Pot
      The Whirl of Life
1918 Men
1919 A Woman's Experience
1920 Blind Love
Bacon, Lillian
1920 Blind Love
Bacon, Lloyd
1919 The Blue Bonnet
      The Feud
      The House of Intrigue
      Square Deal Sanderson
      Vagabond Luck
      Wagon Tracks
1920 The Broken Gate
      The Girl in the Rain
      The Kentucky Colonel
      The Midlanders
      Miss Nobody
Badaracco, Jacob A. *same as*
   Badaracco, J.; Badaracco, Jacob;
   Badaracco, Jake; Badarraco, J.;
   Badarraco, Jake
1918 The Inn of the Blue Moon
      Love's Law
      Wild Honey
1919 Bullin' the Bullsheviki
      Coax Me
      Miss Crusoe
      The Poison Pen
      The Steel King
      The Woman of Lies
1920 Nothing but Lies
      Nothing but the Truth
      The Very Idea
Badarracco, Amelia
1914 The House of Bondage
Bade, Annette
1920 A Woman's Business
Badger, Charles J.
1913 Victory
Badger, Clarence G. *same as* **Badger,**
   Clarence
1916 A Modern Enoch Arden
1918 The Floor Below
      Friend Husband
      The Kingdom of Youth
      A Perfect Lady
      The Venus Model
1919 Almost a Husband
      Daughter of Mine
      Day Dreams
      Jubilo
      Leave It to Susan
      Sis Hopkins
      Strictly Confidential
      Through the Wrong Door
1920 Cupid, the Cowpuncher
      Honest Hutch
      Jes' Call Me Jim
      The Man Who Lost Himself*
      The Strange Boarder
      Water, Water Everywhere
Badger, Robert
1919 The Four-Flusher
Badgley, Gerald
1917 The Heart of Ezra Greer
      Pots-and-Pans Peggy
      The Streets of Illusion
Badgley, Helen
1915 Milestones of Life
      The Price of Her Silence
1916 The Stolen Triumph
1917 The Candy Girl
      The Fires of Youth
      The Heart of Ezra Greer
      A Modern Monte Cristo
      Pots-and-Pans Peggy
Badgley, Lieut. Frank
1918 Too Fat to Fight
Baer, Arthur "Bugs" *same as* **Baer,**
   Bugs
1917 The Baseball Revue of 1917
1920 Headin' Home
      Up in Mary's Attic

Bageard, Jeanette *same as* **Berergard,**
   Jeanette
1915 The Fight
      Sunday
Baggot, King *same as* **Baggott, King**
1913 Ivanhoe
1914 Absinthe
1915 The Marble Heart
      The Suburban
1916 Half a Rogue
      The Man from Nowhere
1918 Kildare of Storm
1918-19
      The Missionary*
1919 The Man Who Stayed at Home
1920 The Cheater
      The Dwelling Place of Light
      The Forbidden Thing
      Life's Twist
      The Thirtieth Piece of Silver
Bagley, Edward
1918 Tell It to the Marines
Bagley, James
1915 How Molly Malone Made
      Good
Bail, Ben *same as* **Bail, Benjamin**
1919 Evangeline
1920 Are All Men Alike?
      From Now On
      The Strongest
Bailey, Bill *see* **Bailey, William**
Bailey, Consuelo
1914 The Gangsters
Bailey, Dan *could be same as* **Bailey,**
   Don
1917 His Old-Fashioned Dad
Bailey, Don *same as* **Baily, Don;** *could*
   be same as **Bailey, Dan**
1916 Redeeming Love
1917 The Blood of His Fathers
      Jack and Jill
      Money Madness
      Out of the Wreck
1918 Three X Gordon
1919 Blackie's Redemption
      Married in Haste
      The Shepherd of the Hills
      Should a Woman Tell?
1920 The Great Accident
Bailey, George
1916 Overalls
Bailey, Grace Helen
1917 Polly Put the Kettle On
      Sirens of the Sea
Bailey, Joseph
1914 The Banker's Daughter
Bailey, Oliver D.
1915 The Melting Pot
      The Whirl of Life
1920 Blind Love
Bailey, William *same as* **Bailey, Bill;**
   Bailey, W. N. "Bill"; Bailey,
   William "Bill"; Bailey, William N.
1914 The Banker's Daughter
      The Boundary Rider
1915 Conscience
      From the Valley of the Missing
      The Suburban
      When It Strikes Home
1916 A Coney Island Princess
      Man and His Soul
      A Million a Minute
      The Red Mouse
      War Brides
1917 The Inevitable
      On Dangerous Ground
      The Pride of New York
      Richard, the Brazen
1918 The Blind Adventure
      Bonnie Annie Laurie
      I'll Say So
      Leap to Fame
1919 Break the News to Mother
      Shadows of Suspicion
      Speedy Meade
      Three Black Eyes
Bain, Agnes Fletcher *same as* **Bain,**
   Agnes L.
1915 Maciste
1917 The Mystic Hour
1920 Sophy of Kravonia; Or, The
      Virgin of Paris

Bainbridge (full name unknown)
1919 Where's Mary?
Bainbridge, Mr.
1918 The Talk of the Town
Bainbridge, Rolinda
1914 One of Our Girls
1917 Chris and His Wonderful
      Lamp
1918 Social Quicksands
Bainbridge, Sherman
1915 Coral
1916 The Heart of Tara
1917 The Girl Who Won Out
Bainbridge, W. H. *same as* **Bainbridge,**
   William; Bainbridge, William H.
1917 The Bond Between
      The Desire of the Moth
      The Door Between
      The Marcellini Millions
      The Promise
      The Savage
      Under Handicap
1918 A Broadway Scandal
      Hands Down
      Hungry Eyes
      The Kaiser, the Beast of Berlin
      Mystic Faces
1919 Desert Gold
      Heart O' the Hills
1920 Bonnie May
      In Folly's Trail
      Seeing It Through
Baird, Leah
1913 Ivanhoe
1914 Absinthe
1916 The Lights of New York
      The People vs. John Doe
1917 The Devil's Pay Day
      The Fringe of Society
      One Law for Both
      Sins of Ambition
1918 Life or Honor?
      Moral Suicide
1919 As a Man Thinks
      The Capitol
      The Echo of Youth
      The Volcano
1920 Cynthia-of-the-Minute
Baird, Stewart
1915 The Incorrigible Dukane
      The Moth and the Flame
      The Runaway Wife
Baker, Mr.
1914 Mother
Baker, Mrs.
1913 Shadows of the Moulin Rouge
Baker, C. Graham
1920 The Vice of Fools
Baker, Dan
1915 Camille
1916 The Salamander
1918 Pay Day
Baker, Doris *same as* **Baker, Baby**
   Doris
1915 The Heart of Maryland
      Kilmeny
1916 The Hidden Law
1917 Glory
1918 Little Orphant Annie
1920 The Secret Gift
      Youth's Desire
Baker, Friend F. *same as* **Baker, Friend**
1915 The Long Chance
1916 Love Never Dies
      A Stranger from Somewhere
      20,000 Leagues Under the Sea
      What Love Can Do
1917 Bringing Home Father
      The Car of Chance
      The Clean-Up
      The Clock
      The Devil's Pay Day
      The Man Who Took a Chance
1918 The Bird of Prey
      The Devil's Wheel
      Her American Husband
      Kultur
      Nobody's Wife
      Painted Lips
      The Scarlet Road
      The Strange Woman
1919 Broken Commandments
      The Call of the Soul
      Chasing Rainbows

      Hell Roarin' Reform
      The Rebellious Bride
      The Sneak
      Thieves
      The Wilderness Trail
1920 Flame of Youth
      The Girl of My Heart
      Merely Mary Ann
      Trumpet Island
      Two Moons
Baker, G. B.
1920 Starvation
Baker, George D.
1915 The Dust of Egypt
      How Cissy Made Good
      A Price for Folly
1916 A Night Out
      The Pretenders
      The Shop Girl
      The Tarantula
      The Two Edged Sword
      The Wager
      The Wheel of the Law
1917 The Duchess of Doubt
      The End of the Tour
      His Father's Son
      The Lifted Veil
      Outwitted
      A Sleeping Memory
      Sowers and Reapers
      The White Raven
1918 The Demon
      Her Inspiration
      Hitting the High Spots
      In Judgment Of
      No Man's Land
      The Only Road
      The Return of Mary
      Revelation
      The Shell Game
      The Testing of Mildred Vane
      Toys of Fate
      Unexpected Places
1919 As the Sun Went Down
      Castles in the Air
      The Cinema Murder
      Faith
      In for Thirty Days
      The Lion's Den
      One-Thing-at-a-Time O'Day
      Peggy Does Her Darndest
      The Spender
      The Uplifters
1920 Heliotrope
      The Man Who Lost Himself
Baker, Graham
1917 The Flaming Omen
      The Grell Mystery
1918 The King of Diamonds
      Love Watches
1919 Daring Hearts
      The Girl Problem
1920 The Broadway Bubble
      The Fortune Hunter
      The Whisper Market
Baker, Harold
1913 The Star of India
Baker, Hettie Gray *same as* **Baker,**
   Hettie Grey
1914 Burning Daylight: The
      Adventures of "Burning
      Daylight" in Alaska
      Burning Daylight: The
      Adventures of "Burning
      Daylight" in Civilization
      The Chechako
      John Barleycorn
      An Odyssey of the North
      The Valley of the Moon
1915 A Fool There Was*
1916 A Daughter of the Gods
1917 The Honor System
Baker, Home Run
1917 The Baseball Revue of 1917*
Baker, Joseph
1914 The Marked Woman
1915 The Unbroken Road
1916 My Country First
Baker, Lee
1918 Just a Woman
      The Kingdom of Youth

27

Baker, Maude
1917 The Princess of Patches
Baker, Newton D. *same as* **Baker, Newton**
1918 The Men of the Hour*
1919 The Girl Who Stayed Home*
Baker, Richard Foster
1915 A Bunch of Keys
1916 The Little Girl Next Door
1918 Kidder and Ko
Baker, Robert M. *same as* **Baker, Robert**
1916 Flirting with Fate
The Flying Torpedo
1919 Counterfeit
Baker, Tarkington
1920 Her Five-Foot Highness
Human Stuff
Baker, Willis
1917 Little Miss Nobody
Baldridge, Sidney A. *same as* **Baldridge, S. A.**
1919 The Hellion
Yvonne from Paris
1920 The Blue Moon
The Gamesters
The Honey Bee
The House of Toys
A Light Woman
Their Mutual Child
Baldwin, Curley
1917 Fighting Back
1918 Desert Law
Little Red Decides
Wolves of the Border
Baldwin, Forrest
1918 Little Miss Hoover*
Baldwin, Frank D.
1914 The Indian Wars
1917 The Adventures of Buffalo Bill
Baldwin, G.
1915 Should a Mother Tell?
Baldwin, Kitty
1914 The Banker's Daughter
1915 Are You a Mason?
Over Night
1917 Magda
Baldwin, Ruth Ann
1914 Damon and Pythias
1917 '49-'17
A Wife on Trial
1919 Broken Commandments
Chasing Rainbows
Cheating Herself
The Sneak
1920 The Devil's Riddle
Balfore, Sue *see* **Balfour, Sue**
Balfour, Mrs. *see* **Balfour, Sue**
Balfour, Augustus *same as* **Balfour, August**
1914 The Lost Paradise
The Port of Missing Men
The Pride of Jennico
1915 The Curious Conduct of Judge Legarde
The Runaway Wife
1916 The Ruling Passion
1920 The Valley of Night
Balfour, Elsie
1915 The Bigger Man
The Governor's Boss
1916 The Straight Way
Balfour, Sue *same as* **Balfore, Sue; Balfour, Mrs.; Balfour, Mrs. Sue**
1914 The Little Gray Lady
The Ordeal
Springtime
1915 All for a Girl
The Avalanche
The Concealed Truth
Life Without Soul*
The Unbroken Road
1916 The Fortunate Youth
1917 Alias Mrs. Jessop
Draft 258
Miss Robinson Crusoe
The Slacker (Metro Pictures Corp.)
1918 Cyclone Higgins, D.D.
1919 The Indestructible Wife

Balfour, William
1917 A Son of the Hills
Ball, Miss *see* **Ball, Leona**
Ball, Eustace Hale
1913 Checkers
Ball, Leona *same as* **Ball, Miss**
1916 The Chaperon
The Return of Eve
Sherlock Holmes
Ballard, Alberta
1918 Revenge
Ballin, Hugo
1917 Baby Mine
The Cinderella Man
Fighting Odds
Nearly Married
The Spreading Dawn
Thais
1918 All Woman
Back to the Woods
The Beloved Traitor
The Danger Game
Dodging a Million
The Face in the Dark
The Fair Pretender
Fields of Honor
The Floor Below
Friend Husband
The Glorious Adventure
Hidden Fires
Just for Tonight
The Kingdom of Youth
Laughing Bill Hyde
Money Mad
Our Little Wife
Peck's Bad Girl
A Perfect Lady
The Service Star
The Splendid Sinner
Thirty a Week
The Turn of the Wheel
The Venus Model
1919 Bonds of Love
The Crimson Gardenia
Daughter of Mine
The Eternal Magdalene
Lord and Lady Algy
Shadows
Sis Hopkins
Strictly Confidential
The Stronger Vow
Upstairs
The World and Its Woman
1920 Help Yourself
Pagan Love
Ballin, Mabel
1917 For Valour
The Spreading Dawn
1918 The Danger Game
The Glorious Adventure
Laughing Bill Hyde
The Service Star
The Turn of the Wheel
1919 The Illustrious Prince
Lord and Lady Algy
The Quickening Flame
The White Heather
1920 Pagan Love
Under Crimson Skies
Ballou, Edward S.
1918 The King of Diamonds
Bally, George
1916 The Man from Manhattan
Balshofer, Fred J.
1915 Rosemary
The Silent Voice*
1916 The Come-Back
A Corner in Cotton
The Masked Rider
Pidgin Island
1917 The Avenging Trail
The Haunted Pajamas
The Hidden Spring
Paradise Garden
The Promise
The Square Deceiver
Under Handicap
1918 Broadway Bill
The Landloper
Lend Me Your Name
1919 A Man of Honor
1920 An Adventuress

Bambrick, Elsa
1917 The Bondage of Fear
Bambrick, Gertrude
1914 Liberty Belles
The Rejuvenation of Aunt Mary
1915 Divorçons
Bancroft, Miss
1914 The House of Bondage
Bancroft, George
1914 Il Trovatore
Bangs, Frank
1917 The Beautiful Adventure
The Runaway
The Unforseen
Banker, Emily
1917 The Last Sentence
Bankhead, Tallulah
1918 Thirty a Week
When Men Betray
Who Loved Him Best?
1919 The Trap
Banks, Bessie
1915 The House of a Thousand Scandals
1916 Dulcie's Adventure
Youth's Endearing Charm
Banks, Elton *see* **Fairbanks, Douglas**
Banks, Estar *same as* **Banks, Esta**
1916 Saints and Sinners
1917 At First Sight
1918 The Clutch of Circumstance
Her Mistake
Hit-the-Trail Holliday
The Love Net
The Sins of the Children
A Woman of Impulse
Banks, F. L.
1919 Injustice
Banks, Monte
1920 Too Much Johnson
Banks, Otis
1919 Injustice
Banks, Mrs. Otis
1919 Injustice
Banks, Perry
1915 The House of a Thousand Scandals
1916 Dulcie's Adventure
Faith
Land O' Lizards
Life's Blind Alley
The Man from Manhattan
Overalls
The Overcoat
1917 Melissa of the Hills
The Sea Master
Snap Judgement
1918 Ann's Finish
Powers That Prey
1919 Eve in Exile
Six Feet Four
A Sporting Chance (American Film Co.)
1920 The House of Toys
Banta, George W.
1920 Beware of the Bride
Bara, Theda
1915 Carmen (Fox Film Corp.)
The Clemenceau Case
Destruction
The Devil's Daughter
A Fool There Was
The Galley Slave
Kreutzer Sonata
Lady Audley's Secret
Sin
The Two Orphans
1916 East Lynne
The Eternal Sapho
Gold and the Woman
Her Double Life
Romeo and Juliet (Fox Film Corp.)
The Serpent
Under Two Flags
The Vixen
1917 Camille
Cleopatra
The Darling of Paris
Du Barry
Heart and Soul
Her Greatest Love

The Rose of Blood
The Tiger Woman
1918 The Forbidden Path
Salome
The She-Devil
The Soul of Buddha
Under the Yoke
When a Woman Sins
1919 La Belle Russe
Kathleen Mavourneen
The Light
Lure of Ambition
The Siren's Song
When Men Desire
A Woman There Was
Barbee, Richard
1916 Her Great Price
Barber, George I.
1915 The Devil's Daughter
Barber, La Verne
1915 The Billionaire Lord
Barbier, Peter *same as* **Barbierre, Peter**
1917 The Eternal Temptress
1918 The Fall of the Romanoffs
1920 The World and His Wife
Barbour, Edwin
1914 The Fortune Hunter
The House Next Door
The Wolf
Barclay, Lila *could be same as* **Barclay, Lola**
1914 The Sign of the Cross
1915 Prohibition
A Royal Family
The Sentimental Lady
Barclay, Lola *could be same as* **Barclay, Lila**
1915 Seven Sisters
Bardine, Mabel *same as* **Bordine, Mabel**
1917 The Barker
Mother Love and the Law
The Night Workers
1918 Beyond the Law
Rough and Ready
1920 The Bromley Case
The Place of Honeymoons
Thoughtless Women
Baring, Mathilde *same as* **Baring, Mathilda; Baring, Matilda**
1914 Fantasma
1916 According to Law
As a Woman Sows
Feathertop
The Haunted Manor
1918 Love's Law
The Panther Woman
Baring, Nancy
1916 The Soul of a Child
Barker, Mr.
1915 Du Barry
Barker, Adelaide *could be same as* **Barker, Adella**
1918 The Unchastened Woman
Barker, Adella *could be same as* **Barker, Adelaide**
1915 Time Lock Number 776
1916 Hypocrisy
Romeo and Juliet (Quality Pictures Corp.)
1917 One of Many
Red, White and Blue Blood
1918 With Neatness and Dispatch
Barker, B. *could be same as* **Barker, Bradley**
1915 The Little Gypsy
Barker, Barclay
1916 One Day
Barker, Bradley *same as* **Barker, H. Bradley; could be same as* **Barker, B.**
1915 The Earl of Pawtucket
The Luring Lights
The Moth and the Flame
What Happened to Jones
1916 The City of Illusion
Common Sense Brackett
Her American Prince
Her Husband's Wife
A Woman's Honor
1917 Billy and the Big Stick
The Jury of Fate
Little Miss Fortune
A Man and the Woman

Barrows, James O. *same as* **Barrows, James**
1919 Brothers Divided
  The Lord Loves the Irish
1920 Dangerous to Men
  Down Home
  The Inferior Sex
  Unseen Forces
  The Untamed
  When Dawn Came
  The White Dove

Barrows, John
1919 Common Clay

Barrows, William
1915 The Prince and the Pauper

Barry, Miss
1916 The Green-Eyed Monster

Barry, Claire Kane *could be same as* **Barry, Claire Lillian**
1920 The Invisible Divorce

Barry, Claire Lillian *could be same as* **Barry, Claire Kane**
1916 Playing with Fire
  The Soul Market
  The Spell of the Yukon

Barry, Eddie
1920 His Pajama Girl

Barry, Eleanor
1914 The Lion and the Mouse
  Michael Strogoff
  Through Fire to Fortune
1915 The Climbers
  The Great Ruby
  Heartaches
  The Nation's Peril
1916 The Flames of Johannis
1920 The Flaming Clue
  The Gauntlet

Barry, Gertrude
1918 Her Great Chance

Barry, Herbert
1913 Across the Continent
1916 Kennedy Square
1917 Panthea

Barry, J. A. (*dir, producing assistant*) *same as* **Barry, John A.**
1915 The Birth of a Nation*
1916 Intolerance*
1919 The Betrayal
  The Fear Woman
1920 Passion's Playground
  The Turning Point

Barry, John (*actor*)
1920 The Invisible Divorce

Barry, John A. *see* **Barry, J. A.** (*dir, producing assistant*)

Barry, Margaret
1919 Dawn
  The Moonshine Trail
1920 The Blood Barrier
  Respectable by Proxy

Barry, Pauline
1916 Gold and the Woman
  A Modern Thelma
  Sins of Men

Barry, Richard
1916 Lovely Mary
1917 Threads of Fate

Barry, Viola
1913 The Sea Wolf
1914 John Barleycorn
  Martin Eden
1916 The Flying Torpedo

Barry, Wesley
1918 Amarilly of Clothes-Line Alley
  How Could You, Jean?
  Johanna Enlists
1919 Daddy-Long-Legs
  Her Kingdom of Dreams
  Male and Female
  The Unpardonable Sin
  A Woman of Pleasure
1920 The County Fair
  Dinty
  Don't Ever Marry
  Go and Get It
  The White Circle

Barrymore, Ethel
1914 The Nightingale
1915 The Final Judgment
1916 The Awakening of Helena
  Richie
  The Kiss of Hate

1917 An American Widow
  The Call of Her People
  The Eternal Mother
  The Greatest Power
  Life's Whirlpool
  The Lifted Veil
  National Red Cross Pageant
  The White Raven
1918 Our Mrs. McChesney
1919 The Divorcee

Barrymore, John
1914 An American Citizen
  The Man from Mexico
1915 Are You a Mason?
  The Dictator
  The Incorrigible Dukane
1916 The Lost Bridegroom
  Nearly a King
  The Red Widow
1917 National Red Cross Pageant
  Raffles, the Amateur
   Cracksman
1918 On the Quiet
1919 Here Comes the Bride
  The Test of Honor
1920 Dr. Jekyll and Mr. Hyde
   (Famous Players-Lasky
   Corp.)

Barrymore, Katherine Harris
1918 The House of Mirth

Barrymore, Lionel
1914 Classmates
  The Seats of the Mighty
  The Span of Life
  The Power of the Press
  Under the Gaslight
  The Woman in Black
1915 The Curious Conduct of Judge
   Legarde
  Dora Thorne
  The Flaming Sword
  A Modern Magdalen
  Wildfire
  A Yellow Streak
1916 The Brand of Cowardice
  Dorian's Divorce
  The Quitter
  The Upheaval
1917 The End of the Tour
  His Father's Son
  Life's Whirlpool
  The Millionaire's Double
  National Red Cross Pageant
1920 The Copperhead
  The Devil's Garden
  The Master Mind
  The Valley of Night

Barstar, A. H.
1914 The Last Volunteer

Barter, H. H.
1916 20,000 Leagues Under the Sea

Barthelmess, Richard *same as* **Barthelmess, Richard S.**
1916 Just a Song at Twilight
  War Brides
1917 Bab's Burglar
  Bab's Diary
  The Eternal Sin
  For Valour
  The Moral Code
  Nearly Married
  The Seven Swans
  The Soul of a Magdalen
  The Streets of Illusion
  The Valentine Girl
1918 Hit-the-Trail Holliday
  The Hope Chest
  Rich Man, Poor Man
  Sunshine Nan
  Wild Primrose
1919 Boots
  Broken Blossoms
  The Girl Who Stayed Home
  I'll Get Him Yet
  Peppy Polly
  Scarlet Days
  Three Men and a Girl
1920 The Idol Dancer
  The Love Flower
  Way Down East

Bartholomae, Philip
1916 The Serpent
1917 The Cigarette Girl
  The Mark of Cain

  Stranded in Arcady
  The Streets of Illusion
  Sylvia of the Secret Service
1918 The Other Woman

Bartholomew, Miss
1914 Brewster's Millions

Bartlett, Capt.
1914 Rescue of the Stefansson Arctic
   Expedition

Bartlett, Aline
1916 The Fourth Estate

Bartlett, Charles E. *same as* **Bartlett, Charles; Bartlett, Charles Earl**
1916 The Bruiser
  The Craving
  The Girl Who Doesn't Know
  The Thoroughbred (American
   Film Co.)
1917 Hell Hath No Fury
1920 Dangerous Love

Bartlett, Don
1918 A Diplomatic Mission
1920 The Fortune Hunter

Bartlett, Harry
1917 The Little Duchess
1918 Her Mistake
  Wanted, a Mother
1919 The Volcano
1920 The Copperhead

Bartlett, Lanier
1914 The Spoilers
1915 The Rosary
1916 A Gamble in Souls
  Jim Grimsby's Boy
  The Ne'er-Do-Well
1917 Princess of the Dark
1918 Madame Sphinx
  The Man Above the Law
  Marked Cards
  Tongues of Flame
1920 The Servant in the House

Bartlett, Richard
1915 The Pretenders

Bartley, Henry
1920 The Woman God Sent

Barton, Charles
1920 The County Fair

Barton, Grace
1917 Great Expectations
  The Raggedy Queen
1918 Madame Jealousy
1919 Heart of Gold
1920 The Harvest Moon

Barton, John
1920 The Sin That Was His

Barton, Julien
1917 Burning the Candle
  Filling His Own Shoes
  The Night Workers

Bary, Leon
1918 The Yellow Ticket
1920 Kismet

Basi, Philip
1916 Fruits of Desire

Basil, Joe
1919 Bullin' the Bullsheviki

Baskette, Lena
1917 The Gates of Doom
  Polly Put the Kettle On
1919 The Weaker Vessel

Bass, J. B.
1919 Injustice

Bassett, Russell
1914 Behind the Scenes
  Such a Little Queen
1915 The Commanding Officer
  Fanchon the Cricket
  The Fatal Card
  The Heart of Jennifer
  Jim the Penman
  Little Pal
  The Masqueraders
  May Blossom
  The Morals of Marcus
  Sold
1916 A Coney Island Princess
  Diplomacy
  Hulda from Holland
  Less Than the Dust
  Little Lady Eileen
  Nearly a King
  The Quest of Life
  The Traveling Salesman

1917 Broadway Jones
  The Honeymoon
  The Public Be Damned
  Seven Keys to Baldpate
1918 Hit-the-Trail Holliday

Baston, J. Thornton *same as* **Baston, Thornton**
1918 Empty Pockets
1920 The Fighting Kentuckians
  The Good-Bad Wife
  The Tiger's Cub
  The White Moll

Bateman, Helen
1917 The Planter

Bateman, Victory
1915 Kilmeny*
1916 The Power of Evil
  Romeo and Juliet (Fox Film
   Corp.)
1918 The Service Star
1920 Beautifully Trimmed
  Cinderella's Twin

Bates, Arthur W. *same as* **Bates, Arthur**
1915 The Alster Case
  The Man Trail
1916 The Phantom Buccaneer
  Vultures of Society
1917 The Night Workers
1918 Uneasy Money

Bates, Blanche
1918 The Border Legion

Bates, Frank
1916 The Dawn of Love
1917 The Avenging Trail

Bates, Granville
1917 The Kill-Joy
  Young Mother Hubbard

Bates, J. C.
1918 Her Boy

Bates, Jack
1913 Ivanhoe

Bates, Les
1920 Skyfire

Bates, Louise *same as* **Bates, Louise Emerald; Bates, Louise M.**
1915 Inspiration
1916 Her Father's Gold
  The Men She Married
  Silas Marner
1917 Arms and the Girl
  The Easiest Way
  Wrath of Love
1918 The Marionettes

Bates, Mae
1917 The Rise of Jennie Cushing

Bates, Tom
1916 Her Father's Son
  The Parson of Panamint
  A Son of Erin
1917 Little Lost Sister
  The Varmint
1918 Huck and Tom; Or, The
   Further Adventures of Tom
   Sawyer
  A Petticoat Pilot
  The Spirit of '17
1919 Children of Banishment
  The Home Town Girl
  An Innocent Adventuress
  Who Cares?
1920 An Arabian Knight
  Burglar Proof
  The Devil's Riddle
  Huckleberry Finn
  The Invisible Divorce

Battista, Archie
1917 Sister Against Sister

Battista, Miriam
1918 Eye for Eye
1920 Humoresque

Battista, William
1917 Sister Against Sister

Bauchens, Anne *same as* **Bauchens, Ann**
1918 The Squaw Man
1919 Don't Change Your Husband
  For Better, for Worse

Bauer, Arthur *same as* **Bower, A.; Bower, Arthur**
1914 Cardinal Richelieu's Ward
1915 God's Witness
  The Last Concert
  Milestones of Life
  The Mill on the Floss

The Squaw Man
Too Many Millions
The Whispering Chorus
The White Man's Law
1919 Everywoman
In Mizzoura
Johnny Get Your Gun
Louisiana
The Red Lantern
Under the Top
The Valley of the Giants
A Very Good Young Man
The Woman Next Door
1920 Dinty
The Fighting Shepherdess
Go and Get It
Love Madness
The Mark of Zorro
The Mutiny of the Elsinore
The Sagebrusher
The Scoffer
The Sea Wolf
Why Tell?

Beery, Noah, Jr. (1884-1946) *see* **Beery, Noah** (1884-1946)
Beery, Noah, Jr. (*born* 1915) son of **Beery, Noah** (1884-1946)
1920 The Mark of Zorro

Beery, Wallace
1915 The Slim Princess
1918 Johanna Enlists
1919 Behind the Door
The Life Line
The Love Burglar
Soldiers of Fortune
The Unpardonable Sin
Victory
1920 813
The Last of the Mohicans
The Mollycoddle
Rookie's Return
The Round-Up
The Virgin of Stamboul

Beery, William
1917 The Spirit of '76

Begeman, Dwight
1917 The Duchess of Doubt

Beggs, Lee
1913 Ten Nights in a Barroom
1914 The Folks from Way Down East
Winning His First Case

Begley, Ed
1918 Marriages Are Made

Behrens, Arthur
1919 Where Bonds Are Loosed
1920 Dad's Girl

Behrens, William
1916 Whispering Smith

Beitel, Dr.
1915 The Woman

Beith, Ian Hay *same as* **Hay, Ian**
1917 The Little American
1919 Male and Female*

Bekum, Frank *see* **Dekum, Frank**

Belasco, David
1914 A Good Little Devil
Rose of the Rancho
1915 The Case of Becky
The Fighting Hope
The Girl of the Golden West
The Governor's Lady
The Warrens of Virginia*
The Woman

Belasco, Jay
1915 Lord John in New York
1916 Bobbie of the Ballet
The Gilded Spider
The Grasp of Greed
The Grip of Jealousy
The Price of Silence
Tangled Hearts
1917 Lorelei of the Sea
1918 Three X Gordon
1919 Life's a Funny Proposition
1920 Dollar for Dollar
Help Wanted—Male
Jenny Be Good
The Palace of Darkened Windows
Smoldering Embers

Belasco, Walter
1915 Judge Not; Or, The Woman of Mona Diggings
A Little Brother of the Rich
Lord John in New York
1916 The Eagle's Wing
From Broadway to a Throne
The Grip of Jealousy
John Needham's Double
What Love Can Do
1917 The Car of Chance
A Jewel in Pawn
1918 Alias Mary Brown
The Kaiser, the Beast of Berlin

Belcher, Charles
1920 The Mark of Zorro

Belcher, Frank *same as* **Belcher, Frank H.**
1915 The Danger Signal
The Green Cloak
Keep Moving
The Sentimental Lady
1916 The Devil's Prayer-Book
The Final Curtain
Wild Oats
1917 Mrs. Balfame
The Recoil
1918 On the Quiet

Belford, Hazel
1916 The Deserter

Belgrade, Adele
1917 Happiness

Bell, Charles
1918 The Sunset Princess

Bell, Digby
1914 The Education of Mr. Pipp
1915 Father and the Boys

Bell, Emma
1917 The Undying Flame

Bell, F. Gatenbery *same as* **Bell, F. G.**
1915 An Enemy to Society
1918 The Make-Believe Wife

Bell, Gaston
1913 The Third Degree
1914 The Daughters of Men
The Fortune Hunter
The Gamblers
The House Next Door
The Lion and the Mouse
The Wolf
1915 Destruction
1919 The Heart of a Gypsy

Bell, Gladys
1919 Stripped for a Million

Bell, Hank
1920 The Last Straw

Bell, Ralph
1918 Denny from Ireland
1919 The Four-Flusher
Please Get Married

Bell, Tula *see* **Belle, Tula**

Bella, Della
1915 The Eternal City

Bellairs, Betty
1915 The Spanish Jade
1917 God's Man

Bellamy, Madge
1920 The Riddle: Woman

Bellamy, Quex
1918 The Spreading Evil

Belle, Tula *same as* **Bell, Tula**
1916 A Bird of Prey
The Brand of Cowardice
1917 Over the Hill
The Vicar of Wakefield
The Woman and the Beast
1918 At the Mercy of Men
The Blue Bird
A Doll's House
1919 Deliverance
Gates of Brass
1920 Old Dad

Belleville, Frederic de *same as* **Belleville, Frederick de**
1915 The Daughter of the People
A Trade Secret

Bellew, Warren G.
1916 La Vie de Boheme*

Bellinger, Roberta
1918 The Splendid Sinner

Bellingford, William
1917 Sudden Jim

Bellon, Andre
1917 The Amazons

Belmar, Henry
1916 The Raiders
1917 The Desert Man
Whither Thou Goest

Belmont, Baldy
1919 Yankee Doodle in Berlin
1920 Love, Honor and Behave

Belmont, Joseph
1915 The Martyrs of the Alamo
1918 The Return of Mary
Up Romance Road

Belmont, Mrs. Morgan
1920 Way Down East

Belmore, Daisy
1915 The Stubbornness of Geraldine
1917 Bab's Burglar
Bab's Matinee Idol
The Seven Swans
1919 His Bridal Night

Belmore, Lionel
1915 The Greater Will
1916 Britton of the Seventh
The Supreme Sacrifice
1917 Shame
1918 The Beautiful Mrs. Reynolds
His Royal Highness
Leap to Fame
Wanted, a Mother
The Wasp
1920 Duds
Godless Men
The Great Lover
Jes' Call Me Jim
Madame X
The Man Who Had Everything
Milestones
The Strange Boarder

Belwin, Alma
1915 The Ivory Snuff Box

Bencivenga, Edoardo
1915 Du Barry

Bendel, Henri
1919 Shadows*

Bender, Chief
1917 The Baseball Revue of 1917*

Benedetta, Marie
1918 The Rose of the World

Benedict XV
1914 His Holiness, the Late Pope Pius X, and the Vatican

Benedict, Edgar Ellis
1917 Man and Beast

Benedict, Kingsley
1915 Judge Not; Or, The Woman of Mona Diggings
1916 The Bugler of Algiers
The Crippled Hand
Love Never Dies
What Love Can Do
1917 Man and Beast
The Plow Woman
1918 After the War
1919 Who Will Marry Me?

Benham, Dorothy
1916 The Fugitive
The Path of Happiness
1917 Weavers of Life

Benham, Grace
1915 Lord John in New York
1916 Alien Souls
The Flirt

Benham, Harry
1913 Moths
Robin Hood
1914 Frou Frou
1916 The Man Inside
The Mischief Maker
Pamela's Past
The Path of Happiness
1917 The Dancer's Peril
The Last of the Carnabys
The Outsider
Putting the Bee in Herbert
The Warfare of the Flesh
When You and I Were Young
1918 Cecilia of the Pink Roses
Convict 993
1920 The Dangerous Paradise
For Love or Money

Polly with a Past
The Prey
The Victim

Benham, Leland
1915 Milestones of Life
1916 The Path of Happiness

Benner, Yale
1915 Vanity Fair
The Way Back
1916 The Catspaw
Other People's Money
The Pillory
1917 A Wife by Proxy

Bennet, John D. *see* **Bennett, John Drew**

Bennett, Alma
1919 The Right to Happiness

Bennett, Arnold *same as* **Bernot, Arnold**
1918 Battling Jane

Bennett, Belle
1914 Mrs. Wiggs of the Cabbage Patch
1915 Mignon
1916 Sweet Kitty Bellairs
1917 Ashes of Hope
Because of a Woman
The Bond of Fear
The Charmer
Fires of Rebellion
The Fuel of Life
1918 The Atom
The Last Rebel
The Lonely Woman
The Reckoning Day
A Soul in Trust
1919 The Mayor of Filbert

Bennett, Billie
1917 Mothers of Men
1919 The Girl from Outside
1920 The Courage of Marge O'Doone
Fighting Cressy
The Parish Priest

Bennett, Charles
1914 Tillie's Punctured Romance
1917 The Rainbow Girl
1918 The Bride of Fear
1919 All Wrong

Bennett, Chester
1917 The Lair of the Wolf
1919-20 When a Man Loves
1920 Captain Swift
A Master Stroke
The Purple Cipher
The Romance Promoters

Bennett, Constance
1914 Fighting Death

Bennett, Enid
1917 The Girl Glory
Happiness
The Little Brother
The Mother Instinct
Princess of the Dark
They're Off
1918 The Biggest Show on Earth
Coals of Fire
A Desert Wooing
Fuss and Feathers
Keys of the Righteous
The Marriage Ring
Naughty, Naughty!
The Vamp
When Do We Eat?
1919 Happy Though Married
The Haunted Bedroom
The Law of Men
Partners Three
Stepping Out
The Virtuous Thief
What Every Woman Learns
1920 The False Road
Hairpins
Her Husband's Friend
Silk Hosiery
The Woman in the Suitcase

Bennett, Frank *same as* **Bennett, Frank Fisher**
1914 The Dishonored Medal
1916 Casey at the Bat
Gretchen, the Greenhorn
The Heiress at Coffee Dan's
Intolerance
Reggie Mixes In
A Sister of Six

Sold for Marriage
Stranded
1917 Her Official Fathers
The Jury of Fate
The Little Yank
Lost in Transit
Stagestruck
1918 The Eyes of Mystery
1919 The Man Who Stayed at Home

Bennett, H. J.
1917 The Car of Chance

Bennett, John Drew *same as* **Bennet, John D.**
1916 The Blue Envelope Mystery
1917 One Touch of Nature

Bennett, Joseph *same as* **Bennett, Joe**
1917 Indiscreet Corinne
1918 Crown Jewels
Faith Endurin'
The Golden Fleece
The Grey Parasol
The Last Rebel
Limousine Life
The Love Brokers
Marked Cards
The Reckoning Day
1919 The Feud
Man's Desire
1920 The Gamesters
The Terror
Their Mutual Child
Youth's Desire

Bennett, Margaret
1918 An American Live Wire

Bennett, Margery *same as* **Bennett, Marjorie**
1917 The Girl Glory
1918 Hugon, the Mighty
The Midnight Patrol
Naughty, Naughty!

Bennett, Richard
1914 Damaged Goods
1916 And the Law Says
Philip Holden—Waster
The Sable Blessing
The Valley of Decision
1917 The Gilded Youth
National Red Cross Pageant*
1919 The End of the Road
Secret Marriage

Bennett, Robert
1920 Forty-Five Minutes from Broadway

Bennett, Whitman
1920 The Devil's Garden
The Master Mind
The Truth About Husbands

Bennett, Wilda
1914 A Good Little Devil
1920 Love, Honor and Obey

Bennington, Marshall Bruce
1918 The Danger Zone

Bennison, Louis
1914 Damaged Goods
1915 Pretty Mrs. Smith
1918 Oh, Johnny!
1919 High Pockets
A Misfit Earl
The Road Called Straight
Sandy Burke of the U-Bar-U
Speedy Meade

Benny, B. H.
1916 Vengeance Is Mine

Benoit, Georges *same as* **Benoit, George**
1915 Carmen (Fox Film Corp.)
Regeneration
1916 Blue Blood and Red
The Serpent
1917 The Broadway Sport
The Derelict
The Honor System
The Scarlet Letter
When False Tongues Speak
1920 The Little 'Fraid Lady
On with the Dance
The Scarlet Dragon
The Stealers
The Wonder Man

Benoit, Victor
1914 The Greyhound
1915 Children of the Ghetto
The Devil's Daughter
A Fool There Was

1916 The Chain Invisible
The Fourth Estate
1917 Little Shoes
1918 Woman and Wife

The Bensings
1914 Mrs. Wiggs of the Cabbage Patch

Benson, Clyde
1915 The Circular Staircase
The Long Chance
1916 The Beast
Civilization's Child
If My Country Should Call
The Mainspring
1917 The Clean-Up
The Flashlight
Triumph
1918 The Girl Who Wouldn't Quit
Green Eyes
More Trouble
The Romance of Tarzan
The Savage Woman
1919 The Best Man
A Daughter of the Wolf
The False Code
Gates of Brass
Jane Goes A-Wooing
Maggie Pepper
The Sheriff's Son
1920 Live Sparks
The Virgin of Stamboul

Benson, Juliette
1920 The Shadow of Rosalie Byrnes

Benson, Millard
1916 The Red Widow

Benson, William Shepherd
1913 Victory

Benton, Curtis
1915 Conscience
1916 Jealousy
The Strength of the Weak
20,000 Leagues Under the Sea
1917 The Siren

Benton, Marie
1916 The Question

Benton, Viola
1916 The World Against Him

Benyon, George *see* **Beynon, George W.**

Benzing, Alma Speer
1918 The Divine Sacrifice

Beranger, Charles S. *see* **Beranger, Clara S.**

Beranger, Clara S. *same as* **Beranger, Clara; Beranger, Charles S.**
1915 Anna Karenina
From the Valley of the Missing
The Galley Slave
Her Mother's Secret*
Princess Romanoff
1916 Sudden Riches*
1917 The Debt
The Dormant Power
The Greater Woman*
Mary Moreland
The Mirror
Mrs. Balfame*
Motherhood (Frank Powell Producing Corp.)
The Slave Market
1918 The Appearance of Evil
The Beloved Blackmailer
By Hook or Crook
Dolly Does Her Bit
The Golden Wall
The Grouch
The Interloper
The Love Net
Milady O' the Beanstalk
The Voice of Destiny
The Way Out
Winning Grandma
1919 The Bluffer
Bringing Up Betty
Come Out of the Kitchen
Dust of Desire
The Firing Line
Girls
The Hand Invisible
Heart of Gold
Hit or Miss
The Little Intruder
Phil-for-Short
The Praise Agent
Sadie Love

The Unveiling Hand
Wanted—A Husband
1920 Blackbirds
Civilian Clothes
The Cost
Dr. Jekyll and Mr. Hyde (Famous Players-Lasky Corp.)
The Fear Market
Flames of the Flesh
Half an Hour
Judy of Rogue's Harbor
White Youth

Beranger, George A. *same as* **Beranger, George; Beranger, George Andre; Beringer, J. A.; Berranger, George A.; Berringer, George**
1914 The Avenging Conscience
Home, Sweet Home
1915 The Absentee
The Birth of a Nation
1916 Flirting with Fate
The Good Bad Man
The Half-Breed
Intolerance
Manhattan Madness
Mixed Blood
Pillars of Society
1917 A Daughter of the Poor
A Love Sublime
The Spotted Lily
Those Without Sin
Time Locks and Diamonds
1918 Sandy
1919 Broken Blossoms
1920 A Manhattan Knight
Uncle Sam of Freedom Ridge

Berenson, Meyer
1918 Come On In

Berergard, Jeanette *see* **Bageard, Jeanette**

Beresford, Miss
1915 A Continental Girl

Beresford, Florence
1917 Rasputin, the Black Monk
1918 The Beautiful Mrs. Reynolds
Her Final Reckoning

Beresford, Frank S. *same as* **Beresford, Frank; Beresford, Frank G.**
1915 The Earl of Pawtucket
The Man of Shame
1917 Outcast
1918 The Border Raiders
Innocent's Progress
1919 The Bishop's Emeralds
Carolyn of the Corners
The Devil's Trail
Impossible Catherine
Paid in Full

Beresford, Vera
1918 A Daughter of the Old South
The Divine Sacrifice
1919 Paid in Full

Beresford, Vincent
1917 The Martinache Marriage

Berg, Geraldine
1916 Rose of the Alley

Berg, Irene
1916 Romeo and Juliet (Quality Pictures Corp.)

Berg, S. M. *same as* **Berg, Samuel**
1915 The Battle Cry of Peace
1916 Romeo and Juliet (Quality Pictures Corp.)
1917 Within the Law

Bergen, Gertrude H.
1919 The Unknown Quantity*

Bergen, Thurlow
1914 The Boundary Rider
A Prince of India
1915 The Little Gypsy
Prohibition
The Running Fight
1916 The City
The Lottery Man
A Woman's Fight
1919 The Love Auction
Lure of Ambition
1920 Blind Love

Berger, Rea
1916 Bluff
The Craving
A Million for Mary

The Overcoat
Purity
Three Pals
The Undertow*
The Valley of Decision
The Voice of Love
1918 Danger Within
The Magic Eye

Bergère, Ouida
1915 At Bay
Via Wireless
1916 Arms and the Woman
Big Jim Garrity
New York
The Romantic Journey
1917 The Iron Heart
Kick In
The On-the-Square-Girl
1918 The Hillcrest Mystery
Innocent
A Japanese Nightingale
More Trouble
The Narrow Path
1919 The Avalanche
The Broken Melody
Common Clay
Counterfeit
The Cry of the Weak
Our Better Selves
The Profiteers
A Society Exile
The Witness for the Defense
1920 Idols of Clay
On with the Dance
The Right to Love

Bergere, Valerie
1917 The Wild Girl

Bergman, Aleene
1920 The Flapper

Bergman, Helmer Walton *same as* **Bergman, H. W.; Bergman, Helmer W.**
1916 An Enemy to the King
1917 Aladdin from Broadway
The Man of Mystery
The Stolen Treaty
Womanhood, the Glory of the Nation
1920 You Never Can Tell

Bergman, Henry *same as* **Bergman, Henri**
1915 Destiny; Or, The Soul of a Woman
An Enemy to Society
The House of Tears
The Melting Pot
One Million Dollars
The Right of Way
1916 In the Diplomatic Service
Man and His Angel
1917 The Black Stork

Bergman, Leo
1916 The Spell of the Yukon

Bergman, Neil
1916 The Devil at His Elbow
1917 Bridges Burned
The Secret of Eve

Bergquist, Henry *could be same as* **Bergquist, Rudolph J.**
1919 The Red Lantern*

Bergquist, Rudolph J. *same as* **Bergquist, R. J.; Bergquist, Rudolph; could be same as Bergquist, Henry**
1915 The White Sister
1916 The Half Million Bribe
In the Diplomatic Service
Romeo and Juliet (Quality Pictures Corp.)
The Stolen Triumph
1917 The Adopted Son
Red, White and Blue Blood
Their Compact
The Voice of Conscience
1918 The Brass Check
His Bonded Wife
A Pair of Cupids
Social Quicksands
Under Suspicion
1919 After His Own Heart
The Four-Flusher
Full of Pep
The Great Romance
In His Brother's Place
Shadows of Suspicion

The Way of the Strong
1920 Billions
The Heart of a Child
Madame Peacock
Stronger Than Death
Beringer, J. A. see **Beranger, George A.**
Berkeley, Mr.
1916 The Flower of No Man's Land
Berkeley, Gertrude
1915 The Soul of Broadway
The Two Orphans
1916 War Brides
1917 The Iron Heart
Over There
1918 Just Sylvia
The Song of Songs
1919 Break the News to Mother
The Way of a Woman
Berkeley, Mowbray
1919 Fires of Faith
Berlin, Minnie
1915 The Last Concert
Berliner, Rudolph
1920 The Great Shadow
Berlinger, Milton
1920 Birthright
Bern, Paul
1920 Greater Than Love
The North Wind's Malice
Women Men Forget
Bernard, Barney
1916 Intolerance
Phantom Fortunes
A Prince in a Pawnshop
1919 The Mother and the Law
Bernard, Dick
1915 Poor Schmaltz
Bernard, Dorothy
1915 The Broken Law
The District Attorney
Dr. Rameau
Gambier's Advocate
The Little Gypsy
Princess Romanoff
A Soldier's Oath
The Song of Hate
1916 The Bondman
Fighting Blood
A Man of Sorrow
Sins of Men
Sporting Blood
1917 The Accomplice
The Final Payment
The Rainbow
1918 Les Miserables
1920 The Great Shadow
Bernard, Edward
1918 A Perfect 36
1920 Help Yourself
Bernard, Harry
1916 Bluff
Bernard, Josephine
1920 Way Down East
Bernard, Lester
1916 Phantom Fortunes
A Prince in a Pawnshop
Bernard, Sam
1915 Poor Schmaltz
Berner, Bernice
1914 The Tangle
1915 What Happened to Father
Bernhardt, Sarah
1919 It Happened in Paris
Bernot, Arnold see **Bennett, Arnold**
Bernoudy, Jane
1915 A Little Brother of the Rich
1917 The Girl in the Checkered Coat
Mr. Opp
Bernstein, Isadore same as **Bernstein, Isidore**
1913 Buried Alive in a Coal Mine*
1917 Loyalty
Who Knows?
1918 Humility
The Romance of Tarzan
Tarzan of the Apes
Berranger, George A. see **Beranger, George A.**
Berrell, George same as **Berrell, George W.; Berrill, George** could be same as **Berrill, Mr.**

1916 Bettina Loved a Soldier
Drugged Waters
The People vs. John Doe
The Three Godfathers
1917 The Flashlight
The Lair of the Wolf
The Man from Montana
Straight Shooting
1919 As the Sun Went Down
Hell Roarin' Reform
In for Thirty Days
1920 The Barbarian
The City of Masks
The Dwelling Place of Light
Pollyanna
The U.P. Trail
Berri, Maud Lillian
1917 Glory
Berrill, Mr. could be same as **Berrell, George**
1915 The Long Chance
Berrill, George see **Berrell, George**
Berringer, George see **Beranger, George A.**
Berry, W. T.
1915 The Pageant of San Francisco
Berse, Lillian
1918 When Men Betray
Berst, J. A.
1920 Women Men Forget
Bert, Mabel
1920 Blackbirds
Berte, Genevieve
1920 The Galloping Devil
Berthelet, Arthur
1916 The Chaperon
The Havoc
The Misleading Lady
The Return of Eve
Sherlock Holmes
1917 The Golden Idiot
Little Shoes
Pants
The Saint's Adventure
Young Mother Hubbard
1918 Beauty and the Rogue
Men Who Have Made Love to Me
Bertholon, George
1917 Thais
1918 Our Little Wife
Bertholon, George, Jr.
1920 The Little 'Fraid Lady
Bertona, Daniel
1914 Forgiven; Or, The Jack of Diamonds
1916 The Sunbeam
Bertram, Helen
1914 The Lightning Conductor
Bertram, William
1914 Damaged Goods
1917 The Little Patriot
Tears and Smiles
The Understudy
1918 Cupid by Proxy
Daddy's Girl
A Daughter of the West
Dolly Does Her Bit
Dolly's Vacation
Milady O' the Beanstalk
The Voice of Destiny
Winning Grandma
1919 The Arizona Cat Claw
The Old Maid's Baby
The Sawdust Doll
Bertsch, Marguerite
1914 Captain Alvarez
A Florida Enchantment
A Million Bid
My Official Wife
1915 The Cave Man
The Man Behind the Door
Mortmain
1916 The Dawn of Freedom
The Devil's Prize
For a Woman's Fair Name
The Law Decides
Salvation Joan
Through the Wall
The Vital Question
The Writing on the Wall
1917 The Glory of Yolanda
The Soul Master

1919 The Painted World
Shadows of the Past
The Wreck
Berwin, Isabel same as **Berwin, Isabelle**
1916 Miss Petticoats
1917 The Social Leper
The Strong Way
Sunshine Alley
The Woman Beneath
1918 The Beloved Blackmailer
The Interloper
Love's Conquest
Prunella
Beryll, Eddie
1919 Open Your Eyes
Besley, Captain J. Campbell
1914 The Captain Besley Expedition
1915 In the Amazon Jungles with the Captain Besley Expedition
Besserer, Eugenie
1915 The Carpet from Bagdad
The Circular Staircase
I'm Glad My Boy Grew Up to Be a Soldier
The Rosary
1916 The Crisis
The Garden of Allah
The Ne'er-Do-Well*
Thou Shalt Not Covet
1917 Beware of Strangers
The Curse of Eve
Little Lost Sister
Who Shall Take My Life?
1918 The City of Purple Dreams
The Eyes of Julia Deep
A Hoosier Romance
Little Orphant Annie
The Road Through the Dark
The Sea Flower
The Still Alarm
1919 Auction of Souls
The Greatest Question
Scarlet Days
Turning the Tables
1920 The Brand of Lopez
Fickle Women
The Fighting Shepherdess
For the Soul of Rafael
Forty-Five Minutes from Broadway
The Gift Supreme
The Scoffer
Seeds of Vengeance
What Happened to Rosa
Bessie, a bear
1919 It's a Bear
Best, George
1916 The Land Just Over Yonder
Best, H. M.
1916 Ramona
The Years of the Locust
Best, Louise
1920 Oil
Best, Lucille
1920 Neptune's Bride
Best, Martin same as **Best, Martyn**
1918 The Seal of Silence
Unexpected Places
1920 The Chorus Girl's Romance
Betchel, William see **Bechtel, William**
Bethew, Herbert
1920 Beautifully Trimmed
Under Northern Lights
Bettelheim, The Misses
1920 April Folly
Betts, Dorothy
1920 A Dark Lantern
Betts, Matthew L. (actor) same as **Betz, Matthew; Betz, Matthew L.**
1919 Checkers
Putting One Over
1920 Good References
High Speed
The Stealers
Betts, Peggy
1918 Empty Pockets
Betz, Fredie
1916 The Female of the Species
The Sorrows of Love

Betz, Matthew L. see **Betts, Matthew L.** (actor)
Betz, Matthew von (dir)
1917 Modern Mother Goose
Bevan, Billy
1920 Love, Honor and Behave
Beveridge, Phyllis
1918 The Triumph of Venus
Bevis, Ted
1918 Tarzan of the Apes*
Bey, Terza
1915 The Slim Princess
Beyers, Clara same as **Byers, Clara**
1914 Salomy Jane
1915 The Lily of Poverty Flat
Mignon
Under Southern Skies
1916 Autumn
Half a Rogue
The Narrow Path
The Strength of the Weak
Temptation and the Man
1917 Little Miss Nobody
1918 Sporting Life
1919 L'Apache
1920 What Women Want
Beyfuss, Alexander E. same as **Beyfuss, Alex E.**
1914 Salomy Jane
1915 Mignon
1916 The Unwritten Law*
Beynon, George W. same as **Benyon, George; Beynon, George**
1915 The Gentleman from Indiana
Jane
Peer Gynt
The Reform Candidate
The Yankee Girl
1916 The Corner
Tongues of Men
1918 Among the Cannibal Isles of the South Pacific
The Girl of My Dreams
1919 In Old Kentucky
Biala, Sara
1919 The Heart of a Gypsy
1920 The Fear Market
The Law of the Yukon
Bianca, Yolanda
1915 The Fairy and the Waif
Bianchi, Katherine same as **Bianchinne, Baby**
1917 The Last Sentence
1918 The Blue Bird
Bianchinne, Baby see **Bianchi, Katherine**
Biccary, Violet de see **De Biccari, Violet**
Bickel, George
1915 The Fixer
Keep Moving
The Politicians
Bickers, H. Sheridan
1918 Her Body in Bond
Biddle, Bruce
1918 Dodging a Million
Biddolph, Mathew see **Biddulph, Matthew**
Biddough, Matthew see **Biddulph, Matthew**
Biddulph, Matthew same as **Biddolph, Mathew; Biddough, Matthew**
1919 A Fugitive from Matrimony
The Long Arm of Mannister
1920 Hitchin' Posts
Bierman, Emil
1916 Ramona
Big Otto
1915 Vengeance of the Wilds
Big Tree, Chief
1917 The Spirit of '76
Bigelow, Arthur
1913 The Tonopah Stampede for Gold
Bigson, Tom
1917 High Speed
Billings, Billie
1916 The Dawn of Freedom
The Enemy
The Girl Philippa
The Hunted Woman
The Redemption of Dave Darcey
Thou Art the Man

Blackton, J. Stuart, Jr.
1920 The Blood Barrier
Blackton, Paula
1919 The Littlest Scout
Blackton, Violet
1919 The Common Cause
A House Divided
The Littlest Scout
The Moonshine Trail
Blackwell, Carlyle
1914 The Key to Yesterday
The Man Who Could Not Lose
The Spitfire
Such a Little Queen
1915 The Case of Becky
The High Hand
Mr. Grex of Monte Carlo
The Puppet Crown
The Secret Orchard
1916 Broken Chains
The Clarion
His Brother's Wife
The Madness of Helen
The Ocean Waif
Sally in Our Alley
The Shadow of a Doubt
A Woman's Way
1917 The Burglar
The Crimson Dove
The Good for Nothing
The Marriage Market
National Association's All-Star
Picture
On Dangerous Ground
The Page Mystery
The Price of Pride
The Social Leper
A Square Deal
The Volunteer
Youth
1918 The Beautiful Mrs. Reynolds
The Beloved Blackmailer
By Hook or Crook
The Cabaret
The Golden Wall
His Royal Highness
Hitting the Trail
Leap to Fame
The Road to France
Stolen Orders
The Way Out
1919 Courage for Two
Hit or Miss
Love in a Hurry
Three Green Eyes
1920 The Restless Sex
The Third Woman
Blackwell, Irene
1918 The Glorious Adventure
Vengeance
1920 Empty Arms
Honor Bound
Blackwell, J. could be same as
Blackwell, James
1918 The Man Who Woke Up
Blackwell, James same as **Blackwell,**
Jim; could be same as **Blackwell, J.**
1914 The Only Son
1919 Over the Garden Wall
The Thunderbolt
1920 The Misfit Wife
Blackwood, John H.
1919 Easy to Make Money
Blackwood, Peggy
1920 Smiling All the Way
Blainey, Mr.
1916 Wall Street Tragedy
Blair, Helen
1917 The Spreading Dawn
Blair, Lottie May
1918 Hearts of Love
Blair, Nan
1919 Whom the Gods Would
Destroy
Blair, Ruth
1916 The Fourth Estate
Blair, Sidney
1917 Her Sister
Blair, Sofia
1914 The Dollar Mark

Blaisdell, Charles
1917 The Climber
The Inspirations of Harry
Larrabee
The Mainspring
Blaising, Harry
1915 The Long Chance
Blaize, Joe
1917 Chris and His Wonderful
Lamp
Blake, A. D. same as **Blake, Alva;**
Blake, Alva D.
1916 The Children in the House
The Heiress at Coffee Dan's
A Knight of the Range
Where Are My Children?
Blake, Anita see **Blake, Nina**
Blake, Ben K.
1920 Uncle Sam of Freedom Ridge
Blake, Grace
1917 Mothers of Men
Blake, J.
1918 The Heart of a Girl
Blake, Loretta
1915 The Absentee
Ghosts
The Sable Lorcha
1916 The Eternal Grind
His Picture in the Papers
1917 The Little Princess
1920 Just Out of College
Blake, Lucy
1917 The Devil's Bait
Sold at Auction
The Stolen Play
Blake, Marguerite
1916 The Supreme Temptation
Blake, Nina same as **Blake, Anita;**
Blake, Wina
1915 The Primrose Path
Blake, Tom same as **Blake, Thomas;**
Blake, Thomas F.
1915 Children of Eve
1917 The Avenging Trail
Knights of the Square Table
Rosie O'Grady
1918 Broadway Bill
A Pair of Cupids
1919 Out of the Fog
1920 Flying Pat
Marooned Hearts
The Wonderful Chance
Blake, Wina see **Blake, Nina**
Blakely, Walter
1917 The Lincoln Cycle
Blakemore, Donald
1918 Viviette
Blakemore, Harry same as **Blakemore,**
H. D.; Blakemore, Harry D.
1913 Arizona
1914 The Education of Mr. Pipp
In Mizzoura
Rip Van Winkle
1915 Always in the Way
Under Southern Skies
1916 In the Diplomatic Service
Life's Shadows
Lovely Mary
The Traveling Salesman
Blanc, Julia
1915 Monsieur Lecoq
The Seventh Noon
Blanc, Margaret
1918 The Scarlet Trail
Blanchard, Agnes
1917 Lorelei of the Sea
Blanchard, Dudley
1916 The Lash
Oliver Twist
1917 Freckles
The Jaguar's Claws
Rebecca of Sunnybrook Farm
Blanchard, Eleanore
1916 Life's Whirlpool
Blanchette, Dell
1915 The Cowpuncher
Blancke, Kate same as **Blanke, Kate**
1915 Should a Mother Tell?
The Whirl of Life
1916 The Brand of Cowardice
The Pretenders

1917 The Duchess of Doubt
The End of the Tour
A Sleeping Memory
Sowers and Reapers
The Tiger Woman
The Trail of the Shadow
1918 The Danger Game
Lest We Forget
A Successful Adventure
1920 Heart Strings
Blandick, Clara
1914 Mrs. Black Is Back
1916 The Stolen Triumph
1917 Peggy, the Will O' the Wisp
Blaney, Charles E.
1914 The Dancer and the King
Blanke, Kate see **Blancke, Kate**
Blatch, Harriot Stanton
1913 Eighty Million Women Want-?
Blau, Leila
1916 The Crown Prince's Double
Bleecker, Katherine Russel
1919 Sing-Sing and Great Meadows
Prison*
Blessing, Christine
1914 Dope
Bletcher, William
1919 The Love Hunger
Blevins, Malcolm
1915 The Reform Candidate
1916 The Eagle's Wing
From Broadway to a Throne
1917 The Terror
1918 An American Live Wire
Blind, Eric
1916 Jaffery
Then I'll Come Back to You
The Woman in 47
Blinn, B. F.
1920 The Blooming Angel
Common Sense
Blinn, Genevieve same as **Blynn,**
Genevieve
1916 The Spider and the Fly
A Wife's Sacrifice
1917 American Methods
Cleopatra
Conscience
Du Barry
The Rose of Blood
Tangled Lives
1918 The Rainbow Trail
Salome
True Blue
When a Woman Sins
1919 In Search of Arcady
The Last of the Duanes
When Fate Decides
Wings of the Morning
The Woman Next Door
1920 The Path She Chose
Sundown Slim
The Tattlers
Blinn, Holbrook
1915 The Boss
A Butterfly on the Wheel
The Family Cupboard
The Ivory Snuff Box
1916 The Ballet Girl
The Hidden Scar
Husband and Wife
Life's Whirlpool
The Prima Donna's Husband
The Unpardonable Sin
The Weakness of Man
1917 The Empress
Pride
The Seventh Sin
Blinn, Marjorie same as **Blynn,**
Marjorie
1916 Where Are My Children?
The Whirlpool of Destiny
1917 The Girl Who Couldn't Grow
Up
Bliss, George
1915 The Rights of Man: A Story of
War's Red Blotch
Bliss, Leila
1915 Pretty Mrs. Smith
1919 The Loves of Letty

Block, Sheridan
1914 The Sign of the Cross
1915 The Soul of Broadway
The Two Orphans
1916 The Dragon
Blonkhall, H.
1919 Virtuous Men
Blood, Adele
1916 The Devil's Toy
1920 The Riddle: Woman
Bloom, Abraham
1915 Hearts Aflame*
Bloome, A. J.
1919 The Greater Sinner
Bloomer, J.
1915 The Heights of Hazard
Bloomer, Raymond
1916 Kennedy Square
1918 Out of a Clear Sky
The Prodigal Wife
A Woman of Impulse
1919 The Belle of New York
Break the News to Mother
1920 The Vice of Fools
Blossom, Henry Martyn same as
Blossom, Henry
1913 Checkers
1915 In the Shadow
Blossom, Marjorie
1915 What Happened to Jones
Blount, Frank M. same as **Blount,**
Frank
1919 Behind the Door
The Grim Game
1920 Down Home
Blow, Grace
1917 Vera, the Medium
Blow, Lila same as **Blow, Leila**
1916 The Lights of New York
1917 The Natural Law
1918 The Menace
Social Quicksands
1919 The Miracle of Love
Blue, Monte
1916 The Matrimaniac*
The Microscope Mystery
1917 Betrayed
Betsy's Burglar
Hands Up!
Jim Bludso
The Man from Painted Post
The Ship of Doom
1918 Johanna Enlists
M'liss
The Only Road
The Red, Red Heart
Riders of the Night
The Romance of Tarzan
The Squaw Man
Till I Come Back to You
1919 Everywoman
In Mizzoura
Pettigrew's Girl
Romance and Arabella
Rustling a Bride
Told in the Hills
1920 A Cumberland Romance
Something to Think About
The Thirteenth Commandment
Too Much Johnson
1921 The Jucklins
"Blue Grass," the horse
1915 Blue Grass
Blum, Sam
1918 The Blue Bird
1920 Headin' Home
Blumenfeld, Jack
1920 The Wonder Man
Blynn, Genevieve see **Blinn, Genevieve**
Blynn, Marjorie see **Blinn, Marjorie**
Blythe, Betty
1917 His Own People
1918 All Man
The Business of Life
A Game with Fate
The Green God
Hoarded Assets
The King of Diamonds
The Little Runaway
Miss Ambition
A Mother's Sin
Over the Top
Tangled Lives

1919 Beating the Odds
Beauty-Proof
Dust of Desire
Fighting Destiny
The Man Who Won
Silent Strength
The Undercurrent
1920 Burnt Wings
The Mischief Man
Nomads of the North
Occasionally Yours
The Silver Horde
The Third Generation

Blythe, Samuel G.
1920 Go and Get It

Boardman, Dixon
1917 Trooper 44

Boardman, True
1915 The Barnstormers
The Pitfall
1918 Danger Within
The Doctor and the Woman
Molly, Go Get 'Em
Tarzan of the Apes

Boardman, Virginia
1919 The House of Intrigue

Bob, the dog
1919 Blind Husbands

Bobo, a puppy
1917 Pants

Boch, Frida
1914 Thou Shalt Not

Bock, Frederick
1914 The Port of Missing Men

Boeger, Arthur
1915 The Devil's Daughter
1917 The Debt
1919 The Forfeit
The Unbroken Promise
1920 Honeymoon Ranch

Boehm, Vera
1919 The Undercurrent

Bogart, Harvey
1917 Life's Whirlpool

Bogel, Claus
1916 Saint, Devil and Woman

Bohamar, Miss
1919 The Bramble Bush

Bohan, Elizabeth Baker
1916 The Argonauts of
California—1849

Boland, Mary
1915 The Edge of the Abyss
1916 The Price of Happiness
The Stepping Stone
1917 Mountain Dew
1918 The Prodigal Wife
1919 The Perfect Lover
A Woman's Experience
1920 His Temporary Wife

Bolder, Robert *same as* **Bolder, Bobbie;
Bolder, Bobby; Boulder, Bobby;
Boulder, Robert**
1914 One Wonderful Night
1915 The Victory of Virtue*
1917 The Dream Doll
Fools for Luck
Sadie Goes to Heaven
Young Mother Hubbard
1918 Arizona
1919 A Gentleman of Quality
The Highest Trump
His Official Fiancée
Strictly Confidential
Upstairs
Words and Music By—
1920 The Beggar Prince
Burning Daylight
The Furnace
The Girl in Number 29
Her Beloved Villain
Sick Abed

Bolles, Florence C. *same as* **Bolles,
Florence**
1917 The Dormant Power
The False Friend
The Social Leper
1918 The Fair Pretender
1919 The American Way

Bolling, Robert
1917 Hate

Bolton, Guy
1918 Marriage

Bolton, Henry
1919 The Girl Alaska

Bonavita, Captain Jack
1917 The Woman and the Beast*

Bond, Clark
1920 The Sagebrusher

Bond, Frank
1920 An Adventuress*

Bond, Fred *same as* **Bond, Frederick**
1918 Me und Gott
The She-Devil
1919 The Lost Princess
1920 Fickle Women
The Hell Ship

Bond, Lucille
1920 Dangerous Trails

Bond, Raymond
1913 Tess of the D'Urbervilles
1914 In Mizzoura

Bondhill, Gertrude
1915-16
The Sins That Ye Sin
1916 The Awakening of Bess Morton
The Unborn
1919 Miss Arizona

Bonelli, William
1915 An American Gentleman

Bongini, R.
1920 Lifting Shadows

Boniel, Bessie
1916 The Innocence of Lizette

Bonn, Frank *same as* **Bonn, Frank A.**
1916 Ben Blair
The Code of Marcia Gray
David Garrick
Madame La Presidente
1918 Who Killed Walton?

Bonnell, Harry
1915 The Warning*

Bonner, Frank
1919 Hawthorne of the U.S.A.
1920 Terror Island

Bonner, Marjorie
1914 The Master Cracksman
The Seats of the Mighty

Bonner, Priscilla
1920 Homer Comes Home
Honest Hutch
The Man Who Had Everything
Officer 666

Booker, Beulah
1918 The Finger of Justice
1919 The Boomerang
1920 The Dwelling Place of Light
The Saphead

Boone, Charles
1916 The Light of Happiness

Boone, Daniel E.
1915 The Turn of the Road

Boone, Dell
1917 Shame
1918 On the Quiet
1919 Other Men's Wives
1920 The Honey Bee
Through Eyes of Men

Boone, John *could be same as* **Boone,
John A.**
1915 Alias Jimmy Valentine

Boone, John A. *could be same as*
Boone, John
1919 The Right to Lie
1920 Birthright

Booth, Anita
1920 The Shadow of Rosalie Byrnes

Booth, Edwin
1916 The Seekers

Booth, Elmer
1914 Mrs. Black Is Back

Booth, Evangeline
1919 Fires of Faith*

Booth, Mary
1916 The Pawn of Fate

Booth, Sydney
1914 Your Girl and Mine: A
Woman Suffrage Play

Boots, the dog
1920 Occasionally Yours

Borden, Eugene
1917 Draft 258
The Slacker (Metro Pictures
Corp.)
Think It Over
1918 Cyclone Higgins, D.D.
The Liar
Revelation
1920 The Stealers

Bordine, Mabel *see* **Bardine, Mabel**

Borein, Edward *could be same as*
Boring, Edward *or* **Boring, Edwin**
1916 The World Against Him

Bori, Rita
1916 The Smugglers
1917 The Heart of a Lion

Boring, Edward *could be same as*
Borein, Edward *or* **Boring, Edwin**
1916 A Daughter of the Gods
The Ruling Passion

Boring, Edwin *could be same as* **Borein,
Edward** *or* **Boring, Edward**
1915 The Bigger Man
1916 Romeo and Juliet (Quality
Pictures Corp.)
1917 Draft 258
1918 The Birth of a Race

Boros, Ferike
1918 Her Boy

Borrero, Inez
1920 His House in Order

Borrup, Doan
1918 Ruling Passions

Borzage, Frank
1914 Samson*
The Typhoon
The Wrath of the Gods
1915 Aloha Oe
The Cup of Life
1916 Immediate Lee
Land O' Lizards
1917 Fear Not
Flying Colors
A Mormon Maid
A School for Husbands
Until They Get Me
Wee Lady Betty
1918 The Curse of Iku
The Ghost Flower
The Gun Woman
An Honest Man
Innocent's Progress
The Shoes That Danced
Society for Sale
Who Is to Blame?
1919 Prudence on Broadway
Toton
Whom the Gods Would
Destroy
1920 Humoresque

Bosburg, Jack
1917 Princess Virtue*

Bosch, Mr.
1915 Mistress Nell

Bosco, Wallace
1913 Ivanhoe

Boshell, Ada
1915 Not Guilty
1917 The Beautiful Adventure
1920 Blackbirds

Boshell, William
1920 In Search of a Sinner

Boss, Yale
1917 Knights of the Square Table

Bost, Herbert
1919 Injustice

Bostwick, Edith
1914 Samson

Bostwick, Elwood Fleet
1914 A Factory Magdalen

Bostwick, Herbert *same as* **Boswick,
Herbert**
1914 Doc
1915 Cap'n Eri
1917 Strife

Bostwick, Phyllis
1914 Frou Frou

Boswick, Herbert *see* **Bostwick, Herbert**

Bosworth, Hobart
1913 The Sea Wolf
1914 Burning Daylight: The
Adventures of "Burning
Daylight" in Alaska
Burning Daylight: The
Adventures of "Burning
Daylight" in Civilization
The Chechako
The Country Mouse
John Barleycorn
Martin Eden
An Odyssey of the North
The Pursuit of the Phantom
The Valley of the Moon
1915 The Beachcomber
Buckshot John
Business Is Business
Colorado
Fatherhood
Help Wanted
A Little Brother of the Rich
Little Sunset
Nearly a Lady
Pretty Mrs. Smith
The Scarlet Sin
Tainted Money
'Twas Ever Thus
The White Scar
1916 Doctor Neighbor
The Iron Hand
Joan the Woman
Oliver Twist
The Target
Two Men of Sandy Bar
The Way of the World
The Yaqui
1917 Betrayed
The Devil-Stone
Freckles
The Inner Shrine
The Little American
A Mormon Maid
Unconquered
What Money Can't Buy
The Woman God Forgot
1918 The Border Legion
1919 Behind the Door
1920 Below the Surface
The Brute Master
His Own Law
A Thousand to One

Boteler, Wade
1919 23 1/2 Hours' Leave
A Very Good Young Man
1920 The Cup of Fury
The False Road
Lahoma
Let's Be Fashionable
An Old Fashioned Boy
She Couldn't Help It
Water, Water Everywhere

Bottomley, Roland
1915 The Green Cloak
1916 The Black Crook

Boucicault, Rene
1916 His Picture in the Papers

Boughton, Beryle
1915 The Long Chance

Boulden, Edward *same as* **Boulden,
Eddie; Bouldon, Edward; Bouldon,
Edwin**
1916 Somewhere in Georgia
1918 The Venus Model
1920 Bachelor Apartments
The Plunger

Boulder, Bobby *see* **Bolder, Robert**

Bouldon, Edwin *see* **Boulden, Edward**

Bourgeois, Paul
1913 A Prisoner in the Harem

Bourke, Fan *same as* **Bourke, Fanny**
1914 Beating Back
1915 Right off the Bat
1920 The Love Expert

Bourke, Ina *see* **Rorke, Ina**

Bouton, Betty
1919 Daddy-Long-Legs
The Final Close-Up
Heart O' the Hills
A Man's Fight
Three Men and a Girl
1920 Don't Ever Marry
The Hell Ship

The Mollycoddle
Bowden, Marjorie Claire
1918 The Star Prince
Bowell, Charles
1919 The Profiteer
Bower, A. see **Bauer, Arthur**
Bower, Lulu May same as **Bowers, Lulu**
1916 The Matrimonial Martyr
1917 When a Man Sees Red
Bowers, John same as **Bowers, John E.**
1915 The Little Dutch Girl
      The Woman Pays
1916 Destiny's Toy
      The Eternal Grind
      Hulda from Holland
      Madame X
      The Reward of Patience
1917 Betsy Ross
      The Bondage of Fear
      Darkest Russia
      The Divorce Game
      Easy Money
      Maternity
      A Self-Made Widow
      Shall We Forgive Her?
      The Strong Way
      The Tenth Case
1918 The Cabaret
      Heredity
      Joan of the Woods
      Journey's End
      The Oldest Law
      The Sea Waif
      The Spurs of Sybil
      Stolen Hours
      T'Other Dear Charmer
      The Way Out
      A Woman of Redemption
1919 Daughter of Mine
      Day Dreams
      The Loves of Letty
      The Pest
      Sis Hopkins
      Strictly Confidential
      Through the Wrong Door
      What Love Forgives
1920 A Cumberland Romance
      Godless Men
      Out of the Storm
      The Woman in Room 13
Bowers, Lulu see **Bower, Lulu May**
Bowers, Robert Hood
1916 A Daughter of the Gods
      War Brides
Bowes, Clifford
1920 Up in Mary's Attic
Bowes, Edward J.
1915 The Kindling
Bowker, Virginia
1917 The Trufflers
1918 A Pair of Sixes
      Uneasy Money
Bowles, Donald
1917 The Squaw Man's Son
Bowman, Laura
1920 The Brute
Bowman, Palmer
1914 The Royal Box
Bowman, William J. same as **Bowman, William**
1915 Pennington's Choice
      Rosemary
      The Second in Command
      The Silent Voice
1916 The Bait
      From Broadway to a Throne
      The Heart of Tara
1919 The False Faces
Bowser, Charles
1916 The Wager
1917 The Price She Paid
      Yankee Pluck
Boyd, Charles A.
1917 A Mother's Ordeal
Boyd, Marguerite
1915 Stop Thief!
Boyd, Marie
1914 The Governor's Ghost
1915 In the Shadow

Boyd, William (actor, died 1935) same as **Boyd, William H.**
1913 The Star of India
1915 The Ringtailed Rhinoceros
      Stop Thief!
1916 The Kiss of Hate
1918 Marriages Are Made
      Virtuous Wives
1920 Blackbirds
      The City of Masks
      A City Sparrow
      The Six Best Cellars
1921 The Jucklins
Boyle, Francis J.
1915 The Chocolate Soldier
Boyle, Irene
1914 The School for Scandal
1915 Children of the Ghetto
1918 Heart of the Sunset
1920 The Dead Line
      Other Men's Shoes
Boyle, John (actor)
1916 The Yellow Passport
1917 Kick In
Boyle, John (cam) see **Boyle, John W.**
Boyle, John W. (cam) same as **Boyle, John** (cam); **Boyle, John William**
1915 Greater Love Hath No Man
      Her Great Match
      My Madonna
1916 The Fall of a Nation
1917 Cleopatra
      Du Barry
      Kick In
      The Rose of Blood
1918 The Forbidden Path
      Salome
      The She-Devil
      The Soul of Buddha
      Under the Yoke
      When a Woman Sins
1919 The Last of the Duanes
      The Lone Star Ranger
      The Siren's Song
      When Men Desire
      Wings of the Morning
      A Woman There Was
1920 The Adventurer
      Drag Harlan
      Heart Strings
      If I Were King
      The Joyous Troublemaker
      The Orphan
      The Scuttlers
Boyle, John William see **Boyle, John W.**
Boyle, Joseph C. same as **Boyle, Joe; Boyle, Joseph**
1915 The Cowardly Way
      Sealed Lips
1916 The Struggle
1917 The Planter*
1919 In Mizzoura
      Rose O' the River
      Secret Service
      The Woman Thou Gavest Me
1920 Civilian Clothes
Brabin, Charles J. same as **Brabin, Charles**
1915 The House of the Lost Court
      The Raven
1916 The Price of Fame
      That Sort
1917 The Adopted Son
      Babette
      Persuasive Peggy
      Red, White and Blue Blood
      The Sixteenth Wife
1918 Breakers Ahead
      Buchanan's Wife
      Gay and Festive Claverhouse
      His Bonded Wife
      A Pair of Cupids
      The Poor Rich Man
      Social Quicksands
1919 La Belle Russe
      God's Outlaw*
      Kathleen Mavourneen
      Thou Shalt Not
1920 Blind Wives
      While New York Sleeps
Brace, Fred S. same as **Brace, Freddie; Brace, Frederick S.**
1917 The Awakening of Ruth
      Builders of Castles

The Courage of the Common
      Place
      Cy Whittaker's Ward
      The Lady of the Photograph
      The Last Sentence
      The Royal Pauper
1919 Ginger
Bracey, Clara T.
1915 The Gambler of the West
Bracey, Sydney see **Bracy, Sidney**
Bracken, Bertram same as **Bracken, Bert**
1915 Beulah
      Comrade John
1916 East Lynne
      The Eternal Sapho
      The Shrine of Happiness
      Sporting Blood
1917 The Best Man
      A Branded Soul
      Conscience
      For Liberty
      The Inspirations of Harry
      Larrabee
      The Martinache Marriage
      The Primitive Call
1918 And a Still Small Voice
      Code of the Yukon
      The Moral Law
1919 The Boomerang
      In Search of Arcady
      The Long Arm of Mannister
1920 The Confession
      Harriet and the Piper
      Parted Curtains
Bracken, Mildred
1916 The Fall of a Nation
Bracy, Sidney same as **Bracey, Sidney; Bracey, Sydney; Bracy, Sid; Bracy, Sydney**
1913 Robin Hood
1915 God's Witness
1916 Elusive Isabel
      A Huntress of Men
      Little Miss Happiness
      The Man Inside
      Merely Mary Ann
      The Path of Happiness
      The Ragged Princess
      Temptation and the Man
1917 Crime and Punishment
      The Deemster
      The Long Trail
1918 The House of Mirth
      A Man's World
      The Million Dollar Mystery
      My Own United States
1919 Reclaimed: The Struggle for a
      Soul Between Love and Hate
1920 An Amateur Devil
      Food for Scandal
Bradbury, Mrs.
1917 The Captain of the Gray Horse
      Troop
Bradbury, Frederick
1920 The Cradle of Courage
Bradbury, James
1915 A Black Sheep
1916 At Piney Ridge
      The Garden of Allah
      The Valiants of Virginia
1919 The Pest
1920 Deadline at Eleven
Bradbury, Kitty
1918 You Can't Believe Everything
1920 The Brand of Lopez
Bradbury, R. see **Bradbury, Ronald**
Bradbury, R. S. see **Bradbury, Ronald**
Bradbury, Robert see **Bradbury, Ronald**
Bradbury, Robert North (prod, dir, writer)
1918 Nobody's Wife
1919 The Faith of the Strong
      Jacques of the Silver North
      The Last of His People
1920 The Courage of Marge
      O'Doone
      Into the Light
Bradbury, Ronald (actor, scen) same as **Bradbury, R.; Bradbury, R. S.; Bradbury, Robert**
1915 Colorado
      The White Scar

1916 A Gutter Magdalene
      The Race
      The Target
      Tennessee's Pardner
      To Have and to Hold
1917 When Men Are Tempted
1918 By the World Forgot
      Cavanaugh of the Forest
      Rangers
      The Wild Strain
Bradden, John D. same as **Braddon, John D.**
1916 A Daughter of the Gods
1918 Les Miserables
1919 Reclaimed: The Struggle for a
      Soul Between Love and Hate
1920 Blind Wives
      The Fortune Teller
      The Thief
      The Wonder Man
Bradford, Gardner
1920 Outside the Law
Bradford, Mr. see **Bradford, James C.**
Bradford, James C. same as **Bradford, Mr.; Bradford, James R.**
1918 The Blue Bird
      Wanted for Murder
1919 The Heart of Humanity
1920 Isobel; Or, The Trail's End
      Parted Curtains
      So Long Letty
      The Stealers
Bradley, Alma
1913 Arizona
Bradley, George
1917 Cy Whittaker's Ward
Bradley, Juliet
1918 The Triumph of Venus
Bradley, Ruth
1918 The Triumph of Venus
Bradley, Samuel R.
1920 Women Men Love
Bradley, W. Bruce
1918 The Birth of a Race
      My Own United States
Bradley, Willard King same as **Bradley, Will**
1920 Bitter Fruit
      Empty Arms
      The Scarlet Dragon
Bradshaw, Herbert
1919 The Fighting Roosevelts
      The Scar
Bradshaw, William H.
1917 A Trip Through Japan
Brady, Alice
1914 As Ye Sow
1915 The Boss
      The Lure of Woman
1916 The Ballet Girl
      Bought and Paid For
      The Gilded Cage
      Miss Petticoats
      The Rack
      Tangled Fates
      Then I'll Come Back to You
      La Vie de Boheme
      The Woman in 47
1917 Betsy Ross
      The Dancer's Peril
      Darkest Russia
      The Divorce Game
      Her Silent Sacrifice
      A Hungry Heart
      The Maid of Belgium
      Maternity
      National Association's All-Star
      Picture
      A Self-Made Widow
      A Woman Alone
1918 At the Mercy of Men
      The Better Half
      The Death Dance
      Her Great Chance
      In the Hollow of Her Hand
      The Knife
      The Ordeal of Rosetta
      The Spurs of Sybil
      The Trap
      The Whirlpool
      Woman and Wife
1919 The End of the Road
      His Bridal Night

The Indestructible Wife
Marie, Ltd.
Redhead
The World to Live In
1920 A Dark Lantern
The Fear Market
The New York Idea
Sinners

Brady, Cyrus Townsend
1915 A Child of God
The Heights of Hazard
1916 The Hero of Submarine D-2
My Lady's Slipper
Whom the Gods Destroy
1917 For France
The Marriage Speculation
Sunlight's Last Raid
Transgression
Womanhood, the Glory of the
Nation
1918 The Girl from Beyond
1919 Daring Hearts
1920 The Blood Barrier
Children of Destiny

Brady, Edwin J. *same as* **Brady, E. J.;**
Brady, Ed; Brady, Edward; Brady,
Edward J.
1916 The Mainspring
Spellbound
The Sultana
The Twin Triangle
1917 The Devil's Bait
Double Room Mystery
Fires of Rebellion
The Flame of Youth
God's Crucible
The High Sign
Indiscreet Corinne
The Learnin' of Jim Benton
Mutiny
The Reed Case
The Spindle of Life
The Stolen Play
Wild Sumac
1918 Beyond the Shadows
Deuce Duncan
Everywoman's Husband
Faith Endurin'
The Grey Parasol
The Gun Woman
Marked Cards
Old Hartwell's Cub
The Shoes That Danced
Who Killed Walton?
Wild Life
1919 Almost a Husband
Diane of the Green Van
The False Code
When Bearcat Went Dry
1920 The Kentucky Colonel
Terror Island
The Yellow Typhoon

Brady, Frank
1919 The Undercurrent

Brady, Jasper Ewing *same as* **Brady, J.**
E.
1914 The Little Angel of Canyon
Creek
The Tangle
1915 Hearts and the Highway
The Island of Regeneration
1916 Britton of the Seventh
The Hero of Submarine D-2
The Island of Surprise
My Lady's Slipper
The Surprises of an Empty
Hotel
1919 The Divorce Trap

Brady, W. J.
1917 The Accomplice

Brady, William (*actor*)
1917 The Regenerates

Brady, William A. (*prod*)
1913 Mexican War Pictures
1914 A Gentleman from Mississippi
1915 The Boss
A Butterfly on the Wheel
1916 All Man
The Almighty Dollar
The Ballet Girl
Bought and Paid For
The Crucial Test
The Gilded Cage
The Heart of a Hero

The Hidden Scar
His Brother's Wife
Husband and Wife
The Madness of Helen
The Man Who Stood Still
The Men She Married
Miss Petticoats
Paying the Price
The Perils of Divorce
The Rail Rider
The Revolt
Sally in Our Alley
The Scarlet Oath
Tangled Fates
The Velvet Paw
La Vie de Boheme
The Weakness of Man
A Woman's Power
A Woman's Way
The World Against Him
1917 The Adventures of Carol
As Man Made Her
The Awakening
The Beloved Adventuress
Betsy Ross
The Bondage of Fear
The Brand of Satan
The Burglar
The Corner Grocer
The Crimson Dove
The Dancer's Peril
Darkest Russia
Diamonds and Pearls
The Divorce Game
The Dormant Power
Easy Money
The False Friend
The Family Honor
Forget-Me-Not
A Girl's Folly
The Good for Nothing
The Guardian
Her Hour
The Iron Ring
The Little Duchess
The Maid of Belgium
The Man Who Forgot
Man's Woman
The Marriage Market
Maternity
Moral Courage
On Dangerous Ground
The Page Mystery
The Price of Pride
Rasputin, the Black Monk
The Red Woman
A Self-Made Widow
Shall We Forgive Her?
The Social Leper
Souls Adrift
A Square Deal
The Stolen Paradise
The Strong Way
The Tenth Case
The Tides of Fate
Tillie Wakes Up
The Volunteer
The Web of Desire
A Woman Alone
The Woman Beneath
Yankee Pluck
Youth
1918 The Beautiful Mrs. Reynolds
Broken Ties
The Cross Bearer
The Divine Sacrifice
Gates of Gladness
The Golden Wall
His Royal Highness
The Spurs of Sybil
Stolen Hours
Wanted, a Mother
The Wasp
Whims of Society
1919 Little Women

Bragdon, John
1916 Intolerance

Braham, Harry
1915 The Fight

Braham, Horace
1920 Twisted Souls

Braham, Lionel
1915 The Battle Cry of Peace
1916 Snow White

Braidon, Thomas A.
1919 Good Gracious, Annabelle

Braidwood, Flora
1919 Deliverance

Braidwood, Frank
1919 The Heart of Humanity
1920 Down Home
Going Some
Hearts Up
West Is West

Brainard, Francis
1920 The Heart of a Woman

Brainerd, Edith Rathbone Jacobs *see*
Rath, E. J.

Brainerd, J. Chauncey Corey *see* **Rath,**
E. J.

Brainerd, William
1916 God's Country and the Woman

Braithwaite, Shirley
1917 Chris and His Wonderful
Lamp

Brammall, Jack *same as* **Brammall,**
John; Brammel, Jack
1915 The Gambler of the West
The Wolf Man
1916 A House Built upon Sand
The Little School Ma'am
Macbeth
The Missing Links
The Wharf Rat
1917 A Love Sublime
1918 Confession
The Girl Who Came Back
Her Inspiration
1919 The Master Man
Rose O' the River
Six Feet Four
1920 The Skywayman
Terror Island

Brand, Anna Fielder
1916 Her Father's Son

Brandeis, Madeline
1918 The Star Prince

Brandt, Alfred
1913 The Battle of Gettysburg
1915 The Alien
1916 Civilization
Peggy

Brandt, Charles *same as* **Brandt,**
Charles C.; Brant, Charles
1914 The Fortune Hunter
The Wolf
1915 The Climbers
The College Widow
The District Attorney
The Great Ruby
The Rights of Man: A Story of
War's Red Blotch
The Sporting Duchess
1916 The Evangelist
Friday the Thirteenth
Nanette of the Wilds
The Soul Market
1918 The Beautiful Mrs. Reynolds
The Cross Bearer
The Gulf Between
1919 As a Man Thinks
A Misfit Earl
1920 The Master Mind

Brandt, Edwin
1914 The Millon Dollar Robbery

Brant, Charles *see* **Brandt, Charles**

Branton, William
1914 The Man Who Could Not Lose

Braughall, Jack
1920 Bright Skies

Braun, Gertrude
1918 The Birth of a Race
When Men Betray

Braun, Leo H. *same as* **Braun, Leo**
1920 Below the Surface
The Brute Master
Hairpins
Her Husband's Friend
His Own Law
Homer Comes Home
Homespun Folks
The Jailbird
The Leopard Woman
Let's Be Fashionable

Love
Love Madness
Rookie's Return
Silk Hosiery
A Thousand to One

Brautigam, Otto *same as* **Brautigan,**
George; Brautigan, Otto
1915 Vanity Fair
1916 The Flight of the Duchess
1918 The Triumph of Venus
1919 The Common Cause
Life's Greatest Problem
1920 Duds
Milestones

Brautigan, George *see* **Brautigam, Otto**

Bravo, Colonel Antonio
1915 Carmen (Fox Film Corp.)*

Brawn, Jack
1915 The Dust of Egypt
The Island of Regeneration
The Juggernaut
The Making Over of Geoffrey
Manning
1916 For a Woman's Fair Name
The Supreme Temptation

Bray, Helen
1917 Big Timber
Little Miss Optimist

Bray, Will H. *same as* **Bray, William**
H.
1917 Master of His Home
A Strange Transgressor
Wooden Shoes

Bray, William (*child actor*)
1918 My Cousin

Breakstone, Ben
1913 The Daughter of the Hills

Breamer, Sylvia *same as* **Bremer, Sylvia**
1917 The Cold Deck
The Millionaire Vagrant
The Narrow Trail
The Pinch Hitter
Sudden Jim
1918 The Family Skeleton
Missing
The Temple of Dusk
We Can't Have Everything
1919 The Common Cause
Dawn
A House Divided
The Moonshine Trail
1920 The Blood Barrier
My Husband's Other Wife
My Lady's Garter
Respectable by Proxy
Unseen Forces

Bredell, Elwood
1917 Southern Justice
Up or Down?

Bredesen, Henry *same as* **Bredeson,**
Henry
1915 Right off the Bat
1917 Polly Ann
1918 The Turn of a Card

Breen, Elizabeth
1919 Counterfeit

Breese, Edmund
1914 The Master Mind
The Walls of Jericho
1915 The Shooting of Dan McGrew
The Song of the Wage Slave
1916 The Lure of Heart's Desire
The Spell of the Yukon
The Weakness of Strength
1919 Someone Must Pay
1920 Chains of Evidence
A Common Level
His Temporary Wife

Breil, Joseph Carl *same as* **Breil, J. C.;**
Breil, Joseph C.; Briel, Joseph C.
1913 The Prisoner of Zenda
1915 The Birth of a Nation
Double Trouble
The Lily and the Rose
The Martyrs of the Alamo
The Penitentes
1916 Intolerance
The Wood Nymph
1918 The Birth of a Race
1919 The Betrayal*

Bremer, Sylvia see **Breamer, Sylvia**
Brennan, Mr.
1920 Sooner or Later
Brennan, Edward same as **Brenon, Edward**
1915 Black Fear
Fighting Bob
The Right of Way
The Woman Pays
1916 The Black Butterfly
Man and His Soul
The Quitter
The Red Mouse
The Wall Between
1919 The Woman Under Oath
Brennan, George
1915 The House of Tears
Brennan, Hazel see **Brennon, Hazel**
Brennan, J.
1920 The Hidden Light
Brennan, John
1916 The Devil's Needle
Brenner, Marjorie
1920 The Deep Purple
Brennon, Hazel same as **Brennan, Hazel**
1919 In Mizzoura
1920 The Paliser Case
Brenon, C. H.
1915 The High Road
Brenon, Edward see **Brennan, Edward**
Brenon, Herbert
1913 Ivanhoe
1914 Absinthe
Neptune's Daughter
1915 The Clemenceau Case
The Heart of Maryland
Kreutzer Sonata
Sin
The Soul of Broadway
The Two Orphans
1916 A Daughter of the Gods
The Marble Heart
The Ruling Passion
War Brides
1917 The Eternal Sin
The Lone Wolf
1918 Empty Pockets
The Fall of the Romanoffs
Brenon, Juliet
1917 The Eternal Sin
The Lone Wolf
Brent, Evelyn
1915 The Shooting of Dan McGrew*
1916 The Iron Woman
The Lure of Heart's Desire
Playing with Fire
The Soul Market
The Spell of the Yukon
The Weakness of Strength
1917 The Millionaire's Double
Raffles, the Amateur Cracksman
To the Death
Who's Your Neighbor?
1918 Daybreak
1919 Fool's Gold
The Glorious Lady
Help! Help! Police!
The Other Man's Wife
Bresee, Mr. see **Bresee, R. A.**
Bresee, R. A. same as **Bresee, Mr.**
1915 Emmy of Stork's Nest
A Yellow Streak
1916 The Child of Destiny
Her Debt of Honor
His Great Triumph
Bret, Tom (title writer)
1915 The Battles of a Nation
1916 America Preparing
1918 The Accidental Honeymoon
The Birth of a Race
The Face in the Dark
Lest We Forget
Pay Day
Rich Man, Poor Man
The Sunset Princess
Wives of Men
1920 Blind Love
The Sacred Flame
Breter, Lucille
1920 Neptune's Bride

Brett (full name unknown)
1915 The Fairy and the Waif*
Brett, Tommy (juvenile actor)
1917 Apartment 29
Brettone, May
1919 Redhead
Breuil, Betta
1918 A Daughter of France
Life or Honor?
When a Woman Sins
Brewer, Thurlow
1916 The Phantom Buccaneer
1917 Burning the Candle
Brewster, Eugene V.
1916 The Two Edged Sword
Breyer, Maggie same as **Breyer, Mrs.**
1916 The Sunbeam
1917 The Voice of Conscience
1918 Flower of the Dusk
Kildare of Storm
Social Hypocrites
Briac, Jean de
1920 The Frisky Mrs. Johnson
Brian, Donald
1915 The Voice in the Fog
1916 The Smugglers
Briand, Anna F.
1919 When Doctors Disagree
Brice, Betty see **Brice, Rosetta**
Brice, Rosetta same as **Brice, Betty**
1914 The Fortune Hunter
Michael Strogoff
The Wolf
1915 The Climbers
The College Widow
The District Attorney
A Man's Making
The Rights of Man: A Story of War's Red Blotch
The Sporting Duchess
1916 The Evangelist
The Gods of Fate
Her Bleeding Heart
Love's Toll
1917 Loyalty
Who Knows?
1918 Humility
1920 A Beggar in Purple
The Money-Changers
The Sagebrusher
The Spenders
The Third Generation
Brickert, Carl same as **Brickett, Carl**
1916 The Half Million Bribe
A Million a Minute
1917 Daughter of Maryland
1918 The Embarrassment of Riches
Briden, Garland
1916 The Sign of the Poppy
Bridges, Winona
1918 The Uphill Path
Briel, Joseph C. see **Breil, Joseph C.**
Brierley, Lloyd could be same as **Brierley, Thomas A.**
1920 813
Brierley, Thomas A. same as **Brierley, Thomas; Brierly, Thomas;** could be same as **Brierley, Lloyd**
1917 The Lust of the Ages
1918 The Border Wireless
Branding Broadway
Selfish Yates
The Tiger Man
1919 Breed of Men
John Petticoats
The Money Corral
Square Deal Sanderson
1920 The Toll Gate
Briggs, David
1920 The Miracle of Money
Briggs, M. J.
1917 The Eternal Sin
Briggs, Oscar
1917 The Slacker's Heart
Brille, William
1920 The Dangerous Paradise
Brinley, Charles
1920 Under Northern Lights
Brisbane, Arthur
1920 Go and Get It

Briscoe, Mr. see **Briscoe, J. F.**
Briscoe, J. F. same as **Briscoe, Mr.; Briscoe**
1915 Buckshot John*
1916 The Three Godfathers
1917 Fighting for Love
Briscoe, Lottie
1918 The House of Mirth
Bristol, Frank
1914 The Patchwork Girl of Oz
Bristow, Ninita
1913 The Inside of the White Slave Traffic
Britton, Edna
1919 A Scream in the Night
Britton, Leon D.
1920 Chains of Evidence
Broad, Kid
1918 A Romance of the Underworld
1918-19 Once to Every Man
1919 Love in a Hurry
Wanted—A Husband
1920 Easy to Get
Broadhurst, George
1914 The Call of the North
Broadley, Edward
1917 The Runaway
Broadwell, Robert B. same as **Broadwell, Robert**
1916 A Law unto Himself
Vengeance Is Mine
The Wasted Years
1917 The Painted Lie
1918 Branding Broadway
Brock, William
1919 The Perfect Lover
Brockwell, Gladys
1914 The Typhoon
1915 Double Trouble
A Man and His Mate
On the Night Stage
Up from the Depths
1916 The Crippled Hand
The End of the Trail
The Fires of Conscience
The Price of Power
Sins of Her Parent
1917 A Branded Soul
Conscience
For Liberty
Her Temptation
The Honor System
One Touch of Sin
The Price of Her Soul
The Soul of Satan
To Honor and Obey
1918 The Bird of Prey
The Devil's Wheel
Her One Mistake
Kultur
The Moral Law
The Scarlet Road
The Strange Woman
1919 Broken Commandments
The Call of the Soul
Chasing Rainbows
The Divorce Trap
The Forbidden Room
Pitfalls of a Big City
The Sneak
Thieves
1920 The Devil's Riddle
Flames of the Flesh
The Mother of His Children
The Rose of Nome
A Sister to Salome
White Lies
Brockwell, Lillian V.
1916 A Law unto Himself
Broderick, Robert
1913 Arizona
The Stranglers of Paris
1914 The Better Man
The Eagle's Mate
In the Name of the Prince of Peace
The Last Volunteer
One of Millions
The Redemption of David Corson
The Ring and the Man

1915 The Daughter of the People
The Dictator
Gambier's Advocate
Poor Schmaltz
The Prince and the Pauper
Still Waters
The White Pearl
1916 Arms and the Woman
One Day
1917 Bridges Burned
Daughter of Destiny
The Guardian
Youth
1918 Hit-the-Trail Holliday
Just for Tonight
The Sea Waif
1919 The Bishop's Emeralds
Me and Captain Kidd
The Open Door
The Rough Neck
1920 The Eternal Mother
The Shark
Brodie, Anne
1920 Headin' Home
Brodin, Norbert same as **Brodin, Norbert F.**
1919 Almost a Husband
The Gay Lord Quex
Toby's Bow
1920 Dollars and Sense
Going Some
The Great Accident
Officer 666
Stop Thief!
Brodsky, Benjamin
1917 A Trip Through China
Brodsky, Samuel
1919 The House Without Children
1920 Hidden Charms
Brody, Anne same as **Brody, Ann; Brody, Anna; Brody, Annie**
1916 The Suspect
1917 The Indian Summer of Dry Valley Johnson
Next Door to Nancy
The Princess of Park Row
The Soul Master
Who Goes There!
1918 One Thousand Dollars
1920 A Fool and His Money
Brody, Sally
1919 The Misleading Widow*
Broek, John van den same as **Broeck, John v. d.; Broeck, John Van de; Broek, John v. d.; Broek, John V. de; Vanderbroeck, John**
1916 The Rail Rider
The Velvet Paw
1917 Barbary Sheep
Exile
A Girl's Folly
The Law of the Land
The Poor Little Rich Girl
The Pride of the Clan
The Rise of Jennie Cushing
The Undying Flame
The Whip
1918 The Blue Bird
A Doll's House
Prunella
The Rose of the World
Sporting Life
Woman
Broening, Edward see **Broening, H. Lyman**
Broening, H. Lyman same as **Broenig, H. Lyman; Broening, Edward; Broening, Henry; Broening, Henry Lyman; Broening, Lyman**
1913 Caprice
Chelsea 7750
In the Bishop's Carriage
Leah Kleschna
1914 The County Chairman
The Lost Paradise
Marta of the Lowlands
Wildflower
1915 The Dancing Girl
David Harum
Heléne of the North
May Blossom
The Pretty Sister of Jose
Still Waters

Straight Shooting
1920 Common Sense
The Little Shepherd of
Kingdom Come
Water, Water Everywhere
Brown, Sedley
1916 The Mediator
1917 One Touch of Sin
1920 The Joyous Troublemaker
Brown, Virginia
1920 An Old Fashioned Boy
Brown, W. H. see **Brown, William H.**
Brown, William H. same as **Brown, Bill;**
Brown, W. H.; Brown, William
1915 The Wolf Man
A Yankee from the West
1916 Casey at the Bat
Don Quixote
Hell-to-Pay Austin
Hoodoo Ann
A House Built upon Sand
Intolerance
Little Meena's Romance
The Rummy
The Wharf Rat
1917 The Bad Boy
Cheerful Givers
1918 M'liss
The Whispering Chorus
1919 In Mizzoura
The Mother and the Law
The Valley of the Giants
1920 Big Happiness
The Dancin' Fool
The Fighting Chance
The Peddler of Lies
The Tree of Knowledge
Brown, Willis same as **Brown, Judge**
Willis
1914 A Boy and the Law
1917 The Girl Who Won Out
The Saint's Adventure
1918 The Spirit of '17
1920 Love and the Law
Brown, Winona
1915 Captain Courtesy
Brown, Yolande
1917 Her Hour
Browne, Betty could be same as **Brown,**
Betty
1920 What Women Want
Browne, Bothwell
1919 Yankee Doodle in Berlin
Browne, Earle same as **Brown, Earle**
1920 The Deep Purple
Headin' Home
Browne, Harry C. same as **Brown,**
Harry; Brown, Harry C.
1914 The Eagle's Mate
1915 The Heart of Jennifer
1916 The Big Sister
The Flower of No Man's Land
1917 Scandal
1918 The Inn of the Blue Moon
1919 The Battler
Browne, John B. (asst dir) same as
Brown, John (asst dir); **Browne,**
John
1918 The Honor of His House
The Mystery Girl
Old Wives for New
One More American
The White Man's Law
The Widow's Might
Browne, Kenneth
1915 Rumpelstiltskin
Browne, Lewis Allen
1918 The Soap Girl
1919 Spotlight Sadie
1920 The Dangerous Paradise
Marooned Hearts
The Road of Ambition
Browne, Pearl
1917 An American Widow
Browne, Porter Emerson
1918 Joan of Plattsburg
1919 The Fighting Roosevelts
Browne, W. Grahame
1915 Mrs. Plum's Pudding

Browne-Decker, Kathryn same as
Decker, Kathryn Browne; could be
same as Brown, Kitty
1915 The Beloved Vagabond
The Closing Net
The Fifth Commandment
1916 The Prima Donna's Husband
1917 The Pride of the Clan
Brownell, Miss
1915 Jewel
Brownell, John C.
1916 The Honor of Mary Blake
1917 The Boy Girl
The Girl by the Roadside
Little Miss Nobody
The Raggedy Queen
Susan's Gentleman
Brownell, Louise
1916 Bullets and Brown Eyes
The Conqueror
The Corner
The Green Swamp
The Honorable Algy
The Moral Fabric
Not My Sister
Shell Forty-Three
The Sin Ye Do
1918 Oh, Johnny!
Browning, Tod
1916 Atta Boy's Last Race
Intolerance
Sunshine Dad
1917 Hands Up!
Jim Bludso
The Jury of Fate
A Love Sublime
Peggy, the Will O' the Wisp
1918 The Brazen Beauty
The Deciding Kiss
The Eyes of Mystery
The Legion of Death
Petticoats and Politics*
Revenge
Set Free
Which Woman?
The Winding Trail*
1919 Bonnie, Bonnie Lassie
The Exquisite Thief
The Mother and the Law
The Petal on the Current
The Pointing Finger
The Unpainted Woman
The Wicked Darling
1920 Outside the Law
The Virgin of Stamboul
Browning, Will
1915 The Better Woman
Brownlee, Frank
1916 The Half-Breed
Intolerance
Sold for Marriage
1917 The Best Man
The Double Standard
The Inspirations of Harry
Larrabee
The Little Pirate
The Martinache Marriage
Mentioned in Confidence
The Mysterious Mr. Tiller
The Mysterious Mrs. M.
The Phantom Shotgun
The Ship of Doom
Wild Sumac
1918 The Empty Cab
$5,000 Reward
Her Moment
Me und Gott
The Return of Mary
The Vanity Pool
1919 Brass Buttons
The Brute Breaker
Desert Gold
The Girl from Nowhere
The Lincoln Highwayman
Miss Adventure
The Mother and the Law
Paid in Advance
1920 Hearts Are Trumps
His Own Law
The Man Who Dared
Riders of the Dawn
Shore Acres
Under Crimson Skies
The Valley of Tomorrow

Brownwell, Laline
1914 Soldiers of Fortune
Bruce, Becky
1916 The Other Girl
1919 The Volcano
Bruce, Belle
1915 The Battle Cry of Peace
The Making Over of Geoffrey
Manning
1916 For a Woman's Fair Name
In the Diplomatic Service
A Night Out
The Redemption of Dave
Darcey
Salvation Joan
1917 The Slacker (Metro Pictures
Corp.)
A Son of the Hills
1919 God's Outlaw
Bruce, Beverly
1920 Empty Arms
Bruce, Clifford
1914 The Royal Box
When Rome Ruled
1915 The Devil's Daughter
A Fool There Was
From the Valley of the Missing
Lady Audley's Secret
Princess Romanoff
A Woman's Past
1916 The Devil at His Elbow
The Fourth Estate
The Weakness of Strength
1917 The Barricade
Blue Jeans
The Final Payment
Passion
The Sin Woman
The Siren
1918 Breakers Ahead
The Racing Strain
Riders of the Night
A Weaver of Dreams
The Winding Trail
1919 Woman, Woman!
Bruce, Cyril
1914 McVeagh of the South Seas
Bruce, David
1915 Children of the Ghetto
Bruce, Ethel
1916 The Spider and the Fly*
Bruce, Kate
1914 Judith of Bethulia
1916 Betty of Graystone
Gretchen, the Greenhorn
A House Built upon Sand
Intolerance
The Marriage of Molly-O
The Microscope Mystery
Susan Rocks the Boat
1917 Betsy's Burglar
Madame Bo-Peep
Souls Triumphant*
The Stainless Barrier
Time Locks and Diamonds
A Woman's Awakening
1918 The Greatest Thing in Life
Hearts of the World
The Hun Within
1919 The Fall of Babylon
The Girl Who Stayed Home
The Mother and the Law
A Romance of Happy Valley
Scarlet Days
True Heart Susie
1920 Flying Pat
The Idol Dancer
Mary Ellen Comes to Town
Way Down East
Brugger, George
1915 A Continental Girl
Brulatier (full name unknown)
1916 20,000 Leagues Under the Sea*
Brule, Frank
1916 The Supreme Temptation
Brule, Shirley
1919 Fortune's Child
Brullier, N. de see **De Brullier, Nigel**
Brun, Edna
1914 The Education of Mr. Pipp

Brundage, Mathilde same as **Brundage,**
Mrs.; Brundage, Bertha; Brundage,
Mrs. J. H.; Brundage, Mrs. J. J.;
Brundage, Mrs. M.; Brundage,
Mathilda; Brundage, Mrs. Mathilde;
Brundage, Matilda;
1914 The Crucible
1915 The Beloved Vagabond
Dr. Rameau
Emmy of Stork's Nest
A Royal Family
A Woman's Resurrection
Wormwood
1916 The City of Illusion
The Great Problem
Half a Rogue
Her Debt of Honor
The Lords of High Decision
The River of Romance
1917 Bridges Burned
Enlighten Thy Daughter
A Hungry Heart
The Little Terror
Raffles, the Amateur
Cracksman
Reputation
The Secret of the Storm
Country
The Slacker (Metro Pictures
Corp.)
The Soul of a Magdalen
Thou Shalt Not Steal
The Waiting Soul
Wife Number Two
1918 The Liar
The Life Mask
Life or Honor?
The Light Within
Neighbors
The Silent Woman
Suspicion
Tempered Steel
Wives of Men
A Woman of Impulse
1919 The Career of Katherine Bush
The Heart of a Gypsy
Her Game
Three Green Eyes
1920 Cynthia-of-the-Minute
Dangerous Business
The Good-Bad Wife
The Man Who Lost Himself
The Silent Barrier
Thoughtless Women
Brundage, Sarah
1916 Love's Pilgrimage to America
Brunette, Fritzi
1914 Forgiven; Or, The Jack of
Diamonds
1916 At Piney Ridge
Unto Those Who Sin
1917 Beware of Strangers
The Jaguar's Claws
Who Shall Take My Life?
1918 And a Still Small Voice
The City of Purple Dreams
Playthings
The Still Alarm
The Velvet Hand
1919 Jacques of the Silver North
The Lord Loves the Irish
The Railroader
The Sealed Envelope
A Sporting Chance (American
Film Co.)
Whitewashed Walls
The Woman Thou Gavest Me
The Woman Under Cover
1920 The Coast of Opportunity
The Devil to Pay
The Dream Cheater
The Green Flame
The House of Whispers
Live Sparks
Number 99
$30,000
Bruno, the bear
1917 A Roadside Impresario
Bruns, Julia
1917 At First Sight
The Honeymoon

Brunswick, Earl
1917 Draft 258
Brunton, George
1914 The Key to Yesterday
Brunton, Robert same as **Brunton, Robert A.**
1916 Bawbs O' Blue Ridge
The Criminal
The Dawn Maker
The Devil's Double
The Eye of the Night
A Gamble in Souls
Honor Thy Name
The Honorable Algy
Jim Grimsby's Boy
The Jungle Child
Lieutenant Danny, U.S.A.
The Patriot
The Payment
Plain Jane
Shell Forty-Three
The Wolf Woman
1917 Alimony
Back of the Man
Blood Will Tell
The Bride of Hate
The Cold Deck
The Dark Road
The Gun Fighter
Happiness
The Hater of Men
The Iced Bullet
The Little Brother
Paddy O'Hara
The Snarl
The Square Deal Man
Sweetheart of the Doomed
The Weaker Sex
Wolf Lowry
1918 A Burglar for a Night
Carmen of the Klondike
The Goddess of Lost Lake
The Heart of Rachael
Honor's Cross
A Law unto Herself
Madam Who
Maid O' the Storm
A Man's Man
Rose O' Paradise
Twenty-One
Two-Gun Betty
Wedlock
With Hoops of Steel
Within the Cup
1919 Adele
Are You Legally Married?
The Lord Loves the Irish
A Man in the Open
Playthings of Passion
A White Man's Chance
1920 The Devil to Pay
The House of Whispers
Live Sparks
$30,000
Brunton, William same as **Brunton, Will; Brunton, William G.**
1914 The Boer War
1915 The Barnstormers
The High Hand
1916 The Diamond Runners
Judith of the Cumberlands
The Manager of the B. and A.
Medicine Bend
Whispering Smith
1918 The Cruise of the Make-Believes
The Squaw Man
1919 As the Sun Went Down
The Valley of the Giants
Bryan, Paul M.
1916 According to Law
The Idol of the Stage
The Isle of Love
Bryan, Ruth
1914 The Fortune Hunter
The Lion and the Mouse
The Wolf
1915 The Climbers
The College Widow
The District Attorney
The Great Ruby
The Sporting Duchess
1916 The Evangelist

Bryan, Vincent
1920 What Women Love
Bryan, William Jennings
1915 Prohibition*
19-- Official Motion Pictures of the Panama Pacific Exposition Held at San Francisco, Calif.*
Bryant, Mrs.
1919 The Witness for the Defense
Bryant, Charles same as **Bryant, G. Charles**
1915 The Battle of Ballots
The Masqueraders
1916 War Brides
1918 Eye for Eye
Revelation
Toys of Fate
1919 The Brat
Out of the Fog
1920 Billions
The Heart of a Child
Stronger Than Death
Bryant, G. Charles see **Bryant, Charles**
Bryant, Grace
1919 The Phantom Honeymoon
Bryce, Jack
1915 Her Atonement
Bryson, J. J.
1919 The Last of His People
Bryson, Winifred
1915 Peer Gynt
Buchanan, Donald I.
1915 The Juggernaut
The Sins of the Mothers*
1916 Lost Souls
Should a Baby Die?*
A Woman's Honor
1917 The Siren
1918 The Girl from Beyond
Buchanan, Lillian
1914 One of Millions
Buchanan, Thompson
1916 A Woman's Way
1919 The World and Its Woman
1920 Dangerous Days
Jes' Call Me Jim
Buck, Inez
1916 The Gods of Fate
Her Bleeding Heart
Love's Toll
Sorrows of Happiness
The Test
Buckingham, Tom same as **Buckingham, Thomas**
1917 Indiscreet Corinne
The Maternal Spark
1918 The Atom
Captain of His Soul
Everywoman's Husband
The Reckoning Day
A Soul in Trust
The Vortex
1920 Up in Mary's Attic
Buckland, Frank M.
1915 American Game Trails
Buckland, Wilfred
1914 The Call of the North
The Man on the Box
Rose of the Rancho
1915 Blackbirds
The Captive
Carmen (Jesse L. Lasky Feature Play Co.)
The Cheat
Chimmie Fadden
The Girl of the Golden West
The Secret Sin
Young Romance
1916 Anton the Terrible
The Clown
Joan the Woman
The Plow Girl
Public Opinion
Pudd'nhead Wilson
The Ragamuffin
The Selfish Woman
The Soul of Kura-San
Sweet Kitty Bellairs
The Trail of the Lonesome Pine
The Victoria Cross
1917 The American Consul
The Call of the East

The Crystal Gazer
The Devil-Stone
The Little American
The Little Princess
On Record
Reaching for the Moon
A Romance of the Redwoods
Wild and Woolly
The Woman God Forgot
1918 Amarilly of Clothes-Line Alley
The City of Dim Faces
The Cruise of the Make-Believes
The Girl Who Came Back
The Goat
Her Country First
Johanna Enlists
Less Than Kin
M'liss
Old Wives for New
One More American
Sandy
The Source
Stella Maris
Such a Little Pirate
We Can't Have Everything
The Whispering Chorus
The Widow's Might
1919 Don't Change Your Husband
Hawthorne of the U.S.A.
Male and Female
The Roaring Road
Something to Do
The Woman Next Door
You're Fired
1920 Always Audacious
The City of Masks
A City Sparrow
Conrad in Quest of His Youth
Crooked Streets
A Cumberland Romance
The Dancin' Fool
Eyes of the Heart
The Fourteenth Man
The Furnace
Held by the Enemy
A Lady in Love
Mrs. Temple's Telegram
Thou Art the Man
You Never Can Tell
Buckley, F. R. see **Buckley, Frederic Robert**
Buckley, Floyd
1917 The Avenging Trail
God's Law and Man's
1920 Love Without Question
Buckley, Frederic Robert same as **Buckley, F. R.; Buckley, Frederick; Buckley, Frederick R.**
1917 A Night in New Arabia
1918 By the World Forgot
A Gentleman's Agreement
The Other Man
The Song of the Soul
1919 The Undercurrent
The Unknown Quantity
Buckley, J. P.
1914 The Line-Up at Police Headquarters
Buckley, Ora
1914 The Last Egyptian
Buckley, William same as **Buckly, William**
1915 Esmeralda
1917 S.O.S.
1919 Fair and Warmer
When Doctors Disagree
1919-20 When a Man Loves
1920 The Devil's Claim
The House of Toys
Just Pals
Under Northern Lights
What's Your Husband Doing?
Buckly, William see **Buckley, William**
Buckridge, Della
1914 The House of Bondage
Buckstone, Roland
1916 An Enemy to the King
Bucus, Gene
1919 Checkers

Budd (pseud. of Robert Hull)
1917 The Tenth Case
Budd, Ruth
1919 A Scream in the Night
Budd, William H.
1920 A Manhattan Knight
Buddie, the dog
1920 Love's Harvest
Buehler, Mrs.
1917 The Bond Between
Buel, Kenean same as **Buel, Keanan; Buel, Keenan; Buel, Keenan J.**
1914 The School for Scandal
Wolfe; Or, The Conquest of Quebec
1915 The Runaway Wife
1916 Blazing Love
Daredevil Kate
Hypocrisy
The Marble Heart
The War Bride's Secret
1917 The Bitter Truth
The New York Peacock
She
Troublemakers
Two Little Imps
1918 American Buds
Doing Their Bit
We Should Worry
The Woman Who Gave
1919 A Fallen Idol
My Little Sister
Woman, Woman!
1920 The Place of Honeymoons
The Veiled Marriage
Buffington, Adele
1919 L'Apache
Buhler, Richard
1914 The Thief
1915 Evidence
A Man's Making
The Rights of Man: A Story of War's Red Blotch
1916 The Gods of Fate
Her Bleeding Heart
Love's Toll
Bulger, Jack
1915 C.O.D.
1918 Five Thousand an Hour
Bull, Chief Short see **Short Bull, Chief**
Bull, Chief Sitting see **Sitting Bull, Chief**
Bull, Chief Tall see **Tall Bull, Chief**
Bull, Little see **Little Bull**
Bull, Short see **Short Bull, Chief**
Buller, the human fish
1917 The Submarine Eye
Buller, Mrs.
1918 The Great Love*
Bullivant, Cecil Henry
1917 Whose Wife?
Bunce, Miss
1917 Within the Law
Bundy, Bruce F.
1916 The Impersonation
Bunnell, Charles E. same as **Bunnell, Charles**
1914 When Rome Ruled
1916 Madame X
Bunnell, Ed
1917 Cy Whittaker's Ward
Bunny, Frank
1916 A Night Out
Bunny, George
1915 Cap'n Eri
1918 A Camouflage Kiss
Caught in the Act
Friend Husband
The Heart of Romance
1919 A Broadway Saint
Dawn
The Poison Pen
1919-20 Piccadilly Jim
Bunny, Grace
1918 The Vigilantes
Bunting, Mary
1916 The Making of Maddalena

Bunyea, Mabel
1918 Brave and Bold
 Hitting the Trail
Buquette, Yolande
1918 At the Mercy of Men
Burbank, Mrs. *see* **Burbank, Zadee**
Burbank, Betty
1918 Me und Gott
Burbank, Luther
19-- Official Motion Pictures of the
 Panama Pacific Exposition
 Held at San Francisco,
 Calif.*
Burbank, Zadee *same as* **Burbank, Mrs.;**
Burbank, Sadee; Burbank, Zaidee
1916 What Will People Say?
1917 A Man and the Woman
1918 A Soul Without Windows
 The Wasp
 Whims of Society
1920 Bachelor Apartments
 The Triple Clue
Burbeck, Frank
1916 Blazing Love
 What Happened at 22
1919 Who's Your Brother?
Burbidge, William
1913 Traffic in Souls
Burbridge, Charles
1916 The Man Inside
Burbridge, Elizabeth
1915 Matrimony
 Rumpelstiltskin
 The Winged Idol
1916 Charity
 Tongues of Men
1917 Captain Kiddo
 Tears and Smiles
1918 Milady O' the Beanstalk
Burdell, Elwood
1918 The Magic Eye
Burgarth, Theodore
1913 Tortures Within Prison Walls
Burgermaster, W.
1916 Plain Jane
Burgermeister, Augusta *see* **Burgmester,**
Auguste
Burgess, Gelett
1917 The Countess Charming
 The Mysterious Miss Terry
Burgess, William
1914 The School for Scandal
1917 The Scarlet Pimpernel
1918 The Talk of the Town
Burkart, Theodore
1913 The Star of India
Burke, Billie
1916 Peggy
1917 Arms and the Girl
 The Land of Promise
 The Mysterious Miss Terry
1918 Eve's Daughter
 In Pursuit of Polly
 Let's Get a Divorce
 The Make-Believe Wife
1919 Good Gracious, Annabelle
 The Misleading Widow
 Sadie Love
 Wanted—A Husband
1920 Away Goes Prudence
 The Frisky Mrs. Johnson
Burke, Daniel
1916 The Quest of Life
Burke, David Lewis
1915 Her Atonement*
Burke, J. Frank
1914 The Bargain
1915 The Alien
 Aloha Oe
 The Despoiler
 The Forbidden Adventure
 The Italian
 The Winged Idol
1916 Bawbs O' Blue Ridge
 The Beckoning Flame
 Civilization
 The Dawn Maker
 Hell's Hinges
 The No-Good Guy
 The Vagabond Prince
 The Waifs

1917 Blood Will Tell
 An Even Break
 The Iced Bullet
 Madcap Madge
 Princess of the Dark
 The Square Deal Man
 A Strange Transgressor
 Whither Thou Goest
 Wooden Shoes
Burke, James L.
1920 The Veiled Marriage
Burke, Joseph *same as* **Burke, Joe**
1915 The Senator
1916 The City of Illusion
 A Fool's Paradise
 The Immortal Flame
1917 The Awakening of Ruth
 Billy and the Big Stick
 Chris and His Wonderful
  Lamp
 The Customary Two Weeks
 Kidnapped
 The Little Chevalier
 Outwitted
1918 Cecilia of the Pink Roses
 Come On In
 De Luxe Annie
 Good-Bye, Bill
 The Green God
 Life or Honor?
 Opportunity
 The Whirlpool
1919 The Girl-Woman
 Help! Help! Police!
 Oh, You Women
 Through the Toils
 The Trap
 The Winchester Woman
1920 Heritage
 The Perfect Woman
 The Silent Barrier
19-- Barnaby Lee
Burke, Marie
1918 The Girl and the Judge
1919 The Glorious Lady
 The Gray Towers Mystery
 Help! Help! Police!
 A House Divided
 The Love Defender
 My Little Sister
1920 A Dark Lantern
 His House in Order
 Little Miss Rebellion
 The New York Idea
 Remodelling Her Husband
 Sooner or Later
Burke, Peggy
1917 It Happened to Adele
1918 The House of Glass
Burke, Tom
1919 Should a Husband Forgive?
Burke, Winifred
1914 Lena Rivers (Cosmos Feature
 Film Corp.)
Burkell, John
1917 On Dangerous Ground
 The Small Town Girl
1918 Lafayette, We Come!
1920 The Wonder Man
Burkett, Bartine
1920 The Turning Point
Burkey, J. R.
1917 The Bronze Bride
Burkhardt, Harry
1916 The Marble Heart
 The Masked Rider
 The Ruling Passion
 The Stolen Triumph
1917 The Law of Compensation
 More Truth Than Poetry
1918 Life or Honor?
1920 Oil
Burks, Hattie
1916 Sins of Men
Burleson, Amelia
1919 Out of the Fog
Burlingham, Martha
1917 Strife
Burlock, William E. *same as* **Burlock,**
William
1915 Excuse Me*
1916 Madame X*

Burmeister, Mrs. *see* **Burmester,**
Auguste
Burmester, Auguste *same as*
Burgermeister, Augusta; Burmeister,
Mrs.; Burmeister, Augusta;
Burmeister, Auguste; Burmester,
Augusta
1914 The Burglar and the Lady
 The School for Scandal
1915 Stop Thief!
1916 The Man Who Stood Still
 The Ocean Waif
 The Revolt
1917 The Dancer's Peril
 Mary Moreland
 Think It Over
1919 A Broadway Saint
Burnell, Gene
1917 The Soul of a Magdalen
1918 The Life Mask
 The Panther Woman
Burnell, Lotta
1917 The Maid of Belgium
Burner, Ethel
1918 The Divine Sacrifice
Burnett, Jessie
1916 The Wasted Years
1917 The Planter*
Burnett, Lois
1914 Officer 666
Burnett, Rexford *same as* **Burnett, Rex**
1914 The Master Cracksman
1917 The Skylight Room
Burnett, Tom L.
1920 Frontier Days
Burnett, Mrs. Tom L.
1920 Frontier Days
Burnham, Beatrice
1916 Ramona
1917 The Eyes of the World
 Her Temptation
 Jack and Jill
1919 The Petal on the Current
 Upstairs
1920 Bullet Proof
 Burnt Wings
 Hitchin' Posts
Burnham, Frances
1916 The Love Thief
1917 Lorelei of the Sea
1918 On the Jump
1919 As the Sun Went Down
 The Price Woman Pays
1920 Who's Your Servant?
Burnham, Julia
1917 The Adventures of Carol
 The Little Duchess
 The Volunteer
1918 A Soul Without Windows
 Wanted, a Mother
1919 The Call of the Soul
 The Love Auction
 Love, Honor and—?
 Lure of Ambition
1920 The Fatal Hour
Burnham, Louise
1920 Lahoma
Burnham, Nicholas
1920 Uncle Sam of Freedom Ridge
Burns, Beulah
1916 Children of the Feud
 The Fall of a Nation
 Gretchen, the Greenhorn
 Let Katie Do It
 A Sister of Six
1918 Six Shooter Andy
Burns, Blanche
1917 God of Little Children
Burns, Bob *see* **Burns, Robert**
Burns, David
1918 De Luxe Annie
Burns, Edward *same as* **Burns, Ed;**
Burns, Edward J.
1916 Intolerance
1917 Diamonds and Pearls
 Her Hour
 The Slave
 Up or Down?
 Wild and Woolly
1918 The Danger Mark
 Headin' South
 The Life Mask
 Love Watches

 Morgan's Raiders
 The Ordeal of Rosetta
 The Queen of Hearts
 The Soap Girl
 Under the Greenwood Tree
 The Wasp
1919 The Love Burglar
 Male and Female
 Marriage for Convenience
 Miss Adventure
 A Very Good Young Man
1920 Eyes of the Heart
 One Hour Before Dawn
 Pegeen
 To Please One Woman
 The Virgin of Stamboul
Burns, Fred
1915 The Birth of a Nation
 Jordan Is a Hard Road
 The Martyrs of the Alamo
1916 Ben Blair
 The Good Bad Man
 Sold for Marriage
1917 The Eyes of the World
 The Hero of the Hour
 Sunlight's Last Raid
1918 Bound in Morocco
Burns, Jack
1913 Ben Bolt
1914 The Million Dollar Robbery
1915 Barbara Frietchie
1917 God of Little Children
1918 My Own United States
Burns, James
1916 Intolerance
Burns, Lillian
1914 A Florida Enchantment
1915 The Cave Man
1916 Green Stockings
 The Shop Girl
Burns, Mary
1917 The Eyes of the World
Burns, Neal
1920 Mary's Ankle
Burns, Paul
1920 The Mollycoddle
Burns, Robert *same as* **Burns, Bob**
1917 The Captain of the Gray Horse
  Troop
 The Eyes of the World
 The Little Yank
1918 The Girl from Beyond
Burns, Thelma
1916 Children of the Feud
 Macbeth
 A Man of Sorrow
 The Wasted Years
Burns, Tod
1917 Borrowed Plumage
 The Mother Instinct
1920 The Little Shepherd of
  Kingdom Come
Burns, Tommy
1917 The Plow Woman
Burns, Vinnie *see* **Daye, June**
Burns, William (actor) *could be same*
as **Burns, William W.**
1917 S.O.S.
 Unknown 274
Burns, William J. (detective)
1914 The $5,000,000 Counterfeiting
  Plot
Burns, William W. (actor) *could be*
same as **Burns, William** (actor)
1916 Vultures of Society
Burr, Charles C.
1920 The Silent Barrier
Burr, Eugene *same as* **Burr, Gene**
1917 Fanatics
 Framing Framers
 The Fuel of Life
1918 Alias Mary Brown
 The Atom
 Captain of His Soul
 Daughter Angele
 Heiress for a Day
 Irish Eyes
 Madame Sphinx
 Nancy Comes Home
 Old Hartwell's Cub
 The Painted Lily
 The Pretender
 The Vortex

1919 The Final Close-Up
The Girl with No Regrets
Restless Souls

Burrell, Mrs. Hamer
1919 Injustice

Burress, Bill see **Burress, William**

Burress, William same as **Burress, Bill**
1915 A Bunch of Keys
1916 The Battle of Hearts
The End of the Trail
The Fires of Conscience
The Man from Bitter Roots
A Man of Sorrow
1917 The Book Agent
The Island of Desire
A Soul for Sale
The Soul of Satan
The Spy
1918 Kultur
The Rainbow Trail
1919 The Forbidden Room
Heartsease
Lord and Lady Algy
Paid in Advance

Burris, Jim
1920 The Symbol of the
Unconquered

Burrough, James
1920 The Symbol of the
Unconquered

Burrough, Tom same as **Burroughs, Tom**
1916 Caprice of the Mountains
The Ragged Princess
Sins of Men
The Unwelcome Mother
1917 God's Man
Miss U.S.A.
She
The Sunshine Maid
Unknown 274
1918 A Romance of the Air
1920 The Fighting Kentuckians
The Key to Power

Burroughs, John
1914 Born Again

Burroughs, Tom see **Burrough, Tom**

Burston, Louis
1919 Crimson Shoals

Burt, Laura
1919 Love and the Woman
The Social Pirate

Burt, Nellie
1920 The Scarlet Dragon

Burt, Willard
1920 Do the Dead Talk?

Burt, William P. same as **Burt, William**
1916 Her Father's Gold
1917 The Penny Philanthropist
The Streets of Illusion
1920 Rogues and Romance

Burton, Charlotte
1914 Damaged Goods
1916 The Bruiser
The Craving
The Highest Bid
Lone Star
The Love Hermit
The Man Who Would Not Die
Soul Mates
The Strength of Donald
McKenzie
The Thoroughbred (American
Film Co.)
The Torch Bearer
The Twinkler
1918 Hearts or Diamonds?
Up Romance Road
1919 Man's Desire
1920 Polly of the Storm Country

Burton, Clarence
1916 Bluff
A Dream or Two Ago
Faith
Lying Lips
The Overcoat
Philip Holden—Waster
Purity
Reclamation
The Sign of the Spade
The Twinkler
1917 Beloved Rogues
The Frame Up

High Play
My Fighting Gentleman
New York Luck
Periwinkle
Pride and the Man
The Sea Master
Snap Judgement
1918 Beauty and the Rogue
A Bit of Jade
Fame and Fortune
The Midnight Trail
The Mystery Girl
Powers That Prey
The Return of Mary
1919 Castles in the Air
Hawthorne of the U.S.A.
Hearts of Men
The Last of the Duanes
Male and Female
Six Feet Four
The Spender
Venus in the East
Wings of the Morning
1920 Burglar Proof
The Fighting Chance
The Six Best Cellars
Thou Art the Man
What's Your Hurry?
1921 The Jucklins

Burton, David
1915 The Galloper
Madame Butterfly

Burton, Frederick same as **Burton, Fred**
1914 Forgiven; Or, The Jack of
Diamonds
1918 Arizona
Ruggles of Red Gap
1919 Anne of Green Gables
The Career of Katherine Bush
Cheating Cheaters
Getting Mary Married
The Teeth of the Tiger
1920 The Fear Market
The Fortune Teller
Heliotrope
Yes or No

Burton, G. Marion
1919 Miss Dulcie from Dixie
Thin Ice
The Unknown Quantity
The Wishing Ring Man
1920 The Woman Game

Burton, George
1917 The Little Boy Scout

Burton, Gideon
1914 In Mizzoura

Burton, Grace
1918 The Studio Girl

Burton, J. W.
1914 The Ghost Breaker

Burton, John
1916 The Making of Maddalena
1917 The Bond Between
The Cook of Canyon Camp
The Fair Barbarian
The Heir of the Ages
A Kiss for Susie
The Lonesome Chap
The Spirit of Romance
The World Apart
1918 Boston Blackie's Little Pal
Hidden Pearls
Huck and Tom; Or, The
Further Adventures of Tom
Sawyer
Mile-a-Minute Kendall
M'liss
A Petticoat Pilot
The Spirit of '17
Unexpected Places
Up Romance Road
The Whispering Chorus
1919 You Never Saw Such a Girl
1920 In the Heart of a Fool
Pinto
The Scoffer

Burton, Mary
1918 Little Red Riding Hood

Burton, Ned
1914 Detective Craig's Coup
The Man of the Hour
1915 Her Great Match
1916 Somewhere in Georgia
The Velvet Paw

War Brides
1917 The Auction Block
Man's Woman
1918 The Danger Game
The Power and the Glory
Ruler of the Road
The Song of Songs
1919 The Moral Deadline
Thou Shalt Not
Thunderbolts of Fate
1920 A Daughter of Two Worlds
Tarnished Reputations

Burton, S. J.
1917 Daughter of Maryland

Burton, W. H. same as **Burton,
William; Burton, William H.**
1913 Across the Continent
1916 Romeo and Juliet (Quality
Pictures Corp.)
1917 Cy Whittaker's Ward
Thou Shalt Not Steal
Wife Number Two
1919 The Lion and the Mouse
The Mystery of the Yellow
Room

Burton, William see **Burton, W. H.**

Busby, Mr.
1920 Footlights and Shadows

Busby, A. H. same as **Busby, Albert;
Busby, Bert; Busby, Burt; Bushy,
Bert**
1914 When Rome Ruled
1915 Under Southern Skies
1916 The River of Romance
Temptation and the Man
1918 Parentage
Who Loved Him Best?
1919 Let's Elope
1920 The Rich Slave

Busby, Bert see **Busby, A. H.**

Busby, Jack
1916 The Light of Happiness

Busby, William
1919 The Great Victory, Wilson or
the Kaiser? The Fall of the
Hohenzollerns

Busch, Mae
1917 The Fair Barbarian
1919 The Grim Game
1920 The Devil's Passkey
Her Husband's Friend

Busch, Mary
1919 The Beloved Cheater*

Busch, Ulrich
1919 The Beloved Cheater*

Bush, Cedric
1917 The Last Sentence

Bush, Pauline
1914 Richelieu

Bush, W. Stephen
1914 The Coliseum in Films
Pagan Rome

Bushman, Francis X.
1914 One Wonderful Night
1915 Graustark
Pennington's Choice
Richard Carvel*
The Second in Command
The Silent Voice
The Slim Princess
1916 In the Diplomatic Service
Man and His Soul
A Million a Minute
The Red Mouse
Romeo and Juliet (Quality
Pictures Corp.)
The Wall Between
1917 The Adopted Son
National Association's All-Star
Picture
Red, White and Blue Blood
Their Compact
The Voice of Conscience
1918 The Brass Check
Cyclone Higgins, D.D.
Gay and Festive Claverhouse
A Pair of Cupids
The Poor Rich Man
Social Quicksands
Under Suspicion
With Neatness and Dispatch
1919 Daring Hearts
God's Outlaw

Bushman, Ralph
1920 It's a Great Life

Bushy, Bert see **Busby, A. H.**

Buskirk, Mrs. see **Buskirk, Hattie**

Buskirk, Bessie
1916 A House Built upon Sand
Macbeth
1917 Cheerful Givers
Her Official Fathers

Buskirk, Hattie same as **Buskirk, Mrs.;
Buskirk, Mrs. Hattie**
1917 The Tenderfoot
1918 Cavanaugh of the Forest
Rangers
A Gentleman's Agreement
The Girl from Beyond
The Wild Strain
1919 Fighting for Gold

Bussell, Walter
1917 Her Father's Keeper

The Bustanoby Girls
1915 Midnight at Maxim's

Butler (full name unknown)
1915 The Fairy and the Waif*

Butler, Alexander
1920 The Night Riders

Butler, Charles could be same as **Butler,
Charley**
1915 Are You a Mason?
Zaza
1916 His Picture in the Papers

Butler, Charley could be same as
Butler, Charles
1915 John Glayde's Honor

Butler, David same as **Butler, David W.**
1915 The Deathlock
1918 The Greatest Thing in Life
1919 Better Times
Bonnie, Bonnie Lassie
The Girl Who Stayed Home
Nugget Nell
The Other Half
The Petal on the Current
The Pointing Finger
The Unpainted Woman
Upstairs and Down
1920 The County Fair
Don't Ever Marry
Fickle Women
Girls Don't Gamble
Smiling All the Way
The Triflers

Butler, Edward
1917 The Submarine Eye

Butler, F. R.
1920 Behold My Wife

Butler, Fred J. same as **Butler,
Frederick J.**
1915 The Deathlock
1916 The Flying Torpedo
Little Meena's Romance
Susan Rocks the Boat
1920 Fickle Women
Girls Don't Gamble
Smiling All the Way

Butler, H. E. could be same as **Butler,
H. J.**
1915 The Pageant of San Francisco
1917 The Sin Woman

Butler, H. J. could be same as **Butler,
H. E.**
1917 The Fringe of Society
Runaway Romany

Butler, Jim
1913 The Tonopah Stampede for
Gold

Butler, Johnny
1920 Red Foam

Butler, Kathleen
1914 McVeagh of the South Seas

Butler, W. J. same as **Butler, William;
Butler, William J.**
1915 The Gambler of the West
1916 I Accuse
The Isle of Love
Rolling Stones
Susie Snowflake
1917 At First Sight
A Girl Like That
The Girl Who Didn't Think

Butler, W. W.
1918 The World for Sale
Butler, Wade
1919 Crooked Straight
Butt, Lawson *see* **Butt, W. Lawson**
Butt, W. Lawson *same as* **Butt, Lawson**
1915 Don Caesar de Bazan
      The Woman Next Door
1916 Romeo and Juliet (Quality
      Pictures Corp.)
1917 The Danger Trail
1918 The Goddess of Lost Lake
      Her Man
      The One Woman
      Shackled
1919 Desert Gold
      It Happened in Paris
      The Loves of Letty
      The Miracle Man
      Playthings of Passion
      The World and Its Woman
1920 Dangerous Days
      Earthbound
      Out of the Storm
      The Street Called Straight
      The Tiger's Coat
Butterfield, Everett
1915 Forbidden Fruit
      The Magic Skin
      The Seventh Noon
Butterfield, Henry A.
1917 The Deemster
      Persuasive Peggy
Butterworth, Ernest, Jr.
1917 The Crab
1918 Selfish Yates
1920 A Beggar in Purple
      The Luck of the Irish
      The Soul of Youth
      What's Your Hurry?
Butterworth, Ernest, Sr.
1916 The Fall of a Nation
      Intolerance*
      Joan the Woman
1918 Arizona
      The Greatest Thing in Life
      Mr. Fix-It
      Say, Young Fellow!
1919 Broken Blossoms
      The Knickerbocker Buckaroo
Butterworth, Frank *same as*
   Butterworth, F.
1918 Amarilly of Clothes-Line Alley
      Till I Come Back to You
1919 The Enchanted Barn
Butterworth, Joe
1920 A Woman Who Understood
Buzard, A. J.
1917 Alaska Wonders in Motion*
Buzzi, Pietro *same as* **Buzzi, Signor**
1917 The Bond Between
      The Gown of Destiny
      The Lonesome Chap
      The Wax Model
1918 The Devil's Wheel
      Maid O' the Storm
      One More American
Byers, Clara *see* **Beyers, Clara**
Byers, Frances Fisher
1915 Seeing America First
Byers, Ruth
1920 Deadline at Eleven
Byram, Ronald *same as* **Byrem, Robert**
1919 A Gentleman of Quality
      The Highest Trump
      Out of the Shadow
Byrd, Anthony
1917 The Voice of Conscience
1918 The Eyes of Mystery
      The Heart of a Girl
      Her Boy
      The Interloper
      Pals First
      A Successful Adventure
Byrd, Beau
1917 The Girl of the Timber Claims
Byrd, Robert
1920 From Now On
Byrem, Robert *see* **Byram, Ronald**

Byrne, Andrew
1918 Eight Bells
Byrne, Francis
1914 The Conspiracy
1917 Blind Man's Luck
Byrne, James A.
1918 Eight Bells
Byrne, John F.
1918 Eight Bells
Byrnes, J.
1915 The Song of the Wage Slave
Byron, Jack
1920 Fixed by George
1921 The Jucklins
Byron, Nina
1917 The Heir of the Ages
      Truthful Tulliver
1918 The Cruise of the
      Make-Believes
      The Source
1919 The Boomerang
      The Broken Butterfly
      The Dub
      Johnny Get Your Gun
Byron, Paul
1915 The Second in Command
1916 The Black Sheep of the Family
      A Child of Mystery
      The Flirt
      For the Defense
      The Heritage of Hate
      The Seekers
1917 Heart Strings
Byron, Royal
1915 The Sins of Society
1916 The Quest of Life
      Where Love Leads
1917 The Girl by the Roadside
      The Lady of the Photograph
Byron, Ruth
1917 The Dazzling Miss Davison
      Hedda Gabler
      Motherhood (Frank Powell
      Producing Corp.)
Bytell, Doc *see* **Bytell, Walter**
Bytell, Walter *same as* **Bytell, Doc;**
   Bytell, Dr. Walter
1917 Wild and Woolly
1920 Once a Plumber
      Whispering Devils
Bytell, William
1918 Her Moment

C

Cabanne, William Christy *same as*
   Cabanne, Christy; Cabanne, W.
   Christy
1914 The Dishonored Medal
      The Great Leap; Until Death
      Do Us Part
      The Life of General Villa
1915 The Absentee
      Double Trouble
      Enoch Arden
      The Failure
      The Lamb
      The Lost House
      The Martyrs of the Alamo
      The Outlaw's Revenge
1916 Daphne and the Pirate
      Diane of the Follies
      Flirting with Fate
      The Flying Torpedo
      Reggie Mixes In
      Sold for Marriage
1917 Draft 258
      Miss Robinson Crusoe
      National Red Cross Pageant
      One of Many
      The Slacker (Metro Pictures
      Corp.)
1918 Cyclone Higgins, D.D.
1919 The Beloved Cheater
      Fighting Through
      God's Outlaw
      The Mayor of Filbert
      The Pest
      A Regular Fellow
1920 Burnt Wings
      Life's Twist
      The Notorious Mrs. Sands

      The Stealers
      The Triflers
Cabot, Harry
1917 The Avenging Trail
Cade, Rose
1920 A City Sparrow
Cadeux, Mrs. Madeline
1918 The Marionettes
Cadwell, A. A. *same as* **Cadwell, A.;**
   Cadwell, Arthur; Cadwell, Arthur A.
1914 Salomy Jane
1915 A Royal Family
1916 The Child of Destiny
      The Dawn of Love
      The Kiss of Hate
      The Sunbeam
1917 A Wife by Proxy
1918 Laughing Bill Hyde
      Too Fat to Fight
1919 As a Man Thinks
      The Lost Battalion
      A Scream in the Night
      Three Black Eyes
1920 Clothes
      Even As Eve
      Madonnas and Men
      A Woman's Business
Cahill, Lily
1915 Colonel Carter of Cartersville
Cahill, Marie
1915 Judy Forgot
Cahill, William
1914 Threads of Destiny
1916 Her Great Price
Cain, George
1917 The Best Man
Cain, Robert
1915 The Bachelor's Romance
      The Dawn of a Tomorrow
      Lydia Gilmore
      The Running Fight
      The White Pearl
1916 The Eternal Grind
      The Innocent Lie
      My Lady Incog.
1917 The Co-Respondent
      Envy
      The Hungry Heart
      Kidnapped
1918 The Death Dance
      Her Final Reckoning
      Men
      A Woman of Impulse
1919 Eastward Ho!
      The End of the Road
      In Mizzoura
      Male and Female
      Paid in Full
      Secret Service
      A Woman's Experience
1920 Heart Strings
      Held by the Enemy
      Shod with Fire
      Unseen Forces
Cain, Viola
1917 One Touch of Nature
Caine, Derwent Hall
1917 Crime and Punishment
      The Deemster
1918 Huns Within Our Gates
Calcagni, David
1915 The Devil's Daughter
1916 Charity
1917 American Maid
      The Auction Block
      The Eternal Sin
      The Final Payment
1918 Daybreak
      For the Freedom of the East
      Oh, Johnny!
1919 A Misfit Earl
      The Road Called Straight
      Sandy Burke of the U-Bar-U
      Speedy Meade
Caldara, Orme
1917 The Spreading Dawn
Caldwell, Golda *see* **Colwell, Goldie**
1918 Code of the Yukon
Caldwell, M. J. "Mickey"
1920 The Kentucky Colonel

Caldwell, Marie
1920 The Mysteries of Paris
Caldwell, Virginia
1919 Lombardi, Ltd.
1920 The Desperate Hero
      The Palace of Darkened
      Windows
      The Right of Way
      The U.P. Trail
Calhoun, Miss
1917 The Last Sentence
Calhoun, Alice
1919 Everybody's Business
1920 Captain Swift
      Deadline at Eleven
      Human Collateral
      The Sea Rider
Calhoun, Catherine *same as* **Calhoun,**
   Katherine
1915 The Daughter of the Sea
      From the Valley of the Missing
1916 A Circus Romance
      The Dragon
      Playing with Fire
Calhoun, Harold Gilmore
1915 The Man Who Couldn't Beat
      God
Calhoun, Jean *same as* **Calhoun, Jeanne;**
   Calhoune, Jean
1918 High Tide
      The Man Who Woke Up
1919 Alias Mike Moran
      The Exquisite Thief
      The False Code
      The Feud
      The Splendid Sin
      Thieves
      The Winning Girl
1919-20
      When a Man Loves
1920 His Own Law
      Officer 666
      The Phantom Melody
Calhoun, Julia
1916 The Human Orchid
1919 The Man Who Stayed at Home
Calhoun, Katherine *see* **Calhoun,**
   Catherine
Calhoun, Patrick
1916 The Discard
      The Truant Soul
1917 Burning the Candle
      Little Shoes
      Mother Love and the Law
      On Trial
      The Saint's Adventure
      The Trufflers
1918 Blindfolded
      The Law That Divides
      My Unmarried Wife
      Whatever the Cost
Calhoun, William
1916 The Price of Malice
1917 The Courage of the Common
      Place
      The Lady of the Photograph
      The Princess' Necklace
1918 Little Miss No-Account
      The Little Runaway
      Over the Top
      The Wasp
19-- Our Daily Bread
Calhoune, Jean *see* **Calhoun, Jean**
Call, Mildred
1917 Polly of the Circus
Call, Zella *same as* **Caull, Zella**
1916 A Corner in Cotton
1918 The Doctor and the Woman
Callaghan, Andrew J.
1920 Bonnie May
      The Midlanders
Callahan, Cordelia
1919 When Fate Decides
1920 Cupid, the Cowpuncher
      What Would You Do?
Callahan, Tom
1913 The Prisoner of Zenda
Callender, A. Romaine *same as*
   Callender, Romaine
1918 The Floor Below
      My Wife

The Snowbird
The Sunbeam
The Upstart
1917 The Barricade
The Greatest Power
Her Fighting Chance
Their Compact
The Trail of the Shadow
The Voice of Conscience
1918 The House of Gold
Pals First
The Splendid Sinner
The Trail to Yesterday
1919 Easy to Make Money
False Evidence
The Great Romance
The Right to Lie
Shadows of Suspicion
The Way of the Strong
1920 Isobel; Or, The Trail's End
Rio Grande
The Web of Deceit
1921 Habit

Carey, Daniel
1919 Out of the Fog

Carey, Harry same as **Carey, H. D.;**
Carey, Harry D.
1914 Judith of Bethulia
McVeagh of the South Seas
The Master Cracksman
1915 Judge Not; Or, The Woman of
Mona Diggings
Just Jim
1916 Behind the Lines
A Knight of the Range
Love's Lariat
Secret Love
The Three Godfathers
1917 Bucking Broadway
The Fighting Gringo
A Marked Man
The Secret Man
Straight Shooting
1918 Hell Bent
The Phantom Riders
The Scarlet Drop
Thieves' Gold
Three Mounted Men
Wild Women
A Woman's Fool
1919 The Ace of the Saddle
Bare Fists
A Fight for Love
A Gun Fightin' Gentleman
Marked Men
The Outcasts of Poker Flats
The Rider of the Law
Riders of Vengeance
Roped
1920 Blue Streak McCoy
Bullet Proof
Hearts Up
Human Stuff
Overland Red
Sundown Slim
West Is West

Carey, Olive see **Golden, Olive Fuller**

Carey, Thomas same as **Carey, Tommy**
1917 The Penny Philanthropist
1918 A Pair of Sixes

Cargill, Henry
1916 The Pursuing Vengeance

Carlbeck, Philip same as **Carlberk, B.**
P.; Carlbert, Philip
1919 The Heart of Youth
An Innocent Adventuress
Louisiana

Carle, Richard
1915 Mary's Lamb

Carleton, Carle E. see **Carlton, Carle E.**

Carleton, George M.
1920 Dad's Girl

Carleton, H. O. see **Carleton, Herbert**
O.

Carleton, Harry Guy see **Carlton, Henry**
Guy

Carleton, Herbert O. same as **Carleton,**
H. O.; Carleton, Herbert Oswald;
Carlton, Herbert; Carlton, Herbert
O.
1914 The Three of Us
1915 The Bigger Man
Fighting Bob
The High Road

One Million Dollars
The Right of Way
Satan Sanderson
1916 The Awakening of Helena
Richie
The Brand of Cowardice
The Light of Happiness
Man and His Soul
The Red Mouse
The Wall Between
1917 The Beautiful Lie
The Call of Her People
A Magdalene of the Hills
The Power of Decision
Shame
1917-18
The Devil's Playground
1918 The Birth of a Race
My Own United States

Carleton, Jane
1920 Sooner or Later

Carleton, John T.
1920 Mountain Madness

Carleton, Lloyd B. same as **Carleton, L.**
B.; Carleton, Lloyd
1914 The Idler
Michael Strogoff
The Ragged Earl
Through Fire to Fortune
The Walls of Jericho
1915 The Girl I Left Behind Me
1916 Barriers of Society
Black Friday
The Devil's Bondwoman
Doctor Neighbor
The Morals of Hilda
Two Men of Sandy Bar
The Unattainable
The Way of the World
The Yaqui
A Yoke of Gold
1917 The Curse of Eve*
1920 The Amazing Woman
Mountain Madness

Carleton, W. C. (1871-1941) same as
Carleton, Will C.; could be same
as Carleton, William or **Carleton,**
William, Sr.
1916 The Final Curtain
1918 At the Mercy of Men

Carleton, W. P. see **Carleton, William**
P.

Carleton, W. P., Jr.
1919 The World to Live In

Carleton, W. T. see **Carleton, William**
T.

Carleton, William could be same as
Carleton, W. C. (1871-1941) or
Carleton, William T. (1859-1930)
1918 Tempered Steel

Carleton, William, Sr. could be same
as Carleton, W. C. (1871-1941);
Carleton, William P. (1873-1947)
or Carleton, William T.
(1859-1930)
1915 The Whirl of Life

Carleton, William P. (1873-1947) same
as Carleton, W. P.; Carlton,
William P.; could be same as
Carleton, William or **Carleton,**
William, Sr.
1917 Scandal
1919 A Society Exile
1920 The Amateur Wife
The Copperhead
The Flapper
His House in Order
The Riddle: Woman
Sinners

Carleton, William T. (1859-1930) same
as Carleton, W. T.; Carlton, W. T.;
Carlton, Will T.; Carlton, William
T.; could be same as Carleton,
William; or Carleton, William, Sr.
1914 Fantasma
The Idler
1915 The Fairy and the Waif
The Greater Will
The Incorrigible Dukane
Madame Butterfly
The Running Fight
1916 Poor Little Peppina
1917 The Antics of Ann
At First Sight

Daughter of Maryland
Fighting Odds
Sunshine Alley
1918 The Beloved Blackmailer
The Better Half
The Danger Mark
Everybody's Girl
Eye for Eye
The Heart of a Girl
The Love Net
The Racing Strain
1919 His Father's Wife
Home Wanted
The Lion and the Mouse
Me and Captain Kidd
A Society Exile*
1920 The Amateur Wife
The Copperhead
His Temporary Wife
Human Collateral
Sinners*

Carlisle, Alexandra
1917 The Tides of Fate

Carlisle, Grace see **Carlyle, Grace**

Carlisle, Helen
1919 The Usurper

Carlock, William
1915 Colorado

Carlos, C. M.
1918 Two-Gun Betty

Carlson, Robert
1920 The Mysteries of Paris

Carlton, Arma
1917 The Climber

Carlton, Carle E. same as **Carleton,**
Carle E.
1918 The Grain of Dust
A Romance of the Air

Carlton, Henry Guy same as **Carleton,**
Harry Guy
1919 The Phantom Honeymoon
1920 The Place of Honeymoons

Carlton, Herbert O. see **Carleton,**
Herbert O.

Carlton, Rena
1916 The Voice of Love
1917 The Sea Master

Carlton, William, Jr. not the same as
Carleton, W. C. (1871-1941);
Carleton, William; Carleton,
William, Sr.; Carleton, William P.
(1873-1947); or **Carleton, William**
T. (1859-1930)
1919 The Spark Divine

Carlton, William P. see **Carleton,**
William P.

Carlton, William T. see **Carleton,**
William T.

Carlyle, Francis
1913 Arizona
1914 Detective Craig's Coup

Carlyle, G. H.
1920 Man and Woman (A. H.
Fischer Features, Inc.)

Carlyle, Grace same as **Carlisle, Grace**
1916 The Eagle's Wing
An International Marriage
The Place Beyond the Winds
1917 Please Help Emily
1918 My Wife
1919 Bringing Up Betty

Carlyle, Hugh
1918 Arizona

Carlyle, Jack same as **Carlyle, J.**
Montgomery; Carlyle, John;
Carlysle, Jack
1917 The Midnight Man
1919 The Arizona Cat Claw
Flame of the Desert
A Girl in Bohemia
1920 The Forbidden Thing
The Girl Who Dared
Lahoma
The Penalty
The Star Rover
Twin Beds

Carlyle, Richard
1915 The Bridge of Sighs
An Enemy to Society
1919 Spotlight Sadie
1920 The Copperhead
The Stolen Kiss

Carlyle, Sidney
1920 Humoresque

Carlysle, Jack see **Carlyle, Jack**

Carmen, Jewel same as **Carman, Jewell**
1916 American Aristocracy
The Children in the House
Daphne and the Pirate
Flirting with Fate
The Half-Breed
Manhattan Madness
Sunshine Dad
1917 American Methods
The Conquerer
A Tale of Two Cities
To Honor and Obey
When a Man Sees Red
1918 The Bride of Fear
Confession
The Fallen Angel
The Girl with the Champagne
Eyes
Lawless Love
Les Miserables

Carmen, La Belle
1914 Mrs. Wiggs of the Cabbage
Patch

Carmen, Sybil
1918 A Romance of the Underworld

Carnahan, Thomas, Jr. same as
Carnahan, Junior; Carnahan, T. B.,
Jr.; Carnahan, Thomas
1915 Dr. Rameau
1916 The Sex Lure
1917 Chris and His Wonderful
Lamp
1918 Uncle Tom's Cabin

Carney, Augustus
1915 The Absentee
The Failure
The Martyrs of the Alamo
1916 Blue Blood and Red

Carney, Lucille same as **Carney, Lucile**
1914 Cinderella
1918 Eve's Daughter
1919 My Little Sister
1920 The Dark Mirror

Carpenter, Betty (actress)
1918 The Kaiser, the Beast of Berlin

Carpenter, Edward Childs
1918 The Make-Believe Wife

Carpenter, Elizabeth R. (scen)
1919 The Quickening Flame

Carpenter, Florence
1917 The World Apart
1918 Face Value
A Pair of Silk Stockings
Uncle Tom's Cabin
1919 Jinx
Some Bride
1920 The Testing Block

Carpenter, Francis
1915 The Commanding Officer
1916 The Children in the House
Going Straight
Gretchen, the Greenhorn
Let Katie Do It
Macbeth
Martha's Vindication
The Patriot
A Sister of Six
1917 Aladdin and the Wonderful
Lamp
The Babes in the Woods
Jack and the Beanstalk
1918 Fan Fan
The Girl with the Champagne
Eyes
Treasure Island
True Blue
1919 The Forbidden Room

Carpenter, George M.
1919 Lombardi, Ltd.
1920 The Best of Luck
The Right of Way
The Willow Tree

Carpenter, Grant
1916 Bobbie of the Ballet
A Child of the Paris Streets
1920 The Woman Gives

Carpenter, H. B. see **Carpenter, Horace**
B.

Carpenter, H. C.
1918 The Border Raiders
1919 The Devil's Trail
Carpenter, Horace B. (*actor*) *same as*
Carpenter, H. B.; Carpenter, Horace
1914 The Call of the North
The Ghost Breaker
The Man from Home
The Man on the Box
The Virginian
1915 The Arab
Armstrong's Wife
Carmen (Jesse L. Lasky
Feature Play Co.)
The Country Boy
The Explorer
The Goose Girl
Mr. Grex of Monte Carlo
The Puppet Crown
Stolen Goods
The Unknown
1916 Anton the Terrible
The Blacklist
The Clown
Common Ground
For the Defense
The Golden Chance
The Heir to the Hoorah
Joan the Woman
Maria Rosa
The Plow Girl
The Race
The Selfish Woman
The Sowers
Sweet Kitty Bellairs
The Thousand Dollar Husband
1917 Castles for Two
The Cost of Hatred
The Devil-Stone
The Ghost House
The Jaguar's Claws
Nan of Music Mountain
The Winning of Sally Temple
1918 Jules of the Strong Heart
One More American
Carpenter, Horace P. (*writer*)
1917 Wild and Woolly
Carpenter, James
1919 A Gentleman of Quality
Carpenter, Merta
1914 The Only Son
What's His Name
Carpenter, Richie
1917 The Blood of His Fathers
Carpenter, Theo-Alice
1920 The Luck of Geraldine Laird
Carpenter, William
1916 The Adventures of Kathlyn
Carpentier, Georges
1920 The Wonder Man
Carr, "Baby"
1918 My Own United States
Carr, Billie (*asst dir*)
1915 Scandal
1916 The Dumb Girl of Portici
Honor Thy Name
Carr, Billy (*child actor*)
1918 The Triumph of the Weak
Carr, Catherine *same as* **Carr,**
Catharine; Carr, Katharine
1914 The Coming Power
The Span of Life
The Spirit of the Poppy
1915 The Melting Pot
The Whirl of Life
1916 A Huntress of Men
The Narrow Path
Temptation and the Man
1917 The Primrose Ring
The Regenerates
1918 The Atom
The Ghost Flower
High Tide
I Love You
Irish Eyes
The Lonely Woman
The Painted Lady
Secret Code
Shifting Sands
A Soul in Trust
Station Content
1919 The Game's Up
Prudence on Broadway
Toton

The Usurper
1920 The Corsican Brothers
The Forgotten Woman
Carr, Dixie *same as* **Carr, Dixey**
1914 False Colours
1915 The Hypocrites
Jewel
1916 The Grip of Jealousy
Secret Love
Carr, Ernest
1915 The Fight
Carr, Harry
1914 The Boundary Rider
1919 I'll Get Him Yet
1920 Flying Pat
Little Miss Rebellion
1922 The Cynic Effect
Carr, John *same as* **Carr, Johnny**
1917 Over the Hill
Polly of the Circus
Carr, Katharine *see* **Carr, Catherine**
Carr, Louella
1920 Over the Hill to the Poorhouse
Carr, Mary *same as* **Carr, Mrs.; Carr,**
Mary K.; Carr, Mary Kennavan;
Carr, Mary Kennevan; Carr, Mary
Kennevean; Carr, Mrs. William
1916 The City of Failing Light
The Flames of Johannis
Her Bleeding Heart
Light at Dusk
Love's Toll
Souls in Bondage
1917 The Barrier
1918 The Birth of a Race
My Own United States
The Sign Invisible
To the Highest Bidder
1919 Calibre 38
The Lion and the Mouse
Mrs. Wiggs of the Cabbage
Patch
The Spark Divine
1920 Over the Hill to the Poorhouse
Carr, Maybeth
1920 Over the Hill to the Poorhouse
Carr, Peter
1920 The Invisible Divorce
Carr, Rosemary
1916 The Flames of Johannis
1920 Over the Hill to the Poorhouse
Carr, Stephen
1917 Polly of the Circus
1918 Little Miss No-Account
The Mating
The Song of the Soul
The Street of Seven Stars
To the Highest Bidder
1919 The Littlest Scout
1920 The Key to Power
Over the Hill to the Poorhouse
The Restless Sex
Carr, Thomas
1918 Virtuous Wives
1919 Through the Toils
1920 The Idol Dancer
Carr, W. H. (*property master*)
1915 Help Wanted
Carr, William (*actor*)
1913 The Battle of Shiloh
1915 The Rights of Man: A Story of
War's Red Blotch
1920 The Veiled Marriage
Carr, Mrs. William *see* **Carr, Mary**
Carrara, Ray
1917 A Hungry Heart
Carré, Ben *same as* **Carré, Benjamin**
1915 Trilby
1917 Barbary Sheep
Exile
The Poor Little Rich Girl
The Pride of the Clan
The Rise of Jennie Cushing
The Undying Flame
The Whip
1918 The Blue Bird
A Doll's House
Prunella
The Rose of the World
Sporting Life
Woman
1919 In Old Kentucky
The Life Line

Victory
1920 Dinty
For the Soul of Rafael
Go and Get It
The River's End
Stronger Than Death
Carrera, Liane Held
1918 The Liar
Carrick, Allyn B.
1920 Her Story
Carrigan, Thomas J. *same as* **Carrigan,**
Thomas; Carrigan, Tom
1914 The Royal Box
1916 Dimples
Lovely Mary
Rose of the Alley
1917 Peggy, the Will O' the Wisp
Somewhere in America
1919 Checkers
Dust of Desire
1920 In Walked Mary
Love's Flame
The Tiger's Cub
The Truth
Carrillo, Diana
1918 Station Content
Carrington, Evelyn C.
1920 In Search of a Sinner
Carrington, Frank
1914 The $5,000,000 Counterfeiting
Plot
Carrington, Phyllis
1915 The Morals of Marcus
Carrington, Reginald
1917 Life's Whirlpool
Outcast
1918 To Him That Hath
The Zero Hour
1919 The Unveiling Hand
Carrol, Ajax
1918 Peg of the Pirates
Carroll, Albert
1920 39 East
Carroll, Alice
1917 Two-Bit Seats
Carroll, Frank J.
1918 The Woman the Germans Shot
Carroll, Harry W.
1919 A Romance of Seattle
Carroll, James C. *same as* **Carroll,**
James
1917 Fools for Luck
The Penny Philanthropist
Skinner's Baby
Skinner's Bubble
Skinner's Dress Suit
Carroll, Joseph
1917 The Love That Lives
Carroll, Marcelle
1920 Love's Flame
Nothing but the Truth
Carroll, Richard Field
1919 Reclaimed: The Struggle for a
Soul Between Love and Hate
Carroll, William *same as* **Carroll, W.**
A.; Carroll, William A.
1915 The End of the Road
The Lonesome Heart
The Quest
1916 And the Law Says
The Courtesan
A Dream or Two Ago
Dulcie's Adventure
Embers
The Girl O' Dreams
Lord Loveland Discovers
America
Powder
Purity
Revelations
The Twinkler
A Woman's Daring
1917 John Ermine of the
Yellowstone
Molly Entangled
My Fighting Gentleman
A Roadside Impresario
1918 Danger Within
The Magic Eye
A Woman's Fool
1919 Bill Henry
The Blue Bonnet
Cheating Cheaters

Married in Haste
One-Thing-at-a-Time O'Day
Carson, Mr.
1916 Tempest and Sunshine
Carson, Mrs.
1916 Tempest and Sunshine
Carson, Adele
1915 The Garden of Lies
Carson, Carola
1918 Love Watches
Carson, Ella Stuart
1917 His Mother's Boy
Love Letters
The Price Mark
1918 The Claws of the Hun
Green Eyes
The Law of the North
1919 The Law of Men
1920 A Fool and His Money
Carson, Robert (*actor*)
1917 The Avenging Trail
1918 Cyclone Higgins, D.D.
Carson, Robert (*cam*) *see* **Carson,**
Robert L.
Carson, Robert L. (*cam*) *same as*
Carson, Robert (*cam*)
1914 Where the Trail Divides
1916 The Adventures of Kathlyn
The Woman Who Dared
1919 Children of Banishment
Jacques of the Silver North
The Price Woman Pays
1920 Mountain Madness
Carson, Willie May
1920 Silk Hosiery
Carter, A. A.
1920 Partners of the Night
Carter, Calvert
1918 Less Than Kin
1919 Six Feet Four
1920 Cinderella's Twin
The Fighting Shepherdess
Carter, Calvin
1917 Wild and Woolly
Carter, Catherine
1914 The Greyhound
The Lost Paradise
Carter, Dorothy Elizabeth
1920 Remodelling Her Husband
Carter, Douglas S.
1920 The Poor Simp
Carter, Harry
1915 The Frame-Up
Judge Not; Or, The Woman of
Mona Diggings
The Silent Command
1916 The Beckoning Trail
Langdon's Legacy
The Measure of a Man
The Pool of Flame
The Right to Be Happy
Secret Love
The Silent Battle
The Social Buccaneer
A Son of the Immortals
A Youth for Fortune
1917 Beloved Jim
The Circus of Life
Even As You and I
A Kentucky Cinderella
1918 After the War
Beans
The Bride's Awakening
The Girl in the Dark
The Kaiser, the Beast of Berlin
Kiss or Kill
The Marriage Lie
Three Mounted Men
Which Woman?
1919 After His Own Heart
1920 Thou Art the Man
Carter, Mrs. Leslie
1915 Du Barry
The Heart of Maryland
Carter, Lucy
1917 Madame Sherry
Carter, Nan
1916 The Serpent
Carter, W. N.
1917 The Lady in the Library

Cartmell, Mayor N. M.
1920 The Copperhead
Carton, Leone
1918 Shifting Sands
Cartwright, Peggy
1920 Love
     The Third Generation
Cartwright, William
1919 The Ace of the Saddle
Carufel, Fred
1916 The Valiants of Virginia
Caruso, Enrico
1918 My Cousin
1919 The Splendid Romance
Carvil, Henry J. *same as* **Carvil, Henry;**
   Carvill, H.; Carvill, H. J.; Carvill,
   Harry; Carvill, Henry
1915 The Greater Will
1918 Just a Woman
     To Hell with the Kaiser
     The Turn of the Wheel
1919 The Great Victory, Wilson or
     the Kaiser? The Fall of the
     Hohenzollerns
1920 The Branded Woman
     Guilty of Love
     If I Were King
Cary, Nadia *see* **Gary, Nadia**
Case, Anna
1919 The Hidden Truth
Case, Helen
1915 The Cowboy and the Lady
Case, Willard
1916 The City of Illusion
     The Immortal Flame
     The Ransom
Caseneuve, Paul *see* **Cazeneuve, Paul**
Casey, Kenneth
1920 The Adventurer
Casey, Leslie *same as* **Casey, Lesley**
1919 Good Gracious, Annabelle
     The Other Man's Wife
The Casino Players
1916 Cousin Jim*
Cassady, James
1915 The Great Ruby
1916 The Flames of Johannis
Cassavant, Nina
1920 Dangerous Business
Cassidy, Ellen *same as* **Cassity, Ellen**
1916 The Kiss
1918 Caught in the Act
     Marriages Are Made
     Milady O' the Beanstalk
     The Voice of Destiny
1919 Checkers
     Love, Honor and—?
     The Other Man's Wife
     Through the Toils
1920 Broadway and Home
     Passers-By
     The Vice of Fools
Cassidy, J. M.
1915 The Goose Girl
Cassinelli, Dolores
1918 Lafayette, We Come!
     The Million Dollar Dollies
     Zongar
1919 The Right to Lie
     The Unknown Love
     The Virtuous Model
1920 The Hidden Light
     Tarnished Reputations
     The Web of Deceit
Cassity, Ellen *see* **Cassidy, Ellen**
Castelet, William
1915 A Bunch of Keys
Castellanos, Joseph
1916 Half a Rogue
Castillo, Francisco
1917 The Ghost of Old Morro
Castle, Irene *same as* **Castle, Mrs.**
   Vernon
1915 The Whirl of Life
1917 The Mark of Cain
     Stranded in Arcady
     Sylvia of the Secret Service
     Vengeance Is Mine
1918 Convict 993
     The First Law
     The Girl from Bohemia
     The Hillcrest Mystery

     The Mysterious Client
1919 The Common Cause
     The Firing Line
     The Invisible Bond
1920 The Amateur Wife
Castle, Vernon
1915 The Whirl of Life
Castleman, Mary
1919 A Romance of Happy Valley
Castleton, Barbara
1914 The Ordeal
1917 For the Freedom of the World
     God's Man
     Her Good Name
     On Trial
     Sins of Ambition
1918 Empty Pockets
     The Heart of a Girl
     Heredity
     Just Sylvia
     Parentage
     Vengeance
1919 The Man Who Turned White
     Peg O' My Heart
     The Rough Neck
     The Silver King
     What Love Forgives
1920 The Branding Iron
     Dangerous Days
     Dangerous Hours
     Out of the Storm
Castlewood, Rosebud
1919 Give and Take
Caswell, Nancy
1918 The Blindness of Divorce
     The Moral Law*
     Riders of the Purple Sage
1919 The Call of the Soul
     The Day She Paid
1920 The Mother of His Children
     Shore Acres
     Under Crimson Skies
     Would You Forgive?
Catlin, Alice
1918 Which Woman?*
Catlin, George
1920 The Symbol of the
     Unconquered
Caulfield, H. P.
1920 What Women Love
Caulfield, Ward
1918 False Ambition
     Irish Eyes
     Station Content
Caull, Zella *see* **Call, Zella**
Cavalieri, Lina
1914 Manon Lescaut
1917 The Eternal Temptress
1918 Love's Conquest
     A Woman of Impulse
1919 The Two Brides
Cavanaugh, Lucille
1920 Leave It to Me
Cavanaugh, William *same as*
   Cavanaugh, William H.
1913 Traffic in Souls
1914 The $5,000,000 Counterfeiting
     Plot
     Rip Van Winkle
     The Seats of the Mighty
1918 Morgan's Raiders
     The Sign Invisible
1919 Calibre 38
     The Open Door
1920 The Bromley Case
     Love's Plaything
Cavender, Glen
1915 A Submarine Pirate
Cavin, R. A.
1916 Kinkaid, Gambler
Cawood, Al *same as* **Cawood, Albert E.**
1914 Shannon of the Sixth
1917 Fear Not
     A Soul for Sale
Cazeneuve, Paul *same as* **Caseneuve,**
   Paul
1919 His Wife's Friend
1920 The Adventurer
     Heart Strings
     Her Honor the Mayor
     The Iron Heart
     The Spirit of Good
     The Square Shooter

     Sunset Sprague
Cecil, Edward *same as* **Cecil, Edwin**
1914 The Burglar and the Lady
1916 The Beast
     The Love Thief
1917 Conscience
     The Show Down
     The Yankee Way
1918 After the War
     Bread
     The Danger Zone
     Fast Company
     The Kaiser's Shadow, or the
     Triple Cross
     The Man Who Wouldn't Tell
     Restitution
     The Risky Road
     The Wildcat of Paris
1919 A Girl in Bohemia
     The Lost Princess
     The Solitary Sin
     The Woman Under Cover
1920 Blackmail
     Cinderella's Twin
     Parted Curtains
     The Price of Redemption
     Sink or Swim
     The Third Generation
Cecil, Mary
1917 Persuasive Peggy
Cecil, Nora *same as* **Cecile, Nora;**
   Cecile, Norah
1915 The Arrival of Perpetua
1917 The Little Duchess
     Royal Romance
     The Wild Girl
1918 American Buds
     The Appearance of Evil
     By Hook or Crook
     The Love Net
     The Power and the Glory
     Prunella
     The Zero Hour
1919 Miss Crusoe
     Woman, Woman!
1920 The Daughter Pays
Cecil, Robert
1918 The Vigilantes
Cecile, Nora *see* **Cecil, Nora**
Cederberg, E. J.
1920 Brain Cinema
Ceillie, Jean
1915 Judge Not; Or, The Woman of
     Mona Diggings
     The Man of Shame
Cello, Mary du *see* **Du Cello, Countess**
Cervi, Nora
1916 Poor Little Peppina
Chadwick, Cyril
1914 Doc
     Mrs. Black Is Back
1915 Marrying Money
1916 The Smugglers
1917 Bab's Matinee Idol
1918 Mrs. Dane's Defense
     On the Quiet
     The Richest Girl
1919 Out Yonder
1920 Clothes
     His Wife's Money
     The Misleading Lady
Chadwick, Helene *same as* **Chadwick,**
   Helen
1916 The Challenge
1917 The Angel Factory
     Blind Man's Luck
     The Iron Heart
     The Last of the Carnabys
     Vengeance Is Mine
1918 Convict 993
     For Sale
     The Naulahka
     The Yellow Ticket
1919 An Adventure in Hearts
     Caleb Piper's Girl
     Girls
     Go Get 'Em Garringer
     Heartsease
     The Long Arm of Mannister
     The Solitary Sin
     A Very Good Young Man
1920 The Cup of Fury
     Cupid, the Cowpuncher
     Godless Men

     Scratch My Back
Chailee, F. T.
1919 Anne of Green Gables
Chailee, Joseph S. *same as* **Chailee,**
   Joseph; Chaille, Joe; Chailles,
   Joseph
1915 The Fight
1916 The Spell of the Yukon
1917 The Lone Wolf
1920 Beyond the Great Wall
Chailles, Charles
1916 War Brides
Chailles, Joseph *see* **Chailee, Joseph S.**
Challenger, Percy
1917 Ashes of Hope
     The Flame of Youth
     Flirting with Death*
     The Medicine Man
     The Spirit of Romance
     The Sudden Gentleman
     Wild Sumac
1918 Captain of His Soul
     The Flames of Chance
     The Fly God
     The Law's Outlaw
     Little Red Decides
     The Lonely Woman
     Nancy Comes Home
     Old Hartwell's Cub
     The Pretender
1919 Blind Husbands
     One Week of Life
     What Every Woman Wants
1920 The Cheater
     The Heart of Twenty
     In the Heart of a Fool
     Trumpet Island
     Uncharted Channels
Chamberlain, Ray
1915 The Great Divide
1916 Those Who Toil
1918 The Sign Invisible
Chamberlain, Riley
1916 Prudence the Pirate
1917 Her New York
Chamberlain, William *could be same*
   as **Chamberlain, Winthrop** *or*
   Chamberlin, William C.
1914 Rip Van Winkle
Chamberlain, Winthrop *could be same*
   as **Chamberlain, William** *or*
   Chamberlin, William C.
1914 Soldiers of Fortune
1915 Marrying Money
Chamberlin, J. R.
1917 The Bar Sinister
Chamberlin, William C. *could be same*
   as **Chamberlain, William** *or*
   Chamberlain, Winthrop
1915 Wildfire
Chambers, Hugh
1915 The Cowpuncher
Chambers, Lyster *same as* **Chambers,**
   Lester
1914 The Span of Life
1915 At Bay
     The Broken Law
     Divorced
     Fine Feathers
     Gretna Green
     Marse Covington
1916 Big Jim Garrity
     The Wager
1919 Bringing Up Betty
     A Fallen Idol
     The Jungle Trail
     My Little Sister
     Should a Husband Forgive?
Chambers, Marie *same as* **Chambers,**
   Mary
1916 Fifty-Fifty
     The Woman in the Case
1917 Maternity
1919 The Gay Old Dog
     The Virtuous Model
Chambers, Robert W.
1918 The Girl of Today
1920 The Song of the Soul
Champlain, Polly
1915 The Labyrinth

The Rack
Sudden Riches
1917 The Eternal Temptress
The Family Honor
The Fires of Youth
Forget-Me-Not
The Heart of Ezra Greer
A Hungry Heart
Magda
The Man Who Forgot
Under False Colors
The Web of Desire
1918 A Daughter of the Old South
Her Final Reckoning
The House of Glass
The Marionettes
The Ordeal of Rosetta
Under the Greenwood Tree
1919 Eyes of the Soul
His Parisian Wife
The Marriage Price
The Mystery of the Yellow
Room
Out of the Shadow
Paid in Full
1920 The Invisible Foe
Chenault, Jack
1920 Within Our Gates
Chenault, Lawrence
1920 The Brute
The Symbol of the
Unconquered
Cherney, Mr.
1915 Du Barry
Cherry, Charles
1915 The Mummy and the
Humming Bird
1916 Passers By
Cherryman, Rex
1919 In for Thirty Days
1920 Madame Peacock
Chesebro, George same as **Chesboro,
George; Cheseborough, George;
Chesbro, George; Cheseboro,
George; Chesebro, George N.**
1915 Mignon
Money
1916 Humanizing Mr. Winsby
The Land Just Over Yonder
1917 Because of a Woman
Broadway Arizona
Indiscreet Corinne
Mr. Opp
The Show Down
The Spirit of '76
Wild Sumac
1918 Modern Love
Riders of the Night
The Risky Road
1919 The She Wolf
1920 The Jungle Princess
Wanted at Headquarters
Cheshire, Mildred
1916 The Madness of Helen
1918 The Struggle Everlasting
1919 The Woman Under Oath
1920 The Flapper
Chester, George Randolph
1915 The Juggernaut*
The Sins of the Mothers*
1916 The Enemy
1917 The Message of the Mouse
The More Excellent Way*
1918 Twenty-One
The Wild Strain
1919 The Climbers
From Headquarters
The Painted World
Shadows of the Past
The Third Degree
Two Women
The Vengeance of Durand
The Wreck
1920 The Birth of a Soul
Dead Men Tell No Tales
Slaves of Pride
Trumpet Island
Chester, Mrs. George Randolph see
Chester, Lillian
Chester, L. C.
1916 America Preparing

Chester, Lila
1913 The Legend of Provence
Moths
1914 Cardinal Richelieu's Ward
1915 The Little Mademoiselle
The Sins of Society
1916 Miss Petticoats
The Unpardonable Sin
1917 The Page Mystery
A Self-Made Widow
1918 The Million Dollar Mystery
Stolen Hours
Vengeance
Chester, Lillian same as **Chester, Mrs.
George Randolph; Chester, Lillian
Randolph**
1915 The Juggernaut*
The Sins of the Mothers*
1916 The Enemy
1917 The Message of the Mouse
The More Excellent Way*
1918 The Wild Strain
1919 The Climbers
The Painted World
Shadows of the Past
The Third Degree
Two Women
The Vengeance of Durand
The Wreck
1920 The Birth of a Soul
Dead Men Tell No Tales
Slaves of Pride
Trumpet Island
Chester, Ruth
1916 Her Great Price
Chester, Virginia
1918 The Demon
Restitution
The Vanity Pool
Chester, William
1918 The Girl Who Wouldn't Quit
The Spirit of '17
Chesterton, Cecil
1918 Her Man*
Cheung, Louie
1919 The Girl from Outside
1920 The Branding Iron
Chevalier, Bliss
1917 The Gown of Destiny
On Record
What Money Can't Buy
1918 Betty Takes a Hand
The Biggest Show on Earth
The Mask
You Can't Believe Everything
Chevalier, Yvonne
1917 The Fortunes of Fifi
Members of the Chicago White Sox
1914 The Giants-White Sox Tour
Chichester, Cecil
1918 Her Man
A Romance of the Underworld
1919 A Stitch in Time
Too Many Crooks
Chichester, Emily
1919 God's Outlaw
Nobody Home
Nugget Nell
Peppy Polly
1920 Burglar Proof
Miss Hobbs
Once to Every Woman
The Woman in Room 13
Child, Ogden see **Childe, Ogden**
Child, Richard Washburn
1919 Faith
Love Is Love
The Merry-Go-Round
Childe, Ogden same as **Child, Ogden;
Child, Master Ogden; Child, Ogden,
Jr.**
1914 The Gangsters
The Sign of the Cross
The Span of Life
1915 The Dawn of a Tomorrow
Divorced
Four Feathers
The Warning
1916 The Undertow
Childers, Hazel
1915 The Cheat

Childers, Naomi
1914 Mr. Barnes of New York
The Tangle
1915 The Dust of Egypt
The Island of Regeneration
The Man Who Couldn't Beat
God
The Turn of the Road
1916 The Devil's Prize
Fathers of Men
The Footlights of Fate
The Price of Fame
The Writing on the Wall
1917 The Auction of Virtue
Womanhood, the Glory of the
Nation
1919 After His Own Heart
Blind Man's Eyes
The Divorcee
The Gay Lord Quex
Human Desire
Lord and Lady Algy
Shadows of Suspicion
The World and Its Woman
1920 Duds
Earthbound
The Street Called Straight
Ching, Hoo
1917 The War of the Tongs
Chira, Harry
1916 The Haunted Manor
The Idol of the Stage
Chisholm, William
1917 The Conquerer
Chong, Joe
1918 For the Freedom of the East
Chrider, Leota
1915 A Bunch of Keys
Chrisman, Pat
1918 Ace High
Western Blood
1919 The Coming of the Law
Rough Riding Romance
The Wilderness Trail
1920 The Daredevil
The Texan
The Untamed
Christensen, Miss
1919 The Gray Towers Mystery
Christian, Mr.
1919 Injustice
Christian, William S.
1918 Hearts of Love
Christians, Broerken
1920 Deep Waters
Christians, Margarete
1916 Audrey
Christians, Rudolph
1920 Burnt Wings
Her Five-Foot Highness
Human Stuff
The Secret Gift
Christie, Al E. same as **Christie, Al**
1915 Mrs. Plum's Pudding
1920 So Long Letty
Christie, Charles
1920 813
Christie, George Stuart same as
Christie, George Stewart
1917 The Duchess of Doubt
Sowers and Reapers
Christie, Ivan see **Christy, Ivan**
Christie, Nan see **Christy, Nan**
Christine, Baby
1916 Should a Baby Die?
Christy, Ivan same as **Christie, Ivan**
1917 Salt of the Earth
1918 The Glorious Adventure
1919 Coax Me
Christy, Nan same as **Christie, Nan**
1915 The End of the Road
An Eye for an Eye
The Quest
1916 The Leopard's Bride
The Love Liar
1917 The Single Code
Unto the End
1918 On the Quiet
Chung, Liu
1918 Mystic Faces

Chung, Walter
1920 Dinty
Church, Fred
1915 The Long Chance
1916 The End of the Rainbow
The Flirt
The Girl of the Lost Lake
It Happened in Honolulu
A Romance of Billy Goat Hill
The Secret of the Swamp
The Wrong Door
1917 The Clever Mrs. Carfax
Du Barry
The Phantom's Secret
Southern Justice
1918 Angel Child
The Blindness of Divorce
1919 The Son-of-a-Gun!
Church, Thornton
1918 The Brazen Beauty
The Deciding Kiss
Churchill, Burton
1919 The Road Called Straight
Churchill, Grant
1916 The Argonauts of
California—1849
The Daughter of the Don
1918 The Vigilantes
Cianelli, Eduardo same as **Ciannelli,
Eduardo**
1917 The Food Gamblers
Cicotte, Eddie
1917 The Baseball Revue of 1917*
Cills, Norbert
1915 Money
Cladwell, Lee
1915 The Cowpuncher
Clair, George same as **Claire, George,
Jr.; Clare, George**
1916 A Law unto Himself
The Soul's Cycle
1920 Below the Surface
Clair, Mildred
1918 Treason
Clair, Roy
1916 The Child of Destiny
Life's Shadows
Claire, Madame
1914 The Three of Us
Claire, Clairet see **Clare, Clarette**
Claire, George, Jr. see **Clair, George**
Claire, Gertrude
1915 The Coward
1916 The Apostle of Vengeance
The Aryan
The Criminal
The Female of the Species
Honor Thy Name
The Jungle Child
Lieutenant Danny, U.S.A.
The Market of Vain Desire
The Payment
Peggy
The Wolf Woman
1917 The Crab
Golden Rule Kate
Happiness
His Mother's Boy
Madcap Madge
The Mother Instinct
The Silent Man
Wooden Shoes
1918 Blue Blazes Rawden
Keys of the Righteous
A Nine O'Clock Town
When Do We Eat?
1919 Blind Man's Eyes
Brothers Divided
The Crimson Gardenia
Hard Boiled
Jinx
Little Comrade
The Petal on the Current
Romance and Arabella
Stepping Out
Widow by Proxy
1920 The Cradle of Courage
Dollar for Dollar
The Forbidden Thing
Her Beloved Villain
Into the Light
Madame Peacock
The Money-Changers

1920 Her Unwilling Husband
Uncharted Channels
Clarke, Lillian *same as* **Clarke, Lilly;**
Clarke, Lily
1918 The Hun Within
Tongues of Flame
The Yellow Dog
Clarke, Marion
1916 The Missing Links*
Clarke, Redfield *same as* **Clark,**
Redfield
1914 The Spitfire
1917 The Greatest Power
Pardners
The Web of Life
1918 The Grain of Dust
Clarke, Richard *could be same as*
Clark, Dick
1917 Betsy Ross
The Burglar
The Iron Ring
The Little Duchess
The Maid of Belgium
A Self-Made Widow
1918 A Soul Without Windows
The Spurs of Sybil
Stolen Hours
Clarke, Wallace *same as* **Clark,**
Wallace; Clark, Wally
1916 Elusive Isabel
20,000 Leagues Under the Sea
1917 Cy Whittaker's Ward
1918 The Whirlpool
Clarke, William *see* **Clark, William**
Clary, Charles
1915 The Carpet from Bagdad
A Man's Prerogative
The Penitentes
The Rosary
Strathmore
1916 The Adventures of Kathlyn
The Blacklist
Each Pearl a Tear
Joan the Woman
The Price of Power
Tennessee's Pardner
1917 The Conqueror
Du Barry
For Liberty
High Finance
The Honor System
The Innocent Sinner
The Price of Silence
The Rose of Blood
The Silent Lie
The Soul of Satan
The Spy
A Tale of Two Cities
To Honor and Obey
1918 The Blindness of Divorce
The Fallen Angel
Kultur
Riders of the Purple Sage
The Scarlet Road
The Strange Woman
True Blue
1919 Bonds of Love
The Call of the Soul
The Day She Paid
Extravagance
A Girl Named Mary
The Girl with No Regrets
The Last of the Duanes
The Lone Star Ranger
The Man Hunter
The Splendid Sin
Under Suspicion
Wolves of the Night
1920 A Connecticut Yankee at King
Arthur's Court
A Light Woman
The Penalty
The Street Called Straight
The Woman in Room 13
Clauson (full name unknown)
1915 The Fairy and the Waif*
Clawson, Dal
1914 The Merchant of Venice
1915 Captain Courtesy
The Gentleman from Indiana*
The Hypocrites
It's No Laughing Matter
Pretty Mrs. Smith*
The Rosary

Scandal
Sunshine Molly
The Yankee Girl
1916 The Call of the Cumberlands
Civilization
The Dumb Girl of Portici
The Female of the Species
Honor Thy Name
The Honorable Algy
The Love Thief
The Phantom
Somewhere in France
The Vagabond Prince
1917 Betrayed
The Conqueror
The Innocent Sinner
One Touch of Sin
The Pride of New York
The Silent Lie
This Is the Life
The Weaker Sex
1918 For Husbands Only
The Red, Red Heart
1919 Bonds of Honor
The Courageous Coward
Eve in Exile
Forbidden
A Heart in Pawn
Her Kingdom of Dreams
Mary Regan
A Midnight Romance
When a Girl Loves
1920 The Corsican Brothers
Clawson, Elliott J. *same as* **Clawson, E.**
J.; Clawson, Elliot; Clawson, Elliott
1914 The Truth Wagon
1915 Jack Chanty
The Yankee Girl
1916 Bettina Loved a Soldier
The Bugler of Algiers
Davy Crockett*
The Evil Women Do
From Broadway to a Throne
The Heritage of Hate
Madame La Presidente
The Right to Be Happy
Tongues of Men
1917 The Circus of Life
The Cricket
The Desire of the Moth
The Door Between
Double Room Mystery
The Double Standard
The Field of Honor
The Gift Girl
A Kentucky Cinderella
The Little Orphan
The Little Pirate
Mother O' Mine
My Little Boy
The Mysterious Mr. Tiller
Polly Redhead
The Savage
The Silent Lady
A Soul for Sale
1918 Beauty in Chains
Fires of Youth
Hands Down
The Kaiser, the Beast of Berlin
Midnight Madness
The Yellow Dog
1919 Common Property
Destiny
The Man in the Moonlight
The Sleeping Lion
1920 The Little Shepherd of
Kingdom Come
Clay, Celia
1915 York State Folks
Clay, Ten Eyck
1916 The Other Girl
Clay, Velma
1919 The Little Diplomat
Clayton, Arthur
1920 The Hope
In Folly's Trail
Clayton, Donald
1918 Rich Man, Poor Man
Clayton, Ethel
1914 The Daughters of Men
The Fortune Hunter
The Gamblers
The House Next Door
The Lion and the Mouse

The Wolf
1915 The College Widow
The Great Divide
The Sporting Duchess
1916 Broken Chains
Dollars and the Woman
The Hidden Scar
His Brother's Wife
Husband and Wife
The Madness of Helen
A Woman's Way
1917 The Bondage of Fear
The Dormant Power
Easy Money
Man's Woman
National Association's All-Star
Picture
Souls Adrift
The Stolen Paradise
The Volunteer
The Web of Desire
The Woman Beneath
Yankee Pluck
1918 The Girl Who Came Back
Journey's End
The Man Hunt
The Mystery Girl
A Soul Without Windows
Stolen Hours
Whims of Society
The Witch Woman
Women's Weapons
1919 Maggie Pepper
Men, Women and Money
More Deadly Than the Male
Pettigrew's Girl
A Sporting Chance (Famous
Players-Lasky Corp.)
The Woman Next Door
1920 A City Sparrow
Crooked Streets
The Ladder of Lies
A Lady in Love
The Sins of Rosanne
The Thirteenth Commandment
Young Mrs. Winthrop
Clayton, Frederic
1920 The Sacred Flame
Clayton, Lucille
1918 Virtuous Wives
Clayton, Marguerite
1915 The Birthmark
The Black Heart
A Daughter of the City
1916 According to the Code
The Prince of Graustark
Vultures of Society
1917 The Dream Doll
The Night Workers
Two-Bit Seats
1918 Hit-the-Trail Holliday
Inside the Lines
The Man of Bronze
1919 Bullin' the Bullsheviki
The New Moon
1920 Pleasure Seekers
Cleary, J. F.
1915 American Game Trails
Cleethorpe, George
1919 The Son-of-a-Gun!
Clemens, James H.
1916 Ben Blair
Clement, Miss *see* **Clement, Eloise**
Clement, Clay *could be same as*
Clement, Clay, Jr.
1918 The Power and the Glory
The Purple Lily
Stolen Honor
1919 Forest Rivals
The Steel King
Clement, Clay, Jr. *could be same as*
Clement, Clay
1918 The Appearance of Evil
The Heart of a Girl
The Sea Waif
Clement, Eloise *same as* **Clement, Miss**
1915 The Daughter of the Sea
1917 The Tenth Case
1918 The Burden of Proof
The Cross Bearer
Just Sylvia
The Oldest Law
1919 The Love Defender

Clement, Joseph I. *same as* **Clement,**
Joseph
1918 Wild Honey
1919 Twilight
Clemento, Steve *same as* **Clements,**
Steve
1917 The Secret Man
1918 The Scarlet Drop
1919 The Arizona Cat Claw
1920 The Girl Who Dared
Clements, Dudley
1920 Yes or No
Clements, Flo *could be same as*
Clements, Foy
1920 The Brute*
Within Our Gates
Clements, Foy *could be same as*
Clements, Flo
1920 The Brute
Clements, Hal
1914 The Man Who Could Not Lose
1915 Armstrong's Wife
The End of the Road
The House of a Thousand
Scandals
The Immigrant
The Lure of the Mask
Out of the Darkness
The Secret Sin
Secretary of Frivolous Affairs
The Unknown
1917 Miss Jackie of the Army
1918 An American Live Wire
Molly, Go Get 'Em
1919 An Innocent Adventuress
The Lamb and the Lion
Other Men's Wives
Clements, Renee *see* **Clemmons, Renee**
Clements, Roy
1918 Crown Jewels
The Light of Western Stars
The Reckoning Day*
1920 King Spruce
The Tiger's Coat
Clements, Steve *see* **Clemento, Steve**
Clemmons, Renee *same as* **Clements,**
Renee; Clemons, Renee
1916 The Chaperon
The Misleading Lady
The Return of Eve
Clerget, Paul
1917 A Crooked Romance
Over the Hill
1918 Mrs. Slacker
Woman
1920 My Lady's Garter
Cleveland, Anna
1919 The Stream of Life
Cleveland, Val
1919 A Dangerous Affair
1920 The Scoffer
Clevenger, Beatrice
1914 Dan
Cliffe, Mrs. Cooper
1915 The Greater Will
Cliffe, H. Cooper
1915 An Enemy to Society
The Face in the Moonlight
The Final Judgment
Her Reckoning
1916 Arms and the Woman
Extravagance
Gold and the Woman
The Kiss of Hate
A Parisian Romance
1917 The Argyle Case
Raffles, the Amateur
Cracksman
1920 The Blue Pearl
The Devil's Garden
Half an Hour
Clifford, Jack
1914 Threads of Destiny
Clifford, Kathleen
1918 Angel Child
The Law That Divides
1919 When the Clouds Roll By
Clifford, Ruth
1916 Behind the Lines
1917 The Desire of the Moth
The Door Between
Eternal Love
A Kentucky Cinderella

Mother O' Mine
The Mysterious Mr. Tiller
Polly Put the Kettle On
The Savage
1918 The Cabaret Girl
Fires of Youth
The Guilt of Silence
Hands Down
Hungry Eyes
The Kaiser, the Beast of Berlin
The Lure of Luxury
Midnight Madness
The Red, Red Heart
1919 The Black Gate
The Game's Up
The Millionaire Pirate
1920 The Amazing Woman
Clifford, Thomas E.
1920 The Mysteries of Paris
Clifford, W. H. see Clifford, William H.
(scen, dir)
Clifford, William (actor)
1915 Rosemary
The Second in Command
The Silent Voice
1916 The Bait
A Corner in Cotton
The Heart of Tara
The Hidden Law
The Leopard's Bride
Sins of Her Parent
1917 The Avenging Trail
The Island of Desire
Out of the Wreck
Paradise Garden
Pay Me
The Square Deceiver
A Tale of Two Cities
Under Handicap
Young Mother Hubbard
1918 Broadway Bill
The Landloper
1919 Gambling in Souls
The Long Arm of Mannister
A Man of Honor
1920 An Adventuress
The Confession
The Notorious Miss Lisle
Parted Curtains
The Turning Point
Clifford, William (scen) **see Clifford, William H.**
Clifford, William H. (scen, dir), same as Clifford, W. H.; Clifford, William (scen)
1914 The Bargain
Shorty Escapes Marriage
Threads of Destiny
The Wrath of the Gods
1916 The Eternal Grind
The Man from Nowhere
My Lady Incog.
Nearly a King
Out of the Drifts
The Spider
1918 Denny from Ireland
The Pen Vulture
The Ranger
1920 The Confession
The Dwelling Place of Light
The Money-Changers
Riders of the Dawn
The Sagebrusher
The U.P. Trail
Clift, Denison
1918 The Danger Zone
His Birthright
The Midnight Patrol
Wedlock
Wolves of the Rail
1919 The Call of the Soul
The Coming of the Law
The Divorce Trap
Gambling in Souls
A Girl in Bohemia
The Girl with No Regrets*
Lost Money
The Love That Dares
Rose of the West
Snares of Paris
The Speed Maniac
The Splendid Sin
When Fate Decides

1920 The Challenge of the Law
Firebrand Trevison
The Hell Ship
Her Honor the Mayor
The Iron Heart
The Last Straw
The Little Wanderer
The Spirit of Good
The Square Shooter
The Tattlers
What Would You Do?
Clifton, Adele
1916 Atta Boy's Last Race
Diane of the Follies
1917 Nina, the Flower Girl
An Old Fashioned Young Man
Clifton, Arthur Shaw
1914 The Idler
The Ragged Earl
1915 The Girl I Left Behind Me
Clifton, Elmer
1914 Burning Daylight: The
Adventures of "Burning
Daylight" in Alaska
John Barleycorn
Martin Eden
1915 The Birth of a Nation
The Fox Woman
The Lily and the Rose
The Lost House
The Sable Lorcha
1916 Acquitted
Intolerance
The Little School Ma'am
The Missing Links
The Old Folks at Home
1917 The Flame of Youth
Flirting with Death
Her Official Fathers
The High Sign
High Speed
The Man Trap
The Midnight Man
Nina, the Flower Girl
A Stormy Knight
1918 Battling Jane
Brace Up
The Eagle
The Flash of Fate
The Guilt of Silence
The Hope Chest
Kiss or Kill
Smashing Through
The Two-Soul Woman
Winner Takes All
1919 Boots
The Fall of Babylon
I'll Get Him Yet
Nobody Home
Nugget Nell
Peppy Polly
Turning the Tables
1920 Mary Ellen Comes to Town
Way Down East*
Clifton, Emma Bell
1917 More Truth Than Poetry
1918 Conquered Hearts
1919 The Little Diplomat
1920 The Blue Pearl
Clifton, Harry
1917 Man and Beast
Clifton, Lotta
1916 Intolerance
Clifton, Wallace C. same as Clifton, Wallace; Clifton, Wallace O.
1916 The Black Butterfly
The Devil at His Elbow
The Eternal Question
Extravagance
The Iron Woman
The Spell of the Yukon
Vanity
The Weakness of Strength
1917 Bridges Burned
The Secret of Eve
The Silence Sellers
The Waiting Soul
1918 Convict 993
The Interloper
Merely Players
Tinsel
To Him That Hath
T'Other Dear Charmer

1919 The American Way
The Hand Invisible
Love in a Hurry
The Oakdale Affair
Three Green Eyes
1920 The Marriage Pit
Wanted at Headquarters
Clifton, William F.
1917 The Kill-Joy
Clisbee, Edward
1914 The Boer War
Shannon of the Sixth
1915 The Pitfall
Clive, Henry
1917 Fighting Odds
Her Silent Sacrifice
1918 I Want to Forget
On the Jump
We Should Worry
1919 As a Man Thinks
When the Clouds Roll By
Clive, Mrs. Henry
1919 The Glorious Lady
Clogg, V. V.
1920 If I Were King
Clonblough, G. Butler see Seyffertitz, Gustav von
Clouston, J. Storer
1917 The Mystery of Number 47
Clovelly, Cecil
1920 Dr. Jekyll and Mr. Hyde
(Famous Players-Lasky
Corp.)
Cloy, May
1916 Bluff
Lonesome Town
A Million for Mary
Peck O' Pickles
Three Pals
1917 Beloved Rogues
Glory
Clugston, Robert
1916 The Isle of Love
1917 The Hunting of the Hawk
Kick In
Little Miss Nobody
The Little Terror
The Siren
Clulow, John
1915 The Eternal City
Clune, W. H.
1916 Ramona
Cluxon, Frank
1919 L'Apache
Clymer, John B. same as Clymer, John
1916 Ashes of Embers
The Drifter
In the Diplomatic Service
1917 The Duchess of Doubt
His Sweetheart
The Moth
On Record
Reputation
Weavers of Life
A Wife by Proxy
1918 Beans
Everywoman's Husband
Gates of Gladness
The Landloper
Lend Me Your Name
1919 The Blinding Trail
Broken Commandments
Go Get 'Em Garringer
In Search of Arcady
The Little Boss
What Am I Bid?
1920 The Riddle: Woman
Coakley, John
1914 Damon and Pythias
1915 The Frame-Up
The Spanish Jade
1916 Langdon's Legacy
The Pool of Flame
1920 Democracy
Coakley, Marion
1919 The Lost Battalion
Coan, M. Blair
1916 The Little Girl Next Door
1918 The Curse of Iku

Coates, Franklin B.
1914 The Captain Besley Expedition
1915 Always in the Way
In the Amazon Jungles with
the Captain Besley
Expedition
1916 The Price of Fame
The Spider and the Fly
A Wife's Sacrifice
1918 A Romance of the Air
1920 The Return of Tarzan
Coates, Hazel
1919 What Love Forgives
Cobb, Agnes Egan
1916 America Preparing*
Cobb, C. Lang, Jr.
1917 The Test of Womanhood
Cobb, Edmund F. same as Cobb,
Edmund; could be same as Cobb,
Edwin
1916 Captain Jinks of the Horse
Marines
1917 Moral Courage
1918 Social Briars
1920 The Desert Scorpion
Wolves of the Street
Cobb, Edwin could be same as Cobb,
Edmund F.
1918 The Deciding Kiss
Cobb, Irvin S.
1915 The Arab
1916 The Dollar and the Law
1917 Fighting Odds
1920 Go and Get It
Cobb, Ty
1916 Somewhere in Georgia
1917 The Baseball Revue of 1917*
Coburn, Gladys
1916 The Battle of Life
The Black Crook
Madame X
1917 The Primitive Call
1919 The Firing Line
1920 The Fatal Hour
Heart Strings
Out of the Snows
Voices
Coburn, W.
1918 The Kaiser, the Beast of Berlin
Coburn, Wallace G.
1918 The Sunset Princess
Cochran, R. H. see Cochrane, R. H.
Cochrane, George
1917 The Spindle of Life
Cochrane, R. H. same as Cochran, R.
H.
1915 The Arrival of Perpetua*
1919 The Exquisite Thief
Cody, Albert same as Cody, Albert R.
1916 The Honorable Algy
1918 The Bells
The Turn of a Card
Two-Gun Betty
1919 All of a Sudden Norma
The Joyous Liar
1920 Madame Peacock
Unseen Forces
Cody, Lewis J. same as Cody, Lew;
Cody, Lewis
1915 Comrade John
The Mating
Should a Wife Forgive?
1916 The Cycle of Fate
1917 A Branded Soul
The Bride's Silence
A Game of Wits
Southern Pride
1918 Beans
Borrowed Clothes
The Bride's Awakening
Daddy's Girl
The Demon
For Husbands Only
Mickey
Painted Lips
Playthings
Treasure of the Sea
1919 Are You Legally Married?
As the Sun Went Down
The Beloved Cheater
The Broken Butterfly
Don't Change Your Husband
The Life Line

       Men, Women and Money
       Our Better Selves
1920 The Butterfly Man
       Occasionally Yours
       Wait for Me

Cody, William F. *same as* **Cody, William Frederick**
1914 The Indian Wars
1917 The Adventures of Buffalo Bill
       The Buffalo Bill Show
19-- Official Motion Pictures of the Panama Pacific Exposition Held at San Francisco, Calif.*

Coe, Arthur J.
1920 The Mollycoddle*

Coer, Mrs. Carlotta
1918 Caught in the Act

Coffee, Lenore J. *same as* **Coffee, Leonore**
1919 The Better Wife
1920 The Forbidden Woman

Coffey, Cameron
1919 The Heart of Youth
       The Woman Michael Married

Coffin, Estelle
1914 The Floor Above
       The Littlest Rebel

Coffin, Jay
1918 Mr. Logan, U.S.A.

Coffray, Frank
1917 The Birth of Patriotism

Coffyn, Pauline
1920 Passers-By

Cogan, Fanny *same as* **Cogan, Fannie; Cogan, Mrs. Fanny**
1918 The Cross Bearer
       The Shell Game
1919 The Great Victory, Wilson or the Kaiser? The Fall of the Hohenzollerns
       The Woman of Lies
1920 The Shadow of Rosalie Byrnes
       The Woman God Sent

Cogan, Mrs. J.
1917 The Cinderella Man

Cogan, James
1917 Draft 258

Coghlan, Charles
1915 Thou Shalt Not Kill

Coghlan, Gertrude
1914 The Royal Box

Coghlan, Lawrence
1919 The Shepherd of the Hills*

Coghlan, Rose
1915 The Sporting Duchess
       Thou Shalt Not Kill
1916 The Faded Flower
       Her Surrender

Cogley, Nick *same as* **Cogley, Nicholas**
1915 The Coward
1918 Inside the Lines
       Madam Who
       Maid O' the Storm
1919 Sis Hopkins
       Toby's Bow
1920 Honest Hutch
       Jes' Call Me Jim
       The Little Shepherd of Kingdom Come

Cohan, George M.
1917 Broadway Jones
       Over There*
       Seven Keys to Baldpate
1918 Hit-the-Trail Holliday

Cohen, Baby
1918 Cheating the Public

Cohen, Bennett R. *same as* **Cohen, Bennett; Cohn, Ben; Cohn, Bennett**
1916 The Love Thief
1917 For Liberty
       Her Temptation
       The Man Who Took a Chance
       The Scarlet Pimpernel
1918 The Bride of Fear
       The Fallen Angel
       Fame and Fortune
1919 Pitfalls of a Big City
1920 Unseen Forces

Cohen, Fannie
1916 The Prince Chap
1917 The Barker

Cohen, Master Isadore
1920 When Dawn Came

Cohen, Jack *see* **Cohn, Jack**

Cohen, Octavus Roy
1916 The Matrimaniac
1917 The Strong Way
1920 Dollars and Sense

Cohill, John
1918 The Silent Woman

Cohill, William *same as* **Cohill, W.; Cohill, W. W.; Cohill, William W.**
1915 Life Without Soul
1916 The Crucial Test
       The Fortunate Youth
1917 Her Fighting Chance
1918 Eye for Eye
       Five Thousand an Hour
1919 The Great Victory, Wilson or the Kaiser? The Fall of the Hohenzollerns
       Virtuous Men

Cohn, Ben *see* **Cohen, Bennett R.**

Cohn, Jack *same as* **Cohen, Jack**
1918 Crashing Through to Berlin
1920 The Victim

Cohn, Martin
1915 Forbidden Fruit*
1916 A Fool's Paradise*

Cohn, Sally
1920 The Confession

Coigne, Frank B.
1915 The Battle of Ballots

Coit, Sam
1914 Soldiers of Fortune
1917 The Honeymoon

Colbert, Suzanne
1919 The Thirteenth Chair

Colby, William
1917 The Spirit of '76

"Cold Molasses"
1920 The County Fair

Coldewey, Anthony W. *same as* **Coldewey, A. W.; Coldeway, Anthony; Coldeway, Anthony W.; Coldewey, A. W.**
1915 Captivating Mary Carstairs
       The Tale of the Night Before
1916 The Morals of Hilda
       The Sable Blessing
1917 The Gilded Youth
1918 Which Woman?

Cole, Blanche Dougan
1916 The Road to Love

Cole, George
1915 The Slim Princess*

Coleman, Charles
1915 The Mummy and the Humming Bird
       When We Were Twenty-One
1919 The Love Cheat
1920 The Place of Honeymoons

Coleman, Cherrie
1917 Crime and Punishment

Coleman, Edward *same as* **Coleman, Ed**
1917 The Apple-Tree Girl
       The Last Sentence

Coleman, J. W.
1919 Injustice

Coleman, John
1919 The Lost Battalion

Coleman, Marion
1914 The House of Bondage

Coleman, Vincent
1918 The Prodigal Wife
       The Scarlet Trail
1919 The Law of Nature
       Should a Husband Forgive?
1920 Good References
       Partners of the Night

Collens, Dick *see* **Collins, Dick**

Collette, Augustus
1914 Over Niagara Falls

Collier, Buster *see* **Collier, William, Jr. (actor, born 1902)**

Collier, Constance
1916 The Code of Marcia Gray
       Macbeth
       Tongues of Men

Collier, Fern
1916 Going Straight

Collier, Harry
1914 Thou Shalt Not

Collier, William *(actor, born 1868)*
1916 The No-Good Guy
1920 The Servant Question

Collier, William, Jr. *(actor, born 1902), same as* **Collier, Buster**
1916 The Bugle Call
1920 Everybody's Sweetheart
       The Servant Question
       The Soul of Youth

Collinge, Claire
1920 Love's Plaything

Collins, Ann Austin
1920 The Mysteries of Paris

Collins, Arthur
1914 The Only Son

Collins, C. E.
1918 Restitution

Collins, Cora
1920 Love's Plaything*

Collins, Courtney
1913 In the Stretch

Collins, Dick *same as* **Collens, Dick; Collins, Richard**
1917 Shall We Forgive Her?
1919 Love in a Hurry
       The Oakdale Affair

Collins, Eddie
1917 The Baseball Revue of 1917*

Collins, Emile
1917 The Barricade
       The Beautiful Lie

Collins, Frederick L.
1919 The Fighting Roosevelts

Collins, Jack *(actor)*
1919 Six Feet Four

Collins, John H. *(dir)*
1915 Children of Eve
       Cohen's Luck
       Gladiola
       On Dangerous Paths
       The Ploughshare
1916 The Cossack Whip
       The Flower of No Man's Land
       The Gates of Eden
       The Innocence of Ruth
       The Light of Happiness
1917 Aladdin's Other Lamp
       Blue Jeans
       The Girl Without a Soul
       God's Law and Man's
       Lady Barnacle
       The Mortal Sin
       Rosie O'Grady
       A Wife by Proxy
1918 Flower of the Dusk
       Opportunity
       Riders of the Night
       A Weaver of Dreams
       The Winding Trail
1919 The Gold Cure
       Satan Junior

Collins, Jose
1915 The Impostor
1916 The Light That Failed
       A Woman's Honor

Collins, Kathleen
1922 The Cynic Effect

Collins, Marie
1915 The Commuters

Collins, Monty
1920 The Jailbird

Collins, Regis
1920 His House in Order

Collins, Richard *see* **Collins, Dick**

Collins, Tom
1920 The Bromley Case
       Circumstantial Evidence
       The Scrap of Paper
       The Trail of the Cigarette
       The Triple Clue
       The Unseen Witness
       The Wall Street Mystery

Collosse, Pierre
1920 Mothers of Men

Collucci, Guido *see* **Colucci, Guido**

Colone, Pierre
1916 An Enemy to the King

Colton, John
1919 The She Wolf
1920 Risky Business
       Two Kinds of Love

Colucci, Guido *same as* **Collucci, Guido**
1915 The Mystery of Room 13
1916 The City of Illusion
       Her Husband's Wife
       The Purple Lady
       When Love Is King
1917 The Master Passion
       Pride
       The Tell-Tale Step

Colvin, Marion
1920 The Branding Iron
       The Cup of Fury

Colvin, William
1918 The Ranger
1920 The Turning Point

Colwell, Goldie *same as* **Caldwell, Golda; Caldwell, Goldie**
1916 The Adventures of Kathlyn
       The Yaqui
1917 The Heart of Texas Ryan
1919 The Railroader

Coman, Morgan
1920 Blind Love

Combe, Boyce
1917 Runaway Romany

Comer, Adila
1916 Love's Pilgrimage to America

Comer, Miriam
1917 The Varmint*

Comfort, Dan
1919 The Poison Pen
1920 The Sporting Duchess

Comiskey, Charles A.
1914 The Giants-White Sox Tour

Commerford, Thomas
1914 One Wonderful Night
1915 Graustark
       In the Palace of the King
       The White Sister
1916 The Sting of Victory

Comont, Mathilda *same as* **Comont, Mathilde; Comount, Mme.**
1919 A Rogue's Romance
1920 Kismet

Compson, Betty
1918 The Border Raiders
1919 The Devil's Trail
       The Light of Victory
       The Little Diplomat
       The Miracle Man
       The Prodigal Liar

Compton, Charles
1916 Big Jim Garrity
       The Sphinx

Compton, Dixie
1914 The Man O' Warsman
       The Trail of the Lonesome Pine
1915 The Family Stain
       The Senator

Compton, Frank
1920 Lone Hand Wilson

Compton, Viola
1917 Polly of the Circus

Comstock, Clark
1915 The Eagle's Nest
1916 The Unborn
1919 The Westerners
1920 A Broadway Cowboy

Comstock, Daniel F.
1918 The Gulf Between*

Comstock, Ray S.
1916 The Battle of Hearts
       Fighting Blood
       The Man from Bitter Roots
       A Man of Sorrow

Concord, Lillian
1916 The Heritage of Hate
       The Isle of Life
       The Woman in 47
1917 The Girl from Rector's
       Troublemakers

Conde, Syn de *see* **De Conde, Syn**

Condon, Frank
1915 Sealed Lips
1918 Mlle. Paulette
       Who Killed Walton?

Cook, John B. *see* Cooke, John B.
Cook, John J. *see* Cooke, Johnnie
Cook, Johnnie *see* Cooke, Johnnie
Cook, Lillian
1914 Mother
1915 Camille
1916 As in a Looking Glass
The Common Law
Sudden Riches
A Woman's Power
1917 The Beloved Adventuress
Betsy Ross
The Corner Grocer
Darkest Russia
Her Hour
The Honeymoon
Rasputin, the Black Monk
The Submarine Eye
1917-18
The Devil's Playground
1918 The Blue Bird
Cook, M.
1915 Colorado
Cook, W.
1919 The Unknown Love
Cook, Warren *same as* **Cook, C.**
Warren; Cooke, Warren
1915 Children of Eve
1916 Slander
The Snowbird
The Unwelcome Mother
1917 The Avenging Trail
Draft 258
Exile
Infidelity
One Hour
The Pride of the Clan
Seven Keys to Baldpate
The Streets of Illusion
The Undying Flame
The Whip
1918 The Challenge Accepted
A Doll's House
Five Thousand an Hour
Her Final Reckoning
The Interloper
The Sins of the Children
Suspicion
The Whirlpool
Woman
1919 A Dangerous Affair
His Wife's Friend
Me and Captain Kidd*
Reclaimed: The Struggle for a
Soul Between Love and Hate
The Right to Lie
The Unveiling Hand
1920 April Folly
Broadway and Home
Civilian Clothes
The Flapper
Lady Rose's Daughter
A Manhattan Knight
My Lady's Garter
The Point of View
Whispers
The Woman God Sent
The Wonderful Chance
Cook, William
1914 The Patchwork Girl of Oz
Cooke, Caroline Frances *same as* **Cook,**
Caroline
1914 The Envoy Extraordinary
1916 The Island of Surprise
Cooke, Ed
1917 Fools for Luck
Cooke, Ethyle *same as* **Cook, Ethyl;**
Cook, Ethyle
1915 Inspiration
1916 The Fear of Poverty
The Fugitive
The Pillory
Saint, Devil and Woman
1917 Her Life and His
Her New York
Patsy
The Small Town Girl
When Love Was Blind
1918 Convict 993
Cooke, George, Jr.
1914 Soldiers of Fortune*

Cooke, John *see* Cooke, Johnnie
Cooke, John B. *same as* Cook, John B.
1920 The Gray Brother
The Triple Clue
Cooke, Johnnie *same as* **Cook, John;**
Cook, John J.; Cook, Johnnie;
Cooke, John
1916 Gloriana
The Right to Be Happy
The Shine Girl
1917 Like Wildfire
1918 The Romance of Tarzan
Thieves' Gold
1919 The Blinding Trail
Common Property
The Girl from Nowhere
A Gun Fightin' Gentleman
Hoop-La
The Little White Savage
The Pointing Finger
The Weaker Vessel
What Am I Bid?
1920 Alias Miss Dodd
Eyes of the Heart
Just Pals
The Prince of Avenue A
Cooke, Warren *see* **Cook, Warren**
Cooksey, Curtis
1915 Shadows from the Past
1916 My Partner
1917 Diamonds and Pearls
A Self-Made Widow
Sloth
The Woman Beneath
1918 The Trap
1920 Life
The Silver Horde
Cooley, Florence Maule
1913 Eighty Million Women Want-?
Cooley, Hallam *same as* **Cooley, Hal**
1916 The Courtesan
The Daughter of the Don
1917 The Cricket
The Planter*
1918 The Deciding Kiss
The Guilty Man
1919 The Girl Dodger
The Girl from Outside
Happy Though Married
The Long Arm of Mannister
More Deadly Than the Male
One of the Finest
Upstairs
1920 Beware of the Bride
Leave It to Me
A Light Woman
An Old Fashioned Boy
Pinto
Trumpet Island
Cooley, James
1914 The Little Gray Lady
Wildflower
1915 The Concealed Truth
The Coquette
Forbidden Fruit
The Price
1916 The Eternal Sapho
A Fool's Paradise
The Immortal Flame
1920 The Common Sin
The Discarded Woman
Cooley, Willard
1918 The Burden of Proof
The Firebrand
1920 The Sacred Ruby
Coolidge, John T.
1914 Common Beasts of Africa*
Coolidge, Karl R. *same as* **Coolidge,**
Karl
1916 Lying Lips
The Voice of Love
1917 The Flame of Youth
Like Wildfire
The Spindle of Life
1918 A Bit of Jade
The Man of Bronze
Cooling, Maud
1917 The Boy Girl
Susan's Gentleman
1918 Fields of Honor
1919 The Eternal Magdalene

Coombs, Guy
1914 A Celebrated Case
The School for Scandal
Wolfe; Or, The Conquest of
Quebec
1915 Barbara Frietchie
The Call of the Dance
My Madonna
1917 Bab's Burglar
Bab's Diary
Two Men and a Woman
1918 Flower of the Dusk
Loaded Dice
The Uphill Path
1920 The Wrong Woman
Coombs, Jack
1917 The Baseball Revue of 1917*
Coombs, Royce
1917 The Cinderella Man
Royal Romance
Coombs, Slats
1920 Down Home
Coonleu, Mrs.
1918 Stella Maris
Coonley, Lou *see* **Conley, Lou**
Coonly, Irma
1920 Her Beloved Villain
Cooper, Mrs.
1914 The Nightingale
Cooper, Ashley
1920 Go and Get It
Cooper, Bigelow
1915 Eugene Aram
The Magic Skin
The Ploughshare
Shadows from the Past
The Truth About Helen
Vanity Fair
1916 The Heart of the Hills
The Martyrdom of Philip
Strong
A Message to Garcia
When Love Is King
1917 The Bottom of the Well
The Ghost of Old Morro
God of Little Children
The Great Bradley Mystery
Light in Darkness
The Master Passion
Passion
Pride and the Devil
The Tell-Tale Step
Where Love Is
1918 The Make-Believe Wife
Revelation
Wild Primrose
The Wooing of Princess Pat
1919 The Country Cousin
Shadows of Suspicion
The Test of Honor
1920 The Law of the Yukon
Cooper, Claude
1914 The Nightingale
Three Weeks
1915 The Garden of Lies
When It Strikes Home
1917 The Woman in White
1918 My Own United States
Cooper, Courtney Ryley
1917 The Secret of the Storm
Country
Cooper, Edna Mae
1918 Old Wives for New
Rimrock Jones
Sauce for the Goose
The Whispering Chorus
1919 Male and Female
Men, Women and Money
Putting It Over
The Third Kiss
You Never Saw Such a Girl
1920 Why Change Your Wife?
Cooper, George
1915 Mother's Roses
The Wheels of Justice
1916 The Hunted Woman
A Night Out
The Suspect
Thou Art the Man
The Vital Question
1917 The Auction Block
Her Secret

1918 Fields of Honor
Her Man
The Struggle Everlasting
1919 The Dark Star
1920 The Birth of a Soul
Chains of Evidence
The Very Idea
Cooper, Grant
1920 She Loves and Lies
Cooper, J. Gordon
1916 Blue Blood and Red
1917 The Honor System
Cooper, James
1914 The School for Scandal
Cooper, Joseph
1920 Humoresque
Cooper, Lenore
1918 The Sins of the Children
Cooper, Marion *could be same as*
Cooper, Miriam
1913 Across the Continent
Cooper, Miriam *could be same as*
Cooper, Marion
1913 Across the Continent*
1914 The Avenging Conscience*
The Dishonored Medal
Home, Sweet Home
1915 The Birth of a Nation
1916 Intolerance
1917 Betrayed
The Honor System
The Innocent Sinner
The Silent Lie
1918 The Prussian Cur
Woman and the Law
1919 Evangeline
The Mother and the Law
Should a Husband Forgive?
1920 The Deep Purple
Cooper, Ollie
1918 The Brass Check
Cooper, Sammy
1918 Our Mrs. McChesney
Cooper, Texas
1918 Lest We Forget
Cooper, William
1917 The Crimson Dove
The Danger Trail
For the Freedom of the World
Youth
1918 The Sunset Princess
1920 The Way Women Love
Cope, James
1918 You Can't Believe Everything
Corbaley, Kate
1918 Real Folks
1919 The False Code
Gates of Brass
1920 Smoldering Embers
Corbell, A. G. *same as* **Corbell, Atillio**
G.; Corbell, Attilio; Corbelle, A. G.
1918 The Beautiful Mrs. Reynolds
The Golden Wall
My Cousin
The Power and the Glory
Corbett, Mrs.
1915 The Old Homestead
Corbett, Ben
1920 Under Northern Lights
Corbett, E. Lord
1920 His Wife's Money*
Out of the Snows
Corbett, Edward
1917 The Sin Woman
Corbett, James J.
1913 The Man from the Golden
West
1914 The Burglar and the Lady
1916 The Other Girl
1920 The Prince of Avenue A
Corbett, Olive
1916 The War Bride's Secret
1917 The Little Samaritan
Corbett, William *same as* **Corbett, W.**
D.; Corbett, Will
1915 The Senator
1916 Somewhere in Georgia
Souls in Bondage
1920 The Discarded Woman
The Face at Your Window
Uncle Sam of Freedom Ridge

Corbin, Louise
1914 Sins of the Parents
Corbin, Virginia Lee *same as* **Corbin, Virginia**
1917 Aladdin and the Wonderful Lamp
The Babes in the Woods
Heart Strings
Jack and the Beanstalk
1918 Ace High
Fan Fan
Six Shooter Andy
Treasure Island
1919 The Forbidden Room
1920 The White Dove
Corcoran, E.
1918 The Kaiser, the Beast of Berlin
Corcoran, Ethel
1915 C.O.D.
The Dust of Egypt
A Price for Folly
1916 A Night Out
The Surprises of an Empty Hotel
Corcoran, Frances G.
1915 The Arrival of Perpetua
Corcoran, Jane
1914 Mother
Cordoba, Pedro de *see* **De Cordoba, Pedro**
Cordova, Joseph
1914 The School for Scandal
Cordova, Leander de *see* **De Cordova, Leander**
Cordova, Rienzi de *see* **De Cordova, Rienzi**
Cordova, Rudolph de *see* **De Cordova, Rudolph**
Corey, Eugene *same as* **Corey, Jean**
1918 The Argument
Captain of His Soul*
The Flames of Chance
The Hopper
The Law of the Great Northwest
Restitution
The Velvet Hand
1920 The Great Lover
Corey, Jean *see* **Corey, Eugene**
Corker, Hazel
1918 Miss Innocence
Corless, Tom
1918 The Blue Bird
Cornell, Bert H.
1920 The Mysteries of Paris
Cornell, Ed *same as* **Cornell, Edwin**
1920 The Mysteries of Paris
Cornell, Frances
1919 The Great Victory, Wilson or the Kaiser? The Fall of the Hohenzollerns
Cornish, John R.
1919 Nugget Nell
Cornwall, Anne
1918 The Knife
1919 The Firing Line
The Indestructible Wife
The World to Live In
1920 The Copperhead
Everything but the Truth
The Girl in the Rain
La La Lucille
The Path She Chose
Corrigan, Emmett
1915 Greater Love Hath No Man
1916 Husband and Wife
1920 Partners of the Night
Corrigan, James
1920 The Jack-Knife Man
Corsan, Maude Erve
1917 Out of the Wreck
Cort, Edward
1915 The Whirl of Life
Cort, Elsie
1915 The Gentleman from Indiana
Corteaux, Marie
1917 The Painted Lie
The Single Code

Cortes, Mrs.
1914 The House of Bondage
Cortes, Armand *same as* **Cortes, Armand F.; Cortez, Armand**
1914 The House of Bondage
1915 How Molly Malone Made Good
1916 The Big Sister
A Woman's Honor
1917 The Angel Factory
Her Better Self
The Road Between
Seven Keys to Baldpate
1918 Dodging a Million
1920 His Temporary Wife
The Return of Tarzan
The Servant Question
The Victim
Cortez, Anita
1918 The Birth of a Race
Oh, Johnny!
Cortez, Armand *see* **Cortes, Armand**
Corwin, Carlos Edwin *same as* **Corwin, Edwin**
1914 The Trail of the Lonesome Pine
1915 Over Night
Cosgrave, Jack *same as* **Cosgrove, Jack; could be same as** **Cosgrove, John**
1916 Daphne and the Pirate
Intolerance
1917 The Spirit of '76
1918 Hearts of the World
Restitution
1919 Whitewashed Walls
1920 Smiling All the Way
Cosgrove, Jack *see* **Cosgrove, Jack**
Cosgrove, John *could be same as* **Cosgrave, Jack**
1919 Deliverance
Cossar, Fanny
1920 Jenny Be Good
Cossar, John *same as* **Cossar, John H.; Cossar, John Hay**
1914 One Wonderful Night
1915 The Alster Case
The Blindness of Virtue
The Crimson Wing
The Man Trail
The White Sister
1916 The Chaperon
The Little Shepherd of Bargain Row
The Misleading Lady
The Prince of Graustark
The Return of Eve
1917 The Dream Doll
The Fibbers
Fools for Luck
Gift O' Gab
On Trial
Pants
Satan's Private Door
The Trufflers
Two-Bit Seats
1918 Beans
Her Country First
The Marriage Ring
A Pair of Sixes
1919 Common Clay
The Feud
The Game's Up
The Highest Trump
Home
The Long Arm of Mannister
Love Insurance
Love Is Love
Thieves
Vagabond Luck
When Fate Decides
Whom the Gods Would Destroy
1920 That Something
Cossard, Ernest
1916 The Pursuing Vengeance
Costello (full name unknown)
1916 The Daughter of the Don
Costello, Mrs.
1915 When a Woman Loves
1917 Her Right to Live
The Money Mill

Costello, Arline
1915 Maciste
Costello, Dolores
1915 How Cissy Made Good
Costello, Helene
1915 How Cissy Made Good
Costello, Jack
1920 The Valley of Doubt
Costello, James
1919 Silent Strength
Costello, John
1916 The Lights of New York
The Man Behind the Curtain
The Redemption of Dave Darcey
The Shop Girl
1917 Blind Man's Holiday
The Princess of Park Row
Womanhood, the Glory of the Nation
1918 The Embarrassment of Riches
The Scarlet Trail
1920-21 The House of Mystery
Costello, Maurice
1914 Mr. Barnes of New York
1915 The Man Who Couldn't Beat God
1916 The Crown Prince's Double
1919 The Cambric Mask
The Captain's Captain
The Girl-Woman
The Man Who Won
1919-20 The Tower of Jewels
1920 Deadline at Eleven
Human Collateral
Cota, Louis
1919 When a Man Rides Alone
Cotton, Billie
1920 Earthbound
Cotton, Lucy
1915 Divorced
Life Without Soul
1918 The Prodigal Wife
1919 The Broken Melody
The Miracle of Love
Roses and Thorns
1920 Blind Love
The Invisible Foe
The Misleading Lady
The Sin That Was His
Cotton, Richardson
1916 The Little Shepherd of Bargain Row
The Sting of Victory
Cotton, Roulef E.
1917 The Silent Witness
Couderc, Pierre
1914 His Majesty, the Scarecrow of Oz
The Patchwork Girl of Oz
1920 The Bromley Case
Coudert, Charles
1918 Peg O' the Sea
Coudert, George C. *same as* **Coudert, George**
1914 The Span of Life
1915 All for a Girl
The Fixer
The Labyrinth
1917 Hate
One Hour
1920 The Fighting Kentuckians
Coudray, Peggy
1916 A Knight of the Range
Coulson, Roy
1919 For a Woman's Honor
1920 An Arabian Knight
The Forgotten Woman
Coulter, Mme.
1915 The Frame-Up
Coulter, Frazer *same as* **Coulter, Fraser**
1913 The Prisoner of Zenda
1915 Body and Soul
1920 The Face at Your Window
Counihan, William J.
1914 The Line-Up at Police Headquarters

Countiss, Catherine
1914 The Idler
1915 The Avalanche
A Modern Magdalen
Courelle, Rose Marie de
1920 The Price of Redemption
Court, Florence
1920 The Fatal Hour
Courtenay, William
1915 Sealed Lips
1916 The Island of Surprise
The Ninety and Nine
The Romantic Journey
1917 The Hunting of the Hawk
Kick In
The Recoil
Courtleigh, William, Jr. *same as* **Courtleigh, William**
1914 The Better Man
The Nightingale
1916 The Birth of Character
The Innocent Lie
Out of the Drifts
The Rainbow Princess
Susie Snowflake
Under Cover
1917 The Heart of a Lion
Miss U.S.A.
The Sunshine Maid
1918 By Right of Purchase
1919 Eyes of Youth
1920 Children of Destiny
Madame X
Moon Madness
Pollyanna
Courtney, George
1913 Ivanhoe
Courtney, Helen
1917 The Unforseen
Courtney, Jane
1918 The Firebrand
Courtney, William B. *same as* **Courtney, Will; Courtney, William**
1916 Artie, the Millionaire Kid
1917 The Defeat of the City
The Duplicity of Hargraves
The Flaming Omen
For France
1920 The Flaming Clue
The Garter Girl
Slaves of Pride
Courtot, Charlotte
1915 The Pretenders
Courtot, Marguerite
1914 A Celebrated Case
1915 The Pretenders
The Vanderhoff Affair
1916 The Dead Alive
Feathertop
The Kiss
Rolling Stones
1917 Crime and Punishment
The Natural Law
1918 The Unbeliever
1919 The Perfect Lover
The Teeth of the Tiger
The Undercurrent
1920 Rogues and Romance
19-- Our Daily Bread
Courtright, Mrs. Jennie Lee
1919 Bill Henry
Courtright, William *same as* **Courtright, Billy; Courtwright, Billy; Courtwright, William**
1918 Hitting the High Spots
1919 Hard Boiled
The Home Town Girl
The Lady of Red Butte
1920 The Blooming Angel
Forty-Five Minutes from Broadway
The Jailbird
Paris Green
Peaceful Valley
Rookie's Return
Water, Water Everywhere
Cousins (full name unknown)
1915 The Fairy and the Waif*
Cove, O. M.
1916 The Corner

Coventry, Florence
1915 The Danger Signal
1916 The Final Curtain
1918 The Golden Wall
     The Heart of a Girl
     Merely Players
1919 What Love Forgives
Coventry, Tom
1916 The Devil's Prayer-Book
Coverdale, Mary
1919 Out Yonder
Covert, Fred
1920 An Adventuress
Covington, Z. Wall *same as* **Covington, Zell; Covington, Zella**
1919 The Poor Boob
1920 A Full House
     She Couldn't Help It
1921 The Jucklins
Cowan, Sada
1920 Seeds of Vengeance
     Why Change Your Wife?
Coward, Noel
1918 Hearts of the World
Cowell, George (*writer*)
1918 Mlle. Paulette
Cowl, George (*actor*) *same as* **Cowle, George**
1914 Dan
     When Broadway Was a Trail
1916 The Closed Road
     The Rack
1917 The Beloved Adventuress
     Betsy Ross
     The Corner Grocer
     The Crimson Dove
     Her Hour
     The Iron Ring
     The Stolen Paradise
     Youth
1919 The Mystery of the Yellow Room
1920 Love, Honor and Obey
     The Shadow of Rosalie Byrnes
Cowl, Jane
1915 The Garden of Lies
1917 The Spreading Dawn
Cowle, George *see* **Cowl, George** (*actor*)
Cowles, Mr.
1915 Emmy of Stork's Nest
Cowles, Albert
1917 Ten of Diamonds
1919 A Dangerous Affair
1920 High Speed
Cowles, Jules *same as* **Cowles, J. D.; Cowles, Julius D.**
1915 A Royal Family
1916 The Girl Philippa
     His Great Triumph
     The Quitter
1917 The Bar Sinister
     The Fringe of Society
     Persuasive Peggy
1918 All Woman
     The Poor Rich Man
     The Service Star
     To the Highest Bidder
1919 The Cambric Mask
     The Clouded Name
     The Oakdale Affair
1920 A Fool and His Money
Cowley, Harry
1914 The Greyhound
Cowper, William *same as* **Cowper, William C.**
1914 The Redemption of David Corson
1915 Emmy of Stork's Nest
     An Enemy to Society
     A Yellow Streak
1916 Dimples
Cox, Doran H. *same as* **Cox, Doran**
1918 Fuss and Feathers
     The Law of the North
1919 Happy Though Married
1920 The Leopard Woman
Cox, George L.
1919 The Hellion
     The Tiger Lily
1920 The Blue Moon
     The Dangerous Talent
     The Gamesters

The House of Toys
A Light Woman
Their Mutual Child
The Thirtieth Piece of Silver
The Week-End
Cox, Harriet
1919 The Phantom Honeymoon
Cox, Ruby
1915 Coral
1916 The Girl of the Lost Lake
Coxen, Edward *same as* **Coxen, Ed**
1916 The Voice of Love
     A Woman's Daring
1917 Beware of Strangers
     The Curse of Eve
     Who Shall Take My Life?
1918 The Bells
     Blindfolded
     Carmen of the Klondike
     The Crime of the Hour
     Go West, Young Man
     The Heart of Rachael
     Honor's Cross
     A Law unto Herself
     Madam Who
     A Man's Man
     Quicksand
     The White Lie
     Within the Cup
1919 The Betrayal
     Desert Gold
     In Old Kentucky
1920 The Amazing Woman
     Honor Bound
     Mountain Madness
     The Path She Chose
     Witch's Gold
Coyle, Walter V.
1920 Love's Plaything
Coyle, William Jennings
1916 The Other Girl
Cozine, Arthur
1914 My Official Wife
1915 A Price for Folly
1916 The Lights of New York
     A Night Out
     Rose of the South
1917 The Danger Trail
Cozzat, Eleanor
1920 Man and Woman (A. H. Fischer Features, Inc.)
Craft, Robert
1920 The White Rider
Craft, Virginia
1915 Rosemary
Craft, William J.
1920 Love's Battle
     The White Rider
Craig, Miss B. *could be same as* **Craig, Blanche**
1914 The Gangsters
Craig, Blanche *could be same as* **Craig, Miss B.**
1915 The Dawn of a Tomorrow
1916 The City of Illusion
1917 Her Silent Sacrifice
1918 The Accidental Honeymoon
     Come On In
     The Love Net
Craig, Charles
1916 The Serpent
     Under Two Flags
     Where Love Leads
1917 The Poor Little Rich Girl
     A Rich Man's Plaything
     Royal Romance
1918 The Blue Bird
     The Fall of the Romanoffs
     Sporting Life
     Under the Greenwood Tree
     The Uphill Path
     We Should Worry
1919 The Firing Line
     The Gray Towers Mystery
     Sadie Love
     Should a Husband Forgive?
     Three Men and a Girl
1919-20
     The Tower of Jewels
1920 The Flapper
     A Fool and His Money
     My Lady's Garter
     Nothing but the Truth

The Wonder Man
Youthful Folly
Craig, Nell *same as* **Craig, Nelle**
1913 The Battle of Shiloh
1914 When Rome Ruled
1915 In the Palace of the King
1916 The Breaker
1917 The Trufflers
1919 Common Property
1920 The Desperate Hero
     Her First Elopement
     Passion's Playground
     The Poor Simp
     The Triflers
Crain, Earl *see* **Crane, Erle**
Cramer, Sam
1915 The Man Trail
Crampton, Howard
1913 Traffic in Souls
1915 Conscience
     Courtmartialed
     The White Terror
1916 The Chalice of Sorrow
     The Great Problem
     Half a Rogue
     20,000 Leagues Under the Sea
1917 Black Orchids
     Like Wildfire
     The Scarlet Car
1918 The Border Raiders
     Humdrum Brown
     The Voice of Destiny
     The Wife He Bought
     With Hoops of Steel
1919 The Devil's Trail
     In His Brother's Place
     The Lion's Den
1920 Hearts Are Trumps
     Someone in the House
Cranby, Joseph
1916 The Victim
Crane, Miss
1914 The House of Bondage
Crane, Cap *same as* **Crane, Captain**
1917 The Learnin' of Jim Benton
     The Medicine Man
     One Shot Ross
1918 The Law's Outlaw
Crane, Doc *same as* **Crane, H. F.; Crane, Harry F.**
1915 The College Orphan
     Father and the Boys
     Lord John in New York
1916 Drugged Waters
     Mixed Blood
     What Love Can Do
     A Youth of Fortune
1917 The Blood of His Fathers
     Flirting with Death
     The Hidden Spring
     The Spirit of Romance
Crane, Edwin
1915 The House of Tears
Crane, Erle *same as* **Crain, Earl**
1920 Drag Harlan
     The Joyous Troublemaker
     The Orphan
     The Scuttlers
Crane, Florence
1917 Maternity
Crane, Dr. Frank (*clergyman*) *not the same as* **Crane, Frank** (*dir*) *or* **Crayne, Frank** (*juvenile actor*)
1920 Empty Arms
Crane, Frank (*dir*) *same as* **Crane, Frank H.; Crane, Frank Hall;** *not the same as* **Crane, Dr. Frank** (*clergyman*) *or* **Crayne, Frank** (*juvenile actor*)
1913 Leah Kleschna
1914 As Ye Sow
1915 The Family Cupboard
     The Gray Mask
     The Man Who Found Himself
     The Moonstone
     Old Dutch
     The Stolen Voice
1916 As in a Looking Glass
     Fate's Boomerang
     The Man Who Stood Still
     Paying the Price
     Whoso Findeth a Wife
     The World Against Him

1917 An Alabaster Box
     The Mark of Cain*
     Stranded in Arcady
     Thais
     Vengeance Is Mine
1918 The Life Mask
     Neighbors
     Wanted for Murder
1919 Her Game
     His Father's Wife
     Miss Crusoe
     The Praise Agent
     The Scar
     The Unveiling Hand
Crane, H. F. *see* **Crane, Doc**
Crane, Hamilton
1914 The Path Forbidden
1915 The Bulldogs of the Trail
Crane, Harold
1914 The Last Volunteer
1915 The Beloved Vagabond
     The Melting Pot
Crane, James L.
1919 His Bridal Night
     The Misleading Widow
     Sadie Love
     Wanted—A Husband
1920 A Dark Lantern
     Sinners
Crane, Juliet
1919 Checkers
Crane, Ogden
1913 Caprice
1915 Lord John in New York
1916 Davy Crockett*
     The End of the Trail
     The Flirt
     The Man from Bitter Roots
     The Parson of Panamint
1917 The Cloud
1918 The Light of Western Stars
     When a Woman Sins
1919 The Hornet's Nest
     Jinx
     The Sealed Envelope
     Soldiers of Fortune
     The Valley of the Giants
1920 The Corsican Brothers
     The Dwelling Place of Light
     Her Five-Foot Highness
19-- Sic-Em
Crane, Ward
1919 The Dark Star
     Soldiers of Fortune
1920 The Frisky Mrs. Johnson
     Harriet and the Piper
     In the Heart of a Fool
     The Luck of the Irish
     The Scoffer
     Something Different
     The Yellow Typhoon
Crane, William H.
1915 David Harum
1920 The Saphead
Crank, Commander R. K.
1916 The Hero of Submarine D-2
Crary, Billy
1918 A Petticoat Pilot
Craven, W. Scott *could be same as* **Craven, Walter**
1913 Ivanhoe
Craven, Walter *could be same as* **Craven, W. Scott**
1914 The Unwelcome Mrs. Hatch
1915 Alias Jimmy Valentine
     The Deep Purple
     The Destroying Angel
     The Dictator
     The Eternal City
     The Greater Will
     The White Pearl
     Zaza
1917 Kidnapped
1918 The Great Adventure
Crawford, Alice
1918 False Ambition
Crawford, Clifton
1915 The Galloper
Crawford, Florence
1916 The Man Inside
     The Path of Happiness

Crawford, Henry
1917 The Secret of Black Mountain
Crawford, Jack
1915 The Battle Cry of Peace
Crawley, Constance
1914 Charlotte Corday
The Fatal Night
Jess
Thais
The Virgin of the Rocks
The Volunteer Parson
1916 Embers
Lord Loveland Discovers
America
Powder
Revelations
1917 A Jewel in Pawn
Crayne, Frank (*juvenile actor*) *not the*
same as **Crane, Dr. Frank**
(*clergyman*) *or* **Crane, Frank** (*dir*)
1917 Arsene Lupin
The Girl Philippa
The Grell Mystery
The Maelstrom
The Skylight Room
1918 The Street of Seven Stars
1920 A Master Stroke
Crazy Thunder
1917 The Judgement House
1918 The World for Sale
Creel, George
1918 Our Bridge of Ships
Pershing's Crusaders*
Crehan, Joseph
1916 Under Two Flags
Cressman, Babe
1917 Durand of the Bad Lands
Creswick, William
1920 Sophy of Kravonia; Or, The
Virgin of Paris
Creutz, Laurence T.
1920 Are All Men Alike?
The Invisible Divorce
The Palace of Darkened
Windows
Crews, Laura Hope
1915 Blackbirds
The Fighting Hope
Crimans, W. W. *same as* **Crimans,**
William W.; *could be same as*
Crimmins, William
1915 The Fight
1917 All for a Husband
1918 The Daredevil
Crimmins, Dan
1915 The Commuters
Keep Moving
1916 The Final Curtain
1919 Johnny Get Your Gun
1920 Once to Every Woman
Pink Tights
Crimmins, Robert
1917 Grafters
Crimmins, William *could be same as*
Crimans, W. W.
1914 The Coming Power
Criner, Gennette *see* **Criner, Janette**
Criner, Janette *same as* **Criner,**
Gennette
1919 Injustice
A Man's Duty
Crinley, Adele
1920 Suds
Crinley, William A. *same as* **Crinley,**
William
1915 Just Jim
1920 Suds
Cripe, Malcolm
1920 Twins of Suffering Creek
Crisman, Pat
1918 Six Shooter Andy
Crisp, Donald *same as* **Needham, James**
1914 The Battle of the Sexes
The Escape
The Great Leap; Until Death
Do Us Part
Home, Sweet Home
The Mountain Rat
1915 The Birth of a Nation
The Commanding Officer
A Girl of Yesterday
The Love Route

May Blossom
1916 Ramona
1917 The Bond Between
The Clever Mrs. Carfax
The Cook of Canyon Camp
The Countess Charming
The Eyes of the World
His Sweetheart
Lost in Transit
The Marcellini Millions
A Roadside Impresario
1918 Believe Me Xantippe
The Firefly of France
The Goat
The House of Silence
Jules of the Strong Heart
Less Than Kin
Rimrock Jones
The Way of a Man with a
Maid
1919 Broken Blossoms
It Pays to Advertise
Johnny Get Your Gun
Love Insurance
The Poor Boob
Putting It Over
Something to Do
Under the Top
Venus in the East
A Very Good Young Man
Why Smith Left Home
1920 The Barbarian
Held by the Enemy
Miss Hobbs
The Six Best Cellars
Too Much Johnson
Criswell, Eliza Helen
1918 The Street of Seven Stars
Critchley, Ben
1920 Alias Jimmy Valentine*
The Right of Way
Crittenden, T. D. *same as* **Crittenden,**
Dwight; Crittenden, Trockwood D.;
Crittendon, T. D.
1915 Jewel
Lord John in New York
1916 From Broadway to a Throne
The Isle of Life
Love Never Dies
The Mark of Cain
1917 The Fighting Gringo
The Lash of Power
Polly Put the Kettle On
The Saintly Sinner
The Winged Mystery
1918 The Devil's Wheel
A Mother's Secret
Real Folks
1919 The False Code
Home
The Hoodlum
The Rescuing Angel
The Veiled Adventure
1920 The Cup of Fury
The Little Shepherd of
Kingdom Come
Pinto
The Star Rover
Crittenden, William
1919 Home*
Crittendon, T. D. *see* **Crittenden, T. D.**
Croghan, Fred H.
1920 Something New*
Crolius, Louise
1915 The Alster Case
Crolly, William *same as* **Crolly, William**
L.; Crolly, William S.; *could be*
same as **Crowley, Mr.** *or* **Crowley,**
William
1917 Daughter of Maryland
Her Sister
Please Help Emily
The Unforseen
1918 The Girl and the Judge
The Inn of the Blue Moon
The Street of Seven Stars
1919 The Gay Old Dog
The Hidden Truth
The Other Man's Wife*
Crompton, Charles
1917 Rasputin, the Black Monk
1918 A Doll's House

Crone, George (*ed*) *could be same as*
Crone, George J. (*asst dir*)
1920 Old Dad
Twin Beds
Crone, George J. (*asst dir*) *could be*
same as **Crone, George** (*ed*)
1920 Let's Be Fashionable
Cronin, F. A.
1917 The Public Defender
Cronin, Tim
1915 The Fight
Cronjager, Henry *same as* **Cronjager,**
H.
1914 Lord Chumley
The Rejuvenation of Aunt
Mary
1916 The Combat*
The Ninety and Nine*
1917 Crime and Punishment
The Deemster
For France*
The Warfare of the Flesh
1918 The Caillaux Case
Moral Suicide
Why America Will Win
1919 Daddy-Long-Legs
Three Men and a Girl
The Unpardonable Sin
1920 Don't Ever Marry
The River's End
Cronjager, Jules
1916 The Combat
The Destroyers
His Wife's Good Name
The Ninety and Nine
1917 The Bottom of the Well
For France
Intrigue
1918 The Beloved Impostor
The Mating
A Nymph of the Foothills
Wild Primrose
1919 The Girl-Woman
Miss Dulcie from Dixie
A Stitch in Time
Too Many Crooks
1920 Greater Than Fame
The Greatest Love
Marooned Hearts
The Shadow of Rosalie Byrnes
Youthful Folly
Crosby, Gene
1917 The Blood of His Fathers
The Eye of Envy
Crosby, Harry
1915 York State Folks
Crosby, Jack
1917 Sloth
1920 Black Is White
A Daughter of Two Worlds
The Fatal Hour
The Stealers
The Wrong Woman
Crosby, James *same as* **Crosby, James**
A.; Crosby, Jim
1914 The Patchwork Girl of Oz
1916 The Beckoning Flame
1917 Lorelei of the Sea
Crosby, Zelda
1918 A Doll's House
1919 The Marriage Price
1920 The Desperate Hero
Crosier, Jacques
1914 The War of Wars; Or, The
Franco-German Invasion
Crosland, Alan
1917 The Apple-Tree Girl
Chris and His Wonderful
Lamp
Kidnapped
Knights of the Square Table
Light in Darkness
The Little Chevalier
1918 The Unbeliever
The Whirlpool
1919 The Country Cousin
1920 Broadway and Home
The Flapper
Greater Than Fame
The Point of View
Youthful Folly
19-- Jennie

Crosman, Henrietta
1914 The Unwelcome Mrs. Hatch
1915 How Molly Malone Made
Good
The Supreme Test
Cross, H. A.
1920 Do the Dead Talk?
Cross, Wellington
1918 The Grey Parasol
Crothers, Rachel
1916 The Perils of Divorce
Crow, Tote du *see* **Du Crow, Tote**
Crowder, E. H.
1919 The Girl Who Stayed Home*
Crowe, Eleanor
1916 The End of the Trail
The Fires of Conscience
1917 The Price of Her Soul
1918 The Turn of a Card
Crowe, Howard
1916 The Voice of Love
Crowell, Josephine *same as* **Crowell,**
Josephine B.
1914 Home, Sweet Home
The Mountain Rat
1915 The Birth of a Nation
A Man and His Mate
The Penitentes
A Yankee from the West
1916 A Child of the Paris Streets
A House Built upon Sand
Intolerance
The Little School Ma'am
Martha's Vindication
The Old Folks at Home
Pillars of Society
The Wharf Rat
1917 The Bad Boy
Betsy's Burglar
Cheerful Givers
The Fair Barbarian
Rebecca of Sunnybrook Farm
1918 The Bravest Way
Hearts of the World
Me und Gott
Stella Maris
Women's Weapons
1919 Diane of the Green Van
Give and Take
The Greatest Question
The House of Intrigue
Josselyn's Wife
Peppy Polly
Puppy Love
Rose O' the River
The Woman Next Door
1920 Crooked Streets
Dangerous to Men
Flames of the Flesh
Half a Chance
Held by the Enemy
The Six Best Cellars
White Lies
Crowell, William
1920 Beyond the Great Wall
Crowley, Mr. *could be same as* **Crolly,**
William *or* **Crowley, William**
1917 Reputation
Crowley, Frances
1918 Blue-Eyed Mary
The Heart of Romance
Miss Innocence*
Crowley, William *could be same as*
Crolly, William *or* **Crowley, Mr.**
1919 The Other Man's Wife
Cruez, Lottie *see* **Kruse, Lottie**
Crute, Sally *same as* **Crute, Sallie**
1915 The House of the Lost Court
The Magic Skin
1916 The Cossack Whip
Her Husband's Wife
Light at Dusk
1917 The Avenging Trail
The Awakening of Ruth
The Beautiful Lie
Blue Jeans
The Law of Compensation
The Law of the North
The Peddler
The Power of Decision
The Tell-Tale Step
A Wife by Proxy

Cruz, Jose de la
1918 The Belgian
    Eye for Eye
    Opportunity
    The Poor Rich Man
    When Men Betray
1919 Atonement
    A Broadway Saint
    A House Divided
    Twilight
1920 Even As Eve
    The Garter Girl
    The Greatest Love
1921 Miss 139

Cruz, Jose de la
1920 The Night Riders

Cruz, Juan de la *see* **De La Cruz, Juan**

Cruze, James
1913 The Legend of Provence
1914 Cardinal Richelieu's Ward
    Frou Frou
    Joseph in the Land of Egypt
1915 Armstrong's Wife
    The Patriot and the Spy
1916 The Snowbird
1917 The Call of the East
    Her Temptation
    Nan of Music Mountain
    On the Level
    The Web of Life
    What Money Can't Buy
1918 Believe Me Xantippe
    The City of Dim Faces
    Hidden Pearls
    Less Than Kin
    The Million Dollar Mystery
    The Source
    Too Many Millions
    Wild Youth
1919 An Adventure in Hearts
    Alias Mike Moran
    The Dub
    Hawthorne of the U.S.A.
    Johnny Get Your Gun
    The Lottery Man
    The Love Burglar
    The Roaring Road
    Under the Top
    The Valley of the Giants
    You're Fired
1920 Always Audacious
    Food for Scandal
    A Full House
    Mrs. Temple's Telegram
    The Sins of St. Anthony
    Terror Island
    What Happened to Jones
19-- The Slave Mart

Cruze, Lottie *see* **Kruse, Lottie**

Cruze, May
1916 The Impersonation

Cudahy, Anne
1920 The Barbarian

Cudahy, Michael
1920 The Barbarian

Cugnet, Eugene J. *same as* **Cugnet, Eugene**
1915 The Battle of Ballots
    The Whirl of Life
1916 The Woman's Law

Cullen, Edward
1920 The Place of Honeymoons

Cullen, James F. *same as* **Cullen, James**
1920 Blind Love
    Chains of Evidence

Cullen, Captain William J.
1919 The Lost Battalion

Culley, John C.
1915 Pennington's Choice

Cullington, Margaret
1918 Betty Takes a Hand
    Little Red Decides
    The Strange Woman
1919 The Game's Up
1920 Three Gold Coins

Cullison, Webster
1915 The Bludgeon
1916 Idols
1919 False Evidence
    In for Thirty Days
    One-Thing-at-a-Time O'Day

Culp, A.
1916 A Daughter of the Gods

Cumberland, John
1917 Baby Mine
1919 The Gay Old Dog

Cumming, Dorothy *same as* **Cumming, Dorothy G.; Cummings, Dorothy**
1916 Snow White
1920 Idols of Clay
    The Notorious Miss Lisle
    The Notorious Mrs. Sands
    The Thief
    The Woman and the Puppet
    A Woman Who Understood

Cumming, Marion
1917 God's Man

Cummings, Charles
1916 The Chalice of Sorrow
1917 Heart Strings
    The Hidden Children

Cummings, Dick *see* **Cummings, Richard**

Cummings, Dorothy *see* **Cumming, Dorothy**

Cummings, George
1918 The Light of Western Stars

Cummings, Irving
1914 The Last Volunteer
    The Three of Us
    Uncle Tom's Cabin
1915 The Lure of the Mask
1916 The Feud Girl
    The Gilded Cage
    The Hidden Scar
    Pamela's Past
    The Saleslady
    The World's Great Snare
1917 An American Widow
    A Man's Law
    Rasputin, the Black Monk
    Royal Romance
    Sister Against Sister
    The Whip
    Wrath of Love
1918 The Debt of Honor
    The Heart of a Girl
    The Interloper
    Merely Players
    The Million Dollar Mystery
    The Struggle Everlasting
    Toys of Fate
    The Woman Who Gave
1919 Auction of Souls
    The Better Wife
    The Bluffer
    Everywoman
    The Greater Sinner
    Her Code of Honor
    Mandarin's Gold
    Men, Women and Money
    The Scar
    Secret Service
    Some Bride
    The Unveiling Hand
    What Every Woman Learns
1920 Beautifully Trimmed
    Harriet and the Piper
    The Ladder of Lies
    Old Dad
    The Round-Up
    The Saphead
    Sex
    The Thirteenth Commandment
    The Tree of Knowledge

Cummings, Mrs. Irving
1920 Wait for Me

Cummings, J.
1919 Under the Top

Cummings, Jack
1916 The Invisible Enemy

Cummings, Janice
1919 The Painted World

Cummings, Kate
1915 From the Valley of the Missing

Cummings, Richard *same as* **Cummings, Dick**
1915 Bred in the Bone
    A Child of God
    Double Trouble
    The Wolf Man
1916 Daphne and the Pirate
1917 The Bad Boy
    Her Official Fathers
    A Mormon Maid

    Reaching for the Moon
1918 The Man of Bronze
    A Petticoat Pilot
1919 Blind Husbands
    Common Property
    The Delicious Little Devil
    Little Comrade
    The Little White Savage
    The Valley of the Giants
1920 The Adorable Savage
    The City of Masks
    The Devil's Riddle
    Pinto
    The Prince of Avenue A
    Sherry
    What Happened to Jones

Cummings, Robert *same as* **Cummings, Robert W.**
1914 The Jungle
    The Little Gray Lady
    The Spitfire
1915 Alias Jimmy Valentine
    Camille
    The Cub
    From the Valley of the Missing
    The Heart of the Blue Ridge
    The Ivory Snuff Box
    The Running Fight
1916 The Awakening of Helena
     Richie
    The Brand of Cowardice
    Fruits of Desire
    A Million a Minute
    Paying the Price
    Romeo and Juliet (Quality
     Pictures Corp.)
    The Wall Between
    The Yellow Passport
1917 Betsy Ross
    Crime and Punishment
    The Law of Compensation
    A Rich Man's Plaything
1917-18
    The Devil's Playground
1918 The Song of Songs
    The Trap
1919 The Golden Shower
    Virtuous Men
1920 The Face at Your Window

Cummins, Miss
1917 American—That's All

Cummins, Samuel
1919 Wild Oats

Cunard, Grace
1914 The Phantom Violin
    Washington at Valley Forge
1915 The Campbells Are Coming
1917 Society's Driftwood
1918 After the War
    Hell's Crater
1920 The Woman of Mystery

Cunard, Mina
1916 Is Any Girl Safe?
    The Sign of the Poppy
    What Love Can Do

Cuneo, Lester
1915 Graustark
    Pennington's Choice
    The Second in Command
    The Silent Voice
    The Slim Princess
1916 Big Tremaine
    The Come-Back
    A Corner in Cotton
    The Masked Rider
    Mister 44
    Pidgin Island
    The River of Romance
1917 The Haunted Pajamas
    The Hidden Children
    The Hidden Spring
    Paradise Garden
    The Promise
    Under Handicap
1920 Are All Men Alike?
    Desert Love
    Food for Scandal
    Lone Hand Wilson
    The Terror

Cunningham, Jack
1917 The Medicine Man
    The Stainless Barrier
    A Stormy Knight
    Wild Sumac

1918 The Argument
    The Bells
    Betty Takes a Hand
    The Border Raiders
    A Burglar for a Night
    The Ghost of the Rancho
    The Goddess of Lost Lake
    The Heart of Rachael
    The Hopper
    A Law unto Herself
    Limousine Life
    Little Red Decides
    More Trouble*
    The Narrow Path
    Real Folks
    The Shoes That Danced
    Two-Gun Betty
    Winning Grandma
1919 Adele
    All of a Sudden Norma
    All Wrong
    The False Code
    Gates of Brass
    It Happened in Paris
    The Joyous Liar
    The Master Man
    The Midnight Stage
    Playthings of Passion
    The Silver Girl
    Todd of the Times
    The World Aflame
1920 Big Happiness
    The Devil to Pay
    The Dream Cheater
    The Green Flame
    The House of Whispers
    Live Sparks
    Number 99
    $30,000
    The Tiger's Coat

Cunningham, James
1915 Blue Grass

Curley, Miss
1916 The Girl Philippa
1917 Intrigue

Curley, James
1916 Intolerance
1919 The Fall of Babylon

Curley, Pauline
1915 Life Without Soul
    The Unbroken Road
1917 A Case at Law
    Cassidy
    The Square Deceiver
1918 Bound in Morocco
    The Fall of the Romanoffs
    Her Boy
    His Daughter Pays
    The Landloper
    Lend Me Your Name
1919 The Man Beneath
    The Solitary Sin
    The Turn in the Road
1920 The Valley of Tomorrow

Curran, T. *could be same as* **Curran, Thomas A.**
1914 Three Weeks

Curran, Thomas A. *same as* **Curran, Thomas; could be same as* **Curran, T.**
1915 The Earl of Pawtucket
    Greater Love Hath No Man
    Inspiration
    The Price of Her Silence
1916 Silas Marner
    The World and the Woman
1917 An Amateur Orphan
    The Candy Girl
    The Heart of Ezra Greer
    A Modern Monte Cristo
    The Vicar of Wakefield
    When Love Was Blind
1918 The Girl and the Judge

Curran, William
1920 The Toll Gate

Currie, John
1919 In Old Kentucky

Currier, C. B.
1920 Smiling All the Way

Currier, Frank
1915 The Juggernaut
    Mother's Roses
1916 The Conflict
    Fifty-Fifty

Green Stockings
His Wife's Good Name
The Hunted Woman
The Ninety and Nine
The Wager
1917 The Barricade
Cassidy
The Duchess of Doubt
The End of the Tour
God's Law and Man's
Grafters
The Greatest Power
Her Father's Keeper
His Father's Son
Outwitted
Panthea
Sowers and Reapers
The Trail of the Shadow
1918 The Brass Check
His Bonded Wife
Opportunity
Revelation
Social Hypocrites
A Successful Adventure
Sylvia on a Spree
To Hell with the Kaiser
Toys of Fate
The Winning of Beatrice
With Neatness and Dispatch
1919 Almost Married
Blackie's Redemption
Blind Man's Eyes
The Brat
Easy to Make Money
The Great Romance
The Great Victory, Wilson or
the Kaiser? The Fall of the
Hohenzollerns
Her Kingdom of Dreams
It Pays to Advertise
Peggy Does Her Darndest
The Red Lantern
Satan Junior
Should a Woman Tell?
1920 The Cheater
Clothes
Don't Ever Marry
The Fatal Hour
The Misleading Lady
Pleasure Seekers
Polly with a Past
The Right of Way
Rookie's Return

Currier, R. C.
1920 The One Way Trail
Curry, Cecelia Wheat
1920 Love's Protegé
Curtis, Cathrine
1919 The Shepherd of the Hills
Curtis, Edward S.
1914 In the Land of the Head
Hunters
1916 Seeing America
Curtis, Elinor
1920 Should a Wife Work?
Curtis, J. could be same as **Curtis, Jack**
1915 Tainted Money
Curtis, Jack same as **Curtis, Master
Jack;** could be same as **Curtis, J.**
1915 The Long Chance
Lydia Gilmore
1916 The End of the Rainbow
The Girl of the Lost Lake
The House of Mirrors
The Iron Hand
It Happened in Honolulu
A Romance of Billy Goat Hill
Secret Love
The Secret of the Swamp
Two Men of Sandy Bar
The Way of the World
The Woman's Law
The Yaqui
1917 Broadway Arizona
The Firefly of Tough Luck
God's Crucible
The Greater Law
Mr. Opp
Mutiny
Southern Justice
Until They Get Me
Up or Down?
1918 Free and Equal
The Golden Fleece

The Hard Rock Breed
The Last Rebel
Little Red Decides
Marked Cards
Wolves of the Border
1919 The Brute Breaker
The Coming of the Law
Hell Roarin' Reform
Man's Desire
The Pest
The Speed Maniac
Treat 'Em Rough
1920 The Courage of Marge
O'Doone
Desert Love
The Gift Supreme
The Hell Ship
Seeds of Vengeance
The Servant in the House
Curtis, Marie
1917 Her Greatest Love
Curwood, James Oliver
1916 Fathers of Men
The Last Man
Thou Shalt Not Covet
Unto Those Who Sin
1917 Clover's Rebellion
Soldiers of Chance
The Soul Master
1918 Such a Little Pirate
Tangled Lives
1919 Beauty-Proof
Two Women
1920 Nomads of the North
Cusack, Faye see **Cusick, Faye**
Cushing, Bartley
1916 The Fall of a Nation
Cushing, Laura Woods
1915 The Rug Maker's Daughter
1916 The Victory of Conscience
Cushing, Sidney
1916 The Wall Between
Cushing, Tom
1917 A Crooked Romance
1918 Annexing Bill
The Yellow Ticket
1919 Caleb Piper's Girl
Love, Honor and—?
1920 The Key to Power
Cusick, Faye same as **Cusack, Faye;
Cusic, Faye**
1914 The Chimes
The Mystery of Edwin Drood
1916 The Lotus Woman
Custer, Peggy
1917 The Lair of the Wolf
Cutler, Marty
1920 The Brute
Cutting, Justine
1916 The Revolt
1917 Betsy Ross
The Burglar
The Corner Grocer
Her Hour
Man's Woman
A Self-Made Widow
A Woman Alone
1918 The Spurs of Sybil
Cytron, Maurice same as **Cytron,
Morris**
1915 Pennington's Choice
Rosemary
1916 The Bait
Czar, an Irish setter
1917 The Eyes of the World

D

Dadmun, Leon same as **Dadman, L. E.**
1919 The Phantom Honeymoon
1920 The Place of Honeymoons
Dagmar, Florence
1914 The Call of the North
The Circus Man
Ready Money
1915 Blackbirds
Chimmie Fadden Out West
The Country Boy
A Gentleman of Leisure
The Kindling
Snobs
Young Romance

1916 The Clown
Pudd'nhead Wilson
Dague, Roswell
1917 A Girl Like That
The Jaguar's Claws
Dahl, Helen
1916 God's Half Acre
Mice and Men
Molly Make-Believe
1917 Heart's Desire
The Secret of the Storm
Country
Sleeping Fires
1918 The Floor Below
Dahlberg, Madame see **Dalberg, Camille**
Dailey, Joseph see **Daly, Joe**
Daintry (full name unknown)
1915 The Fairy and the Waif*
Dakin, Raymond E.
1917 Salt of the Earth
1918 Uneasy Money
Dalberg, Camille same as **Dahlberg,
Madame; Dalberg, Camilla;
Dalburg, Mme. C.**
1913 In the Bishop's Carriage
Tess of the D'Urbervilles
1914 The Brute
One of Our Girls
1915 One Million Dollars
Seven Sisters
The Woman Next Door
1916 Should a Baby Die?
1917 Draft 258
1918 Just a Woman
1920 The Chamber Mystery
D'Albrook, Sidney
1915 All for a Girl
The Governor's Boss
1916 The Gilded Cage
1917 The Bitter Truth
The Dancer's Peril
Draft 258
God's Man
Somewhere in America
Two Little Imps
1918 The Challenge Accepted
Heart of the Wilds
Under Suspicion
With Neatness and Dispatch
1919 Life's Greatest Problem
The Lost Battalion
Three Men and a Girl
1920 The Flaming Clue
The Gray Brother
The Mutiny of the Elsinore
Roman Candles
Dalby, Edmund
1917 Passion
Dale, Billy could be same as **Dale,
William**
1918 Love's Pay Day
Dale, Jack
1916 The Sting of Victory
Dale, June
1914 The Spitfire
1916 The Lost Bridegroom
Dale, Margaret
1920 The World and His Wife
Dale, Tommie
1917 The Gates of Doom
Dale, William could be same as **Dale,
Billy**
1916 The Race
1917 The Evil Eye
Daley, Marcella see **Daly, Marcella**
Dallas, Gertrude
1917 The Woman in White
Dallett, M.
1920 Chains of Evidence
Dallzell, Paul
1915 Marse Covington
Dalmores, Aimee
1917 The On-the-Square-Girl
Scandal
Dalton, Charles
1917 Fighting Odds
1919 The Eternal Magdalene
Dalton, Dorothy
1914 Across the Pacific
Pierre of the Plains
1915 The Disciple

1916 The Captive God
Civilization's Child
D'Artagnan
The Female of the Species
A Gamble in Souls
The Jungle Child
The Raiders
The Vagabond Prince
1917 Back of the Man
Chicken Casey
The Dark Road
The Flame of the Yukon
Love Letters
The Price Mark
Ten of Diamonds
The Weaker Sex
Wild Winship's Widow
1918 "Flare-Up" Sal
Green Eyes
The Kaiser's Shadow, or the
Triple Cross
Love Me
The Mating of Marcella
Quicksand
Tyrant Fear
Vive La France!
1919 L'Apache
Extravagance
Hard Boiled
His Wife's Friend
The Homebreaker
The Lady of Red Butte
The Market of Souls
Other Men's Wives
1920 Black Is White
The Dark Mirror
Guilty of Love
Half an Hour
A Romantic Adventuress
Dalton, Emmett
1918 Beyond the Law
Dalton, Eric
1919 The Oakdale Affair
Dalton, Louis
1917 Lorelei of the Sea*
Daly, Arnold
1914 The Port of Missing Men
1915 An Affair of Three Nations
The House of Fear
The Menace of the Mute
1916 Idols
The King's Game
1918 My Own United States
Daly, Bernard
1914 The Lure
Daly, Hazel
1917 Filling His Own Shoes
Satan's Private Door
Skinner's Baby
Skinner's Bubble
Skinner's Dress Suit
1918 Brown of Harvard
1919 The Gay Lord Quex
The Little Rowdy
A Wild Goose Chase
1920 Stop Thief!
Daly, James
1913 The Battle of Shiloh
1914 The Daughters of Men
The Fortune Hunter
1915 The Sporting Duchess
1916 Sorrows of Happiness
Daly, Joe same as **Daily, Joseph; Daly,
Joseph**
1915 What Happened to Jones
1916 Driftwood
The Lords of High Decision
Romeo and Juliet (Quality
Pictures Corp.)
1917 The Avenging Trail
1918 Daybreak
The Gulf Between
Daly, Lee F.
1917 The Seven Swans
Daly, Marcella same as **Daley,
Marcella**
1918 Her Country First
1920 Leave It to Me
The Star Rover
Trumpet Island

Daly, Orlando
1915 The Bigger Man
 The Call of the Dance
 The Runaway Wife
Daly, Robert
1920 Down Home
Daly, William Robert
1914 Forgiven; Or, The Jack of
 Diamonds
 Uncle Tom's Cabin
1916 At Piney Ridge
 Unto Those Who Sin
Dalzell, Lydia
1917 Filling His Own Shoes
1918 Brown of Harvard
Dana, Gordon
1917 The Seven Swans
1919 Good Gracious, Annabelle
Dana, Viola *same as* **Flugrath, Virginia**
1915 Children of Eve
 Cohen's Luck
 Gladiola
 The House of the Lost Court
 On Dangerous Paths
1916 The Cossack Whip
 The Flower of No Man's Land
 The Gates of Eden
 The Innocence of Ruth
 The Light of Happiness
1917 Aladdin's Other Lamp
 Blue Jeans
 The Girl Without a Soul
 God's Law and Man's
 Lady Barnacle
 The Mortal Sin
 Rosie O'Grady
 Threads of Fate
1918 Breakers Ahead
 Flower of the Dusk
 The Only Road
 Opportunity
 Riders of the Night
 A Weaver of Dreams
 The Winding Trail
1919 False Evidence
 The Gold Cure
 The Microbe
 The Parisian Tigress
 Please Get Married
 Satan Junior
 Some Bride
1920 Blackmail
 The Chorus Girl's Romance
 Cinderella's Twin
 Dangerous to Men
 The Willow Tree
Dane, Karl *same as* **Dane, Carl**
1918 Her Final Reckoning
 My Four Years in Germany
 To Hell with the Kaiser
 The Triumph of Venus
1919 Daring Hearts
 The Great Victory, Wilson or
 the Kaiser? The Fall of the
 Hohenzollerns
Dane, Rita
1918 Dodging a Million
Danes, Harry
1916 The Ballet Girl
Danforth, William
1917 The Seven Swans
Danforth, Rev. William F.
1916 The Gates of Eden
Dangerfield, George
1917 The Bar Sinister
Dangman, William
1916 The Ninety and Nine
Daniel, H. B. *same as* **Daniels, H. B.**
1917 Indiscreet Corinne
1918 Honor's Cross
 Humdrum Brown
 The Thing We Love
1920 $30,000
Daniel, M. G.
1918 Humdrum Brown
 The Thing We Love
Daniel, Viora
1920 The Fourteenth Man
 The Life of the Party
 The Sins of St. Anthony
 Thou Art the Man
 Young Mrs. Winthrop

Daniels, Bebe
1919 Everywoman
 Male and Female
1920 The Dancin' Fool
 The Fourteenth Man
 Oh, Lady, Lady
 She Couldn't Help It
 Sick Abed
 Why Change Your Wife?
 You Never Can Tell
Daniels, Frank
1915 Crooky
 What Happened to Father
Daniels, H. B. *see* **Daniel, H. B.**
Daniels, Josephus
1913 Victory
1915 The Nation's Peril*
 Prohibition*
1918 The Men of the Hour*
 The Spreading Evil
 Your Fighting Navy at Work
 and at Play*
Daniels, Nixola
1915 Destruction
Daniels, Phyllis
1917 The World Apart
Danks, Hart Pease
1915 Silver Threads Among the
 Gold*
Dansey, Herbert
1917 One Hour
1918 The Impostor
Danuff, Irving R.
1920 Empty Arms
Danvers, Minnie
1918 Cupid by Proxy
Danzig (full name unknown)
1915 The Fairy and the Waif*
Danziger, Abraham J.
1913 The Lure of New York
Darby, Rhy
1919 Male and Female
Darclay, Louis
1918 The Wildcat of Paris
1919 L'Apache
 The Parisian Tigress
 The Shepherd of the Hills
D'Arcy, Camille
1915 A Daughter of the City
 The White Sister
1916 Captain Jinks of the Horse
 Marines
 The Prince Chap
D'Arcy, Hugh
1918 The Brass Check
Darden, Tasmania
1919 A Man's Duty
Dare, Doris
1920 It Might Happen to You
Dare, Virginia
1917 The Moth
Dare, Walter
1915 The Little Gypsy*
Dark, Stanley
1914 The Education of Mr. Pipp
1916 Green Stockings
 Jaffery
 Man and His Angel
1917 Moral Courage
Dark Cloud *same as* **Dark Cloud, Chief;
 Darkcloud, John**
1914 The Dishonored Medal
1915 Captain Macklin
 The Penitentes
1917 John Ermine of the
 Yellowstone
 The Spirit of '76
1919 What Am I Bid?
1920 The Woman Untamed
Dark Cloud, Mrs.
1919 Desert Gold
Dark Cloud, William
1916 Intolerance
Darkcloud, John *see* **Dark Cloud**
Darley, Brian
1914 The House of Bondage
1918 A Romance of the Air
1919 The Capitol

Darling, Bonita
1915 The Yankee Girl
Darling, Caroline
1913 Tess of the D'Urbervilles
Darling, Grace
1919 False Gods
 Virtuous Men
1920 The Common Sin
 The Discarded Woman
 Even As Eve
Darling, Ida
1914 The Adventures of Kitty Cobb
 The Nightingale
1915 Heléne of the North
 The Masqueraders
 The Morals of Marcus
1916 The Big Sister
 Davy Crockett
 Hypocrisy
 The Lost Bridegroom
 The Test
 Under Cover
1917 Broadway Jones
 Heart's Desire
 Scandal
 When Love Was Blind
1918 By Right of Purchase
 The Ghosts of Yesterday
 The Girl of Today
 The Make-Believe Wife
 Marriage
 Men
 Mrs. Dane's Defense
 Out of the Night
 T'Other Dear Charmer
1919 False Gods
 Life's Greatest Problem
 The Man Who Stayed at Home
 The Miracle of Love
 Three Men and a Girl
1919-20
 When a Man Loves
1920 The Dangerous Paradise
 Marooned Hearts
 She Loves and Lies
 Whispers
 The Woman Game
Darling, Jack
1914 The Brute
Darling, Ruth
1916 Fifty-Fifty
 Intolerance
 Manhattan Madness
1919 The Fall of Babylon
Darling, W. Scott
1920 813
 His Pajama Girl
 So Long Letty
Darmond, Grace
1914 Your Girl and Mine: A
 Woman Suffrage Play
1915 A Black Sheep
 The House of a Thousand
 Candles
 The Millionaire Baby
 A Texas Steer
1917 In the Balance
 When Duty Calls
1918 An American Live Wire
 The Crucible of Life
 A Diplomatic Mission
 The Girl in His House
 The Gulf Between
 The Man Who Wouldn't Tell
 The Other Man
 The Seal of Silence
1919 The Highest Trump
 The Valley of the Giants
 What Every Woman Wants
1920 Below the Surface
 The Invisible Divorce
 So Long Letty
Darrow, Clarence
1913 From Dusk to Dawn
D'Art, E. Clement *same as* **d'Art,
 Clement**
1917 The Apple-Tree Girl
 The Customary Two Weeks
 The Little Chevalier
 The Princess' Necklace
 Putting the Bee in Herbert
19-- Barnaby Lee

Darwell, Jane
1914 The Man on the Box
 The Master Mind
 The Only Son
 Ready Money
 Rose of the Rancho
1915 After Five
 The Goose Girl
 The Reform Candidate
 The Rug Maker's Daughter
Darwin, Margaret
1916 The Path of Darkness
Dashiell, Willard
1918 The Face in the Dark
 The Floor Below
 Joan of Plattsburg
 My Four Years in Germany
Daube, Belle
1914 The Education of Mr. Pipp
Daube, Harda
1919 A Virtuous Vamp
D'Aubrey, Diane
1916 The Half Million Bribe
Daugherty, Jack
1920 Neptune's Bride
D'Auray, Jacques
1920 813
Davenport, Alice
1915 My Valet
1918 Little Red Decides
1919 Spotlight Sadie
Davenport, Blanche
1915 Her Own Way
1916 The Heart of New York
1917 American—That's All
 The Crimson Dove
 The Man Who Made Good
1918 The Belgian
 Peck's Bad Girl
 The Unbeliever
1919 The Lost Battalion
 Marriage for Convenience
 The Miracle of Love
1920 Bab's Candidate
 Madonnas and Men
 The White Moll
 The Woman Game
Davenport, Charles E.
1913 Arizona
1919 Broken Barriers
Davenport, Dorothy
1915 The Explorer
 Mr. Grex of Monte Carlo
 The Unknown
1916 Barriers of Society
 Black Friday
 The Devil's Bondwoman
 Doctor Neighbor
 The Unattainable
 The Way of the World
 A Yoke of Gold
1917 The Girl and the Crisis
 Mothers of Men
 The Scarlet Crystal
 The Squaw Man's Son
 Treason
1920 The Fighting Chance
Davenport, Edgar L. *same as*
 Davenport, E. L.
1914 His Last Dollar
 The Little Gray Lady
 The Thief
 Wildflower
1915 Four Feathers
 Her Reckoning
 Samson
 Simon, the Jester
 A Woman's Resurrection
 Wormwood
1916 The Blindness of Love
 Dorian's Divorce
 The Salamander
 The Upheaval
1917 The Black Stork
 The Great White Trail
Davenport, Harry
1915 C.O.D.
 Father and the Boys
 The Island of Regeneration
 The Making Over of Geoffrey
 Manning
1916 For a Woman's Fair Name
 The Supreme Temptation

The Wheel of the Law
1917 The False Friend
A Man's Law
The Millionaire's Double
The Planter
A Son of the Hills
Sowers and Reapers
Tillie Wakes Up
A Woman Alone
1919 Dawn
A Girl at Bay
The Unknown Quantity

Davenport, Mrs. Harry *same as*
Davenport, Mrs. H.
1916 Ramona
1917 The Planter*
1918 Tony America
1920 The Sleep of Cyma Roget

Davenport, Kate
1915 The Making Over of Geoffrey
Manning
1916 The Supreme Temptation

Davenport, Milla
1918 Social Briars
1919 The Brat
Daddy-Long-Legs
In Mizzoura
The Solitary Sin
1920 Faith
The Forbidden Woman
Leave It to Me
She Couldn't Help It
Stronger Than Death
You Never Can Tell

Davenport, Nettie
1919 The Stream of Life

Davenport, R. J.
1920 Girls Don't Gamble

Davey, Allen M. *same as* **Davey, Allan;**
Davey Allan M.; Davey Allan N.;
Davey, Allen N.
1916 The Soul of Kura-San
The Three Godfathers
1917 Each to His Kind
The Golden Fetter
The Heir of the Ages
The Lonesome Chap
The Prison Without Walls
The Squaw Man's Son
1919 The Blue Bonnet
The Weaker Vessel
1920 The Kentucky Colonel

David, William
1917 Arms and the Girl
1919 The Girl Problem
Here Comes the Bride
1920 The Copperhead

Davide
1920 Witch's Gold

Davidge, Helen
1920 The Road to Divorce

Davidson, Carter
1916 The Mainspring*

Davidson, Charles
1916 The Green-Eyed Monster

Davidson, Dore
1918 Joan of the Woods
Merely Players
Stolen Orders
1920 The Daughter Pays
Humoresque

Davidson, John *same as* **Davidson, J.**
W.; Davidson, Jack
1915 The Alien
The Danger Signal
The Green Cloak
The Sentimental Lady
1916 The Brand of Cowardice
Man and His Soul
A Million a Minute
The Pawn of Fate
The Red Mouse
Romeo and Juliet (Quality
Pictures Corp.)
The Wall Between
1917 The Awakening
The Beautiful Lie
The Power of Decision
Shame
Souls Adrift
The Wild Girl
1918 The Grouch
The Spurs of Sybil

The Winning of Beatrice
1919 The Black Circle
The Bluffer
Forest Rivals
The Stronger Vow
Through the Toils
1920 The Great Lover
Romance
The Tiger's Cub
A Woman's Business

Davidson, Max
1916 Don Quixote
The Heiress at Coffee Dan's
Intolerance
Mr. Goode, the Samaritan
Sunshine Dad
1917 A Daughter of the Poor
1918 The Hun Within
1919 The Hoodlum
The Mother and the Law

Davidson, William B. *same as* **Davidson,**
William
1915 A Yellow Streak
1916 The Child of Destiny
Dorian's Divorce
Her Debt of Honor
In the Diplomatic Service
The Pretenders
The Price of Malice
Thou Art the Man
1917 American Maid
The Call of Her People
The Greatest Power
Her Second Husband
Lady Barnacle
The Lifted Veil
A Magdalene of the Hills
Mary Lawson's Secret
More Truth Than Poetry
Persuasive Peggy
The White Raven
1918 Ashes of Love
Friend Husband
In Pursuit of Polly
Our Little Wife
The Whirlpool
Why I Would Not Marry
1919 La Belle Russe
The Capitol
The Gold Cure
Impossible Catherine
Lure of Ambition
A Woman There Was
1920 A Child for Sale
Partners of the Night
The Valley of Doubt

Davidson, Wynn
1915 The Bulldogs of the Trail

Davies, Acton
1915 Tillie's Tomato Surprise

Davies, Daniel
1917 The Hidden Children

Davies, David
1913 The Daughter of the Hills
1917 The Awakening of Ruth
1918 A Soul Without Windows
1919 His Father's Wife

Davies, Edward *see* **Davis, Edwards**

Davies, Edyna
1920 The Stolen Kiss

Davies, H. *could be same as* **Davies,**
Howard; Davis, H. O. *or* **Davis,**
Howard
1916 Sudden Riches

Davies, Howard *could be same as*
Davies, H.; Davis, H. O. *or* **Davis,**
Howard
1914 The Last Egyptian
1915 The Gentleman from Indiana
Jane
Kilmeny
The Reform Candidate
The Rug Maker's Daughter
The Spanish Jade
The Yankee Girl
1916 The American Beauty
The Call of the Cumberlands
The Code of Marcia Gray
Davy Crockett
The Heart of Paula
The Intrigue
Madame La Presidente
The Making of Maddalena
The Parson of Panamint

Tongues of Men
1917 Her Own People
The Hidden Children
The Silent Lie
1918 The Argument
Boston Blackie's Little Pal
Hearts or Diamonds?
His Birthright
The Spreading Evil
1919 Auction of Souls
It's a Bear
A Sporting Chance (Famous
Players-Lasky Corp.)
A White Man's Chance
1920 Love in the Wilderness
One Hour Before Dawn

Davies, Marion
1917 Runaway Romany
1918 The Burden of Proof
Cecilia of the Pink Roses
1919 The Belle of New York
The Cinema Murder
The Dark Star
Getting Mary Married
1920 April Folly
The Restless Sex

Davies, Marshall
1916 The Colored American
Winning His Suit

Davies, Reine
1915 Sunday
1917 The Sin Woman

Davis (full name unknown)
1915 The Fairy and the Waif*

Davis, Miss
1915 A Continental Girl

Davis, Allan *same as* **Davis, Al**
1917 The Ship of Doom
1920 Oil

Davis, Ann
1920 Parted Curtains

Davis, Charles J. (*cam*) *same as* **Davis,**
Charles
1916 The Chattel
An Enemy to the King
1917 The Man of Mystery
1918 The Girl of Today
The Menace
1919 The Fighting Roosevelts
1920 The Broadway Bubble
Captain Swift
Slaves of Pride
The Sporting Duchess
The Whisper Market

Davis, Charlie (*actor*)
1919 A Romance of Seattle

Davis, Clayton
1920 The Hidden Code

Davis, Delbert L.
1914 A Mother's Heart
Sins of the Parents
1918 Restitution
1920 Mountain Madness

Davis, Edwards *same as* **Davies,**
Edward; Davies, Edwards; Davis,
Edward
1915 Her Mother's Secret
1916 A Circus Romance
The Daughter of MacGregor
The Strength of the Weak
1917 The Question
Transgression
1918 De Luxe Annie
Kildare of Storm
1919 The Love Cheat
1920 The Gray Brother
The New York Idea
Wings of Pride

Davis, Ethel
1915 Jack Chanty
1916 The Phantom Buccaneer

Davis, George H. (*prod*)
1920 Isobel; Or, The Trail's End

Davis, George W. (*actor*)
1919 Out of the Fog

Davis, Grif
1919 Twilight

Davis, Gunnis *see* **Davis, James**

Davis, H. O. *could be same as* **Davies,**
H.; Davies, Howard *or* **Davis,**
Howard
1917 Bringing Home Father
The Little Orphan

A Phantom Husband
1918 High Stakes
1920 The Servant in the House

Davis, Howard *could be same as*
Davies, H.; Davies, Howard *or*
Davis, H. O.
1916 He Fell in Love with His Wife
1920 Dice of Destiny
Wanted at Headquarters

Davis, J. Gunnis *see* **Davis, James**

Davis, James *same as* **Davis, Gunnis;**
Davis, J. G.; Davis, J. Gunnis
1914 The Pit
1917 The Little Duchess
1918 Peg of the Pirates
The Road to France
Stolen Orders
1919 Bolshevism on Trial
The Rough Neck

Davis, Jeff
1915 The Bridge of Sighs

Davis, Katharine Bement
1919 The End of the Road

Davis, Lizzie
1918 A Soul in Trust

Davis, Lou
1916 Soul Mates

Davis, Margaret
1920 Honeymoon Ranch

Davis, Mary *could be same as* **Davis,**
Mary B.; Davis, Mary G. *or* **Davis,**
Mary I.
1918 Rich Man, Poor Man
1919 Mrs. Wiggs of the Cabbage
Patch

Davis, Mary B. *could be same as* **Davis,**
Mary; Davis, Mary G. *or* **Davis,**
Mary I.
1919 An Amateur Widow

Davis, Mary G. *could be same as* **Davis,**
Mary; Davis, Mary B. *or* **Davis,**
Mary I.
1916 The Haunted Manor

Davis, Mary I. *could be same as* **Davis,**
Mary; Davis, Mary B. *or* **Davis,**
Mary G.
1916 I Accuse

Davis, Mildred
1917 Fighting Mad
1918 A Weaver of Dreams
1919 All Wrong

Davis, Myra
1918 Maid O' the Storm

Davis, Norton (Doc)
1915 Lady Audley's Secret

Davis, Owen
1914 The Marked Woman
1915 The Green Cloak
Hearts in Exile
The Sentimental Lady

Davis, Ruby
1920 Bachelor Apartments

Davis, Ulysses
1915 Tainted Money
The White Scar
1916 The Iron Hand
The Soul's Cycle

Davis, Violet
1916 The Salamander

Davis, Will S. *same as* **Davis, Will;**
Davis, Will H.; Davis, William;
Davis, William S.
1913 In the Stretch
1914 The Criminal Path
The Governor's Ghost
The Ordeal
Springtime
Thou Shalt Not
Through Dante's Flames
The War of Wars; Or, The
Franco-German Invasion
1915 The Avalanche
The Curious Conduct of Judge
Legarde
Destruction
Dr. Rameau
The Family Stain
A Modern Magdalen
1916 The Fool's Revenge
Jealousy
Slander
The Straight Way

A Tortured Heart
The Victim
1917 Alias Mrs. Jessop
The Cloud
A Mother's Ordeal
1918 The Brass Check
In Judgment Of
No Man's Land
Under Suspicion
With Neatness and Dispatch
1920 The Eternal Mother
Davison, Grace
1917 Hell Hath No Fury
1918 Suspicion
When Destiny Wills
Wives of Men
Zongar
1919 Atonement
1920 The Hidden Code
Man's Plaything
Davison, Mrs. H. P.
1917 National Red Cross Pageant
Davril, Lena
1915 The Mystery of Room 13
Vanity Fair
1916 The Innocence of Ruth
1917 The Last Sentence
Daw, Marjorie
1915 The Chorus Lady
Out of the Darkness
The Puppet Crown
The Secret Orchard
The Unafraid
1916 The House with the Golden
Windows
Joan the Woman
1917 Conscience
The Jaguar's Claws
A Modern Musketeer
Rebecca of Sunnybrook Farm
1918 Arizona
He Comes Up Smiling
Mr. Fix-It
Say, Young Fellow!
The Sunset Princess
1919 His Majesty, the American
The Knickerbocker Buckaroo
1920 Dinty
Don't Ever Marry
The Great Redeemer
The River's End
Dawkins, Irma
1915 The Hungarian Nabob
Dawley, Bert same as **Dawley, Burt**
1920 The Harvest Moon
The Silent Barrier
Dawley, De Forrest
1914 The House of Bondage
Dawley, Hubert
1915 Children of Eve
Dawley, J. Searle same as **Dawley, J. S.**
1913 An Hour Before Dawn
Caprice
Chelsea 7750
The Daughter of the Hills
In the Bishop's Carriage
Leah Kleschna
The Port of Doom
Tess of the D'Urbervilles
1914 An American Citizen
The Day of Days
In the Name of the Prince of
Peace
The Lost Paradise
Marta of the Lowlands
The Mystery of the Poison Pool
The Next in Command
One of Millions
The Pride of Jennico
A Woman's Triumph
1915 Always in the Way
The Daughter of the People
Four Feathers
Heléne of the North
Still Waters
1916 Little Lady Eileen
Mice and Men
Miss George Washington
Molly Make-Believe
Out of the Drifts
The Rainbow Princess
Silks and Satins
Snow White

1917 Bab's Burglar
Bab's Diary
Bab's Matinee Idol
Conscience
The Mysterious Miss Terry
The Seven Swans
The Valentine Girl
1918 The Death Dance
The Lie
Rich Man, Poor Man
Uncle Tom's Cabin
1919 Everybody's Business
Married in Haste
The Phantom Honeymoon
The Spirit of Lafayette
Twilight
When Men Desire
1920 The Harvest Moon
Dawley, James
1914 The Bargain
Dawley, Janet
1916 The Martyrdom of Philip
Strong
1917 The Last Sentence
Dawn, Hazel
1914 One of Our Girls
1915 The Fatal Card
Gambier's Advocate
The Heart of Jennifer
The Masqueraders
Niobe
1916 The Feud Girl
My Lady Incog.
The Saleslady
Under Cover
1917 The Lone Wolf
National Red Cross Pageant
Dawn, Norman
1919 Lasca
The Right to Happiness
1920 The Adorable Savage
A Tokio Siren
White Youth
Dawson, Albert K. same as **Dawson, A. K.**
1915 The Battle and Fall of
Przemysl
The Battles of a Nation
Friends and Foes
System, the Secret of Success*
The Warring Millions
1916 The Fighting Germans
Dawson, Frank
1917 The Law of Compensation
Dawson, Ivo
1919 The Broken Melody
1920 Footlights and Shadows
Love Without Question
A Romantic Adventuress
The Truth About Husbands
Day, Mr.
1919 The Wreck
Day, Cynthia
1915 The Model
Day, Edith
1918 The Grain of Dust
A Romance of the Air
1920 Children Not Wanted
Day, Gerald
1918 My Own United States
Day, Joel
1915 The Man of Shame
1916 Caprice of the Mountains
1917 The Pride of the Clan
1918 The Challenge Accepted
Vengeance
1919 Hit or Miss
Day, Juliette
1914 The Master Cracksman
1917 Betty and the Buccaneers
The Calendar Girl
The Rainbow Girl
Day, June see **Daye, June**
Day, Shannon
1920 The Man Who Had Everything
Day, Vernon
1914 The Indian Wars
Daye, June same as **Burns, Vinnie; Day, June**
1912 Oliver Twist
1913 The Rogues of Paris
1914 The Chimes
The Million Dollar Robbery

The Mystery of Edwin Drood
The Temptations of Satan
The Woman of Mystery
1915 Heartaches
1916 Sorrows of Happiness
1917 The Derelict
Trooper 44
1918 Wild Honey
1920 The Rich Slave
Dayton, Ethel
1917 The End of the Tour
The White Raven
Dayton, Frank
1915 The White Sister
Dayton, James
1914 Called Back
Damon and Pythias
Samson
The Spy
1915 Mrs. Plum's Pudding
The Scarlet Sin
The Suburban
1919 The Hornet's Nest
Dayton, Lewis
1918 Woman and the Law
Dazey, Charles Turner same as **Dazey, C. T.; Dazey, Charles; Dazey, Charles T.**
1915 The Making Over of Geoffrey
Manning
The Suburban
1916 The Flower of Faith
Manhattan Madness
The Redemption of Dave
Darcey
1917 Behind the Mask
Her Country's Call
New York Luck
Peggy Leads the Way
Wolf Lowry
1918 Danger Within
The Midnight Trail
The Mysterious Client
Shifting Sands
The Testing of Mildred Vane
1920 The Fighting Kentuckians
The Prince of Avenue A
The Silent Barrier
Women Men Love
Dazey, Frank M. same as **Dazey, Frank**
1915 The House of Tears
1916 The Flower of Faith
A Night Out
1917 New York Luck
Peggy Leads the Way
1918 Danger Within
1920 The Fighting Shepherdess
Polly of the Storm Country
The Prince of Avenue A
Silk Hosiery
The Woman Game
Women Men Love
Dazie, Mlle.
1920 The Scarlet Dragon
Dean, Byron
1917 The Boy Girl
Dean, Daisy
1917 The Sawdust Ring
Dean, Dora
1915 Silver Threads Among the Gold
Time Lock Number 776
Dean, Faxon M. same as **Dean, F.**
1917 The Clever Mrs. Carfax
The Cook of Canyon Camp
The Countess Charming
Lost in Transit
The Marcellini Millions
A Roadside Impresario
1918 Jules of the Strong Heart
Rimrock Jones
1919 The Invisible Bond
1920 The Copperhead
A Cumberland Romance
The Fighting Chance
Dean, Jack same as **Dean, John**
1915 The Cheat
The Marriage of Kitty
1916 Each Pearl a Tear
For the Defense
A Gutter Magdalene
Tennessee's Pardner
Witchcraft
The Years of the Locust

1917 Betty to the Rescue
The Crystal Gazer
Her Strange Wedding
On the Level
A School for Husbands
Unconquered
The Winning of Sally Temple
1919 Sealed Hearts
Dean, John see **Dean, Jack**
Dean, Julia
1915 How Molly Malone Made
Good
Judge Not; Or, The Woman of
Mona Diggings
Matrimony
1916 The Ransom
1917 Rasputin, the Black Monk
1918 Ruling Passions
1919 A Society Exile
Dean, Louis
1917 The Darling of Paris
The Tiger Woman
1918 The Birth of a Race
The Kaiser's Finish
My Four Years in Germany
Queen of the Sea
1919 The Common Cause
The Moonshine Trail
1920 The Blood Barrier
Man and His Woman
Dean, Martha
1917 Her Sister
1919 Crimson Shoals
Dean, Priscilla
1914 Mother
1917 Beloved Jim
Even As You and I
The Hand That Rocks the
Cradle
1918 The Brazen Beauty
Kiss or Kill
She Hired a Husband
The Two-Soul Woman
Which Woman?
The Wildcat of Paris
1919 The Exquisite Thief
Forbidden
Paid in Advance
Pretty Smooth
The Silk Lined Burglar
The Wicked Darling
1920 Outside the Law
The Virgin of Stamboul
Dean, Miss R.
1915 The Fairy and the Waif*
Dean, Ralph
1915 The Fairy and the Waif
1916 The Conquest of Canaan
1917 The Accomplice
Madame Sherry
The Rainbow
A Song of Sixpence
1918 The Birth of a Race
Dean, Raye same as **Dean, Ray**
1916 The Stolen Triumph
1920 The Greatest Love
Madonnas and Men
Wings of Pride
Dean, Rosemary
1916 The Clarion
Life's Whirlpool
Dean, Sidney see **Deane, Sydney**
Dean, Ted
1916 Then I'll Come Back to You
Deane (full name unknown)
1915 The Immigrant
Deane, Sydney same as **Dean, Sidney; Dean, Sydney; Deane, Sidney**
1914 Brewster's Millions
The Call of the North
The Making of Bobby Burnit
Ready Money
Rose of the Rancho
The Virginian
What's His Name
1915 The Arab
A Gentleman of Leisure
The Girl of the Golden West
The Goose Girl
The Secret Orchard
Stolen Goods
The Warrens of Virginia

1916 The Evil Women Do
1917 Beloved Jim
     A Doll's House
     The Field of Honor
     Melting Millions
     The Reed Case
     Sirens of the Sea
1918 Breakers Ahead
     The Midnight Trail
     No Man's Land
     The Wife He Bought
1919 The Crimson Gardenia
     Male and Female
     A Man and His Money
1920 The Last of the Mohicans
     The Midlanders
     Once a Plumber
     The Strange Boarder
     Treasure Island

De Anquinos, Alexander
1915 Virtue

Dear, Frank L.
1914 At the Cross Roads

Dearholt, Ashton
1916 The Innocence of Lizette
     Lone Star
     The Love Hermit
     Purity
1917 The Bride's Silence
     The Calendar Girl
     Charity Castle
     Her Country's Call
     High Play
     The Masked Heart
     Snap Judgement
     Souls in Pawn
1918 The Bride's Awakening
     The Cabaret Girl
     The Girl in the Dark
     The Spirit of '17
     The Two-Soul Woman
1919 Pitfalls of a Big City
     The Silk Lined Burglar
1920 The Luck of Geraldine Laird
     Out of the Storm

Dearing, Ann
1918 My Four Years in Germany
1919 The Career of Katherine Bush

Dearing, M. V.
1918 Wild Life

Deaver, Nancy
1920 The Law of the Yukon

Deaves, Ada
1916 Mice and Men

De Beck, George
1915 The Cave Man
     The Heights of Hazard

De Becker, Harold
1915 The Right of Way

De Biccari, Violet same as **Biccari, Violet de; Biccary, Violet de**
1915 Life Without Soul
1916 The Battle of Life
     The Unwelcome Mother
1917 The Princess of Patches
1919 The Spirit of Lafayette

De Brullier, Nigel same as **Brouillet, N.; Brullier, N. de; De Brulier, Nigel; De Bruillier, Nigel; De Brullier, Mr.**
1914 The Pursuit of the Phantom
1915 The Spanish Jade
1916 The Dumb Girl of Portici
     The Girl O' Dreams
     Pasquale
     Purity
     Ramona
1917 The Bond Between
1918 The Kaiser, the Beast of Berlin
     Kultur
     Me und Gott
     The Romance of Tarzan
     The Testing of Mildred Vane
1919 The Boomerang
     Sahara
1920 The Dwelling Place of Light
     Flames of the Flesh
     His Pajama Girl
     The Mother of His Children
     That Something
     The Virgin of Stamboul

De Camp, Frank
1919 The Woman Under Oath

De Carlton, George
1914 Captain Swift
     The Greyhound
     Northern Lights
     The Ordeal
     The Thief
1915 A Gilded Fool
     Life Without Soul
     The Nigger
     The Plunderer
     Samson
1918 The Grouch
     The Gulf Between
     The Road to France
     Tinsel
     To Him That Hath
1919 The Rough Neck

De Carlton, Grace
1916 Betrayed
     The Five Faults of Flo
     The World and the Woman
1917 An Amateur Orphan
     The Vicar of Wakefield

De Castro, Roland
1914 The Master Cracksman

Decker, Harry L. same as **Decker, Harry**
1920 Forty-Five Minutes from Broadway
     Homer Comes Home
     Mary's Ankle
     What's Your Husband Doing?

Decker, Kathryne Browne see **Browne-Decker, Kathryn**

DeComathiere, A. B.
1920 The Brute

De Conde, Syn same as **Conde, Syn de**
1918 The Brass Check
     Revelation
1919 Flame of the Desert
     The Girl Who Stayed Home
     Mary Regan
     Out of the Shadow
1920 Rouge and Riches

De Cordoba, Señorita
1919 The Nature Girl

De Cordoba, Pedro same as **Cordoba, Pedro de**
1915 Carmen (Jesse L. Lasky Feature Play Co.)
     Temptation
1916 Just a Song at Twilight
     Maria Rosa
1917 Barbary Sheep
     One Law for Both
     Runaway Romany
     Sapho
1918 A Daughter of the Old South
1919 The New Moon
1920 The Dark Mirror
     The Sin That Was His
     The World and His Wife

De Cordova, Leander same as **Cordova, Leander de**
1916 Romeo and Juliet (Quality Pictures Corp.)
1918 Her Boy
     The House of Mirth
     Social Hypocrites
1919 The Lost Battalion
     A Scream in the Night
1920 Love, Honor and Obey
     Polly with a Past

De Cordova, Reinzi same as **Cordova, Reinzi de; De Cordova, R.; Cordova, Rienzi de**
1914 The Sign of the Cross
1915 Flame of Passion
     The Pearl of the Antilles
     The Pursuing Shadow

De Cordova, Rudolph same as **Cordova, Rudolph de**
1916 Romeo and Juliet (Quality Pictures Corp.)
     Whoso Findeth a Wife
1917 The Greatest Power
1918 The Birth of a Race
     The Brass Check
     A Daughter of the Old South
1919 The Firing Line
1920 Trumpet Island

De Cordova, Tessie
1915 The Pearl of the Antilles

De Costa, Louise
1918 The Gulf Between*

De Costa, Olga
1917 The Golden Rosary

Dee, Dorothy
1919 Three Green Eyes

Deeley, Ben see **Deely, Ben**

Deely, Barbara La Marr see **La Marr, Barbara**

Deely, Ben same as **Deeley, Ben**
1914 The Patchwork Girl of Oz
1916 East Lynne
1918 In Pursuit of Polly
1919 Victory
1920 Flames of the Flesh
     The Iron Heart
     A Sister to Salome
     The Tattlers
     Would You Forgive?

Deery, Alfred
1917 Madame Sherry

De Felice, Carlotta same as **De Felico, Carlotta**
1914 The Christian
1915 One Million Dollars
     When a Woman Loves
1916 The Price of Happiness

DeFoe, Annette
1917 Indiscreet Corinne
1918 Fame and Fortune
1920 Lone Hand Wilson

De Forest, Charlie see **De Forrest, Charlie**

De Forest, Marian
1919 Erstwhile Susan*

De Forest, Patsey same as **De Forest, Patsy; DeForest, Patsy**
1917 An Alabaster Box
     Her Secret
     The Love Doctor
     A Night in New Arabia
1919 Bullin' the Bullsheviki
1920 The Square Shooter
     Sunset Sprague

De Forrest, Charles same as **De Forest, Charlie**
1914 Lena Rivers (Cosmos Feature Film Corp.)
1916 The Black Crook
1918-19 Once to Every Man

De Forrest, Hal
1916 A Daughter of the Gods
     The Marble Heart

De Gaetano, Alfred
1916 Love and Hate
     Romeo and Juliet (Fox Film Corp.)
     The War Bride's Secret

De Garde, Adele
1914 Mr. Barnes of New York
1916 Green Stockings
     The Lights of New York
     Phantom Fortunes
1917 The Bottom of the Well
     The Love Doctor
     Within the Law
1918 The Triumph of the Weak

De Gonzales, Carmen
1913 The Daughter of the Hills

De Grasse, Joseph same as **DeGrasse, Joseph; Grasse, Joseph de**
1915 Father and the Boys
1916 Bobbie of the Ballet
     The Gilded Spider
     The Grasp of Greed
     The Grip of Jealousy
     If My Country Should Call
     The Mark of Cain
     The Place Beyond the Winds
     The Price of Silence
     Tangled Hearts
1917 Anything Once
     A Doll's House
     The Girl in the Checkered Coat
     Hell Morgan's Girl
     Pay Me
     The Piper's Price
     The Scarlet Car
     Triumph
     The Winged Mystery

1918 After the War
     A Broadway Scandal
     The Fighting Grin
     The Rough Lover
     The Wildcat of Paris
1919 L'Apache
     His Wife's Friend
     The Market of Souls
1920 Bonnie May
     The Brand of Lopez
     Forty-Five Minutes from Broadway
     The Midlanders
     Nineteen and Phyllis

De Grasse, Sam same as **DeGrasse, Sam; DeGrasse, Samuel; Grasse, Sam de**
1915 The Birth of a Nation
     A Child of God
     A Man and His Mate
     The Martyrs of the Alamo
1916 Acquitted
     Children of the Feud
     Cross Currents
     Diane of the Follies
     The Good Bad Man
     The Half-Breed
     An Innocent Magdalene
     Intolerance
     The Price of Power
1917 Anything Once
     Her Official Fathers
     Jim Bludso
     Madame Bo-Peep
     An Old Fashioned Young Man
     The Scarlet Car
     Wild and Woolly
     The Winged Mystery
1918 Brace Up
     The Guilt of Silence
     The Hope Chest
     A Law unto Herself
     The Mortgaged Wife
     The Narrow Path
     Six Shooter Andy
     Smashing Through
     Winner Takes All
     A Woman's Fool
1919 Blind Husbands
     The Exquisite Thief
     Heart O' the Hills
     The Mother and the Law
     The Silk Lined Burglar
     Sis Hopkins
1920 The Broken Gate
     The Devil's Passkey
     The Little Grey Mouse
     Moon Madness
     The Skywayman
     Uncharted Channels
     Unseen Forces

De Gray, Sidney see **De Grey, Sidney**

De Gresac, Mme. Fred same as **De Grissac, Mme.**
1916 The Kiss of Hate
1917 The Eternal Temptress

De Grey, Sidney same as **De Gray, Sidney; De Grey, Sydney; Grey, Syd de**
1915 Jane
     The Yankee Girl
1918 Alias Mary Brown
     His Birthright
     The Reckoning Day
1919 Almost a Husband
1920 The Chorus Girl's Romance
     Jes' Call Me Jim
     The Mark of Zorro
     Water, Water Everywhere

De Grissac, Mme. see **De Gresac, Mme. Fred**

De Groff, Etta
1915 John Glayde's Honor
1916 The Witching Hour

De Haven, Carter
1915 The College Orphan
1916 From Broadway to a Throne
     The Wrong Door
     A Youth of Fortune
1920 Twin Beds

De Haven, Flora Parker same as **De Haven, Flora; DeHaven, Flora Parker**

1915 The College Orphan
1916 The Madcap
The Seekers
The Whirlpool of Destiny
The Wrong Door
A Youth of Fortune
1920 Twin Beds
Deione, Madame
1920 The Luck of the Irish
Deitrich, Theodore C.
1918 The Street of Seven Stars
Wild Honey
1920 The Harvest Moon
De Jarnette, Jessie
1919 In His Brother's Place
De Klade, Louis
1917 The Fringe of Society*
Dekum, Frank *same as* **Bekum, Frank**
1915 Madame Butterfly
De La Cruz, Juan *same as* **Cruz, Juan de la**
1915 The Gentleman from Indiana
Peer Gynt
1916 The Flirt
Hop, the Devil's Brew
The House of Lies
The Making of Maddalena
Where Are My Children?
1918 A Gentleman's Agreement
1919 An Adventure in Hearts
1920 Food for Scandal
For the Soul of Rafael
Pegeen
De Lacy, Ralph
1920 A Connecticut Yankee at King
Arthur's Court
De Lacy, Robert
1920 Held in Trust
De La Mothe, Leon
1920 Vengeance and the Girl
De La Motte, Marguerite *same as* **LaMotte, Marguerite de; Motte, Marguerite de la**
1918 Arizona
1919 Dangerous Waters
For a Woman's Honor
In Wrong
Josselyn's Wife
The Pagan God
A Sage Brush Hamlet
1920 The Broken Gate
The Hope
The Mark of Zorro
The Sagebrusher
Trumpet Island
The U.P. Trail
Delaney (full name unknown)
1915 The Fairy and the Waif*
Delaney, Bernard *same as* **Delaney, Bert**
1915 Inspiration
1916 The Net
1917 The Small Town Girl
Delaney, E. L.
1916 The Thousand Dollar Husband
Delaney, Jerry
1919 A Regular Girl
Delaney, Leo
1915 The Island of Regeneration
1916 The Surprises of an Empty
Hotel
Susie Snowflake
The Vital Question
Whoso Findeth a Wife
1917 Love's Law
Pride and the Devil
The Slacker (Metro Pictures
Corp.)
1919 False Gods
The Great Victory, Wilson or
the Kaiser? The Fall of the
Hohenzollerns
The Moonshine Trail
1920 Circumstantial Evidence
The Scrap of Paper
The Unseen Witness
The Wall Street Mystery
Delano, Edith Barnard
1915 The Heart of Jennifer
Rags
Still Waters
The White Pearl
1916 Hulda from Holland

1918 The Velvet Hand
De La Parelle, L.
1919 Stripped for a Million
De la Parelle, M.
1914 The Hoosier Schoolmaster
Delaro, Hattie *same as* **Barnes, Hattie Delaro; Lara, Hattie de;**
1914 The Pit
Uncle Tom's Cabin
1915 The Heights of Hazard
1916 The Awakening of Helena
Richie
The Eternal Sapho
Kennedy Square
1917 A Night in New Arabia
Sloth
1918 Marriage
1919 False Gods
Human Desire
Mind the Paint Girl
1920 April Folly
Delaro, Hazlan
1917 A Night in New Arabia*
Delatore, Sallie *could be same as* **Dillatore, Calla**
1917 The Rise of Jennie Cushing
DeLavalade, Herman
1920 In the Depths of Our Hearts
Delavanti, Edward
1920 Bright Skies
D'Elba, Henri *same as* **D'Elba, Count H.; D'Elba, H.**
1917 Framing Framers
1918 Alias Mary Brown
Marked Cards
DeLeon, Pedro
1920 The Joyous Troublemaker
De Leon, Walter
1920 Democracy
DeLesque, Lillian
1912 Oliver Twist
De Lewis, Del *could be same as* **Lewis, Del**
1914 Hearts of Oak
Delfino, Mildred
1917 Framing Framers
1918 Without Honor
DeLima, Charles
1916 American Aristocracy
1920 The Deep Purple
De Linsky, Victor
1916 His Great Triumph
The Kiss of Hate
1917 Thou Shalt Not Steal
1918 The Kaiser's Finish
1919 Bullin' the Bullsheviki
The New Moon
De Lint, Fritz
1916 The Soul Market
What Will People Say?
De Lisle, June
1918 Betty Takes a Hand
Dell, Howard
1919 Virtuous Men*
Delmar, Joseph *same as* **Delmar, J.**
1915 Business Is Business
Judge Not; Or, The Woman of
Mona Diggings
Delmar, Thomas *same as* **Delmar, Tom**
1914 The Man Who Could Not Lose
1915 My Best Girl
1916 The Lash
Undine
The Victory of Conscience
1917 Their Compact
1919 Eastward Ho!
1920 A Broadway Cowboy
Delmar, William
1918 Rose O' Paradise
Delmont, Baldy
1920 White Youth
Delmore, Herbert
1916 Broken Chains
Delmore, Ralph
1915 The Sins of Society
1916 The Conquest of Canaan
Fruits of Desire
The Hand of Peril
1917 The Man Who Forgot
1918 The Grain of Dust
1920 The Gray Brother

De Loan, Frank
1919 Gates of Brass
DeLois, Del
1915 Destiny; Or, The Soul of a
Woman
De Lontan, Natalie
1915 The Chalice of Courage
Delorez, Claire
1920 The Joyous Troublemaker
The Scuttlers
Del Ruth, Hampton
1914 Tillie's Punctured Romance*
1915 A Submarine Pirate
1918 Mickey*
Delva, Yvonne
1919 The Thirteenth Chair
Del Val, Merry
1914 His Holiness, the Late Pope
Pius X, and the Vatican
De Maine, Gordon
1914 The Path Forbidden
The Toll of Mammon
When Fate Leads Trump
1915 In the Shadow
Demarest, George F.
1918 Her Boy
De Masber, Sloane
1918 The Rose of the World
De Matteis, Pierre
1917 The Eternal Temptress
De Me, Shirley
1915 Bondwomen
De Mel, Carl
1919 The Great Victory, Wilson or
the Kaiser? The Fall of the
Hohenzollerns
De Merstina, Countess
1913 A Prisoner in the Harem
1914 When Rome Ruled
De Metz, Mae
1915 The Woman Pays
1916 Dimples
de Mille, Agnes
1916 The Ragamuffin
de Mille, Beatrice C.
1916 Each Pearl a Tear
The Heir to the Hoorah
The Storm
Unprotected
The Years of the Locust
1917 Betty to the Rescue
Castles for Two
The Devil-Stone
Forbidden Paths
The Inner Shrine
The Jaguar's Claws
Sacrifice
Unconquered
DeMille, Cecil B.
1912 Cleopatra*
1914 Brewster's Millions
The Call of the North
The Ghost Breaker
The Man from Home
The Master Mind
The Only Son
Rose of the Rancho
The Squaw Man
The Trail of the Lonesome
Pine*
The Virginian
What's His Name
1915 After Five
The Arab
The Captive
Carmen (Jesse L. Lasky
Feature Play Co.)
The Cheat
Chimmie Fadden
Chimmie Fadden Out West
The Explorer*
A Gentleman of Leisure*
The Girl of the Golden West
The Kindling
Snobs*
Temptation
The Unafraid
The Warrens of Virginia
The Wild Goose Chase
1916 The Dream Girl
The Golden Chance
The Heart of Nora Flynn
Joan the Woman

The Love Mask
Maria Rosa
The Ragamuffin*
The Trail of the Lonesome Pine
1917 The Devil-Stone
The Little American
Nan of Music Mountain*
A Romance of the Redwoods
The Woman God Forgot
1918 Old Wives for New
The Squaw Man
Till I Come Back to You
We Can't Have Everything
The Whispering Chorus
1919 Don't Change Your Husband
For Better, for Worse
Male and Female
1920 Something to Think About
Why Change Your Wife?
de Mille, Cecilia
1914 The Virginian
de Mille, William C.
1914 The Only Son
1915 After Five
Carmen (Jesse L. Lasky
Feature Play Co.)
The Explorer
The Goose Girl
The Governor's Lady
The Puppet Crown
The Secret Orchard
Stolen Goods*
The Wild Goose Chase
Young Romance
1916 Anton the Terrible
The Blacklist
The Clown
Common Ground
The Heir to the Hoorah
Maria Rosa
The Ragamuffin
The Sowers
1917 The Ghost House
Hashimura Togo
The Secret Game
1918 The Honor of His House
Mirandy Smiles
The Mystery Girl
One More American
We Can't Have Everything
The Widow's Might
1919 For Better, for Worse
Peg O' My Heart
1920 Conrad in Quest of His Youth
Jack Straw
The Prince Chap
The Tree of Knowledge
Why Change Your Wife?
1921 Midsummer Madness
Deming, Walter
1918 Love's Law
De Mise, Raphael
1918 The Street of Seven Stars
De More, Harry *same as* **De More, H. C.**
1916 The People vs. John Doe
Vengeance Is Mine
1917 The Car of Chance
The Hand That Rocks the
Cradle
The Plow Woman
1918 The Empty Cab
1919 Paid in Advance
Dempsey, Josephine
1920 Women Men Love
Dempsey, Julie
1919 His Father's Wife
Dempsey, Patrick
1915 The Deathlock
Dempsey, Pauline
1917 The Voice of Conscience
1918 The Eyes of Mystery
Pals First
A Successful Adventure
1919 An Amateur Widow
The Great Victory, Wilson or
the Kaiser? The Fall of the
Hohenzollerns
Me and Captain Kidd
1920 The Good-Bad Wife
Youthful Folly

69

Devereaux, Ora
1920 The Peddler of Lies
Deverez, Mildred
1915 The Pearl of the Antilles*
Deverich, Nat
1914 His Last Dollar
1917 The Little Princess
1918 Amarilly of Clothes-Line Alley
The Firefly of France
The House of Silence
Less Than Kin
Stella Maris
1919 Johnny Get Your Gun
Under the Top
1920 The Invisible Divorce
Witch's Gold
De Vernon, Frank same as **DeVernon, Frank; Vernon, Frank de**
1915 All for a Girl
The Concealed Truth
Wormwood
1916 Lovely Mary
The Turmoil
1917 Darkest Russia
Souls Adrift
The Woman Beneath
1918 Pals First
The Unbeliever
1919 Little Women
The Way of a Woman
Devi, Mlle. Nila
1920 The Place of Honeymoons
Devine, James
1920 The Adventurer
Devine, Jerry
1920 Over the Hill to the Poorhouse
DeVinna, Clyde same as **Vinna, Clyde de**
1916 Bawbs O' Blue Ridge
The Beggar of Cawnpore
The Captive God
Civilization
A Corner in Colleens
D'Artagnan
The Raiders
1917 Blood Will Tell
The Dark Road
The Flame of the Yukon
The Hater of Men
The Little Brother
Princess of the Dark
Whither Thou Goest
Wild Winship's Widow
1918 Blindfolded
The Heart of Rachael
Madam Who
Maid O' the Storm
The One Woman
Patriotism
Rose O' Paradise
The White Lie
Within the Cup
1919 Adele
All Wrong
The Lincoln Highwayman
Playthings of Passion
1920 The Challenge of the Law
The Iron Rider
Leave It to Me
The Man Who Dared
Twins of Suffering Creek
Devlin, Donald
1915 The Arrival of Perpetua
Devoe, Olga
1915 The College Orphan*
De Vonde, Chester
1920 Even As Eve
The Good-Bad Wife
Voices
Devore, Dorothy
1920 Forty-Five Minutes from Broadway
Devries, Henry see **Vries, Henri de**
Dewey (full name unknown)
1919 Love in a Hurry
Dewey, Charles
1918 The Sea Waif
1919 The Oakdale Affair
Dewey, Mrs. Charles
1920 The Amateur Wife

Dewey, Elmer
1920 Girls Don't Gamble
Dewey, George
1915 The Battle Cry of Peace*
DeWitt, Clarence
1920 Forty-Five Minutes from Broadway
Dewitt, Jack
1920 Lone Hand Wilson
De Wolf, Miss
1917 The Last Sentence
De Wolfe, Elsie
1920 Democracy
DeWolfe, Marie
1918 The Kingdom of Youth
De Wolfe, Vivian
1914 The House of Bondage
DeWolff, Dorothy
1915 The Climbers
1916 The City of Failing Light
Dexter, Elliott same as **Dexter, Elliot**
1915 Heléne of the North
The Masqueraders
1916 The American Beauty
Daphne and the Pirate
Diplomacy
The Heart of Nora Flynn
An International Marriage
The Lash
The Plow Girl
Public Opinion
The Victory of Conscience
1917 Castles for Two
The Eternal Temptress
The Inner Shrine
Lost and Won
The Rise of Jennie Cushing
A Romance of the Redwoods
Stranded in Arcady
Sylvia of the Secret Service
The Tides of Barnegat
Vengeance Is Mine
1918 The Girl Who Came Back
Old Wives for New
The Squaw Man
We Can't Have Everything
The Whispering Chorus
Woman and Wife
Women's Weapons
1919 A Daughter of the Wolf
Don't Change Your Husband
For Better, for Worse
Maggie Pepper
1920 Behold My Wife
Something to Think About
Dey, Frederic Van Rensselaer
1920 The Flaming Clue
Diane, Mlle.
1915 The Siren's Song
Díaz, General Armando
1918 Lafayette, We Come!*
Under Four Flags
Dickerson, Jennie same as **Dickerson, Jenny**
1916 The Rise of Susan
1918 The Kingdom of Youth
1919 Kathleen Mavourneen
1920 The Fatal Hour
Dickey, Basil
1920 Blind Love
The Gray Brother
Dickinson, W.
1915 Are You a Mason?
Dickson, Charles
1915 Little Miss Brown
The Siren's Song
Sunday
1917 An American Widow
Dickson, Dorothy
1919 Eastward Ho!
Dickson, Lydia
1916 Hypocrisy
Diem, Roy
1919 A Daughter of the Wolf
Dierker, Hugh E.
1920 When Dawn Came
Dierker, Mrs. Hugh E.
1920 When Dawn Came
Diestal, Edith same as **Diestal, Miss; Diestel, Edith**
1915 The Flaming Sword

1916 King Lear
Dietz, Carl
1917 Daughter of Destiny
Dietz, Charles
1914 The Strange Story of Sylvia Gray
Dietz, Loan Star
1919 Fool's Gold
Dill, Jack same as **Dill, J. Webster; Dill, Jack W.**
1917 The Edge of the Law
Follow the Girl
Should She Obey?
1918 Fame and Fortune
Mr. Logan, U.S.A.
1919 The Coming of the Law
1920 The One Way Trail
West Is West
Dill, Max M. same as **Dill, Max**
1916 Bluff
Lonesome Town
A Million for Mary
Peck O' Pickles
Three Pals
1917 Beloved Rogues
Glory
Dillatore, Calla could be same as **Delatore, Sallie**
1917 Sister Against Sister
Dillenback, George P.
1915 A Price for Folly
1917 The Love Doctor
Diller, Phyllis
1920 Over the Hill to the Poorhouse
Dillion, John Webb (actor, 1877-1949) same as **Dillion, Jack; Dillon, John W.; Dillon, John Webb;** not the same as **Dillon, J. Francis** or **Dillon, Jack**
1914 Sins of the Parents
Three Weeks
1916 By Whose Hand?
Her American Prince
Hypocrisy
One Day
Romeo and Juliet (Fox Film Corp.)
The Unwelcome Mother
The Woman's Law
1917 Alma, Where Do You Live?
The Darling of Paris
Heart and Soul
The Primitive Call
The Tiger Woman
1918 Joan of Plattsburg
The Queen of Hearts
1919 A Scream in the Night
1920 Cynthia-of-the-Minute
The Law of the Yukon
Dillman, Hugh
1919 An Amateur Widow
Dillon, Edward
1914 Home, Sweet Home
1916 Don Quixote
The Heiress at Coffee Dan's
Intolerance
Mr. Goode, the Samaritan
Sunshine Dad
1917 The Antics of Ann
A Daughter of the Poor
Might and the Man
1918 The Embarrassment of Riches
Our Little Wife
1919 Help! Help! Police!
Luck and Pluck
The Mother and the Law
Never Say Quit
Putting One Over
The Winning Stroke
1920 The Amateur Wife
The Frisky Mrs. Johnson
Parlor, Bedroom and Bath
Dillon, Irving
1916 The Flames of Johannis
Dillon, J. Francis (dir, actor, 1884-1934) same as **Dillon, Jack** for some films; not the same as **Dillon, Jack** (actor, 1866-1937)
1914 The Gangsters
The Key to Yesterday
1917 Indiscreet Corinne
1918 Beans
Betty Takes a Hand

Heiress for a Day
Limousine Life
The Love Swindle
Nancy Comes Home
She Hired a Husband
1919 Burglar by Proxy
The Follies Girl
Love's Prisoner
The Silk Lined Burglar
A Taste of Life
1920 Blackbirds
The Right of Way
Suds
Dillon, Jack (actor, 1866-1937) same as **Dillon, John T.;** not the same as **Dillion, John Webb** or **Dillon, J. Francis** (dir, actor, 1884-1934, who was also called **Dillon, Jack**)
1913 Robin Hood
1914 Home, Sweet Home
Shannon of the Sixth
1915 The Martyrs of the Alamo
The Outcast
1916 Destiny's Toy
The Lost Bridegroom
1917 A Case at Law
A Girl Like That
A Rich Man's Plaything
1918 All Woman
The Embarrassment of Riches
1919 Putting One Over
Wanted—A Husband
1920 She Loves and Lies
Dillon, Julian
1916 Seventeen
1918 Wanted—A Brother
Dillon, Robert A.
1914 The Key to Yesterday
1916 The Stain in the Blood
1920 The Last of the Mohicans
Dills, William
1920 The Deceiver
The Golden Trail
Dilworth, Lillian
1915 Wormwood
Dintenfass, Mark M.
1918 My Four Years in Germany
Dinwiddie, R.
1915 The Adventures of a Boy Scout
Dion, Hector
1914 The $5,000,000 Counterfeiting Plot
Forgiven; Or, The Jack of Diamonds
1916 The Fugitive
King Lear
Saint, Devil and Woman
Silas Marner
1917 Fighting Mad
1918 One More American
Painted Lips
The Wolf and His Mate
1919 Auction of Souls
1920 The Jungle Princess
Dione, Rose same as **Dion, Mlle.; Dion, Rose; Dione, Madame**
1919 It Happened in Paris
The Secret Garden
The World and Its Woman
1920 The Great Lover
The Land of Jazz
Silk Hosiery
Suds
The Woman and the Puppet
Ditline, Rene
1915 Sealed Valley
Ditmars, Raymond L. same as **Dittmars, Raymond**
1914 The Book of Nature
1916 Race Suicide
Ditrichstein, Leo
1915 How Molly Malone Made Good
Ditt, Josephine
1914 Damaged Goods
1915 The House of a Thousand Scandals
Secretary of Frivolous Affairs
Dittmar, Harry
1920 The Broadway Bubble
The Sea Rider

Dittmars, Raymond see Ditmars,
  Raymond L.
Dix, Beulah Marie
  1917 The Call of the East
       The Cost of Hatred
       The Ghost House
       The Girl at Home
       The Hostage
       The Land of Promise*
       Nan of Music Mountain
       The Prison Without Walls
       The Sunset Trail
       What Money Can't Buy
  1918 The Girl Who Came Back
       Hidden Pearls
       The Squaw Man
       Wild Youth
       Women's Weapons
  1919 Fires of Faith
       The Heart of Youth
       In Mizzoura
       Men, Women and Money
       Secret Service
       The Woman Thou Gavest Me
  1920 Held by the Enemy
       Judy of Rogue's Harbor*
       Sweet Lavender
Dix, Richard
  1917 One of Many
Dixey, Henry E.
  1913 Chelsea 7750
  1916 Father and Son
Dixon, Charles
  1915 Are You a Mason?
Dixon, Florence
  1918 Too Fat to Fight
  1919 Never Say Quit
  1920 Captain Swift
       Hidden Charms
       The Road of Ambition
       The Silent Barrier
Dixon, Henry P.
  1917 The Man Who Made Good
Dixon, Jane
  1919 The Darkest Hour
Dixon, Ralph H. same as Dixon, Ralph
  1919 Bill Henry
       Hay Foot, Straw Foot
       His Wife's Friend
       The Lady of Red Butte
       The Lone Wolf's Daughter
       Stepping Out
  1920 The Brute Master
       His Own Law
       The Leopard Woman
       Love
       Love Madness
       Sex
       A Thousand to One
Dixon, Roy
  1917 A Wife on Trial
Dixon, Thomas
  1915 The Birth of a Nation*
  1916 The Fall of a Nation
  1918 The One Woman*
D'Juria, Mme. I.
  1917 The Inner Shrine
Doane, Frank
  1918 By Hook or Crook
  1920 The Truth
Dobble, Ivan
  1917 The Little Duchess
       The Stolen Paradise
Dobbs, Beverly B.
  1912 Atop of the World in Motion
  1919 A Romance of Seattle
Dobson, Fred
  1914 The Banker's Daughter
  1915 The Gentleman from Indiana
       The Reform Candidate
  1916 Tongues of Men
Dobson, Miles
  1919 Are You Legally Married?
       Flame of the Desert
Dockstader, Lew
  1914 Dan
Dodd, Rev. Neal
  1920 The Furnace
Dodge, Anna
  1915 The Circular Staircase
       The Rosary
  1917 The Devil Dodger
       Framing Framers

       Indiscreet Corinne
       Polly Put the Kettle On
       Until They Get Me
  1918 Betty Takes a Hand
       The Flames of Chance
       Heiress for a Day
       The Last Rebel
       The Lonely Woman
       Mlle. Paulette
       Nancy Comes Home
       The Shoes That Danced
       Without Honor
  1919 Hearts Asleep
  1920 The Gift Supreme
Dodge, M. A.
  1920 Witch's Gold
Dodge, Mary
  1920 Neptune's Bride
Dodson, Mitchell
  1915 Are You a Mason?
Dodsworth, Betty
  1917 Trooper 44
Dolan, Viola
  1919 Castles in the Air
Dolive, Jenkyns
  1920 The Sleep of Cyma Roget
Doll, Dixie
  1918 Paying His Debt
Dolly, Roszika same as Dolly, Rozsika
  1915 The Lily and the Rose
  1918 The Million Dollar Dollies
Dolly, Yancsi
  1915 The Call of the Dance
  1918 The Million Dollar Dollies
Dolores, Miss
  1915 The Spendthrift*
Dominguez, Beatrice
  1919 The Light of Victory
       The Sundown Trail
  1920 Under Crimson Skies
Don, the dog
  1917 The Island of Desire
Don, D. L.
  1919 The Hidden Truth
Don, R. G.
  1915 The Unwelcome Wife
Donahue, Joseph A.
  1919 The Undercurrent
Donahue, Lucy
  1918 The Strange Woman
  1919 The Microbe
Donald, James
  1917 The Planter
Donald, Sherwood
  1917 Bab the Fixer
Donald, Walter
  1920 The Triple Clue
Donaldson, Mrs.
  1916 Should a Baby Die?
Donaldson, Arthur
  1914 The Day of Days
       The Land of the Lost
       Over Niagara Falls
       Three Weeks
       Wolfe; Or, The Conquest of
       Quebec
  1915 Hearts of Men
       The Moth and the Flame
  1916 The Faded Flower
       Her American Prince
       The Salamander
       Should a Baby Die?
       A Woman's Honor
  1917 Babbling Tongues
       The Danger Trail
       Enlighten Thy Daughter
       For France
       His Own People
       I Will Repay
       Who Goes There!
  1918 Find the Woman
       The Golden Goal
       The Green God
       Over the Top
  1919 The A.B.C. of Love
       Atonement
       The Captain's Captain
       Coax Me
       Daring Hearts
       Fighting Destiny
       Me and Captain Kidd
       Mind the Paint Girl

       Miss Dulcie from Dixie
       The Undercurrent
  1920 Greater Than Fame
       The Hidden Light
       A Modern Salome
       Mothers of Men
Donaldson, Dick
  1918 A Good Loser
Donaldson, Howard
  1920 Up in Mary's Attic
Donaldson, Lyn same as Donelson, Lyn
  1916 The Ocean Waif
  1917 The Empress
  1918 The Blue Bird
       The Inn of the Blue Moon
       Woman
Donaldson, R. M.
  1918 His Enemy, the Law
Donelson, Lyn see Donaldson, Lyn
Doner, Martin J. same as Doner, M.;
  Doner, Martin L.
  1916 The Captive God
  1918 The Girl of My Dreams
       The Romance of Tarzan
       Tarzan of the Apes
  1919 In Search of Arcady
       The Love Call
Dones, Sidney P. same as Dones, Sidney
  Preston
  1919 Injustice
  1920 Reformation
Donlin, Mike
  1915 Right off the Bat
  1917 Raffles, the Amateur
       Cracksman
  1918 Jack Spurlock, Prodigal
       The Unchastened Woman
Donlin, Rita Ross
  1915 Right off the Bat
Donnelly, Dorothy
  1914 The Thief
  1915 Sealed Valley
  1916 Madame X
Donnelly, Jim
  1919 Cupid Forecloses
Donnelly, Thomas
  1918 My Own United States
  1919 The Indestructible Wife
Donohue, Doc
  1916 The Daring of Diana
Donohue, Joseph same as Donohue, Joe
  1917 Within the Law
  1918 The World for Sale
  1920 Bachelor Apartments
Donough, John J.
  1915 A Yellow Streak
  1916 Dimples
Donovan, Frank P.
  1919 Bullin' the Bullsheviki
Donovan, Jack
  1920 The Midlanders
       Milestones
Dooley, Johnny
  1920 Skinning Skinners
Doquette, Yolande same as Douquette,
  Yolande
  1917 The Adventurer
       House of Cards
       A Man and the Woman
Doralinda, Mme. same as Doralinda
  1918 The Naulahka
  1920 The Woman Untamed
Dore, Alma
  1918 Suspicion
Dore, Gladys
  1917 A Modern Monte Cristo
  1918 What Becomes of the
       Children?
Doreau, Robert
  1916 The Sign of the Spade
Dorfman, Nat
  1919 Broken Barriers
Dorhan, Ed
  1918 Berlin Via America
Doria, Vera
  1916 The Madcap
  1918 A Lady's Name
       Mrs. Leffingwell's Boots
       A Pair of Silk Stockings
       Salome
       Sauce for the Goose
       Women's Weapons

  1919 Life's a Funny Proposition
       The Veiled Adventure
Dorian, Charles
  1918 All Night
       The Answer
       Hell's End
       Innocent's Progress
       The Red-Haired Cupid
       Society for Sale
  1919 The Sealed Envelope
Dorland, John
  1918 The Star Prince
Dorner, August C.
  1914 La Belle Russe*
Doro, Marie
  1915 The Morals of Marcus
       The White Pearl
  1916 Common Ground
       Diplomacy
       The Heart of Nora Flynn
       The Lash
       Oliver Twist
       The Wood Nymph
  1917 Castles for Two
       Heart's Desire
       Lost and Won
Dorrance, Ethel
  1918 The Law's Outlaw
Dorrance, James
  1918 The Law's Outlaw
Dorrington, Lucile
  1917 Corruption
       The Inevitable
       Little Miss Fortune
       The Little Samaritan
  1918 A Man's World
Dorris, Albert same as Dorris, A.
  1916 La Vie de Boheme*
  1918 Missing
  1919 The Invisible Bond
Dorris, Bert
  1916 Driftwood
  1920 A Cumberland Romance
       The Fighting Chance
D'Orsay, Lawrence
  1915 The Earl of Pawtucket
  1918 Ruggles of Red Gap
Dorsey, Dee
  1917 The Jury of Fate
Dorsey, Dr. George A.
  1915 China
       Japan
  1918 Our Navy
Dorsey, Richard
  1919 The Great Victory, Wilson or
       the Kaiser? The Fall of the
       Hohenzollerns
Doscher, Doris
  1918 The Birth of a Race
Doti, Carlotta
  1913 The Third Degree
  1914 The Lion and the Mouse
Doty, Douglas
  1920 Beautifully Trimmed
       Risky Business
       Two Kinds of Love
Doubble, Graham
  1917 The Apple-Tree Girl
Doubble, Ivan
  1919 The Mystery of the Yellow
       Room
Doucet, Paul
  1914 Sins of the Parents
  1915 The Devil's Daughter
  1916 Jaffery
  1917 The Judgement House
       Shame
  1918 The Danger Game
       The Fair Pretender
       The Knife
       The Million Dollar Dollies
  1919 The Scar
       The Virtuous Model
Doud, Jack
  1920 Oh, Lady, Lady
Dougherty, George S.
  1914 The Line-Up at Police
       Headquarters
Dougherty, Lee
  1919 The Oakdale Affair

Dougherty, Victor
1918 Hearts of Love
Doughty, Francis Worcester
1914 Hook and Hand
Douglas, Blanche
1915 The Price
1918 The Ghosts of Yesterday
Douglas, Byron
1919 The Winning Stroke
1920 The Plunger
Douglas, Gilbert
1918 Five Thousand an Hour
1919 Good Gracious, Annabelle
Douglas, Royal
1915 A Bunch of Keys
Douglas, Tom
1922 The Cynic Effect
Douglass, Charles
1914 The Ring and the Man
Douglass, Leon F.
1918 Cupid Angling
Douquette, Yolande see **Doquette, Yolande**
Doux, Julian
1914 Sport and Travel in Central Africa
Dovey, Alice
1915 The Commanding Officer
1916 The Romantic Journey
Dow, T. J.
1915 The Vanderhoff Affair
Dowlan, William C. same as **Dowlan, W. C.; Dowlan, William**
1914 Richelieu
1915 The College Orphan
1916 Drugged Waters
The Light
The Madcap
Youth's Endearing Charm
1917 The Outsider
Somewhere in America
1918 The Atom
Daughter Angele
Irish Eyes
1919 Cowardice Court
Loot
Restless Souls
Under Suspicion
1920 The Chorus Girl's Romance
Dangerous to Men
Locked Lips
The Peddler of Lies
Dowling, Edward
1920 The Greatest Love
Dowling, George
1919 The Gold Cure
1920 A Fool and His Money
Dowling, Joseph J. same as **Dowling, J. J.; Dowling, Joe; Dowling, Joseph**
1915 The Brink
The Iron Strain
The Man from Oregon
1916 The Apostle of Vengeance
Bawbs O' Blue Ridge
The Beckoning Flame
Bullets and Brown Eyes
The Criminal
The Deserter
Home
Somewhere in France
The Stepping Stone
The Thoroughbred (New York Motion Picture Corp.; Kay-Bee)
1917 Alimony
The Gun Fighter
The Iced Bullet
Master of His Home
Paddy O'Hara
The Pinch Hitter
The Square Deal Man
Sudden Jim
Wooden Shoes
The Yankee Way
1918 An Alien Enemy
And a Still Small Voice
The Bells
Blindfolded
Carmen of the Klondike
Free and Equal
The Ghost of the Rancho
The Goddess of Lost Lake
His Robe of Honor

Honor's Cross
Humdrum Brown
A Law unto Herself
A Little Sister of Everybody
Madam Who
Maid O' the Storm
A Man's Man
More Trouble
One Dollar Bid
Patriotism
Social Ambition
Wedlock
With Hoops of Steel
1919 Adele
All of a Sudden Norma
Beckoning Roads
The False Code
Her Purchase Price
Josselyn's Wife
The Joyous Liar
Kitty Kelly, M.D.
The Long Lane's Turning
The Lord Loves the Irish
A Man in the Open
A Man's Country
The Master Man
The Midnight Stage
The Miracle Man
Todd of the Times
A Trick of Fate
A White Man's Chance
1920 Big Happiness
The Devil to Pay
The Dream Cheater
Everybody's Sweetheart
The House of Whispers
The Kentucky Colonel
Live Sparks
Riders of the Dawn
Sink or Swim
The Spenders
A Splendid Hazard
$30,000
The U.P. Trail
Dowling, Sydell
1916 Temptation and the Man
Dowling, Walter could be same as **Downing, Walter**
1918 The Daredevil
1920 The Sacred Ruby
Downing, Helen
1913 Ivanhoe
Downing, Walter could be same as **Dowling, Walter**
1920 The Hidden Light
Downs, Olga
1919 Good Gracious, Annabelle
Downs, Rex
1916 The Impersonation
1917 North of Fifty-Three
1918 Cavanaugh of the Forest Rangers
Dowst, Henry Payson
1919 Redhead
Doyle, Sir Arthur Conan
1914 The $5,000,000 Counterfeiting Plot
Doyle, Gertrude
1920 Two Weeks
Doyle, Johnny
1914 Without Hope
Doyle, Larry
1917 The Baseball Revue of 1917*
Doyle, Mary
1917 The Bar Sinister
The Barricade
The Golden God
Drageauson, Lt. Marcel
1919 The Day She Paid
Draham, Edward
1917 The Avenging Trail
Drain, Lillian
1920 An Arabian Knight
Drake, Dorothy
1917 Cleopatra
Du Barry
The Saintly Sinner
1919 Lure of Ambition
1920 The Adventurer
Drake, Eugenia
1920 That Something

Drake, Mrs. Jane
1920 The Sacred Ruby
Drake, Josephine
1914 Clothes
1916 Bought and Paid For
1917 National Red Cross Pageant*
Drake, Mrs. Whitney
1920 Woman's Man
Drane, Sam D.
1916 The Crisis
Dranet, Leontine
1914 The Patchwork Girl of Oz
Draper, T. W. M. same as **Draper, T. Waln-Mogan**
1915 The Curious Conduct of Judge Legarde
A Price for Folly
1920 The Valley of Night
Draper, W. J.
1915 A Royal Family
Dray, Rosa
1916 Ramona
Drehle, Henry
1917 The Burglar
Dressler, Marie
1914 Tillie's Punctured Romance
1915 Tillie's Tomato Surprise
1917 Tillie Wakes Up
Drew, Mrs. could be same as **Drew, Lillian**
1915 The Beachcomber
1919 The Love Hunger
Drew, Ann
1915 The Silent Voice
Drew, Cora same as **Drew, Mrs. Cora; Drew, Cora Rankin**
1914 The Opened Shutters
1915 It's No Laughing Matter
The Lily and the Rose
1916 Where Are My Children?
The Wood Nymph
1917 The Calendar Girl
Hell Hath No Fury
The Honor System
Southern Pride
When a Man Sees Red
1918 The Moral Law
A Weaver of Dreams*
1919 Under Suspicion
1920 Black Shadows
The Kentucky Colonel
Nineteen and Phyllis
The Prince of Avenue A
Drew, Dionna
1917 The Lair of the Wolf
Drew, Donna
1917 '49-'17
1918 Madame Spy
Drew, Florence
1918 Denny from Ireland
Drew, Gladys S. Rankin see **Cameron, George**
Drew, John
1915 The Second in Command*
Drew, Lillian could be same as **Drew, Mrs.**
1915 In the Palace of the King
1916 Vultures of Society
1918 Ruggles of Red Gap
Uneasy Money
Drew, Little
1914 One Wonderful Night
Drew, Philip Yale
1919 Fruits of Passion
The Root of Evil
Water Lily
Drew, S. Rankin
1914 Mr. Barnes of New York
1915 The Island of Regeneration
1916 The Daring of Diana
The Girl Philippa
The Hunted Woman
Kennedy Square
The Suspect
Thou Art the Man
The Vital Question
Who Killed Joe Merrion?
1917 Who's Your Neighbor?
1919 The Belle of the Season

Drew, Sidney
1914 A Florida Enchantment
1915 Playing Dead
1918 Pay Day
Drew, Mrs. Sidney (died 1914) see **Cameron, George**
Drew, Mrs. Sidney (died 1925) same as **McVey, Lucille; Morrow, Jane**
1914 A Florida Enchantment
1915 Playing Dead
1918 Pay Day
1919 The Gay Old Dog
Drew, Violet
1915 Young Romance
Dreyfus, Miss
1919 Injustice
Drinkwitz, Neta
1916 Purity
Driscole, Henry see **Driscoll, Henry**
Driscoll, G. C.
1918 Restitution
Driscoll, Geneva
1916 Purity
Driscoll, Harold Quintin
1918 Restitution
Driscoll, Henry
1914 The Education of Mr. Pipp
The $5,000,000 Counterfeiting Plot
Driscoll, Tex same as **Driscol, Tex**
1914 The Virginian
1915 The Country Boy
The Girl of the Golden West
Driskell, Evelyn
1917 A Phantom Husband
Drogheda, Countess of
1918 The Great Love*
Dromgold, George same as **Drumgold, George C.**
1919 In Wrong
The Web of Chance
1920 Dinty
Go and Get It
The Little Shepherd of Kingdom Come
Drouart, Hazlan
1917 A Night in New Arabia
Drouet, Robert
1913 The Battle of Shiloh
1915 The Gambler of the West
Druce, Hubert same as **Druce, Herbert**
1917 Please Help Emily
1918 My Wife
1920 Life
Drum, Harry C.
1917 The Planter
Drumier, Jack same as **Drumier, John; Drumiere, Jack**
1914 The $5,000,000 Counterfeiting Plot
The Woman in Black
1916 The Madness of Helen
1917 The Adventures of Carol
The Beloved Adventuress
The Burglar
The Dancer's Peril
Darkest Russia
The Divorce Game
Easy Money
The False Friend
The Little Duchess
The Marriage Market
The Volunteer
1918 The Appearance of Evil
The Beautiful Mrs. Reynolds
The Beloved Blackmailer
By Hook or Crook
The Golden Wall
Heredity
Journey's End
Just Sylvia
The Love Net
The Man Hunt
The Power and the Glory
The Road to France
A Soul Without Windows
Stolen Hours
Vengeance
The Way Out
Whims of Society
The Witch Woman
1919 An Amateur Widow
The Black Circle

Dundas, Don
1916 The Sex Lure
1917 Two Men and a Woman
Dungan, Charles *same as* **Dungan, C. W.**
1914 As Ye Sow
    The Man of the Hour
1915 After Dark
    The Earl of Pawtucket
    The Man Who Found Himself
1916 What Will People Say?
1917 Behind the Mask
    Diamonds and Pearls
    The Man Without a Country
    The Silence Sellers
    The Tenth Case
1918 The Beloved Blackmailer
    The Divine Sacrifice
    T'Other Dear Charmer
1919 The Scar
Dungan, John
1918 The Man Hunt
Dunham, Mary
1916 Purity
Dunham, Maudie
1920 Love in the Wilderness
    The Night Riders
    The Ugly Duckling
Dunham, Phil
1918 Playthings
    The Romance of Tarzan
Dunkinson, Harry *same as* **Dunkinson, Harry Leopold; Dunkinson, Henry**
1915 The Blindness of Virtue
    The Crimson Wing
    In the Palace of the King
    The Raven
    The Slim Princess
1916 The Misleading Lady
1917 The Edge of the Law
    Follow the Girl
    Skinner's Dress Suit
    A Soul for Sale
    The Trufflers
1918 Danger Within
    Kidder and Ko
    Selfish Yates
1919 Chasing Rainbows
    The Coming of the Law
    The Forbidden Room
    Love Is Love
    The Rebellious Bride
    A Rogue's Romance
1920 Beware of the Bride
    The Daredevil
    Forbidden Trails
    Husband Hunter
    The Land of Jazz
    Molly and I
    Officer 666
    Prairie Trails
    Rouge and Riches
    The Willow Tree
Dunlap, Louise
1914 Tess of the Storm Country
Dunlap, Scott *same as* **Dunlap, Scotty**
1915 The College Orphan
    The Long Chance
1919 Be a Little Sport
    The Lost Princess
    Love Is Love
    Vagabond Luck
    Words and Music By—
1920 The Challenge of the Law
    Forbidden Trails
    The Hell Ship
    Her Elephant Man
    The Iron Rider
    Twins of Suffering Creek
    Would You Forgive?
Dunmyre, Louis H. *same as* **Dunmyre, Louis, Dunmyre, Louis J.**
1916 Dollars and the Woman
1917 Her Good Name
1918 The Service Star
1920 A Child for Sale
    The Fatal Hour
Dunn, D. L.
1915 The Unwelcome Wife*
Dunn, Dorothy
1918 The Uphill Path

Dunn, Eddie *same as* **Dunn, Edward**
1916 The Shop Girl
1918 My Own United States
1919 Dawn
    The Moonshine Trail
1920 The Blood Barrier
Dunn, Eleanor
1914 The Ragged Earl
1916 The Evangelist
Dunn, Emma
1914 Mother
1920 Old Lady 31
Dunn, J. Allen
1918 For the Freedom of the East
1919 Sandy Burke of the U-Bar-U
Dunn, J. C.
1919 The Great Victory, Wilson or the Kaiser? The Fall of the Hohenzollerns
Dunn, J. J. *see* **Dunn, John**
Dunn, J. Malcolm
1917 Arms and the Girl
1920 Dr. Jekyll and Mr. Hyde (Famous Players-Lasky Corp.)
Dunn, James
1919 Deliverance
Dunn, John *same as* **Dunn, J. J.; Dunn, John J.; could be same as* **Dunne, J. J. or Dunne, James J.**
1914 The Spirit of the Poppy*
1915 The Bludgeon
1916 Charity
    The Soul of a Child
1917 Corruption
    The Eternal Mother
    Shame
1918 Social Quicksands
1920 The Key to Power
Dunn, John W.
1918 The Great Adventure
Dunn, Marie
1920 A Double Dyed Deceiver
Dunn, Stanley
1916 Fathers of Men
    The Girl Philippa
1917 His Own People
    Who Goes There!
Dunn, William *same as* **Dunn, W. R.; Dunn, William, Dunne, William**
1914 The Spirit of the Poppy
    The Spitfire
1915 C.O.D.
    The Juggernaut
    On Her Wedding Night
1916 Artie, the Millionaire Kid
    For a Woman's Fair Name
    The Man Behind the Curtain
    Mrs. Dane's Danger
    The Surprises of an Empty Hotel
1917 Babette
    Clover's Rebellion
    His Own People
    I Will Repay
    Mary Jane's Pa
    The Princess of Park Row
1918 Beyond the Law
    I Want to Forget
    The Little Runaway
    Social Quicksands
    The Wooing of Princess Pat
1919 The Undercurrent
    Woman, Woman!
    The Wreck
1920 The Blood Barrier
    Forbidden Valley
    The House of the Tolling Bell
    Respectable by Proxy
Dunn, Winifred
1918 And the Children Pay
    Peg O' the Sea
1919 Human Passions
    It Happened in Paris
    The Red Viper
    Thunderbolts of Fate
1920 Man and Woman (Tyrad Pictures, Inc.)
Dunne, Elenore
1914 The Wolf

Dunne, J. J. *could be same as* **Dunn, John or Dunne, James J.**
1918 Under Suspicion
Dunne, James J. *could be same as* **Dunn, John or Dunne, J. J.**
1918 The Eyes of Mystery
1919 Full of Pep
Dunne, William *see* **Dunn, William**
Dupont, Miss
1920 Bonnie May
Dupont, Edwin
1915 The Fairy and the Waif
Dupont, Max
1919 A Gentleman of Quality
    A Rogue's Romance
    The Wolf
1920 Blind Youth
    The Invisible Divorce
    Just a Wife
    The Palace of Darkened Windows
Dupont, Richard
1915 The Fairy and the Waif
Dupont, Mrs. W.
1915 The Fairy and the Waif*
DuPre, Louise
1918 A Mother's Sin
1919 The Moral Deadline
Dupree, George
1918 The Woman the Germans Shot
1919 The Avalanche
1920 Bachelor Apartments
Duprez, Charles J.
1919 His Father's Wife*
    The Oakdale Affair*
    The Steel King
1920 The Blue Pearl*
Duque, T. Gabriel
1920 The Eternal Union of the Seas
DuRae, Zoe *see* **Rae, Zoe**
Durall, William
1918 Inside the Lines
Durand, Edouard *same as* **Durand, Edward**
1914 The Conspiracy
1915 The Devil's Daughter
1919 Love, Honor and—?
1920 Blind Love
    The Branded Woman
Durant, Harry R. *same as* **Durant, H. R.**
1917 The Red Woman
1918 The Girl and the Judge*
    A Perfect Lady
    The Richest Girl
    Treason
    The Venus Model
Durborough, Wilbur H.
1915 On the Firing Line with the Germans
Durfee, Minta
1914 Tillie's Punctured Romance*
1918 Mickey
Durham, Louis *same as* **Durham, Bill; Durham, Bull; Durham Lewis; Durham, Lou; Durnham, Louis**
1915 The Brink
1916 The Conscience of John David
    A Law unto Himself
    The Waifs
1917 An Even Break
    The Iced Bullet
    Love or Justice
    One Shot Ross
    The Pinch Hitter
    The Regenerates
1918 Closin' In
    The Hard Rock Breed
    Hell's End
    The Hopper
    The Law of the Great Northwest
    The Law's Outlaw
    Wolves of the Border
1919 The Busher
    Flame of the Desert
    The Mayor of Filbert
    A Regular Fellow
1920 The Silver Horde
    The Strange Boarder

Durkin, James
1915 The Celebrated Scandal
    The Incorrigible Dukane
    The Mummy and the Humming Bird
    The Running Fight
1916 By Whose Hand?
    The Clarion
    The Red Widow
Durling, E. V.
1919 Almost Married
    Forbidden
Durnham, Louis *see* **Durham, Louis**
Durning, Bernard *same as* **Durning, Bernard J.**
1918 Gay and Festive Claverhouse
1919 Blackie's Redemption
    The Unwritten Code
    When Bearcat Went Dry
1920 The Gift Supreme
    The Scoffer
    Seeds of Vengeance
DuRoy, Harry *see* **De Roy, Harry**
1916 A Man of Sorrow
1919 The Man in the Moonlight
Durpee, G.
1919 Eyes of the Soul
Du Souchet, Henry A.
1917 Betsy Ross
D'Usseau, Leon *same as* **d'Usseau, Leon**
1919 The Miracle of Love
1920 The Restless Sex
Duvalle, William *see* **De Vault, William**
DuVaul, B. *could be same as* **De Vaull, William**
1919 Life's a Funny Proposition
Du Vaull, William P. *see* **De Vault, William**
Du Vaulle, Lottie
1918 Limousine Life
Duvel, Arthur C.
1918 My Four Years in Germany
Duvoisin, Yvette
1918 Hearts of the World
Dwan, Allan *same as* **Dwan, Alan; Dwan, Allen**
1914 The Conspiracy
    Richelieu
    The Straight Road
    Wildflower
1915 The Commanding Officer
    A Girl of Yesterday
    Jordan Is a Hard Road
    The Love Route
    May Blossom
    The Pretty Sister of Jose
1916 Betty of Graystone
    Fifty-Fifty
    The Good Bad Man
    The Habit of Happiness
    The Half-Breed
    An Innocent Magdalene
    Manhattan Madness
1917 American—That's All
    A Case at Law
    Fighting Odds
    The Food Gamblers
    For Valour
    Grafters
    Her Excellency, the Governor
    The Man Hater
    The Man Who Made Good
    A Modern Musketeer
    Panthea
1918 Bound in Morocco
    From Two to Six
    He Comes Up Smiling
    Headin' South
    Mr. Fix-It
1919 Cheating Cheaters
    The Dark Star
    Getting Mary Married
    Sahara
    Soldiers of Fortune
1920 The Forbidden Thing
    In the Heart of a Fool
    The Luck of the Irish
    The Scoffer
    A Splendid Hazard
Dwan, Norman
1919 Destiny

Dwiggins, Jay *same as* **Dwiggens, Jay**
- 1915 The Dust of Egypt
- 1918 Bound in Morocco
  - He Comes Up Smiling
  - High Tide
  - Unexpected Places
  - The Way of a Man with a Maid
- 1919 Everywoman
  - His Majesty, the American
  - In for Thirty Days
  - The Man Who Turned White
  - The Poor Boob
  - Whitewashed Walls

Dwight, Mabel
- 1915 June Friday
  - Through Turbulent Waters
  - The Way Back
- 1916 The Catspaw
- 1917 Builders of Castles
  - The Last Sentence

Dwight, Marquita
- 1914 The Dancer and the King

Dwyer, John
- 1920 Over the Hill to the Poorhouse

Dwyer, Ruth
- 1920 The Stealers

Dyas, Dave
- 1920 Pink Tights

Dycke, Van
- 1920 The Price of Silence

Dye, Florence
- 1917 Money Magic
  - The Tenderfoot

Dyer, Bill *see* **Dyer, William**

Dyer, E.
- 1919 The Exquisite Thief

Dyer, Jack
- 1918 The Family Skeleton

Dyer, Madge
- 1916 Macbeth

Dyer, Marion
- 1919 You Never Know Your Luck

Dyer, Percy
- 1913 From the Manger to the Cross

Dyer, William *same as* **Dyer, Bill; Dyer, William J.**
- 1916 Broken Fetters
  - The Great Problem
- 1917 Anything Once
  - Black Orchids
  - Come Through
  - The Pulse of Life
  - The Reward of the Faithless
  - The Spotted Lily*
  - Triumph
- 1918 All Night
  - The Law of the Great Northwest
  - Madame Sphinx
  - Paying His Debt
  - The Shoes That Danced
  - A Soul in Trust
- 1919 The Little White Savage
  - The Love Call
  - Man's Desire
  - The Mayor of Filbert
  - Who Will Marry Me?
  - Whom the Gods Would Destroy
- 1920 The Courage of Marge O'Doone

E

Eagels, Jeanne *same as* **Eagles, Jeanne**
- 1915 The House of Fear
- 1916 The World and the Woman
- 1917 The Fires of Youth
  - Under False Colors
- 1918 The Cross Bearer

Eagle, Oscar
- 1914 The Royal Box
- 1915 The Cotton King
  - The Dictator
  - The Little Mademoiselle
  - The Sins of Society
- 1916 Fruits of Desire
- 1917 The Frozen Warning

Eagle Eye *could be same as* **Eagle Eye, Charles** *or* **Eagle Eye, William**
- 1914 The Great Leap; Until Death Do Us Part
- 1915 The Lamb
  - The Outlaw's Revenge
- 1918 Untamed
- 1920 The Mollycoddle

Eagle Eye, Charles *could be same as* **Eagle Eye**
- 1916 Intolerance

Eagle Eye, William *could be same as* **Eagle Eye**
- 1918 Hitting the High Spots

Eagle Feather, Nigura
- 1915 The Iron Strain

Eagle Shirt, William
- 1917 The Conqueror
  - The Silent Lie

Eagler, Paul E. *same as* **Eagler, Paul**
- 1917 Because of a Woman
  - The Bond of Fear
  - The Clodhopper
  - The Millionaire Vagrant
  - The Pinch Hitter
  - The Son of His Father
  - Sudden Jim
- 1919 The False Faces

Eagles, Jeanne *see* **Eagels, Jeanne**

Eakins, Guy
- 1919 The Feud

Eames, Henry Purmort
- 1920 The Blue Moon
  - The Gamesters

Eames, Virginia
- 1918 The Light of Western Stars
- 1919 The Railroader

Earl, Miss
- 1914 The House of Bondage

Earl, Arthur *see* **Earle, Arthur**

Earl, Edna *see* **Earle, Edna**

Earl, Edward *see* **Earle, Edward**

Earlcott, Gladys
- 1917 The Red Woman

Earle, Arthur *same as* **Earl, Arthur**
- 1919 The Dark Star
- 1920 Stolen Moments

Earle, Edna *same as* **Earl, Edna**
- 1918 The Eagle
  - How Could You, Caroline?
  - The Model's Confession
  - The Studio Girl

Earle, Edward *same as* **Earl, Edward; Earle, Edward C.**
- 1915 Eugene Aram
  - The Great Divide
  - Ranson's Folly
  - Through Turbulent Waters
- 1916 The Flames of Johannis
  - The Gates of Eden
  - The Innocence of Ruth
  - Light at Dusk
  - The Light of Happiness
- 1917 The Bar Sinister
  - The Barrier
  - The Beautiful Lie
  - For France
  - God's Man
  - The Great Bradley Mystery
  - The Last Sentence*
- 1918 The Blind Adventure
  - The Little Runaway
  - One Thousand Dollars
  - The Sign Invisible
- 1919 A Dangerous Affair
  - The Heart of a Gypsy
  - His Bridal Night
  - Love, Honor and—?
  - The Miracle of Love
  - Thunderbolts of Fate
  - A Woman's Experience
- 1920 A Beggar in Purple
  - Blind Love
  - High Speed
  - Lahoma
  - The Law of the Yukon
  - Sherry

Earle, Elsie
- 1917 Mrs. Balfame

Earle, F. C.
- 1918 My Own United States

Earle, Ferdinand Pinney
- 1917 Within the Law
  - Womanhood, the Glory of the Nation
- 1918 The Birth of a Race
  - The Embarrassment of Riches
  - Pals First
  - To Hell with the Kaiser
  - Toys of Fate
- 1918-19 Once to Every Man
- 1919 The Better Wife
  - Bill Apperson's Boy
  - Daddy-Long-Legs
  - His Majesty, the American
  - The Miracle Man
  - Shadows of Suspicion
- 1920 The Money-Changers
  - Out of the Dust

Earle, Frank
- 1920 La La Lucille

Earle, Josephine
- 1916 The Blue Envelope Mystery
  - The Dollar and the Law
  - Hesper of the Mountains
  - The Shop Girl
  - The Two Edged Sword
  - The Writing on the Wall
- 1917 The Awakening
  - A Hungry Heart
  - Indiscretion
  - The More Excellent Way

Earle, Laddie
- 1920 The Money-Changers

Earle, William P. S.
- 1916 The Law Decides
  - Whom the Gods Destroy
- 1917 The Courage of Silence
  - His Own People
  - I Will Repay
  - Mary Jane's Pa
  - Who Goes There!
  - Within the Law
  - Womanhood, the Glory of the Nation
- 1918 Heredity
  - Little Miss No-Account
  - The Little Runaway
  - T'Other Dear Charmer
  - The Wooing of Princess Pat
- 1919 The Better Wife
  - The Broken Melody
  - The Lone Wolf's Daughter
  - The Love Hunger
- 1920 The Dangerous Paradise
  - The Road of Ambition
  - Whispers
  - The Woman Game

Eason, Reaves *same as* **Eason, Breezy; Eason, Reeves**
- 1916 Pay Dirt
- 1917 Hell Hath No Fury
- 1918 Nine-Tenths of the Law
- 1919 The Right to Happiness
- 1920 Blue Streak McCoy
  - Human Stuff
  - Pink Tights
  - Two Kinds of Love

Eason, Reaves, Jr. *(child actor)* *same as* **Reeves, Breezy; Reeves, Master Breezy, Jr.**
- 1918 Nine-Tenths of the Law
- 1919 The Thunderbolt
- 1920 Pink Tights
  - Two Kinds of Love

Easthope, Ida
- 1918 The Eyes of Julia Deep

Eastin, Madeline
- 1917 A Bit O' Heaven

Eastman, Orlo
- 1918 The Kaiser, the Beast of Berlin

Eaton, Elwin
- 1916 Romeo and Juliet (Fox Film Corp.)

Eaton, Jay
- 1920 Her First Elopement

Eaton, Jean
- 1920 The Mother of His Children

Eaton, Robert
- 1917 Motherhood (Frank Powell Producing Corp.)

Eberle, Ray
- 1918 Me und Gott
- 1919 Give and Take

Eburne, Maude
- 1918 A Pair of Sixes
- 1919 Taxi

Eckhart, Fred
- 1917 The Barker
  - The Mystery of Number 47

Eckstein, William
- 1914 A Boy and the Law

Eckstrom, Carl
- 1917 The Derelict
  - When False Tongues Speak

Eddinger, Wallace
- 1914 The Great Diamond Robbery
- 1915 A Gentleman of Leisure

Eddy, Helen Jerome *same as* **Eddy, Helen; Eddy, Helene Jerome**
- 1915 The Gentleman from Indiana
- 1916 The Code of Marcia Gray
  - Her Father's Son
  - Madame La Presidente
  - Pasquale
  - Redeeming Love
  - Tongues of Men
- 1917 As Men Love
  - The Cook of Canyon Camp
  - The Fair Barbarian
  - His Sweetheart
  - Lost in Transit
  - The Marcellini Millions
  - Rebecca of Sunnybrook Farm
  - The Wax Model
- 1918 Breakers Ahead
  - Jules of the Strong Heart
  - Old Wives for New
  - One More American
  - The Spirit of '17
  - Winner Takes All
- 1919 The Blinding Trail
  - The Boomerang
  - The Man Beneath
  - The Tong Man
  - The Trembling Hour
  - The Turn in the Road
  - A Very Good Young Man
- 1920 A City Sparrow
  - The County Fair
  - The Forbidden Thing
  - The House of Toys
  - A Light Woman
  - Miss Hobbs
  - Pollyanna

Eddy, Mary Baker
- 1918 And a Still Small Voice*

Eden, Mrs.
- 1915 Du Barry

Edeson, Arthur
- 1914 The Dollar Mark
- 1915 The Deep Purple
  - Hearts in Exile
  - The Master Hand
- 1916 Bought and Paid For
  - The Devil's Toy
  - The Gilded Cage
  - His Brother's Wife
  - Miss Petticoats
- 1917 Baby Mine
  - Nearly Married
  - The Page Mystery
  - The Price of Pride
  - The Social Leper
  - Souls Adrift
  - A Square Deal
  - The Stolen Paradise
  - A Woman Alone
- 1918 The Road Through the Dark
  - The Savage Woman
- 1919 The Better Wife
  - Cheating Cheaters
  - The Hushed Hour
- 1920 For the Soul of Rafael
  - The Forbidden Woman
  - Mid-Channel

Edeson, Robert
- 1914 The Call of the North
  - Where the Trail Divides
- 1915 The Absentee
  - The Cave Man
  - The Girl I Left Behind Me

How Molly Malone Made
Good
A Man's Prerogative
Mortmain
On the Night Stage
1916 Big Jim Garrity
Fathers of Men
For a Woman's Fair Name
The Light That Failed
1917 The Public Defender
The Royal Pauper*
1919 Eyes of Youth
Sealed Hearts

Edgard, Lewis *same as* **Edgard, Louis**
1915 In the Palace of the King
1917 The False Friend
The Marriage Market

Edgelow, Thomas
1917 The Stolen Treaty
1919 All of a Sudden Norma

Edginton, May
1919 The Love Auction

Edgren, Robert
1920 Go and Get It

Edhler, Charles *see* **Edler, Charles**

Edis, Joan
1917 Draft 258

Edison, Thomas A. *same as* **Edison,
Thomas Alva**
1915 Cohen's Luck
Gladiola
The House of the Lost Court
June Friday
Shadows from the Past
1917 Cy Whittaker's Ward
19-- Official Motion Pictures of the
Panama Pacific Exposition
Held at San Francisco,
Calif.*

Edler, Charles *same as* **Edhler, Charles;
Ehler, Charles; Elder, Charles**
1916 The Love Thief
1917 The Clean Gun
Feet of Clay
One Touch of Sin
The Yankee Way
1918 Cheating the Public
The Girl with the Champagne
Eyes
Her Inspiration
1919 Carolyn of the Corners
The Heart of Wetona
1920 Huckleberry Finn
Seeds of Vengeance
Sink or Swim

Edler, William
1917 Zollenstein

Edlin, Ted
1915 Mignon

Edmond, Bob
1919 The Light of Victory

Edmond, W. M. *see* **Edmond, William
M.**

Edmond, William H.
1914 The Quest of the Sacred Jewel

Edmond, William M. *same as* **Edmond,
William; Edmond, W. M.**
1918 Desert Law
1920 The Cheater
Held in Trust
Parlor, Bedroom and Bath

Edmonde, Frances
1920 The Unfortunate Sex

Edmondson, Al *same as* **Edmondson,
Albert; Edmundson, Al**
1915 The Butterfly
1918 Hitting the High Spots
1920 The Devil's Passkey
Officer 666

Edmondson, Harry *same as* **Edmonson,
Harry**
1914 Washington at Valley Forge
1916 The Man from Manhattan

Edmundson, Mr.
1915 Just Jim

Edmundson, Al *see* **Edmondson, Al**

Edney, Florence
1916 Hazel Kirke

Edney, Sylvia
1919 Give and Take

Edward, Donald
1920 His Pajama Girl

Edward, Walter *see* **Edwards, Walter**

Edwardes-Hall, George *see* **Hall, George
E.**

Edwards, Miss
1915 The College Orphan

Edwards, Aaron
1917 The Firefly of Tough Luck
The Medicine Man
Mountain Dew
The Ship of Doom
Wolf Lowry
1918 The Boss of the Lazy Y
The Fly God
The Hand at the Window
The Hard Rock Breed
The Red-Haired Cupid
1920 Burning Daylight
A World of Folly

Edwards, Alan *same as* **Edwards, Allan;
Edwards, Allen**
1916 Rose of the Alley
1917 The Girl by the Roadside
1919 Help! Help! Police!
The Social Pirate

Edwards, C. *see* **Edwards, Charles**

Edwards, Carol
1919 The Rescuing Angel

Edwards, Charles *same as* **Edwards, C.**
1915 C.O.D.
1916 The Immortal Flame
The Velvet Paw
The Victim
1917 Her Sister
The Last Sentence
1918 Five Thousand an Hour
1919 The Clouded Name
The Great Victory, Wilson or
the Kaiser? The Fall of the
Hohenzollerns
1920 The Master Mind
19-- Barnaby Lee

Edwards, David M.
1920 Merely Mary Ann

Edwards, Donald
1917 The Gilded Youth

Edwards, Grant
1920 Within Our Gates

Edwards, Harry
1920 His Pajama Girl

Edwards, J. Gordon
1914 Life's Shop Window
St. Elmo
1915 Anna Karenina
The Blindness of Devotion
The Galley Slave
Should a Mother Tell?
The Song of Hate
The Unfaithful Wife
A Woman's Resurrection
1916 A Daughter of the Gods
The Green-Eyed Monster
Her Double Life
Romeo and Juliet (Fox Film
Corp.)
The Spider and the Fly
Under Two Flags
The Vixen
A Wife's Sacrifice
1917 Camille
Cleopatra
The Darling of Paris
Du Barry
Heart and Soul
Her Greatest Love
The Rose of Blood
Tangled Lives
The Tiger Woman
1918 The Forbidden Path
Salome
The She-Devil
The Soul of Buddha
Under the Yoke
When a Woman Sins
1919 The Last of the Duanes
The Light
The Lone Star Ranger
The Siren's Song
When Men Desire
Wings of the Morning
Wolves of the Night
A Woman There Was

1920 The Adventurer
Drag Harlan
Heart Strings
If I Were King
The Joyous Troublemaker
The Orphan
The Scuttlers

Edwards, J. Harrison
1920 The Fighting Kentuckians

Edwards, Jack
1920 High Speed

Edwards, John
1914 The Folks From Way Down
East

Edwards, Margaret
1915 The Hypocrites
Sunshine Molly

Edwards, Mattie
1920 The Brute
Within Our Gates

Edwards, Neely
1920 You Never Can Tell

Edwards, Rowland G.
1920 Heart Strings

Edwards, Ruth
1915 C.O.D.
1919 From Headquarters

Edwards, Sam
1920 The Chamber Mystery

Edwards, Snitz
1915 The Fixer
Keep Moving
The Politicians
1917 The Price She Paid
1920 The City of Masks
Going Some

Edwards, Thornton
1916 The Eye of the Night
Lieutenant Danny, U.S.A.
1917 Fighting Back
Indiscreet Corinne
The Learnin' of Jim Benton
Wee Lady Betty
1918 The Gun Woman
The Hard Rock Breed
1919 The False Faces
1920 813
Neptune's Bride

Edwards, Viva
1916 A Modern Enoch Arden

Edwards, Walter *same as* **Edward,
Walter**
1915 The Edge of the Abyss
1916 Civilization
The Corner
The Dividend
The Eye of the Night
A Gamble in Souls
Honor's Altar
The Jungle Child
The Last Act
Lieutenant Danny, U.S.A.
The No-Good Guy
The Sin Ye Do
1917 Ashes of Hope
The Bride of Hate
The Crab
The Fuel of Life
Idolators
The Last of the Ingrams
Love or Justice
Master of His Home
Paddy O'Hara
Time Locks and Diamonds
1918 The Argument
Good Night, Paul
The Gypsy Trail
I Love You
A Lady's Name
The Man from Funeral Range
Mrs. Leffingwell's Boots
A Pair of Silk Stockings
Real Folks
Sauce for the Goose
Viviette
Without Honor
1919 The Final Close-Up
A Girl Named Mary
Girls
Happiness à la Mode
Luck in Pawn
The Rescuing Angel
Romance and Arabella

The Veiled Adventure
Who Cares?
Widow by Proxy
1920 All-of-a-Sudden-Peggy
Easy to Get
A Lady in Love
Young Mrs. Winthrop

Edwards, Zelma
1920 Dangerous Love

Edwin, Arthur
1919 The Love Hunger

Edwin, Walter
1915 The Danger Signal
The Green Cloak
The Sentimental Lady
The Spendthrift
The Woman Next Door
1917 A Mute Appeal

Effee, William *see* **Ehfe, William**

Egan, Gladys
1913 Ten Nights in a Barroom

Egleston, Ann *same as* **Egelston, Ann;
Eggleston, Mrs.; Eggleston, Ann;
Eglestone, Ann**
1918 Wanted for Murder
We Should Worry
1919 His Father's Wife
Phil-for-Short
1920 The Gray Brother

Ehfe, William *same as* **Effee, William;
Ephe, William**
1915 The End of the Road
The House of a Thousand
Scandals
Secretary of Frivolous Affairs
1916 The Argonauts of
California—1849
Big Tremaine
The Daughter of the Don
1917 The Best Man
The Inspirations of Harry
Larrabee
1918 Code of the Yukon
The Vigilantes

Ehler, Charles *see* **Edler, Charles**

Ehrich, D. E.
1917 The Penny Philanthropist

Eichman, Charles
1916 The Land Just Over Yonder

Elder, Charles *see* **Edler, Charles**

Elder, Ruth
1917 Triumph
1918 Thirty a Week

Eldridge, Charles
1914 The Strange Story of Sylvia
Gray
1915 The Cave Man
Crooky
Hearts and the Highway
The Man Who Couldn't Beat
God
The Wheels of Justice
1916 As in a Looking Glass
The Pretenders
The Surprises of an Empty
Hotel
The Wheel of the Law
1917 The Duchess of Doubt
The End of the Tour
His Father's Son
Polly of the Circus
1918 The Challenge Accepted
Eye for Eye
The Grain of Dust
Sporting Life
Sunshine Nan
1919 Redhead
1920 The Birth of a Soul
Broken Hearts
The Gauntlet
The Woman Game

Eldridge, Frances
1920 The Little Outcast

Eldridge, Helen
1916 The Five Faults of Flo

Eline, Marie
1914 Uncle Tom's Cabin

Elinor, Carli D.
1915 The Alien*
1918 The Great Love
Hearts of the World

Shall We Forgive Her?
The Social Leper
A Square Deal
The Strong Way
The Tenth Case
The Volunteer
The Whip
Youth
1918 The Appearance of Evil
The Beautiful Mrs. Reynolds
Broken Ties
The Cabaret
Joan of the Woods
The Oldest Law
The Power and the Glory
Stolen Orders
The Way Out
A Woman of Redemption
The Zero Hour
1919 The Bluffer
Coax Me
His Father's Wife
Love and the Woman
The Love Defender
The Moral Deadline
The Poison Pen
The Quickening Flame
The Social Pirate
The Steel King
Three Green Eyes
The Woman of Lies
1920 The Law of the Yukon
Elwell, George
1916 The Raiders
Ely, G. W.
1919 Brothers Divided
Ely, Gilbert
1914 The Gamblers
Emerson, Aaron
1915 Colonel Carter of Cartersville
Emerson, Agnes
1916 John Needham's Double
1920 Wanted at Headquarters
Emerson, Billy
1918 Headin' South
Emerson, Charlie same as **Emerson, Charles**
1915 Colonel Carter of Cartersville
1917 It Happened to Adele
Emerson, E.
1920 The Great Shadow
Emerson, Edna same as **Emerson, Eda**
1918 Berlin Via America
1919 Crimson Shoals
Emerson, John
1914 The Conspiracy
1915 The Bachelor's Romance
The Failure
Old Heidelberg
1916 The Flying Torpedo
His Picture in the Papers
Less Than the Dust
Macbeth
The Matrimaniac*
The Social Secretary
1917 The Americano
Down to Earth
In Again—Out Again
Reaching for the Moon
Wild and Woolly
1918 Come On In
Good-Bye, Bill
Hit-the-Trail Holliday
Let's Get a Divorce
1919 Getting Mary Married
The Isle of Conquest
Oh, You Women
A Temperamental Wife
Under the Top
A Virtuous Vamp
1920 Dangerous Business
In Search of a Sinner
The Love Expert
The Perfect Woman
Emerson, Kathleen
1915 Rule G
1917 The Gown of Destiny
1918 The Dream Lady
Her American Husband
1919 The Rebellious Bride

Emery, Maude same as **Emory, Maud; Emory, Maude; Taylor, Maud Emery**
1917 The Greater Law
The Planter*
1918 Madame Spy
Mr. Logan, U.S.A.
1920 For the Soul of Rafael
Emery, Thomas V.
1914 The Price He Paid
Emlay, Earl
1915 The Pageant of San Francisco
A Phyllis of the Sierras
Salvation Nell
Emmons, Mrs. could be same as **Emmons, Louise A.** or **Emmons, Marion**
1916 Mixed Blood
Emmons, Bob
1915 The Commanding Officer
Emmons, Buster
1916 John Needham's Double
Emmons, Louise A. could be same as **Emmons, Mrs.**
1916 The Stronger Love
Emmons, Marion could be same as **Emmons, Mrs.**
1914 Samson
1916 The Measure of a Man
1918 Hearts of the World
Emory, Maude see **Emery, Maude**
Emory, May could be same as **Emory, Ray**
1919 A Taste of Life
Emory, Ray could be same as **Emory, May**
1919 The Chosen Path
Empey, Guy same as **Empey, Arthur Guy**
1918 Over the Top
1919 The Undercurrent
1920 Oil
Empress, Marie
1915 Old Dutch
The Stubbornness of Geraldine
When We Were Twenty-One
The Woman Pays
1916 Behind Closed Doors
The Girl Who Doesn't Know
Encinas, L.
1917 The Planter
Engel, Joseph
1918 Pay Day
Enger, Charles van see **Van Enger, Charles**
England, Frank
1920 The Mollycoddle*
Engler, Gustav Adolf
1916 The Fighting Germans*
Engleton, E. N.
1916 Black Friday
English, Bessie Mar
1918 Wives of Men
English, Fred
1913 The Star of India
English, Harry
1915 Playing Dead
Ensminger, Robert same as **Ensminger, Bert**
1917 The Climber
The Girl Angle
The Mainspring
1918 The Midnight Burglar
Wanted—A Brother
Whatever the Cost
Enstedt, Howard
1919 The Ace of the Saddle
Bare Fists
Entwistle, Harold same as **Entwhistle, H.; Entwistle, H. E.; Entwistle, Harold**
1914 Mrs. Wiggs of the Cabbage Patch
Salomy Jane
1916 The Beggar of Cawnpore
The Summer Girl
1917 Miss Robinson Crusoe
One of Many
1918 In the Hollow of Her Hand
Too Fat to Fight
1919 The Divorcee
The Woman Under Oath

Entwistle, Robert
1917 The Beautiful Adventure
Ephe, William see **Ehfe, William**
Ephran, Lorretta
1914 Salomy Jane
Erb, Ludwig same as **Erb, Mr.; Erb, Ludwig G. B.**
1915 The Footsteps of Capt. Kidd
On the Spanish Main
Pirate Haunts
1917 The Road Between
1920 The Victim
Erckmann, Emile
1918 The Bells*
Eric, Fred
1915 The Builder of Bridges
Divorced
1917 The Woman and the Beast
Erickson, Baby
1915 The Millionaire Baby
Erickson, A. F.
1920 Down Home
Erics, Finnstron
1920 A Fool and His Money
Erlanger, Frank
1916 The Power of Evil
Spellbound
The Sultana
1917 The Climber
Feet of Clay
The Girl Angle
The Understudy
The Yellow Bullet
Zollenstein
1918 The Midnight Burglar
Erlicher, Elsa
1920 Neptune's Bride
Errol, Eileen
1917 Her Sister
Erskine, Mrs. Wallace
1915 The House of the Lost Court
The Mystery of Room 13
The Truth About Helen
The Way Back
1916 The Light of Happiness
1917 The Last Sentence
Eschrich, Julius
1920 Conrad in Quest of His Youth
Esmelton, Frederick same as **Esmelton, Fred**
1916 The Prima Donna's Husband
1917 The Law of Compensation
1918 Out of the Night
1919 The Avalanche
Come Out of the Kitchen
The Misleading Widow
Esmond, Baby could be same as **Esmond, Eve** or **Esmond, Elsie**
1914 Lola
Esmond, Elsie could be same as **Esmond, Baby** or **Esmond, Eve**
1914 The Boundary Rider
A Prince of India
1916 The City
The Lottery Man
1917 The Black Stork
Esmond, Merceita same as **Esmond, Merceita; Esmonde, Merceita; Northrup, Mrs. Henry**
1916 Less Than the Dust
1917 The Beautiful Adventure
1919 Oh, You Women
1920 Thoughtless Women
Estabrook, Howard
1914 Officer 666
1915 The Butterfly
The Closing Net
Four Feathers
M'liss
1917 Giving Becky a Chance
The Highway of Hope
The Wild Girl
Este, Louis
1919 The Winning Stroke
Ethier, Alphonse
1915 Monsieur Lecoq
The Patriot and the Spy
1917 The Woman and the Beast
1918 The Forbidden Path
I Want to Forget
Oh, Johnny!
Rough and Ready

1919 Sandy Burke of the U-Bar-U
Evans, Arthur
1914 The Dancer and the King
Evans, Eileen
1916 The Struggle
Evans, Estelle could be same as **Evans, Esther**
1918 The Man Who Woke Up
1920 Black Shadows
The Return of Tarzan
The Walk-Offs
Evans, Esther could be same as **Evans, Estelle**
1916 Vanity
1917 Reputation
Evans, Franck Taylor not the same as **Evans, Frank**
1916 The Hero of Submarine D-2
Evans, Frank not the same as **Evans, Franck Taylor**
1914 The Woman in Black
1915 Destruction
The Family Stain
1916 The Battle of Life
Her Maternal Right
The Madness of Helen
The Unwelcome Mother
The World's Great Snare
1917 The Argyle Case
The Love That Lives
Miss U.S.A.
1918 Conquered Hearts
The Knife
Peg of the Pirates
1919 High Pockets
The Open Door
1920 The Flaming Clue
The Tiger's Cub
Evans, H. could be same as **Evans, Herbert**
1916 East Lynne
Evans, Herbert could be same as **Evans, H.**
1916 Where Love Leads
1917 All for a Husband
The Customary Two Weeks
Her Sister
The Undying Flame
The Wild Girl
1918 A Daughter of France
The Firebrand
Who Loved Him Best?
1919 The Third Degree
1920 The Place of Honeymoons
Evans, John William same as **Evans, Jack; Evans, John William, Jr.**
1920 Bab's Candidate
The Garter Girl
The Vice of Fools
Evans, Larry
1917 High Finance
1918 His Own Home Town
Evans, Louise
1916 The Question
Evans, Madge
1914 Shore Acres
1915 The Master Hand
Seven Sisters
1915-16 The Little Church Around the Corner
1916 Broken Chains
The Devil's Toy
The Hidden Scar
Husband and Wife
The Revolt
Seventeen
Sudden Riches
1917 The Adventures of Carol
The Beloved Adventuress
The Burglar
The Corner Grocer
The Little Duchess
Maternity
The Volunteer
The Web of Desire
1918 Gates of Gladness
The Golden Wall
Heredity
The Love Net
Neighbors
The Power and the Glory
Stolen Orders
Vengeance

Wanted, a Mother
1919 Home Wanted
The Love Defender
Three Green Eyes
Evans, Captain Michael P.
1916 The Breaker*
Evans, Millicent
1914 The Seats of the Mighty
Under the Gaslight
The Woman in Black
1915 Dora Thorne
1916 Father and Son
Evans, Perry
1920 Down on the Farm
Love, Honor and Behave
Evans, Robert
1920 Kismet
Evans, Tom
1918 Wanted, a Mother
Evans, William
1916 The Heart of New York
Evans, William A.
1914 The Education of Mr. Pipp
Evart, Lawrence
1918 The Grain of Dust
Eve, Marie
1918 The Death Dance
1919 The Darkest Hour*
The Golden Shower
Evelyn, Fay
1919 The Heart of a Gypsy
1920 High Speed
Evelynne, Mary
1917 S.O.S.
Everdale, Ruth
1917 Snap Judgement
Souls in Pawn
Everets, John Allen
1915 The Warring Millions*
Everett, Agnes
1915 Samson
1920 Sinners
The Stolen Kiss
The Vice of Fools
Everett, Grace
1915 Should a Mother Tell?
Everett, Jack
1915 The Warring Millions
Everett, M.
1917 Money Madness
Everett, Reginald
1917 The Book Agent
Everett, W. J.
1917 The Lust of the Ages
Evers, Arthur
1914 In the Name of the Prince of
Peace
One of Millions
1915 Always in the Way
Four Feathers
Still Waters
1916 One Day
The Snowbird
Evers, E. P.
1916 Drugged Waters
Evers, Ernest
1914 The Jungle
Everton, Paul
1915 Black Fear
1916 A Message to Garcia
The Quitter
1917 The Debt
The Last of the Carnabys
Life's Whirlpool
The Mirror
Motherhood (Frank Powell
Producing Corp.)
Outwitted
Seven Keys to Baldpate
1918 Convict 993
Friend Husband
1919 Ginger
1920 From Now On
Eville, Mrs.
1915 The Fairy and the Waif*
Eville, Martin E.
1915 The Fairy and the Waif
Eville, William
1915 The Fairy and the Waif
1916 The Witching Hour
1919 A Virtuous Vamp

1920 Oil
Evison, Millicent
1917 Next Door to Nancy
1918 The Mating
1919 Over the Garden Wall
Ewens, James
1916 Fruits of Desire
1917 The Fires of Youth
Ewers, Edward
1916 Romeo and Juliet (Quality
Pictures Corp.)
Ewing, Howard M. same as **Ewing,
Howard**
1916 Joan the Woman
1920 Don't Ever Marry
The River's End
Ewing, Jean
1919 The Mystery of the Yellow
Room
Eyerman, Captain
1916 The Girl Philippa
Eyre, Agnes see **Ayres, Agnes**
Eyre, Elizabeth
1915 The Plunderer
Eytinge, Harry
1916 The Catspaw
1917 God's Man
Eyton, Alice
1916 The Feud Girl*
1919 Experimental Marriage
A Girl Named Mary
Girls
Happiness à la Mode
Little Comrade
Louisiana
Luck in Pawn
1920 A Full House
Her Beloved Villain
A Lady in Love
The Thirteenth Commandment
Eyton, Bessie
1914 In the Days of the Thundering
Herd
The Spoilers
1916 The Crisis
The Cycle of Fate
The Prince Chap
1917 Beware of Strangers
The Heart of Texas Ryan
Little Lost Sister
Who Shall Take My Life?
1918 The City of Purple Dreams
Lend Me Your Name
The Still Alarm
The Way of a Man with a
Maid
1919 Children of Banishment
A Man of Honor
The Usurper

F

Fables, William
1914 Fantasma
1917 The Barker
The Last Sentence
Fair, Elinor could be same as **Fair,
Lenore**
1918 The Road Through the Dark
1919 Be a Little Sport
The End of the Game
The Lost Princess
Love Is Love
Married in Haste
The Miracle Man
Tin Pan Alley
Vagabond Luck
Words and Music By—
1920 Broadway and Home
The Girl in Number 29
Kismet
The Mischief Man
Occasionally Yours
Wait for Me
Fair, Joyce
1917 The Apple-Tree Girl
Over the Hill
Redemption
Shame
Vera, the Medium
1918 The Woman the Germans Shot

1919 The End of the Road
1920 The Victim
Fair, Lenore could be same as **Fair,
Elinor**
1918 The Reckoning Day
Fair, Otis B.
1916 The Unborn
Fairbanks, Douglas same as **Banks,
Elton**
1915 Double Trouble
The Lamb
The Martyrs of the Alamo
1916 American Aristocracy
Flirting with Fate
The Good Bad Man
The Habit of Happiness
The Half-Breed
His Picture in the Papers
Manhattan Madness
The Matrimaniac
Reggie Mixes In
1917 The Americano
Down to Earth
In Again—Out Again
The Man from Painted Post
A Modern Musketeer
National Association's All-Star
Picture
Reaching for the Moon
Wild and Woolly
1918 Arizona
Bound in Morocco
He Comes Up Smiling
Headin' South
Mr. Fix-It
Say, Young Fellow!
1919 His Majesty, the American
The Knickerbocker Buckaroo
When the Clouds Roll By
1920 The Mark of Zorro
The Mollycoddle
Fairbanks, Eleanor
1915 Tillie's Tomato Surprise
Fairbanks, Gladys
1914 Shore Acres
1917 The Outsider
The Poor Little Rich Girl
The Road Between
Who's Your Neighbor?
Fairbanks, John
1918 Headin' South*
Fairbanks, Madeline
1914 Beating Back
1915 The Flying Twins
1916 A Bird of Prey
Fairbanks, Marion
1915 The Flying Twins
Fairbanks, Robert
1919 When the Clouds Roll By
1920 The Mollycoddle
Fairchild, Dorothy
1915 The Face in the Moonlight
The Flash of an Emerald
The Impostor
The Little Dutch Girl
The Sins of Society
1916 Fruits of Desire
Fairchild, Ray
1916 A Message to Garcia
Faire, Virginia
1920 Under Northern Lights
Fairfax, Marion
1915 The Chorus Lady
The Immigrant
Mr. Grex of Monte Carlo
1916 Anton the Terrible
The Blacklist
The Clown
Common Ground
The Sowers
Tennessee's Pardner
1917 The Crystal Gazer
Freckles
Hashimura Togo
On the Level
The Primrose Ring
The Secret Game
1918 The Honor of His House
Less Than Kin
The Mystery Girl
The White Man's Law
The Widow's Might

1919 A Daughter of the Wolf
Love Insurance
Putting It Over
The Roaring Road
The Secret Garden
The Valley of the Giants
The Woman Next Door
You Never Saw Such a Girl
1920 Dinty
Don't Ever Marry
Go and Get It
Judy of Rogue's Harbor*
The River's End
Fairfax, Virginia
1915 An American Gentleman
Fallon, Thomas F. same as **Fallon,
Thomas**
1918 Blue-Eyed Mary
Miss Innocence
1919 Sacred Silence
1920 The Plunger
The Shark
While New York Sleeps
"The Famous Tarzan Lion"
1920 It Might Happen to You
Fang, Charles same as **Fang, Charles
A.; Fang, Charlie**
1916 Broken Fetters
In the Diplomatic Service
1917 The Jury of Fate
The Slacker (Metro Pictures
Corp.)
1918 Cyclone Higgins, D.D.
1919 Checkers
God's Outlaw
Mandarin's Gold
1920 Pagan Love
Fariss, Evelyn same as **Farriss, Evelyn**
1915 The Masqueraders
1920 The Return of Tarzan
Farjean, Herbert same as **Farjeon,
Herbert**
1916 The Captive God
Farley, Mrs. see **Farley, Dot**
Farley, Dot same as **Farley, Mrs.;
Farley, Dorothea**
1914 Even unto Death
The Lust of the Red Man
1916 Inherited Passions
Farley, James same as **Farley, James
Lee; Farley, Jim; could be same as
Farley, James G.**
1916 Sins of Her Parent
1917 The Bride's Silence
The Highway of Hope
1918 Believe Me Xantippe
Desert Law
Her Country First
A Lady's Name
The Spirit of '17
The White Lie
1919 An Innocent Adventuress
Nugget Nell
Rustling a Bride
Sue of the South
You Never Saw Such a Girl
1920 Alias Jimmy Valentine
The Challenge of the Law
The Fourteenth Man
The Girl in the Rain
That Something
Farley, James G. could be same as
Farley, James
1917 The Stainless Barrier
Farley, James Lee see **Farley, James**
Farley, Jim see **Farley, James**
Farley, Cardinal John Murphy
1914 His Holiness, the Late Pope
Pius X, and the Vatican
Farley, Linda
1918 Pay Day
Farmer, Jacques
1920 Our Christianity and Nobody's
Child
Farnham, Henry Allen same as
Farnham, Allen
1913 Arizona
From the Manger to the Cross
1915 The Garden of Lies
The Rights of Man: A Story of
War's Red Blotch
1916 The Fighting Chance
Her Bleeding Heart

Farnham, Joseph W. *same as* **Farnham, Joe; Farnham, Joseph; Farnham, Joseph White**
1915 The Rights of Man: A Story of War's Red Blotch*
1918-19
     Once to Every Man
1919 Bullin' the Bullsheviki
     Deliverance
1920 Bachelor Apartments
     The Little 'Fraid Lady
     Sky Eye
     The Wonder Man
Farnsworth, Louise
1915 Maciste
Farnum, Dorothy
1915 The Cub
     Over Night
1919 The Broken Melody
1920 Good References
Farnum, Dustin
1914 Cameo Kirby
     The Lightning Conductor
     Soldiers of Fortune
     The Squaw Man
     The Virginian
1915 Captain Courtesy
     The Gentleman from Indiana
     The Iron Strain
1916 Ben Blair
     The Call of the Cumberlands
     David Garrick
     Davy Crockett
     The Parson of Panamint
     A Son of Erin
1917 Durand of the Bad Lands
     North of Fifty-Three
     The Scarlet Pimpernel
     The Spy
1918 The Light of Western Stars
1919 A Man in the Open
     A Man's Fight
1920 Big Happiness
     The Corsican Brothers
Farnum, Franklyn *same as* **Farnum, Franklin**
1916 Love Never Dies
     A Stranger from Somewhere
1917 Anything Once
     Bringing Home Father
     The Car of Chance
     The Clean-Up
     The Clock
     The Devil's Pay Day
     The Man Who Took a Chance
     National Association's All-Star Picture
     The Scarlet Car
     A Stormy Knight
     The Winged Mystery
1918 The Empty Cab
     Fast Company
     The Fighting Grin
     $5,000 Reward
     In Judgment Of
     The Rough Lover
     The Vanity Pool
1919 Go Get 'Em Garringer
     The Virtuous Model
1920 The Galloping Devil
     The Land of Jazz
     Vengeance and the Girl
Farnum, Marshall
1915 Lady Audley's Secret
     Wormwood
1916 Driftwood
     The House of Mirrors
1917 The Tides of Fate
Farnum, William
1914 The Redemption of David Corson
     The Sign of the Cross
     The Spoilers
1915 The Broken Law
     A Gilded Fool
     The Nigger
     The Plunderer
     Samson
     A Soldier's Oath
     The Wonderful Adventure
1916 The Battle of Hearts
     The Bondman
     The End of the Trail
     Fighting Blood

     The Fires of Conscience
     The Man from Bitter Roots
     A Man of Sorrow
1917 American Methods
     The Conquerer
     The Heart of a Lion
     The Price of Silence
     A Tale of Two Cities
     When a Man Sees Red
1918 For Freedom
     Les Miserables
     The Rainbow Trail
     Riders of the Purple Sage
     Rough and Ready
     True Blue
1919 The Jungle Trail
     The Last of the Duanes
     The Lone Star Ranger
     The Man Hunter
     Wings of the Morning
     Wolves of the Night
1920 The Adventurer
     Drag Harlan
     Heart Strings
     If I Were King
     The Joyous Troublemaker
     The Orphan
     The Scuttlers
Farrar, Geraldine
1915 Carmen (Jesse L. Lasky Feature Play Co.)
     Temptation
1916 Joan the Woman
     Maria Rosa
1917 The Devil-Stone
     The Woman God Forgot
1918 The Hell Cat
     The Turn of the Wheel
1919 Flame of the Desert
     Shadows
     The Stronger Vow
     The World and Its Woman
1920 The Riddle: Woman
     The Woman and the Puppet
Farrell, Mr.
1920 Footlights and Shadows
Farrell, H.
1920 Pagan Love
Farrell, Jack
1916 Powder
     Revelations
1918 Rosemary Climbs the Heights
1919 Yvonne from Paris
Farrell, James
1915 The Great Ruby
Farrell, Jane
1919 Paid in Full
Farrell, Robert
1917 Peggy, the Will O' the Wisp*
Farren, George
1917 The Cinderella Man
Farrington, Adele
1914 The Country Mouse
     False Colours
1915 Help Wanted
     The Hypocrites
     It's No Laughing Matter
     Scandal
     Sunshine Molly
     The Supreme Test
1916 The Devil's Bondwoman
     Doctor Neighbor
     Her Bitter Cup
     If My Country Should Call
     The Love Girl
     The Morals of Hilda
     A Soul Enslaved
     The Way of the World
     What Love Can Do
1917 The Heir of the Ages
     The Inner Shrine
     The Marcellini Millions
     The Mate of the Sally Ann
     The Price Mark
     The Price of a Good Time
     A Roadside Impresario
1918 Honor's Cross
     The House of Silence
     Such a Little Pirate
     Wild Youth
1919 A Fugitive from Matrimony
     In Old Kentucky
     Putting It Over
     Something to Do

1920 A Connecticut Yankee at King Arthur's Court
     Don't Ever Marry
     The Girl in the Web
     The Mollycoddle
     One Hour Before Dawn
     The Palace of Darkened Windows
     Rio Grande
     The Spenders
     Too Much Johnson
Farrington, Doris
1915 Right off the Bat
Farrington, Frank
1914 Beating Back
1915 Through Turbulent Waters
1916 The Cossack Whip
     Pamela's Past
1917 The Long Trail
1918 The Million Dollar Mystery
     To Hell with the Kaiser
1919 The Scar
1920 The Face at Your Window
Farris, Evelyn *see* **Fariss, Evelyn**
Farris, William
1915 Pennington's Choice
Fassatt, Malcolm
1919 His Father's Wife
Fatherree, Mr.
1917 The Blackmailers
Faulkner, Ralph *same as* **Faulkner, Ralph C.**
1918 On the Jump
     The Prussian Cur
     Why America Will Win
Fausett, James
1917 Unto the End
Faust, Martin J. *same as* **Faust, Martin; Faust, Marty**
1914 Lena Rivers (Whitman Features Co.)
     The Line-Up at Police Headquarters
     The Toll of Love
1915 Emmy of Stork's Nest
     A Yellow Streak
1916 The Child of Destiny
     The Dawn of Love
     His Great Triumph
     The Kiss of Hate
1917 The Blue Streak
     The Slave
     Thou Shalt Not Steal
     Wife Number Two
1918 Find the Woman
     The Woman the Germans Shot
1919 The Cambric Mask
Faversham, William
1915 One Million Dollars
     The Right of Way
1919 The Silver King
1920 The Man Who Lost Himself
     The Sin That Was His
Faviere, Guy
1917 National Red Cross Pageant*
Favor, Edward M. *same as* **Favor, E. M.; Favor, Ed**
1917 Cy Whittaker's Ward
1918 Peck's Bad Girl
     The Soap Girl
1920 Bachelor Apartments
Fawcett, George
1915 The Frame-Up
     The Majesty of the Law
1916 Betty of Graystone
     The Corner
     The Country That God Forgot
     The Crisis
     The Habit of Happiness
     The Prince Chap
1917 The Cinderella Man
     The Heart of Texas Ryan
     Little Lost Sister
     Panthea
     Shirley Kaye
1918 The Beloved Traitor
     The Great Love
     Hearts of the World
     The Hope Chest
     The Hun Within
     The Talk of the Town
1919 The Fall of Babylon
     The Girl Who Stayed Home

     The Greatest Question
     I'll Get Him Yet
     Nobody Home
     The Railroader
     A Romance of Happy Valley
     Scarlet Days
     True Heart Susie
     Turning the Tables
1920 Bab's Candidate
     The Branded Woman
     Dangerous Business
     Deadline at Eleven
     Idols of Clay
     Little Miss Rebellion
     Two Weeks
Fawcett, Margaret
1916 The Prince Chap
Fay, Billy
1920 Two Moons
Fay, Hugh
1919 Almost Married
     Better Times
     A Favor to a Friend
     Please Get Married
Fay, Joseph C.
1914 Three Weeks
Faye, Julia
1916 Don Quixote
1917 A Roadside Impresario
1918 Mrs. Leffingwell's Boots
     Old Wives for New
     Sandy
     The Squaw Man
     Till I Come Back to You
1919 Don't Change Your Husband
     It Pays to Advertise
     Male and Female
     Stepping Out
     Venus in the East
     A Very Good Young Man
1920 The Life of the Party
     The Six Best Cellars
     Something to Think About
Fazenda, Louise
1920 Down on the Farm
     Married Life
Fealy, Maude
1913 The Legend of Provence
     Moths
1914 Frou Frou
1915 Bondwomen
1916 The Immortal Flame
     Pamela's Past
1917 The American Consul
Fearnley, Jane
1913 The Stranglers of Paris
1914 The Christian
     The Little Gray Lady
     The Scales of Justice
1915 The Marble Heart
1917 The Black Stork
     The Eternal Sin
Featherstone, Eddie *see* **Fetherston, Edward A.**
Feday, Suzanne
1917 S.O.S.
Feder, I.
1915 Seven Sisters
Fedris, John
1918 The Triumph of Venus
Feeney, Francis
1918 Berlin Via America
Feinberg, Silas
1916 The Yellow Passport
Fellowes, Rockcliffe *same as* **Fellowes, Rockliffe**
1915 Regeneration
1916 Where Love Leads
1917 The Bondage of Fear
     The Easiest Way
     Man's Woman
     The Web of Desire
1918 Friend Husband
     The Man Hunt
     The Panther Woman
     The Wasp
1920 The Cup of Fury
     In Search of a Sinner
     Pagan Love
     The Point of View
     Yes or No

Findlay, J.
1920 Birthright

Findlay, J.
1915 The Bachelor's Romance

Findlay, Ruth *same as* **Finley, Ruth**
1915 The Man Who Found Himself
The Moonstone
A Soldier's Oath
1916 The Fool's Revenge
The Salamander
The World Against Him
1919 The Scar

Findlay, Thomas J.
1920 Heliotrope

Fine Arts Kiddies
1917 Cheerful Givers

Fine, Lieut. R. P.
1919 Brothers Divided

Finlay, Ned *see* **Finley, Ned**

Finlayson, James
1920 Down on the Farm
Married Life

Finley, Ned *same as* **Finlay, Ned**
1915 Hearts and the Highway
The Making Over of Geoffrey
Manning
1916 Britton of the Seventh
The Hunted Woman
The Kid
1917 The Blue Streak
The Bottom of the Well
The Little Terror
Soldiers of Chance
The White Raven
1918 Buchanan's Wife
The Menace

Finley, Ruth *see* **Findlay, Ruth**

Finley, William
1920 The Woman Above Reproach

Finn, Arthur
1915 On the Russian Frontier

Finnegan, Frank X.
1918 Jules of the Strong Heart
Rimrock Jones

Fischbeck, Harry *same as* **Fishbeck, Harry; Fishbeck, Harry A.**
1914 Life's Shop Window
1916 The Ninety and Nine
1917 The Lincoln Cycle
1918 Wives of Men
1919 Her Code of Honor
1920 The Hidden Code
Woman's Man

Fischer, Alice
1917 National Red Cross Pageant*

Fischer, David G.
1919 The Law of Nature
Where Bonds Are Loosed
1920 Dad's Girl
In the Shadow of the Dome

Fischer, Dorothea
1920 Man and Woman (A. H.
Fischer Features, Inc.)

Fischer, George
1920 His Pajama Girl*

Fischer, Gustave
1917 The Submarine Eye

Fischer, Harry *could be same as* **Fisher, Harry**
1917 The Bad Boy
1919 Fruits of Passion

Fischer, Leonard
1917 Motherhood (Minerva Motion
Picture Co.)

Fischer, Maggie *see* **Fisher, Maggie Halloway**

Fischer, Margarita *see* **Fisher, Margarita**

Fischer, Robert *could be same as* **Fisher, Robert**
1915 Excuse Me
1916 Madame X
1918 From Two to Six
1919 Heart of Gold

Fischter, W. D. *same as* **Fichter, W. D.; Fischter, Walter**
1914 As Ye Sow
Dan
1918 The House of Mirth

Fishback, Charles
1919 Virtuous Men*

Fishbeck, Harry *see* **Fischbeck, Harry**

Fishenden, J. S.
1918 Her American Husband

Fisher (full name unknown)
1915 The Fairy and the Waif*

Fisher, Mrs.
1917 The Defeat of the City
The Duplicity of Hargraves

Fisher, Alfred
1915 The Prince and the Pauper
1919 The House of Intrigue
1920 Beautifully Trimmed
Sherry

Fisher, Blanche
1914 The Crucible
1915 Zaza

Fisher, George
1915 The Darkening Trail
Rumpelstiltskin
1916 Civilization
D'Artagnan
Home
Honor Thy Name
Shell Forty-Three
Somewhere in France
The Thoroughbred (New York
Motion Picture Corp.;
Kay-Bee)
Three of Many
1917 Alimony
Annie-for-Spite
Environment
The Gentle Intruder
Periwinkle
Pride and the Man
The Promise
The Rainbow Girl
The Sea Master
The Spirit of Romance
The Wax Model
1918 And a Still Small Voice
Blue Blood
Fires of Youth
A Little Sister of Everybody
Maid O' the Storm
Mrs. Leffingwell's Boots
Within the Cup
1919 Gates of Brass
Hearts Asleep
Luck and Pluck
Rose O' the River
1920 The Devil to Pay
The Heart of a Woman
The Land of Jazz
The Prince of Avenue A
The Woman in His House
The Yellow Typhoon

Fisher, Harry *same as* **Fisher, Harry, Jr.; could be same as* **Fischer, Harry**
1914 The Man on the Box
The Master Mind
1915 The Yankee Girl
1916 The Dollar and the Law
The Rummy
Somewhere in Georgia

Fisher, Harvey A.
1920 Bab's Candidate

Fisher, Kathie
1918 The Vigilantes

Fisher, Lucille
1918 Little Red Riding Hood

Fisher, Maggie Halloway *same as* **Fischer, Maggie; Fisher, Maggie; Fisher, Maggie H.; Fisher, Maggie Holloway**
1915 The Bachelor's Romance
1916 Ashes of Embers
Little Lady Eileen
Mice and Men
1917 The Valentine Girl
1918 Out of a Clear Sky
1919 The Lost Princess
Three Men and a Girl
1920 All-of-a-Sudden-Peggy
Jenny Be Good
The Luck of Geraldine Laird
Sherry

Fisher, Margarita *same as* **Fischer, Margarita**
1915 The Girl from His Town
Infatuation
The Lonesome Heart
The Miracle of Life
The Quest
1916 The Dragon
Miss Jackie of the Navy
The Pearl of Paradise
1917 The Butterfly Girl
The Devil's Assistant
The Girl Who Couldn't Grow
Up
Miss Jackie of the Army
1918 Ann's Finish
Fair Enough
Impossible Susan
Jilted Janet
The Mantle of Charity
Molly, Go Get 'Em
Money Isn't Everything
The Primitive Woman
The Square Deal
1919 Charge It to Me
The Hellion
Molly of the Follies
Put Up Your Hands
The Tiger Lily
Trixie from Broadway
1920 The Dangerous Talent
The Gamesters
Their Mutual Child
The Thirtieth Piece of Silver
The Week-End

Fisher, Millicent
1917 Draft 258
The Slacker (Metro Pictures
Corp.)
1919 Fighting Through
The Mayor of Filbert
A Regular Fellow
1920 Alarm Clock Andy

Fisher, Robert *could be same as* **Fischer, Robert**
1915 Hearts of Men
1917 The Lone Wolf
Rasputin, the Black Monk
1919 The American Way

Fisher, Ross
1919 The Blue Bonnet*
The Love Call
1920 His Pajama Girl
Twin Beds

Fisher, Sallie
1916 The Little Shepherd of Bargain
Row

Fisher, Stewart
1919 The American Way

Fiske, Mrs. *same as* **Fiske, Minnie Maddern**
1913 Tess of the D'Urbervilles
1915 Vanity Fair

Fitch, George
1916 A Daughter of the Gods
War Brides
1917 The Eternal Sin
The Lone Wolf
The Warfare of the Flesh
1918 The Fall of the Romanoffs

Fitzallen, Adelaide
1920 Heritage

Fitzer, James
1919 Crimson Shoals

Fitzgerald, Mrs.
1916 Common Sense Brackett

Fitzgerald, Betty T.
1916 A Circus Romance
Little Lady Eileen
Silks and Satins

Fitzgerald, Cissy *same as* **Fitzgerald, Cissie; Fitz-Gerald, Cissy**
1914 The Win(k)some Widow
1915 The Dust of Egypt
How Cissy Made Good
Keep Moving
The Man Behind the Door

Fitzgerald, Dallas M.
1914 The Ordeal*
1916 Common Sense Brackett
1919 The Open Door
1920 Blackmail
Chains of Evidence

Cinderella's Twin
The Price of Redemption

Fitzgerald, George
1919 The Witness for the Defense

Fitzgerald, J. A. *see* **Fitzgerald, James A.**

Fitzgerald, James (*actor*)
1914 Hearts of Oak

Fitzgerald, James A. (*dir*) *same as* **Fitzgerald, J. A.**
1916 Ignorance
1920 Brain Cinema

Fitzgerald, Rita
1916 The Fortunate Youth

Fitzhugh, Ida
1916 Rolling Stones
1919 Oh, You Women

Fitzhugh, Venita
1918 Restitution

Fitzmaurice, George
1914 The Corsair
The Quest of the Sacred Jewel
When Rome Ruled
1915 At Bay
The Commuters
The Money Master
Stop Thief!
Via Wireless
Who's Who in Society
1916 Arms and the Woman
Big Jim Garrity
New York
The Romantic Journey
The Test
1917 Blind Man's Luck
The Hunting of the Hawk
The Iron Heart
Kick In
The Mark of Cain
The On-the-Square-Girl
The Recoil
Sylvia of the Secret Service
Vengeance Is Mine
1918 The Hillcrest Mystery
Innocent
A Japanese Nightingale
The Narrow Path
The Naulahka
1919 The Avalanche
Common Clay
Counterfeit
The Cry of the Weak
Our Better Selves
The Profiteers
A Society Exile
The Witness for the Defense
1920 Idols of Clay
On with the Dance
The Right to Love

Fitzroy, Emily
1916 East Lynne
The Return of Eve
Sins of Men
1919 A Broadway Saint
The Climbers
1920 Deadline at Eleven
The Frisky Mrs. Johnson
The Man Who Lost Himself
The New York Idea
Oil
Way Down East

Fitzroy, Louis
1917 The Planter
1918 The Strange Woman
1919 Blind Husbands
The Four-Flusher
1920 A Beggar in Purple
The Devil's Riddle
Flames of the Flesh
Two Moons

Fitzsimmons, R. H.
1919 The Red Viper

Fjorde, Madame
1915 How Molly Malone Made
Good

Flanagan, D. J. *same as* **Flanagan, David; Flannigan, D. J.**
1915 Alias Jimmy Valentine
Trilby
1916 The Common Law
Fruits of Desire
La Vie de Boheme

1917 One Hour
        Sloth
1920 The Blue Pearl
Flanagan, Joseph *same as* **Flanagan, Joe**
1920 Marooned Hearts
        The Wonderful Chance
Flanigan, J.
1919 Eyes of the Soul
Flannigan, D. J. *see* **Flanagan, D. J.**
Flannigan, E. F.
1914 Springtime
Flateau, George *same as* **Flateau,
    Georges; Slatteau, George**
1917 The Mad Lover
1918 Lest We Forget
Fleck, Fred
1914 The Littlest Rebel
Fleming, Alice
1919 The Beloved Cheater
1920 Women Men Love
Fleming, Asta
1917 Draft 258
Fleming, Augustus
1920 The Daughter Pays
Fleming, Bob *same as* **Fleming, Robert;
    Flemming, Bob**
1915 The Immigrant
1916 The House with the Golden
        Windows
        The Love Mask
        The Selfish Woman
        To Have and to Hold
1918 Six Shooter Andy
1919 Nugget Nell
Fleming, C. S. *see* **Fleming, Caryl S.**
Fleming, Carlyle *see* **Fleming, Caryl S.**
Fleming, Carroll *(actor) same as*
    Flemming, Carroll
1915 The Master Hand
1920 Milestones
Fleming, Caryl S. *(dir, actor) same as*
    **Fleming, C. S.; Fleming, Carlyle;
    Fleming, Caryl; Fleming, Caryl
    Stacy**
1914 The Floor Above
        Beating Back
1915 York State Folks
1916 The Devil's Prayer-Book
        My Country First
1919 The Clouded Name
        Wild Oats
Fleming, Claude
1915 Hearts in Exile
1916 The Light That Failed
        The Test
Fleming, Ethel
1916 East Lynne
        The Kiss
        Under Cover
1917 Putting the Bee in Herbert
1918 The Pretender
        The Silent Rider
        Untamed
1919 Love Insurance
        Modern Husbands
        Smiles
Fleming, James
1920 Oil
Fleming, John
1917 The Argyle Case
Fleming, Robert *see* **Fleming, Bob**
Fleming, Una
1918 The Talk of the Town
Fleming, Victor *same as* **Fleming, Vic**
1917 The Americano
        Down to Earth
        In Again—Out Again
        The Man from Painted Post
        A Modern Musketeer*
        Reaching for the Moon
        Wild and Woolly
1919 His Majesty, the American
        When the Clouds Roll By
1920 The Mollycoddle
Flemming, Bob *see* **Fleming, Bob**
Flemming, Carroll *see* **Fleming, Carroll**
Fletcher, Mr.
1915 Buckshot John*

Fletcher, Billy *see* **Fletcher, William**
Fletcher, Cecil
1917 The Price She Paid
        Red, White and Blue Blood
1918 The Grain of Dust
        The Song of Songs
Fletcher, Frank Friday
1915 The Nation's Peril*
Fletcher, W. K. *could be same as*
    Fletcher, William
1916 Vengeance Is Mine
Fletcher, William *same as* **Fletcher,
    Billy; could be same as* **Fletcher,
    W. K.**
1920 Her Honor the Mayor
Fleury, Yahne
1915 My Madonna
Flinn, Florence *same as* **Flynn, Florence**
1916 The Big Sister
1918 Eve's Daughter
1919 Little Women
        Woman, Woman!
Flint, Helen
1920 Uncle Sam of Freedom Ridge
Florence (full name unknown)
1915 Hearts of Men
Florence, Grace
1916 The Soul Market
Flores, Joseph *same as* **Flores, Joe**
1915 Fatherhood
1917 John Ermine of the
        Yellowstone
Flower, Sidney R.
1919 Whom the Gods Would
        Destroy
Flowers, Eleanor *same as* **Flowers,
    Elenore**
1913 Leah Kleschna
1915 Heléne of the North
Flowers, Sergeant Sidney
1919 The Heart of Humanity
Floyd, Henrietta
1918 Too Fat to Fight
1920 The Branded Woman
Flugrath, Leonie *see* **Mason, Shirley**
Flugrath, Virginia *see* **Dana, Viola**
Flynn, E. J. *see* **Flynn, Emmett J.**
Flynn, Emmett J. *same as* **Flynn, E. J.**
1914 The Pursuit of the Phantom
1917 Alimony
1918 The Racing Strain
1919 A Bachelor's Wife
        The Bondage of Barbara
        Eastward Ho!
        The Lincoln Highwayman
        Virtuous Sinners
        Yvonne from Paris
1920 A Connecticut Yankee at King
        Arthur's Court
        Leave It to Me
        The Man Who Dared
        Shod with Fire
        The Untamed
        The Valley of Tomorrow
Flynn, Florence *see* **Flinn, Florence**
Flynn, Joseph
1919 The Son-of-a-Gun!
Flynn, Lefty *see* **Flynn, M. B.**
Flynn, M. B. *same as* **Flynn, Lefty;
    Flynn, M. B. (Lefty); Flynn,
    Maurice B.; Flynn, Maurice Bennett**
1919 Oh, Boy!
1920 Going Some
        The Great Accident
        Just Out of College
        Officer 666
        The Silver Horde
        Stop Thief!
Flynn, Ray
1920 A Connecticut Yankee at King
        Arthur's Court
Flynn, Thomas
1917 Mother Love and the Law
Foch, General Ferdinand
1918 Lafayette, We Come!*
        Under Four Flags
Foley, John J.
1919 Eastward Ho!
1920 A Manhattan Knight
        The Shark

Foley, Louis B.
1916 Tempest and Sunshine
1917 Aladdin's Other Lamp
        The Mortal Sin
Folger, Miriam
1917 Her Second Husband
1918 Who Loved Him Best?
Folsey, George
1919 His Bridal Night
1920 The Fear Market
        The Frisky Mrs. Johnson
        Sinners
        The Stolen Kiss
Foltz, Virginia
1915 The Gentleman from Indiana*
1916 Ben Blair
        The Call of the Cumberlands
        Gloriana
1918 The Argument*
        Limousine Life
1919 Girls
        His Official Fiancée
        The Man in the Moonlight
        The Valley of the Giants
1920 All-of-a-Sudden-Peggy
        The Paliser Case
Fonda, Gloria
1915 The College Orphan
1916 Drugged Waters
Fontaine, Evan-Burrows *same as*
    Fontaine, Evan Burroughs
1920 Madonnas and Men
        Women Men Love
Fontaine, Gerard
1920 Sophy of Kravonia; Or, The
        Virgin of Paris
Foote, Courtenay *same as* **Foote,
    Courtenay**
1914 False Colours
        Home, Sweet Home
        The Pursuit of the Phantom
1915 Buckshot John
        The Caprices of Kitty
        Captain Courtesy
        The Hypocrites
        Up from the Depths
1916 Cross Currents
        An International Marriage
1918 Love's Conquest
        Love's Law
1919 His Parisian Wife
        The Two Brides
1920 The Star Rover
Forbes, Arthur
1915 Heartaches
Forbes, Harry W. *same as* **Forbes,
    Harry; Forbes, Henry W.**
1915 The Victory of Virtue
1917 Little Miss Nobody
        The Little Terror
1918 Morgan's Raiders
        Rough and Ready
        Stolen Honor
        Together
1919 Reclaimed: The Struggle for a
        Soul Between Love and Hate
Forbes, Henry W. *see* **Forbes, Harry W.**
Forbes, James
1916 The Traveling Salesman
Forbes, Mary Elizabeth
1915 God's Witness
1917 Cy Whittaker's Ward
        The Warfare of the Flesh
Force, Charles
1920 Her Honor the Mayor
        The Square Shooter
Ford, Captain *see* **Ford, Sterrett**
Ford, Mr. *see* **Ford, Sterrett**
Ford, Mrs. *could be same as* **Ford, Mrs.
    L.; Ford, Lettie; Ford, Lottie**
1914 Lena Rivers (Whitman
        Features Co.)
Ford, Elsie
1917 John Ermine of the
        Yellowstone
Ford, Eugene *same as* **Forde, Eugene**
1916 The Innocence of Lizette
Ford, Eugenie *see* **Forde, Eugenie**
Ford, Francis
1914 The Phantom Violin
        Washington at Valley Forge

1915 The Campbells Are Coming
1917 The Avenging Trail
        John Ermine of the
        Yellowstone
        Who Was the Other Man?
1918 Berlin Via America
        The Craving
1919 Crimson Shoals
1920 The Man from Nowhere
        The Woman of Mystery
Ford, Frank A. *could be same as* **Ford,
    Frank**
1918 The Menace
Ford, Frank *same as* **Ford, Frank W.;
    could be same as* **Ford, Frank A.**
1917 The Dazzling Miss Davison
        The Greater Woman
        Hedda Gabler
        Mary Moreland
        The Mirror
        Motherhood (Frank Powell
        Producing Corp.)
Ford, Hal *see* **Forde, Hal**
Ford, Harrison
1915 Excuse Me
1916 Anton the Terrible
1917 The Crystal Gazer
        Molly Entangled
        The Mysterious Mrs. M.
        On the Level
        A Roadside Impresario
        The Sunset Trail
        The Tides of Barnegat
1918 The Cruise of the
        Make-Believes
        Good Night, Paul
        A Lady's Name
        Mrs. Leffingwell's Boots
        A Pair of Silk Stockings
        A Petticoat Pilot
        Sauce for the Goose
        Such a Little Pirate
        Unclaimed Goods
        Viviette
1919 Experimental Marriage
        Girls
        Happiness à la Mode
        Hawthorne of the U.S.A.
        The Lottery Man
        Romance and Arabella
        The Third Kiss
        The Veiled Adventure
        Who Cares?
        You Never Saw Such a Girl
1920 Easy to Get
        Food for Scandal
        Her Beloved Villain
        A Lady in Love
        Miss Hobbs
        Oh, Lady, Lady
        Young Mrs. Winthrop
Ford, Harry
1916 Dimples
Ford, Henry
19-- Official Motion Pictures of the
        Panama Pacific Exposition
        Held at San Francisco,
        Calif.*
Ford, Hugh
1914 The Crucible
        Such a Little Queen
1915 Bella Donna
        The Eternal City
        Lydia Gilmore
        The Morals of Marcus
        Niobe
        The Old Homestead
        Poor Schmaltz
        The Prince and the Pauper
        Sold
        When We Were Twenty-One
        The White Pearl
        Zaza
1916 Diplomacy
        The Feud Girl*
        The Innocent Lie
        Little Lady Eileen*
        Mice and Men
        Molly Make-Believe
        The Moment Before
        The Red Widow
        Saints and Sinners
        Silks and Satins*
        The Woman in the Case

The World's Great Snare*
1917 Sapho
Seven Keys to Baldpate
The Slave Market
Sleeping Fires
1918 The Danger Mark
Mrs. Dane's Defense
1919 In Mizzoura
Let's Elope*
Mrs. Wiggs of the Cabbage
Patch
Secret Service
The Woman Thou Gavest Me
1920 Civilian Clothes
His House in Order
Lady Rose's Daughter
Ford, Jack *same as* **Ford, John**
1917 Bucking Broadway
A Marked Man
The Secret Man
Straight Shooting
1918 The Craving
Hell Bent
The Phantom Riders
The Scarlet Drop
Thieves' Gold
Three Mounted Men
Wild Women
A Woman's Fool
1919 The Ace of the Saddle
Bare Fists
A Fight for Love
A Gun Fightin' Gentleman
Marked Men
The Outcasts of Poker Flats
The Rider of the Law
Riders of Vengeance
Roped
1920 The Girl in Number 29
Hitchin' Posts
Just Pals
The Prince of Avenue A
Ford, Mrs. L. *could be same as* **Ford, Mrs.; Ford, Lettie; Ford, Lottie**
1918 Flower of the Dusk
Ford, Lettie *same as* **Ford, Mrs. Lettie; Ford, Letty; could be same as Ford, Mrs.; Ford, Mrs. L.; Ford, Lottie**
1916 Half a Rogue
1917 The Avenging Trail
1919 Courage for Two
1920 The Web of Deceit
Ford, Lottie *could be same as* **Ford, Mrs.; Ford, Mrs. L.; Ford, Lettie**
1917 The Waiting Soul
1918 The Beautiful Mrs. Reynolds
Ford, Maude *same as* **Forde, Maude**
1916 The Madness of Helen
1917 Barbary Sheep
Magda
Ford, Sterrett *same as* **Ford, Capt.; Ford, Captain; Ford, Mr.; Ford, Starrett**
1916 Joan the Woman
The Soul of Kura-San
1917 Each to His Kind
The Golden Fetter
The Prison Without Walls
The Squaw Man's Son
Forde, Arthur
1917 The Price of a Good Time
Forde, Eugene *see* **Ford, Eugene**
Forde, Eugenie *same as* **Ford, Eugenie**
1916 The Courtesan
The Girl O' Dreams
The Innocence of Lizette
The Light
Lonesome Town
Lying Lips
Purity
True Nobility
The Undertow
The White Rosette
1917 Annie-for-Spite
Charity Castle
Conscience
The Gentle Intruder
The Upper Crust
1918 Cupid's Roundup
Fair Enough
Wives and Other Wives
1919 Bonnie, Bonnie Lassie
Sis Hopkins
Strictly Confidential

1920 The Road to Divorce
A Tokio Siren
The Virgin of Stamboul
19-- Sic-Em
Forde, Hal *same as* **Ford, Hal**
1915 The Primrose Path
The Vanderhoff Affair
1916 Saints and Sinners
1917 Mayblossom
Forde, Maude *see* **Ford, Maude**
Forde, Rae
1914 At the Cross Roads
Forde, Victoria
1916 The Country That God Forgot
1917 The Heart of Texas Ryan*
1918 Western Blood
Fordyce, Al
1916 April
The Bruiser
The Courtesan
Fordyce, Madeline
1916 Revelations
Fordyce, Virginia
1915 The Buzzard's Shadow
Foreman, Grant *same as* **Forman, Grant**
1915 The Crimson Wing
The Raven
1917 S.O.S.
1920 Do the Dead Talk?
Forest, Alan *see* **Forrest, Allan**
Forest, B.
1914 Shannon of the Sixth
Forest, Hal de
1917 Tangled Lives
Forestelle, W. H. *same as* **Forsythe, W. H.; could be same as Forsyth, W. S.**
1918 La Tosca
Forman, Grant *see* **Foreman, Grant**
Forman, Harry H.
1914 Lena Rivers (Whitman
Features Co.)
Forman, Tom *same as* **Foreman, Thomas**
1915 Chimmie Fadden
Chimmie Fadden Out West
The Explorer
The Fighting Hope
A Gentleman of Leisure
The Governor's Lady
The Kindling
The Marriage of Kitty
Out of the Darkness
The Puppet Crown
Stolen Goods*
The Unknown
The Wild Goose Chase
The Woman
Young Romance
1916 The Clown
Public Opinion
The Ragamuffin
Sins of Her Parent
Sweet Kitty Bellairs
The Thousand Dollar Husband
To Have and to Hold
Unprotected
The Yellow Pawn
1917 The American Consul
The Cost of Hatred
The Evil Eye
Forbidden Paths
Hashimura Togo
Her Strange Wedding
The Jaguar's Claws
A Kiss for Susie
On Record
Those Without Sin
The Tides of Barnegat
The Trouble Buster
1919 For Better, for Worse
The Heart of Youth
Told in the Hills
1920 The Ladder of Lies
The Round-Up
The Sea Wolf
The Sins of Rosanne
The Tree of Knowledge
Formes, Karl *same as* **Formes, Carl; Formes, Carl, Jr.; Formes, Karl, Jr.**
1915 Old Heidelberg
1916 Macbeth

1918 His Own Home Town
Keys of the Righteous
Up the Road with Sallie
1919 The Little Boss
A Rogue's Romance
1920 A Connecticut Yankee at King
Arthur's Court
Felix O'Day
Flame of Youth
The Red Lane
Forrest, Allan *same as* **Forest, Alan; Forrest, Alan ; Forrest, Allen**
1914 Called Back
1915 Captivating Mary Carstairs
Heritage
The Silent Command
1916 And the Law Says
Dulcie's Adventure
Peck O' Pickles
The Sign of the Spade
The Torch Bearer
1917 American Methods
Charity Castle
Glory
Her Country's Call
The Mate of the Sally Ann
Melissa of the Hills
Peggy Leads the Way
Periwinkle
1918 Beauty and the Rogue
A Bit of Jade
The Eyes of Julia Deep
The Ghost of Rosy Taylor
Powers That Prey
Rosemary Climbs the Heights
Social Briars
1919 The Amazing Impostor
A Bachelor's Wife
The Great Air Robbery
The Intrusion of Isabel
Over the Garden Wall
Yvonne from Paris
1920 The Forgotten Woman
Li Ting Lang
The Purple Cipher
Forrest, Ann
1918 The Rainbow Trail
1919 The Grim Game
1920 Behold My Wife
Dangerous Days
The Great Accident
The Prince Chap
A Splendid Hazard
Forrest, Edith
1919 The Imp
Forrest, Marguerite *same as* **Forrest, Margaret**
1916 The Fortunate Youth
The Pursuing Vengeance
1917 The Renaissance at Charleroi
Forrest, Martha
1920 The Rich Slave
Forrester, Fred
1917 The Tenderfoot
Forrester, Izola
1916 The Quitter
1917 Anything Once
1918 How Could You, Caroline?
In Pursuit of Polly
The Woman Who Gave
1919 The Fear Woman
The Four-Flusher
The Stronger Vow
The Unveiling Hand
1920 Easy to Get
Forsberg, Edwin *same as* **Fosberg, Edwin**
1914 Forgiven; Or, The Jack of
Diamonds
1916 Madame X
1917 The Silent Witness
1918 The Crucible of Life
A Romance of the Underworld
Forsell, J. H.
1919 The Great Victory, Wilson or
the Kaiser? The Fall of the
Hohenzollerns
Forshay, Harold *see* **Foshay, Harold**
Forst, E. *same as* **Forst, Elmer; Forst, Emil**
1918 Sylvia on a Spree
1919 The Social Pirate
The Splendid Sin

1920 Occasionally Yours
Forster, Oscar W.
1915 Vanity Fair
1916 The Flight of the Duchess
1917 The Vicar of Wakefield
Forsyth, Robert *same as* **Forsythe, Robert**
1916 The Supreme Sacrifice
1917 The Beloved Adventuress
Betsy Ross
Moral Courage
The Stolen Paradise
1918 The Beautiful Mrs. Reynolds
1920 The Rich Slave
Forsyth, W. S. *same as* **Forsythe, William S.; could be same as Forestelle, W. H.; Forsythe, W. H.**
1915 The Stubbornness of Geraldine
1920 Roman Candles
Forsythe (full name unknown)
1916 The Code of Marcia Gray*
Forsythe, Hattie
1913 The Port of Doom
1916 Destiny's Toy
Forsythe, Robert *see* **Forsyth, Robert**
Forsythe, W. H. *see* **Forestelle, W. H.**
Forsythe, William S. *see* **Forsyth, W. S.**
Fortescue, Viola A.
1917 The White Raven
Forth, George J. *same as* **Forth, George**
1917 The Awakening of Ruth
The Heart of Ezra Greer
I Will Repay
The Sixteenth Wife
1918 Our Little Wife
Fortier, Herbert
1915 A Man's Making
The Nation's Peril
The Ringtailed Rhinoceros
1916 The City of Failing Light
Dollars and the Woman
Race Suicide
Those Who Toil
1918 The Gulf Between
1919 Who's Your Brother?
1920 A Connecticut Yankee at King
Arthur's Court
Fortney, Jimmie
1919 The Egg Crate Wallop
Fortson, Robert
1919 Injustice
Fosberg, Edwin *see* **Forsberg, Edwin**
Foshay, Harold *same as* **Forshay, Harold**
1916 The Hunted Woman
Kennedy Square
The Shop Girl
The Tarantula
Thou Art the Man
1918 The Desired Woman
The Soap Girl
1919 The Girl Problem
1920 Dr. Jekyll and Mr. Hyde
(Pioneer Film Corp.)
Other Men's Shoes
Voices
Foshida, M.
1919 Bonds of Honor
Foss, Darrell *same as* **Foss, Darrel**
1917 An Even Break
The Firefly of Tough Luck
The Girl Glory
The Pinch Hitter
Polly Ann
The Regenerates
The Square Deal Man
Time Locks and Diamonds
1918 Closin' In
Her American Husband
Her Decision
The Man Who Woke Up
The Return of Mary
A Soul in Trust
The Testing of Mildred Vane
Without Honor
You Can't Believe Everything
1919 The Brat
Loot
The Parisian Tigress
The Red Lantern
Rose O' the River
1920 Held in Trust
The Walk-Offs

Foss, Eugene Noble
19-- Official Motion Pictures of the Panama Pacific Exposition Held at San Francisco, Calif.*

Foster, Billy same as **Foster, William** (cam); **Foster, William C.**
1916 Sins of Her Parent
1917 American Methods
    The Heart of a Lion
    The Price of Silence
    A Tale of Two Cities
    When a Man Sees Red
1918 The Blindness of Divorce
    For Freedom
    Les Miserables
    The Rainbow Trail
    Riders of the Purple Sage
    True Blue
1919 The Man Hunter
    The Man Who Turned White
    The Pagan God
    A Woman of Pleasure
1920 The Corsican Brothers
    The Silver Horde
    When Dawn Came

Foster, C. A.
1916 Vengeance Is Mine

Foster, Cecil
1920 Cinderella's Twin

Foster, Fern
1914 McVeagh of the South Seas
    The Master Cracksman

Foster, J. Morris same as **Foster, J. M.; Foster, J. Maurice; Foster, Morris;** could be same as **Foster, J. W.**
1914 Cardinal Richelieu's Ward
1915 The Flying Twins
    God's Witness
1916 The Innocent Lie
1917 Beloved Jim
    High Speed
    The Secret Man
1918 All the World to Nothing
    The Fighting Grin
    Money Isn't Everything
    The Voice of Destiny
    Winning Grandma
1919 Blind Man's Eyes
    Who Cares?
    You Never Saw Such a Girl
1920 Overland Red
    The Parish Priest
    Sundown Slim
    What Happened to Jones

Foster, J. W. could be same as **Foster, J. Morris**
1918 A Daughter of the West

Foster, John
1920 The Little Shepherd of Kingdom Come

Foster, Lorena
1918 Breakers Ahead

Foster, Martha D.
1917 Bab's Diary

Foster, Maximillian
1919 Something to Do
    A Taste of Life

Foster, May
1920 Forty-Five Minutes from Broadway
    Milestones
    Two Moons

Foster, Morris see **Foster, J. Morris**

Foster, William (black film pioneer)
1919 The Homesteader*

Foster, William (cam) see **Foster, Billy**

Fouche, Marion could be same as **Fouche, Miriam**
1917 God's Man

Fouche, Miriam could be same as **Fouche, Marion**
1917 She
    Soldiers of Chance
1918 Private Peat

Fovieri, Ninon same as **Fovieri, Nino**
1916 The Children in the House
    Going Straight
    Let Katie Do It

Fowler, B. L.
1916 The Dupe

Fowler, Brenda
1918 Thirty a Week

Fowler, Caroline
1916 Undine

Fowler, Harry same as **Fowler, Harry M.**
1918 Tarzan of the Apes
1919 Hoop-La
1920 Hearts Up
    Sundown Slim
    West Is West

Fowler, Lawrence
1919 Deliverance

Fox, Earl see **Foxe, Earle**

Fox, Edmund K.
1920 In the Shadow of the Dome

Fox, Edward Lyell
1915 The Battle and Fall of Przemysl
    Friends and Foes
    System, the Secret of Success*
    The Warring Millions

Fox, Elsa
1916 The Land Just Over Yonder

Fox, Finis
1917 The Jury of Fate
    The Voice of Conscience
1919 Blackie's Redemption
    Easy to Make Money
    False Evidence
    Fools and Their Money
    The Great Romance
    The Parisian Tigress
    Please Get Married
    Shadows of Suspicion
    Should a Woman Tell?
    The Way of the Strong
1920 Alias Jimmy Valentine
    Isobel; Or, The Trail's End
    The Web of Deceit

Fox, George
1919 The House Without Children
1920 Hidden Charms

Fox, Gladys
1918 Bread

Fox, John, Jr.
1918 Why America Will Win

Fox, Lucy
1918 Just for Tonight
    Why I Would Not Marry
1919 The Bishop's Emeralds
    The Winchester Woman
1920 The Empire of Diamonds
    The Flaming Clue
    Something Different
    Women Men Forget

Fox, Patricia
1920 Haunting Shadows

Fox, Stephen see **Furthman, Jules**

Fox, William
1914 The Idler
    St. Elmo
    The Thief
1915 The Blindness of Devotion
    The Broken Law
    The Celebrated Scandal
    Children of the Ghetto
    Destruction
    The Devil's Daughter
    Dr. Rameau
    From the Valley of the Missing
    The Galley Slave
    A Gilded Fool
    The Girl I Left Behind Me
    The Nigger
    Regeneration
    Samson
    Should a Mother Tell?
    The Song of Hate
    A Woman's Resurrection
1916 A Daughter of the Gods
    Jealousy
    The Mischief Maker
    Romeo and Juliet (Fox Film Corp.)
    A Wife's Sacrifice
    The Witch
1917 Aladdin and the Wonderful Lamp
    American Methods
    The Book Agent

    A Branded Soul
    For Liberty
    Heart and Soul
    Her Temptation
    High Finance
    The Honor System
    Jack and the Beanstalk
    A Modern Cinderella
    One Touch of Sin
    The Price of Silence
    The Scarlet Letter
    The Scarlet Pimpernel
    The Silent Lie
    Some Boy!
    To Honor and Obey
    When a Man Sees Red
    Wrath of Love
1918 Ali Baba and the Forty Thieves
    American Buds
    The Bird of Prey
    Bonnie Annie Laurie
    The Caillaux Case
    Caught in the Act
    Confession
    The Debt of Honor
    The Forbidden Path
    The Girl with the Champagne Eyes
    A Heart's Revenge
    Her One Mistake
    I Want to Forget
    I'll Say So
    Jack Spurlock, Prodigal
    The Kid Is Clever
    Kultur
    Les Miserables
    Miss Innocence
    Mr. Logan, U.S.A.
    On the Jump
    Other Men's Daughters
    The Prussian Cur
    The Queen of Hearts
    Queen of the Sea
    The Rainbow Trail
    Riders of the Purple Sage
    Rough and Ready
    Salome
    Six Shooter Andy
    Stolen Honor
    Swat the Spy
    True Blue
    Under the Yoke
    We Should Worry
    When a Woman Sins
    Why I Would Not Marry
    Woman and the Law
    The Woman Who Gave
1919 The Divorce Trap
    The Feud
    The Forbidden Room
    The Girl with No Regrets
    Hell Roarin' Reform
    The Last of the Duanes
    The Lone Star Ranger
    Love Is Love
    The Love That Dares
    Luck and Pluck
    The Man Hunter
    Married in Haste
    Snares of Paris
    Tin Pan Alley*
    When Men Desire
    Words and Music By—
1920 Black Shadows*
    Blind Wives
    A Connecticut Yankee at King Arthur's Court
    The Face at Your Window
    Firebrand Trevison
    Flame of Youth
    The Girl of My Heart
    The Hell Ship
    Her Elephant Man
    If I Were King
    Just Pals
    Love's Harvest
    The Orphan
    Prairie Trails
    The Shark
    A Sister to Salome
    The Skywayman
    The Spirit of Good
    The Strongest
    The Terror
    The Thief

    Three Gold Coins
    The Tiger's Cub
    Twins of Suffering Creek
    Two Moons
    The Untamed
    The White Moll

Foxe, Earle same as **Fox, Earl**
1914 The Floor Above
    Home, Sweet Home
1916 Alien Souls
    Ashes of Embers
    The Dream Girl
    The Love Mask
    Public Opinion
    The Trail of the Lonesome Pine
    Unto Those Who Sin
1917 Blind Man's Luck
    The Honeymoon
    Outwitted
    Panthea
1918 From Two to Six
    Peck's Bad Girl
    The Studio Girl

Foxhall, George
1917 The Climber

Foy, Mrs. see **Foy, Mrs. Patrick**

Foy, Patrick same as **Foy, Pat**
1916 Sally in Our Alley
1917 The Little Duchess
1918 T'Other Dear Charmer

Foy, Mrs. Patrick same as **Foy, Mrs.**
1916 Sally in Our Alley
1917 Thou Shalt Not Steal

Frame, Park same as **Frame, Park B.; Frame, Parke**
1919 Dangerous Waters
    For a Woman's Honor
    The Gray Wolf's Ghost
    The Man Who Turned White
    The Mints of Hell
    The Pagan God
    Whitewashed Walls
1920 The Forgotten Woman

Framer, Samuel
1919 God's Outlaw

France, Charles H.
1917 The Natural Law

France, Floyd
1917 The Princess' Necklace
    Putting the Bee in Herbert

France, Herminia
1920 Do the Dead Talk?

France, J. J. see **Franz, Joseph J.**

Frances, Alec see **Francis, Alec B.**

Francis (full name unknown)
1915 The Fairy and the Waif*

Francis, Alec B. same as **Frances, Alec; Francis, Alec; Francis, Alexander**
1914 Lola
    The Man of the Hour
    The Pit
    When Broadway Was a Trail
    The Wishing Ring; An Idyll of Old England
1915 After Dark
    Alias Jimmy Valentine
    The Arrival of Perpetua
    The Impostor
    The Model
    The Sins of Society
1916 All Man
    The Ballet Girl
    Fruits of Desire
    The Gilded Cage
    The Heart of a Hero
    Human Driftwood
    Husband and Wife
    Miss Petticoats
    The Pawn of Fate
    The Perils of Divorce
    Tangled Fates
    A Woman's Way
    The Yellow Passport
1917 The Auction Block
    The Cinderella Man
    The Family Honor
    Forget-Me-Not
    A Hungry Heart
    The Page Mystery
1918 The Beautiful Mrs. Reynolds
    Broken Ties
    The Cross Bearer
    The Face in the Dark

Francis, Alma
The Glorious Adventure
Hidden Fires
Leap to Fame
The Marionettes
Money Mad
Thirty a Week
The Venus Model
Wanted, a Mother
1919 The City of Comrades
The Crimson Gardenia
Day Dreams
Flame of the Desert
Heartsease
Her Code of Honor
Lord and Lady Algy
The Pest
The Probation Wife
Spotlight Sadie
When Doctors Disagree
The World and Its Woman
1920 The Butterfly Man
Earthbound
Godless Men
The Man Who Had Everything
The Paliser Case
The Street Called Straight

Francis, Alma
1920 An Adventuress*

Francis, Charles
1915 The Greater Will
1916 Broken Fetters

Francis, Enid
1916 The Price of Happiness

Francis, Eva
1916 A Coney Island Princess

Francis, Helen
1914 The Taint

Francisco, Betty
1920 A Broadway Cowboy
The Furnace
1921 Midsummer Madness
19-- Sic-Em

Franck, J. L.
1916 Ramona
1918 Her Moment

Frank, Alexander F. *same as* **Frank, Alexander**
1914 A Suspicious Wife
1918 The Liar
1920 The Bromley Case
The Sacred Ruby
The Scrap of Paper
The Trail of the Cigarette
The Triple Clue
The Unseen Witness
The Wall Street Mystery
1920-21
The House of Mystery

Frank, Bert S. *could be same as* **Frank, J. Herbert**
1914 The Littlest Rebel

Frank, Herbert *see* **Frank, J. Herbert**

Frank, J. Herbert *same as* **Frank, Herbert; could be same as** **Frank, Bert S.**
1915 The Breath of Araby
Destruction
The Dust of Egypt
Mortmain
1916 Ashes of Embers
The Crucial Test
Who Killed Joe Merrion?
1917 The Brand of Satan
Darkest Russia
The End of the Tour
The Fringe of Society
The Iron Ring
Scandal
The Secret of the Storm
Country
1918 Dodging a Million
For Freedom
Good-Bye, Bill
Tempered Steel
1920 April Folly
Empty Arms
The Scarlet Dragon

Frank, Sam
1919 The Microbe*

Franke, Grover
1918 A Soul in Trust
You Can't Believe Everything

Frankenburg, Julius *same as* **Frankenberg, Julius**
1916 Humanizing Mr. Winsby
The Land Just Over Yonder
1918 Nine-Tenths of the Law

Frankenfield, Laura
1916 Captain Jinks of the Horse Marines

Franklin, C. M. *same as* **Franklin, Chester M.**
1916 The Children in the House
Going Straight
Gretchen, the Greenhorn
Let Katie Do It
The Little School Ma'am
Martha's Vindication
A Sister of Six
1917 Aladdin and the Wonderful Lamp
The Babes in the Woods
Jack and the Beanstalk
1918 Ali Baba and the Forty Thieves
Fan Fan
The Girl with the Champagne Eyes
Six Shooter Andy
Treasure Island
1920 You Never Can Tell

Franklin, Edgar *same as* **Stearns, Edgar Franklin**
1918 More Trouble
1920 Alias Miss Dodd
The Desperate Hero
Once a Plumber

Franklin, George
1917 The Savage

Franklin, Harry L.
1918 Kildare of Storm
A Successful Adventure
Sylvia on a Spree
The Winning of Beatrice
1919 After His Own Heart
The Four-Flusher
Full of Pep
In His Brother's Place
Johnny-on-the-Spot
That's Good
1920 Alias Miss Dodd
Her Five-Foot Highness
Rouge and Riches
The Secret Gift

Franklin, Irene
1918 Wanted for Murder

Franklin, John E.
1918 The Prussian Cur

Franklin, Martha
1916 The Haunted Manor

Franklin, S. A. *same as* **Franklin, Sid; Franklin, Sidney; Franklin, Sidney A.; Franklin, Sydney; Franklin, Sydney A.**
1916 The Children in the House
Going Straight
Gretchen, the Greenhorn
Let Katie Do It
The Little School Ma'am
Martha's Vindication
A Sister of Six
1917 Aladdin and the Wonderful Lamp
The Babes in the Woods
Jack and the Beanstalk
1918 Ali Baba and the Forty Thieves
The Bride of Fear
Confession
Fan Fan
The Forbidden City
Her Only Way
The Safety Curtain
Six Shooter Andy
Treasure Island
1919 Heart O' the Hills
The Heart of Wetona
The Hoodlum
The Man in the Moonlight
The Probation Wife
A Rogue's Romance
The Sleeping Lion
1920 The Blue Moon
Down Home
Drag Harlan*
Two Weeks
Unseen Forces

Franklyn, Beth
1920 Nothing but the Truth

Frankman, Charles
1917 Panthea

Franz, Joseph J. *same as* **France, J. J.; Franz, J. J.; Franz, Joseph**
1918 The Pretender
1919 Bare-Fisted Gallagher
The Blue Bandanna
The Devil's Trail
The End of the Game
Life's a Funny Proposition
The Mints of Hell
A Sage Brush Hamlet
1920 A Broadway Cowboy
The Parish Priest

Franzen, Nell
1916 The Courtesan
Embers
Life's Blind Alley
Lord Loveland Discovers America
Purity
Revelations
The Strength of Donald McKenzie

Fraser, Harry
1916 The Man Who Stood Still
1918 The Divine Sacrifice

Fraunholz, Fraunie *same as* **Fraunholtz, Fraunie; Fraunholz, Fraunie French**
1913 Ben Bolt
A Prisoner in the Harem
The Rogues of Paris
Shadows of the Moulin Rouge
The Star of India
1914 Beneath the Czar
The Burglar and the Lady
The Dream Woman
The Lure
The Millon Dollar Robbery
The Temptations of Satan
The Woman of Mystery
1915 The Avalanche
Barbara Frietchie
Her Own Way
The Song of the Wage Slave
1916 The Ocean Waif
Other People's Money
The Soul Market
What Will People Say?
1917 The Little Boy Scout
1919 The Thirteenth Chair

Frawley, William
1916 Lord Loveland Discovers America

Frayne, Frank *same as* **Frayne, Frank, Jr.**
1915 Right off the Bat
1917 Motherhood (Frank Powell Producing Corp.)

Frazer, Elizabeth
1916 The Kiss

Frazer, Gene
1915 Sweet Alyssum

Frazer, George P.
1919 The Chosen Path

Frazer, Nitra
1915 The Man Behind the Door

Frazer, Robert *same as* **Frazer, Robert W.**
1915 The Lone Star Rush
1916 The Ballet Girl
The Dawn of Love
The Decoy
The Feast of Life
Light at Dusk
1919 Bolshevism on Trial
The Bramble Bush
Her Code of Honor

Frederic, Alma
1915 A Soldier's Oath

Frederic, William *same as* **Frederick, William; could be same as** **Fredericks, William** *or* **Frederics, William**
1915 The Prince and the Pauper
1916 Common Sense Brackett
The Pursuing Vengeance
1917 Richard the Brazen
1918 Five Thousand an Hour
Heart of the Sunset
His Bonded Wife

The Poor Rich Man
1919 Never Say Quit

Frederici, Blanche
1920 39 East

Frederick, John
1920 Bullet Proof

Frederick, Pauline
1915 Bella Donna
The Eternal City
Lydia Gilmore
Sold
Zaza
1916 Ashes of Embers
Audrey
The Moment Before
Nanette of the Wilds
The Spider
The Woman in the Case
The World's Great Snare
1917 Double Crossed
Her Better Self
The Hungry Heart
The Love That Lives
Sapho
The Slave Market
Sleeping Fires
1918 A Daughter of the Old South
Fedora
Her Final Reckoning
Madame Jealousy
Mrs. Dane's Defense
Resurrection
La Tosca
1919 Bonds of Love
The Fear Woman
The Loves of Letty
One Week of Life
Out of the Shadow
Paid in Full
The Peace of Roaring River
The Woman on the Index
1920 Madame X
The Paliser Case
A Slave of Vanity
The Woman in Room 13

Frederick, Walter S. *see* **Fredericks, Walter S.**

Frederick, William *see* **Frederic, William**

Fredericks, Helene
1917 Next Door to Nancy

Fredericks, Walter S. *same as* **Frederick, Walter S.**
1916 The Making of Maddalena

Fredericks, William *could be same as* **Frederic, William** *or* **Frederics, William**
1918 Joan of Plattsburg
1919 The Imp
The Volcano
1920 The Scrap of Paper
The Trail of the Cigarette
Two Weeks
The Unseen Witness
The Woman God Sent

Frederics, William *could be same as* **Frederic, William** *or* **Fredericks, William**
1917 God's Man

Freedman, I. K.
1915 Richard Carvel*
The Silent Voice

Freeland, A.
1918 The Triumph of Venus

Freeman, Helen
1915 Are You a Mason?
The Morals of Marcus

Freeman, William
1915 The Birth of a Nation
1917 The Spirit of '76
1918 Mirandy Smiles

Freemont, W. J.
1916 Acquitted

Freise, Jack
1915 Environment

Fremont, Al *same as* **Frement, Al; Fremont, A.; Fremont, Alfred**
1917 Du Barry
1918 The Blindness of Divorce
Kultur
Salome
When a Woman Sins

1919 The Forbidden Room
      The Girl with No Regrets
      Happiness à la Mode
      Pitfalls of a Big City
      The Siren's Song
      Vagabond Luck
      Wolves of the Night
1920 Drag Harlan
      The Girl of My Heart
      The Joyous Troublemaker
      The Orphan
      The Scuttlers
      The Square Shooter
Fremont, Marian
1919 True Heart Susie
Fremyear, Mabel
1915 A Fool There Was
1918 Social Quicksands
French, Caroline same as **French, Carolyn**
1914 Forgiven; Or, The Jack of Diamonds
      The Nightingale
      Paid in Full
      Il Trovatore
1915 The Avalanche
French, Charles K. same as **French, Charles**; could be same as **French, Charles W.**
1915 The Coward
      The Despoiler
      The Disciple
      The Iron Strain
1916 The Aryan
      Civilization
      A Corner in Colleens
      The Criminal
      A Gamble in Souls
      The Honorable Algy
      The No-Good Guy
      The Patriot
      The Phantom
      Shell Forty-Three
      The Vagabond Prince
1917 The Clodhopper
      An Even Break
      The Hater of Men
      Love or Justice
      Paws of the Bear
      The Son of His Father
      The Weaker Sex
      Wee Lady Betty
1918 A Burglar for a Night
      Free and Equal
      Fuss and Feathers
      Green Eyes
      The Guilty Man
      The Hired Man
      His Own Home Town
      The Kaiser's Shadow, or the Triple Cross
      The Law of the North
      The Marriage Ring
      The Midnight Patrol
      Three X Gordon
      The Tiger Man
      The Vamp
1919 Come Again Smith
      Happy Though Married
      Jubilo
      The Mints of Hell
      The Sheriff's Son
      Six Feet Four
      The Speed Maniac
      This Hero Stuff
      What Every Woman Wants
      Whom the Gods Would Destroy
1920 The Daredevil
      Desert Love
      Flames of the Flesh
      Haunting Shadows
      Prairie Trails
      The Square Shooter
      The Terror
      The Texan
      The Untamed
      What Would You Do?
      White Lies
French, Charles W. could be same as **French, Charles K.**
1920 Stronger Than Death

French, Eugene De Tousard
1918 What Becomes of the Children?
1920 Oil
French, F.
1920 Lifting Shadows
French, George
1918 Tarzan of the Apes
1920 His Pajama Girl
French, Georgia
1916 The Mark of Cain
      Tangled Hearts
1918 Restitution
      The Wolf and His Mate
French, Herbert
1916 The Social Secretary
French, Mrs. R. E.
1915 Silver Threads Among the Gold
Frere, Eve
1915 Old Dutch*
Freuderman, A. E. same as **Freudemann, Alfred E.**
1914 The Banker's Daughter
1920 The Chorus Girl's Romance
      Dangerous to Men
Freulich, Jack
1919 The Silk Lined Burglar
Freyer (full name unknown)
1917 The Lincoln Cycle
Friebus, Theodore
1917 The Warfare of the Flesh
Fried, Abe same as **Fried, A.**
1919 The Lost Battalion
      A Scream in the Night*
1920 Even As Eve
      The Good-Bad Wife
      Man and Woman (A. H. Fischer Features, Inc.)
Fried, Eleanor
1919 Blind Husbands
Friedgen, Ray
1919 Broken Barriers
Friedley, Vinton
1919 A Dangerous Affair
Friel, Thornton
1915 Right off the Bat
Frink, Lola
1919 The Praise Agent
Friquet, Jules
1918 Captain of His Soul
      Limousine Life
Fritz
1917 The Narrow Trail
Froest, Frank
1917 The Maelstrom
Frohman (full name unknown)
1915 The Fairy and the Waif*
Frohman, Charles
1914 The Conspiracy
1915 Are You a Mason?
      David Harum
      The Morals of Marcus
1917 The Beautiful Adventure
1918 Lest We Forget*
Frohman, Daniel
1913 Chelsea 7750
      The Daughter of the Hills
      Leah Kleschna
      The Port of Doom
      The Prisoner of Zenda
      Tess of the D'Urbervilles
1914 Aftermath
      Aristocracy
      Behind the Scenes
      The Brute
      Cinderella
      The Crucible
      The Day of Days
      A Good Little Devil
      Hearts Adrift
      His Last Dollar
      A Lady of Quality
      The Lost Paradise
      The Man from Mexico
      Marta of the Lowlands
      Mrs. Black Is Back
      One of Our Girls
      The Redemption of David Corson
      The Sign of the Cross
      The Spitfire
      The Straight Road

      Such a Little Queen
      The Unwelcome Mrs. Hatch
      Wildflower
      A Woman's Triumph
1915 The Bachelor's Romance
      The Commanding Officer
      The Dancing Girl
      The Dawn of a Tomorrow
      Esmeralda
      The Eternal City
      Fanchon the Cricket
      The Fatal Card
      Gambier's Advocate
      A Girl of Yesterday
      Gretna Green
      The Heart of Jennifer
      Heléne of the North
      The Incorrigible Dukane
      Jim the Penman
      Little Pal
      The Love Route
      Lydia Gilmore
      Madame Butterfly
      The Masqueraders
      May Blossom
      Mistress Nell
      The Moth and the Flame
      Niobe
      The Old Homestead
      The Pretty Sister of Jose
      The Prince and the Pauper
      Rags
      Seven Sisters
      Sold
      When We Were Twenty-One
      The White Pearl
1916 The Daughter of MacGregor
      The Eternal Grind
      The Foundling
      The Kiss
      The Lost Bridegroom
      Mice and Men
      The Rainbow Princess
      Seventeen
      The Spider
      The Traveling Salesman
1917 The Dummy
      The Fortunes of Fifi
      A Girl Like That
      Great Expectations
      Sapho
      The Slave Market
      Sleeping Fires
Frohman, Gustave same as **Frohman, Gustav**
1915 The Builder of Bridges
      The Fairy and the Waif
      Just Out of College
Frohman, Marie Hubert
1915 The Fairy and the Waif
Frommer, Henry G.
1915 The Master of the House
      The Senator
1916 Man and His Angel
1918 Conquered Hearts
Froom, Albert same as **Froome, Albert**
1914 Beating Back
1915 The Song of the Wage Slave
1917 The Deemster
Frost, Leila
1916 The Fall of a Nation
1917 The Heart of Ezra Greer
Frost, Lorraine
1916 God's Half Acre
      The Light of Happiness
1920 The Deep Purple
      Sinners
      The Truth About Husbands
Frost, Walter Archer
1917 The Siren
Fruen, Patricia
1920 Way Down East
Frusta, Arrigo
1915 Du Barry
Fryer, Richard
1914 America
1918 His Daughter Pays
1920 The Miracle of Money
Fuhr, Charles
1919 The Red Lantern*

Fujita, Toyo
1919 Bonds of Honor
      The Courageous Coward
      The Dragon Painter
      The Illustrious Prince
      The Tong Man
1920 A Tokio Siren
Fullen, Donald could be same as **Fuller, Donald**
1917 Fanatics
Fuller, Donald could be same as **Fullen, Donald**
1917 The Sudden Gentleman
Fuller, Emily
1920 The Mysteries of Paris
Fuller, Haidee
1914 The Squaw Man
Fuller, Mary
1915 Under Southern Skies
      The Woman Who Lied
1916 A Huntress of Men
      The Strength of the Weak
      Thrown to the Lions
1917 The Long Trail
      The Public Be Damned
Fulton, Helen
1915 Vanity Fair
1916 The Unpardonable Sin
Fulton, James F. same as **Fulton, James**
1917 The Kill-Joy
      The Mystery of Number 47
      The Small Town Guy
1918 Ruggles of Red Gap
      Uneasy Money
Fuqua, John W.
1920 Before the White Man Came
Furey, Barney same as **Fury, Barney**
1916 A Stranger from Somewhere
1917 A Branded Soul
      Feet of Clay
      The Lady in the Library
      The Phantom Shotgun
1918 True Blue
      Western Blood
1919 The Long Arm of Mannister
1920 The Confession
Furey, J. A. same as **Furey, J. S.**; **Furey, James**; **Furey, James A.**; **Fury, J. A.**
1915 Destruction
1916 The Awakening of Helena Richie
      Whoso Findeth a Wife
1917 Forget-Me-Not
      Over There
      Panthea
      Sunshine Alley
1918 The Beloved Traitor
      My Own United States
      Neighbors
      The Panther Woman
      The Queen of Hearts
      Sunshine Nan
      Under the Greenwood Tree
1919 The Climbers
      Dawn
      The Great Victory, Wilson or the Kaiser? The Fall of the Hohenzollerns
      Phil-for-Short
1920 Greater Than Fame
      On with the Dance
      Pleasure Seekers
Furey, James see **Furey, J. A.**
Furness, Lucille
1918 The Wildcat of Paris
Furry, Elda
1916 The Battle of Hearts
1917 Seven Keys to Baldpate
Furry, George
1919 L'Apache
Fursman, Georgia May same as **Fursman, Georgia**
1915 The Flash of an Emerald
      Seven Sisters
Fursman, Lucille
1915 Sold
Furst, William
1916 The Green Swamp
      Joan the Woman
      Let Katie Do It

Furthman, Jules *same as* **Fox, Stephen;**
  Furthman, Jules G.; Furthman,
  Julius G.; Furthmann, Jules Grinnell;
  Furthmann, Julius Grinnell
1917 The Frame Up
      High Play
      The Masked Heart
      Shackles of Truth
      Souls in Pawn
1918 All the World to Nothing
      A Camouflage Kiss
      Hobbs in a Hurry
      A Japanese Nightingale
      The Mantle of Charity
      More Trouble*
      Up Romance Road
      Wives and Other Wives
1919 The Beloved Cheater
      Brass Buttons
      The Lincoln Highwayman
      Six Feet Four
      Some Liar
      A Sporting Chance (American
        Film Co.)
      This Hero Stuff
      Victory
      When a Man Rides Alone
      Where the West Begins
1920 The Great Redeemer
      The Iron Rider
      The Land of Jazz
      Leave It to Me
      The Man Who Dared
      A Sister to Salome
      The Skywayman
      The Texan
      Treasure Island
      Twins of Suffering Creek
      The Valley of Tomorrow
      The White Circle
      Would You Forgive?
Fury, Barney *see* **Furey, Barney**
Fury, J. A. *see* **Furey, J. A.**

G

Gabourie, Fred
1919 A Woman of Pleasure
Gaden, Alexander
1913 The Daughter of the Hills
      Leah Kleschna
1914 An American Citizen
      A Lady of Quality
1915 The Unbroken Road
1916 As a Woman Sows
      The Drifter
      I Accuse
      The Quality of Faith
1919 The Bandbox
      The Capitol
1920 Cynthia-of-the-Minute
Gaffney, William
1919 The Great Victory, Wilson or
      the Kaiser? The Fall of the
      Hohenzollerns
Gahris, Roy
1915 The Game of Three
1917 Trooper 44
Gail, Jane
1913 Traffic in Souls
1916 20,000 Leagues Under the Sea
1917 The Girl Who Didn't Think
1920 Bitter Fruit
Gailer, Eddie *see* **Gheller, Edward**
Gaillard, F. *could be same as* **Gaillard,**
  Robert
1915 The Eternal City
Gaillard, Robert *same as* **Gaillord,**
  Robert; *could be same as* **Gaillard,**
  F.
1912 Cleopatra
1914 Mr. Barnes of New York
1915 The Man Who Couldn't Beat
      God
      The Turn of the Road
1916 The Alibi
      Fathers of Men
      Hesper of the Mountains
      The Kid
      Phantom Fortunes
      The Redemption of Dave
      Darcey

      The Surprises of an Empty
        Hotel
      The Two Edged Sword
      The Writing on the Wall
1917 The Bottom of the Well
      The Courage of Silence
      The Grell Mystery
      In the Balance
      Indiscretion
      The Maelstrom
      The Message of the Mouse
      A Son of the Hills
      The Stolen Treaty
      Within the Law
1918 All Man
      The Clutch of Circumstance
      A Game with Fate
      The Golden Goal
      The Green God
      Hoarded Assets
1919 The Adventure Shop
      Beating the Odds
      Beauty-Proof
      The Darkest Hour
      In Honor's Web
      The Man Who Won
      Silent Strength
1920 The Birth of a Soul
      The Broadway Bubble
      The Flaming Clue
      The Gauntlet
Gaines, Al
1920 The Brute
Galaher, Donald *see* **Gallaher, Donald**
Galanta, Ketty
1918 Empty Pockets
      The Fall of the Romanoffs
Gale, Alice
1916 Romeo and Juliet (Fox Film
        Corp.)
      Sins of Men
1917 Camille
      The Darling of Paris
      Heart and Soul
      Her Greatest Love
      Magda
      The New York Peacock
      To-Day
1918 The Birth of a Race
1919 L'Apache
Gale, Clita
1919 Riders of Vengeance
Gale, Marguerite *same as* **Gale,**
  Margaret
1915 How Molly Malone Made
      Good
1917 The Man Hater
1918 The Beautiful Mrs. Reynolds
      Joan of the Woods
1919 The Hand Invisible
      Mandarin's Gold
      The Poison Pen
1920 In the Shadow of the Dome
Gale, Minna *same as* **Haines, Mina**
  Gale; Haines, Minna; Haynes,
  Minna Gale
1913 The Prisoner of Zenda
1914 Clothes
      The Port of Missing Men
      The Unwelcome Mrs. Hatch
1915 The Dancing Girl
      A Fool There Was
Galezio, L.
1915 American Game Trails
Gallagher, D. *see* **Gallaher, Donald**
Gallagher, Raymond *same as* **Gallagher,**
  Ray
1919 His Divorced Wife
1920 The Phantom Melody
Gallaher, Donald *same as* **Galaher,**
  Donald; Gallagher, D.
1917 Draft 258
      The Silent Master
1918 Eye for Eye
1919 The Eternal Magdalene
Gallatin, Alberta
1914 The Christian
      Mr. Barnes of New York
1915 The Fifth Commandment
      Fine Feathers
      Little Miss Brown

Gallery, Tom
1920 Bright Skies
      The Chorus Girl's Romance
      Dinty
      The Heart of Twenty
Galloway, James T.
1918 Her Boy
Gally, David B.
1920 Overland Red
Gamble, Fred *same as* **Gamble,**
  Frederick
1915 The Girl from His Town
1918 A Broadway Scandal
1919 The Woman Under Cover
1920 Bullet Proof
      Fixed by George
      Homespun Folks
      La La Lucille
      The Secret Gift
Gamble, Warburton
1917 The Unforseen
1918 Thirty a Week
1919 As a Man Thinks
      La Belle Russe
      The Invisible Bond
      The Silver King
      A Society Exile
      The Two Brides
1920 The Cost
      The Law of the Yukon
      The Paliser Case
Gandolfi, Alfred E. *same as* **Gandolfi,**
  Alfred; Gandolfi, Alfredo; Gondolfi,
  Alfred; Gondolfi, Alfred E.;
  Gondolfi, Alfredo
1915 After Five
      The Little Gypsy
1916 The Battle of Hearts
      The End of the Trail
      The Man from Bitter Roots
      A Man of Sorrow
1918 The Grouch
1919 Bringing Up Betty
      The Crook of Dreams
      The Little Intruder
      Me and Captain Kidd
      The Oakdale Affair
      The Rough Neck
      The Thunderbolt
1920 The Greatest Love
      The Woman God Sent
Gane, Gladys
1917 The Last Sentence
Gane, Nolan
1914 Cardinal Richelieu's Ward
1915 The Last Concert
Gant, Harry A. *same as* **Gant, Harry**
1916 Behind the Lines
      The Secret of the Swamp
1919 A Man's Duty
Ganz, Pearl
1915 The Unwelcome Wife*
Garbutt, Frank *see* **Garbutt, Frank E.**
  (cam)
Garbutt, Frank A. *(executive)*
1913 The Sea Wolf
Garbutt, Frank E. *(cam) same as*
  Garbutt, Frank; *not the same as*
  Garbutt, Frank A. *(executive)*
1918 The Gypsy Trail*
      Her Country First
      Mile-a-Minute Kendall
      Mirandy Smiles
      Up the Road with Sallie
1919 Experimental Marriage
      The Home Town Girl
      An Innocent Adventuress
      Little Comrade
      Louisiana
      Peppy Polly*
      The Poor Boob
      The Third Kiss
      You Never Saw Such a Girl
1920 Huckleberry Finn
Garcia, Al *same as* **Garcia, Al Ernest;**
  Garcia, Alfred; Garcia, Ernest;
  Garcia, Ernesto
1914 The Valley of the Moon
1915 After Five
      The Country Boy
      Her Atonement
      The Unafraid
      Young Romance

1917 The Single Code
      Sunlight's Last Raid
1918 Baree, Son of Kazan
      A Gentleman's Agreement
      Restitution
1919 The Lamb and the Lion
      Six Feet Four
1920 The Golden Trail
      Skyfire
Garcia, May
1916 Casey at the Bat
1919 The Lady of Red Butte
Gard, Sumner
1915 The Impostor
Gardelle, Yvonne
1920 Occasionally Yours
      The Prince Chap
      The Tree of Knowledge
Garden, Mary
1917 Thais
1918 The Splendid Sinner
Gardner, Amelia
1919 Lure of Ambition
Gardner, Bert
1914 Springtime
Gardner, Charles *same as* **Gardner,**
  Charles T.
1916 The Quality of Faith
1917 The Frozen Warning
1918 Uneasy Money
Gardner, Cyril
1918 Prisoners of the Pines
1920 Greater Than Fame
      Whispers
Gardner, George
1916 The Narrow Path
Gardner, Helen
1912 Cleopatra
1913 A Princess of Bagdad
      A Sister to Carmen
1914 Pieces of Silver; A Story of
        Hearts and Souls
      The Strange Story of Sylvia
        Gray
1915 The Breath of Araby
1920 The Sleep of Cyma Roget
Gardner, Jack
1917 Gift O' Gab
      The Land of Long Shadows
      Men of the Desert
      The Night Workers
      Open Places
      The Range Boss
Gardner, Lois
1918 Restitution
Gardner, Louis B.
1915 The Glory of Youth
Gardner, Orra
1919 The Last of the Duanes
Garey, James R.
1916 The Battle of Life
      Love and Hate
1917 Wrath of Love
Garland, F. H. *could be same as*
  Garland, Franklyn
1915 Jack Chanty
Garland, Franklyn *could be same as*
  Garland, F. H.
1920 Shore Acres
Garmes, Lee
1918 The Hope Chest
1919 I'll Get Him Yet
      Nobody Home
      Nugget Nell
Garnett *(full name unknown)*
1917 The Alien Blood
Garon, Pauline
1920 A Manhattan Knight
Garrick, Richard
1914 Tess of the Storm Country
1916 According to Law
      The Drifter
      The Idol of the Stage
      The Quality of Faith
1917 Daughter of Destiny
Garrison, Mrs.
1918 Miss Innocence
1919 The Other Man's Wife
Garrison, Elizabeth
1918 Caught in the Act
      Other Men's Daughters

George, Grace
1915 Tainted Money
George, John
1917 Black Orchids
George, Maude *same as* **George, Maud**
1915 Business Is Business
     The Frame-Up
     A Little Brother of the Rich
1916 The Beckoning Trail
     The Gay Lord Waring
     Idle Wives
     The Iron Hand
     Langdon's Legacy
     The People vs. John Doe
     The Pool of Flame
     The Silent Battle
     The Social Buccaneer
     A Son of the Immortals
     The Target
     A Youth of Fortune
1917 Even As You and I
     The Fighting Gringo
     Heart Strings
     The Piper's Price
1918 Blue Blazes Rawden
     The Marriage Ring
1919 The Lamb and the Lion
     The Midnight Stage
     A Rogue's Romance
1920 The Devil's Passkey
     Madame X
George, Peggy
1916 The Heart of Nora Flynn
George, William
1919 The Homesteader
Georgina, Mae *same as* **Georgine, Mae**
1915 Prohibition
     Time Lock Number 776
Geraci, May *see* **Giraci, May**
Geraghty, Tom J. *same as* **Geraghty, Thomas; Geraghty, Thomas J.; Geraghty, Tom**
1917 The American Consul
     Those Without Sin
1918 Her Inspiration
     A Man's Man
     One Dollar Bid
     Social Ambition
     The Turn of a Card
     With Hoops of Steel
1919 The Courageous Coward
     Diane of the Green Van
     A Heart in Pawn
     In for Thirty Days
     In Old Kentucky
     A Man's Fight
     When the Clouds Roll By
1920 An Adventuress
     Always Audacious
     Burglar Proof
     The Mollycoddle
     Too Much Johnson
     You Never Can Tell
Gerald, Pete *same as* **Gerald, Peter**
1918 The Craving
1919 Crimson Shoals
Gerald, William *same as* **Gerard, William; could be same as* **Jerald, William**
1916 The Spider and the Fly*
     A Wife's Sacrifice
1917 Tangled Lives
Gerard, Alice
1919 Break the News to Mother
Gerard, Carl *same as* **Gerrard, Carl; could be same as* **Girard, Carl**
1915 The Family Stain
1916 The Vixen
1917 Crime and Punishment
     The Little Samaritan
1920 Body and Soul
     The Secret Gift
     The Silver Horde
Gerard, Charles *same as* **Gerard, Charles K.; Gerard, Charlie; Gerrard, Charles**
1916 The Country That God Forgot
     Miss Petticoats
     The Plow Girl
     The Prince Chap
1917 Down to Earth
     The Fair Barbarian
     The Heart of Texas Ryan
     Little Miss Optimist

     Melting Millions
     A Woman's Awakening
1918 Beans
     The Demon
     The Hun Within
     The Legion of Death
     Playthings
     She Hired a Husband
1919 Counterfeit
     The Isle of Conquest
     The New Moon
     The Pest
     Pettigrew's Girl
     Something to Do
     The Teeth of the Tiger
     Venus in the East
1920 Blackbirds
     Mary Ellen Comes to Town
     Whispers
     Why Women Sin
     The World and His Wife
Gerard, James W.
1919 Beware
Gerard, Rene
1920 The Scarlet Dragon
Gerard, William *see* **Gerald, William**
Gerber, Neva
1914 The Criminal Code
1915 An Eye for an Eye
     The High Hand
1916 Idle Wives
     The Impersonation
1917 Like Wildfire
     Mr. Opp
     The Spindle of Life
1918 Hell Bent
     Three Mounted Men
1919 A Fight for Love
     Pitfalls of a Big City
     Roped
Gerdes, Emma
1917 Rebecca of Sunnybrook Farm
1918 How Could You, Jean?
     A Lady's Name
1919 Puppy Love
Gereghty, Frank L. *same as* **Gereghty, Frank**
1914 Cardinal Richelieu's Ward
1915 The Patriot and the Spy
1916 Silas Marner
1920 The Leopard Woman
     $30,000
Gerhardt, George *see* **Gebhardt, George**
Germaine, Mary
1914 Wildflower
Germonprez, Valerie
1919 Blind Husbands
     The Heart of Humanity
Gernon, George
1917 The Poor Little Rich Girl
Gerold, Herman
1919 The Great Victory, Wilson or the Kaiser? The Fall of the Hohenzollerns
Gerrard, Carl *see* **Gerard, Carl**
Gerrard, Charles *see* **Gerard, Charles**
Gerrard, Douglas
1914 The Merchant of Venice
     Shannon of the Sixth
1915 The Commanding Officer
     The High Hand
1916 Bettina Loved a Soldier
     The Dumb Girl of Portici
     The Evil Women Do
     Naked Hearts
     A Soul Enslaved
     Undine
1917 Conscience
     Eternal Love
     Polly Put the Kettle On
1918 The Cabaret Girl
     The Empty Cab
     $5,000 Reward
     Madame Spy
     A Mother's Secret
     Playthings
     The Velvet Hand
1919 His Divorced Wife
     The Sealed Envelope
1920 The Forged Bride
     The Phantom Melody

Gerry, Charles
1918 The Wasp
Gerstad, Harry *same as* **Gerstad, Harry W.; Gersted, Harry**
1914 The Spoilers
1915 The Rosary
1916 Little Mary Sunshine
     The Man from Bitter Roots
     The Ne'er-Do-Well
1917 Aladdin and the Wonderful Lamp
     The Babes in the Woods
     Jack and the Beanstalk
1918 The Danger Zone
     Salome
     The She-Devil
     Treasure Island
     Under the Yoke
1919 Gambling in Souls
     The Prince and Betty
1920 A Broadway Cowboy
     The Parish Priest
     Women Men Love
Gerstedt, Merritt
1920 The Poor Simp
Gerstle, Edward
1918 Lest We Forget
Gesell, Henry *see* **Sell, Henry G.**
Gest, Morris
1915 Blackbirds
     Carmen (Jesse L. Lasky Feature Play Co.)
Gettinger, Billy *same as* **Gettinger, Bill; Gettinger, William**
1916 A Knight of the Range
1917 Bucking Broadway
     The Fighting Gringo
     Her Own People
     A Marked Man
     The Secret Man
1918 The Phantom Riders
1920 The Misfit Wife
     The Stranger
Gheller, Edward *same as* **Gailer, Eddie; Gheller, Eddie**
1916 The Moment Before
     The World's Great Snare
1917 The Sudden Gentleman
     Wild Sumac
1918 The Craving
1919 Bonds of Love
     The Fear Woman
     The Loves of Letty
     One Week of Life
     The Peace of Roaring River
     The Woman on the Index
1920 The Paliser Case
Ghent, Derrick
1920 Silk Hosiery
Gibbons, Cedric
1919 The Unwritten Code
1920 Earthbound
Gibbons, Rose
1914 Samson
Gibbs, George
1916 The Madcap
Gibbs, Harrington
1915 The Rug Maker's Daughter
Gibbs, Leah
1917 The Climber
     Mentioned in Confidence
     Zollenstein
Gibbs, Robert Paton *same as* **Gibbs, R. Paton; Gibbs, R. Payton; Gibbs, Robert Patton; Gibbs, Robert Payton**
1914 The Jungle
1916 Robinson Crusoe
1917 The Beloved Adventuress
     Her Silent Sacrifice
1918 Conquered Hearts
     The Fall of the Romanoffs
1919 Lure of Ambition
     The Man Who Stayed at Home
1920 Even As Eve
Gibbs, Walter
1913 Robin Hood
Giblyn, Charles
1914 The Voice at the Telephone
1916 Civilization's Child
     Honor Thy Name
     Not My Sister
     Peggy

     The Phantom
     Somewhere in France
     The Sorrows of Love
     The Vagabond Prince
1917 The Honeymoon
     The Price She Paid
     Scandal
1918 Just for Tonight
     The Lesson
     Let's Get a Divorce
     Peck's Bad Girl
     A Perfect 36
     The Studio Girl
     Sunshine Nan
1919 The Spite Bride
     Upstairs and Down
1920 Black Is White
     The Dark Mirror
     The Thief
     The Tiger's Cub
Gibson, Charles
1917 Greed
Gibson, Florence
1919 A Sage Brush Hamlet
Gibson, Helen
1917 Fighting Mad
1919 Loot
Gibson, Hoot *same as* **Gibson, Ed**
1915 Buckshot John*
1916 A Knight of the Range
1917 The Secret Man
     Straight Shooting
1918 Headin' South
Gibson, James *could be same as* **Gibson, James E.**
1915 Old Heidelberg
Gibson, James E. *could be same as* **Gibson, James**
1920 Deep Waters
Gibson, Lorell
1916 The Question
Gibson, Margaret *same as* **Gibson, Marguerite**
1915 The Coward
1916 The Bait
     The Heart of Tara
     The Hidden Law
     The Leopard's Bride
     A Soul Enslaved
     The Soul's Cycle
1917 The Island of Desire
Gibson, Tom
1917 The Midnight Man
1920 Wolves of the Street
Gibson, W. H.
1919 The Volcano
Gibson, Wiley J.
1916 The Fall of a Nation*
Gibson-Gowland, T. H. *see* **Gowland, Gibson**
Giegerich, Charles J., Jr.
1916 The Redemption of Dave Darcey
Giesman, Henry
1918 Vengeance
Giesy, J. U. *same as* **Geisy, J. U.**
1916 The Matrimaniac
1918 The Cabaret
1920 Pink Tights
Giffen, C. M.
1915 The Cowpuncher
1918 The Sunset Princess
Gifford, Ada
1914 A Florida Enchantment
Gilbert, Dent
1916 The Dupe
     Public Opinion
     The Storm
     The Victory of Conscience
     Witchcraft
1917 Betty to the Rescue
     The Black Wolf
     Castles for Two
     The Inner Shrine
     Sacrifice
     Unconquered
Gilbert, Ella
1917 A Bit O' Heaven
Gilbert, Florence
1920 Down Home

Glaser, Lulu
1915 How Molly Malone Made
Good
1916 Love's Pilgrimage to America
Glass, Gaston
1919 Let's Elope
The Lost Battalion
Oh, You Women
Open Your Eyes
The Woman of Lies
1920 The Branded Woman
Humoresque
Mothers of Men
The World and His Wife
Glassmire, Albert
1919 Smiles
Glassner, Izzie
1919 The Egg Crate Wallop
Glaum, Louise
1915 The Cup of Life
The Darkening Trail
The Forbidden Adventure
The Iron Strain
Matrimony
The Reward
The Toast of Death
1916 The Aryan
D'Artagnan
Hell's Hinges
Home
Honor Thy Name
The Return of Draw Egan
Somewhere in France
The Wolf Woman
1917 Golden Rule Kate
Idolators
Love or Justice
A Strange Transgressor
Sweetheart of the Doomed
The Weaker Sex
1918 An Alien Enemy
The Goddess of Lost Lake
A Law unto Herself
Shackled
Staking His Life
Wedlock
1919 The Lone Wolf's Daughter
Sahara
1920 Greater Than Love
The Leopard Woman
Love
Love Madness
Sex
Glavey, John J. same as **Glavey, John C.**
1920 Chains of Evidence
High Speed
The Veiled Marriage
Gleason, Adda same as **Gleason, Ada**
1915 The Rosary
Saved from the Harem
The Voice in the Fog
1916 Ramona
1917 Fanatics
Shackles of Truth
Snap Judgement
The Spirit of '76
1918 The One Woman
That Devil, Bateese
True Blue
1919 The Thunderbolt
Gleason, Joe see **Gleason, Joseph**
Gleason, John J.
1914 The Giants-White Sox Tour
Gleason, Joseph same as **Gleason, Joe**
1916 The Big Sister
Miss George Washington
1918 The Beloved Impostor
1919 Fortune's Child
Miss Dulcie from Dixie
Gleason, Mina
1919 The Price Woman Pays
Glendinning, Ernest
1915 The Seventh Noon
Glendon, J. Frank same as **Glendon, Frank**
1915 Her Reckoning
1916 Her American Prince
The House of Mirrors
The Price of Malice
The Salamander
1917 The Defeat of the City
The Duplicity of Hargraves
Light in Darkness
A Night in New Arabia

The Renaissance at Charleroi
Wrath of Love
1918 By the World Forgot
The Changing Woman
The Dawn of Understanding
The Wooing of Princess Pat
1919 The Enchanted Barn
The Wishing Ring Man
1920 For the Soul of Rafael
The Forgotten Woman
Mid-Channel
Roman Candles
Glenn, Claire
1916 Boots and Saddles
Glennon, Bert (cam) same as **Glennon, Bert L.**
1916 Ramona
1917 The Eyes of the World
1918 The Family Skeleton
1920 The Kentucky Colonel
Glennon, Herbert (actor)
1914 The Patchwork Girl of Oz
Glennon, Ione
1917 Jack and the Beanstalk
Glenwood, Emma
1915 A Black Sheep
The House of a Thousand
Candles
Glickman, Ellis F.
1915 The Last Concert
Glover, Gertrude
1916 The Chaperon
The Discard
The Phantom Buccaneer
Glynn, Arthur
1918 Cheating the Public
Gobbett, D. W. same as **Gobbett, David**
1914 The Master Cracksman
1917 Madame Sherry
Godfrey, Rae
1918 Irish Eyes
Marked Cards
The Mask
Tony America
Godowsky, Dagmar
1919 Bonds of Honor
1920 The Forged Bride
Hitchin' Posts
Honor Bound
The Marriage Pit
The Path She Chose
The Peddler of Lies
Goebel, O. E. same as **Goebel, Otto E.**
1918 The Transgressor
1919 The Burning Question
The Eternal Light
1920 Luring Shadows
The Victim
Goethals, Stanley
1920 Outside the Law
Goethe, Mrs.
1915 The Fairy and the Waif*
Goethe, J.
1915 The Fairy and the Waif*
Goetz, Ben
1917 The Inevitable
Goetzl, Dr. Anselm
1919 Deliverance
Goff, John
1917 The Frame Up
Goldberg, Alfred
1920 Humoresque
Goldburg, Jesse J.
1915 The Curious Conduct of Judge
Legarde
Life Without Soul
1918 Huns Within Our Gates
1919 The Profiteer
Golden, Ella
1916 The Love Liar
Golden, Joseph A. same as **Golden, Joseph**
1913 The Count of Monte Cristo
1914 Hearts and Flowers
1915 The Better Woman
Divorced
Fine Feathers
The Master of the House
Not Guilty
The Price
The Senator

1916 Behind Closed Doors
The Libertine
The Prima Donna's Husband
1917 The Law of Compensation
Redemption
Golden, Mignonne
1920 Hearts Up
Golden, Olive Fuller same as **Carey, Olive; Golden, Olive**
1914 Tess of the Storm Country
1915 The Frame-Up
Just Jim
1916 A Knight of the Range
Love's Lariat
Golden, Ruth Fuller same as **Golden, Ruth**
1919 Cupid Forecloses
Over the Garden Wall
1920 Blue Streak McCoy
Human Stuff
Pegeen
Goldin, Sidney M. same as **Golden, Sidney M.**
1912 The Adventures of Lieutenant
Petrosino*
1914 Escaped from Siberia
Uriel Acosta
1915 Hear Ye, Israel
The Jewish Crown
The Last of the Mafia
The Period of the Jew
Goldman, Mayer C.
1917 The Public Defender
Goldsmith, Frank
1915 The Clemenceau Case
The Two Orphans
1916 As in a Looking Glass
Blazing Love
Fate's Boomerang
The Velvet Paw
1917 Love's Law
Man's Woman
The New York Peacock
The Page Mystery
Reputation
The Rise of Jennie Cushing
Vera, the Medium
1918 The Debt of Honor
The Divine Sacrifice
A Heart's Revenge
Oh, Johnny!
Other Men's Daughters
1919 Wanted—A Husband
Woman, Woman!
1920 A Fool and His Money
Goldstein, Robert
1917 The Spirit of '76
Goldsworthy, John same as **Goldsworthy, J. H.; Goldsworthy, John H.; Goldworthy, J. H.**
1915 After Dark
The Bigger Man
A Yellow Streak
1916 A Corner in Cotton
Her Debt of Honor
1917 Thou Shalt Not Steal
Wife Number Two
1919 The Career of Katherine Bush
The Divorcee
Life's Greatest Problem
1920 Even As Eve
The Sporting Duchess
Goldwyn, Samuel
1918 Go West, Young Man
1919 The Bondage of Barbara
The City of Comrades
Daughter of Mine
Day Dreams
The Eternal Magdalene
The Fear Woman
The Girl from Outside
Jinx
Leave It to Susan
The Loves of Letty
A Man and His Money
One of the Finest
One Week of Life
The Pest
Shadows
Spotlight Sadie
Strictly Confidential
The Stronger Vow
Through the Wrong Door
Toby's Bow

When Doctors Disagree
The Woman on the Index
The World and Its Woman
1920 The Branding Iron
The Cup of Fury
Dangerous Days
A Double Dyed Deceiver
Going Some
The Great Accident
Jes' Call Me Jim
The Little Shepherd of
Kingdom Come
Milestones
The North Wind's Malice
Out of the Storm
The Paliser Case
Partners of the Night
The Penalty
Pinto
The Silver Horde
Stop Thief!
The Strange Boarder
The Truth
Gollan, Campbell see **Gullan, Campbell**
Goltz, Capt. Horst von der
1918 The Prussian Cur
Gomez, Inez
1916 Ramona
1920 Hell's Oasis
Gomp, Mr.
1912 Richard III
Gondolfi, Alfredo see **Gandolfi, Alfred E.**
Gonzales, Lillian
1915 Secretary of Frivolous Affairs
Gonzalez, Myrtle
1914 Captain Alvarez
1915 The Chalice of Courage
1916 The End of the Rainbow
The Girl of the Lost Lake
It Happened in Honolulu
A Romance of Billy Goat Hill
The Secret of the Swamp
1917 God's Crucible
The Greater Law
Mutiny
The Show Down
Southern Justice
Good, Frank same as **Good, F. B.; Good, Frank B.**
1915 The Birth of a Nation*
1916 The Children in the House
Going Straight
Let Katie Do It
1917 Jack and the Beanstalk
1918 The Fallen Angel
Fan Fan
Lawless Love
Treasure Island
1919 A Girl in Bohemia
The Love That Dares
The Merry-Go-Round
Rose of the West
The Web of Chance
When Fate Decides
1920 The Cyclone
Desert Love
Prairie Trails
The Terror
The Texan
Three Gold Coins
The Untamed
Goodall, Grace
1914 Fantasma
Goodall, Richard
1916 Vultures of Society
1920 The Trail of the Cigarette
Goodboy, Joe
1915 The Iron Strain
1916 The Bugle Call
The Dawn Maker
The Patriot
Goode, Lizzie
1915 Seven Sisters
Goodell, Walter J.
1920 The Blue Moon
The Gamesters
Gooden, Arthur H. same as **Gooden, Arthur Henry**
1916 A Dream or Two Ago
The Highest Bid
The Innocence of Lizette
The Torch Bearer

1918 The Ghost of the Rancho
1920 Below the Deadline
Goodfriend, Pliny
1917 The Divorcee
1920 Old Dad
The Woman in His House
Goodleigh, Ernee
1920 A Lady in Love
Goodman, Daniel Carson
1913 Sapho
1914 The Battle of the Sexes
The Escape*
Imar the Servitor
1915 Heartaches
1916 The Gods of Fate
Her Bleeding Heart
Love's Toll
Souls in Bondage
Those Who Toil
1918 Irish Eyes
1919 The Mayor of Filbert
A Regular Fellow
1920 Thoughtless Women
The Wonder Man
Goodman, Henrietta
1913 The Port of Doom
1914 A Lady of Quality
Goodman, Jack
1917 Draft 258
1918 Jack Spurlock, Prodigal
Goodman, Jules Eckert
1916 Anton the Terrible
Goodman, Kenneth S.
1916 Cousin Jim
Goodman, Ludloe
1915 'Twas Ever Thus
Goodman, Robert
1914 The Murders in the Rue
Morgue
Goodnow, Judge Charles N.
1918 And the Children Pay
Goodrich, Charles
1916 The Awakening of Helena
Richie
Goodrich, Dorothy
1915 Old Dutch*
Goodrich, Edna
1915 Armstrong's Wife
1916 The House of Lies
The Making of Maddalena
1917 American Maid
Daughter of Maryland
Her Second Husband
Queen X
Reputation
1918 Her Husband's Honor
Treason
Who Loved Him Best?
Goodrich, Katherine
1916 The Diamond Runners
Goodstadt, Mitzi
1919 The Parisian Tigress
Goodstadt, Nini
1914 The Dollar Mark
Goodwin, Gloria
1918 Her Great Chance
Woman
Goodwin, Harold
1917 The Sawdust Ring
The Silent Man
1918 Set Free
A Society Sensation
1919 Heart O' the Hills
Puppy Love
The Winning Girl
1920 The Family Honor
Overland Red
Suds
Sweet Lavender
You Never Can Tell
Goodwin, Nat C.
1912 Oliver Twist
1915 Business Is Business
The Master Hand
1916 The Marriage Bond
Wall Street Tragedy
Goodwins, Fred
1916 The Leopard's Bride
The Love Liar
1917 Down to Earth
1918 Amarilly of Clothes-Line Alley
For Husbands Only

Hitting the High Spots
Mr. Fix-It
Mrs. Leffingwell's Boots
The Testing of Mildred Vane
The Way of a Man with a
Maid
1919 Common Clay
Forbidden
Goose, Elizabeth Foster
1917 Polly Put the Kettle On*
Gordon, Mrs.
1915 When We Were Twenty-One
1916 Ramona
Gordon, Alice
1915 Marrying Money
1916 The Wall Between
1918 Brown of Harvard
1920 The Common Sin
Gordon, Bruce
1920 Forbidden Valley
The House of the Tolling Bell
Gordon, Carl
1916 The Rainbow Princess
Gordon, Charles
1920 Bonnie May
A Connecticut Yankee at King
Arthur's Court
Gordon, Dorothy
1920 The Chorus Girl's Romance
The Price of Silence
Gordon, Lady Duff
1916 The Misleading Lady
1918 The Reason Why
Gordon, Edward
1916 The Leopard's Bride
Gordon, Eva
1918 Under Suspicion
1919 The Black Circle
1920 Bachelor Apartments
Chains of Evidence
She Loves and Lies
The White Moll
Gordon, Frances
1916 The Scarlet Woman
Gordon, George A.
1920 The Mysteries of Paris
Gordon, Gerald
1916 The Redemption of Dave
Darcey
Gordon, Gilbert could be same as
Gordon, Robert
1918 The Hired Man
Gordon, Grace
1917 Mrs. Balfame
1920 Lone Hand Wilson
Gordon, Gwendoline
1919 Injustice
Gordon, Harris
1914 The Million Dollar Robbery
1915 God's Witness
Milestones of Life
The Mill on the Floss
The Price of Her Silence
1916 The Five Faults of Flo
Her Father's Gold
The Oval Diamond
1917 Double Crossed
The Honeymoon
The Image Maker
Vera, the Medium
When Love Was Blind
1918 Beyond the Law
The Prodigal Wife
Why America Will Win
1919 Suspense
1920 Stop Thief!
Gordon, Huntley
1916 The Conflict
The Destroyers
His Wife's Good Name
1918 The Beloved Impostor
The Eleventh Commandment
Men
The Million Dollar Dollies
Our Mrs. McChesney
1919 Atonement
The Common Cause
The Glorious Lady
The Invisible Bond
Out Yonder
Too Many Crooks
The Unknown Quantity

1920 The Dark Mirror
The Frisky Mrs. Johnson
Out of the Snows
Red Foam
Gordon, Jack
1914 At the Cross Roads
Gordon, James same as Gordon, Jim
1913 Caprice
Hoodman Blind
The Stranglers of Paris
Tess of the D'Urbervilles
1914 The Mystery of the Poison Pool
The Next in Command
1919 Behind the Door
Experimental Marriage
The Final Close-Up
Jacques of the Silver North
The Thunderbolt
When Doctors Disagree
1920 The Blue Moon
Excuse My Dust
Homespun Folks
The Last of the Mohicans
Mary's Ankle
The Sea Wolf
Gordon, Julia Swayne
1914 A Million Bid
1915 The Battle Cry of Peace
The Juggernaut
The Sins of the Mothers
1916 The Daring of Diana
The Enemy
The Island of Surprise
My Lady's Slipper
The Suspect
1917 Arsene Lupin
Clover's Rebellion
The Hawk
Her Right to Live
In the Balance
The Maelstrom
The Message of the Mouse
Soldiers of Chance
A Son of the Hills
The Soul Master
1918 The Desired Woman
Love Watches
Over the Top
The Soap Girl
1919 The Bramble Bush
The Captain's Captain
The Girl Problem
The Girl-Woman
Miss Dulcie from Dixie
The Moonshine Trail
The Painted World
Shadows of the Past
A Stitch in Time
Two Women
1920 A Child for Sale
For Love or Money
Greater Than Fame
Heliotrope
Lifting Shadows
Gordon, Kilbourn
1917 The Debt
Gordon, Kitty
1916 As in a Looking Glass
The Crucial Test
Her Maternal Right
1917 The Beloved Adventuress
Diamonds and Pearls
Forget-Me-Not
Her Hour
National Red Cross Pageant*
Vera, the Medium
The Volunteer
1918 The Divine Sacrifice
The Interloper
Merely Players
The Purple Lily
Stolen Orders
Tinsel
The Wasp
1919 Adele
Mandarin's Gold
Playthings of Passion
The Scar
The Unveiling Hand
Gordon, Lawrence
1914 La Belle Russe

Gordon, Leo
1916 Then I'll Come Back to You
1917 Pardners
The Royal Pauper
Gordon, Maude Turner same as **Gordon, Maud Turner**
1914 The Idler
1916 Miss George Washington
1917 Her Better Self
The Honeymoon
1918 The Danger Mark
Just for Tonight
The Lie
Mrs. Dane's Defense
The Ordeal of Rosetta
The Service Star
The Turn of the Wheel
1919 Bringing Up Betty
The Divorcee
Home Wanted
The Oakdale Affair
1920 Away Goes Prudence
Civilian Clothes
Gordon, Paul
1915 The Flash of an Emerald
1916 The Pretenders
Vanity
The Woman in the Case
1917 The Great White Trail
Gordon, Richard
1920 The Truth About Husbands
Gordon, Robert could be same as
Gordon, Gilbert
1917 The Little American
Tom Sawyer
The Varmint
1918 Blue Blazes Rawden
The Hired Man*
Huck and Tom; Or, The
Further Adventures of Tom
Sawyer
The Kaiser, the Beast of Berlin
Missing
A Pair of Silk Stockings
1919 Captain Kidd, Jr.
Dawn
The Moonshine Trail
A Yankee Princess
1920 The Blood Barrier
Dollars and the Woman
My Husband's Other Wife
Respectable by Proxy
The Vice of Fools
Gordon, Russell
1920 The Night Riders
Gordon, Sadie
1920 Old Lady 31
Gordon, Vera
1920 The Greatest Love
Humoresque
The North Wind's Malice
Gordon, Walter
1920 Sophy of Kravonia; Or, The
Virgin of Paris
Gordon, Warren
1920 Woman's Man
Gore, Rosa same as Gore, Rose
1915 Keep Moving
1916 The Final Curtain
1920 La La Lucille
Once to Every Woman
Pink Tights
Gorey, Lou
1918 A Pair of Cupids
1919 His Father's Wife
Gorgas, Alice
1920 The Brute
Gorman, Charles
1915 The Gambler of the West
1916 Children of the Feud
Let Katie Do It
A Sister of Six
1918 The Bride of Fear
Confession
The Girl with the Champagne
Eyes
Treasure Island
Gorman, Em same as Gorman, Baby;
Gorman, Baby Em; Gorman, Emmie
1914 Hearts of Oak
1916 Little Miss Nobody
The Soul of a Child

1918 The Secret Trap
1920 The Little Outcast
Gorman, Jack *same as* **Gorman, John**
1915 An American Gentleman
1916 Little Miss Nobody
     The Soul of a Child
1917 Corruption
Gorman, James J.
1915 Wildfire
Gorman, John *see* **Gorman, Jack**
Gormely, Miss
1914 The House of Bondage
Gosden, Alfred *same as* **Gosden, A. G.;**
    Gosden, Alfred G.
1916 Don Quixote
     Mr. Goode, the Samaritan
     Sunshine Dad
     The Wharf Rat
1917 Jim Bludso
     Might and the Man
     Princess Virtue
     Time Locks and Diamonds
1918 Beauty in Chains
     The Brazen Beauty
     The City of Tears
     Face Value
     A Mother's Secret
     New Love for Old
     Old Hartwell's Cub
     Set Free
1919 The Exquisite Thief
     The Game's Up
     Pretty Smooth
     The Spitfire of Seville
     The Trembling Hour
     The Wicked Darling
     The Woman Under Cover
1920 The Breath of the Gods
     Burnt Wings
     Everything but the Truth
     Fixed by George
     The Girl in the Rain
     La La Lucille
     Once a Plumber
Gotch, J. H.
1917 Wooden Shoes
Gotthold, Charles *same as* **Gotthold,**
    Charles F.
1916 The Blindness of Love
     The Challenge
     Fate's Boomerang
1917 The Secret of the Storm
     Country
1920 Bitter Fruit
Gottschalk, Ferdinand *(actor)*
1917 Please Help Emily
1918 My Wife
Gottschalk, Louis F. *(composer, co-dir)*
same as **Gottschalk, L. F.;**
    Gottschalk, Louis
1914 The Patchwork Girl of Oz
1916 Honor's Altar
1917 The Curse of Eve
1918 The Great Love
1919 Broken Blossoms
     The Mother and the Law
     The Shepherd of the Hills
1920 A Splendid Hazard
Gough, John
1916 A Dream or Two Ago
     Dulcie's Adventure
     Faith
     Soul Mates
1917 The Calendar Girl
     Melissa of the Hills
     Sands of Sacrifice
     The Upper Crust
1918 Ann's Finish
     Hearts or Diamonds?
     Wives and Other Wives
1919 The Amazing Impostor
     A Fugitive from Matrimony
     Six Feet Four
     Some Liar
1920 Half a Chance
     Risky Business
Gould, Bobby
1914 The Patchwork Girl of Oz
Gould, D. H.
1916 The City of Illusion

Gould, Milton S.
1914 Should a Woman Divorce?
Gould, Mitzi
1918 Captain of His Soul
Gould, Rita
1915 A Black Sheep
Gould, Walter *same as* **Gould, Walter J.**
1915 Forbidden Fruit
1917 Enlighten Thy Daughter
     One Law for Both
Goulding, Edmund
1916 Little Lady Eileen*
1917 The Silent Partner
1918 The Ordeal of Rosetta
1919 The Glorious Lady
     The Imp
     The Perfect Lover
     A Regular Girl
     Sealed Hearts
1920 The Dangerous Paradise
     A Daughter of Two Worlds
     Madonnas and Men
     The Sin That Was His
Gow, Lee
1917 The War of the Tongs
Gowland, Gibson *same as* **Gibson-**
    Gowland, T. H.; Gowland, G. H.;
    Gowland, T. H.; Gowland, T. H.
    Gibson; *could be same as* **Gowland,**
    T. W.
1917 The Climber
     Molly Entangled
     The Phantom Shotgun
     The Promise
     The Secret of Black Mountain
     Under Handicap
1918 Breakers Ahead
1919 Behind the Door
     Blind Husbands
1920 The Fighting Shepherdess
     The Right of Way
Gowland, T. W. *could be same as*
    Gowland, Gibson
1915 Jewel
Goyette, Frank
1918 Parentage
Grace-Boon, Margaret
1919 Injustice
Grady, Al
1915 All for a Girl
Grady, Henry
1915 Right off the Bat
Grafton, Edward L.
1916 The Argonauts of
     California—1849
Graham, Ben
1915 The Better Woman
     The Senator
1917 The Lone Wolf
1918 Empty Pockets
Graham, Charles *same as* **Graham,**
    Charles E.
1913 Arizona
     Checkers
1914 The $5,000,000 Counterfeiting
     Plot
     The Seats of the Mighty
1915 An American Gentleman
     The Curious Conduct of Judge
     Legarde
     A Modern Magdalen
     One Million Dollars
     The Unbroken Road
1916 The Bondman
     Driftwood
     Feathertop
     The Fortunate Youth
     The Human Orchid
1917 The Auction Block
     The Tides of Fate
1918 The Birth of a Race
     His Daughter Pays
     My Own United States
1920 The Song of the Soul
     The Valley of Night
     The Wall Street Mystery
     Why Tell?
Graham, Clara
1917 For Liberty
Graham, Dorothy
1917 The Ghost of Old Morro
     The Princess' Necklace

Graham, Fred
1916 The Wood Nymph
1917 The Silent Witness
Graham, Mildred Carl
1918 A Bit of Jade
Graham, Robert *same as* **Graham, R.**
    E.; Graham, Robert, Jr.; Graham,
    Robert E., Jr.
1913 The Battle of Shiloh
     The Third Degree
1914 The Great Diamond Robbery
     The Wolf
Gramlich, Charles
1920 When Quackel Did Hide
Gran, Albert
1915 The Fight
1916 Caprice of the Mountains
     Out of the Drifts
     Where Love Leads
1918 American Buds
1920 Civilian Clothes
Granby, Joseph
1916 Jealousy
     The Man from Nowhere
     Temptation and the Man
1917 The Accomplice
     The Awakening
     Rasputin, the Black Monk
1918 Peck's Bad Girl
1919 The Great Romance
     The Imp
1920 Black Is White
     Chains of Evidence
Grandin, Elmer
1919 Getting Mary Married
Grandin, Ethel
1913 Traffic in Souls
Grandon, Francis J. *same as* **Grandon,**
    F. J.; Grandon, Francis
1915 Strathmore
1916 The Adventures of Kathlyn
     Cross Currents
     The Lure of Heart's Desire
     The Narrow Path
     Playing with Fire
     The Soul Market
1917 The Dummy
     Glory
     Heart's Desire
     The Little Boy Scout
1918 Conquered Hearts
     The Daredevil
     Love's Law
     Wild Honey
1919 The Lamb and the Lion
     Modern Husbands
1920 Miss Nobody
Grange, Maud *(scen)* *same as* **Grange,**
    Maude
1916 The Eagle's Wing
     The Measure of a Man
1917 The Bronze Bride
     Even As You and I
     John Ermine of the
     Yellowstone
Granger, Maude *(actress)* *same as*
    Granger, Maud
1915 The Runaway Wife
     The White Pearl
     Zaza
Granger, Willis
1916 The Heart of New York
Grant, Carew
1918 The Impostor
Grant, Corinne
1915 The Adventures of a Madcap
     Beulah
1918 The Lady of the Dugout
     The Law That Divides
     Whatever the Cost
Grant, Edwin J.
1918 The Panther Woman
Grant, Frances Miller *same as* **Grant,**
    Frances; Grant, Frances M.
1918 The Beloved Impostor
     The Mating
1919 Come Out of the Kitchen
1920 Bab's Candidate
     In Walked Mary
Grant, Harry *(cam)*
1917 The Man from Montana

Grant, Henry *(actor)*
1914 The School for Scandal
1917 Panthea*
Grant, Lawrence
1915 The Eternal City
1918 To Hell with the Kaiser
1920 The Chorus Girl's Romance
     Held in Trust
     Someone in the House
Grant, Marie
1919 Out of the Fog
Grant, Nellie
1915 Children of Eve
     The Magic Skin
     Shadows from the Past
1916 The Innocence of Ruth
     Just a Song at Twilight
1917 Aladdin's Other Lamp
     Builders of Castles
     Chris and His Wonderful
     Lamp
     Lady Barnacle
     The Last Sentence
     The Royal Pauper
     The Tell-Tale Step
     Threads of Fate
Grant, S. *(dir)*
1917 How Uncle Sam Prepares
Grant, Sydney *(actor)*
1915 Jane
Grant, Valentine
1915 The Melting Pot
1916 The Daughter of MacGregor
     The Innocent Lie
1918 The Belgian
Granville, Charlotte
1917 The Antics of Ann
     The Red Woman
     A Square Deal
1918 The Floor Below
     The Girl and the Judge
     The Impostor
1919 A Damsel in Distress
Granville, Fred Le Roy *same as*
    Granville, Fred; Granville, Fred L.;
    Granville, Le Roy
1914 Rescue of the Stefansson Arctic
     Expedition
1916 The Beast
     Undine
1917 Man and Beast
     Money Madness
1918 The Bride's Awakening
     Her Body in Bond
     The Mortgaged Wife
     The Talk of the Town
1919 The Coming of the Law
     The Divorce Trap
     The Heart of Humanity
     Loot
     Rough Riding Romance
     The Speed Maniac
1920 Once to Every Woman
     The Price of Silence
Granville, V. L.
1917 Outcast
Grassby, Bertram *same as* **Grasby, Bert;**
    Grasby, Bertram
1915 The Circular Staircase
1916 The Gay Lord Waring
     The Girl of the Lost Lake
     It Happened in Honolulu
     Langdon's Legacy
     The Pool of Flame
     A Son of the Immortals
     The Whirlpool of Destiny
     A Youth of Fortune
1917 American Methods
     Conscience
     Even As You and I
     For Liberty
     Her Temptation
     The Mysterious Mrs. M.
     The Scarlet Pimpernel
     The Soul of Satan
     To Honor and Obey
1918 Battling Jane
     The Blindness of Divorce
     Cheating the Public
     The Devil's Wheel
     The Hope Chest
     The Moral Law
     Salome

Greenleaf, Charles L.
1920 The Inner Voice
     The Way Women Love
Greenleaf, Charles L.
1916 The Little Girl Next Door
Greenwood, Barnett
1916 Ambition
Greenwood, Charlotte
1915 Jane
Greenwood, Claire
1919 Pretty Smooth
Greenwood, Herbert
1920 The White Dove
Greenwood, Reeva
1914 The Price He Paid
1918 The Embarrassment of Riches
Greenwood, Winifred *same as*
     Greenwood, Winnifred
1916 Dust
     The Inner Struggle
     Lying Lips
     Reclamation
     The Voice of Love
     A Woman's Daring
1917 The Alien Blood
     The Crystal Gazer
     The Inspirations of Harry
       Larrabee
     Lorelei of the Sea
1918 Believe Me Xantippe
     Danger Within
     The Deciding Kiss
     The Goat
     M'liss
     Too Many Millions
1919 An Adventure in Hearts
     Come Again Smith
     The Lottery Man
     Maggie Pepper
     Men, Women and Money
     Putting It Over
1920 Are All Men Alike?
     The Life of the Party
     Sick Abed
     Young Mrs. Winthrop
Greeson, Elsie
1917 The Curse of Eve
Gregg, Arnold
1920 The Broken Gate
     Love's Protegé
     White Youth
Gregory, Anne
1917 Under False Colors
Gregory, Carl Louis *same as* **Gregory,**
     Carl L.
1914 Thirty Leagues Under The Sea
1915 An Enemy to Society
     The Patriot and the Spy
     The Woman Pays
1918 Queen of the Sea
1920 Love's Flame
Gregory, Edna
1920 Up in Mary's Attic
Gregory, Jackson
1917 The Man from Painted Post
Gregory, Mildred
1913 The Battle of Shiloh
1915 Bondwomen
     The Climbers
     The Valley of Lost Hope
1916 According to Law
     Common Sense Brackett
     The Lords of High Decision
Gregory, Zoe
1914 Under the Gaslight
1916 The Perils of Divorce
Greiner, Samuel
1917 Cy Whittaker's Ward
Grenier, George *same as* **Grenier,**
     George G.
1916 Fighting Blood
     The Man from Bitter Roots
1917 The Conquerer
     The Honor System
Grenville, Claire *same as* **Grenville,**
     Clare
1919 The Great Romance
     The Right to Lie
Gresham, Edith
1920 39 East

Greuze, Lillian
1917 The Recoil
Grey, Albert L.
1920 Romance
Grey, Alice
1915 Vanity Fair
Grey, Betty *see* **Gray, Betty**
Grey, Doris
1917 Her Beloved Enemy
     The Streets of Illusion
Grey, Sir Edward
1918 Hearts of the World*
Grey, Hetty
1915 Buckshot John
Grey, Jack *see* **Grey, John W.**
Grey, Jane
1914 The Little Gray Lady
1915 The Flaming Sword
     The Right of Way
1916 The Flower of Faith
     Let Katie Do It
     Man and His Angel
     The Test
     The Waifs
1917 Her Fighting Chance
1918 The Birth of a Race
     The Guilty Wife
1919 When My Ship Comes In
Grey, John W. *(scen, actor) same as*
     Grey, Jack; *could be same as* **Gray,**
     John *(actor)*
1917 The Little Patriot
     Sunshine Alley
1918 Daddy's Girl
     Kidder and Ko
1919 The Grim Game
1920 Terror Island
Grey, Lionel
1917 The Fettered Woman
Grey, Margaret
1917 The Greater Woman
Grey, Mary *could be same as* **Gray,**
     Mary
1918 Parentage
Grey, Olga *same as* **Gray, Olga**
1915 The Absentee
     Double Trouble
     The Failure
1916 Intolerance
     The Little Liar
     Macbeth
     Pillars of Society
     The Wild Girl of the Sierras
1917 Fanatics
     The Ghost House
     The Girl at Home
     Jim Bludso
     Love's Law
     The Woman God Forgot
1919 The Mayor of Filbert
     Modern Husbands
     Trixie from Broadway
     When a Man Rides Alone
Grey, Phyllis *same as* **Gray, Phyllis**
1914 The Strange Story of Sylvia
       Gray
     The Tangle
1915 Her Atonement
Grey, R. Henry *(born in Oakland, CA)*
     same as **Gray, R. Henry; Grey,**
     Robert; *not the same as* **Gray,**
     Robert *(born in Houlton, ME)*
1916 Boots and Saddles
     The Girl Who Doesn't Know
     The Matrimonial Martyr
     Shadows and Sunshine
     Spellbound
     The Sultana
     The Twin Triangle
1917 Bab the Fixer
     Brand's Daughter
     The Checkmate
     Feet of Clay
     Mentioned in Confidence
     The Phantom Shotgun
     Twin Kiddies
     Zollenstein*
1918 No Children Wanted
     Petticoats and Politics
1919 All of a Sudden Norma

Grey, Richard
1915 The Chorus Lady
Grey, Robert *see* **Grey, R. Henry**
Grey, Syd de *see* **De Grey, Sidney**
Grey, Miss Yaha
1915 The Spendthrift*
Grey, Zane
1917 The Heart of Texas Ryan*
Gribbon, Eddie
1920 Love, Honor and Behave
     Married Life
Gribbon, Harry
1920 Down on the Farm
     Up in Mary's Attic
Griffen, C. A.
1920 His Pajama Girl
Griffith, Mrs.
1918 Face Value
     The Talk of the Town
1919 A Rogue's Romance
Griffin, Alex
1920 Our Christianity and Nobody's
       Child
Griffin, C. Elliott
1915 The Girl from His Town
Griffin, Frank C.
1916 Where Love Leads
Griffin, Gerald
1916 Feathertop
     The Sunbeam
1917 Lady Barnacle
1918 A Pair of Cupids
Griffin, Ted
1916 Gold and the Woman
Griffin, Walter L. *same as* **Griffin, W.;**
     Griffin, Walter
1917 The Spotted Lily
1918 The Girl of My Dreams
     Inside the Lines
     The Man of Bronze
1919 The Boomerang
     The Long Arm of Mannister
     The Long Lane's Turning
     Modern Husbands
1920 The Confession
     Nomads of the North
     Parted Curtains
Griffin, William
1919 The Lamb and the Lion
Griffith *(full name unknown)*
1916 The Code of Marcia Gray*
Griffith, Beverly
1918 Cheating the Public
Griffith, Cecelia
1916 His Great Triumph
Griffith, Clark
1917 The Baseball Revue of 1917*
Griffith, Corinne
1916 The Last Man
     Through the Wall
1917 I Will Repay
     The Love Doctor
     The Stolen Treaty
     Transgression
     Who Goes There!
1918 The Clutch of Circumstance
     The Girl of Today
     Love Watches
     The Menace
     Miss Ambition
1919 The Adventure Shop
     The Bramble Bush
     The Climbers
     A Girl at Bay
     The Girl Problem
     Thin Ice
     The Unknown Quantity
1919-20
     The Tower of Jewels
1920 Bab's Candidate
     The Broadway Bubble
     Deadline at Eleven
     The Garter Girl
     Human Collateral
     The Whisper Market
Griffith, D. W. *same as* **Griffith, David**
     W.; Griffith, David Wark; Marier,
     Captain Victor; Tolignac, M.
     Gaston de; Warwick, Granville
1914 The Avenging Conscience
     The Battle of the Sexes
     The Dishonored Medal

     The Escape
     The Floor Above
     The Gangsters
     The Great Leap; Until Death
       Do Us Part
     Home, Sweet Home
     Judith of Bethulia
     The Life of General Villa
1915 The Birth of a Nation
     Double Trouble
     Enoch Arden
     Ghosts
     Jordan Is a Hard Road
     The Lamb
     The Lily and the Rose
     The Martyrs of the Alamo
     Old Heidelberg
     The Penitentes
     The Sable Lorcha
1916 Betty of Graystone
     Cross Currents
     Daphne and the Pirate
     Diane of the Follies
     Don Quixote
     The Flying Torpedo
     Hoodoo Ann
     An Innocent Magdalene
     Intolerance
     Let Katie Do It
     Little Meena's Romance
     Macbeth
     The Marriage of Molly-O
     The Missing Links
     The Wood Nymph
1918 Battling Jane*
     The Great Love
     The Greatest Thing in Life
     Hearts of the World
     The Hun Within
1919 Broken Blossoms
     The Fall of Babylon
     The Girl Who Stayed Home
     The Greatest Question
     I'll Get Him Yet*
     The Mother and the Law
     Nugget Nell*
     A Romance of Happy Valley
     Scarlet Days
     True Heart Susie
1920 The Idol Dancer
     The Love Flower
     Way Down East
Griffith, Edward H. *same as* **Griffith, E.**
     H.; Griffith, Edward
1917 The Awakening of Ruth
     Billy and the Big Stick
     The Last Sentence
     The Law of the North
     One Touch of Nature
1919 The Betrayal*
     The End of the Road
     Fit to Win
1920 Bab's Candidate
     The Garter Girl
     The Vice of Fools
19-- Barnaby Lee
Griffith, Gordon
1915 Kilmeny
     Little Sunset
1916 Ben Blair
     The Code of Marcia Gray*
     Gloriana
     If My Country Should Call
     Naked Hearts
1917 The Price of Silence
1918 Hitting the High Spots
     The Romance of Tarzan
     Tarzan of the Apes
1919 Cupid Forecloses
     The Solitary Sin
     Under the Top
1920 Huckleberry Finn
     The Kentucky Colonel
     That Something
     To Please One Woman
Griffith, H. L. *could be same as*
     Griffith, Harry *or* **Griffith, Henry**
1914 Tess of the Storm Country
Griffith, Harry *could be same as*
     Griffith, H. L. *or* **Griffith, Henry**
1916 The Beckoning Trail
     Kinkaid, Gambler
     Shoes
1917 Mothers of Men

Hackett, Mrs. James K.
1919 Should a Husband Forgive?
Hackett, Jeanette
1915 The Great Ruby
Hackett, Lillian
1920 Once a Plumber
Hackett, Norman
1917 The Crimson Dove
Hackett, Raymond
1915 The Ringtailed Rhinoceros
1919 Ginger
1922 The Cynic Effect
Hackett, William A.
1918 The Spreading Evil
Haddock, William F. *same as* **Haddock, William**
1914 The Banker's Daughter
Paid in Full
Soldiers of Fortune
1915 A Trade Secret
1916 As a Woman Sows
I Accuse
1917 The Girl Who Didn't Think
Hadfield, Harry *could be same as* **Hatfield, Harry**
1915 Chimmie Fadden Out West
Hadley, A. C.
1918 Revelation
Hadley, Arthur Twining
1917 The Courage of the Common Place
Hadley, Bert
1915 The Cowboy and the Lady
The Fox Woman
The Heart of Maryland
Little Pal
1916 Casey at the Bat
A Child of the Paris Streets
1917 Nina, the Flower Girl
An Old Fashioned Young Man
The Scarlet Pimpernel
1918 Her Moment
Madam Who
A Petticoat Pilot
1919 The House of Intrigue
1920 The Beggar Prince
Down Home
Three Gold Coins
Hadley, Hopp
1914 His Majesty, the Scarecrow of Oz*
1918 The Lost Chord
Hadley, Raymond C.
1918 Broadway Bill
Hadley, Thomas
1919 Please Get Married
Hagan, Dorothy *same as* **Hagar, Dorothy; Hagar, Dot; Haggar, Dorothy**
1918 Hell's End
His Enemy, the Law
Mlle. Paulette
Old Hartwell's Cub
The Painted Lily
Wild Life
1919 The Westerners
Who Cares?
The Wishing Ring Man
1920 The Forged Bride
One Hour Before Dawn
Haganey, Frank *see* **Hagney, Frank**
Hagar, Dorothy *see* **Hagan, Dorothy**
Hage, Robert
1917 The Golden God
Haggar, Dorothy *see* **Hagan, Dorothy**
Haggin, Ben Ali
1917 National Red Cross Pageant*
Haggin, Mrs. Ben Ali
1917 National Red Cross Pageant
Hagin, John
1920 Honeymoon Ranch
Hagney, Frank *same as* **Haganey, Frank**
1919 The Battler
1920 The Gauntlet
Hagy, Eugene H.
1914 The Flooding and Opening of the Panama Canal
Hahn, Louis
1918 Dolly Does Her Bit

Hahn, Philip
1914 The Nightingale
The Price He Paid
1915 The Bachelor's Romance
The Garden of Lies
The Senator
Wormwood
1916 The Clarion
Playing with Fire
The Scarlet Oath
The Woman's Law
1917 The Dancer's Peril
Haidez, Sara
1917 The Greater Woman
Haig, Field Marshal Douglas
1918 Lafayette, We Come!*
Under Four Flags
Haight, Dorothy
1920 The Girl with the Jazz Heart
Haily, Bert
1920 Reformation
Haine, Horace *same as* **Hain, Horace; Haine, Horace J.**
1915 The Coquette
1917 A Hungry Heart
Kidnapped
1919 The Woman of Lies
1920 The Truth
Haines, Marie *see* **Haynes, Marie**
Haines, Rhea *same as* **Haynes, Rhea**
1914 Burning Daylight: The Adventures of "Burning Daylight" in Alaska
The Country Mouse
John Barleycorn*
Martin Eden
An Odyssey of the North
The Pursuit of the Phantom
The Valley of the Moon
1915 The Beachcomber
Buckshot John
Little Sunset
1916 The Chalice of Sorrow
1917 Hands Up!
The Man from Painted Post
Nina, the Flower Girl
1919 Scarlet Days
Turning the Tables
1920 Always Audacious
Girls Don't Gamble
Mary Ellen Comes to Town
A Master Stroke
Smiling All the Way
Haines, Robert T.
1916 The Heart of New York
1919 The Capitol
1920 The Victim
Haiselden, Dr. Harry J.
1917 The Black Stork
Haisman, Irene
1915 Niobe
Hakeem, William
1918 Beauty in Chains
Halbert, Burton
1920 La La Lucille
Haldorn, Francis
1920 The Copperhead
Hale, Alan *(actor)*
1913 The Prisoner of Zenda*
1914 The Power of the Press
The Woman in Black
1915 Dora Thorne
1916 The Love Thief
Pudd'nhead Wilson
The Purple Lady
Rolling Stones
The Scarlet Oath
The Woman in the Case
1917 The Eternal Temptress
Life's Whirlpool
One Hour
The Price She Paid
1918 Moral Suicide
1920 The Barbarian
Hale, Albert W. *(prod)*
1913 The Prisoner of Zenda
Hale, Allene *(actress)*
1919 The Love Hunger
Hale, Creighton
1914 The Taint
The Three of Us
1915 A Fool There Was
The Old Homestead

1916 Charity
Hazel Kirke
Snow White
1918 Annexing Bill
For Sale
His Bonded Wife
Mrs. Slacker
Waifs
The Woman the Germans Shot
1919 The Black Circle
A Damsel in Distress
The Great Victory, Wilson or the Kaiser? The Fall of the Hohenzollerns
The Love Cheat
Oh, Boy!
The Thirteenth Chair
1920 A Child for Sale
The Idol Dancer
Way Down East
Hale, Ethelbert
1915 The Garden of Lies
Hale, J. S.
1914 The Dollar Mark
Hale, Richard
1916 Caprice of the Mountains
Hale, Walter
1913 The Prisoner of Zenda
1914 The Lightning Conductor
Hale, William
1919 The Greatest Question
Haley, Merton
1914 The Tangle
Hall, Al *see* **Hall, Alex**
Hall, Albert *(actor)*
1918 The Struggle Everlasting
Hall, Albert J. *(writer)*
1920 The Heart of a Woman
Hall, Alex *(actor) same as* **Hall, Al; Hall, Alexander**
1917 The Deemster
Miss U.S.A.
1918 Doing Their Bit
Hall, Ben
1918 Empty Pockets
The Fall of the Romanoffs
Hall, Lieut. Bert
1918 A Romance of the Air
Hall, Danny
1920 The Midlanders
Smiling All the Way
Hall, Donald
1914 The Christian
A Million Bid
Mr. Barnes of New York
The Win(k)some Widow
1915 Hearts and the Highway
Mortmain
Playing Dead
1916 Hesper of the Mountains
The Law Decides
Mrs. Dane's Danger
Salvation Joan
The Sex Lure
1917 Alias Mrs. Jessop
The Awakening of Ruth
The Moth
The On-the-Square-Girl
The Raggedy Queen
1918 The Face in the Dark
The Great Adventure
1919 The Broken Melody
The Chosen Path
Fruits of Passion
Love and the Woman
Water Lily
The Wreck
1920 The Great Shadow
The Greatest Love
In the Shadow of the Dome
A Woman's Business
Hall, Ella
1914 The Spy
1915 Heritage
Jewel
The Silent Command
1916 The Bugler of Algiers
The Crippled Hand
Little Eve Edgarton
The Love Girl
Secret Love
1917 The Charmer
Her Soul's Inspiration

A Jewel in Pawn
The Little Orphan
My Little Boy
National Association's All-Star Picture
Polly Redhead
The Spotted Lily
1918 Beauty in Chains
The Heart of Rachael
A Mother's Secret
New Love for Old
Which Woman?
1919 Under the Top
Hall, Emmett Campbell
1913 The Battle of Shiloh
1916 Human Driftwood
The Madness of Helen
1917 Polly of the Circus
Hall, Frank G. *(dist)*
1917 The Bar Sinister*
1919 A Dangerous Affair
A House Divided
The Other Man's Wife
When My Ship Comes In
Hall, Franklyn *(actor) same as* **Hall, Franklin**
1913 Tess of the D'Urbervilles
1916 The Adventures of Kathlyn
Where Are My Children?
1917 A Branded Soul
1918 Code of the Yukon
The Moral Law*
1919 The Boomerang
The Long Arm of Mannister
1920 The Confession
Parted Curtains
Hall, George E. *same as* **Edwardes-Hall, George; Hall, George; Hall, George Edward; Hall, George Edwardes; Hall, George Edwards**
1915 Tainted Money
1916 The Iron Hand
Under Two Flags
1917 Babbling Tongues
The Eternal Sin
The Lone Wolf
1918 Empty Pockets
The Fall of the Romanoffs
The Unchastened Woman
1919 Atonement
Reclaimed: The Struggle for a Soul Between Love and Hate
1919-20
When a Man Loves
1920 The Luck of Geraldine Laird
Hall, Helen
1914 The Crucible
Hall, Howard
1916 According to Law
The Clarion
The Crown Prince's Double
The Human Orchid
1917 Alias Mrs. Jessop
The Barrier
The Hungry Heart
The Natural Law
Weavers of Life
1918 Flower of the Dusk
Mrs. Dane's Defense
Treason
1919 The Echo of Youth
The Gold Cure
The Price of Innocence
Hall, Iris
1919 The Homesteader
1920 The Symbol of the Unconquered
Hall, J. Albert *same as* **Hall, J. A.; Hall, James**
1914 The Eagle's Mate
1915 Children of the Ghetto
The Eternal City
The Girl I Left Behind Me
Gretna Green
Mistress Nell
When It Strikes Home
1916 The Big Sister
The Eternal Grind
The Ransom
The Salamander
1918 The Wooing of Princess Pat
1920 Love's Flame

Hamilton, Laura
1915 The Apaches of Paris
Hamilton, Lloyd
1920 The Mischief Man
Occasionally Yours
Hamilton, Louise
1917 Souls Triumphant
1918 The Impostor
Hamilton, Mahlon
1914 Three Weeks
1915 The Final Judgment
1916 The Black Butterfly
The Eternal Question
Extravagance
Molly Make-Believe
1917 Bridges Burned
Exile
The Law of the Land
More Truth Than Poetry
The Red Woman
The Silence Sellers
The Soul of a Magdalen
To the Death
The Undying Flame
The Waiting Soul
1918 The Danger Mark
The Death Dance
The Sins of the Children
1919 Adele
Daddy-Long-Legs
Her Kingdom of Dreams
In Old Kentucky
Playthings of Passion
1920 The Deadlier Sex
Earthbound
Half a Chance
The Third Generation
Hamilton, May
1920 The Mysteries of Paris
Hamilton, Reed *same as* **Hamilton, Reid**
1918 The Forbidden City
Love's Law
When Men Betray
Hamilton, Shorty
1914 Shorty Escapes Marriage
1915 On the Night Stage
1918 Denny from Ireland
The Pen Vulture
The Prisoner of War
The Ranger
The Snail
1919 When Arizona Won
Hamilton, Vincent C.
1920 Peaceful Valley
Hamlin, Charles
1916 The Unborn
Hamm, Harry *see* **Ham, Harry**
Hammer, Ben
1918 Six Shooter Andy
Hammer, Ina
1915 The House of Fear
1916 King Lear
Hammerstein, Elaine
1915 The Moonstone
1917 The Argyle Case
The Co-Respondent
The Mad Lover
1918 The Accidental Honeymoon
Her Man
Wanted for Murder
1919 The Country Cousin
1920 The Daughter Pays
Greater Than Fame
Pleasure Seekers
The Point of View
The Shadow of Rosalie Byrnes
Whispers
The Woman Game
Hammerstein, Reginald
1919 The Imp
Hammerstein, Stella
1915 Anna Karenina
1918 Social Hypocrites
Hammett, Melville
1920 The Wonderful Chance
Hammond, C. Norman *same as*
Hammond, C. N.; Hammond, C.
Norton
1915 The Gentleman from Indiana
1916 The Black Sheep of the Family
The Evil Women Do
The Grasp of Greed
It Happened in Honolulu

The Place Beyond the Winds
The Way of the World
What Love Can Do
Where Are My Children?
1918 Restitution
Wolves of the Rail
1920 The Midlanders
Hammond, Charles
1914 Manon Lescaut
1916 Hop, the Devil's Brew
1918 An Alien Enemy
1919 You Never Know Your Luck
Hammond, Gilmore
1916 The Black Sheep of the Family
Bobbie of the Ballet
The Gilded Spider
The Mark of Cain
Hammond, Kathleen
1914 Without Hope
Hammond, Lynn
1919 Little Women
Hammond, Virginia
1916 The Discard
The Kiss
Vultures of Society
1919 The Battler
The Crook of Dreams
The Hand Invisible
Miss Crusoe
The World to Live In
1920 A Manhattan Knight
Hammons, E. W.
1920 The Key to Power
Hampden, Burford
1916 Sherlock Holmes
Hampden, Charles
1917 Outcast
Hampden, Walter
1917 The Warfare of the Flesh
Hamper, Genevieve
1915 The Blindness of Devotion
The Unfaithful Wife
1916 The Green-Eyed Monster
The Spider and the Fly
A Wife's Sacrifice
1917 Tangled Lives
Hampton, Benjamin B.
1917 The Barrier
1919 Desert Gold
The Westerners
1920 The Dwelling Place of Light
The Money-Changers
Riders of the Dawn
The Sagebrusher
The U.P. Trail
Hampton, Eloise
1919 Water Lily
Hampton, Grace
1916 The Pursuing Vengeance
Hampton, Hope
1920 A Modern Salome
Hampton, Jesse D.
1918 Prisoners of the Pines
Three X Gordon
1919 Bare-Fisted Gallagher
The Best Man
The Blue Bandanna
Come Again Smith
Dangerous Waters
The Drifters
The End of the Game
For a Woman's Honor
A Fugitive from Matrimony
The Man Who Turned White
The Mints of Hell
The Pagan God
The Prince and Betty
The Prodigal Liar
A Sage Brush Hamlet
What Every Woman Wants
Whitewashed Walls
A Woman of Pleasure
1920 A Broadway Cowboy
Dice of Destiny
Felix O'Day
Fighting Cressy
The Girl in the Web
Haunting Shadows
Help Wanted—Male
Her Unwilling Husband
Their Mutual Child
Uncharted Channels

Hamrick, Burwell *same as* **Hamerick,**
Burwell; Hemerick, Burwell
1917 The Devil-Stone
John Ermine of the
Yellowstone
The Little Pirate
1918 How Could You, Jean?
A Law unto Herself
1919 The Brute Breaker
Under Suspicion
1920 Seeds of Vengeance
Shore Acres
Smoldering Embers
Hanaway, Joseph *could be same as*
Henaway, Joe
1920 The Dead Line
Hancock, Elinor *same as* **Hancock,**
Eleanor
1917 The Fair Barbarian
A Kiss for Susie
Master of His Home
The Spirit of Romance
1918 A Desert Wooing
Love Me
Mirandy Smiles
A Petticoat Pilot
1919 The Better Wife*
Cheating Cheaters
Little Comrade
A Midnight Romance
The Splendid Sin
1920 The Barbarian
The Cup of Fury
Out of the Storm
Rookie's Return
The Tattlers
A Tokio Siren
Hancock, Mrs. H. R.
1918 Mr. Fix-It
Hand, Frederick
1915 The Millionaire Baby
Handforth, Maude
1918 Little Red Decides
Handforth, Ruth
1916 Going Straight
Intolerance
The Little Liar
1917 The Fair Barbarian
1918 The Atom
The Wild Strain
1919 The Siren's Song
1920 A Slave of Vanity
Handschiegl, Max
1916 Joan the Woman*
Handworth, Harry
1914 The Path Forbidden
The Toll of Mammon
When Fate Leads Trump
1915 In the Shadow
1916 Artie, the Millionaire Kid
The Question
Handworth, Octavia
1914 The Path Forbidden
The Toll of Mammon
When Fate Leads Trump
1915 The Great Ruby
In the Shadow
1916 The City of Failing Light
Race Suicide
Handyside, Clarence *same as*
Handysides, Clarence; Handysides,
J. Clarence
1914 The Jungle
One of Our Girls
1916 His Picture in the Papers
Mice and Men
Saints and Sinners
The Saleslady
Silks and Satins
The Woman in the Case
1917 Double Crossed
1918 From Two to Six
The Rose of the World
The Turn of the Wheel
A Woman of Impulse
Hanford, Ray *same as* **Hanford,**
Raymond
1916 The Beckoning Trail
Behind the Lines
Her Bitter Cup
The Silent Battle
1917 The Price of Silence
1918 Desert Law
Hell's Crater

Hanford, Ruth
1917 The Calendar Girl
Hanft, Jules
1919 One-Thing-at-a-Time O'Day
Hankin, Lieut.
1919 Injustice
Hanks, Frederick O.
1917 The Bar Sinister
Hanley, Marguerite
1915 Flame of Passion
Hanley, William J.
1914 La Belle Russe
Hanlon, Alma
1915 The Fixer
Keep Moving
The Politicians
1916 The Devil's Prayer-Book
The Faded Flower
The Final Curtain
Gold and the Woman
The Libertine
The Weakness of Man
Wild Oats
1917 God of Little Children
The Golden God
The Great Bradley Mystery
The Law That Failed
The Mystic Hour
Pride and the Devil
The Public Defender
When You and I Were Young
The Whip
1918 The Sins of the Children
1919 The Profiteer
Hanlon, Dan
1916 The Great Problem
The River of Romance
20,000 Leagues Under the Sea
Hanlon, George, Jr.
1914 Fantasma
Hanlon, Michael J.
1919 Home Wanted
Hann, Harry *could be same as* **Ham,**
Harry
1915 The Penitentes*
Hanna, Franklyn *same as* **Hanna,**
Frank; Hanna, Franklin; Hannah,
Frank
1915 Black Fear
1916 My Lady Incog.
The Scarlet Woman
The Upheaval
1917 The Cloud
Kidnapped
The Message of the Mouse
One Hour
Richard, the Brazen
Who's Your Neighbor?
1918 Doing Their Bit
Just Sylvia
Under Suspicion
1919 The American Way
The Belle of New York
Break the News to Mother*
The Gold Cure
The Great Romance
1920 Democracy
The Fortune Teller
The Web of Deceit
Hannafy, M. E.
1914 Il Trovatore
Hannah, Frank *see* **Hanna, Franklyn**
Hannan, Patricia
1919 Lombardi, Ltd.
Hanneford, John
1917 Her Father's Keeper
Hannon, Peggy
1920 The Return of Tarzan
Hanoki
1914 The Wrath of the Gods
Hansell, Howell *same as* **Hansel, Howell**
1913 Ben Bolt
1915 Colonel Carter of Cartersville
Tillie's Tomato Surprise
1917 The Deemster
The Long Trail
1918 The Million Dollar Mystery
Hansen, Grace
1919 Bringing Up Betty

Hansen, Juanita *same as* **Hanson, Wahneta; Hanson, Wahnetta**
1914 The Patchwork Girl of Oz
1915 The Absentee
    Betty in Search of a Thrill
    The Failure
    The Love Route
    The Martyrs of the Alamo
1916 The Mediator
1917 Glory
1918 Broadway Love
    Fast Company
    The Mating of Marcella
    The Risky Road
    The Rough Lover
    The Sea Flower
1919 Breezy Jim
    Devil McCare
    Lombardi, Ltd.
    A Midnight Romance
    The Poppy Girl's Husband
    Rough Riding Romance
1920 The Jungle Princess

Hansen, Philip *same as* **Hansen, M. Philip**
1917 Lorelei of the Sea
    The Planter*

Hansen, Speed
1919 The Valley of the Giants

Hanshaw, Dale
1916 The Flower of Faith
    The Spell of the Yukon
1918 The Grain of Dust

Hanson, Blanche
1916 The Innocence of Lizette
    The Valley of Decision

Hanson, Gladys
1914 The Straight Road
1915 The Climbers
    The Primrose Path
1916 The Evangelist
    The Havoc
1917 National Red Cross Pageant

Hanson, Wahneta *see* **Hansen, Juanita**

Haragan, J. D.
1917 The Law of the Land

Harbaugh, Carl
1915 Carmen (Fox Film Corp.)
    Regeneration
1916 Arms and the Woman
    Big Jim Garrity
    The Iron Woman
    The Serpent
    The Test
1917 All for a Husband
    The Broadway Sport
    The Derelict
    A Rich Man's Plaything
    The Scarlet Letter
    When False Tongues Speak
1918 Brave and Bold
    Jack Spurlock, Prodigal
    Marriages Are Made
    Other Men's Daughters
1919 The Other Man's Wife
1920 The North Wind's Malice

Harbon, John W.
1918 The Prussian Cur

Harcourt, Miss
1915 A Continental Girl

Harcourt, George
1915 A Continental Girl

Harcourt, W. *could be same as* **Harcourt, William**
1919 Out of the Shadow

Harcourt, William *could be same as* **Harcourt, W.**
1920 It Might Happen to You

Harde, Harry D.
1919 The A.B.C. of Love
    Go Get 'Em Garringer
    The Twin Pawns
1920 A Modern Salome

Hardenberg, Count von *see* **Von Hardenburg, Count**

Hardenburg, Fritz von *could be same as* **Von Hardenberg, Count**
1918 Inside the Lines

Harder, Emil
1916 What the World Should Know*

Hardin, Neil *same as* **Hardin, Neal**
1917 Sunshine and Gold
    The Understudy
    The Yellow Bullet
1918 Angel Child
    Little Miss Grown-Up
    The Midnight Burglar
    No Children Wanted
1919 Johnny-on-the-Spot
    Modern Husbands
1920 The Dangerous Talent
    The Girl in the Rain

Harding, Lorraine
1919 The Bandbox

Hards, Ira M.
1920 The Rich Slave

Hardy, Frank
1914 The Great Diamond Robbery
    Manon Lescaut

Hardy, Sam B. *same as* **Hardy, Sam; Hardy, Sam T.; Hardy, Samuel B.**
1915 Judy Forgot
    Over Night
1917 At First Sight
1919 His Father's Wife
    A Woman's Experience

Hare, Lumsden *same as* **Hare, F. Lumsden; Hare, Francis Lumsden**
1916 Arms and the Woman
    As in a Looking Glass
    Love's Crucible
    The Test
1917 Barbary Sheep
    Envy
    National Red Cross Pageant
1918 The Light Within
1919 The Avalanche
    The Country Cousin
1920 The Blue Pearl
    Children Not Wanted
    The Frisky Mrs. Johnson
    Mothers of Men
    Thoughtless Women

Harford, Harry
1915 The Battle of Ballots

Hargan, D. T.
1914 The Indian Wars

Harigan, Pat *see* **Hartigan, P. C.**

Harkins, W. S.
1920 The Plunger

Harkness, Carter B. *same as* **Harkness, Carter**
1916 Gold and the Woman
1917 Cy Whittaker's Ward
1918 The Birth of a Race

Harkness, Frank
1919 The Great Victory, Wilson or the Kaiser? The Fall of the Hohenzollerns

Harlam, Macey *same as* **Harlam, Macy; Harlan, Macey; Harlan, Macy; Harlon, Macy**
1915 The Eternal City
1916 Betty of Graystone
    The Habit of Happiness
    Manhattan Madness
    Nanette of the Wilds
    The Perils of Divorce
    The Romantic Journey
    The Witch
1917 Barbary Sheep
1918 Money Mad
1919 L'Apache
    False Gods
    Flame of the Desert
    Toby's Bow
1920 The Right to Love
    The Woman and the Puppet

Harlan, Miss
1914 At the Cross Roads

Harlan, Kenneth
1917 Betsy's Burglar
    Cheerful Givers
    The Flame of the Yukon
    The Lash of Power
    The Price of a Good Time
1918 Bread
    Her Body in Bond
    The Law That Divides
    A Man's Man
    The Marriage Lie
    Midnight Madness
    The Model's Confession

    My Unmarried Wife
    The Wife He Bought
    The Wine Girl
1919 The Hoodlum
    The Microbe
    The Trembling Hour
1920 Dangerous Business
    Dollars and Sense
    Going Some
    Love, Honor and Obey
    The Penalty
    The Turning Point

Harlan, Macey *see* **Harlam, Macey**

Harlan, Otis
1915 A Black Sheep
1920 The Romance Promoters

Harlan, Rita
1918 Angel Child
1919 The Way of the Strong

Harland, Eva
1920 The Mysteries of Paris

Harley, Edwin *same as* **Harley, Ed**
1915 Blackbirds
    The Girl of the Golden West
    Jack Chanty
1916 Martha's Vindication
    Susan Rocks the Boat
1918 Treasure Island

Harlon, Macy *see* **Harlam, Macey**

Harman, Henry *see* **Harmon, Henry**

Harmon, Denver
1919 The Beloved Cheater

Harmon, Henry *same as* **Harman, Henry**
1919 Out of the Fog
1920 Love, Honor and Obey
    Old Lady 31
    The Right of Way
    Stronger Than Death

Harnman, Pat
1920 Firebrand Trevison

Harolds, Ralph
1920 Headin' Home

Harper, Mrs. Florence Ann
1916 War As It Really Is

Harrigan, William
1915 An Affair of Three Nations

Harriman, W. H.
1915 The Last Concert

Harrington, A.
1916 The Rail Rider

Harrington, Fred
1917 Mutiny

Harris, Adele
1917 As Men Love
    The Happiness of Three Women
    The Spirit of Romance

Harris, Caroline
1915 Madame Butterfly
    Wormwood
1916 The Eternal Sapho
    Gold and the Woman
    The Honor of Mary Blake
    The Ragged Princess
1917 The Boy Girl
    One of Many
1918 The Gulf Between

Harris, Charles K.
1915 Always in the Way
    Hearts of Men
    The Raven
    When It Strikes Home
1916 Should a Baby Die?
1917 The Barker

Harris, Clarence J. *same as* **Harris, Rev. Clarence J.**
1915 Barbara Frietchie
1916 Caprice of the Mountains
    Daredevil Kate
    Little Miss Happiness
1917 Little Miss Fortune
    The Little Samaritan

Harris, E. *(painter)*
1919 Virtuous Men*

Harris, E. W. *(actor)*
1916 A Law unto Himself

Harris, Elmer *(scen)*
1915 Help Wanted
    The Wild Olive
1919 An Adventure in Hearts
    It Pays to Advertise

    The Lottery Man
    The Love That Dares
    Why Smith Left Home
1920 Jack Straw
    Miss Hobbs
    Mrs. Temple's Telegram
    The Sins of St. Anthony
    The Six Best Cellars
    What Happened to Jones

Harris, Frank W.
1917 The Public Defender

Harris, George
1916 The Wasted Years

Harris, H. B. *see* **Harris, Harry B.**

Harris, Harry *(actor, boxer)*
1918 Sporting Life

Harris, Harry B. *(cam, dir) same as* **Harris, H. B.; Harris, Harry; Harris, Harry V.**
1915 Captain Macklin
    Her Shattered Idol
    The Outcast
1916 Through the Wall
    Vanity
1917 Daughter of Destiny
    Maternity
    More Truth Than Poetry
    Raffles, the Amateur Cracksman
    The Silence Sellers
    The Soul of a Magdalen
    To the Death
1918 Her Boy
    Hugon, the Mighty
    The Life Mask
    Tempered Steel
1919 The Light of Victory
    The Mints of Hell
    The Right to Happiness
    Whitewashed Walls
1920 In Folly's Trail
    The Mother of His Children
    Risky Business
    The Rose of Nome
    A Sister to Salome
    White Lies

Harris, Harry V. *see* **Harris, Harry B.**

Harris, Helen
19-- Sic-Em

Harris, J. *see* **Harris, Joe**

Harris, James
1915 Children of Eve
    Ranson's Folly
1916 The Catspaw
    When Love Is King
1917 The Barker
    Rosie O'Grady

Harris, Joe *same as* **Harris, J.; Harris, Joel; Harris, Joseph**
1915 The Girl from His Town
1916 The Dragon
    The Pearl of Paradise
1917 The Devil's Assistant
    The Girl Who Couldn't Grow Up
1918 Hell Bent
    Humdrum Brown
    Three Mounted Men
1919 The Ace of the Saddle
    Bare Fists
    A Fight for Love
    A Gun Fightin' Gentleman
    Marked Men
    The Outcasts of Poker Flats
    The Rider of the Law
    Riders of Vengeance
1920 Bullet Proof
    Hitchin' Posts
    Human Stuff
    Overland Red
    Sundown Slim
    West Is West
    The White Rider

Harris, Katherine
1916 The Lost Bridegroom
    Nearly a King

Harris, Mrs. L. C.
1918 A Mother's Secret
1919 The Thunderbolt

Harris, Lena *could be same as* **Harris, Leonore**
1917 The Stainless Barrier

Harris, Leonore same as **Harris, Lenore**; could be same as **Harris, Lena**
1916 Betty of Graystone
     The Decoy
     Friday the Thirteenth
     Human Driftwood
1917 The Iron Heart
     To-Day

Harris, Louise
1917 The Trouble Buster

Harris, Lucretia
1917 A Kentucky Cinderella
1918 Captain of His Soul
     The Last Rebel
1919 Creaking Stairs
     The Feud
     The Intrusion of Isabel

Harris, M. A.
1915 The Voice in the Fog
1916 The Clown
     The Ragamuffin
     The Sowers

Harris, Marcia
1916 The Foundling
     Susie Snowflake
1917 Every Girl's Dream
     Great Expectations
     The Little Boy Scout
     The Poor Little Rich Girl
1918 Madame Jealousy
     Marriage
     Prunella
     A Romance of the Underworld
1919 Anne of Green Gables
     The Bishop's Emeralds
     Day Dreams
     Kathleen Mavourneen
     Putting One Over
1920 The Flapper
     The Right to Love

Harris, Martin
1916 Common Ground

Harris, Mildred same as **Chaplin, Mrs. Charlie; Chaplin, Mildred Harris**
1914 His Majesty, the Scarecrow of Oz
     The Magic Cloak of Oz
     The Patchwork Girl of Oz
1915 The Absentee
     The Warrens of Virginia
1916 Hoodoo Ann
     Intolerance
     The Old Folks at Home
1917 The Bad Boy
     The Cold Deck
     Golden Rule Kate
     A Love Sublime
     The Price of a Good Time
     Time Locks and Diamonds
1918 Borrowed Clothes
     Cupid by Proxy
     The Doctor and the Woman
     For Husbands Only
1919 The Fall of Babylon
     Forbidden
     Home
     When a Girl Loves
1920 The Inferior Sex
     Old Dad
     Polly of the Storm Country
     The Woman in His House
1921 Habit

Harris, Mitchell
1920 The Web of Deceit

Harris, Sadie
1914 The Day of Days

Harris, Sherry same as **Harris, Sherrie**
1920 The Best of Luck
     Old Lady 31

Harris, Theodosia
1915 The House of a Thousand Scandals
1916 The Heart of Tara
     The Hidden Law
     The Leopard's Bride
     The Soul's Cycle

Harris, Virginia
1920 The Spenders

Harris, W. see **Harris, Wadsworth**

Harris, W. B. (cam)
1917 Mary Lawson's Secret

Harris, Wadsworth (actor) same as **Harris, W.**
1915 The Scarlet Sin
     Tainted Money
1916 The Dumb Girl of Portici
     The Love Girl
     Love Never Dies
     The Right to Be Happy
1917 The Gift Girl
     The Hero of the Hour
1918 All Night
     The Kaiser, the Beast of Berlin
     Kidder and Ko
     Madame Spy
1919 Loot
     The Midnight Stage
1920 The Iron Rider

Harris, Winifred same as **Harris, Winnifred**
1916 The Crucial Test
     The Iron Hand
1917 The Co-Respondent
     The Dazzling Miss Davison
     Panthea
1918 The Crucible of Life
1920 A Daughter of Two Worlds

Harrison, Bertram
1914 The $5,000,000 Counterfeiting Plot

Harrison, C. Sanford
1918 The Vigilantes

Harrison, Ida
1920 The Place of Honeymoons

Harrison, Irma
1919 The Red Viper
1920 The Fighting Kentuckians

Harrison, James
1917 The Bad Boy
     Madame Bo-Peep
     Should She Obey?

Harrison, Kay
1920 Under Northern Lights

Harrison, Louis Reeves
1914 The Greyhound
     Paid in Full
     The Price He Paid
     Shore Acres
1915 The Garden of Lies
     The Rights of Man: A Story of War's Red Blotch
1917 The Law That Failed
1920 Love's Flame

Harrison, Mark
1914 A Suspicious Wife

Harrison, Saul
1916 The Cossack Whip
1917 The Customary Two Weeks
     Salt of the Earth

Harrison, Stanley
1915 The Stubbornness of Geraldine

Harrison, W. F.
1915 The Beachcomber

Harrison, William
1918 The Prussian Cur

Harron, Mrs.
1918 Hearts of the World

Harron, Jessie
1918 Hearts of the World

Harron, Johnny
1918 Hearts of the World

Harron, Mary
1918 Hearts of the World

Harron, Robert
1914 The Avenging Conscience
     The Battle of the Sexes
     The Escape
     The Great Leap; Until Death Do Us Part
     Home, Sweet Home
     Judith of Bethulia
1915 The Birth of a Nation
     Her Shattered Idol
     The Outcast
     The Outlaw's Revenge
1916 A Child of the Paris Streets
     Hoodoo Ann
     Intolerance
     The Little Liar
     The Marriage of Molly-O
     The Missing Links
     The Wharf Rat

     The Wild Girl of the Sierras
1917 The Bad Boy
     An Old Fashioned Young Man
     Sunshine Alley
1918 The Great Love
     The Greatest Thing in Life
     Hearts of the World
1919 The Girl Who Stayed Home
     The Greatest Question
     The Mother and the Law
     A Romance of Happy Valley
     True Heart Susie

Harrower, John Booth
1920 The Family Honor

Harsell, Norman
1920 The Hidden Code

Hart, Albert same as **Hart, Al; Hart, Albert S.**
1915 The Siren's Song
     Sunday
1916 Human Driftwood
     Tangled Fates
1917 The Brand of Satan
     The Page Mystery
     The Secret of the Storm Country
     The Slave Market
1918 The Beautiful Mrs. Reynolds
     The Cross Bearer
     The Grouch
     The Heart of a Girl*
     Joan of the Woods
     The Man Hunt
     The Power and the Glory
     The Road to France
     A Woman of Redemption
1919 The Challenge of Chance
     The Little Intruder
     Miss Crusoe
     The Oakdale Affair
     The Quickening Flame
     The Rough Neck
1920 The Dead Line
     Why Women Sin

Hart, Betty see **Harte, Betty**

Hart, Charles S.
1918 Our Bridge of Ships
     Pershing's Crusaders*

Hart, Florence
1920 The Prince Chap
     A Tokio Siren

Hart, Gypsy see **Harte, Gypsy**

Hart, L. O.
1916 The Bondman

Hart, Lallah
1919 Men, Women and Money

Hart, Lew could be same as **Hart, Louis V.**
1917 The Stolen Paradise
1918 The Unbeliever

Hart, Louis V. could be same as **Hart, Lew**
1915 A Soldier's Oath

Hart, Neal
1916 Love's Lariat
1917 The Man from Montana
1918 Smashing Through
1919 When the Desert Smiles
1920 Hell's Oasis
     The Lumber Jack
     Skyfire

Hart, William S.
1914 The Bargain
1915 The Darkening Trail
     The Disciple
     On the Night Stage
1916 The Apostle of Vengeance
     The Aryan
     Between Men
     The Captive God
     The Dawn Maker
     The Devil's Double
     Hell's Hinges
     The Patriot
     The Primal Lure
     The Return of Draw Egan
1917 The Cold Deck
     The Desert Man
     The Gun Fighter
     The Narrow Trail
     The Silent Man
     The Square Deal Man
     Truthful Tulliver

     Wolf Lowry
1918 Blue Blazes Rawden
     The Border Wireless
     Branding Broadway
     A Lion of the Hills
     Riddle Gawne
     Selfish Yates
     Shark Monroe
     Staking His Life
     The Tiger Man
     Wolves of the Rail
1919 Breed of Men
     John Petticoats
     The Money Corral
     The Poppy Girl's Husband
     Square Deal Sanderson
     Wagon Tracks
1920 The Cradle of Courage
     Sand!
     The Testing Block
     The Toll Gate

Hartberg, Carl
1913 Checkers

Harte, Betty same as **Hart, Betty; Harte, Bettie**
1913 Hoodman Blind
1914 The Mystery of the Poison Pool
     The Next in Command
     The Pride of Jennico
     The Spy*
     A Woman's Triumph
1915 The Bridge of Sighs
     The Buzzard's Shadow
1916 The Bait
     The Heritage of Hate
     The Man from Bitter Roots

Harte, Gypsy same as **Hart, Gypsy**
1917 The Flower of Doom
     The Pulse of Life

Hartford, David M. same as **Hartford, David**
1914 Tess of the Storm Country
     The Voice at the Telephone
1916 Civilization
     The Sin Ye Do
1917 Blood Will Tell
     The Bride of Hate
1918 Inside the Lines
     Madam Who
     The Man of Bronze
     Rose O' Paradise
     The Turn of a Card
1919 It Happened in Paris
1920 Nomads of the North

Hartigan, P. C. same as **Hartigan, Pat; Hartigan, Pat J.; Hartigan, Patrick**
1917 The Planter
1918 The Prussian Cur
     Swat the Spy
     Why America Will Win
1919 A Fallen Idol
1920 The Adventurer
     Out of the Snows
     The Wonder Man

Hartigan, William
1915 The Menace of the Mute

Hartley, Charles
1915 Barbara Frietchie
1917 The Crimson Dove
     A Hungry Heart
     The Little Duchess
     The Submarine Eye
1918 Neighbors
     Prunella
     To Hell with the Kaiser
1919 An Amateur Widow
     Oh, Boy!

Hartley, Joseph
1918 Cheating the Public

Hartley, Nellie
1917 The Mystery of Number 47

Hartman, Ferris
1917 Framing Framers
     A Phantom Husband

Hartman, Fred G.
1919 Crimson Shoals
1920 The Amazing Woman
     King Spruce

Hartman, Gretchen same as **Hartman, Greta; Markova, Sonia**
1916 The Love Thief
     The Purple Lady
     Rolling Stones

1920 Black Shadows
The Cyclone
Her Elephant Man
The Joyous Troublemaker
The Orphan
Sunset Sprague
Twins of Suffering Creek
Heck, Frederick *same as* **Heck, Fred**
1915 Barbara Frietchie
1916 The Half Million Bribe
Rose of the Alley
1920 An Adventuress*
Heck, Louis
1913 From the Manger to the Cross*
Heck, Stanley *could be same as* **Heck, Stanton**
1918 A Heart's Revenge
Heck, Stanton *could be same as* **Heck, Stanley**
1918 Broadway Bill
Hitting the High Spots
The Landloper
Lend Me Your Name
Unexpected Places
1919 Easy to Make Money
A Man of Honor
One-Thing-at-a-Time O'Day
1920 A Beggar in Purple
Dangerous Days
Firebrand Trevison
Forbidden Trails
The Money-Changers
The Rose of Nome
Heck, William
1916 The Price of Malice
Hedges, John
1920 The Isle of Destiny
Hedman, Martha
1915 The Cub
Hedrick, Richard
1920 The Woman in His House
Heerman, Victor
1920 Don't Ever Marry
The Poor Simp
The River's End
Heffron, Thomas N. *same as* **Heffron, T. N.; Heffron, Thomas**
1914 Aristocracy
The Brute
His Last Dollar
The Man from Mexico
The Million
Mrs. Black Is Back
One of Our Girls
The Only Son
The Scales of Justice
1915 Are You a Mason?
A Black Sheep
Gretna Green
The House of a Thousand Candles
The Millionaire Baby*
1916 Into the Primitive
Lonesome Town
Peck O' Pickles
The Valiants of Virginia
1917 Mountain Dew
The Planter
The Stainless Barrier
The Sudden Gentleman
1918 Deuce Duncan
The Hopper
The Lonely Woman
Madame Sphinx
The Mask
Old Hartwell's Cub
The Painted Lady
The Price of Applause
The Sea Panther
Tony America
Who Killed Walton?
1919 The Best Man
Life's a Funny Proposition
A Man's Fight
The Prodigal Liar
Whitewashed Walls*
1920 The City of Masks
Firebrand Trevison
Sunset Sprague
Thou Art the Man

Heidloff, William *same as* **Heidoff, William**
1915 Under Southern Skies
The Waif
The Woman Who Lied
Heins, Grace
1916 Diane of the Follies
Heisey, Mart
1914 The Wolf
1915 For $5,000 a Year
Held, Anna
1916 Madame La Presidente
Held, Fred
1915 On Her Wedding Night
1916 The Devil's Prize
Fathers of Men
The Footlights of Fate
1917 The Glory of Yolanda
The Soul Master
1918 An American Live Wire
The Girl in His House
1920 The Key to Power
Held, Maxwell *same as* **Held, Max**
1916 The Lights of New York
1917 Love's Law
Held, Tom
1920 Dinty
The River's End
Hellis, Lieut. W. R.
1919 Turning the Tables*
Hellman, George S.
1920 Pagan Love
Helms, Ruth
1920 The Fighting Chance
Helt, Lincoln *see* **Lincoln, Elmo**
Helton, Percy
1915 The Fairy and the Waif
1916 The Flower of Faith
Hemerick, Burwell *see* **Hamrick, Burwell**
Heming, Alfred *see* **Hemming, Alfred**
Heming, Violet
1915 The Running Fight
1917 The Danger Trail
The Judgement House
1918 The Turn of the Wheel
1919 The Common Cause
Everywoman
1920 The Cost
Hemment, John C.
1912 Paul J. Rainey's African Hunt
Hemmer, Edward
1920 Birthright
Hemming, Alfred *same as* **Heming, Alfred**
1914 The Chimes
1915 Flame of Passion
The Pursuing Shadow
1916 My Country First
Society Wolves
1917 God's Man
A Song of Sixpence
The Whip
Hemming, Arthur
1914 The Mystery of Edwin Drood
Hemming, Elwood D.
1916 The Unattainable
Hemmingway, John A.
1918 The Service Star
Henabery, Joseph
1915 The Birth of a Nation
The Penitentes*
1916 Children of the Feud
Intolerance
1917 Her Official Fathers
The Man from Painted Post
1918 Say, Young Fellow!
1919 His Majesty, the American
The Knickerbocker Buckaroo
1920 The Fourteenth Man
The Inferior Sex
The Life of the Party
Love Madness
Henaway, Joe *could be same as* **Hanaway, Joseph**
1918 All Woman
Henderson, Charles
1917 Soldiers of Chance
Henderson, Dell *same as* **Henderson, Del**
1914 Liberty Belles
The Rejuvenation of Aunt Mary

1915 Divorçons
1916 A Coney Island Princess
The Kiss
Rolling Stones
1917 The Beautiful Adventure
A Girl Like That
Her Second Husband
Outcast
Please Help Emily
The Runaway
1918 The Beloved Blackmailer
By Hook or Crook
The Golden Wall
Hitting the Trail
The Impostor
My Wife
The Road to France
Who Loved Him Best?
1919 Courage for Two
Hit or Miss
Love in a Hurry
The Social Pirate
Three Green Eyes
1920 The Dead Line
The Plunger
The Servant Question
The Shark
Henderson, Grace
1913 In the Bishop's Carriage
1917 Pots-and-Pans Peggy
Royal Romance
War and the Woman
1918 Thirty a Week
The Zero Hour
1919 Day Dreams
Henderson, Hazel
1915 Beulah
Henderson, Jack
1916 Charlie Chaplin's Burlesque on "Carmen"
Henderson, Lucius
1914 Salomy Jane
1915 Under Southern Skies
The Woman Who Lied
1916 A Huntress of Men
The Strength of the Weak
Thrown to the Lions
Henderson, Ralf
1914 Sins of the Parents
Henderson, V. T.
1916 Nancy's Birthright
Henderson-Bland, Robert
1913 From the Manger to the Cross
Hendricks, Adeline
1920 Dad's Girl
Hendricks, Ben *same as* **Hendricks, Ben, Sr.**
1915 The Galley Slave
John Glayde's Honor
Just Out of College
1916 The Challenge
The Conquest of Canaan
Jaffery
1918 The Birth of a Race
Life or Honor?
A Perfect Lady
1919 The Capitol
My Little Sister
A Temperamental Wife
The Woman on the Index
1920 Heliotrope
Nothing but the Truth
The Rich Slave
Hendricks, Ben, Jr. *same as* **Hendricks, Benjamin, Jr.**
1918 For the Freedom of the East
1919 The Capitol
Hendricks, Ben, Sr. *see* **Hendricks, Ben**
Hendricks, Dudley
1920 The Little Shepherd of Kingdom Come
Hendricks, John
1916 The Red Widow
Hendricks, Louis *same as* **Hendricks, Lewis**
1914 The Taint
1915 The Family Stain
1916 Sins of Men
1918 Come On In
1919 The Silver King
1920 The Bromley Case

Hendrix, Elizabeth Chandler
1917 Polly Put the Kettle On
Hendryx, James B.
1920 Prairie Trails
Henkel, Charles V. *same as* **Henkel, C. V.**
1914 The Three Musketeers
1919 The Red Peril
Henkle, Edith
1914 An American Citizen
Henley, Hobart
1915 Courtmartialed
A Little Brother of the Rich
The White Terror
1916 A Child of Mystery
The Evil Women Do
The Sign of the Poppy
Temptation and the Man
1917 Double Room Mystery
1918 All Woman
The Face in the Dark
The Glorious Adventure
Laughing Bill Hyde
Mrs. Slacker
Money Mad
Parentage
Too Fat to Fight
1919 The Gay Old Dog
One Week of Life
The Peace of Roaring River
The Woman on the Index
1920 The Miracle of Money
The Sin That Was His
Henley, Rosina
1914 The Lightning Conductor
The Sign of the Cross
1917 The Adventures of Carol
The Burglar
The Strong Way
1918 Gates of Gladness
Wanted, a Mother
1919 Courage for Two
1920 Guilty of Love
A Romantic Adventuress
Hennessy, John
1918 Why America Will Win
Henry, Mr.
1915 Mistress Nell
Henry, Miss C. *could be same as* **Henry, Catherine**
1915 The Silent Voice
Henry, Catherine *could be same as* **Henry, Miss C.**
1917 Paradise Garden
1918 The Rough Lover
Henry, George
1915 The Game of Three
Right off the Bat
When It Strikes Home
1916 The Come-Back
The Sex Lure
Should a Baby Die?
Where Is My Father?
1917 American Maid
One Touch of Nature
Putting the Bee in Herbert
1918 Berlin Via America
The Grain of Dust
The Ordeal of Rosetta
1919 The Gray Towers Mystery
1920 The Little Outcast
Henry, Jack
1914 Tess of the Storm Country
Henry, John, Jr.
1920 Down on the Farm
Henry, Judge Lyman I.
1917 The Chosen Prince, or the Friendship of David and Jonathan
Henry, Katherine
1914 Your Girl and Mine: A Woman Suffrage Play
Henry, Marion
1915 The Making Over of Geoffrey Manning
The Man Who Couldn't Beat God
1916 Britton of the Seventh
The Shop Girl
The Two Edged Sword

Henry, R. J.
1914 The Eagle's Mate
Henry-Houry see **Houry, Henry**
Herbert, A. J. same as **Herbert, Alexander; Herbert, Alexander J.; Herbert, Alexandre; Herbert, Alexandre J.**
1916 Romeo and Juliet (Quality Pictures Corp.)
1917 The Silent Witness
1918 In Pursuit of Polly
In the Hollow of Her Hand
1919 As a Man Thinks
Coax Me
The Man Who Stayed at Home
1920 Romance
Herbert, H. E. see **Herbert, Holmes E.**
Herbert, Henry J. see **Hebert, Henry J.**
Herbert, Holmes E. same as **Herbert, H. E.**
1915 His Wife
1917 Her Life and His
The Man Without a Country
1918 The Death Dance
A Doll's House
The Whirlpool
1919 The A.B.C. of Love
The Divorcee
The Market of Souls
Other Men's Wives
The Rough Neck
The White Heather
1920 Black Is White
Dead Men Tell No Tales
His House in Order
Lady Rose's Daughter
My Lady's Garter
The Right to Love
The Truth About Husbands
Herbert, J. could be same as **Herbert, J. W.** or **Herbert, Jack**
1918 Less Than Kin
Herbert, J. W. could be same as **Herbert, J.** or **Herbert, Jack**
1918 Rich Man, Poor Man
Herbert, Jack could be same as **Herbert, J.** or **Herbert, J. W.**
1918 How Could You, Jean?
The Squaw Man
1919 A Daughter of the Wolf
Told in the Hills
1920 Excuse My Dust
1921 The Jucklins
Herbert, Joseph
1917 The Divorce Game
The Dormant Power
The Strong Way
1918 Laughing Bill Hyde
Stolen Hours
1919 The Teeth of the Tiger
Herbert, Lillian
1914 The Tangle
1915 The Island of Regeneration
The Mystery of Room 13
1917 Forget-Me-Not
Herbert, Nina
1915 Salvation Nell
1916 The Unwritten Law
1920 The New York Idea
Herbert, Sydney same as **Herbert, Sidney**
1920 The Branded Woman
The Thief
Herbert, Victor
1915 In the Shadow
1916 The Fall of a Nation
Herbert, W. J.
1915 The Little Gypsy
Herblin, David
1917 The Painted Madonna
1918 The Clutch of Circumstance
A Heart's Revenge
1919 The Scar
Herford, Will
1920 The Marriage Pit
Heriot, J. D. H. see **Herriot, J. D. H.**
Heritage, Clarence
1916 A Parisian Romance
1918 Her Husband's Honor
The Light Within
The Shell Game
Treason

1920 The Bromley Case
Heritage, Dora
1916 Driftwood
Herlinger, Carl
1918 Inside the Lines
Herman, Jay
1916 The Birth of a Man
Herman, Rutherford
1916 Society Wolves
Hern, Fred
1918 My Four Years in Germany
Hernandez, Anna
1916 Hoodoo Ann
1919 Leave It to Susan
1920 An Amateur Devil
Seeing It Through
Hernandez, George same as **Hernandez, George F.**
1914 The Making of Bobby Burnit
1915 The Circular Staircase
The Rosary
Rosemary
1916 The End of the Rainbow
The Girl of the Lost Lake
It Happened in Honolulu
A Romance of Billy Goat Hill
The Secret of the Swamp
A Son of the Immortals
Unto Those Who Sin
1917 Broadway Arizona
God's Crucible
The Greater Law
Mr. Opp
Mutiny
The Show Down
Southern Justice
Up or Down?
1918 Betty Takes a Hand
The Hopper
Mlle. Paulette
The Man Who Woke Up
The Vortex
You Can't Believe Everything
1919 Be a Little Sport
The Courageous Coward
The Lost Princess
Mary Regan
Miss Adventure
The Rebellious Bride
The Silver Girl
A Taste of Life
Tin Pan Alley
1920 The Daredevil
The Honey Bee
The House of Toys
Just Out of College
The Money-Changers
Seeds of Vengeance
The Third Woman
The Village Sleuth
Hernandez, Mrs. George
1920 Darling Mine
The Jack-Knife Man
The Servant in the House
Hernandez, Lola
1919 Mrs. Wiggs of the Cabbage Patch
Heron, Joseph
1918 The Sign Invisible
Heron-Maxwell, Beatrice
1916 Who Killed Joe Merrion?
Herring, Aggie same as **Herring, Agnes**
1915 The Despoiler
1916 A Corner in Colleens
The Eye of the Night
The Female of the Species
Home
Honor Thy Name
The Vagabond Prince
1917 Madcap Madge
The Millionaire Vagrant
The Snarl
Wee Lady Betty
1918 The Cast-Off
More Trouble
Wedlock
The White Lie
Within the Cup
1919 Cupid Forecloses
A Girl Named Mary
The Hoodlum
The Lord Loves the Irish
A Man's Fight
Todd of the Times

A Yankee Princess
1920 Big Happiness
Down Home
The Dream Cheater
The Dwelling Place of Light
Hairpins
The Little Shepherd of Kingdom Come
Rookie's Return
The Sagebrusher
Unseen Forces
Herring, Jess same as **Herring, Jesse**
1918 A Law unto Herself
One Dollar Bid
1920 Homespun Folks
Peaceful Valley
Herriot, J. D. H. same as **Heriot, J. D. H.; Herriot, J. D.**
1916 The Payment
Plain Jane
The Wolf Woman
Herron, Stella Wynne
1917 Double Room Mystery
Hersholt, Allen
1920 The Golden Trail
Hersholt, Jean
1916 Hell's Hinges
1917 Fighting for Love
'49-'17
The Greater Law
Love Aflame
Princess Virtue
The Show Down
Southern Justice
A Stormy Knight
The Terror
1918 The Answer
Little Red Decides
Madame Spy
1919 Whom the Gods Would Destroy
1920 The Deceiver
The Golden Trail
Merely Mary Ann
The Red Lane
The Servant in the House
Herz, Ralph
1916 The Purple Lady
1917 The Mystery of Number 47
Herzinger, C. W.
1920 Honor Bound
Herzog, Buck
1917 The Baseball Revue of 1917*
Herzog, F. could be same as **Herzog, Frederick**
1914 The Gangsters
Herzog, Frederick same as **Herzog, Fred; Herzog, Frederic; could be same as Herzog, F.**
1918 My Own United States
1919 The Last of the Duanes
The Lone Star Ranger
1920 Faith
Forbidden Trails
King Spruce
The Red Lane
Hese, Alfred
1916 The Pursuing Vengeance
Hesser, Edwin Bower
1917 For the Freedom of the World
1918 The Triumph of Venus
Hester, James
1914 Mrs. Black Is Back
Heustis, Reed
1917 Man and Beast
The Price of Her Soul
1920 What Women Love
Hevener, Gerald
1915 All for a Girl
Simon, the Jester
Hewitt, Russell
1919 Anne of Green Gables
1920 The Flapper
Heyes, Herbert same as **Hayes, Herbert**
1916 The Final Curtain
The Straight Way
Under Two Flags
The Victim
The Vixen
Wild Oats
1917 The Darling of Paris
The Outsider
The Slave

Somewhere in America
The Tiger Woman
1918 The Bird of Prey
The Fallen Angel
The Heart of Rachael
Heart of the Sunset
Her Inspiration
The Lesson
Salome
1919 Children of Banishment
Deliverance
Gambling in Souls
More Deadly Than the Male
1920 The Land of Jazz
Heywood, Doris
1915 The Devil's Daughter
Heywood, W. L.
1920 The Brute Master
Hairpins
Her Husband's Friend
His Own Law
Homer Comes Home
The Jailbird
The Leopard Woman
Let's Be Fashionable
Love Madness
Mary's Ankle
Rookie's Return
Sex
Silk Hosiery
Hiatt, Ruth
1918 The Vigilantes
Hibbard, Edna
1915 The Apaches of Paris
The Fight
1917 Weavers of Life
Hick, Bob
1920 Everybody's Sweetheart
Hick, Emil
1916 Thrown to the Lions
Hickman, Alfred
1915 Are You a Mason?
A Woman's Past
1916 The Chain Invisible
The Flames of Johannis
The Fourth Estate
The Iron Woman
The Witch
1917 The Final Payment
Greed
Hedda Gabler
The Lone Wolf
Mrs. Balfame
The Zeppelin's Last Raid
1918 The Fall of the Romanoffs
Fedora
In Pursuit of Polly
Little Miss Hoover
The Make-Believe Wife
On the Quiet
The Venus Model
1919 Erstwhile Susan
False Gods
Here Comes the Bride
The Love Cheat
1919-20 Piccadilly Jim
1920 Civilian Clothes
The Fear Market
The Shadow of Rosalie Byrnes
Hickman, Charles H. same as **Hickman, Charles**
1915 Colorado
1916 Doctor Neighbor
Two Men of Sandy Bar
The Yaqui
Hickman, Frank
1914 The Circus Man
Hickman, Howard same as **Hickman, Howard C.**
1914 The Making of Bobby Burnit
1915 The Cup of Life
The Man from Oregon
Matrimony
1916 Civilization
The Female of the Species
The Honorable Algy
The Jungle Child
The Moral Fabric
The Sin Ye Do
Somewhere in France
The Wolf Woman
1917 Blood Will Tell
Chicken Casey

The Snarl
Those Who Pay
Wooden Shoes
1918 Blue Blood
The Cast-Off
The Heart of Rachael
Madam Who
Maid O' the Storm
Rose O' Paradise
Social Ambition
Two-Gun Betty
The White Lie
1919 All of a Sudden Norma
Beckoning Roads
Hearts Asleep
Her Purchase Price
Josselyn's Wife
Kitty Kelly, M.D.
Tangled Threads
A Trick of Fate
1920 Just a Wife
Hickman, Roberta
1915 Betty in Search of a Thrill
Nearly a Lady
Sunshine Molly
Hickok, Lida *same as* **Hikox, Lida**
1915 Flame of Passion
1916 Society Wolves
Hickok, Rodney
1914 The Mystery of Edwin Drood
1915 The Pearl of the Antilles
Hicks, Gaspard
1920 Voices
Hicks, Maxine Elliott *same as* **Hicks, Maxine**
1917 The Crimson Dove
The Eternal Mother
The Little Duchess
The Poor Little Rich Girl
1918 Neighbors
1919 The Right to Happiness
1920 Double Speed
The Gilded Dream
Hicks, May
1920 Footlights and Shadows
Hiers, Walter
1915 Just Out of College
The Labyrinth
1916 Common Sense Brackett
The Conquest of Canaan
Seventeen
1917 The End of the Tour
God's Man
Life's Whirlpool
The Mysterious Miss Terry
Over There
1918 The Accidental Honeymoon
Brown of Harvard
The Daredevil
The Lesson
A Man's World
Marriage
Mrs. Slacker
A Nymph of the Foothills
Our Little Wife
Waifs
1919 Bill Henry
Experimental Marriage
The Fear Woman
Hard Boiled
It Pays to Advertise
The Lamb and the Lion
Leave It to Susan
Spotlight Sadie
When Doctors Disagree
Why Smith Left Home
1920 A City Sparrow
The Fourteenth Man
Going Some
Held by the Enemy
Miss Hobbs
Mrs. Temple's Telegram
Oh, Lady, Lady
So Long Letty
The Turning Point
What's Your Husband Doing?
Young Mrs. Winthrop
Higbee, Mary Jane *see* **Higby, Mary**
Higbee, Wilbur *see* **Higby, Wilbur**
Higby, Mrs. *could be same as* **Higby, Mary**
1917 Nina, the Flower Girl

Higby, Mary *same as* **Higbee, Mary Jane; could be same as* **Higby, Mrs.**
1914 Where the Trail Divides
1915 The Reform Candidate
Higby, W. J. *see* **Higby, Wilbur**
Higby, Walter
1919 True Heart Susie
1920 Homer Comes Home
Higby, Wilbur *same as* **Higbee, Wilbur; Higby, W. J.; could be same as* **Higby, William**
1915 Strathmore
1916 Diane of the Follies
Flirting with Fate
Hoodoo Ann
Intolerance*
The Mainspring
The Matrimaniac
Mixed Blood
The Old Folks at Home
Reggie Mixes In
The Sign of the Poppy
1917 The Girl of the Timber Claims
The Medicine Man
The Midnight Man
Might and the Man
An Old Fashioned Young Man
The Tar Heel Warrior
Until They Get Me
Wild Sumac
1918 By Proxy
The Flames of Chance
Keith of the Border
Madame Sphinx
The Vortex
1919 Brass Buttons
Broken Blossoms
I'll Get Him Yet
The Mayor of Filbert
Nugget Nell
True Heart Susie*
1920 Girls Don't Gamble
Homer Comes Home
The Jailbird
Let's Be Fashionable
The Lone Hand
The Price of Redemption
The Terror
Higby, William *could be same as* **Higby, Wilbur**
1916 The Missing Links
1917 The Mysterious Mr. Tiller
Higgins, Audelle
1918 The Argument
Higgins, David
1914 His Last Dollar
1916 The Conquest of Canaan
1918 Rough and Ready
Higgins, Howard
1919 Don't Change Your Husband
1920 Why Change Your Wife?
Higginson, Percy
1919 The Forfeit
The Unbroken Promise
Hikox, Lida *see* **Hickok, Lida**
Hilburn, Betty
1920 Girl of the Sea
Heart Strings
Heliotrope
Hilburn, Jewel
1915 Little Miss Brown
Hilburn, Percy
1915 The Explorer
The Goose Girl
The Puppet Crown
1916 Each Pearl a Tear
A Gutter Magdalene
The House with the Golden Windows
The Race
The Selfish Woman
Tennessee's Pardner
To Have and to Hold
The Years of the Locust
The Yellow Pawn
1917 The Call of the East
The Cost of Hatred
The Crystal Gazer
The Evil Eye
Her Strange Wedding
On the Level
A School for Husbands
The Sunset Trail
The Winning of Sally Temple

1918 The Hell Cat
Innocent
A Japanese Nightingale
The Narrow Path
The Turn of the Wheel
1919 Flame of the Desert
The Girl from Outside
The Pest
Shadows
Sis Hopkins
The Stronger Vow
When Doctors Disagree
The World and Its Woman
1920 The Branding Iron
Dangerous Days
Godless Men
The Woman and the Puppet
Hildreth, Kathryn
1920 Civilian Clothes
Hill, Miss
1916 The Heart of New York
Hill, Arthur
1914 A Good Little Devil
Hill, Ben
1920 The Border Raiders
Dangerous Trails
The Unknown Ranger
Hill, Bob *see* **Hill, Robert F.**
Hill, Bonnie
1919 The Amateur Adventuress
The Brat
Cowardice Court
The Microbe
The Woman Michael Married
1920 Billions
The Peddler of Lies
The Road to Divorce
Silk Hosiery
Three Gold Coins
Hill, Dudley
1917 The Lady of the Photograph
1918 My Wife
Hill, Ethel
1918 The Eagle
1919 The Faith of the Strong
Hill, George W. *same as* **Hill, George; Hill, George William**
1913 The Sea Wolf
1914 Burning Daylight: The Adventures of "Burning Daylight" in Alaska
Burning Daylight: The Adventures of "Burning Daylight" in Civilization
Martin Eden
The Pursuit of the Phantom
1915 Buckshot John
The Hypocrites
Pretty Mrs. Smith
1916 Less Than the Dust
Macbeth
1917 The Cinderella Man
Polly of the Circus
Sunshine Alley
The Waiting Soul
1918 The Beloved Traitor
Fields of Honor
Our Little Wife
1919 Turning the Tables
1920 Mary Ellen Comes to Town
Remodelling Her Husband
Hill, Gus
1914 The Line-Up at Police Headquarters
Hill, Helen
1915 The Woman
Hill, James
1919 Impossible Catherine
Hill, Josephine
1919 Love and the Law
1920 Burnt Wings
Parlor, Bedroom and Bath
Hill, Kenneth
1915 The Arrival of Perpetua
1920 The Truth
Hill, Lee *same as* **Hill, Rollo Lee**
1916 Behind the Lines
1917 The Fuel of Life
Idolators
When Baby Forgot
1918 False Ambition
A Good Loser
The Lonely Woman

The Love Brokers
Old Love for New
The Sea Panther
A Soul in Trust
Station Content
1919 The Challenge of Chance
Girls
A Sporting Chance (American Film Co.)
1920 The Deceiver
A Master Stroke
Hill, Maud *same as* **Hill, Maude**
1915 The Cowardly Way
1916 The Blindness of Love
1917 The End of the Tour
The Lifted Veil
Sister Against Sister
1918 A Daughter of France
The House of Gold
To Hell with the Kaiser
1919 The End of the Road
When Men Desire
1920 The Dangerous Paradise
The Sacred Flame
Whispers
Hill, Raymond C. *same as* **Hill, Raymond G.**
1914 The Coming Power
1919 The Black Circle
1920 The Green Flame
Hill, Robert *see* **Hill, Robert F.**
Hill, Robert E.
1917 Babbling Tongues
Hill, Robert F. *same as* **Hill, Bob; Hill, Robert**
1916 Temptation and the Man
1917 The Girl by the Roadside
The Raggedy Queen
1918 Crown Jewels
Heiress for a Day
Nancy Comes Home
The Reckoning Day
The Trap
1919 Full of Pep
Jubilo
Upstairs
1920 Water, Water Everywhere
Hill, Robert Lee
1916 Man and His Angel
Hill, Walter
1920 Little Miss Rebellion
Hill, Wycliffe A.
1917 The Curse of Eve
Hiller, Lejaren a'
1920 The Sleep of Cyma Roget
Hilliard, Harry *same as* **Hilliard, Harry S.**
1916 Caprice of the Mountains
Gold and the Woman
Little Miss Happiness
Merely Mary Ann
A Modern Thelma
The Ragged Princess
Romeo and Juliet (Fox Film Corp.)
The Strength of the Weak
1917 Every Girl's Dream
Heart and Soul
Her Greatest Love
The New York Peacock
Patsy
1918 Set Free
A Successful Adventure
1919 Cheating Herself
Destiny
The Little Rowdy
The Little White Savage
The Sneak
1920 The Dangerous Talent
The Girl in Number 29
Hillier, Claire
1915 The Alien
The Song of the Wage Slave
Hilliker, Mrs. Belle *see* **Hilliker, Katharine**
Hilliker, Katharine *same as* **Hilliker, Belle**
1920 Cynthia-of-the-Minute
What Women Love
Hillis, W. A.
1917 Alaska Wonders in Motion*

Hillman, Gertrude
1919 Marie, Ltd.
1920 Something Different
Hills (full name unknown)
1915 The Fairy and the Waif*
Hills, W. R.
1919 Turning the Tables*
Hillyer, Lambert
1917 The Desert Man
An Even Break
The Little Brother
Love or Justice
The Mother Instinct
The Narrow Trail
One Shot Ross
The Silent Man*
The Snarl
Strife
They're Off
1918 Riddle Gawne
1919 Breed of Men
John Petticoats
The Money Corral
The Poppy Girl's Husband
Square Deal Sanderson
Wagon Tracks
1920 The Cradle of Courage
Sand!
The Testing Block
The Toll Gate
Hilton, Frank
1918 On the Quiet
1919 The Moonshine Trail
Hilton, Harold
1917 Somewhere in America
Hilton, Helen
1914 The Brute
1915 How Molly Malone Made
Good
Himes, A. B.
1916 The World Against Him
Himm, Carr
1920 Molly and I
Hinckle, Edith *same as* **Hinkle, Edith**
1914 The Price He Paid
1918 The Life Mask
Tempered Steel
Hinckley, William *same as* **Hinckley,
William L.**
1915 Bred in the Bone
The Lily and the Rose
The Wolf Man
1916 The Children in the House
Martha's Vindication
1917 The Amazons
Reputation
The Secret of Eve
Hincus, Charles
1918 Ali Baba and the Forty Thieves
Hines, Blanche
1918 Blue-Eyed Mary
Hines, Charles
1917 The Argyle Case
Hines, John *same as* **Hines, Johnnie;
Hines, Johnny**
1914 As Ye Sow
The Man of the Hour
The Wishing Ring; An Idyll of
Old England
1915 Alias Jimmy Valentine
The Arrival of Perpetua
A Butterfly on the Wheel
The Cub
The Family Cupboard
The Gray Mask
Little Miss Brown
A Price for Folly
1916 All Man
Miss Petticoats
The Pawn of Fate
The Weakness of Man
1917 The Dancer's Peril
A Girl's Folly
Man's Woman
Tillie Wakes Up
Yankee Pluck
Youth
1918 The Golden Wall
Just Sylvia
Merely Players
Neighbors
The Power and the Glory
The Studio Girl

Sunshine Nan
1919 Eastward Ho!
Heart of Gold
The Little Intruder
Three Green Eyes
What Love Forgives
Hines, Sam
1914 Across the Pacific
Hing, Tom
1917 The War of the Tongs
Hinkle, Edith *see* **Hinckle, Edith**
Hipp, Dorothy
1920 A Tokio Siren
Hipp, Young
1920 Dinty
Hippe, Lewis
1920 The Mollycoddle
Hirsh, Nathan
1920 The Evolution of Man
The Woman Above Reproach
Hitchcock, Charles *(actor) could be
same as* **Hitchcock, Charles
Webster** *(scen, dir)*
1914 One Wonderful Night
Hitchcock, Charles Webster *(scen, dir)
same as* **Hitchcock, C. W.;** *could be
same as* **Hitchcock, Charles** *(actor)*
1916 Cousin Jim
1918 The Sunset Princess
Hitchcock, Harry
1914 The Chimes
Hitchcock, Raymond
1915 My Valet
The Ringtailed Rhinoceros
Hitchcock, Walter
1914 The Idler
Uncle Tom's Cabin
1915 The Celebrated Scandal
The Climbers
Destiny; Or, The Soul of a
Woman
The Girl I Left Behind Me
The Great Ruby
Her Reckoning
The House of Tears
1916 The Blindness of Love
The Half Million Bribe
The Libertine
The Prima Donna's Husband
The Snowbird
1917 The Auction Block
The Moral Code
Vera, the Medium
The White Raven
1919 The Belle of the Season
Hively, George
1917 Bucking Broadway
The Devil's Pay Day
A Marked Man
The Secret Man
Straight Shooting
1918 Deuce Duncan
The Phantom Riders
The Scarlet Drop
Thieves' Gold
Wild Women
A Woman's Fool
1919 The Ace of the Saddle
The Great Air Robbery
Hoadley, C. B.
1915 Wildfire
1916 Unto Those Who Sin
1920 Fixed by George
Once a Plumber
Hoadley, Hal
1919 The Day She Paid
A Gun Fightin' Gentleman
1920 Burnt Wings
Dangerous Love
The Forged Bride
Her Five-Foot Highness
Rouge and Riches
The Triflers
Hoag, C. Tracy
1919 Bill Henry
Hay Foot, Straw Foot
The Homebreaker
The Market of Souls
Stepping Out
The Virtuous Thief
What Every Woman Learns
1920 What's Your Husband Doing?

Hoagland, Herbert C.
1918 Pershing's Crusaders
Hoban, Stella
1915 The Luring Lights
Hobart, C. D. *see* **Hobart, Doty**
Hobart, Doty *same as* **Hobart, C. D.;
Hobart, C. Doty**
1915 The Pretenders
1916 Molly Make-Believe
Under Cover
Woman in the Case
1917 Baby Mine
Charity Castle
Great Expectations
The Inevitable
Sapho
1918 A Woman of Redemption
1919 Sacred Silence*
Hobart, George V.
1918 Madame Jealousy
1919 The Jungle Trail
Hoberg, Hildor
1917 The Princess of Patches
Hobson, Homer
1920 The Family Honor*
Hobson, Richmond Pearson
1915 Prohibition*
1919 The Law of Nature
Hoch, Emil *same as* **Hach, Emil; Hoch,
Emile**
1915 The Earl of Pawtucket
1916 The Pursuing Vengeance
1917 Sloth
1918 A Romance of the Air
To Hell with the Kaiser
1919 The Dark Star
The Great Victory, Wilson or
the Kaiser? The Fall of the
Hohenzollerns
1920 The Girl with the Jazz Heart
Hocky, Harry
1920 The New York Idea
Hodge, Rex *same as* **Hodge, Rex E.**
1916 Behind the Lines
Nancy's Birthright
Where Are My Children?
1919 The Fire Flingers
His Divorced Wife
The Millionaire Pirate
The Sleeping Lion
1920 The Phantom Melody
Hodges, Maxine
1914 The Jungle
Hodges, Runa
1915 A Fool There Was
Should a Mother Tell?
The Unfaithful Wife
1916 The House of Mirrors
1917 Enlighten Thy Daughter
Hodgkins, Bert
1920 The Rich Slave
Hoerle, Helen Christine
1919 His Father's Wife
Hoffman, Miss
1916 Joan the Woman
Hoffman, Aaron
1914 The Tigress
1915 The Heart of a Painted Woman
My Madonna
The Politicians
The Shadows of a Great City*
The Song of the Wage Slave
1916 Bluff
The Devil at His Elbow
The Eternal Question
Extravagance
The Lure of Heart's Desire
A Million for Mary
Playing with Fire
The Sable Blessing
The Scarlet Woman
The Soul Market
The Spell of the Yukon
Vanity
The Weakness of Strength
A Woman's Fight
1917 Beloved Rogues
The Clock
The Gilded Youth
Glory
The Secret of Eve
The Waiting Soul

Hoffman, Alpharetta *same as*
Hoffmann, Alpharetta
1918 Old Wives for New
The Way of a Man with a
Maid
Hoffman, C. W. *see* **Hoffman, Charles
W.**
Hoffman, Carl von
1916 The Marriage Bond
Hoffman, Charles W. *same as* **Hoffman,
C. W.; Hoffman, Charles**
1916 Divorce and the Daughter
The Fear of Poverty
The Fugitive
Master Shakespeare, Strolling
Player
1917 Her Life and His
The Jury of Fate
1918 The Challenge Accepted
Hoffman, George
1917 The Son of His Father
Hoffman, Hugh
1917 The Terror
Hoffman, M. H.
1918 Suspicion
Hoffman, Margaretta
1919 Don't Change Your Husband
Hoffman, Nell *see* **Holman, Nell**
Hoffman, Otto
1915 The White Terror
1917 The Secret of Black Mountain
1918 The Family Skeleton
His Own Home Town
The Kaiser's Shadow, or the
Triple Cross
A Nine O'Clock Town
String Beans
1919 Behind the Door
The Busher
The City of Comrades
Crooked Straight
The Egg Crate Wallop
Greased Lightning
The Haunted Bedroom
The Sheriff's Son
1920 The Great Accident
Homer Comes Home
It's a Great Life
The Jailbird
Just Out of College
Paris Green
Silk Hosiery
Hoffman, Ruby
1914 The Million
The Taint
1915 Children of the Ghetto
The Danger Signal
The Dictator
The Fixer
Keep Moving
Mistress Nell
The Politicians
Poor Schmaltz
1916 The Devil's Prayer-Book
Her American Prince
The Perils of Divorce
The Summer Girl
Wild Oats
A Woman's Honor
1917 The Dummy
Passion
The Slave Market
1918 Uncle Tom's Cabin
1919 Upside Down
1920 Cynthia-of-the-Minute
The Tiger's Cub
Hoffman, William
1917 Love Letters
Hoffmann, Alpharetta *see* **Hoffman,
Alpharetta**
Hoffner, J. C. *same as* **Hoffner, Cal**
1920 The Cradle of Courage
The Toll Gate
Hogaboom, Winfield
1916 The Argonauts of
California—1849
The Daughter of the Don
Hogan, Danny *same as* **Hogan, Daniel;
Hogan, Daniel B. "Kid"; Hogan,
Danny "Kid"**
1914 A Good Little Devil*
Such a Little Queen*

A Tortured Heart
Under Two Flags
A Wife's Sacrifice
The Witch
1917 The Broadway Sport
The Derelict
Love's Law
The Scarlet Letter
Tangled Lives
The Test of Womanhood
The Wild Girl
1918 The Ghosts of Yesterday
The Poor Rich Man
A Romance of the Air
The Sins of the Children
Treason
When Men Betray
1919 A Dangerous Affair
Dust of Desire
The Little Intruder
Love, Honor and—?
The New Moon
The Other Man's Wife
The Way of a Woman
1920 Body and Soul
Lifting Shadows
Man's Plaything

Holmes, Taylor
1917 Efficiency Edgar's Courtship
Fools for Luck
The Small Town Guy
Two-Bit Seats
1918 A Pair of Sixes
Ruggles of Red Gap
Uneasy Money
1919 It's a Bear
A Regular Fellow
Taxi
Three Black Eyes
Upside Down
1920 Nothing but Lies
Nothing but the Truth
The Very Idea

Holt, Edwin
1916 The Pretenders
Romeo and Juliet (Fox Film Corp.)
The Wheel of the Law
1917 Heart and Soul
The Tiger Woman
Two Little Imps

Holt, George
1914 Captain Alvarez
The Little Angel of Canyon Creek
1915 The Chalice of Courage
1916 God's Country and the Woman
Through the Wall
1917 Aladdin from Broadway
1918 Hugon, the Mighty
1920 Dangerous Trails

Holt, Gloria
1920 The Road to Divorce
A Woman Who Understood

Holt, Jack same as **Holt, John**
1915 Jewel
1916 The Black Sheep of the Family
The Dumb Girl of Portici
Naked Hearts
Saving the Family Name
1917 The Call of the East
The Cost of Hatred
Giving Becky a Chance
The Inner Shrine
The Little American
Sacrifice
The Secret Game
1918 The Claw
A Desert Wooing
Green Eyes
Hidden Pearls
The Honor of His House
Love Me
The Marriage Ring
One More American
The Road Through the Dark
The Squaw Man
The White Man's Law
1919 Cheating Cheaters
For Better, for Worse
Kitty Kelly, M.D.
The Life Line
A Midnight Romance
A Sporting Chance (Famous Players-Lasky Corp.)

Victory
The Woman Michael Married
The Woman Thou Gavest Me
1920 The Best of Luck
Crooked Streets
Held by the Enemy
The Sins of Rosanne
1921 Midsummer Madness

Holte, Helen
1920 The Saphead

Holton, Betty
1916 The Fortunate Youth

Holubar, Allen same as **Holubar, Alan;**
Holubar, Allan; Holubar, Allen J.
1915 Conscience
Courtmartialed
The White Terror
1916 20,000 Leagues Under the Sea
1917 Fear Not
The Field of Honor
Heart Strings
The Reed Case
Sirens of the Sea
A Soul for Sale
Treason
1918 The Mortgaged Wife
The Talk of the Town
1919 The Heart of Humanity
Paid in Advance
The Right to Happiness
1920 Once to Every Woman

Homans, Robert
1917 Madame Sherry

Honey, Bert
1918 His Royal Highness

Hong, Fong
1920 Firebrand Trevison

Hood, H.
1913 Barbarous Mexico*

Hooper, John
1920 That Something

Hooper, Lewis
1914 Neptune's Daughter

Hoops, Arthur
1914 Aristocracy
The Better Man
The Lost Paradise
The Straight Road
Such a Little Queen
1915 The Danger Signal
Esmeralda
Gretna Green
Mistress Nell
The Mummy and the Humming Bird
Should a Mother Tell?
The Song of Hate
When We Were Twenty-One
A Woman's Resurrection
1916 The Devil's Prayer-Book
The Eternal Question
Extravagance
The Final Curtain
The Lure of Heart's Desire
Playing with Fire
The Scarlet Woman
The Soul Market
The Spell of the Yukon
1917 Bridges Burned
The Secret of Eve

Hooser, William S.
1916 The Highest Bid

Hoover, Billy
1920 The Fortune Hunter

Hoover, Herbert
1917 The Public Be Damned

Hope, Charles
1918 A Nymph of the Foothills

Hope, Evelyn
1913 Ivanhoe

Hope, Florence
1920 Two Weeks

Hope, Gloria
1917 Time Locks and Diamonds
1918 $5,000 Reward
Free and Equal
The Great Love
The Guilty Man
The Heart of Rachael
The Law of the North
Naughty, Naughty!
1919 Bill Apperson's Boy
Burglar by Proxy

The Gay Lord Quex
The Hushed Hour
The Outcasts of Poker Flats
The Rider of the Law
1920 The Desperate Hero
Prairie Trails
Seeds of Vengeance
The Texan
The Third Woman
Too Much Johnson

Hope, J. could be same as **Hope, William J.**
1916 A Youth of Fortune

Hope, William J. could be same as **Hope, J.**
1916 Where Are My Children?

Hopkins, Arthur
1917 Fighting Odds
1919 The Eternal Magdalene

Hopkins, B. W. could be same as **Hopkins, Ben**
1919 Secret Marriage

Hopkins, Ben could be same as **Hopkins, B. W.**
1917 Whither Thou Goest

Hopkins, Clyde same as **Hopkins, Clyde E.**
1916 Hell-to-Pay Austin
Intolerance
The Matrimaniac
The Price of Power
The Rummy
Susan Rocks the Boat
1917 Betsy's Burglar
The Girl of the Timber Claims
Might and the Man
1918 The Kid Is Clever
1919 The Mother and the Law
The Trembling Hour

Hopkins, Ed
1915 The Cowardly Way

Hopkins, George (art dir)
1920 Polly of the Storm Country

Hopkins, George (cowboy)
1918 The Hell Cat

Hopkins, George (prod mgr, writer)
same as **Hopkins, George S.**
1917 The Spirit of Romance
1920 The Furnace

Hopkins, Georgia
1920 Bachelor Apartments

Hopkins, Jack same as **Hopkins, John**
1912 Oliver Twist
1914 The Adventures of Kitty Cobb
The Criminal Path
The Governor's Ghost
The Seats of the Mighty
1915 Life Without Soul
1916 The Black Butterfly
A Circus Romance
The Conquest of Canaan
My Country First
1917 American Maid
The Bitter Truth
Daughter of Maryland
Queen X
The Rainbow
1918 The Challenge Accepted
The Inn of the Blue Moon
The Street of Seven Stars
The Unchastened Woman
Wild Honey
Zongar
1919 Open Your Eyes
1920 The Dead Line
A Manhattan Knight

Hopkins, May
1915 The Deep Purple
1917 The Easiest Way
1918 Everybody's Girl
1919 Bolshevism on Trial
The Social Pirate
The Virtuous Model

Hopkins, Neje
1918 The She-Devil

Hopkins, Peggy
1916 Dimples
1918 Woman and the Law

Hopkins, Tom J.
1920 Parted Curtains

Hopkins, Una Nixson same as **Hopkins, Una Nixon**
1917 The Spirit of Romance
1919 More Deadly Than the Male
1920 Burglar Proof
Food for Scandal
A Full House
Her First Elopement
Jenny Be Good
Judy of Rogue's Harbor
Nurse Marjorie
Oh, Lady, Lady

Hopkins, William H. (actor)
1916 The Haunted Manor

Hopkins, Willie (art titles)
1919 Everywoman

Hopp, George
1918 The Lure of Luxury

Hopper, De Wolf
1916 Casey at the Bat
Don Quixote
Intolerance*
Mr. Goode, the Samaritan
Stranded
Sunshine Dad

Hopper, E. Mason
1915 The Labyrinth
1916 Gloriana
The Right Direction
The Selfish Woman
1917 As Men Love
The Firefly of Tough Luck
The Hidden Spring
The Prison Without Walls
The Regenerates
The Spirit of Romance
The Tar Heel Warrior
The Wax Model
1918 The Answer
Boston Blackie's Little Pal
Her American Husband
The Love Brokers
Love's Pay Day
Mystic Faces
Unexpected Places
Wife or Country
Without Honor
1919 As the Sun Went Down
Come Again Smith
1920 It's a Great Life

Hopper, Edna Wallace
1916 By Whose Hand?
The Perils of Divorce

Hopper, Hedda same as **Hopper, Mrs. De Wolf**
1917 Nearly Married
1918 The Beloved Traitor
Virtuous Wives
1919 The Isle of Conquest
Sadie Love
The Third Degree
1920 The Man Who Lost Himself
The New York Idea

Hopper, William De Wolf, Jr.
1916 Sunshine Dad

Horan, Charles same as **Horan, Charles T.**
1915 Fighting Bob
Her Reckoning
The Right of Way
When a Woman Loves
1916 The Blindness of Love
The Quitter
Rose of the Alley
The Upheaval
1917 Polly of the Circus
Somewhere in America*
1918 The Birth of a Race
1919 Three Black Eyes
1920 Man's Plaything

Horine, Alice
1914 The Gangsters

Horkheimer, E. D. same as **Horkheimer, Elwood D.**
1915 Should a Wife Forgive?
1916 Boots and Saddles
Pay Dirt
The Power of Evil
Spellbound
1917 Bab the Fixer
The Best Man
Betty Be Good
A Bit of Kindling
Brand's Daughter

Howe, Eliot *same as* **Howe, Elliot**
1915 Matrimony
1918 Blue Blood
      With Hoops of Steel
1919 The Silver Girl
      Todd of the Times
1920 Dice of Destiny
      Dollar for Dollar
Howe, Marjorie
1916 I Accuse
Howe, Maude
1920 Neptune's Bride
Howell, George
1920 The New York Idea
Howell, Hazel
1920 Fixed by George
      Forty-Five Minutes from
        Broadway
      A Full House
      Old Dad
Howey, Walter C.
1917 Should She Obey?
Howland, E.
1916 Whispering Smith
Howland, Jobyna
1918 Her Only Way
1919 The Way of a Woman
Howland, Louis *same as* **Howland, Lou;
Howland, Louis A.**
1918 The Girl Who Came Back
      Rimrock Jones
      Women's Weapons
1919 Maggie Pepper
      Men, Women and Money
      Pettigrew's Girl
      The Secret Garden
      A Sporting Chance (Famous
        Players-Lasky Corp.)
      The Winning Girl
      The Woman Next Door
Howley, Irene
1914 Under the Gaslight
1915 The Heart of Jennifer
      The Moth and the Flame
      A Yellow Streak
1916 Life's Shadows
      The Purple Lady
1917 Her Father's Keeper
      His Father's Son
Howson, Albert *same as* **Howson, Albert
S.**
1915 My Madonna
      The Vampire
1916 The Devil's Prize
1917 The Soul Master
Hoxan, Art *same as* **Hoxen, Art**
1919 The Love Call
Hoxen, Edward
1919 More Deadly Than the Male
Hoxie, Hart
1915 Fatherhood
      The Scarlet Sin
1916 The Dumb Girl of Portici
      The Three Godfathers
      A Youth of Fortune
1917 Jack and Jill
      Nan of Music Mountain
1918 Blue Blazes Rawden
      His Majesty, Bunker Bean
      Nobody's Wife
      The Wolf and His Mate
1919 Johnny Get Your Gun
      Told in the Hills
      The Valley of the Giants
Hoxie, Jack
1915 Captain Courtesy
1920 The Man from Nowhere
Hoyt, Arthur
1916 The Lash*
      Love Never Dies
      A Stranger from Somewhere
1917 Bringing Home Father
      The Man Who Took a Chance
      Mr. Opp
      The Show Down
1918 Her American Husband
      High Stakes
      Station Content
      The Yellow Dog
1919 Cowardice Court
      The Grim Game
1920 The Desperate Hero
      The Girl in Number 29

In the Heart of a Fool
Nurse Marjorie
A Slave of Vanity
The Triflers
Trumpet Island
Hoyt, Edward N. *same as* **Hoyt,
Edward; Hoyt, Edwin; Hoyt, Edwin
N.**
1914 The Last Volunteer
1915 Greater Love Hath No Man
      Sealed Lips
1916 Little Miss Happiness
      Merely Mary Ann
      Society Wolves
1917 The Crimson Dove
      The Scarlet Letter
      Vengeance Is Mine
1918 The Struggle Everlasting
Hoyt, Fanny
1915 The Mill on the Floss
Hoyt, Harry O.
1916 The Blindness of Love
      The Child of Destiny
      Dimples
      The Half Million Bribe
      Rose of the Alley
1917 The Moth
      Somewhere in America*
      Weavers of Life
1918 The Beloved Blackmailer
      By Hook or Crook
      By Right of Purchase
      Gates of Gladness
      The Girl of Today
      Hitting the Trail
      I Want to Forget
      Just Sylvia
      Neighbors
      The Power and the Glory
      The Queen of Hearts
      The Road to France
      The Sea Wolf
      The Zero Hour
1919 The Battler
      A Broadway Saint
      Courage for Two
      Forest Rivals
      The Hand Invisible
      Hit or Miss
      The Rough Neck
      Through the Toils
Hoyt, Mrs. William
1916 One Day
Hubbard, Hazel
1916 Race Suicide
Hubbard, Lucien
1917 The Angel Factory
      The Awakening of Ruth
1918 The Beloved Blackmailer
1919 The Black Gate
      The Climbers
      The Gamblers
      Mandarin's Gold
      The Moral Deadline
1919-20
      The Tower of Jewels
1920 Bab's Candidate
      Captain Swift
      Deadline at Eleven
      Dollars and the Woman
      The Garter Girl
      A Master Stroke
      Outside the Law
      The Sporting Duchess
Hubbard, Philip E.
1919 The Merry-Go-Round
Huber, Herbert
1915 The Eternal City
Hubert, Harold
1915 The Battle Cry of Peace
Hubley, Russell
1917 The Avenging Trail
Huddleston, Jack
1920 Alias Jimmy Valentine*
      The Right of Way
Huddleston, Josephine
1919 Where's Mary?
Hudson, E.
1917 The Submarine Eye
Hudson, Edgar
1920 Whispers

Hudson, Eric
1916 Romeo and Juliet (Quality
        Pictures Corp.)
1917 Fighting Odds
      Seven Keys to Baldpate
Hudson, Hazel
1920 The Isle of Destiny
Hudson, Virginia Tyler *same as*
Hudson, Virginia
1915 Inspiration
1916 The Flight of the Duchess
1917 The Burglar
      The Darling of Paris*
1918 The Cabaret
      Gates of Gladness
      The Man Hunt
      The Oldest Law
      Wanted, a Mother
      A Woman of Redemption
Hudson, Wilbur *same as* **Hudson,
Wilbur C.**
1913 Across the Continent
1914 Born Again
      Hearts of Oak
1915 An American Gentleman
      The Fight
Huff, Justina
1913 Tess of the D'Urbervilles
1916 The Man Inside
Huff, Louise
1915 For $5,000 a Year
      Marse Covington
      The Old Homestead
1916 Blazing Love
      Destiny's Toy
      The Ransom
      The Reward of Patience
      Seventeen
      The Sphinx
1917 Freckles
      The Ghost House
      Great Expectations
      Jack and Jill
      The Lonesome Chap
      The Varmint
      What Money Can't Buy
1918 His Majesty, Bunker Bean
      Mile-a-Minute Kendall
      Sandy
      The Sea Waif
      T'Other Dear Charmer
      Wild Youth
1919 The Crook of Dreams
      Heart of Gold
      The Little Intruder
      Oh, You Women
1920 The Dangerous Paradise
      What Women Want
Huggins, Bob
1917 The Tell-Tale Step
Huggins, Miller
1917 The Baseball Revue of 1917*
Hughes, Frank
1916 Casey at the Bat
Hughes, Gareth *same as* **Hughes,
Garreth**
1918 And the Children Pay
      Every Mother's Son
1919 Eyes of Youth
      Ginger
      The Isle of Conquest
      Mrs. Wiggs of the Cabbage
        Patch
      The Red Viper
      The Woman Under Oath
      Woman, Woman!
1920 Broken Hearts*
      The Chorus Girl's Romance
      The Eternal Mother
      The Woman in His House
Hughes, Leonore
1919 The Indestructible Wife
Hughes, Lloyd
1918 Impossible Susan
1919 The Haunted Bedroom
      The Heart of Humanity
      An Innocent Adventuress
      Satan Junior
      The Turn in the Road
      The Virtuous Thief
1920 Below the Surface
      Dangerous Hours
      The False Road
      Homespun Folks

Hughes, Mae
1919 The Woman Next Door
Hughes, Morris
1920 The Mollycoddle
Hughes, Rupert
1916 The Old Folks at Home
1920 The Cup of Fury*
      Scratch My Back
Hughes, Warren
1916 Tempest and Sunshine
1917 The Courage of the Common
        Place
      Cy Whittaker's Ward
Hughston, Regan
1916 Behind Closed Doors
1917 Fighting Odds
      Her Excellency, the Governor
Hugo, Adelbert
1919 A Scream in the Night
Huhn, A. O.
1917 A Man's Law
Hulette, Gladys
1915 Eugene Aram
1916 The Flight of the Duchess
      Other People's Money
      Prudence the Pirate
      The Shine Girl
      The Traffic Cop
1917 The Candy Girl
      The Cigarette Girl
      A Crooked Romance
      Her New York
      The Last of the Carnabys
      Miss Nobody
      Over the Hill
      Pots-and-Pans Peggy
      The Streets of Illusion
1918 Annexing Bill
      For Sale
      Mrs. Slacker
      Waifs
1920 High Speed
      The Silent Barrier
Huling, Lorraine
1914 The Straight Road
      The Unwelcome Mrs. Hatch
1915 Are You a Mason?
      The Bachelor's Romance
      The Dancing Girl
      The Flying Twins
      His Wife
1916 The Fall of a Nation
      King Lear
1917 Even As You and I*
Hull, Alexander
1920 Homer Comes Home
Hull, Arthur
1913 Victory
Hull, Frank E.
1920 Just Out of College
      The Little Shepherd of
        Kingdom Come
      Out of the Storm
      The Penalty
      The Street Called Straight
Hull, George C.
1920 Hitchin' Posts
      The Secret Gift
      West Is West
      White Youth
Hull, Henry
1917 The Family Honor
      Rasputin, the Black Monk
      A Square Deal
      The Volunteer
1919 Little Women
Hull, Jack
1918 Ali Baba and the Forty Thieves
      All Night
1921 The Jucklins
Hull, Robert *see* **Budd** (pseud. of Robert
Hull)
Hull, Shelly
1913 Sapho
Human, William *same as* **Human, Bill;
Human, Billy**
1916 Behind the Lines
1917 The Clean-Up
1919 The Forfeit
      The Unbroken Promise

Hutchinson, Betty
1919 Dust of Desire
The Man Who Stayed at Home
Me and Captain Kidd
The Undercurrent
Hutchinson, Charles same as **Hutchison, Charles**
1914 Lena Rivers (Cosmos Feature Film Corp.)
The Little Angel of Canyon Creek
1915 The Better Woman
Divorced
The Master of the House
Not Guilty
1916 War Brides
1917 God of Little Children
The Golden God
The Mystic Hour
Pride and the Devil
1918 The Desired Woman
Hutchinson, Jack
1918 My Unmarried Wife
Hutchinson, James C.
1919 The Open Door
1920 The Return of Tarzan
Hutchinson, Louise
1916 In the Web of the Grafters
1918 Sandy
Hutchinson, Samuel S.
1916 The Abandonment
The Man Who Would Not Die
Whispering Smith
1917 Her Country's Call
The Mate of the Sally Ann
Sands of Sacrifice
Snap Judgement
1918 Molly, Go Get 'Em
1920 The Dangerous Talent
The Valley of Tomorrow
Hutchinson, William
1917 The Fair Barbarian
The Happiness of Three Women
1918 The Strange Woman
Hutchinson, Belle see **Hutchinson, Belle**
Hutchison, Charles see **Hutchinson, Charles**
Hutchison, Kathryn
1917 The Square Deceiver
Hutt, L. C.
1915 The Lily of Poverty Flat
Hutton, F. Laws
1919 Diane of the Green Van
Hutton, L. H.
1917 The Saintly Sinner
Hutton, Leona
1914 The Typhoon
1916 The Man Who Would Not Die
The Market of Vain Desire
Soul Mates
1917 The Snarl
Hutton, Lucille
1919 The Miracle Man
Huxley, Shirley
1919 A House Divided
Hyde (full name unknown)
1915 The Fairy and the Waif*
Hyde, Harry
1919 Fool's Gold
1920 Homer Comes Home
Hyde, Mabel
1918 The Law That Divides
Hydell, Dorothy
1917 The Slacker (Metro Pictures Corp.)
Hyder, Glenn L.
1920 Frontier Days
Hyland, John
1916 Love's Crucible
Hyland, Peggy
1916 The Chattel
The Enemy
Rose of the South
Saints and Sinners
1917 Babette
Her Right to Live
Intrigue
Persuasive Peggy
The Sixteenth Wife
Womanhood, the Glory of the Nation

1918 Bonnie Annie Laurie
Caught in the Act
The Debt of Honor
Marriages Are Made
Other Men's Daughters
The Other Woman
Peg of the Pirates
1919 Cheating Herself
Cowardice Court
A Girl in Bohemia
The Girl with No Regrets
The Merry-Go-Round
Miss Adventure
The Rebellious Bride
The Web of Chance
1920 Black Shadows
Faith
The Price of Silence
Hymer, John B.
1914 The Path Forbidden
When Fate Leads Trump*
Hyson, Carl
1919 Eastward Ho!

I

Iliff, R. M.
1916 Vengeance Is Mine
Iliodor
1918 The Fall of the Romanoffs
Illington, Margaret could be same as **Illington, Martha**
1917 The Inner Shrine
Sacrifice
Illington, Martha could be same as **Illington, Margaret**
1915 An American Gentleman
Ince, John same as **Ince, John E.**
1913 The Battle of Shiloh
1915 The Cowardly Way
Sealed Lips
1916 The Crucial Test
Her Maternal Right
The Struggle
1917 The Planter*
1918 Her Man
Secret Strings
1919 Blackie's Redemption
Blind Man's Eyes
A Favor to a Friend
One-Thing-at-a-Time O'Day
Please Get Married
Should a Woman Tell?
1920 Held in Trust
Old Lady 31
Someone in the House
Ince, Ralph same as **Ince, Ralph W.**
1914 A Million Bid
1915 The Juggernaut
The Sins of the Mothers
1916 The Combat
The Conflict
The Destroyers
His Wife's Good Name
My Lady's Slipper
The Ninety and Nine
1917 The Argyle Case
The Co-Respondent
To-Day
1918 The Eleventh Commandment
Fields of Honor
Five Thousand an Hour
Her Man
Our Mrs. McChesney
The Panther Woman
Tempered Steel
1919 From Headquarters
Out Yonder
The Painted World
The Perfect Lover
Sealed Hearts
Shadows of the Past
A Stitch in Time
Too Many Crooks
Two Women
Virtuous Men
The Wreck
1920 His Wife's Money
Out of the Snows
Red Foam

Ince, Thomas H. same as **Ince, Thomas; Ince, Thomas Harper**
1913 The Battle of Gettysburg
1914 The Bargain
Shorty Escapes Marriage
The Typhoon
The Voice at the Telephone
The Wrath of the Gods
1915 The Alien
Aloha Oe
The Coward
The Cup of Life
The Darkening Trail
The Despoiler
The Devil
The Disciple
The Edge of the Abyss
The Forbidden Adventure
The Golden Claw
The Iron Strain
The Italian
The Man from Oregon
The Mating
Matrimony
On the Night Stage
The Reward
Rumpelstiltskin
The Toast of Death
The Winged Idol
1916 The Apostle of Vengeance
The Aryan
Bawbs O' Blue Ridge
The Beckoning Flame
The Beggar of Cawnpore
Between Men
Bullets and Brown Eyes
Civilization
Civilization's Child
The Conqueror
The Corner
A Corner in Colleens
The Criminal
D'Artagnan
The Dawn Maker
The Deserter
The Dividend
The Female of the Species
A Gamble in Souls
Hell's Hinges
Jim Grimsby's Boy
The Jungle Child
The Last Act
Lieutenant Danny, U.S.A.
The Moral Fabric
The Patriot
Peggy
The Primal Lure
The Raiders
The Return of Draw Egan
Shell Forty-Three
The Sin Ye Do
Somewhere in France
The Sorrows of Love
The Stepping Stone
The Thoroughbred (New York Motion Picture Corp.; Kay-Bee)
Three of Many
The Vagabond Prince
The Waifs
The Wolf Woman
1917 Ashes of Hope
Back of the Man
Blood Will Tell
Borrowed Plumage
The Bride of Hate
Chicken Casey
The Clodhopper
The Cold Deck
The Crab
The Dark Road
The Desert Man
The Flame of the Yukon
The Girl Glory
The Gun Fighter
Happiness
The Hater of Men
His Mother's Boy
The Iced Bullet
The Last of the Ingrams
The Little Brother
Love Letters
Love or Justice
Madcap Madge
The Millionaire Vagrant

The Narrow Trail
Paddy O'Hara
Paws of the Bear
The Pinch Hitter
The Price Mark
Princess of the Dark
The Sawdust Ring
The Silent Man
The Snarl
The Son of His Father
The Square Deal Man
A Strange Transgressor
Sweetheart of the Doomed
Those Who Pay
Time Locks and Diamonds
Truthful Tulliver
The Weaker Sex
Whither Thou Goest
Wild Winship's Widow
Wolf Lowry
The Zeppelin's Last Raid
1918 The Biggest Show on Earth
Blue Blazes Rawden
The Border Wireless
Branding Broadway
The Cast-Off
The Claws of the Hun
Coals of Fire
A Desert Wooing
The Family Skeleton
"Flare-Up" Sal
Fuss and Feathers
Green Eyes
The Guilty Man
The Hired Man
His Own Home Town
The Kaiser's Shadow, or the Triple Cross
Keys of the Righteous
The Law of the North
Love Me
The Marriage Ring
The Mating of Marcella
The Midnight Patrol
Naughty, Naughty!
A Nine O'Clock Town
Playing the Game
Quicksand
Riddle Gawne
Selfish Yates
Shark Monroe
String Beans
The Tiger Man
Tyrant Fear
The Vamp
Vive La France!
When Do We Eat?
Wolves of the Rail
1919 L'Apache
Behind the Door
Bill Henry
Breed of Men
The Busher
Crooked Straight
The Egg Crate Wallop
Extravagance
The False Faces
The Girl Dodger
Greased Lightning
Happy Though Married
Hard Boiled
The Haunted Bedroom
Hay Foot, Straw Foot
His Wife's Friend
The Homebreaker
John Petticoats
The Lady of Red Butte
The Law of Men
Let's Elope
The Market of Souls
The Money Corral
Other Men's Wives
Partners Three
The Poppy Girl's Husband
Red Hot Dollars
The Sheriff's Son
Square Deal Sanderson
Stepping Out
23 1/2 Hours' Leave
The Virtuous Thief
Wagon Tracks
What Every Woman Learns
1920 Alarm Clock Andy
Below the Surface
Black Is White

Dangerous Hours
The Dark Mirror
The False Road
Hairpins
Her Husband's Friend
Homer Comes Home
Homespun Folks
The Jailbird
Let's Be Fashionable
Mary's Ankle
An Old Fashioned Boy
Paris Green
Rookie's Return
Silk Hosiery
The Village Sleuth
What's Your Husband Doing?
The Woman in the Suitcase

The Indian Players
1913 Hiawatha
Inescourt, Elaine
1920 An Arabian Knight
Ingerson, William
1920 Partners of the Night
Ingleton, E. Magnus same as **Ingleton, E. M.; Ingleton, Eugenie Magnus**
1915 After Dark
A Butterfly on the Wheel
The Impostor
The Ivory Snuff Box
The Little Dutch Girl
The Model
The Moonstone
Trilby
1916 The Almighty Dollar
Broken Chains
Life's Whirlpool
1917 Because of a Woman
The Birth of Patriotism
Eternal Love
The Girl in the Checkered Coat
Heart Strings
The Lair of the Wolf
The Pulse of Life
The Reward of the Faithless
1918 Alias Mary Brown
The Answer
False Ambition
Her American Husband
The Mask
Mystic Faces
Who Is to Blame?
1919 The Blue Bonnet
The Lamb and the Lion
The Long Lane's Turning
The Love Call
Love's Prisoner
1920 Below the Surface
Black Is White
The Dark Mirror
His Own Law
Miss Nobody
Ingleton, George
1914 The Pit
1915 The Sins of Society
1920 Mid-Channel
Ingraham, Harrish
1914 Lena Rivers (Whitman Features Co.)
The Million Dollar Robbery
The Toll of Love
1917 The Blood of His Fathers
The Eye of Envy
The Painted Lie
The Single Code
Unto the End
When Baby Forgot
1919 Child of M'sieu
A Sage Brush Hamlet
Ingraham, Lloyd
1915 The Fox Woman
The Sable Lorcha
The Spanish Jade
1916 American Aristocracy
Casey at the Bat
A Child of the Paris Streets
The Children Pay
Hoodoo Ann
Intolerance
The Little Liar
The Missing Links
Stranded
1917 Charity Castle
Her Country's Call
Miss Jackie of the Army

Nina, the Flower Girl
An Old Fashioned Young Man
Peggy Leads the Way
1918 Ann's Finish
The Eyes of Julia Deep
Impossible Susan
Jilted Janet
Molly, Go Get 'Em
The Primitive Woman
Rosemary Climbs the Heights
The Square Deal
Wives and Other Wives
1919 The Amazing Impostor
The House of Intrigue
The Intrusion of Isabel
Man's Desire
The Mother and the Law
1920 The Jailbird
Let's Be Fashionable
Mary's Ankle
Old Dad
Twin Beds
What's Your Husband Doing?
Ingraham, Mary Louise
1920 The Mysteries of Paris
Ingram, Rex
1915 The Blindness of Devotion
Should a Mother Tell?
The Song of Hate
A Woman's Past
The Wonderful Adventure
1916 Broken Fetters
The Chalice of Sorrow
The Great Problem
1917 Black Orchids
The Flower of Doom
The Little Terror
The Pulse of Life
The Reward of the Faithless
1918 His Robe of Honor
Humdrum Brown
1919 The Day She Paid
1920 Hearts Are Trumps
Shore Acres
Under Crimson Skies
Inokuchi, Makoto
1914 Officer 666
1917 The Stolen Play
Ireland, Frederick J.
1917 The Slacker's Heart
Irish, R. E.
1915 Judge Not; Or, The Woman of Mona Diggings
1916 The Crippled Hand
The Eagle's Wing
Little Eve Edgarton
1917 The Book Agent
Fighting for Love
Love Aflame
The Saintly Sinner
Some Boy!
The Stainless Barrier
The Sudden Gentleman
The Terror
1918 The Empty Cab
The Reckoning Day
1920 The Tiger's Coat
Irrah, Tatjana
1920 The Little Outcast
Man and Woman (A. H. Fischer Features, Inc.)
1921 Miss 139
Irvine, Clarke
1916 Barriers of Society
The Love Hermit
Irvine, W.
1915 The Builder of Bridges*
Irving, Miss
1915 The Fairy and the Waif*
1918 Why America Will Win
Irving, Mrs.
1915 The Fairy and the Waif*
Irving, Buster
1917 The Desert Man
1918 The Mating of Marcella
1919 Breed of Men
The Heart of Youth
Irving, Ethelyn
1920 Under Crimson Skies
Irving, George same as **Irving, George H.; Irving, George Henry**
1914 Dan
The Education of Mr. Pipp

The Jungle
Paid in Full
1915 Body and Soul
The Builder of Bridges
The Fairy and the Waif
John Glayde's Honor
Just Out of College
1916 The Conquest of Canaan
Jaffery
Then I'll Come Back to You
What Happened at 22
The Witching Hour
The Woman in 47
1917 Daughter of Destiny
God's Man
Raffles, the Amateur Cracksman
1918 Back to the Woods
Her Boy
Hidden Fires
The Landloper
To Hell with the Kaiser
1919 As a Man Thinks
The Capitol
The Glorious Lady
The Silver King
The Volcano
1920 The Blue Pearl
Children of Destiny
The Misleading Lady
Irving, Mary Jane
1917 The Square Deal Man
1918 An Alien Enemy
The Heart of Rachael
The One Woman
Patriotism
The Temple of Dusk
The White Lie
1919 The Brand
Desert Gold
The Gray Horizon
Tangled Threads
The Westerners
The Woman Michael Married
1920 Live Sparks
The Luck of Geraldine Laird
A Woman Who Understood
Irving, Dr. Montgomery
1917 National Red Cross Pageant*
Irving, Paul
1916 Behind Closed Doors
Irving, William J. same as **Irving, W. J.; Irving, William**
1918 Till I Come Back to You
1920 Billions
The Heart of a Child
Love's Protegé
Someone in the House
Twin Beds
Irvins, Beth see **Ivins, Beth**
Irwin, Boyd
1920 The Gilded Dream
A Lady in Love
The Luck of Geraldine Laird
The Marriage Pit
Milestones
Irwin, Caroline same as **Irwin, Carolyn**
1917 Pants
Young Mother Hubbard
1920 A Dark Lantern
Irwin, Charles
1915 The Cowpuncher
Irwin, Frank
1915 The Cowpuncher
Irwin, May
1914 Mrs. Black Is Back
Irwin, Wallace
1916 Thrown to the Lions
Isham, Frederick
1920 The Marriage Pit
Ito, Corley T.
1920 The Breath of the Gods
Itow, Michio
1917 National Red Cross Pageant*
Ivan, Rosalind
1916 Arms and the Woman
1917 The Bondage of Fear
Ivans, Beth see **Ivins, Beth**
Ivans, Elaine
1914 The Littlest Rebel
1915 The Devil's Daughter
John Glayde's Honor

1917 The Last Sentence
Iver, Jeanne
1916 One Day
Ivers, Ann
1914 Martin Eden
Ivers, Julia Crawford same as **Ivers, J. C.; Ivers, Julia C.**
1915 The Gentleman from Indiana*
The Majesty of the Law
The Rug Maker's Daughter
1916 The American Beauty
Ben Blair
The Call of the Cumberlands
He Fell in Love with His Wife
The Heart of Paula
The Intrigue
The Parson of Panamint
The Right Direction
A Son of Erin
1917 The Bond Between*
The Cook of Canyon Camp
Her Own People
A Kiss for Susie
Lost in Transit
A Roadside Impresario*
Tom Sawyer
The World Apart
1918 Good Night, Paul
The Gypsy Trail
His Majesty, Bunker Bean
Huck and Tom; Or, The Further Adventures of Tom Sawyer
A Lady's Name
Sauce for the Goose
The Spirit of '17
Up the Road with Sallie
Viviette
1919 The Final Close-Up
More Deadly Than the Male
The Veiled Adventure
Who Cares?
Widow by Proxy
1920 Easy to Get
The Furnace
Huckleberry Finn
Jenny Be Good
Nurse Marjorie
The Soul of Youth
Ives, Charlotte
1914 Clothes
1915 The Dictator
1916 A Prince in a Pawnshop
1917 The Man of Mystery
The Warfare of the Flesh
Ivins, Beth same as **Irvins, Beth; Ivans, Beth**
1918 Doing Their Bit
Queen of the Sea
The Scarlet Trail
1920 In Folly's Trail
Live Sparks

J

Jaccard, Jacques
1916 Is Any Girl Safe?
A Knight of the Range
1919 The Great Air Robbery
1920 Desert Love
Honor Bound
The Terror
Under Northern Lights
Jack, The Man-Ape
1920 The Evolution of Man
Jack, T. C.
1917 Little Lost Sister
Jackman, Fred
1918 Mickey
1919 Yankee Doodle in Berlin
1920 Down on the Farm
Love, Honor and Behave
Married Life
Jacks, S. T.
1920 Within Our Gates
Jackson (full name unknown)
1915 The Fairy and the Waif*
Jackson, Lieut.
1919 Injustice

The Tiger Lily
Trixie from Broadway
The Woman Next Door
1920 Children of Destiny
Husband Hunter
Polly of the Storm Country
She Couldn't Help It
The Walk-Offs
Johnson, Eva
1919 A Man's Duty
Johnson, F. A. see **Johnston, F. A.**
Johnson, Gladys E.
1917 Easy Money
1919 The Game's Up
Johnson, Grace
1915 Scandal
1916 Wanted—A Home
Johnson, Harold
1919 Secret Marriage
Johnson, Hiram W.
19-- Official Motion Pictures of the
Panama Pacific Exposition
Held at San Francisco,
Calif.*
Johnson, Howard
1918 The Make-Believe Wife
Johnson, Isabelle see **Johnston, Isabel**
Johnson, J. W. see **Johnston, J. W.**
Johnson, Jack W. see **Johnston, J. W.**
Johnson, James
1914 The Millon Dollar Robbery*
The Yellow Traffic
Johnson, Jugo C.
1916 The Scarlet Road
Wild Oats
Johnson, Julianne see **Johnston, Julianne**
Johnson, Julian
1918 High Stakes
1920 Who's Your Servant?
Johnson, Katherine see **Johnston,**
Katherine
Johnson, Kitty
1917 Diamonds and Pearls
1918 His Royal Highness
Neighbors
Johnson, L. S.
1916 The Girl Philippa
Johnson, Lawrence
1918 The Fall of the Romanoffs
1919 Mrs. Wiggs of the Cabbage
Patch
The Silver King
1920 Guilty of Love
His House in Order
The Right to Love
Johnson, Lorimer see **Johnston, Lorimer**
Johnson, Lou
1916 The Daring of Diana
Johnson, Mabel
1916 Plain Jane
Johnson, Margaret
1918 Little Red Riding Hood
Johnson, Martin E. same as **Johnson,**
Martin
1913 Jack London's Adventures in
the South Sea Islands
1918 Among the Cannibal Isles of
the South Pacific
Johnson, Max
1920 Our Christianity and Nobody's
Child
Johnson, Noble
1916 Kinkaid, Gambler
1917 Fighting for Love
The Hero of the Hour
Love Aflame
Mr. Dolan of New York
The Terror
1920 The Adorable Savage
The Leopard Woman
Sunset Sprague
Under Crimson Skies
Johnson, Nora same as **Johnson, Norine**
1919 Happy Though Married
The Homebreaker
Johnson, Norris
1920 An Amateur Devil
Let's Be Fashionable
Paris Green
What's Your Husband Doing?

Johnson, Olive
1915 The Commanding Officer
Johnson, Orrin
1915 Fighting Bob
The Penitentes
Satan Sanderson
1916 D'Artagnan
Light at Dusk
The Price of Power
1917 Whither Thou Goest
Johnson, Osa
1918 Among the Cannibal Isles of
the South Pacific
Johnson, R. L. (asst dir)
1920 The City of Masks
Johnson, Ralph (actor)
1917 The Frozen Warning
Johnson, Richard same as **Johnson,**
Dick
1914 The Will O' the Wisp
1916 The Birth of a Man
The Sultana
1917 His Old-Fashioned Dad
1919 The Boomerang
1920 The Fourteenth Man
The Life of the Party
The Unfortunate Sex
Johnson, Roswell J.
1915 The Model
Johnson, Sheldon
1918 The Vigilantes
Johnson, Tefft
1915 The Battle Cry of Peace
C.O.D.
The Turn of the Road
1916 Who Killed Joe Merrion?
The Writing on the Wall
1917 Love's Law
1918 The Love Net
The Panther Woman
1919 Home Wanted
Love and the Woman
The Love Defender
Johnson, Vida
1916 Driftwood
1920 Alias Miss Dodd
The Desert Scorpion
Wolves of the Street
Johnson, Walter
1917 The Baseball Revue of 1917*
Johnson, William could be same as
Johnson, Willie
1920 Suds
Johnson, Willie could be same as
Johnson, William
1917 The Courage of Silence
Johnston, Agnes C. same as **Johnson,**
Agnes; Johnson, Agnes C.; Johnston,
Agnes; Johnston, Agnes Christine
1916 Divorce and the Daughter
The Fear of Poverty
God's Country and the Woman
Prudence the Pirate
The Shine Girl
1917 An Amateur Orphan
The Fires of Youth
Her New York
It Happened to Adele
Pots-and-Pans Peggy
When Love Was Blind
1918 The Great Adventure
How Could You, Caroline?
Mrs. Slacker
1919 Daddy-Long-Legs
The Old Maid's Baby
The Sawdust Doll
Trixie from Broadway
23 1/2 Hours' Leave
1920 Alarm Clock Andy
Her Husband's Friend
Homer Comes Home
An Old Fashioned Boy
Silk Hosiery
The Village Sleuth
Johnston, Constance see **Johnson,**
Constance
Johnston, F. A. same as **Johnson, F. A.**
1916 Vengeance Is Mine
1917 The Single Code
Johnston, Captain George W.
1917 Womanhood, the Glory of the
Nation

Johnston, Isabel same as **Johnson,**
Isabelle; Johnston, Isabel M.;
Johnston, Isabelle
1915 Carmen (Fox Film Corp.)*
The Turn of the Road
1918 Cupid by Proxy
1920 Forty-Five Minutes from
Broadway
Her Elephant Man
Love's Harvest
Molly and I
Peaceful Valley
A Woman Who Understood
Johnston, J. W. same as **Johnson, J.**
W.; Johnson, Jack; Johnson, Jack
W.; Johnston, Jack W.; could be
same as **Johnstone, Jack**
1914 The Ghost Breaker
The Man on the Box
Rose of the Rancho
The Virginian
Where the Trail Divides
1915 Sealed Valley
1916 Destiny's Toy
Fifty-Fifty
God's Half Acre
Molly Make-Believe
The Moment Before
Out of the Drifts
Should a Baby Die?
1917 The Adopted Son
As Men Love
The Cost of Hatred
The Eternal Mother
The Land of Promise
1918 At the Mercy of Men
On the Quiet
The Reason Why
The Spirit of '17
Uncle Tom's Cabin
The Woman the Germans Shot
1919 Out of the Shadow
The Praise Agent
The Price of Innocence
Speedy Meade
The Test of Honor
The Twin Pawns
1920 Man's Plaything
Why Women Sin
Johnston, Julianne same as **Johnson,**
Julanne; Johnstone, Julianne
1919 Better Times
1920 Fickle Women
Miss Hobbs
Seeing It Through
Johnston, Katherine same as **Johnson,**
Katherine
1917 The Beloved Adventuress
The Brand of Satan
The Good for Nothing
The Iron Ring
Shall We Forgive Her?
1918 Whims of Society
1919 A Damsel in Distress
The Love Cheat
1920 The Flapper
Johnston, L.
1917 Apartment 29
Johnston, Lamar see **Johnstone, Lamar**
Johnston, Lorimer same as **Johnson,**
Lorimer
1914 The Envoy Extraordinary
1916 The Island of Surprise*
1917 The Blood of His Fathers*
1919 Breezy Jim
Devil McCare
Johnston, Ralph (child actor)
1915 Should a Mother Tell?
Johnston, Renita
1920 If I Were King
Johnstone, Belle Stoddard
1920 The Marriage Pit
Johnstone, Calder
1916 The Crippled Hand
A Yoke of Gold
1917 Twin Kiddies
1920 The Prey
Johnstone, Harold
1918 The Midnight Patrol
Johnstone, Jack could be same as
Johnston, J. W.
1919 The Broken Melody

Johnstone, Julianne see **Johnston,**
Julianne
Johnstone, Justine same as **Johnstone,**
Justina
1914 The Crucible
1920 Blackbirds
Nothing but Lies
Johnstone, Lamar same as **Johnston,**
Lamar
1916 Ben Blair
The Impersonation
The Ne'er-Do-Well
Tongues of Men
1917 The Calendar Girl
The Planter
1918 The Girl of My Dreams
That Devil, Bateese
1919 Diane of the Green Van
The Last of the Duanes
The Lone Star Ranger
A Man in the Open
The Sheriff's Son
The Spite Bride
Wolves of the Night
Jolivet, Rita
1915 The Unafraid
1916 Her Redemption
An International Marriage
Love's Sacrifice
1917 National Red Cross Pageant
One Law for Both
1918 Lest We Forget
Jonasson, Frank
1914 The Invisible Power
1915 The Barnstormers
The Pitfall
1920 A Full House
The Sins of St. Anthony
What Happened to Jones
Jones, Alida same as **Jones, Alida D.**
1918 Her Moment
1920 White Youth
Jones, Buck same as **Jones, Charles**
1918 The Rainbow Trail
Riders of the Purple Sage
True Blue
Western Blood
1919 The Sheriff's Son
The Speed Maniac
1920 Firebrand Trevison
Forbidden Trails
Just Pals
The Last Straw
The Square Shooter
Sunset Sprague
Two Moons
Jones, Ed (actor) same as **Jones,**
Edward
1918 Wild Women
A Woman's Fool
1920 Sundown Slim
Jones, Edgar (dir, actor)
1913 The Battle of Shiloh
1915 An Enemy to Society
The Woman Pays
1916 Dimples
The Half Million Bribe
Lovely Mary
The Turmoil
1917 The Girl Angle
The Lady in the Library
Mentioned in Confidence
Zollenstein
1918 The Girl Who Wouldn't Quit
A Rich Man's Darling
Wild Honey
1919 One Against Many
Jones, Edward see **Jones, Ed** (actor)
Jones, F. Richard same as **Jones,**
Richard
1918 Mickey
1919 Yankee Doodle in Berlin
1920 Down on the Farm
Flying Pat
Love, Honor and Behave
1922 The Cynic Effect
Jones, Fielder
1917 The Baseball Revue of 1917*
Jones, Fred same as **Jones, Fred C.;**
Jones, Frederick
1915 The Destroying Angel
1916 The Flower of No Man's Land
The Gates of Eden
The Straight Way

Kelly, Eddie
1918 Sporting Life
1918-19
      Once to Every Man
Kelly, Fanny
1920 Love, Honor and Behave
Kelly, Frank
1915 The College Orphan
      The Long Chance
Kelly, Gladys
1917 All for a Husband
      A Rich Man's Plaything
Kelly, Harry A.
1913 One Hundred Years of
      Mormonism*
Kelly, Helen
1918 M'liss
Kelly, John T.
1915 The Cave Man
1916 Artie, the Millionaire Kid
      Green Stockings
Kelly, M. A.
1920 Beyond the Great Wall
Kelly, Mabel
1915 C.O.D.
      The Turn of the Road
1916 Who Killed Joe Merrion?
      The Writing on the Wall
Kelly, Margot
1920 The Sport of Kings
Kelly, Paul
1917 Knights of the Square Table
1919 Anne of Green Gables
      Fit to Win
1920 Uncle Sam of Freedom Ridge
Kelly, R. H.
1917 The Princess of Patches
      The Unforseen
Kelly, Renee
1915 All for a Girl
      The Bigger Man
Kelly, Robert *same as* **Kelley, Robert**
1917 Her Secret
      Richard, the Brazen
Kelly, Thomas (*actor*)
1919 The Son-of-a-Gun!
Kelly, Thomas J. (*writer*)
1917 The Bondage of Fear
Kelly, William J.
1915 A Woman's Resurrection
1918 Secret Strings
1919 When My Ship Comes In
Kelsey, Fred *same as* **Kelsey Fred A.**
1917 The Fighting Gringo
1918 The Empty Cab
      A Society Sensation
      The Yellow Dog
1919 The Fire Flingers
      The Light of Victory
      The Silk Lined Burglar
1920 Alias Jimmy Valentine
      Blackmail
      The One Way Trail
      The Third Generation
Kelso, Bobby
1920 The Jack-Knife Man
Kelso, Lou
1915 A Black Sheep
Kelso, Mayme *same as* **Kelso, Maym**
1914 The Three of Us
1915 The Bigger Man
      Dr. Rameau
      The Family Stain
      One Million Dollars
      The Warning
1916 Man and His Angel
      Slander
1917 Castles for Two
      The Cost of Hatred
      Lost and Won
      The Primrose Ring
      Rebecca of Sunnybrook Farm
      The Secret Game
      The Silent Partner
      Those Without Sin
1918 The Cruise of the
      Make-Believes
      His Birthright
      The Honor of His House
      Mirandy Smiles
      The Mystery Girl
      Old Wives for New

      The Thing We Love
      The White Man's Law
      The Widow's Might
1919 Cheating Cheaters
      Experimental Marriage
      In for Thirty Days
      Johnny Get Your Gun
      Male and Female
      Men, Women and Money
      Peg O' My Heart
      A Very Good Young Man
      Why Smith Left Home
      You Never Saw Such a Girl
1920 The Brand of Lopez*
      Conrad in Quest of His Youth
      Don't Ever Marry
      The Furnace
      Help Wanted—Male
      The Hope
      Seeing It Through
      Simple Souls
      The Week-End
      Why Change Your Wife?
Kelson, George
1917 The Strong Way
      The Tenth Case
1918 The Purple Lily
      Stolen Orders
      The Way Out
1919 Bolshevism on Trial
      Little Women
Kelvah, Princess
1920 Empty Arms
Kemble, Lillian
1916 The House of Mirrors
Kemble, William H.
1916 America Preparing
      The Zeppelin Raids on London
      and the Siege of Verdun
1918 The Men of the Hour
Kendall, E. K.
1919 The Shepherd of the Hills
Kendall, Harry
1914 The Win(k)some Widow
      Without Hope
1916 The Witch
1918 Miss Ambition
1920 Dollar for Dollar
      Haunting Shadows
Kendall, Messmore
1920 The Song of the Soul
Kendall, Preston
1919 Heads Win
Kendig, Walter
1915 Wildfire
Kendrick, Frank
1912 Oliver Twist
Kendrick, Ruby
1919 Blind Husbands
Kenley, Thelma
1920 Sky Eye
Kennard, Pop
1918 Cyclone Higgins, D.D.
Kennard, Victor
1917 Betsy Ross
      The Burglar
      The Iron Ring
      The Volunteer
      Youth
1918 Journey's End
      The Soul of Buddha
      A Soul Without Windows
      Stolen Hours
      The Wasp
Kennedy, A. M.
1918 Dodging a Million
Kennedy, Ann
1918 Dodging a Million*
Kennedy, Arthur
1918 Prunella
Kennedy, Aubrey M.
1918 Dodging a Million*
1920 Sky Eye
Kennedy, Clara Genevieve *same as* **Kennedy, Clara G.**
1919 An Innocent Adventuress
      You're Fired
1920 A City Sparrow
      The Dancin' Fool
      Double Speed
      Eyes of the Heart
      Sick Abed

Kennedy, Ed
1917 The Blue Streak
Kennedy, Edith *same as* **Kennedy, Edith M.**
1917 The Bond of Fear
      The Fair Barbarian
      Giving Becky a Chance
      The Marcellini Millions
      Molly Entangled
1918 The Bravest Way
      The Cruise of the
      Make-Believes
      Her Country First
      Mirandy Smiles
      Mrs. Leffingwell's Boots
      A Pair of Silk Stockings
      Sandy
      The Way of a Man with a
      Maid
1919 His Official Fiancée
      The Home Town Girl
      Jane Goes A-Wooing
      The Rescuing Angel
      Romance and Arabella
      Rustling a Bride
      The Third Kiss
1920 All-of-a-Sudden-Peggy
      Crooked Streets
      Food for Scandal
      Her First Elopement
      The Ladder of Lies
      Oh, Lady, Lady
      Young Mrs. Winthrop
Kennedy, Elizabeth
1916 A Modern Thelma
1918 The Road to France
1919 Who's Your Brother?
Kennedy, Jack
1917 Persuasive Peggy
Kennedy, Kathryn
1917 Sadie Goes to Heaven
Kennedy, Lem F. *same as* **Kennedy, L. F.**
1917 Thou Shalt Not Steal
      Wife Number Two
1920 The Key to Power
Kennedy, Leo A. *same as* **Kennedy, Leo**
1914 The War of Wars; Or, The
      Franco-German Invasion
1916 Little Miss Happiness
Kennedy, Madge
1917 Baby Mine
      Nearly Married
1918 The Danger Game
      The Fair Pretender
      Friend Husband
      The Kingdom of Youth
      Our Little Wife
      A Perfect Lady
      The Service Star
1919 Daughter of Mine
      Day Dreams
      Leave It to Susan
      Strictly Confidential
      Through the Wrong Door
1920 The Blooming Angel
      Dollars and Sense
      The Girl with the Jazz Heart
      Help Yourself
      The Truth
Kennedy, Mary
1918 The Blue Bird
Kennedy, Norman
1920 Hearts Are Trumps
Kennedy, Tom *same as* **Kennedy, Thomas**
1915 Double Trouble
1918 Mickey
1919 The Island of Intrigue
1920 Kismet
      The Poor Simp
Kenneth, Harry
1915 The Eagle's Nest
Kenney, Edward *could be same as* **Kenny, Edward**
1916 The Stolen Triumph
Kenny, Colin
1918 The Romance of Tarzan
      The Seal of Silence
      Tarzan of the Apes
      Unexpected Places
1919 The Girl from Outside
      Toby's Bow

      Upstairs
      The Wishing Ring Man
1920 Blind Youth
      Darling Mine
      813
      The Last Straw
      The Triflers
Kenny, Edward *could be same as* **Kenney, Edward**
1916 D'Artagnan
Kensel, Lieut. Frederick, U.S.M.C.
1918 The Unbeliever
Kent, Bertha
1918 The Lie
Kent, Bruce
1916 Captain Jinks of the Horse
      Marines
Kent, Charles
1914 The Christian
      A Florida Enchantment
      A Million Bid
      Mr. Barnes of New York
      The Strange Story of Sylvia
      Gray
1915 The Battle Cry of Peace
      Hearts and the Highway
      The Heights of Hazard
      On Her Wedding Night
      A Price for Folly
1916 The Blue Envelope Mystery
      Britton of the Seventh
      The Chattel
      The Enemy
      The Island of Surprise
      Kennedy Square
      Rose of the South
      The Supreme Temptation
      The Tarantula
      The Vital Question
      Whom the Gods Destroy
1917 The Duplicity of Hargraves
      Kitty MacKay
      The Marriage Speculation
      The Money Mill
      The Question
      Soldiers of Chance
1918 Tangled Lives
      Wild Primrose
      The Wooing of Princess Pat
1919 Counterfeit
      Daring Hearts
      The Gamblers
      Miss Dulcie from Dixie
      Thin Ice
1920 The Birth of a Soul
      Forbidden Valley
      Human Collateral
      Man and His Woman
Kent, Craufurd *same as* **Kent, Craufurd; Kent, Crawford**
1915 The Deep Purple
      Greater Love Hath No Man
      Little Miss Brown
      Nedra
      The Pretenders
      Simon, the Jester
1916 Dollars and the Woman
      The Evil Thereof
      The Heart of the Hills
      Her Bleeding Heart
      Love's Toll
      Sorrows of Happiness
1917 The Antics of Ann
      Broadway Jones
      Double Crossed
      Thais
      The Woman Beneath
1918 The Better Half
      The Danger Mark
      The Inn of the Blue Moon
      Kildare of Storm
      The Knife
      The Ordeal of Rosetta
      The Song of Songs
      The Trap
1919 The Career of Katherine Bush
      Come Out of the Kitchen
      Good Gracious, Annabelle
      The Splendid Romance
      Thou Shalt Not
1920 Clothes
      Dollars and the Woman
      The Love Flower
      Other Men's Shoes

King, Carlton *same as* King, Carleton;
  King, Carleton S.
1915 The Mystery of Room 13
     The Ring of the Borgias
     The Truth About Helen
     The Way Back
1916 Just a Song at Twilight
     Tempest and Sunshine
     When Love Is King
1917 Blind Man's Holiday
     The Indian Summer of Dry
       Valley Johnson
     The Skylight Room
1918 All Man
     Little Miss No-Account
     The Wooing of Princess Pat
King, Charles A. *same as* King, Charles
1914 The Indian Wars
1917 The Adventures of Buffalo Bill
King, Clara
1917 The Flaming Omen
King, Claude
1920 Idols of Clay
King, Clo
1920 Judy of Rogue's Harbor
     The Spirit of Good
King, Emmett *same as* King, Emmet C.;
  King, Emmett C.
1917 Mary Jane's Pa
1918 The Fair Pretender
     Lafayette, We Come!
     Out of the Night
1919 Beckoning Roads
     The Fear Woman
     Fools and Their Money
     In His Brother's Place
     Please Get Married
1920 The Best of Luck
     Billions
     The Desperate Hero
     Kismet
     Number 99
1921 Habit
King, F.
1916 The Colored American
       Winning His Suit
King, George
1918 The City of Dim Faces
1919 Satan Junior
King, Gerald
1914 The House of Bondage
King, Helen
1914 The Will O' the Wisp
King, Henry
1915 Should a Wife Forgive?
1916 Joy and the Dragon
     Little Mary Sunshine
     Pay Dirt
     The Power of Evil
     Shadows and Sunshine
1917 The Bride's Silence
     The Climber
     The Devil's Bait
     A Game of Wits
     The Mainspring
     The Mate of the Sally Ann
     New York Luck*
     Souls in Pawn
     Southern Pride
     Sunshine and Gold
     Told at Twilight
     Twin Kiddies
1918 All the World to Nothing
     Beauty and the Rogue
     The Ghost of Rosy Taylor*
     Hearts or Diamonds?
     Hobbs in a Hurry
     The Locked Heart
     No Children Wanted*
     Powers That Prey
     Social Briars
     Up Romance Road
1919 Brass Buttons
     A Fugitive from Matrimony
     Six Feet Four
     Some Liar
     A Sporting Chance (American
       Film Co.)
     This Hero Stuff
     23 1/2 Hours' Leave
     When a Man Rides Alone
     Where the West Begins
1920 Dice of Destiny
     Haunting Shadows

     Help Wanted—Male
     One Hour Before Dawn
     Uncharted Channels
     The White Dove
King, J. A.
1919 The Lost Battalion
King, J. C.
1920 The Deep Purple
King, Joe *same as* King, Joseph
1916 Her Bitter Cup*
     The Selfish Woman
     Sweet Kitty Bellairs
1917 Betty and the Buccaneers
     Big Timber
     Du Barry
     Hell Hath No Fury
     The Rose of Blood
     Sands of Sacrifice
     The Sea Master
     Until They Get Me
     Wild Winship's Widow
1918 The Answer
     Everywoman's Husband
     The Hand at the Window
     Heiress for a Day
     Irish Eyes
     The Last Rebel
     The Price of Applause
     Secret Code
     Shifting Sands
     The Vortex
     When Destiny Wills
1919 False Evidence
     The Imp
     Love's Prisoner
     The Right to Lie
     The Way of the Strong
1920 The Broadway Bubble
     Children Not Wanted
     The Girl with the Jazz Heart
     Man and Woman (A. H.
       Fischer Features, Inc.)
     The North Wind's Malice
     The Woman God Sent
King, Leslie
1919 Here Comes the Bride
     The Witness for the Defense
1920 Idols of Clay
King, Lewis *same as* King, Louis
1917 The Secret of Black Mountain
1918 Rosemary Climbs the Heights
1919 The Forbidden Room
1920 The Valley of Tomorrow
King, Lucille
1917 The Planter
King, Mollie
1916 All Man
     Fate's Boomerang
     The Summer Girl
     A Woman's Power
1917 Blind Man's Luck
     Kick In
     The On-the-Square-Girl
1918 Human Clay
1919 Suspense
1920 Greater Than Love
     Women Men Forget
King, Nellie
1918 Wild Honey
King, Ruth
1917 The Blood of His Fathers
     The Evil Eye
     The Land of Long Shadows
     Men of the Desert
     Open Places
     The Range Boss
1918 The Pen Vulture
     Winning Grandma
1920 Alias Miss Dodd
     A Beggar in Purple
     Dangerous Love
     The Devil's Passkey
     For the Soul of Rafael
King, Stanley
1917 The Seven Swans
King, Ward
1918 The Eagle
King, Webb
1919 A Man's Duty
1920 Reformation

Kingdon, Dorothy *same as* Van Raven,
  Baroness Dorothy
1915 The Battle of Ballots
     The Governor's Boss
1919 The Profiteer
Kingdon, Frank
1917 The Easiest Way
     The Moth
1918 Mrs. Dane's Defense
1920 Partners of the Night
     Remodelling Her Husband
Kingsbury, Charles J. (cam)
1918 The Love Swindle
Kingsbury, Jacob (actor)
1919 The Volcano
1920 The Whisper Market
Kingsley, Ada
1917 The Skylight Room
Kingsley, Ethel
1919 Sealed Hearts
Kingsley, Florida *same as* Kingsley,
  Flora
1916 The Turmoil
1917 The Boy Girl
1918 Hidden Fires
     Money Mad
1919 Thou Shalt Not
     The Woman on the Index
     The Woman Under Oath
1920 Dangerous Business
     Greater Than Fame
     Youthful Folly
Kingsley, Frank
1915 What Happened to Father
1919 The Bishop's Emeralds
     The Girl Problem
Kingsley, Harry
1917 The Public Defender
Kingsley, Mona
1916 The Light of Happiness
1919 The Glorious Lady
     The Lion and the Mouse
     The Oakdale Affair
Kingsley, Pierce
1914 After the Ball
     The House of Bondage
1915 The Magic Toy Maker
     Silver Threads Among the Gold
1920 The Wall Street Mystery
Kingston, Winifred
1914 Brewster's Millions
     The Call of the North
     Cameo Kirby
     Paid in Full
     Soldiers of Fortune
     The Squaw Man
     The Virginian
     Where the Trail Divides
1915 Captain Courtesy
     The Gentleman from Indiana
     The Love Route
     The Seventh Noon
1916 Ben Blair
     The Call of the Cumberlands
     David Garrick
     Davy Crockett
     The Parson of Panamint
     A Son of Erin
1917 Durand of the Bad Lands
     North of Fifty-Three
     The Scarlet Pimpernel
     The Spy
1918 The Light of Western Stars
1920 The Corsican Brothers
Kinkead, Eleanor Talbot
1918 Captain of His Soul
Kinkel, George
1916 Through the Wall
Kinmaird, Marian
1917 Alma, Where Do You Live?
Kinney, Martin
1916 Blue Blood and Red
Kino, Goro *same as* Keeno, Gordo;
  Kino; Kino, G.; Kino, Gordo
1916 The Honorable Friend
1917 The Flower of Doom
     The Haunted Pajamas
1918 The Bravest Way
     Little Red Decides
     The Midnight Patrol
1920 The Purple Cipher
     A Tokio Siren

Kinsella, Frank
1915 Bred in the Bone
Kipling, Richard
1920 The Lone Hand
Kirby, Andrew
1914 The Rejuvenation of Aunt
       Mary
Kirby, David
1917 The Girl in the Checkered Coat
1918 Blindfolded
     The White Lie
1919 The Poppy Girl's Husband
     Virtuous Sinners
Kirby, Frank *see* Kugler, Frank
Kirby, Madge
1915 The Hungarian Nabob
1918 The Flash of Fate
Kirby, Ollie *see* Kirkby, Ollie
Kirk, Evans
1920 The Gamesters
     Husband Hunter
     White Lies
Kirkby, Ollie *same as* Kirby, Ollie
1914 The Key to Yesterday
1915 The Barnstormers
1917 The Fringe of Society
Kirkham, Cathleen *see* Kirkham,
  Kathleen
Kirkham, Correan
1920 Black Shadows
     Madame X
     Milestones
     The Tattlers
Kirkham, Katherine *could be same as*
  Kirkham, Kathleen
1918 Social Ambition
1920 The Triflers
Kirkham, Kathleen *same as* Kirkham,
  Cathleen; *could be same as*
  Kirkham, Katherine *or* Kirkman,
  Kathleen
1916 The House of Lies
1917 Brand's Daughter
     The Calendar Girl
     The Clean Gun
     The Devil's Assistant
     The Eyes of the World
     His Sweetheart
     The Masked Heart
     A Modern Musketeer
     The Phantom Shotgun
1918 Arizona
     A Diplomatic Mission
     For Husbands Only
     He Comes Up Smiling
     The Married Virgin
     The Seal of Silence
     Tarzan of the Apes
1919 The Beauty Market
     The Beloved Cheater
     The Gay Lord Quex
     In Search of Arcady
     Josselyn's Wife
     The Master Man
     The Third Kiss
     Upstairs and Down
1920 Dollar for Dollar
     Her Five-Foot Highness
     The Little 'Fraid Lady
     Number 99
     Parlor, Bedroom and Bath
     When Dawn Came
Kirkland, David
1916 The Crippled Hand
1919 A Temperamental Wife
     A Virtuous Vamp
1920 In Search of a Sinner
     The Love Expert
     Nothing but the Truth
     The Perfect Woman
Kirkland, Hardee *same as* Kirkland,
  Hardie; Kirkland, Hardy
1915 The Galley Slave
1916 The Feud Girl
     The Lost Bridegroom
1917 When False Tongues Speak
1918 Eye for Eye
     Five Thousand an Hour
     Her Great Chance
     Les Miserables
1919 In Wrong
     Johnny-on-the-Spot
     The Master Man

Konishi, Horin
  1917 Hashimura Togo
  1920 Isobel; Or, The Trail's End
Konnella, Sam
  1920 White Youth
Korach, Milton W. *same as* **Korach, Milton**
  1919 The House Without Children
  1920 Women Men Love
Korlin, Boris
  1915 The Beloved Vagabond
  1916 The Scarlet Oath
  1917 Darkest Russia
         The Soul of a Magdalen
         To the Death
Kortman, Robert
  1916 The Captive God
         Hell's Hinges
         Lieutenant Danny, U.S.A.
         The No-Good Guy
         The Waifs
  1917 The Narrow Trail
  1919 Through the Wrong Door
  1920 Godless Men
Koser, Mr. *could be same as* **Koser, H. E.; Koser, Henry S.** *or* **Kosher, Harry**
  1915 Mistress Nell
Koser, H. E. *could be same as* **Koser, Mr; Koser, Henry S.** *or* **Kosher, Harry**
  1918 Good-Bye, Bill
Koser, Henry S. *could be same as* **Koser, Mr.; Koser, H. E.** *or* **Kosher, Harry**
  1919 The Mystery of the Yellow Room
Kosher, Harry *could be same as* **Koser, Mr.; Koser, H. E.** *or* **Koser, Henry S.**
  1919 Out of the Shadow
Kosloff, Alexis
  1917 The Dancer's Peril
  1920 The Garter Girl*
Kosloff, Theodore
  1917 The Woman God Forgot
  1920 The City of Masks
         The Prince Chap
         Something to Think About
         The Tree of Knowledge
         Why Change Your Wife?
Kost, Emma
  1916 The Argonauts of California—1849
Kotani, Henry *same as* **Katoni, Henry**
  1914 The Typhoon
  1915 The Fox Woman
         The Sable Lorcha
  1917 The Hostage
  1918 Believe Me Xantippe
         The Firefly of France
         The Goat
         The House of Silence
         Less Than Kin
         The Way of a Man with a Maid
  1919 The Heart of Youth
         Jane Goes A-Wooing
         Johnny Get Your Gun
         Puppy Love
         Rustling a Bride
         The Secret Garden
         Told in the Hills
         Under the Top
  1920 Mrs. Temple's Telegram
         Young Mrs. Winthrop
Kotlowsky, Benjamin S. *see* **Kutler, Benjamin S.**
Koupal, T. Morse *same as* **Koupal, T. M.**
  1919 Out of the Fog
  1920 The Fortune Teller
Krafft, John W.
  1920 A Connecticut Yankee at King Arthur's Court
Kraft, Virginia
  1916 The Valiants of Virginia
Krakauer, David
  1915 The Last of the Mafia*

Krakauer, Minnie
  1916 The Man Behind the Curtain
Kramer, Wright
  1915 John Glayde's Honor
         Just Out of College
Kraus, Charles *same as* **Kraus, Fred; Krauss, Charles**
  1914 One of Our Girls
  1915 An Affair of Three Nations
         The House of Fear
         Seven Sisters
  1918 Just a Woman
Kreiss, Ludwig
  1916 Sherlock Holmes
Krelle, Mark
  1919 Stripped for a Million
Kroell, Adrienne
  1914 The Royal Box
Kromarm, Ann *same as* **Kroman, Ann; Kroman, Anne; Kronan, Ann**
  1917 The Birth of Patriotism
         The Flame of Youth
         The Medicine Man
         The Midnight Man
         The Tar Heel Warrior
  1918 Her Decision
         An Honest Man
         Marked Cards
         The Shoes That Danced
Krotoshinsky, Private Abraham
  1919 The Lost Battalion
Krows, Arthur Edwin
  1919 The Winchester Woman
         The Woman Thou Gavest Me*
  1920 The Birth of a Soul
Kruger, Otto
  1915 A Mother's Confession
         The Runaway Wife
Kruse, Lottie *same as* **Cruez, Lottie; Cruze, Lottie; Kruze, Lottie**
  1917 The Planter
         The Spirit of '76
  1918 The City of Tears
         The Deciding Kiss
  1919 The Girl Alaska
Krushe, Emil
  1915 Mignon
Kruze, Lottie *see* **Kruse, Lottie**
Kuan, Moru
  1917 The Lady in the Library
Kugel, Lee
  1915 How Molly Malone Made Good
Kugler, Frank *same as* **Kirby, Frank; Kirby, Frank Gordon; Kugler, Frank C.; Kugler, Frank G.**
  1914 The Ordeal
  1915 The Plunderer
  1916 Daredevil Kate
         My Country First
         The War Bride's Secret
  1917 The Bitter Truth
         The New York Peacock
         She
         The Wild Girl
  1918 A Daughter of France
         Her Price
  1919 The Price of Innocence
         Wild Oats
  1920 Life
Kull, Edward *same as* **Kull, Ed; Kull, Ed J.; Kull, Eddie**
  1916 The Mainspring
         The Measure of a Man
         The Social Buccaneer
         The Whirlpool of Destiny
  1917 The Charmer
         The Desire of the Moth
         Her Soul's Inspiration
         A Jewel in Pawn
         The Little Orphan
         Polly Redhead
  1918 $5,000 Reward
         Hungry Eyes
         The Kaiser, the Beast of Berlin
         The Lure of Luxury
         Midnight Madness
  1919 Creaking Stairs
         The Fire Flingers
         The Pointing Finger
         The Sleeping Lion
         The Sundown Trail

Kull, George
  1916 Bobbie of the Ballet
  1918 Playthings
Kull, Jacob
  1917 The Lair of the Wolf
  1918 The Lonely Woman
         Who Killed Walton?
Kulz, Frederic
  1916 The Scarlet Oath
Kummer, Frederic Arnold
  1917 Motherhood (Frank Powell Producing Corp.)
  1918 The Belgian
Kunkel, George
  1914 Captain Alvarez
  1915 The Chalice of Courage
  1916 God's Country and the Woman
  1917 The Magnificent Meddler
  1918 By the World Forgot
         The Changing Woman
         The Dawn of Understanding
         Unclaimed Goods
  1919 A Fighting Colleen
         Leave It to Susan
  1920 Forbidden Trails
         The Girl in the Rain
         Pinto
Kunkel, Glenn
  1920 Chains of Evidence
Kunkel, Robert
  1919 The Brand
Kurihara, Thomas *same as* **Kurahara, Thomas; Kurahara, Tom; Kurichari, Thomas; Kurikara, Thomas**
  1914 The Typhoon
         The Wrath of the Gods
  1915 The Forbidden Adventure
  1916 The Soul of Kura-San
  1917 The Square Deal Man
  1918 The Bravest Way
         Her American Husband
         The Honor of His House
         The Hopper
         Wolves of the Rail
Kurrle, Robert B. *same as* **Kurrle, Robert**
  1916 Her Great Price
  1918 Boston Blackie's Little Pal
         Hitting the High Spots
         No Man's Land
         The Trail to Yesterday
         Unexpected Places
  1919 Blackie's Redemption
         Blind Man's Eyes
         Easy to Make Money
         Faith
         The Lion's Den
         Lombardi, Ltd.
         One-Thing-at-a-Time O'Day
         The Red Lantern*
         The Spender
  1920 Isobel; Or, The Trail's End
         The Right of Way
         Rio Grande
  1921 Habit
Kusell, Maurice
  1916 Love Never Dies
Kuszewski, Hedda
  1916 Light at Dusk
Kutler, Benjamin S. *same as* **Kotlowsky, Benjamin S.**
  1914 The Jungle
         Michael Strogoff
         Pierre of the Plains
         The Ragged Earl
  1917 The Outsider
  1918 A Daughter of France
Kuwa, George *same as* **Kuwa, Mr.; Kuwa, George K.**
  1916 The Soul of Kura-San
         The Yellow Pawn
  1917 The Bottle Imp
         The Countess Charming
  1918 Rimrock Jones
  1919 Toby's Bow
  1920 Officer 666
         The Round-Up
         Sick Abed
         The Willow Tree
  1921 Midsummer Madness

Kuwa, Mrs. George
  1917 The Countess Charming
Kuwuhara (full name unknown)
  1917 Hashimura Togo
Kyle, Alexander
  1919 A Society Exile
Kyle, Edward
  1915 Samson
Kyle, Howard
  1917 National Red Cross Pageant*
  1918 The Purple Lily
         Wild Honey
Kyle, William
  1917 Betty and the Buccaneers
Kyne, Peter B.
  1915 Judge Not; Or, The Woman of Mona Diggings
Kyson, Charles H. *same as* **Kyson, Charles; Kyson, Charles J.**
  1920 The Brute Master
         Her Husband's Friend
         His Own Law
         Homespun Folks
         In the Heart of a Fool
         The Jailbird
         The Leopard Woman
         Love
         Love Madness
         The Luck of the Irish
         Rookie's Return
         Silk Hosiery
         A Splendid Hazard
         A Thousand to One

L

La Badie, Florence
  1914 Cardinal Richelieu's Ward
  1915 God's Witness
         Monsieur Lecoq
         The Price of Her Silence
  1916 Divorce and the Daughter
         The Fear of Poverty
         The Five Faults of Flo
         The Fugitive
         Master Shakespeare, Strolling Player
         The Pillory
         Saint, Devil and Woman
  1917 Her Life and His
         The Man Without a Country
         War and the Woman
         When Love Was Blind
         The Woman in White
  1918 The Million Dollar Mystery
La Brandt, Gertrude *see* **Le Brandt, Gertrude**
La Cheur, Estelle *same as* **Lacheur, Estelle**
  1917 The Fuel of Life
         A Phantom Husband
Lack, A. Lloyd
  1917 Think It Over
  1919 The Man Who Stayed at Home
Lackaye, Helen
  1918 The Knife
Lackaye, James
  1914 The Christian
  1915 York State Folks
  1916 The Upstart
  1918 Pals First
Lackaye, Ruth
  1916 The Twin Triangle
  1917 Bab the Fixer
         The Climber
         The Girl Angle
         The Lady in the Library
         The Stolen Play
         Twin Kiddies
         The Yellow Bullet
  1918 The Law That Divides
         The Midnight Burglar
         Miss Mischief Maker
         No Children Wanted
         Petticoats and Politics
         Wanted—A Brother
Lackaye, Wilton
  1914 The Pit
  1915 Children of the Ghetto
         The Man of Shame
         Trilby

1920 Body and Soul
1921 Habit
Lawrence, Walter same as **Lawrence, Walter M.**
1918 The Prussian Cur
1920 The Deep Purple
Headin' Home
Lawrence, William see **Lawrence, W. E.**
Lawshe, Er
1916 His Brother's Wife*
Lawson, Eleanor same as **Lawson, Elsie**
1917 The Amazons
The Renaissance at Charleroi
1918 A Mother's Sin
Lawton, Jack
1916 Her Father's Son
Lawton, Mary
1915 John Glayde's Honor
Lawton, Thais
1915 The Battle Cry of Peace
Layman, Gene
1920 Forbidden Valley
Layton, Miss
1917 As Man Made Her
Layton, Verne
1920 Dangerous Love
Lazzarini, Lorenza
1920 Sick Abed
The Sins of St. Anthony
Thou Art the Man
Lea, D. P.
1917 The Blood of His Fathers
Lea, John A.
1914 Prince Edward Island in
Motion; Home of the Silver
Black Fox Industry*
Leach, H. Alderson same as **Leach, A.;**
Leach, Al; Leach, Henry A.
1917 Miss U.S.A.
1918 Blue-Eyed Mary
Bonnie Annie Laurie
A Camouflage Kiss
Parentage
Tell It to the Marines
1919 The Love Auction
Lure of Ambition
Putting One Over
The Winning Stroke
1920 The Law of the Yukon
Leach, John
1916 Dorian's Divorce
Leach, Nat
1918 Miss Innocence
Leach, Ollie same as **Leach, Olie**
1916 The Man from Nowhere
1917 Unknown 274
Lean, Kathryn
1918 Ruler of the Road
1920 Girl of the Sea
Learn, Bessie same as **Lern, Bessie**
1915 The Ploughshare
Through Turbulent Waters
1919 The Lost Battalion
Leary, Glide
1915 The Seventh Noon
Leary, Mildred
1918 Wild Honey
Leaske, Emily
1916 The Shop Girl
Leavitt, Harvey C. same as **Leavitt, R.**
V. C.
1920 The Brute Master
Hairpins
Her Husband's Friend
His Own Law
Homer Comes Home
Homespun Folks
The Jailbird
The Leopard Woman
Let's Be Fashionable
Love
Love Madness
Mary's Ankle
Rookie's Return
Sex
Silk Hosiery
A Thousand to One
Le Blanc, Paul
1916 A Child of the Paris Streets
The Devil's Needle

Le Brandt, Gertrude same as **La Brandt,**
Gertrude; Le Brant, Gertrude
1916 A Dream or Two Ago
Dulcie's Adventure
Faith
Youth's Endearing Charm
1917 Annie-for-Spite
Melissa of the Hills
1918 Doing Their Bit
The Rose of the World
1919 Through the Toils
Wild Oats
Le Brandt, Joseph
1920 The Prey
Le Brant, Gertrude see **Le Brandt,**
Gertrude
LeBrun, Mignon
1917 Betty Be Good
The Secret of Black Mountain
Twin Kiddies
1918 Wanted—A Brother
Le Croix, Emile see **La Croix, Emile**
Ledbetter, Bud
1915 Passing of the Oklahoma
Outlaw
Lederer, George W.
1915 The Fight
The Siren's Song
Sunday
1916 The Decoy
1917 Runaway Romany
The Sin Woman
Lederer, Gretchen
1915 Business Is Business
Lord John in New York
1916 Black Friday
Bobbie of the Ballet
Doctor Neighbor
The Grasp of Greed
If My Country Should Call
Little Eve Edgarton
The Mark of Cain
The Morals of Hilda
Two Men of Sandy Bar
The Way of the World
The Yaqui
A Yoke of Gold
1917 Bondage
The Cricket
The Greater Law
A Kentucky Cinderella
The Lair of the Wolf
The Little Orphan
The Little Pirate
My Little Boy
Polly Redhead
Princess Virtue
The Rescue
The Silent Lady
The Spotted Lily
1918 After the War
Beauty in Chains
Hungry Eyes
The Kaiser, the Beast of Berlin
The Model's Confession
New Love for Old
The Red, Red Heart
Riddle Gawne
Wife or Country
Lederer, Otto
1914 Captain Alvarez
The Little Angel of Canyon
Creek
1915 The Chalice of Courage
1916 The Last Man
Through the Wall
1917 Aladdin from Broadway
By Right of Possession
The Captain of the Gray Horse
Troop
Dead Shot Baker
The Flaming Omen
The Magnificent Meddler
When Men Are Tempted
1918 By the World Forgot
Cavanaugh of the Forest
Rangers
The Changing Woman
The Wild Strain
1919 Cupid Forecloses
The Enchanted Barn
The Little Boss
Over the Garden Wall

1920 The Spenders
Lee, Al
1916 The Sunbeam
1918 Marriages Are Made
Lee, Alberta
1915 Bred in the Bone
The Wolf Man
1916 Children of the Feud
Intolerance
Little Meena's Romance
Martha's Vindication
Reggie Mixes In
A Sister of Six
1917 The Fuel of Life
The Little Yank
An Old Fashioned Young Man
The Sudden Gentleman
1918 Alias Mary Brown
Beyond the Shadows
Closin' In
False Ambition
Keith of the Border
Limousine Life
The Lonely Woman
Love's Pay Day
The Man Who Woke Up
The Painted Lily
Real Folks
1919 The Mother and the Law
Prudence on Broadway
The Red Viper
Whom the Gods Would
Destroy
The Wishing Ring Man
1920 The Butterfly Man
The Cheater
The Road to Divorce
Rouge and Riches
Lee, Alice
1919 Mandarin's Gold
Lee, Betty
1918 The Triumph of Venus
Lee, Bob see **Lee, Robert** (asst dir)
Lee, Carey same as **Lee, Carrey; Lee,**
Carrie
1915 The Concealed Truth
The Family Stain
A Gilded Fool
The Nigger
Samson
1916 The Bondman
Her Double Life
1917 The Darling of Paris
Reputation
1918 Queen of the Sea
1920 The Miracle of Love
Lee, Carolyn same as **Lee, Caroline**
1916 The Flight of the Duchess
It May Be Your Daughter
The Lottery Man
1917 The Awakening of Ruth
1919 Anne of Green Gables
My Little Sister
1920 The Copperhead
Lee, Carrie see **Lee, Carey**
Lee, Catherine see **Lee, Katherine**
Lee, Charles
1915 The Absentee
The Sable Lorcha
1916 Hoodoo Ann
1917 The Girl of the Timber Claims
Her Official Fathers
Jim Bludso
An Old Fashioned Young Man
Lee, Clara
1920 Someone in the House
Lee, Dick same as **Lee, Richard**
1915 The Bigger Man
Fanchon the Cricket
Seven Sisters
Silver Threads Among the Gold
1916 Seventeen
1917 Polly of the Circus
1918 The Birth of a Race
1920 Passers-By
Lee, Dixie
1919 The Law of Nature
Where Bonds Are Loosed
1920 In the Shadow of the Dome
Lee, Doris see **May, Doris**

Lee, Dorothy
1920 Her Elephant Man
Lee, Duke same as **Lee, Duke R.**
1917 The Savage
Straight Shooting
1918 Hell Bent
1919 The Ace of the Saddle
A Gun Fightin' Gentleman
The Pointing Finger
The Rider of the Law
1920 Hitchin' Posts
Just Pals
Sundown Slim
Lee, Edward
1918 For the Freedom of the East
Lee, Eldridge
1919 Injustice
Lee, Florence
1914 The Rejuvenation of Aunt
Mary
1915 Divorçons
Lee, Frank (actor)
1918 The Kaiser, the Beast of Berlin
Love's Conquest
Lee, Frankie (child actor) same as **Lee,**
Francis
1916 The Right to Be Happy
A Romance of Billy Goat Hill
1917 The Bronze Bride
Durand of the Bad Lands
The Field of Honor
God's Crucible
One Touch of Sin
The Soul of Satan
1918 The Boss of the Lazy Y
Cheating the Public
Quicksand
1919 Bonds of Love
Daddy-Long-Legs
The Law of Men
The Miracle Man
Rough Riding Romance
The Westerners
1920 Judy of Rogue's Harbor
Moon Madness
Nurse Marjorie
An Old Fashioned Boy
Lee, Mrs. George Griffin same as **Lee,**
Mrs. George
1918 Dolly's Vacation
The King of Diamonds
Lee, Harry same as **Lee, Henry**
1916 Destiny's Toy
Little Lady Eileen
The Rainbow Princess
1917 Arms and the Girl
A Girl Like That
Heart's Desire
The Little Boy Scout
1918 Eve's Daughter
Out of the Night
A Romance of the Underworld
Uncle Tom's Cabin
1919 Twilight
The Undercurrent
Upside Down
1920 Oil
Lee, Irene
1916 A Daughter of the Gods
Lee, Jane same as **Lee, Little Jane; Lee,**
Janey; Lee, Little Janey
1915 The Clemenceau Case
The Devil's Daughter
The Galley Slave
The Magic Toy Maker
Silver Threads Among the Gold
The Soul of Broadway
1916 Daredevil Kate
A Daughter of the Gods
Her Double Life
Love and Hate
The Ragged Princess
The Spider and the Fly
The Unwelcome Mother
A Wife's Sacrifice
1917 A Child of the Wild
Patsy
Sister Against Sister
The Small Town Girl
Tangled Lives
Troublemakers
Two Little Imps
1918 American Buds
Doing Their Bit

Swat the Spy
Tell It to the Marines
We Should Worry
1919 Smiles
Lee, Jennie *same as* **Lee, Jenny**
1915 The Birth of a Nation
Her Shattered Idol
1916 A Child of the Paris Streets
The Children Pay
An Innocent Magdalene
The Little Liar
1917 The Clever Mrs. Carfax
Her Official Fathers
The Innocent Sinner
Madame Bo-Peep
Nina, the Flower Girl
Souls Triumphant*
Stagestruck
A Woman's Awakening
1918 Sandy
1919 The Rider of the Law
Riders of Vengeance
1920 The Secret Gift
Lee, Jesse M.
1914 The Indian Wars
1917 The Adventures of Buffalo Bill
Lee, Joseph
1919 Mandarin's Gold
Lee, Katherine *same as* **Lee, Catherine;**
Lee, Little Katherine
1914 Neptune's Daughter
The Scales of Justice
1915 The Bludgeon
The Last of the Mafia
The Magic Toy Maker
The Master Hand
Silver Threads Among the Gold
1916 Daredevil Kate
A Daughter of the Gods
Her Double Life
Love and Hate
The Ragged Princess
The Unwelcome Mother
1917 Troublemakers
Two Little Imps
1918 American Buds
Doing Their Bit
Swat the Spy
Tell It to the Marines
We Should Worry
1919 Smiles
Lee, Lila
1918 The Cruise of the
Make-Believes
Such a Little Pirate
1919 A Daughter of the Wolf
Hawthorne of the U.S.A.
The Heart of Youth
Male and Female
Puppy Love
Rose O' the River
Rustling a Bride
The Secret Garden
1920 The Prince Chap
The Soul of Youth
Terror Island
1921 Midsummer Madness
Lee, Lois
1919 The Lincoln Highwayman
1920 The Phantom Melody
Lee, Louise
1918 On the Quiet
The Whirlpool
1920 The Fortune Hunter
Lee, Lucille *see* **Stewart, Lucille Lee**
1915 The Sins of the Mothers
Lee, Madge
1919 Forest Rivals
Lee, Marian *same as* **Lee, Marion**
1918 The Ghost of Rosy Taylor*
1919 Put Up Your Hands
Lee, Mildred
1919 The Game's Up
Lee, Moe
1920 The Good-Bad Wife
Lee, Nancy
1920 The Fortune Hunter
Lee, Raymond *same as* **Lee, Ray**
1917 Aladdin and the Wonderful
Lamp
1918 Ali Baba and the Forty Thieves
Six Shooter Andy

Lee, Richard *see* **Lee, Dick**
Lee, Robert (*asst dir*) *same as* **Lee, Bob**
1920 A City Sparrow
The Dancin' Fool
Excuse My Dust
Her First Elopement
Lee, Robert Morton (*scen*)
1917 The Frozen Warning
Lee, Rowland *same as* **Lee, Roland; Lee,**
Rowland V.
1917 The Maternal Spark
The Mother Instinct
Polly Ann
The Stainless Barrier
They're Off
Time Locks and Diamonds
Wild Winship's Widow
1920 Dangerous Days
Her Husband's Friend
His Own Law
A Thousand to One
Water, Water Everywhere
The Woman in the Suitcase
Lee, Veronica
1919 Mandarin's Gold
Lee, Virginia
1917 The Terror
1918 Beyond the Law
The Gulf Between
Oh, Johnny!
The Whirlpool
1919 Luck and Pluck
Sandy Burke of the U-Bar-U
1920 A Daughter of Two Worlds
For Love or Money
The Fortune Teller
The Servant Question
Leech, John
1916 My Partner
Leezer, John, *same as* **Leezer, J. W.;**
Leezer, John W.
1915 The Lily and the Rose
1916 Hell-to-Pay Austin
The Marriage of Molly-O
Susan Rocks the Boat
The Wood Nymph
1917 Cheerful Givers
The Girl of the Timber Claims
1918 The Hope Chest
Indian Life
The Kid Is Clever
1919 Boots
The Feud
I'll Get Him Yet
Nobody Home
Nugget Nell
Peppy Polly
1920 Bright Skies
The Heart of Twenty
The Triflers
Lefler, Velma
1916 The Heart of Paula
Leggett, J. Alexander
1916 The Island of Happiness
Le Guere, George *same as* **La Guere,**
George; Le Guerre, George
1915 The Bachelor's Romance
The Blindness of Virtue
The Commuters
Destiny; Or, The Soul of a
Woman
One Million Dollars
The Seventh Noon
1916 The Blindness of Love
The Evil Thereof
The Turmoil
The Upstart
1917 Envy
Greed
Passion
Pride
The Seventh Sin
Sloth
Strife
Wrath
1918 The Birth of a Race
Cecilia of the Pink Roses
The Woman the Germans Shot
1919 The Hand Invisible
The Way of a Woman
1920 Blind Love

Le Guerie, Albert
1918 The Embarrassment of Riches
Le Guerre, George *see* **Le Guere, George**
Lehnberg, John
1916 A Bird of Prey
Lehr, Anna *same as* **Lehr, Anne**
1913 The Stranglers of Paris
Victory
1914 Should a Woman Divorce?
1915 Colorado
Heritage
The White Scar
1916 The Bugle Call
Civilization's Child
Ramona
The Target
1917 Grafters
The Man Hater
1918 The Birth of a Race
For Freedom
Laughing Bill Hyde
Men
My Own United States
The Other Woman
Parentage
The Yellow Ticket
1919 The Darkest Hour
Home Wanted
The Jungle Trail
The Open Door
Thunderbolts of Fate
Upside Down
1920 Chains of Evidence
A Child for Sale
The Truth About Husbands
The Valley of Doubt
The Veiled Marriage
Leiber, Fritz *same as* **Lieber, Fritz**
1916 Romeo and Juliet (Quality
Pictures Corp.)
1917 Cleopatra
The Primitive Call
1920 If I Were King
The Song of the Soul
Leibfreed, Edwin
1919 Deliverance
Leibrand, Lela *same as* **Liebrand, Lela**
1917 The Climber
The Lady in the Library
The Little Patriot
The Understudy
1918 Bonnie Annie Laurie
Cupid by Proxy
Leigh, Anne
1915 The Alster Case
1916 The Sting of Victory
Leigh, Bert
1919 The Quickening Flame
1920 Blind Love
Leigh, Frank
1917 Life's Whirlpool
On Dangerous Ground
1918 Crown Jewels
Stolen Orders
1919 All of a Sudden Norma
Common Property
The Homebreaker
Lord and Lady Algy
A Regular Fellow
Rose of the West
The Sleeping Lion
Snares of Paris
The Usurper
1920 The Cup of Fury
Dangerous Days
Help Wanted—Male
The Mother of His Children
Nurse Marjorie
One Hour Before Dawn
Leigh, Grace
1914 The Seats of the Mighty
1915 The Spendthrift
Leigh, Lisle
1916 Caprice of the Mountains
1918 The Forbidden Path
1919 The American Way
Leigh, Philip
1918 Virtuous Wives
Leighton, Daniel
1916 The Crown Prince's Double
The Supreme Temptation
1917 The Phantom's Secret

Leighton, Fred
1916 The Colored American
Winning His Suit
Leighton, Harry
1916 The Dragon
Leighton, Lillian
1916 Joan the Woman
The Plow Girl
Witchcraft
1917 Betty to the Rescue
Castles for Two
The Devil-Stone
Freckles
The Ghost House
The Hostage
The Little American
The Prison Without Walls
The Tides of Barnegat
1918 Her Country First
A Lady's Name
The Married Virgin*
Old Wives for New
The Road Through the Dark
Till I Come Back to You
1919 A Girl Named Mary
Louisiana
Male and Female
Men, Women and Money
Poor Relations
Secret Service
1920 All-of-a-Sudden-Peggy
The Barbarian
A City Sparrow
The Dancin' Fool
A Full House
Held by the Enemy
Her Beloved Villain
The House of Toys
The Jack-Knife Man
The Prince Chap
The Thirtieth Piece of Silver
Thou Art the Man
The Week-End
What Happened to Jones
1921 Midsummer Madness
Leighton, Winifred
1918 The Golden Wall
1919 Home Wanted
The Social Pirate
Through the Toils
Leinsky, N.
1919 23 1/2 Hours' Leave
Leisen, Mitchell *same as* **Leisen, James**
Mitchell
1919 Male and Female
1920 The Prince Chap
Why Change Your Wife?
Leitzbach, Adeline *same as* **Leitzbach,**
Adelaine
1917 Diamonds and Pearls
1918 The Heart of Romance
Her Price
The Liar*
Miss Innocence*
Stolen Honor
Leland, Georgette
1914 Il Trovatore
Leland, Lea
1914 Should a Woman Divorce?
Le Marr Deely, Barbara *see* **La Marr,**
Barbara
Le May, Lester
1919 Under the Top
LeMay, Pierre *same as* **LeMae, P. J.**
1916 Her Great Hour
Playing with Fire
The Reapers
A Woman's Way
Lemontier, Jules
1918 Hearts of the World
Le Moyne, Charles *same as* **Le Moyne,**
Charles J.
1915 Vengeance of the Wilds
1916 The Country That God Forgot
1917 The Lad and the Lion
The Princess of Patches
1918 Mr. Logan, U.S.A.
1919 The Brute Breaker
The Coming of the Law
His Divorced Wife
Marked Men
The Rebellious Bride
Treat 'Em Rough

1920 Blue Streak McCoy
Bullet Proof
Hearts Up
Human Stuff
The Last Straw
Overland Red
Sundown Slim
West Is West

Lemport, Fay
1919 Daddy-Long-Legs
The Heart of Youth
1920 Huckleberry Finn

Lena, Al
1919 Eyes of the Soul
The Marriage Price
Out of the Shadow
Paid in Full*

Le Nard, Madeleine
1916 Her Double Life
Love and Hate
Sporting Blood

Lennon, Stephen
1915 C.O.D.

Lenone, Col.
1917 Jack and Jill

Le None, C. F.
1914 The Man on the Box

Lenot, Gene
1918 The Uphill Path

Lenox, Frank
1918 Love's Law

Lenox, Fred
1918 The Burden of Proof

Lenz, A. Francis
1917 The Barker

Leo, a lion
1916 Sunshine Dad

Leon, Bertha
1915 The Flying Twins

Leon, Pedro same as **Leon, Peter; Leone, Pedro**
1914 Washington at Valley Forge
1916 Love's Lariat
1920 Just Pals

Leonard (full name unknown)
1915 The Fairy and the Waif*

Leonard, Ann
1917 The Master Passion

Leonard, Foster
1920 Dinty

Leonard, Frank
1915 The Call of the Dance
1916 The Black Crook

Leonard, Gus
1920 Homer Comes Home

Leonard, Irene
1917 Grafters

Leonard, J. N.
1917 His Sweetheart

Leonard, Jack
1916 Macbeth
1920 The Return of Tarzan

Leonard, Marie same as **Leonhard, Marie**
1914 The Pride of Jennico
1915 Niobe

Leonard, Marion
1913 The Seed of the Fathers
1914 The Light Unseen
Mother Love
1915 The Vow

Leonard, Robert Z. same as **Leonard, Robert**
1915 Heritage
Judge Not; Or, The Woman of Mona Diggings
The Silent Command
1916 The Crippled Hand
Little Eve Edgarton
The Love Girl
The Plow Girl
Secret Love
1917 At First Sight
A Mormon Maid
On Record
The Primrose Ring
Princess Virtue
1918 The Bride's Awakening
Danger—Go Slow
Face Value
Her Body in Bond
Modern Love

1919 The Big Little Person
The Delicious Little Devil
The Miracle of Love
The Scarlet Shadow
The Way of a Woman
What Am I Bid?
1920 April Folly
The Restless Sex

Leonard, Sadie
1919 Marriage for Convenience

Leone, Henry same as **Leone, Henri; Leoni, Harry**
1915 The Blindness of Devotion
Cohen's Luck
The Galley Slave
The Melting Pot
The Model
The Ploughshare
Should a Mother Tell?
1916 The Eternal Question
The Green-Eyed Monster
The Heart of the Hills
Hypocrisy
The Spider and the Fly
A Wife's Sacrifice
The Witch*
1917 Arsene Lupin
Daughter of Destiny
Lady Barnacle
The Mortal Sin
The Silence Sellers
Tangled Lives
To the Death
1918 The Belgian
Her Price
My Cousin
The Ordeal of Rosetta
Prunella
The Song of Songs

Leone, Pedro see **Leon, Pedro**

Leong, Gilbert
1918 For the Freedom of the East

Leonhard, Marie see **Leonard, Marie**

Leoni, Harry see **Leone, Henry**

Le Picard, Marcel same as **Le Picard, Marcel A.**
1915 The Outlaw's Revenge
1916 A Daughter of the Gods
The Faded Flower
Her Surrender
The House of Mirrors
The Sex Lure
The Sphinx
1917 Babbling Tongues
Enlighten Thy Daughter
One Law for Both
Sins of Ambition
Two Men and a Woman
1918 Ashes of Love
Conquered Hearts
Life or Honor?
A Perfect Lady
When Men Betray
1919 Almost a Husband
Daughter of Mine
Day Dreams
Jubilo
Leave It to Susan
Strictly Confidential
Through the Wrong Door
1920 Cupid, the Cowpuncher
Honest Hutch
Jes' Call Me Jim
The Strange Boarder
Water, Water Everywhere

Lerch, Theodore
1920 The Last of the Mohicans

Le Reno, Richard see **La Reno, Dick**

Lern, Bessie see **Learn, Bessie**

Le Roy, Elizabeth
1916 The Child of Destiny

Le Roy, Maude
1919 Reclaimed: The Struggle for a Soul Between Love and Hate

Le Roy, Victor
1917 The Beautiful Adventure

Lertora, Joseph
1918 A Romance of the Air

Le Saint, Edward J. same as **Le Saint, E. J.; Le Saint, Edward; Le Sainte, Edward**
1915 The Circular Staircase
The Long Chance

Lord John in New York
The Supreme Test
1916 The Honorable Friend
The Soul of Kura-San
The Three Godfathers
The Victoria Cross
1917 Each to His Kind
Fighting Mad
The Golden Fetter
The Heir of the Ages
The Lonesome Chap
The Squaw Man's Son
1918 The Bird of Prey
Cupid's Roundup
The Devil's Wheel
Her One Mistake
Kultur
Nobody's Wife
Painted Lips
The Scarlet Road
The Strange Woman
The Wolf and His Mate
1919 The Call of the Soul
The Feud
Fighting for Gold
Hell Roarin' Reform
The Sneak
The Speed Maniac
The Wilderness Trail
1920 Flames of the Flesh
The Girl of My Heart
Merely Mary Ann
The Mother of His Children
The Rose of Nome
A Sister to Salome
Two Moons
White Lies

Leslie (full name unknown)
1915 The Fairy and the Waif*

Leslie, Arthur
1916 The Marble Heart

Leslie, Elgin see **Lessley, Elgin**

Leslie, Gladys
1915 Ranson's Folly
1916 Betrayed
1917 An Amateur Orphan
Her Beloved Enemy
His Own People
It Happened to Adele
The Vicar of Wakefield
When Love Was Blind
1918 The Beloved Impostor
Little Miss No-Account
The Little Runaway
The Mating
A Nymph of the Foothills
The Soap Girl
Wild Primrose
The Wooing of Princess Pat
1919 Fortune's Child
The Girl-Woman
The Golden Shower
The Gray Towers Mystery
Miss Dulcie from Dixie
A Stitch in Time
Too Many Crooks
1920 A Child for Sale
The Midnight Bride

Leslie, Helen
1916 If My Country Should Call

Leslie, James
1915 Salvation Nell
1916 The Woman Who Dared

Leslie, John
1919 The Winning Stroke

Leslie, Lilie same as **Leslie, Lila; Leslie, Lily**
1913 The Third Degree
1914 The Daughters of Men
The Gamblers
The Lion and the Mouse
1915 The Warning
1916 The Fortunate Youth
A Modern Thelma
1918 The Silent Woman
1919 Johnny-on-the-Spot
A Little Brother of the Rich
The Man Who Stayed at Home
Satan Junior
1920 The Best of Luck
Blue Streak McCoy
The Butterfly Man
Love's Harvest
Molly and I

Number 99
Would You Forgive?

Leslie, Marguerite
1915 Jim the Penman
1916 The Question
1919 The Chosen Path

Leslie, Martin
1916 The Code of Marcia Gray*

Leslie, Richard
1915 Mother's Roses

Lesly, Elgin see **Lessley, Elgin**

Lesser, Sol
1916 The Ne'er Do Well
1919 Yankee Doodle in Berlin
1920 Sky Eye
What Women Love

Lessey, George same as **Lessey, George A.**
1915 Cap'n Eri
The Marble Heart
The Suburban
1916 The Purple Lady
1918 To Him That Hath
1919 Twilight
1920 The Harvest Moon
Wits vs. Wits

Lessing, Bruno
1916 The Scarlet Road

Lessing, Edith M.
1918 His Majesty, Bunker Bean

Lessing, Naida
1918 The Ghost Flower

Lessley, Elgin same as **Leslie, Elgin; Lesly, Elgin; Lessly, Elgin**
1917 Framing Framers
A Phantom Husband
1918 Alias Mary Brown
The Atom
Daughter Angele
Her Decision
High Stakes
Irish Eyes
Little Red Decides
Marked Cards
Station Content
You Can't Believe Everything
1920 The Servant in the House

Lesta, William
1919 You're Fired

Lester, Mrs. see **Lester, Louise**

Lester, Edward
1915 Who's Who in Society
1919 Wanted—A Husband
1920 The Very Idea

Lester, Kate
1916 A Coney Island Princess
Destiny's Toy
The Kiss
The Reward of Patience
The Social Secretary
1917 The Adventures of Carol
Betsy Ross
Darkest Russia
The Divorce Game
The Fortunes of Fifi
God's Man
The Good for Nothing
To-Day
The Volunteer
1918 Annexing Bill
Broken Ties
The Cross Bearer
Doing Their Bit
The Golden Wall
The Heart of a Girl
His Royal Highness
The Love Net
The Reason Why
The Unbeliever
The Way Out
1919 Bonds of Love
The City of Comrades
The Crimson Gardenia
The Crook of Dreams
The Gay Lord Quex
The Hand Invisible
Little Women
Lord and Lady Algy
A Man and His Money
The Solitary Sin
The Stronger Vow
Through the Wrong Door
Upstairs

1920 The Cup of Fury
Earthbound
Officer 666
The Paliser Case
Simple Souls
Stop Thief!
The Woman in Room 13

Lester, Louise same as **Lester, Mrs.**
1914 Damaged Goods
1916 April
Dust
1918 The Reckoning Day
1919 The Mayor of Filbert
1920 The Luck of the Irish

Lestina, Adolphe same as **Lestina, Adolph**
1916 Fruits of Desire
The Yellow Passport
1918 Battling Jane
The Greatest Thing in Life
Hearts of the World
The Hun Within
1919 The Girl Who Stayed Home
A Romance of Happy Valley
Scarlet Days
1920 The Idol Dancer
The Love Flower
Mary Ellen Comes to Town

Le Strange, Dick same as **La Strang, Richard; La Strange, Dick; L'Estrange, Dick; Le Strange, G. S.; Lestrange, Richard**
1914 The Ghost Breaker
The Master Mind
The Squaw Man
What's His Name
1915 The Girl of the Golden West
The Warrens of Virginia
1916 The Call of the Cumberlands
Fighting Blood
Madame La Presidente
The Right to Be Happy
The Trail of the Lonesome Pine
1917 The Square Deceiver
1919 The Unbroken Promise
1920 The Hidden Code
The Woman God Sent

L'Estrange, Julian
1915 Bella Donna
The Morals of Marcus
Sold
Zaza
1916 The Girl with the Green Eyes
The Quest of Life
1918 Daybreak

Leverage, Henry
1916 The Twinkler

Levering, Jack
1920 Seeds of Vengeance
Someone in the House
The Very Idea

Levering, James
1916 The Dead Alive
Feathertop
I Accuse
The Idol of the Stage
1917 The Deemster
Kidnapped
1918 My Own United States

Levering, Joseph
1913 Ben Bolt
The Fight for Millions
Shadows of the Moulin Rouge
The Star of India
1914 The Line-Up at Police
Headquarters
The Temptations of Satan
1916 The Haunted Manor
A Tortured Heart
1917 Little Miss Fortune
The Little Samaritan
The Road Between
1918 The Transgressor
1920 His Temporary Wife
Husbands and Wives
Luring Shadows
The Victim

Levey, Harry
1918 Keep the Home Fires Burning
1919 Heads Win
1920 Uncle Sam of Freedom Ridge

Levi, Maurice
1915 Silver Threads Among the Gold

Le Vien, Arthur
1916 Divorce and the Daughter

Levien, Sonya
1919 Who Will Marry Me?

Levier, Pearl
1920 The Corsican Brothers

Levigne, Maurice
1920 Humoresque

Levin, Edwina
1920 The Devil's Riddle
Help Wanted—Male

Levine, Charles
1919 Virtuous Men*
1920 His Wife's Money

Le Viness, Carl
1917 The Spirit of '76
1918 To the Highest Bidder
1920 The Love Expert

Le Vino, Albert Shelby same as **Le Vino, A. S.; Le Vino, A. Shelby; Le Vino, Albert S.**
1915 Right off the Bat
1916 The Woman's Law
1917 The Adopted Son
Alias Mrs. Jessop
An American Widow
The Greatest Power
The Lifted Veil
A Sleeping Memory
Their Compact
1918 Boston Blackie's Little Pal
Her Boy
No Man's Land
The Only Road
The Poor Rich Man
Riders of the Night
Treasure of the Sea
Under Suspicion
Unexpected Places
1919 After His Own Heart
The Four-Flusher
Full of Pep
The Great Victory, Wilson or
the Kaiser? The Fall of the
Hohenzollerns
In His Brother's Place
The Island of Intrigue
1920 The Best of Luck
Blackmail
Burning Daylight
The Hope
The Mutiny of the Elsinore
The Star Rover

Levy, Ethyl
1917 Modern Mother Goose

Levy, Lorraine
1914 Salomy Jane

Levy, Morris
1916 Intolerance

Levy, Sol
1914 His Majesty, the Scarecrow of
Oz*
1917 The Bar Sinister

Lewenhaupt, Count
1916 The Black Butterfly

Lewin, Ben
1919 Thunderbolts of Fate

Lewin, William
1915 Flame of Passion

Lewis, Miss
1915 The Fairy and the Waif*

Lewis, Mrs.
1915 The Fairy and the Waif*

Lewis, A. Lloyd same as **Lewis, Atwood Lloyd; Lewis, Lloyd**
1916 Slander
The Straight Way
A Tortured Heart
The Victim
1917 The Blue Streak
The Slave*
1918 Just for Tonight

Lewis, Ada
1917 Her Own People

Lewis, Albert
1915 The Fairy and the Waif
A Royal Family

Lewis, Arthur
1917 An American Widow
1918 Wild Primrose

Lewis, Ben
1916 A Sister of Six
1917 The Spirit of '76
1918 Beyond the Shadows
The Flames of Chance
High Stakes
Marked Cards
1920 The Fighting Shepherdess
The Life of the Party

Lewis, Catherine see **Lewis, Katharine**

Lewis, Daddy
1915 Forbidden Fruit

Lewis, Del could be same as **De Lewis, Del**
1915 Black Fear

Lewis, E. B. see **Lewis, Eugene B.**

Lewis, Edgar
1914 Captain Swift
The Littlest Rebel
Northern Lights
The Thief
1915 A Gilded Fool
The Great Divide
The Nigger
The Plunderer
Samson
1916 The Bondman
The Flames of Johannis
Light at Dusk
Souls in Bondage
Those Who Toil
1917 The Bar Sinister
The Barrier
1918 The Sign Invisible
Wives of Men
1919 Calibre 38
Love and the Law
1920 A Beggar in Purple
Lahoma
Other Men's Shoes
Sherry

Lewis, Edward
1915 The Country Boy

Lewis, Elsie
1916 The Kiss

Lewis, Eugene B. same as **Lewis, E. B.**
1916 The Unattainable
1917 The Car of Chance
The Hero of the Hour
The Saintly Sinner
1918 The Eagle
Fast Company
Hell Bent*
A Rich Man's Darling
The Rough Lover*
Three Mounted Men
1919 Bare Fists
The Blue Bandanna
A Fight for Love
Riders of Vengeance
Roped
What Every Woman Learns
1920 Haunting Shadows
Uncharted Channels

Lewis, Eva
1917 The Chosen Prince, or the
Friendship of David and
Jonathan

Lewis, Frederick same as **Lewis, Fred**
1915 Bought
The Lily of Poverty Flat
1916 An Enemy to the King

Lewis, George
1918 The Talk of the Town

Lewis, Grace
1917 The Planter*

Lewis, Ida
1915 The Alien
The Mating
1917 Alimony
The Painted Lie
The Single Code
Unto the End
Whither Thou Goest
1918 The Bells
Blue Blood
Humdrum Brown
Inside the Lines
Maid O' the Storm
A Man's Man

More Trouble
Patriotism
Wedlock
1919 Bill Henry*
Dangerous Waters
1920 Mary's Ankle
Paris Green
Peaceful Valley

Lewis, J. H.
1916 Her Husband's Wife

Lewis, Jack
1919 The House Without Children

Lewis, Jane
1915 The Dust of Egypt
1916 The Chattel
An Enemy to the King
The Law Decides
My Lady's Slipper

Lewis, Mrs. Jeffrey
1919 A Regular Girl

Lewis, Jerome
1920 The Heart of a Woman

Lewis, Jessie same as **Lewis, Jesse**
1914 The Pit
1915 The Butterfly
The Cub
Over Night
1916 The Ballet Girl
Broken Chains
The Dark Silence
Love's Crucible
The Supreme Sacrifice

Lewis, Joy
1917 Her Own People
1919 The Son-of-a-Gun!

Lewis, Katharine same as **Lewis, Catherine; Lewis, Katherine**
1916 The Footlights of Fate
1917 The Hawk
Indiscretion
The More Excellent Way
The Soul Master
1918 Virtuous Wives
The Woman Between Friends
1920 Everything but the Truth
Twin Beds
The Unfortunate Sex

Lewis, Kid
1918 A Romance of the Underworld

Lewis, Lloyd see **Lewis, A. Lloyd**

Lewis, Mitchell
1916 The Come-Back
The Flower of No Man's Land
1917 The Bar Sinister
The Barrier
1918 Code of the Yukon
The Million Dollar Mystery
Nine-Tenths of the Law
The Sign Invisible
1919 Calibre 38
Children of Banishment
The Faith of the Strong
Fool's Gold
Jacques of the Silver North
The Last of His People
Life's Greatest Problem
1920 Burning Daylight
King Spruce
The Mutiny of the Elsinore

Lewis, Pearl
1918 Her Aviator

Lewis, Philip
1914 The War of the World

Lewis, Ralph
1914 The Avenging Conscience
The Escape
The Floor Above
The Gangsters
The Great Leap; Until Death
Do Us Part
Home, Sweet Home
1915 The Birth of a Nation
Jordan Is a Hard Road
The Outcast
The Wolf Man
1916 The Children Pay
The Flying Torpedo
Going Straight
Gretchen, the Greenhorn
Hell-to-Pay Austin
Intolerance
Let Katie Do It
Macbeth

Martha's Vindication
A Sister of Six
1917 Her Temptation
Jack and the Beanstalk
The Silent Lie
A Tale of Two Cities
This Is the Life
1918 Cheating the Public
Fires of Youth
The Kid Is Clever
Revenge
1919 The Dub
Eyes of Youth
The Hoodlum
The Long Lane's Turning
The Mother and the Law
The Valley of the Giants
When the Clouds Roll By
1920 Common Sense
813
Outside the Law
What Women Love

Lewis, Randolph
1917 Miss U.S.A.
A Rich Man's Plaything
The Soul of Satan
1918 The Kid Is Clever
1920 Forbidden Valley

Lewis, Samuel
1920 The Eternal Union of the Seas

Lewis, Sheldon
1915 An Affair of Three Nations
The House of Fear
The Menace of the Mute
1916 Charity
The King's Game
The Pursuing Vengeance
1917 The Warfare of the Flesh
1919 The Bishop's Emeralds
Impossible Catherine
1920 Dr. Jekyll and Mr. Hyde
(Pioneer Film Corp.)
The Silent Barrier

Lewis, Sinclair
1919 The Unpainted Woman

Lewis, Ted, and his band
1920 The Scarlet Dragon

Lewis, Tom
1920 Passers-By

Lewis, Vera
1915 Betty in Search of a Thrill
The Caprices of Kitty
Sunshine Molly
1916 The Argonauts of
California—1849
Cross Currents
Intolerance
The Price of Power
1917 Jack and the Beanstalk
Lost in Transit
The Trouble Buster
1918 A Bit of Jade
The Vigilantes
A Weaver of Dreams
1919 As the Sun Went Down
The Lamb and the Lion
Lombardi, Ltd.
The Long Lane's Turning
The Merry-Go-Round
The Mother and the Law
The Pest
Yvonne from Paris
1920 The Blooming Angel
The Devil's Riddle
A Full House
Nurse Marjorie
The Poor Simp
She Couldn't Help It

Lewis, Victor
1915 The Man of Shame

Lewis, Walter same as **Lewis, Walter P.; Lewis, Walter Pratt**
1915 Divorçons
The Gambler of the West
1916 The Eternal Sapho
1917 The Avenging Trail
Trooper 44
1918 Joan of the Woods
Out of a Clear Sky
Pals First
To Hell with the Kaiser
Uncle Tom's Cabin
1920 The Birth of a Soul
The Bromley Case

The White Moll

Lewyn, Louis
1920 Sky Eye

Leyva, Chief
1920 The Joyous Troublemaker

Liddy, James
1920 The Girl in the Rain

Lidel, Frank same as **Lidell, Frank**
1915 The Case of Becky
The Chorus Lady
The Clue
Mr. Grex of Monte Carlo
The Secret Orchard
The Secret Sin
1916 Pudd'nhead Wilson

Lieb, Herman
1914 Dope
1918 Daybreak

Liebe, Hapsburg
1918 The Last Rebel
1919 Bill Apperson's Boy

Lieber, Fritz see **Leiber, Fritz**

Liebrand, Lela see **Leibrand, Lela**

Light, Blanche
1915 Secretary of Frivolous Affairs

Light Moon, Susie
1917 Master of His Home

Liguori, Al same as **Ligouri, Al; Liquori, Al**
1916 The Daughter of MacGregor
The Innocent Lie
The Smugglers
1918 The Belgian
The Grain of Dust
A Romance of the Air
1919 The Firing Line
Marie, Ltd.
Redhead
The Silver King
The Teeth of the Tiger
The World to Live In
1920 The World and His Wife

Lija, Carolina
1920 Wits vs. Wits

Likes, Don same as **Likes, Don (Fat Boy); Lykes, Don**
1917 A Phantom Husband
Wooden Shoes
1918 The Kid Is Clever
Sandy

Lillford, Harry
1914 The $5,000,000 Counterfeiting Plot

Lillibridge, DeWitt
1916 Out of the Drifts

Lima, C. A. de
1918 Her Great Chance
1920 The Strongest

Lince, John
1917 The Bond of Fear
The Devil Dodger
Framing Framers
The Regenerates
The Stainless Barrier
1918 Beyond the Shadows
By Proxy
I Love You
Love's Pay Day
Madame Sphinx
Mlle. Paulette
Untamed
1920 Stop Thief!

Lincoln, Alpheus
1915 Shadows from the Past
1917 The Master Passion

Lincoln, E. K.
1914 The Littlest Rebel
A Million Bid
1916 The Almighty Dollar
The Fighting Chance
The World Against Him
1917 For the Freedom of the World
1918 The Beloved Traitor
Lafayette, We Come!
1919 Desert Gold
Fighting Through
The Painted World
Shadows of the Past
The Unknown Love
Virtuous Men
The Wreck
1920 The Inner Voice

19-- The Girl from Alaska

Lincoln, Elmo same as **Helt, Lincoln; Lincoln, Otto; Linkenhelt, Otto Elmo; Linkenhelt, Oscar**
1914 Burning Daylight: The
Adventures of "Burning
Daylight" in Alaska*
Burning Daylight: The
Adventures of "Burning
Daylight" in Civilization*
John Barleycorn*
Judith of Bethulia
1915 The Absentee
The Birth of a Nation
Buckshot John
Her Shattered Idol
Jordan Is a Hard Road
1916 Children of the Feud
Hoodoo Ann
Intolerance
1917 Aladdin and the Wonderful
Lamp
The Bad Boy
Might and the Man
1918 The Greatest Thing in Life
The Kaiser, the Beast of Berlin
The Road Through the Dark
The Romance of Tarzan
Tarzan of the Apes
Treasure Island
1919 Deliverance
The Fall of Babylon
1920 Under Crimson Skies

Lincoln, Natalie S.
1920 Black Shadows

Lincoln, Otto see **Lincoln, Elmo**

Lincoln, Samuel
1917 They're Off

Lind, Billie
1920 The Heart of Twenty

Lind, Jenny
1919 Deliverance

Lind, Myrtle
1918 Nancy Comes Home

Lind, Sarah
1919 Deliverance

Lind, Viola
1920 In Folly's Trail

Lindblom, Miss E. O.
1915 The Black Heart

Linden, Edwin
1917 Modern Mother Goose

Linden, Einar
1915 Carmen (Fox Film Corp.)
The Family Stain
1916 The Eternal Sapho
The Iron Woman
Romeo and Juliet (Fox Film
Corp.)
1917 Hedda Gabler

Linden, H.
1915 Should a Mother Tell?

Linden, Margaret
1918 The Grouch
1919 A Virtuous Vamp
Wanted—A Husband
1920 His House in Order
The New York Idea

Lindley, Bert
19-- Sic-Em

Lindley, Betty
1920 Duds

Lindley, H. M.
1920 Lahoma

Lindner, Pearl
1920 The Heart of Twenty*

Lindreth, Helen see **Lindroth, Helen**

Lindreth, Nellie could be same as
Lindrich, Nellie
1917 At First Sight

Lindrich, Nellie could be same as
Lindreth, Nellie
1917 Shirley Kaye

Lindroth, Helen same as **Lindreth, Helen**
1914 Wolfe; Or, The Conquest of
Quebec
1915 Don Caesar de Bazan
The Luring Lights
The Pretenders
The Vanderhoff Affair

1916 Audrey
The Black Crook
The Daughter of MacGregor
The Innocent Lie
Seventeen
1917 The Hungry Heart
Little Miss Nobody
1918 At the Mercy of Men
The House of Gold
Kildare of Storm
Woman and Wife
1919 The Great Romance
Shadows of Suspicion
1920 The Gray Brother
The Point of View

Lindroth, Louise
1920 The Flapper

Lindsay, Herald
1919 Soldiers of Fortune

Lindsey, Judge Ben
1920 The Soul of Youth

Lindsey, Mrs. Ben
1920 The Soul of Youth

Lindsey, Harry
1918 The Empty Cab

Lindsey, Nina
1915 The Masqueraders
The Mummy and the
Humming Bird

Lines, Marie
1916 The Foolish Virgin

Ling (full name unknown)
1915 Buckshot John*

Ling, Richie
1915 The Green Cloak
The Sentimental Lady
The Woman Next Door
1918 Come On In
The Impostor

Ling, Wong
1913 Arizona

Lingham, Thomas same as **Lingham, Thomas G.**
1914 Shannon of the Sixth
1915 The Pitfall
1916 The Diamond Runners
Judith of the Cumberlands
The Manager of the B. and A.
Medicine Bend
Whispering Smith

Link, Adolph
1915 The Siren's Song
Sunday

Linkenhelt, Oscar see **Lincoln, Elmo**

Linkey, Harry
1916 The Masked Rider

Linn, Louise
1915 Secretary of Frivolous Affairs

Linson, Harry same as **Linsen, Harry**
1915 The Magic Skin
The Truth About Helen
1916 The Gates of Eden
Life's Shadows
The Light of Happiness
1917 Lady Barnacle
The Last Sentence
1918 The Silent Woman

Linton, Cora
1915 The Ring of the Borgias

Lionel, C. J. could be same as **Lionel, Cecil**
1917 The Land of Long Shadows

Lionel, Cecil could be same as **Lionel, C. J.**
1918 A Petticoat Pilot

Lippert, William H. same as **Lippert, W. H.**
1916 Gloriana
The Lords of High Decision
A Woman's Daring
1917 The Yellow Bullet

Lipton, Lewis
1920 Outside the Law

Liquori, Al see **Liguori, Al**

Lisa, Mona same as **Liza, Mona**
1920 Good References
To Please One Woman

Lisette, Madame
1920 Way Down East*

Liston, Mrs. *same as* **Lyston, Mrs. Hudson**
1912 Oliver Twist
1913 Traffic in Souls
Liston, Hudson
1912 Oliver Twist
1916 Love's Pilgrimage to America
Liston, J.
1913 Tess of the D'Urbervilles
Liston, Milly *same as* **Liston, Millicent; Liston, Millie**
1914 Neptune's Daughter
1916 A Daughter of the Gods
The Ruling Passion
1917 Tangled Lives
Liston, S.
1919 The Probation Wife
Liten, Carlo
1920 The Strongest
Litson, M. N.
1915 The Patriot and the Spy
1916 The Eternal Question
The Heart of a Hero
Paying the Price
1917 The Poor Little Rich Girl
The Pride of the Clan
Littell, Eddie
1916 The Cycle of Fate
Little (full name unknown)
1915 The Fairy and the Waif*
Little, Ann *same as* **Little, Anna**
1914 Called Back
Damon and Pythias
The Opened Shutters
The Voice at the Telephone
1916 Immediate Lee
Land O' Lizards
1917 Nan of Music Mountain
The Silent Master
Under Handicap
1918 Believe Me Xantippe
The Firefly of France
The House of Silence
Less Than Kin
The Man from Funeral Range
Rimrock Jones
The Source
The Squaw Man
The World for Sale
1919 Alias Mike Moran
The Roaring Road
Something to Do
Square Deal Sanderson
Told in the Hills
1920 The Cradle of Courage
Excuse My Dust
Little, Thomas K.
1918 Within the Cup
Little Bear
1917 The Conquerer
Little Bull
1915 The Cowpuncher
Littlefield, Lon D.
1920 The Discarded Woman
Littlefield, Lucien
1914 The Ghost Breaker
1915 A Gentleman of Leisure
Mr. Grex of Monte Carlo
The Warrens of Virginia
The Wild Goose Chase
1916 The Blacklist
To Have and to Hold
1917 The Cost of Hatred
The Golden Fetter
The Hostage
The Jaguar's Claws
The Squaw Man's Son
1919 Everywoman
1920 Double Speed
Eyes of the Heart
The Fourteenth Man
The Furnace
Her First Elopement
Jack Straw
The Round-Up
Sick Abed
The Sins of St. Anthony
Why Change Your Wife?
Litton, Morgia
1914 Il Trovatore

Livingston, H. A. *same as* **Livingstone, H. A.; could be same as** **Livingston, Harold**
1914 The Truth Wagon
1915 Jack Chanty
Livingston, Harold *could be same as* **Livingston, H. A.**
1914 Wolfe; Or, The Conquest of Quebec
Livingston, Jack *same as* **Livingstone, Jack**
1915 Captivating Mary Carstairs
1916 The American Beauty
The Heart of Paula
A Son of Erin
The Stronger Love
1917 Ashes of Hope
Back of the Man
Because of a Woman
The Dark Road
The Desert Man
The Eyes of the World
Flying Colors
In Slumberland
Madcap Madge
The Stainless Barrier
Ten of Diamonds
Wooden Shoes
1918 The Cast-Off
Everywoman's Husband
The Hard Rock Breed
His Enemy, the Law
Innocent's Progress
The Price of Applause
Who Is to Blame?
1919 Cowardice Court
1920 The Golden Trail
Mid-Channel
The Misfit Wife
The Saphead
A Tokio Siren
Livingston, Marguerite *same as* **Livingston, Margaret**
1916 The Chain Invisible
1917 Alimony
1919 All Wrong
1920 The Brute Master
Hairpins
Haunting Shadows
The Parish Priest
Water, Water Everywhere
What's Your Husband Doing?
Livingstone, H. A. *see* **Livingston, H. A.**
Livingstone, Jack *see* **Livingston, Jack**
Liza, Mona *see* **Lisa, Mona**
Lloyd, Ethel
1914 A Florida Enchantment
1915 Little Miss Brown
Mother's Roses
1916 The Ransom
Lloyd, Frank
1914 Damon and Pythias
The Opened Shutters
The Spy
1915 The Gentleman from Indiana
Jane
The Reform Candidate
1916 The Code of Marcia Gray
David Garrick
An International Marriage
The Intrigue
Madame La Presidente
The Making of Maddalena
Sins of Her Parent
The Stronger Love
Tongues of Men
1917 American Methods
The Heart of a Lion
The Price of Silence
A Tale of Two Cities
When a Man Sees Red
1918 The Blindness of Divorce
For Freedom
Les Miserables
The Rainbow Trail
Riders of the Purple Sage
True Blue
1919 The Loves of Letty
The Man Hunter
Pitfalls of a Big City
The World and Its Woman
1920 The Great Lover
Madame X
The Silver Horde

The Woman in Room 13
Lloyd, Harold (*actor, 1893-1971*) *not the same as* **Lloyd, Harold Warner** (*asst dir, actor*)
1914 Samson*
Lloyd, Harold Warner (*asst dir, actor*) *not the same as* **Lloyd, Harold** (*actor, 1893-1971*); *same as* **Lloyd, Harry**
1916 The Dumb Girl of Portici
Judith of the Cumberlands
Medicine Bend
Whispering Smith
Lloyd, Harry *see* **Lloyd, Harold Warner** (*asst dir, actor*)
Lloyd, Rollo
1915 The Call of the Dance
Midnight at Maxim's
1918 Pals First
Lloyd, William
1914 The County Chairman
Richelieu
1915 The Dancing Girl
The Eternal City
Little Pal
The Pretty Sister of Jose
1917 Panthea
The Scarlet Car
1918 $5,000 Reward
1919 The Fire Flingers
1920 Their Mutual Child
Lobel, Mme. Malvine
1915 The Unwelcome Wife
Lobert, John Bernard "Hans"
1914 The Giants-White Sox Tour
Locke, E. A.
1914 The Master Cracksman
Locke, Ralph J.
1919 Putting One Over
Locke, William
1920 While New York Sleeps
Lockhart, Anne
1917 Mr. Opp
Lockhart, Tom
1916 The Evil Women Do
Locklear, Lieut. Ormer
1919 The Great Air Robbery
1920 The Skywayman
Lockney, J. P. *same as* **Lockney, John P.**
1916 Civilization's Child
D'Artagnan
The Eye of the Night
Jim Grimsby's Boy
The Return of Draw Egan
Shell Forty-Three
1917 The Bride of Hate
The Crab
Flying Colors
The Girl Glory
Golden Rule Kate
The Gun Fighter
In Slumberland
Polly Ann
The Silent Man
The Son of His Father
The Tar Heel Warrior
Wee Lady Betty
1918 Coals of Fire
A Desert Wooing
"Flare-Up" Sal
Fuss and Feathers
The Guilty Man
String Beans
The Tiger Man
The Vamp
1919 Behind the Door
The Egg Crate Wallop
Greased Lightning
Hay Foot, Straw Foot
Partners Three
The Sheriff's Son
1920 Below the Surface
A Broadway Cowboy
Dice of Destiny
Down Home
813
The Family Honor
The Mutiny of the Elsinore
Uncharted Channels
What's Your Husband Doing?

Lockwood, Earl
1919 The Career of Katherine Bush
Lockwood, Harold
1914 The Conspiracy
The County Chairman
The Crucible
The Man from Mexico
The Scales of Justice
Such a Little Queen
Tess of the Storm Country
The Unwelcome Mrs. Hatch
Wildflower
1915 Are You a Mason?
The Buzzard's Shadow
David Harum
The End of the Road
The House of a Thousand Scandals
Jim the Penman
The Love Route
The Lure of the Mask
Secretary of Frivolous Affairs
1916 Big Tremaine
The Come-Back
Life's Blind Alley
The Masked Rider
Mister 44
The Other Side of the Door
Pidgin Island
The River of Romance
1917 The Avenging Trail
The Haunted Pajamas
The Hidden Children
The Hidden Spring
National Association's All-Star Picture
Paradise Garden
The Promise
The Square Deceiver
Under Handicap
1918 Broadway Bill
The Landloper
Lend Me Your Name
Pals First
1919 The Great Romance
A Man of Honor
Shadows of Suspicion
Lockwood, J. R.
1919 Yankee Doodle in Berlin
1920 Love, Honor and Behave
Lodge, Ben
1917 The Deemster
Loeb, Sophie Irene
1920 The Woman God Sent
Loew, Jeanne *same as* **Loew, Jean**
1918 Journey's End
1919 The Poison Pen
Loftus, Alexander
1920 The Little Outcast*
Loftus, Cecilia
1914 A Lady of Quality
Logan, Anna
1915 The Governor's Boss
Logan, Eugene Winfield
1914 Sitting Bull—The Hostile Sioux Indian Chief
Logan, Paul
1916 Britton of the Seventh*
Logan, Rosanna
1914 Under the Gaslight
Logan, Tom
1919 Whom the Gods Would Destroy
Logue, Charles A. *same as* **Logue, A.**
1916 Ashes of Embers
The Feud Girl
1917 The Duchess of Doubt
Outwitted
Their Compact
The White Raven
A Wife by Proxy
1918 Just for Tonight
The Kingdom of Youth
My Four Years in Germany
The Service Star
Too Fat to Fight
1919 Beware
Flame of the Desert
The Lost Battalion
A Scream in the Night
1920 Even As Eve
Man and Woman (A. H. Fischer Features, Inc.)

1921 Miss 139

Logue, G.
1918 Everywoman's Husband

Lohmeyer, Robert
1916 The Children Pay

Lois, Will
1915 A Soldier's Oath

London, Babe
1920 Merely Mary Ann

London, Charmian
1920 The Brute Master

London, Jack
1913 Jack London's Adventures in the South Sea Islands
     The Sea Wolf
1914 The Valley of the Moon

London, Mrs. Jack
1918 Among the Cannibal Isles of the South Pacific

London, Samuel H.
1913 The Inside of the White Slave Traffic
1918 Her Moment

London, Tom
1919 The Heart of Humanity*

Lonergan, Lloyd same as **Lonergan, Lloyd F.**
1913 Moths
     Robin Hood
1914 Beating Back
     Frou Frou
1915 The Price of Her Silence
1916 The Five Faults of Flo
     Other People's Money
     The Traffic Cop
1917 The Heart of Ezra Greer
     Her Beloved Enemy
     Hinton's Double
     The Man Without a Country
     Mary Lawson's Secret
     A Modern Monte Cristo
     Under False Colors
     The Woman in White
1918 The Million Dollar Mystery
1920 A Common Level
     My Lady's Garter
     The Rich Slave
     Why Women Sin

Lonergan, Philip
1915 The Mill on the Floss
1916 Betrayed
     A Bird of Prey
     The Five Faults of Flo
     The Fugitive
     King Lear
     The Pillory
     Saint, Devil and Woman
     Silas Marner
     The Woman in Politics
     The World and the Woman
1917 The Candy Girl
     Her Life and His
     War and the Woman
1919 Coax Me
     His Father's Wife
     Love and the Woman
     Mandarin's Gold
1920 The Girl with the Jazz Heart
     The Penalty

Long, Helen
1918 A Heart's Revenge

Long, J. A.
1916 How Life Begins

Long, Louise
1917 Filling His Own Shoes

Long, Nicholas (actor)
1917 The Adventures of Carol

Long, Nick, Jr. (child actor) same as **Long, Nicholas, Jr.**
1915 Hearts of Men
1917 The Corner Grocer
1919 The Oakdale Affair

Long, Walter same as **Long, W. H.**
1914 The Escape
     Home, Sweet Home
1915 The Birth of a Nation
     Jordan Is a Hard Road
     A Man and His Mate
     The Martyrs of the Alamo
     The Outlaw's Revenge
1916 The Children in the House
     Daphne and the Pirate
     Intolerance

Joan the Woman
Let Katie Do It
The Marriage of Molly-O
Sold for Marriage
Unprotected
The Years of the Locust
1917 The Cost of Hatred
     Each to His Kind
     The Evil Eye
     The Golden Fetter
     Hashimura Togo
     The Little American
     The Winning of Sally Temple
     The Woman God Forgot
1919 An Adventure in Hearts
     Chasing Rainbows
     Desert Gold
     The Mother and the Law
     The Poppy Girl's Husband
     Scarlet Days
1920 Excuse My Dust
     The Fighting Shepherdess
     Go and Get It
     Held in Trust
     The Sea Wolf
     The Third Woman
     What Women Love

Longacre, Frank same as **Longacre, Master Frank**
1915 Hearts of Men
     The Warning

Longman, Edward G. same as **Longman, Ed; Longman, Edward**
1915 All for a Girl
1917 Builders of Castles
     The Last Sentence

Lonsdale, Harry same as **Lonsdale, Harry G.; Lounsdale, H.**
1915 The Carpet from Bagdad
     The Rosary
     Sweet Alyssum
1916 The Garden of Allah
     Into the Primitive
     The Ne'er-Do-Well
     The Valiants of Virginia
1917 Beware of Strangers
     Conscience
     Little Lost Sister
     Who Shall Take My Life?
1918 The City of Purple Dreams
     The Girl in His House
     Little Orphant Annie
1919 Cowardice Court
     Fighting for Gold
     The Illustrious Prince
     The Last of His People
     The Shepherd of the Hills
1920 The Return of Tarzan
     The Week-End

Loomis, Fred
1914 Il Trovatore

Loomis, Madge could be same as **Loomis, Margaret**
1914 At the Cross Roads

Loomis, Margaret could be same as **Loomis, Madge**
1917 The Call of the East
     Hashimura Togo
1918 Hidden Pearls
1919 Everywoman
     Told in the Hills
     The Veiled Adventure
     Who Cares?
     Why Smith Left Home
1919-20
     When a Man Loves
1920 Always Audacious
     Conrad in Quest of His Youth
     The Sins of St. Anthony
     Three Gold Coins
     What Happened to Jones

Looney, Jere F. same as **Looney, Jere**
1917 The Brand of Satan
     The Rainbow Girl
1918 Kildare of Storm

Loos, Anita
1916 American Aristocracy
     His Picture in the Papers
     Intolerance
     The Little Liar
     The Matrimaniac*
     The Social Secretary
     Stranded
     The Wharf Rat

The Wild Girl of the Sierras
1917 The Americano
     A Daughter of the Poor
     Down to Earth
     In Again—Out Again
     Reaching for the Moon
     Wild and Woolly
1918 Come On In
     Good-Bye, Bill
     Hit-the-Trail Holliday
     Let's Get a Divorce
     The Marionettes*
1919 Getting Mary Married
     The Isle of Conquest
     Oh, You Women
     A Temperamental Wife
     Under the Top
     A Virtuous Vamp
1920 The Branded Woman
     Dangerous Business
     In Search of a Sinner
     The Love Expert
     The Perfect Woman

Lopez, Baby Anita
1920 The Dead Line

Lopez, John E. (scen) could be same as **Lopez, John S.** (scen, dir)
1916 The Girl Who Doesn't Know

Lopez, John S. (scen, dir) could be same as **Lopez, John E.** (scen)
1918 The Sins of the Children

Loraine, Emily see **Lorraine, Emily**

Lord, John
1916 The Woman Who Dared

Loreno, Richard see **La Reno, Dick**

Lorenz, John
1915 The Man Trail
1916 The Sting of Victory
     That Sort

Lorimer, Elsa same as **Larimer, Elsie; Lorimer, Elsie; Lorrimer, Elsa**
1914 The Good-for-Nothing
1916 The Jungle Child
1919 Other Men's Wives
1920 The Gilded Dream
     A Lady in Love
     The Six Best Cellars
     Too Much Johnson

Loring, Alfred
1916 The Struggle

Loring, Cleo
1916 Kinkaid, Gambler

Loring, Hope
1918 The Cabaret Girl
     A Society Sensation

Loring, Luke J.
1914 Forgiven; Or, The Jack of Diamonds

Lorna, Baby
1917 The Law of Compensation

Lorraine, Emily same as **Loraine, Emily**
1914 Captain Swift
1917 Cy Whittaker's Ward
1918 The Accidental Honeymoon
     Pay Day
1919 The Gay Old Dog

Lorraine, Harry
1920 Kismet
     The Last of the Mohicans
     The Slim Princess

Lorraine, Leota
1917 Feet of Clay
     The Girl Who Couldn't Grow Up
     The Martinache Marriage
     The Promise
1918 A Daughter of the West
     Desert Law
     The Finger of Justice
     Her American Husband
     The Kaiser's Shadow, or the Triple Cross
     Playing the Game
1919 Be a Little Sport
     The Girl Dodger
     The Loves of Letty
     Luck in Pawn
     The Pest
1920 Her Five-Foot Highness
     The Misfit Wife
     The Turning Point

Lorraine, Lillian
1915 Should a Wife Forgive?

Lorrimer, Elsa see **Lorimer, Elsa**

Lorrimore, Frances could be same as **Larrimore, Francine**
1915 A Woman's Resurrection

Loryea, Milton
1916 20,000 Leagues Under the Sea

Losee, Frank
1915 The Eternal City
     Heléne of the North
     The Masqueraders
     The Old Homestead
1916 Ashes of Embers
     Diplomacy
     The Evil Thereof
     Hulda from Holland
     The Innocent Lie
     Less Than the Dust
     Miss George Washington
     The Moment Before
     The Spider
     Under Cover
1917 Bab's Burglar
     Bab's Diary
     Bab's Matinee Idol
     The Dummy
     Great Expectations
     Sapho
     Seven Keys to Baldpate
     The Valentine Girl
1918 In Pursuit of Polly
     Madame Jealousy
     Mrs. Dane's Defense
     On the Quiet
     The Reason Why
     The Song of Songs
     La Tosca
     Uncle Tom's Cabin
1919 The Firing Line
     Good Gracious, Annabelle
     Here Comes the Bride
     His Parisian Wife
     Marie, Ltd.
     Paid in Full
1920 Broadway and Home
     Civilian Clothes
     The Fear Market
     Half an Hour
     Lady Rose's Daughter
     The Riddle: Woman
     The Right to Love
     Sinners
     The Stolen Kiss

Lott, Jack
1916 The Whirlpool of Destiny
1918 The Finger of Justice
     A Petticoat Pilot
1920 Mountain Madness

Lotus, Elys
1915 A Continental Girl

Lou-Tellegen see **Tellegen, Lou**

Louis, Mrs.
1919 After His Own Heart

Louis, Hermina
1916 The End of the Trail

Louis, Maude same as **Louis, Maud**
1920 Madame X
     A Slave of Vanity

Louis, Willard
1916 The Battle of Hearts
     The End of the Trail
     Fighting Blood
     The Fires of Conscience
     The Love Thief
     The Man from Bitter Roots
     A Man of Sorrow
1917 American Methods
     The Book Agent
     A Branded Soul
     Du Barry
     For Liberty
     High Finance
     The Island of Desire
     One Touch of Sin
     The Price of Her Soul
     The Scarlet Pimpernel
     A Tale of Two Cities
     To Honor and Obey
1918 The Bird of Prey
     The Blindness of Divorce
     Her One Mistake
     Kultur

1919 Jubilo
Love Insurance
The Loves of Letty
The Merry-Go-Round
The Scarlet Shadow
The Unpainted Woman
What Am I Bid?
1920 Dollars and Sense
Going Some
The Great Accident
Madame X
A Slave of Vanity

Louise, Mary
1917 A Bit O' Heaven

Lounsdale, H. see Lonsdale, Harry

Lovci, Pearl
1919 Little Comrade

Love, Bessie
1916 Acquitted
The Aryan
The Flying Torpedo
The Good Bad Man
The Heiress at Coffee Dan's
Hell-to-Pay Austin
Intolerance
Reggie Mixes In
A Sister of Six
Stranded
1917 Cheerful Givers
A Daughter of the Poor
Nina, the Flower Girl
Polly Ann
The Sawdust Ring
Wee Lady Betty
1918 The Dawn of Understanding
The Great Adventure
How Could You, Caroline?
A Little Sister of Everybody
1919 Carolyn of the Corners
Cupid Forecloses
The Enchanted Barn
A Fighting Colleen
The Little Boss
Over the Garden Wall
The Wishing Ring Man
A Yankee Princess
1920 Bonnie May
The Midlanders
Pegeen

Love, Montagu same as Love, Montague
1915 The Antique Dealer
The Face in the Moonlight
The Greater Will
Hearts in Exile
A Royal Family
Sunday
1916 Bought and Paid For
The Challenge
The Devil's Toy
Friday the Thirteenth
The Gilded Cage
The Hidden Scar
Husband and Wife
The Men She Married
The Scarlet Oath
A Woman's Way
1917 The Awakening
The Brand of Satan
The Dancer's Peril
The Dormant Power
Forget-Me-Not
The Guardian
Rasputin, the Black Monk
The Volunteer
Yankee Pluck
1918 Broken Ties
The Cabaret
The Cross Bearer
The Grouch
Stolen Orders
To Him That Hath
Vengeance
1919 A Broadway Saint
The Hand Invisible
The Quickening Flame
The Rough Neck
The Steel King
Three Green Eyes
Through the Toils
1920 Man's Plaything
The Place of Honeymoons
The Riddle: Woman
The World and His Wife
The Wrong Woman

Lovell, Grace could be same as Lowell, Grace
1916 The Soul of a Child

Lovelle, Laurie
1919 Anne of Green Gables

Lovely, Louise
1916 Bettina Loved a Soldier
Bobbie of the Ballet
The Gilded Spider
The Grasp of Greed
The Grip of Jealousy
The Measure of a Man
The Social Buccaneer
Tangled Hearts
1917 The Field of Honor
The Gift Girl
The Reed Case
Sirens of the Sea
1918 The Girl Who Wouldn't Quit
Nobody's Wife
Painted Lips
A Rich Man's Darling
The Wolf and His Mate
1919 Johnny-on-the-Spot
The Last of the Duanes
Life's a Funny Proposition
The Lone Star Ranger
The Man Hunter
The Usurper
Wings of the Morning
Wolves of the Night
1920 The Butterfly Man
The Joyous Troublemaker
The Little Grey Mouse
The Orphan
The Skywayman
The Third Woman
Twins of Suffering Creek

Loveridge, Marguerite
1914 Without Hope

Lovett, Josephine
1916 His Wife's Good Name
The Ninety and Nine
1920 Away Goes Prudence

Lovett, Shaw
1919 Erstwhile Susan
The Firing Line
Sadie Love
1920 Dr. Jekyll and Mr. Hyde
(Famous Players-Lasky
Corp.)

Lowe, Alice
1920 Should a Wife Work?

**Lowe, E. C. see Lowe, Edward T., Jr.
(scen)**

**Lowe, E. T., Jr. see Lowe, Edward T.,
Jr. (scen)**

Lowe, Edmund (actor)
1915 The Wild Olive
1917 The Spreading Dawn
1918 Vive La France!
1919 Eyes of Youth
1920 Madonnas and Men
Someone in the House
The Woman Gives
A Woman's Business

**Lowe, Edward T., Jr. (scen) same as
Lowe, E. C.; Lowe, E. T., Jr.; Lowe,
Edward; Lowe, Edward T.**
1915 The Slim Princess
1917 Little Shoes
1918 Men Who Have Made Love to
Me
1919 Bonds of Love
Toby's Bow
The World and Its Woman
1920 A Double Dyed Deceiver
It's a Great Life
Jes' Call Me Jim
Scratch My Back
The Street Called Straight

Lowe, Jessie
1917 Who Was the Other Man?

Lowe, Maude
1918 The Burden of Proof

Lowell, Aubrey
1919 The Great Victory, Wilson or
the Kaiser? The Fall of the
Hohenzollerns

**Lowell, Grace could be same as Lovell,
Grace**
1915 An American Gentleman

Lowell, Helen
1919 The Virtuous Model

Lowell, John
1919 The Clouded Name

Lowenhaupt, Karl
1919 The Golden Shower

**Lowery, William A. same as Lowery,
W. E.; Lowery, William ; Lowery,
William E.; Lowry, William E.**
1915 Captain Macklin
Double Trouble
The Lamb
1916 Reggie Mixes In
Sold for Marriage
1917 The Man from Painted Post
The Spy
1918 Her Moment

Lowry, Emma
1918 The Blue Bird
Conquered Hearts

Lowry, Eugene
1919 Eve in Exile

Lowry, Ira M.
1916 Race Suicide
1917 For the Freedom of the World
1918 For the Freedom of the East
Oh, Johnny!
1919 High Pockets
A Misfit Earl
The Road Called Straight
Sandy Burke of the U-Bar-U
Speedy Meade

Lowry, L.
1918 Hearts of the World

Lowry, Lilla May
1919 The Undercurrent

Lowry, Ludwig
1918 Her American Husband
Tony America

**Lowry, William E. see Lowery, William
A.**

Loyer, Georges
1918 Hearts of the World

Lubin, Herbert
1919 Virtuous Men
1920 Love, Honor and Obey

Luby, Edna
1916 The Immortal Flame

Lucas, Charles D.
1919 The Homesteader
1920 Within Our Gates

Lucas, Clara
1917 The Hidden Children

Lucas, Lieut. Eugene
1919 Injustice

Lucas, Sam
1914 Uncle Tom's Cabin

Lucas, Wilfred
1915 The Lily and the Rose
The Spanish Jade
1916 Acquitted
Hell-to-Pay Austin
Macbeth
The Microscope Mystery
The Rummy
The Wild Girl of the Sierras
The Wood Nymph
1917 The Co-Respondent
The Food Gamblers
Hands Up!
Her Excellency, the Governor
Jim Bludso
The Judgement House
A Love Sublime
Sins of Ambition
Souls Triumphant
1918 Morgan's Raiders
The Red, Red Heart
The Return of Mary
The Romance of Tarzan
The Testing of Mildred Vane
1919 The Girl from Nowhere
The Hushed Hour
Soldiers of Fortune
The Westerners
What Every Woman Wants
A Woman of Pleasure

Luckett, Edith
1914 The Coming Power
The Spirit of the Poppy
1916 The Other Girl

Lucy, Arnold
1916 The Devil's Toy
1917 In Again—Out Again
1918 A Nymph of the Foothills
1920 Good References
In Search of a Sinner
The Love Expert

Luke, Lucas C.
1920 White Youth

Luke, Norman W.
1916 Boots and Saddles

Lummis, Charles F.
1915 The Penitentes*

**Lund, O. A. C. same as Lund, Oscar;
Lund, Oscar A. C.**
1914 The Dollar Mark
The Marked Woman
When Broadway Was a Trail
1915 The Butterfly
Just Jim
M'liss
Pennington's Choice
1916 Autumn
Dorian's Divorce
The Price of Malice
1917 Her New York
Mother Love and the Law
The Painted Madonna
The Trail of the Shadow
1918 The Debt of Honor
A Heart's Revenge
Pals First
Peg of the Pirates
Together
1919 The Nature Girl

Lundeen, Peggy
1918 The Embarrassment of Riches

Luneska, Gene
1915 The Senator

Lunton, Mayne
1915 Seven Sisters

Lusk, Norbert
1916 Thrown to the Lions

Lusk, Robert
1915 Lord John in New York*

**Luther, Anna same as Luther, Ann;
Luther, Anne**
1914 The Wolf
1915 I'm Glad My Boy Grew Up to
Be a Soldier
The Pursuing Shadow
1916 The Beast
1917 The Island of Desire
Melting Millions
1918 Her Moment
Moral Suicide
1919 The Jungle Trail
Woman, Woman!
1920 Why Women Sin

**Luttrell, Helen same as Luttrell, Helen;
Luttrelle, Helen**
1914 Soldiers of Fortune
1915 Gretna Green
Lydia Gilmore
When We Were Twenty-One

Luxford, Nola
1920 The Tiger's Coat

Luzon, Octave same as Luzon, Octav
1913 Across the Continent
1914 Born Again

Lybarger, Lee Francis
1920 Democracy

Lydford, S.
1915 Lady Mackenzie's Big Game
Pictures

Lykes, Don see Likes, Don

Lyle, Edith same as Lyle, Edythe
1916 The Girl with the Green Eyes
1919 Deliverance

Lyle, Prudence
1920 Through Eyes of Men

Lyle, Warren E.
1916 The Folly of Revenge

Lyman, Laura
1916 Merely Mary Ann

Lynard, Lenore
1920 What Would You Do?
Whispering Devils

Lynbrook, Billy
1916 The War Bride's Secret

McCarthy, Myles *same as* McCarthy,
Miles
1917 Fear Not
The Silence Sellers
1918 Daughter Angele
1919 Auction of Souls
The False Code
The Highest Trump
A Man's Fight
1920 The Green Flame
The House of Whispers
The Tiger's Coat
McCarty, J. P.
1916 Flirting with Fate
McCauley, David
1915 Life Without Soul
1916 Driftwood
McCauley, Jack
1915 Hearts of Men
McChesney, Alice *same as*
MacChesney, Alice
1916 The Little Shepherd of Bargain
Row
1917 Satan's Private Door
The Trail of the Shadow
McChesney, L. W.
1919 The Unwritten Code
Macchia, Vincent
1920 The World and His Wife
McChord, Mrs. *see* McCord, Mrs.
Lewis
McClain, A.
1919 The Heart of Humanity
McClellan, Donald *see* McClennan,
Donald
McClennan, Donald *same as* McClellan,
Donald; MacClennan, Donald
1917 The Awakening of Ruth*
Knights of the Square Table
McCloskey, Brooks
1915 The Sporting Duchess
McCloskey, Justin H. *same as*
McCloskey, Justin; McClosky,
Justin; McClosky, Justin H.
1918 Madame Spy
1919 When Bearcat Went Dry
Whom the Gods Would
Destroy
1920 The Gift Supreme
McCloskey, Lawrence
1914 The Daughters of Men
1915 Bought
The Ringtailed Rhinoceros
1916 Pasquale
1917 The Adventurer
The Corner Grocer
His Sweetheart
The Magnificent Meddler
Nearly Married
Pride and the Devil
The Question
1918 The Golden Goal
Shackled
1919 Impossible Catherine
Silent Strength
1920 The Discarded Woman
The Frisky Mrs. Johnson
McClosky, Justin H. *see* McCloskey,
Justin H.
McCloud, Norma
1918 The Caillaux Case
McClung, Hugh C. *same as* McClung,
H. C.; McClung, Hugh
1915 A Child of God
The Lily and the Rose
A Man and His Mate
The Sable Lorcha
1916 Caprice of the Mountains
Little Miss Happiness
Merely Mary Ann
A Modern Thelma
1917 A Modern Musketeer
The Spirit of '76*
1918 Arizona
Bound in Morocco
He Comes Up Smiling
Headin' South
Mickey
Mr. Fix-It
Say, Young Fellow!
1919 The Knickerbocker Buckaroo
1920 Bullet Proof
Fickle Women

Girls Don't Gamble
Overland Red
Smiling All the Way
McClure, A. W.
1916 Intolerance
1919 The Mother and the Law
MacClure, Gladys
1919 The Love Auction
McClure, Laura
1916 The Ballet Girl
McCollough, Mrs.
1917 A Jewel in Pawn*
McCollough, Philip *see* McCullough,
Philo
McCollum, H. H. *see* McCullum, H. H.
McComas, Carroll *same as* McComas,
Carol
1916 When Love Is King
1920 Jack Straw
McConnell, Clay
1916 A House Built upon Sand*
McConnell, Guy W. *same as*
McConnell, Guy
1917 Cinderella and the Magic
Slipper
The Penny Philanthropist
McConnell, Harriet
1918 The Street of Seven Stars
McConnell, Marie
1918 The Street of Seven Stars
McConnell, Mollie *same as*
MacConnell, Mollie; McConnell,
Molly
1915 Beulah
Should a Wife Forgive?
1916 Joy and the Dragon
Little Mary Sunshine
Pay Dirt
Shadows and Sunshine
The Twin Triangle
1917 Bab the Fixer
The Best Man
Betty Be Good
The Checkmate
The Climber
The Girl Angle
His Old-Fashioned Dad
The Martinache Marriage
The Understudy
The Wildcat
1918 The Claws of the Hun
The Demon
Go West, Young Man
Little Miss Grown-Up
Missing
No Man's Land
The Primitive Woman
Set Free
1919 Bare Fists
Cheating Herself
The Feud
Fools and Their Money
His Official Fiancée
The Homebreaker
One of the Finest
Red Hot Dollars
Roped
1920 Dangerous to Men
Let's Be Fashionable
Nurse Marjorie
McConnell, Parker *same as*
MacConnell, Parker
1920 The Romance Promoters
The Six Best Cellars
Smiling All the Way
McConville, Bernard
1916 Children of the Feud
Going Straight
Gretchen, the Greenhorn
The Heiress at Coffee Dan's
Let Katie Do It
The Little School Ma'am
The Missing Links
The Price of Power
A Sister of Six
Susan Rocks the Boat
1917 Aladdin and the Wonderful
Lamp
The Babes in the Woods
The Rose of Blood
1918 Ali Baba and the Forty Thieves
The Deciding Kiss
Fan Fan

The Girl with the Champagne
Eyes
Rosemary Climbs the Heights
Six Shooter Andy
That Devil, Bateese
Treasure Island
1919 Bare Fists
Heart O' the Hills
The Sleeping Lion
A Yankee Princess
1920 Bonnie May
A Connecticut Yankee at King
Arthur's Court
Forty-Five Minutes from
Broadway
Nineteen and Phyllis
McCord, Mrs. Lewis *same as* McChord,
Mrs.; McCord, Mrs. Louis
1915 Armstrong's Wife
Chimmie Fadden
Chimmie Fadden Out West
The Chorus Lady
The Country Boy
The Immigrant
The Kindling
The Marriage of Kitty
Stolen Goods*
The Warrens of Virginia
Young Romance
1916 Common Ground
The Heart of Nora Flynn
The Race
The Ragamuffin
Unprotected
1917 The Ghost House
The Golden Fetter
McCord, Vera
1920 The Good-Bad Wife
McCormack, Mr.
1917 The Money Mill
McCormack, Claire
1916 The Shop Girl
1917 Sowers and Reapers
McCormack, Frank
1917 Motherhood (Frank Powell
Producing Corp.)
MacCormack, George E.
1920 Forty-Five Minutes from
Broadway
McCormack, Miles
1918 Cheating the Public
McCormick, Langdon
1914 The Burglar and the Lady
McCormick, Mrs. Medill
1914 Your Girl and Mine: A
Woman Suffrage Play*
McCormick, R. R.
1915 Russian Battlefields
McCormick, S. Barret
1915 The Disciple
McCoy, Bill *see* McCoy, William
McCoy, Gertrude
1915 The House of the Lost Court
June Friday
The Ploughshare
Through Turbulent Waters
1916 The Isle of Love
The Lash of Destiny
1917 Madame Sherry
The Silent Witness
1918 The Blue Bird
The Danger Mark
His Daughter Pays
Men
To Him That Hath
1920 Out of the Darkness
McCoy, H. *could be same as* McCoy,
Harry
1915 Regeneration
McCoy, Harry *could be same as*
McCoy, H.
1918 Fair Enough
A Hoosier Romance
1919 Sis Hopkins
McCoy, Kid *see* Selby, Norman
McCoy, William (*cam*) *same as*
McCoy, Bill; McCoy, William H.
1915 The Man Who Couldn't Beat
God
1916 The Island of Surprise
1917 The Bottom of the Well
1919 Daring Hearts

1920 Bab's Candidate
The Midnight Bride
The Sea Rider
McCoy, William M. (*writer*)
1917 The Jaguar's Claws
1919 Hearts of Men
McCready, Jack
1917 The Spirit of '76
1918 Me und Gott
McCree, Junie
1915 The Man Who Beat Dan Dolan
McCulley, May
1920 The Gilded Dream
McCullom, Bartley *see* McCullum,
Bartley
McCullough (full name unknown)
1915 The Fairy and the Waif*
McCullough, Campbell
1915 The Adventures of a Boy Scout
MacCullough, Jack
1920 Do the Dead Talk?
McCullough, Philo *same as*
McCollough, Philip; McCullough, P.
H.; McCullough, P. M.
1915 The Adventures of a Madcap
1916 Pay Dirt
The Power of Evil
1917 Captain Kiddo
The Martinache Marriage
The Secret of Black Mountain
Tears and Smiles
1918 Daughter Angele
The Dream Lady
The Girl Who Wouldn't Quit
The Goat
The Legion of Death
Modern Love
Quicksand
A Rich Man's Darling
1919 Child of M'sieu
Extravagance
The Gay Lord Quex
Happy Though Married
Johnny-on-the-Spot
Lord and Lady Algy
The Market of Souls
Soldiers of Fortune
Spotlight Sadie
1920 Flame of Youth
The Great Accident
In the Heart of a Fool
The Little Grey Mouse
The Scoffer
A Splendid Hazard
The Untamed
A World of Folly
McCullough, Ralph
1920 Homer Comes Home
One Hour Before Dawn
McCullough, Walter
1916 A Daughter of the Gods
The Marble Heart
A Wife's Sacrifice
McCullum, Bartley *same as* McCullom,
Bartley
1913 The Third Degree
1914 The Lion and the Mouse
1915 The College Widow
1916 Dollars and the Woman
The Evangelist
Sorrows of Happiness
McCullum, H. H. *same as* McCullom,
H. H.; MacCullom, H. H.
1915 Keep Moving
1916 The Final Curtain
McCutcheon, John T.
1916 Cousin Jim
McCutcheon, Wallace
1918 The Floor Below
1919 A Virtuous Vamp
1920 The Thief
McDaniel, George *same as* MacDaniel,
George; McDaniel, George E.;
McDaniels, George; McDaniels,
George A.
1917 The Door Between
The Hidden Children
The Little Princess
1918 Beauty in Chains
Hell's Crater
Hungry Eyes
The Man from Funeral Range
The Price of Applause

Mack, Hughie

　　Impossible Susan
　　The Winding Trail
1919　Fighting Through
　　It Happened in Paris
　　Love Is Love
　　Put Up Your Hands
　　Some Liar
　　The Speed Maniac
　　Thieves
1920　Burglar Proof
　　The Gamesters
　　The Girl in the Web
　　Going Some
　　The Land of Jazz

Mack, Hughie
1914　The Win(k)some Widow
1915　C.O.D.
　　The Dust of Egypt
　　A Price for Folly
1916　A Night Out
1920　Seeing It Through

Mack, James
1916　Fruits of Desire
1917　The Secret of the Storm
　　　　Country
1920　The Shark

Mack, Joseph P.
1918　Wild Honey
1920　Chains of Evidence

Mack, Violet
1920　It Might Happen to You

Mack, Walter
1917　Alma, Where Do You Live?

Mack, Wayne
1920　Bubbles

Mack, Willard
1915　Aloha Oe
　　The Edge of the Abyss
1916　All Man
　　A Child of Mystery
　　The Conqueror
　　The Corner
　　Her Maternal Right
　　The Lost Bridegroom
　　Mixed Blood
　　Nanette of the Wilds
　　The Saleslady
1917　The Highway of Hope
　　Two Men and a Woman
　　Who's Your Neighbor?
　　A Woman Alone
　　The Woman Beneath
　　Yankee Pluck
1918　Go West, Young Man
　　The Hell Cat
　　Laughing Bill Hyde
　　The Wasp
　　The Witch Woman
1919　One Week of Life
　　Shadows
　　The Woman on the Index
1920　Heritage
　　The Valley of Doubt

Mack, William B.
1919　Virtuous Men
1920　The Deep Purple
　　Heliotrope

Mackay, Charles same as **MacKay,
　Charles; Mackay, Charles D.**
1916　The Unpardonable Sin
　　The Velvet Paw
　　The Weakness of Man
1919　Me and Captain Kidd
　　The Oakdale Affair
　　The Poison Pen
　　The Steel King
　　The Woman of Lies
1920　Love Without Question

Mackay, Edward same as **MacKay,
　Edward; Mackey, Edward**
1914　Clothes
　　The Coming Power
　　The Port of Missing Men
　　The Span of Life
　　The Spirit of the Poppy
1915　The Clue
　　The Secret Orchard
1916　The Faded Flower
　　Her Husband's Wife
　　Man and His Angel
1918　Life or Honor?

McKay, Grant
1920　Risky Business
McKay, James
1916　The Ruling Passion
　　War Brides
1917　The Eternal Sin
　　The Lone Wolf
Mackay, John
1919　The Weaker Vessel
Mackay, Marshall see **Mackaye,
　Marshall**
McKay, Windsor
1918　Crashing Through to Berlin
Mackaye, Elsie
1920　Nothing but the Truth
MacKaye, Fred
1915　Time Lock Number 776
Mackaye, Marshall same as **Mackay,
　Marshall**
1915　Kilmeny
　　Young Romance
1917　A Jewel in Pawn
McKean, F. H.
1918　Crashing Through to Berlin
McKee, John
1916　Robinson Crusoe
McKee, L. D. could be same as **McKee,
　L. S.** or **McKee, Lafayette**
1918　The Silent Rider
McKee, L. S. could be same as **McKee,
　L. D.** or **McKee, Lafayette**
1919　Charge It to Me
1920　The Daredevil
　　Lone Hand Wilson
McKee, Lafayette could be same as
　McKee, L. D. or **McKee, L. S.**
1916　The Adventures of Kathlyn
1917　The Lad and the Lion
1918　The City of Purple Dreams
　　Little Orphant Annie
McKee, Raymond same as **McKee, Ray;
　McKee, Sergt. Raymond**
1916　The Heart of the Hills
　　The Sunbeam
　　The Wheel of the Law
1917　The Apple-Tree Girl
　　Billy and the Big Stick
　　Kidnapped
　　The Lady of the Photograph
　　The Last Sentence
　　The Little Chevalier
　　The Master Passion
　　Where Love Is
1918　The Unbeliever
1919　The End of the Road
　　Fit to Win
　　Kathleen Mavourneen
　　Me and Captain Kidd
1920　Flame of Youth
　　The Fortune Teller
　　The Girl of My Heart
　　The Little Wanderer
　　Love's Harvest
McKee, Scott
1916　Macbeth
1917　The Babes in the Woods
1920　Sherry
　　West Is West
McKeen, Marie
1916　The Daughter of the Don
1917　The Island of Desire
McKeever, Rodney
1919　The Quickening Flame
McKenna, William J.
1918　The Crucible of Life
McKennon, John
1916　The Victory of Conscience
McKenzie, Bob
1920　Bullet Proof
MacKenzie, Donald same as **McKenzie,
　Donald**
1915　The Galloper
　　Mary's Lamb
　　The Spender
1916　The Challenge
　　The Precious Packet
McKenzie, G. (cam)
1916　The Crisis
McKenzie, George (actor)
1916　Macbeth
1918　The Widow's Might

Mackenzie, Lady Grace
1915　Lady Mackenzie's Big Game
　　　　Pictures
Mackenzie, Jack same as **MacKenzie,
　Jack; McKenzie, Jack; Mackenzie,
　John**
1916　The Heritage of Hate
　　The Isle of Life
1917　Anything Once
　　Eternal Love
1918　False Ambition
　　The Fighting Grin
　　The Ghost Flower
　　The Girl Who Wouldn't Quit
　　The Last Rebel
　　The Love Brokers
　　Madame Spy
　　A Rich Man's Darling
1919　Toton
　　When Bearcat Went Dry
　　Whom the Gods Would
　　　　Destroy
1920　Captain Swift
　　The Gift Supreme
　　The Honey Bee
　　The Romance Promoters
McKenzie Twins
1919　Jane Goes A-Wooing
McKeogh, Lt. Arthur F.
1919　The Lost Battalion
McKeown, Wally
1918　Caught in the Act
Mackey, Edward see **Mackay, Edward**
McKey, William same as **MacKey,
　William**
1915　The Warning
1916　Mice and Men
　　The Ransom
McKim, Edwin same as **McKim,
　Edward; McKim, Edward J.**
1912　Oliver Twist
1914　Should a Woman Divorce?
1915　A Mother's Confession
　　The Unwelcome Wife*
McKim, Robert
1915　The Disciple
　　The Edge of the Abyss
1916　Between Men
　　The Captive God
　　The Devil's Double
　　Hell's Hinges
　　Honor's Altar
　　Jim Grimsby's Boy
　　The Last Act
　　The Phantom
　　The Primal Lure
　　The Raiders
　　The Return of Draw Egan
　　The Stepping Stone
1917　Blood Will Tell
　　The Dark Road
　　The Iced Bullet
　　The Last of the Ingrams
　　Master of His Home
　　Paddy O'Hara
　　Paws of the Bear
　　The Silent Man
　　The Son of His Father
　　Time Locks and Diamonds
　　The Weaker Sex
1918　Blue Blazes Rawden
　　The Claws of the Hun
　　Fuss and Feathers
　　Green Eyes
　　The Law of the North
　　Love Me
　　The Marriage Ring
　　Playing the Game
　　The Vamp
　　When Do We Eat?
1919　The Brand
　　Greased Lightning
　　Her Kingdom of Dreams
　　Partners Three
　　Wagon Tracks
　　The Westerners
　　The Wolf
1920　Bullet Proof
　　The Devil to Pay
　　The Dwelling Place of Light
　　The Mark of Zorro
　　The Money-Changers
　　Out of the Dust
　　Riders of the Dawn

　　The Silver Horde
　　The Spenders
　　The U.P. Trail
　　The Woman in Room 13
Mackin, John E. same as **Mackin, John;
　could be same as Macklin, Jack** or
　Macklin, John
1915　Don Caesar de Bazan
　　The Pretenders
1916　Common Sense Brackett
　　The Haunted Manor
　　The Idol of the Stage
　　The Lotus Woman
　　The Quality of Faith
1917　Little Miss Nobody
　　The New York Peacock
1919　The Belle of the Season
Mackin, Laurie same as **Mackin,
　Laura; could be same as Macklan,
　Laura**
1915　The Battle of Ballots
1917　The Secret of Eve
Mackin, Louise
1915　A Soldier's Oath
McKinney, C. R.
1917　Red, White and Blue Blood
McKinnon (full name unknown)
1916　The Code of Marcia Gray*
McKinnon, Mr.
1913　Victory
McKinnon, Al
1916　The Woman Who Dared
1919　Cowardice Court
1920　Neptune's Bride
MacKinnon, John same as **McKinnon,
　John**
1916　The Stronger Love
　　Tongues of Men
1917　The Winning of Sally Temple
1918　The Cruise of the
　　　　Make-Believes
　　The Girl Who Came Back
1920　The Forbidden Woman
　　The Fourteenth Man
　　Her First Elopement
McKinnon, Roger
1919　Strictly Confidential
Mackintosh, Louis
1920　The Deep Purple
Macklan, Laura could be same as
　Mackin, Laurie
1916　The Heart of New York
Mackley, Mrs. see **Mackley, Mrs.
　Arthur**
Mackley, Arthur same as **Mackley, J.
　Arthur**
1917　The Honor System
1919　The Feud
　　Loot
Mackley, Mrs. Arthur same as
　Mackley, Mrs.
1916　Intolerance
1918　Daughter Angele
1919　The Mother and the Law
Mackley, J. Arthur see **Mackley, Arthur**
Macklin, Albert
1916　According to Law
　　The Drifter
　　I Accuse
Macklin, Jack could be same as
　Mackin, John E. or **Macklin, John**
1917　God's Man
Macklin, John could be same as
　Mackin, John E. or **Macklin, Jack**
1916　I Accuse
Macklyn, Frederick
1915　The Closing Net
MacLane, Mary
1918　Men Who Have Made Love to
　　　　Me
MacLaren, Mrs.
1917　The Last Sentence
MacLaren, Katherine same as
　McLaren, Katherine
1917　Tears and Smiles
1918　Daddy's Girl
1919　Child of M'sieu
MacLaren, Mary
1916　Idle Wives
　　Saving the Family Name
　　Shoes
　　Wanted—A Home

McRae, Duncan
- 1915 Cohen's Luck
- The House of the Lost Court
- June Friday
- Through Turbulent Waters
- 1916 The Flower of No Man's Land
- The Lash of Destiny
- That Sort
- The Woman's Law
- 1917 Red, White and Blue Blood
- 1918 The Daredevil
- My Own United States

McRae, Henry
- 1915 Coral
- 1916 Behind the Lines
- 1917 The Bronze Bride
- Man and Beast
- Money Madness
- 1918 The Phantom Riders

McRayne, Tom
- 1919 The Perfect Lover

MacTammany, Ruth
- 1917 Alma, Where Do You Live?
- The Girl from Rector's

McVeigh, John
- 1914 The Line-Up at Police Headquarters

McVey, Lucille *see* **Drew, Mrs. Sidney** *(died 1925)*

McVey, Viola
- 1920 The Mysteries of Paris

McVicker, Sarah *same as* **McVickar, Sara**
- 1915 Tillie's Tomato Surprise
- 1917 The Sin Woman
- 1918 We Should Worry

McWade, Mrs. *could be same as* **McWade, Margaret**
- 1919 The Red Lantern

McWade, Edward *same as* **McWade, Eddie**
- 1914 Uncle Tom's Cabin
- 1919 The Hornet's Nest
- 1919-20
- When a Man Loves
- 1920 Dangerous Days
- The Great Accident
- Husband Hunter
- Stop Thief!

McWade, Margaret *could be same as* **McWade, Mrs.**
- 1917 Blue Jeans
- 1918 Flower of the Dusk
- To Hell with the Kaiser
- 1919 Broken Commandments
- The Great Victory, Wilson or the Kaiser? The Fall of the Hohenzollerns
- 1919-20
- When a Man Loves
- 1920 Alias Miss Dodd
- The Blue Moon
- The Confession
- Darling Mine
- Food for Scandal
- Her Beloved Villain
- Shore Acres
- Stronger Than Death

MacWilliams, Glen *same as* **McWilliams, Glen; McWilliams, Glenn**
- 1917 Wild and Woolly
- 1918 Arizona
- Headin' South
- Say, Young Fellow!
- 1919 His Majesty, the American
- The Knickerbocker Buckaroo
- 1920 Kismet
- The Luck of the Irish
- The Poor Simp
- A Splendid Hazard

Macy, Mrs. Anne Sullivan *same as* **Sullivan, Anne**
- 1919 Deliverance

Macy, Carleton *same as* **Macey, Carleton; Macy, Carlton**
- 1915 Destruction
- A Woman's Past
- 1916 Big Jim Garrity
- The City of Illusion
- Gold and the Woman
- The Scarlet Oath

- 1917 Seven Keys to Baldpate
- 1918 The Eleventh Commandment
- The Firebrand
- Her Man
- Miss Innocence
- Peg of the Pirates

Macy, H. R.
- 1914 Tess of the Storm Country

Macy, Maud Hall *same as* **Macey, Maud Hall**
- 1914 A Mother's Heart
- 1916 Where Love Leads

Madden, Edward
- 1916 The Devil's Toy

Madden, Golda
- 1917 Fires of Rebellion
- Flying Colors
- 1918 Jilted Janet
- 1919 Lombardi, Ltd.
- 1920 The Mother of His Children
- The Woman in Room 13

Maddock, Jeanne
- 1918 The Light of Western Stars

Maddox, Miss *see* **Mattox, Martha**

Madigan, Virginia
- 1917 Baby Mine

Madin, Captain
- 1914 Sport and Travel in Central Africa

Madison, Cleo
- 1914 Damon and Pythias
- Samson
- 1916 The Chalice of Sorrow
- Her Bitter Cup
- A Soul Enslaved
- 1917 Black Orchids
- 1918 The Romance of Tarzan
- 1919 The Girl from Nowhere
- 1920 The Price of Redemption

Madsen, Chris
- 1915 Passing of the Oklahoma Outlaw

Mae, Leola *could be same as* **May, Lola**
- 1917 Broadway Arizona

Mae, Neola *see* **Neola May, Princess**

Maedler, Richard W. *same as* **Maedler, Richard**
- 1919 Checkers
- Eastward Ho!
- Evangeline
- Kathleen Mavourneen
- The Last of the Duanes
- Lure of Ambition
- Sacred Silence
- Should a Husband Forgive?
- Wings of the Morning
- 1920 A Connecticut Yankee at King Arthur's Court

Mageroni, George *see* **Majeroni, George**

Magner, William
- 1920 The Woman God Sent

Magowan, Robert
- 1919 The Devil's Trail

Magrane, Thomas *same as* **McGrane, T. J.; McGrane, Thomas; McGrane, Thomas J.; Magrane, Tom**
- 1916 The Dragon
- 1917 A Mute Appeal
- 1919 The Hidden Truth
- Too Many Crooks
- 1920 The Way Women Love

Maguire, Harry *same as* **MacGuire, Harry; Maguire, H. H.;** *could be same as* **Maguire, Micky**
- 1916 Mixed Blood
- The Sign of the Poppy
- 1917 The Gates of Doom
- The Phantom's Secret
- The Plow Woman
- The Scarlet Crystal

Maguire, Micky *could be same as* **Maguire, Harry**
- 1919 The Red Lantern*

Maguire, Tom *could be same as* **McGuire, Tom**
- 1920 Half a Chance

Mahamet, Tarah Ben
- 1920 Twisted Souls

Mahon, John
- 1916 The Lure of Heart's Desire

Mahoney, Elizabeth
- 1917 The Mate of the Sally Ann
- 1918 Ann's Finish
- Beauty and the Rogue
- The Eyes of Julia Deep
- Fair Enough
- The Ghost of Rosy Taylor
- Impossible Susan
- Jilted Janet
- The Square Deal
- 1920 The Golden Trail

Mahoney, John
- 1914 Over Niagara Falls

Mahony, J. J.
- 1915 The Man Who Beat Dan Dolan

Mahring, Anne
- 1916 The Crown Prince's Double

Maier, Julia
- 1918 The Wolf and His Mate

Maigne, Charles
- 1916 The Brand of Cowardice
- 1917 Barbary Sheep
- The Bottle Imp
- The Golden Fetter
- Her Strange Wedding
- The Hungry Heart
- The Rise of Jennie Cushing
- The Squaw Man's Son
- 1918 The Blue Bird
- The Danger Mark
- Heart of the Wilds
- Her Great Chance
- In the Hollow of Her Hand
- The Knife
- The Lie
- Out of a Clear Sky
- Prunella
- The Rose of the World
- 1919 The Firing Line
- The Hushed Hour
- The Indestructible Wife
- The Invisible Bond
- Redhead
- The World to Live In
- 1920 The Copperhead
- A Cumberland Romance
- The Fighting Chance

Mailes, Charles Hill *same as* **Mailes, Charles; Mailes, Charles H.**
- 1914 Lord Chumley
- The Woman in Black
- 1915 Dora Thorne
- The Hungarian Nabob
- 1916 The Eagle's Wing
- The People vs. John Doe
- The Seekers
- The Whirlpool of Destiny
- 1917 Beloved Jim
- The Bronze Bride
- The Clock*
- Come Through
- The Girl Who Won Out
- The Lair of the Wolf
- The Lash of Power
- Money Madness
- The Mysterious Mrs. M.
- Polly Redhead
- Southern Justice
- The Spotted Lily
- The Winged Mystery
- 1918 Danger Within
- The Fighting Grin
- The Girl Who Wouldn't Quit
- The Magic Eye
- The Talk of the Town
- Three Mounted Men
- 1919 Fools and Their Money
- Full of Pep
- Our Better Selves
- Red Hot Dollars
- The Speed Maniac
- 1920 Go and Get It
- Haunting Shadows
- Homespun Folks
- The Mark of Zorro
- Treasure Island
- Witch's Gold

Mailly, M.
- 1920 The Empire of Diamonds

Mainhall, Harry
- 1914 One Wonderful Night

Maiori, Mrs. A.
- 1916 Poor Little Peppina

Maiori, Antonio
- 1916 Poor Little Peppina

Maison, Edna *same as* **Maison, Elsie**
- 1914 The Merchant of Venice
- Richelieu
- The Spy
- 1916 The Dumb Girl of Portici
- Undine
- 1917 Mr. Opp
- 1918 The Mysterious Mr. Browning
- A Rich Man's Darling

Maison, Elsie *see* **Maison, Edna**

Maison Bernard
- 1917 Daughter of Destiny

Maitland, Gertrude
- 1917 On Record

Maja, Zelma
- 1920 Live Sparks
- The Six Best Cellars

Majerino, Mario *see* **Majeroni, Mario**

Majeroni, George *same as* **Mageroni, George; Majeroni, Georgio; Majeroni, Giorgini; Majeroni, Giorgio**
- 1914 The Sign of the Cross
- 1915 Bella Donna
- The Eternal City
- The Gray Mask
- The Stolen Voice
- 1916 As in a Looking Glass
- Diplomacy
- The Feud Girl
- My Lady Incog.
- Paying the Price
- 1917 Stranded in Arcady
- Who's Your Neighbor?
- 1918 All Man
- The Belgian
- The Caillaux Case
- The Green God
- Hoarded Assets
- The King of Diamonds
- Stolen Honor
- Tangled Lives
- The Woman the Germans Shot
- 1919 Beating the Odds
- Beauty-Proof
- The Darkest Hour
- Fighting Destiny
- The Gamblers
- In Honor's Web
- The Invisible Bond
- Marriage for Convenience

Majeroni, Mario *same as* **Majerino, Mario; Majerone, Mario;** *could be same as* **Maroney, Mario**
- 1914 The Nightingale
- 1915 The Cotton King
- The Dictator
- The Little Mademoiselle
- 1916 Less Than the Dust
- Sherlock Holmes
- 1917 The Broadway Sport
- The Hawk
- Heart's Desire
- A Sleeping Memory
- The White Raven
- 1920 Children Not Wanted
- From Now On
- Love Without Question
- Partners of the Night

Makarenko, Daniel
- 1914 Michael Strogoff

Malaidy, James C. *same as* **Malaide, James C.; Malaidy, James**
- 1916 The Upheaval
- 1917 Outcast
- The Runaway

Malatesta, Fred *same as* **Malatesta, Fred M.; Malatesta, Frederic**
- 1916 Sherlock Holmes
- 1918 The Border Raiders
- The Claim
- The Demon
- The Legion of Death
- 1919 The Devil's Trail
- The Four-Flusher
- Full of Pep

1920 The Best of Luck
Big Happiness
The Challenge of the Law
Risky Business
The Sins of Rosanne
The Valley of Tomorrow
Malette, Arthur *see* **Mallette, Arthur**
Maley, Denman
1915 The Old Homestead
1916 Rolling Stones
Mallette, Arthur *same as* **Malette, Arthur**
1918 Without Honor
1919 Bare-Fisted Gallagher
Whitewashed Walls
Mallory, Viola *same as* **Lawrence, Viola**
1917 Within the Law
1919 The Heart of Humanity
His Divorced Wife
Loot
Malloy, Dan
1918 Out of the Night
Malloy, Tom *same as* **Malloy, Thomas F.**
1917 Clover's Rebellion
The Judgement House
1919 The Adventure Shop
The Bramble Bush
The Climbers
A Girl at Bay
The Girl Problem
Thin Ice
The Unknown Quantity
1920 The Fortune Hunter
Malone, Ann
1919 The Secret Garden
Malone, Florence
1915 The Master Hand
1918 The Sea Waif
1919 The Battler
1920 The Strongest
Malone, Helen
1915 The Suburban
Malone, Marty
1916 Man and His Soul
The Red Mouse
Malone, Molly
1917 Bucking Broadway
The Car of Chance
A Marked Man
The Phantom's Secret
The Pulse of Life
The Rescue
Straight Shooting
1918 The Phantom Riders
The Scarlet Drop
Thieves' Gold
Wild Women
A Woman's Fool
1919 The Spite Bride
1920 It's a Great Life
Just Out of College
Stop Thief!
Malone, Violet
1914 The Little Angel of Canyon Creek
1916 Alien Souls
1920 Woman's Man
Maloney, Gertrude
1918 The Landloper
Maloney, Leo D. *same as* **Maloney, Leo**
1916 The Diamond Runners
Judith of the Cumberlands
The Manager of the B. and A.
Medicine Bend
Whispering Smith
1919 The Arizona Cat Claw
The Spitfire of Seville
Malvern, Corinne
1915 The Luring Lights
Malvern, Henry
1917 The Varmint
Mammy Lou
1918 The Glorious Adventure
Man, Frankie
1914 Through Fire to Fortune
Mandell, Winthrop
1916 The Combat
Mandeville, William *same as* **Manderville, William**
1914 Without Hope

1915 Cap'n Eri
What Happened to Jones
1917 The Call of Her People
The Girl Who Didn't Think
Manley, Del
1917 A Trip Through Japan
Manly, G. Burnell *same as* **Manly, J. B.**
1919 Through the Wrong Door
1920 Held in Trust
Mann, Mrs.
1917 The Skylight Room
Mann, Alice
1918 A Pair of Sixes
1919 Fruits of Passion
Help! Help! Police!
Water Lily
Mann, Bertha
1918 The Blindness of Divorce
Mann, Ernest
1917 Knights of the Square Table
Mann, Frankie *same as* **Mann, Frances**
1913 The Battle of Shiloh
1914 The House Next Door
The Wolf
1915 The Climbers
The Great Ruby
The Sporting Duchess
1916 The Evangelist
Her Surrender
The Sex Lure
1919 Fortune's Child
Fruits of Passion
The Root of Evil
Water Lily
1920 The Place of Honeymoons
Mann, Hank
1916 A Modern Enoch Arden
Mann, Harry
1916 Kinkaid, Gambler
What Love Can Do
1917 The Flame of Youth
Mr. Dolan of New York
1918 A Rich Man's Darling
1919 The Red Lantern
Mann, Louis
1914 Your Girl and Mine: A Woman Suffrage Play
Mann, Margaret *same as* **Mann, Mrs. Margaret**
1919 The Heart of Humanity
The Right to Happiness
1920 Once to Every Woman
Mann, Virginia
1913 The Inside of the White Slave Traffic
Mann, Walter
1920 A Manhattan Knight
Manners, Lady Diana
1918 The Great Love*
Manning, Aileen
1919 A Regular Fellow
1920 Everybody's Sweetheart
The Heart of Twenty
Her Husband's Friend
The Little Shepherd of Kingdom Come
Manning, Amy
1916 The Rainbow Princess
Manning, Jack
1920 The Love Flower
Manning, Joseph
1915 Little Pal
Rags
Manning, Mildred
1916 An Enemy to the King
1917 The Marriage Speculation
Mary Jane's Pa
Next Door to Nancy
The Princess of Park Row
1918 The Unchastened Woman
1919 Kitty Kelly, M.D.
The Westerners
Manning, R. J.
1920 Marooned Hearts
Manon, Marcia *same as* **Ankewich, Camille**
1917 The Hostage
The Prison Without Walls
1918 The Border Wireless
The Claw
The Girl Who Came Back
Old Wives for New

One More American
The Savage Woman
Stella Maris
1919 Captain Kidd, Jr.
A Daughter of the Wolf
In Old Kentucky
The Lottery Man
Maggie Pepper
The Test of Honor
The Woman Michael Married
1920 The Forbidden Thing
Life's Twist
Mansfield, Duncan
1918 Fuss and Feathers
String Beans
When Do We Eat?
1919 L'Apache
The Broken Melody
Happy Though Married
Hard Boiled
The Homebreaker
The Market of Souls
Partners Three
The Virtuous Thief
What Every Woman Learns
1920 Everybody's Sweetheart
Hairpins
His Wife's Money
The Poor Simp
Mansfield, Etta
1916 Driftwood
Man and His Soul
The Red Mouse
1918 And the Children Pay
Mansfield, Martha
1918 Broadway Bill
1919 The Hand Invisible
The Perfect Lover
Should a Husband Forgive?
1920 Civilian Clothes
Dr. Jekyll and Mr. Hyde (Famous Players-Lasky Corp.)
Mothers of Men
Women Men Love
The Wonderful Chance
Manson, F. M.
1917 The Planter
Mantell, Ethel
1916 Romeo and Juliet (Quality Pictures Corp.)
The Spider and the Fly
Mantell, Mary
1916 My Partner
Mantell, R. B., Jr. *see* **Mantell, Robert B., Jr.**
Mantell, Robert B. *same as* **Mantell, Robert**
1915 The Blindness of Devotion
The Unfaithful Wife
1916 The Green-Eyed Monster
The Spider and the Fly
A Wife's Sacrifice
1917 Tangled Lives
Mantell, Robert B., Jr. *same as* **Mantell, R. B., Jr.; Mantell, Robert, Jr.**
1915 The Boss
The Sins of Society
1917 When You and I Were Young
Mantle, Burns
1915 How Molly Malone Made Good
1919 The Silver King
1920 The Branded Woman
A Dark Lantern
Good References
Lady Rose's Daughter
Yes or No
Mantley, Clay
1917 The Marriage Market
Mantz, Al F. G.
1920 Blackmail
Cinderella's Twin
When Dawn Came
Mapes, Agnes
1914 Il Trovatore
1915 The Glory of Youth
1916 The Foolish Virgin
Mapes, Victor
1920 The Saphead

Maple, John E.
1918 Indian Life*
1920 Before the White Man Came
Marba, Joseph
1920 Wits vs. Wits
Marbe, Fay
1920 The Very Idea
Marburg, Bertram *see* **Marburgh, Bertram**
Marburgh, Benjamin *could be same as* **Marburgh, Bertram**
1915 A Soldier's Oath
Marburgh, Bertram *same as* **Marburg, Bertram; could be same as* **Marburgh, Benjamin**
1915 After Dark
The Broken Law
The Stolen Voice
1916 The Rail Rider
1919 Checkers
The Social Pirate
You Never Know Your Luck
1920 The Greatest Love
Marc, Agnes
1915 The Commuters
1916 Where Is My Father?
1918 A Perfect Lady
Marc, Alice
1914 The Jungle
1917 Nan of Music Mountain
Marceau, Emily
1919 Open Your Eyes
Wild Oats
Marceau, Grace
1919 The Great Victory, Wilson or the Kaiser? The Fall of the Hohenzollerns
Marcel, Mlle.
1919 The Common Cause
Marcel, Inez
1914 Cinderella
1916 The Mischief Maker
1917 The Small Town Girl
Unknown 274
1918 The Appearance of Evil
The Power and the Glory
The Transgressor
1919 The Burning Question
The Gay Old Dog
1920 The Victim
Marcel, Sonia *see* **Marcelle, Sonia**
Marcelle, Mademoiselle
1916 A Daughter of the Gods
The Marble Heart
Marcelle, Sonia *same as* **Marcel, Sonia**
1916 Elusive Isabel
Should a Baby Die?
1917 Baby Mine
1918 The Fall of the Romanoffs
March, General Peyton Conway
1919 The Girl Who Stayed at Home*
Marche, Gazelle
1916 Should a Baby Die?
1917 The Argyle Case
Marcil, Isadore
1915 Playing Dead
Marcin, Max
1916 The Devil's Prayer-Book
1920 The Face at Your Window
The Thief
Marcus, James *same as* **Marcus, J. A.; Marcus, James A.**
1915 Carmen (Fox Film Corp.)
Regeneration
1916 Blue Blood and Red
The Mediator
The Serpent
1917 Betrayed
The Conqueror
The Honor System
The Pride of New York
This Is the Life
1918 The Kid Is Clever
On the Jump
The Prussian Cur
1919 Evangeline
Should a Husband Forgive?
1920 From Now On
Headin' Home
The Strongest

Mardiganian, Aurora
1919 Auction of Souls
Mardo, Estelle
1915 The Man Who Couldn't Beat
God
To Cherish and Protect
Margolies, Florence
1918 For Freedom
Marguerite, Mlle.
1915 Business Is Business
Mari, Febo
1920 A Common Level
Mariani, Elizabeth J.
1918 The Beloved Impostor
Marie, Bonnie same as **Katz, Bonnie Marie**
1918 The Triumph of Venus
Marier, Captain Victor see **Griffith, D. W.; Taylor, S. E. V.**
Marigold, Col. Todhunter
1920 The Cyclone
Marinoff, Fania
1914 One of Our Girls
1915 The Galloper
The Money Master
Nedra
1916 Life's Whirlpool
New York
1917 The Rise of Jennie Cushing
Marion, Arthur
1918 The Marionettes
1919 The Imp
Marion, Ernest
1918 Battling Jane
1919 Life's a Funny Proposition
Marion, Frances (scen)
1915 Camille
The Daughter of the Sea
A Girl of Yesterday
1916 The Battle of Hearts
The Crucial Test
The Feast of Life
The Foundling
Friday the Thirteenth
The Gilded Cage
The Heart of a Hero
The Hidden Scar
The Revolt
The Social Highwayman
The Summer Girl
Tangled Fates
La Vie de Boheme
A Woman's Way
The Yellow Passport
1917 The Amazons
As Man Made Her
The Beloved Adventuress
Forget-Me-Not
A Girl's Folly
A Hungry Heart
The Little Princess
The Poor Little Rich Girl
Rebecca of Sunnybrook Farm
The Social Leper
A Square Deal
The Stolen Paradise
Tillie Wakes Up
The Web of Desire
A Woman Alone
1918 Amarilly of Clothes-Line Alley
The City of Dim Faces
The Goat
He Comes Up Smiling
How Could You, Jean?
Johanna Enlists
M'liss
The Rise of Susan
Stella Maris
The Temple of Dusk
1919 Anne of Green Gables
Captain Kidd, Jr.
The Cinema Murder
The Dark Star
The Misleading Widow
A Regular Girl
1920 The Flapper
Humoresque
Pollyanna
The World and His Wife
Marion, Francis (child actor)
1918 Hearts of the World
The Legion of Death

1919 The World and Its Woman
Marion, Frank J. (prod)
1913 From the Manger to the Cross
Marion, George F.
1915 Excuse Me
1916 Madame X
Marion, Sidney
1919 The Winning Stroke
Marion, William
1915 The Boss
1917 One Hour
The Streets of Illusion
1920 The Devil to Pay
Their Mutual Child
Wanted at Headquarters
Mariott, Crittenden
1916 Her Father's Gold
Marix, Admiral
1915 The Battle Cry of Peace*
Marker, H., Jr. see **Marker, William H., Jr.**
Marker, William H., Jr. same as **Marker, H., Jr.; Marker, William H.**
1920 Her Husband's Friend
The Jailbird
Rookie's Return
Silk Hosiery
Markey, Enid
1915 Aloha Oe
The Cup of Life
The Darkening Trail
The Despoiler
The Iron Strain
The Mating
1916 Between Men
The Captive God
Civilization
The Conqueror
The Devil's Double
The Female of the Species
Jim Grimsby's Boy
Lieutenant Danny, U.S.A.
The No-Good Guy
The Phantom
Shell Forty-Three
1917 Blood Will Tell
The Curse of Eve
The Yankee Way
The Zeppelin's Last Raid
1918 Cheating the Public
The Romance of Tarzan
Six Shooter Andy
Tarzan of the Apes
1920 Sink or Swim
Markham, Kirah
1914 The Lure
Markova, Sonia see **Hartman, Gretchen**
Marks, Lou
1919 Bullin' the Bullsheviki
Marks, Maurice E.
1916 The Devil's Toy
Marks, Willis
1916 Her Bitter Cup
The People vs. John Doe
Secret Love
1917 The Clock
The Mysterious Mrs. M.
1918 The Flash of Fate
The Man from Funeral Range
The Vanity Pool
1919 Greased Lightning
Over the Garden Wall
The Trembling Hour
The Virtuous Thief
When a Girl Loves
The Wishing Ring Man
You Never Saw Such a Girl
1920 The Dancin' Fool
Everything but the Truth
The Family Honor
Homespun Folks
The Jack-Knife Man
The Little Grey Mouse
Markwell, Milton
1919 The Blinding Trail
1920 The Barbarian
The Phantom Melody
Marlborough, Miss could be same as **Marlborough, Helen**
1916 Tongues of Men

Marlborough, Helen could be same as **Marlborough, Miss**
1915 Jack Chanty*
The Wild Goose Chase
Marley, Jay
1919 A Fighting Colleen
Marlo, George could be same as **Merlo, George**
1915 Inspiration
The Mill on the Floss
1916 The Fear of Poverty
The Fugitive
The Pillory
The Woman in Politics
1917 Pots-and-Pans Peggy
Marlo, Zada
1917 The Devil's Bait
Marlowe, Miss
1916 The Code of Marcia Gray*
Marmont, Percy
1918 In the Hollow of Her Hand
The Lie
The Rose of the World
The Turn of the Wheel
1919 The Climbers
The Indestructible Wife
Three Men and a Girl
The Vengeance of Durand
The Winchester Woman
1920 Away Goes Prudence
The Branded Woman
Dead Men Tell No Tales
Slaves of Pride
The Sporting Duchess
Maroney, Mario could be same as **Majeroni, Mario**
1915 Prohibition
Marquard, Rube
1917 The Baseball Revue of 1917*
Marquis, Joseph
1920 The Gray Brother
The Little Outcast
Marr, Gordon
1919 Fools and Their Money
The Island of Intrigue
Marr, William
1917 High Finance
Marriam, H.
1916 Sins of Men
Marriott, Charles same as **Marriot, Charles**
1914 False Colours
1915 It's No Laughing Matter
Sunshine Molly
The Wild Olive
1916 Tongues of Men
Wanted—A Home
1917 Betty and the Buccaneers
Marsh, Mrs.
1917 Betty Be Good
Marsh, "Mother"
1918 Fields of Honor
Marsh, Betty
1914 Home, Sweet Home
1915 The Martyrs of the Alamo
Marsh, George
1917 Southern Justice
Marsh, Mae
1914 The Avenging Conscience
The Escape
The Great Leap; Until Death
Do Us Part
Home, Sweet Home
Judith of Bethulia
1915 The Birth of a Nation
Her Shattered Idol
The Outcast
The Outlaw's Revenge
1916 A Child of the Paris Streets
Hoodoo Ann
Intolerance
The Little Liar
The Marriage of Molly-O
The Wharf Rat
The Wild Girl of the Sierras
1917 The Cinderella Man
Polly of the Circus
Sunshine Alley
1918 All Woman
The Beloved Traitor
The Face in the Dark
Fields of Honor
The Glorious Adventure

Hidden Fires
Money Mad
The Racing Strain
1919 The Bondage of Barbara
The Mother and the Law
Spotlight Sadie
1920 The Little 'Fraid Lady
Marsh, Marguerite same as **Marsh, Margaret**
1914 Threads of Destiny
1916 Casey at the Bat
The Devil's Needle
Intolerance
Little Meena's Romance
Mr. Goode, the Samaritan
The Price of Power
1918 Conquered Hearts
Fields of Honor
Our Little Wife
1919 The Eternal Magdalene
The Mother and the Law
The Phantom Honeymoon
A Royal Democrat
1920 Wits vs. Wits
Women Men Love
Marsh, Mildred
1918 The Daredevil
1922 The Cynic Effect
Marsh, Oliver T. same as **Marsh, Oliver**
1918 All Woman
Dodging a Million
The Floor Below
Hidden Fires
Joan of Plattsburg
Money Mad
The Racing Strain
1919 The Bondage of Barbara
The Brand
The Crimson Gardenia
The Girl from Outside
A Temperamental Wife
A Virtuous Vamp
1920 Dangerous Business
Good References
In Search of a Sinner
The Love Expert
The North Wind's Malice
The Perfect Woman
The Point of View
Something Different
Two Weeks
Marshall, Betty
1915 The Man Who Beat Dan Dolan
A Trade Secret
Marshall, Boyd
1915 The Flying Twins
The Mill on the Floss
1916 Hidden Valley
King Lear
The World and the Woman
1917 A Modern Monte Cristo
The Vicar of Wakefield
When Love Was Blind
Marshall, Carol
1920 The Jack-Knife Man
Marshall, Charles
1918 The Song of Songs
Marshall, Clark
1919 The World Aflame
1920 The Little Shepherd of
Kingdom Come
Marshall, Dixie
1916 Vanity
Marshall, Dorothy
1917 The Gown of Destiny
Marshall, George same as **Marshall, George E.**
1916 Love's Lariat
1917 The Man from Montana
1920 Prairie Trails
Marshall, Josephine
1915 Life Without Soul*
Marshall, Madeline
1918 From Two to Six
Loaded Dice
The Sins of the Children
1920 April Folly
Marshall, Capt. Robert
1917 Her Sister*
Marshall, Roy same as **Marshall, Roy H.**
1916 The Plow Girl

1917 The Call of the East
The Crystal Gazer
Her Strange Wedding
A Mormon Maid
On the Level
The Sunset Trail
1919 A Daughter of the Wolf
The Grim Game
The Other Half
Poor Relations
Rustling a Bride
1920 The Brute Master
Marshall, Ruby
1917 Fighting for Love
Marshall, Thomas Riley
19-- Official Motion Pictures of the
Panama Pacific Exposition
Held at San Francisco,
Calif.*
Marshall, Tina
1916 The Honor of Mary Blake
The Man Inside
1917 The Boy Girl
Marshall, Tully
1914 Paid in Full
1915 The Sable Lorcha
1916 A Child of the Paris Streets
The Devil's Needle
Intolerance
Joan the Woman
Let Katie Do It
Martha's Vindication
Oliver Twist
1917 The Countess Charming
The Devil-Stone
The Golden Fetter
A Modern Musketeer
A Romance of the Redwoods
Unconquered
1918 Bound in Morocco
The Man from Funeral Range
M'liss
Old Wives for New
The Squaw Man
The Thing We Love
Too Many Millions
We Can't Have Everything
The Whispering Chorus
1919 Cheating Cheaters
The Crimson Gardenia
Daughter of Mine
Everywoman
The Fall of Babylon
The Girl Who Stayed Home
The Grim Game
Hawthorne of the U.S.A.
Her Kingdom of Dreams
The Lady of Red Butte
The Life Line
Maggie Pepper
1920 The Dancin' Fool
Double Speed
Excuse My Dust
The Gift Supreme
Her Beloved Villain
Honest Hutch
The Little 'Fraid Lady
Sick Abed
The Slim Princess
What Happened to Rosa
Marshall, William same as **Marshall, William C.**
1916 A Daughter of the Gods
Dust
The Reward of Patience
Under Cover
1917 The Amazons
Arms and the Girl
The Clean Gun
Feet of Clay
The Fortunes of Fifi
Great Expectations
The Land of Promise
The Little Boy Scout
The Phantom Shotgun
Shirley Kaye
1918 The Danger Mark
In Pursuit of Polly
Let's Get a Divorce*
Little Miss Hoover
The Make-Believe Wife
On the Quiet
The Song of Songs
The Whirlpool

1919 A Girl Named Mary
Hawthorne of the U.S.A.
In Mizzoura
Mrs. Wiggs of the Cabbage
Patch
Rose O' the River
Secret Service
The Woman Thou Gavest Me
1920 All-of-a-Sudden-Peggy
Crooked Streets
Eyes of the Heart
The Ladder of Lies
A Lady in Love
Sweet Lavender
Terror Island
Marsten, Lawrence see **Marston, Lawrence**
Marstini, Rosita
1917 The Babes in the Woods
The Clever Mrs. Carfax
Du Barry
High Finance
The Innocent Sinner
A Tale of Two Cities
1918 Good Night, Paul
The Moral Law
Rosemary Climbs the Heights
1919 The Tiger Lily
The Veiled Adventure
Widow by Proxy
1920 Flames of the Flesh
The Luck of Geraldine Laird
Marston, A. C.
1915 Dora Thorne
1916 Love's Pilgrimage to America
Marston, Mrs. A. C.
1914 Under the Gaslight
1915 The Millionaire Baby
Marston, Lawrence same as **Marsten, Lawrence; Marston, Laurence**
1914 Under the Gaslight
The Woman in Black
1915 The Millionaire Baby
1916 Love's Pilgrimage to America
The Marriage Bond
Wall Street Tragedy
1917 The Warfare of the Flesh
1918 The Border Legion
Marston, Mrs. Lawrence
1913 Moths
1914 The Woman in Black
Marston, Theodore
1915 The Cave Man
Mortmain
Mother's Roses
The Primrose Path
The Wheels of Justice
1916 The Dawn of Freedom
The Surprises of an Empty
Hotel
1917 The Girl by the Roadside
Greed
The Raggedy Queen
Sloth
Wrath
1918 Beyond the Law
1919 The Black Gate
Marten, Florence could be same as **Martin, Florence**
1916 Miss George Washington
Marten, Helen see **Martin, Helen**
Martimprey, Comtesse Floria de
1918 Too Fat to Fight
Martin, Master
1914 At the Cross Roads
Martin, Mr.
1918 Caught in the Act
Martin, Alice
1918 Flower of the Dusk
Martin, Alma
1915 The Spender
Martin, Bob
1920 Girls Don't Gamble
Smiling All the Way
Martin, C. H. see **Martin, Charles** (actor)
Martin, Charles (actor) same as **Martin, C. H.; Martin, Charles H.**
1917 Daughter of Maryland
Exile
The Last Sentence
Light in Darkness
More Truth Than Poetry

The Public Defender
1918 Her Price
Who Loved Him Best?
A Woman of Redemption
1920 Dad's Girl
Martin, Charles (cam)
1914 Native Life in the Philippines
Martin, Charles H. see **Martin, Charles** (actor)
Martin, Charles W.
1917 The Undying Flame
Martin, E. A.
1917 The Heart of Texas Ryan
1920 The Jungle Princess
Martin, Earl
1920 Fixed by George
Martin, Ed could be same as **Martin, Edward** or **Martin, Edwin**
1919 The Grim Game
The Woman Next Door
Martin, Edward could be same as **Martin, Ed** or **Martin, Edwin**
1917 Framing Framers
1918 Jules of the Strong Heart
Martin, Edwin could be same as **Martin, Ed** or **Martin, Edward**
1915 Destiny; Or, The Soul of a
Woman
Martin, Ethel
1918 The Rose of the World
Martin, Florence same as **Martin, Florence Evelyn; could be same as Marten, Florence**
1917 The Tiger Woman
1918 The Forbidden Path
The Soul of Buddha
1919 The Light
The Undercurrent
When Men Desire
1920 Oil
Martin, Glenn
1915 A Girl of Yesterday
Martin, H. Kinley same as **Martin, Kinley**
1920 An Amateur Devil
Food for Scandal
A Full House
Oh, Lady, Lady
She Couldn't Help It
What Happened to Jones
Martin, Helen same as **Marten, Helen**
1915 The Song of the Wage Slave
1916 According to Law
I Accuse
The Idol of the Stage
The Man from Nowhere
1917 Corruption
Martin, Irvin J. same as **Martin, I. V.**
1918 The Border Wireless
The Claws of the Hun
A Desert Wooing
Fuss and Feathers
Green Eyes
His Own Home Town
The Kaiser's Shadow, or the
Triple Cross
The Law of the North
The Marriage Ring
A Nine O'Clock Town
The Vamp
Vive La France!
When Do We Eat?
1919 L'Apache
Bill Henry
Breed of Men
Happy Though Married
Hard Boiled
Hay Foot, Straw Foot
His Wife's Friend
The Homebreaker
The Lady of Red Butte
The Market of Souls
The Money Corral
Partners Three
Sahara
Square Deal Sanderson
Stepping Out
The Virtuous Thief
What Every Woman Learns
1920 The Isle of Destiny
Mary's Ankle
Out of the Snows
What's Your Husband Doing?

Martin, Jack (asst dir, actor) could be same as **Martin, John** (actor) or **Martin, John W.** (actor)
1918 The Heart of Romance
1919 Dawn
The Moonshine Trail
Martin, Joe, an ape
1917 Black Orchids
Man and Beast
1919 The Merry-Go-Round
1920 The Return of Tarzan
Martin, John (actor) could be same as **Martin, Jack** (asst dir, actor) or **Martin, John W.** (actor)
1918 Revelation
Martin, John W. (actor) could be same as **Martin, Jack** (asst dir, actor) or **Martin, John** (actor)
1919 Life's Greatest Problem
Martin, Kinley see **Martin, H. Kinley**
Martin, Mary same as **Martin, Mary G.**
1915 The Broken Law
Greater Love Hath No Man
The Vampire
The Wonderful Adventure
1916 Daredevil Kate
The Eternal Sapho
Hazel Kirke
The Vixen
1917 The Derelict
The Heart of a Lion
The Scarlet Letter
The Tiger Woman
Martin, Millicent
1920 A Daughter of Two Worlds
Martin, Rea
1915 The Coquette
Martin, Richard
1920 Beyond the Great Wall
Martin, Vivian
1914 The Wishing Ring; An Idyll of
Old England
1915 The Arrival of Perpetua
A Butterfly on the Wheel
The Little Dutch Girl
The Little Mademoiselle
Little Miss Brown
Old Dutch
Over Night
1916 Her Father's Son
Merely Mary Ann
A Modern Thelma
The Right Direction
The Stronger Love
1917 The Fair Barbarian
Forbidden Paths
The Girl at Home
Giving Becky a Chance
A Kiss for Susie
Little Miss Optimist
Molly Entangled
The Spirit of Romance
The Sunset Trail
The Trouble Buster
The Wax Model
1918 Her Country First
Mirandy Smiles
A Petticoat Pilot
Unclaimed Goods
Viviette
1919 His Official Fiancée
The Home Town Girl
An Innocent Adventuress
Jane Goes A-Wooing
Little Comrade
Louisiana
The Third Kiss
You Never Saw Such a Girl
1920 Husbands and Wives
The Song of the Soul
Martindel, Edward same as **Martindale, Edward; Martindell, Edward**
1916 The Devil at His Elbow
The Eternal Question
Extravagance
The Foundling
The Scarlet Woman
Vanity
1917 A Rich Man's Plaything
1920 Captain Swift
The Furnace
The Misfit Wife
Unseen Forces
The Very Idea

You Never Can Tell

Martine, Mortimer see **Martini, Mortimer**

Martinelli, Arthur same as **Martinelli, Mr.**
1916 God's Half Acre
The Purple Lady
1917 Alias Mrs. Jessop
The End of the Tour
The Greatest Power
Her Fighting Chance
The Trail of the Shadow
The White Raven
1918 Kildare of Storm
Pay Day
A Successful Adventure
Sylvia on a Spree
The Winning of Beatrice
1919 The Amateur Adventuress
Fair and Warmer
A Favor to a Friend
Fools and Their Money
Johnny-on-the-Spot
The Red Lantern*
That's Good
1920 Love, Honor and Obey
The Misleading Lady
Polly with a Past
The Walk-Offs

Martini (full name unknown)
1915 The Fairy and the Waif*

Martini, Mortimer same as **Martine, Mortimer**
1912 Oliver Twist
1914 The Port of Missing Men
1916 The Other Girl
1918 The Unbeliever

Martyn, Wyndham
1920 Wait for Me

Marvin, Miss
1917 Eternal Love

Marvin, Alice
1917 Tom Sawyer
1918 Huck and Tom; Or, The Further Adventures of Tom Sawyer

Marvin, Betty
1917 The Square Deceiver

Marvin, Grace
1916 The Love Girl
1918 The Mask

Marvin, Marion
1918 Cactus Crandall

Mary, Queen of England, 1897-1965
1920 The Fatal Hour*

Maschke, Paul E. same as **Maschke, Paul**
1916 Whom the Gods Destroy
1917 The Barrier
1920 Democracy

Masi, Philip W. same as **Masi, Phil; Masi, Philip; Masse, Philip**
1916 As in a Looking Glass
The River of Romance
1917 The Awakening
Diamonds and Pearls
The Undying Flame
The Whip
1918 The Cross Bearer
Stolen Orders
1919 A Damsel in Distress
1920 The Shadow of Rosalie Byrnes

Mason, Alice
1919 Miss Adventure

Mason, Ann
1919 Deliverance

Mason, Bessie
1920 Dinty

Mason, Betty
1920 Man and Woman (Tyrad Pictures, Inc.)

Mason, Billy same as **Mason, "Smiling" Billy**
1914 A Prince of India
1916 The Right Direction
1919 Some Bride
A Taste of Life
The Wolf
1920 It Might Happen to You

Mason, C. W.
1919 Hard Boiled

Mason, Charles (actor) same as **Mason, Charles E.**
1916 The Clarion
1917 The Boy Girl
1919 The Love Auction
1920 Li Ting Lang

Mason, Charles Post (prod)
1916 Greater New York by Day and by Night; The Wonder City of the World

Mason, Dan
1917 The Broadway Sport
The Derelict
Every Girl's Dream
Over the Hill
The Scarlet Letter
The Slave
Thou Shalt Not Steal
Unknown 274
Wife Number Two
1918 All Woman
Brave and Bold
Jack Spurlock, Prodigal
Laughing Bill Hyde
Marriages Are Made
On the Quiet
The Yellow Ticket
1919 Lure of Ambition
1920 Skinning Skinners

Mason, Eliza
1914 The Chimes

Mason, Elsie
1917 A Mute Appeal

Mason, Flora
1915 The Earl of Pawtucket

Mason, Frank
1917 Apartment 29

Mason, Grace Sartwell
1918 Waifs

Mason, J. M. could be same as **Mason, James; Mason, James L.; Mason, James P.** or **Mason, Jim**
1918 Little Miss Hoover

Mason, James could be same as **Mason, J. M.; Mason, James L.; Mason, James P.** or **Mason, Jim**
1918 The Border Wireless
Headin' South
1919 A Daughter of the Wolf
Jubilo
Pettigrew's Girl
Something to Do
1920 Godless Men
The Penalty
Something to Think About
The Strange Boarder

Mason, James L. could be same as **Mason, J. M.; Mason, James; Mason, James P.** or **Mason, Jim**
1920 The Red Lane

Mason, James P. could be same as **Mason, J. M.; Mason, James; Mason, James L.** or **Mason, Jim**
1917 Nan of Music Mountain
On the Level

Mason, Jim could be same as **Mason, J. M.; Mason, James; Mason, James L.** or **Mason, James P.**
1915 Scandal
1918 The Squaw Man
1919 Flame of the Desert

Mason, John
1915 The Fatal Card
Jim the Penman
1916 The Libertine
The Reapers
1918 Moral Suicide

Mason, Lillian
1919 The Valley of the Giants
You're Fired

Mason, Margery Land
1918 By Right of Purchase

Mason, Marie
1914 Lena Rivers (Cosmos Feature Film Corp.)

Mason, Reginald
1917 Vengeance Is Mine
1920 Two Weeks

Mason, Sarah Y.
1920 Bright Skies
The Heart of Twenty
Held in Trust
The Poor Simp*

Mason, Shirley same as **Flugrath, Leonie**
1915 Shadows from the Past
Vanity Fair
1917 The Apple-Tree Girl
The Awakening of Ruth
Cy Whittaker's Ward
Envy
Greed
The Lady of the Photograph
The Law of the North
Light in Darkness
The Little Chevalier
Passion
Pride
The Seventh Sin
Sloth
The Tell-Tale Step
Where Love Is
Wrath
1918 Come On In
Good-Bye, Bill
1919 The Final Close-Up
Putting It Over
The Rescuing Angel
Secret Service
The Unwritten Code
The Winning Girl
1920 Flame of Youth
The Girl of My Heart
Her Elephant Man
The Little Wanderer
Love's Harvest
Merely Mary Ann
Molly and I
Treasure Island

Mason, Sidney same as **Mason, Sidney L.; Mason, Sydney**
1915 The Builder of Bridges
John Glayde's Honor
A Mother's Confession
Seven Sisters
1916 The Daughter of MacGregor
The Dead Alive
Feathertop
The Honor of Mary Blake
I Accuse*
1917 The Boy Girl
Little Miss Nobody
The Little Terror
The Painted Madonna
The Peddler
Susan's Gentleman
1918 Bonnie Annie Laurie
The Forbidden Path
Moral Suicide
Peg of the Pirates
The Prussian Cur
1919 A Fallen Idol
The Trap
The Unbroken Promise
1919-20 The Marriage Blunder
1920 Birthright
The Good-Bad Wife
A Modern Salome

Mason, Smiling Billy see **Mason, Billy**

Mason, Stanley G.
1919 The Law of Nature
Where Bonds Are Loosed

Mason, Sue
1920 West Is West

Mason, Sydney see **Mason, Sidney**

Massarene, Countess of
1918 The Great Love*

Masse, Philip see **Masi, Philip W.**

Massell, Sonia
1915 The Fight

Massey, Joe
1916 Her Father's Son
The Road to Love

Masters, Eleanor
1918 The Blue Bird

Mastine, Mme.
1920 The Corsican Brothers

Masuroff, Giacomo
1919 Broken Barriers

Matheis, Jack same as **Mathes, Jack**
1919 Blind Husbands
1920 The Devil's Passkey
The Romance Promoters

Mather, Charles
1915 Flame of Passion
The Pearl of the Antilles*
Right off the Bat

Mather, Sidney
1917 Miss Nobody

Mathes, Jack see **Matheis, Jack**

Mathews, Dorcas see **Matthews, Dorcas**

Mathews, Junius
1917 The Silent Witness

Mathewson, Christy same as **Mathewson, Christopher**
1914 The Giants-White Sox Tour
1917 The Baseball Revue of 1917*

Mathis, Miss
1915 The Fairy and the Waif*

Mathis, Mrs.
1915 The Fairy and the Waif*

Mathis, June
1916 The Dawn of Love
God's Half Acre
Her Great Price
The Purple Lady
The Sunbeam
The Upstart
1917 Aladdin's Other Lamp
The Barricade
The Beautiful Lie
Blue Jeans
The Call of Her People
Draft 258
His Father's Son
The Jury of Fate
Lady Barnacle
A Magdalene of the Hills
The Millionaire's Double
Miss Robinson Crusoe
The Power of Decision
Red, White and Blue Blood
Somewhere in America
Threads of Fate
The Trail of the Shadow
The Voice of Conscience
A Wife by Proxy
1918 The Brass Check
The Claim
Daybreak
Eye for Eye
The Eyes of Mystery
Five Thousand an Hour
Gay and Festive Claverhouse
His Bonded Wife
The House of Gold
The House of Mirth
Kildare of Storm
The Legion of Death
A Man's World
Secret Strings
The Silent Woman
Social Hypocrites
Social Quicksands
A Successful Adventure
Sylvia on a Spree
To Hell with the Kaiser
Toys of Fate
The Trail to Yesterday
The Winding Trail
The Winning of Beatrice
With Neatness and Dispatch
1919 Almost Married
The Amateur Adventuress
Blind Man's Eyes
The Brat
The Divorcee
Fair and Warmer
The Great Victory, Wilson or the Kaiser? The Fall of the Hohenzollerns
The Island of Intrigue
Johnny-on-the-Spot
Lombardi, Ltd.
The Man Who Stayed at Home
The Microbe
Out of the Fog
The Parisian Tigress
The Red Lantern
Satan Junior
Some Bride

The Way of the Strong
1920 Hearts Are Trumps
     Old Lady 31
     Parlor, Bedroom and Bath
     Polly with a Past
     The Price of Redemption
     The Right of Way
     The Saphead
     The Walk-Offs
     The Willow Tree
Mathison, Edith Wynne see **Matthison, Edith Wynne**
Mathot, Leon
1920 The Empire of Diamonds
Matiesen, Otto
1920 The Golden Trail
Matsumato, M.
1916 The Honorable Friend
Matters, Dolly Ledgerwood
1917 Mother Love and the Law
Matthews, Lieut.
1919 Injustice
Matthews, Arthur same as **Matthews, Arthur W.**
1913 The Battle of Shiloh
1914 The Daughters of Men
     Through Fire to Fortune
1915 The College Widow
     The Nation's Peril
     The Ringtailed Rhinoceros
1916 The Evangelist
     Ignorance
1917 Shall We Forgive Her?
1918 Broken Ties
Matthews, Cecilia
1916 Idle Wives
Matthews, Dorcas same as **Mathews, Dorcas**
1916 The Captive God
     Honor Thy Name
     The Jungle Child
1917 Borrowed Plumage
     Idolators
     The Little Brother
     Love Letters
     Love or Justice
     Madcap Madge
     The Millionaire Vagrant
     The Price Mark
     The Silent Man
     A Strange Transgressor
     The Tar Heel Warrior
     Ten of Diamonds
     Those Who Pay
1918 The Cast-Off
     The Claws of the Hun
     Love Me
     A Nine O'Clock Town
1919 Beckoning Roads
     The Haunted Bedroom
     The Law of Men
     The Market of Souls
     The Virtuous Thief
1920 The Luck of Geraldine Laird
     Out of the Dust
     The Woman in the Suitcase
Matthews, O. A.
1914 The Man O' Warsman
Matthews, Sis
1915 Scandal
Matthison, Edith Wynne same as **Mathison, Edith Wynne**
1915 The Governor's Lady
1917 National Red Cross Pageant*
Mattox, M. could be same as **Mattox, Martha**
1915 Buckshot John*
Mattox, Martha same as **Maddox, Miss;** could be same as **Mattox, M.**
1915 The Caprices of Kitty
1917 The Charmer
     The Clean-Up
     The Lair of the Wolf
     Polly Put the Kettle On
1918 The Rough Lover
     The Scarlet Drop
     Thieves' Gold
     Wild Women
1919 Eve in Exile
     The Scarlet Shadow
     The Sealed Envelope
1920 The Butterfly Man
     A Cumberland Romance

Everybody's Sweetheart
Firebrand Trevison
The Girl of My Heart
Huckleberry Finn
Old Lady 31
Matus, Kalman
1916 Fathers of Men
     The Wheel of the Law
Matzen, Madeline (writer)
1918 The Ghost Flower
Matzene, M. (cam)
1919 It Happened in Paris
Maude, Arthur
1914 Charlotte Corday
     The Fatal Night
     Jess
     Thais
     The Virgin of the Rocks
     The Volunteer Parson
1915 The Brink
     The Cup of Life
     The Devil
     The Reward
1916 The Courtesan
     D'Artagnan
     Embers
     Lord Loveland Discovers America
     Powder
     Revelations
1917 Borrowed Plumage
     A Jewel in Pawn
1919 The Blinding Trail
     Common Property
     The Microbe
1920 The Thirteenth Commandment
Maude, Beatrice
1915 The Final Judgment
Maude, Cyril
1915 The Greater Will
     Peer Gynt
Maupain, Ernest same as **Maupin, Ernest**
1915 A Daughter of the City
     Graustark
     In the Palace of the King
     The Man Trail
     The Raven
     The White Sister
1916 The Breaker
     Captain Jinks of the Horse Marines
     The Discard
     The Prince of Graustark
     Sherlock Holmes
     That Sort
     Vultures of Society
1917 The Dream Doll*
     Efficiency Edgar's Courtship
     The Man Who Was Afraid
     The Trufflers
1918 Lafayette, We Come!
     Lest We Forget
     The Million Dollar Dollies
     A Mother's Sin
     The Trail to Yesterday
     The Turn of the Wheel
     Why America Will Win
Maurese, Mrs. see **Maurice, Mary**
Maurice (dancer)
1916 The Quest of Life
Maurice, Mrs. see **Maurice, Mary**
Maurice, M. (gown designer)
1916 The Hero of Submarine D-2
Maurice, Mary (actress) same as **Maurese, Mrs.; Maurice, Mrs.**
1915 The Battle Cry of Peace
     How Cissy Made Good
     The Man Who Couldn't Beat God
     Mother's Roses
     The Sins of the Mothers
1916 Black Friday
     The Dollar and the Law
     The Mainspring
     Phantom Fortunes
     The Price of Fame
     The Redemption of Dave Darcey
     Rose of the South
     The Supreme Temptation
     Whom the Gods Destroy
1917 For France
     Her Secret

I Will Repay
Mary Jane's Pa
Transgression
Who Goes There!
Womanhood, the Glory of the Nation
1918 The Little Runaway
     Over the Top
     The Woman Between Friends
Maurice, Richard
1920 Our Christianity and Nobody's Child
Maurice, Ruth
1919 Castles in the Air
1920 The Honey Bee
Maurice, Vivian
1920 Our Christianity and Nobody's Child
Maus, Marion P.
1914 The Indian Wars
1917 The Adventures of Buffalo Bill
Mawden, Golda
1918 The Girl of My Dreams
Mawson, Edward R. same as **Mawson, Edward**
1915 The Builder of Bridges
1916 The Return of Eve
Maxam, Louella same as **Maxam, Lola; Maxim, Luella**
1917 Because of a Woman
1918 Deuce Duncan
     The Mantle of Charity
1920 Vengeance and the Girl
The Maxim Cabaret Girls
1915 Midnight at Maxim's
Maxim, Hudson
1915 The Battle Cry of Peace
Maxim, Luella see **Maxam, Louella**
Maxon, Eric
1915 After Dark
Maxwell, Anne
1918 The Cross Bearer
1919 Little Women
Maxwell, Barry
1916 Romeo and Juliet (Quality Pictures Corp.)
Maxwell, Joe
1918 The Married Virgin
Maxwell, Theresa
1920 The Daughter Pays
May, Alice
1917 The Bitter Truth
     A Mother's Ordeal
May, Ann
1919 Lombardi, Ltd.
     Marriage for Convenience
1920 An Amateur Devil
     Paris Green
     Peaceful Valley
May, Doris same as **Lee, Doris**
1917 His Mother's Boy
1918 Green Eyes
     The Hired Man
     The Law of the North
     Playing the Game
1919 The Girl Dodger
     Hay Foot, Straw Foot
     23 1/2 Hours' Leave
1920 The Jailbird
     Let's Be Fashionable
     Mary's Ankle
     Rookie's Return
     What's Your Husband Doing?
May, Edna
1916 Salvation Joan
May, Helen
1917 The Silent Witness
May, Jimsy see **Maye, Jimsy**
May, Lola could be same as **Mae, Leola**
1914 The Lure
1916 The Beggar of Cawnpore
     Civilization
     The Green Swamp
     The Heart of Nora Flynn
     Honor's Altar
1918 A Camouflage Kiss
May, Mildred
1917 The Courage of Silence
     The Soul Master

May, Neola see **Neola May, Princess**
May, Peggy
1919 The House of Intrigue
Mayall, Herschel same as **Mayall, Herschall; Mayall, Herschell; Mayall, Hershal; Mayall, Hershall; Mayall, Hershel**
1914 The Voice at the Telephone
1915 The Forbidden Adventure
     The Man from Oregon
     On the Night Stage
     The Toast of Death
1916 The Aryan
     The Beast
     Civilization
     The Road to Love
     Sins of Her Parent
     The Sorrows of Love
1917 The Babes in the Woods
     Cleopatra
     Du Barry
     High Finance
     The Island of Desire
     The Rose of Blood
     Some Boy!
     A Tale of Two Cities
1918 Carmen of the Klondike
     The Heart of Rachael
     Honor's Cross
     Maid O' the Storm
     The One Woman
     Patriotism
     Shackled
     Treasure Island
     Wedlock
1919 Bonds of Honor
     The Divorce Trap
     A Man in the Open
     The Money Corral
     The Silver Girl
     The Sleeping Lion
     Todd of the Times
     Wings of the Morning
1920 The Coast of Opportunity
     Drag Harlan
     Kismet
     The Scuttlers
Mayburn, Margaret
1916 What Love Can Do*
Maye, Jimsy same as **May, Jimsy**
1918 Nine-Tenths of the Law
1920 Two Kinds of Love
Mayer, Hy
1918 The Hillcrest Mystery
Mayer, Joseph
1920 The White Rider
Mayer, Louis could be same as **Mayer, Louis B.**
1920 Dr. Jekyll and Mr. Hyde (Pioneer Film Corp.)
Mayer, Louis B. could be same as **Mayer, Louis**
1918 Virtuous Wives
1919 Her Kingdom of Dreams
     Human Desire
     In Old Kentucky
     Mary Regan
     A Midnight Romance
1920 The Fighting Shepherdess
     Harriet and the Piper
     The Inferior Sex
     Old Dad
     Polly of the Storm Country
     The Woman in His House
     The Yellow Typhoon
1921 Habit
Mayer, Max
1914 America
Mayers, Mr.
1916 Joan the Woman
Mayfield, Charline
1916 Jealousy
Mayne, Eric
1914 The Dollar Mark
     The Man of the Hour
1915 The Beloved Vagabond
     The Cotton King
1917 Her Hour
     The New York Peacock
     The Slave
     The Submarine Eye
     The Tenth Case
     Thou Shalt Not Steal
     Wife Number Two

1918 The Debt of Honor
The Girl and the Judge
A Heart's Revenge
Other Men's Daughters
Peg of the Pirates
1919 The Gamblers
The Greater Sinner
Help! Help! Police!
A House Divided
The Oakdale Affair
The Scar
Should a Husband Forgive?
1920 Man's Plaything
Marooned Hearts
Twisted Souls

Mayo, Miss
1914 The War of Wars; Or, The
Franco-German Invasion

Mayo, Albert F.
1915 Tillie's Tomato Surprise

Mayo, Christine *same as* **Mayo,**
Chrystine
1915 The Broken Law
A Mother's Confession
The Warning
1916 A Fool's Paradise
The Iron Woman
The Spell of the Yukon
The Supreme Sacrifice
1917 Raffles, the Amateur
Cracksman
Two Men and a Woman
Who's Your Neighbor?
1918 The House of Mirth
The Life Mask
A Successful Adventure
1919 Fair and Warmer
A Fugitive from Matrimony
The Little Intruder
The Thirteenth Chair
1920 An Amateur Devil
Don't Ever Marry
Duds
The Girl in the Web
The Palace of Darkened
Windows

Mayo, Edna
1914 Aristocracy
The Key to Yesterday
The Million
The Quest of the Sacred Jewel
1915 The Blindness of Virtue
Graustark
The Warning
1916 The Chaperon
The Misleading Lady
The Return of Eve
1918 Hearts of Love

Mayo, Frank
1915 The Adventures of a Madcap
1917 Betsy Ross
The Bronze Bride
The Burglar
The Checkmate
Easy Money
Glory
Sold at Auction
Sunny Jane
1918 The Appearance of Evil
The Interloper
Journey's End
The Power and the Glory
The Purple Lily
A Soul Without Windows
Stolen Hours
Tinsel
The Trap
Whims of Society
The Witch Woman
The Zero Hour
1919 The Amazing Wife
The Bluffer
The Brute Breaker
The Crook of Dreams
Lasca
A Little Brother of the Rich
The Love Defender
Mary Regan
The Moral Deadline
The Rough Neck
1920 Burnt Wings
The Girl in Number 29
Hitchin' Posts
Honor Bound
The Marriage Pit

The Peddler of Lies
The Red Lane
Through Eyes of Men

Mayo, Harry
1916 The Destroyers
The Wager

Mayo, Henry Thomas
1915 The Nation's Peril*

Mayo, Margaret
1917 Baby Mine
1919 The Poor Boob

Mayo, Martha
1919 My Little Sister

Mayo, Melvin
1915 Saved from the Harem
1917 Brand's Daughter
Mentioned in Confidence
Tears and Smiles

Mayo, Rose
1918 Ruggles of Red Gap

Mayon, Florence *could be same as*
Mayon, Mrs.
1917 Bringing Home Father
Down to Earth

Mayon, Mrs. *could be same as* **Mayon,**
Florence
1920 Alias Jimmy Valentine*

Mea, Madame
1918 The Accidental Honeymoon

Mead, Tommy
1915 Blue Grass

Meade, Harold B. *same as* **Meade,**
Harold
1914 Salomy Jane
1915 Mignon

Meade, J. Walter
1917 Hate

Meader, Albert
1920 The Mysteries of Paris

Mealand, Walter D.
1916 The Rainbow Princess

Mears, Mary
1920 The Forbidden Thing

Mechtold, Mary Rider
1914 The Mountain Rat

Medan, Leopold
1915 Beulah

Meech, William
1915 The Incorrigible Dukane

Meehan, William E.
1917 When False Tongues Speak

Meek, Kate *same as* **Meeks, Kate**
1915 The Builder of Bridges
David Harum

Meeker, Leeward
1920 Life

Meeks, Kate *see* **Meek, Kate**

Megargee, Lon
1920 The Round-Up

Megin, Mae
1918 Peg O' the Sea

Megrue, Roi Cooper
1917 Fighting Odds

Mei, Lady Tsen
1918 For the Freedom of the East

Meighan, Johnny
1918 A Man's Man

Meighan, Thomas
1915 Armstrong's Wife
Blackbirds
The Fighting Hope
The Immigrant
The Kindling
Out of the Darkness
The Secret Sin
1916 The Clown
Common Ground
The Dupe
The Heir to the Hoorah
Pudd'nhead Wilson
The Sowers
The Storm
The Trail of the Lonesome Pine
1917 Arms and the Girl
The Evil Eye*
Her Better Self
The Land of Promise
The Mysterious Miss Terry
Sapho
The Silent Partner
The Slave Market

Sleeping Fires
1918 Eve's Daughter
The Forbidden City
Heart of the Wilds
In Pursuit of Polly
Madame Jealousy
Missing
M'liss
Out of a Clear Sky
1919 The Heart of Wetona
Male and Female
The Miracle Man
Peg O' My Heart
The Probation Wife
The Thunderbolt
1920 Civilian Clothes
Conrad in Quest of His Youth
The Prince Chap
Why Change Your Wife?

Meinke, William V.
1919 Whom the Gods Would
Destroy

Mel, Carl dec
1917 Draft 258

Melancon (full name unknown)
1915 The Fairy and the Waif*

Melfield, Richard
1920 Neptune's Bride

Melford, George *same as* **Melford,**
George H.
1914 The Boer War
The Invisible Power
Shannon of the Sixth
1915 Armstrong's Wife
The Explorer
The Fighting Hope
A Gentleman of Leisure
The Governor's Lady
The Immigrant
The Marriage of Kitty
Out of the Darkness
The Puppet Crown
Stolen Goods
The Unknown
The Woman
Young Romance
1916 Each Pearl a Tear
A Gutter Magdalene
The House with the Golden
Windows
The Race
The Selfish Woman
Tennessee's Pardner
To Have and to Hold
The Years of the Locust
The Yellow Pawn
1917 The Call of the East
The Cost of Hatred
The Crystal Gazer
The Evil Eye
Her Strange Wedding
Nan of Music Mountain
On the Level
A School for Husbands
The Sunset Trail
The Winning of Sally Temple
1918 The Bravest Way
The City of Dim Faces
The Cruise of the
Make-Believes
Hidden Pearls
Sandy
The Source
Such a Little Pirate
Wild Youth
1919 Everywoman
Good Gracious, Annabelle
Jane Goes A-Wooing
Men, Women and Money
Pettigrew's Girl
A Sporting Chance (Famous
Players-Lasky Corp.)
Told in the Hills
1920 Behold My Wife
The Round-Up
The Sea Wolf
1921 The Jucklands

Mellinino, Ardita *see* **Mellonino, Ardita**

Mellish, Fuller
1915 The Dancing Girl
Esmeralda
The Eternal City
Four Feathers
Gambier's Advocate

A Royal Family
1916 A Tortured Heart
1917 Mayblossom
The Power of Decision
The Trail of the Shadow
The Unforseen
1920 The Inner Voice
The Silent Barrier

Mellish, Vera Fuller
1917 The Beautiful Adventure

Mellonino, Ardita *same as* **Mellinino,**
Ardita; Mellonino, Ardito
1919 Deliverance
The Shepherd of the Hills
Tin Pan Alley
1920 Her Elephant Man

Melville, Jose *see* **Melville, Jose**

Melody, John
1916 The Snowbird

Meltzer, Harold
1915 Always in the Way
1916 When Love Is King

Melville, Emilie
1915 The White Sister

Melville, Fred
1918 The Woman the Germans Shot

Melville, George *same as* **Melville,**
George D.
1915 An Affair of Three Nations
The Menace of the Mute
Vanity Fair
1916 The Gates of Eden
The Light of Happiness
The Woman in 47
1917 Chris and His Wonderful
Lamp
The Last Sentence
A Wife by Proxy

Melville, Harry
1920 Sophy of Kravonia; Or, The
Virgin of Paris

Melville, Jose *same as* **Mellville, Jose;**
Melville, Josie
1917 A Roadside Impresario
1919 The Winning Girl
1920 Treasure Island

Melville, Wilbert
1915 Saved from the Harem

Melvin, Mae
1917 The Cloud

Menasco, Milton
1918 His Birthright
The Temple of Dusk
1919 The Courageous Coward
The Dragon Painter
The Tong Man
Whom the Gods Would
Destroy
1920 The Butterfly Man
The Notorious Miss Lisle

Mendel, Katherine
1915 The Man of Shame

Mendoza, Jean *see* **Acker, Jean**

Menessier, Henri *same as* **Menessier,**
Henry
1916 The Common Law
1917 The Price She Paid
1918 Eye for Eye
Lest We Forget
The Million Dollar Dollies
1919 A Damsel in Distress
The Love Cheat
Out of the Fog
The Red Lantern
The Virtuous Model

Menjou, Adolphe *same as* **Menjou,**
Adolph
1916 The Crucial Test
The Devil at His Elbow
The Kiss
The Price of Happiness
The Reward of Patience
1917 The Moth
The Valentine Girl

Menke, William
1915 China
Japan

Menzies, William Cameron *same as*
Menzies, William
1919 The Teeth of the Tiger
1920 The Deep Purple

Merbreier, E. A.
1915 For $5,000 a Year
Mercer, Beryl
1916 The Final Curtain
Meredith, Anita
1920 Neptune's Bride
Meredith, Anne
1915 The Money Master
Meredith, Bess see **Meredyth, Bess**
Meredith, Charles
1919 Luck in Pawn
The Other Half
Poor Relations
1920 The Family Honor
Judy of Rogue's Harbor
The Ladder of Lies
The Little 'Fraid Lady
The Perfect Woman
A Romantic Adventuress
Simple Souls
That Something
The Thirteenth Commandment
Meredith, J. Jackson see **Meredith, Jack**
Meredith, Jack same as **Meredith, J. Jackson**
1915 The Man Trail
1916 The Almighty Dollar
Vultures of Society
1917 The Frozen Warning
The Golden Rosary
The Man Hater
Panthea
Poppy
Sloth
Meredith, Jane
1915 Her Mother's Secret
1916 The Pursuing Vengeance
Meredith, Lois
1914 The Conspiracy
Dan
The Seats of the Mighty
1915 An Enemy to Society
The Greater Will
Help Wanted
My Best Girl
The Woman
1916 The Precious Packet
Spellbound
1917 In the Hands of the Law
Sold at Auction
1918 Her Mistake
On the Quiet
Over the Top
Meredith, Madeline
1917 Her Sister
Meredith, Peggy
1915 The Raven
Meredyth, Bess same as **Meredith, Bess**
1916 Spellbound
The Twin Triangle
1917 Bringing Home Father
The Little Orphan
The Midnight Man
Pay Me
Scandal
1918 The Grain of Dust
The Man Who Wouldn't Tell
Morgan's Raiders
The Red, Red Heart
The Romance of Tarzan
That Devil, Bateese
1919 The Big Little Person
The Girl from Nowhere
Meriam (full name unknown)
1915 The Fairy and the Waif*
Merill, Maitland
1918 Just a Woman
Merket, Bert
1916 The Unborn
Merkyl, John
1918 The Burden of Proof
A Man's World
Merkyl, Wilmuth same as **Merkyl, W.; Merkyll, Wilmuth**
1915 The Celebrated Scandal
Gretna Green
Niobe
The Price
The Victory of Virtue
1916 Blazing Love
The Fortunate Youth
Her Surrender
The Soul Market

1918 Fedora
Let's Get a Divorce
Suspicion
Merlin, Iva
1914 A Good Little Devil
Merlo, Anthony same as **Merlo, Anthony J.; Merlo, Tony**
1916 The Black Butterfly
Is Any Girl Safe?
The Narrow Path
Seventeen
1917 The Eternal Sin
The Maid of Belgium
More Truth Than Poetry
1918 The Cross Bearer
A Daughter of France
Just Sylvia
Neighbors
The Sea Waif
The Soul of Buddha
Tinsel
1919 Atonement
Heart of Gold
Mandarin's Gold
Phil-for-Short
The Unveiling Hand
1920 The Thief
The White Moll
Merlo, George could be same as **Marlo, George**
1917 Magda
Merlo, Tony see **Merlo, Anthony**
Merollo, Ralph
1915 Fatherhood
Merriam, Charlotte
1919 The Blue Bonnet
1920 The Honey Bee
Merrick, Frederick
1917 The Seven Swans
Merrick, George M.
1914 Over Niagara Falls
1916 It May Be Your Daughter
1919 The Open Door
1920 The Return of Tarzan
Merrick, William
1920 The Ugly Duckling
Merriman, Hale
1919 Be a Little Sport
Merritt, Paula
1920 For the Soul of Rafael
Merriwell, Charles
1915 The Fight
Merry, the dog
1916 Molly Make-Believe
Merryman, A. N., Jr.
1920 Love Madness
Mersch, Mary
1916 Common Ground
David Garrick
The Dream Girl
The Making of Maddalena
1917 Her Own People
One of Many
The Trouble Buster
1918 Blue Blood
The Claw
A Mother's Secret
The Rainbow Trail
Riders of the Purple Sage
Rimrock Jones
Who Killed Walton?
Mersereau, Claire
1915 The Avalanche
Right off the Bat
When It Strikes Home
1920 Black Is White
Mersereau, Vera could be same as **Mersereau, Verne**
1919 Secret Marriage
Mersereau, Violet
1914 The Spitfire
1915 The Avalanche
The Wolf of Debt
1916 Autumn
Broken Fetters
The Great Problem
The Honor of Mary Blake
The Narrow Path
The Path of Happiness
1917 The Boy Girl
The Girl by the Roadside
Little Miss Nobody
The Little Terror

The Raggedy Queen
Susan's Gentleman
1918 Morgan's Raiders
Together
1919 The Nature Girl
Mervale, Gaston
1914 Dope
1915 The Stubbornness of Geraldine
Mescall, John
1920 It's a Great Life
Mesereau, Verne could be same as **Mersereau, Vera**
1918 Cupid's Roundup
Mesick, W. K.
1919 Please Get Married
Mesreau, Charlotte
1919 Deliverance
Messenger, Buddy see **Messinger, Buddy**
Messenger, Dorothy
1920 The Sins of Rosanne
Messenger, Frank
1920 The Virgin of Stamboul
Messenger, Gertrude see **Messinger, Gertrude**
Messenger, Marie see **Messinger, Marie**
Messenger, Melvin
1919 The Hoodlum
Messick, Homer I.
1920 The Money-Changers
Messimore, Howard see **Missimer, Howard**
Messinger, Buddy same as **Messenger, Buddy; Messinger, Bud; Messinger, Buddie**
1916 Gloriana
1917 Aladdin and the Wonderful Lamp
The Babes in the Woods
Jack and the Beanstalk
1918 Ali Baba and the Forty Thieves
Fan Fan
Six Shooter Andy
Treasure Island
1919 The Hoodlum
Messinger, Gertrude same as **Messenger, Gertrude; Messinger, Gertie**
1917 A Bit O' Heaven
Aladdin and the Wonderful Lamp
1918 Ali Baba and the Forty Thieves
Fan Fan
The Girl with the Champagne Eyes
1919 Miss Adventure
1920 The Luck of the Irish
Messinger, Marie same as **Messenger, Marie**
1917 Aladdin and the Wonderful Lamp
1918 Ali Baba and the Forty Thieves
1920 Riders of the Dawn
Messmore, Herbert
1916 A Daughter of the Gods
1920 Oil
Mestayer, Harry
1915 The House of a Thousand Candles
I'm Glad My Boy Grew Up to Be a Soldier
The Millionaire Baby
Stop Thief!
1918 The Atom
High Tide
Wife or Country
1919 False Gods
Metcalfe, Arthur
1917 Filling His Own Shoes
The Golden Idiot
Pants
Metcalfe, Earl same as **Metcalf, Earl; Metcalfe, Earle; Metcalfe, Edward**
1914 The Daughters of Men
The Gamblers
1915 The Nation's Peril
The Ringtailed Rhinoceros
1916 Ignorance
Race Suicide
1917 Her Good Name
1919 The Battler
Coax Me
The Poison Pen

The Woman of Lies
The World to Live In
1920 The Chamber Mystery
The Face at Your Window
The Fortune Hunter
The Garter Girl
While New York Sleeps
Meter, Harry see **Von Meter, Harry**
Methol, Minnie
1918 Queen of the Sea
Meusel, Irish
1920 The Best of Luck
Meyer, Baroness de
1920 The Devil's Passkey
Meyer, Arthur
1916 Intolerance
Meyer, Henry see **Myers, Harry C.**
Meyer, Louis
1919 The Bishop's Emeralds
Impossible Catherine
Meyer Brothers
1918 My Four Years in Germany
Meyers, Eddie
1918 Sylvia on a Spree
Meyers, Harry see **Myers, Harry C.**
Meyers, Helen
1919 The Silver King
Meyers, Otto
1920 Sundown Slim
Meyers, William S.
1918 Marriage
Michael, the studio cat
1918 Dodging a Million
Micheaux, Oscar
1919 The Homesteader
1920 The Brute
The Symbol of the Unconquered
Within Our Gates
Michelena, Beatriz
1914 Mrs. Wiggs of the Cabbage Patch
Salomy Jane
1915 The Lily of Poverty Flat
Mignon
A Phyllis of the Sierras
Salvation Nell
1916 The Unwritten Law
The Woman Who Dared
1919 The Heart of Juanita
Just Squaw
The Price Woman Pays
1920 The Flame of Hellgate
Michelena, Teresa
1914 Uncle Tom's Cabin
Michelena, Vera
1916 Driftwood
1917-18
The Devil's Playground
Michelson, Charles
1916 According to the Code
The Discard
Mickey, the dog
1920 Two Kinds of Love
Middlemass, Robert same as **Middlemas, Robert**
1918 Five Thousand an Hour
Other Men's Daughters
1919 The Winchester Woman
Middleton, Mrs. could be same as **Middleton, Mrs. E.**
1914 Lena Rivers (Whitman Features Co.)
Middleton, Charles
1920 Wits vs. Wits
Middleton, Mrs. E. could be same as **Middleton, Mrs.**
1915 The Flaming Sword
Middleton, Edwin same as **Middleton, E.**
1914 Rip Van Winkle
1915 The Flaming Sword
Wildfire
1916 The Haunted Manor
The Isle of Love
Middleton, George (writer, actor) could be same as **Middleton, George E.** (dir) or **Middleton, George W.** (actor)
1914 Born Again
1917 At First Sight
The Girl at Home

151

Sleeping Fires
The World Apart
1918 Tempered Steel
1920 What Women Want
Middleton, George E. (*dir*) *could be same as* **Middleton, George** (*writer, actor*)
1914 Mrs. Wiggs of the Cabbage Patch
1915 The Lily of Poverty Flat
Mignon
A Phyllis of the Sierras
Salvation Nell
1916 The Unwritten Law
The Woman Who Dared
1919 The Heart of Juanita
Just Squaw
The Price Woman Pays*
1920 The Flame of Hellgate
Middleton, George W. (*actor*) *could be same as* **Middleton, George** (*writer, actor*)
1914 Hearts of Oak
1915 An American Gentleman
The Soul of Broadway
Middleton, Roy
1919 Calibre 38
Middleton, Scudder
1917 The Love That Lives
Middleton, Thomas B. (*dir*)
1914 Damaged Goods
Middleton, Tom (*cam*)
1918 Milady O' the Beanstalk
1919 The Old Maid's Baby
Midgely, Fannie *see* **Midgley, Fannie**
Midgely, Florence
1920 Eyes of the Heart
Midgley, Fannie *same as* **Midgeley, Fannie; Midgely, Fannie; Midgley, Miss; Midgley, Fanny**
1914 Shorty Escapes Marriage
1915 The Alien
The Despoiler
The Man from Oregon
1916 The Apostle of Vengeance
Civilization
Jim Grimsby's Boy
Plain Jane
Somewhere in France
The Waifs
1917 Blood Will Tell
1918 Cheating the Public
The Goat
How Could You, Jean?
Madam Who
The Vigilantes
1919 The Heart of Youth
The Lottery Man
Secret Service*
1920 Always Audacious
The Corsican Brothers
Crooked Streets*
Seeing It Through
1921 The Jucklins
Midland, Roy
1918 The Sign Invisible
Miehlesfield, Al
1920 Up in Mary's Attic*
Miggins, Benny
1920 While New York Sleeps
Mignonne
1920 Sundown Slim
West Is West
Milady, James
1920 The Dead Line
Milar, A. C. *could be same as* **Milar, Adolph**
1920 Man and Woman (A. H. Fischer Features, Inc.)
Milar, Adolph *same as* **Milar, Adolf; Millar, Adolph; could be same as Milar, A. C.**
1919 The Black Circle
1920 The Road of Ambition
The Silent Barrier
Something Different
Milasch, Robert *same as* **Milasch, R. E.; Milash, R.; Milash, R. E.; Milash, Robert**
1915 The Arrival of Perpetua
1918 Under the Greenwood Tree
1919 Dawn
Mrs. Wiggs of the Cabbage Patch

The Moonshine Trail
The Rough Neck
The Two Brides
1920 The Flaming Clue
The Fourteenth Man
Milburn, James
1916 20,000 Leagues Under the Sea
Miles, Joseph R.
1917 The Test of Womanhood
Miles, Miriam
1917 The Grell Mystery
In the Balance
1918 The Beloved Impostor
A Mother's Sin
1919 Fortune's Child
Miles, Nelson Appleton
1914 The Indian Wars
1917 The Adventures of Buffalo Bill
Miles, Norbig *see* **Myles, Norbert**
Milford, Bliss
1915 The Beloved Vagabond
The Closing Net
1916 The House of Mirrors
1918 And the Children Pay
Flower of the Dusk
Sylvia on a Spree
Milham, Guy
1920 A Full House
A Light Woman
Milholland, Cora
1916 The Soul Market
Milholland, Helen *same as* **Mulholland, Helen; Mulhuland, Helen**
1915 The Runaway Wife
1917 The Girl Who Didn't Think
1918 My Own United States
Millais, Warren
1920 Whispering Devils
Millar (full name unknown)
1914 Across the Pacific
Millar, Adolph *see* **Milar, Adolph**
Millar, Elda
1917 The Food Gamblers
Her Excellency, the Governor
Millarde, Harry *same as* **Millard, Harry**
1914 A Celebrated Case
1915 Don Caesar de Bazan
1916 Elusive Isabel
The Lotus Woman
1917 Every Girl's Dream
Little Miss Nobody
Miss U.S.A.
The Sunshine Maid
Unknown 274
1918 Blue-Eyed Mary
Bonnie Annie Laurie
A Camouflage Kiss
Caught in the Act
The Heart of Romance
Miss Innocence
1919 Gambling in Souls
The Girl with No Regrets
The Love That Dares
Rose of the West
Sacred Silence
When Fate Decides
1920 Man and Woman (A. H. Fischer Features, Inc.)
Over the Hill to the Poorhouse
The White Moll
Mille, Agnes de *see* **de Mille, Agnes**
Mille, Beatrice C. de *see* **de Mille, Beatrice C.**
Mille, William C. de *see* **de Mille, William C.**
Miller, Mrs.
1917 The Auction of Virtue
A Man and the Woman
Miller, Arthur C. *same as* **Miller, A. C.; Miller, Arthur**
1916 Arms and the Woman
1917 Blind Man's Luck
The Hunting of the Hawk
The Iron Heart
Kick In
The Mark of Cain
The On-the-Square-Girl
The Recoil
Sylvia of the Secret Service
1918 Convict 993
The Hillcrest Mystery
A Japanese Nightingale

1919 Counterfeit
The Cry of the Weak
Our Better Selves
The Profiteers
A Society Exile
1920 His House in Order
Idols of Clay
Lady Rose's Daughter
On with the Dance
The Right to Love
Miller, Ashley
1915 An Affair of Three Nations
The House of Fear
The Menace of the Mute
1916 The King's Game
The Quest of Life
1917 Infidelity
The Marriage Speculation
The Moral Code
The Princess of Park Row
1920 To-Morrow
Miller, Bota
1919 Stepping Out
Miller, Carl
1917 A Bit O' Heaven
1918 The Doctor and the Woman
1919 Mary Regan
1920 The Parish Priest
Miller, Charles *same as* **Miller, Charles F.**
1916 Bawbs O' Blue Ridge
The Corner
A Corner in Colleens
The Market of Vain Desire
The Moral Fabric
The Payment
Plain Jane
1917 Blood Will Tell
The Dark Road
The Flame of the Yukon
The Hater of Men
The Little Brother
Polly Ann
Princess of the Dark
The Sawdust Ring
The Secret of the Storm Country
Wee Lady Betty
Wild Winship's Widow
1918 At the Mercy of Men
By Right of Purchase
The Fair Pretender
The Ghosts of Yesterday
The Service Star
1919 Common Clay
A Dangerous Affair
The Great Victory, Wilson or the Kaiser? The Fall of the Hohenzollerns
The Heart of a Gypsy
Love, Honor and—?
1920 High Speed
The Law of the Yukon
Miller, Clarkson
1916 The Scarlet Road*
1919 The Day She Paid
Miller, Ethel Browning
1918 Revelation
Miller, Eugene
1920 The Mark of Zorro
Miller, Florence
1917 Daughter of Maryland
Miller, Frances
1916 A Tortured Heart
1917 The Adventures of Carol
The Bondage of Fear
Diamonds and Pearls
Troublemakers
1918 Broken Ties
Miller, Dr. Francis Trevelyan
1919 Deliverance
Miller, Fred
1919 The Test of Honor
Miller, Gertie
1914 The House of Bondage
Miller, Harold A. (*actor*) *same as* **Miller, Harold**
1919 Upstairs and Down
1920 The Forged Bride
Her Five-Foot Highness
In the Heart of a Fool
Mountain Madness
The Peddler of Lies

Miller, Harold Louis (*cam*) *same as* **Miller, Harold L.**
1914 Three Weeks
1915 Hearts of Men
When It Strikes Home
1916 Her American Prince
The Romantic Journey
Should a Baby Die?
Miller, Harry B.
1918 And the Children Pay
Miller, Harvey
1919 The Price Woman Pays
Miller, Henry, Jr.
1918 In the Hollow of Her Hand
1919 The Gay Lord Quex
1920 The Desperate Hero
Parlor, Bedroom and Bath
Someone in the House
Miller, Hugh S.
1917 Her Official Fathers
Miller, J. Clarkson
1918 Back to the Woods
The Daredevil
Her Husband's Honor
Hidden Fires
Just for Tonight
The Kingdom of Youth
Love's Law
Thirty a Week
Treason
The Venus Model
1919 Me and Captain Kidd
Miss Crusoe
One of the Finest
The Poison Pen
The Woman of Lies
1920 Chains of Evidence
The Scarlet Dragon
Miller, Jack (*cam*)
1918 Kiss or Kill
Miller, Jack, Jr. (*actor*)
1919 A Favor to a Friend
Miller, Jane
1915 The Devil's Daughter
From the Valley of the Missing
1916 The Witch
1917 The Final Payment
1918 Heart of the Sunset
High Stakes
1919 The Forfeit
The Unbroken Promise
1920 Beware of the Bride
Husband Hunter
Miller, Jessie
1916 The Conflict
His Wife's Good Name
Miller, Katherine
1917 The Eyes of the World
Miller, Leon
1920 High Speed
Miller, Liza
1916 In the Diplomatic Service
Miller, M. A.
1919 Fool's Gold
Miller, Peck
1920 Sky Eye
Miller, Robert
1916 The Craving
The Sign of the Spade
1918 Powers That Prey
Miller, Victor *see* **Milner, Victor**
Miller, Virgil E. *same as* **Miller, V. E.; Miller, Virgil**
1917 Flirting with Death
The Man Trap
A Stormy Knight
1918 Brace Up
The Eagle
The Flash of Fate
The Guilt of Silence
Smashing Through
Winner Takes All
1920 Pink Tights
The Silent Barrier
Two Kinds of Love
Miller, Walter (*actor*) *same as* **Miller, Walter C.**
1914 Lord Chumley
1915 The Family Stain
1916 The Human Orchid
The Marble Heart
The Spider and the Fly
The Toll of Justice

A Wife's Sacrifice
1917 The Cloud
Draft 258
Miss Robinson Crusoe
A Mother's Ordeal
The Slacker (Metro Pictures
Corp.)
Tangled Lives
1918 The Eleventh Commandment
The Mysterious Mr. Browning
With Neatness and Dispatch
1919 A Girl at Bay
The Open Door
Thin Ice
1920 The Invisible Divorce
The Return of Tarzan
The Stealers
The Way Women Love
Why Tell?
Miller, Walter (*jockey*)
1915 Winning the Futurity
Miller, Walter C. see Miller, Walter
(*actor*)
Miller, William same as **Miller, William V.**
1917 The Deemster
God of Little Children
1918 The Beautiful Mrs. Reynolds
My Own United States
Millett, A. B. could be same as **Millett, Arthur**
1920 A Beggar in Purple
Millett, Arthur same as **Millet, Arthur; Millett, Arthur N.; Millette, Arthur; could be same as Millett, A. B.**
1916 Humanizing Mr. Winsby
The Land Just Over Yonder
1917 Framing Framers
The Hidden Spring
The Ship of Doom
1918 Alias Mary Brown
A Good Loser
The Hand at the Window
Her American Husband
Madame Sphinx
Paying His Debt
The Sea Panther
Shifting Sands
Station Content
1919 The Egg Crate Wallop
Todd of the Times
1920 Bubbles
Drag Harlan
Hearts Up
King Spruce
Live Sparks
Love Madness
The Scuttlers
$30,000
West Is West
Millhauser, Bertram
1916 The Challenge
Millington, Miss
1915 The Fairy and the Waif*
Millington, Mrs.
1915 The Fairy and the Waif*
Millington, Noris
1915 The Fairy and the Waif
Millman, Bird
1920 The Deep Purple
The Law of the Yukon
Mills, Berry
1919 The Solitary Sin
Mills, C. W.
1916 Vengeance Is Mine
Mills, David
1917 Unknown 274
Mills, Frank
1915 The Edge of the Abyss
The Golden Claw
1916 The Flower of Faith
The House of Mirrors
The Moral Fabric
The Wheel of the Law
1917 As Man Made Her
The Eternal Mother
House of Cards
The Price of Pride
A Sleeping Memory
To-Day
1918 De Luxe Annie
The Silent Woman
The Unchastened Woman

Wild Honey
Wives of Men
1919 The Bramble Bush
Let's Elope
The Misleading Widow
The Right to Lie
Twilight
1920 Women Men Forget
Mills, Jerry
1919 The Homesteader
Mills, Marie
1917 Castles for Two
Mills, Thomas R. same as **Mills, Thom; Mills, Thomas; Mills, Tom**
1915 The Making Over of Geoffrey
Manning
The Man Who Couldn't Beat
God
1916 The Crown Prince's Double
The Dawn of Freedom
The Dollar and the Law
The Hero of Submarine D-2
The Shop Girl
Whom the Gods Destroy
1917 The Defeat of the City
The Duplicity of Hargraves
Indiscretion
Kitty MacKay
A Night in New Arabia
The Renaissance at Charleroi
Sally in a Hurry
1918 An American Live Wire
The Girl in His House
A Mother's Sin
The Seal of Silence
1919 A Girl at Bay
The Girl-Woman
Thin Ice
The Unknown Quantity
1920 Duds
The Invisible Divorce
Mills, Varnum
1919 Coax Me
Millsfield, Charles
1920 An Adventuress
Deep Waters
Millum, George
1919 Vagabond Luck
Milne, Margaret
1916 The Lash of Destiny
Milne, Minnie
1916 The Mischief Maker
Milner, Victor same as **Miller, Victor**
1913 Hiawatha
1917 The Inspirations of Harry
Larrabee
1918 The Cabaret Girl
The Velvet Hand
1919 A Fugitive from Matrimony
The Sealed Envelope
1920 Dice of Destiny
Felix O'Day
Half a Chance
Haunting Shadows
Her Unwilling Husband
One Hour Before Dawn
Out of the Dust
Uncharted Channels
The White Dove
Miltern, John same as **Miltern, John T.**
1916 New York
1917 The Black Stork
1918 Her Final Reckoning
Innocent
Let's Get a Divorce
1919 The Profiteers
1920 On with the Dance
Milton, John
1917 The Accomplice
God's Man
Milton, Captain Louis M.
1916 The Hero of Submarine D-2
Milton, Marjorie
1920 In Search of a Sinner
Milton, Maud
1914 Damaged Goods
Mineau, Charlotte
1915 A Bunch of Keys
1918 Rosemary Climbs the Heights
1919 Carolyn of the Corners
1920 Love, Honor and Behave
Married Life

Mineugh, Louise
1917 The Cost of Hatred
Mink, Emil
1920 Forbidden Valley
Minne-ha-ha see **Provost, Minnie**
Minnerly, Nelson H. same as **Minnerly, Nelson**
1917 The Price of Pride
1918 Gates of Gladness
Stolen Orders
1919 Phil-for-Short
Minot, Robert
1919 The Career of Katherine Bush
Minter, Mary Miles
1915 Always in the Way
Barbara Frietchie
Emmy of Stork's Nest
The Fairy and the Waif
1916 Dimples
A Dream or Two Ago
Dulcie's Adventure
Faith
The Innocence of Lizette
Lovely Mary
Rose of the Alley
Youth's Endearing Charm
1917 Annie-for-Spite
Charity Castle
Environment
The Gentle Intruder
Her Country's Call
The Mate of the Sally Ann
Melissa of the Hills
National Association's All-Star
Picture
Peggy Leads the Way
Periwinkle
Somewhere in America
1918 Beauty and the Rogue
A Bit of Jade
The Eyes of Julia Deep
The Ghost of Rosy Taylor
Powers That Prey
Rosemary Climbs the Heights
Social Briars
Wives and Other Wives
1919 The Amazing Impostor
Anne of Green Gables
A Bachelor's Wife
The Intrusion of Isabel
Yvonne from Paris
1920 A Cumberland Romance
Eyes of the Heart
Jenny Be Good
Judy of Rogue's Harbor
Nurse Marjorie
Sweet Lavender
Minter, Sam B.
1917 The Girl by the Roadside
Mintone, A.
1918 Why America Will Win
Minty, C. B.
1919 Open Your Eyes
Mirabeau, the dog
1917 The Hidden Spring
Missimer, Howard same as **Messimore, Howard**
1913 In the Bishop's Carriage
1914 The Adventures of Kitty Cobb
An American Citizen
The $5,000,000 Counterfeiting
Plot
Mrs. Black Is Back
1915 The College Widow
Missimer, Howard
1916 The Eternal Question
Mitchel, Arthur
1916 The Oval Diamond*
Mitchell, Mr. see **Mitchell, Claude**
Mitchell, Aaron
1920 Dinty
Mitchell, Abbie
1920 Eyes of Youth
Mitchell, Beekman
1916 Romeo and Juliet (Quality
Pictures Corp.)*
1917 The White Raven*
Mitchell, Bess
1920 Old Dad

Mitchell, Bruce
1915 Captivating Mary Carstairs
The Tale of the Night Before
Mitchell, Charles
1916 A Woman's Power
Mitchell, Claude same as **Mitchell, Mr.; Mitchell, C. H.; Mitchell, Claude H.**
1915 The Explorer
The Unknown
1916 Each Pearl a Tear
A Gutter Magdalene
The House with the Golden
Windows
Joan the Woman
The Race
The Selfish Woman
Tennessee's Pardner
The Years of the Locust
The Yellow Pawn
1917 The Clever Mrs. Carfax
The Cost of Hatred
The Countess Charming
The Evil Eye
Nan of Music Mountain
A School for Husbands
What Money Can't Buy
The Winning of Sally Temple
1918 The Bravest Way
The City of Dim Faces
The Cruise of the
Make-Believes
Hidden Pearls
Sandy
The Source
Such a Little Pirate
Wild Youth
1919 Jane Goes A-Wooing
1920 Seeing It Through
Mitchell, Dodson
1914 The Conspiracy
1916 Fifty-Fifty
1918 Toys of Fate
1920 Deadline at Eleven
Nothing but Lies
Mitchell, Doris
1915 An Affair of Three Nations
Mitchell, Earle
1917 The End of the Tour
1919 The Moral Deadline
The Praise Agent
Mitchell, Edmund
1915 The Lone Star Rush
Mitchell, Ethel
1915 The Pearl of the Antilles
Mitchell, Evert
1920 The Corsican Brothers
Mitchell, Frank
1920 Humoresque
Mitchell, Grant
1916 The Misleading Lady
Mitchell, Howard M.
1915 The Great Ruby
1916 Betrayed
The Traffic Cop
1918 The Law That Divides
Petticoats and Politics
1919 A Girl in Bohemia
Snares of Paris
The Splendid Sin
1920 Beware of the Bride
Black Shadows
Faith
Flame of Youth
Husband Hunter
The Little Wanderer
Love's Harvest
Molly and I
The Tattlers
Mitchell, Nellie G.
1916 The Flower of No Man's Land
Mitchell, Rhea
1914 Shorty Escapes Marriage
1915 The Brink
The Devil
On the Night Stage
1916 The Beckoning Flame
D'Artagnan
Don Quixote
The Man from Manhattan
Overalls
The Overcoat
Philip Holden—Waster
The Sable Blessing

Mitchell, Ruth Comfort
1917 The Gilded Youth
Whither Thou Goest
1918 The Blindness of Divorce
Boston Blackie's Little Pal
The Ghost of the Rancho
The Goat
Honor's Cross
Social Ambition
Unexpected Places
1919 The Money Corral
The Sleeping Lion
1920 The Devil's Claim
The Scoffer

Mitchell, Ruth Comfort
1916 The Blindness of Love
The Price of Happiness

Mitchell, Susan
1917 The Master Passion
The Princess' Necklace

Mitchell, W.
1917 Even As You and I

Mitchell, Yvette
1917 The Flower of Doom
The Reward of the Faithless
1919 The Last of His People
1920 Lahoma
The Virgin of Stamboul

Mitsoras, D. *same as* **Mitsoras, D. J.;**
Mitsoras, Demetrius; Mitsoris,
Demetrius
1914 Salomy Jane
1915 The Lily of Poverty Flat
Mignon
Salvation Nell
1916 The Woman Who Dared
1919 The Amazing Impostor
Just Squaw
When a Man Rides Alone
1920 The Challenge of the Law
The Flame of Hellgate

Mix, Emmett *see* **Mixx, Emmet**

Mix, Tom
1914 In the Days of the Thundering
Herd
1917 Durand of the Bad Lands
The Heart of Texas Ryan
1918 Ace High
Cupid's Roundup
Fame and Fortune
Mr. Logan, U.S.A.
Six Shooter Andy
Western Blood
1919 The Coming of the Law
The Feud
Fighting for Gold
Hell Roarin' Reform
Rough Riding Romance
The Speed Maniac
Treat 'Em Rough
The Wilderness Trail
1920 The Cyclone
The Daredevil
Days of Daring
Desert Love
Prairie Trails
The Terror
The Texan
Three Gold Coins
The Untamed

Mixx, Emmet *same as* **Mix, Emmett;**
Mixx, Emmett
1916 Hidden Valley
1917 The Image Maker
The Vicar of Wakefield
The Woman and the Beast

Mizner, Wilson
1917 The Law of Compensation

Modjeska, Felix
1914 Charlotte Corday

Modotti, Tina
1920 The Tiger's Coat

Moey, Rosie
1918 For the Freedom of the East

Mohr, Hal
1918 Restitution
1920 The Deceiver
The Golden Trail

Mojean, Olga
1920 White Youth

Mollineaux, Constance *same as*
Molineux, Constance
1914 The Redemption of David
Corson

1915 The Senator

Molloy, Thomas F.
1915 The Island of Regeneration
1916 The Blue Envelope Mystery
The Dollar and the Law
Hesper of the Mountains
The Kid
The Ordeal of Elizabeth
Salvation Joan
1917 Indiscretion
Kitty MacKay
Sally in a Hurry
1918 A Mother's Sin
One Thousand Dollars
Over the Top
1919-20
The Tower of Jewels
1920 Oil

Molter, Bennett A. *same as* **Molter,**
Bennett; Moulter, Bennett A.
1916 Half a Rogue
The Man from Nowhere
Mister 44
The River of Romance

Monet, M.
1914 The Nightingale

Mong, William V. *same as* **Mong, W.**
V.; Mong, William
1915 Tainted Money
1916 Her Bitter Cup
The Iron Hand
Shoes
Two Men of Sandy Bar
1917 The Chosen Prince, or the
Friendship of David and
Jonathan
Fanatics
The Girl and the Crisis
Wild Sumac
1918 The Hopper
The Law of the Great
Northwest
The Man Who Woke Up
The Painted Lily
1919 After His Own Heart
The Amateur Adventuress
The Delicious Little Devil
The Follies Girl
Fools and Their Money
Love's Prisoner
The Master Man
Put Up Your Hands
The Spender
1920 Burning Daylight
The Chorus Girl's Romance
The Coast of Opportunity
A Connecticut Yankee at King
Arthur's Court
The County Fair
The Dwelling Place of Light
813
Life's Twist
The Luck of Geraldine Laird
The Mutiny of the Elsinore
Number 99
The Turning Point

Monley, Frederick
1920 The Blue Moon

Monro, Chief Engineer
1914 Rescue of the Stefansson Arctic
Expedition

Monroe, Frank
1915 The Gray Mask
1917 Vengeance Is Mine

Monroe, Isette
1917 Yankee Pluck

Monsch, Lavine
1918 The Fallen Angel

Mont, Monte du
1920 Jack Straw

Montague, Hon. Mrs.
1918 The Great Love*

Montague, Mr. *see* **Montague, Frederick**

Montagne, Edward J. *same as*
Montagne, Edward; Montague,
Edward J.
1915 The Wheels of Justice
1916 The Combat
The Conflict
The Destroyers
Fathers of Men
His Wife's Good Name
My Lady's Slipper

The Ninety and Nine
1917 Apartment 29
The Maelstrom
The Message of the Mouse
Sunlight's Last Raid
Transgression
1918 The Clutch of Circumstance
The Dawn of Understanding
The Desired Woman
A Game with Fate
Hoarded Assets
A Mother's Sin
To the Highest Bidder
1919 Beating the Odds
Beauty-Proof
Cupid Forecloses
The Darkest Hour
Fighting Destiny
The Girl-Woman
The Lion and the Mouse
The Man Who Won
Out Yonder
A Stitch in Time
Too Many Crooks
1920 Children of Destiny
The Daughter Pays
The Greatest Love
Pleasure Seekers
The Point of View
Red Foam

Montague, Fred *same as* **Montague,**
Mr.; Montague, Frederick
1914 The Call of the North
Cameo Kirby
The Circus Man
The Ghost Breaker
The Man from Home
The Man on the Box
The Master Mind
Ready Money
The Squaw Man
What's His Name
Where the Trail Divides
1915 A Gentleman of Leisure
1916 The Bait
Barriers of Society
The Conscience of John David
The Hidden Law
The Leopard's Bride
1917 The Clock
The Flame of Youth
The Gift Girl
God's Crucible
The Reed Case
The Saintly Sinner
The Winged Mystery
1918 Fast Company
The Fighting Grin
His Robe of Honor
The Rough Lover
1919 All Wrong
The Best Man
His Debt

Montana, Bull
1917 Down to Earth
In Again—Out Again
Snap Judgement
1918 The Border Legion
Fair Enough
He Comes Up Smiling
In Bad
1919 Brass Buttons
Charge It to Me
Cowardice Court
Easy to Make Money
The Hellion
His Majesty, the American
In for Thirty Days
One-Thing-at-a-Time O'Day
The Unpardonable Sin
Victory
1920 The Girl in Number 29
Go and Get It
Hearts Are Trumps
Treasure Island
What Women Love

Montana, Joy
1919 Deliverance

Monteran, Jacques *same as* **Monteran,**
J.; Monteran, Jack; Monteron,
Jacques
1914 America
1915 The Fairy and the Waif
1916 The Common Law
The Foolish Virgin

What Happened at 22
1917 The Easiest Way
The Guardian
The Marriage Market
Rasputin, the Black Monk
Shall We Forgive Her?
1918 Broken Ties
Come On In
Good-Bye, Bill
Heredity
Neighbors
The Oldest Law
Stolen Orders
T'Other Dear Charmer
The Way Out
1919 Come Out of the Kitchen
His Bridal Night
Oh, You Women
The Test of Honor
1920 The Fortune Teller

Monterey, Carlotta
1920 The Cost

Montero, David
1920 A Dark Lantern

Monteron, Jacques *see* **Monteran,**
Jacques

Montgomery, Frank
1916 The Awakening of Helena
Richie
The Brand of Cowardice
Her Debt of Honor
His Great Triumph
The Kiss of Hate
Life's Shadows
1917 The Call of Her People
A Magdalene of the Hills
The Spirit of '76
1918 Under Suspicion
1919 Forest Rivals

Montgomery, James
1914 The Ghost Breaker*
1916 Not My Sister

Montgomery, Mabel
1916 Father and Son

Montgomery, Nadyne
1920 Suds

Montjoy, Louis
1918 The Gulf Between

Montrose, Helene *same as* **Montrose,**
Helen
1918 The Death Dance
Out of a Clear Sky
1919 The Bandbox
The Career of Katherine Bush
Counterfeit
The Country Cousin
Sadie Love

Montrose, Vivian
1919 Nobody Home

Mood, Frank
1919 The Great Victory, Wilson or
the Kaiser? The Fall of the
Hohenzollerns

Moody, Carl
1917 All for a Husband

Moody, Harry
1918 The Legion of Death
1920 Lone Hand Wilson

Moody, Lieut. John
1919 Brothers Divided

Moomaw, L. H.
1920 The Deceiver
The Golden Trail

Moon, Arthur
1918 Without Honor

Moon, Donna
1917 The Flame of Youth

Mooney, Margaret
1916 Intolerance
1919 The Fall of Babylon

Mooney, William A.
1917 Hate

Moore (full name unknown)
1915 The Fairy and the Waif*

Moore, Carlyle
1918 The Fair Pretender

Moore, Charles C.
19-- Official Motion Pictures of the
Panama Pacific Exposition
Held at San Francisco,
Calif.*

Moore, Charles S.
1919 The Homesteader
Moore, Colleen
1917 The Bad Boy
Hands Up!
An Old Fashioned Young Man
The Savage
1918 A Hoosier Romance
Little Orphant Annie
1919 The Busher
Common Property
The Egg Crate Wallop
The Man in the Moonlight
The Wilderness Trail
1920 The Cyclone
The Devil's Claim
Dinty
So Long Letty
When Dawn Came
Moore, Eugene same as **Moore, Eugene W.; Moore, W. Eugene**
1914 Joseph in the Land of Egypt
1915 God's Witness
The Mill on the Floss
1916 Her Father's Gold
The Oval Diamond
The Woman in Politics
The World and the Woman
1917 The Candy Girl
Captain Kiddo
The Girl Who Won Out
Her New York
The Image Maker
A Modern Monte Cristo
Pots-and-Pans Peggy
When Baby Forgot
1919 Sue of the South
Moore, Eunice same as **Moore, Eunice Murdock; Van Moore, Eunice**
1918 The Cruise of the Make-Believes
The Strange Woman
1919 Carolyn of the Corners
1920 Fighting Cressy
Huckleberry Finn
Just Pals
The Soul of Youth
Two Moons
Moore, Evelyn
1914 An American Citizen
Moore, F. see **Moore, Fred**
Moore, Florence
1916 The Weakness of Strength
1917 The Secret of Eve
Moore, Frank
1914 His Majesty, the Scarecrow of Oz
The Last Egyptian
The Patchwork Girl of Oz
1917 The Soul of a Magdalen
Moore, Fred same as **Moore, F.**
1919 Bill Henry
The Egg Crate Wallop
1920 The Man from Nowhere
Moore, Jacqueline
1914 Damaged Goods
Moore, Joe same as **Moore, Joseph**
1914 Hearts of Oak
Three Weeks
1920 Love's Battle
The White Rider
Moore, Joyce
1915 Beulah
1916 The Birth of a Man
The Twin Triangle
1919 A Gentleman of Quality
Moore, Juliette
1917 The Silent Master
1918 When Men Betray
Moore, Leighton
1920 Risky Business
Moore, Lucia
1914 The Lure
1916 Her Double Life
Little Miss Happiness
1917 The Courage of the Common Place
The Small Town Girl
1920 39 East
Moore, Marceau
1916 The Invisible Enemy

Moore, Marcia
1915 The Heart of Maryland
The Second in Command
1916 The Grip of Jealousy
1917 Her Soul's Inspiration
Moore, Margaret
1915 The Rights of Man: A Story of War's Red Blotch
Moore, Mary
1914 The Brute
Lena Rivers (Whitman Features Co.)
Lola
1915 The Great Divide
Prohibition
The Stubbornness of Geraldine
Under Southern Skies
1916 A Million a Minute
1917 Miss Deception
The Warfare of the Flesh
Moore, Matt
1913 Traffic in Souls
1916 20,000 Leagues Under the Sea
1917 The Pride of the Clan
Runaway Romany
1918 Heart of the Wilds
1919 The Bondage of Barbara
The Dark Star
Getting Mary Married
The Glorious Lady
A Regular Girl
Sahara
The Unpardonable Sin
The Unwritten Code
A Wild Goose Chase
1920 Don't Ever Marry
Hairpins
Love Madness
The Sport of Kings
Whispers
Moore, Mickey same as **Moore, Master Micky; Moore, Micky**
1919 The Unpainted Woman
1920 Out of the Dust
Parted Curtains
Polly of the Storm Country
The Price of Redemption
Something to Think About
Moore, Milton same as **Moore, Milton Mark**
1916 Love's Lariat
1918 The Grand Passion
1919 The Great Air Robbery
1920 Skyfire
Moore, Nora
1916 The King's Game
Moore, Owen
1913 Caprice
1914 Aftermath
The Battle of the Sexes
Cinderella
The Escape
Home, Sweet Home
1915 Betty in Search of a Thrill
Help Wanted
Jordan Is a Hard Road
Mistress Nell
Nearly a Lady
Pretty Mrs. Smith
'Twas Ever Thus
1916 Betty of Graystone
A Coney Island Princess
The Kiss
Little Meena's Romance
Rolling Stones
Susan Rocks the Boat
Under Cover
1917 A Girl Like That
The Little Boy Scout
1919 The Crimson Gardenia
1919-20
Piccadilly Jim
1920 The Desperate Hero
The Poor Simp
Sooner or Later
Moore, Pat same as **Moore, Master Pat**
1918 The Seal of Silence
The Squaw Man
Women's Weapons
1919 Fires of Faith
His Divorced Wife
Luck in Pawn
A Rogue's Romance
Sahara

The Sleeping Lion
1920 Out of the Dust
Their Mutual Child
The Turning Point
Moore, Ray same as **Moore, R. C.**
1919 Strictly Confidential
When Doctors Disagree
Moore, Tom
1916 Dollars and the Woman
1917 The Cinderella Man
The Jaguar's Claws
Little Miss Optimist
The Primrose Ring
The Wild Girl
1918 Brown of Harvard
The Danger Game
Dodging a Million
The Fair Pretender
The Floor Below
Go West, Young Man
Just for Tonight
The Kingdom of Youth
The Lesson
Thirty a Week
1919 The City of Comrades
The Gay Lord Quex
Heartsease
Lord and Lady Algy
A Man and His Money
One of the Finest
Toby's Bow
1920 Duds
The Great Accident
Officer 666
Stop Thief!
Moore, Vernol
1920 Reformation
Moore, Victor
1915 Chimmie Fadden
Chimmie Fadden Out West
Snobs
1916 The Clown
The Race
Moore, Vin
1919 Captain Kidd, Jr.
Moore, W. Eugene see **Moore, Eugene**
Moore, W. Scott
1919 The Cinema Murder
Moores, Clara
1919 Three Black Eyes
Mooser, George
1920 The Girl with the Jazz Heart
Moran (full name unknown)
1916 The Code of Marcia Gray*
Moran, Lee
1915 Mrs. Plum's Pudding
1920 Everything but the Truth
Fixed by George
La La Lucille
Once a Plumber
Moran, Neil
1917 For the Freedom of the World
1918 Fields of Honor
For the Freedom of the East
1919 High Pockets
A Misfit Earl
Speedy Meade
Moran, Tom
1917 Pride and the Man
Moran, William F. same as **Moran, William**
1919 Please Get Married
1920 A Beggar in Purple
The Green Flame
Into the Light
The Path She Chose
Morange, Edward A.
1914 The Great Diamond Robbery
Mordant, Edwin
1915 The Moth and the Flame
A Royal Family
Seven Sisters
1916 Molly Make-Believe
Poor Little Peppina
1917 The Undying Flame
1920 The Cost
Moree, Maxfield
1915 Keep Moving
Morel, Franklyn
1920 Sophy of Kravonia; Or, The Virgin of Paris

Moreland, Beatrice
1912 Oliver Twist
1914 The Scales of Justice
Moreland, Margaret
1917 National Red Cross Pageant*
Moreno, Antonio
1915 The Dust of Egypt
The Island of Regeneration
On Her Wedding Night
A Price for Folly
1916 The Devil's Prize
Kennedy Square
Rose of the South
The Shop Girl
The Supreme Temptation
The Tarantula
1917 Aladdin from Broadway
The Angel Factory
By Right of Possession
The Captain of the Gray Horse Troop
Her Right to Live
The Magnificent Meddler
The Mark of Cain
Money Magic
A Son of the Hills
1918 The First Law
The Naulahka
Moret, Neil
1918 Mickey*
Moreville, Harry
1916 The Spell of the Yukon
Morey, Harry T. same as **Morey, Harry**
1914 A Million Bid
My Official Wife
1915 Crooky
The Making Over of Geoffrey Manning
The Man Behind the Door
The Man Who Couldn't Beat God
A Price for Folly
To Cherish and Protect
1916 For a Woman's Fair Name
The Law Decides
Salvation Joan
Whom the Gods Destroy
1917 The Courage of Silence
Her Secret
His Own People
The Question
Richard, the Brazen
Who Goes There!
Within the Law
Womanhood, the Glory of the Nation
1918 All Man
A Bachelor's Children
The Desired Woman
A Game with Fate
The Golden Goal
The Green God
Hoarded Assets
The King of Diamonds
The Other Man
Tangled Lives
1919 Beating the Odds
Beauty-Proof
The Darkest Hour
Fighting Destiny
The Gamblers
In Honor's Web
The Man Who Won
Shadows of the Past
Silent Strength
The Wreck
1920 The Birth of a Soul
The Flaming Clue
The Gauntlet
The Sea Rider
Morgan, Beatrice
1915 The Great Ruby
1918 Sylvia on a Spree
Morgan, Byron
1920 What's Your Hurry?
Morgan, Charles could be same as **Morgan, Charles B.**
1917 Easy Money
Morgan, Charles B. could be same as **Morgan, Charles**
1914 The Dollar Mark

155

Morrison, W. H.
1916 Vengeance Is Mine
Morrison, William
1919 The Mystery of the Yellow Room
Morrissey, Edward same as **Morrisey, Edward**
1916 A House Built upon Sand
1917 Stagestruck
1919 The Pointing Finger
Morrissey, Grace
1916 The Catspaw
1917 The Tell-Tale Step
Morrissey, Tommy
1917 The Flower of Doom
Morrow, Cleo
1916 The Sin Ye Do
Morrow, Jane see **Drew, Mrs. Sidney** (died 1925)
Morse, Beatrice
1917 Who Knows?
1918 Humility
Morse, Clara
1914 The Envoy Extraordinary
Morse, Grace
1920 Burglar Proof
Hairpins
Let's Be Fashionable
An Old Fashioned Boy
The Sins of Rosanne
The Soul of Youth
Morse, John P. same as **Morse, J. P.**
1920 Dangerous to Men
The Hope
Shore Acres
Morse, Josephine
1917 The Co-Respondent
The Runaway
1918 Her Man
Morse, Myrtle
1920 The Stealers
Morse, Samuel same as **Morse, Sam**
1917 Daughter of Maryland
The Last of the Carnabys
Morse, Stanley C.
1920 The Leopard Woman
Morse, William A. same as **Morse, William**
1915 Barbara Frietchie
Greater Love Hath No Man
Her Own Way
The Shooting of Dan McGrew
The Song of the Wage Slave
The Vampire
1916 The Ocean Waif
What Will People Say?
1917 The Empress
Morsell, H. Tudor
1915 The Grandee's Ring
Mortemer, Ellen
1918 And the Children Pay
Mortensen, C. N.
1916 D'Artagnan
Mortimer, Captain
1918 Virtuous Wives
Mortimer, Edmund same as **Mortimer, Edwin**
1914 As Ye Sow
Neptune's Daughter
1915 The Moonstone
1918 The Road Through the Dark
The Savage Woman
1919 The Hushed Hour
1920 Alias Jimmy Valentine
The Misfit Wife
Mortimer, Henry same as **Mortimer, Harry**
1916 Her Great Price
The Pursuing Vengeance
1917 Their Compact
1919 His Wife's Friend
The Road Called Straight
1920 The Fear Market
Mortimer, Lewis J.
1920 Sophy of Kravonia; Or, The Virgin of Paris
Mortimer, William
1920 Hidden Charms
Morton (full name unknown)
1914 The Temptations of Satan

Morton, Howard E.
1918 The Border Wireless
Morton, Luther
1917 Feet of Clay
Morton, Walter
1914 The Temptations of Satan*
The Wishing Ring; An Idyll of Old England
1915 The Chocolate Soldier
1916 The Folly of Revenge
Morville, Guy
1916 Broken Fetters
Moscowitz, Mrs.
1916 Phantom Fortunes
Moses, Albert see **Moses, Alfred**
Moses, Alfred same as **Moses, Albert; Moses, Alfred, Jr.; Moses, Alfred E.; Moses, Alfred Huger, Jr.**
1914 Joseph in the Land of Egypt
1916 Life's Shadows
The Social Secretary
Whoso Findeth a Wife
1917 The Little Duchess
The Sin Woman
1918 By Right of Purchase
De Luxe Annie
Her Only Way
His Royal Highness
The Love Net
Men
The Safety Curtain
1919 The Hand Invisible
The Quickening Flame
Mosher, Clara
1916 Judith of the Cumberlands
Mosley, Thomas M.
1916 The Colored American Winning His Suit
Moss, B. S.
1914 Three Weeks
1916 Boots and Saddles
In the Hands of the Law
One Day
1918 The Scarlet Trail*
1919 Break the News to Mother
Moss, George
1913 In the Bishop's Carriage
1914 As Ye Sow
The House of Bondage
Marta of the Lowlands
The Pride of Jennico
A Woman's Triumph
1915 Four Feathers
1916 Fruits of Desire
1917 The Black Stork
The Web of Life
1918 A Daughter of France
Les Miserables
The Street of Seven Stars
Moss, Howard S.
1917 The Dream Doll
1918 Movie Marionettes
Moss, Stewart B. same as **Moss, Stewart Belfield**
1917 Big Timber
1920 Empty Arms
The Riddle: Woman
The Stealers
Mostyn, Hallen
1917 The Eternal Temptress
Mott, Valentine
1919 God's Outlaw
Motte, Marguerite de la see **De La Motte, Marguerite**
Moulter, Bennett A. see **Molter, Bennett A.**
Moulton, Lucille
1920 The Adorable Savage
Moussel, Miss
1915 The Model
Mowbray, Henry same as **Mowbray, Harry**
1919 The Stream of Life
1920 Should a Wife Work?
Mowbray, Robert
1919 Beating the Odds
Mower, Jack
1916 The Last Man
Miss Jackie of the Navy
1917 The Butterfly Girl
The Devil's Assistant
The Girl Who Couldn't Grow Up

The Lust of the Ages
Miss Jackie of the Army
1918 Ann's Finish
Fair Enough
Impossible Susan
Jilted Janet
The Mantle of Charity
Molly, Go Get 'Em
Money Isn't Everything
The Primitive Woman
The Square Deal
1919 The Beloved Cheater
The Island of Intrigue
The Millionaire Pirate
Molly of the Follies
1920 Bubbles
Life
Mowschine, Michel
1916 The Crisis
Moyers, Bertie Badger
1916 Fate's Boomerang
Moyles, Dan
1914 Officer 666
1915 The Commuters
Stop Thief!
Who's Who in Society
Mudge, Elizabeth
1916 Autumn
Mueller, Floyd
1916 The Bait
1919 Victory
1920 Deep Waters
The Great Redeemer
The Last of the Mohicans
Treasure Island
The White Circle
Mueller, Lillian
1917 The Heart of Ezra Greer
Muir, Helen
1919 Strictly Confidential
Muldoon, William
1916 The Other Girl
Mulhall, Jack
1914 The Rejuvenation of Aunt Mary
1916 The Place Beyond the Winds
The Price of Silence
Wanted—A Home
The Whirlpool of Destiny
1917 Fighting for Love
The Flame of Youth
The Hero of the Hour
High Speed
Love Aflame
The Midnight Man
Mr. Dolan of New York
The Saintly Sinner
Sirens of the Sea
The Terror
1918 Danger—Go Slow
The Flames of Chance
The Grand Passion
Madame Spy
Wild Youth
1919 Creaking Stairs
A Favor to a Friend
Fools and Their Money
The Merry-Go-Round
Should a Woman Tell?
The Solitary Sin
The Spite Bride
Whom the Gods Would Destroy
1920 All-of-a-Sudden-Peggy
The Hope
Miss Hobbs
You Never Can Tell
Mulhall, Mrs. Jack
1919 Cheating Herself
Cowardice Court
Mulhuland, Helen see **Milholland, Helen**
Mullally, Jode
1914 The Call of the North
Cameo Kirby
The Circus Man
The Ghost Breaker
The Man from Home
Ready Money
1915 After Five
Snobs
1917 The Blood of His Fathers
The Eye of Envy
Unto the End

Mullaly (full name unknown)
1916 The Code of Marcia Gray*
Mullen, Eugene see **Mullin, Eugene**
Mullen, Gordon
1919 Crooked Straight
1920 Dangerous Hours
The False Road
Paris Green
Mullen, Paul
1919 Brothers Divided
The Hoodlum
Muller, Alma
1917 Patsy
Mullin, Eugene same as **Mullen, Eugene**
1914 The Christian
A Florida Enchantment
Mr. Barnes of New York
1915 The Heights of Hazard
On Her Wedding Night
1916 Green Stockings
Who Killed Joe Merrion?
1917 The Bottom of the Well
Within the Law
1919 The Cambric Mask
The Third Degree
Mulvane, Margaret
1915 Beulah
Mumper, Norris M.
1920 The Dwelling Place of Light
The Money-Changers
Riders of the Dawn
The Sagebrusher
Mundon, Abe
1915 Jewel
Scandal
Mundy, Jack
1917 Madame Sherry
Munier, Ferdinand
1918 Ruggles of Red Gap
Munro, Izeth same as **Munro, Iseth**
1918 The Spurs of Sybil
1919 Suspense
Munsey, Edna
1917 Patsy
Munson, Audrey
1915 Inspiration
1916 The Girl O' Dreams
Purity
Munson, Byron
1920 Harriet and the Piper
Honest Hutch
Muratore, Lucien
1914 Manon Lescaut
1918 A Woman of Impulse
Murdock, Ann same as **Murdock, Anna**
1915 A Royal Family
1916 Captain Jinks of the Horse Marines
1917 The Beautiful Adventure
Envy
Outcast
Please Help Emily
The Seventh Sin
Where Love Is
1918 The Impostor
My Wife
The Richest Girl
Murdock, Bobby
1915 Buckshot John*
Murdock, Frank same as **Murdock, Frank J.**
1919 A Regular Girl
Sealed Hearts
1920 The Veiled Marriage
Murdock, George
1919 The Forfeit
Murfin, Jane
1919 Marie, Ltd.
The Right to Lie
1920 The Amateur Wife
Murillo, Mary
1915 The Little Gypsy
A Soldier's Oath
The Unfaithful Wife
1916 Ambition
Blazing Love
East Lynne
The Eternal Sapho
Gold and the Woman
The Green-Eyed Monster
Her Double Life
Love and Hate

A Parisian Romance
Sins of Men
The Unwelcome Mother
The Vixen
The War Bride's Secret
1917 The Avenging Trail
The Bitter Truth
The Eternal Mother
Jack and the Beanstalk
Love's Law
The New York Peacock
Outwitted
The Secret of the Storm
Country
She
Sister Against Sister
Tangled Lives
Two Little Imps
Wrath of Love
1918 Cheating the Public
The Forbidden City
Her Only Way
The Panther Woman
The Reason Why
1919 The Heart of Wetona
The Other Man's Wife
1920 Mothers of Men
The New York Idea
The Wonderful Chance
Yes or No

Murnane, Allan *same as* **Murnane, Allen**
1916 The City
Hazel Kirke
The Lottery Man
1917 The Black Stork
Murphy, Mr.
1916 The Adventures of Kathlyn
Murphy, A. N. *same as* **Murphy, A. M.**
1913 The Tonopah Stampede for
Gold
Murphy, Charles B. *same as* **Murphy,
C. B.**
1920 The Dwelling Place of Light
The U.P. Trail
Murphy, Edna
1918 To the Highest Bidder
1920 The Branded Woman
The North Wind's Malice
Over the Hill to the Poorhouse
Murphy, Francis *could be same as*
Murphy, Frank
1919 The Sealed Envelope
Murphy, Frank *could be same as*
Murphy, Francis
1917 The Upper Crust
Murphy, George E.
1919 The Oakdale Affair
Murphy, Harlem Tommy
1919-20
Piccadilly Jim
Murphy, J. D. *see* **Murphy, John Daly**
Murphy, Joe
1920 Nurse Marjorie
Murphy, John Daly *same as* **Murphy, J.
D.; Murphy, John D.**
1914 The Million
1915 A Black Sheep
The Two Orphans
1918 The Ghosts of Yesterday
Oh, Johnny!
Our Mrs. McChesney
Secret Strings
1919 The Road Called Straight
Murphy, Martin
1916 20,000 Leagues Under the Sea
Murphy, Richard
1913 The Prisoner of Zenda
1917 The Antics of Ann
Murphy, Steve *same as* **Murphy, S.**
1916 A Law unto Himself
Vengeance Is Mine
Murphy, Will C.
1919 Coax Me
Murray, Charles *same as* **Murray,
Charlie**
1919 Puppy Love
Yankee Doodle in Berlin
1920 Love, Honor and Behave
Married Life

Murray, Edgar, Jr.
1917 The Mystery of Number 47
Murray, Frank
1918 My Own United States
Murray, J. K.
1916 Little Lady Eileen
1917 The Fortunes of Fifi
1918 Madame Jealousy
1919 Oh, Boy!
Murray, Jack
1915 A Continental Girl
Time Lock Number 776
1916 Her Debt of Honor
Murray, James E.
1920 The Mysteries of Paris
Murray, Mae
1916 The Big Sister
The Dream Girl
The Plow Girl
Sweet Kitty Bellairs
To Have and to Hold
1917 At First Sight
A Mormon Maid
On Record
The Primrose Ring
Princess Virtue
1918 The Bride's Awakening
Danger—Go Slow
Face Value
Her Body in Bond
Modern Love
1919 The A.B.C. of Love
The Big Little Person
The Delicious Little Devil
The Scarlet Shadow
The Twin Pawns
What Am I Bid?
1920 Idols of Clay
On with the Dance
The Right to Love
Murray, Raymond
1915 The Little Gypsy
Murray, T. Henderson
1917 Hate
1918 Back to the Woods
Murray, T. J.
1920 The Valley of Doubt
Muse, Dion
1918 A Successful Adventure
Musgrave, William *same as* **Musgrave,
Billy; Musgrave, W. F.**
1916 The Black Sheep of the Family
1917 Society's Driftwood
1918 Crown Jewels
The Midnight Patrol
1919 Blackie's Redemption
Musgrove, Lon
1914 The Patchwork Girl of Oz
Mussalli, Hassan
1916 The Awakening of Helena
Richie
1917 The Greater Woman
One Law for Both
1918 The Splendid Sinner
The Triumph of Venus
Mussett, Charles *same as* **De Massett,
Charles; Mussett, Charles de;
Muzitt, Charles**
1916 An Enemy to the King
1917 American—That's All
Knights of the Square Table
Sloth
1918 The Impostor
Musson, Bennet *same as* **Musson,
Bennett**
1914 Forgiven; Or, The Jack of
Diamonds
1918 Marriage
Out of the Night
The Struggle Everlasting
The Uphill Path
1919 Marriage for Convenience
Muzitt, Charles *see* **Mussett, Charles**
Myers (full name unknown)
1920 The Virgin of Stamboul*
Myers, Amos
1919 Please Get Married
Should a Woman Tell?
1920 Old Lady 31

Myers, Carmel
1917 A Daughter of the Poor
The Haunted Pajamas
The Lash of Power
A Love Sublime
Might and the Man
Sirens of the Sea
1918 All Night
A Broadway Scandal
The City of Tears
The Dream Lady
The Girl in the Dark
The Marriage Lie
My Unmarried Wife
A Society Sensation
The Wife He Bought
The Wine Girl
1919 The Little White Savage
Who Will Marry Me?
1920 Beautifully Trimmed
The Gilded Dream
In Folly's Trail
Myers, Harry C. *same as* **Meyer,
Henry; Meyers, Harry; Myers,
Harry**
1915 The Earl of Pawtucket
The Man of Shame
1918 Conquered Hearts
The Face in the Dark
Out of the Night
1920 A Connecticut Yankee at King
Arthur's Court
Forty-Five Minutes from
Broadway
La La Lucille
The Notorious Mrs. Sands
Peaceful Valley
Sky Eye
Myers, Ray
1914 Martin Eden
Myles, Norbert *same as* **Miles, Norbig;
Myles, N. A.; Myles, Norbert A.**
1916 In the Web of the Grafters
Nancy's Birthright
The Stain in the Blood
1917 For Liberty
The Planter*
Should She Obey?
Some Boy!
The Soul of Satan
Truthful Tulliver
1920 The Daughter of Dawn
Myll, Louis
1915 Keep Moving
Myott, Florence
1920 Respectable by Proxy
Myton, Fred
1916 Barriers of Society
The Devil's Bondwoman
The Isle of Life
Kinkaid, Gambler
The Social Buccaneer
1917 The Charmer
Come Through
The Devil's Pay Day
Fear Not
Fighting for Love
Fighting Mad
Follow the Girl
Heart Strings
The Lash of Power
Love Aflame
Mr. Dolan of New York
Princess Virtue
The Spotted Lily
The Terror
Triumph
1918 All Night
Blue Blood
The Cabaret Girl*
The Dream Lady
Face Value
Fires of Youth
Kultur
The Love Swindle
The Lure of Luxury
Maid O' the Storm
Shackled
1919 Desert Gold
A Fugitive from Matrimony
The Gray Wolf's Ghost
Hearts Asleep
Josselyn's Wife
A Man in the Open

The Prince and Betty
The Silk Lined Burglar
Tangled Threads
A Taste of Life
A Trick of Fate
Who Will Marry Me?
1920 The Deadlier Sex
Dice of Destiny
Felix O'Day
Fighting Cressy
Half a Chance
One Hour Before Dawn
Simple Souls

N

Nagel, Conrad
1919 The Lion and the Mouse
Little Women
Redhead
1920 The Fighting Chance
Unseen Forces
1921 Midsummer Madness
Nagy, Anton
1917 Polly Put the Kettle On
1918 The Answer
Betty Takes a Hand
Limousine Life
1920 813
So Long Letty
Naldi, Nita
1920 The Common Sin
Dr. Jekyll and Mr. Hyde
(Famous Players-Lasky
Corp.)
Life
Nally, William G.
1920 The Shark
Namara, Marguerite
1920 Stolen Moments
Nana, Mme.
1920 Why Women Sin
Nannery, Edward
1915 Prohibition
Nansen, Betty
1915 Anna Karenina
The Celebrated Scandal
Should a Mother Tell?
The Song of Hate
A Woman's Resurrection
Nanson, Deborah
1916 The Almighty Dollar
Nares, P. W.
1913 The Daughter of the Hills
Narin, Robert
1919 Sandy Burke of the U-Bar-U
Nash, Alice
1918 Love Watches
Nash, Dorothy
1916 The Stain in the Blood
Nash, Edna
1918 Love Watches
Nash, Florence
1914 Springtime
Nash, George
1914 The Jungle
1915 The Cotton King
Nash, J. E.
1919 The Loves of Letty
1920 The Great Lover
Madame X
Out of the Storm
The Silver Horde
Nash, Mary
1915 The Unbroken Road
1916 Arms and the Woman
Nash, Nadine
1920 The Law of the Yukon
Nash, Thomas S.
1914 The Mysterious Man of the
Jungle
1915 Unto the Darkness
Nash, William
1917 The Bondage of Fear
Nason, Flora *same as* **Naso, Flora**
1914 The Criminal Path
1916 A Modern Thelma
1917 Behind the Mask

Nathan, George G.
1914 The $5,000,000 Counterfeiting Plot

Natho, Louis
1919 Tin Pan Alley
1920 The Devil's Riddle

Natol, Florence
1915 The Man Who Couldn't Beat God
1916 The Destroyers
1917 His Father's Son

Natteford, J. F.
1915 Forbidden Fruit*
1916 A Fool's Paradise*

Nau, Marie
1918 Tinsel

Naulty, J. N.
1920 The Copperhead

Navaro, Anita
1917 The Painted Madonna

Navarro, Mary same as **Navaro, Mary**
1914 Hearts of Oak
When Broadway Was a Trail
1915 The Battle of Ballots
1918 Eve's Daughter
Mrs. Dane's Defense

Navarro, Ralph
1916 The Challenge

Nawn, Tom
1915 Keep Moving

Nazimova same as **Nazimova, Madame; Nazimova, Alla**
1916 War Brides
1918 Eye for Eye
Revelation
Toys of Fate
1919 The Brat
Out of the Fog
The Red Lantern
1920 Billions
The Heart of a Child
Madame Peacock
Stronger Than Death

Neal, Richard see **Neill, Richard**

Nealand, Walter D. could be same as **Neeland, Walter**
1916 One Day

Nedell, Ben same as **Nedell, Benny**
1918 Leap to Fame
1920 Bachelor Apartments

Needham, James see **Crisp, Donald**

Neeland, Walter could be same as **Nealand, Walter D.**
1920 The Dark Mirror

Neery, Joe
1916 Atta Boy's Last Race

Neff, Mr. (actor)
1916 The Grip of Jealousy

Neff, M. A. (prod)
1915 The Battle of Ballots

Neff, Pauline
1914 The Man from Mexico

Nehli-Kalini, Thais
1919 Injustice

Nehls, R. R.
1920 The Blue Moon

Neice, Alice
1916 Humanizing Mr. Winsby

Neil, James see **Neill, James**

Neil, Richard see **Neill, Richard**

Neilan, Marshall same as **Neilan, Marshal; Neilan, Marshall A.**
1914 Classmates
1915 The Commanding Officer
The Country Boy
A Girl of Yesterday
Little Pal
The Love Route
Madame Butterfly
May Blossom
Rags
1916 The Country That God Forgot
The Crisis
The Cycle of Fate
Mice and Men
The Prince Chap
1917 The Bottle Imp
Freckles
The Girl at Home
The Jaguar's Claws
The Little Princess
Rebecca of Sunnybrook Farm

The Silent Partner
Those Without Sin
The Tides of Barnegat
1918 Amarilly of Clothes-Line Alley
Heart of the Wilds
Hit-the-Trail Holliday
Out of a Clear Sky
Stella Maris
1919 Daddy-Long-Legs
Her Kingdom of Dreams
In Old Kentucky
Three Men and a Girl
The Unpardonable Sin
1920 Dinty
Don't Ever Marry
Go and Get It
The River's End

Neilan, Martin
1920 Pink Tights

Neill, James same as **Neil, James**
1914 Cameo Kirby
The Circus Man
The Man on the Box
Ready Money
Richelieu
Rose of the Rancho
Where the Trail Divides
1915 After Five
The Case of Becky
The Cheat
The Clue
The Explorer
The Goose Girl
The Governor's Lady
Mr. Grex of Monte Carlo
The Warrens of Virginia
The Woman
1916 The Dream Girl
For the Defense
A Gutter Magdalene
The House with the Golden Windows
Joan the Woman
The Lash
Maria Rosa
Oliver Twist
The Ragamuffin
Sweet Kitty Bellairs
Tennessee's Pardner
The Thousand Dollar Husband
To Have and to Hold
1917 Betty to the Rescue
The Black Wolf
The Bottle Imp
The Devil-Stone
Forbidden Paths
The Ghost House
The Girl at Home
The Little American
On the Level
The Prison Without Walls
A School for Husbands
Those Without Sin
The Trouble Buster
What Money Can't Buy
The Woman God Forgot
1918 The Girl Who Came Back
Jules of the Strong Heart
Less Than Kin
A Petticoat Pilot
Sandy
Say, Young Fellow!
Too Many Millions
The Way of a Man with a Maid
We Can't Have Everything
The Whispering Chorus
The Widow's Might
Women's Weapons
1919 A Daughter of the Wolf
Don't Change Your Husband
Everywoman
Fires of Faith
Her Kingdom of Dreams
His Official Fiancée
Men, Women and Money
Peg O' My Heart
The Rescuing Angel
Romance and Arabella
The Secret Garden
1920 A Double Dyed Deceiver
The Little Shepherd of Kingdom Come
The Paliser Case

Neill, Mrs. James
1916 The Selfish Woman

Neill, R. R. see **Neill, Richard**

Neill, R. William same as **Neill, Roy; Neill, Roy W.; Neill, Roy William**
1916 A Corner in Colleens
1917 The Girl Glory
Love Letters
The Mother Instinct
The Price Mark
They're Off
1918 "Flare-Up" Sal
Free and Equal
Green Eyes
The Kaiser's Shadow, or the Triple Cross
Love Me
The Mating of Marcella
Tyrant Fear
Vive La France!
1919 The Bandbox
The Career of Katherine Bush
Charge It to Me
Puppy Love
Trixie from Broadway
1920 Dangerous Business
Good References
The Inner Voice
Something Different
The Woman Gives
Yes or No

Neill, Richard same as **Neal, Richard; Neil, Richard; Neill, R. R.; Neill, Richard R.**
1914 Fantasma
1915 The Broken Law
Colonel Carter of Cartersville
The Labyrinth
1916 The Battle of Life
The Fool's Revenge
God's Half Acre
A Modern Thelma
The Ragged Princess
Wall Street Tragedy
1917 A Child of the Wild
The Co-Respondent
Her Second Husband
Love's Law
Unknown 274
The Woman in White
1918 Doing Their Bit
Pals First
The Road to France
1919 His Wife's Friend
Hit or Miss
1920 The Dead Line
The Plunger

Neill, Roy William see **Neill, R. William**

Neilsen, Agnes same as **Neilson, Agnes; Nielsen, Agnes; Nilson, Agnes**
1917 The Girl Who Didn't Think
1918 Woman and the Law
1920 April Folly

Neilson, Alec see **Nilson, Alec**

Neilson, Anna not the same as **Nilsson, Anna Q.**
1919 Checkers

Neilson, Frances (actor)
1919 The Gay Old Dog

Neilson, Francis (scen)
1916 The Martyrdom of Philip Strong

Neissen, M. P.
1916 The Love Thief

Neitz, Alvin J.
1917 Fighting Back
The Learnin' of Jim Benton
The Medicine Man
1918 The Boss of the Lazy Y
The Gun Woman
High Stakes
Keith of the Border
The Law's Outlaw
Paying His Debt
The Pretender
Wolves of the Border
1920 The Lone Hand
Three Gold Coins

Nelson, Miss
1914 The House of Bondage

Nelson, Mr.
1915 Business Is Business

Nelson, C. A.
1916 As a Woman Sows
The Haunted Manor

Nelson, Charles
1919 Virtuous Men*

Nelson, Edgar
1915 The House of a Thousand Candles
1920 Way Down East

Nelson, Frances
1915 Conscience
Courtmartialed
The Family Cupboard
The Sins of Society
The Stolen Voice
The White Terror
1916 The Almighty Dollar
The Decoy
Human Driftwood
Love's Crucible
The Revolt
What Happened at 22
1917 The Beautiful Lie
One of Many
The Power of Decision

Nelson, Frank
1919 The Oakdale Affair
You Never Know Your Luck

Nelson, Howard
1920 Our Christianity and Nobody's Child

Nelson, Jack
1914 The Envoy Extraordinary
1915 The Alien
Business Is Business*
Colorado*
The Long Chance
1916 If My Country Should Call
Pasquale
Undine
1917 A Kiss for Susie
The Lash of Power
The Man Trap
The Scarlet Pimpernel
The Spotted Lily
1918 The Biggest Show on Earth
The Cabaret Girl
The Flash of Fate
Riders of the Purple Sage
When Do We Eat?
Winner Takes All
1919 The Busher
Fighting for Gold
The Girl Dodger
The Girl with No Regrets
The Haunted Bedroom
Rose of the West
Rough Riding Romance
23 1/2 Hours' Leave
The Wilderness Trail
1920 Love Madness
Rookie's Return

Nelson, Jennie
1913 The Battle of Shiloh

Nelson, Marjorie
1915 A Modern Magdalen
Seven Sisters

Nelson, Otto
1916 The Man from Manhattan
1920 West Is West

NeMoyer, Frances
1919 The Law of Nature

Neola May, Princess same as **Mae, Neola; May, Neola; Neola, Princess**
1917 The Captain of the Gray Horse Troop
1918 The Red, Red Heart
1919 A Fight for Love
1920 The Silver Horde

Neong, Lin
1917 The War of the Tongs

Nesbit, Evelyn same as **Nesbit-Thaw, Evelyn; Thaw, Evelyn Nesbit**
1914 Threads of Destiny
1917 Redemption
1918 Her Mistake
I Want to Forget
The Woman Who Gave
1919 A Fallen Idol
My Little Sister
Thou Shalt Not

Woman, Woman!
Nesbit, Pinna
1917 The Beloved Adventuress
The Corner Grocer
The False Friend
The Good for Nothing
The Little Duchess
The Page Mystery
The Price of Pride
Rasputin, the Black Monk
The Stolen Paradise
1918 The Beautiful Mrs. Reynolds
Broken Ties
Let's Get a Divorce
Merely Players
A Soul Without Windows
Whims of Society
1919 Bolshevism on Trial
1920 Partners of the Night
Nesbit-Thaw, Evelyn see **Nesbit, Evelyn**
Nesbitt, Miriam
1915 The Way Back
1916 The Catspaw
1917 Builders of Castles
Infidelity
The Last Sentence
Nesmith, Miriam
1920 Twisted Souls
Nesmith, Ottola
1915 Still Waters
1918 Rich Man, Poor Man
Neuman, Bobby
1919 Bullin' the Bullsheviki
Neuman, Harry see **Neumann, Harry**
Neuman, Myrtle
1915 Salvation Nell
Neumann, Harry same as **Neuman, Harry**
1917 The Lad and the Lion
1918 A Hoosier Romance
The Still Alarm
The Yellow Dog
Neville, Ada
1914 Officer 666
1916 The Witch
1920 The Stolen Kiss
Neville, George
1920 Way Down East
Neville, Harry
1916 The Blindness of Love
The Pretenders
1917 The Man Hater
New York Giants
1914 The Giants-White Sox Tour
Newall, Marie same as **Newell, Marie**
1919 Men, Women and Money
1920 Dangerous Trails
The Unknown Ranger
Newberg, Frank see **Newburg, Frank**
Newberry, Frank
1918 Unexpected Places
Newburg, F. H. could be same as
Newburg, Frank or **Newburg, Fred**
1917 The Fuel of Life
Newburg, Frank same as **Newberg,
Frank**; could be same as **Newburg,
F. H.** or **Newburg, Fred**
1914 The Spirit of the Conqueror
1915 Business Is Business
Tainted Money
The White Scar
1916 Inherited Passions
The Iron Hand
1917 The Maternal Spark
1918 The Married Virgin
Unexpected Places*
1919 Whom the Gods Would
Destroy
Newburg, Fred could be same as
Newburg, F. H. or **Newburg, Frank**
1917 When Baby Forgot
Newcomb, Robert
1916 Madame La Presidente
Newcomb, Warren A.
1920 The Isle of Destiny
Newcomer, Judge John R.
1918 And the Children Pay
Newell, Marie see **Newall, Marie**
Newhard, Guy
1918 His Robe of Honor

Newhard, Robert same as **Newhard,
Robert S.; Newhardt, Robert;
Newhart, Robert**
1915 The Coward
The Iron Strain
On the Night Stage
1916 Civilization
Where Love Leads
1917 Back of the Man
The Crab
Golden Rule Kate
Happiness
The Iced Bullet
Paws of the Bear
Sweetheart of the Doomed
1918 Carmen of the Klondike
Fuss and Feathers
His Birthright
Social Ambition
When Do We Eat?
With Hoops of Steel
1919 Diane of the Green Van
Happy Though Married
A Man in the Open
A Man's Country
A Man's Fight
1920 Big Happiness
Dollar for Dollar
Everybody's Sweetheart
Smoldering Embers
The Street Called Straight
Newman, A.
1919 Devil McCare
Newman, Horace
1915 The Old Homestead
1916 Saints and Sinners
Newman, Laura
1919 The Other Man's Wife
Newman, Nell
1920 The Heart of a Child
Newman, Walter
1915 The Long Chance
1919 The Bishop's Emeralds
Newmann, J. E.
1918 The Legion of Death
Newton, Mr.
1916 The Innocence of Lizette
Newton, Ashton
1919 The Law of Nature
1920 Cynthia-of-the-Minute
Newton, Charles
1916 April
Immediate Lee
Lord Loveland Discovers
America
The Sable Blessing
True Nobility
A Woman's Daring
1917 Annie-for-Spite
The Frame Up
My Fighting Gentleman
Snap Judgement
1920 Two Kinds of Love
Newton, Dodo
1916 A Dream or Two Ago
A Million for Mary
Soul Mates
Newton, Frank
1918 Rough and Ready
Newton, Jack
1916 Elusive Isabel
1917 Alma, Where Do You Live?
Miss Deception
1918 Berlin Via America
The Brass Check
Stolen Orders
Under Suspicion
1920 The Sacred Ruby
Uncle Sam of Freedom Ridge
Newton, Marie
1914 The Woman in Black
1915 Dora Thorne
1919 A Fallen Idol
Niblack, Sam same as **Niblack, Samuel;
Niblack, Samuel N.**
1916 Divorce and the Daughter
The Five Faults of Flo
The Fugitive
1917 Her Life and His
Kidnapped
Light in Darkness
19-- Barnaby Lee

Niblo, Fred
1918 Coals of Fire
Fuss and Feathers
The Marriage Ring
When Do We Eat?
1919 Happy Though Married
The Haunted Bedroom
The Law of Men
Partners Three
Stepping Out
The Virtuous Thief
What Every Woman Learns
1920 Dangerous Hours
The False Road
Hairpins
Her Husband's Friend
The Mark of Zorro
Sex
Silk Hosiery
The Woman in the Suitcase
Nicholls, Fred
1914 The House of Bondage
Nicholls, George see **Nichols, George**
Nicholls, Robert
1914 In the Name of the Prince of
Peace*
Nichols, George same as **Nicholls,
George; Nichols, George O.;
Nichols, George P.**
1915 Ghosts
A Man's Prerogative
1917 The Silent Man
The Son of His Father
1918 Battling Jane
Borrowed Clothes
Fame and Fortune
Hearts of the World
Keys of the Righteous
Mickey
1919 Bill Apperson's Boy
Children of Banishment
The Coming of the Law
The Greatest Question
The Light of Victory
The Rebellious Bride
A Romance of Happy Valley
The Turn in the Road
Victory
When Doctors Disagree
The Wolf
1920 Deep Waters
The Family Honor
The Iron Rider
The Joyous Troublemaker
Love's Protegé
Nineteen and Phyllis
The Orphan
Pinto
The River's End
Nichols, Guy
1915 David Harum
Nichols, Margaret see **Nichols,
Marguerite**
Nichols, Marguerite same as **Nichols,
Margaret**
1915 Beulah
1916 Dust
The Girl O' Dreams
Little Mary Sunshine
The Matrimonial Martyr
Pay Dirt
The Power of Evil
Reclamation
The Strength of Donald
McKenzie
The Torch Bearer
Youth's Endearing Charm
1917 Sold at Auction
When Baby Forgot
Nichols, Norma
1916 The Ne'er-Do-Well
1917 The Tides of Barnegat
1918 The Legion of Death
Nichols, R. W.
1917 In Again—Out Again
Nicholson, Capt. J. E. same as
**Nicholson, Capt.; could be same as
Nicholson, John**
1917 The Best Man
The Phantom Shotgun

Nicholson, John could be same as
Nicholson, Capt. J. E.
1915 The Fixer
The Politicians
The Spendthrift
The Woman Next Door
1917 Kidnapped
The Planter
Wrath
1920 The Discarded Woman
Nicholson, Meredith
1916 Langdon's Legacy
Nicholson, Paul
1917 Princess Virtue
Nickerson, Clark R.
1916 The Law Decides
Whom the Gods Destroy
1917 The Courage of Silence
The Sixteenth Wife
Within the Law
Womanhood, the Glory of the
Nation
Niederaur, Lillian
1915 The Game of Three
Nielsen, Agnes
1917 The Girl Who Didn't Think
Nielsen, F. O.
1915 Guarding Old Glory
Nielson, Agnes see **Neilsen, Agnes**
Niemeyer, Bernard
1917 The Little Samaritan
Nietz, Alvin J. see **Neitz, Alvin J.**
Nigh, William could be same as **Nye,
William**
1914 Salomy Jane
1915 Emmy of Stork's Nest
Mignon
A Royal Family
A Yellow Streak
1916 The Child of Destiny
Her Debt of Honor
His Great Triumph
The Kiss of Hate
Life's Shadows
1917 The Blue Streak
The Slave
Thou Shalt Not Steal
Wife Number Two
1918 The Kaiser's Finish
My Four Years in Germany
1919 Beware
The Fighting Roosevelts
1920 Democracy
Skinning Skinners
Nigh, Mrs. William
1916 His Great Triumph
Nillson, Carlotta
1913 Leah Kleschna
Nilson, Alex same as **Neilson, Alec;
Nilson, Alec**
1917 The Corner Grocer
1918 To Him That Hath
Nilsson, Anna Q. same as **Nilsson,
Anna; not the same as Neilson,
Anna**
1914 Wolfe; Or, The Conquest of
Quebec
1915 Barbara Frietchie
Regeneration
1916 Her Surrender
The Scarlet Road
The Supreme Sacrifice
1917 The Inevitable
Infidelity
The Moral Code
Over There
Seven Keys to Baldpate
1918 Heart of the Sunset
In Judgment Of
No Man's Land
The Trail to Yesterday
The Vanity Pool
1919 Auction of Souls
Cheating Cheaters
Her Kingdom of Dreams
The Love Burglar
Soldiers of Fortune
A Sporting Chance (Famous
Players-Lasky Corp.)*
Venus in the East
A Very Good Young Man
The Way of the Strong

1920 The Brute Master
　　　The Fighting Chance
　　　The Figurehead
　　　In the Heart of a Fool
　　　The Luck of the Irish
　　　One Hour Before Dawn
　　　The Thirteenth Commandment
　　　The Toll Gate

Nix, E. D.
1915 Passing of the Oklahoma
　　　Outlaw

Noa, J.
1918 The Gulf Between

Noar, Florence
1916 The Seekers

Noble, G. M.
1915 Rule G

Noble, John W.
1914 The Three of Us
1915 The Bigger Man
　　　Black Fear
　　　Fighting Bob
　　　The High Road
　　　One Million Dollars
　　　The Right of Way
　　　Satan Sanderson
1916 The Awakening of Helena
　　　Richie
　　　The Brand of Cowardice
　　　Man and His Soul
　　　A Million a Minute
　　　The Red Mouse
　　　Romeo and Juliet (Quality
　　　Pictures Corp.)
　　　The Wall Between
1917 The Beautiful Lie
　　　The Call of Her People
　　　A Magdalene of the Hills
　　　The Power of Decision
　　　Shame
　　　Sunshine Alley
1918 The Birth of a Race
　　　My Own United States
1919 The Golden Shower
　　　The Gray Towers Mystery
1920 Footlights and Shadows
　　　The Song of the Soul

Nobles, Milton
1917 The Courage of Silence
　　　The Price of Pride

Nobles, W. W. see **Nobles, William**

Nobles, William same as **Nobles, W. W.**
1917 The Little Patriot
1919 Child of M'sieu
1920 The Man from Nowhere

Noel, Miss
1920 The Mysteries of Paris

Noel, Renee
1915 The Blindness of Virtue

Noell, William
1920 The Wonder Man

Nolan, Edward
1920 Down Home

Noldie, Baby Doris
1920 Women Men Love

Nomis, Leo
1916 Joan the Woman

Nood, A. Voorhees could be same as
　　Wood, A. Voorhees
1918 The Glorious Adventure

Noonan, Francis J.
1919 The Fighting Roosevelts

Norcross, Frank same as **Norcross, F.**
1915 The Magic Toy Maker
1916 East Lynne
　　　The Eternal Sapho
　　　The Final Curtain
1917 The Master Passion
　　　The Stolen Paradise
1918 The Accidental Honeymoon
　　　The Blind Adventure
　　　The Oldest Law
　　　The Other Man
　　　The Soap Girl
1919 Beating the Odds
　　　Beware
　　　Fortune's Child
　　　The Girl-Woman
　　　The Spark Divine
　　　The Undercurrent
1920 The Fortune Hunter
　　　Nineteen and Phyllis
　　　The Sea Rider

Nord, Hilda
1917 The Web of Life

Norden, Virginia
1916 The Combat
　　　The Destroyers
1918 Virtuous Wives
1919 Mind the Paint Girl

Nordine, Miss
1915 The Great Ruby

Nordquist, Pete
1918 The Hell Cat

Nordyke, Kenneth
1918 Cupid by Proxy
　　　The Ranger

Norman (full name unknown)
1915 The Fairy and the Waif*

Norman, Gertrude
1914 One of Millions
　　　The Unwelcome Mrs. Hatch
1915 Fanchon the Cricket
　　　A Girl of Yesterday
　　　May Blossom
　　　The Pretty Sister of Jose
1916 The Feud Girl
　　　Molly Make-Believe
　　　The Reward of Patience
1917 The Adopted Son
　　　Heart's Desire
　　　Persuasive Peggy
1918 The Studio Girl
　　　The Unbeliever
1919 An Innocent Adventuress
　　　Strictly Confidential
　　　Widow by Proxy
1920 The Brand of Lopez

Norman, Grace
1915 The Game of Three

Norman, Henry
1916 Love's Pilgrimage to America

Norman, Karin
1915 Mortmain
　　　Mother's Roses
1916 The Ordeal of Elizabeth

Norman, Vera
1916 The Dollar and the Law

Norman, Victor
1916 The Dollar and the Law

Normand, Mabel
1914 Tillie's Punctured Romance
1915 My Valet
1918 Back to the Woods
　　　Dodging a Million
　　　The Floor Below
　　　Joan of Plattsburg
　　　Mickey
　　　Peck's Bad Girl
　　　A Perfect 36
　　　The Venus Model
1919 Jinx
　　　The Pest
　　　Sis Hopkins
　　　Upstairs
　　　When Doctors Disagree
1920 Pinto
　　　The Slim Princess
　　　What Happened to Rosa

Norris, Joseph L.
1916 The Vital Question

Norris, Richard
1919 The Boomerang

Norris, William
1914 A Good Little Devil

North, Bobby
1917 Daughter of Destiny
1918 The Life Mask

North, Wilfrid same as **North, Wilfred**
1915 The Battle Cry of Peace
　　　Hearts and the Highway
1916 The Blue Envelope Mystery
　　　The Dollar and the Law
　　　Green Stockings
　　　Hesper of the Mountains
　　　The Kid
　　　Mrs. Dane's Danger
　　　The Ordeal of Elizabeth
　　　Salvation Joan
1917 Clover's Rebellion
　　　Indiscretion
　　　Kitty MacKay
　　　Sally in a Hurry
1918 Over the Top
1919 Human Desire
　　　Mind the Paint Girl

　　　The Undercurrent
1920 Oil

Northmore, Mary
1918 Little Miss Grown-Up

Northrup, Ethel
1917 The Renaissance at Charleroi

Northrup, H. S. see **Northrup, Harry S.**

Northrup, Harry S.
1914 The Christian
1915 Hearts and the Highway
　　　To Cherish and Protect
1916 The Blue Envelope Mystery
　　　Britton of the Seventh
　　　Fathers of Men
　　　Fifty-Fifty
　　　My Lady's Slipper
　　　The Traveling Salesman
1917 The Beautiful Lie
　　　The Greatest Power
　　　Greed
　　　The Millionaire's Double
　　　Their Compact
　　　The Trail of the Shadow
　　　The Voice of Conscience
1918 Arizona
　　　The Eyes of Mystery
　　　In Judgment Of
　　　The Trail to Yesterday
1919 As the Sun Went Down
　　　The Brute Breaker
　　　The Fear Woman
　　　The Hushed Hour
　　　The Painted World
　　　Two Women
　　　The Way of the Strong
1920 The Blue Moon
　　　The Luck of the Irish
　　　Polly of the Storm Country
　　　The Prince of Avenue A
　　　The White Circle

Northrup, Mrs. Henry see **Esmond, Merceita**

Norton, Edgar
1916 The Ocean Waif
1917 The Amazons
　　　The Beautiful Adventure
1918 A Pair of Cupids
1920 The New York Idea

Norton, Katherine
1920 The Forbidden Thing

Norton, Mary
1916 Wall Street Tragedy

Norton, Pearlie
1920 Isobel; Or, The Trail's End

Norton, S. M. see **Norton, Stephen S.**

Norton, Stephen S. same as **Norton, S. M.; Norton, S. S.; Norton, Stephen; Norton, Steve; Norton, Steve S.**
1915 The Silent Command
1916 The Eye of God
　　　Gloriana
　　　John Needham's Double
　　　The Seekers
　　　Shoes
　　　Where Are My Children?
1917 Double Room Mystery
　　　The Double Standard
　　　A Wife on Trial
1918 Beyond the Shadows
　　　Closin' In
　　　The Grey Parasol
　　　Heiress for a Day
　　　Hell's End
　　　The Man Who Woke Up
　　　Nancy Comes Home
　　　Wild Life
1919 The Follies Girl
　　　Love's Prisoner
　　　Restless Souls
1920 Bubbles
　　　The Peddler of Lies
　　　Shore Acres

Norton, William A.
1916 The Unpardonable Sin

Norwood, John
1919 The Right to Lie

Norworth, Ned
1919 The Microbe

Noskowski, Lawrence see **Nowskowski, L. de**

Nosler, Lloyd same as **Nosler, Lloyd L.**
1919 The Great Air Robbery
1920 Desert Love

Nounnan, Frazier
1920 The Key to Power

Nova, Hedda
1917 The Bar Sinister
1918 By the World Forgot
　　　The Changing Woman
　　　The Sign Invisible
1919 Calibre 38
　　　The Crimson Gardenia
　　　Mary Regan
　　　The Spitfire of Seville
1920 The Turning Point

Novak, Eva
1919 The Feud
　　　The Speed Maniac
1920 The Daredevil
　　　Desert Love
　　　Silk Husbands and Calico
　　　Wives
　　　The Testing Block
　　　Up in Mary's Attic
　　　Wanted at Headquarters

Novak, Jane
1915 A Little Brother of the Rich
　　　The Scarlet Sin
　　　Tainted Money
　　　The White Scar
1916 The Iron Hand
　　　The Target
1917 The Eyes of the World
　　　The Innocent Sinner
　　　The Spirit of '76
1918 The Claws of the Hun
　　　A Nine O'Clock Town
　　　Selfish Yates
　　　String Beans
　　　The Temple of Dusk
　　　The Tiger Man
1919 Behind the Door
　　　The Fire Flingers
　　　His Debt
　　　Man's Desire
　　　The Money Corral
　　　Treat 'Em Rough
　　　Wagon Tracks
　　　The Wolf
1920 The Barbarian
　　　The Golden Trail
　　　The Great Accident
　　　Isobel; Or, The Trail's End
　　　The River's End

Nowell, Wedgwood
1915 The Disciple
　　　The Golden Claw
　　　Matrimony
　　　The Winged Idol
1916 The Beggar of Cawnpore
　　　Between Men
　　　The Chalice of Sorrow
　　　The Conqueror
　　　D'Artagnan
　　　The Deserter
　　　The Sorrows of Love
1917 Black Orchids
　　　The Flower of Doom
　　　The Hand That Rocks the
　　　Cradle
　　　The Mysterious Mr. Tiller
　　　The Pulse of Life
　　　The Reward of the Faithless
1918 Money Isn't Everything
　　　The Velvet Hand
1919 Adele
　　　The Beauty Market
　　　Diane of the Green Van
　　　Her Purchase Price
　　　Kitty Kelly, M.D.
　　　The Lord Loves the Irish
　　　The Man Beneath
　　　The Man Who Turned White
　　　A Man's Fight
1920 The Corsican Brothers
　　　The Dream Cheater
　　　813

Nowland, Alice
1919 The Lion's Den

Nowland, Eugene
1915 Vanity Fair
1916 A Bird of Prey
　　　The Flight of the Duchess

1917 Threads of Fate
1918 Peg O' the Sea
Nowskowski, L. de *same as* **Noskowski, Lawrence**
1916 Macbeth
1917 Polly Put the Kettle On
Noyes, Beatrice
1916 The Sphinx
Nurnberger, Joseph E. *same as* **Nurnberger, J. E.; Nurnberger, Prof. J. E.; Nurnberger, Joseph**
1915 Aloha Oe
      The Edge of the Abyss
      The Iron Strain*
      Matrimony
      The Winged Idol
1916 Between Men
      D'Artagnan
Nutt, Lieut. C. C.
1920 Sky Eye
Nye, G. Raymond
1916 Is Any Girl Safe?
1917 The Curse of Eve
      When a Man Sees Red
1918 Ali Baba and the Forty Thieves
      For Freedom
      The Girl with the Champagne Eyes
      Salome
      The Strange Woman
      True Blue
      Under the Yoke
1919 Broken Commandments
      The Jungle Trail
      The Last of the Duanes
      The Lone Star Ranger
      When Men Desire
      Wings of the Morning
      Wolves of the Night
1920 Drag Harlan
      The Joyous Troublemaker
      The Orphan
      Sand!
      The Scuttlers
Nye, Ned
1915 A Mother's Confession
      The Unwelcome Wife
Nye, Oscar
1916 The Victim
Nye, William *could be same as* **Nigh, William**
1918 The Rainbow Trail

O

Oaker, John
1915 The Majesty of the Law
1916 The Conscience of John David
      The Hidden Law
      Joan the Woman
      The Soul's Cycle
      The Wasted Years
1917 Lorelei of the Sea
      The Single Code
1918 The Finger of Justice
1919 The Sneak
Oakland (full name unknown)
1915 The Fairy and the Waif*
Oakland, Ethelmary
1915 Always in the Way
      Hearts of Men
1916 Divorce and the Daughter
      The Shine Girl
      The World and the Woman
1917 The Dummy
Oakland, Vivian
1915 Destiny; Or, The Soul of a Woman
Oakley, Laura
1915 Lord John in New York
1916 The Dumb Girl of Portici
1918 Two-Gun Betty
Oakman, Gertrude
1917 The Lad and the Lion
Oakman, Wheeler
1914 In the Days of the Thundering Herd
      The Spoilers
1915 The Carpet from Bagdad
      The Rosary
      Sweet Alyssum

1916 The Battle of Hearts
      The Cycle of Fate
      The Ne'er-Do-Well
1917 Betrayed
      Princess Virtue
1918 The Claim
      Face Value
      I Love You
      Mickey
      Revenge
1919 Eve in Exile
      False Evidence
      The Splendid Sin
      A Woman of Pleasure
1920 Outside the Law
      The Virgin of Stamboul
      What Women Love
O'Beck, Ferdinand
1915 The Great Divide
Oberle, Florence
1915 A Daughter of the City
      The White Sister
1916 According to the Code
      The Little Shepherd of Bargain Row
      The Prince of Graustark
      Vultures of Society
1917 Skinner's Dress Suit
1918 Her Country First
1920 Haunting Shadows
O'Brien, Eugene
1915 Just Out of College
      The Moonstone
1916 The Chaperon
      Poor Little Peppina
      The Return of Eve
      The Rise of Susan
      The Scarlet Woman
1917 The Moth
      National Red Cross Pageant*
      Poppy
      Rebecca of Sunnybrook Farm
1918 By Right of Purchase
      De Luxe Annie
      The Ghosts of Yesterday
      Her Only Way
      Little Miss Hoover
      A Romance of the Underworld
      The Safety Curtain
      Under the Greenwood Tree
1919 The Broken Melody
      Come Out of the Kitchen
      Fires of Faith
      The Perfect Lover
      Sealed Hearts
1920 Broadway and Home
      The Figurehead
      A Fool and His Money
      His Wife's Money
      The Wonderful Chance
O'Brien, Geraldine
1914 A Lady of Quality
1915 Excuse Me
      His Wife
1916 A Woman's Fight
O'Brien, Gypsy
1916 The Soul Market
1919 Wanted—A Husband
1920 The Master Mind
      Nothing but Lies
O'Brien, John B. *same as* **O'Brien, Jack; O'Brien, John; O'Brien, John D.** *could be same as* **O'Brien, John J.**
1915 Captain Macklin
      Her Shattered Idol
      The Outcast
1916 The Big Sister
      Destiny's Toy
      The Eternal Grind
      The Flying Torpedo
      The Foundling
      Hulda from Holland
      Vanity
1917 Bab's Diary
      The Buffalo Bill Show*
      Daughter of Maryland
      Her Sister
      Mary Lawson's Secret
      Maternity
      Queen X
      Reputation
      Souls Triumphant
      The Unforseen

1918 The Girl and the Judge
      The Inn of the Blue Moon
      The Street of Seven Stars
1919 The Bishop's Emeralds
      Impossible Catherine
1920 The Stealers
      Wings of Pride
O'Brien, John J. *could be same as* **O'Brien, John B.**
1917 The Buffalo Bill Show
O'Brien, Thomas E. *same as* **O'Brien, Thomas; O'Brien, Tom**
1914 The Escape*
1915 The Birth of a Nation
1919 The Mints of Hell
      Square Deal Sanderson
1920 The Sagebrusher
      Their Mutual Child
Obrock, Herman, Jr.
1916 Passers By
      Sally in Our Alley
O'Brody, John
1916 Sally in Our Alley
O'Connell, Cardinal William Henry
1914 His Holiness, the Late Pope Pius X, and the Vatican
O'Connell, L. W. *see* **O' Connell, William**
O'Connell, Peggy
1917 Whither Thou Goest
1918 His Majesty, Bunker Bean
O'Connell, William *same as* **O'Connell, L. W.**
1916 The Victory of Conscience
      Witchcraft
1918 Missing
1920 The Little Grey Mouse
      Suds
O'Connor (full name unknown)
1916 The Code of Marcia Gray*
O'Connor, A.
1915 God's Witness
O'Connor, Edward *same as* **O'Connor, Eddie**
1915 The Woman Next Door
1916 Hazel Kirke
      The Man Who Stood Still
1917 The Courage of the Common Place
      One Touch of Nature
1918 Cecilia of the Pink Roses
1919 Kathleen Mavourneen
O'Connor, Frank *could be same as* **O'Connor, Frank L. A.**
1918 The Crucible of Life
      Little Miss No-Account
1919 The Unwritten Code
1920 Blind Love
      The Furnace
O'Connor, Frank L. A. *could be same as* **O'Connor, Frank**
1917 Madame Sherry
      The Silent Witness
O'Connor, Harry M. *same as* **O'Connor, H. M.**
1918 Blindfolded
1919 The Dub
      The Long Lane's Turning
O'Connor, J.
1919 Out of the Fog
O'Connor, Jack
1915 Rule G
O'Connor, James
1916 East Lynne
O'Connor, John
1917 Cassidy
O'Connor, Kathleen
1918 Missing
1919 A Gun Fightin' Gentleman
1920 Bullet Proof
      The Path She Chose
      Prairie Trails
O'Connor, Lew *same as* **O'Connor, L. J.; O'Connor, Louis J.**
1920 A Manhattan Knight
      Partners of the Night
O'Connor, Loyola
1915 The Country Boy
      The Lily and the Rose
      Out of the Darkness
      The Secret Orchard
      The Secret Sin*

1916 Atta Boy's Last Race
      A Child of the Paris Streets
      The Children Pay
      Hoodoo Ann
      Intolerance
      The Little Liar
      The Missing Links
      Stranded
1917 Cheerful Givers
      Nina, the Flower Girl
      An Old Fashioned Young Man
1919 The Fall of Babylon
      The Love Burglar
      True Heart Susie
1920 Eyes of the Heart
      Harriet and the Piper
      Old Dad
      The Tree of Knowledge
O'Connor, Mary H. *same as* **O'Connor, Mary**
1915 Infatuation
      Jordan Is a Hard Road*
      The Lonesome Heart
      The Lure of the Mask
      The Penitentes
      Up from the Depths
      A Yankee from the West
1916 Cross Currents
      Hell-to-Pay Austin
      A House Built upon Sand
1917 Cheerful Givers
      The Girl of the Timber Claims
      Nina, the Flower Girl
      Souls Triumphant
1920 The Sins of Rosanne
O'Day, William
1919 The Silver King
Odd, Charles
1916 The Beast
Oddie, Gov. Tasker L.
1913 The Tonopah Stampede for Gold
Odell, George *same as* **Odell, George R.**
1916 The Vixen
1917 Bab's Burglar
      Bab's Diary
      Bab's Matinee Idol
      Fighting Odds
      The Planter
1918 The Wolf and His Mate
O'Dell, H.
1915 Pennington's Choice
Odell, Maude
1915 Gambier's Advocate
      Niobe
Odell, Robert A.
1920 The Little 'Fraid Lady
      Occasionally Yours
O'Donnell, Gene
1920 Man and Woman (A. H. Fischer Features, Inc.)
O'Donnell, George
1916 My Lady's Slipper
1917 Cy Whittaker's Ward
1919 A Stitch in Time
      Too Many Crooks
O'Donnell, Joseph
1914 Neptune's Daughter
O'Donnell, Thomas
1920 The Woman God Sent
O'Donohue, M. T.
1915 The Arrival of Perpetua
O'Farrell, Broderick
1920 The Golden Trail
Offatt, Edith
1915 York State Folks
Offerd, Bert
1917 Flying Colors
Offerman, George
1917 S.O.S.
Ogden (full name unknown)
1915 The Fairy and the Waif*
Ogden, Vivia *same as* **Ogden, Viva**
1917 The Corner Grocer
1919 Mrs. Wiggs of the Cabbage Patch
1920 Way Down East
Ogle, Charles
1915 Under Southern Skies
      The Woman Who Lied
1916 The Heir to the Hoorah
      The Years of the Locust

1917 The Cost of Hatred
Nan of Music Mountain
On Record
Rebecca of Sunnybrook Farm
A Romance of the Redwoods
The Secret Game
The Sunset Trail
Those Without Sin
1918 Believe Me Xantippe
The Firefly of France
The Goat
Jules of the Strong Heart
Less Than Kin
M'liss
Rimrock Jones
The Source
The Squaw Man
The Thing We Love
Too Many Millions
We Can't Have Everything
Wild Youth
1919 Alias Mike Moran
A Daughter of the Wolf*
The Dub
Everywoman
Fires of Faith
Hawthorne of the U.S.A.
The Heart of Youth
Men, Women and Money
The Poor Boob
Something to Do
Told in the Hills
Under the Top
The Valley of the Giants
1920 Conrad in Quest of His Youth
Jack Straw
The Prince Chap
Treasure Island
What's Your Hurry?
Young Mrs. Winthrop
1921 The Jucklins
Midsummer Madness

O'Hara, George
1920 Love, Honor and Behave

O'Hara, John
1915 An Enemy to Society

O'Hara, W. A.
1917 Over There

Ohlson, Albert J. *same as* **Ohlson, Al J.**
1917 Womanhood, the Glory of the
Nation
1918 A Diplomatic Mission

Ojeda, Manuel *same as* **Ojeda, Michael R.**
1918 The Law of the North
1919 The Man Who Turned White
Rustling a Bride
1920 A Double Dyed Deceiver
Pinto
The Scuttlers

O'Keefe, John
1917 The Public Defender
1918 Suspicion

O'Keefe, Thomas *same as* **O'Keefe, Tom**
1914 Captain Swift
1915 The Curious Conduct of Judge
Legarde
The Plunderer*
The Unbroken Road
1916 The Kiss
Vanity
1917 A Girl Like That
1920 The Valley of Night

Okuga, Otto
1918 On the Quiet

Oland, Warner
1915 Destruction
Sin
The Unfaithful Wife
1916 The Eternal Question
The Eternal Sapho
The Reapers
The Rise of Susan
1917 The Cigarette Girl
1918 Convict 993
The Mysterious Client
The Naulahka
The Yellow Ticket
1919 The Avalanche
Mandarin's Gold
The Twin Pawns
The Witness for the Defense

Olcott, Sidney
1913 From the Manger to the Cross
1915 Madame Butterfly
The Moth and the Flame
Seven Sisters
1916 The Daughter of MacGregor
Diplomacy
The Innocent Lie
My Lady Incog.
Poor Little Peppina
The Smugglers
1918 The Belgian
1919 Marriage for Convenience
1920 The Gray Brother
Scratch My Back

Old Rosebud, a horse
1919 Checkers

Olesen, Ellen *could be same as* **Olson, Ellen**
1920 The Harvest Moon

Oliver, Clarence
1918 Laughing Bill Hyde
The Racing Strain
The Service Star

Oliver, Guy
1915 The Carpet from Bagdad
The Circular Staircase
I'm Glad My Boy Grew Up to
Be a Soldier
1916 Into the Primitive
Thou Shalt Not Covet
The Valiants of Virginia
1917 The Bottle Imp
The Call of the East
Each to His Kind
Freckles
The Golden Fetter
The Hostage
The Little American
Nan of Music Mountain
Those Without Sin
1918 The Bravest Way
Jules of the Strong Heart
Less Than Kin
M'liss
Rimrock Jones
The Squaw Man
Such a Little Pirate
The Whispering Chorus
1919 Alias Mike Moran
The Dub
Hawthorne of the U.S.A.
The Heart of Youth
In Mizzoura
It Pays to Advertise
Male and Female
The Poor Boob
Putting It Over
The Roaring Road
Rustling a Bride
Secret Service
Told in the Hills
Under the Top
The Valley of the Giants
Venus in the East
1920 Always Audacious
A Cumberland Romance
Double Speed
Excuse My Dust
The Round-Up
The Sins of Rosanne
The Sins of St. Anthony
1921 The Jucklins

Oliver, Harold G.
1919 Behind the Door
The Grim Game
1920 Below the Surface
Down Home

Olmstead, Stanley *same as* **Olmsted, Stanley**
1918 Find the Woman
One Thousand Dollars
1919 Cupid Forecloses
Dawn
The Moonshine Trail
1920 The Blood Barrier
Man and His Woman
My Husband's Other Wife
Passers-By
Respectable by Proxy

O'Loughlin, Jack
1918 Beyond the Law

Olson, Ellen *could be same as* **Olesen, Ellen**
1920 The Amateur Wife

Olsson, Robert A.
1918 Beyond the Law

O'Madigan, Isabel
1916 Merely Mary Ann
A Parisian Romance
1917 Bab's Burglar
Bab's Diary
Bab's Matinee Idol
1918 The Better Half
Five Thousand an Hour
Madame Jealousy
The Make-Believe Wife
The Studio Girl
Sylvia on a Spree
1919 Courage for Two
The Love Defender
Love in a Hurry
Suspense

O'Malley, Pat *same as* **O'Malley, Patrick**
1915 Gladiola
On Dangerous Paths
1917 The Adopted Son
The Barker
The Law of the North
The Love That Lives
The Tell-Tale Step
1918 Her Boy
Hit-the-Trail Holliday
The Prussian Cur
She Hired a Husband
1919 False Evidence
The Heart of Humanity
1920 The Blooming Angel
The Breath of the Gods
Dinty
Go and Get It
The Heart of a Woman
Sherry

O'Malley, Thomas F. *same as* **O'Malley, Thomas**
1917 The Deemster
Peggy, the Will O' the Wisp
1920 The Law of the Yukon

O'Mara, Jack
1918 The Way Out

O'Moore, Charles
1919 The Shepherd of the Hills*

O'Neil, Mr.
1915 The Fairy and the Waif*

O'Neil, Mrs.
1915 The Fairy and the Waif*

O'Neil, Barry
1913 The Third Degree
1914 The House Next Door
The Lion and the Mouse
The Fortune Hunter
The Wolf
1915 Bought
The Climbers
The College Widow
The District Attorney
The Great Ruby
The Sporting Duchess
1916 The Evangelist
The Hidden Scar
Husband and Wife
Life's Whirlpool
The Revolt
The Unpardonable Sin
The Weakness of Man
A Woman's Way

O'Neil, Frank
1914 A Florida Enchantment

O'Neil, Jim (*Western actor*)
1914 The Lure
1919 Miss Arizona
1920 Two Moons
West Is West

O'Neil, Nance
1915 Kreutzer Sonata
Princess Romanoff
A Woman's Past
1916 The Flames of Johannis
The Iron Woman
Souls in Bondage
Those Who Toil
The Witch
1917 The Final Payment
Greed
Hedda Gabler

Mrs. Balfame
The Seventh Sin
1918 The Fall of the Romanoffs

O'Neil, Peggy (*actress and model; could be two persons of the same name*)
1913 The Battle of Shiloh
1915 Old Dutch*
1917 The Penny Philanthropist
1920 The Sleep of Cyma Roget

O'Neill, George Kerr
1916 The Unpardonable Sin

O'Neill, James (*actor, born* U.S. *ca. 1870*) *same as* **O'Neill, James, Jr.** *not the same as* **O'Neill, James** (*actor, born* Ireland, *1847*) *Note: Some films listed below may have been the work of one or more other actors with this name who worked during the teens.*
1913 Ben Bolt
The Star of India
1914 A Fight for Freedom; Or,
Exiled to Siberia
The Million Dollar Robbery
The Temptations of Satan
1915 Her Own Way
My Madonna
1916 The Honor of Mary Blake
The Traveling Salesman
1917 The Boy Girl
God of Little Children
House of Cards
Little Miss Nobody
The Raggedy Queen
Susan's Gentleman
1918 The Grain of Dust
1920 Captain Swift
The Courage of Marge
O'Doone
King Spruce
The Red Lane
The Whisper Market

O'Neill, James (*actor, born* Ireland, *1847*)
1913 The Count of Monte Cristo

O'Neill, Thomas
1916 The Honor of Mary Blake

O'Neill, William
1916 Whoso Findeth a Wife
1917 Susan's Gentleman

Ong, Dana
1915 The Cheat
1916 Wanted—A Home
1917 Broadway Arizona
1918 The Flash of Fate

Ongley, Amy
1920 The Deep Purple

Onslow, Alex
1920 Footlights and Shadows

Onzevdo, Louis
1919 Out of the Fog

Oppenheim, Arthur
1915 The Eternal City

Oppenheim, Howard
1918 A Successful Adventure

Oppenheim, James
1916 The Cossack Whip
1917 The Ghost of Old Morro

Opperman, Frank
1915 My Valet

O'Ramie, Georgia
1914 The $5,000,000 Counterfeiting
Plot

Ordynski, Richard
1917 The Rose of Blood

O'Reilly, Tex
1920 Honeymoon Ranch

Orlamond, Ruth *could be same as* **Orlamonde, Mrs.**
1919 Johnny-on-the-Spot

Orlamond, William *same as* **Orlamond, William H.;could be** *same as* **Orlemond, W. A.**
1919 A Rogue's Romance
1920 Body and Soul
Madame Peacock
Stronger Than Death

Orlamonde, Mrs. *could be same as* **Orlamond, Ruth**
1920 The Amazing Woman
The Yellow Typhoon

Orlando, Nicholas
1919 The Spirit of Lafayette
Orlemond, W. A. *could be same as* **Orlamond, William**
1914 The Pit
Ormand, Robert
1915 Maciste
Ormonde, Eugene
1915 Bella Donna
    The Dancing Girl
    The Morals of Marcus
1916 Betty of Graystone
    Manhattan Madness
    Slander
1917 A Modern Musketeer
    Reaching for the Moon
1918 The Caillaux Case
    The Woman Who Gave
1919 The Light
Ormont, James
1916 The House of Mirrors
Ormston, Frank *same as* **Ormston, Frank D.; Ormstrom, Frank D.**
1914 Damon and Pythias
    The Merchant of Venice
    Richelieu
    Samson
1915 The College Orphan
    Colorado
    The Hypocrites
    The Long Chance
1916 The Dumb Girl of Portici
    20,000 Leagues Under the Sea
1917 The Price of a Good Time
1918 For Husbands Only
    A Japanese Nightingale
1919 The Beloved Cheater
    The Man Beneath
1920 Kismet
Ormstrom, Frank D. *see* **Ormston, Frank**
O'Rourke, Eugene
1917 Within the Law
O'Rourke, Jane
1918 The Finger of Justice
Orr, Stanley
1919 The Love Hunger
Ortego, Art *same as* **Ortego, Arthur; Ortego, Artie**
1915 The Girl of the Golden West
1916 American Aristocracy
1917 The Avenging Trail
1918 Broadway Bill
1920 Skyfire
Ortego, John
1915 The Girl of the Golden West
Orth, Dorothy
1919 Checkers
Orth, Louise
1919 Three Black Eyes
Orth, Marion
1917 The Price of a Good Time
1918 Borrowed Clothes
Ortlieb, Alfred
1915 Greater Love Hath No Man
    The Heart of a Painted Woman
    The Shooting of Dan McGrew
1918 Annexing Bill
    Lafayette, We Come!
    Waifs
1919 The A.B.C. of Love
    The Thirteenth Chair
    The Twin Pawns
    The Unknown Love
1920 Deep Waters
    Lifting Shadows
    A Modern Salome
    The White Circle
Osborne, Mr.
1912 Cleopatra
Osborne, Bud
1916 A Knight of the Range
    Love's Lariat
1920 The Galloping Devil
    Vengeance and the Girl
Osborne, Hugh R.
1919 Nugget Nell*
Osborne, Jefferson *same as* **Osborne, Jeff**
1914 The Last Egyptian
1920 Homespun Folks
    Once a Plumber

Osborne, Leon T.
1919 The Arizona Cat Claw
1920 The One Way Trail
Osborne, Baby Marie *same as* **Osborne, Baby; Osborne, Baby Helen Marie; Osborne, Marie**
1915 Should a Wife Forgive?
1916 Joy and the Dragon
    Little Mary Sunshine
    Shadows and Sunshine
1917 Captain Kiddo
    The Little Patriot
    Sunshine and Gold
    Tears and Smiles
    Told at Twilight
    Twin Kiddies
    When Baby Forgot
1918 Cupid by Proxy
    Daddy's Girl
    A Daughter of the West
    Dolly Does Her Bit
    Dolly's Vacation
    Milady O' the Beanstalk
    The Voice of Destiny
    Winning Grandma
1919 Child of M'sieu
    The Little Diplomat
    The Old Maid's Baby
    The Sawdust Doll
Osborne, Ralph
1920 The Hidden Code
Osborne, Roland
1915 Mortmain
1919 The Undercurrent
Osborne, Thomas Mott
1915 Alias Jimmy Valentine*
1920 The Gray Brother
Osborne, Vivienne *same as* **Osborne, Vivian**
1920 The Gray Brother
    In Walked Mary
    Love's Flame
    Over the Hill to the Poorhouse
    The Restless Sex
O'Shea, James *same as* **O'Shea, James F.**
1915 The Spanish Jade
1916 Acquitted
    Hell-to-Pay Austin
    Little Meena's Romance
    The Marriage of Molly-O
    The Microscope Mystery
    The Rummy
    Susan Rocks the Boat
    The Wild Girl of the Sierras
1917 Jim Bludso
    A Love Sublime
    The Yankee Way
1920 Sink or Swim
Oskima, Mr.
1919 The Unwritten Code
Osmun, Leighton
1916 Each Pearl a Tear
    The Heir to the Hoorah
    The Storm
    Unprotected
    The Years of the Locust
1917 Betty to the Rescue
    Castles for Two
    The Devil-Stone
    Forbidden Paths
    The Inner Shrine
    The Jaguar's Claws
    Sacrifice
    Unconquered
1918 The Claim
    Treasure of the Sea
1920 The Woman Game
Osterman, Kathryn
1915 The Bludgeon
Ostland, Louis *same as* **Ostland, Lewis; Ostland, Lewis G.; Ostland, Louis G.**
1916 The Honor of Mary Blake
    The Narrow Path
1917 The Boy Girl
    Diamonds and Pearls*
    Her Hour
    The Marriage Market
    Susan's Gentleman
1918 The Beloved Blackmailer
    By Hook or Crook
    The Golden Wall
    Hitting the Trail
    The Purple Lily

    The Road to France
    The Wasp
Ostriche, Muriel
1915 The Daughter of the Sea
    Mortmain
    When It Strikes Home
1916 By Whose Hand?
    A Circus Romance
    Kennedy Square
    The Men She Married
    Sally in Our Alley
1917 The Dormant Power
    The Good for Nothing
    Moral Courage
    A Square Deal
    The Volunteer
    Youth
1918 Hitting the Trail
    Journey's End
    Leap to Fame
    Merely Players
    The Purple Lily
    The Road to France
    Tinsel
    The Way Out
1919 The Bluffer
    The Hand Invisible
    The Moral Deadline
    What Love Forgives
1920 The Sacred Flame
Ostrom, Harold
1914 The Patchwork Girl of Oz
Oswald, Emma K.
1916 The Invisible Enemy
Oswald, Howard
1919 The Pointing Finger
1920 The Peddler of Lies
Otis, Elita Proctor *same as* **Otis, Olita; Ottis, Oleta**
1914 The Great Diamond Robbery
    The Greyhound
1920 The Six Best Cellars
    The Triflers
    Under Northern Lights
Otte, Henri Rolf
1920 The Key to Power
Otten, Alice Morton
1916 Ramona
Ottinger, Leonora *same as* **von Ottinger, Leonora**
1916 The Narrow Path
1917 The Tell-Tale Step
1920 The Frisky Mrs. Johnson
Ottke, Ernest
1916 Tempest and Sunshine
Otto, Big *see* **Big Otto**
Otto, Frank
1917 The Raggedy Queen
    Shirley Kaye
1918 Who Loved Him Best?
Otto, Henry
1916 Big Tremaine
    Half a Rogue
    The Man from Nowhere
    Mister 44
    The River of Romance
    Undine
1917 The Butterfly Girl
    Lorelei of the Sea
1918 Angel Child
    Wild Life
1919 The Amateur Adventuress
    Fair and Warmer
    The Great Romance
    The Island of Intrigue
    The Microbe
    Some Bride
1920 The Cheater
    A Slave of Vanity
    The Willow Tree
Otto, Lorraine
1915 Vengeance of the Wilds
Outtrim, Irene
1915 Salvation Nell
1916 The Unwritten Law
1919 The Heart of Juanita
Overbaugh, Roy *same as* **Overbaugh, Roy F.**
1917 American—That's All
    A Case at Law
    Cassidy
    Grafters
    Her Father's Keeper

    The Man Who Made Good
    Panthea
1918 On the Jump
    The Prussian Cur
    Woman and the Law
1919 Erstwhile Susan
    The Misleading Widow
    Wanted—A Husband
1920 Away Goes Prudence
    A Dark Lantern
    Dr. Jekyll and Mr. Hyde
     (Famous Players-Lasky
     Corp.)
    39 East
Overstreet, Tommy
1918 The Hell Cat
Overton, Evart
1915 The Battle Cry of Peace
    Crooky
1916 The Enemy
    Hesper of the Mountains
    The Man Behind the Curtain
    The Ordeal of Elizabeth
    The Supreme Temptation
    The Two Edged Sword
1917 The Bottom of the Well
    The Glory of Yolanda
    The Love Doctor
    The Money Mill
    National Association's All-Star
     Picture
    Soldiers of Chance
1918 The Menace
1919 Mind the Paint Girl*
Owen, Cecil *same as* **Owens, Cecil**
1915 The Victory of Virtue
1917 The Girl by the Roadside
    The Greatest Power
    The Spreading Dawn
1918 A Pair of Sixes
1920 Hidden Charms
    The Wonder Man
Owen, Eugene
1917 Anything Once*
    Bondage
    The Hero of the Hour
1918 Her Moment
Owen, Myrtle
1920 The Third Woman
Owen, Seena *same as* **Aüen, Signe**
1915 Bred in the Bone
    The Fox Woman
    A Yankee from the West
    The Lamb
    The Penitentes
1916 Intolerance
    Martha's Vindication
1917 Madame Bo-Peep
    A Woman's Awakening
1918 Branding Broadway
1919 Breed of Men
    The City of Comrades
    The Fall of Babylon
    A Fugitive from Matrimony
    The Life Line
    A Man and His Money
    One of the Finest
    Riders of Vengeance
    The Sheriff's Son
    Victory
1920 The Gift Supreme
    The House of Toys
    The Price of Redemption
    Sooner or Later
Owens, Cecil *see* **Owen, Cecil**
Owens, Robert C.
1919 Injustice
Owens, Mrs. Wilhelmina
1919 Injustice
Ozuman, Dorothy
1915 Midnight at Maxim's

P

Paanakker, M. B.
1918 Up the Road with Sallie
Packard, Frank L.
1920 From Now On
    The Iron Rider

The Virgin of Stamboul
Parker-Spaulding, Nellie
1918 Her Great Chance
The House of Mirth
Parkhurst, C. H.
1916 Warning! The S.O.S. Call of Humanity
Parks, Frances
1919 The Girl Who Stayed Home
1920 The Figurehead
Jack Straw
Parks, George
1916 The King's Game
Parks-Jones, J. *see* **Jones, J. Parks**
Parkyn, Mary
1916 The Truant Soul
Parr, Charles T.
1918 The Kaiser's Finish
Parr, Peggy
1917 The Duchess of Doubt
Sowers and Reapers
1918 Sylvia on a Spree
The Winning of Beatrice
1919 The Cinema Murder
Lure of Ambition
1920 Love Without Question
Parsons, Agnes
1920 The Virgin of Stamboul*
Parsons, William *same as* **Parsons, William E.**
1915 The Tale of the Night Before
1916 The Argonauts of California—1849
The Invisible Enemy
1917 The Innocent Sinner
1918 Tarzan of the Apes
The Vigilantes
1919 The Blue Bonnet
1920 Eyes of the Heart
Pascal, Jane
1917 The Serpent's Tooth
Pasha, Kalla *same as* **Pascha, Kalla**
1919 The Wicked Darling
1920 Love, Honor and Behave
Married Life
Pasque, Ernest *same as* **Pasque, E.; Pasque, Ernst**
1918 A Man's Man
Too Many Millions
1919 The False Faces
The Fear Woman
Love Insurance
Upstairs and Down
1920 The Romance Promoters
Pastrone, Giovanni
1915 Maciste
Pasztor, John J.
1917 The Slacker's Heart
Patch, a dog
1920 The Mutiny of the Elsinore
Patch, Katherine
1917 Strife
Pathé, Polly *same as* **Green, Grace Wheeler**
1915 Seeing America First
Paton, Goldwin
1916 My Partner
Paton, Marie
1920 Sophy of Kravonia; Or, The Virgin of Paris
Paton, Stuart
1915 Conscience
Courtmartialed
The White Terror
1916 Elusive Isabel
The Mark of Cain
20,000 Leagues Under the Sea
1917 Beloved Jim
Like Wildfire
1918 The Border Raiders
The Girl in the Dark
The Marriage Lie
The Wine Girl
1919 The Blinding Trail
The Devil's Trail
The Little Diplomat
1920 Wanted at Headquarters
Patrick, Jerome
1919 Three Men and a Girl
1920 The Furnace
Her First Elopement
Officer 666

Pattee, Herbert *same as* **Pattee, H. H.; Pattee, Herbert Horton**
1916 The Salamander
1917 The Greater Woman
The Millionaire's Double
The Royal Pauper
The Skylight Room
The White Raven
1918 And the Children Pay
The Business of Life
For the Freedom of the East
Neighbors
1919 The Cambric Mask
The Darkest Hour
Sandy Burke of the U-Bar-U
Silent Strength
The Vengeance of Durand
1920 Captain Swift
The Prey
Patten, Gilbert
1916 The Crown Prince's Double
Patterson, Charles P.
1919 The Phantom Honeymoon
Patterson, Elmer
1917 The Eternal Sin
Patterson, Isabel
1916 Broken Fetters
Patterson, Joseph Medill
1914 On the Belgian Battlefield*
Patteson, Starke
1920 Sweet Lavender
Patton, Bill
1918 The Boss of the Lazy Y
Wild Life
1919 Bare-Fisted Gallagher
Leave It to Susan
A Sage Brush Hamlet
Patton, F. G.
1918 Peck's Bad Girl
Patton, Frank
1914 The Education of Mr. Pipp
Patton, William
1920 Sand!
Paul, Agnes
1917 Modern Mother Goose
Paul, Ellis
1917 Modern Mother Goose
The Saint's Adventure
Paul, Franklin
1915 The Man of Shame
Paul, Jack
1917 Little Shoes
Modern Mother Goose
Paul, Logan
1915 The Island of Regeneration
The Making Over of Geoffrey Manning
1916 Britton of the Seventh
Fathers of Men
The Island of Surprise
Kennedy Square
The Price of Fame
The Redemption of Dave Darcey
The Two Edged Sword
Whom the Gods Destroy
1917 Arsene Lupin
The Money Mill
The Streets of Illusion
1919 The Bandbox
Virtuous Men
Wild Oats
Paul, R. Holmes
1917 Alimony
1918 The Turn of a Card
Paul, Val
1915 The College Orphan
1916 The End of the Rainbow
The Girl of the Lost Lake
It Happened in Honolulu
A Romance of Billy Goat Hill
The Secret of the Swamp
1917 God's Crucible
The Lair of the Wolf
Mutiny
1918 Fame and Fortune
Mr. Logan, U.S.A.
M'liss
The Red, Red Heart
The Square Deal
1919 The Girl from Nowhere
Hoop-La
Smiles

Treat 'Em Rough
1920 Hearts Up
Sundown Slim
West Is West
Pauncefort, George *same as* **Pauncefote, George**
1915 The Running Fight
1916 Her Great Price
The Precious Packet
The Purple Lady
1919 Dawn
Marriage for Convenience
1920 The Key to Power
The White Moll
Pauzdrovna, Lola
1919 Calibre 38
Pavis, Marie
1914 Mrs. Black Is Back
1920 An Arabian Knight
Silk Hosiery
Pavis, Yvonne
1918 High Tide
1920 The Walk-Offs
Pavlowa, Anna
1916 The Dumb Girl of Portici
Pawelson, Arthur *see* **Powelson, Arthur**
Pawn, Doris
1916 Blue Blood and Red
Little Eve Edgarton
1917 The Book Agent
High Finance
Some Boy!
The Spirit of '76
1918 The City of Dim Faces
The Kid Is Clever
1919 The Beloved Cheater
Toby's Bow
1920 Li Ting Lang
Out of the Storm
The Strange Boarder
What Happened to Rosa
Paxton, George
1913 Shadows of the Moulin Rouge
Payne, Clarence
1919 The Price Woman Pays
1920 Who's Your Servant?
Payne, Herbert
1915 The Pageant of San Francisco
Payne, Louis
1915 Du Barry
Payne, Sidney
1920 The Brand of Lopez
The Corsican Brothers
The Devil's Claim
Payne, Will
1920 The Strange Boarder
Paynter, Corone
1918 Every Mother's Son
Payson, Blanche
1920 The Land of Jazz
Payson, William Farquhar
1917 Periwinkle
Payton, Claude *same as* **Peyton, Claude;** *could be same as* **Peyton, C.; Peyton, Charles**
1919 A Woman There Was
1920 Dice of Destiny
If I Were King
The Man Who Lost Himself
The Soul of Youth
Payton, Gloria
1917 A Branded Soul
Brand's Daughter
The Phantom Shotgun
The Yellow Bullet
1919 The Faith of the Strong
1920 Sunset Sprague
Payton, Lucy *same as* **Peyton, Lucy**
1915 The Last Concert
The Lure of the Mask
Secretary of Frivolous Affairs
1916 The Love Liar
Pamela's Past
Shadows and Sunshine
Where Are My Children?
1917 His Old-Fashioned Dad
The Yellow Bullet
Peacock, Lillian
1917 The Little Pirate

Peacocke, Capt. Leslie T. *same as* **Peacock, Captain Leslie; Peacock, Leslie T.**
1914 Neptune's Daughter
1915 Salvation Nell
1916 The Unwritten Law
The Woman Who Dared
1917 The Alien Blood
Bab the Fixer
Betty Be Good
Brand's Daughter
The Checkmate
The Clean Gun
Innocence
Mentioned in Confidence
1918 Angel Child
Whatever the Cost
1919 The Heart of Juanita
Injustice
The Price Woman Pays*
Shadows of Suspicion
1920 Neptune's Bride
Reformation
Peal, Henry
1918 Cheating the Public
Pearce, Betty
1918 Little Red Decides
The Love Brokers
Madame Sphinx
Real Folks
Pearce, George *same as* **Pierce, George**
1914 Three Weeks
1915 The Gambler of the West
The Sable Lorcha
1916 The Children in the House
Daphne and the Pirate
Let Katie Do It
Little Meena's Romance
The Little School Ma'am
Martha's Vindication
1917 Because of a Woman
'49-'17
Framing Framers
A Jewel in Pawn
The Reed Case
Treason
A Wife on Trial
1918 Closin' In
Crown Jewels
Desert Law
Everywoman's Husband
Little Red Decides
The Love Brokers
Mlle. Paulette
The Man Who Woke Up
Nancy Comes Home
Old Love for New
Real Folks
The Sea Flower
1919 A Gentleman of Quality
Man's Desire
The Mayor of Filbert
Whom the Gods Would Destroy
A Yankee Princess
1920 Her Husband's Friend
Pearce, Georgia
1916 Intolerance
Pearce, Harry C.
1917 The Spirit of '76*
Pearce, Jack
1915 Coral*
Pearce, Peggy
1918 False Ambition
The Golden Fleece
A Good Loser
The Red-Haired Cupid
1919 The Ace of the Saddle
False Evidence
More Deadly Than the Male
1920 Love Madness
Sex
A Tokio Siren
Pearl, Lloyd *see* **Perl, Lloyd**
Pearl, Queen
1916 The Rainbow Princess
Pearse, Thomas H. *same as* **Pearse, Tom** *could be same as* **Persse, Thomas D.**
1918 Hugon, the Mighty
1920 It's a Great Life

Pearson, F. M.
1917 Might and the Man
Pearson, H. B.
1917 High Speed
Pearson, Nannie
1915 The Valley of Lost Hope
Pearson, Virginia
1914 Aftermath
1915 The Turn of the Road
1916 Blazing Love
      Daredevil Kate
      The Hunted Woman
      Hypocrisy
      Thou Art the Man
      A Tortured Heart
      The Vital Question
      The War Bride's Secret
      The Writing on the Wall
1917 All for a Husband
      The Bitter Truth
      Royal Romance
      Sister Against Sister
      Thou Shalt Not Steal
      When False Tongues Speak
      Wrath of Love
1918 Buchanan's Wife
      A Daughter of France
      The Firebrand
      Her Price
      The Liar
      The Queen of Hearts
      Stolen Honor
1919 The Bishop's Emeralds
      Impossible Catherine
      The Love Auction
Pearson, W. B.
1916 Love's Lariat
1917 The Bronze Bride
1918 The Flash of Fate
      Hell's Crater
Pearson, William
1920 An Adventuress*
Peat, Harold R.
1918 Private Peat
Pecheur, Ruth
1920 Bitter Fruit
Peck, Charles Mortimer
1916 The Sting of Victory
1917 The Kill-Joy
      Pants
      Young Mother Hubbard
1918 The Law of the Great
          Northwest
      You Can't Believe Everything
1919 The Arizona Cat Claw
      Cheating Herself
      The Follies Girl
1920 The One Way Trail
Peck, Gladys
1915 Hearts of Men
      When It Strikes Home
Peck, Leah
1917 The Natural Law
Peckre, Maurice
1920 Humoresque
Pedlar, Gertrude
1920 White Youth
Peel, Edward J. see Peil, Edward
Peel, Hal
1917 Miss Deception
Peer, Richard
1915 The Ploughshare
Pegg, Vester same as **Pegg, Vesta**
1917 Bucking Broadway
      The Fighting Gringo
      A Marked Man
      The Secret Man
      Straight Shooting
1918 Hell Bent
      The Phantom Riders
      The Scarlet Drop
      Thieves' Gold
      Wild Women
      A Woman's Fool
1919 The Ace of the Saddle
      Bare Fists
      The Rider of the Law
1920 The Galloping Devil
      Vengeance and the Girl
Peggy, a dog
1919 A Man and His Money

Peil, Edward same as **Peel, Edward;
    Peel, Edward J.; Peil, Ed; Peil,
    Edward J.; Pell, Edward; Piel, E. J.;
    Piel, Edward; Piel, Edward J.;** not
    the same as **Peil, Edward, Jr.**
1914 The Ragged Earl
      Through Fire to Fortune
1916 At Piney Ridge
      The Stronger Love
      Unto Those Who Sin
      The Valiants of Virginia
1917 The Eyes of the World
      High Play
      The Man from Montana
      New York Luck
      The Serpent's Tooth
      Souls in Pawn
      The Upper Crust
      Whose Wife?
1918 Borrowed Clothes
      Cheating the Public
      False Ambition
      The Fly God
      The Greatest Thing in Life
      Jilted Janet
      The Primitive Woman
      The Shuttle
      You Can't Believe Everything
1919 Boots
      Broken Blossoms
      The Dragon Painter
      The Girl Who Stayed Home
      I'll Get Him Yet
      The Illustrious Prince
      The Lincoln Highwayman
      The Pagan God
      Peppy Polly
      Prudence on Broadway
      A Sage Brush Hamlet
1920 Fighting Cressy
      Haunting Shadows
      Isobel; Or, The Trail's End
      The Money-Changers
      The Road to Divorce
      The Rose of Nome
      The Servant in the House
      Two Moons
Pellissier, G.
1916 Whispering Smith*
Pelly, William Dudley
1917 A Case at Law
Pember, Clifford
1920 Way Down East
Pemberton, Henry W. same as
    Pemberton, Henry
1916 The Dead Alive
      The Haunted Manor
      I Accuse
      The Quality of Faith
1917 One Hour
1920 The Dead Line
      The Shark
      The Way Women Love
Pemberton, Nell
1917 A Song of Sixpence
Pembroke, P. L. could be same as
    Pembroke, P. S.; Pembroke, Percy
    or **Pembroke, Stanley**
1917 The Girl Who Won Out
Pembroke, P. S. could be same as
    Pembroke, P. L.; Pembroke, Percy
    or **Pembroke, Stanley**
1919 Sue of the South
Pembroke, Percy could be same as
    Pembroke, P. L.; Pembroke, P. S.
    or **Pembroke, Stanley**
1919 The Son-of-a-Gun!
Pembroke, Stanley could be same as
    Pembroke, P. L.; Pembroke, P. S.
    or **Pembroke, Percy**
1918 The Law That Divides
      Whatever the Cost
Pendleton, Edna
1915 The Curious Conduct of Judge
          Legarde
1916 20,000 Leagues Under the Sea
1920 The Valley of Night
Penn, M. O.
1914 The Corsair
      A Prince of India
      The Taint

Pennel, H. G.
1919 The Better Wife*
Pennell, Daniel same as **Pennell, Dan**
1916 The Daughter of MacGregor
      Nanette of the Wilds
1919 His Bridal Night
      The Silver King
1920 The Harvest Moon
      Sinners
Pennell, J. O.
1918 A Petticoat Pilot
Pennell, R. O.
1918 The Legion of Death
Pennington, Ann
1916 The Rainbow Princess
      Susie Snowflake
1917 The Antics of Ann
      The Little Boy Scout
1918 Sunshine Nan
Pennington, Edna
1920 Mountain Madness
Penny, Catharine
1920 The Stranger
Penwarden, Duncan
1919 The Imp
1920 The Woman God Sent
Pepper, the cat comedian
1920 Down on the Farm
Pepprell, Mrs. see **Pepprell, Ethel**
Pepperell, Ethel same as **Pepprell, Mrs.;
    Pepprell, Ethel**
1917 The Mainspring
1918 Little Miss Grown-Up
      The Midnight Burglar
      Miss Mischief Maker
Pepperell, Jane same as **Pepprell, Jane**
1917 The Lady in the Library
      Zollenstein
Percival, G. Harold same as **Percival, G.
    H.**
1916 The Fall of a Nation
1917 The Cold Deck
      The Flame of the Yukon
      His Mother's Boy
      Love Letters
      The Price Mark
      The Son of His Father
      Wee Lady Betty
1918 The Biggest Show on Earth
      Blue Blazes Rawden
      The Claws of the Hun
      A Desert Wooing
      The Family Skeleton
      "Flare-Up" Sal
      Fuss and Feathers
      Green Eyes
      The Guilty Man
      The Hired Man
      His Own Home Town
      The Kaiser's Shadow, or the
          Triple Cross
      Keys of the Righteous
      The Law of the North
      Love Me
      The Marriage Ring
      The Mating of Marcella
      Naughty, Naughty!
      A Nine O'Clock Town
      Playing the Game
      Riddle Gawne
      Tyrant Fear
      The Vamp
      Vive La France!
      When Do We Eat?
1919 Happy Though Married
      Hard Boiled
      The Lady of Red Butte
      Partners Three
Percival, J. W. could be same as
    Percival, Walter
1917 Sylvia of the Secret Service
Percival, Walter same as **Percival, W.
    I.; Percival, Walter I.;** could be
    same as **Percival, J. W.**
1918 Our Mrs. McChesney
      Sylvia on a Spree
1919 Almost Married
      Castles in the Air
Percy, Lieutenant
1918 Why America Will Win

Percy, Eileen same as **Persey, Eileen**
1917 Down to Earth
      The Man from Painted Post
      Panthea*
      Reaching for the Moon
      Wild and Woolly
1918 The Empty Cab
      Hitting the High Spots
1919 The Beloved Cheater
      Brass Buttons
      Desert Gold
      The Gray Horizon
      In Mizzoura
      One-Thing-at-a-Time O'Day
      Some Liar
      Told in the Hills
      Where the West Begins
1920 Beware of the Bride
      Her Honor the Mayor
      Husband Hunter
      The Land of Jazz
      Leave It to Me
      The Man Who Dared
Percy, Thelma
1920 The Beggar Prince
      The Star Rover
Percyval, Wigney
1917 She
Perdue, Leon
1918 The Locked Heart
Pereda, Cristina
1920 The Woman and the Puppet
Perez, Marcel
1920 The Way Women Love
Perez, Paul
1917 The Apple-Tree Girl
1918 Just a Woman
Periolat, George
1914 Samson
1916 And the Law Says
      Philip Holden—Waster
      The Sable Blessing
      The Valley of Decision
1917 Annie-for-Spite
      Environment
      A Game of Wits
      The Gilded Youth
      Her Country's Call
      The Mate of the Sally Ann
      Melissa of the Hills
      Periwinkle
      Sands of Sacrifice
      Southern Pride
1918 Beauty and the Rogue
      The Eyes of Julia Deep
      The Ghost of Rosy Taylor
      Rosemary Climbs the Heights
      Social Briars
      Wives and Other Wives
1919 The Amazing Impostor
      Beckoning Roads
      Eve in Exile
      The Hellion
      The Intrusion of Isabel
      Put Up Your Hands
      A Sporting Chance (American
          Film Co.)
      The Tiger Lily
      Trixie from Broadway
1920 The Dangerous Talent
      Judy of Rogue's Harbor
      Life's Twist
      The Mark of Zorro
      Nurse Marjorie
      Parlor, Bedroom and Bath
Perkins, David
1915 The Running Fight
Perkins, J. E.
1916 Whispering Smith
Perkins, Katherine
1919 The Phantom Honeymoon
Perkins, Walter same as **Perkins, W.**
1917 Wee Lady Betty
1918 The Atom
      Faith Endurin'
      The Gun Woman
      The Lonely Woman
      Paying His Debt
      The Pretender
      Without Honor*
1919 Bill Henry
      The Mayor of Filbert
      Whom the Gods Would
          Destroy

1920 Peaceful Valley
Perl, Lloyd *same as* **Pearl, Lloyd**
1916 Let Katie Do It
    A Sister of Six
1917 Aladdin and the Wonderful
    Lamp
1918 Ace High
    The Girl with the Champagne
    Eyes
    Treasure Island
Perley, Charles
1914 A Suspicious Wife
1915 The Gambler of the West
1917 The Chosen Prince, or the
    Friendship of David and
    Jonathan
    The Devil's Pay Day
    The Girl and the Crisis
    The Man Who Took a Chance
1918 Her One Mistake
    Playing the Game
Perret, Léonce
1917 The Mad Lover
    The Silent Master
1918 The Accidental Honeymoon
    Lafayette, We Come!
    Lest We Forget
    The Million Dollar Dollies
1919 The A.B.C. of Love
    The Thirteenth Chair
    The Twin Pawns
    The Unknown Love
1920 The Empire of Diamonds
    Lifting Shadows
    A Modern Salome
    Tarnished Reputations
Perret, Valentine Petit *see* **Petit,**
Valentine
Perrier, Gaby
1918 Lest We Forget
Perrin, Jack
1919 Blind Husbands
    Toton
1920 The Adorable Savage
    Lahoma
    Pink Tights
Perry, Albert
1917 Her Excellency, the Governor
Perry, Anna Day
1917 Little Miss Fortune
Perry, Augusta
1918 Love's Law
    The Silent Woman
1920 The Bromley Case
    Heritage
    The Wall Street Mystery
Perry, Fayette
1916 Silks and Satins
Perry, Frederick
1915 Dr. Rameau
    The Family Stain
    Jim the Penman
1917 Poppy
    Raffles, the Amateur
    Cracksman
1918 Innocent
Perry, Harry
1920 The Sins of Rosanne
Perry, Katherine
1920 Sooner or Later
Perry, Lester
1915 Jordan Is a Hard Road
Perry, Pansy
1918 The Girl Who Came Back
Perry, Paul *same as* **Perry, Paul P.**
1916 The Lash
    Sweet Kitty Bellairs
    The Thousand Dollar Husband
    Unprotected
1917 Forbidden Paths
    The Ghost House
    Lost and Won
    Nan of Music Mountain
    What Money Can't Buy
1918 The Bravest Way
    The City of Dim Faces
    The Cruise of the
     Make-Believes
    Hidden Pearls
    Sandy
    The Source
    Such a Little Pirate
    Wild Youth

1919 Everywoman
    Good Gracious, Annabelle
    Jane Goes A-Wooing
    Men, Women and Money
    Pettigrew's Girl
    A Sporting Chance (Famous
     Players-Lasky Corp.)
    Told in the Hills
1920 Behold My Wife
    The Round-Up
    The Sea Wolf
1921 The Jucklands
Perry, Pauline
1917 A Kiss for Susie
Perry, Ralph
1917 The Reward of the Faithless
Perry, Vivian
1916 When Love Is King
Perry, Walter
1916 A Corner in Colleens
    The Thoroughbred (New York
     Motion Picture Corp.;
     Kay-Bee)
1917 In Slumberland
    The Learnin' of Jim Benton
    The Sudden Gentleman
    Truthful Tulliver
    Until They Get Me
1918 By Proxy
    Faith Endurin'
    The Fly God
    Little Red Decides
    Mlle. Paulette
    Prisoners of the Pines
    The Red-Haired Cupid
    Three X Gordon
1919 Come Again Smith
    Dangerous Waters
    The Drifters
    The End of the Game
    A Fugitive from Matrimony
    The Man Who Turned White
    The Mints of Hell
    The Pagan God
    The Prince and Betty
    The Prodigal Liar
    A Sage Brush Hamlet
    Whitewashed Walls
1920 Fighting Cressy
    The Parish Priest
    The U.P. Trail
Persee, Thomas *see* **Persse, Thomas**
Persey, Eileen *see* **Percy, Eileen**
Pershing, General John J.
1918 Lafayette, We Come!*
    Pershing's Crusaders*
    Under Four Flags
Persons, Thomas
1916 The Adventures of Kathlyn
Persse, Thomas D. *same as* **Persse,**
Thomas; Persse, Thomas H.; Persse,
Thomas; Persse, Thomas H. *could*
be same as **Pearse, Thomas H.**
1918 A Pair of Silk Stockings
    The Shuttle
    Up the Road with Sallie
1919 Girls
    Happiness à la Mode
    The Home Town Girl
    Luck in Pawn
    The Third Kiss
    Tin Pan Alley
1920 Uncharted Channels
Pesce, Albert
1919 The Greatest Question
Peters, Edward *same as* **Peters, E. T.;**
Peters, Eddie
1916 The Power of Evil
    Spellbound
    The Sultana
1918 Wild Life
Peters, Fred W. *same as* **Peters, Fred**
1918 A Mother's Sin
1919 Reclaimed: The Struggle for a
    Soul Between Love and Hate
Peters, George *same as* **Peters, George**
W.
1916 The Foolish Virgin
    The Soul Market
1918 Wanted for Murder
1919 Taxi
    Upside Down

1919-20
    Piccadilly Jim
1920 The Girl with the Jazz Heart
    The North Wind's Malice
    Sooner or Later
Peters, Hattie
1920 White Youth
Peters, House
1913 Chelsea 7750
    An Hour Before Dawn
    In the Bishop's Carriage
    Leah Kleschna
    The Port of Doom
1914 The Brute
    Clothes
    A Lady of Quality
    Mrs. Wiggs of the Cabbage
     Patch
    The Pride of Jennico
    Salomy Jane
1915 The Captive
    The Girl of the Golden West
    The Great Divide
    Mignon
    Stolen Goods
    The Unafraid
    The Warrens of Virginia
    The Winged Idol
1916 Between Men
    The Closed Road
    The Hand of Peril
    The Rail Rider
    The Velvet Paw
1917 As Men Love
    The Happiness of Three
     Women
    The Heir of the Ages
    The Highway of Hope
    The Lonesome Chap
1919 The Forfeit
    Thunderbolts of Fate
    You Never Know Your Luck
1920 The Great Redeemer
    Isobel; Or, The Trail's End
    The Leopard Woman
    Silk Husbands and Calico
     Wives
Peters, Jay
1920 Her Beloved Villain
Peters, Rev. Madison C.
1915 The Governor's Boss
Peters, Page *same as* **Peters, P. E.**
1915 The Captive
    The Clue
    The Gentleman from Indiana
    The Goose Girl
    The Unafraid
    The Warrens of Virginia
1916 The Call of the Cumberlands
    The Code of Marcia Gray*
    Davy Crockett
    He Fell in Love with His Wife
    An International Marriage
    Madame La Presidente
    Pasquale
Peters, Thomas J.
1916 Fate's Chessboard
    The Toll of Justice
Peters, William F.
1920 Way Down East
Petersen, Cecile B.
1915 What Happened to Father
Petersen, Gus
1917 The Girl and the Crisis
Peterson, Betty K. *same as* **Peterson,**
Betty
1916 Sally in Our Alley
1918 The Beautiful Mrs. Reynolds
1919 Fools and Their Money
Peterson, Elinor O.
1913 The Inside of the White Slave
    Traffic
Peterson, Elmer
1914 At the Cross Roads
1915 Samson
Peterson, Gus *same as* **Peterson, C. G.;**
Peterson, G. C.; Peterson, G. E.;
Peterson, Gus C.
1914 The Chechako
    An Odyssey of the North
1915 The Beachcomber
1917 Ashes of Hope
    The Fuel of Life

1918 The Argument
    A Good Loser
    The Hand at the Window
    His Enemy, the Law
    I Love You
    Mlle. Paulette*
    Old Love for New
    Real Folks
1919 Her Purchase Price
1920 Rouge and Riches
Peterson, Lieut. Harold
1920 Sky Eye
Peterson, Verne
1917 Framing Framers
Petit, Valentine *same as* **Perret,**
Valentine Petit; Petit, Valentin
1917 The Mad Lover
    The Silent Master
1918 Lafayette, We Come!
Petit, Wanda *see* **Hawley, Wanda**
Petrosino, Joseph
1912 The Adventures of Lieutenant
    Petrosino*
Petrova, Olga *same as* **Petrova,**
Madame
1914 The Tigress
1915 The Heart of a Painted Woman
    My Madonna
    The Vampire
1916 The Black Butterfly
    The Eternal Question
    Extravagance
    Playing with Fire
    The Scarlet Woman
    The Soul Market
    What Will People Say?
1917 Bridges Burned
    Daughter of Destiny
    Exile
    The Law of the Land
    More Truth Than Poetry
    National Association's All-Star
     Picture
    The Secret of Eve
    The Silence Sellers
    The Soul of a Magdalen
    To the Death
    The Undying Flame
    The Waiting Soul
1918 The Life Mask
    The Light Within
    The Panther Woman
    Tempered Steel
Petrucelli, Anonia
1920 The Place of Honeymoons
Pette, Graham *see* **Pettie, Graham**
Pettengill, Mrs. C.
1916 The Woman in the Case
Pettibone, Henry *same as* **Pettibone,**
Harry
1918 The Splendid Sinner
1919 The Great Victory, Wilson or
    the Kaiser? The Fall of the
    Hohenzollerns
Pettie, Graham *same as* **Pette, Graham**
1915 The Deathlock
1917 Up or Down?
1918 Betty Takes a Hand
    Beyond the Shadows
    The Boss of the Lazy Y
    Closin' In
    Faith Endurin'
    The Golden Fleece
    A Good Loser
    Heiress for a Day
    High Tide
    His Enemy, the Law
    An Honest Man
    Innocent's Progress
    Old Hartwell's Cub
    The Pretender
    Untamed
    Wild Life
1919 The Westerners
1920 An Amateur Devil
    The Misfit Wife
    Old Lady 31
    Parlor, Bedroom and Bath
    Smoldering Embers
    You Never Can Tell

Pike, Grace
1920 Jenny Be Good
Mountain Madness
Pike, J. W.
1914 The Spy
Pike, Wallace
1916 The Clown
Pike, William
1914 Mrs. Wiggs of the Cabbage
Patch
Salomy Jane
1915 Mignon
A Phyllis of the Sierras
Salvation Nell
1916 The Unwritten Law
The Woman Who Dared
1918 We Should Worry
1919 The Heart of Juanita
Just Squaw
The Price Woman Pays*
1920 The Flame of Hellgate
Pilcer, Harry
1915 Her Triumph
Pilcer, Ray could be same as **Pilcher,
Roy** or **Pilser, Roy**
1916 The Hand of Peril
Pilcher, Roy could be same as **Pilcer,
Ray** or **Pilser, Roy**
1915 The Spendthrift
1916 Betrayed
The Black Butterfly
Where Is My Father?
1917 The Waiting Soul
Pilkerton, Paul
1914 The Littlest Rebel
Pillsbury, Helen
1915 Mortmain
A Price for Folly
1920 The Misfit Wife
Pilser, Roy could be same as **Pilcer,
Ray** or **Pilcher, Roy**
1914 A Lady of Quality
Pino, Chris
1917 The Kill-Joy
Pinto, Effingham
1915 Destiny; Or, The Soul of a
Woman
The House of a Thousand
Candles
1920 Life
Pinto, J. E.
1914 Il Trovatore
Piper, Teddy
1920 The Strongest
Pirnikoff, Leo
1915 Midnight at Maxim's
Pitt, Margaret
1918 The Struggle Everlasting
Pittman, Martha
1919 Boots
Pitts, Ella
1917 The Lady in the Library
Pitts, ZaSu same as **Pitts, Zasu**
1917 The Little Princess
1918 How Could You, Jean?
A Lady's Name
A Society Sensation
The Talk of the Town
1919 As the Sun Went Down
Better Times
Men, Women and Money
The Other Half
Poor Relations
1920 Bright Skies
The Heart of Twenty
Seeing It Through
Pius X, Pope
1914 His Holiness, the Late Pope
Pius X, and the Vatican
Pivar, Maurice
1920 Love's Plaything
Pixley, Gus
1915 The Hungarian Nabob
1918 A Soul Without Windows
Plaisetty, Rene
1915 Her Great Match
Plank, Jack
1918 Six Shooter Andy
Plank, Vivian
1918 Six Shooter Andy

Planta, Carl de see **De Planta, Charles**
Plater, Harry
1920 The Brute
Platt, George Foster
1915 His Wife
Inspiration
1916 The Five Faults of Flo
The Net
1919 Deliverance
Platz, Mildred
1916 The Devil's Prize
1917 Her Right to Live
Player, Mrs.
1915 Coral
Player, Wellington same as **Player,
Wellington A.;** could be the same
as **Prater, Wellington**
1913 The Daughter of the Hills
1914 An American Citizen
The County Chairman
His Last Dollar
The Lost Paradise
The Man from Mexico
Marta of the Lowlands
Mrs. Black Is Back
The Ring and the Man
A Woman's Triumph
1915 Business Is Business
Coral
The Morals of Marcus
Pennington's Choice
1916 The Soul of a Child
1917 Glory
Polly of the Circus
The Sin Woman
The Slave Market
1918 The Struggle Everlasting
1919 Fool's Gold
In Search of Arcady
Spotlight Sadie
The Wicked Darling
Plimpton, Harry G. see **Plimpton,
Horace G., Jr.**
Plimpton, Horace G. same as **Plympton,
Horace G.**
1918 The Menace*
1919 The Stream of Life
1920 Should a Wife Work?
Plimpton, Horace G., Jr. same as
**Plimpton, H. G., Jr.; Plimpton,
Harry G.; Plimpton, Horace;
Plimpton, Horace G.; Plimpton,
Howard**
1918 Why I Would Not Marry
The Wooing of Princess Pat*
1919 Checkers
The Jungle Trail
The Winning Stroke*
1920 The Face at Your Window
Plimpton, Jennie B.
1919 The Stream of Life
Plowden, Dore
1917 The Dazzling Miss Davison
The Runaway
Plumer, Lincoln
1918 The Floor Below
1920 The Deep Purple
Plunkett, Joseph L.
1918 The Woman the Germans Shot
Pluto, Mr.
1915 The Dust of Egypt
Plympton, George H. same as
**Plympton, George; Plympton,
George Holcombe**
1916 The Alibi
The Shop Girl
1917 Dead Shot Baker
The Question
Soldiers of Chance
The Tenderfoot
When Men Are Tempted
1918 The Blind Adventure
The Home Trail
The Little Runaway
The Menace
Miss Ambition
The Wild Strain
The Wooing of Princess Pat
1919 The Adventure Shop
1920 A Broadway Cowboy
Help Wanted—Male

Plympton, Horace G. see **Plimpton,
Horace G., Jr.**
Poe, Jeanne
1920 The Unfortunate Sex
Poff, Lon same as **Poff, Lou**
1918 The Light of Western Stars
1919 The Shepherd of the Hills
1920 Bonnie May
The Last Straw
The Man Who Dared
Sand!
The Square Shooter
Poffley, Edwin
1919 The Phantom Honeymoon
Pogue, Baby
1918 Her Aviator
Poland, Joseph F. same as **Poland,
Joseph; Poland, Joseph Francis;
Poland, Joseph Franklin**
1916 Hesper of the Mountains
Rose of the South
1917 The Auction of Virtue
The Beautiful Adventure
The Cloud
Daughter of Maryland
Intrigue
Miss Deception
Patsy
Please Help Emily
The Runaway
A Son of the Hills
1918 Closin' In
Impossible Susan
Love's Law
The Mating of Marcella
The Rough Lover
Set Free
Wild Primrose
1919 An Amateur Widow
The Amazing Impostor
A Bachelor's Wife
The Girl Problem
The Intrusion of Isabel
The Spitfire of Seville
The Tiger Lily
Yvonne from Paris
1920 Beware of the Bride
Husband Hunter
A Thousand to One
The Triflers
Polini, Emilie
1915-16
The Little Church Around the
Corner
Polito, Sol same as **Polito, Salvador**
1914 Rip Van Winkle
1915 The Butterfly
A Butterfly on the Wheel
The Cotton King
M'liss
The Sins of Society
Wildfire
1916 Fate's Boomerang
Fruits of Desire
The Man Who Stood Still
Paying the Price
The World Against Him
1917 Her Second Husband
The Runaway
1918 The Heart of a Girl
Her Husband's Honor
The Impostor
Ruling Passions
Treason
Who Loved Him Best
1919 Are You Legally Married?
Bill Apperson's Boy
Burglar by Proxy
In Wrong
The Love Defender
Should a Woman Tell?
Soldiers of Fortune
What Love Forgives
1920 Alias Jimmy Valentine
The Misleading Lady
The Price of Redemption
The Right of Way
Polk, Edwin
1915 Black Fear
Pollar, Gene
1920 The Return of Tarzan

Pollard, Harry
1915 The Girl from His Town
Infatuation
The Miracle of Life
The Quest
1916 The Dragon
Miss Jackie of the Navy
The Pearl of Paradise
1917 The Devil's Assistant
The Girl Who Couldn't Grow
Up
1918 The Danger Game
The Reckoning Day
Which Woman?
Pollard, William
1918 Doing Their Bit
Pollock, Channing
1914 The Pit
1916 By Whose Hand?
The Dawn of Love
The Evil Thereof
The Final Curtain
The Pretenders
1917 His Father's Son
Lost and Won
The Mortal Sin*
Pollock, E.
1920 Democracy
Pollock, Gabriel
1915 The Circular Staircase
1916 The Crisis
The Garden of Allah
The Ne'er-Do-Well
Pollock, J. L.
1920 Isobel; Or, The Trail's End
Pollock, Josephine see **Gray, Stella**
Polo, Eddie
1917 The Bronze Bride
A Kentucky Cinderella
Money Madness
The Plow Woman
Polo, Sam
1920 The Man from Nowhere
Poloskova, Karva
1916 Her Bleeding Heart
Love's Toll
Ponci, Caesar
1915 The Devil's Daughter
Pope, James
1920 The Family Honor*
Pope, Sybilla
1915 The Bachelor's Romance
Porches, C.
1918 At the Mercy of Men
Porter, David
1917 Down to Earth
Porter, Edward
1917 Her Fighting Chance
The Little Terror
Porter, Edwin S. same as **Porter, Edwin
Stanton**
1913 The Count of Monte Cristo
In the Bishop's Carriage
The Prisoner of Zenda
1914 The Crucible
A Good Little Devil
Hearts Adrift
The Spitfire
Such a Little Queen
Tess of the Storm Country
1915 Bella Donna
The Eternal City
Jim the Penman
Lydia Gilmore
The Morals of Marcus
Niobe
The Prince and the Pauper
Sold
When We Were Twenty-One
The White Pearl
Zaza
Porter, Jean
1917 Bondage
Porter, Pansy
1920 The Man from Nowhere
Porter, Reba
1918 The Forbidden Path
Porter, Verne Hardin
1918 Winner Takes All

Posey, A. C.
1915 Rule G

Post, Buddy same as **Post, Bud; Post, Budd; Post, Charles "Buddy"**
1918 M'liss
1919 Charge It to Me
The Courageous Coward
Todd of the Times
Upstairs
1920 The Beggar Prince
Blind Youth

Post, Lee
1917 The Deemster

Postance, William
1916 The Iron Woman
Sherlock Holmes

Potapovitch, S. E.
1918 The Blue Bird

Potel, Victor
1914 The Good-for-Nothing
1919 The Amateur Adventuress
Captain Kidd, Jr.
Full of Pep
In Mizzoura
The Petal on the Current
1920 Billions
The Heart of a Child
Mary's Ankle
Water, Water Everywhere

Potter, Herbert
1918 The Desired Woman

Potter, Paul same as **Potter, Paul M.**
1914 The War of Wars; Or, The Franco-German Invasion
1916 The Victoria Cross

Pouget, Mr.
1915 Du Barry

Pouyet, Eugène
1918 Hearts of the World

Powel, Soldine
1915 Stop Thief!

Powell (full name unknown)
1915 The Fairy and the Waif*

Powell, A. Van Buren
1917 An Alabaster Box
Babette
The Captain of the Gray Horse Troop
Clover's Rebellion
Kitty MacKay
The Marriage Speculation
Mary Jane's Pa
Money Magic
The Money Mill
The Princess of Park Row
Richard, the Brazen
Sally in a Hurry
The Sixteenth Wife
Who Goes There!
1918 The Beloved Impostor
Everybody's Girl
Little Miss No-Account
The Mating
Wild Primrose
1919 The Captain's Captain
The Girl-Woman

Powell, Curtiss G.
1919 Brothers Divided

Powell, David
1914 One of Our Girls
1915 The Dawn of a Tomorrow
The Fatal Card
Fine Feathers
1916 Less Than the Dust
1917 The Beautiful Adventure
Her Sister
Maternity
Outcast
The Price She Paid
The Unforseen
1918 The Better Half
The Girl and the Judge
Her Great Chance
Her Husband's Honor
The Impostor
The Lie
The Make-Believe Wife
Marriage
The Richest Girl
A Romance of the Underworld
1919 Counterfeit
The Firing Line
His Parisian Wife

The Teeth of the Tiger
The Woman Under Oath
1920 Idols of Clay
Lady Rose's Daughter
On with the Dance
The Right to Love

Powell, Ernest
1916 One Day

Powell, F. Templar same as **Templer-Powell, F.**
1920 Behold My Wife
Her Beloved Villain

Powell, Frank same as **Powell, Frank E.**
1914 The Corsair
Officer 666
1915 Children of the Ghetto
The Devil's Daughter
A Fool There Was
From the Valley of the Missing
Princess Romanoff
A Woman's Past
1916 The Chain Invisible
Charity
The Fourth Estate
The Scarlet Oath
The Witch
1917 The Dazzling Miss Davison
The Debt
The Final Payment
The Greater Woman
Hedda Gabler
Mary Moreland
The Mirror
Mrs. Balfame
Motherhood (Frank Powell Producing Corp.)
1918 Heart of the Sunset
1919 The Forfeit
The Unbroken Promise
You Never Know Your Luck

Powell, Henry
1919 The House Without Children

Powell, Louise
1920 The Woman God Sent

Powell, Paul
1915 Bred in the Bone
The Lily and the Rose
Up from the Depths
The Wolf Man
1916 Acquitted
Hell-to-Pay Austin
Little Meena's Romance
The Marriage of Molly-O
The Matrimaniac
The Microscope Mystery
The Rummy
Susan Rocks the Boat
The Wild Girl of the Sierras
The Wood Nymph
1917 Betsy's Burglar
Cheerful Givers
The Girl of the Timber Claims
The Sawdust Ring
1918 All Night
Indian Life
The Kid Is Clever
A Society Sensation
1919 The Blinding Trail
Common Property
The Little White Savage
The Man in the Moonlight
The Weaker Vessel
Who Will Marry Me?
1920 Crooked Streets
Eyes of the Heart
Pollyanna
Sweet Lavender

Powell, Russ same as **Powell, Russell**
1915 The Tale of the Night Before
1919 Brothers Divided
1920 The Slim Princess
Smoldering Embers
The Soul of Youth

Powelson, Arthur same as **Pawelson, Arthur; Powelson, A.**
1914 Mrs. Wiggs of the Cabbage Patch
Salomy Jane
1915 Mignon
The Pageant of San Francisco
1917 Glory
Who Knows?

Power, Jule
1915 Her Mother's Secret

Power, Tyrone (1869-1931)
1914 Aristocracy
1915 Sweet Alyssum
A Texas Steer
1916 The Eye of God
John Needham's Double
Thou Shalt Not Covet
Where Are My Children?
1917 Lorelei of the Sea
National Red Cross Pageant
The Planter
1919 Fool's Gold*
1920 The Great Shadow

Power, Mrs. Tyrone
1915 A Texas Steer

Power, William H.
1914 The Master Cracksman
1915 Who's Who in Society

Powers, Mr.
1916 The Place Beyond the Winds

Powers, Edwin
1916 The Unborn

Powers, Francis
1914 Clothes
The Little Gray Lady
The Port of Missing Men
The Redemption of David Corson
The Ring and the Man
1920 Out of the Dust
The White Rider

Powers, John
1916 The Man Who Stood Still

Powers, Leonard S. same as **Powers, Len**
1916 Blue Blood and Red
1917 The Honor System
1918 Headin' South

Powers, Maurine same as **Powers, Maureen**
1918 To Hell with the Kaiser
1919 Beware
1920 Democracy
Skinning Skinners

Powers, P. A.
1919 A Fight for Love
The Outcasts of Poker Flats

Powers, Pauline
1920 The Mysteries of Paris

Powers, Tom
1917 The Auction Block

Powers, William
1913 Traffic in Souls
1915 Wildfire
1918-19 Once to Every Man

Poy, Lee
1918 For the Freedom of the East

Poynter, Beulah
1914 Born Again
Hearts and Flowers
Lena Rivers (Cosmos Feature Film Corp.)
The Little Girl That He Forgot
The Ordeal
1915 Hearts of Men

Prater, Wellington could be same as **Playter, Wellington**
1919 The Littlest Scout

Pratt, Miss A.
1917 The Last Sentence

Pratt, Aurora
1917 A Kentucky Cinderella

Pratt, Jack see **Pratt, John H.**

Pratt, Jessie
1917 The Spindle of Life

Pratt, John H. same as **Pratt, Jack; Pratt, John; Pratt, John D.**
1913 Victory
1914 America
Dan
The Jungle
Shore Acres
Soldiers of Fortune
1915 The Garden of Lies
A Man's Making
The Rights of Man: A Story of War's Red Blotch
1916 The Gods of Fate
Her Bleeding Heart

Love's Toll
1917 Loyalty
Who Knows?
1918 Humility
1920 Bright Skies
The Heart of a Woman
The Heart of Twenty
The Little Wanderer
Roman Candles
The Third Generation
The Woman Untamed
19-- The Girl from Alaska

Pratt, Miss M.
1917 The Last Sentence

Pratt, Purnell B. same as **Pratt, Purnell**
1914 The Great Diamond Robbery
1917 Seven Keys to Baldpate

Preer, Evelyn
1919 The Homesteader
1920 The Brute
Within Our Gates

Prem, Joseph
1919 Virtuous Men*

Prendergast, Betty
1917 A Modern Cinderella

Prentice, Beatrice
1916 Nearly a King

Prentis, Jean
1918 Johanna Enlists

Prentis, June
1918 Johanna Enlists

Prescott, John same as **Prescott, Jack**
1914 The Key to Yesterday
1915 The Martyrs of the Alamo
1916 The Highest Bid
The Love Hermit
The Man from Manhattan
The Man Who Would Not Die
Overalls
Powder
Soul Mates
The Strength of Donald McKenzie
The Thoroughbred (American Film Co.)
The Torch Bearer
1918 Cyclone Higgins, D.D.

Prescott, Vivian
1915 The Unwelcome Wife

Prestell, Mae
1915 Beulah

Preston, Clinton
1914 The Seats of the Mighty
1915 The Family Cupboard

Preston, Stanley J.
1917 The Clean Gun

Pretty, Arline
1915 The Man Who Found Himself
1916 The Dawn of Freedom
The Surprises of an Empty Hotel
1917 In Again—Out Again
1919 The Challenge of Chance
1920 Life
The Valley of Doubt

Prevost, Marie same as **Provost, Marie**
1916 Unto Those Who Sin
1919 Yankee Doodle in Berlin
1920 Down on the Farm
Love, Honor and Behave

Prevost, Minna see **Provost, Minna**

Prevost, Peggy
1918 Lend Me Your Name

Price, Ada
1916 The Revolt

Price, Ed
1920 Sundown Slim

Price, Kate
1914 A Million Bid
1916 A Night Out
The Ordeal of Elizabeth
1918 Amarilly of Clothes-Line Alley
Arizona
The Ghost of Rosy Taylor
Humdrum Brown
The Mantle of Charity
Money Isn't Everything
The Seal of Silence
1919 Put Up Your Hands
Tin Pan Alley
1920 Bright Skies
The Devil's Riddle

Dinty
The Figurehead
Price, Mark
1914 The Lost Paradise
The Scales of Justice
1916 A Daughter of the Gods
The Marble Heart
Price, May
1916 Ambition
Price, Mechtilde
1920 Roman Candles
Price, Paul
1920 The Good-Bad Wife
The Little Outcast
Prichard, Walter C.
1914 The Lion and the Mouse
"Prince," an animal
1918 Code of the Yukon
Prince, a dog
1919 Carolyn of the Corners
Prince, Adelaide
1917 National Red Cross Pageant*
1920 Captain Swift
Prince, Alador
1918 Men Who Have Made Love to Me
Prince, Charles same as **Prince, Charles H.**
1915 Emmy of Stork's Nest
A Royal Family
1916 Man and His Soul
A Million a Minute
The Quitter
The Turmoil
The Wall Between
Prince Charles, the chimpanzee
1918 Tarzan of the Apes
Princess of Monaco
1918 The Great Love*
Pring, Gerald
1917 The Lady of the Photograph
1920 Milestones
The Palace of Darkened Windows
Pringle, Aileen
1919 Redhead*
1920 Stolen Moments*
Pringle, Della
1917 The Butterfly Girl
Printy, Florence
1917 The Single Code
Unto the End
Printzlau, Olga same as **Clark, Olga Printzlau**
1915 Coral
The Scarlet Sin
The Woman Who Lied
1916 John Needham's Double
Naked Hearts
The Seekers
A Soul Enslaved
Two Men of Sandy Bar
The Wrong Door
1917 To Honor and Obey
1918 Believe Me Xantippe
The City of Tears
Lawless Love
One More American
1919 Peg O' My Heart
1920 Conrad in Quest of His Youth
Jack Straw
The Prince Chap
Why Change Your Wife?
1921 Midsummer Madness
Prior, Herbert same as **Pryor, Herbert**
1915 Eugene Aram
The Magic Skin
The Truth About Helen
1916 The Heart of the Hills
The Martyrdom of Philip Strong
A Message to Garcia
Miss George Washington
1917 The Bottom of the Well
The Ghost of Old Morro
Great Expectations
The Last Sentence
The Poor Little Rich Girl
1918 After the War
A Burglar for a Night
The Menace
Mrs. Leffingwell's Boots
The Model's Confession

Society for Sale
1919 After His Own Heart
Creaking Stairs
Heartsease
Her Kingdom of Dreams
The Love Hunger
That's Good
You're Fired
1920 The Fighting Chance
The House of Whispers
The Little 'Fraid Lady
Pollyanna
The Poor Simp
The Rose of Nome
Stronger Than Death
Prisee, Allan
1917 The Last Sentence
Pritchard, Walter
1920 His Temporary Wife
Probert, George
1915 Nedra
The Spender
1916 The King's Game
1920 Madame Peacock
Probet, Fred
1916 Autumn
Proctor, Catherine
1914 Without Hope
1915 Not Guilty
1916 The Foolish Virgin
Proctor, George D. same as **Proctor, G. D.; Proctor, George; Proctor, George DuBois; Proctor, George du Boise**
1915 One Million Dollars
1916 I Accuse
The Lash
The Other Girl
1917 Each to His Kind
The Evil Eye
Framing Framers
The Maternal Spark
On Record
A Phantom Husband
The Silent Partner
Those Without Sin
1918 The Heart of a Girl
Heredity
1919 The Crook of Dreams
The Love Defender
The Spark Divine
What Love Forgives
1920 The Fortune Teller
In Walked Mary
Other Men's Shoes
Whispers
Prouty, Jed
1919 Her Game
Sadie Love
Provost, Marie see **Prevost, Marie**
Provost, Minnie same as **Ha Ha, Minnie; Minne-ha-ha**
1918 Mickey
1919 A Daughter of the Wolf
Rose of the West
1920 Food for Scandal
Up in Mary's Attic
Pruce (full name unknown)
1915 The Fairy and the Waif*
Pruden, A. Sears could be same as **Sears, A. D.**
1915 The Grandee's Ring
Prussing, Louise
1919 Out Yonder
1920 A Fool and His Money
His Wife's Money
Prussing, Margaret
1914 The Mystery of Edwin Drood
1915 On Dangerous Paths
The Ploughshare
The Ring of the Borgias
Pryer, Carl DeForest same as **Pryer, Carl D.**
1916 Following the Flag in Mexico*
United States Marines Under Fire in Haiti
Pryor, Arthur
1919 Soldiers of Fortune*
Pryor, Charles A.
1913 The Tonopah Stampede for Gold

Pryor, Herbert see **Prior, Herbert**
Puffer, Frank V.
1920 Mothers of Men
Pulliam, Pauline
1919 A Girl Named Mary
Pulver, Mary Brecht
1917 The Man Who Was Afraid*
Purdee, Stephen
1915 The Luring Lights
Purdon, Richard
1914 The School for Scandal
Pursell, Roni
1920 A Dark Lantern
Purviance, Edna
1916 Charlie Chaplin's Burlesque on "Carmen"
The Essanay-Chaplin Revue of 1916
1918 Chase Me Charlie
Putnam, Nina Wilcox
1919 It's a Bear
1920 Democracy
Putnam, O. G.
1917 God's Man
Putnam, R. M. S.
1916 The Ordeal of Elizabeth
Pyke, Wallace
1916 A Son of Erin

Q

Quealy, H. J.
1917 Madame Sherry
Quillan, Frances
1918 Innocent's Progress
Quin, Philip see **Quinn, Philip**
Quincy, Dorothy
1914 The Man from Home
1917 All for a Husband
Quincy, Stockton
1915 Don Caesar de Bazan
1916 The Drifter
Quinlan, Charles
1919 Out of the Fog
Quinn, Mr. see **Quinn, Philip**
Quinn, Alan same as **Quinn, Alen**
1914 The Fortune Hunter
1915 The Climbers
The Great Ruby
The Sporting Duchess
Quinn, Arthur T. same as **Quinn, Arthur**
1915 The Battle Cry of Peace
Mortmain
1916 The Daring of Diana
The Girl Philippa
The Hunted Woman
Kennedy Square
The Suspect
Thou Art the Man
1917 Her Secret
The More Excellent Way
The Question
Richard, the Brazen
1919 Daring Hearts
1920 Blackbirds
Quinn, Fred
1916 The Colored American Winning His Suit
Quinn, John (actor)
1917 The Last Sentence
Quinn, John Philip (gambler)
1915 Gambling Inside and Out
Quinn, Philip same as **Quin, Philip; Quinn, Mr.; Quinn, Phil**
1915 The Ploughshare
Vanity Fair
1916 The Price of Fame
1918 Over the Top
1919 The Undercurrent
1920 Oil
Quinn, Regina
1917 The Pride of New York
1918 American Buds
Brave and Bold
I'll Say So
Other Men's Daughters
1919 Beware
A Dangerous Affair
The Other Man's Wife

1920 From Now On
The Wrong Woman
Quinn, William same as **Quinn, William J.**
1914 Called Back
1916 Drugged Waters
The Heritage of Hate
Is Any Girl Safe?
Love's Lariat
1917 The Curse of Eve
Sirens of the Sea
1918 A Daughter of the West
The Grey Parasol
The Marriage Lie
Winning Grandma
1919 The Arizona Cat Claw
The Devil's Trail
The Old Maid's Baby
The Sawdust Doll
1920 The Chorus Girl's Romance
Hell's Oasis
Occasionally Yours
Skyfire
Quirk, Billy same as **Quirk, William A.**
1915 What Happened to Father
1917 The Web of Life
Quong, Frank could be same as **Quong, I.**
1919 The Quickening Flame
Quong, I. could be same as **Quong, Frank**
1918 The Interloper

R

Rabbell, Du Vernet
1920 His Wife's Money
Raboch, Alfred same as **Raboch, Al; Rabock, Al; Rabock, Alfred**
1916 The Girl Philippa
The Suspect
1918 His Bonded Wife
To Hell with the Kaiser
1920 While New York Sleeps
Racey, Charles
1916 Vultures of Society
Radcliffe, E. J. same as **Ratcliffe, E. J.**
1915 In the Palace of the King
1918 Out of a Clear Sky
The Struggle Everlasting
Tempered Steel
1919 The Divorcee
The Fighting Roosevelts
The Imp
1920 A Daughter of Two Worlds
The Discarded Woman
Even As Eve
Help Yourself
Love, Honor and Obey
Why Women Sin
1921 Miss 139
Radcliffe, Fred same as **Ratcliffe, Fred**
1915 The Butterfly
1916 The Ballet Girl
1917 The Submarine Eye
The Warfare of the Flesh
1918 A Heart's Revenge
Love's Conquest
Men
Revelation
1920 The Key to Power
Radcliffe, R. see **Ratcliffe, Rawland**
Radcliffe, Sadie
1920 The Adventurer
Radcliffe, Violet
1916 The Children in the House
Children of the Feud
Going Straight
Gretchen, the Greenhorn
Let Katie Do It
A Sister of Six
1917 Aladdin and the Wonderful Lamp
The Babes in the Woods
Jack and the Beanstalk
1918 Fan Fan
Six Shooter Andy
Treasure Island
Radford, Mazie
1916 Little Meena's Romance
The Wild Girl of the Sierras

1917 Might and the Man
Stagestruck
Radin, Sonia
1919 Broken Barriers
Radinoff, Florence
1916 The Blue Envelope Mystery
The Chattel
1917 A Son of the Hills
Rae, Alice see **Wilson, Alice**
Rae, Joseph see **Ray, Joe**
Rae, Mab
1914 The Banker's Daughter
Rae, Thomas see **Rea, Thomas**
Rae, Zoe same as **DuRae, Zoe; Rae, Little Zoe**
1916 Bettina Loved a Soldier
Gloriana
1917 The Circus of Life
The Cricket
Heart Strings
A Kentucky Cinderella
The Little Pirate
My Little Boy
Polly Put the Kettle On
The Silent Lady
1918 Danger Within
The Kaiser, the Beast of Berlin
The Magic Eye
The Star Prince
1919 The Ace of the Saddle
The Weaker Vessel
1920 Twinkle Twinkle Little Star
Raffi, Leo
1918 American Buds
Ragep, Micheline
1915 His Turning Point
Rags (*animal performer*)
1916 The Patriot
Ragsdale, James Henry
1915 The Life of Sam Davis: A Confederate Hero of the Sixties*
Rahawanaku, Mr.
1915 The Beachcomber
Raines, Anna
1917 Mrs. Balfame
Rainey, Paul J.
1912 Paul J. Rainey's African Hunt
1914 Rainey's African Hunt
Raker, Lorin
1919 The Mystery of the Yellow Room
Rale, M. W. same as **Rale, Michael**
1915 The Final Judgment
Lydia Gilmore
Madame Butterfly
1920 Away Goes Prudence
Raleigh, Mrs. Cecil
1915 Body and Soul
The Clemenceau Case
The Two Orphans
1916 A Parisian Romance
A Woman's Honor
Rallow, P. J.
1917 A Man and the Woman
Ralph, George
1915 A Butterfly on the Wheel
1916 Her Maternal Right
Ralph, Jessie
1915 The Galloper
Mary's Lamb
1916 New York
Ralston, Esther
1920 Huckleberry Finn
Whispering Devils
Ralston, Henry
1920 Stop Thief!
Ralston, Howard
1920 Pollyanna
Rambeau, Lillian
1918 The Lesson
1920 Jenny Be Good
Occasionally Yours
Rambeau, Marjorie
1917 The Dazzling Miss Davison
The Debt
The Greater Woman
Mary Moreland
The Mirror
Motherhood (Frank Powell Producing Corp.)
National Red Cross Pageant

1919 The Common Cause
1920 The Fortune Teller
Ramirez-Torres, M.
1918 Daddy's Girl
Kidder and Ko
Ramona, the mule
1915 Chimmie Fadden Out West
The Unknown
Ramsay (full name unknown)
1915 The Fairy and the Waif*
Ramsey, Alicia same as **Ramsay, Alicia**
1918 A Daughter of the Old South
1919 The Spark Divine
The Two Brides
Ramsey, E. R.
1915 Wheat and Tares; A Story of Two Boys Who Tackle Life on Diverging Lines*
Ramsey, John
1918 The Scarlet Trail
Rancourt, Jules
1917 At First Sight
Rand, John
1916 Charlie Chaplin's Burlesque on "Carmen"
Randall, Bernard same as **Randall, Barney**
1915 The House of Tears
1916 The Question
1917 The Auction Block
Within the Law
1918 Blue-Eyed Mary
Come On In
The Song of the Soul
Together
1919 Life's Greatest Problem
Oh, You Women
1920 The Master Mind
Whispers
Wits vs. Wits
Randall, C. R. could be same as **Randall, W. R.; Randall, William R.**
1913 The Prisoner of Zenda
Randall, Mon
1918 The Romance of Tarzan
Randall, Thomas
1920 Lone Hand Wilson
Randall, W. L.
1918 Peg of the Pirates
Randall, W. R. could be same as **Randall, C. R.; Randall, William R.**
1919 Miss Crusoe
Randall, William R. could be same as **Randall, C. R.; Randall, W. R.**
1913 The Prisoner of Zenda*
Randolf, Anders same as **Randolph, Anders**
1915 Hearts and the Highway
Mother's Roses
The Wheels of Justice
1916 The Crown Prince's Double
The Daring of Diana
The Girl Philippa
The Hero of Submarine D-2
The Island of Surprise
The Suspect
The Vital Question
1917 The Courage of Silence
Daughter of Destiny
One Law for Both
Sins of Ambition
Who's Your Neighbor?
Within the Law
1918 The Belgian
The Safety Curtain
The Splendid Sinner
1919 The Cinema Murder
Erstwhile Susan
From Headquarters
The Lion and the Mouse
The Price of Innocence
Reclaimed: The Struggle for a Soul Between Love and Hate
The Third Degree
Too Many Crooks
1920 The Common Sin
The Idol Dancer
The Love Flower
Madonnas and Men
Randolph, Beverly
1918 Wedlock
1919 Who Cares?

Randolph, Mrs. T.
1918 A Daughter of the Old South
Rankin, Arthur same as **Rankin, Arthur L.**
1916 Silas Marner
1920 The Amateur Wife
The Copperhead
Romance
The Truth About Husbands
Rankin, Caroline same as **Rankin, Caroline "Spike"; Rankin, Carolyn**
1914 Lena Rivers (Cosmos Feature Film Corp.)
Without Hope
1915 What Happened to Jones
1917 Some Boy!
1918 A Nine O'Clock Town
1919 Bare-Fisted Gallagher
The Lottery Man
The Uplifters
1920 What Happened to Jones
Rankin, Doris
1920 The Copperhead
The Devil's Garden
Rankin, Grace
1916 Betty of Graystone
The Habit of Happiness
Rankin, Mildred
1918 The Unchastened Woman
Ranous, William V.
1914 The Little Angel of Canyon Creek
1915 The Chalice of Courage
Ransom, John
1914 The $5,000,000 Counterfeiting Plot
Rapf, Harry
1917 The Argyle Case
The Mad Lover
One Hour
To-Day
1918 The Accidental Honeymoon
The Struggle Everlasting
Wanted for Murder
1920 Blind Youth
The Greatest Love
The Invisible Divorce
Rappe, Virginia same as **Rappae, Virginia**
1917 Paradise Garden
1920 An Adventuress
Rarvey, Dadie
1920 Neptune's Bride
Raskolnikoff, Fedor
1916 The Sowers
Rasmussen, Maurine
1914 Brewster's Millions
Ratcliffe, Fred see **Radcliffe, Fred**
Ratcliffe, Rawland same as **Radcliffe, R.**
1914 The Marked Woman
1916 The Other Girl
Rath, E. J. same as **Brainerd, Edith Rathbone Jacobs; Brainerd, J. Chauncey Corey**
1916 The River of Romance
Rath, Frederick
1917 Behind the Mask
The Golden God
The Mystic Hour
The Public Defender
When You and I Were Young
Rathbone, Bill
1917 The Reward of the Faithless
Rattenberry, Harry same as **Ratteberry, Harry; Rattenbury, Harry**
1915 Mrs. Plum's Pudding
1916 Oliver Twist
1917 '49-'17
High Speed
Indiscreet Corinne
The Learnin' of Jim Benton
A Marked Man
The Mysterious Mr. Tiller
1918 The Law's Outlaw
Limousine Life
Playing the Game
1919 Almost Married
The Delicious Little Devil
Hearts of Men
1920 Huckleberry Finn
His Pajama Girl
The Poor Simp

Raucourt, Jules same as **Raucort, Jules**
1917 Outcast
The Outsider
Please Help Emily
Somewhere in America
1918 My Wife
Prunella
La Tosca
Rausher, William
1916 Dimples
Raven, Charles
1918 Wanted for Murder
Raver, Harry same as **Raver, Harry B.; Raver, Harry R.**
1914 His Holiness, the Late Pope Pius X, and the Vatican
1916 The Fortunate Youth*
1917 God of Little Children
The Golden God
The Law That Failed
The Public Defender
1919 As a Man Thinks
The Volcano
1920 Sophy of Kravonia; Or, The Virgin of Paris
Rawlinson, Miss
1915 Du Barry
Rawlinson, Herbert
1913 The Sea Wolf
1914 Called Back
Damon and Pythias
Martin Eden
The Opened Shutters
The Spy
1916 The Eagle's Wing
Little Eve Edgarton
1917 Come Through
Flirting with Death
The High Sign
Like Wildfire
The Man Trap
The Scarlet Crystal
1918 Back to the Woods
Brace Up
The Flash of Fate
Kiss or Kill
The Mating
Out of the Night
Smashing Through
The Turn of the Wheel
1919 The Common Cause
A Dangerous Affair
Good Gracious, Annabelle
A House Divided
1920 Man and His Woman
Passers-By
Ray, Adele same as **Rey, Adele**
1914 Springtime
1915 The Moth and the Flame
Sealed Lips
Ray, Albert same as **Ray, Al**
1918 More Trouble
When Do We Eat?
1919 Be a Little Sport
The Game's Up
Home
The Lost Princess
Love Is Love
Married in Haste
Tin Pan Alley
Vagabond Luck
Words and Music By—
1920 The Honey Bee
The Night Riders
The Ugly Duckling
Ray, Allene
1920 Honeymoon Ranch
Ray, Bennie
1919 Soldiers of Fortune
Ray, Charles
1915 The Coward
The Cup of Life
The Forbidden Adventure
The Painted Soul
1916 A Corner in Colleens
The Deserter
The Dividend
Home
Honor Thy Name
The Honorable Algy
Peggy
Plain Jane
The Wolf Woman

1917 Back of the Man
The Clodhopper
His Mother's Boy
The Millionaire Vagrant
The Pinch Hitter
The Son of His Father
Sudden Jim
The Weaker Sex
1918 The Claws of the Hun
The Family Skeleton
The Hired Man
His Own Home Town
The Law of the North
A Nine O'Clock Town
Playing the Game
Staking His Life
String Beans
1919 Bill Henry
The Busher
Crooked Straight
The Egg Crate Wallop
The Girl Dodger
Greased Lightning
Hay Foot, Straw Foot
Red Hot Dollars
The Sheriff's Son
1920 Alarm Clock Andy
Forty-Five Minutes from
Broadway
Homer Comes Home
Nineteen and Phyllis
An Old Fashioned Boy
Paris Green
Peaceful Valley
The Village Sleuth

Ray, Joe *same as* **Rae, Joseph; Ray,
Joseph**
1914 John Barleycorn
The Valley of the Moon
1915 Buckshot John*
The Gentleman from Indiana
Little Sunset
'Twas Ever Thus
The Yankee Girl
1916 The Call of the Cumberlands
1918 The Vigilantes
1919 The Master Man
A White Man's Chance
1920 Firebrand Trevison
King Spruce
The Man Who Dared
The Phantom Melody
Twins of Suffering Creek

Ray, Julia
1917 Mr. Dolan of New York

Ray, Rex
1920 Dangerous Trails
The Unknown Ranger

Ray, Wallace
1920 Bitter Fruit
The Bromley Case
Chains of Evidence
Over the Hill to the Poorhouse

Rayle, Michael
1918 The Forbidden City

Raymond (full name unknown)
1915 The Fairy and the Waif*

Raymond, Dean
1917 The Boy Girl
The Cinderella Man
Little Miss Nobody
Strife
Who's Your Neighbor?
The Wild Girl
1918 Conquered Hearts
To Him That Hath
The Winning of Beatrice

Raymond, Earle
1915 The Sable Lorcha

Raymond, Frances (actress) *same as*
**Raymond, Frankie; Raymond,
Francis** (actress); *not the same as*
Raymond, Francis (actor)
1916 The Chaperon
A Law unto Himself
The Misleading Lady
1917 Burning the Candle
Fools for Luck
The Man Who Was Afraid
Sadie Goes to Heaven
The Saint's Adventure
Skinner's Dress Suit
1919 The Best Man
The Last of the Duanes

Love Insurance
The Other Half
1920 The Best of Luck
The City of Masks
The Forged Bride
A Lady in Love
Li Ting Lang
A Light Woman
The Midlanders
Miss Hobbs
Seeing It Through
Smiling All the Way
Smoldering Embers

Raymond, Francis (actor) *not the same
as* **Raymond, Francis** (actress)
1916 The Conscience of John David

Raymond, Frankie *see* **Raymond,
Frances**

Raymond, Helen
1920 Dangerous to Men
She Couldn't Help It
Twin Beds

Raymond, Jack *could be same as*
Raymond, John
1917 American—That's All
Her Father's Keeper
The Little Terror
The Millionaire's Double
Red, White and Blue Blood
1918 Caught in the Act
The Heart of Romance
T'Other Dear Charmer
1919 The Bluffer
1920 The Blue Pearl
Dad's Girl
Dangerous Business
The Dangerous Paradise
A Manhattan Knight
The Silent Barrier

Raymond, John *could be same as*
Raymond, Jack
1917 The Land of Promise

Raymond, Pete *same as* **Raymond,
Peter**
1920 Birthright
Democracy
The Fighting Kentuckians

Raymond, Roma
1916 The Wheel of the Law
1919 The Darkest Hour

Raymond, Whitney
1913 Caprice*

Raymond, William
1916 The Woman in 47
1917 The Recoil

Raynale, Marjorie
1919 Peppy Polly

Raynes, J. A.
1915 The Lily and the Rose
The Sable Lorcha
1916 Cross Currents
The Flying Torpedo
The Price of Power

Raynor, C. Edward
1919 The Shepherd of the Hills

Razeto, Stella *same as* **Razetto, Stella**
1915 The Circular Staircase
The Long Chance
Lord John in New York
The Supreme Test
1916 The Three Godfathers
1917 Out of the Wreck

Rea, Isabel
1914 Fire and Sword
Under the Gaslight
1915 Dora Thorne
1917 The Siren

Rea, Thomas *same as* **Rae, Thomas**
1919 Lasca
1920 The Adorable Savage
A Tokio Siren
White Youth

Read, Daniel
1912 Oliver Twist

Read, J. Parker, Jr. *same as* **Read, J.
Parker; Reed, J. Parker**
1913 The Stranglers of Paris
Victory
1916 Civilization
1918 The Gulf Between*
1919 The Lone Wolf's Daughter
Sahara

1920 The Brute Master
His Own Law
The Leopard Woman
Love
Love Madness
Sex
A Thousand to One

Read, John T.
1918 Restitution

Reader, Anna
1915 The Green Cloak
The Sentimental Lady

Reagan, Martin
1914 The Littlest Rebel
1915 Gretna Green
1917 She

Reals, Grace
1915 The Fifth Commandment
The Master of the House
1916 Sherlock Holmes
1918 Mrs. Dane's Defense
1919 The Hidden Truth
Oh, Boy!
The Right to Lie

Reals, Irene *see* **Reels, Frances Irene**

Reardon, Mildred
1919 Everywoman
Male and Female
Upstairs and Down
1920 Silk Husbands and Calico
Wives

Reardon, Ned
1915 The Marble Heart

Reardon, Stephen
1915 The Bridge of Sighs

Reckly, Jane
1918 Sauce for the Goose

The Rector Girls
1915 Midnight at Maxim's

Red Eagle
1920 Out of the Snows

Red Wing, Chief *same as* **Red Wing**
1914 In the Days of the Thundering
Herd
1915 The Cowpuncher

Red Wing, Princess *same as* **Redwing,
Miss**
1914 The Squaw Man
1915 Fighting Bob
1916 Ramona

Redden, Arthur
1919 The Other Half
The Way of the Strong
1920 The Road to Divorce
Smiling All the Way

Redding, Ernest
1913 Robin Hood

Redding, Eugene
1916 The Red Widow

Redding, Henry *same as* **Redding,
Harry**
1916 Fate's Boomerang
The Other Girl

Reddway, Eddie
1916 The Sunbeam

Redman, Frank
1920 Rogues and Romance

Redmond, Douglas *same as* **Redmond,
Douglas, Jr.**
1918 The Appearance of Evil
A Doll's House
1919 The Stream of Life
1920 Guilty of Love

Redmond, Harry
1917 Outcast

Redwing, Miss *see* **Red Wing, Princess**

Reed, Arthur
1919 The Light*

Reed, Cora *see* **Reed, Nora**

Reed, Mrs. Crystal
1919 Injustice

Reed, Edward *could be same as* **Reed,
Edwin E.**
1917 The Stolen Paradise

Reed, Edwin E. *could be same as* **Reed,
Edward**
1918 The Blue Bird

Reed, Florence
1915 At Bay
The Cowardly Way
The Dancing Girl

Her Own Way
1916 New York
The Woman's Law
1917 The Eternal Sin
To-Day
1918 The Struggle Everlasting
Wives of Men
1919 Her Code of Honor
Her Game
The Woman Under Oath
1920 The Eternal Mother

Reed, George
1920 Huckleberry Finn

Reed, J. Parker *see* **Read, J. Parker, Jr.**

Reed, J. Theodore
1919 When the Clouds Roll By

Reed, Katherine *same as* **Reed,
Katharine; Reed, Katharine S.;
Reed, Katherine S.; Reed, Katherine
Speer; Reed, Kathryn**
1917 Blind Man's Holiday
The Indian Summer of Dry
Valley Johnson
The Renaissance at Charleroi
The Skylight Room
1918 The Business of Life
The Girl in His House
1919 The Bramble Bush
The Enchanted Barn
A Girl at Bay
Let's Elope
1920 Blind Youth
Greater Than Fame
The Invisible Divorce
Just a Wife
Nothing but the Truth
The Palace of Darkened
Windows

Reed, Langford
1918 Chase Me Charlie

Reed, Luther *same as* **Reed, Luther A.;
Reed, Lieutenant Luther A.**
1918 A Pair of Cupids
With Neatness and Dispatch
1919 Almost Married
The Amateur Adventuress
Behind the Door
A Favor to a Friend
In for Thirty Days
The Light
Some Bride
1920 Below the Surface
Cinderella's Twin
Let's Be Fashionable
Mary's Ankle

Reed, Mary
1916 The Spell of the Yukon

Reed, Nora *same as* **Reed, Cora; Reed,
Norah**
1919 The Career of Katherine Bush
Injustice
1920 The Dangerous Paradise
The Fear Market
Sinners

Reed, Opie
1920 Birthright

Reed, Robert Ralston
1916 Witchcraft

Reed, Theodore *same as* **Reed, Ted**
1918 Arizona
He Comes Up Smiling
Say, Young Fellow!
1919 His Majesty, the American
The Knickerbocker Buckaroo
1920 The Mark of Zorro
The Mollycoddle

Reed, Violet *same as* **Reed, Violet B.**
1915 The Gambler of the West
1916 The Black Butterfly
1917 Exile
The Eyes of the World
More Truth Than Poetry
The Silence Sellers
The Soul of a Magdalen
To the Death
The Undying Flame
1918 The Panther Woman
The Power and the Glory
1919 The Right to Lie
1920 The Man Who Lost Himself

Revelle, Hamilton
1915 Du Barry
An Enemy to Society
1916 The Half Million Bribe
The Price of Malice
1917 The Black Stork
Thais
1918 Lest We Forget
The Splendid Sinner
1920 Kismet
Revelle, Johnnie
1920 The Confession
Revier, Harry
1915 The Siren's Song*
1916 The Eternal Question*
The Weakness of Strength
1917 The Lust of the Ages
1918 The Grain of Dust
A Romance of the Air
1919 The Challenge of Chance
What Shall We Do with Him?
1920 The Return of Tarzan
Rex, a dog
1914 A Factory Magdalen
1916 Out of the Drifts
Rexford, Eben E.
1915 Silver Threads Among the
Gold*
Rey, Adele see **Ray, Adele**
Reybo, P.
1918 To Hell with the Kaiser
Reynold, Genevieve
1916 Little Miss Happiness
Reynolds, Ben F. same as **Reynolds, B.
F.; Reynolds, Ben**
1917 Bucking Broadway
1918 Beans
Hell Bent
The Phantom Riders
The Scarlet Drop
Thieves' Gold
Three Mounted Men
Wild Women
A Woman's Fool
1919 Blind Husbands
A Fight for Love
The Silk Lined Burglar*
Under Suspicion
1920 Alias Miss Dodd
The Devil's Passkey
Reynolds, Carrie
1915 A Mother's Confession
Reynolds, Charles
1918 The Prussian Cur
Reynolds, D. W.
1920 Woman's Man
Reynolds, Ernest same as **Reynolds, E.
M.**
1919 The House Without Children
1920 Hidden Charms
Reynolds, Genevieve
1916 Romeo and Juliet (Quality
Pictures Corp.)
Reynolds, George
1920 Bachelor Apartments
Reynolds, Harrington
1914 The Voice at the Telephone
Reynolds, Lynn F. same as **Reynolds,
Lynn**
1916 The End of the Rainbow
The Girl of the Lost Lake
It Happened in Honolulu
A Romance of Billy Goat Hill
The Secret of the Swamp
1917 Broadway Arizona
God's Crucible
The Gown of Destiny
The Greater Law
Mr. Opp
Mutiny
The Show Down
Southern Justice
Up or Down?
1918 Ace High
Fame and Fortune
Fast Company
Mr. Logan, U.S.A.
Western Blood
1919 The Brute Breaker
The Forbidden Room
A Little Brother of the Rich
Miss Adventure
The Rebellious Bride

Treat 'Em Rough
1920 Bullet Proof
Overland Red
The Red Lane
The Texan
Reynolds, Tuck
1919 Leave It to Susan
Reynolds, William
1916 The Flower of Faith
Reynolds, Wilson
1917 The Inevitable
Rheinhard, Cyril
1915 The Warning
Rheinhardt, Louis
1919 Heart of Gold
Rhino, William see **Ryno, William**
Rhoads, Mildred
1919 The Capitol
Rhodes, Billie
1918 The Girl of My Dreams
1919 The Blue Bonnet
Hoop-La
In Search of Arcady
The Lamb and the Lion
The Love Call
1920 Miss Nobody
His Pajama Girl
Rhodes, Elizabeth
1919 The Shepherd of the Hills
Rhodes, Eugene Manlove same as
Rhodes, Eugene M.
1917 The Desire of the Moth
1920 West Is West
Rial, Louise
1916 A Daughter of the Gods
The Marble Heart
The Spider and the Fly
A Wife's Sacrifice
1917 Tangled Lives
1919 My Little Sister
Riaume, Helen
1916 Where Are My Children?
Ricardo, Captain
1917 The Lad and the Lion
Ricciardi, Joseph
1918 My Cousin
Rice, Edward E.
1913 The Prisoner of Zenda*
Rice, Fanny same as **Rice, Fannie**
1919 Dawn
The Moonshine Trail
1920 My Husband's Other Wife
Rice, Frank
1914 Richelieu
Rice, Grantland
1916 Somewhere in Georgia
Rice, Herbert
1916 The Rainbow Princess
Rice, Josephine
1916 Big Tremaine
The Lash
Undine
Rice, Philip S.
1919 The Firing Line
Rice, Roy Hiram same as **Rice, Roy**
1915 The Lily and the Rose
Up from the Depths
1916 The Wood Nymph
1917 The Honor System
The Planter*
Rich, H. Thompson
1920 A Master Stroke
Stolen Moments
Rich, Irene
1918 The Girl in His House
A Law unto Herself
1919 The Blue Bonnet
Castles in the Air
Diane of the Green Van
Her Purchase Price
The Lone Star Ranger
A Man in the Open
The Silver Girl
The Sneak
The Spite Bride
Todd of the Times
Wolves of the Night
1920 Godless Men
Jes' Call Me Jim
Just Out of College
Stop Thief!
The Strange Boarder

The Street Called Straight
Water, Water Everywhere
Rich, Lillian
1919 The Day She Paid
1920 Dice of Destiny
Felix O'Day
Half a Chance
One Hour Before Dawn
The Red Lane
Rich, Vivian
1917 Beware of Strangers
A Branded Soul
The Man from Montana
The Price of Silence
1918 Code of the Yukon
The Crime of the Hour
1919 The Mints of Hell
1920 The Last Straw
A World of Folly
Would You Forgive?
Richard, Albert
1917 A Crooked Romance
The Last of the Carnabys
Over the Hill
The Streets of Illusion
1918 For Sale
Mrs. Slacker
The Mysterious Client
Richards, Miss
1919 The Two Brides
Richards, C.
1916 A Daughter of the Gods
Richards, Mabel
1918 Old Hartwell's Cub
Richards, Mary
1918 The Burden of Proof
Richards, Lieut. Percy
1916 Autumn
Richards, Regina
1914 Doc
Richards, Tom
1915 The Chocolate Soldier
1916 Love's Pilgrimage to America
Richardson, Anna Steese
1918 Hell's End
Richardson, Frank
1918 How Could You, Jean?
Johanna Enlists
The Way of a Man with a
Maid
1919 Captain Kidd, Jr.
Love Insurance
The Poor Boob
Venus in the East
A Very Good Young Man
Why Smith Left Home
1920 The Six Best Cellars
Too Much Johnson
Richardson, J. C.
1918 The Legion of Death
Richardson, Jack
1916 Immediate Lee
Land O' Lizards
1917 Ashes of Hope
Beware of Strangers
Fighting Back
Giving Becky a Chance
Golden Rule Kate
Love or Justice
Mountain Dew
One Shot Ross
The Sawdust Ring
The Sudden Gentleman
1918 Captain of His Soul
Desert Law
Free and Equal
Go West, Young Man
His Enemy, the Law
The Man Above the Law
The Painted Lily
The Reckoning Day
The Sea Panther
Wife or Country
You Can't Believe Everything
1919 The End of the Game
The Long Lane's Turning
The Mayor of Filbert
The Mints of Hell
The Old Maid's Baby
The She Wolf
Whitewashed Walls
1920 Dangerous Hours
Dangerous Love

Duds
The Heart of a Woman
The Strange Boarder
The Toll Gate
Richardson, Walter
1920 Alias Miss Dodd
Richelavie, George
1919 The Unpardonable Sin
Richelle, Myrtle
1919 Girls
Happiness à la Mode
Luck in Pawn
Richman, Charles
1914 The Idler
The Man from Home
1915 The Battle Cry of Peace
The Heights of Hazard
1916 The Dawn of Freedom
The Hero of Submarine D-2
The Surprises of an Empty
Hotel
1917 The More Excellent Way
Over There
The Public Be Damned
1919 The Echo of Youth
Everybody's Business
The Hidden Truth
1920 Curtain
Half an Hour
Harriet and the Piper
Richmond, J. A.
1917 The Barker
Richmond, Warner same as **Richmond,
W. P.; Richmond, Warner P.**
1914 Springtime
1915 The Great Divide
Lady Audley's Secret
1916 Betty of Graystone
Fifty-Fifty
Her Maternal Right
Manhattan Madness
1918 Brown of Harvard
A Romance of the Air
Sporting Life
Woman
1919 The Gray Towers Mystery
1920 My Lady's Garter
A Woman's Business
Richtel, Rose
1914 The Avenging Conscience*
Richter, George
1916 Blue Blood and Red
Fighting Blood
1917 The Honor System
One Touch of Sin
1918 Ace High
Fan Fan
Richter, Mildred
1917 Draft 258
National Red Cross Pageant
The Slacker (Metro Pictures
Corp.)
1918 Cyclone Higgins, D.D.
Rickert, Frank
1917 Souls in Pawn
Whose Wife?
Ricketts, G. M.
1917 The Greater Law
Ricketts, George
1914 The House of Bondage
Ricketts, Thomas same as **Ricketts,
Thomas R.; Ricketts, Tom**
1914 Damaged Goods
1915 The Buzzard's Shadow
The End of the Road
The House of a Thousand
Scandals
The Lure of the Mask
Secretary of Frivolous Affairs
1916 The Other Side of the Door
1917 The Painted Lie*
The Single Code
1918 The Crime of the Hour
1919 Girls
His Official Fiancée
Please Get Married
Secret Marriage
1920 All-of-a-Sudden-Peggy
The Desperate Hero
The Great Lover
The Paliser Case
The Parish Priest
The Spenders

Roberson, Jessylee
1917 The Lady in the Library
Roberts, Miss
1916 Vengeance Is Mine
Roberts, Mr.
1917 The Man of Mystery
Roberts, B. K.
1915 The Valley of Lost Hope
Roberts, Chester L.
1919 The Miracle Man
Roberts, Edith
1918 Beans
The Deciding Kiss
The Love Swindle
Set Free
1919 Bill Henry
Lasca
Sue of the South
A Taste of Life
1920 The Adorable Savage
Alias Miss Dodd
Her Five-Foot Highness
The Triflers
White Youth
Roberts, Edward
1916 The Heart of Tara
Roberts, Florence
1913 Sapho
Roberts, Frederic
1914 Should a Woman Divorce?
Roberts, Hans
1917 The Great White Trail
Roberts, J. K. *could be same as*
Roberts, Jack *or* **Roberts, James**
1916 The Devil at His Elbow
1917 The Law That Failed
The Public Defender
Roberts, Jack *could be same as*
Roberts, J. K.
1918 A Soul Without Windows
Roberts, James *could be same as*
Roberts, J. K.
1920 The Woman Above Reproach
Roberts, Lolita *see* **Robertson, Lolita**
Roberts, R. A.
1919 The Painted World
Roberts, Theodore
1914 The Call of the North
The Circus Man
The Ghost Breaker
The Making of Bobby Burnit
The Man from Home
Ready Money
What's His Name
Where the Trail Divides
1915 After Five
The Arab
The Captive
The Case of Becky
The Fighting Hope
The Girl of the Golden West
The Governor's Lady
The Immigrant
Mr. Grex of Monte Carlo
The Secret Orchard
Stolen Goods
Temptation
The Unafraid
The Unknown
The Wild Goose Chase
The Woman
1916 Anton the Terrible
Common Ground
The Dream Girl
Joan the Woman
The Plow Girl
Pudd'nhead Wilson
The Sowers
The Storm
The Thousand Dollar Husband
The Trail of the Lonesome Pine
Unprotected
1917 The American Consul
The Cost of Hatred
The Devil-Stone
The Little Princess
Nan of Music Mountain
The Varmint
What Money Can't Buy
1918 Arizona
The Girl Who Came Back
Hidden Pearls
M'liss

Old Wives for New
A Petticoat Pilot
The Source
The Squaw Man
Such a Little Pirate
We Can't Have Everything
Wild Youth
1919 Don't Change Your Husband
Everywoman
Fires of Faith
For Better, for Worse
Hawthorne of the U.S.A.
Love Insurance
Male and Female
The Poor Boob
The Roaring Road
Secret Service
What Every Woman Learns
The Winning Girl
The Woman Thou Gavest Me
You're Fired
1920 Double Speed
Excuse My Dust
The Furnace
Judy of Rogue's Harbor
Something to Think About
Sweet Lavender
Roberts, Walter
1915 A Texas Steer
Robertson (full name unknown)
1915 The Fairy and the Waif*
Robertson, Mrs.
1919 Counterfeit
Robertson, Charles
1919 The She Wolf
Robertson, Clifford
1919 Sis Hopkins
Robertson, Forest
1918 The Mating
Robertson, Helen
1915 The Celebrated Scandal
Robertson, J. S. *see* **Robertson, John S.**
Robertson, James
1917 The Inevitable
Little Miss Fortune
The Road Between
Robertson, Jean
1920 Children Not Wanted
Robertson, John S. *same as* **Robertson,**
J. S.; Robertson, John
1916 The Combat
The Conflict
The Destroyers
An Enemy to the King
His Wife's Good Name
The Supreme Temptation
1917 Baby Mine
The Bottom of the Well
Her Right to Live
Intrigue
The Maelstrom
The Money Mill
1918 The Better Half
The Girl of Today
Little Miss Hoover
The Make-Believe Wife
The Menace
1919 Come Out of the Kitchen
Erstwhile Susan
Here Comes the Bride
Let's Elope
The Misleading Widow
Sadie Love
The Test of Honor
1920 Away Goes Prudence
A Dark Lantern
Dr. Jekyll and Mr. Hyde
(Famous Players-Lasky
Corp.)
39 East
Robertson, Lolita *same as* **Roberts,**
Lolita
1914 The Hoosier Schoolmaster
The Man on the Box
The Truth Wagon
What's His Name
1915 Jack Chanty
Robertson, Marie
1917 The Rainbow Girl
Robeson, Andrew *see* **Robson, Andrew**

Robeson, Phil *see* **Robson, Philip**
Robins, Charles A. *see* **Robbins, Charles**
Robins, Walt
1920 Three Gold Coins
Robinson, Miss
1915 Du Barry
Robinson, Mr. *could be same as*
Robinson, Sam
1917 The Moral Code
Robinson, A. J.
1915 The Seventh Noon
Robinson, Alan *same as* **Robinson, Allan**
1916 According to Law
The Idol of the Stage
The Quality of Faith
Robinson, Billy
1915 The Raven
Robinson, Clark
1920 Dr. Jekyll and Mr. Hyde
(Famous Players-Lasky
Corp.)
Way Down East
Robinson, Daisy
1914 The County Chairman
Rip Van Winkle
1916 Intolerance*
The Price of Power
1917 The Clever Mrs. Carfax
The Happiness of Three
Women
The Spirit of Romance
1918 The Fallen Angel
1919 Please Get Married
When the Clouds Roll By
1920 Fixed by George
The Price of Silence
A Slave of Vanity
A World of Folly
Robinson, Eileen
1920 Mid-Channel
Robinson, Forrest
1915 The Dawn of a Tomorrow
The Fifth Commandment
The House of a Thousand
Candles
1918 From Two to Six
Just a Woman
Little Miss Hoover
The Mating*
1919 Break the News to Mother
The Hidden Truth
1920 His House in Order
Robinson, Fred *same as* **Robinson, Fred**
J.
1919 Widow by Proxy
1920 Crooked Streets
Easy to Get
A Lady in Love
Robinson, George
1917 The Moral Code*
Robinson, Gertrude
1914 Classmates
1915 The Arab
The Concealed Truth
The Gambler of the West
May Blossom
1916 As a Woman Sows
The Haunted Manor
The Quality of Faith
1918 A Woman of Impulse
1919 The Gay Old Dog
1920 Milestones
Robinson, Harry
1918 Huns Within Our Gates
Robinson, Helen
1917 The Amazons
Robinson, Sam *could be same as*
Robinson, Mr.
1917 The Little Samaritan
Robinson, Spike
1917 In Again—Out Again
1919 Thieves
Robson, Andrew *same as* **Robeson,**
Andrew
1914 Mrs. Wiggs of the Cabbage
Patch
Salomy Jane
1915 The Lily of Poverty Flat
Mignon
A Phyllis of the Sierras
Salvation Nell
1916 The Unwritten Law
The Woman Who Dared

1918 Branding Broadway
A Broadway Scandal
The Devil's Wheel
That Devil, Bateese
Which Woman?
1919 The Beloved Cheater
The Gray Horizon
The Heart of Juanita
Just Squaw
The Law of Men
The Light of Victory
Square Deal Sanderson
Upstairs and Down
The Virtuous Thief
1920 Alarm Clock Andy
The Amazing Woman
The Butterfly Man
The Corsican Brothers
Cupid, the Cowpuncher
The Great Accident
Scratch My Back
Their Mutual Child
Who's Your Servant?
Robson, Mary
1915 The House of a Thousand
Candles
Robson, May
1915 How Molly Malone Made
Good
1916 A Night Out
Robson, Philip *same as* **Robeson, Phil;**
Robson, Phil
1914 The Banker's Daughter
Captain Swift
The Greyhound
1915 The Running Fight
1916 The Conquest of Canaan
Life's Whirlpool
Robson, Stuart
1920 The Harvest Moon
Should a Wife Work?
Robson, Mrs. Stuart
1914 At the Cross Roads
The Trail of the Lonesome Pine
1918 Gates of Gladness
The Prodigal Wife
1919 A Broadway Saint
His Bridal Night
The Lost Battalion
Robyn, Alfred G.
1915 The Galloper*
Roccardi, Albert
1914 Mr. Barnes of New York
The Win(k)some Widow
1915 The Man Behind the Door
1916 Artie, the Millionaire Kid
A Modern Thelma
My Lady's Slipper
1918 The Liar
Tangled Lives
1919 The Virtuous Model
1920 Greater Than Fame
Love's Flame
Roche, J. Anthony *see* **Roach, J.**
Anthony
Roche, M. Paul
1918 The Triumph of Venus
Rock, William
1917 National Red Cross Pageant
Rockett, Albert
1918 Miss Mischief Maker
Rockwell, Florence
1915 Body and Soul
A Man and His Mate*
1916 He Fell in Love with His Wife
Rockwell, Gladys *see* **Brockwell, Gladys**
Rockwell, Violet
1916 The Ruling Passion
Roden, Robert F.
1917 Little Miss Nobody
1920 Greater Than Love
Rodgers, Ann
1913 Across the Continent
Rodgers, Dora *same as* **Rogers, Dora**
1916 A Modern Enoch Arden
1918 After the War
Who Killed Walton?
Rodgers, Walter L. *see* **Rogers, Walter**
Rodier, Alice
1915 Midnight at Maxim's
1917 The Defeat of the City

Rosenberg, Irving
1917 The Darling of Paris
Heart and Soul
Her Greatest Love
The Spreading Dawn
Tangled Lives
The Tiger Woman
1918 The Light Within
1919 The Brute Breaker
The Eternal Magdalene
Fool's Gold
A Little Brother of the Rich
The Love Hunger
The Miracle Man
1920 Are All Men Alike?
The Greatest Love
The Path She Chose
The Road to Divorce
Under Crimson Skies

Rosenberg, Irving
1919 The Feud
1920 A Connecticut Yankee at King
Arthur's Court
The Untamed

Rosenberg, Sol A.
1914 The Murders in the Rue
Morgue

Rosener, George M.
1917 The Wild Girl

Rosenfeld, Sydney
1915 The Senator

Rosenstock, A.
1920 The Misleading Lady

Rosenthal, Boris
1920 The Face at Your Window

Rosher, Charles *same as* **Rosher,
Charles G.**
1914 The Mystery of the Poison Pool
1915 Blackbirds
The Voice in the Fog
1916 Anton the Terrible
The Blacklist
The Clown
Common Ground
The Heir to the Hoorah
The Plow Girl
The Sowers
1917 At First Sight
Hashimura Togo
A Mormon Maid
On Record
The Primrose Ring
The Secret Game
1918 The Honor of His House
How Could You, Jean?
Johanna Enlists
One More American
Too Many Millions
The White Man's Law
The Widow's Might
1919 Captain Kidd, Jr.
Daddy-Long-Legs
The Dub
Heart O' the Hills
The Hoodlum
1920 Dinty
Pollyanna
Suds
The White Circle

Rosher, Dorothy
1918 How Could You, Jean?
Women's Weapons
1920 Thou Art the Man
Young Mrs. Winthrop

Rosine, Lillian *same as* **Rosine, Lilyan**
1917 The Cost of Hatred
Hell Morgan's Girl

Roskam, Edward M.
1914 The Banker's Daughter
The Ordeal
Springtime
1920 Why Pick on Me?

Ross, Arthur
1918 The Clutch of Circumstance
Love Watches
Miss Ambition
1919 The Girl-Woman
1920 Deadline at Eleven

Ross, Charles J.
1914 The Great Diamond Robbery
1915 How Molly Malone Made
Good
The Senator
1916 By Whose Hand?

Ross, Lieut. Clinton
1919 Injustice

Ross, Daniel
1920 The Mysteries of Paris

Ross, Etna *same as* **Ross, Little Etna**
1919 Deliverance
1920 The Restless Sex

Ross, George
1918 The Rainbow Trail

Ross, H. Milton
1917 Golden Rule Kate
1919 Pretty Smooth
1920 Dangerous Days
Duds
813
The Little Shepherd of
Kingdom Come

Ross, Harriet
1918 The Embarrassment of Riches
Eve's Daughter
The Inn of the Blue Moon

Ross, Irva
1916 The Human Orchid
The Toll of Justice
1920 Why Tell?

Ross, Jackson T.
1917 The Frozen Warning

Ross, James B.
1914 A Celebrated Case
The School for Scandal
1915 Don Caesar de Bazan
1916 The Lotus Woman

Ross, Mary Taylor *same as* **Ross, Mary**
1914 The School for Scandal
1915 Don Caesar de Bazan

Ross, Milton *same as* **Ross, Milton L.**
1916 The Green Swamp
The Patriot
1917 The Desert Man
The Gun Fighter
Idolators
The Narrow Trail
The Silent Man
The Square Deal Man
Time Locks and Diamonds
Truthful Tulliver
1918 "Flare-Up" Sal
His Own Home Town
The Mating of Marcella
A Nine O'Clock Town
Riddle Gawne
The Tiger Man
1919 The End of the Game
The Exquisite Thief
The False Faces
Flame of the Desert
A Woman of Pleasure
1920 The Penalty
The Woman and the Puppet

Ross, Mina
1918 Les Miserables

Ross, Master Richard
1916 One Day

Ross, Robert
1915 The Frame-Up

Ross, Samuel
1919 A Misfit Earl

Ross, Thomas W.
1913 Checkers
1914 The Only Son
1920 The Fatal Hour

Ross, Virginia
1919 False Evidence
The Red Lantern

Rosselli, Rex de *see* **De Rosselli, Rex**

Rossi, Leo
1917 Troublemakers
1918 Her Great Chance
In the Hollow of Her Hand
We Should Worry
1919 The Challenge of Chance

Rossi, Tina
1916 Children of the Feud
1917 A Daughter of the Poor

Rossier, Ben
1917 Betty Be Good

Rossom, Queenie *see* **Rosson, Queenie**

Rosson, Arthur *same as* **Rosson, Arthur
H.**
1917 American—That's All
A Case at Law
Cassidy

Grafters
Her Father's Keeper
The Man Who Made Good
Panthea
1918 Headin' South
1919 The Coming of the Law
Married in Haste
Rough Riding Romance
Sahara
Soldiers of Fortune
1920 Polly of the Storm Country

Rosson, Dick *same as* **Rosson, Richard**
1914 The Patchwork Girl of Oz
Richelieu
1915 My Best Girl
The Pretty Sister of Jose
1916 Seventeen
1917 American—That's All
A Case at Law
Cassidy
Her Father's Keeper
The Man Who Made Good
Panthea
1918 Alias Mary Brown
Arizona*
The Ghost Flower
A Good Loser
High Stakes
Madame Sphinx
The Shoes That Danced
1919 Chasing Rainbows
Peggy Does Her Darndest
Playthings of Passion
The Poor Boob
The Secret Garden

Rosson, Harold *same as* **Rosson, Hal**
1916 The Honorable Friend
Oliver Twist
The Victoria Cross
1917 The American Consul
Lost and Won
1919 The Cinema Murder
1920 Heliotrope
Polly of the Storm Country

Rosson, Helene *same as* **Rosson, Helen**
1915 The End of the Road
1916 The Abandonment
April
The Craving
The Light
The Sign of the Spade
True Nobility
The Undertow
The White Rosette
1917 The Price of a Good Time
1918 Borrowed Clothes

Rosson, Queenie *same as* **Rossom,
Queenie**
1914 The Patchwork Girl of Oz*
1916 The Love Hermit

Rosson, Richard *see* **Rosson, Dick**

Rotell, Joe
1920 Live Sparks

Roth, Arthur
1916 The Dawn of Freedom

Rothacker, Watterson
1918 The Life Mask
1919 Whom the Gods Would
Destroy

Rothapfel, S. L. *same as* **Rothapfel,
Samuel L.**
1914 The Avenging Conscience
1915 The Battle Cry of Peace
Carmen (Jesse L. Lasky
Feature Play Co.)
Trilby*
1918 Too Fat to Fight*
Under Four Flags
1919 False Gods

Rothe, Anita
1915 The Fairy and the Waif
1917 Her Sister
1918 The Impostor

Rothe, Bert
1919 The Perfect Lover

Rothe, Celeste
1915 The Fairy and the Waif

Rothschild, Baroness
1918 The Great Love*

Rothschild, Edith
1918 The Star Prince

Rothschild, Julius
1917 American Maid

Rotoli, Francesca
1914 In Mizzoura

Rottenthal, Baroness Irmgard von
1915 Midnight at Maxim's

Rottger, Herman
1917 Womanhood, the Glory of the
Nation

Rottman, Victor
1917 The Spotted Lily

Roubert, Matty
1914 John Barleycorn
1915 The Waif
1916 The Big Sister
1918 Parentage
1920 Heritage

Roubert, William *same as* **Roubert,
William L.**
1915 The Waif
1920 Heritage

Rounds, Steve *same as* **Rounds, S.;
Rounds, Stephen; Rounds, Steven**
1915 Business Is Business
The Frame-Up
1916 Bettina Loved a Soldier
The Bugler of Algiers
The Evil Women Do
The Right to Be Happy
1917 The Cricket
The Gift Girl
A Kentucky Cinderella
The Little Pirate
My Little Boy
The Mysterious Mr. Tiller
1918 The Boss of the Lazy Y
By Proxy
Cactus Crandall
Faith Endurin'
The Fly God
Hands Down
Keith of the Border
Paying His Debt
The Pretender
The Red-Haired Cupid
The Silent Rider
Untamed
Wolves of the Border
1919 The Day She Paid
The She Wolf
1920 Scratch My Back
So Long Letty

Rouse, Mr.
1915 Mistress Nell

Rousseau, Victor
1916 The Truant Soul

Roussillon, Marcelle
1919 Her Code of Honor

Routh, George
1915 Saved from the Harem
1917 For Liberty
1918 Two-Gun Betty

Rover, the dog
1918 Huns Within Our Gates

Row, Arthur
1915 Vanity Fair

Rowell, Maj. Ross E.
1918 The Unbeliever

Rowland, Clarence
1917 The Baseball Revue of 1917*

Rowland, Richard A.
1918 Eye for Eye
Pay Day
1919 The Brat
Out of the Fog
The Red Lantern
1920 Stronger Than Death

Roy, Harry de *see* **De Roy, Harry**

Royal, Lee
1919 The Lamb and the Lion
Modern Husbands
1920 Fickle Women

Royce, Brigham
1915 Heléne of the North

Royce, Ray L.
1915 York State Folks

Royce, Ruth
1920 Blue Streak McCoy
The Girl in Number 29

Ruada, Arthur
1920 Hearts Are Trumps
Rube, Slim
1919 The Moonshine Trail
Rubel, Laurence
1917 Uncle Sam, Awake!
Rubens, Alma same as **Reuben, Alma;**
  Reubens, Alma; Ruben, Alma;
  Rueben, Alma; Ruebens, Alma
1916 The Children Pay
    The Half-Breed
    Intolerance
    Reggie Mixes In
1917 The Americano
    The Cold Deck
    The Firefly of Tough Luck
    The Gown of Destiny
    Master of His Home
    The Regenerates
    Truthful Tulliver
    A Woman's Awakening
1918 The Answer
    False Ambition
    The Ghost Flower
    I Love You
    The Love Brokers
    Madame Sphinx
    The Painted Lily
1919 Diane of the Green Van
    The Fall of Babylon
    A Man's Country
    Restless Souls
1920 Humoresque
    Thoughtless Women
    The World and His Wife
Rubinstein, Irving see **Ruby, Irving**
Rubinstein, Leon J.
1913 The Shame of the Empire State
Ruby, Irving same as **Rubinstein, Irving**
1919 Broken Barriers
1920 Uncle Sam of Freedom Ridge
Ruby, Mary
1915 Peer Gynt
    The Reform Candidate
    The Rug Maker's Daughter
    The Wild Olive
1916 Drugged Waters
    A Man of Sorrow
Rudisill, Ivan
1915 The Battle Cry of Peace
Rue, Baby de see **De Rue, Carmen**
Rue, Romena
1918 The Oldest Law
Rueben, Alma see **Rubens, Alma**
Ruge, Billy could be same as **Ruge,**
  William
1919 Bullin' the Bullsheviki
Ruge, William could be same as **Ruge,**
  Billy
1914 Fantasma
Ruggles, Charles
1915 The Majesty of the Law
    Peer Gynt
    The Reform Candidate
Ruggles, Wesley same as **Ruggles,**
  Wesley H.
1915 A Submarine Pirate
1916 Charlie Chaplin's Burlesque on
    "Carmen"
1917 For France
    Outcast
1918 The Blind Adventure
1919 The Winchester Woman
1919-20
    Piccadilly Jim
1920 The Desperate Hero
    The Leopard Woman
    Love
    Sooner or Later
Rule, Beverly C.
1920 The Fourth Face*
Rumhauser, Judge
1916 A Youth of Fortune
Rumplestilzen, a duck
1919 Day Dreams
Ruoff, Allen
1920 The Heart of a Child
Rupert could be animal actor
1916 Jim Grimsby's Boy

Rush, Charles O.
1917 The Cold Deck
    The Square Deal Man
Rush, Dick
1920 Three Gold Coins
    The Village Sleuth
Russell, Mr.
1918 Mr. Fix-It
Russell, Bob
1919 The Usurper
Russell, Byron same as **Russell, Bryson**
1920 The Daughter Pays
    The World and His Wife
Russell, Charles Edward
1918 The Fall of the Romanoffs
Russell, Ethel
1920 The Bromley Case
    The Sacred Ruby
    The Trail of the Cigarette
    The Triple Clue
1920-21
    The House of Mystery
Russell, Evelyn
1914 La Belle Russe
Russell, Frank
1916 The Witch
19-- Our Daily Bread
Russell, Gordon
1916 The Heart of Tara
1917 Betty and the Buccaneers
    Charity Castle
1918 A Diplomatic Mission
    The Mantle of Charity
1919 Put Up Your Hands
    Some Liar
    When a Man Rides Alone
1920 The Sagebrusher
    The Testing Block
Russell, H. C.
1917 A Bit of Kindling
    The Secret of Black Mountain
Russell, Harry could be same as
  Russell, Harry J. or **Russell, Henry**
1919 The Little Boss
Russell, Harry J. could be same as
  Russell, Harry or **Russell, Henry**
1917 The Avenging Trail
Russell, Hattie
1914 Paid in Full
Russell, Helen
1918 The Sea Waif
Russell, Henry could be same as
  Russell, Harry or **Russell, Harry J.**
1919 Deliverance
Russell, Herbert
1914 McVeagh of the South Seas
    The Master Cracksman
Russell, J. Gordon
1916 Miss Jackie of the Navy
    The Pearl of Paradise
1917 The Butterfly Girl
1920 A Thousand to One
Russell, Capt. James C.
1919 Through Hell and Back with
    the Men of Illinois
Russell, John L.
1919 Fruits of Passion
Russell, L. Case same as **Russell, Lulu**
  Case; Russell, Mrs. L. Case
1916 The Black Butterfly
    Somewhere in Georgia
    The Two Edged Sword
1917 The Soul of a Magdalen
    To the Death
1918 The Life Mask
    The Light Within
    Merely Players
    Tempered Steel
1919 The Clouded Name
    Fruits of Passion
    Water Lily
Russell, Lillian
1915 Wildfire
Russell, Lorna
1914 Il Trovatore
Russell, Lulu Case see **Russell, L. Case**
Russell, Marcella
1917 Mothers of Men

Russell, Raymond
1914 His Majesty, the Scarecrow of
    Oz
    The Patchwork Girl of Oz
1915 The Heart of Maryland
Russell, Stuart
1916 A Modern Thelma
Russell, William same as **Russell,**
  William E.
1913 Moths
    Robin Hood
1914 The Straight Road
    Under the Gaslight
1915 The Dancing Girl
    Dora Thorne
    The Garden of Lies
1916 The Bruiser
    The Craving
    The Highest Bid
    Lone Star
    The Love Hermit
    The Man Who Would Not Die
    Soul Mates
    The Strength of Donald
      McKenzie
    The Thoroughbred (American
      Film Co.)
    The Torch Bearer
    The Twinkler
1917 The Frame Up
    High Play
    The Masked Heart
    My Fighting Gentleman
    New York Luck
    Pride and the Man
    Sands of Sacrifice
    The Sea Master
    Shackles of Truth
    Snap Judgement
1918 All the World to Nothing
    Hearts or Diamonds?
    Hobbs in a Hurry
    In Bad
    The Midnight Trail
    Up Romance Road
1919 Brass Buttons
    Eastward Ho!
    The Lincoln Highwayman
    Sacred Silence
    Six Feet Four
    Some Liar
    A Sporting Chance (American
      Film Co.)
    This Hero Stuff
    When a Man Rides Alone
    Where the West Begins
1920 The Challenge of the Law
    The Iron Rider
    Leave It to Me
    The Man Who Dared
    Shod with Fire
    Twins of Suffering Creek
    The Valley of Tomorrow
Ruth, George Herman "Babe" same as
  Ruth, Babe
1917 The Baseball Revue of 1917*
1920 Headin' Home
Rutherford, John
1920 The Great Shadow
Ruttenberg, Joseph same as **Ruttenberg,**
  Joe
1917 The Blue Streak
    The Painted Madonna
    The Slave
    Thou Shalt Not Steal
    Wife Number Two
1918 The Debt of Honor
    Doing Their Bit
    A Heart's Revenge
    The Woman Who Gave
1919 A Fallen Idol
    My Little Sister
    Woman, Woman!
1920 From Now On
    The Shark
    The Thief
    The Tiger's Cub
Rutter, Louise
1915 An Affair of Three Nations
    The Menace of the Mute
    Milestones of Life

Rutter, Mabel
1917 The Broadway Sport
Ryan, Dick see **Ryan, Richard**
Ryan, Gertrude
1915 The Rosary
1920 The Rose of Nome
Ryan, Hugh see **Conway, Jack**
Ryan, J. W.
1917 Dead Shot Baker
Ryan, James
1916 My Partner
Ryan, James A.
1921 Miss 139
Ryan, Joe same as **Ryan, Joseph**
1916 The End of the Rainbow
1917 The Girl Angle
    The Tenderfoot
Ryan, Mary
1915 Stop Thief!
Ryan, Mona
1914 The Education of Mr. Pipp
1916 The Other Girl
Ryan, Richard same as **Ryan, Dick**
1916 The Isle of Life
1917 Her Soul's Inspiration
    The Scarlet Crystal
1920 David and Jonathan
Ryan, Sam
1914 The Taint
1915 The Galloper
    The Spender
1918 The Love Net
1919 High Pockets
Ryan, Sam J. same as **Ryan, Samuel J.**
1916 Charity
    The Fourth Estate
1917 Peggy, the Will O' the Wisp
1919 The Open Door
Ryder, J. P.
1920 The Invisible Divorce
Ryder, Pidgie
1920 The Invisible Divorce
Ryder, Walter
1917 The Tides of Fate
Ryecroft, Leslie
1919 Beware
Ryland, Cpl. Bob
1918 The Unbeliever
Ryley, James could be same as **Riley,**
  James
1916 By Whose Hand?
Ryley, Phil
1918 Just for Tonight
    Uncle Tom's Cabin
Ryno, William same as **Rhino, William;**
  Ryno, Bill; Ryno, W. H.
1914 The Spoilers
1915 The Cowboy and the Lady
    My Best Girl
1917 For Liberty
    The Heart of Texas Ryan
    This Is the Life
1919 The Boomerang
    Love Is Love
    Vagabond Luck
1920 Bullet Proof
    The Hell Ship
    Twins of Suffering Creek

S

Saalman, Nell
1918 Miss Mischief Maker
Sabin, Ruth
1920 Humoresque
Sabine, Martin
1915 An Affair of Three Nations
    The House of Fear
    The Menace of the Mute
1916 The Pursuing Vengeance
Sabo, G.
1914 Rip Van Winkle
Sachs, Nat see **Sack, Nathaniel**
Sachs, Ruth Buchanan
1920 Woman's Man
Sack, Nathaniel same as **Sachs, Nat;**
  Sack, Nathan; Saxe, Nathaniel
1914 The Man from Mexico
1915 The Glory of Youth
    The Luring Lights

Mistress Nell
The Prince and the Pauper
1916 Less Than the Dust
The Social Secretary
1917 Peggy, the Will O' the Wisp
1918 Innocent

Sacker, Amy E.
1918 The Ghost Flower
Shifting Sands

Sackson, Hugh
1920 Sand!

Sackville, Effie
1916 The Adventures of Kathlyn

Sackville, Gordon
1914 An Odyssey of the North
1915 Beulah
1916 Boots and Saddles
Pay Dirt
The Power of Evil
The Shrine of Happiness
The Sultana
1917 The Best Man
The Devil's Bait
The Girl Angle
Mentioned in Confidence
Zollenstein*
1918 Angel Child
The Law That Divides
Petticoats and Politics
Three X Gordon
Whatever the Cost
1919 The Arizona Cat Claw
The Boomerang
1920 The Girl Who Dared
Homespun Folks
Honor Bound
The One Way Trail

Sadlek, Charles
1917 The Crimson Dove

Sadler, Josie
1915 What Happened to Jones
1918 The House of Glass

Sage, Stuart
1916 The War Bride's Secret
1917 Troublemakers
Two Little Imps
1920 The Deep Purple

Sainpolis, John same as **Sainpolis, John M.; Saintpolis, John**
1914 Joseph and His Coat of Many Colors
Soldiers of Fortune
1915 Bondwomen
Wormwood
1916 The Salamander
The Social Highwayman
The World Against Him
The Yellow Passport
1917 The Fortunes of Fifi
The Love That Lives
The Mark of Cain
The Mystic Hour
The Public Defender
Sapho
Sleeping Fires
1918 All Woman
Laughing Bill Hyde
Money Mad
Resurrection
1919 The Poison Pen
1920 The Great Lover
Old Dad

St. Bau, Clio
1919 His Father's Wife

St. Clair, Mal
1919 Yankee Doodle in Berlin

St. Claire, Ada
1917 The Runaway

St. Gaudens, Homer
1920 The Truth About Husbands

St. George, Jenny
1917 Sadie Goes to Heaven

St. James, William H. same as **St. James, W. H.**
1917 The Runaway
1918 Our Mrs. McChesney

St. John, Adela Rogers see **St. Johns, Adela Rogers**

St. John, Mary
1917 Anything Once

St. Johns, Adela Rogers same as **St. John, Adela Rogers**
1918 Marked Cards
Old Love for New
Secret Code

St. Leger, H. P.
1918 Lest We Forget

St. Leonard, Florence
1917 The Bar Sinister

Sainty, L.
1915 The Frame-Up
The Long Chance

Sais, Marin
1914 The Boer War
Shannon of the Sixth
1915 The Barnstormers
The Pitfall
1918 The City of Dim Faces
His Birthright
The Vanity Pool
1919 Bonds of Honor

Salinger, Helen
1917 Polly of the Circus

Salisbury, Dr. Edward A. same as **Salisbury, Edward A.**
1915 On the Spanish Main
Pirate Haunts
Wild Life of America in Films

Salisbury, Monroe
1914 Brewster's Millions
The Man from Home
The Master Mind
Ready Money
Rose of the Rancho
The Squaw Man
1915 After Five
Double Trouble
A Gentleman of Leisure
The Goose Girl
The Lamb
1916 Ramona
1917 The Cook of Canyon Camp
The Desire of the Moth
The Devil's Assistant
The Door Between
The Eyes of the World
The Price of Her Soul
The Savage
The Silent Lie
Zollenstein
1918 The Eagle
The Guilt of Silence
Hands Down
Hugon, the Mighty
Hungry Eyes
The Red, Red Heart
That Devil, Bateese
Winner Takes All
1919 The Blinding Trail
His Divorced Wife
The Light of Victory
The Man in the Moonlight
The Millionaire Pirate
The Sleeping Lion
The Sundown Trail
1920 The Barbarian
The Phantom Melody

Sally, the chimpanzee
1918 Tarzan of the Apes

Sally, Janet
1918 The Lure of Luxury

Salter, Harold
1919 The Law of Nature

Salter, Lou
1915 Matrimony
1918 Tyrant Fear
1919 Spotlight Sadie

Salter, Thelma
1915 The Alien
The Disciple
Matrimony
1916 The Wasted Years
1917 The Crab
Happiness
In Slumberland
The Last of the Ingrams
1918 Selfish Yates
1920 Huckleberry Finn
The Kentucky Colonel

Saltus, Edgar
1920 The Paliser Case

Salzen, Gussie von
1918 The Vigilantes

Sam, a lion
1917 Man and Beast

Sambo same as **Sambo, Little**
1918 Dolly Does Her Bit
Dolly's Vacation
Milady O' the Beanstalk
The Voice of Destiny
Winning Grandma
1919 The Little Diplomat
The Old Maid's Baby

Sambrook, J. W.
1914 The Christian

Samms, Gladys
1915 The House of a Thousand Candles

Samoloff, Leonid
1914 Should a Woman Divorce?

Sampson, Manuel
1917 The Frame Up

Sampson, Teddy
1914 Home, Sweet Home
1915 The Fox Woman
The Outlaw's Revenge
The Pretty Sister of Jose
1916 As in a Looking Glass
Cross Currents
The Weakness of Man
1918 Her American Husband
1919 Fighting for Gold

Samuelson, G. B.
1920 David and Jonathan
Her Story
Love in the Wilderness
The Night Riders
The Price of Silence
The Ugly Duckling

San Martin, Carlos
1920 The Dancin' Fool

Sanborn, Robert A.
1918 The Changing Woman

Sanders, W. H.
1919 A Man's Duty

Sanderson, Grace Marbury
1918 The Finger of Justice

Sanderson, Julia
1917 The Runaway

Sands, Mary
1917 More Truth Than Poetry

Sandway, Mary
1916 The Devil at His Elbow

Sanford, J. Fred
1917 The Road Between

Sanford, Phil same as **Sanford, Philip**
1917 His Father's Son
The White Raven
1918 Revelation
The Sign Invisible
1919 Broken Barriers
Sandy Burke of the U-Bar-U
1920 Heritage
Other Men's Shoes

Sanford, Roy S.
1918 Within the Cup

Sanford, Stanley
1919 After His Own Heart

Sanger, Mr.
1916 My Partner

Sanger, Margaret
1916 Where Are My Children?*
1917 Birth Control

Sankey, Bess
1915 Blue Grass
1916 The Heart of New York

Sanson, Frances
1917 The Lust of the Ages

Santell, Al same as **Santel, Al**
1916 Bluff
Lonesome Town
A Million for Mary
Three Pals
1917 Beloved Rogues
1920 It Might Happen to You

Santschi, Thomas same as **Santschi, Tom**
1914 The Spoilers
1916 The Adventures of Kathlyn
The Country That God Forgot
The Crisis
The Garden of Allah

1917 Beware of Strangers
Who Shall Take My Life?
1918 The City of Purple Dreams
Code of the Yukon
The Hell Cat
Little Orphant Annie
The Still Alarm
1919 Broken Commandments
Eve in Exile
Her Kingdom of Dreams
In Search of Arcady
The Love That Dares
The Railroader
Rose of the West
Shadows
The Stronger Vow
1920 The Cradle of Courage
The North Wind's Malice

Sap, J. Shakespeare
1920 The Poor Simp

Sargeant, Louis see **Sargent, Lewis**

Sargeantson, Kate see **Sergeantson, Kate**

Sargent, George L. same as **Sargent, George**
1914 A Gentleman from Mississippi
1915 The Call of the Dance
Midnight at Maxim's
1916 The Fall of a Nation
Philip Holden—Waster
The Sable Blessing
1917 The Gilded Youth
High Speed
1920 The Broadway Bubble
The Prey
The Whisper Market

Sargent, Leo
1917 High Speed

Sargent, Lewis same as **Sargeant, Louis; Sargent, Lew**
1917 Aladdin and the Wonderful Lamp
1918 Ace High
Ali Baba and the Forty Thieves
Fan Fan
Six Shooter Andy
Treasure Island
1919 The Coming of the Law
The Heart of Youth
Miss Adventure
1920 Huckleberry Finn
The Soul of Youth

Sarjeanston, Kate see **Sergeantson, Kate**

Sarlabous, Marie de
1916 A Prince in a Pawnshop
1917 The Flaming Omen

Sarle, Regina
1919 Nugget Nell

Sarno, Hector V. same as **Sarno, Hector; Sarno, Victor**
1914 Under the Gaslight
The Woman in Black
1915 The Hungarian Nabob
1916 The Black Sheep of the Family
The Isle of Life
1917 Cleopatra
Du Barry
The Island of Desire
The Plow Woman
The Rose of Blood
Some Boy!
This Is the Life
1918 Go West, Young Man
A Little Sister of Everybody
1919 The Crimson Gardenia
For a Woman's Honor
The Forfeit
Give and Take
The Gray Wolf's Ghost
The Island of Intrigue
The Right to Happiness
1920 Rio Grande
Roman Candles
The Silver Horde

Sartov, Hendrick
1920 Way Down East

Sarver, Charles
1916 Anton the Terrible
The House with the Golden Windows
The Plow Girl
The Soul of Kura-San
1917 The Little Boy Scout
A Mormon Maid
Shall We Forgive Her?

1918 Kidder and Ko
A Little Sister of Everybody
T'Other Dear Charmer
1919 Bringing Up Betty
Forest Rivals
Sarver, Lucy
1918 Dolly Does Her Bit
1919 Heart of Gold
Home Wanted
Saskin, A. could be same as **Saskins, Alex**
1920 The Amateur Wife
Saskins, Alex could be same as **Saskin, A.**
1920 Blackbirds
Satherwaite, Lillian see **Southerwaite, Lucille**
Satterthwaite, Lucille see **Southerwaite, Lucille**
Sauerman, Carl same as **Sauermann, Carl**
1917 The Beautiful Adventure
1918 My Wife
1919 The American Way
The Black Circle
Saum, Clifford P. same as **Saum, Clifford**
1914 The $5,000,000 Counterfeiting Plot
1915 The Blindness of Devotion
1918 The Kaiser's Finish
Lest We Forget
My Four Years in Germany
Saums, Grace same as **Saum, Grace**
1917 Her Greatest Love
Sowers and Reapers
Saunders, Alice
1918 Dolly Does Her Bit
Saunders, Eddie could be same as **Saunders, Edward**
1917 The Clean Gun
Saunders, Edward could be same as **Saunders, Eddie**
1918 Little Miss Grown-Up
Miss Mischief Maker
No Children Wanted
Saunders, Jackie
1914 Ill Starred Babbie
The Will O' the Wisp
1915 The Adventures of a Madcap
Pearls of Temptation
1916 Rose of the Alley
The Shrine of Happiness
The Twin Triangle
1917 Bab the Fixer
Betty Be Good
A Bit of Kindling
The Checkmate
Somewhere in America*
Sunny Jane
The Wildcat
1919 The Miracle of Love
Muggsy
Someone Must Pay
1920 Dad's Girl
Drag Harlan
The Scuttlers
Saunders, Lucille
1915 The Chocolate Soldier
Savage, Aileen
1920 The Cost
The Sport of Kings
Stolen Moments
Savage, Henry W.
1914 The County Chairman
The Million
1915 Excuse Me
1916 Madame X
Savage, Jim
1919 Bolshevism on Trial
La Savillas
1914 Mrs. Wiggs of the Cabbage Patch
Saville, DeSacia could be same as **Saville, Gus**
1919 The Virtuous Model
Saville, Gus C. same as **Saville, Gus; Soville, Gus;** could be same as **Saville, DeSacia**
1918 Irish Eyes
1919 Almost a Husband
The Brand
The Girl from Outside

1920 King Spruce
Sunset Sprague
Two Moons
Savold, James
1920 The World and His Wife
Savoy, Viola
1915 Alice in Wonderland
The Spendthrift
Sawyer, Arthur H. same as **Sawyer, Arthur**
1919 Virtuous Men
1920 Love, Honor and Obey
Sawyer, Carl
1920 The Best of Luck
Sawyer, Doris
1916 The Hand of Peril
Jaffery
The Libertine
Tangled Fates
Sawyer, Joan
1917 Love's Law
Sawyer, Laura
1913 Chelsea 7750
The Daughter of the Hills
An Hour Before Dawn
The Port of Doom
1914 In the Name of the Prince of Peace
One of Millions
A Woman's Triumph
1915 The Daughter of the People
1917 The Valentine Girl
Saxe, Florentine
1915 Business Is Business
Saxe, Nathaniel see **Sack, Nathaniel**
Saxe, Templer same as **Saxe, Templar**
1915 The Breath of Araby
1916 The Dawn of Freedom
The Devil's Prize
The Footlights of Fate
Hesper of the Mountains
The Man Behind the Curtain
The Ordeal of Elizabeth
The Shop Girl
The Supreme Temptation
The Tarantula
1917 Babette
The Fettered Woman
In the Balance
Intrigue
Mary Jane's Pa
The Sixteenth Wife
Womanhood, the Glory of the Nation
1918 The Business of Life
Miss Ambition
One Thousand Dollars
The Triumph of the Weak
The Wooing of Princess Pat
1919 Fighting Destiny
From Headquarters
Human Desire
The Lion and the Mouse
Mind the Paint Girl
The Teeth of the Tiger
1920 The Dangerous Paradise
Oil
Slaves of Pride
The Sleep of Cyma Roget
Two Weeks
Whispers
Saxman, Alice Fair see **Saxmar, Alice von**
Saxman, Robert
1920 The Return of Tarzan
Saxmar, Alice von same as **Saxman, Alice Fair**
1915 Sunshine Molly
1916 The Stronger Love
Saxon, Hugh
1919 The Other Half
1920 Body and Soul
The Heart of Twenty
Her Five-Foot Highness
Skyfire
Sayre, Caroline
1920 Live Sparks
Scammon, P. R.
1918 My Own United States
Scanlon, Edward
1920 It Might Happen to You

Scar Face
1916 The World Against Him
Scarborough, George same as **Scarborough, George M.**
1915 The Final Judgment
1917 All for a Husband
The Painted Madonna
Unknown 274
When False Tongues Speak
1918 Cupid's Roundup
The Forbidden City
A Heart's Revenge
Her One Mistake
Her Only Way
Her Price
The Liar*
Stolen Honor
Under the Yoke
1919 The Heart of Wetona
Luck and Pluck
Scarborough, Harry
1917 The Cinderella Man
Scardon, Paul
1914 Uncle Tom's Cabin
1915 The Battle Cry of Peace
The Breath of Araby
The Juggernaut
The Sins of the Mothers
1916 The Alibi
The Dawn of Freedom
The Enemy
The Hero of Submarine D-2
The Island of Surprise
Phantom Fortunes
A Prince in a Pawnshop
The Redemption of Dave Darcey
Rose of the South
1917 Apartment 29
Arsene Lupin
The Grell Mystery
The Hawk
Her Right to Live
In the Balance
The Love Doctor
The Maelstrom
Soldiers of Chance
The Stolen Treaty
Transgression
1918 All Man
A Bachelor's Children
The Desired Woman
A Game with Fate
The Golden Goal
The Green God
Hoarded Assets
The King of Diamonds
The Other Man
Tangled Lives
1919 Beating the Odds
Beauty-Proof
The Darkest Hour
Fighting Destiny
The Gamblers
In Honor's Web
The Man Who Won
Silent Strength
1920 The Broken Gate
Children Not Wanted
Her Unwilling Husband
Milestones
Partners of the Night
Scervin, Margaret see **Skirvin, Marguerite**
Schable, Robert
1919 The Firing Line
The Marriage Price
Redhead
The Test of Honor
The World to Live In
1920 On with the Dance
A Romantic Adventuress
Sinners
The Stolen Kiss
Schade, Betty
1914 The Opened Shutters
1915 After Five
1916 The Dumb Girl of Portici
The Heritage of Hate
The Love Girl
The Man from Bitter Roots
1917 The Bronze Bride
The Edge of the Law
Fighting Mad

The Reward of the Faithless
The Scarlet Crystal
1918 The Girl in the Dark
The Guilt of Silence
Nobody's Wife
Painted Lips
The Scarlet Drop
The Scarlet Road
Winner Takes All
The Wolf and His Mate
A Woman's Fool
1919 Bare Fists
Bonds of Love
The Crimson Gardenia
Deliverance
The Divorce Trap
A Girl in Bohemia
Happiness à la Mode
Spotlight Sadie
Through the Wrong Door
Who Will Marry Me?
Whom the Gods Would Destroy
1920 Darling Mine
Flame of Youth
Shod with Fire
The Soul of Youth
The Village Sleuth
Schaefer, Anne same as **Schaefer, Ann; Schaeffer, Ann; Schaeffer, Anna; Schaeffer, Anne; Schaffer, Anne**
1915 The Chalice of Courage
1916 Through the Wall
1917 The Little Princess
Melissa of the Hills
Periwinkle
The Price of a Good Time
1918 The Demon
The Ghost of Rosy Taylor
Her Moment
Impossible Susan
Johanna Enlists
Social Briars
Unclaimed Goods
1919 Cupid Forecloses
A Fighting Colleen
The Jungle Trail
Over the Garden Wall
Six Feet Four
The Solitary Sin
The Weaker Vessel
1920 The Chorus Girl's Romance
The City of Masks
Mrs. Temple's Telegram
Pegeen
Schaefer, Earl
1920 The Unfortunate Sex
Schaefer, Fred
1920 The Gauntlet
The Sea Rider
Schaefer, Herman A. "Germany"
1914 The Giants-White Sox Tour
Schaeffer, Ann see **Schaefer, Anne**
Schaeffer, Sadie
1918 A Soul Without Windows
Schafer, Mellie see **Shafer, Molly**
Schaffer, Anne see **Schaefer, Anne**
Schaffer, Peggy
1918 A Law unto Herself
Schalenberg (full name unknown)
1915 Buckshot John*
Schayer, E. Richard same as **Schayer, Richard**
1916 Sudden Riches
1917 Rasputin, the Black Monk
1918 Blindfolded
The One Woman
1919 Brothers Divided
The Dragon Painter
Flame of the Desert
The House of Intrigue
The Illustrious Prince
A Man's Country
The Tong Man
The Westerners
1919-20 When a Man Loves
1920 An Arabian Knight
The Beggar Prince
The Brand of Lopez
The Cup of Fury
Li Ting Lang
The Spenders
The Woman in Room 13

Scheff, Fritzi
1915 Pretty Mrs. Smith
Schelderfer, Joe see **Shelderfer, Joe**
Schellinger, H. B.
1916 The Ragged Princess
Schellinger, Joe
1919 The Cambric Mask
Schellinger, Rial B. same as **Schellinger, R.; Schellinger, R. B.; Schellinger, Rial**
1916 East Lynne
The Eternal Sapho
The Mischief Maker
Sporting Blood
1917 Camille
Cleopatra
Du Barry
A Modern Cinderella
The Primitive Call
The Rose of Blood
The Small Town Girl
1918 The Kaiser's Finish
My Four Years in Germany
1919 The Fighting Roosevelts
Never Say Quit
1920 Cynthia-of-the-Minute
The Master Mind
Schenck, Earl same as **Schenck, Earl O.**
1916 The Haunted Manor
The Isle of Love
The Madness of Helen
1917 The False Friend
Weavers of Life
1918 The Kaiser's Finish
My Four Years in Germany
Ruling Passions
To Hell with the Kaiser
The Unbeliever
1919 The Great Victory, Wilson or the Kaiser? The Fall of the Hohenzollerns
The Spirit of Lafayette
A Stitch in Time
The Trap
1920 The Blue Pearl
The Harvest Moon
The Sacred Flame
Schenck, Harry
1914 The Line-Up at Police Headquarters
Schenck, Joseph M. same as **Schenck, Joseph**
1917 The Law of Compensation
The Moth
Panthea
Poppy
The Secret of the Storm Country
1918 By Right of Purchase
De Luxe Annie
The Forbidden City
The Ghosts of Yesterday
Her Only Way
Just a Woman
The Safety Curtain
1919 The Heart of Wetona
The Isle of Conquest
The New Moon
The Probation Wife
A Temperamental Wife
A Virtuous Vamp
The Way of a Woman
1920 The Branded Woman
Dangerous Business
A Daughter of Two Worlds
Good References
The Perfect Woman
She Loves and Lies
The Woman Gives
Scherer, Will
1912 Oliver Twist
Scherr, Harry
1915 Cohen's Luck
Schertzinger, Victor L. same as **Schertzinger, Victor**
1915 The Edge of the Abyss
The Winged Idol
1916 The Beckoning Flame
Between Men
Civilization
The Conqueror
D'Artagnan
Peggy

1917 The Clodhopper
His Mother's Boy
The Millionaire Vagrant
The Pinch Hitter
Princess of the Dark
The Son of His Father
Sudden Jim
1918 The Claws of the Hun
Coals of Fire
The Family Skeleton
The Hired Man
His Own Home Town
A Nine O'Clock Town
Playing the Game
Quicksand
String Beans
1919 Extravagance
Hard Boiled
The Homebreaker
Jinx
The Lady of Red Butte
Other Men's Wives
The Peace of Roaring River
Sahara
The Sheriff's Son
Upstairs
When Doctors Disagree
1920 The Blooming Angel
Pinto
The Slim Princess
What Happened to Rosa
Scheurich, Alex
1916 The Argonauts of California—1849
Scheurich, Victor
1916 The Argonauts of California—1849
Schiller, Carl von see **Von Schiller, Carl**
Schiller, Kate
1919 Devil McCare
Schmidt, Adolph
1916 The Dumb Girl of Portici
Schnall, Ida
1916 Undine
Schneider, Carl
1920 Below the Surface
The Brute Master
Hairpins
Her Husband's Friend
His Own Law
Homer Comes Home
Homespun Folks
The Jailbird
The Leopard Woman
Let's Be Fashionable
Love
Love Madness
Rookie's Return
Sex
Silk Hosiery
A Thousand to One
Schneider, James
1914 The Key to Yesterday
Schneider, Louis
1917 The Stainless Barrier
Schneider, Max
1916 The Hidden Scar
Husband and Wife
The Madness of Helen
The Revolt
The Weakness of Man
A Woman's Way
1917 Betsy Ross
The Bondage of Fear
The Dancer's Peril
Darkest Russia
The Divorce Game
The Dormant Power
Easy Money
Man's Woman
A Self-Made Widow
The Woman Beneath
1918 The Appearance of Evil
The Heart of a Girl*
Journey's End
The Power and the Glory
A Soul Without Windows
The Spurs of Sybil
Stolen Hours
Whims of Society
The Witch Woman
1919 An Amateur Widow
The American Way
The Battler

The Black Circle
Bringing Up Betty*
Phil-for-Short
The Praise Agent
The Unveiling Hand
1920 The Blue Pearl
The Riddle: Woman
Schneiderman, George
1915 Carmen (Fox Film Corp.)
A Fool There Was
1917 Cleopatra
A Tale of Two Cities
1918 The Great Love
Les Miserables
Salome
1919 The Lost Princess
Love Is Love
Vagabond Luck
1920 A Connecticut Yankee at King Arthur's Court
Flame of Youth
The Hell Ship
Her Elephant Man
Just Pals
The Little Wanderer
Love's Harvest
Molly and I
Over the Hill to the Poorhouse
Sunset Sprague
Schoedsack, Fred
1920 Moon Madness
Schoenbaum, C. Edgar same as **Schoenbaum, Charles; Schoenbaum, Charles E.; Schoenbaum, Charles Edgar; Schoenbaum, Charles Edward; Schoenbaum, Charles F.; Shoenbaum, C. Edward**
1918 The Girl Who Came Back
The Mystery Girl
The Way of a Man with a Maid
Women's Weapons
1919 An Adventure in Hearts
The Best Man
Fires of Faith
Hawthorne of the U.S.A.
It Pays to Advertise
Love Insurance
Something to Do
Venus in the East
A Very Good Young Man
Why Smith Left Home
The Winning Girl
The Woman Next Door
1920 Always Audacious
Burglar Proof
Held by the Enemy
Miss Hobbs
The Six Best Cellars
Too Much Johnson
Schofield, Paul
1920 Just Pals
The Rose of Nome
Smiling All the Way
The Tiger's Coat
Scholl, Olga Linek same as **Scholl, Olga**
1919 The Heart of Humanity
The Right to Happiness
1920 Once to Every Woman
Scholtz, Abraham same as **Scholtz, A.; Scholtz, Abe**
1918 The Border Legion
1919 Desert Gold
1920 The Cup of Fury
Schomer, Abraham S. same as **Schomer, Abraham**
1916 The Yellow Passport
1918 Ruling Passions
1920 The Chamber Mystery
The Hidden Light
The Sacred Flame
Schooler, Louis
1920 The Brute
Schram, Violet
1916 What Love Can Do
1919 The Gray Wolf's Ghost
Toby's Bow
1920 Big Happiness
Riders of the Dawn
White Lies
Schramm, Karla
1920 The Return of Tarzan

Schrock, Raymond L. same as **Schrock, Raymond**
1915 Courtmartialed
Judy Forgot
The White Terror
1916 Elusive Isabel
The Man Inside
The Sphinx
1917 Her Hour
1918 Caught in the Act
His Royal Highness
In Bad
Leap to Fame
Madame Sphinx
Marriages Are Made
Swat the Spy
1919 Ginger
The Girl with No Regrets
Help! Help! Police!
The Love Auction
Luck and Pluck
Never Say Quit
Putting One Over
The She Wolf
The Winning Stroke
1920 The Third Woman
Schrode, George
1914 Fantasma
Schroeder, Doris
1917 My Fighting Gentleman
The Serpent's Tooth
1918 The Girl Who Wouldn't Quit
A Mother's Secret
My Unmarried Wife
The Price of Applause
Tony America
The Wolf and His Mate
1919 The Trembling Hour
Under Suspicion
1920 The Adorable Savage
The Gilded Dream
The Girl in the Rain
In Folly's Trail
The Path She Chose
A Tokio Siren
Schroell, Nicholas
1920 The Copperhead
Schuette, Oswald F.
1915 On the Firing Line with the Germans*
Schulberg, B. P. same as **Schulberg, Ben**
1913 In the Bishop's Carriage
1914 Tess of the Storm Country
Schulter, Edward J. see **Shulter, Ed J.**
Schultz, Gladys
1915 Just Out of College
Schulze, Jack same as **Schulze, John D.**
1918 My Four Years in Germany
1920 Skinning Skinners
Schuman, Bennie
1917 The Girl of the Timber Claims
Schumann, Milton
1917 Her Official Fathers
The Varmint
Schumen-Heink, Henry
1917 Flirting with Death*
Schumm, Harry
1914 Washington at Valley Forge
1915 The Campbells Are Coming
1916 The Wrong Door
1920 The Path She Chose
Schuyler, David
1918 The Service Star
Schwartz, Abraham
1919 Daughter of Mine
Schwartz, Ira B.
1918 The Prodigal Wife
Schwed, Blanche
1915 The Alien
Scoll, George
1916 A Child of Mystery
Scott, Agnes
1920 Twisted Souls
Scott, Anita d'Este
1916 The Woman's Law
Scott, Betty
1915 The Alster Case
The Blindness of Virtue
The Crimson Wing
A Daughter of the City
The Man Trail

Scott, Cyril
1913 Arizona
1914 The Day of Days
1915 How Molly Malone Made
    Good
    Not Guilty
1916 The Lords of High Decision
Scott, Fred
1920 Reformation
Scott, George W.
1917 Mr. Dolan of New York
Scott, Helen
1920 Smiling All the Way
Scott, Homer
1914 The Key to Yesterday
    The Man Who Could Not Lose
1915 The Clue
    The Secret Orchard
1916 Davy Crockett
    Her Father's Son
    The House of Lies
    The Parson of Panamint
    Pasquale
    Redeeming Love
    The Right Direction*
1917 As Men Love
    Big Timber
    The Happiness of Three
      Women
    Jack and Jill
    Out of the Wreck
    The Prison Without Walls*
    The Spirit of Romance*
    Tom Sawyer
    The Varmint
    The World Apart
1918 His Majesty, Bunker Bean
    Huck and Tom; Or, The
      Further Adventures of Tom
      Sawyer
    The Light of Western Stars
    The Spirit of '17
1919 The Shepherd of the Hills
1920 Deep Waters
Scott, Howard
1916 Intolerance
1919 The Fall of Babylon
1920 Neptune's Bride
    The Tattlers
    White Lies
Scott, Jack (asst dir)
1917 In Again—Out Again
Scott, Joe
1916 The Final Curtain
Scott, John (actor)
1913 Shadows of the Moulin Rouge
Scott, Leigh R.
1919 I'll Get Him Yet
Scott, LeRoy
1920 Partners of the Night
Scott, Lois
1918 Berlin Via America
Scott, Mabel could be same as **Scott, Mabel Julienne**
1915 A Continental Girl
Scott, Mabel Julienne same as **Scott, Mabel Juliene; Scott, Mabel Juline;** could be same as **Scott, Mabel**
1916 The Lash of Destiny
1917 The Barrier
1918 Ashes of Love
    The Sign Invisible
1919 Reclaimed: The Struggle for a
    Soul Between Love and Hate
1920 Behold My Wife
    The Round-Up
    The Sea Wolf
1921 The Jucklins
Scott, Ovid
1919 Injustice
Scott, Rica
1917 The Siren
Scott, W. K. see **Scott, Walter K.**
    (cam)
Scott, Wallace
1914 The Lure
    Rip Van Winkle
1915 Barbara Frietchie
    The Song of the Wage Slave
    The Vampire

Scott, Walter (actor)
1921 The Jucklins
Scott, Walter K. (cam) same as **Scott, W. K.**
1916 Other People's Money
1918 Your Fighting Navy at Work
    and at Play
Scott, William
1916 At Piney Ridge
    A Man of Sorrow
1918 Amarilly of Clothes-Line Alley
    The City of Purple Dreams
    The Devil's Wheel
    Her One Mistake
    Kultur
    Riders of the Purple Sage
    The Scarlet Road
    The Still Alarm
    The Strange Woman
    True Blue
1919 Broken Commandments
    The Call of the Soul
    Chasing Rainbows
    The Divorce Trap
    The Forbidden Room
    Pitfalls of a Big City
    The Price Woman Pays
    The Sneak
    Thieves
1920 The Devil's Riddle
    Flames of the Flesh
    The Mother of His Children
    The Rose of Nome
    A Sister to Salome
    White Lies
    Who's Your Servant?
Scovelle, Phil see **Scoville, Phillip**
Scovill, Ada
1919 Out of the Fog
Scoville, Phillip same as **Scovelle, Phil**
1913 In the Stretch
1914 The Criminal Path
Scudiford, Grace
1920 Something Different
Scully, William J. same as **Scully, William; Scully, William Joseph**
1917 Her Better Self
1918 The Reason Why
1919 The Avalanche
    The Country Cousin
    A Society Exile
    The Witness for the Defense
1920 The Flapper*
    Greater Than Fame
Scutt, W. E.
1920 The Whisper Market
Seabury, Forrest same as **Seaberry, Forrest; Seabury, Forest**
1917 The Girl and the Crisis
    Wild and Woolly
1918 The Honor of His House
    Such a Little Pirate
    The White Man's Law
1919 The Secret Garden
Seacombe, Belle
1918 The Birth of a Race
Seager, Mrs. James B.
1919 Injustice
Sealey, Lewis see **Sealy, Lewis**
Sealock, Jack
1916 The Microscope Mystery
Sealy, Lewis same as **Sealey, Lewis; Sealy, Louis; Sealy, Louis**
1915 Barbara Frietchie
1916 The Unborn
    The Witching Hour
1917 Draft 258
    The Primitive Call
1920 The Fatal Hour
    His House in Order
Searight, Frank
1915 Midnight at Maxim's
Searl, Veta
1916 Charity
1917 Over There
Searles, Sam
1917 The Island of Desire
Sears, A. D. same as **Sears, Al; Sears, Allan; Sears, Allan D.; Sears, Allen** could be same as **Pruden, A. Sears**
1915 The Absentee
    The Birth of a Nation
    The Failure

    The Lost House
    The Martyrs of the Alamo
    The Penitentes
1916 Children of the Feud
    Diane of the Follies
    Hell-to-Pay Austin
    Intolerance
    Reggie Mixes In
    The Rummy
    A Sister of Six
    Sold for Marriage
1917 The Desire of the Moth
    The Girl of the Timber Claims
    The Gown of Destiny
    The Little Yank
    Madame Bo-Peep
    The Regenerates
    The Savage
    A Woman's Awakening
1918 The City of Purple Dreams
    Her Inspiration
    The Kaiser, the Beast of Berlin
    The Red, Red Heart
1919 The Amateur Adventuress
    The Big Little Person
    Destiny
    Heart O' the Hills
1920 Judy of Rogue's Harbor
    Rio Grande
Sears, Laura
1916 Land O' Lizards
    The Voice of Love
1917 The Firefly of Tough Luck
    Flying Colors
    Framing Framers
    In Slumberland
    Time Locks and Diamonds
1918 Without Honor
Sears, Zelda
1920 The Truth
Seaward, Sydney
1914 Doc
    Officer 666
    Pierre of the Plains
Seay, Charles same as **Seay, Charles M.**
1914 Fantasma
1915 Blue Grass
    The Daughter of the Sea
1916 A Circus Romance
1917 The Great Bradley Mystery*
Sebastian, Charles E.
1917 The Downfall of a Mayor
Seddon, Margaret same as **Sedden, Margaret; Sidden, Marguerite**
1915 The Dawn of a Tomorrow
    The Old Homestead
1917 The Girl Without a Soul
    The Land of Promise
    Miss Robinson Crusoe
1919 The Country Cousin
    The Unveiling Hand
1920 Headin' Home
    The Miracle of Money
    Wings of Pride
Sedgwick, "Babe" see **Sedgwick, Eileen**
Sedgwick, Edward same as **Sedgwick, Ed**
1917 The Haunted Pajamas
    The Varmint
    The Yankee Way
1918 Cheating the Public
    Rough and Ready
    Why I Would Not Marry
1919 Checkers
    The Jungle Trail
    The Winning Stroke
1920 The Face at Your Window
    Sink or Swim
Sedgwick, Eileen same as **Sedgwick, "Babe"**
1915 The Eagle's Nest
1916 The Heritage of Hate
    The Isle of Life
1917 Man and Beast
1918 Hell's Crater
1920 Love's Battle
    The White Rider
Sedgwick, Josie
1917 Ashes of Hope
    Fighting Back
    Indiscreet Corinne
    The Maternal Spark
    One Shot Ross

1918 Beyond the Shadows
    The Boss of the Lazy Y
    Hell's End
    Keith of the Border
    The Man Above the Law
    Paying His Debt
    Wild Life
    Wolves of the Border
1919 Jubilo
    The She Wolf
1920 The Lone Hand
Sedgwick, Lloyd
1917 The Mystery of Number 47
1920 Wanted at Headquarters
Sedley, Henry same as **Sedley, Henry J.**
1917 Corruption
1918 The Daredevil
    The Embarrassment of Riches
    His Daughter Pays
    Just for Tonight
1919 Marriage for Convenience
    Taxi
    Thunderbolts of Fate
1920 Birthright
    The Hidden Light
    Voices
See, Ed
1917 Sunshine Alley
Seeley, James
1916 The Pillory
Seeling, Charles R. same as **Seeling, Charles**
1918 Baree, Son of Kazan
    The Dawn of Understanding
    A Gentleman's Agreement
    The Girl from Beyond
    That Devil, Bateese
1919 The Enchanted Barn
    The Wishing Ring Man
1920 Pegeen
    The Third Generation
Seessel, Charles O. same as **Seessel, Charles Osborn; Seessel, Charles Osborne**
1919 Anne of Green Gables
    L'Apache
1920 The Amateur Wife
    Dr. Jekyll and Mr. Hyde
    (Famous Players-Lasky
    Corp.)
    Easy to Get
    Way Down East
Segurola, Andres de
1916 A Prince in a Pawnshop
1917 The Flaming Omen
Seibert, Lavilla
1920 Marooned Hearts
Seiden, Joseph same as **Seiden, Joe**
1915 The Siren's Song
1916 The Eternal Question
    The Question
    The Weakness of Strength
1917 The Lust of the Ages
1918 The Grain of Dust
Seifert, Norma
1918 The Panther Woman
Seigel, Bernard see **Siegel, Bernard**
Seigmann, George see **Siegmann, George**
Seiter, William A.
1920 The Kentucky Colonel
Seitz, Alvin J.
1920 The Girl Who Dared
Seitz, George B. same as **Seitz, George Brackett**
1914 Detective Craig's Coup
1915 The Beloved Vagabond
    The Closing Net
    The Galloper
    Nedra
    Simon, the Jester
    The Spender
1916 The King's Game
    The Light That Failed
    The Precious Packet
1917 Blind Man's Luck
    The Hunting of the Hawk
    The Last of the Carnabys
1918 The Naulahka
1920 Rogues and Romance
Seitz, John same as **Seitz, John F.**
1917 The Serpent's Tooth
    Souls in Pawn
    Whose Wife?

Seivel, Bert
1918 Beauty and the Rogue
     Powers That Prey
1919 The Westerners
1920 Hearts Are Trumps
     The Sagebrusher

Seivel, Bert *see* **Siebel, Bert**

Seke, M. *see* **Seki, Misao**

Seki, Frank *could be same as* **Seki, Misao**
1920 The Purple Cipher

Seki, Misao *same as* **Seke, M.; Seki, Missao;** *could be same as* **Seki, Frank**
1918 Her American Husband
     Mystic Faces
1920 The Breath of the Gods

Selbie, Evelyn
1914 The Good-for-Nothing
1916 The People vs. John Doe
     The Price of Silence
1917 The Flashlight
     The Flower of Doom
     The Hand That Rocks the
        Cradle
     The Mysterious Mrs. M.
     Pay Me
     Sirens of the Sea
     The Terror
1918 The Grand Passion
     The Two-Soul Woman
1920 A Broadway Cowboy
     The Broken Gate
     The Devil to Pay
     Seeds of Vengeance
     Uncharted Channels

Selby, George
1916 Blazing Love

Selby, Gertrude
1916 A Child of Mystery
     The Sign of the Poppy
1917 Double Room Mystery
1918 Kidder and Ko
     Twenty-One
1919 Easy to Make Money

Selby, Norman *same as* **McCoy, Kid; Selby, Kid**
1916 Betty of Graystone
1918 The House of Glass
1919 Broken Blossoms
     Eyes of Youth
     The Hushed Hour
     Secret Service
1920 The Fourteenth Man
     The Honey Bee

Selig, William N. *same as* **Selig, W. N.**
1914 The Spoilers
     Your Girl and Mine: A
        Woman Suffrage Play
1916 The Adventures of Kathlyn
     The Crisis
     The Garden of Allah
     The Ne'er-Do-Well
1917 The Barker
     Beware of Strangers
     The Danger Trail
     Who Shall Take My Life?
1918 Brown of Harvard
     The City of Purple Dreams
     A Hoosier Romance
     Little Orphant Annie
     The Still Alarm
1919 Auction of Souls
1920 The Galloping Devil
     The Jungle Princess

Sell, Henry G. *same as* **Gesell, Henry; Gsell, Henry**
1915 Fine Feathers
1919 The House Without Children
     Thin Ice
     The Twin Pawns
1920 The Empire of Diamonds

Sellers, Ollie L.
1919 When Bearcat Went Dry
     Whom the Gods Would
        Destroy
1920 The Gift Supreme
     Seeds of Vengeance

Sellery, William
1915 The Cave Man
     What Happened to Father

Selman, Joseph
1920 The Place of Honeymoons

Selman, Richard
1915 The Waif
1916 One Day

Seltzer, Charles Alden
1918 Riddle Gawne
1920 Drag Harlan

Selwyn, Clarissa *see* **Selwynne, Clarissa**

Selwyn, Edgar
1914 Pierre of the Plains
1915 The Arab
1918 Dodging a Million
1919 For Better, for Worse

Selwynne, Clarissa *same as* **Selwyn, Clarrisa; Selwyn, Clarisse; Selwynn, Clarissa; Selwynne, Miss; Selwynne, Clara**
1915 The Flash of an Emerald
     Hearts in Exile
     Her Great Match
     Her Own Way
     The Master Hand
     The Running Fight
1916 The Come-Back
     Driftwood
     Gloriana
     The Masked Rider
1917 The Calendar Girl
     The Curse of Eve
     The Double Standard
     Princess Virtue
     The Wax Model
1918 The Bride's Awakening
     Face Value
     The Love Swindle
     Smashing Through
     The Talk of the Town
     A Weaver of Dreams
     The White Man's Law
1919 The Big Little Person
     The Black Gate
     Bonnie, Bonnie Lassie
     Creaking Stairs
     Girls
     Home
     The Parisian Tigress
     The Scarlet Shadow
1920 The Cup of Fury
     Dangerous Days
     Out of the Storm

Selznick, Lewis J.
1914 The Seats of the Mighty
1916 The Common Law
1917 The Honeymoon
     Scandal
1918 Good Night, Paul
     A Lady's Name
     The Lesson
     Mrs. Leffingwell's Boots
     A Pair of Silk Stockings
     Sauce for the Goose
     The Shuttle
     The Studio Girl
     Up the Road with Sallie
1919 Experimental Marriage
     Happiness à la Mode
     Romance and Arabella
     The Veiled Adventure
     Who Cares?
1920 The Amazing Woman
     Blind Youth
     The Dangerous Paradise
     Darling Mine
     The Desperate Hero
     Everybody's Sweetheart
     The Greatest Love
     Out of the Snows
     Pleasure Seekers
     The Poor Simp
     The Road of Ambition
     Sooner or Later
     Whispers
     The Woman Game
     Youthful Folly

Selznick, Myron
1919 The Spite Bride
     Upstairs and Down
1920 The Flapper

Semels, Harry *same as* **Semmels, Harry**
1919 The American Way
     A Fallen Idol
     Here Comes the Bride

1920 Rogues and Romance

Seng, Frank J.
1918 Parentage

Sennett, Mack
1914 Tillie's Punctured Romance
1915 My Valet
     A Submarine Pirate
1916 A Modern Enoch Arden
1918 Mickey
1919 Yankee Doodle in Berlin
1920 Down on the Farm
     Love, Honor and Behave
     Married Life

Sensabaugh, Roy S. *same as* **Sensabaugh, Roy**
1917 Youth
1918 Journey's End
1919 Miss Crusoe

Serena, Ja. A.
1915 Wheat and Tares; A Story of
     Two Boys Who Tackle Life
     on Diverging Lines*

Sergeantson, Kate *same as* **Sargeantson, Kate; Sarjeantson, Kate**
1915 Who's Who in Society
1916 Passers By
1917 The Beautiful Adventure
     Outcast

Serino, Josef de
1919 Deliverance

Serrano, Vincent
1915 Lydia Gilmore
1917 A Modern Monte Cristo
     One Law for Both
1919 Eyes of Youth
     The Virtuous Model
1920 The Branded Woman
     The Deep Purple
     Silk Husbands and Calico
        Wives

Serruys, Mlle. Marguerite
1919 Fool's Gold

Sershon, Rosalie
1919 A Sage Brush Hamlet

Serwill, Lucille
1917 The Devil's Bait

Seville, Emily
1920 Kismet

Sexton, Hazel
1919 The American Way
     Anne of Green Gables

Seybolt, Eleanor
1917 Her Sister
1918 The Impostor

Seyffertitz, Gustav von *same as* **Clonblough, G. Butler; Clonbough, G. Butler; Clonebough, G. Butler; Seyffertitz, G. V.; Seyffertitz, George von; Seyffertitz, Gustav; Seyffertitz, Gustave von; Von Seyffertitz, Gustav**
1917 The Countess Charming
     The Devil-Stone
     Down to Earth
     The Little Princess
1918 Hidden Pearls
     His Majesty, Bunker Bean
     Less Than Kin
     Old Wives for New
     Rimrock Jones
     The Source
     Till I Come Back to You
     The Whispering Chorus
     The Widow's Might
1919 The Dark Star
     The Secret Garden
     The Vengeance of Durand
1920 Dead Men Tell No Tales
     Even As Eve
     Madonnas and Men
     Slaves of Pride
     The Sporting Duchess

Seymour, Carol
1916 The Half Million Bribe

Seymour, Clarine
1917 It Happened to Adele
1919 The Girl Who Stayed Home
     Scarlet Days
     True Heart Susie
1920 The Idol Dancer

Seymour, Pauline
1914 Three Weeks

Seymour, Walter R.
1914 When Rome Ruled

Shade, Betty
1919 The Girl with No Regrets

Shafer, Molly *same as* **Schafer, Mellie**
1916 Dulcie's Adventure
     Purity
1918 Nine-Tenths of the Law

Shaffer, Marie
1920 The Fatal Hour

Shaffner, Lillian
1916 The Sunbeam

Shafroth, John F.
1915 Prohibition*

Shaklein, Bessie
1915 The Waif

Shalet, Edmund
1915 Bella Donna

Shallenberger, W. E.
1915 The Buzzard's Shadow*
1917 The Deemster
1918 Her Aviator*

Shannon, Alex *same as* **Shannon, A.; Shannon, Alex K.; Shannon, Alexander**
1916 The Battle of Life
     Daredevil Kate
     The Velvet Paw
     War Brides
1917 Barbary Sheep
     The Eternal Sin
     The Man Who Forgot
     Royal Romance
     Unknown 274
1918 A Doll's House
     The Road to France
     Stolen Orders
     A Woman of Redemption
1919 The Social Pirate
     The Steel King
     The Woman of Lies
1920 Dr. Jekyll and Mr. Hyde
     (Pioneer Film Corp.)
     Girl of the Sea
     The Little Outcast
     Stolen Moments

Shannon, Effie
1914 After the Ball
1916 The Sphinx
1918 Ashes of Love
     Her Boy
1919 The Common Cause

Shannon, Eleanor
1917 S.O.S.

Shannon, Ethel
1919 Easy to Make Money
     John Petticoats
1920 Beware of the Bride
     The Breath of the Gods
     The Master Stroke
     An Old Fashioned Boy

Shannon, Frank
1913 The Prisoner of Zenda

Shannon, Inez
1917 The Beloved Adventuress
1918 The Heart of a Girl
     The Road to France
1920 The Plunger

Shannon, Norris
1917 Her Temptation
     The Little Pirate
1918 The Magic Eye

Shannon, Zyllah
1919 The World to Live In

Shanor, Peggy
1918 The Queen of Hearts
1919 The Echo of Youth

Sharkey, Bert
1915 Hearts in Exile

Sharkey, Jack *same as* **Sharkey, John**
1914 The $5,000,000 Counterfeiting
     Plot
1915 The Game of Three
1916 Those Who Toil
1920 Other Men's Shoes
     The Trail of the Cigarette

Sharp, Henry
1920 Homespun Folks

Sherwin, Louis
1917 Back of the Man
Blood Will Tell
Borrowed Plumage
Fanatics
Flying Colors
The Fuel of Life
The Gown of Destiny
The Iced Bullet
Love or Justice
Madcap Madge
The Millionaire Vagrant
The Snarl
The Stainless Barrier
A Strange Transgressor
Ten of Diamonds
The Weaker Sex
1918 The Argument
The Hard Rock Breed
Her Decision
High Stakes
Real Folks
The Reckoning Day
Secret Code
A Soul in Trust
Who Killed Walton?
1919 The Black Gate
Extravagance
The Forbidden Room
A Gun Fightin' Gentleman
A Little Brother of the Rich
A Man's Fight
Mary Regan
The Master Man
The Mayor of Filbert
Restless Souls
This Hero Stuff
The Tiger Lily
Yvonne from Paris
1920 The Barbarian
The Breath of the Gods
Darling Mine
Dinty
The Forged Bride
Go and Get It
Occasionally Yours
The Phantom Melody
The River's End

Sherwin, Louis
1918 The Better Half
Her Great Chance
1919 Bonds of Love
1920 Milestones

Sherwood, Billy see **Sherwood, William**

Sherwood, Robert
1915 The Millionaire Baby

Sherwood, William same as **Sherwood, Billy**
1915 The Danger Signal
1916 Broken Chains
The Spell of the Yukon
1917 The Beloved Adventuress
The Corner Grocer
The Good for Nothing
The Jury of Fate
Who's Your Neighbor?
1918 The Triumph of Venus

Shields, Ernest same as **Shields, Ernie**
1914 Washington at Valley Forge
1916 Wanted—A Home
The Wrong Door
1917 The Birth of Patriotism
Double Room Mystery
The Little Orphan
Mr. Dolan of New York
The Reed Case
1919 The Speed Maniac
1920 The Purple Cipher
The Square Shooter

Shields, Harry
1917 The Chosen Prince, or the
Friendship of David and
Jonathan

Shields, Sidney same as **Shields, Sydney**
1915 The Bulldogs of the Trail
The Clemenceau Case

Shilling, Arthur
1918 Cheating the Public

Shilling, S. K.
1918 A Broadway Scandal

Shilling, William
1920 The Woman God Sent

Shillingford, Margaret
1917 The Fuel of Life
The Sudden Gentleman

Shindler, Walter
1916 The Precious Packet

Shine, John L. same as **Shine, John**
1916 Little Lady Eileen
1918 The Lie
Mrs. Dane's Defense
1919 The Greater Sinner
1920 Even As Eve
Man and Woman (A. H.
Fischer Features, Inc.)
1921 Miss 139

Shinn, Everett P.
1917 The Spreading Dawn
Sunshine Alley

Shipman, Edna
1919 The Trembling Hour

Shipman, Gertrude
1913 Arizona
Checkers
1914 The Price He Paid

Shipman, Nell
1913 One Hundred Years of
Mormonism
1916 The Fires of Conscience
God's Country and the Woman
Through the Wall
1917 The Black Wolf
My Fighting Gentleman
1918 Baree, Son of Kazan
Cavanaugh of the Forest
Rangers
A Gentleman's Agreement
The Girl from Beyond
The Home Trail
The Wild Strain
1919 Tiger of the Sea
1920 Something New

Shirley, Arthur
1916 Bawbs O' Blue Ridge
The Fall of a Nation
The Valiants of Virginia
1917 Bab the Fixer
Betty Be Good
A Bit of Kindling
The Wildcat
1918 Branding Broadway
Modern Love
1919 Roped
1920 The Triflers

Shirley, Jessie
1917 The Man Hater

Shirley, Robert
1916 Fifty-Fifty
1917 American—That's All
The Food Gamblers
For Valour
Her Excellency, the Governor
Her Father's Keeper
The Man Who Made Good

Shoenbaum, C. Edward see
Schoenbaum, C. Edgar

Short, Antrim same as **Short, Master
Antrim**
1914 John Barleycorn
Where the Trail Divides
1915 The Gambler of the West
Jack Chanty*
1916 The Flirt
Nancy's Birthright
1917 A Jewel in Pawn
Pride and the Man
Tom Sawyer
1918 Amarilly of Clothes-Line Alley
Cupid by Proxy
Huck and Tom; Or, The
Further Adventures of Tom
Sawyer
Hugon, the Mighty
The Narrow Path
A Petticoat Pilot
The Yellow Dog
1919 Destiny
Please Get Married
Romance and Arabella
The Thunderbolt
1920 Fighting Cressy
Old Lady 31
The Right of Way

Short, Don
1920 The Little Shepherd of
Kingdom Come
The Penalty

Short, Florence
1914 Damaged Goods
1915 Destiny; Or, The Soul of a
Woman
1917 The Golden God
The Great Bradley Mystery
The Law That Failed
The Mystic Hour
The Outsider
The Public Defender
When You and I Were Young
1918 Five Thousand an Hour
The Great Adventure
Kildare of Storm
A Man's World
Pay Day
1919 The Great Victory, Wilson or
the Kaiser? The Fall of the
Hohenzollerns
Love, Honor and—?
Phil-for-Short
1920 The Idol Dancer
The Love Flower
Way Down East

Short, Gertrude
1914 The Little Angel of Canyon
Creek
1915 The Cowboy and the Lady
1917 A Bit O' Heaven
The Hostage
The Little Princess
1918 Amarilly of Clothes-Line Alley
The Only Road
Riddle Gawne
1919 Blackie's Redemption
The Heart of Youth
In Mizzoura
1920 Cinderella's Twin
She Couldn't Help It
You Never Can Tell

Short, Hassard
1917 The Moth
1918 The Turn of the Wheel
1919 The Stronger Vow
The Way of a Woman

Short, Joe
1914 An American Citizen

Short, John W.
1918 A Good Loser

Short, Lew same as **Short, Lewis W.**
1915 The Campbells Are Coming
1918 Branding Broadway
1920 Once a Plumber

Short Bull, Chief
1914 The Indian Wars
1917 The Adventures of Buffalo Bill

Shotwell, Marie
1915 Under Southern Skies
1916 The Pillory
The Witching Hour
1917 Enlighten Thy Daughter
Married in Name Only
The Warfare of the Flesh
The Woman and the Beast
1918 Miss Innocence
1919 The Echo of Youth
The Thirteenth Chair
1920 Blackbirds
Chains of Evidence
Civilian Clothes
The Harvest Moon
The Master Mind

Shropshire, C.
1914 The House of Bondage

Shubert, Lee
1918 Just a Woman

Shulter, Edward J. same as **Schulter,
Ed; Schulter, Ed J.; Schulter,
Edward J.; Shulter, E. J.; Shulter,
Edward**
1916 The Light of Happiness
The Purple Lady
Romeo and Juliet (Quality
Pictures Corp.)
The Sunbeam
The Upheaval
1917 The Greatest Power
The Lifted Veil
Peggy, the Will O' the Wisp

1918 Revelation
Social Hypocrites
1919 Satan Junior
1920 Madame Peacock
The Mutiny of the Elsinore
The Right of Way
The Star Rover

Shumate, Harold M. same as **Shumate,
Harry**
1917 Fighting Back
1920 Hitchin' Posts

Shumway, L. C. same as **Shumway,
Leonard C.**
1915 Saved from the Harem
1916 Behind the Lines
1917 The Gates of Doom
Miss Jackie of the Army
The Phantom's Secret
The Plow Woman
1918 The Bird of Prey
The Bride of Fear
Confession
The Fallen Angel
The Girl with the Champagne
Eyes
The Scarlet Road
Two-Gun Betty
1919 Eve in Exile
A Girl in Bohemia
The Love Hunger
Rustling a Bride
The Siren's Song
The Speed Maniac
1920 A Beggar in Purple
The Daredevil
The Gamesters
To Please One Woman
Wanted at Headquarters
When Dawn Came

Shumway, Walter
1918 What Becomes of the
Children?

Sibley, Earl
1915 The Gentleman from Indiana
1916 The Call of the Cumberlands

Sibole, Douglas
1915 An American Gentleman
For $5,000 a Year
The Great Ruby

Sickles, H. G.
1914 The Indian Wars
1917 The Adventures of Buffalo Bill

Sidden, Marguerite see **Seddon,
Margaret**

Siddon, Charles
1915 The Millionaire Baby

Siddons, Herbert J. same as **Siddons, H.
J.**
1914 The Sign of the Cross
1916 The Feud Girl

Sidney, Basil
1920 Romance

Sidney, Scott
1915 Matrimony
The Painted Soul
The Winged Idol
1916 Bullets and Brown Eyes
The Deserter
The Green Swamp
The Road to Love
The Waifs
1917 Her Own People
1918 Tarzan of the Apes
1920 813

Sidwell, Alfred
1913 Checkers
1914 Paid in Full

Sidwell, Frank
1914 The Mystery of the Poison Pool
The Next in Command

Siebel, Bert same as **Seivel, Bert; Siebel,
Bert S.**
1918 Vive La France!
1919 Hard Boiled
1920 Black Is White
The Tiger's Cub

Siebert, William
1916 Sold for Marriage

Siegel, Bernard same as **Seigel, Bernard;
Siegel, Mr.; Siegle, Bernard**
1913 The Third Degree
1914 The Daughters of Men
The Fortune Hunter

Slatteau, George *see* Flateau, George
Slattery, Charles *same as* Slattery,
    Charles J.
1917 The Raggedy Queen
1918 The Death Dance
    The Fair Pretender
    Swat the Spy
    Tell It to the Marines
1919 Shadows
1920 A Daughter of Two Worlds
    A Manhattan Knight
    The White Moll
Slattery, Nellie *same as* Slattery, Nell
1915 Under Southern Skies
1916 The Mischief Maker
    The Narrow Path
1917 Royal Romance
    The Submarine Eye
    Wrath of Love
Slattery, William
1917 The Last Sentence
Slaven, John *could be same as* Slavin,
    John
1918 For Freedom
Slaven, M. J.
1917 Draft 258
Slavin, John *could be same as* Slaven,
    John
1915 A Bunch of Keys
Slevin, James
1914 His Holiness, the Late Pope
    Piux X, and the Vatican
Slider, William
1915 The Avalanche
Sloan, Jeffrey
1920 The Valley of Tomorrow
Sloan, William *same as* Sloane, William
1914 The Rejuvenation of Aunt
    Mary
1915 What Happened to Father
1916 Love's Pilgrimage to America
1918 The Embarrassment of Riches
1920 Down Home
Sloane, June
1918 The Rose of the World
Sloane, Paul H. *same as* Sloan, Paul
1916 The Cossack Whip
1917 The Lady of the Photograph
    Pardners
    The Royal Pauper
1919 The Wolf
1920 The Dead Line
    A Manhattan Knight
    Over the Hill to the Poorhouse
    The Scuttlers
    The Thief
    The Tiger's Cub
Sloane, William *see* Sloan, William
Sloman, Edward *same as* Sloman,
    Edward S.
1916 Dust
    The Inner Struggle
    Lone Star
    Lying Lips
    Philip Holden—Waster*
    Reclamation
    The Twinkler
    A Woman's Daring
1917 The Frame Up
    High Play
    The Masked Heart
    My Fighting Gentleman
    New York Luck
    Pride and the Man
    Sands of Sacrifice
    The Sea Master
    Shackles of Truth
    Snap Judgement
1918 A Bit of Jade
    Fair Enough
    The Ghost of Rosy Taylor
    In Bad
    The Mantle of Charity
    The Midnight Trail
    Money Isn't Everything
    Social Briars
1919 Molly of the Follies
    Put Up Your Hands
    The Westerners
1920 Blind Youth
    Burning Daylight
    The Luck of Geraldine Laird
    The Mutiny of the Elsinore

The Sagebrusher
The Star Rover
Sloman, Hilda Hollis
1915 Jewel
Slow, Edward
1919 Marriage for Convenience
Slye, Edward
1920 The Mysteries of Paris
Small, Howard
1917 House of Cards
Small, Sam, Jr.
1917 Satan's Private Door
1918 The Curse of Iku
Smalley, Phillips
1914 False Colours
    The Merchant of Venice
    The Traitor
1915 Betty in Search of a Thrill
    The Caprices of Kitty
    Captain Courtesy
    The Galloper*
    Jewel
    Scandal
    Sunshine Molly
1916 The Dumb Girl of Portici
    The Eye of God
    The Flirt
    Hop, the Devil's Brew
    Idle Wives
    John Needham's Double
    Saving the Family Name
    Shoes
    Wanted—A Home
    Where Are My Children?
1917 The Double Standard
    The Hand That Rocks the
    Cradle
    The Price of a Good Time
1918 Borrowed Clothes
    The Doctor and the Woman
    For Husbands Only
1919 Forbidden
    When a Girl Loves
Smalley, Mrs. Phillips *see* Weber, Lois
Smallwood, Ray C. *same as* Smallwood,
    Ray
1917 Outwitted
    A Sleeping Memory
1918 Revelation
1920 The Best of Luck
    Billions
    The Heart of a Child
    Madame Peacock
Smaney, Edward P.
1918 Little Miss No-Account
Smart, W. G.
1920 Madonnas and Men
Smiley, Charles
1919 Out of the Fog
1920 The False Road
    Smiling All the Way
    The Spirit of Good
Smiley, Joe *see* Smiley, Joseph
Smiley, John *same as* Smiley, John A.;
    Smiley, John H.
1913 The Battle of Shiloh
1915 The Climbers
1916 The Fortunate Youth
    God's Half Acre
    The Half Million Bribe
    The Upheaval
1917 The Adopted Son
    The Millionaire's Double
    Patsy
    Their Compact
1918 The Beautiful Mrs. Reynolds
    The Brass Check
    Secret Strings
    The Trail to Yesterday
1919 Out Yonder
    The Price of Innocence
    The Unbroken Promise
1920 The Woman Gives
Smiley, Joseph *same as* Smiley, Joe;
    Smiley, Joseph W.
1913 The Battle of Shiloh
1914 Threads of Destiny
1915 Life Without Soul
1916 Energetic Eva
    The Fortunate Youth
1917 Broadway Jones
    Double Crossed
    The Public Be Damned

Seven Keys to Baldpate
Sleeping Fires
1918 Dodging a Million
    The Face in the Dark
    The Heart of a Girl
    Heart of the Wilds
    Her Final Reckoning
    Heredity
    Hitting the Trail
    Joan of Plattsburg
    The Lesson
    The Queen of Hearts
    The Road to France
1919 As a Man Thinks
    Break the News to Mother
    The Isle of Conquest
    Luck and Pluck
    The Moral Deadline
    Never Say Quit
    The Poison Pen
    What Love Forgives
1920 A Daughter of Two Worlds
    The Law of the Yukon
    The Rich Slave
Smith (full name unknown)
1915 The Fairy and the Waif*
1916 The Storm
Smith, Lieutenant
1919 The Heart of Humanity
Smith, Al Ira *same as* Smith, Al I.
1917 Alaska Wonders in Motion
1919 The Girl Alaska
Smith, Albert E.
1914 A Million Bid
1915 The Battle Cry of Peace
    Crooky
    The Heights of Hazard
    The Island of Regeneration
    On Her Wedding Night
    Playing Dead
1916 The Devil's Prize
    Fathers of Men
    The Girl Philippa
    Green Stockings
1917 Dead Shot Baker
    The Marriage Speculation
    The Princess of Park Row
    The Question
    Sunlight's Last Raid
    Who Goes There!
    Womanhood, the Glory of the
    Nation
1918 An American Live Wire
    A Bachelor's Children
    The Beloved Impostor
    The Blind Adventure
    Cavanaugh of the Forest
    Rangers
    The Changing Woman
    The Clutch of Circumstance
    The Dawn of Understanding
    The Desired Woman
    A Diplomatic Mission
    Everybody's Girl
    Find the Woman
    A Game with Fate
    A Gentleman's Agreement
    The Girl from Beyond
    The Girl in His House
    The Girl of Today
    The Golden Goal
    The Green God
    Hoarded Assets
    The Home Trail
    The King of Diamonds
    Little Miss No-Account
    Love Watches
    The Man Who Wouldn't Tell
    The Mating
    The Menace
    Miss Ambition
    A Mother's Sin
    A Nymph of the Foothills
    One Thousand Dollars
    The Other Man
    Over the Top
    The Seal of Silence
    The Soap Girl
    The Song of the Soul
    Tangled Lives
    To the Highest Bidder
    The Triumph of the Weak
    Wild Primrose
    The Wild Strain
    The Woman Between Friends

The Wooing of Princess Pat
1919 The Adventure Shop
    The Captain's Captain
    The Common Cause
    Daring Hearts
    The Darkest Hour
    The Enchanted Barn
    Fortune's Child
    The Gamblers
    The Girl-Woman
    The Highest Trump
    The Lion and the Mouse
    Mind the Paint Girl
    A Rogue's Romance
    Silent Strength
    Too Many Crooks
    The Vengeance of Durand
    The Wolf
1920 Bab's Candidate
    The Courage of Marge
    O'Doone
    Dead Men Tell No Tales
    Dollars and the Woman
    The Garter Girl
    The Gauntlet
    The Midnight Bride
    The Prey
    The Purple Cipher
    Trumpet Island
    The Whisper Market
Smith, Governor Alfred E.
1919 The Volcano
Smith, Alice
1917 His Old-Fashioned Dad
1918 Mr. Fix-It
Smith, Allen
1920 Hell's Oasis
Smith, Art
19-- Official Motion Pictures of the
    Panama Pacific Exposition
    Held at San Francisco,
    Calif.*
Smith, Bertha
1916 The Five Faults of Flo
Smith, Bruce
1916 Pay Dirt
    The Shrine of Happiness
    Spellbound
1917 The Climber
    Feet of Clay
    Mentioned in Confidence
    The Phantom Shotgun
    The Understudy
    The Yellow Bullet
1918 Whatever the Cost
Smith, C., Jr.
1918 The Changing Woman
Smith, C. Aubrey
1915 The Builder of Bridges
    John Glayde's Honor
1916 Jaffery
    The Witching Hour
Smith, Cameron
1920 The Walk-Offs
Smith, Charles
1917 The Co-Respondent
1920 Dinty
Smith, Clara
1914 Your Girl and Mine: A
    Woman Suffrage Play
Smith, Cliff *same as* Smith, Clifford
1917 The Devil Dodger
    The Learnin' of Jim Benton
    The Medicine Man
    One Shot Ross
1918 The Boss of the Lazy Y
    By Proxy
    Cactus Crandall
    Faith Endurin'
    The Fly God
    Keith of the Border
    The Law's Outlaw
    Paying His Debt
    The Pretender
    The Red-Haired Cupid
    The Silent Rider
    Untamed
    Wolves of the Border
1919 The She Wolf
1920 The Cyclone
    The Girl Who Dared
    The Lone Hand
    Three Gold Coins

Smith, David
1918 Baree, Son of Kazan
By the World Forgot
The Changing Woman
The Dawn of Understanding
A Gentleman's Agreement
1919 Cupid Forecloses
The Enchanted Barn
A Fighting Colleen
The Little Boss
Over the Garden Wall
The Wishing Ring Man
A Yankee Princess
1920 The Courage of Marge
O'Doone
Pegeen

Smith, Dudley
1918 The Hell Cat

Smith, Ethel
1916 The Argonauts of
California—1849

Smith, Frank (*actor*) *same as* **Smith, Frank Wilson**
1915 The Marble Heart
The Suburban
1916 Broken Fetters
The Man from Nowhere

Smith, Frank (*scen*) *see* **Smith, Frank Leon**

Smith, Frank J. (*pres*)
1918 The Curse of Iku*

Smith, Frank Leon (*scen*) *same as* **Smith, Frank** (*scen*)
1918 Waifs
1919 Go Get 'Em Garringer
1920 One Hour Before Dawn*

Smith, Fred
1918 In Bad
Jilted Janet
Miss Ambition
1919 The Adventure Shop
Fortune's Child

Smith, George
1919 Shadows

Smith, Gerald O.
1917 The Mysterious Miss Terry

Smith, H. Cameron
1918 Eve's Daughter

Smith, H. J. *see* **Smith, Harry Jay "Doc"**

Smith, Hamilton
1916 In the Diplomatic Service
1917 American Maid
The Barricade
Her Second Husband
1918 I Want to Forget
Just Sylvia
Neighbors
The Power and the Glory
The Sea Wolf
The Zero Hour
1919 Courage for Two
The Scar

Smith, Harry (*actor*) *could be same as* **Smith, Harry Jay "Doc"** (*asst dir, actor*)
1914 The Three of Us

Smith, Harry J. *see* **Smith, Harry Jay "Doc"** (*asst dir, actor*)

Smith, Harry Jay "Doc" (*asst dir, actor*) *same as* **Smith, H. J.**; **Smith, Harry J.**; *could be same as* **Smith, Harry** (*actor*)
1914 The Sign of the Cross
Three Weeks
1915 Vanity Fair
1916 Nearly a King
1917 The Winning of Sally Temple

Smith, Helen G.
1920 Mary Ellen Comes to Town

Smith, Henry
1918 Lest We Forget

Smith, Inez
1919 The Homesteader

Smith, James
1914 The Avenging Conscience*
1920 The Sins of Rosanne
Way Down East

Smith, Jay
1918 The Kaiser, the Beast of Berlin

Smith, John
1916 Immediate Lee

Smith, Joseph
1915 The Apaches of Paris

Smith, Lee Orean
1919 What Love Forgives

Smith, Leigh R. *same as* **Smith, Leigh**
1919 I'll Get Him Yet
Nobody Home
Peppy Polly
1920 Way Down East*

Smith, Leonard *same as* **Smith, Leonard M.**
1915 The Battle Cry of Peace
1916 Bullets and Brown Eyes
For a Woman's Fair Name
The Supreme Temptation

Smith, Lola
1920 Roman Candles

Smith, Luella
1917 The Flaming Omen

Smith, Mrs. M. S.
1914 An American Citizen

Smith, Mark
1915 Zaza
1917 Nearly Married
1918 Annexing Bill
1919 A Damsel in Distress
The Vengeance of Durand
1920 Something Different

Smith, Mary
1915 Old Dutch*

Smith, Minnie
1916 The Colored American
Winning His Suit

Smith, Oliver
1919 Bringing Up Betty

Smith, Reverend Paul
1918 The Finger of Justice

Smith, R. Cecil
1917 Flying Colors
Madcap Madge
Master of His Home
The Maternal Spark
Polly Ann
The Sudden Gentleman
1918 The Claws of the Hun
Coals of Fire
Free and Equal
Green Eyes
The Law of the North
The Marriage Ring
The Mating of Marcella
Playing the Game
Quicksand
Tyrant Fear
1919 L'Apache
The Busher
The Country Cousin
Extravagance
Hard Boiled
His Wife's Friend
The Homebreaker
Sealed Hearts
1920 Broadway and Home
The Daughter Pays
The Figurehead
Footlights and Shadows
His Wife's Money
The Shadow of Rosalie Byrnes
Sooner or Later
The Valley of Doubt
What's Your Husband Doing?

Smith, Robert *same as* **Smith, Robert C.**
1916 The Iron Woman
The People vs. John Doe
Playing with Fire
The Scarlet Woman

Smith, Roscoe
1916 Public Opinion

Smith, Rose
1920 Way Down East

Smith, Russell E.
1915 Captain Macklin
The Daughter of the Sea
Ghosts
The Painted Soul
1916 The Dragon
The Female of the Species
The Strength of Donald
McKenzie
1918 For the Freedom of the East
The Man Hunt*

Smith, Sidney
1915 The Rosary
1916 The Ne'er-Do-Well
1920 Kismet

Smith, Veronica
1919 Injustice

Smith, Vola
1916 The Eagle's Wing
The Price of Silence

Smith, Rev. W. S.
1916 The Colored American
Winning His Suit

Smith, W. Steve, Jr. *same as* **Smith, W. Stephen, Jr.**
1914 The Little Angel of Canyon
Creek
1917 Dead Shot Baker
Money Magic
The Tenderfoot

Smith, Walter
1919 The Career of Katherine Bush

Smith, Wesley
1917 Modern Mother Goose

Smith, Will E. (*cam*)
1916 The Chaperon
The Return of Eve
The Sting of Victory
1917 Burning the Candle

Smith, William (*actor*)
1919 The Great Victory, Wilson or
the Kaiser? The Fall of the
Hohenzollerns

Smith, Winchell
1920 The Saphead

Smithfield, George F.
1917 National Red Cross Pageant*

Smollen, Bradley J. *same as* **Smollen, J. Bradley**
1916 The Hunted Woman
1917 The Night Workers

Smoller, Dorothy
1919 Out of the Fog

Smythe, Florence *same as* **Smyth, Florence**
1915 The Fighting Hope
The Voice in the Fog
The Wild Goose Chase
1916 Common Ground
1917 The Silent Partner
The Winning of Sally Temple

Snead, Mrs. E.
1916 The Colored American
Winning His Suit

Snead, Edgar
1916 The Colored American
Winning His Suit

Snead, Florence
1916 The Colored American
Winning His Suit

Sneeze, Mr.
1915 The Dust of Egypt

Snell, Earle
1919 The Busher
The Heart of Juanita
Just Squaw
1920 The Flame of Hellgate

Snively, Vernon
1916 The Valiants of Virginia

Snook, Fred
1914 Salomy Jane

Snow, Marguerite
1914 Joseph in the Land of Egypt
1915 The Patriot and the Spy
Rosemary
The Second in Command
The Silent Voice
1916 A Corner in Cotton
The Faded Flower
The Half Million Bribe
His Great Triumph
The Upstart
1917 Broadway Jones
The Hunting of the Hawk
1918 The First Law
The Million Dollar Mystery
1918-19
The Missionary*
1919 In His Brother's Place
1920 Felix O'Day
Rouge and Riches
The Woman in Room 13

Snow, William F.
1919 Fit to Win*

Snyder, Clarence
1918 The Hell Cat

Snyder, George
1916 The Crisis

Snyder, Jack
1917 Cassidy
The Food Gamblers
1918 Les Miserables

Snyder, Lillian
1918 Hearts of Love

Snyder, M. (*cam*)
1918 The Woman the Germans Shot

Snyder, Matt (*actor*) *same as* **Snyder, Matt B.**; *could be same as* **Snyder, Nat**
1914 Salomy Jane
1915 The Heart of Maryland
Money
1916 The Crisis
The Garden of Allah
The Unwritten Law

Snyder, Nat *could be same as* **Snyder, Matt**
1915 The Lily of Poverty Flat

Soders, Walter
1920 The Miracle of Money

Sohn, Kathryn
1919 His Official Fiancée

Solman, Alfred
1916 The Mischief Maker
Miss Jackie of the Navy
1917 Little Miss Nobody

Solter, Harry *same as* **Solter, Harry L.**
1917 The Spotted Lily
1918 The Wife He Bought

Somers, Amy *could be same as* **Summers, Amy**
1918 From Two to Six

Somers, Harry
1917 The Lash of Power

Somerville, Roy *same as* **Sommerville, Roy**
1916 Acquitted
The Children in the House
The Devil's Needle
An Innocent Magdalene
Reggie Mixes In
1917 Her Official Fathers
The Little Yank
Stagestruck
1918 The Danger Game
The Embarrassment of Riches
The First Law
The Grain of Dust
Hitting the Trail
The Mysterious Client
Our Little Wife
1919 The Bandbox
The Challenge of Chance
Eastward Ho!
Sacred Silence
The Teeth of the Tiger
What Shall We Do with Him?
1920 The Orphan

Sonnenblick, David
1919 From Headquarters

Sonntag, Emil B.
1920 Before the White Man Came

Sontag, George
1915 The Folly of a Life of Crime

Soon-goot
1913 Hiawatha

Sorelle, William J. *same as* **Sorell, William**; **Sorelle, William**; **Sorrell, William**; **Sorrell, William F.**; **Sorrelle, William**; **Sorrille, William J.**
1914 The Littlest Rebel
Northern Lights
1915 A Continental Girl
The Mummy and the
Humming Bird
The Prince and the Pauper
1916 Common Sense Brackett
Where Is My Father?
1917 The Fortunes of Fifi
1918 Private Peat
1919 The Hand Invisible

19-- The Slave Mart

191

Sorenson, Harriet
1917 Castles for Two
Sorrelle, William *see* **Sorelle, William J.**
Sorrille, William J. *see* **Sorelle, William J.**
Sorter, A. B.
1915 The Long Chance
Sorter, Irma
1916 A Soul Enslaved
1917 A Bit O' Heaven
Sorter, William
1915 Colorado
Sose, Pedro *see* **Sosso, Pietro**
Sosso, Pietro *same as* **Sose, Pedro**
1916 The Garden of Allah
1917 Giving Becky a Chance
Lost in Transit
The Marcellini Millions
1918 The Kaiser, the Beast of Berlin
1919 The Home Town Girl
Sothern, E. H.
1916 The Chattel
An Enemy to the King
1917 The Man of Mystery
National Red Cross Pageant
Sothern, Elsie
1918 All Woman
Sothern, Harry *same as* **Southern, Harry**
1916 Romeo and Juliet (Quality Pictures Corp.)
1919 The New Moon
1920 Blind Wives
While New York Sleeps
Sothern, Jean
1915 Dr. Rameau
Should a Mother Tell?
The Two Orphans
1916 Whoso Findeth a Wife
1917 The Cloud
Her Good Name
Miss Deception
A Mother's Ordeal
A Mute Appeal
1918 Peg O' the Sea
Sothern, Louise
1916 Unto Those Who Sin
1917 The Clean Gun
Sothern, Sam
1919 Eyes of Youth
His Majesty, the American
1920 The Dream Cheater
Silk Husbands and Calico Wives
Whispering Devils
Sottong, Florence
1918 Life or Honor?
Soule, Mrs.
1916 The Shop Girl
Sousa, John Philip
19-- Official Motion Pictures of the Panama Pacific Exposition Held at San Francisco, Calif.*
Soutar, Andrew
1917 Souls Adrift
The Streets of Illusion
1919 The Sealed Envelope
Southard, Bennett
1915 The Cowardly Way
1916 The Dragon
Southard, H. D. *see* **Southard, Harry**
Southard, Harry *same as* **Southard, H. D.; Southard, Howard D.**
1916 Secret Love
1917 God's Man
The Small Town Girl
The Stolen Play
1918 American Buds
1920 The Adventurer
Southard, Howard D. *see* **Southard, Harry**
Southard, Irving
1914 Paid in Full
Southerland, Roy
1917 The Princess of Patches
Southern, Eve
1917 Conscience
1918 Broadway Love

Southern, Harry *see* **Sothern, Harry**
Southern, Virginia
1916 Big Tremaine
Black Friday
1918 Coals of Fire
Southerwaite, Lucille *same as* **Satherwaite, Lillian; Satterthwaite, Lucille**
1917 Polly of the Circus
1918 American Buds
Woman and the Law
Southwell, Harry
1917 Intrigue
Southwick, Mildred
1919 You Never Know Your Luck
Souzade, Richard
1918 The Border Legion
Soville, Gus *see* **Saville, Gus**
Spahn, Anna
1918 Little Red Riding Hood
Spalding, Eleanor
1915 The Flying Twins
Spanuth, H. A.
1912 Oliver Twist
1917 The Frozen Warning
Sparks, Frances
1919 A Romance of Happy Valley
Sparks, Ned *same as* **Sparks, Ned A.**
1915 Little Miss Brown
1919 The Social Pirate
A Temperamental Wife
A Virtuous Vamp
1920 Good References
In Search of a Sinner
Nothing but the Truth
The Perfect Woman
Spaulding, G. S.
1917 Molly Entangled
Spaulding, Georgie D.
1917 The Hostage
Spaulding, Nellie Parker *same as* **Spaulding, Nellie; Spaulding, Mrs. Nellie; Spaulding, Nellie P.; Spaulding, Mrs. Nellie Parker**
1916 The Flight of the Duchess
The Pillory
1917 Her Good Name
The Lust of the Ages
Reputation
1918 The Business of Life
Love Watches
1920 Good References
The Love Expert
The Midnight Bride
Speaker, Tris
1917 The Baseball Revue of 1917*
Spear, Gil
1917 The Auction Block
1919 High Pockets
Spear, Rita
1916 The Kiss
1918 The Death Dance
1919 Come Out of the Kitchen
Speare, Edith
1917 Her Excellency, the Governor
1918 The Woman Between Friends
Spellman, Leora
1920 Wits vs. Wits
Spence, Annie Laurie
1919 A Broadway Saint
Spence, Edna
1915 The Unbroken Road
Spence, Ralph H. *same as* **Spence, Ralph**
1917 The Pride of New York
This Is the Life
The Yankee Way
1918 A Camouflage Kiss
I'll Say So
Jack Spurlock, Prodigal
Miss Innocence*
On the Jump
1919 Never Say Quit
Smiles
1920 Husband Hunter
Roman Candles
Sink or Swim
Spencer, Charles F.
1916 Lonesome Town

Spencer, Elizabeth
1917 Infidelity
Spencer, Ernest
1919 The Girl from Outside
Spencer, George Soule
1913 The Third Degree
1914 The Daughters of Men
The Fortune Hunter
The Gamblers
The House Next Door
The Lion and the Mouse
The Wolf
1915 Blue Grass
The Climbers
The College Widow
The District Attorney
The Great Ruby
The Sporting Duchess
1916 The Clarion
The Evangelist
1917 Trooper 44
The Web of Life
Spencer, Jean
1920 The Devil's Passkey
Spencer, Marvel
1916 The Bait
From Broadway to a Throne
The Heart of Tara
1917 A Bit O' Heaven
Polly Put the Kettle On
Spencer, Nell
1917 The Skylight Room
Spencer, Richard V. *same as* **Spencer, R. V.**
1914 The Voice at the Telephone
1916 The Deserter
Pidgin Island
1917 The Hidden Spring
Paradise Garden
The Promise
The Square Deceiver
Under Handicap
Spencer, Tom
1916 Gretchen, the Greenhorn
Spencer, Walter
1916 The Heart of Tara
Spencer, William
1916 The Twinkler
1917 The Frame Up*
Peggy Leads the Way
Spere, Charles
1918 A Desert Wooing
The Man Who Wouldn't Tell
1919 A Bachelor's Wife
A Fighting Colleen
The Hellion
The Lamb and the Lion
The Solitary Sin
1920 Pegeen
The Tiger's Coat
Sperl, Edna May
1920 Other Men's Shoes
Spiegel (full name unknown)
1915 The Fairy and the Waif*
Spier, Angelica
1916 A Parisian Romance
Spike, the dog
1919 The Lincoln Highwayman
Spingler, Harry *same as* **Spingler, Henry; Springer, Harry; Springer, Harry**
1914 The Banker's Daughter
Captain Swift
The Greyhound
The Idler
Northern Lights
The Ordeal
The Thief
1915 From the Valley of the Missing
A Gilded Fool
The Plunderer
Samson
1916 The Bondman
Driftwood
Her Surrender
The House of Mirrors
1917 The Spreading Dawn
1917-18 The Devil's Playground
1918 Les Miserables
A Perfect Lady
1919 The Black Gate
The Lincoln Highwayman

The Woman Under Cover
1920 Flames of the Flesh
Merely Mary Ann
The Scuttlers
Sherry
Spitalny, Phil
1918 Virtuous Wives
Spitzer, Nellie
1917 Intrigue
Spong, Hilda
1915 Divorced
Spooner, Cecil
1914 The Dancer and the King
Nell of the Circus
Spooner, F. E.
1919 As the Sun Went Down
Spoor, George K.
1917 Efficiency Edgar's Courtship
Pants
Two-Bit Seats
1918 Men Who Have Made Love to Me
A Pair of Sixes
Uneasy Money
Spottswood, James C. *same as* **Spottswood, James**
1919 The Climbers
1920 The Love Expert
Spraggins, Virginia
1917 The Defeat of the City
Sprague, A. C.
1919 The Beloved Cheater
Sprague, Arthur E.
1920 The Sacred Ruby
Sprague, Norah
1918 Dodging a Million
Springer, Harry *see* **Spingler, Harry**
Sprotte, Bert *same as* **Sprotte, B.; Sprotte, Berthold**
1918 The Border Wireless
Selfish Yates
Shark Monroe
Vive La France!
1919 Breed of Men
The Brute Breaker
The Girl from Outside
The Shepherd of the Hills
Wagon Tracks
The World Aflame
1920 Below the Deadline
The Deceiver
The Golden Trail
Jes' Call Me Jim
Out of the Dust
Two Moons
Sprotti, G.
1917 Paradise Garden
Squire, Harry
1917 Salt of the Earth
Stabler, Harry S.
1917 Brand's Daughter
Stafford, Frank
1912 Oliver Twist
Stafford, H. G.
1915 Heritage
Stafford, John
1917 The Lincoln Cycle
Stafford, Marvel
1916 The Apostle of Vengeance
Stagg, Clinton H.
1916 A Gutter Magdalene
The Race
Stahl, John M.
1917 The Lincoln Cycle
1918 Suspicion
Wives of Men
1919 Her Code of Honor
The Woman Under Oath
1920 Greater Than Love
The Woman in His House
Women Men Forget
Stahl, Walter Richard
1917 Hate
Stall, Fred
1917 Shame
Stallard, Ernest
1917 An American Widow
Stallings, George
1917 The Baseball Revue of 1917*

Stamford, Henry
1918 Uncle Tom's Cabin
Stammers, Frank
1916 Peck O' Pickles
Stan, Rita
1914 The Lost Paradise
Stanard, Ethel
1917 The Adventurer
Standing, Mr. *could be same as*
Standing, Sir Guy; Standing,
Herbert *(born* 1846*);* **Standing,**
Herbert, Jr. *(born* 1887*);* **Standing,**
Jack; Standing, Percy *or* **Standing,**
Wyndham
1914 Alone in New York
Standing, Blanche
1919 Let's Elope
The Witness for the Defense
Standing, Gordon H. *same as* **Standing,**
Gordon
1919 Three Black Eyes
1920 The Little Outcast
Man and Woman (A. H.
Fischer Features, Inc.)
1921 Miss 139
Standing, Sir Guy *could be same as*
Standing, Mr.
Standing, Mrs. Guy
1913 Across the Continent
Standing, H. *could be same as*
Standing, Herbert, Jr. *(born* 1887*)*
1915 Buckshot John*
Standing, Herbert *(born* 1846*) could be*
same as **Standing, Mr.**
1914 False Colours
1915 Betty in Search of a Thrill
Buckshot John
The Caprices of Kitty
Captain Courtesy
The Gentleman from Indiana
Help Wanted
The Hypocrites
Jane
Kilmeny
The Majesty of the Law
Peer Gynt
The Rug Maker's Daughter
Sunshine Molly
The Wild Olive
The Yankee Girl
1916 Ben Blair
The Call of the Cumberlands
The Code of Marcia Gray
David Garrick
Davy Crockett
The Heart of Paula
Her Father's Son
The House of Lies
An International Marriage
The Intrigue
Madame La Presidente
Redeeming Love
The Right Direction
The Stronger Love
Tongues of Men
1917 Down to Earth
The Hidden Spring
The Little Patriot
The Man from Painted Post
The Spirit of Romance
1918 Amarilly of Clothes-Line Alley
Daddy's Girl
He Comes Up Smiling
How Could You, Jean?
In Judgment Of
The Squaw Man
Stella Maris
The White Man's Law
1919 Almost a Husband
Beware*
The Home Town Girl
Jane Goes A-Wooing
Lord and Lady Algy
A Rogue's Romance
A Sporting Chance (Famous
Players-Lasky Corp.)
Strictly Confidential
Through the Wrong Door
You Never Saw Such a Girl
1920 The Blue Moon
The Cup of Fury
Her First Elopement
Judy of Rogue's Harbor
Man and Woman (A. H.
Fischer Features, Inc.)

She Couldn't Help It
Standing, Herbert, Jr. *(born* 1887*)*
could be same as **Standing, Mr.** *or*
Standing, H.
1918 A Romance of the Air
Wild Honey
1919 Beware
A Misfit Earl
My Little Sister
1920 Don't Ever Marry
Heritage
The Rich Slave
Simple Souls
Standing, Jack *could be same as*
Standing, Mr.
1914 Detective Craig's Coup
The Price He Paid
1915 The Blindness of Devotion
Fanchon the Cricket
1916 Civilization's Child
The Evangelist
Hell's Hinges
1917 The Curse of Eve
The Innocent Sinner
One Touch of Sin
The Price of Her Soul
Standing, Jack, Jr. *(child actor,* son *of*
Standing, Jack)
1918 With Hoops of Steel
Standing, Joan
1919 The Loves of Letty
1920 The Branding Iron
Silk Hosiery
Standing, Percy *same as* **Standing, P.**
D.; Standing, Percy D.; Standing,
Percy Darrell; Standing, Percy G.;
could be same as **Standing, Mr.**
1914 The Great Diamond Robbery
1915 The Final Judgment
Life Without Soul
York State Folks
1916 The Fall of a Nation
1917 Her Fighting Chance
1918 The Blind Adventure
The Business of Life
Every Mother's Son
Everybody's Girl
A Game with Fate
The Kaiser's Finish
My Four Years in Germany
The Song of the Soul
To the Highest Bidder
The Triumph of Venus
1919 Bonds of Love
The Captain's Captain
The Miracle of Love
Should a Husband Forgive?
1920 A Modern Salome
Standing, Wyndham *could be same as*
Standing, Mr.
1915 Business Is Business
The Supreme Test
1916 The Beggar of Cawnpore
The Bugle Call
Bullets and Brown Eyes
Redeeming Love
The Wolf Woman
1917 The Auction of Virtue
Exile
The Law of the Land
The Silence Sellers
The Soul of a Magdalen
To the Death
The Waiting Soul
1918 The Glorious Adventure
The Hillcrest Mystery
The Life Mask
The Rose of the World
1919 Eyes of the Soul
The Hushed Hour
The Isle of Conquest
The Marriage Price
The Miracle of Love
Out of the Shadow
Paid in Full
A Temperamental Wife
The Witness for the Defense
The Woman on the Index
1920 Blackmail
Earthbound
Lifting Shadows
A Modern Salome
My Lady's Garter

Standing Bear, Chief
1916 Ramona
1919 Bolshevism on Trial
Standish, Joseph
1914 Threads of Destiny
Stanford, Arthur
1915 The Whirl of Life
Stanford, Henry
1917 Where Love Is
Stange, Stanislaus
1915 The Chocolate Soldier
1917 A School for Husbands
Stanhope, Frederick
1914 The Christian
Stanhope, Ida
1916 Souls in Bondage
Stanley, Edwin
1916 Divorce and the Daughter
The Fear of Poverty
King Lear
1917 The Dummy
The Law of Compensation
Miss Deception
1918 Every Mother's Son
Just a Woman
Marriages Are Made
1919 The Love Auction
1920 Life
Stanley, Forrest
1915 Jane
Pretty Mrs. Smith
The Reform Candidate
The Rug Maker's Daughter
The Wild Olive
The Yankee Girl
1916 The Code of Marcia Gray
He Fell in Love with His Wife
The Heart of Paula
Madame La Presidente
The Making of Maddalena
Tongues of Men
1919 His Official Fiancée
Other Men's Wives
The Rescuing Angel
The Thunderbolt
Under Suspicion
What Every Woman Wants
1920 The Misfit Wife
The Notorious Mrs. Sands
The Thirtieth Piece of Silver
The Triflers
A Woman Who Understood
Stanley, George *same as* **Stanley,**
George S.
1914 Captain Alvarez
The Little Angel of Canyon
Creek
1916 The Soul's Cycle
1920 The Courage of Marge
O'Doone
Pegeen
Stanley, Henry *not the same as* **Stanley,**
Sir Henry
1915 Beulah
1916 The Birth of a Man
The Girl Who Doesn't Know
1920 The Confession
Stanley, Sir Henry *not the same as*
Stanley, Henry
1918 The Great Love*
Stanley, Maxfield *same as* **Stanley,**
Max
1915 The Birth of a Nation
1916 Intolerance
1917 The Double Standard
Southern Justice
The Varmint
1918 Beauty in Chains
The Great Love
1919 23 1/2 Hours' Leave
1920 Just Out of College
The Poor Simp
Stanton, Edward *not the same as*
Stanton, Edwin M.
1920 Humoresque
Stanton, Edwin M. *not the same as*
Stanton, Edward
1917 Queen X
Stanton, Ely
1919 Flame of the Desert

Stanton, Frederick *same as* **Stanton,**
Fred; Stanton, Fred R.
1916 Daredevil Kate
1918 De Luxe Annie
1919 The Great Victory, Wilson or
the Kaiser? The Fall of the
Hohenzollerns
1920 The Chamber Mystery
The Fighting Chance
Jenny Be Good
The Silver Horde
The Spirit of Good
Stanton, John
1917 Redemption
Stanton, Paul
1918 The Girl and the Judge
The Glorious Adventure
Her Price
Stanton, Richard *same as* **Stanton,**
Richard S.
1914 Shorty Escapes Marriage
1915 Aloha Oe
1916 The Beast
The Love Thief
1917 Durand of the Bad Lands
Her Temptation
North of Fifty-Three
One Touch of Sin
The Scarlet Pimpernel
The Spy
The Yankee Way
1918 The Caillaux Case
Cheating the Public
Rough and Ready
Stolen Honor
Why America Will Win
Why I Would Not Marry
1919 Checkers
The Jungle Trail
1920 The Face at Your Window
Sink or Swim
Stanwood, Louise B.
1915 Kilmeny
Stanwood, Rita
1914 The Ghost Breaker
1916 The Deserter
1919 The Gray Wolf's Ghost
Stapler, Maurice
1919 Injustice
Staples, Frank
1920 Under Northern Lights
Star, Sally
1918 The Flash of Fate
Stark, Ardine *see* **Stark, Ordean**
Stark, Audrine *see* **Stark, Ordean**
Stark, Jack
1917 Her Own People
The Inner Shrine
Stark, Julia N.
1919 Under the Top
Stark, Leighton
1914 Soldiers of Fortune
1916 Daredevil Kate
Society Wolves
Stark, Lowell Randall
1915 The Call of the Dance
Stark, Ordean *same as* **Stark, Ardine;**
Stark, Audrine
1914 Hearts of Oak
Should a Woman Divorce?
1915 The Shooting of Dan McGrew
The Unwelcome Wife
Stark, Pauline *see* **Starke, Pauline**
Starke, Pauline *same as* **Stark, Pauline**
1916 Intolerance
The Rummy
The Wharf Rat
1917 Cheerful Givers
Madame Bo-Peep
The Regenerates
Until They Get Me
1918 Alias Mary Brown
The Argument
The Atom
Daughter Angele
Innocent's Progress
Irish Eyes
The Man Who Woke Up
The Shoes That Danced
1919 The Broken Butterfly
Eyes of Youth
The Fall of Babylon
The Life Line

Soldiers of Fortune
Whom the Gods Would
Destroy
1920 A Connecticut Yankee at King
Arthur's Court
The Courage of Marge
O'Doone
Dangerous Days
The Forgotten Woman
The Little Shepherd of
Kingdom Come
Seeds of Vengeance
The Untamed

Starkey, Bert
1914 The Dollar Mark
The Man of the Hour
The Pit
1915 The Boss
The Cub
1916 The Come-Back
1917 The Dazzling Miss Davison
1918 Broadway Bill
Convict 993
The Landloper
Lend Me Your Name
1919 A Man of Honor
1920 The Dark Mirror

Starkey, Buckley
1915 The Gray Mask
1916 Dorian's Divorce
The World's Great Snare

Starkey, John
1915 Alias Jimmy Valentine*
Time Lock Number 776

Starks, William
1920 Within Our Gates

Starling, John
1917 A Bit O' Heaven

Starr, Bobby
1919 Thieves

Starr, Frederick same as **Starr, Fred;
Starr, Frederic**
1914 The Only Son
1918 The Sea Flower
Vive La France!
The Yellow Dog
1919 The Poppy Girl's Husband
A Woman of Pleasure
1920 Crooked Streets
The Life of the Party
Moon Madness
Riders of the Dawn
The Square Shooter
The U.P. Trail

Starr, Helen
1917 High Speed

Starr, Phoebe
1918 A Successful Adventure

Starr, Sally
1917 The Man Trap
1918 The Risky Road
Smashing Through

Statter, Arthur F. same as **Statter, A.
F.**
1919 The Best Man
1920 Honest Hutch
Just Out of College
The Man Who Had Everything
The Truth

Staulcup, M. P.
1919 The Brat
Lombardi, Ltd.
1920 The Fatal Hour
Love, Honor and Obey
The Willow Tree

Steadman, Lincoln see **Stedman, Lincoln**

Steadman, Vera
1920 813

Stearn, Al (actor)
1917 The Golden God

Stearns, Albert (writer)
1917 Chris and His Wonderful
Lamp

Stearns, Baby Virginia
1920 Up in Mary's Attic

Stearns, Edgar Franklin see **Franklin,
Edgar**

Stearns, Louis see **Stern, Louis**

Stearns, M. M.
1918 The Hope Chest
1919 Boots
Peppy Polly

Stearns, W. H.
1918 Daughter Angele

Stears, Larry
1919 Cowardice Court

Stechhan, H. O. same as **Stechan, H.
O.; Strachhan, H. O.**
1917 His Old-Fashioned Dad*
The Stolen Play*

Steck, H. Tipton
1915 Graustark
1916 The Phantom Buccaneer
1917 The Fibbers
Gift O' Gab
The Golden Idiot
The Man Who Was Afraid
The Small Town Guy
1918 The Sea Flower
1919 The Broken Butterfly
Marked Men
The Outcasts of Poker Flats
The Rider of the Law
1920 The Leopard Woman
Love
The Mischief Man
Occasionally Yours
Wait for Me

Stecker, Ray
1920 The Road to Divorce

Stedman, Mr. see **Stedman, Marshall**

Stedman, Lincoln same as **Steadman,
Lincoln**
1917 The Charmer
1918 The Atom
1919 Anne of Green Gables
Puppy Love
Through the Toils
The Winning Girl
1920 Nineteen and Phyllis
Out of the Storm
Peaceful Valley

Stedman, Marshall same as **Stedman,
Mr.**
1914 The Country Mouse
1915 The Beachcomber
Buckshot John
Little Sunset
1919 Three Black Eyes

Stedman, Myrtle
1914 Burning Daylight: The
Adventures of "Burning
Daylight" in Civilization
The Chechako
The Country Mouse
Martin Eden
The Pursuit of the Phantom
The Valley of the Moon
1915 The Caprices of Kitty
Help Wanted
The Hypocrites
It's No Laughing Matter
Jane
Kilmeny
The Majesty of the Law
Nearly a Lady
Peer Gynt
The Reform Candidate
'Twas Ever Thus
The Wild Olive
1916 The American Beauty
The Call of the Cumberlands
Pasquale
The Soul of Kura-San
1917 As Men Love
The Happiness of Three
Women
The Prison Without Walls
The World Apart
1918 In the Hollow of Her Hand
1919 In Honor's Web
The Teeth of the Tiger
1920 Harriet and the Piper
Old Dad
Sex
The Silver Horde
The Tiger's Coat

Steel, Vernon see **Steele, Vernon**

Steele, Edward
1917 The Man from Montana

Steele, Geraldine
1920 Reformation

Steele, R. Vernon see **Steele, Vernon**

Steele, Radcliffe
1920 The Man Who Lost Himself
Nothing but the Truth

Steele, Robert
1919 Human Desire

Steele, Rufus
1916 The Eagle's Wing
1917 The Divorcee

Steele, Vernon same as **Steel, Vernon;
Steele, R. Vernon**
1915 Hearts in Exile
Her Great Match
The Stubbornness of Geraldine
The Vampire
1916 Little Lady Eileen
Silks and Satins
The Supreme Sacrifice
1917 Bab's Matinee Idol
Polly of the Circus
1918 Fields of Honor
The Panther Woman
1919 The Eternal Magdalene
The Firing Line
The Phantom Honeymoon
The Witness for the Defense
1920 His House in Order

Steele, Victor
1919 Mind the Paint Girl

Steers, L. T. could be same as **Steers,
Larry**
1919 The Hushed Hour

Steers, Larry same as **Steers, L. W.;
could be same as Steers, L. T.**
1917 The Happiness of Three
Women
1918 The City of Dim Faces
Her Country First
Mystic Faces
A Pair of Silk Stockings
The Widow's Might
1919 Heartsease
Little Comrade
Mary Regan
The Secret Garden
1920 Dollar for Dollar
The Right of Way

Stefansky, Frank
1919 Suspense

Stefansson, Vilhjamur
1914 Rescue of the Stefansson Arctic
Expedition

Steger, Julius
1915 The Fifth Commandment
The Master of the House
The Warning*
1916 The Blindness of Love
The Libertine
The Price of Happiness*
The Prima Donna's Husband
The Stolen Triumph
1917 The Law of Compensation
Redemption
1918 The Burden of Proof
Cecilia of the Pink Roses
Her Mistake
Just a Woman
1919 The Belle of New York
Break the News to Mother
The Hidden Truth

Stein, Geoffrey
1915 An Affair of Three Nations
1920 Life

Steiner, Walter
1919 A Romance of Seattle

Steiner, William
1915 How Molly Malone Made
Good
Prohibition
1920 The Bromley Case
The Trail of the Cigarette
The Way Women Love

Stellson, Carol
1916 Undine

Stengard, Arthur
1915 The Victory of Virtue

Stephens, Charles
1916 A Sister of Six

Stephens, Oscar
1914 The Only Son*

Stephens, Walter
1920 The Midlanders

Stephenson, Henry same as **Stephenson,
Harry**
1917 The Spreading Dawn
1919 A Society Exile
1919-20
The Tower of Jewels

Stephenson, Marian
1917 Corruption

Steppling, John same as **Stepling, John**
1913 In the Bishop's Carriage
Tess of the D'Urbervilles
1914 Damaged Goods
1917 The Butterfly Girl
The Girl Who Couldn't Grow
Up
The Promise
1918 Cupid by Proxy
Good Night, Paul
The Guilty Man
Johanna Enlists
A Lady's Name
A Man's Man
Restitution
The Road Through the Dark
1919 The Better Wife*
The Divorce Trap
Fools and Their Money
Life's a Funny Proposition
Lombardi, Ltd.
Luck in Pawn
The Rescuing Angel
1920 Billions
The County Fair
The Heart of a Child
Husband Hunter
The Inferior Sex
Live Sparks
Madame Peacock
Number 99
Sick Abed

Sterett, Capt. Thomas
1918 The Unbeliever

Sterling, Edythe same as **Sterling, Edith**
1916 In the Web of the Grafters
Nancy's Birthright
The Stain in the Blood
1917 The Planter*
The Secret Man
1919 The Arizona Cat Claw
1920 The Girl Who Dared
The One Way Trail

Sterling, Ford
1919 Yankee Doodle in Berlin
1920 Love, Honor and Behave
Married Life

Sterling, Jane
1918 The Road to France
1919 The Moral Deadline
1920 The Heart of a Child
The Street Called Straight

Sterling, Joseph
1916 My Country First
1917 The Seven Swans

Sterling, Marie
1915 The Great Divide
The Rights of Man: A Story of
War's Red Blotch
1916 Sorrows of Happiness

Sterling, Meta
1920 Up in Mary's Attic

Sterling, Paul
1914 The Mystery of Edwin Drood

Sterling, Richard
1916 The Madcap
Ramona
The Storm
1920 The Ladder of Lies*

Stern, G. B.
1918 For Husbands Only

Stern, Louis same as **Stearns, Louis;
Stern, Lew; Sterns, Louis**
1916 Blazing Love
Gold and the Woman
1917 Bridges Burned
The Greater Woman
The Public Defender
When You and I Were Young
1918 Eye for Eye
1919 Break the News to Mother
The Great Romance
The Great Victory, Wilson or
the Kaiser? The Fall of the
Hohenzollerns

Stewart, Vera
1920 Thirty Years Between

Stewart, Victor A. *same as* **Stewart, Victor; Stuart, V.**
1916 The Unborn
1917 Apartment 29
      Within the Law
1918 Everybody's Girl
      Find the Woman
1919 The Adventure Shop
      The Undercurrent
1920 Oil

Stewart, Violet *see* **Stuart, Violet**
Stewart, William T. *see* **Stuart, William T.**

Stibgen, Beatrice
1918 Little Red Riding Hood

Stiles, James A.
1917 Hell Hath No Fury

Stillwell, George *same as* **Stillwell, G. A.; Stillwell, George A.**
1914 In the Name of the Prince of Peace
      Soldiers of Fortune
1915 The Eternal City
      Gretna Green

Stine, Charles J. *same as* **Stine, Charles**
1915 In the Palace of the King
1916 Captain Jinks of the Horse Marines
      The Discard
      The Misleading Lady
      Vultures of Society

Stinson, Bessie
1918 Out of the Night
1920 Birthright
      The Good-Bad Wife
      Respectable by Proxy
      The Wrong Woman

Stirling, Ada
1915 Over Night

Stockbridge, Fanny Y.
1915 Peer Gynt
      The Reform Candidate

Stockbridge, Robert Bronson
1919 Who's Your Brother?

Stockdale, Carl
1914 The Good-for-Nothing
1915 My Best Girl
1916 Atta Boy's Last Race
      Casey at the Bat
      A Child of the Paris Streets
      The Children Pay
      Don Quixote
      Hoodoo Ann
      Intolerance
      The Little Liar
      Oliver Twist
      Stranded
1917 The Americano
      A Daughter of the Poor
      The Land of Long Shadows

Lost and Won
Men of the Desert
Might and the Man
New York Luck
Open Places
Peggy Leads the Way
The Range Boss
1918 The Bells
      The Biggest Show on Earth
      The Eyes of Julia Deep
      Hearts or Diamonds?
      Hobbs in a Hurry
      In Bad
      Kidder and Ko
      The Lady of the Dugout
      The Midnight Trail
      Rosemary Climbs the Heights
      Up Romance Road
      Wives and Other Wives
1919 The Amazing Impostor
      Brass Buttons
      The Fall of Babylon
      For a Woman's Honor
      The Intrusion of Isabel
      The Pagan God
      The Pointing Finger
      The Spitfire of Seville*
      The Sundown Trail
      The Unpainted Woman
      When a Man Rides Alone
      Where the West Begins
      The Woman Under Cover
1920 The Coast of Opportunity
      $30,000

Stockton, Edith
1919 The House Without Children
      The Open Door
      Putting One Over
      Who's Your Brother?
1920 The Fear Market
      Should a Wife Work?

Stockwell, B. Edgar
1920 Deep Waters

Stoermer, William *same as* **Stormer, William**
1916 The Invisible Enemy
1918 The Tidal Wave

Stokes, Olive
1917 The Single Code

Stone, Agnes
1912 Oliver Twist

Stone, E. *could be same as* **Stone, Elinor**
1915 The Gambler of the West

Stone, Elinor *could be same as* **Stone, E.**
1916 The Missing Links

Stone, Frank
1915 The Game of Three*
1918 My Four Years in Germany

Stone, Fred
1915 Destiny; Or, The Soul of a Woman
1918 The Goat
1919 Johnny Get Your Gun
      Under the Top

Stone, George
1916 Children of the Feud
      The Patriot
1917 In Slumberland
      Sudden Jim
1918 The Gypsy Trail
      Six Shooter Andy
      Till I Come Back to You
1919 The Poppy Girl's Husband
      The Speed Maniac
1920 Fighting Cressy
      The Scoffer

Stone, George *(child actor) same as* **Stone, Georgie**
1915 The Game of Three
1916 The Children in the House
      Going Straight
      Gretchen, the Greenhorn
      Let Katie Do It
      The Little School Ma'am
      Martha's Vindication
      A Sister of Six
1917 The Gun Fighter
      Jim Bludso
1918 Ali Baba and the Forty Thieves
1919 The Jungle Trail
1920 Just Pals
      Rio Grande

Seeds of Vengeance
Stone, George E. *(prod)*
1916 How Life Begins
1920 The Living World

Stone, Georgie *see* **Stone, George** *(child actor)*

Stone, Helen
1920 Twins of Suffering Creek

Stone, LeRoy *same as* **Stone, Le Roy**
1916 Civilization
1920 The Cradle of Courage
      Sand!
      The Testing Block
      The Toll Gate

Stone, Lewis S. *same as* **Stone, Lewis**
1916 According to the Code
      The Havoc
      Honor's Altar
1918 Inside the Lines
      The Man of Bronze
1919 Man's Desire
1920 Held by the Enemy
      Milestones
      Nomads of the North
      The River's End

Stone, William
1918 Social Quicksands

Stonehouse, Ruth
1915 The Alster Case
      The Crimson Wing
      The Slim Princess
1916 Kinkaid, Gambler
      Love Never Dies
1917 The Edge of the Law
      Fighting for Love
      Follow the Girl
      Love Aflame
      A Phantom Husband
      The Saintly Sinner
1919 The Four-Flusher
      The Red Viper
1920 Are All Men Alike?
      Cinderella's Twin
      The Hope
      The Land of Jazz
      Parlor, Bedroom and Bath

Stopp, Wallace
1915 The Shooting of Dan McGrew

Storey, Edith
1914 Captain Alvarez
      The Christian
      A Florida Enchantment
1915 The Dust of Egypt
      How Cissy Made Good
      The Island of Regeneration
      On Her Wedding Night
      A Price for Folly
1916 An Enemy to the King
      The Shop Girl
      The Tarantula
      The Two Edged Sword
1917 Aladdin from Broadway
      The Captain of the Gray Horse Troop
      Money Magic
      National Association's All-Star Picture
1918 The Claim
      The Demon
      The Eyes of Mystery
      The Legion of Death
      Revenge
      The Silent Woman
      Treasure of the Sea
1919 As the Sun Went Down
1920 Moon Madness

Storey, Jack
1916 A Night Out

Storey, Minnie *same as* **Storey, Mrs. M.**
1915 C.O.D.
1916 The Ordeal of Elizabeth

Storm, Jerome
1915 The Cup of Life
1916 Civilization
      The Honorable Algy
      The Primal Lure
      Somewhere in France
1917 The Bride of Hate
      His Mother's Boy
      The Iced Bullet
      The Pinch Hitter
1918 The Biggest Show on Earth
      A Desert Wooing

Keys of the Righteous
Naughty, Naughty!
The Vamp
1919 Bill Henry
      The Busher
      Crooked Straight
      The Egg Crate Wallop
      The Girl Dodger
      Greased Lightning
      Hay Foot, Straw Foot
      Red Hot Dollars
1920 Alarm Clock Andy
      Homer Comes Home
      An Old Fashioned Boy
      Paris Green
      Peaceful Valley
      The Village Sleuth

Stormer, William *see* **Stoermer, William**
Storrer, Arnold
1916 The Dollar and the Law
1919 Love and the Law

Storrs, Marguerite C.
1920 Beautifully Trimmed

Story, Frederick
1914 Rip Van Winkle

Stover, Florence
1915 Shadows from the Past
      Vanity Fair
1917 Builders of Castles
      The Last Sentence

Stowe, Leslie *same as* **Stowe, Leslie A.; could be same as* **Stowe, Lester**
1915 The Impostor
1916 The Closed Road
      The Dawn of Love
      Driftwood
      La Vie de Boheme
1917 The Adopted Son
1918 Social Quicksands
1919 Bolshevism on Trial
1920 The Copperhead
      The Good-Bad Wife

Stowe, Lester *could be same as* **Stowe, Leslie**
1916 Autumn

Stowell, William
1915 The Buzzard's Shadow
      The End of the Road
1916 The Girl O' Dreams
      Immediate Lee
      The Love Hermit
      The Man from Manhattan
      The Other Side of the Door
      Overalls
      The Overcoat
      The White Rosette
1917 Bondage
      A Doll's House
      Fighting Mad
      Fires of Rebellion
      The Flashlight
      The Girl in the Checkered Coat
      Hell Morgan's Girl
      Pay Me
      The Piper's Price
      The Rescue
      Triumph
1918 Broadway Love
      The Grand Passion
      The Mortgaged Wife
      The Risky Road
      The Talk of the Town
1919 Destiny
      The Heart of Humanity
      The Man in the Moonlight
      Paid in Advance
      The Right to Happiness
      When a Girl Loves

Stowers, Frederick
1920 The Coast of Opportunity
      Nineteen and Phyllis

Strachhan, H. O. *see* **Stechhan, H. O.**
Stradling, Harry
1920 The Devil's Garden
      The Stolen Kiss

Stradling, Walter
1914 Captain Alvarez
1915 The Case of Becky
      The Chorus Lady
      A Gentleman of Leisure
      Mr. Grex of Monte Carlo
      The Secret Orchard
      The Secret Sin
      Young Romance

196

1918 The Blind Adventure
　　　To Him That Hath
1920 The Return of Tarzan
Sturgeon, Rollin S. *same as* **Sturgeon, Rollin**
1914 Captain Alvarez
　　　The Little Angel of Canyon
　　　　Creek
1915 The Chalice of Courage
1916 God's Country and the Woman
　　　Through the Wall
1917 The American Consul
　　　Betty and the Buccaneers
　　　The Calendar Girl
　　　The Rainbow Girl
　　　The Serpent's Tooth
　　　The Upper Crust
　　　Whose Wife?
1918 Hugon, the Mighty
　　　A Petticoat Pilot
　　　The Shuttle
　　　Unclaimed Goods
1919 Destiny
　　　Pretty Smooth
　　　The Sundown Trail
1920 The Breath of the Gods
　　　The Gilded Dream
　　　The Girl in the Rain
　　　In Folly's Trail
　　　Risky Business
Sturgis, Edwin *same as* **Sturgis, Ed;
Sturgis, Eddie; Sturgis, Edward**
1916 Destiny's Toy
　　　The Lost Bridegroom
　　　The Moment Before
　　　The Rainbow Princess
1917 At First Sight
　　　A Case at Law
　　　Cassidy
　　　A Girl Like That
　　　Heart's Desire
1918 Doing Their Bit
　　　Just for Tonight
　　　Madame Jealousy
　　　Peck's Bad Girl
　　　The Racing Strain
　　　We Should Worry
1919 The Bondage of Barbara
　　　The Dark Star
　　　A Man and His Money
　　　Miss Crusoe
　　　The Oakdale Affair
　　　One of the Finest
　　　The Peace of Roaring River
1920 The Deep Purple
　　　Man and Woman (A. H.
　　　　Fischer Features, Inc.)
Sturgis, Fowler H.
1920 The Spenders
Sturz, Louis
1918 The Woman the Germans Shot
Styler, Beatrice
1915 The Alster Case
Sues, S. A.
1916 Judith of the Cumberlands
Sugden, Dr. Leonard S.
1915 The Lure of Alaska
Sullivan, Anne *see* **Macy, Mrs. Anne
Sullivan**
Sullivan, Arthur
1917 The Cigarette Girl
Sullivan, Billy *see* **Sullivan, William A.**
Sullivan, C. Gardner
1915 The Cup of Life
　　　The Darkening Trail
　　　The Edge of the Abyss
　　　The Forbidden Adventure
　　　The Golden Claw
　　　The Iron Strain
　　　The Italian
　　　The Man from Oregon
　　　The Mating
　　　Matrimony
　　　On the Night Stage
　　　The Reward
　　　The Toast of Death
　　　The Winged Idol
1916 The Aryan
　　　The Beckoning Flame
　　　The Beggar of Cawnpore
　　　Between Men
　　　The Bugle Call
　　　Civilization
　　　Civilization's Child

　　　The Conqueror
　　　The Corner
　　　A Corner in Colleens
　　　The Criminal
　　　The Dawn Maker
　　　The Dividend
　　　The Eye of the Night
　　　The Green Swamp
　　　Hell's Hinges
　　　Home
　　　Honor's Altar
　　　The Last Act
　　　The Market of Vain Desire
　　　The Moral Fabric
　　　The No-Good Guy
　　　Not My Sister
　　　The Payment
　　　Peggy
　　　Plain Jane
　　　The Return of Draw Egan
　　　Shell Forty-Three
　　　The Stepping Stone
　　　The Thoroughbred (New York
　　　　Motion Picture Corp.;
　　　　Kay-Bee)
　　　Three of Many
　　　The Wolf Woman
1917 The Crab
　　　The Girl Glory
　　　Happiness
　　　The Hater of Men
　　　The Iced Bullet
　　　The Pinch Hitter
　　　Those Who Pay
　　　The Zeppelin's Last Raid
1918 The Border Wireless
　　　Branding Broadway
　　　The Cast-Off
　　　Keys of the Righteous
　　　Love Me
　　　Naughty, Naughty!
　　　Selfish Yates
　　　Shark Monroe
　　　The Vamp
　　　Vive La France!
　　　When Do We Eat?
　　　Without Honor
1919 Happy Though Married
　　　The Haunted Bedroom
　　　John Petticoats
　　　The Lady of Red Butte
　　　The Market of Souls
　　　Other Men's Wives
　　　The Poppy Girl's Husband
　　　Sahara
　　　Stepping Out
　　　The Virtuous Thief
　　　Wagon Tracks
1920 Dangerous Hours
　　　The False Road
　　　Hairpins
　　　Love Madness
　　　Sex
　　　The Woman in the Suitcase
Sullivan, Danny *same as* **Sullivan, Dan;
Sullivan, Daniel; Sullivan, Daniel J.**
1916 The Kiss of Hate
1917 The Blue Streak
　　　Thou Shalt Not Steal
　　　Wife Number Two
1918 Cecilia of the Pink Roses
1919 The Other Man's Wife
Sullivan, Edward *same as* **Sullivan, E.
P.; Sullivan, Edward P.**
1915 The Governor's Boss
　　　How Molly Malone Made
　　　　Good
　　　Time Lock Number 776
1916 The Black Crook
Sullivan, Fred *(actor)*
1915 The White Terror
Sullivan, Frederic *(dir)*
1916 The Fear of Poverty
　　　Master Shakespeare, Strolling
　　　　Player
　　　The Pillory
　　　Saint, Devil and Woman
19-- Sic-Em
Sullivan, Frederick *(dir)*
1916 Divorce and the Daughter
　　　The Fugitive
1917 Her Life and His
　　　When Love Was Blind
1919 The Solitary Sin

Sullivan, George
1915 Right off the Bat
Sullivan, Helene *same as* **Sullivan, Helen**
1919 The False Code
　　　A Girl Named Mary
　　　The House of Intrigue
1920 Common Sense
　　　For the Soul of Rafael
　　　Mid-Channel
　　　Parlor, Bedroom and Bath
　　　Rouge and Riches
　　　The Tiger's Coat
Sullivan, Irene
1920 Jack Straw
Sullivan, J. *(actor) could be same as*
Sullivan, James E. *or* **Sullivan,
Joseph**
1917 The Broadway Sport
Sullivan, J. *(chief electrician)*
1916 A Daughter of the Gods
Sullivan, James E. *same as* **Sullivan,
James; could be same as* **Sullivan, J.**
1917 A Crooked Romance
　　　The Public Defender
Sullivan, Joe *see* **Sullivan, Joseph**
Sullivan, John J.
1919 A Romance of Seattle
Sullivan, Joseph *same as* **Sullivan, Joe;
could be same as* **Sullivan, J.**
1914 The $5,000,000 Counterfeiting
　　　　Plot
　　　The Life of Big Tim Sullivan;
　　　　Or, From Newsboy to
　　　　Senator
1915 The Coquette
1920 The Scrap of Paper
　　　The Unseen Witness
Sullivan, Paddy
1916 Broken Fetters
Sullivan, Ruth
1920 A Child for Sale
　　　Children Not Wanted
Sullivan, William A. *same as* **Sullivan,
Billy; Sullivan, W. A.; Sullivan,
William**
1917 Over the Hill
1918 The House of Mirth
　　　What Becomes of the
　　　　Children?
1920 A Manhattan Knight
Sulzer, Gov. William
1913 The Shame of the Empire State
1915 The Governor's Boss
Sumers, Amy *see* **Summers, Amy**
Summer, Frederick *same as* **Summer,
Frederic; Sumner, Frederic; Sumner,
Frederick**
1915 Bondwomen
1916 The Turmoil
　　　The Upstart
Summers, Amy *same as* **Sumers, Amy;
could be same as* **Somers, Amy**
1914 The County Chairman
　　　The Lost Paradise
Summerville, Amelia
1915 Just Out of College
1918 How Could You, Caroline?
　　　Mrs. Dane's Defense
1919 Getting Mary Married
　　　My Little Sister
　　　The Probation Wife
　　　The Witness for the Defense
1920 April Folly
　　　Romance
Sumner, Frederic *see* **Summer, Frederick**
Sumner, G. Lynn
1919 Heads Win
Sunderland, John
1917 Shirley Kaye
1918 The Kaiser's Finish
　　　The Reason Why
　　　To Hell with the Kaiser
1919 The Silver King
Sundin, Jere
1920 The Chorus Girl's Romance
Suratt, Valeska
1915 The Immigrant
　　　The Soul of Broadway
1916 Jealousy
　　　The Straight Way
　　　The Victim

1917 The New York Peacock
　　　A Rich Man's Plaything
　　　She
　　　The Siren
　　　The Slave
　　　Wife Number Two
Suslow, Benjamin *same as* **Suslow, Ben;
Susslow, Benny**
1917 The Varmint
1918 The Girl of My Dreams
1920 The Devil's Riddle
Sutch, Herbert *same as* **Sutch, Bert**
1917 Should She Obey?
1918 Hearts of the World
　　　The Hun Within
　　　Restitution
1919 Scarlet Days
1920 The Idol Dancer
　　　Way Down East*
Sutherland, A. Mackay
1915 The Pageant of San Francisco
Sutherland, Anne *same as* **Sutherland,
Ann**
1915 A Woman's Resurrection
1917 The Debt
　　　Motherhood (Frank Powell
　　　　Producing Corp.)
Sutherland, Eddie *same as* **Sutherland,
Edward**
1918 Which Woman?
1919 A Girl Named Mary
　　　Love Insurance
　　　The Veiled Adventure
1920 All-of-a-Sudden-Peggy
　　　Conrad in Quest of His Youth
　　　The Paliser Case
　　　The Round-Up
　　　The Sea Wolf
Sutherland, Hugh
1918 Beyond the Shadows
　　　Tongues of Flame
Sutherland, John
1919 The Imp
　　　The Silver King
Sutherland, Victor
1914 The Dancer and the King
1916 Daredevil Kate
　　　The Flames of Johannis
　　　One Day
　　　Those Who Toil
1917 The Bar Sinister
　　　The Barrier
1918 Buchanan's Wife
　　　The Firebrand
　　　Her Price
　　　The Liar
　　　The Queen of Hearts
　　　The Sign Invisible
　　　The Unchastened Woman
1919 Calibre 38
Sutter, Elenore
1916 What Will People Say?
Sutton, Brad *same as* **Sutton, Bradley**
1915 Children of Eve
1916 The Catspaw
　　　The Innocence of Ruth
　　　The Martyrdom of Philip
　　　　Strong
　　　A Message to Garcia
Sutton, Charles *same as* **Sutton, Charles
W.**
1915 Gladiola
　　　Vanity Fair
1916 The Heart of the Hills
　　　A Message to Garcia
　　　The Rainbow Princess
　　　When Love Is King
1917 The Eternal Mother
　　　The Law of the North
　　　Pardners
　　　Persuasive Peggy
　　　The Royal Pauper
　　　The Tell-Tale Step
1918 Flower of the Dusk
　　　Her Boy
　　　The Lie
　　　The Love Net
　　　A Pair of Cupids
　　　Peg O' the Sea
1919 Hit or Miss
　　　Home Wanted
　　　The Steel King
　　　The Stream of Life

1920 Democracy
Sutton, Prince
1916 The Final Curtain
Sutton, Susie
1920 The Brute
Suzanne, Jacques
1916 The Spell of the Yukon
1920 Out of the Snows
Swain, Mack
1914 Tillie's Punctured Romance
1916 A Modern Enoch Arden
Swallow (full name unknown)
1916 The Aryan
Swan, Mark
1915 Just Out of College
The Little Mademoiselle
Poor Schmaltz
1916 Dollars and the Woman
1917 Tillie Wakes Up
Swann, George
1919 Charge It to Me
The Prince and Betty
Swanson, Gloria
1918 Everywoman's Husband
Her Decision
Secret Code
Shifting Sands
Society for Sale
Station Content
Wife or Country
You Can't Believe Everything
1919 Don't Change Your Husband
For Better, for Worse
Male and Female
1920 Something to Think About
Why Change Your Wife?
Swanson, Siska
1920 The Luck of Geraldine Laird
Swayne, Marian same as **Swayne, Marion**
1913 The Fight for Millions
1914 The Adventures of Kitty Cobb
The Line-Up at Police
Headquarters
1916 Behind Closed Doors
The Net
A Tortured Heart
1917 The Adventurer
The Deemster
Little Miss Fortune
The Little Samaritan
The Road Between
1918 The Transgressor
Sweatman, Willis P.
1914 The County Chairman
Sweeney, "Jimmy"
1917 The Duchess of Doubt
Sweeney, Joseph
1918 Sylvia on a Spree
Sweeney, Peggy same as **Sweeny, Peggy**
1916 It May Be Your Daughter
That Sort
Sweet, Blanche
1914 The Avenging Conscience
Classmates
The Escape
Home, Sweet Home
Judith of Bethulia
1915 The Captive
The Case of Becky
The Clue
The Secret Orchard
The Secret Sin
Stolen Goods
The Warrens of Virginia
1916 The Blacklist
The Dupe
Public Opinion
The Ragamuffin
The Sowers
The Storm
The Thousand Dollar Husband
Unprotected
1917 The Evil Eye
The Silent Partner
Those Without Sin
The Tides of Barnegat
1919 The Hushed Hour
The Unpardonable Sin
A Woman of Pleasure
1920 The Deadlier Sex
Fighting Cressy
The Girl in the Web

Help Wanted—Male
Her Unwilling Husband
Simple Souls
Sweezea, Bert
1919 A Romance of Seattle
Swenson, Alfred
1916 Hypocrisy
1917 Strife
Swickard, Charles
1914 Shorty Escapes Marriage
The Typhoon*
1915 Aloha Oe
The Brink
The Devil
The Forbidden Adventure
1916 The Beckoning Flame
The Beggar of Cawnpore
The Captive God
D'Artagnan
Hell's Hinges
Mixed Blood
The Raiders
The Sign of the Poppy
1917 The Gates of Doom
The Lair of the Wolf
The Phantom's Secret
The Plow Woman
The Scarlet Crystal
1918 Hitting the High Spots
The Light of Western Stars
1919 Almost Married
Faith
The Spender
1920 An Arabian Knight
Body and Soul
The Devil's Claim
The Last Straw*
Li Ting Lang
The Third Woman
Swickard, Josef same as **Swickard, Joe;**
Swickard, Joseph
1917 American Methods
Because of a Woman
The Book Agent
His Mother's Boy
The Soul of Satan
A Tale of Two Cities
To Honor and Obey
1918 Keys of the Righteous
The Light of Western Stars
Treasure of the Sea
When a Woman Sins
The White Man's Law
1919 A Girl in Bohemia
The Lady of Red Butte
The Last of His People
Pretty Smooth
Snares of Paris
A Trick of Fate
A Woman of Pleasure
1920 The Beggar Prince
Blind Youth
Moon Madness
The Third Generation
Trumpet Island
Swinburne, Lawrence
1916 Master Shakespeare, Strolling
Player
Swinton, Thomas
1920 The Fighting Kentuckians
Swisher, H. L.
1918 The Legion of Death
Sydney, Basil
1920 Romance
Sydney, Cecilia
1915 A Woman's Resurrection
Sylva, Marguerita
1920 The Honey Bee
Sylvester, Lillian same as **Sylvester, Lillie**
1919 Life's a Funny Proposition
1920 The Slim Princess
Sylvester, Maud
1920 Birthright
Symon, Burke
1919 The Bondage of Barbara
Symonds, Henry
1920 Go and Get It
Synon, Mary
1917 The Innocent Sinner

T

Taafe, Alice see **Terry, Alice**
Taber, Richard same as **Tabor, Richard**
1915 At Bay
1917 Kick In
1919 Miss Crusoe
Taber, Robert same as **Tabor, Robert**
1914 Lena Rivers (Cosmos Feature
Film Corp.)
Should a Woman Divorce?
1918 Heart of the Sunset
1919 The Glorious Lady
The Unbroken Promise
1920 Circumstantial Evidence
The Scrap of Paper
The Unseen Witness
Tabler, P. D. same as **Tabler, P.
Dempsey**
1916 The Captive God
A Gamble in Souls
The Patriot
The Phantom
1919 Love Insurance
1920 The Cheater
The Gamesters
Smiling All the Way
Tabor, Richard see **Taber, Richard**
Tabor, Robert see **Taber, Robert**
Taffe, Alice see **Terry, Alice**
Taft, Lucille
1916 The Drifter
The Idol of the Stage
The Quality of Faith
1917 Queen X
Taft, William Howard
19-- Official Motion Pictures of the
Panama Pacific Exposition
Held at San Francisco,
Calif.*
Taggart, Ben L. same as **Taggart, Ben**
1915 The Fixer
The Sentimental Lady
The Woman Next Door
1917 She
1919 Oh, Boy!
1920 The Hidden Light
Taggart, Marshall W.
1915 The Man Who Beat Dan Dolan
A Trade Secret
Tainguy, Lucien
1912 Cleopatra
1913 Arizona
Checkers
1915 The Boss
1916 All Man
Friday the Thirteenth
The Heart of a Hero
The Rack
1917 The Beloved Adventuress
The Corner Grocer
The Family Honor
Forget-Me-Not
The Good for Nothing
A Hungry Heart
The Man Who Forgot
The Web of Desire
1918 The Beautiful Mrs. Reynolds
His Royal Highness
Hitting the Trail
The Interloper
Leap to Fame
Merely Players
The Purple Lily
The Sea Wolf
Tinsel
1919 Courage for Two
A Damsel in Distress
The Echo of Youth
Hit or Miss
The Love Cheat
Love in a Hurry
Mandarin's Gold
The Scar
1920 In Walked Mary
The North Wind's Malice
The Shadow of Rosalie Byrnes
What Women Want
Taintor, Hal
1919 Lord and Lady Algy

Taka, Martha
1918 Mystic Faces
Takata, Frank
1916 The Land Just Over Yonder
Talbot, Edward
1919 Virtuous Men
Talbot, Frank L.
1919 The Price of Innocence
Talbot, Hayden
1917 Alimony
1918 The Married Virgin
1920 Body and Soul
Talbot, Mary could be same as **Talbot,
May**
1916 Gloriana
Langdon's Legacy
1917 A Bit O' Heaven
The Clean-Up
1918 Cupid by Proxy
The Vanity Pool
1919 Brothers Divided
The Girl from Nowhere
1920 The Dangerous Talent
The Kentucky Colonel
Live Sparks
Talbot, May could be same as **Talbot,
Mary**
1915 Heritage
Talbot, Stella K.
1919 The Price of Innocence
Talbot, Thea
1917 Wrath
1918 Ashes of Love
1919 Lombardi, Ltd.
1920 The Fatal Hour
Taliaferro, Edith
1915 Young Romance
1916 The Conquest of Canaan
1919 Who's Your Brother?
Taliaferro, Mabel
1914 The Three of Us
1916 The Dawn of Love
God's Half Acre
Her Great Price
The Snowbird
The Sunbeam
1917 The Barricade
Draft 258
The Jury of Fate
A Magdalene of the Hills
Peggy, the Will O' the Wisp
A Wife by Proxy
1920 The Rich Slave
Tall Bull, Chief
1917 The Adventures of Buffalo Bill
Tallent, Jane
1920 The Last Straw
Tallman, George
1915 The Chocolate Soldier
Talma, Zola
1917 Outcast
1920 On with the Dance
Talmadge, Mrs.
1917 The Girl of the Timber Claims
Talmadge, Constance
1916 Intolerance
The Matrimaniac
The Microscope Mystery
The Missing Links
1917 Betsy's Burglar
The Girl of the Timber Claims
The Honeymoon
Scandal
1918 Good Night, Paul
A Lady's Name
The Lesson
Mrs. Leffingwell's Boots
A Pair of Silk Stockings
Sauce for the Goose
The Shuttle
The Studio Girl
Up the Road with Sallie
1919 Experimental Marriage
The Fall of Babylon
Happiness à la Mode
Romance and Arabella
A Temperamental Wife
The Veiled Adventure
A Virtuous Vamp
Who Cares?
1920 Dangerous Business
Good References
In Search of a Sinner

The Love Expert
The Perfect Woman
Two Weeks
Talmadge, Natalie
1919 The Isle of Conquest
1920 The Love Expert
Yes or No
Talmadge, Norma
1915 The Battle Cry of Peace
Captivating Mary Carstairs
1916 The Children in the House
The Crown Prince's Double
The Devil's Needle
Fifty-Fifty
Going Straight
Martha's Vindication
The Missing Links
The Social Secretary
1917 The Law of Compensation
The Moth
Panthea
Poppy
The Secret of the Storm
Country
1918 By Right of Purchase
De Luxe Annie
The Forbidden City
The Ghosts of Yesterday
Her Only Way
The Safety Curtain
1919 The Heart of Wetona
The Isle of Conquest
The New Moon
The Probation Wife
The Way of a Woman
1920 The Branded Woman
A Daughter of Two Worlds
She Loves and Lies
The Woman Gives
Yes or No
Tamamoto, T. *same as* **Tamamato, T.;
Tamameto, T.**
1914 Paid in Full
1915 The Mystery of Room 13
1916 The Innocence of Ruth
The Straight Way
When Love Is King
1918 The Sea Waif
The Silent Woman
1919 The Great Victory, Wilson or
the Kaiser? The Fall of the
Hohenzollerns
Tamato, P.
1917 Queen X
Tamison, Ruth
1920 Skyfire
Tams, Irene
1914 Lola
1919 Taxi
Tang, Charles
1916 Broken Fetters
Tanguay, Eva
1916 Energetic Eva
1917 The Wild Girl
Tannehill, Myrtle
1915 The Barnstormers
Tannura, Philip
1917 The Apple-Tree Girl
Knights of the Square Table
The Little Chevalier
1918 The Unbeliever
Tansey, Master *could be same as*
Tansey, John *or* **Tansey, Sheridan**
1915 Destruction
Tansey, Mrs. *could be same as* **Tansey,
Emma**
1917 When You and I Were Young
1918 Joan of the Woods
Tansey, Emma *could be same as*
Tansey, Mrs.
1920 The Little Outcast
Tansey, John *same as* **Tansy, John;
could be same as* **Tansey, Master**
1915 Black Fear
1916 Broken Chains
1917 Knights of the Square Table
1918 The Heart of a Girl
Little Miss Hoover
19-- Barnaby Lee
Tansey, Robert
1917 The Runaway
1918 The Witch Woman

1920 The Girl with the Jazz Heart
The Little Outcast
Tansey, Sheridan *same as* **Tansey,
Sherry; could be same as* **Tansey,
Master**
1916 The Foolish Virgin
1917 The Little Duchess
The Runaway
1918 Conquered Hearts
The Power and the Glory
1919 The Two Brides
1920 Over the Hill to the Poorhouse
Uncle Sam of Freedom Ridge
Tansy, John *see* **Tansey, John**
Tapley, Rose *same as* **Tapley, Rose E.**
1914 My Official Wife
1915 Hearts and the Highway
1916 Britton of the Seventh
The Chattel
Hesper of the Mountains
Rose of the South
Who Killed Joe Merrion?
1918 The Beautiful Mrs. Reynolds
1919 Shadows of the Past
Tarbell, James
1920 The Garter Girl
Tarbutt, Fraser
1916 The Devil's Prayer-Book
1917 Mary Moreland
Tarleton, Dr. W. A.
1919 Injustice
Tate, Cullen *same as* **Tate, Cullen B.**
1916 Joan the Woman
1917 The Devil-Stone
The Little American
A Romance of the Redwoods
The Woman God Forgot
1919 An Adventure in Hearts
Hawthorne of the U.S.A.
The Lottery Man
The Love Burglar
The Valley of the Giants
You're Fired
1920 Always Audacious
Mrs. Temple's Telegram
Terror Island
Tatum, E. G.
1920 The Brute
The Symbol of the
Unconquered
Within Our Gates
Tauber, Samuel
1916 Phantom Fortunes
Tauszky, D. Anthony *same as* **Tauszky,
David Anthony**
1918 Eye for Eye
1919 The Microbe*
Please Get Married
Tavalotti, Reg
1917 The Last Sentence
Tavares, Arthur
1915 The Spanish Jade
1916 Ramona
1917 The Eyes of the World
Mothers of Men
The Savage
1918 Hungry Eyes
Tavernier, Albert *same as* **Travernier,
Albert**
1915 Stop Thief!
1916 Betty of Graystone
The Flower of Faith
Saints and Sinners
1917 God's Man
The Inevitable
The Jury of Fate
The Man Who Made Good
The Painted Madonna
1920 Democracy
The Tiger's Cub
Taylor, Bonnie
1916 The Law Decides
Taylor, Charles A. *same as* **Taylor,
Charles**
1916 A Corner in Cotton
Mister 44
1917 Blue Jeans
Crime and Punishment
The Deemster
The Outsider
1918 Lest We Forget
1920 An Adventuress
Through Eyes of Men

Taylor, E. Forrest
1916 The Abandonment
April
True Nobility
The White Rosette
Taylor, Elizabeth
1917 Whose Wife?
Taylor, Estelle
1919 The Golden Shower
1919-20
The Tower of Jewels
1920 The Adventurer
Blind Wives
The Return of Tarzan
While New York Sleeps
Taylor, Eva
1916 A Night Out
Taylor, Irma *same as* **Taylor, Irma
Whelpley; Taylor, Irma Whipley**
1918 The Menace
The Other Man
1919 Leave It to Susan
Taylor, J. O.
1916 A Son of Erin
1917 The Bond Between
His Sweetheart
The Marcellini Millions*
1919 Behind the Door
A Daughter of the Wolf
The Grim Game
1920 Below the Surface
The Brute Master
His Own Law
A Thousand to One
Taylor, Jean
1915 Just Jim
1916 Two Men of Sandy Bar
Taylor, Jo *see* **Taylor, Josephine**
Taylor, John Lark *see* **Taylor, Lark**
Taylor, Josephine *same as* **Taylor, Jo**
1916 Faith
The Man from Manhattan
Taylor, L. E. *see* **Taylor, Loren**
Taylor, Lark *same as* **Taylor, John
Lark**
1916 The Chattel
The Devil's Prize
Taylor, Loren *same as* **Taylor, L. E.**
1916 Joan the Woman*
1917 Royal Romance
Wrath of Love
1919 Everywoman
Taylor, Marie
1913 Checkers
Taylor, Mary (actress)
1917 The End of the Tour
Taylor, Mary Imlay (scen)
1915 The Ploughshare
Taylor, Maud Emery *see* **Emery, Maude**
Taylor, Pop
1919 As the Sun Went Down
Taylor, Rex
1918 Beans
The Cabaret Girl
The Love Swindle
The Menace
Miss Ambition
A Nymph of the Foothills
The Other Man
She Hired a Husband
Set Free
1919 Leave It to Susan
Strictly Confidential
Through the Wrong Door
1920 Twin Beds
Taylor, Ruth
1918 Jack Spurlock, Prodigal
Wild Honey
1920 Headin' Home
Taylor, S. E. V. *same as* **Marier,
Captain Victor; Taylor, Stanley E.
V.; Taylor, Stanner E. V.**
1913 The Seed of the Fathers
1914 The Light Unseen
Mother Love
1915 The Vow
1916 Her Great Hour
Passers By
1917 The Public Be Damned
1918 The Great Love*
The Hun Within
The Rise of Susan

1919 Boots
The Girl Who Stayed Home
Scarlet Days
1920 The Idol Dancer
Nothing but Lies
The Very Idea
Taylor, Sam
1919 The Gamblers
The Gray Towers Mystery
In Honor's Web
Over the Garden Wall
1920 Human Collateral
The Midnight Bride
Taylor, Stanley E. V. *see* **Taylor, S. E.
V.**
Taylor, Stanner E. V. *see* **Taylor, S. E.
V.**
Taylor, Wilfred *could be same as*
Taylor, Wilton
1918 Wild Women
Taylor, William D. *same as* **Taylor,
William; Taylor, William Desmond**
1914 Captain Alvarez
The Criminal Code
1915 An Eye for an Eye
The High Hand
1916 The American Beauty
Ben Blair
Davy Crockett
He Fell in Love with His Wife
The Heart of Paula
Her Father's Son
The House of Lies
The Parson of Panamint
Pasquale
Redeeming Love
1917 Big Timber
The Happiness of Three
Women
Jack and Jill
The Lonesome Chap*
Out of the Wreck
Tom Sawyer
The Varmint
The World Apart
1918 His Majesty, Bunker Bean
How Could You, Jean?
Huck and Tom; Or, The
Further Adventures of Tom
Sawyer
Johanna Enlists
Mile-a-Minute Kendall
The Spirit of '17
Up the Road with Sallie
1919 Anne of Green Gables
Captain Kidd, Jr.
1920 The Furnace
Huckleberry Finn
Jenny Be Good
Judy of Rogue's Harbor
Nurse Marjorie
The Soul of Youth
Taylor, Wilton *could be same as*
Taylor, Wilfred
1917 The Spotted Lily
1918 The Sea Flower*
1919 Blackie's Redemption
The Girl from Outside
The Lottery Man
The Love Burglar
Love Insurance
Peggy Does Her Darndest
The Prince and Betty
Whom the Gods Would
Destroy
1920 Alias Jimmy Valentine
Half a Chance
One Hour Before Dawn
Outside the Law
Terror Island
Treasure Island
Tchkowski, Ivan
1919 Deliverance
Tead, Phillips
1914 The Lost Paradise
1920 She Loves and Lies
Whispers
Tearle, Conway
1914 The Nightingale
Shore Acres
1915 Heléne of the North
Poor Schmaltz
Seven Sisters

Toner, Bessie *could be same as* **Toner, Miss**
1918 Tarzan of the Apes
Tonge, H. Ashton
1917 Outcast
Tonge, Philip
1915 Still Waters
Tooker, Armin
1914 Springtime
Tooker, William H. *same as* **Tooker, W. H.; Tooker, William**
1914 The Banker's Daughter
       Captain Swift
       Dope
       The Greyhound
       Northern Lights
       The Ordeal
       Springtime
1915 The Avalanche
       The Curious Conduct of Judge Legarde
       The Daughter of the Sea
       How Molly Malone Made Good
       A Modern Magdalen
       Sunday
       The Unbroken Road
1916 Ambition
       East Lynne
       The Fool's Revenge
       Her Surrender
       A Modern Thelma
1917 Alias Mrs. Jessop
       The Bitter Truth
       Draft 258
       Light in Darkness
       Red, White and Blue Blood
1917-18
       The Devil's Playground
1918 Men
       The Woman the Germans Shot
1919 The Lost Battalion
       Woman, Woman!
1920 A Child for Sale
       Greater Than Fame
       The Greatest Love
       Heliotrope
       The Stealers
       The Valley of Night
       The Vice of Fools
       Woman's Man
Torrance, Ernest
1919 A Dangerous Affair
Torrence, David
1913 The Prisoner of Zenda
       Tess of the D'Urbervilles
Torres, Callie *same as* **Terres, Callie; Torrez, Caille**
1917 Her Greatest Love
Torres, M. Ramirez *see* **Ramirez-Torres, M.**
Torrez, Caille *see* **Torres, Callie**
Torti, Ernesto
1916 Poor Little Peppina
Totten, Edyth
1914 A Factory Magdalen
Totten, Joseph Byron
1915 The Blindness of Virtue
Tourneur, Maurice
1914 The Man of the Hour
       Mother
       The Pit
       The Wishing Ring; An Idyll of Old England
1915 Alias Jimmy Valentine
       A Butterfly on the Wheel
       The Cub
       The Ivory Snuff Box
       Trilby
1916 The Closed Road
       The Hand of Peril
       The Pawn of Fate
       The Rail Rider
       The Velvet Paw
1917 Barbary Sheep
       Exile
       A Girl's Folly
       The Law of the Land
       The Poor Little Rich Girl
       The Pride of the Clan
       The Rise of Jennie Cushing
       The Undying Flame
       The Whip

1918 The Blue Bird
       A Doll's House
       Prunella
       The Rose of the World
       Sporting Life
       Woman
1919 The Broken Butterfly
       The Life Line
       Victory
       The White Heather
1920 The County Fair
       Deep Waters
       The Great Redeemer
       The Last of the Mohicans
       My Lady's Garter
       Treasure Island
       The White Circle
Tourneur, Renault
1918 Come On In
1920 Help Yourself
Tovell, Albert
1916 A Modern Thelma
1920 The Sleep of Cyma Roget
Tower, Catherine
1918 The Unchastened Woman
Towne, Charles Hanson
1919 The Fighting Roosevelts
Towne, Elaine
1919 A Romance of Seattle
Townley, Robin H. *same as* **Townley, Robert; Townley, Robin**
1918 Huns Within Our Gates
1918-19
       The Candidates
       Marriage a la Mode
1919 The Profiteer
1920 Honeymoon Ranch
Townsend, Mrs.
1917 A Marked Man
Townsend, Kathleen
1916 The Awakening of Helena Ritchie
       The Quest of Life
       The Stolen Triumph
       Vanity
1917 The Princess' Necklace
Townsend, Margaret
1917 A Song of Sixpence
       Thais
Tracey, Thomas F. *same as* **Tracy, Thomas**
1915 The Senator
1916 Behind Closed Doors
1917 The Food Gamblers
       For Valour
       The Man Hater
1918 From Two to Six
Tracy, Clyde
1915 Rumpelstiltskin
Tracy, Helen *same as* **Tracy, Helen T.**
1916 Romeo and Juliet (Fox Film Corp.)
1917 The Land of Promise
1918 Blue-Eyed Mary
       Let's Get a Divorce
       Sunshine Nan
Tracy, Louis
1916 A Son of the Immortals
Tracy, Nell
1919 The Gay Old Dog
Tracy, Thomas *see* **Tracey, Thomas F.**
Trader, George Henry
1916 Whoso Findeth a Wife
Trado, Della
1915 Prohibition
Trado, Mae *could be same as* **Trado, Marie**
1915 Time Lock Number 776
Trado, Marie *could be same as* **Trado, Mae**
1913 Ten Nights in a Barroom
Trainor, Frank
1917 Builders of Castles
Trant, Joseph H. *same as* **Trant, Joseph**
1915 The Family Stain
1916 According to Law
1917 Sylvia of the Secret Service
Traub, Philip
1914 Shore Acres

Traver, J. G.
1917 Jack and the Beanstalk
Travernier, Albert *see* **Tavernier, Albert**
Travers, Miss *could be same as* **Travers, Beverly; Travers, Mildred Carrie** *or* **Traverse, Madlaine**
1919 Upstairs and Down
Travers, Belle *could be same as* **Travers, Beverly**
1919 The Woman Next Door
Travers, Beverly *same as* **Traverse, Beverly; could be same as* **Travers, Miss; Travers, Belle** *or* **Travis, Beverly**
1918 Impossible Susan
1919 The Fear Woman
       The Girl with No Regrets
       The Illustrious Prince
1920 A Full House
       Their Mutual Child
       The Thirteenth Commandment
       The Week-End
Travers, Charles *see* **Travis, Charles W.**
Travers, Mildred Carrie *could be same as* **Travers, Miss**
1919 The Stream of Life
Travers, Richard C.
1915 In the Palace of the King
       The Man Trail
       The White Sister
1916 Captain Jinks of the Horse Marines
       The Little Shepherd of Bargain Row
       The Phantom Buccaneer
1917 S.O.S.
       The Trufflers
1919 The House Without Children
1920 The White Moll
Traverse, Madlaine *same as* **Traverse, Madeline; could be same as* **Travers, Miss**
1913 Leah Kleschna
1914 Three Weeks
1915 The Closing Net
1916 Fruits of Desire
1917 The Poor Little Rich Girl
       Sins of Ambition
1918 The Caillaux Case
       The Danger Zone
1919 Gambling in Souls
       Lost Money
       The Love That Dares
       Rose of the West
       Snares of Paris
       The Splendid Sin
       When Fate Decides
1920 The Hell Ship
       The Iron Heart
       The Spirit of Good
       The Tattlers
       What Would You Do?
Travis, Beverly *could be same as* **Travers, Beverly**
1919 The Homebreaker
Travis, Charles W. *same as* **Travers, Charles; Travis, C. W.; Travis, Charles**
1914 The Criminal Path
       Springtime
       Thou Shalt Not
1916 According to Law
       As a Woman Sows
       I Accuse
       The Idol of the Stage
       The Isle of Love
       The Quality of Faith
Travis, Norton *same as* **Travis, N. C.**
1916 The Folly of Revenge
1920 Heritage
Traxler, Ernest *same as* **Traxler, E.**
1917 The Ghost House
       Hashimura Togo
       The Primrose Ring
       The Silent Partner
       The Tides of Barnegat
1919 Caleb Piper's Girl
       Go Get 'Em Garringer
Traxler, Valeria
1918 How Could You, Jean?

Treador, Marie
1920 Circumstantial Evidence
       The Sacred Ruby
       The Wall Street Mystery
Trebaol, Edouard *same as* **Trebaol, Eddie**
1920 Honest Hutch
       The Penalty
Trebaol, Jeanette *same as* **Trebol, Jenette**
1919 A Rogue's Romance
1920 Honest Hutch
Trebaol, Yves
1920 Honest Hutch
Trebol, Jenette *see* **Trebaol, Jeanette**
Tree, Sir Herbert Beerbohm
1916 Intolerance*
       Macbeth
       The Old Folks at Home
Trees, James C. Van *see* **Van Trees, James C.**
Tremaine, Tom
1920 The Return of Tarzan
Trent, Viola
1916 The Kiss
       The Man Who Stood Still
Trenton, Pell
1917 The Adventurer
       Stranded in Arcady
1918 A Camouflage Kiss
       The House of Glass
1919 Fair and Warmer
       The False Code
       The Joyous Liar
       The Rebellious Bride
       The Uplifters
1920 Beautifully Trimmed
       The Blue Moon
       Fighting Cressy
       The House of Toys
       The Willow Tree
Treskoff, Countess Olga
1920 The Sleep of Cyma Roget
Tressida, Madame
1920 The Strongest
Trevelyn, Una
1918 The Venus Model
1919 Her Purchase Price
1920 The Devil's Passkey
Treves, Sir Frederick
1918 The Great Love*
Trevor, Norman
1915 After Dark
       The Ivory Snuff Box
1917 National Red Cross Pageant*
       The Runaway
1918 The Daredevil
1920 The Daughter Pays
       Romance
Trevor, Olive
1916 The Haunted Manor
1917 The Derelict
1919 The Other Man's Wife
       Taxi
Trevor, Paul
1914 The Unwelcome Mrs. Hatch
Tricoli, Charles
1914 Il Trovatore
Trimble, George S. *same as* **Trimble, George**
1914 The House Next Door
       Michael Strogoff
1915 The Great Ruby
1916 The Man Who Stood Still
       Sins of Men
1917 Arms and the Girl
       The Crimson Dove
       Light in Darkness
       Polly of the Circus
1917-18
       The Devil's Playground
1918 Our Mrs. McChesney
       To Hell with the Kaiser
1919 A Damsel in Distress
       The Price of Innocence
Trimble, Laurence *same as* **Trimble, Larry; Trimble, Lawrence**
1917 The Auction Block
       The Spreading Dawn
1918 The Light Within
1919 Fool's Gold
       Spotlight Sadie

1920 Darling Mine
Everybody's Sweetheart
Going Some
The Silver Horde
The Woman God Sent

Trinchera, Paul
1918 His Daughter Pays
A Son of Strife

Trinnear, Mabel
1916 The Salamander

Troffey, Alex *same as* **Troffey, Alexander**
1918 The Border Legion
1918-19
Once to Every Man
1920 Earthbound

Trombly, Delia
1916 Anton the Terrible

Troughton, John
1913 Tess of the D'Urbervilles

Trow, Buster
1920 What Happened to Rosa

Trowbridge, Charles
1915 The Fight
Prohibition
The Siren's Song
Sunday
1917 Thais
1919 The Eternal Magdalene
1920 The Fortune Hunter

Troyano, John
1915 The Arrival of Perpetua

Truax, Sarah *could be same as* **Truex, Sarah**
1915 Jordan Is a Hard Road

Truesdale, Fred *see* **Truesdell, Frederick**

Truesdale, Howard *same as* **Truesdell, Harry; Truesdell, Howard**
1915 Destiny; Or, The Soul of a Woman
Marse Covington
1916 The Come-Back
A Corner in Cotton
The Masked Rider
The Pretenders
The Purple Lady
The Upheaval
1918 The Embarrassment of Riches
1919 Bolshevism on Trial
Suspense
1920 Empty Arms
What Women Want
The Whisper Market
Youthful Folly

Truesdell, Frederick *same as* **Truesdale, Fred; Truesdell, Charles Fred; Truesdell, Fred; Truesdell, Fred C.; Truesdell, Frederick C.**
1915 Alias Jimmy Valentine
The Arrival of Perpetua
The Boss
Camille
The Cotton King
The Deep Purple
Hearts in Exile
1916 Love's Crucible
La Vie de Boheme
The World Against Him
1917 The Beloved Adventuress
Daughter of Maryland
The Duchess of Doubt
The Greatest Power
The Man Who Forgot
The Marriage Market
National Red Cross Pageant*
Outwitted
1918 Hearts of Love
A Man's World
My Own United States
The Panther Woman
1919 The Great Victory, Wilson or the Kaiser? The Fall of the Hohenzollerns
Shadows

Truesdell, Howard *see* **Truesdale, Howard**

Truex, Ernest
1913 Caprice
1914 An American Citizen
Dope
A Good Little Devil
The Quest of the Sacred Jewel

1916 Artie, the Millionaire Kid
1918 Come On In
Good-Bye, Bill
1919 Oh, You Women

Truex, Sarah *could be same as* **Truax, Sarah**
1919 Fool's Gold

Truman, California
1919 Who Cares?

Trunnelle, Mabel
1915 The Destroying Angel
Eugene Aram
The Magic Skin
Ranson's Folly
Shadows from the Past
1916 The Heart of the Hills
The Martyrdom of Philip Strong
A Message to Garcia
1917 The Ghost of Old Morro
The Grell Mystery
The Master Passion
Where Love Is

Tsingh, Hurri
1916 The Adventures of Kathlyn

Tucker, George Loane
1913 Traffic in Souls
1917 The Cinderella Man
1918 The Beloved Traitor
Dodging a Million
Joan of Plattsburg
Virtuous Wives
1919 The Miracle Man

Tucker, Harland
1918 Sauce for the Goose
1919 The Loves of Letty

Tucker, Lillian
1915 Evidence
The Mummy and the Humming Bird
1916 The Light That Failed
The Red Widow
1920 The Marriage Pit

Tucker, Richard
1915 The Ring of the Borgias
Vanity Fair
1916 The Cossack Whip
When Love Is King
1917 Babbling Tongues
Behind the Mask
The Cloud
The Law of the North
The Little Chevalier
The Master Passion
The On-the-Square-Girl
Pardners
The Power of Decision
The Royal Pauper
Think It Over
Threads of Fate
1920 The Branding Iron
Darling Mine
Dollars and Sense
The Great Lover
The Woman in Room 13

Tuckerman, Ray
1915 Blue Grass

Tuers, William H. *same as* **Tuers, William**
1917 Alias Mrs. Jessop
An American Widow
Blue Jeans
1919 The Lost Battalion
Out of the Fog
1920 Birthright

Tuey, Bert
1915 All for a Girl
The Governor's Boss
1916 The Soul Market
1918 Secret Strings
Sylvia on a Spree

Tuff, Jimmy
1918 The Hell Cat

Tully, Ethel
1916 The Flames of Johannis
Ignorance
1917 Her Good Name

Tully, May
1918 The Winning of Beatrice
1920 His Wife's Money

Tully, Richard Walton
1914 Rose of the Rancho

Tunis, Fay
1915 Carmen (Fox Film Corp.)

Tupper, Edith Sessions
1920 For Love or Money

Turbett, Ben
1916 When Love Is King
1917 Builders of Castles
The Courage of the Common Place
Cy Whittaker's Ward
The Lady of the Photograph
The Last Sentence
The Royal Pauper

Turin, Mr.
1917 The Glory of Yolanda

Turnbull, Hector
1915 The Cheat
The Marriage of Kitty
Out of the Darkness
Temptation
The Voice in the Fog
1916 Alien Souls
The Dupe
For the Defense
The Heart of Nora Flynn
Less Than the Dust
The Race
The Selfish Woman
1917 The Clever Mrs. Carfax
Double Crossed
The Evil Eye

Turnbull, Margaret
1915 Armstrong's Wife
Blackbirds
The Case of Becky
The Clue
The Fighting Hope
The Secret Sin
Stolen Goods
The Unknown
1916 Alien Souls
The Dupe
For the Defense
Public Opinion
Pudd'nhead Wilson
The Thousand Dollar Husband
To Have and to Hold
The Victoria Cross
The Victory of Conscience
Witchcraft
The Yellow Pawn
1917 Bab's Matinee Idol
The Black Wolf
Her Better Self
Jack and Jill
Lost and Won
Magda
Shirley Kaye
1918 A Daughter of the Old South
Eve's Daughter
The Firefly of France
The House of Silence
Mrs. Dane's Defense
My Cousin
The Shuttle
1919 The Splendid Romance
The Two Brides
The World to Live In
1920 Thou Art the Man
The Tree of Knowledge

Turnbull, Roberto A. *same as* **Turnbull, Robert; Turnbull, Robert A.**
1917 The Blood of His Fathers
The Eye of Envy
The Painted Lie
The Planter*

Turner, Mrs.
1918 A Pair of Cupids
1919 The Two Brides

Turner, Alice
1918 Sylvia on a Spree

Turner, B. M. *see* **Turner, Bowd M.**

Turner, Bert
1917 The Rose of Blood

Turner, Betty
1920 The Return of Tarzan

Turner, Bowd M. *same as* **Turner, B. M.; Turner, Bowditch; Turner, Bowd M. (Smoke)**
1917 Little Shoes

1919 The Coming of the Law
Hell Roarin' Reform
Married in Haste

Turner, D. H. *same as* **Turner, Dave; Turner, David**
1914 Hearts of Oak
1916 The Dawn of Love
Her American Prince
1918 Revelation

Turner, Emmanuel A. *same as* **Turner, E. A.; Turner, Emanuel; Turner, Emanuel A.; Turner, Emmanuel**
1914 The Mystery of the Poison Pool
1916 The Redemption of Dave Darcey
The Tarantula
1917 Sowers and Reapers
1918 The Love Swindle
1920 Are All Men Alike?

Turner, F. A. *same as* **Turner, Fred; Turner, Fred A.**
1914 The Escape
Home, Sweet Home*
The Next in Command
1915 The Lost House
A Man and His Mate
The Penitentes
1916 Acquitted
Atta Boy's Last Race
Children of the Feud
The Devil's Needle
Intolerance
Little Meena's Romance
The Microscope Mystery
Susan Rocks the Boat
1917 Aladdin and the Wonderful Lamp
The Girl of the Timber Claims
Her Official Fathers
The Little Yank
A Love Sublime
Madame Bo-Peep
1918 Playthings
Restitution
She Hired a Husband
The Velvet Hand
1919 As the Sun Went Down
Bonnie, Bonnie Lassie
The Heart of Wetona
The Miracle Man
The Mother and the Law
1920 Eyes of the Heart
The Furnace
The Jack-Knife Man
The Return of Tarzan
Terror Island

Turner, Florence
1919 Fool's Gold
1920 Blackmail
The Brand of Lopez
The Ugly Duckling

Turner, Frank
1917 Rebecca of Sunnybrook Farm

Turner, Fred *see* **Turner, F. A.**

Turner, Joseph Allan *same as* **Turner, J. Alan**
1916 A Daughter of the Gods
The Witch

Turner, K. M.
1914 A Suspicious Wife

Turner, Otis
1914 Called Back
Damon and Pythias
Neptune's Daughter
The Opened Shutters
The Spy
1915 Business Is Business
The Frame-Up
A Little Brother of the Rich
The Scarlet Sin
1916 The Gay Lord Waring
Langdon's Legacy
The Mediator
The Pool of Flame
The Seekers
A Son of the Immortals
The Whirlpool of Destiny
A Youth of Fortune
1917 The Book Agent
High Finance
The Island of Desire
Melting Millions
Some Boy!
The Soul of Satan

To Honor and Obey
Turner, Richard
1916 The Combat
The Conflict
The Destroyers
The Straight Way
1917 Moral Courage
Troublemakers
The Web of Desire
1918 Conquered Hearts
Turner, William H. *same as* **Turner, W. H.; Turner, William**
1913 Traffic in Souls
1914 The Daughters of Men
The Gamblers
1915 The Climbers
The Great Ruby
A Man's Making
The Nation's Peril
1916 The City of Failing Light
The Evangelist
The Gods of Fate
Her Bleeding Heart
Love's Toll
1917 Her Good Name
1920 The Prey
The Sporting Duchess
Turpin, Ben
1916 Charlie Chaplin's Burlesque on "Carmen"
The Essanay-Chaplin Revue of 1916
1919 Yankee Doodle in Berlin
1920 Down on the Farm
Married Life
Tuttle, W. C.
1920 Hell's Oasis
Tyke, John
1920 Hell's Oasis
Tylden, L.
1916 Macbeth
Tyler, Dallas
1914 The Toll of Love
1917-18
The Devil's Playground
Tyler, F. J. *could be same as* **Tyler, Francis** *or* **Tyler, Fred**
1915 The Circular Staircase
Tyler, Francis *could be same as* **Tyler, F. J.**
1915 A Gentleman of Leisure
Tyler, Fred *could be same as* **Tyler, F. J.**
1918 The Brazen Beauty
1919 Bonnie, Bonnie Lassie
The Exquisite Thief
1920 The Virgin of Stamboul
Tyler, G. Vere
1916 A Huntress of Men
Tyler, Odette
1920 The Saphead
Typsy, the puppy
1915 The Golden Claw
Tyrel, Betty
1917 In Again—Out Again
Tyrol, Jacques
1918 And the Children Pay
The Grain of Dust
1919 Human Passions
The Red Viper
Tyrone, Madge
1915 The House of Tears
1916 One Day
1920 Rio Grande
The Woman in His House
1921 Habit
Tyscher, Sallie
1917 The Road Between

U

Ugliest Pup in the World, The
1916 Prudence the Pirate
Ullman, Carl *same as* **Ulman, Carl**
1916 Somewhere in France
1917 The Flame of the Yukon
The Little Brother
The Medicine Man
The Mother Instinct
Wolf Lowry

1918 The Hired Man
1920 The Secret Gift
That Something
What Women Love
Ullman, Edward *same as* **Ullman, E. G.; Ullman, E. J.; Ullman, Eddie**
1915 Father and the Boys
1918 A Broadway Scandal
Fast Company
The Grand Passion*
A Society Sensation
The Wildcat of Paris
1919 The Blinding Trail
The Little White Savage
Ullman, Ethel
1916 Civilization
The Dividend
1917 Whose Wife?
1920 The Honey Bee
Ullman, Sidney
1920 Alias Jimmy Valentine
Are All Men Alike?
Parlor, Bedroom and Bath
Ulman, Carl *see* **Ullman, Carl**
Ulmer, R. W.
1916 Willard-Johnson Boxing Match*
Ulrich, Lenore
1915 The Better Woman
Kilmeny
1916 The Heart of Paula
The Intrigue
The Road to Love
1917 Her Own People
1919 Roses and Thorns
Unander, S. M. *same as* **Unander, C. M.; Unander, Jack; Unander, James**
1917 The Danger Trail
1918 Marriage
Out of the Night
1919 Marriage for Convenience
Underhill, John *same as* **Underhill, J. G.; Underhill, J. J.; Underhill, Jack**
1919 The Better Wife*
The Woman Next Door
1920 The Best of Luck
The Joyous Troublemaker
Underwood, Lawrence
1920 Old Lady 31
That Something
Unger, Red
1917 Flirting with Death
Unsell, Eve *same as* **Unsell, Eva**
1914 The Man from Mexico
One of Our Girls
Wildflower
1915 Are You a Mason?
The Dawn of a Tomorrow
Richard Carvel
The Second in Command
The Silent Voice
1916 Behind Closed Doors
The Honorable Friend
The Ransom
The Reapers
1917 The Crystal Gazer
Double Crossed
The Dummy
The Eternal Temptress
Forbidden Paths
The Fortunes of Fifi
Freckles*
Heart's Desire
Her Silent Sacrifice
The Long Trail
Over There
The Tides of Barnegat
1918 The Debt of Honor
In Pursuit of Polly
Madame Jealousy
The Prodigal Wife
Sunshine Nan
The Whirlpool
A Woman of Impulse
1919 Eyes of the Soul
His Parisian Wife
The Marriage Price
Mrs. Wiggs of the Cabbage Patch
Out of the Shadow
Suspense
The Test of Honor
Three Men and a Girl
The Trap

1920 The Cup of Fury*
Sinners
Urban, Jane
1914 The Last Egyptian
Urban, Joseph
1920 The World and His Wife
Urhe, Clarice
1918 A Petticoat Pilot
Urie, John
1916 The Libertine
The Prima Donna's Husband
1917 The Law of Compensation
Redemption
1918 The Queen of Hearts
Urson, Frank *same as* **Urson, Frank J.**
1917 Miss Jackie of the Army
Nina, the Flower Girl
1918 Ann's Finish
The Eyes of Julia Deep
Jilted Janet
Molly, Go Get 'Em
1919 An Adventure in Hearts
Alias Mike Moran
Hawthorne of the U.S.A.
The Lottery Man
The Love Burglar
The Roaring Road
The Valley of the Giants
You're Fired
Utell, George
1917 Mothers of Men
Uttenhover, M. Harry
1920 The Mark of Zorro*
Uzzell, Corene *same as* **Uzzell, Corine; Uzzell, Corinne; Uzzell, Corrine; Uzzelle, Corinne**
1917 On Trial
Seven Keys to Baldpate
1918 Conquered Hearts
The Daredevil
The Grain of Dust
The Song of Songs
A Woman of Impulse
1919 The Clouded Name
Luck and Pluck
The Oakdale Affair
Thunderbolts of Fate
A Woman's Experience

V

Vail, Edwin
1916 The Dead Alive
Valbel, Henri
1917 The Silent Master
Valderna, Louis A.
1916 The Yaqui
Vale, Louise
1913 The Girl of the Sunny South
1915 The Hungarian Nabob
1916 The Sex Lure
1917 Easy Money
1918 Joan of the Woods
Journey's End
Vengeance
The Witch Woman
Vale, Margaret
1915 A Gilded Fool
Vale, Pamela
1917 Pride and the Devil
Vale, Travers
1913 The Girl of the Sunny South
1915 The Hungarian Nabob
1916 The Madness of Helen
The Men She Married
Sally in Our Alley
The Scarlet Oath
Tangled Fates
1917 Betsy Ross
The Bondage of Fear
The Dancer's Peril
Darkest Russia
The Divorce Game
The Dormant Power
Easy Money
Man's Woman
A Self-Made Widow
The Woman Beneath
1918 Joan of the Woods
Journey's End
Just Sylvia
The Man Hunt

A Soul Without Windows
The Spurs of Sybil
Stolen Hours
Vengeance
Whims of Society
The Witch Woman
A Woman of Redemption
The Zero Hour
1919 The Bluffer
Heart of Gold
The Moral Deadline
The Quickening Flame
1920 Life
Vale, Vola
1917 The Bond Between
Each to His Kind
The Lady in the Library
Mentioned in Confidence
The Secret of Black Mountain
The Silent Man
The Son of His Father
The Winning of Sally Temple
Zollenstein
1918 The Locked Heart
Wolves of the Rail
1919 Happy Though Married
A Heart in Pawn
Hearts Asleep
The Hornet's Nest
Six Feet Four
1920 Alias Jimmy Valentine
Common Sense
The Iron Rider
A Master Stroke
Overland Red
The Purple Cipher
Someone in the House
Valencia, E.
1916 Ramona
Valentina, Rodolfo di *see* **Valentino, Rudolph**
Valentine, Gertrude
1920 $30,000
Valentine, Grace
1915 Black Fear
1916 The Blindness of Love
The Brand of Cowardice
Dorian's Divorce
The Evil Thereof
Man and His Soul
1917 Babbling Tongues
1918 The Unchastened Woman
Valentine, Leila
1920 Passers-By
Valentine, Louiszita
1917 The Mystery of Number 47
1920 The Gauntlet
Polly with a Past
The Sea Rider
Valentine, Maurice
1920 Polly of the Storm Country
Valentine, Rodolph *see* **Valentino, Rudolph**
Valentine, Spencer
1913 The Sea Wolf
Valentine, Vangie
1919 When Bearcat Went Dry
1920 Romance
Valentino, Rudolph *same as* **De Valentina, R.; De Valentina, M. Rodolfo; DeValentino, Rudolph; De Valintine, Rudolpho; Valentina, Rodolfo di; Valentine, Rodolph; Valentine, Rudolph; Valentini, Rodolfo di; Valentino, Rudolfo; Volantino, Rudolph**
1918 All Night
The Married Virgin
A Society Sensation
1919 The Big Little Person
The Delicious Little Devil
Eyes of Youth
Nobody Home
A Rogue's Romance
1920 An Adventuress
Once to Every Woman
Passion's Playground
Stolen Moments
The Wonderful Chance
Valerie, Gladys
1918 The Heart of a Girl
1919 Dawn
Marie, Ltd.

Vance, Louis Joseph
1915 The Spanish Jade
1918 The Inn of the Blue Moon
Wild Honey
1919 The Lone Wolf's Daughter
Twilight
1920 Love

Vanderbroeck, John *see* **Broek, John van den**

Vanderlip, Frank A.
1916 The Dollar and the Law

Vane, Denton
1915 The Man Who Couldn't Beat God
On Her Wedding Night
To Cherish and Protect
1916 An Enemy to the King
Green Stockings
Hesper of the Mountains
The Hunted Woman
The Island of Surprise
The Ordeal of Elizabeth
The Vital Question
Who Killed Joe Merrion?
1917 Apartment 29
The Glory of Yolanda
The Grell Mystery
The Hawk
In the Balance
The Maelstrom
Soldiers of Chance
The Soul Master
The Stolen Treaty
Transgression
1918 A Bachelor's Children
The Beloved Impostor
The Clutch of Circumstance
A Game with Fate
The Golden Goal
Love Watches
Miss Ambition
A Mother's Sin
1919 Beauty-Proof
The Bramble Bush
Fortune's Child
A Girl at Bay
The Man Who Won
Mind the Paint Girl*
1920 The Midnight Bride
Oil
Wings of Pride
Women Men Love

Vardaman, James K.
1915 Prohibition*

Varesi, Gilda *same as* **Varesi, Vilda**
1917 The Man of Mystery
1920 Romance

Vaughan, Arthur
1918 The Birth of a Race

Vaughan, Margaret *same as* **Vaughan, Peggy**
1917 The Girl Without a Soul
1919 Heart of Gold

Vaughan, Roy *see* **Vaughn, Roy**

Vaughan, William H. *see* **Vaughn, William**

Vaughn, Katherine *same as* **Vaughn, Kathryn**
1914 The House of Bondage
1917 The Wax Model

Vaughn, Robert
1913 Ten Nights in a Barroom
1914 After the Ball
A Mother's Heart
1915 Still Waters
1916 The Fear of Poverty
The Fugitive
Master Shakespeare, Strolling Player
1917 The Fires of Youth
Her New York
Mary Lawson's Secret
Under False Colors
The Vicar of Wakefield
1920 The Girl with the Jazz Heart

Vaughn, Roy *same as* **Vaughan, Roy**
1917 The Food Gamblers
For Valour
Her Excellency, the Governor
The Man Hater
1918 From Two to Six
1919 The Lost Battalion
1920 High Speed
The North Wind's Malice

Vaughn, William *same as* **Vaughan, William H.**
1914 The Brute
The Redemption of David Corson
1915 The Man Who Beat Dan Dolan
1916 The Light

Vaull, William de *see* **De Vaull, William**

Vautier, Sidney
1920 Help Yourself

Veiller, Bayard
1919 Pretty Smooth
1920 Blackmail
Cinderella's Twin
The Deadlier Sex
Held in Trust

Vekroff, Perry N. *same as* **Vekroff, Perry**
1914 Three Weeks
1915 Hearts of Men
When It Strikes Home
1916 Should a Baby Die?
1917 Bridges Burned
Her Secret
The More Excellent Way
The Question
Richard, the Brazen
The Secret of Eve
1918 Men
1919 Dust of Desire
In Honor's Web
What Love Forgives
A Woman's Experience
1920 Cynthia-of-the-Minute

Velasquez, Edward
1915 Carmen (Fox Film Corp.)

Velmar, Tom
1920 The Law of the Yukon

Velsey, Graham
1915 Dr. Rameau

Veness, Amy *same as* **Van Ness, Amy**
1917 Please Help Emily
1918 My Wife
1919 The Brat
The Red Lantern

Venturini, Edward D.
1919 The Gay Old Dog

Verdi, Freddie *same as* **Verdi, Fredi**
1915 The Eternal City
1918 The Light Within
Love's Conquest

Vere, Maud de
1917 God's Man

Vermilye, Harold *same as* **Vermilyea, W.**
1914 The Jungle
1917 The Law That Failed
Pride and the Devil

Vermilyea, Lester J. *same as* **Vermilyea, L. J.; Vermilyea, Lester**
1917 The Soul of a Magdalen
1919 The Miracle of Love
1920 The Misleading Lady
Polly with a Past

Vermilyea, W. *see* **Vermilye, Harold**

Verner, Charles E. *see* **Vernon, Charles E.**

Vernon, Mrs.
1916 The Heart of New York

Vernon, Agnes *see* **Vernon, Brownie**

Vernon, Bob
1915 A Little Brother of the Rich

Vernon, Brownie *same as* **Vernon, Agnes; Vernon, Agnes "Brownie"**
1916 A Stranger from Somewhere
Tangled Hearts
1917 Bringing Home Father
The Car of Chance
The Clean-Up
The Clock
Fear Not
Flirting with Death
The High Sign
The Man Who Took a Chance
A Stormy Knight
1919 Bare-Fisted Gallagher
The Coming of the Law
Widow by Proxy

Vernon, Charles E. *same as* **Verner, Charles E.**
1914 The Sign of the Cross

1916 Hulda from Holland

Vernon, Frank de *see* **De Vernon, Frank**

Vernon, Isabel *same as* **Vernon, Isabelle**
1914 Cinderella
1916 The Struggle
1917 An Amateur Orphan
Polly of the Circus
The Rise of Jennie Cushing
1918 Joan of Plattsburg

Vernon, Jane
1916 The Land Just Over Yonder

Vernon, Judson
1920 The Marriage Pit

Vernot, Henry J. *same as* **Vernot, Henry**
1916 The Dead Alive
Feathertop

Victory, Frances
1920 Headin' Home

Vidor, Florence
1916 The Intrigue
1917 American Methods
The Cook of Canyon Camp
The Countess Charming
Hashimura Togo
The Secret Game
1918 The Bravest Way
Hidden Pearls
The Honor of His House
Old Wives for New
Till I Come Back to You
The White Man's Law
The Widow's Might
1919 The Other Half
Poor Relations
1920 The Family Honor
The Jack-Knife Man

Vidor, King *same as* **Vidor, King W.**
1919 Better Times
The Other Half
Poor Relations
The Turn in the Road
1920 The Family Honor
The Jack-Knife Man

Vignola, Robert G. *same as* **Vignola, Robert**
1913 From the Manger to the Cross
1915 Don Caesar de Bazan
The Pretenders
The Vanderhoff Affair
1916 Audrey
The Black Crook
The Evil Thereof
The Moment Before
The Reward of Patience
Seventeen
The Spider
Under Cover
1917 Double Crossed
The Fortunes of Fifi
Great Expectations
Her Better Self
The Hungry Heart
The Love That Lives
1918 The Claw
The Girl Who Came Back
The Knife
Madame Jealousy
The Reason Why
The Savage Woman
Women's Weapons
1919 Experimental Marriage
The Heart of Youth
His Official Fiancée
The Home Town Girl
An Innocent Adventuress
Louisiana
More Deadly Than the Male
The Third Kiss
The Winning Girl
The Woman Next Door
You Never Saw Such a Girl
1920 The Thirteenth Commandment
The World and His Wife

Viliers, Victor de
1918 The Border Legion

Viller, Edgar
1920 The Rich Slave

Vincent, Florence
1916 His Great Triumph
1918 The Biggest Show on Earth

Vincent, James *same as* **Vincent, James R.**
1914 The Land of the Lost
1915 The Melting Pot
1916 Ambition
The Battle of Life
Gold and the Woman
Love and Hate
Sins of Men
The Unwelcome Mother
1917 Royal Romance
Sister Against Sister
Wrath of Love
1919 The Spirit of Lafayette
1920 Stolen Moments

Vinna, Clyde de *see* **DeVinna, Clyde**

Vinna, Padre Francisca de la
1914 Rose of the Rancho

Vinton, Horace
1914 The Line-Up at Police Headquarters
1916 The Other Girl
Romeo and Juliet (Quality Pictures Corp.)
1917 A Night in New Arabia

Viragh-Flower, A. Béla
1920 Empty Arms
The Scarlet Dragon

Virgo, Teddy
1916 The Chaperon

Vitolli, Antonio
1919 The Great Victory, Wilson or the Kaiser? The Fall of the Hohenzollerns

Vivian, Robert
1914 The Chimes
1915 The Eternal City
1916 Green Stockings
Little Miss Happiness
The War Bride's Secret
1917 The Argyle Case
The Man Hater
The Moth
The Scarlet Letter
Troublemakers
1918 Jack Spurlock, Prodigal
Out of a Clear Sky
Under the Greenwood Tree
1919 La Belle Russe
1920 The New York Idea
The Plunger
The Restless Sex

Vivian, T.
1917 The Law of the Land

Viviani, Rene Raphael
1918 Hearts of the World*

Vizard, Harold
1920 Flying Pat

Voegtlin, Arthur
1914 America

Volantino, Rudolph *see* **Valentino, Rudolph**

Volare, Lorna *same as* **Volare, Baby**
1916 The Ransom
The Spell of the Yukon
1917 The Barricade
A Man and the Woman
The Moth
Motherhood (Frank Powell Producing Corp.)
The Secret of the Storm Country
1918 Just a Woman

Volkman, P. Thad.
1916 Lovely Mary
The Quitter
The Stolen Triumph
The Turmoil
The Upheaval
1918 Kildare of Storm
A Successful Adventure
1919 The Divorcee

Vollmer, Margaret
1915 Prohibition

Volnys, Jacques
1920 The Empire of Diamonds

Von Betz, M. C.
1914 One Wonderful Night

Von Eltz, Theodore
1915 His Wife
1916 The Traffic Cop

Von Hardenberg, Count *same as* **Hardenburg, Count;** *could be same as* **Hardenburg, Fritz von**
1917 The Yankee Way
1918 Cheating the Public
1920 Sink or Swim

Von Harder, Armin
1917 Polly Put the Kettle On

Von Meter, Harry *same as* **Meter, Harry; Meter, Harry von; Van Meter, Harry**
1915 The Buzzard's Shadow
The End of the Road
1916 The Abandonment
April
Dulcie's Adventure
Dust
Lone Star
The Love Hermit
The Other Side of the Door
True Nobility
The Undertow
The White Rosette
Youth's Endearing Charm
1917 Beloved Rogues
Captain Kiddo
My Fighting Gentleman
Princess Virtue
Whose Wife?
1918 Broadway Love
The Cabaret Girl
The Dream Lady
His Birthright
The Kaiser, the Beast of Berlin
The Lure of Luxury
The Man of Bronze
A Man's Man
Midnight Madness
1919 The Challenge of Chance
The Day She Paid
Diane of the Green Van
The Girl with No Regrets
A Gun Fightin' Gentleman
A Man's Fight
A Rogue's Romance
1920 Alias Miss Dodd
The Cheater
Dangerous Love
Dollar for Dollar
The Lone Hand
Under Crimson Skies
The Unfortunate Sex

Von Ottinger, Leonora *see* **Ottinger, Leonora**

Von Ritzau, Baron *see* **Ritzau, Erik von**

von Ritzen, E. *see* **Ritzau, Erik von**

Von Schiller, Carl *same as* **Schiller, Carl; Schiller, Carl von**
1915 Buckshot John
Captain Courtesy
Colorado
Help Wanted
A Little Brother of the Rich
Secretary of Frivolous Affairs
1916 If My Country Should Call
A Law unto Himself
Saving the Family Name
Sins of Her Parent
Vengeance Is Mine
1919 Devil McCare

Von Seyffertitz, Gustav *see* **Seyffertitz, Gustav von**

Von Stroheim, Eric *see* **Stroheim, Erich von**

Vonnegut, Marjorie
1918 The Grain of Dust

Vorzimer, Sydney
1917 God's Man

Vosburgh, Alfred *same as* **Vosburg, Alfred; Vosburgh, Al**
1916 Her Father's Son
The Road to Love
1917 The Divorcee
Environment
Money Madness
Princess of the Dark
The Serpent's Tooth
Shackles of Truth

Vosburgh, Harold
1916 My Country First
The Smugglers
1920-21
The House of Mystery

Vosburgh, Jack
1916 A Gamble in Souls
Honor Thy Name
1917 Environment
The Lady in the Library
My Fighting Gentleman
Princess Virtue
Southern Pride

Voshell, John M.
1919 Eyes of Youth
1920 The Forbidden Woman
Silk Husbands and Calico Wives
Whispering Devils

Voute, Dad
1917 Betty Be Good

Vries, Henri de *same as* **Devries, Henry**

Vroom, Frederick *same as* **Vroom, Fred; Vroom, Frederic**
1915 Fighting Bob
A Gentleman of Leisure
1916 The Invisible Enemy
The Jungle Child
1917 The Gown of Destiny
New York Luck
The Serpent's Tooth
Shackles of Truth
1918 Betty Takes a Hand
High Tide
I Love You
Little Red Decides
Restitution
She Hired a Husband
1919 The Beloved Cheater
Devil McCare
Fighting Through
The Island of Intrigue
One of the Finest
Secret Marriage
Upstairs
Where the West Begins
1920 813
The Great Lover
The Kentucky Colonel
The Marriage Pit
The Misfit Wife
The Prince of Avenue A
The Six Best Cellars
A Tokio Siren
The Triflers

W

Wada, F.
1919 The Unwritten Code

Wade, Mrs. J. W.
1919 Her Kingdom of Dreams

Wade, John P. *same as* **Wade, J. P.; Wade, John**
1914 The Seats of the Mighty
1917 A Bit of Kindling
Feet of Clay
Zollenstein
1919 Life's Greatest Problem
The Open Door
The Third Degree
Too Many Crooks
Virtuous Men
1920 Other Men's Shoes
The White Moll
The Woman God Sent

Wade, Lillian
1918 Little Orphant Annie

Wadleigh, Agnes
1916 The Lights of New York

Wadsworth (full name unknown)
1915 The Fairy and the Waif*

Wadsworth, William
1915 Children of Eve
Cohen's Luck
Vanity Fair
1916 The Catspaw
The Cossack Whip
The Martyrdom of Philip Strong
1917 The Apple-Tree Girl
Billy and the Big Stick
Builders of Castles
Chris and His Wonderful Lamp
The Courage of the Common Place

Cy Whittaker's Ward
Envy
Kidnapped
The Last Sentence
Light in Darkness
The Little Chevalier
The Master Passion
Putting the Bee in Herbert
The Royal Pauper
Salt of the Earth
Where Love Is
1918 Rich Man, Poor Man
19-- Barnaby Lee

Wagner, Billie (*actress*)
1918 The Kaiser's Finish

Wagner, Billy (*cam*) *see* **Wagner, William**

Wagner, Carolyn
1917 The Devil Dodger
The Millionaire Vagrant
1918 The Spreading Evil

Wagner, Fred
1919 Where's Mary?

Wagner, Honus
1917 The Baseball Revue of 1917*

Wagner, Jack
1920 The Forbidden Thing
In the Heart of a Fool*

Wagner, Leon
1914 The Land of the Lost*
1915 The Game of Three
1917 The Girl Who Didn't Think*

Wagner, Robert
1916 A Yoke of Gold

Wagner, William *same as* **Wagner, Billy; Wagner, William F.**
1915 The Incorrigible Dukane
1916 Dorian's Divorce
The Pretenders
The Red Widow
1917 The Debt*
The Greater Woman
Mary Moreland
The Mirror
Mrs. Balfame
1919 The Country Cousin
1920 The Dangerous Paradise
Whispers
The Woman Game

Waid, Dan
1915 The Beachcomber

Wain, Dick
1919 Behind the Door

Wainwright, Charles
1915 'Twas Ever Thus

Wainwright, Marie
1918 Secret Strings
Social Hypocrites
1920 Polly with a Past

Waipahu, Lehua
1917 The Bottle Imp

Waite, Mr.
1912 Cleopatra

Wakara, India
1920 Dead Men Tell No Tales

Wakefield, Agnes
1919 Out of the Shadow

Walburn, Raymond
1916 The Tarantula

Walcamp, Marie
1915 Coral
1916 The Flirt
Hop, the Devil's Brew
John Needham's Double
Where Are My Children?
1918 Tongues of Flame

Walck, Ezra
1914 The $5,000,000 Counterfeiting Plot
1918 T'Other Dear Charmer

Walcott, Charles
1919 Phil-for-Short

Walcott, Helen
1916 Diane of the Follies

Walcott, Julia
1914 The Day of Days
The House of Bondage
The Little Gray Lady
1915 Gretna Green

Walcott, William
1918 Hit-the-Trail Holliday
The Inn of the Blue Moon
1919 The Mystery of the Yellow Room
1920 The Girl with the Jazz Heart

Waldermeyer, Jack
1920 Roman Candles

Waldron, Andrew
1919 Under Suspicion

Waldron, Charles
1915 At Bay
Esmeralda
When We Were Twenty-One
1916 Audrey
Mice and Men
1920 The Thief

Waldron, Le Monte
1916 The Last Act*

Wales, Betty
1919 Oh, You Women
1920 King Spruce

Wales, C. H. *same as* **Wales, Claude H. "Bud"**
1916 The Fall of a Nation
1917 Until They Get Me
1918 Deuce Duncan
The Gun Woman
Madame Sphinx
The Mask
The Painted Lady
The Price of Applause
Tony America
1919 The Betrayal

Wales, Ethel
1921 Midsummer Madness

Wales, R. Ellis *same as* **Wales, R. E.**
1916 Intolerance
Macbeth
1919 The Test of Honor

Walheim, L. *see* **Wolheim, Louis**

Walker, Mrs. *could be same as* **Walker, Mrs. Allan**
1916 A Million a Minute
1918 Wanted for Murder

Walker, Allan *same as* **Walker, Allen**
1916 A Modern Thelma
1918 To Hell with the Kaiser

Walker, Mrs. Allan *same as* **Walker, Mrs. Allen; could be same as Walker, Mrs.**
1914 Neptune's Daughter
1915 Black Fear
The Clemenceau Case
1917 The Beautiful Lie
The Call of Her People
The Little Samaritan
1918 Her Price
My Own United States
1920 The World and His Wife

Walker, Antoinette
1916 The Sting of Victory

Walker, Ben
1918 The Silent Woman

Walker, Bob *see* **Walker, Robert**

Walker, Charlotte
1915 The Kindling
Out of the Darkness
1916 The Trail of the Lonesome Pine
1917 Mary Lawson's Secret
Pardners
The Seventh Sin
Sloth
1918 Every Mother's Son
Just a Woman
Men
1919 Eve in Exile

Walker, Christy
1918 The Lesson

Walker, Darbey A.
1919 The Enchanted Barn

Walker, Dorothy
1920 The Chamber Mystery

Walker, Edith Campbell
1916 Diplomacy
A Woman's Way
1917 Hedda Gabler
The Valentine Girl
1920 The Sporting Duchess

Walker, Eileen
1918 Conquered Hearts
Walker, Helen
1914 John Barleycorn*
Walker, Johnnie same as **Walker, J.;**
    Walker, John; Walker, Johnny
1915 Cohen's Luck
    Destruction
    On Dangerous Paths
1916 The Man from Nowhere
1918 Brown of Harvard
    His Daughter Pays
    The Knife
    A Son of Strife
1919 Impossible Catherine
    The Open Door
1920 Bachelor Apartments
    Greater Than Fame
    Over the Hill to the Poorhouse
Walker, Lee
1916 The River of Romance
Walker, Lillian
1915 Hearts and the Highway
1916 The Blue Envelope Mystery
    The Dollar and the Law
    Green Stockings
    Hesper of the Mountains
    The Kid
    The Man Behind the Curtain
    Mrs. Dane's Danger
    The Ordeal of Elizabeth
1917 Indiscretion
    Kitty MacKay
    The Lust of the Ages
    National Association's All-Star
      Picture
    Sally in a Hurry
1918 The Blot*
    The Embarrassment of Riches
    The Grain of Dust
1919 The Better Wife
    The Joyous Liar
    The Love Hunger
    A White Man's Chance
Walker, Nell
1920 The Luck of the Irish
Walker, Ollie
1916 The Ordeal of Elizabeth
Walker, Ralph
1919 The City of Comrades
Walker, Robert same as **Walker, Bob;**
    Walker, Robert D.
1915 Children of Eve
    Don Caesar de Bazan
    The Ploughshare
    The Way Back
1916 Caprice of the Mountains
    The Cossack Whip
    The Gates of Eden
    The Light of Happiness
1917 Aladdin's Other Lamp
    Blue Jeans
    The Girl Without a Soul
    God's Law and Man's
    Lady Barnacle
    The Mortal Sin
    A Wife by Proxy
1918 At the Mercy of Men
    The Fair Pretender
    Miss Innocence
    The Sins of the Children
    The Whirlpool
    The Woman Between Friends
    The Woman Who Gave
1919 Burglar by Proxy
    The Light
    The Merry-Go-Round
1920 Isobel; Or, The Trail's End
    Prairie Trails
    Rouge and Riches
    Shore Acres
    The Texan
    The Woman in His House
Walker, Vernon
1920 Firebrand Trevison
    Forbidden Trails
    The Last Straw
    The Square Shooter
    Would You Forgive?
Walker, Waldo
1916 Madame La Presidente
1920 The Woman Gives

Walker, Walter
1917 American—That's All
    Her Excellency, the Governor
    In Again—Out Again
1920 Blackbirds
Wall, Boots
1913 Caprice
    Tess of the D'Urbervilles
1914 Uncle Tom's Cabin
1915 Always in the Way
Wall, David same as **Wall, Dave**
1913 In the Bishop's Carriage
    The Port of Doom
1914 The Banker's Daughter
    Captain Swift
    The Day of Days
    The Greyhound
    A Lady of Quality
    Northern Lights
    The Port of Missing Men
1915 Four Feathers
    The Garden of Lies
    Heléne of the North
    Prohibition
    Time Lock Number 776
1916 The Price of Happiness
1918 The Birth of a Race
1920 The Bromley Case
    Circumstantial Evidence
    The Sacred Ruby
    The Scrap of Paper
    The Trail of the Cigarette
    The Triple Clue
    The Unseen Witness
    The Wall Street Mystery
Wall, Margaret
1915 Under Southern Skies
Wallace, Baby
1915 Mignon
Wallace, C. R.
1918 The Romance of Tarzan
1919 The Lincoln Highwayman
1920 A Connecticut Yankee at King
    Arthur's Court
    Shod with Fire
Wallace, Catherine same as **Wallace,**
    Katherine
1919 The Sealed Envelope
    Toby's Bow
1920 Cupid, the Cowpuncher
    A Full House*
    Jenny Be Good
Wallace, Dorothy
1918 Secret Code
1919 A Man's Fight
    The Spite Bride
1920 Parlor, Bedroom and Bath
Wallace, Edgar
1920 Wanted at Headquarters
Wallace, Fay
1915 The Cave Man
Wallace, Grant
1917 The Fuel of Life
Wallace, Helene
1915 The Grandee's Ring
Wallace, Irene
1913 Traffic in Souls
19-- Sic-Em
Wallace, Katherine see **Wallace,**
    Catherine
Wallace, Morgan
1919 Bringing Up Betty
1920 Flying Pat
Wallace, Ramsey same as **Wallace,**
    Ramsaye
1918 The Grain of Dust
    Her Only Way
    Woman and the Law
1920 Even As Eve
    Her Beloved Villain
    Her Honor the Mayor
    The Woman in His House
Wallace, Raymond
1918 The Hell Cat
Wallace, Thomas
1918 Who Loved Him Best?
Wallack, Ann same as **Wallick, Ann**
1920 Humoresque
    Nothing but Lies

Wallack, E. N. see **Wallock, Edwin**
Waller, Jane
1915 My Best Girl
Wallick, Ann see **Wallack, Ann**
Wallock, Edwin same as **Wallack, E.**
    N.; Wallock, E. N.; Wallock, Edwin,
    N.
1916 Behind the Lines
1917 The Cold Deck
    Even As You and I
    The Price Mark
1918 Fame and Fortune
1919 Johnny-on-the-Spot
    Square Deal Sanderson
1920 Duds
    The Green Flame
    The Sagebrusher
Wally, Frank
1919 Soldiers of Fortune
Waln, Nora
1919 Auction of Souls
Walpole, Stanley
1914 The Dollar Mark
1916 The Alibi
1917 The Girl Who Didn't Think
1918 A Game with Fate
    The Other Man
    Peg O' the Sea
1919 Fortune's Child
    The Price of Innocence
1920 In Walked Mary
    The Trail of the Cigarette
    The Triple Clue
    A Woman's Business
Walsh, Ed
1917 The Baseball Revue of 1917*
Walsh, George
1916 The Beast
    Blue Blood and Red
    Don Quixote
    Intolerance
    The Mediator
    The Serpent
1917 The Book Agent
    High Finance
    The Honor System
    The Island of Desire
    Melting Millions
    The Pride of New York
    Some Boy!
    This Is the Life
    The Yankee Way
1918 Brave and Bold
    I'll Say So
    Jack Spurlock, Prodigal
    The Kid Is Clever
    On the Jump
1919 Help! Help! Police!
    Luck and Pluck
    Never Say Quit
    Putting One Over
    The Winning Stroke
1920 The Dead Line
    From Now On
    A Manhattan Knight
    The Plunger
    The Shark
    Sink or Swim
Walsh, J. D.
1920 Wings of Pride
    The Woman God Sent
Walsh, Jessie May
1914 The Patchwork Girl of Oz
Walsh, Raoul A. same as **Walsh, R. A.;**
    Walsh, Raoul
1914 The Dishonored Medal
    The Great Leap; Until Death
      Do Us Part
1915 The Birth of a Nation
    Carmen (Fox Film Corp.)
    The Outlaw's Revenge
    Regeneration
1916 Blue Blood and Red
    Pillars of Society
    The Serpent
1917 Betrayed
    The Conquerer
    The Honor System
    The Innocent Sinner
    The Pride of New York
    The Silent Lie
    This Is the Life
1918 Every Mother's Son
    I'll Say So

    On the Jump
    The Prussian Cur
    Woman and the Law
1919 Evangeline
    Should a Husband Forgive?
1920 The Deep Purple
    From Now On
    Headin' Home
    The Strongest
Walsh, Tom same as **Walsh, Thomas**
1915 The Danger Signal
1919 The Bandbox
    Rustling a Bride
1920 From Now On
Walsh, William
1920 Dangerous Love
Walska, Madama Ganna
1916 The Child of Destiny
Walter, Cecil
1914 Manon Lescaut
Walter, Eugene
1914 Tess of the Storm Country
1919 The Belle of New York
    Sealed Hearts
    The Way of a Woman
1920 Love, Honor and Obey
Walter, Lew
1916 Jealousy
Walter, R. W.
1916 The Dumb Girl of Portici
Walter, Wilmer
1918 The Fair Pretender
Walters, Dorothy
1918 The Woman Who Gave
    The Zero Hour
1919 Through the Toils
1920 Away Goes Prudence
    Children Not Wanted
    Good References
    The Veiled Marriage
Walters, Easter
1919 Common Clay
1920 The Devil's Riddle
Walters, Fred
1918 Our Mrs. McChesney
Walters, Mrs. George W.
1914 The Fortune Hunter
    The House Next Door
    The Wolf
Walters, Jack
1919 The Ace of the Saddle
Walters, L. Virginia
1918 Wanted—A Brother
Walters, May
1918 Station Content
Walters, W. R.
1914 Tess of the Storm Country
Walthall, Anna Mae same as **Walthall,**
    Anna May
1916 The Truant Soul
1918 Hearts of the World
    Humdrum Brown*
    With Hoops of Steel
1919 Bare Fists
    The Trembling Hour
Walthall, Henry B. same as **Walthall,**
    Henry
1914 The Avenging Conscience
    Classmates
    The Floor Above
    The Gangsters
    Home, Sweet Home
    Judith of Bethulia
    Lord Chumley
    The Mountain Rat
1915 Beulah
    The Birth of a Nation
    Ghosts
    The Raven
1916 The Birth of a Man
    The Misleading Lady
    Pillars of Society
    The Sting of Victory
    The Truant Soul
1917 Burning the Candle
    Little Shoes
    National Association's All-Star
      Picture
    The Saint's Adventure
1918 And a Still Small Voice
    The Great Love
    His Robe of Honor
    Humdrum Brown

Welles, Lieutenant Roger K.
1916 The Hero of Submarine D-2
Wellesley, Charles *same as* **Wellsley, Charles**
1914 My Official Wife
The Tangle
1915 Hearts and the Highway
The Man Behind the Door
1916 The Daring of Diana
The Enemy
Green Stockings
The Hero of Submarine D-2
The Hunted Woman
The Island of Surprise
Just a Song at Twilight
The Writing on the Wall
1917 Her Better Self
The Poor Little Rich Girl
Redemption
Richard, the Brazen
Wrath
1918 By Right of Purchase
The Heart of a Girl
Her Mistake
Madame Jealousy
The Purple Lily
The Richest Girl
The Song of Songs
1919 The American Way
Wellman, William
1919 The Knickerbocker Buckaroo
Wellmore, Lydia
1919 Out of the Fog
Wells, Alice Stebbins
19-- The Policewoman
Wells, C. U. *could be same as* **Wells, Charles, Wells, Charles B.** *or* **Wells, Charles G.**
1916 Whispering Smith
Wells, Carolyn
1917 The Countess Charming
The Mark of Cain
Wells, Charles *could be same as* **Wells, C. U.; Wells, Charles B.** *or* **Wells, Charles G.**
1915 Young Romance
Wells, Charles B. *could be same as* **Wells, C. U.; Wells, Charles** *or* **Wells, Charles G.**
1918 From Two to Six
Wells, Charles G. *could be same as* **Wells, C. U.; Wells, Charles** *or* **Wells, Charles B.**
1916 The Diamond Runners
Wells, L. M. *same as* **Wells, Louis M.;** *could be same as* **Wells, L. N.**
1916 Behind the Lines
1917 Bucking Broadway
The Girl Who Won Out
Like Wildfire
Man and Beast
Treason
A Wife on Trial
1918 After the War
Impossible Susan
The Square Deal
Thieves' Gold
1919 Sue of the South
1920 The Forgotten Woman
Huckleberry Finn
The Parish Priest
Wells, L. N. *could be same as* **Wells, L. M.**
1918 The Spirit of '17
Wells, Leila Burton
1920 The Invisible Divorce
Wells, Louis M. *see* **Wells, L. M.**
Wells, Mai *see* **Wells, May**
Wells, Marie Edith *same as* **Wells, Marie E.; Wells, Mary Edith**
1915 The Builder of Bridges
Just Out of College
Sealed Lips
1916 The Conquest of Canaan
Then I'll Come Back to You
Wells, May *same as* **Wells, Mai**
1914 His Majesty, the Scarecrow of Oz
The Last Egyptian
1920 The Breath of the Gods
Old Lady 31

Wells, Norman
1920 Birthright
Wells, Raymond *same as* **Wells, Raymond B.**
1915 Old Heidelberg
The Sable Lorcha
1916 The Flying Torpedo
Intolerance
Kinkaid, Gambler
Macbeth
Sunshine Dad
1917 Anything Once
Fanatics
Fighting Back
Fighting for Love
The Hero of the Hour
Love Aflame
Mr. Dolan of New York
The Saintly Sinner
The Terror
1918 The Flames of Chance
The Hand at the Window
The Hard Rock Breed
His Enemy, the Law
The Law of the Great Northwest
Mlle. Paulette
The Man Above the Law
Old Love for New
1919 In the Land of the Setting Sun; Or, Martyrs of Yesterday
Wells, William
1915 The Battle of Ballots
Wellsley, Charles *see* **Wellesley, Charles**
Welsh, Dorothy
1915 The Bridge of Sighs
Welsh, Nanon
1919 Are You Legally Married?
Welsh, Niles *see* **Welch, Niles**
Welsh, William *same as* **Welch, William; Welsh, William J.**
1913 Traffic in Souls
1914 Neptune's Daughter
1915 Conscience
Courtmartialed
The Primrose Path
The White Terror
1916 Elusive Isabel
The Foolish Virgin
The Lords of High Decision
The Narrow Path
20,000 Leagues Under the Sea
1917 The Eternal Sin
1918 Parentage
1919 The Heart of Humanity
The Little Diplomat
1920 Cynthia-of-the-Minute
Over the Hill to the Poorhouse
Wenstrom, Harold
1920 The Best of Luck
The Saphead
Wentworth, Harry
1920 The Love Expert
Wentworth, Isaac
1918 The Service Star
Wentworth, Marion Craig
1916 War Brides
Werden (full name unknown)
1915 The Fairy and the Waif*
Werker, Alfred L. *same as* **Werker, Albert**
1917 The Firefly of Tough Luck
The Regenerates
1919 Heart O' the Hills
The Hoodlum
1920 Pollyanna
Suds
Werner, Carl
1914 'Round the World in 80 Days*
Werner, Marion
1919 The Old Maid's Baby
Wertz, Alfred
1916 The Heritage of Hate
Wescott, W. Burton
1918 The Gulf Between*
Wesner, A. Burt *same as* **Wesner, Bert; Wesner, Burt**
1916 Between Men
1917 When a Man Sees Red
1918 The Kid Is Clever
1919 The Lost Princess

Wessel, John
1918 Fields of Honor
West, Mrs. *could be same as* **West, Isabelle**
1916 The Dollar and the Law
1917 Indiscretion
Sally in a Hurry
West, Beverly
1914 As Ye Sow
West, Billie (*actress*) *not the same as* **West, Billy** (*actor*)
1915 A Man's Prerogative
The Wolf Man
1917 The Hidden Spring
Should She Obey?
West, Blanche
1913 The Battle of Shiloh
West, Charles *same as* **West, Charles H.**
1915 Divorçons
The Gambler of the West
1916 The Dream Girl
A Gutter Magdalene
The Heart of Nora Flynn
Let Katie Do It
Martha's Vindication
The Wood Nymph
1917 The American Consul
Betty to the Rescue
Little Miss Optimist
The Little Pirate
Society's Driftwood
The Trouble Buster
1918 The Flash of Fate
The Ghost Flower
The Girl Who Came Back
The Mystery Girl
Revenge
Shackled
The Source
The White Man's Law
Wife or Country
1919 His Divorced Wife
A Very Good Young Man
The Woman Michael Married
1920 Go and Get It
Parlor, Bedroom and Bath
The Phantom Melody
Polly of the Storm Country
The River's End
A Thousand to One
West, Clare
1920 Why Change Your Wife?
West, De Jalma
1917 The Trail of the Shadow
West, Dorothy
1916 The Eternal Grind
The Habit of Happiness
West, Ed
1914 The Nightingale
West, Ethel
1914 An American Citizen
West, George
1917 The Tar Heel Warrior
West, Harold
1916 It May Be Your Daughter
West, Harry *see* **West, Henry**
West, Hazel
1916 Purity
West, Henry *same as* **West, Harry**
1915 Colonel Carter of Cartersville
The Dictator
1916 All Man
Broken Chains
The Heart of a Hero
The Rail Rider
1917 The Crimson Dove
Youth
1918 The Beautiful Mrs. Reynolds
The Purple Lily
The Road to France
Sporting Life
To Him That Hath
Woman
1919 Courage for Two
The Poison Pen
1920 The North Wind's Malice
West, Irene
1919 The Firing Line*
West, Isabelle *same as* **West, Isabel;** *could be same as* **West, Mrs.**
1916 The Blue Envelope Mystery

1917 Kitty MacKay
Weavers of Life
1919 The Firing Line
West, James
1917 The Kill-Joy
West, Langdon
1915 The Ring of the Borgias
West, Laura
1919 Through the Toils
West, Lillian
1916 Boots and Saddles
The Power of Evil
1917 American Methods
The Gown of Destiny
The Hidden Children
1918 Everywoman's Husband
The Hopper
Innocent's Progress
Limousine Life
Love's Pay Day
The Mask
Society for Sale
A Soul in Trust
Who Is to Blame?
1919 Auction of Souls
The Forbidden Room
The Island of Intrigue
Louisiana
Prudence on Broadway
The Silk Lined Burglar
The Woman of Lies
West, Olive
1915 Madame Butterfly
West, Paul
1915 Crooky
1916 The Chattel
The Dark Silence
The Lash
The Velvet Paw
1917 The Adventurer
The American Consul
Each to His Kind
A Girl Like That
Great Expectations
Her Right to Live
A Kiss for Susie
A Mormon Maid
On Record
The Princess of Park Row
1918 At the Mercy of Men
De Luxe Annie
The Death Dance
The Little Runaway
The Ordeal of Rosetta
The Safety Curtain
The Studio Girl
Woman and Wife
The Zero Hour
1919 A Taste of Life
West, Pearl
1920 Neptune's Bride
West, Raymond B. *same as* **West, Raymond**
1914 The Wrath of the Gods
1915 The Alien
The Cup of Life
The Mating
Rumpelstiltskin
1916 Civilization
The Female of the Species
Home
The Honorable Algy
The Payment
The Wolf Woman
1917 Borrowed Plumage
Chicken Casey
Madcap Madge
The Snarl
Ten of Diamonds
Those Who Pay
The Weaker Sex
Whither Thou Goest
Wooden Shoes
1918 Blindfolded
The Cast-Off
Maid O' the Storm
Patriotism
Within the Cup
1919 All Wrong
West, Roland
1916 A Woman's Honor
1917 The Siren
1918 De Luxe Annie

White, Nita
1917 Love Aflame
White, Olive
1916 David Garrick
An International Marriage
1917 A Tale of Two Cities
1920 The Orphan
White, Pearl
1916 Hazel Kirke
The King's Game
1917 Mayblossom
1920 The Thief
The Tiger's Cub
The White Moll
White, Philip H.
1920 Youth's Desire
White, Robert
1918 The Marionettes
White, Ruth
1916 The Girl Who Doesn't Know
Pay Dirt
White, Sam
1920 Honeymoon Ranch
White, Stewart Edward same as **White, Stuart Edward**
1914 The Call of the North
1919 The Westerners
White, Turner
1917 Burning the Candle
White, Violet
1916 The Making of Maddalena
White, William H.
1915 The Chocolate Soldier
White Eagle
1919 The Heart of Wetona
Whitehead, Grace
1917 The Planter
Whitehead, Hubert
1914 The Circus Man
1916 Ramona
1917 The Chosen Prince, or the Friendship of David and Jonathan
Whitehead, J. V.
1917 The Chosen Prince, or the Friendship of David and Jonathan
Whitehead, V. O.
1916 The Daughter of the Don
Whiteside, Edward
1920 Empty Arms
Whiteside, Walker
1915 The Melting Pot
1918 The Belgian
Whitie (full name unknown)
1920 The Brute
Whiting, Miss
1916 Barriers of Society
Whiting, A. E. see **Witting, A. E.**
Whitlock, Brand
1917 The Double Standard
The Field of Honor
Whitlock, Earl
1920 Curtain
Whitlock, Lloyd same as **Whitlock, Lloyd T.; Whitlock, T. Lloyd**
1917 The Edge of the Law
The Man Who Took a Chance
The Mysterious Mr. Tiller
1919 The Boomerang
The Gray Wolf's Ghost
Lasca
The Love Call
1920 Cupid, the Cowpuncher
Rouge and Riches
Scratch My Back
Whitman, District Attorney
1914 Smashing the Vice Trust
Whitman, Alfred
1917 The Flaming Omen
Sunlight's Last Raid
When Men Are Tempted
1918 Baree, Son of Kazan
Cavanaugh of the Forest Rangers
Desert Law
A Gentleman's Agreement
The Girl from Beyond
The Home Trail
The Sea Flower
Tongues of Flame
The Wild Strain

1919 The Best Man
The End of the Game
A Trick of Fate
Whitman, Charles Seymour
1918 The Girl of Today*
19-- Official Motion Pictures of the Panama Pacific Exposition Held at San Francisco, Calif.*
Whitman, Fred
1915 Should a Wife Forgive?
1916 The Matrimonial Martyr
1917 A Branded Soul
Whitman, Velma
1916 East Lynne
1917 The Book Agent
Melting Millions
The Primitive Call
Some Boy!
1918 The Finger of Justice
1919 The Railroader
Whitman, Walt same as **Whitman, Walter**
1915 The Mating
1916 The Criminal
D'Artagnan
The Honorable Algy
The Sin Ye Do
1917 The Dark Road
The Desert Man
The Firefly of Tough Luck
The Girl Glory
The Last of the Ingrams
The Millionaire Vagrant
Paddy O'Hara
Polly Ann
Princess of the Dark
The Regenerates
The Tar Heel Warrior
They're Off
Wee Lady Betty
1918 The Boss of the Lazy Y
Captain of His Soul
Daughter Angele
Desert Law
Everywoman's Husband
False Ambition
His Enemy, the Law
The Hopper
The Last Rebel
Old Hartwell's Cub
The Price of Applause
Without Honor
1919 The Cry of the Weak
Destiny
The Heart of Humanity
John Petticoats
Pretty Smooth
When Bearcat Went Dry
Whom the Gods Would Destroy
1920 Dangerous Hours
Darling Mine
The Mark of Zorro
Passion's Playground
Whitney, Claire
1913 Ben Bolt
Shadows of the Moulin Rouge
The Star of India
1914 Beneath the Czar
The Burglar and the Lady
The Dream Woman
The Idler
Life's Shop Window
The Lure
The Million Dollar Robbery
The Walls of Jericho
The Woman of Mystery
1915 The Blindness of Devotion
The Galley Slave
The Girl I Left Behind Me
The Nigger
The Plunderer
Should a Mother Tell?
The Song of Hate
1916 East Lynne
The Ruling Passion
The Spider and the Fly
Sporting Blood
The Straight Way
Under Two Flags
The Victim
A Wife's Sacrifice
1917 Camille
Heart and Soul

The New York Peacock
Shirley Kaye
Tangled Lives
Thou Shalt Not Steal
When False Tongues Speak
1918 The Kaiser's Finish
Moral Suicide
Ruling Passions
1919 The Career of Katherine Bush
The Isle of Conquest
The Man Who Stayed at Home
You Never Know Your Luck
1920 The Chamber Mystery
A Common Level
Love, Honor and Obey
Mothers of Men
Why Women Sin
Whitney, F. C.
1915 The Chocolate Soldier
Whitney, Marion
1915 The Apaches of Paris
Whitson, Frank
1915 The Battle of Ballots
The Concealed Truth
When a Woman Loves
1916 Gold and the Woman
If My Country Should Call
The Isle of Life
The Mark of Cain
The Morals of Hilda
One Day
The Price of Silence
1917 The Clock
Sudden Jim
1918 After the War
Boston Blackie's Little Pal
A Daughter of the West
Restitution
Social Briars
1919 The Faith of the Strong
Hearts Asleep
The Love Call
The Son-of-a-Gun!
Square Deal Sanderson
A Trick of Fate
1920 The Tattlers
Three Gold Coins
Whittaker, Charles (actor) same as **Whitaker, Charles** (actor); not the same as **Whitaker, Charles E.** (asst dir) or **Whittaker, Charles E.** (scen)
1916 The End of the Trail
The Man from Bitter Roots
1920 In Search of a Sinner
Whittaker, Charles (scen) see **Whittaker, Charles E.** (scen)
Whittaker, Charles E. (scen, born in Dublin, Ireland) same as **Whittaker, Charles** (scen); **Whittaker, Charles Everard**; not the same as **Whitaker, Charles E.** (asst dir) or **Whittaker, Charles** (actor)
1917 Arms and the Girl
Exile
The Land of Promise
The Law of the Land
The Pride of the Clan
The Undying Flame
The Unforseen
The Whip
1918 The Claw
Fedora
Her Final Reckoning
The House of Glass
Love's Conquest
On the Quiet
Private Peat
Resurrection
Stolen Orders
La Tosca
Woman
1919 The Broken Butterfly
Eyes of Youth
Fires of Faith
Here Comes the Bride
The Life Line
Paid in Full
The White Heather
1920 Billions
For the Soul of Rafael
The Forbidden Woman
Kismet
Mothers of Men

Partners of the Night
Whittaker, Raymond same as **Whitaker, Raymond; Whittaker, Ray**
1916 Kinkaid, Gambler
The Mainspring
1917 Her Soul's Inspiration
Love Aflame
Polly Redhead
The Saintly Sinner
The Scarlet Crystal
Whittell, Josephine
1917 Alimony
1919 The Climbers
Marie, Ltd.
Whittier, Robert
1913 The Third Degree
1916 The Awakening of Helena Richie
Betrayed
A Bird of Prey
King Lear
Master Shakespeare, Strolling Player
1917 The Call of Her People
Threads of Fate
1918 Five Thousand an Hour
1919 The Man Who Stayed at Home
Whitting, A. E. see **Witting, A. E.**
Whitting, Mrs. A. E. see **Witting, Mrs. A. E.**
Whittle, W. E.
1918 Why America Will Win
Whittlesey, Lt. Col. Charles W.
1919 The Lost Battalion
Whitworth, Robert
1915 Body and Soul
1916 The Alibi
War Brides
Whytock, Grant
1917 Sirens of the Sea
1919 Paid in Advance
1920 Hearts Are Trumps
Shore Acres
Under Crimson Skies
Wick, May
1920 The Fighting Kentuckians
Wicki, Norbert same as **Wicke, Norbert**
1917 Darkest Russia
Panthea
1918 The World for Sale
1920 The Scarlet Dragon
19-- Barnaby Lee
Widdicombe, Wallace same as **Widdecombe, Wallace**
1913 Ivanhoe
1920 Cynthia-of-the-Minute
Widen, Amelia
1917 Whose Wife?
Widen, Carl
1916 A Dream or Two Ago
Dulcie's Adventure
Faith
1918 Blue Blood
His Robe of Honor
Widen, Nellie
1916 April
1917 Annie-for-Spite
Her Country's Call
Wiegle, Paul see **Weigel, Paul**
Wierman, Miss could be same as **Weirman, Marie**
1915 The Marble Heart
Wiggin, Mrs. Margaret A. same as **Wiggin, Mrs.; Wiggins, Margaret**
1917 Gift O' Gab
The Mystery of Number 47
The Penny Philanthropist
1919 Sadie Love
Wiggins, Lillian
1915 Her Atonement
1920 The Shadow of Rosalie Byrnes
Wilber, Mabel
1914 The County Chairman
Wilbur, Burke
1917 The Princess of Patches
Wilbur, Crane
1914 The Corsair
1916 The Conscience of John David
A Law unto Himself
The Love Liar
Vengeance Is Mine
The Wasted Years

1915 God's Witness

Williams, J. B. *could be same as*
Williams, J. *or* **Williams, Jeff**
1915 A Woman's Resurrection

Williams, J. J. *see* **Williams, John J.**

Williams, Jeff *same as* **Williams,**
Jeffrey; *could be same as* **Williams,**
J. *or* **Williams, J. B.**
1919 Just Squaw
1920 The Flame of Hellgate
The Saphead

Williams, John J. *same as* **Williams, J.**
J.; *could be same as* **Williams, J.**
1915 Marse Covington
1917 Peggy, the Will O' the Wisp
1918 Little Miss Hoover

Williams, Josephine *could be same as*
Williams, J.
1919 The Crook of Dreams

Williams, Kathlyn
1914 The Spoilers
1915 The Carpet from Bagdad
The Rosary
Sweet Alyssum
1916 The Adventures of Kathlyn
Into the Primitive
The Ne'er-Do-Well
Redeeming Love
Thou Shalt Not Covet
The Valiants of Virginia
1917 Big Timber
The Cost of Hatred
The Highway of Hope
Lost in Transit
Out of the Wreck
1918 The Thing We Love
We Can't Have Everything
The Whispering Chorus
1919 The Better Wife
A Girl Named Mary
Her Kingdom of Dreams
Her Purchase Price
1920 Conrad in Quest of His Youth
Just a Wife
The Prince Chap
The Tree of Knowledge
The U.P. Trail

Williams, Lawrence E. *same as*
Williams, Larry; Williams,
Lawrence
1915 His Wife
Inspiration
1916 The Big Sister
Little Lady Eileen
The Traveling Salesman
1917 Broadway Jones
The Dummy
Heart's Desire
1918 The Accidental Honeymoon
Eve's Daughter
Marriage
Out of the Night
A Romance of the Underworld
The Struggle Everlasting
1919 The Bishop's Emeralds
Impossible Catherine
Marriage for Convenience

Williams, Lottie
1920 A Full House
Twin Beds

Williams, Malcolm
1914 The Brute
1915 The Dancing Girl
1916 The Idol of the Stage
1918 Empty Pockets

Williams, Margot
1914 The Ordeal
1915 The Greater Will
The Master of the House

Williams, Pauline
1916 The Hidden Law

Williams, Percy
1918 Too Many Millions

Williams, Robert
1920 Thoughtless Women

Williams, S. W.
1920 The White Rider

Williams, Stanton
1920 The Forbidden Woman
A Woman Who Understood

Williams, Sumner *same as* **Williams,**
Charles Sumner
1915 Vanity Fair
1916 When Love Is King
1917 Chris and His Wonderful
Lamp
Kidnapped
Knights of the Square Table

Williams, Tom
1919 Love and the Law

Williams, Virgil
1920 The Brute
In the Depths of Our Hearts

Williams, W. A. *see* **Williams, William**
A.

Williams, W. E. (*actor*) *could be same*
as **Williams, Walter** (*actor*)
1918 The Whirlpool

Williams, Walter (*actor*) *could be same*
as **Williams, W. E.**
1914 Salomy Jane

Williams, Walter (*cam*) *same as*
Williams, Walter E.
1917 Jack and the Beanstalk
1919 Lost Money
Snares of Paris
The Splendid Sin
1920 Beware of the Bride
Her Honor the Mayor
Husband Hunter
The Iron Heart
The Land of Jazz
The Spirit of Good
The Tattlers
What Would You Do?

Williams, Walter E. *see* **Williams,**
Walter (*cam*)

Williams, William A. *same as* **Williams,**
W. A.; Williams, William
1913 Checkers
1914 The Path Forbidden
The Toll of Mammon
When Fate Leads Trump
1915 How Molly Malone Made
Good
In the Shadow
1916 The Awakening of Helena
Richie
Silks and Satins
The Woman's Law
1917 The Bar Sinister
The Web of Desire
1918 The Sign Invisible
1919 Calibre 38
Heart of Gold
His Wife's Friend
The Indestructible Wife

Williams, Zack
1920 The Money-Changers

Williams, Zenaide
1916 Divorce and the Daughter
1920 The Servant in the House

Williamson, A. M.
1920 Passion's Playground

Williamson, C. N.
1920 Passion's Playground

Williamson, Captain Charles
1914 Thirty Leagues Under the Sea*

Williamson, George M. *same as*
Williamson, George; *see also*
Williamson Brothers
1914 Thirty Leagues Under the Sea*
1917 The Submarine Eye

Williamson, J. Ernest *see also*
Williamson Brothers
1914 Thirty Leagues Under the Sea
1917 The Submarine Eye
1920 Girl of the Sea

Williamson, Robert
1918 The Brass Check

Williamson, Robin
1915 The Valley of Lost Hope
1919 In Wrong

Williamson Brothers *see also* individual
entries for **Williamson, George M.**
and **Williamson J. Ernest**
1919 The White Heather*

Willink, Max
1920 Honor Bound

Willis, Anthony F. McGrew *see* **Willis,**
F. McGrew

Willis, E. Cooper
1915 The Primrose Path
1916 Love's Pilgrimage to America

Willis, Enid
1916 The Criminal

Willis, Eugene B.
1916 The Whirlpool of Destiny

Willis, F. McGrew *same as* **Willis,**
Anthony F. McGrew; *see also*
Woods, Willis (pseud. of **Willis, F.**
McGrew *and* **Woods, Walter**)
1915 Business Is Business
The Quest
Tainted Money
1916 The Beckoning Trail
The Gay Lord Waring
The Iron Hand
The Pool of Flame
The Silent Battle
The Way of the World
The Whirlpool of Destiny
1917 American Methods
The Book Agent
High Finance
To Honor and Obey
1918 The Bride's Awakening
A Burglar for a Night
The Empty Cab
$5,000 Reward
Modern Love
Playthings
The Velvet Hand
1919 The End of the Game
His Divorced Wife
The Pagan God
1920 The Common Sin
The Phantom Melody

Willis, George
1917 The Devil Dodger

Willis, H. W.
1916 The Masked Rider

Willis, J. Cooper
1916 Wall Street Tragedy

Willis, Leo
1916 Hell's Hinges
The Jungle Child
1917 Framing Framers
One Shot Ross
1918 The Law of the Great
Northwest
Old Love for New
The Silent Rider
1919 A Regular Fellow

Willis, Lloyd
1919 The Greater Sinner

Willis, Paul
1916 The Fall of a Nation
1917 The Haunted Pajamas
The Promise
The Trouble Buster
1919 The Cry of the Weak
The Secret Garden
The Son-of-a-Gun!

Willis, Richard
1915 The High Hand
1917 Lorelei of the Sea

Willis, Sue *could be same as* **Willis,**
Susanne
1914 The House of Bondage

Willis, Susanne *could be same as*
Willis, Sue
1918 Uncle Tom's Cabin

Willis, William
1918 Berlin Via America
1919 The Great Victory, Wilson or
the Kaiser? The Fall of the
Hohenzollerns

Willoughby, Louis *same as* **Willoughby,**
Lewis
1918 Her Country First
Midnight Madness
Mirandy Smiles
The Model's Confession
A Pair of Silk Stockings
Sauce for the Goose
The Temple of Dusk
Treasure of the Sea
1920 Risky Business

Wills, David
1917 Every Girl's Dream

Willsea, Bertha
1918 To Hell with the Kaiser

Wilson, Al W.
1914 The Truth Wagon

Wilson, Alice *same as* **Browning, Mrs.**
Tod; Rae, Alice
1916 The Children in the House
1917 A Love Sublime
Should She Obey?
1918 The Brazen Beauty
The Eyes of Julia Deep
The Face in the Dark
Parentage
1919 La Belle Russe
1920 The Dream Cheater
The Little Wanderer
Passion's Playground
What's Your Husband Doing?
The Willow Tree

Wilson, Ben
1916 Idle Wives
The Mainspring
1917 Even As You and I
The Spindle of Life
1919 The Blue Bonnet
Castles in the Air
1920 The Man from Nowhere

Wilson, Bert
1918 Dolly's Vacation

Wilson, Billie
1916 Susie Snowflake
1919 Broken Barriers
Good Gracious, Annabelle

Wilson, Carey
1920 Madonnas and Men
A Woman's Business

Wilson, Charles J., Jr. *same as* **Wilson,**
Charles; Wilson, Charles, Jr.,
Wilson, Charles J.
1914 Jess of the Mountain Country
1917 The Girl Who Won Out
1918 Beyond the Shadows
Everywoman's Husband
The Grey Parasol
Hell's End
Her Decision
The Love Brokers
Society for Sale
Station Content
Wife or Country
Wild Life
1919 Spotlight Sadie
Sue of the South
1920 Alias Miss Dodd
The Breath of the Gods
The Mother of His Children
The Prince of Avenue A
White Lies

Wilson, Edna Mae *same as* **Wilson,**
Edna; Wilson, Edna May
1916 The Fall of a Nation
1917 Those Without Sin
Who Knows?
1919 Maggie Pepper
A Man's Country
1920 Once a Plumber

Wilson, Elsie Jane
1915 The Lure of the Mask
Temptation
1916 Bettina Loved a Soldier
The Evil Women Do
Oliver Twist
1917 The Circus of Life
The Cricket
A Kentucky Cinderella
The Little Pirate
Mother O' Mine
My Little Boy
The Silent Lady
1918 Beauty in Chains
The City of Tears
The Dream Lady
The Lure of Luxury
New Love for Old
1919 The Game's Up

Wilson, Frank
1919 The Stream of Life

Wilson, Fred L. *same as* **Wilson, Fred;**
not the same as **Wilson, Frederick**
1914 The Man on the Box
The Merchant of Venice

1915 The High Road
Young Romance
1916 Joan the Woman
Pidgin Island
1918 Tarzan of the Apes
1919 The Light of Victory
The Lone Wolf's Daughter
1920 The Confession
Go and Get It
Wilson, Frederick *not the same as*
Wilson, Fred L.
1915 Blackbirds
Kilmeny
Young Romance
Wilson, Georgia
1914 Cinderella
Wilson, Gladys
1918 The Glorious Adventure
The Richest Girl
Wilson, Grace
1916 Intolerance
Wilson, Gustave
1920 The Wonder Man
Wilson, Hal
1915 The Sable Lorcha
1916 Casey at the Bat
Intolerance*
The Little School Ma'am
The Missing Links
1917 Betsy's Burglar
Her Official Fathers
The Little Yank
The Man Trap
The Midnight Man
1918 Cavanaugh of the Forest
Rangers
The Home Trail
1919 Easy to Make Money
1920 Dinty
Everybody's Sweetheart
Hell's Oasis
The Marriage Pit
Suds
Whispering Devils
Wilson, Harold
1917 Betty and the Buccaneers
Wilson, Jack
1915 The Supreme Test
1918 Tarzan of the Apes
Wilson, Janice *same as* **Wilson, Janis**
1919 Pitfalls of a Big City
The World Aflame
1920 The White Circle
Wilson, Jay
1916 Ashes of Embers
1917 The Broadway Sport
Wilson, Jean
1917 Her Hour
Wilson, Jerome N. *same as* **Wilson,
Jerome**
1916 Dorian's Divorce
A Million a Minute
The Pretenders
The Wheel of the Law
1917 Sweetheart of the Doomed
A Wife by Proxy
1920 Woman's Man
Wilson, Lois
1916 The Beckoning Trail
The Gay Lord Waring
Langdon's Legacy
The Morals of Hilda
The Pool of Flame
The Silent Battle
A Son of the Immortals
1917 Alimony
Treason
1918 The Bells
A Burglar for a Night
His Robe of Honor
Maid O' the Storm
A Man's Man
One Dollar Bid
Prisoners of the Pines
Three X Gordon
The Turn of a Card
1919 The Best Man
Come Again Smith
The Drifters
The End of the Game
Gates of Brass
It Pays to Advertise
Love Insurance

A Man's Fight
The Price Woman Pays
Why Smith Left Home
1920 Burglar Proof
The City of Masks
A Full House
Thou Art the Man
Too Much Johnson
What's Your Hurry?
Who's Your Servant?
1921 Midsummer Madness
Wilson, M. K. *see* **Wilson, Millard K.**
Wilson, Mae
1919 The Secret Garden
Wilson, Margery *same as* **Wilson,
Margie; Wilson, Marjorie; Wilson,
Marjory**
1915 Bred in the Bone
Double Trouble
1916 A Corner in Colleens
The Eye of the Night
The Honorable Algy
Intolerance
The Primal Lure
The Return of Draw Egan
The Sin Ye Do
1917 The Bride of Hate
The Clodhopper
The Desert Man
The Gun Fighter
The Last of the Ingrams
The Mother Instinct
Mountain Dew
Wild Sumac
Wolf Lowry
1918 The Flames of Chance
The Hand at the Window
The Hard Rock Breed
The Law of the Great
Northwest
Marked Cards
Old Love for New
Without Honor
1919 Crooked Straight
Desert Gold
Venus in the East
1920 The Blooming Angel
The House of Whispers
That Something
Wilson, Millard K. *same as* **Wilson M.
K.; Wilson, Millard**
1916 In the Web of the Grafters
Nancy's Birthright
The Stain in the Blood
1917 The Field of Honor
Fighting Mad
The Flower of Doom
The Hero of the Hour
The Pulse of Life
1918 The Primitive Woman
The Scarlet Drop
Smashing Through
A Woman's Fool
1919 When Bearcat Went Dry
Whom the Gods Would
Destroy
1920 The Stranger
Wilson, Roberta
1916 The Heritage of Hate
The Isle of Life
The Right to Be Happy
1918 More Trouble
Shackled
Wilson, Stella
1917 Who Knows?
Wilson, Tom *same as* **Wilson, Thomas**
1915 The Birth of a Nation
The Martyrs of the Alamo
A Yankee from the West
1916 Atta Boy's Last Race
The Children Pay
The Half-Breed
Hell-to-Pay Austin
Intolerance
The Little Liar
Reggie Mixes In
1917 The Americano
An Old Fashioned Young Man
Pay Me
Wild and Woolly
The Yankee Way
1918 Amarilly of Clothes-Line Alley
Cheating the Public

1919 The Greatest Question
The Mother and the Law
1920 Dinty
Don't Ever Marry
Isobel; Or, The Trail's End
Sink or Swim
Wilson, William J.
1914 America
Wilson, Woodrow
1915 The Adventures of a Boy
Scout*
1917 How Uncle Sam Prepares*
1918 Lafayette, We Come!*
Stolen Orders*
Wiltermood, Frank *same as*
Wiltermood, F. M.
1916 The Black Sheep of the Family
19-- The Policewoman
Wiltsie, Simeon *same as* **Wiltse,
Simeon; Wiltsie, Sim**
1914 The Pit
The Wishing Ring; An Idyll of
Old England
1916 A Woman's Power
Winant, Forrest
1915 The Brink
1916 New York
1917 The Iron Heart
Winchester, Alice
1917 The Planter
Wincott, Marion
1918 Marriage
Windom, Lawrence C. *same as*
Windom, L. C.; Windom, Lawrence
1916 The Discard
1917 Efficiency Edgar's Courtship
Fools for Luck
The Small Town Guy
Two-Bit Seats
1918 The Appearance of Evil
The Grey Parasol
A Pair of Sixes
The Power and the Glory
Ruggles of Red Gap
Uneasy Money
1919 It's a Bear
Taxi
Upside Down
Wanted—A Husband
1920 The Girl with the Jazz Heart
Headin' Home
Human Collateral
Nothing but Lies
The Truth
The Very Idea
Windsor, Claire
1920 To Please One Woman
Windsor, Stafford
1917 Panthea
Wing, A. W. *could be same as* **Wing,
Ah**
1918 The Girl from Beyond
Wing, Ah *could be same as* **Wing, A.
W.**
1917 The Eyes of the World
1919 The She Wolf
Wing, Ruth
1920 Deep Waters
Wing, W. E. *see* **Wing, William E.**
Wing, Ward
1919 In His Brother's Place
Wing, William E. *same as* **Wing, W. E.**
1916 Casey at the Bat
The Microscope Mystery
Sold for Marriage
1918 The Brazen Beauty
Hugon, the Mighty
Social Ambition
Tarzan of the Apes*
1920 Before the White Man Came
The Galloping Devil
Vengeance and the Girl
Wingfield, H. Conway
1917 The Rainbow
Winick, Hyman
1918 Mickey
Winkler, M.
1915 The Battle Cry of Peace*
Business Is Business
The College Orphan
Colorado
Fatherhood
The Frame-Up

Judge Not; Or, The Woman of
Mona Diggings
The Long Chance
The Man of Shame
1916 The Crippled Hand
The Flirt
The Gay Lord Waring
The Great Problem
The Grip of Jealousy
John Needham's Double
The Ne'er-Do-Well
Secret Love
The Strength of the Weak
Tangled Hearts
Undine
The Wrong Door
The Yaqui
1919 The Belle of New York
1920 The Virgin of Stamboul
Winn, John
1920 The Mark of Zorro
Winslow, Cameron McRae
1915 The Nation's Peril*
Winslow, H. L.
1914 Manon Lescaut
Winslow, Herbert Hall
1914 The Great Diamond Robbery
Manon Lescaut
1915 The Fight
The Siren's Song
Sunday
1917 The Sin Woman
1919 The Millionaire Pirate
Winston, Charles
1916 The Idol of the Stage
Winston, Laura
1917 Aladdin from Broadway
Money Magic
The Planter
Should She Obey?
1918 Cavanaugh of the Forest
Rangers
The Demon
1919 Desert Gold
Victory
1920 The Forgotten Woman
Winston, Nancy
1918 Brown of Harvard
Winter, Miss
1912 Cleopatra
Winter, Louise
1918 The Spurs of Sybil
Winter, Percy
1914 The Daughters of Men
1915 The College Widow
1916 The Other Girl
Winters, Verne *same as* **Winter, Verne;
Winters, Vern**
1920 The Heart of Twenty
The Secret Gift
Silk Hosiery
Winters, Winona
1914 The Man from Mexico
Winthrop, Barbara
1914 The Crucible
1918 Secret Strings
Winthrop, Ethel *same as* **Winthrop,
Mrs. Ethel**
1916 The Lottery Man
1918 Lafayette, We Come!
The Marionettes
Social Hypocrites
Winthrop, Mrs. F. O.
1917 Shirley Kaye
Wirth, Billy *see* **Wirth, William**
Wirth, Leo
1914 Joseph in the Land of Egypt
1915 The Mill on the Floss
Wirth, William *same as* **Wirth, Billy**
1915 Vanity Fair
1917 The Last Sentence
Wischussen, G. H. *same as*
Wisschussen, G. H.
1916 Judith of the Cumberlands
Whispering Smith
Wise, Mrs. *see* **Wise, Mary Lee**
Wise, Harry *same as* **Weiss, Harry;
could be same as* **Weise, Harry**
1917 The Dummy
The End of the Tour
1919 The Avalanche
Out of the Fog

Wise, Mary Lee *same as* **Wise, Mrs.;
Wise, Mary**
1917 The Clever Mrs. Carfax
     The Serpent's Tooth
1918 Restitution
1919 Molly of the Follies
     Our Better Selves
1920 Once to Every Woman
     The Week-End
Wise, Thomas A.
1914 A Gentleman from Mississippi
1915 Blue Grass
Wisschussen, G. H. *see* **Wischussen, G.
H.**
Withee, Mable
1918-19
     Once to Every Man
Withey, Chester
1916 The Devil's Needle
     Don Quixote
     Mr. Goode, the Samaritan
     The Old Folks at Home
     Sunshine Dad
     The Wharf Rat
1917 An Alabaster Box
     The Bad Boy
     Madame Bo-Peep
     Nearly Married
     A Woman's Awakening
1918 The Hun Within
     In Pursuit of Polly
     On the Quiet
1919 Little Comrade
     Maggie Pepper
     The New Moon
     The Teeth of the Tiger
1920 Romance
     She Loves and Lies
Withey, Virginia Philley
1920 Flying Pat
Witt, Elizabeth
1920 Everything but the Truth
Witting, A. E. *same as* **Whiting, A. E.;
Whitting, A. E.; Witting, Arthur
Eugene**
1916 The Fall of a Nation
     Two Men of Sandy Bar
1917 The Charmer
1919 The Son-of-a-Gun!
Witting, Mrs. A. E. *same as* **Whitting,
Mrs. A. E.; Witting, Mrs.; Witting,
Mattie; could be same as* **Wright,
Mrs. A. E.**
1916 Love Never Dies
     Shoes
     The Unattainable
1917 Beloved Jim
     Follow the Girl
     '49-'17
     The Girl in the Checkered Coat
     The Girl Who Won Out
     Heart Strings
     Man and Beast
1918 Painted Lips
1919 The Son-of-a-Gun!
Witting, Mattie *see* **Witting, Mrs. A. E.**
Witwer, H. C.
1916 Where D'Ye Get That Stuff?
Wokoff, Mr.
1918 Wives of Men
Wolbert, Dorothea *same as* **Wolbert,
Ella**
1919 Cupid Forecloses
     The Enchanted Barn
     The Solitary Sin
1920 A Beggar in Purple
     La La Lucille
     Pink Tights
Wolbert, Ella *see* **Wolbert, Dorothea**
Wolbert, William
1915 An Eye for an Eye
1916 The Dumb Girl of Portici
     The Last Man
1917 Aladdin from Broadway
     By Right of Possession
     The Captain of the Gray Horse
      Troop
     The Divorcee
     The Flaming Omen
     The Magnificent Meddler
     Money Magic
     Sunlight's Last Raid
     When Men Are Tempted

1918 Cavanaugh of the Forest
      Rangers
     The Girl from Beyond
     The Home Trail
     That Devil, Bateese
     The Wild Strain
1919 The Light of Victory
Wolcott, Helen
1914 The Pursuit of the Phantom
1915 The Beachcomber
     Buckshot John
     Fatherhood
     Help Wanted
     'Twas Ever Thus
Wolcott, William
1917 Queen X
1918 Marriage
Wolf, Mr.
1917 Cy Whittaker's Ward
Wolf, Jane *see* **Wolfe, Jane**
Wolf, Rennold
1916 By Whose Hand?
     The Dawn of Love
     The Evil Thereof
     The Pretenders
1917 His Father's Son
     Lost and Won
     The Mortal Sin*
Wolfe, Frank E.
1913 From Dusk to Dawn
Wolfe, Jane *same as* **Wolf, Jane; Wolff,
Jane**
1914 The Boer War
     The Invisible Power
     Shannon of the Sixth
1915 Blackbirds
     The Case of Becky
     The Immigrant
     The Majesty of the Law
1916 The Blacklist
     Each Pearl a Tear
     The Lash
     Pudd'nhead Wilson
     The Selfish Woman
     Unprotected
1917 The Call of the East
     Castles for Two
     The Crystal Gazer
     The Fair Barbarian
     On the Level
     Rebecca of Sunnybrook Farm
     Unconquered
1918 The Bravest Way
     The Cruise of the
      Make-Believes
     The Firefly of France
     The Girl Who Came Back
     Less Than Kin
     Mile-a-Minute Kendall
     A Petticoat Pilot
1919 The Grim Game
     An Innocent Adventuress
     Men, Women and Money
     The Poor Boob
     Under the Top
     A Very Good Young Man
     The Woman Next Door
1920 Behold My Wife
     The Round-Up
     The Six Best Cellars
     The Thirteenth Commandment
     Thou Art the Man
     Why Change Your Wife?
Wolff, F.
1914 The Hand of Destiny*
     The Reign of Terror
Wolff, Jane *see* **Wolfe, Jane**
Wolheim, Louis *same as* **Walheim,
Louis; Wolheim, L. Robert;
Wolheim, Louis R.**
1916 The Brand of Cowardice
     Dorian's Divorce
     The Sunbeam
1917 The Avenging Trail
     The End of the Tour
     The Eternal Mother
     The Greatest Power
     The Millionaire's Double
1918 The Eyes of Mystery
     A Pair of Cupids
     Peg of the Pirates
     The Poor Rich Man
1919 The Belle of the Season
     The Darkest Hour

1920 Dr. Jekyll and Mr. Hyde
      (Famous Players-Lasky
      Corp.)
     A Manhattan Knight
Wolkof, Herman *same as* **Wolkof, H.**
1915 The Fool and the Dancer
     Hearts Aflame
Wollnough, James
1919 The Open Door*
Wonderley, W. Carey *see* **Wonderly, W.
Carey**
Wonderly, Frank
1919 The Hidden Truth
     The Nature Girl
Wonderly, W. Carey *same as*
Wonderley, W. Carey
1918 The Love Brokers
1919 The Follies Girl
     The World to Live In
Wong, Gung
1919 Cowardice Court
Wood, A. Voorhees *could be same as*
Nood, A. Voorhees
1918 Prunella
Wood, Anita
1915 Old Dutch*
Wood, Carolyne
1920 Neptune's Bride
Wood, Douglas J.
1917 National Red Cross Pageant*
Wood, F. D.
1917 Mother Love and the Law
Wood, Frank *same as* **Wood, Frank
Sidney; Woods, Frank** *(actor)*
1914 La Belle Russe
1915 The Coquette
     The Luring Lights
1917 The Penny Philanthropist
Wood, Freeman
1919 The Adventure Shop
Wood, Grace
1918 The Strange Woman
Wood, Harry *same as* **Woods, Harry**
1916 The Challenge
1917 The Angel Factory
     Vengeance Is Mine
1920 Rogues and Romance
Wood, Smoky Joe *same as* **Wood, Joe**
1917 The Baseball Revue of 1917*
Wood, Lawrence
1915 Madame Butterfly
Wood, Leonard
1915 The Battle Cry of Peace*
Wood, Lois
1919 The Uplifters
Wood, Marjorie
1917 National Red Cross Pageant*
Wood, N. Z. *same as* **Wood, N. S.;
Wood, N. V.; Woods, N. Z.**
1916 The Manager of the B. and A.
     Medicine Bend
     Whispering Smith
1917 Mary Lawson's Secret
Wood, Peggy
1919 Almost a Husband
Wood, Rose
1918 Sylvia on a Spree
Wood, Sam
1917 Who Knows?
1918 Old Wives for New
     The Squaw Man
     We Can't Have Everything
1919 Don't Change Your Husband
     For Better, for Worse
1920 A City Sparrow
     The Dancin' Fool
     Double Speed
     Excuse My Dust
     Her Beloved Villain
     Her First Elopement
     Sick Abed
     What's Your Hurry?
     Why Change Your Wife?
Wood, Thomas
1915 The Old Homestead
Woodburn, Margaret
1916 The Pursuing Vengeance
Woodbury, Jean *could be same as*
Woodbury, Joane
1916 An International Marriage

Woodbury, Joane *could be same as*
Woodbury, Jean
1916 The Heir to the Hoorah
Woodford, John *same as* **Woodford,
Mr.**
1919 The Winning Stroke
1920 The Tiger's Cub
     The White Moll
Woodhouse, J. Stewart
1920 Double Speed
Woodrow, Martha
1915 Her Mother's Secret
Woodruff, Bert
1917 Hands Up!
     A Love Sublime
1918 Six Shooter Andy
     Vive La France!
1919 Bill Henry
     Greased Lightning
     Virtuous Sinners
1920 Bubbles
     Homer Comes Home
     The Jailbird
     Paris Green
Woodruff, Eleanor
1914 The Last Volunteer
1915 The Heights of Hazard
1916 Big Jim Garrity
     Britton of the Seventh
     The Hero of Submarine D-2
     The Island of Surprise
     Jaffery
     The Weakness of Man
Woodruff, Eunice
1919 Virtuous Sinners
Woodruff, Franklin
1917 The Long Trail
Woodruff, Henry
1915 A Man and His Mate
1916 The Beckoning Flame
Woods, A. H.
1913 Jack London's Adventures in
      the South Sea Islands
1916 Big Jim Garrity
     New York
1918 Free and Equal
     The Guilty Man
     Innocent
     The Narrow Path
1919 Common Clay
1920 Parlor, Bedroom and Bath
Woods, Adelaide
1916 The American Beauty
     An International Marriage
1917 Her Own People
Woods, Charlotte
1919 The Pointing Finger
1920 Oh, Lady, Lady
Woods, Chester
1917 The Slacker's Heart
Woods, Ella Carter *same as* **Woods,
Ella**
1915 Her Shattered Idol
1916 Martha's Vindication
Woods, F. E. *see* **Woods, Frank E.**
Woods, Frank *(actor) see* **Wood, Frank**
Woods, Frank *(scen) see* **Woods, Frank
E.**
Woods, Frank E. *same as* **Woods, F. E.;
Woods, Frank** *(scen)*
1914 The Mountain Rat
1915 The Absentee
     The Birth of a Nation
     A Man's Prerogative
1916 The Children Pay
     The Little School Ma'am
1917 The Bad Boy
     Betsy's Burglar
     An Old Fashioned Young Man
     A Woman's Awakening
Woods, Harry *see* **Wood, Harry**
Woods, Jack
1916 Blue Blood and Red
1919 The Rider of the Law
Woods, Lotta
1920 The Mollycoddle*
Woods, N. Z. *see* **Wood, N. Z.**
Woods, Trevy
1919 The Homesteader

Woods, Walter see also **Woods, Willis** (pseud. of **Willis, F. McGrew** and **Woods, Walter**)
1916 Behind the Lines
The Heritage of Hate
Langdon's Legacy*
Undine
1917 The Book Agent
1918 Smashing Through
1919 The Grim Game
Hawthorne of the U.S.A.
The Love Burglar
A Very Good Young Man
1920 The City of Masks
The Fourteenth Man
The Life of the Party
Terror Island

Woods, Willis pseud. of **Willis, F. McGrew** and **Woods, Walter**
1916 The Devil's Bondwoman
A Stranger from Somewhere
1917 Even As You and I
The Flame of Youth

Woodthorpe, Georgia same as **Woodthorpe, Georgie**
1918 Kultur
1919 Better Times
The Old Maid's Baby
1920 Kismet
Madame Peacock
Merely Mary Ann
The Rose of Nome

Woodward, Mrs. see **Woodward, Eugenie**

Woodward, Eugenie same as **Woodward, Mrs.; Woodward, Eugenia**
1916 As in a Looking Glass
East Lynne
The Hidden Scar
1917 Betsy Ross
Easy Money
The Good for Nothing
The Last of the Carnabys
Man's Woman
The Marriage Market
The Social Leper
The Woman Beneath
1918 A Soul Without Windows
The Spurs of Sybil
T'Other Dear Charmer
1919 An Amateur Widow
1920 Greater Than Fame
Youthful Folly

Woodward, Fred
1914 His Majesty, the Scarecrow of Oz
The Magic Cloak of Oz
The Patchwork Girl of Oz

Woodward, Henry same as **Woodward, H.; Woodward, Henry F.**
1917 The Marcellini Millions
Nan of Music Mountain
On the Level
The Winning of Sally Temple
1918 Believe Me Xantippe
The Claw
The Firefly of France
Hidden Pearls
Lawless Love
The Mystery Girl
The Road Through the Dark
1919 Are You Legally Married?
Forbidden
Hearts Asleep
The Love Burglar
Male and Female
You're Fired
1920 Deep Waters
Her Five-Foot Highness
The Last of the Mohicans
Seeing It Through

Woodward, Jill
1916 My Country First
1920 The Kentucky Colonel

Woody, Wallace M.
1917 Billy and the Big Stick

Wooldridge, Doris
1915 The Unfaithful Wife
1916 The Bondman

Worcester, Dean C.
1914 Native Life in the Philippines

Worden, Walter
1917 One of Many

Woren, Edward
1919 Crimson Shoals

Works, John D.
1915 Prohibition*

Worman, Cliff
1918 Men Who Have Made Love to Me

Worms, Kenneth
1917 The Moth

Wormwood, John
1919 The Right to Lie*

Worne, Duke
1915 The Campbells Are Coming
Just Jim
1916 The Gay Lord Waring
1917 John Ermine of the Yellowstone
Who Was the Other Man?
1918 The Craving

Worris, Stanley J.
1920 The Mysteries of Paris

Worsley, Wallace
1917 Alimony
Borrowed Plumage
Paws of the Bear
1918 An Alien Enemy
The Goddess of Lost Lake
Honor's Cross
A Law unto Herself
Madam Who
A Man's Man
Social Ambition
The Turn of a Card
Wedlock
1919 Adele
Diane of the Green Van
Playthings of Passion
A Woman of Pleasure
1920 The Little Shepherd of Kingdom Come
The Penalty
The Street Called Straight

Worth, Dorothy
1920 Whispers

Worth, Lillian
1920 The Girl with the Jazz Heart
In Search of a Sinner

Worth, Peggy
1919 Checkers
1920 Chains of Evidence
Red Foam

Worthington, Harriet
1913 Checkers

Worthington, William (dir, actor)
1914 Called Back
Damon and Pythias
The Opened Shutters
Samson
The Spy
1916 Love Never Dies
A Stranger from Somewhere
1917 Bringing Home Father
The Car of Chance
The Clean-Up
The Clock
The Devil's Pay Day
The Man Who Took a Chance
1918 The Beloved Traitor
The Ghost of the Rancho
His Birthright
The Temple of Dusk*
Twenty-One
1919 All Wrong
Bonds of Honor
The Courageous Coward
The Dragon Painter
The Gray Horizon
A Heart in Pawn
His Debt
The Illustrious Prince
The Man Beneath
The Tong Man
1920 The Beggar Prince
The Silent Barrier

Worthington, William, Jr. (child actor)
1917 Polly Redhead

Worthley, Althea
1918 How Could You, Jean?
1919 Under the Top

Wortman, Frank "Huck" same as **Wortmann, Frank**
1916 Intolerance
1920 Way Down East

Wray, Joe
1920 The Devil's Claim

Wray, John Griffith
1920 Homespun Folks

Wright, Mrs. A. E. could be same as **Witting, Mrs. A. E.**
1918 Modern Love

Wright, Bert
1920 His Pajama Girl

Wright, Edith
1916 The Martyrdom of Philip Strong
1917 Passion
Where Love Is

Wright, Edmund
1918 Her Boy

Wright, Ethel
1919 Bolshevism on Trial

Wright, Fred E. same as **Wright, Fred**
1915 Graustark
In the Palace of the King
The White Sister
1916 The Breaker
Captain Jinks of the Horse Marines
The Little Shepherd of Bargain Row
The Prince of Graustark
1917 The Fibbers
The Kill-Joy
The Man Who Was Afraid
The Trufflers
1918 For Sale
The Mysterious Client
1919 Love Insurance

Wright, Gene
1920 An Arabian Knight

Wright, George A. same as **Wright, George**
1915 The Destroying Angel
Eugene Aram
The Magic Skin
The Mystery of Room 13
Ranson's Folly
Shadows from the Past
Vanity Fair
The Way Back
1916 The Catspaw
The Heart of the Hills
1917 God's Law and Man's
His Father's Son
The Mysterious Miss Terry
The White Raven
1918 The Blind Adventure

Wright, Haidee
1915 Evidence

Wright, Harold Bell
1917 The Eyes of the World*
1919 The Shepherd of the Hills

Wright, Helen
1915 Heritage
The Scarlet Sin
1916 Is Any Girl Safe?
A Stranger from Somewhere
1917 The Car of Chance
A Doll's House
The Field of Honor
The Lash of Power
Polly Redhead
Sirens of the Sea
Triumph
1918 Her One Mistake
1919 The Speed Maniac
1920 That Something

Wright, Mabel
1914 Should a Woman Divorce?
Sins of the Parents
1915 The Game of Three
Greater Love Hath No Man
Right off the Bat
The Song of the Wage Slave
1916 Wall Street Tragedy
1917 Who's Your Neighbor?
1918 To Hell with the Kaiser
1919 Reclaimed: The Struggle for a Soul Between Love and Hate
1920 Birthright

Wright, Mack
1917 The Bar Sinister

Wright, Nanine same as **Wright, Nannie; Wright, Nannine**
1916 A Child of Mystery
The Flirt
Naked Hearts
Wanted—A Home
The Whirlpool of Destiny
1917 The Phantom's Secret
The Reed Case
1918 Rosemary Climbs the Heights
The Square Deal
1919 Destiny
Whom the Gods Would Destroy
1920 The Luck of Geraldine Laird
Risky Business

Wright, Miss O.
1917 The Last Sentence

Wright, Olive
1916 The Martyrdom of Philip Strong
1917 The Master Passion

Wright, Tenny
1919 Beauty-Proof
1920 The Broken Gate
Milestones
Partners of the Night

Wright, Todd
1914 His Majesty, the Scarecrow of Oz
The Patchwork Girl of Oz

Wright, W. E.
1917 Alaska Wonders in Motion

Wright, Walter
1920 Love's Protegé

Wunderlee, Frank
1915 Midnight at Maxim's
1916 My Lady Incog.

Wupperman, Frank
1916 The Suspect

Wyatt, Fred
1915 A Bunch of Keys

Wycherly, Margaret
1915 The Fight

Wyckoff, Alvin
1914 The Spoilers
The Virginian
1915 The Captive
Carmen (Jesse L. Lasky Feature Play Co.)
The Cheat
The Girl of the Golden West
Temptation
1916 The Dream Girl
Joan the Woman
Maria Rosa
The Trail of the Lonesome Pine
1917 The Devil-Stone
The Little American
A Romance of the Redwoods
The Woman God Forgot
1918 Old Wives for New
The Squaw Man
Till I Come Back to You
We Can't Have Everything
The Whispering Chorus
1919 Don't Change Your Husband
Fires of Faith
For Better, for Worse
Male and Female
1920 Something to Think About
Why Change Your Wife?

Wylie, I. A. R.
1917 The Birth of Patriotism

Wylie, Irene
1918 The Spreading Evil

Wynard, Edward same as **Weynard, Ed; Wynard, Charles; Wynard, Charles E.; Wynard, E.; Wynard, Ed; Wynard, Eddie**
1913 The Tonopah Stampede for Gold
1914 A Woman Who Did
1915 The Earl of Pawtucket
Fanchon the Cricket
The Man of Shame
1916 A Woman's Honor
1917 The Fringe of Society
The Moth
The Siren

CORPORATE NAME INDEX

★ The corporate name index contains listings of production and distribution companies. In addition, it includes laboratories, corporate copyright claimants, and corporate entities connected with individual films in other ways. Personal names have been included here only if the person is listed as a production or distribution entity for a specific film, rather than as a producer or distributor employed by a corporation.

The determination of exact names was as difficult for corporate as personal names, and, in some cases, nearly impossible. Research among reviews, advertisements, and news items often resulted in conflicting information. For these cases, we gave the most credence to the name as it appeared in company records, followed by advertisements, copyright records and studio directories.

The numerous corporate mergers and takeovers which occurred between 1911 and 1920 resulted in seemingly conflicting information about company names. Often after a merger or takeover a company name became a "brand," or "series" name of another company or a newly formed corporation. For example, "Paramount Pictures" became a brand name after Famous Players-Lasky Corp. was created from Paramount Pictures Corp. and other companies. In some cases, when we could not determine if the new brand or series name was actually a continuing corporate entity or not, we included the brand or series name following the corporate entity with which it was connected. For example, we included "World Film Corp.; Shubert" because the Shubert Film Corp. existed at one time, although we were not sure if its involvement in films after a certain time was still that of a separate corporate entity, or merely a brand for World Film Corp.

As a rule, brand or series names are not included in this index as separate entries because the index was designed to list films made by distinct corporate entities. In many cases, brand or series names only represent advertising jargon, but in instances when we have determined that a brand or series name is important or relevant, we have included it with its corporate entity. In those cases in which a brand or series name are connected with a corporate entity, the brand or series will have a cross-reference to the complete entry.

In cases where a company name is only listed in the credits of a film's entry as a copyright claimant, or only in the Notes section, the film's title is listed under the company name with an asterisk following it. A dagger following a film title indicates the company's involvement is questionable and that the company listing in the film entry is followed by a question mark. The notes for each of these films explains the controversy. Claimants who copyrighted scenarios for films, but not the films themselves, are not listed in the index.

CORPORATE NAME INDEX

A

A & W Film Corp.
1916 The Prima Donna's Husband

A. H. Fischer Features, Inc.
1919 A Scream in the Night
1920 Even As Eve
    Man and Woman
1921 Miss 139

A. H. Jacobs Photoplays, Inc.
1917 Her Fighting Chance
1919 When My Ship Comes In

A. H. Woods
1918 Free and Equal

Abo Feature Film Co.
1914 Joliet Prison, Joliet, Ill.

Abrams & Werner see also **Werner and Abrams**
1917 The Bar Sinister

Abrams, Hiram see **Hiram Abrams**

Abrams, Hiram, Productions see **A Hiram Abrams Production**

Abramson, Ivan, Distributing Corp. see **Ivan Abramson Distributing Corp.**

Acme Pictures Corp.
1919 The A.B.C. of Love
    The Thirteenth Chair
    The Twin Pawns

Adanac Producing Co.
1920 The Great Shadow

Advanced Motion Picture Corp.
1917 The Co-Respondent
1918 The Eleventh Commandment
    Her Man

Affiliated Distributors' Corp.
1918 Lafayette, We Come!

Al Ira Smith
1919 The Girl Alaska

Al Jennings Productions Co.
1918 The Lady of the Dugout

Alaska Film Corp.
1915 The Lure of Alaska

Alaskan-Siberian Motion Pictures
1912 The Alaska-Siberian Expedition

Albert Blinkhorn see also **Blinkhorn Photoplays Corp.**
1914 The Capture of a Sea Elephant
    and Hunting Wild Game in
    the South Pacific Islands

Albert Capellani Productions, Inc.
1919 A Damsel in Distress
    The Love Cheat
    Oh, Boy!
    The Right to Lie
    The Virtuous Model
1920 The Fortune Teller
    In Walked Mary

Albuquerque Film Co. see also **Albuquerque Film Mfg. Co.**
1914 Even unto Death

Albuquerque Film Mfg. Co. see also **Albuquerque Film Co.**
1914 The Lust of the Red Man

Alco Film Corp.
1914 The Education of Mr. Pipp
    Michael Strogoff
    The Nightingale
    The Ragged Earl
    Rip Van Winkle
    Salomy Jane
    Shore Acres
    Springtime
    The Three of Us
    The Tigress

Alexander Film Corp.
1920 The Lone Hand

Alkire Productions
1920 Youth's Desire

All Feature Booking Agency
1915 Right off the Bat

All Star Feature Corp. same as **All-Star Feature Corp.**
1913 Arizona
    Checkers
1914 America
    Dan
    The Education of Mr. Pipp
    In Mizzoura
    The Jungle
    The Nightingale
    Paid in Full
    Pierre of the Plains
    Shore Acres
    Soldiers of Fortune
1915 The Garden of Lies

All Star Feature Distributors
1915 Wild Life of America in Films

Allan Dwan Productions
1919 Soldiers of Fortune
1920 The Forbidden Thing
    In the Heart of a Fool
    The Luck of the Irish
    The Scoffer
    A Splendid Hazard

Alliance Films Corp.
1914 At the Cross Roads
    Hearts and Flowers
    His Majesty, the Scarecrow of
    Oz
    The Hoosier Schoolmaster
    Ill Starred Babbie
    The Key to Yesterday
    The Last Egyptian
    McVeagh of the South Seas
    The Man Who Could Not Lose
    The Path Forbidden
    The Truth Wagon
    When Fate Leads Trump
1915 Beulah
    The Chocolate Soldier
    The High Hand
    In the Shadow
    Jack Chanty
    The Lone Star Rush
    The Pageant of San Francisco

Allied Artists
1920 Sophy of Kravonia; Or, The
    Virgin of Paris

Allied Independent Attractions, Inc.
1920 Birthright

Alpha Pictures, Inc.
1919 Reclaimed: The Struggle for a
    Soul Between Love and Hate

American Cinema Corp.
1920 The Inner Voice
    Stolen Moments
    What Women Want
    Women Men Forget

American Commercial Film Co.
1915 The Billionaire Lord

American Committee for Armenian and Syrian Relief
1919 Auction of Souls

American Correspondent Film Co.
1915 The Battle and Fall of
    Przemysl
    The Battles of a Nation
    Friends and Foes
    System, the Secret of Success
    The Warring Millions

1916 The Fighting Germans
American Defense Society
1916 United States Marines Under
    Fire in Haiti
1918 Keep the Home Fires Burning
American Feature Film Corp.
1918 Hearts of Love
American Film Co. see also **American Film Mfg. Co.**
1915 The Buzzard's Shadow
    The End of the Road
    The House of a Thousand
    Scandals
    Infatuation
    The Miracle of Life
1916 The Abandonment
    And the Law Says
    April
    Bluff
    The Bruiser
    The Courtesan
    The Craving
    A Dream or Two Ago
    Dulcie's Adventure
    Dust
    Embers
    Faith
    The Girl O' Dreams
    The Highest Bid
    Immediate Lee
    The Inner Struggle
    The Innocence of Lizette
    Land O' Lizards
    Life's Blind Alley
    The Light
    Lone Star
    Lonesome Town
    Lord Loveland Discovers
    America
    The Love Hermit
    Lying Lips
    The Man from Manhattan
    The Man Who Would Not Die
    A Million for Mary
    The Other Side of the Door
    Overalls
    The Overcoat
    Peck O' Pickles
    Philip Holden—Waster
    Powder
    Purity
    Reclamation
    Revelations
    The Sable Blessing
    The Sign of the Spade
    Soul Mates
    The Strength of Donald
    McKenzie
    The Thoroughbred
    Three Pals
    The Torch Bearer
    True Nobility
    The Twinkler
    The Undertow
    The Valley of Decision
    The Voice of Love
    The White Rosette
    A Woman's Daring
    Youth's Endearing Charm
1917 Annie-for-Spite
    Beloved Rogues
    Betty and the Buccaneers
    The Bride's Silence
    The Calendar Girl
    Charity Castle
    Environment
    The Frame Up
    A Game of Wits

The Gentle Intruder
The Gilded Youth
Her Country's Call
High Play
The Masked Heart
The Mate of the Sally Ann
Melissa of the Hills
Miss Jackie of the Army
My Fighting Gentleman
New York Luck
Peggy Leads the Way
Periwinkle
Pride and the Man
The Rainbow Girl
Sands of Sacrifice
The Sea Master
The Serpent's Tooth
Shackles of Truth
Snap Judgement
Souls in Pawn
Southern Pride
The Upper Crust
Whose Wife?
1918 All the World to Nothing
    Ann's Finish
    Beauty and the Rogue
    A Bit of Jade
    The Eyes of Julia Deep
    Fair Enough
    The Ghost of Rosy Taylor
    Hobbs in a Hurry
    Impossible Susan
    In Bad
    Jilted Janet
    The Mantle of Charity
    The Midnight Trail
    Molly, Go Get 'Em
    Money Isn't Everything
    Powers That Prey
    The Primitive Woman
    Rosemary Climbs the Heights
    Social Briars
    The Square Deal
    Wives and Other Wives
1919 The Amazing Impostor
    A Bachelor's Wife
    Brass Buttons
    Charge It to Me
    Eve in Exile
    The Hellion
    The Intrusion of Isabel
    Molly of the Follies
    Put Up Your Hands
    Six Feet Four
    Some Liar
    A Sporting Chance
    This Hero Stuff
    The Tiger Lily
    Trixie from Broadway
    When a Man Rides Alone
    Where the West Begins
    Yvonne from Paris
1920 The Blue Moon
    The Dangerous Talent
    The Gamesters
    The Honey Bee
    The House of Toys
    A Light Woman
    Their Mutual Child
    The Thirtieth Piece of Silver
    The Valley of Tomorrow
    The Week-End
American Film Mfg. Co. see also **American Film Co.**
1914 Damaged Goods
1915 The Girl from His Town
    The Lonesome Heart
    The Lure of the Mask
    The Quest

Secretary of Frivolous Affairs
American Kineto Corp.
1913 The Girl of the Sunny South
American Lifeograph Co.
1915 Where Cowboy Is King
1920 The Deceiver
The Golden Trail
American Rotograph Co.
1914 Sitting Bull—The Hostile
Sioux Indian Chief
American Social Hygiene Association
1919 Fit to Win
American Standard Motion Picture Corp.
1917 The Blackmailers
The Golden Rosary*
Has Man the Right to Kill?
S.O.S.
America's Feature Film Co.
1913 Barbarous Mexico
Anchor Film Corp.
1917 Hell Hath No Fury
Anderson-Brunton Co. *see also* **Robert Brunton Co.; Robert Brunton Productions** *and* **Robert Brunton Studios, Inc.**
1918 The Bells
The Ghost of the Rancho
A Little Sister of Everybody
More Trouble
Twenty-One
1919 All Wrong
Carolyn of the Corners
The Midnight Stage
The Silver Girl
Andrew J. Callaghan Productions, Inc.
1920 Bonnie May
The Midlanders
Anita Stewart Productions, Inc.
1918 Virtuous Wives
1919 Her Kingdom of Dreams
Human Desire
In Old Kentucky
Mary Regan
A Midnight Romance
Mind the Paint Girl
1920 The Fighting Shepherdess
Harriet and the Piper
The Yellow Typhoon
Anti-Vice Motion Picture Co.
1916 Is Any Girl Safe?
Apex Film Co. *could be same as* **Apex Film Corp.**
1913 The Black Snake
1915 The Man Who Vanished
1920 Out of the Dust*
Apex Film Corp. *could be same as* **Apex Film Co.**
1915 European War Pictures
Apollo Pictures, Inc.
1917 God of Little Children
The Golden God
The Great Bradley Mystery
The Law That Failed
The Mystic Hour
Pride and the Devil
Rosie O'Grady
When You and I Were Young
Aras
1918 An Armenian Crucifixion‡
Arctic Film Co.
1914 Captain F. E. Kleinschmidt's
Arctic Hunt
An Arden Picture
1918 The Challenge Accepted
Ardsley Art Film Corp.
1917 Runaway Romany
Argosy Film Co. *could be same as* **Argosy Films, Inc.**
1918 After the War
Argosy Films, Inc. *could be same as* **Argosy Film Co.**
1916 The People vs. John Doe*
Where D'Ye Get That Stuff?
Argus Enterprises, Inc. *see also* **Argus Motion Picture Co.**
1919 The House Without Children
Argus Motion Picture Co. *see also* **Argus Enterprises, Inc.**
1920 Hidden Charms

Arizona Film Co.
1917 Should She Obey?
Armstrong *see* **World Film Corp.; Armstrong**
Arrow Film Corp.
1915 The Buzzard's Shadow*
Right off the Bat
1916 The Daughter of the Don*
The Woman's Law
1917 Crime and Punishment
The Deemster
The Eyes of the World*
1918 The Finger of Justice
Her Aviator
Huns Within Our Gates
The Million Dollar Mystery
The Mysterious Mr. Browning
The Struggle Everlasting
1919 Fool's Gold
The Greater Victory
The Law of Nature
Miss Arizona
The Profiteer
When the Desert Smiles
1920 Bachelor Apartments
Before the White Man Came
Bitter Fruit
The Bromley Case
The Chamber Mystery
Circumstantial Evidence
The Deceiver
The Desert Scorpion
The Golden Trail
Love's Protegé
The Man from Nowhere
The Sacred Ruby
The Scrap of Paper
The Trail of the Cigarette
The Triple Clue
The Unseen Witness
The Wall Street Mystery
The Way Women Love
Wolves of the Street
Woman's Man
1920-21
The House of Mystery
Art Dramas, Inc.
1916 The Lash of Destiny
Whoso Findeth a Wife
1917 The Accomplice
The Adventurer
The Auction of Virtue
Behind the Mask
The Blood of His Fathers
The Cloud
The Eye of Envy
God of Little Children
The Golden God
The Great Bradley Mystery
Her Good Name
House of Cards
The Inevitable
Infidelity
The Law That Failed
Little Miss Fortune
The Little Samaritan
A Man and the Woman
Miss Deception
The Moral Code
A Mother's Ordeal
A Mute Appeal
The Mystic Hour
The Peddler
Pride and the Devil
The Rainbow
The Road Between
Rosie O'Grady
A Song of Sixpence
Think It Over
Unto the End
When You and I Were Young
1918 Peg O' the Sea
Art Film Co.
1915 The Stubbornness of Geraldine
Art-O-Graf Film Co.
1919 Miss Arizona
1920 The Desert Scorpion
Wolves of the Street
Artclass Pictures Corp.
1919 The Open Door
1920 It Might Happen to You

Artco Productions, Inc. *see also* **Harry Raver, Inc.**
1919 As a Man Thinks
The Capitol
The Volcano
Artcraft Pictures Corp. *Note:* Artcraft was incorporated as a distribution company in 1916. Early in 1918, the corporate name of Artcraft Pictures Corp. was discontinued and Artcraft Pictures became a brand name of Famous Players-Lasky Corp. For films released under the brand name, see **Famous Players-Lasky Corp.; Artcraft Pictures** *and* **Famous Players-Lasky Corp.; Paramount-Artcraft Pictures**
1916 Less Than the Dust
1917 Barbary Sheep
Broadway Jones
The Devil-Stone
Down to Earth
In Again—Out Again
The Little American
The Little Princess
The Man from Painted Post
A Modern Musketeer
The Narrow Trail
The Poor Little Rich Girl
The Pride of the Clan
Reaching for the Moon
Rebecca of Sunnybrook Farm
The Rise of Jennie Cushing
A Romance of the Redwoods
Seven Keys to Baldpate
The Silent Man
Wild and Woolly
The Woman God Forgot
1918 Riddle Gawne
The Rose of the World
Arthur S. Hyman Attractions Co.
1917 The Penny Philanthropist*
Arthur S. Kane
1915 Somewhere in France
Arthur S. Kane Pictures Corp.
1920 Forty-Five Minutes from Broadway
Ascher Productions, Inc.
1920 Below the Deadline
Up in Mary's Attic
Associated Exhibitors, Inc.
1920 The Riddle: Woman
Associated Film Sales Corp.
1915 Her Atonement
His Turning Point
Associated First National Pictures, Inc. *same as* **Associated First National Film Corp.** *see also* **First National Exhibitors Circuit, Inc.**
1919 Human Desire
1920 Dangerous Business
Dinty
Forty-Five Minutes from Broadway
Harriet and the Piper
In the Heart of a Fool
Love, Honor and Behave
Married Life
The Master Mind
Nineteen and Phyllis
Nomads of the North
The Notorious Miss Lisle
Old Dad
Peaceful Valley
The Scoffer
The Truth About Husbands
Unseen Forces
What Women Love
The Yellow Typhoon
1921 Habit
Associated Producers, Inc.
1920 The Forbidden Thing
Homespun Folks
The Last of the Mohicans
The Leopard Woman
Love
A Thousand to One
Astra Film Corp.
1916 Arms and the Woman
The Challenge
The Romantic Journey
The Test
1917 The Angel Factory
Blind Man's Luck

The Cigarette Girl
A Crooked Romance
The Hunting of the Hawk
The Iron Heart
Kick In
The Last of the Carnabys
The Mark of Cain
Mayblossom
Miss Nobody
The On-the-Square-Girl
Over the Hill
The Recoil
Stranded in Arcady
The Streets of Illusion
Sylvia of the Secret Service
Vengeance Is Mine
1918 Annexing Bill
Convict 993
The First Law
For Sale
The Girl from Bohemia
The Hillcrest Mystery
Innocent
A Japanese Nightingale
Mrs. Slacker
The Mysterious Client
The Narrow Path
The Naulahka
The Other Woman
Waifs
The Yellow Ticket
1919 The Beloved Cheater
Caleb Piper's Girl
Common Clay
The Cry of the Weak
Go Get 'Em Garringer
Our Better Selves
The Profiteers
Athletic Feature Films
1917 The Baseball Revue of 1917
Atlantic Distributing Corp.
1917-18
The Devil's Playground*
1918 Nine-Tenths of the Law
Atlas Film Corp.
1920 The Place of Honeymoons
Attractions Distributing Corp.
1919 The Beauty Market
1920 The Notorious Miss Lisle
Passion's Playground
The Turning Point
Aurora Film Plays Corp.
1915 The Waif
Austro-Servian Film Co.
1914 With Serb and Austrian
Authors' Film Co.
1916 Her Redemption
Love's Sacrifice
1917 Madame Sherry
The Silent Witness
1918 The Crucible of Life
Author's Photo-Plays, Inc.
1918 Her Moment
Aywon Film Corp.
1915 Not Guilty*
1916 Behind Closed Doors*
The Ransom*
1919 The Law of Nature*
Roses and Thorns
When the Desert Smiles
1920 Blind Love
The Border Raiders
Dangerous Trails
Days of Daring
The Evolution of Man
Thirty Years Between
The Unknown Ranger
When Quackel Did Hide
Witch's Gold
The Woman Above Reproach
The Woman of Mystery

B

B. A. Rolfe Photoplays, Inc. *see also* **Rolfe Photoplay, Inc.**
1914 Rip Van Winkle
The Three of Us
B. B. Features *see also* **Bessie Barriscale Productions**
1919 All of a Sudden Norma
Beckoning Roads

Hearts Asleep
Her Purchase Price
Josselyn's Wife
Kitty Kelly, M.D.
Tangled Threads
A Trick of Fate
The Woman Michael Married
1920 Life's Twist
The Luck of Geraldine Laird
The Notorious Mrs. Sands
A Woman Who Understood*

B.P.O.E. (Benevolent and Protective Order of Elks)
1919 The Greater Victory

B. S. Moss see also **B. S. Moss Motion Picture Corp.**
1918 The Scarlet Trail*

B. S. Moss Motion Picture Corp. see also **B. S. Moss**
1916 The Birth of a Man
Boots and Saddles
The Girl Who Doesn't Know
One Day
The Power of Evil
The Salamander
1917 Birth Control
One Hour
1920 The Stranger‡

Backer, George, Film Corp. see **George Backer Film Corp.**

Bacon-Backer Film Corp.
1918 Men
1919 A Woman's Experience

Bacon, Gerald F., Productions see **Gerald F. Bacon Productions**

Balboa Amusement Co. see also **Balboa Amusement Producing Co.; Balboa Feature Film Co.; Falcon Features; Horkheimer Bros.; Horkheimer Studios** and **Knickerbocker Star Features**
1916 Joy and the Dragon
Shadows and Sunshine
The Sultana
The Twin Triangle
1917 Sunshine and Gold
Told at Twilight
Twin Kiddies

Balboa Amusement Producing Co. see also **Balboa Amusement Co.; Balboa Feature Film Co.; Falcon Features; Horkheimer Bros.; Horkheimer Studios** and **Knickerbocker Star Features**
1914 Ill Starred Babbie
St. Elmo
The Will O' the Wisp
1915 The Adventures of a Madcap Beulah
Comrade John
1916 The Birth of a Man
Boots and Saddles
The Power of Evil
Spellbound
1917 The Alien Blood
The Best Man*
Betty Be Good
The Devil's Bait
In the Hands of the Law
The Inspirations of Harry Larrabee
Mentioned in Confidence
Sold at Auction
Sunny Jane
Vengeance of the Dead
The Yellow Bullet
1918 Nine-Tenths of the Law
19-- The Policewoman

Balboa Feature Film Co. see also **Balboa Amusement Co.; Balboa Amusement Producing Co.; Falcon Features; Horkheimer Bros.; Horkheimer Studios** and **Knickerbocker Star Features**
1914 The Criminal Code
1915 An Eye for an Eye
Pearls of Temptation
1916 Little Mary Sunshine
The Matrimonial Martyr
The Shrine of Happiness

Ballin, Hugo, Productions, Inc. see **Hugo Ballin Productions, Inc.**

Balshofer, Fred J. see **Fred J. Balshofer**

Barker, Reginald, Productions see **Reginald Barker Productions**

Barriscale, Bessie, Feature Corp. see **Bessie Barriscale Feature Corp.**

Barry MacDonald Film Co.
1915 What Should a Woman Do to Promote Youth and Happiness?

Beach, Corra, Pictures Corp. see **Corra Beach Pictures Corp.**

Beach, Rex see **Rex Beach**

Beach, Rex, Pictures Co. see **Rex Beach Pictures Co.**

Beach, Rex, Productions see **A Rex Beach Production**

Bear State Film Co.
1918 The Vigilantes

Beatriz Michelena Features
1919 Just Squaw
1920 The Flame of Hellgate

Ben Wilson Productions
1920 The Man from Nowhere

Benjamin B. Hampton Productions
1919 The Westerners
1920 The Dwelling Place of Light
The Money-Changers
The Spenders
The U.P. Trail

Bennett, Whitman, Productions see **Whitman Bennett Productions**

Berenstein, Bernard H. see **Bernard H. Berenstein**

Bernard H. Berenstein
1918 A Lion of the Hills

Bernstein Film Productions
1917 Loyalty
Who Knows?
1918 Humility

Bert Lubin
1920 Honeymoon Ranch

Besley, Captain, Motion Picture Co. see **Captain Besley Motion Picture Co.**

Bessie Barriscale Productions see also **B. B. Features**
1918 The Heart of Rachael

Better-Than-Program Distributing Co.
1916 The Woman Who Dared

Betzwood Film Co.
1918 For the Freedom of the East
Oh, Johnny!
1919 High Pockets
A Misfit Earl
The Road Called Straight
Sandy Burke of the U-Bar-U
Speedy Meade

Beverly B. Dobbs
1912 Atop of the World in Motion

Biograph Co.
1914 Classmates
Judith of Bethulia
Liberty Belles
Lord Chumley
The Power of the Press
The Rejuvenation of Aunt Mary
Under the Gaslight
The Woman in Black
1915 Divorçons
Dora Thorne
The Gambler of the West
The Hungarian Nabob

Birth of a Race Photoplay Corp.
1918 The Birth of a Race

Blaché Features, Inc.
1913 The Fight for Millions
The Fortune Hunters
A Prisoner in the Harem
The Star of India
1914 The Dream Woman
Fighting Death
Hook and Hand
The Lure
The War Extra
The Woman of Mystery
The Yellow Traffic

Blackton Productions, Inc. see also **J. Stuart Blackton; J. Stuart Blackton Feature Pictures, Inc.; J. Stuart Blackton Productions** and **J. Stuart Blackton Productions, Inc.**

1918 The World for Sale
1919 The Common Cause
Life's Greatest Problem
The Littlest Scout

Blackton, J. Stuart see **J. Stuart Blackton**

Blackton, J. Stuart, Feature Pictures, Inc. see **J. Stuart Blackton Feature Pictures, Inc.**

Blackton, J. Stuart, Productions see **J. Stuart Blackton Productions**

Blackton, J. Stuart, Productions, Inc. see **J. Stuart Blackton Productions, Inc.**

Blaney see **World Film Corp.; Blaney**

Blaney, Charles E., Productions see **Charles E. Blaney Productions**

Blaney, Charles E., Productions see **Charles E. Blaney Productions**

Blazon Film Producing Co. see also **A Blazon Production**
1915 Rule G

A Blazon Production see also **Blazon Film Producing Co.**
1915 The Deathlock

Blinkhorn Photoplays Corp. see also **Albert Blinkhorn**
1914 Jane Eyre
Lena Rivers

Blue Ribbon Features see **Vitagraph Co. of America**

Bluebird Photoplays, Inc. see also **Universal Film Mfg. Co.** Note: Although an independent corporate entity, Bluebird was connected in some manner with Universal. After Bluebird Photoplays, Inc. was discontinued as a corporate name, Bluebird became a Universal brand name.
1915 Scandal*
1916 Behind the Lines
Bettina Loved a Soldier
Bobbie of the Ballet
Broken Fetters
The Bugler of Algiers
The Chalice of Sorrow
The Crippled Hand
The Eagle's Wing
Elusive Isabel
The End of the Rainbow
The Evil Women Do
The Eye of God
The Flirt
The Gay Lord Waring
The Gilded Spider
The Girl of the Lost Lake
Gloriana
The Grasp of Greed
The Great Problem
The Grip of Jealousy
The Honor of Mary Blake
Hop, the Devil's Brew
John Needham's Double
Little Eve Edgarton
The Love Girl
Love Never Dies
Love's Lariat
The Measure of a Man
Naked Hearts
The Price of Silence
The Right to Be Happy
Saving the Family Name
Secret Love
The Secret of the Swamp
Shoes
The Sign of the Poppy
The Silent Battle
The Social Buccaneer
A Son of the Immortals
A Stranger from Somewhere
The Strength of the Weak
Tangled Hearts
The Target*
The Three Godfathers
The Unattainable
Undine
Wanted—A Home
The Whirlpool of Destiny
The Wrong Door
The Yaqui
1917 Anything Once
Black Orchids
Bondage
The Boy Girl
Bringing Home Father
The Car of Chance

The Charmer
The Clean-Up
The Clock
The Desire of the Moth
The Devil's Pay Day
A Doll's House
The Door Between
Fires of Rebellion
The Flashlight
Flirting with Death
The Gift Girl
The Girl by the Roadside
The Girl in the Checkered Coat
God's Crucible
The Greater Law
Hell Morgan's Girl
Her Soul's Inspiration
A Jewel in Pawn
A Kentucky Cinderella
The Lash of Power
Little Miss Nobody
The Little Orphan
The Little Terror
The Man Trap
The Man Who Took a Chance
Mr. Opp
Mother O' Mine
Mutiny
My Little Boy
The Mysterious Mr. Tiller
The Mysterious Mrs. M.
The Piper's Price
Polly Redhead
Princess Virtue
The Pulse of Life
The Raggedy Queen
The Rescue
The Reward of the Faithless
The Saintly Sinner
The Savage
The Scarlet Car
The Show Down
A Soul for Sale‡
Southern Justice
The Spotted Lily
A Stormy Knight
Susan's Gentleman
Treason
Triumph
The Winged Mystery
1918 After the War
All Night
Beans
Brace Up
The Brazen Beauty
The Bride's Awakening
Broadway Love
A Broadway Scandal
The Cabaret Girl
The City of Tears
The Craving
Danger Within
The Deciding Kiss
The Dream Lady
The Eagle
The Empty Cab
Face Value
Fast Company
The Fighting Grin
Fires of Youth
$5,000 Reward
The Girl in the Dark
The Guilt of Silence
Hands Down
Hugon, the Mighty
Hungry Eyes
The Love Swindle
The Lure of Luxury
The Marriage Lie
Midnight Madness
Morgan's Raiders
A Mother's Secret
My Unmarried Wife
Playthings
The Red, Red Heart
A Rich Man's Darling
The Rough Lover
The Sea Flower
Set Free
She Hired a Husband
A Society Sensation
That Devil, Bateese
Together
Tongues of Flame
The Two-Soul Woman

The Velvet Hand
Which Woman?
The Wife He Bought
The Wine Girl
Winner Takes All
1919　The Game's Up
The Light of Victory
The Little White Savage
The Millionaire Pirate
The Nature Girl
The Sealed Envelope
Sue of the South
A Taste of Life
Who Will Marry Me?
The Wicked Darling*
Boland, J. M. see **J. M. Boland**
Bookertee Film Exchange
1919　Injustice
Boris Thomashefsky Film Co.
1915　Hear Ye, Israel
The Jewish Crown
The Period of the Jew
Bosburn Photoplay Co.
1914　Doc
Boston Motion Picture Co.
1916　The Whaling Industry
Bosworth, Inc. predecessor of **Famous Players-Lasky Corp.** see also **Pallas Pictures** Note: Bosworth, Inc. produced under the name of Pallas Pictures.
1913　The Sea Wolf
1914　Burning Daylight: The Adventures of "Burning Daylight" in Alaska
Burning Daylight: The Adventures of "Burning Daylight" in Civilization
The Chechako
The Country Mouse
False Colours
John Barleycorn
Martin Eden
An Odyssey of the North
The Pursuit of the Phantom
The Traitor
The Valley of the Moon
1915　The Beachcomber
Betty in Search of a Thrill
Buckshot John
The Caprices of Kitty
Captain Courtesy
Help Wanted
The Hypocrites
It's No Laughing Matter
Little Sunset
The Majesty of the Law
Nearly a Lady
Pretty Mrs. Smith
The Rug Maker's Daughter
Sunshine Molly
'Twas Ever Thus
The Wild Olive
1916　He Fell in Love with His Wife
Box Office Attraction Co. predecessor of **Fox Film Corp.** see also **William Fox Vaudeville Co.**
1914　The Criminal Code
The Idler
Kate
Life's Shop Window
St. Elmo
The Thief
The Walls of Jericho
The Will O' the Wisp
1915　Children of the Ghetto
A Fool There Was
A Gilded Fool
The Girl I Left Behind Me
Samson
Bradbury Productions
1920　Into the Light
Bradley Feature Film Co.
1920　Women Men Love
Brady, William A. see **William A. Brady**
Brady, William A., Picture Plays, Inc. see **William A. Brady Picture Plays, Inc.**
Brenon, Herbert, Film Corp. see **Herbert Brenon Film Corp.**

Brentwood Film Corp.
1919　Better Times
The Other Half
Poor Relations
The Turn in the Road
1920　Bright Skies
The Heart of Twenty
Seeing It Through
The Third Generation
British-American Pictures Finance Corp.
1919　The Heart of a Gypsy*
Love, Honor and—?*
The Other Man's Wife*
The Phantom Honeymoon*
1920　Wits vs. Wits*
Broadway Favorites see **Kalem Co.**
Broadway Film Co.
1915　The Bridge of Sighs
The Vow
Broadway Picture Producing Co.
1914　The Man O' Warsman
The Trail of the Lonesome Pine
Broadway Star Features Co. see also **Vitagraph Co. of America.** Note: Although an independent corporate entity, Broadway Star Features Co. was connected in some manner with Vitagraph.
1914　Captain Alvarez
A Florida Enchantment
The Little Angel of Canyon Creek
A Million Bid
Mr. Barnes of New York
My Official Wife
The Strange Story of Sylvia Gray
The Tangle
The Win(k)some Widow
1915　The Breath of Araby
C.O.D.
Hearts and the Highway
How Cissy Made Good
The Island of Regeneration
The Juggernaut
The Man Behind the Door
Mother's Roses
The Sins of the Mothers
The Wheels of Justice
1917　Blind Man's Holiday
The Defeat of the City
The Duplicity of Hargraves
The Indian Summer of Dry Valley Johnson
A Night in New Arabia
The Renaissance at Charleroi
The Skylight Room
Broadway Universal Features see **Universal Film Mfg. Co.**
Broncho Co. see **New York Motion Picture Corp.**
Brunton, Robert, Co. see **Robert Brunton Co.**
Brunton, Robert, Productions see **Robert Brunton Productions**
Brunton, Robert, Studios, Inc. see **Robert Brunton Studios, Inc.**
Buffalo Motion Picture Co. could be same as **Buffalo Motion Picture Corp.**
1920　The Sport of Kings
Buffalo Motion Picture Corp. could be same as **Buffalo Motion Picture Co.**
1919　The Price of Innocence
Burnside, M. J. see **M. J. Burnside**
Burr McIntosh Film Corp.
1915　Colonel Carter of Cartersville
Burton King Productions
1920　The Common Sin
The Discarded Woman
For Love or Money
Butterfly Pictures see **Universal Film Mfg. Co.**

C

C. B. C. Film Sales Corp.
1920　Dangerous Love
The Victim

C. B. Price Co.
1916　The Decoy*
1918　The Prodigal Wife*
1920　His Pajama Girl
C. E. Shurtleff, Inc.
1920　Burning Daylight
The Mutiny of the Elsinore
The Star Rover
C. K. Y. Film Corp. see also **Clara Kimball Young Film Corp. and Clara Kimball Young Picture Co.**
1917　Magda
Shirley Kaye
1918　The Claw
The House of Glass
The Marionettes
The Reason Why
1919　Cheating Cheaters
A C. L. Yearsley Picture
1917　Alimony
C. R. Macauley Photoplays, Inc.
1919　When Bearcat Went Dry
Whom the Gods Would Destroy
1920　The Gift Supreme
Seeds of Vengeance
Cabanne, William Christy, Producing Co. see **William Christy Cabanne Producing Co.**
California Motion Picture Corp.
1914　Mrs. Wiggs of the Cabbage Patch
Salomy Jane
1915　The Lily of Poverty Flat
Mignon
The Pageant of San Francisco
A Phyllis of the Sierras
Salvation Nell
1916　The Unwritten Law
The Woman Who Dared
1917　Innocence
1919　The Heart of Juanita
The Price Woman Pays
Callaghan, Andrew J., Productions, Inc. see **Andrew J. Callaghan Productions, Inc.**
Canyon Pictures Corp.
1920　The Galloping Devil
Vengeance and the Girl
Capellani, Albert, Productions, Inc. see **Albert Capellani Productions, Inc.**
Capital Film Co.
1920　Lone Hand Wilson
Witch's Gold
Captain Besley Motion Picture Co.
1914　The Captain Besley Expedition
1915　In the Amazon Jungles with the Captain Besley Expedition
Captain F. E. Kleinschmidt
1916　War on Three Fronts
Capt. Lewis
1915　Chinatown Pictures
Cardinal Film Corp.
1916　Joan the Woman
Carewe, Edward, Productions, Inc. see **Edward Carewe Productions, Inc.**
A Carl Harbaugh Production
1919　The Other Man's Wife
Carl Ray Motion Picture Co.
1915　Vengeance of the Wilds
Carleton, Lloyd, Productions see **Lloyd Carleton Productions**
Carroll, Frank J. see **Frank J. Carroll**
Carter Cinema Co.
1916　How Life Begins*
Carter De Haven Productions
1920　Twin Beds
Catholic Art Association
1918　The Transgressor
1919　The Burning Question
The Eternal Light
1920　Luring Shadows
The Victim
Celebrated Players Film Co.
1916　The Birth of a Man
Centaur Film Co.
1914　Il Trovatore
1916　The Bait
The Conscience of John David
The Heart of Tara
The Hidden Law

A Law unto Himself
The Leopard's Bride
The Love Liar
The Soul's Cycle
Vengeance Is Mine
The Wasted Years
1917　The Single Code*
Central Film Co.
1914　Under the Black Robe
1915　Russian Battlefields
Wild Life of America in Films
Century Film Co.
1916　Inherited Passions
Chadwick Pictures
1916　The Faded Flower*
A Fool's Paradise*
Champion Sports Exhibition Co.
1916　Willard-Moran Fight
Chandler, Roy, South American Pictures see **Roy Chandler South American Pictures**
Chaplin-Mayer Pictures Co.
1920　The Inferior Sex
Old Dad
Polly of the Storm Country
The Woman in His House
1921　Habit
Character Pictures Corp.
1920　The Isle of Destiny
Charles E. Blaney Productions see also **World Film Corp.; Blaney**
1914　Across the Pacific
The Dancer and the King
Charles Frohman
1915　Bella Donna
The Fatal Card
The Mummy and the Humming Bird
Zaza
Charles K. Harris Feature Film Co.
1915　Hearts of Men
When It Strikes Home
1916　Should a Baby Die?
Charles L. Fuller Dist. Co.
1913　A Princess of Bagdad
A Sister to Carmen
Charles Miller Productions
1919　A Dangerous Affair
The Heart of a Gypsy
Love, Honor and—?
Charles Post Mason Enterprises
1916　Greater New York by Day and by Night; The Wonder City of the World
Charles Ray Pictures Corp. see also **Charles Ray Productions, Inc.**
1920　Nineteen and Phyllis
Charles Ray Productions, Inc. see also **Charles Ray Pictures Corp.**
1920　Forty-Five Minutes from Broadway
Peaceful Valley
Charles Richman Co. see also **Charles Richman Pictures Corp.**
1919　Everybody's Business
Charles Richman Pictures Corp. see also **Charles Richman Co.**
1917　Over There
Charter Features Corp.
1917　The Lincoln Cycle
Chautard, Emile, Pictures Corp. see **Emile Chautard Pictures Corp.**
The Chicago Tribune
1915　The German Side of the War
Russian Battlefields
Chopin Features
1920　The Little Outcast
Christie Film Co.
1920　813
So Long Letty
Cinart
1920　Roman Candles
Cinema Distributing Corp.
1919　Ginger
Circle Film Corp.
1915　Thou Shalt Not Kill
Circle H Film Co.
1919　When the Desert Smiles

Dra-Ko Film Co.
1915 York State Folks
Dramafilms
1920 Bitter Fruit
Dramascope Co.
1914 The $5,000,000 Counterfeiting
      Plot
Dudley Motion Picture Mfg. Co.
1916 Humanizing Mr. Winsby
      The Land Just Over Yonder
Duplex Films, Inc.
1917 Shame
Dustin Farnum Productions, Inc.
1920 Big Happiness
Dwan, Allan, Productions *see* **Allan Dwan
Productions**
Dyreda Art Film Corp.
1914 In the Name of the Prince of
      Peace
      One of Millions
1915 Always in the Way
      The Daughter of the People
      Four Feathers

E

E. D. Horkheimer
1917 Bab the Fixer
      The Wildcat
E. I. S. Motion Picture Corp.
1917 Trooper 44
E. K. O. Film Co.
1916 The Invisible Enemy
Eagle Film Co.
1915 Passing of the Oklahoma
      Outlaw
Eastern Film Corp.
1915 Cap'n Eri
1920 Beyond the Great Wall
Ebony Film Corp. of Chicago
1920 Do the Dead Talk?
Eclair Film Co.
1914 The Kangaroo
Eclectic Film Co.
1914 The Boundary Rider
      The Corsair
      Detective Craig's Coup
      The Giants-White Sox Tour
      The Last Volunteer
      The Money Lender
      The Pawn of Fortune
      A Prince of India
      The Quest of the Sacred Jewel
      The Reign of Terror
      The Taint
      When Rome Ruled
Edgar Lewis Productions, Inc.
1917 The Bar Sinister
1918 The Sign Invisible
1919 Calibre 38
      Love and the Law
1920 A Beggar in Purple
      Lahoma
      Other Men's Shoes
      Sherry
Edison, Thomas A., Inc. *see* **Thomas A.
Edison, Inc.**
Edmonde, Frances, Productions *see*
Frances Edmonde Productions
Educational Films Corp. of America
1915 American Game Trails
1917 Alaska Wonders in Motion
1918 Your Fighting Navy at Work
      and at Play
1920 The Key to Power
Edward A. Salisbury
1915 The Footsteps of Capt. Kidd
      On the Spanish Main
      Pirate Haunts
      Wild Life of America in Films
Edward José Productions
1920 Mothers of Men
Edward Warren Productions
1917 The Warfare of the Flesh
      Weavers of Life
1919 Thunderbolts of Fate
Edwin Carewe Productions, Inc.
1920 Rio Grande
      The Web of Deceit

Edyth Totten Features
1914 A Factory Magdalen
Efanel Film Corp.
1920 The Secret Formula
Eff & Eff Producing Co.
1919 Bullin' the Bullsheviki
Egan Film Co.
1916 America Preparing*
Eight Bells Film Co.
1918 Eight Bells‡
El Dorado Feature Film Co.
1916 The Impersonation
Elk Photoplays, Inc.
1919 Are You Legally Married?
1920 Why Tell?
Ellay Co.
1913 One Hundred Years of
      Mormonism
Elliott, Comstock and Gest
1918 Hearts of the World*
Elm Features
1915 Was She to Blame? Or, Souls
      That Meet in the Dark
Elmer J. McGovern
1920 The Woman Untamed
Emerald Motion Picture Co.
1917 The Slacker's Heart
Emerald Pictures Co.
1918 The Million Dollar Dollies
Emerson, John-Anita Loos Productions
see **John Emerson-Anita Loos
Productions**
Emile Chautard Pictures Corp.
1919 The Mystery of the Yellow
      Room
1920 The Invisible Foe
Eminent Authors Pictures, Inc.
1919 The Girl from Outside
1920 The Cup of Fury
      Dangerous Days
      Going Some
      It's a Great Life
      The North Wind's Malice
      Out of the Storm
      Partners of the Night
      The Penalty
      Scratch My Back
      The Silver Horde
      The Street Called Straight
Emory Film Corp.
1919 The Chosen Path
Empey, Guy, Pictures Corp. *see* **Guy
Empey Pictures Corp.**
Empire All Star Corp. *same as* **Empire
All-Star Corp.**
1917 The Beautiful Adventure
      Her Sister
      Outcast
      Please Help Emily
      The Runaway
      The Unforseen
1918 The Girl and the Judge
      The Impostor
      My Wife
      The Richest Girl
Empire State Film Corp.
1920 The Bromley Case
      The Desert Scorpion*
      The Unseen Witness
      The Wall Street Mystery
En l'Air Cinema, Ltd.
1918 A Romance of the Air
Epoch Producing Corp.
1915 The Birth of a Nation
Equality Photo-Play Corp.
1920 Why Leave Your Husband?
Equitable Motion Pictures Corp.
1915 The Better Woman
      The Bludgeon
      Blue Grass
      The Cowardly Way
      The Daughter of the Sea
      Divorced
      The Labyrinth
      The Master of the House
      Not Guilty
      The Price
      Sealed Lips
      The Senator
      Should a Wife Forgive?
      Trilby
      The Warning

1915-16
      The Little Church Around the
      Corner
1916 Behind Closed Doors
      The Birth of Character
      By Whose Hand?
      The Chain Invisible
      A Circus Romance
      The Clarion
      The Devil's Toy
      The Dragon
      The Heart of New York
      Her Great Hour
      Idols
      Man and His Angel
      Passers By
      The Price of Happiness
      The Question
      The Ransom
      The Reapers
      The Shadow of a Doubt
      The Struggle
      The Twin Triangle
      The Woman in 47
1917 The Tides of Fate
Equity Pictures Corp.
1919 Eyes of Youth
      Who's Your Brother?*
1920 For the Soul of Rafael
      The Forbidden Woman
      Mid-Channel
      Silk Husbands and Calico
      Wives
      Whispering Devils
Erbograph Co.
1917 The Inevitable
      Infidelity
      Little Miss Fortune
      The Little Samaritan
      The Moral Code
      The Road Between
1920 The Victim
Ernest Shipman
1913 From Dusk to Dawn
1918 Berlin Via America
      The Crime of the Hour
      Denny from Ireland
      The Lady of the Dugout
      The Pen Vulture
      The Prisoner of War
      The Ranger
      The Snail
1919 Tiger of the Sea
Essanay Film Mfg. Co.
1914 The Good-for-Nothing
      The Indian Wars
      One Wonderful Night
1915 The Alster Case
      The Blindness of Virtue
      A Bunch of Keys
      The Crimson Wing
      A Daughter of the City
      Graustark
      In the Palace of the King
      The Man Trail
      The Raven
      The Slim Princess
      The White Sister
1916 According to the Code
      The Breaker
      Captain Jinks of the Horse
      Marines
      The Chaperon
      Charlie Chaplin's Burlesque on
      "Carmen"
      The Discard
      The Essanay-Chaplin Revue of
      1916
      The Havoc
      The Little Girl Next Door
      The Little Shepherd of Bargain
      Row
      The Misleading Lady
      The Phantom Buccaneer
      The Prince of Graustark
      The Return of Eve
      Sherlock Holmes
      The Sting of Victory
      That Sort
      The Truant Soul
      Vultures of Society
1917 The Adventures of Buffalo Bill
      Burning the Candle
      The Dream Doll
      Efficiency Edgar's Courtship

      The Fibbers
      Filling His Own Shoes
      Fools for Luck
      Gift O' Gab
      The Golden Idiot
      The Kill-Joy
      The Land of Long Shadows
      Little Shoes
      The Man Who Was Afraid
      Men of the Desert
      The Night Workers
      On Trial
      Open Places
      Pants
      The Range Boss
      Sadie Goes to Heaven
      The Saint's Adventure
      Satan's Private Door
      Skinner's Baby
      Skinner's Bubble
      Skinner's Dress Suit
      The Small Town Guy
      The Trufflers
      Two-Bit Seats
      Young Mother Hubbard
1918 Chase Me Charlie
      The Curse of Iku
      Men Who Have Made Love to
      Me
      Movie Marionettes
      A Pair of Sixes
      Ruggles of Red Gap
      Uneasy Money
Estes, Martin *see* **Martin Estes**
Eugenic Film Co.
1917 Birth
European Film Co.
1916 Fighting for Verdun
Eva Tanguay Film Corp. *see also* **Eva
Tanguay Films**
1917 The Wild Girl
Eva Tanguay Films *see also* **Eva Tanguay
Film Corp.**
1916 Energetic Eva
Excelsior Feature Film Co.
1914 The Path Forbidden
      The Toll of Mammon
      When Fate Leads Trump
1915 In the Shadow
Exclusive Features, Inc.
1915 The Victory of Virtue
1916 The Country That God Forgot*
      Pamela's Past
      The Unwritten Law*
      Where Is My Father?
1919 The Chosen Path
Exclusive Supply Corp.
1913 The Rogues of Paris
Exhibitors Booking Agency
1916 How Life Begins
Exhibitors Mutual Distributing Corp.
same as **Exhibitor's Mutual
Distributing Corp.** *and* **Exhibitors'
Mutual Distributing Corp.**
1918 And a Still Small Voice
      The Girl of My Dreams
      Lafayette, We Come!
1919 All of a Sudden Norma
      Bare-Fisted Gallagher
      Better Times
      The Blue Bandanna
      Bonds of Honor
      The Courageous Coward
      Dangerous Waters
      Diane of the Green Van
      The Dragon Painter
      For a Woman's Honor
      The Gray Horizon
      A Heart in Pawn
      Hearts Asleep
      Her Purchase Price
      His Debt
      Hoop-La
      The House of Intrigue
      In Search of Arcady
      Josselyn's Wife
      Just Squaw
      Kitty Kelly, M.D.
      The Lamb and the Lion
      Life's a Funny Proposition
      The Long Lane's Turning
      The Love Call
      The Man Beneath
      A Man's Country

Pettigrew's Girl
The Poor Boob
Puppy Love
Putting It Over
The Rescuing Angel
The Roaring Road
Rose O' the River
Rustling a Bride
Sadie Love
The Secret Garden
Secret Service
The Silver King
A Society Exile
Something to Do
The Splendid Romance
A Sporting Chance
The Teeth of the Tiger
The Test of Honor
The Third Kiss
Three Men and a Girl
Told in the Hills
The Two Brides
Under the Top
The Valley of the Giants
Venus in the East
A Very Good Young Man
Wanted—A Husband
Why Smith Left Home
Widow by Proxy
The Winning Girl
The Witness for the Defense
The Woman Next Door
The Woman Thou Gavest Me
You Never Saw Such a Girl
You're Fired
1920 Alarm Clock Andy
All-of-a-Sudden-Peggy
Always Audacious
An Amateur Devil
The Amateur Wife
American Catholics in War
   and Reconstruction
Away Goes Prudence
Behold My Wife
Burglar Proof
The City of Masks
A City Sparrow
Civilian Clothes
Conrad in Quest of His Youth
The Copperhead
The Cost
Crooked Streets
The Dancin' Fool
The Dark Mirror
Dr. Jekyll and Mr. Hyde
Double Speed
Easy to Get
Excuse My Dust
The Fighting Chance
The Fourteenth Man
The Frisky Mrs. Johnson
A Full House
Guilty of Love
Half an Hour
Held by the Enemy
His House in Order
Huckleberry Finn
Jack Straw
The Ladder of Lies
A Lady in Love
Lady Rose's Daughter
Life
The Life of the Party
Mrs. Temple's Telegram
On with the Dance
The Prince Chap
A Romantic Adventuress
The Sea Wolf
Sick Abed
Silk Hosiery
The Sins of Rosanne
The Sins of St. Anthony
The Six Best Cellars
Terror Island
The Thirteenth Commandment
Thou Art the Man
Too Much Johnson
The Tree of Knowledge
What Happened to Jones
What's Your Hurry?
Why Change Your Wife?
Young Mrs. Winthrop
1921 Midsummer Madness

Famous Players-Lasky Corp.; Artcraft Pictures see also **Artcraft Pictures Corp.**
1918 Amarilly of Clothes-Line Alley
Arizona
The Blue Bird
Blue Blazes Rawden
The Border Wireless
Bound in Morocco
Branding Broadway
The Danger Mark
A Doll's House
Fuss and Feathers
The Goat
The Great Love
The Greatest Thing in Life
He Comes Up Smiling
Headin' South
Heart of the Wilds
Hit-the-Trail Holliday
How Could You, Jean?
Johanna Enlists
The Lie
Mr. Fix-It
M'liss
My Cousin
Old Wives for New
Say, Young Fellow!
Selfish Yates
Shark Monroe
The Song of Songs
The Squaw Man
Stella Maris
The Tiger Man
Till I Come Back to You
Under the Greenwood Tree
We Can't Have Everything
The Whispering Chorus
Wolves of the Rail
1919 The Avalanche
Breed of Men
Broken Blossoms*
Captain Kidd, Jr.
Don't Change Your Husband
Eyes of the Soul
For Better, for Worse
The Girl Who Stayed at Home
His Parisian Wife
Johnny Get Your Gun
The Knickerbocker Buckaroo
The Marriage Price
The Money Corral
The Poppy Girl's Husband
A Romance of Happy Valley
A Society Exile
The Splendid Romance
Square Deal Sanderson
True Heart Susie
Under the Top
Wagon Tracks
1920 The Cradle of Courage
The Toll Gate

Famous Players-Lasky Corp.; Paramount-Artcraft Pictures see also **Artcraft Pictures Corp.** and **Paramount Pictures Corp.**
1918 The Hun Within
Private Peat
1919 An Adventure in Hearts
L'Apache
Behind the Door
The Career of Katherine Bush
The Cinema Murder
Counterfeit
Crooked Straight
The Dark Star
Everywoman
The False Faces
The Firing Line
A Girl Named Mary
The Grim Game
Hawthorne of the U.S.A.
His Official Fiancée
His Wife's Friend
In Mizzoura
The Invisible Bond
It Pays to Advertise
John Petticoats
Little Women
The Lottery Man
Male and Female
The Market of Souls
The Miracle Man
The Miracle of Love
The Misleading Widow

More Deadly Than the Male
Red Hot Dollars
Sadie Love
Scarlet Days
The Silver King
The Teeth of the Tiger
Told in the Hills
Turning the Tables
23 1/2 Hours' Leave
Victory
Wanted—A Husband
What Every Woman Learns
The White Heather
Why Smith Left Home
Widow by Proxy
The Witness for the Defense
The Woman Thou Gavest Me
1920 Alarm Clock Andy
All-of-a-Sudden-Peggy
The Amateur Wife
April Folly
Away Goes Prudence
Black Is White
The City of Masks
The Copperhead
The Cost
Crooked Streets
The Dancin' Fool
Dangerous Hours
The Dark Mirror
Dr. Jekyll and Mr. Hyde
Double Speed
Easy to Get
Excuse My Dust
The False Road
The Fighting Chance
A Full House
Guilty of Love
Hairpins
His House in Order
Homer Comes Home
Huckleberry Finn
Humoresque
Jack Straw
The Ladder of Lies
A Lady in Love
Lady Rose's Daughter
Let's Be Fashionable
Mary Ellen Comes to Town
Mary's Ankle
Mrs. Temple's Telegram
My Lady's Garter
On with the Dance
Paris Green
The Prince Chap
Remodelling Her Husband
The Right to Love
The Round-Up
Sand!
The Sea Wolf
Sick Abed
The Sins of St. Anthony
The Six Best Cellars
Terror Island
The Thirteenth Commandment
Thou Art the Man
Too Much Johnson
Treasure Island
The Tree of Knowledge
What Happened to Jones
What's Your Husband Doing?
The White Circle
Why Change Your Wife?
The World and His Wife
Young Mrs. Winthrop

Famous Players-Lasky Corp.; Paramount Pictures see also **Paramount Pictures Corp.**
1918 Battling Jane
Believe Me Xantippe
The Biggest Show on Earth
The Bravest Way
The City of Dim Faces
The Claws of the Hun
Coals of Fire
Come On In
The Cruise of the
   Make-Believes
A Daughter of the Old South
A Desert Wooing
Eve's Daughter
The Family Skeleton
Fedora
The Firefly of France
"Flare-Up" Sal

The Girl Who Came Back
Good-Bye, Bill
Green Eyes
The Gypsy Trail
Her Country First
Her Final Reckoning
Hidden Pearls
The Hired Man
His Majesty, Bunker Bean
His Own Home Town
The Honor of His House
The Hope Chest
The House of Silence
Huck and Tom; Or, The
   Further Adventures of Tom
   Sawyer
In Pursuit of Polly
The Kaiser's Shadow, or the
   Triple Cross
Keys of the Righteous
The Law of the North
Less Than Kin
Little Miss Hoover
Love Me
Love's Conquest
Madame Jealousy
The Make-Believe Wife
The Man from Funeral Range
The Marriage Ring
The Mating of Marcella
Mile-a-Minute Kendall
Mirandy Smiles
Missing
The Mystery Girl
Naughty, Naughty!
On the Quiet
One More American
Out of a Clear Sky
A Petticoat Pilot
Playing the Game
Prunella
Resurrection
Rich Man, Poor Man
Rimrock Jones
The Sand Rat
Sandy
The Source
String Beans
Such a Little Pirate
Sunshine Nan
The Thing We Love
Too Many Millions
La Tosca
Tyrant Fear
Unclaimed Goods
Uncle Tom's Cabin
The Vamp
Vive La France!
Viviette
The Way of a Man with a
   Maid
We Can't Have Everything
When Do We Eat?
The Whispering Chorus
The White Man's Law
Wild Youth
A Woman of Impulse
Women's Weapons
1919 Alias Mike Moran
Bill Henry
Boots
The Busher
Come Out of the Kitchen
A Daughter of the Wolf
The Dub
The Egg Crate Wallop
Extravagance
The Final Close-Up
Fires of Faith
The Girl Dodger
Girls
Good Gracious, Annabelle
Greased Lightning
Happy Though Married
Hard Boiled
The Haunted Bedroom
Hay Foot, Straw Foot
The Heart of Youth
Here Comes the Bride
The Home Town Girl
The Homebreaker
I'll Get Him Yet
An Innocent Adventuress
Jane Goes A-Wooing
The Lady of Red Butte

The Soul of Broadway
The Two Orphans
The Unfaithful Wife
A Woman's Past
A Woman's Resurrection
The Wonderful Adventure
Wormwood
1916 Ambition
The Battle of Hearts
The Battle of Life
The Beast
Blazing Love
Blue Blood and Red
The Bondman
Caprice of the Mountains
Daredevil Kate
A Daughter of the Gods
East Lynne
The End of the Trail
The Eternal Sapho
Fighting Blood
The Fires of Conscience
The Fool's Revenge
The Fourth Estate
Gold and the Woman
The Green-Eyed Monster
Her Double Life
Hypocrisy
Jealousy
Little Miss Happiness
Love and Hate
The Love Thief
The Man from Bitter Roots
A Man of Sorrow
The Marble Heart
The Mediator
Merely Mary Ann
The Mischief Maker
A Modern Thelma
A Parisian Romance
The Ragged Princess
Romeo and Juliet
The Ruling Passion
The Serpent
Sins of Her Parent
Sins of Men
Slander
The Spider and the Fly
Sporting Blood
The Straight Way
A Tortured Heart
Under Two Flags
The Unwelcome Mother
The Victim
The Vixen
The War Bride's Secret
Where Love Leads
A Wife's Sacrifice
The Witch
A Woman's Honor
1917 Aladdin and the Wonderful
Lamp
All for a Husband
American Methods
The Babes in the Woods
Betrayed
The Bitter Truth
The Blue Streak
The Book Agent
A Branded Soul
The Broadway Sport
Camille
A Child of the Wild
Cleopatra
The Conqueror
Conscience
The Darling of Paris
The Derelict
Du Barry
Durand of the Bad Lands
Every Girl's Dream
The Final Payment
For Liberty
Heart and Soul
The Heart of a Lion
Her Greatest Love
Her Temptation
High Finance
The Honor System
The Innocent Sinner
The Island of Desire
Jack and the Beanstalk
Love's Law
Melting Millions
Miss U.S.A.

A Modern Cinderella
The New York Peacock
North of Fifty-Three
One Touch of Sin
The Painted Madonna
Patsy
The Price of Silence
The Pride of New York
The Primitive Call
A Rich Man's Plaything
The Rose of Blood
Royal Romance
The Scarlet Letter
The Scarlet Pimpernel
She
The Silent Lie
The Siren
Sister Against Sister
The Slave
The Small Town Girl
Some Boy!
The Soul of Satan
The Spy
The Sunshine Maid
A Tale of Two Cities
Tangled Lives
This Is the Life
Thou Shalt Not Steal
The Tiger Woman
To Honor and Obey
Troublemakers
Two Little Imps
Unknown 274
When a Man Sees Red
When False Tongues Speak
Wife Number Two
Wrath of Love
The Yankee Way
1918 Ace High
Ali Baba and the Forty Thieves
American Buds
The Bird of Prey
The Blindness of Divorce
Blue-Eyed Mary
Bonnie Annie Laurie
Brave and Bold
The Bride of Fear
Buchanan's Wife
The Caillaux Case
A Camouflage Kiss
Caught in the Act
Cheating the Public
Confession
Cupid's Roundup
The Danger Zone
A Daughter of France
The Debt of Honor
The Devil's Wheel
Doing Their Bit
Every Mother's Son
The Fallen Angel
Fame and Fortune
Fan Fan
The Firebrand
For Freedom
The Forbidden Path
The Girl with the Champagne
Eyes
The Heart of Romance
A Heart's Revenge
Her One Mistake
Her Price
I Want to Forget
I'll Say So
Jack Spurlock, Prodigal
The Kid Is Clever
Kultur
Lawless Love
The Liar
Marriages Are Made
Les Miserables
Miss Innocence
Mr. Logan, U.S.A.
The Moral Law
On the Jump
Other Men's Daughters
Peg of the Pirates
The Prussian Cur
The Queen of Hearts
Queen of the Sea
The Rainbow Trail
Riders of the Purple Sage
Rough and Ready
Salome
The Scarlet Road

The Seventy-Five Mile Gun
The She-Devil
Six Shooter Andy
The Soul of Buddha
Stolen Honor
The Strange Woman
Swat the Spy
Tell It to the Marines
Treasure Island
True Blue
Under the Yoke
We Should Worry
Western Blood
When a Woman Sins
Why America Will Win
Why I Would Not Marry
Woman and the Law
The Woman Who Gave
1919 Be a Little Sport
La Belle Russe
Broken Commandments
The Call of the Soul
Chasing Rainbows
Cheating Herself
Checkers
The Coming of the Law
Cowardice Court
The Divorce Trap
Eastward Ho!
Evangeline
A Fallen Idol
The Feud
Fighting for Gold
The Forbidden Room
Gambling in Souls
A Girl in Bohemia
The Girl with No Regrets
Hell Roarin' Reform
Help! Help! Police!
The Jungle Trail
Kathleen Mavourneen
The Last of the Duanes
The Light
The Lincoln Highwayman
The Lone Star Ranger
Lost Money
The Lost Princess
The Love Auction
Love Is Love
The Love That Dares
Luck and Pluck
Lure of Ambition
The Man Hunter
Married in Haste
The Merry-Go-Round
Miss Adventure
My Little Sister
Never Say Quit
Pitfalls of a Big City
Putting One Over
The Rebellious Bride
Rose of the West
Rough Riding Romance
Sacred Silence
Should a Husband Forgive?
The Siren's Song
Smiles
Snares of Paris
The Sneak
The Speed Maniac
The Splendid Sin
Thieves
Thou Shalt Not
Tin Pan Alley
Treat 'Em Rough
Vagabond Luck
The Web of Chance
When Fate Decides
When Men Desire
The Wilderness Trail
Wings of the Morning
The Winning Stroke
Wolves of the Night
A Woman There Was
Woman, Woman!
Words and Music By—
1920 The Adventurer
Beware of the Bride
Black Shadows
Blind Wives
The Challenge of the Law
A Connecticut Yankee at King
Arthur's Court
The Cyclone
The Daredevil

The Dead Line
Desert Love
The Devil's Riddle
Drag Harlan
The Face at Your Window
Faith
Firebrand Trevison
Flame of Youth
Flames of the Flesh
Forbidden Trails
From Now On
The Girl of My Heart
Heart Strings
The Hell Ship
Her Elephant Man
Her Honor the Mayor
Husband Hunter
If I Were King
The Iron Heart
The Iron Rider
The Joyous Troublemaker
Just Pals
The Land of Jazz
The Last Straw
Leave It to Me
The Little Grey Mouse
The Little Wanderer
Love's Harvest
The Man Who Dared
A Manhattan Knight
Merely Mary Ann
Molly and I
The Mother of His Children
The Orphan
Over the Hill to the Poorhouse
The Plunger
Prairie Trails
The Rose of Nome
The Scuttlers
The Shark
Shod with Fire
Sink or Swim
A Sister to Salome
The Skywayman
The Spirit of Good
The Square Shooter
The Strongest
Sunset Sprague
The Tattlers
The Terror
The Texan
The Thief
Three Gold Coins
The Tiger's Cub
Twins of Suffering Creek
Two Moons
The Untamed
What Would You Do?
While New York Sleeps
White Lies
The White Moll
A World of Folly
Would You Forgive?

Fox-Fischer Masterplays, Inc.
1920 In the Shadow of the Dome
Fox, William, Vaudeville Co. *see* **William**
Fox Vaudeville Co.
France Films, Inc.
1917 The Natural Law
Frances Edmonde Productions
1920 The Unfortunate Sex
Frank A. Keeney Pictures Corp.
1918 Marriage
Out of the Night
A Romance of the Underworld
The Uphill Path
1919 Marriage for Convenience
Frank E. Moore
1913 Hiawatha
Frank G. Hall
1917 Her Fighting Chance
1919 The Other Man's Wife
Frank Gersten, Inc.
1920 The Unfortunate Sex
Frank J. Carroll
1917 For the Freedom of the World
1918 The Woman the Germans Shot
Frank Keenan Productions, Inc.
1919 Brothers Divided
The False Code
Gates of Brass
The Master Man
The World Aflame

Glaum, Louise, Organization see **Louise Glaum Organization**

Globe Feature Picture Booking Co.
1915 Vengeance of the Wilds
      Where Cowboy Is King

Gold Medal Photo Players
1917 The Web of Life

Gold Rooster Plays see **Pathé Exchange, Inc.**

Gold Seal Film Corp.
1920 When Quackel Did Hide

Golden West Producing Co. same as **Golden West Photoplay Co.** and **Golden West Productions**
1919 Red Blood and Yellow
      The Son-of-a-Gun!

Goldwyn Distributing Corp. see also **Goldwyn Pictures Corp.**
1917 The Auction Block
      Baby Mine
      The Cinderella Man
      Fighting Odds
      For the Freedom of the World
      Nearly Married
      Polly of the Circus
      The Spreading Dawn
      Sunshine Alley
      Thais
1918 Blue Blood
      The Border Legion
      The Danger Game
      Dodging a Million
      The Face in the Dark
      The Fair Pretender
      The Floor Below
      For the Freedom of the East
      Friend Husband
      The Glorious Adventure
      Go West, Young Man
      Heart of the Sunset
      The Hell Cat
      Hidden Fires
      Honor's Cross
      Joan of Plattsburg
      Just for Tonight
      The Kingdom of Youth
      Laughing Bill Hyde
      Money Mad
      Oh, Johnny!
      Our Little Wife
      Peck's Bad Girl
      A Perfect Lady
      A Perfect 36
      The Racing Strain
      The Service Star
      Thirty a Week
      Too Fat to Fight
      The Turn of the Wheel
      The Venus Model
1919 Almost a Husband
      The Bondage of Barbara
      Bonds of Love
      The Brand
      The City of Comrades
      The Crimson Gardenia
      Daughter of Mine
      Day Dreams
      The Eternal Magdalene
      The Fear Woman
      Flame of the Desert
      The Gay Lord Quex
      The Girl from Outside
      Heartsease
      High Pockets
      Jinx
      Jubilo
      Leave It to Susan
      Lord and Lady Algy
      The Loves of Letty
      A Man and His Money
      A Misfit Earl
      One of the Finest
      One Week of Life
      The Peace of Roaring River
      The Pest
      The Road Called Straight
      Sandy Burke of the U-Bar-U
      Shadows
      Sis Hopkins
      Speedy Meade
      Spotlight Sadie
      Strictly Confidential
      The Stronger Vow
      Through the Wrong Door

Toby's Bow
Upstairs
When Doctors Disagree
The Woman on the Index
The World and Its Woman
1920 The Blooming Angel
      The Branding Iron
      The Cup of Fury
      Cupid, the Cowpuncher
      Dangerous Days
      Dollars and Sense
      A Double Dyed Deceiver
      Duds
      Earthbound
      The Girl with the Jazz Heart
      Godless Men
      Going Some
      The Great Accident
      The Great Lover
      Help Yourself
      His Own Law
      Honest Hutch
      It's a Great Life
      Jes' Call Me Jim
      Just Out of College
      The Little Shepherd of
        Kingdom Come
      Madame X
      The Man Who Had Everything
      Milestones
      The North Wind's Malice
      Officer 666
      Out of the Storm
      The Paliser Case
      Partners of the Night
      The Penalty
      Pinto
      The Return of Tarzan
      Scratch My Back
      The Silver Horde
      The Slim Princess
      The Song of the Soul
      Stop Thief
      The Strange Boarder
      The Street Called Straight
      The Truth
      Water, Water Everywhere
      What Happened to Rosa
      The Woman and the Puppet
      The Woman in Room 13

Goldwyn Pictures Corp. see also **Goldwyn Distributing Corp.**
1917 Baby Mine
      The Cinderella Man
      Fighting Odds
      Nearly Married
      Polly of the Circus
      The Spreading Dawn
      Sunshine Alley
      Thais
1918 All Woman
      Back to the Woods
      The Beloved Traitor
      The Danger Game
      Dodging a Million
      The Face in the Dark
      The Fair Pretender
      Fields of Honor
      The Floor Below
      Friend Husband
      The Glorious Adventure
      Go West, Young Man
      The Hell Cat
      Hidden Fires
      Joan of Plattsburg
      Just for Tonight
      The Kingdom of Youth
      Money Mad
      Our Little Wife
      Peck's Bad Girl
      A Perfect Lady
      A Perfect 36
      The Racing Strain
      Social Ambition
      The Splendid Sinner
      Thirty a Week
      The Turn of the Wheel
      The Venus Model
1919 Almost a Husband
      The Bondage of Barbara
      Bonds of Love
      The Brand
      The City of Comrades
      The Crimson Gardenia
      Daughter of Mine

Day Dreams
The Eternal Magdalene
The Fear Woman
Fit to Win*
Flame of the Desert
The Gay Lord Quex
Heartsease
Jinx
Jubilo
Leave It to Susan
Lord and Lady Algy
The Loves of Letty
A Man and His Money
One of the Finest
One Week of Life
The Peace of Roaring River
The Pest
Shadows
Sis Hopkins
Spotlight Sadie
Strictly Confidential
The Stronger Vow
Through the Wrong Door
Toby's Bow
Upstairs
When Doctors Disagree
The Woman on the Index
The World and Its Woman
1920 The Blooming Angel
      The Branding Iron
      Cupid, the Cowpuncher
      Dollars and Sense
      A Double Dyed Deceiver
      Duds
      Earthbound
      The Girl with the Jazz Heart
      Godless Men
      The Great Accident
      The Great Lover
      Help Yourself
      His Own Law*
      Honest Hutch
      Jes' Call Me Jim
      Just Out of College
      The Little Shepherd of
        Kingdom Come
      Madame X
      The Man Who Had Everything
      Milestones
      Officer 666
      The Paliser Case
      Pinto
      The Slim Princess
      Stop Thief
      The Strange Boarder
      The Truth
      Water, Water Everywhere
      What Happened to Rosa
      The Woman and the Puppet
      The Woman in Room 13

Good Luck Film Co.
1915 The Battle of Ballots

Goodman, Daniel Carson see **Daniel Carson Goodman**

Gordon, Kitty, Film Corp. see **Kitty Gordon Film Corp.**

Gotham Film Co.
1914 The Life of Big Tim Sullivan;
        Or, From Newsboy to
        Senator
1915 The Man Who Beat Dan Dolan
      A Trade Secret

The Governor's Boss Photoplay Co.
1915 The Governor's Boss

Grafton Publishing Film Co.
1916 The Argonauts of
        California—1849

Grand Feature Film Co.
1915 The Footsteps of Capt. Kidd
      On the Spanish Main
      Pirate Haunts

Graphic Features not the same as **Graphic Film Corp.**
1917 The Woman and the Beast

Graphic Film Corp. not the same as **Graphic Features**
1918 Ashes of Love
      Moral Suicide
      When Men Betray
1919 The Echo of Youth
      Someone Must Pay
1920 A Child for Sale
      The Wrong Woman

Great Authors' Pictures, Inc.
1919 The Westerners
1920 The Sagebrusher
      The Spenders

Great Players Feature Film Corp.
1914 Escaped from Siberia
      Uriel Acosta

Great West Film Co.
1918 The Sunset Princess

Greater Vitagraph, Inc. same as **Vitagraph—V-L-S-E, Inc.** see also **Greater Vitagraph (V-L-S-E); Greater Vitagraph (V-L-S-E, Inc.)** and **V-L-S-E, Inc.**
1917 His Own People
      In the Balance
      When Men Are Tempted
1918 All Man
      An American Live Wire
      A Bachelor's Children
      Baree, Son of Kazan
      The Beloved Impostor
      The Blind Adventure
      The Business of Life
      By the World Forgot
      Cavanaugh of the Forest
        Rangers
      The Changing Woman
      The Clutch of Circumstance
      The Dawn of Understanding
      The Desired Woman
      Everybody's Girl
      Find the Woman
      A Game with Fate
      A Gentleman's Agreement
      The Girl from Beyond
      The Girl in His House
      The Girl of Today
      The Golden Goal
      The Green God
      Hoarded Assets
      The Home Trail
      The King of Diamonds
      Little Miss No-Account
      The Little Runaway
      Love Watches
      The Man Who Wouldn't Tell
      The Mating
      The Menace
      Miss Ambition
      A Mother's Sin
      A Nymph of the Foothills
      One Thousand Dollars
      The Other Man
      Over the Top
      The Seal of Silence
      The Soap Girl
      The Song of the Soul
      Tangled Lives
      To the Highest Bidder
      The Triumph of the Weak
      Wild Primrose
      The Wild Strain
      The Woman Between Friends
      The Wooing of Princess Pat
1919 The Adventure Shop
      The Captain's Captain

Greater Vitagraph (V-L-S-E) same as **Vitagraph—V-L-S-E, Inc.** see also **Greater Vitagraph, Inc.; Greater Vitagraph (V-L-S-E, Inc.)** and **V-L-S-E, Inc.**
1917 An Alabaster Box
      The Bottom of the Well
      By Right of Possession
      The Captain of the Gray Horse
        Troop
      Clover's Rebellion
      Dead Shot Baker
      The Divorcee
      The Fettered Woman
      The Flaming Omen
      For France
      The Grell Mystery
      I Will Repay
      The Love Doctor
      The Maelstrom
      The Magnificent Meddler
      The Marriage Speculation
      Mary Jane's Pa
      The Message of the Mouse
      Next Door to Nancy
      The Princess of Park Row
      The Question
      Richard the Brazen

The Sixteenth Wife
Soldiers of Chance
A Son of the Hills
The Soul Master
The Stolen Treaty
Sunlight's Last Raid
The Tenderfoot
Transgression
Who Goes There!
Within the Law

Greater Vitagraph (V-L-S-E, Inc.) same as **Vitagraph—V-L-S-E, Inc.** see also **Greater Vitagraph, Inc.; Greater Vitagraph (V-S-L-E);** and **V-L-S-E, Inc.**
1916 The Blue Envelope Mystery
The Dollar and the Law
The Enemy
An Enemy to the King
The Girl Philippa
The Price of Fame
A Prince in a Pawnshop
Rose of the South
Through the Wall
Whom the Gods Destroy
1917 Aladdin from Broadway
Apartment 29
Arsene Lupin
Babette
The Courage of Silence
The Glory of Yolanda
The Hawk
Her Right to Live
Her Secret
Indiscretion
Intrigue
Kitty MacKay
The Man of Mystery
Money Magic
The Money Mill
The More Excellent Way
Sally in a Hurry
Womanhood, the Glory of the Nation

Green Co.
1915 Winning the Futurity
Grey, Zane, Pictures, Inc. see **Zane Grey Pictures, Inc.**
Griffith, D. W. see **D. W. Griffith**
Griffith, D. W., Inc. see **D. W. Griffith, Inc.**
Griffith, D. W., Service see **D. W. Griffith Service**
Griffith, David W., Corp. see **David W. Griffith Corp.**
Grossman Pictures
1920 Wits vs. Wits
Gruver, P. F. see **P. F. Gruver**
Guy Croswell Smith
1920 The County Fair
Guy Empey Pictures Corp.
1919 The Undercurrent
1920 Oil

H

H. N. Nelson Attractions
1918 The Mysterious Mr. Browning
Hagy Features
1914 The Flooding and Opening of the Panama Canal
Hall, Frank G. see **Frank G. Hall**
Hall, P. J. see **P. J. Hall**
Hallmark Pictures Corp.
1918 The Ghost of Rosy Taylor*
Impossible Susan*
Social Briars
Up Romance Road*
1919 A Dangerous Affair
The Heart of a Gypsy
Love, Honor and—?
The Phantom Honeymoon
1920 Chains of Evidence
The Common Sin
The Discarded Woman
For Love or Money
High Speed
Should a Wife Work?
The Veiled Marriage
Wits vs. Wits

Hall's Western Productions
1920 Frontier Days
Hampton, Benjamin B., Productions see **Benjamin B. Hampton Productions**
Hampton, Hope, Productions, Inc. see **Hope Hampton Productions, Inc.**
Hampton, Jesse D., Features Corp. see **Jesse D. Hampton Features Corp.**
Hampton, Jesse D., Productions see **Jesse D. Hampton Productions**
Hanover Film Corp.
1916 Should a Baby Die?
1917 How Uncle Sam Prepares
Harbaugh, Carl Productions see **A Carl Harbaugh Production**
Harold Bell Wright Story Picture Corp.
1919 The Shepherd of the Hills
Harris, Charles K., Feature Film Co. see **Charles K. Harris Feature Film Co.**
Harry Garson see also **Garson Productions; Garson Studios, Inc.** and **Harry Garson Productions**
1919 The Unpardonable Sin
Harry Garson Productions see also **Garson Productions; Garson Studios, Inc.** and **Harry Garson**
1919 The Hushed Hour
1920 Whispering Devils
Harry Levey Productions
1920 Uncle Sam of Freedom Ridge
Harry McRae Webster Productions, Inc.
1919 Reclaimed: The Struggle for a Soul Between Love and Hate
Harry Rapf Productions
1918 The Sins of the Children
The Struggle Everlasting
Wanted for Murder
Harry Raver, Inc. see also **Artco Productions, Inc.** and **Raver Film Corp.**
1917 The Public Defender
1919 The Volcano
1920 Sophy of Kravonia; Or, The Virgin of Paris
Hart, William S., Co. see **William S. Hart Co.**
Hart, William S., Productions see **William S. Hart Productions**
Hatch, J. Frank, Enterprises see **J. Frank Hatch Enterprises**
Hawk Film Co. see also **Piedmont Pictures Corp.**
1918 A Son of Strife
Haworth Pictures Corp. same as **Haworth Pictures** and **Haworth Studios**
1918 His Birthright
The Temple of Dusk
1919 Bonds of Honor
The Courageous Coward
The Dragon Painter
The Gray Horizon
A Heart in Pawn
His Debt
The House of Intrigue
The Illustrious Prince
The Man Beneath
The Tong Man
1920 An Arabian Knight
The Beggar Prince
The Brand of Lopez
The Devil's Claim
Li Ting Lang
Moon Madness
Hearst newspapers
1915 The History of the World's Greatest War
Hector Film Corp.
1914 Born Again
Hefco Films
1914 The Lightning Conductor
Helen Gardner Film Co. see also **Helen Gardner Picture Players**
1920 Broken Hearts*
Helen Gardner Picture Players see also **Helen Gardner Film Co.**
1912 Cleopatra
1913 A Princess of Bagdad
A Sister to Carmen
1914 Pieces of Silver; A Story of Hearts and Souls

Helen Keller Film Corp.
1919 Deliverance
The Helgar Corp.
1914 Pieces of Silver; A Story of Hearts and Souls
Hemmer Superior Productions, Inc.
1920 Birthright
Henley, Hobart see **Hobart Henley**
Henley, Hobart, Productions see **Hobart Henley Productions**
Henry W. Savage, Inc.
1915 Excuse Me
1916 Madame X
Robinson Crusoe
Herbert Brenon Film Corp.
1916 War Brides
1917 The Eternal Sin
The Lone Wolf
1918 Empty Pockets
Herman J. Garfield
1920 The Parish Priest
Hermann Film Corp.
1920 That Something
High Art Productions, Inc.
1918 The Accidental Honeymoon
The Struggle Everlasting
Hiller & Wilk, Inc.
1917 A Mormon Maid
Raffles, the Amateur Cracksman
1918 Sporting Life
Woman
Hiller, L. L. see **L. L. Hiller**
Hiller, Lejaren a', Productions see **Lejaren a' Hiller Productions**
Hippodrome Film Co.
1916 At the Front with the Allies
Hiram Abrams see also **A Hiram Abrams Production**
1919 America Was Right‡
Hearts of Men
Yankee Doodle in Berlin
A Hiram Abrams Production see also **Hiram Abrams**
1919 Hearts of Men
Hobart Henley see also **Hobart Henley Productions**
1918 Parentage
Hobart Henley Productions see also **Hobart Henley**
1919 The Gay Old Dog
1920 The Miracle of Money
Hodkinson, W. W. see **W. W. Hodkinson**
Hodkinson, W. W., Corp. see **W. W. Hodkinson Corp.**
Hoffman, M. H., Inc. see **M. H. Hoffman, Inc.**
Holmes, Taylor, Productions, Inc. see **Taylor Holmes Productions, Inc.**
Hope Hampton Productions, Inc.
1920 A Modern Salome
Hopkins, Georgia, Picture Co. see **Georgia Hopkins Picture Co.**
Horkheimer Bros. see also **Balboa Amusement Co.; Balboa Amusement Producing Co.; Balboa Feature Film Co.; Falcon Features; Horkheimer Studios** and **Knickerbocker Star Features**
1915 Should a Wife Forgive?
Horkheimer, E. D. see **E. D. Horkheimer**
Horkheimer Studios see also **Balboa Amusement Co.; Balboa Amusement Producing Co.; Balboa Feature Film Co.; Falcon Features; Horkheimer Bros.** and **Knickerbocker Star Features**
1917 A Bit of Kindling
The Checkmate
The Girl Angle
Horsley, David, Productions see **David Horsley Productions**
Hub Cinemagraph Co. of Boston
1920 The Mysteries of Paris
Hudris Film Co.
1919 A Romance of Seattle
Hugh E. Dierker Photo Drama Productions
1920 When Dawn Came

Hugo Ballin Productions, Inc.
1920 Pagan Love
Humanology Film Producing Co.
1914 The Price He Paid
1915 Are They Born or Made?
Humphrey Pictures, Inc.
1919 Atonement
Hyclass Producing Co.
1917 Raffles, the Amateur Cracksman
Hyman, Arthur S., Attractions Co. see **Arthur S. Hyman Attractions Co.**

I

I.S.P. Co.
1914 The Long Arm of the Law
Iliodor Pictures Corp.
1918 The Fall of the Romanoffs
Imp (Independent Moving Picture Co.) see also **Imp Film Co.** and **Universal Film Mfg. Co.; Imp**
1913 Traffic in Souls
1914 Absinthe
1915 The Marble Heart
Imp Film Co. see also **Imp (Independent Moving Picture Co.)** and **Universal Film Mfg. Co.; Imp**
1913 Ivanhoe
Imperial Film Mfg. Co.
1917 Uncle Sam, Awake!*
Ince, Ralph, Film Attractions see **Ralph Ince Film Attractions**
Ince, Thomas H. see **Thomas H. Ince**
Ince, Thomas H., Corp. see **Thomas H. Ince Corp.**
Ince, Thomas H., Inc. see **Thomas H. Ince, Inc.**
Ince, Thomas H., Productions see **Thomas H. Ince Productions**
Ince, Thomas H., Productions, Inc. see **Thomas H. Ince Productions, Inc.**
Independent Films Association
1920 Hell's Oasis
The Lumber Jack
Skyfire
Independent Sales Corp.
1918 A Romance of the Air*
Wanted for Murder
1919 The Challenge of Chance
A Dangerous Affair
False Gods
A House Divided
Life's Greatest Problem
The Littlest Scout
Love, Honor and—?
The Other Man's Wife
Suspense
When My Ship Comes In
A Woman's Experience
Indian Film Co.
1915 Russian Battlefields
Industrial Film Co.
1920 The Little Outcast
Industrial Moving Picture Co. predecessor of **Rothacker Film Mfg. Co.**
1914 Joliet Prison, Joliet, Ill.
1915 On the Firing Line with the Germans
Inland Feature Amusement Co.
1915 The Diamond Robbery
International Correspondence Schools
1919 Heads Win
International Feature Film Co.
1913 Buried Alive in a Coal Mine
International Film Mfg. Co.
1914 Prince Edward Island in Motion; Home of the Silver Black Fox Industry
International Film Service Co. see also **International Film Service, Inc.**
1919 Break the News to Mother
The Cinema Murder
The Dark Star
The Hidden Truth
The Miracle of Love
1920 April Folly
Heliotrope
Humoresque

John Emerson-Anita Loos Productions
1918   Come On In
     Good-Bye, Bill
1919   Oh, You Women
     A Temperamental Wife
     A Virtuous Vamp
1920   The Love Expert
     The Perfect Woman
     Two Weeks

John W. Noble *see also* **A John W. Noble Production**
1917   Shame

A John W. Noble Production *see also* **John W. Noble**
1920   The Song of the Soul

Johnson, Martin, Film Co. *see* **Martin Johnson Film Co.**

Jolivet, Rita, Film Corp. *see* **Rita Jolivet Film Corp.**

Jones, Peter P., Film Co. *see* **Peter P. Jones Film Co.**

José, Edward, Productions *see* **Edward José Productions**

Joseph Conoly
1912   Atop of the World in Motion

Joseph L. Plunkett
1918   The Woman the Germans Shot

Joseph Leon Weiss
1914   What Is to Be Done?

Joseph Levering Productions
1920   His Temporary Wife

Joseph M. Schenck Productions
1920   The Perfect Woman
     Two Weeks

Joseph R. Miles
1917   The Test of Womanhood

Joseph W. Farnham
1916   The Awakening of Bess Morton
     Race Suicide

Jungle Film Co.
1912   Paul J. Rainey's African Hunt

K

K. & R. Film Co.
1915   The Magic Toy Maker
     Silver Threads Among the Gold

K & S Feature Film Co.
1914   A Mother's Heart
     A Woman Who Did

K-E-S-E Service *see also* **George Kleine** *and* **George Kleine System**
1916   The Breaker
     The Chaperon
     The Cossack Whip
     The Country That God Forgot
     The Heart of the Hills
     A Message to Garcia
     The Phantom Buccaneer
     The Prince of Graustark
     The Return of Eve
     The Truant Soul
     World Series Games 1916,
       Boston vs. Brooklyn
1917   The Adventures of Buffalo Bill
     The Apple-Tree Girl
     The Barker
     Billy and the Big Stick
     Builders of Castles
     Burning the Candle
     Chris and His Wonderful
       Lamp
     The Customary Two Weeks
     The Danger Trail
     Efficiency Edgar's Courtship
     Filling His Own Shoes
     The Ghost of Old Morro
     The Golden Idiot
     The Heart of Texas Ryan
     Kidnapped
     Knights of the Square Table
     The Lad and the Lion
     The Lady of the Photograph
     The Land of Long Shadows
     The Last Sentence
     The Law of the North
     Light in Darkness
     The Little Chevalier
     Little Lost Sister
     Little Shoes
     The Man Who Was Afraid

     The Master Passion
     Men of the Desert
     The Mystery of Number 47
     The Night Workers
     One Touch of Nature
     Open Places
     Pants
     The Princess' Necklace
     The Princess of Patches
     Putting the Bee in Herbert
     The Range Boss
     The Royal Pauper
     The Saint's Adventure
     Satan's Private Door
     Skinner's Baby
     Skinner's Bubble
     Skinner's Dress Suit
     The Tell-Tale Step
     The Trufflers

K. C. Booking Co.
1914   Born Again
     The Span of Life
     The Spirit of the Poppy

Kalem Co.
1913   From the Manger to the Cross
1914   The Boer War
     A Celebrated Case
     The Invisible Power
     The School for Scandal
     Shannon of the Sixth
     Wolfe; Or, The Conquest of
       Quebec
1915   The Coquette
     Don Caesar de Bazan
     The Glory of Youth
     The Luring Lights
     Midnight at Maxim's
     The Pitfall
     The Pretenders
1916   The Black Crook
     The Lotus Woman

Kane, Arthur S. *see* **Arthur S. Kane**

Kane, Arthur S., Pictures Corp. *see* **Arthur S. Kane Pictures Corp.**

Kane, Gail, Productions *see* **Gail Kane Productions**

Katherine MacDonald Pictures Corp.
1919   The Beauty Market
     The Thunderbolt
1920   Curtain
     The Notorious Miss Lisle
     Passion's Playground
     The Turning Point

Kay-Bee *see* **New York Motion Picture Corp.; Kay-Bee** *and* **Triangle Film Corp.; Kay-Bee**

Keane, James, Co. *see* **James Keane Co.**

Keane, James, Feature Photo-play Productions *see* **James Keane Feature Photo-play Productions**

Keenan, Frank, Productions, Inc. *see* **Frank Keenan Productions, Inc.**

Keeney, Frank A., Pictures Corp. *see* **Frank A. Keeney Pictures Corp.**

Keller, Helen, Film Corp. *see* **Helen Keller Film Corp.**

Kemble Film Corp.
1916   America Preparing
     The Zeppelin Raids on London
       and the Siege of Verdun

Kendall-Chambers Corp.
1920   The Song of the Soul

Kennedy Features, Inc.
1914   Charlotte Corday
     Jess

Kerrigan, J. Warren, Features Corp. *see* **J. Warren Kerrigan Features Corp.**

Kerrigan, J. Warren, Pictures, Inc. *see* **J. Warren Kerrigan Pictures, Inc.**

Kerrigan Productions Co. *see also* **J. Warren Kerrigan Features Corp.** *and* **J. Warren Kerrigan Pictures, Inc.**
1919   A White Man's Chance

A Kessel & Baumann Production
1920   Headin' Home

Keystone Film Co.
1914   Tillie's Punctured Romance
1915   Mixed Up‡
     My Valet
     A Submarine Pirate

1916   A Modern Enoch Arden

Kinemacolor Co. *see also* **Kinemacolor Co. of America**
1916   Her American Prince

Kinemacolor Co. of America *see also* **Kinemacolor Co.**
1913   The Call of the Blood

Kinetophote Corp.
1914   Born Again
     The Coming Power
     The Little Jewess
     The Span of Life
     The Spirit of the Poppy

King, Burton, Productions *see* **Burton King Productions**

King Vidor Productions
1920   The Family Honor
     The Jack-Knife Man

Kipling, Richard, Enterprises *see* **Richard Kipling Enterprises**

Kismet Feature Film Co.
1914   Fire and Sword

Kitty Gordon Film Corp.
1917   Vera, the Medium

Klaw & Erlanger
1914   Classmates
     Liberty Belles
     Lord Chumley
     The Power of the Press
     The Rejuvenation of Aunt
       Mary
     Under the Gaslight
     The Woman in Black

Kleine-Edison Feature Service *see also* **George Kleine** *and* **K-E-S-E Service**
1915   Bondwomen
     Children of Eve
     The Danger Signal
     The Destroying Angel
     The Fixer
     The Green Cloak
     The Magic Skin
     The Money Master
     The Politicians
     The Sentimental Lady
     Vanity Fair
     The Woman Next Door
1916   The Catspaw
     The Devil's Prayer-Book
     The Final Curtain
     The Innocence of Ruth
     The Scarlet Road
     When Love Is King
     Wild Oats

Kleine, George *see* **George Kleine**

Kleine, George, System *see* **George Kleine System**

Kleinschmidt, Captain F. E. *see* **Captain F. E. Kleinschmidt**

Klotz and Streimer, Inc.
1917   Whither Thou Goest

Knickerbocker Star Features *see also* **Balboa Amusement Co.; Balboa Amusement Producing Co.; Balboa Feature Film Co.; Horkheimer Bros.** *and* **Horkheimer Studios**
1916   Pay Dirt
     Spellbound

Kremer Film Features *see also* **Victor Kremer Film Features**
1915   The Man Trail*
1916   The Little Shepherd of Bargain
       Row*
     The Misleading Lady*
1917   Little Shoes*
     The Range Boss*

Kremer, Victor, Film Features *see* **Victor Kremer Film Features**

Kulee Features, Inc.
1915   How Molly Malone Made
       Good
1916   The Unborn

L

L-Ko Pictures Corp.
1919   Injustice

L. J. Gasnier Productions
1920   The Butterfly Man
     Occasionally Yours

L. L. Hiller
1919   The Price Woman Pays

L. Lawrence Weber Photo Dramas, Inc.
1917   Raffles, the Amateur
       Cracksman
1920   The Blue Pearl

Lady Mackenzie Film Co.
1915   Lady Mackenzie's Big Game
       Pictures

Laemmle Brand *see* **Universal Film Mfg. Co.; Laemmle Brand**

Lamree Film Corp.
1917   The Blackmailers

Lanzke
1915   A Continental Girl*

Lariat Films
1915-16
     The Sins That Ye Sin
1916   The Awakening of Bess Morton

Lasalida Film Corp.
1917   Captain Kiddo
     Tears and Smiles
     When Baby Forgot

Lasky, Jesse L., Feature Play Co. *see* **Jesse L. Lasky Feature Play Co.**

Lasso
1918   The Lone Avenger

Latin-American Republics Film Corp.
1920   The Eternal Union of the Seas

Laurence Rubel Service Co.
1917   Uncle Sam, Awake!

Lea-Bel Co.
1917   Modern Mother Goose

Lederer, George W., Filmotions, Inc. *see* **George W. Lederer Filmotions, Inc.**

Lederer, George W., Stage Filmotions, Inc. *see* **George W. Lederer Stage Filmotions, Inc.**

Leggett-Gruen Corp.
1916   The Island of Happiness

Lejaren a' Hiller Productions
1920   The Sleep of Cyma Roget

Lenox Film Corp.
1915   The Despoiler*

Lenox Producing Corp.
1919   The Betrayal

Leon J. Rubinstein
1914   Protect Us

Leonard, Marion, Film Co. *see* **Marion Leonard Film Co.**

Leonard S. Sugden
1915   The Lure of Alaska

Léonce Perret Productions *see also* **Perret Productions, Inc.**
1919   The A.B.C. of Love
     The Twin Pawns
1920   The Empire of Diamonds
     Lifting Shadows

Leslie's Weekly
1916   War As It Really Is

Lesser, Ira *see* **Ira Lesser**

Lesser, Sol *see* **Sol Lesser**

Lester Cuneo Productions
1920   Lone Hand Wilson

Levering, Joseph, Productions *see* **Joseph Levering Productions**

Levey, Harry, Productions *see* **Harry Levey Productions**

Lew Cody Films Corp.
1919   The Beloved Cheater
1920   Occasionally Yours
     Wait for Me

Lewis, Capt. *see* **Capt. Lewis**

Lewis, Edgar, Productions, Inc. *see* **Edgar Lewis Productions, Inc.**

Lewis J. Selznick Enterprises, Inc. *see also* **Select Pictures Corp.**
1916   The Common Law
     The Foolish Virgin
     War Brides
     War on Three Fronts
1917   The Argyle Case
     The Easiest Way
     The Eternal Sin
     The Law of Compensation
     The Lone Wolf
     The Mad Lover*
     Panthea
     Poppy
     The Price She Paid

Scandal
The Silent Master
Vera, the Medium
The Wild Girl
Lewis, Mitchell, Corp. *see* **Mitchell Lewis Corp.**
Lewis, Mitchell, Producing Co. *see* **Mitchell Lewis Producing Co.**
Lewis S. Stone Productions, Inc.
1919　Man's Desire
Liberty Bell Features *see* **Lubin Mfg. Co.**
Liberty Film Mfg. Co. *not the same as* **Liberty Motion Picture Co.**
1915　The Black Heart
Liberty Motion Picture Co. *not the same as* **Liberty Film Mfg. Co.**
1915　An American Gentleman
　　　For $5,000 a Year
Liebler Co. *see also* **World Film Corp.; A Liebler Feature**
1914　The Christian
　　　The Man from Home
　　　Mrs. Wiggs of the Cabbage Patch
　　　Salomy Jane
Life Photo Film Corp.
1914　The Banker's Daughter
　　　Captain Swift
　　　The Greyhound
　　　Northern Lights
　　　The Ordeal
　　　Springtime
1915　The Avalanche
　　　The Curious Conduct of Judge Legarde
　　　A Modern Magdalen
　　　The Unbroken Road
Lillian Walker Pictures Corp. *see also* **Lillian Walker Pictures, Inc.**
1918　The Embarrassment of Riches
Lillian Walker Pictures, Inc. *see also* **Lillian Walker Pictures Corp.**
1919　The Love Hunger
Lincoln & Parker Co.
1914　Florida Historic Scenes and Florida in Mid-Winter
Lincoln Motion Picture Co.
1919　A Man's Duty
Linick & Melchior
1915　Was She to Blame? Or, Souls That Meet in the Dark
Little Players' Film Co.
1918　The Star Prince
Lloyd Carleton Productions
1917　The Curse of Eve*
1920　The Amazing Woman
　　　Mountain Madness
Lloyd, Frank, Productions *see* **Frank Lloyd Productions**
Loftus Features
1914　Thais
Lois Weber Productions *not the same as* **Weber Productions, Inc.**
1917　Even As You and I
　　　The Price of a Good Time
1918　Borrowed Clothes
　　　The Doctor and the Woman
　　　For Husbands Only
1919　Forbidden
　　　Home
　　　When a Girl Loves
1920　To Please One Woman
Louis B. Mayer Productions
1919　Human Desire
　　　In Old Kentucky
1920　The Fighting Shepherdess
　　　Harriet and the Piper
Louis Tracy Productions, Inc.
1920　The Silent Barrier
Louise Glaum Organization
1918　The Goddess of Lost Lake
Lowell Thomas
1919　With Allenby in Palestine and Lawrence in Arabia
Lowry, Ira M. *see* **Ira M. Lowry**
Loyalty Film Co. *see also* **Democracy Film Co.**
1920　Reformation

Lubin, Bert *see* **Bert Lubin**
Lubin Mfg. Co.
1913　The Battle of Shiloh
　　　Mexican War Pictures
　　　The Third Degree
1914　The Battle of Gettysgoat
　　　Cocaine Traffic; Or, The Drug Terror
　　　The Daughters of Men
　　　The Fortune Hunter
　　　The Gamblers
　　　The House Next Door
　　　The Lion and the Mouse
　　　Michael Strogoff
　　　A Mother's Heart*
　　　Threads of Destiny
　　　Through Fire to Fortune
　　　The Wolf
1915　The Climbers
　　　The College Widow
　　　The District Attorney
　　　The Eagle's Nest
　　　The Evangelist
　　　The Great Divide
　　　The Great Ruby
　　　Heartaches
　　　A Man's Making
　　　The Nation's Peril
　　　The Rights of Man: A Story of War's Red Blotch
　　　The Ringtailed Rhinoceros
　　　Saved from the Harem
　　　The Sporting Duchess
　　　Tillie's Tomato Surprise
　　　The Valley of Lost Hope
1916　The City of Failing Light
　　　Dollars and the Woman
　　　The Flames of Johannis
　　　The Gods of Fate
　　　Her Bleeding Heart
　　　Light at Dusk
　　　Love's Toll
　　　Race Suicide
　　　Sorrows of Happiness
　　　Souls in Bondage
　　　Those Who Toil
19--　The Girl from Alaska‡
Lumen C. Mann
1916　Around the World in Ninety Minutes
Luna Film Co.
1913　The Black Snake
Lynch, S. A., Enterprises *see* **S. A. Lynch Enterprises**
Lyric Films, Inc.
1920　The Way Women Love

M

M-C (Max Cohen) Film Co.
1917　America Is Ready
M. A. Dodge Film Co.
1920　Witch's Gold
M. A. Neff
1915　The Battle of Ballots
M. B. Schlesinger
1920　Into the Light
M. Clark Productions
1919　Three Men and a Girl*
M. H. Hoffman, Inc.
1917　The Fringe of Society
　　　Madame Sherry
　　　One Hour
　　　The Silent Witness
　　　The Sin Woman
1918　After the War
　　　The Cast-Off
　　　The Craving
　　　Humility
　　　Suspicion
M. J. Burnside
1920　Roman Candles
M. L. B. Film Co.
1917　Glory
Mabel Normand Feature Film Co.
1918　Mickey
McCarthy Picture Productions
1920　Out of the Dust

Macauley, C. R., Photoplays, Inc. *see* **C. R. Macauley Photoplays, Inc.**
McClure Pictures, Inc. *not the same as* **McClure Productions, Inc.**
1917　Envy
　　　Greed
　　　Passion
　　　Pride
　　　The Seventh Sin
　　　Sloth
　　　Wrath
McClure Productions, Inc. *not the same as* **McClure Pictures, Inc.**
1919　The Fighting Roosevelts
　　　Fruits of Passion
　　　What Shall We Do with Him?
McCord, Vera, Productions, Inc. *see* **Vera McCord Productions, Inc.**
MacDonald, Barry, Film Co. *see* **Barry MacDonald Film Co.**
MacDonald, Katherine, Pictures Corp. *see* **Katherine MacDonald Pictures Corp.**
McGovern, Elmer J. *see* **Elmer J. McGovern**
McIntosh, Burr, Film Corp. *see* **Burr McIntosh Film Corp.**
Mack Sennett Comedies
1919　Yankee Doodle in Berlin
1920　Down on the Farm
　　　Love, Honor and Behave
　　　Married Life
Mackenzie, Lady, Film Co. *see* **Lady Mackenzie Film Co.**
MacManus Corp. *see also* **MacManus Film Corp.**
1919　The Lost Battalion
MacManus Film Corp. *see also* **MacManus Corp.**
1920　The Gray Brother
Magnet Film Exchange
1919　Broken Barriers
Majestic Motion Picture Co.
1913　Sapho
1914　The Avenging Conscience; Thou Shalt Not Kill
　　　The Battle of the Sexes
　　　The Escape
　　　Home, Sweet Home
　　　Imar the Servitor
1915　The Absentee
　　　The Birth of a Nation*
　　　Captain Macklin
　　　Enoch Arden
　　　The Fox Woman
　　　Ghosts
　　　Her Shattered Idol
　　　The Lost House
　　　The Outcast
　　　A Yankee from the West
1916　Intolerance*
Major Film Corp.
1917-18
　　　Will You Marry Me?‡
Mann, Lumen C. *see* **Lumen C. Mann**
Marine Film Co.
1917　Lorelei of the Sea
Marion Davies Film Co. *see also* **Marion Davies Film Corp.**
1918　Cecilia of the Pink Roses
1919　Getting Mary Married
Marion Davies Film Corp. *see also* **Marion Davies Film Co.**
1918　The Burden of Proof
1919　The Belle of New York
1920　April Folly
Marion Leonard Film Co.
1914　The Light Unseen
　　　Mother Love
Mark Twain Co.
1920　A Connecticut Yankee at King Arthur's Court
　　　Huckleberry Finn
Marshall Neilan Productions
1920　Dinty
　　　Don't Ever Marry
　　　Go and Get It
　　　The River's End
Martin Estes
1915　For the Honor of the Kingdom

Martin Johnson Film Co.
1918　Among the Cannibal Isles of the South Pacific
Mary Pickford Co. *see also* **Famous Players-Mary Pickford Co.; Mary Pickford Film Corp.; A Mary Pickford Production** *and* **Pickford Film Corp.**
1919　Daddy-Long-Legs
　　　Heart O' the Hills
　　　The Hoodlum
1920　Pollyanna
　　　Suds
Mary Pickford Film Corp. *see also* **Famous Players-Mary Pickford Co.; Mary Pickford Co.; A Mary Pickford Production** *and* **Pickford Film Corp.**
1916　Less Than the Dust
1917　The Little American
　　　The Little Princess
　　　The Pride of the Clan
　　　Rebecca of Sunnybrook Farm
　　　A Romance of the Redwoods*
1918　Amarilly of Clothes-Line Alley
A Mary Pickford Production *see also* **Famous Players-Mary Pickford Co.; Mary Pickford Co.; Mary Pickford Film Corp.** *and* **Pickford Film Corp.**
1918　How Could You, Jean?
Mason, Charles Post, Enterprises *see* **Charles Post Mason Enterprises**
Master Drama Features, Inc.
1917　Who's Your Neighbor?
Master Pictures
1920　Roman Candles
Mastercraft Photoplay Corp.
1918　The One Woman
Masterpiece Film Mfg. Co.
1914　The Hoosier Schoolmaster
　　　The Truth Wagon
1915　Jack Chanty
1916　The Bondman*
Matty Roubert Productions, Inc.
1920　Heritage
Maurice Film Co.
1920　Our Christianity and Nobody's Child
Maurice Tourneur Productions, Inc.
1918　Sporting Life
　　　Woman
1919　The Broken Butterfly
　　　The Life Line
　　　Victory
　　　The White Heather
1920　The County Fair
　　　Deep Waters
　　　The Great Redeemer
　　　The Last of the Mohicans
　　　My Lady's Garter
　　　Treasure Island
　　　The White Circle
Maxwell Productions
1918　The Married Virgin
Mayer, Louis B., Productions *see* **Louis B. Mayer Productions**
Mayfair Film Corp.
1917　Persuasive Peggy
Mayflower Photoplay Corp.
1919　Bolshevism on Trial
　　　The Miracle Man
　　　The Mystery of the Yellow Room
　　　Soldiers of Fortune
1920　The Deep Purple
　　　In the Heart of a Fool
　　　The Invisible Foe
　　　The Law of the Yukon
　　　The Luck of the Irish
　　　The Scoffer
　　　A Splendid Hazard
　　　Unseen Forces
Maytrix Photo Plays, Inc.
1918　And the Children Pay
　　　Humility
　　　When Destiny Wills
Meeker, George R. *see* **George R. Meeker**
Mena Film Co.
1918　Restitution
Merit Film Co.
1916　Her Husband's Wife

Moore, Frank E. *see* **Frank E. Moore**
Moral Feature Film Co.
  1913 The Inside of the White Slave
       Traffic
Moral Uplift Society of America
  1916 It May Be Your Daughter
Morosco, Oliver, Photoplay Co. *see* **Oliver**
  Morosco Photoplay Co.
Moss, B. S. *see* **B. S. Moss**
Moss, B. S., Motion Picture Corp. *see* **B.**
  S. Moss Motion Picture Corp.
Motion Drama Co.
  1913 The Stranglers of Paris
Motioncraft
  1917 The Wife Who Wouldn't Tell‡
Multnomah Film Corp.
  1919 In the Land of the Setting Sun;
       Or, Martyrs of Yesterday‡
Mutual Film Corp.
  1913 The Battle of Gettysburg
       The Legend of Provence
       Moths
       Robin Hood
       Sapho*
  1914 The Avenging Conscience;
       Thou Shalt Not Kill
       The Battle of the Sexes
       Beating Back
       Damaged Goods
       The Dishonored Medal
       Dope
       The Escape
       The Floor Above
       Frou Frou
       The Gangsters
       The Great Leap; Until Death
       Do Us Part
       Home, Sweet Home
       Imar the Servitor
       The Life of General Villa
       The Mountain Rat
       Shorty Escapes Marriage
       Thirty Leagues Under the Sea
       The Voice at the Telephone
       The Wrath of the Gods
  1915 The Absentee
       Bred in the Bone
       The Brink
       The Buzzard's Shadow
       Captain Macklin
       A Child of God
       A Continental Girl*
       The Cup of Life
       The Darkening Trail
       The Deathlock
       The Devil
       The End of the Road
       Enoch Arden
       The Failure
       The Flying Twins
       The Forbidden Adventure
       The Fox Woman
       Ghosts
       The Girl from His Town
       God's Witness
       Her Shattered Idol
       His Wife
       The House of a Thousand
       Scandals
       Infatuation
       Inspiration
       The Last Concert
       The Lonesome Heart
       The Lost House
       The Lure of the Mask
       A Man and His Mate
       The Man from Oregon
       A Man's Prerogative
       The Mating
       Milestones of Life
       The Mill on the Floss
       The Miracle of Life
       Monsieur Lecoq
       On the Night Stage
       The Outcast
       The Outlaw's Revenge
       The Painted Soul
       The Patriot and the Spy
       The Price of Her Silence
       The Quest
       The Reward
       Rumpelstiltskin
       Secretary of Frivolous Affairs
       The Seventh Noon

Strathmore
The Toast of Death
Up from the Depths
The Wolf Man
A Yankee from the West
1916 The Abandonment
According to Law
And the Law Says
April
As a Woman Sows
The Bait
Betrayed
A Bird of Prey
Bluff
The Bruiser
The Conscience of John David
The Courtesan
The Craving
The Dead Alive
The Decoy
The Diamond Runners
A Dream or Two Ago
The Drifter
Dulcie's Adventure
Dust
Embers
Faith
Father and Son
Feathertop
The Fighting Chance
The Fighting Germans
The Five Faults of Flo
The Flight of the Duchess
The Haunted Manor
The Heart of Tara
Her American Prince
Her Father's Gold
The Hidden Law
The Highest Bid
The House of Mirrors
I Accuse
The Idol of the Stage
Immediate Lee
In the Web of the Grafters
The Inner Struggle
The Innocence of Lizette
The Isle of Love
Judith of the Cumberlands
Land O' Lizards
A Law unto Himself
The Leopard's Bride
Life's Blind Alley
The Light
Lone Star
Lonesome Town
Lord Loveland Discovers
  America
The Love Hermit
The Love Liar
Lying Lips
The Man from Manhattan
The Man Who Would Not Die
The Manager of the B. and A.
Master Shakespeare, Strolling
  Player
Medicine Bend
A Million for Mary
Miss Jackie of the Navy
My Partner
Nancy's Birthright
The Net
Other People's Money
The Other Side of the Door
The Oval Diamond
Overalls
The Overcoat
The Pearl of Paradise
Peck O' Pickles
Philip Holden—Waster
Powder
Purity
The Quality of Faith
Reclamation
Revelations
The Sable Blessing
The Sign of the Spade
Silas Marner
Society Wolves
Soul Mates
The Soul's Cycle
The Stain in the Blood
The Strength of Donald
  McKenzie
The Thoroughbred
Three Pals

The Torch Bearer
The Traffic Cop
True Nobility
The Twinkler
The Undertow
The Valley of Decision
Vengeance Is Mine
The Voice of Love
Wall Street Tragedy
The Wasted Years
Whispering Smith
The White Rosette
The Woman in Politics
A Woman's Daring
Youth's Endearing Charm
1917 American Maid
Annie-for-Spite
Bab the Fixer
The Beautiful Adventure
Beloved Rogues
Betty and the Buccaneers
Betty Be Good
A Bit of Kindling
The Bride's Silence
The Butterfly Girl
The Calendar Girl
Charity Castle
The Checkmate
Daughter of Maryland
The Dazzling Miss Davison
The Debt
The Devil's Assistant
Environment
The Frame Up
A Game of Wits
The Gentle Intruder
The Gilded Youth
The Girl Angle
The Girl from Rector's
The Girl Who Couldn't Grow
  Up
The Greater Woman
Hedda Gabler
Her Country's Call
Her Second Husband
Her Sister
Heroic France
High Play
Mary Moreland
The Masked Heart
The Mate of the Sally Ann
Melissa of the Hills
The Mirror
Miss Jackie of the Army
Mrs. Balfame
Motherhood
My Fighting Gentleman
New York Luck
Outcast
The Painted Lie
Pardners
Peggy Leads the Way
Periwinkle
The Planter
Please Help Emily
Pride and the Man
Queen X
The Rainbow Girl
Reputation
The Runaway
Sands of Sacrifice
The Sea Master
The Serpent's Tooth
Shackles of Truth
The Single Code
Snap Judgement
Souls in Pawn
Southern Pride
Sunny Jane
The Unforseen
The Upper Crust
Where Love Is
Whose Wife?
The Wildcat
1918 Ann's Finish
Beauty and the Rogue
A Bit of Jade
The Daredevil
The Ghost of Rosy Taylor
The Girl and the Judge
Hearts or Diamonds?
Her Husband's Honor
His Birthright
A Hoosier Romance
Impossible Susan

The Impostor
In Bad
Jilted Janet
Love's Law
The Midnight Trail
Molly, Go Get 'Em
My Wife
Powers That Prey
The Primitive Woman
The Richest Girl
Social Briars
The Square Deal
The Temple of Dusk
Treason
Up Romance Road
Who Loved Him Best?
1918-19
    The Kaiser's Bride
My Four Years in Germany, Inc.
  1918 My Four Years in Germany

N

Nash Motion Picture Co.
  1914 The Mysterious Man of the
       Jungle
  1915 Unto the Darkness
National Association of the Motion
  Picture Industry
  1917 National Association's All-Star
       Picture
National Drama Corp.
  1916 The Fall of a Nation
National Film Corp. of America *same*
  as **National Film Corp.**
  1915 Captivating Mary Carstairs
       The Tale of the Night Before
  1918 And a Still Small Voice
       The Girl of My Dreams
       The Romance of Tarzan
       Tarzan of the Apes
  1919 The Blue Bonnet
       The Boomerang
       The Girl from Nowhere
       Hoop-La
       In Search of Arcady
       The Lamb and the Lion
       The Long Arm of Mannister
       The Long Lane's Turning
       The Love Call
       Modern Husbands
  1920 The Confession
       The Kentucky Colonel
       Miss Nobody
       Parted Curtains
       The Sport of Kings
National Film Distributors
  1919 Broken Barriers
National Movement Motion Picture
  Bureau
  1915 The Adventures of a Boy Scout
National Picture Theatres, Inc.
  1920 Blind Youth
       The Invisible Divorce
       Just a Wife
       Marooned Hearts
       Out of the Snows
       The Palace of Darkened
       Windows
       The Road of Ambition
National Red Cross Pageant Committee
  1917 National Red Cross Pageant
The Nazimova Productions
  1918 Eye for Eye
  1919 The Brat
       The Red Lantern
  1920 Billions
       The Heart of a Child
       Madame Peacock
       Stronger Than Death
Neff, M. A. *see* **M. A. Neff**
Neilan, Marshall, Productions *see*
  Marshall Neilan Productions
Nelson, H. N., Attractions *see* **H. N.**
  Nelson Attractions
Neutral Film Co.
  1915 The Last of the Mafia
Nevada Motion Picture Corp.
  1917 The Planter

Paragon Photo Plays Co. *not the same
as* **Paragon Films, Inc.**
1914 The Murders in the Rue
Morgue
Paralta Plays, Inc.
1917 Alimony
1918 An Alien Enemy
Blindfolded
A Burglar for a Night
The Goddess of Lost Lake*
The Heart of Rachel
His Robe of Honor
Humdrum Brown
A Law unto Herself
Madam Who
Maid O' the Storm
A Man's Man
One Dollar Bid
Patriotism
Rose O' Paradise
Shackled
The Turn of a Card
Wedlock
The White Lie
With Hoops of Steel
Within the Cup

Paramount Pictures Corp. *Note*:
Paramount was incorporated as a
distribution company in 1914. Early
in 1918, Paramount Pictures Corp.
was discontinued as a corporate name
and Paramount Pictures became a
brand name of Famous Players-
Lasky Corp. For films released under
the brand name, see **Famous Players-
Lasky Corp.; Paramount Pictures**
and **Famous Players-Lasky Corp.;
Paramount-Artcraft Pictures**
1914 Aristocracy
The Bargain
Behind the Scenes
Burning Daylight: The
Adventures of "Burning
Daylight" in Alaska
Burning Daylight: The
Adventures of "Burning
Daylight" in Civilization
Cameo Kirby
The Chechako
Cinderella
The Circus Man
The Conspiracy
The Country Mouse
The County Chairman
The Crucible
The Eagle's Mate
False Colours
The Ghost Breaker
His Last Dollar
The Lost Paradise
The Magic Cloak of Oz
The Making of Bobby Burnit
The Man from Home
The Man from Mexico
Marta of the Lowlands
The Million
Mrs. Black Is Back
An Odyssey of the North
The Patchwork Girl of Oz
The Pursuit of the Phantom
Ready Money
Rose of the Rancho
The Sign of the Cross
The Spitfire
The Straight Road
Such a Little Queen
The Typhoon
The Unwelcome Mrs. Hatch
The Virginian
What's His Name
Where the Trail Divides
Wildflower
1915 After Five
The Arab
Are You a Mason?
Armstrong's Wife
The Bachelor's Romance
Bella Donna
Betty in Search of a Thrill
Blackbirds
Buckshot John
The Caprices of Kitty
Captain Courtesy
The Captive
Carmen

The Case of Becky
The Cheat
Chimmie Fadden
Chimmie Fadden Out West
The Chorus Lady
The Clue
The Commanding Officer
The Country Boy
The Dancing Girl
David Harum
The Dawn of a Tomorrow
The Dictator
Esmeralda
The Explorer
Fanchon the Cricket
The Fatal Card
The Fighting Hope
Gambier's Advocate
The Gentleman from Indiana
A Gentleman of Leisure
The Girl of the Golden West
A Girl of Yesterday
The Goose Girl
The Governor's Lady
Gretna Green
The Heart of Jennifer
Heléne of the North
Help Wanted
Her Triumph
The House of the Lost Court
The Hypocrites
The Immigrant
The Incorrigible Dukane
The Italian
It's No Laughing Matter
Jane
Jim the Penman
Kilmeny
The Kindling
Little Pal
Little Sunset
The Love Route
Lydia Gilmore
Madame Butterfly
The Majesty of the Law
The Marriage of Kitty
The Masqueraders
May Blossom
Mr. Grex of Monte Carlo
Mistress Nell
The Morals of Marcus
The Moth and the Flame
The Mummy and the
Humming Bird
Nearly a Lady
Niobe
The Old Homestead
Out of the Darkness
Peer Gynt
Poor Schmaltz
Pretty Mrs. Smith
The Pretty Sister of Jose
The Prince and the Pauper
The Puppet Crown
Rags
The Reform Candidate
The Rug Maker's Daughter
Rule G
The Running Fight
The Secret Orchard
The Secret Sin
Seven Sisters
Snobs
Sold
The Spanish Jade
Still Waters
Stolen Goods
Sunshine Molly
Temptation
'Twas Ever Thus
The Unafraid
The Unknown
The Voice in the Fog
The Warrens of Virginia
When We Were Twenty-One
The White Pearl
The Wild Goose Chase
The Wild Olive
The Woman
The Yankee Girl
Young Romance
Zaza
1916 Alien Souls
The American Beauty
Anton the Terrible

Ashes of Embers
Audrey
Ben Blair
The Big Sister
The Blacklist
The Call of the Cumberlands
The Clown
The Code of Marcia Gray
Common Ground
A Coney Island Princess
The Daughter of MacGregor
David Garrick
Davy Crockett
Destiny's Toy
Diplomacy
The Dream Girl
The Dupe
Each Pearl a Tear
The Eternal Grind
The Evil Thereof
The Feud Girl
For the Defense
The Foundling
The Golden Chance
A Gutter Magdalene
He Fell in Love with His Wife
The Heart of Nora Flynn
The Heart of Paula
The Heir to the Hoorah
Her Father's Son
The Honorable Friend
The House of Lies
The House with the Golden
Windows
Hulda from Holland
The Innocent Lie
An International Marriage
The Intrigue
The Kiss
The Lash
Little Lady Eileen
The Lost Bridegroom
The Love Mask
Madame La Presidente
The Making of Maddalena
Maria Rosa
The Martyrdom of Philip
Strong
Mice and Men
Miss George Washington
Molly Make-Believe
The Moment Before
My Lady Incog.
Nanette of the Wilds
Nearly a King
Oliver Twist
Out of the Drifts
The Parson of Panamint
Pasquale
The Plow Girl
Poor Little Peppina
Public Opinion
Pudd'nhead Wilson
The Quest of Life
The Race
The Ragamuffin
The Rainbow Princess
The Red Widow
Redeeming Love
The Reward of Patience
The Right Direction
The Road to Love
Rolling Stones
Saints and Sinners
The Saleslady
The Selfish Woman
Seventeen
Silks and Satins
The Smugglers
Snow White
A Son of Erin
The Soul of Kura-San
The Sowers
The Spider
The Storm
The Stronger Love
Susie Snowflake
Sweet Kitty Bellairs
Tennessee's Pardner
The Thousand Dollar Husband
To Have and to Hold
Tongues of Men
The Trail of the Lonesome Pine
The Traveling Salesman
Under Cover

Unprotected
The Victoria Cross
The Victory of Conscience
Witchcraft
The Woman in the Case
The World's Great Snare
The Years of the Locust
The Yellow Pawn
1917 The Amazons
The American Consul
The Antics of Ann
Arms and the Girl
As Men Love
At First Sight
Bab's Burglar
Bab's Diary
Bab's Matinee Idol
Betty to the Rescue
Big Timber
The Black Wolf
The Bond Between
The Bottle Imp
The Call of the East
Castles for Two
The Clever Mrs. Carfax
The Cook of Canyon Camp
The Cost of Hatred
The Countess Charming
The Crystal Gazer
Double Crossed
The Dummy
Each to His Kind
The Eternal Temptress
The Evil Eye
Exile
The Fair Barbarian
Forbidden Paths
The Fortunes of Fifi
Freckles
The Ghost House
The Girl at Home
A Girl Like That
Giving Becky a Chance
The Golden Fetter
Great Expectations
The Happiness of Three
Women
Hashimura Togo
Heart's Desire
The Heir of the Ages
Her Better Self
Her Own People
Her Strange Wedding
The Highway of Hope
His Mother's Boy
His Sweetheart
The Hostage
The Hungry Heart
The Inner Shrine
Jack and Jill
The Jaguar's Claws
The Judgement House
A Kiss for Susie
The Land of Promise
The Law of the Land
The Little Boy Scout
Little Miss Optimist
The Lonesome Chap
The Long Trail
Lost and Won
Lost in Transit
Love Letters
The Love That Lives
The Marcellini Millions
Molly Entangled
The Mysterious Miss Terry
Nan of Music Mountain
On Record
On the Level
Out of the Wreck
The Price Mark
The Primrose Ring
The Prison Without Walls
A Roadside Impresario
Sacrifice
Sapho
A School for Husbands
The Secret Game
The Seven Swans
The Silent Partner
The Slave Market
Sleeping Fires
The Son of His Father
The Spirit of Romance
The Squaw Man's Son

The Sunset Trail
Those Without Sin
The Tides of Barnegat
Tom Sawyer
The Trouble Buster
Unconquered
The Undying Flame
The Valentine Girl
The Varmint
The Wax Model
What Money Can't Buy
The Winning of Sally Temple
The World Apart
1918 The Guilty Man
In Pursuit of Polly
Jules of the Strong Heart
Mrs. Dane's Defense
A Nine O'Clock Town
Quicksand
The Spirit of '17
The Widow's Might
The World for Sale

Park-Whiteside Productions
1920 Empty Arms
The Scarlet Dragon

Pasquali American Co.
1914 The Next in Command

Pathé Exchange, Inc. *see also* **Pathé Frères**
1915 The Adventures of a Madcap
An Affair of Three Nations
At Bay
The Beloved Vagabond
The Closing Net
Comrade John
Excuse Me
An Eye for an Eye
The Galloper
The Greater Will
The House of Fear
John Glayde's Honor
Mary's Lamb
The Menace of the Mute
Nedra
Pearls of Temptation
Queen and Adventurer
Seeing America First
Simon, the Jester
The Spender
Via Wireless
1916 Arms and the Woman
Big Jim Garrity
The Challenge
Divorce and the Daughter
The Fear of Poverty
The Fugitive
The Girl with the Green Eyes
Hazel Kirke
Hidden Valley
Joy and the Dragon
King Lear
The King's Game
The Light That Failed
Little Mary Sunshine
Madame X
The Matrimonial Martyr
New York
The Pillory
The Precious Packet
Prudence the Pirate
The Romantic Journey
Saint, Devil and Woman
Shadows and Sunshine
The Shine Girl
The Shrine of Happiness
The Sultana
The Test
A Woman's Fight
The Woman's Law
The World and the Woman
1917 An Amateur Orphan
The Angel Factory
Blind Man's Luck
The Candy Girl
Captain Kiddo
The Cigarette Girl
Crime and Punishment
A Crooked Romance
The Empress
The Fires of Youth
The Heart of Ezra Greer
Her Beloved Enemy
Her Life and His
Her New York
Hinton's Double

The Hunting of the Hawk
The Image Maker
The Iron Heart
It Happened to Adele
Kick In
The Last of the Carnabys
The Little Patriot
The Mad Lover
The Mark of Cain
Mary Lawson's Secret
Mayblossom
Miss Nobody
A Modern Monte Cristo
The On-the-Square-Girl
Over the Hill
Pots-and-Pans Peggy
The Recoil
Runaway Romany
Sold at Auction
Stranded in Arcady
The Streets of Illusion
Sunshine and Gold
Sylvia of the Secret Service
Tears and Smiles
To-Day*
Told at Twilight
Twin Kiddies
Under False Colors
Vengeance Is Mine
The Vicar of Wakefield
War and the Woman
When Baby Forgot
When Love Was Blind
The Woman in White
1918 All the World to Nothing
Annexing Bill
Arms in France‡
The Bells
The Border Raiders
The Challenge Accepted
Convict 993
Cupid by Proxy
Daddy's Girl
A Daughter of the West
Dolly Does Her Bit
Dolly's Vacation
The Eyes of Julia Deep
Fair Enough
The First Law
For Sale
The German Curse in Russia
The Ghost of the Rancho
The Girl from Bohemia
The Great Adventure
Her Man
The Hillcrest Mystery
Hobbs in a Hurry
How Could You, Caroline?
Innocent
A Japanese Nightingale
Kidder and Ko
A Little Sister of Everybody
Loaded Dice
The Mantle of Charity
Milady O' the Beanstalk
Mrs. Slacker
Money Isn't Everything
More Trouble
The Mysterious Client
The Narrow Path
The Naulahka
The Other Woman
Rosemary Climbs the Heights
Ruler of the Road
Twenty-One
Two-Gun Betty
The Voice of Destiny
Waifs
Winning Grandma
Wives and Other Wives
The Yellow Ticket
1919 The A.B.C. of Love
All Wrong
The Amazing Impostor
As a Man Thinks
A Bachelor's Wife
The Bandbox
The Best Man
The Bishop's Emeralds
The Blue Bonnet
Brass Buttons
Brothers Divided
Caleb Piper's Girl
The Capitol
Carolyn of the Corners

Charge It to Me
Come Again Smith
Common Clay
The Cry of the Weak
A Damsel in Distress
Dawn
Desert Gold
The Drifters
The End of the Game
Eve in Exile
The False Code
Fighting Through
The Forfeit
Gates of Brass
The Gay Old Dog
Go Get 'Em Garringer
The Hellion
Impossible Catherine
The Intrusion of Isabel
The Joyous Liar
The Little Diplomat
The Lone Wolf's Daughter
The Lord Loves the Irish
The Love Cheat
The Love Hunger
The Master Man
The Midnight Stage
Molly of the Follies
The Moonshine Trail
Oh, Boy!
The Old Maid's Baby
Our Better Selves
Pagan Love
The Prince and Betty
The Profiteers
Put Up Your Hands
Riders of the Dawn
The Right to Lie
Sahara
The Sawdust Doll
The Silver Girl
Six Feet Four
Some Liar
The Spenders
A Sporting Chance
The Thirteenth Chair
$30,000
This Hero Stuff
Thunderbolts of Fate
The Tiger Lily
The Tiger's Coat
Todd of the Times
Trixie from Broadway
The Twin Pawns
The Unknown Love
The Virtuous Model
The Volcano
The Westerners
When a Man Rides Alone
Where the West Begins
The White Man's Chance
A Woman of Pleasure
The World Aflame
Yvonne from Paris
1920 A Beggar in Purple
The Blood Barrier
The Blue Moon
A Broadway Cowboy
The Broken Gate
The Brute Master
The Dangerous Talent
The Deadlier Sex
The Devil to Pay
Dice of Destiny
Dollar for Dollar
The Dwelling Place of Light
The Empire of Diamonds
Felix O'Day
Fighting Cressy
Forbidden Valley
The Gamesters
The Girl in the Web
The Green Flame
Half a Chance
The Harvest Moon
Help Wanted—Male
Her Unwilling Husband
The Honey Bee
The House of the Tolling Bell
The House of Toys
The House of Whispers
In Walked Mary
The Kentucky Colonel
King Spruce
Lahoma

Lifting Shadows
A Light Woman
Live Sparks
Love Madness
Man and His Woman
The Miracle of Money
The Money-Changers
My Husband's Other Wife
Number 99
One Hour Before Dawn
Other Men's Shoes
Passers-By
Respectable by Proxy
The Riddle: Woman
Rio Grande
Rogues and Romance
The Sagebrusher
Sex
Sherry
The Silent Barrier
Simple Souls
Smoldering Embers
Tarnished Reputations
Their Mutual Child
The Thirtieth Piece of Silver
The Valley of Tomorrow
The Web of Deceit
The Week-End

Pathé Frères *see also* **Pathé Exchange, Inc.**
1914 The Corsair
Detective Craig's Coup
The Last Volunteer
The Quest of the Sacred Jewel
Sport and Travel in Central Africa
The Taint
When Rome Ruled
1915 Queen and Adventurer

Paul J. Rainey
1914 Common Beasts of Africa
Rainey's African Hunt

Paul Smith Pictures Co.
1918 The Finger of Justice

Payne, Clarence *see* **Clarence Payne**

Pearson, Virginia, Photoplays, Inc. *see* **Virginia Pearson Photoplays, Inc.**

Peerless Features Producing Co. *see also* **World Film Corp.; Peerless**
1916 Sally in Our Alley

Peerless Film Exchange
1915 The Exposition's First Romance

Peerless Pictures Co.
1920 The Heart of a Woman

Penn Yan Film Corp.
1915 Wheat and Tares; A Story of Two Boys Who Tackle Life on Diverging Lines‡

Perfection Pictures
1917 The Apple Tree Girl
The Awakening of Ruth
The Courage of the Common Place
Cy Whittaker's Ward
The Dream Doll
The Fibbers
Fools for Luck
Gift O' Gab
The Kill-Joy
The Lady of the Photograph
Men of the Desert
Sadie Goes to Heaven
Salt of the Earth
The Small Town Guy
Two-Bit Seats
Young Mother Hubbard
1918 Brown of Harvard
Chase Me Charlie
The Curse of Iku
Men Who Have Made Love to Me
A Pair of Sixes
Ruggles of Red Gap
The Unbeliever
The Unchastened Woman
Uneasy Money

Perret, Léonce, Productions *see* **Léonce Perret Productions**

Perret Productions, Inc. *see also* **Léonce Perret Productions**
1918 Lafayette, We Come!
1919 The Unknown Love

1920 Tarnished Reputations

Peter P. Jones Film Co.
1917 The Slacker

Petrova Picture Co.
1917 Daughter of Destiny
1918 The Life Mask
      The Light Within
      The Panther Woman
      Tempered Steel

Phoenix Film Co.
1914 The Spirit of the Conqueror

Photo Drama Co. see also **Photo Drama Motion Picture Co.**
1913 Ten Nights in a Barroom
1914 After the Ball
1915 How Molly Malone Made Good
      Prohibition
      Time Lock Number 776

Photo Drama Motion Picture Co. see also **Photo Drama Co.**
1914 The Folks from Way Down East
      The House of Bondage
      Winning His First Case

Photo Products Export Co.
1915 The Destroying Angel*
      The Spendthrift*
1916 The Final Curtain*
      When Love Is King*
1920 Beyond the Great Wall
      The Rich Slave

Photodramas, Inc.
1920 Bitter Fruit*

Photoplay Libraries
1920 Empty Arms
      The Scarlet Dragon

Photoplay Productions Co.
1914 The Littlest Rebel

Physical Culture Photoplays, Inc.
1918 Zongar

Pickford Film Corp. see also **Famous Players-Mary Pickford Co.; Mary Pickford Co.; Mary Pickford Film Corp.** and **A Mary Pickford Production**
1918 Johanna Enlists
      M'liss
      Stella Maris
1919 Captain Kidd, Jr.

Pickford, Jack, Film Co. see **Jack Pickford Film Co.**

Pickford, Jack, Productions see **Jack Pickford Productions**

Pickford, Mary, Co. see **Mary Pickford Co.**

Pickford, Mary, Film Corp. see **Mary Pickford Film Corp.**

Pickford, Mary, Productions see **A Mary Pickford Production**

Picture Finance Corp.
1919 Suspense*

Picture Playhouse Film Co.
1914 The Mystery of the Poison Pool
      The Next in Command
1915 The Bulldogs of the Trail
      Flame of Passion
      The Grandee's Ring
      History of the Great European War
      The Pearl of the Antilles
      The Pursuing Shadow

Piedmont Film Co. not the same as **Piedmont Pictures Corp.**
1916 The Mirror of Life

Piedmont Pictures Corp. see also **Hawk Film Co.** not the same as **Piedmont Film Co.**
1918 His Daughter Pays
      A Son of Strife

Pike's Peak Photoplay Co.
1915-16
      The Sins That Ye Sin
1916 The Awakening of Bess Morton

Pilot Films Corp.
1913 Across the Continent
      Hoodman Blind

Pinnacle Productions
1920 Hell's Oasis
      Skyfire

Pioneer Feature Film Corp. see also **Pioneer Film Corp.**
1916 The Soul of a Child
1919 Atonement
      The Long Arm of Mannister

Pioneer Film Corp. see also **Pioneer Feature Film Corp.**
1918 Little Orphant Annie
      The Prodigal Wife
      The Sins of the Children
      The Still Alarm
      Wives of Men
1919 The Boomerang
      The Girl from Nowhere
      Virtuous Sinners
1920 The Barbarian
      Bubbles
      Dr. Jekyll and Mr. Hyde
      The Forgotten Woman*
      The Hidden Code
      Oil
      The Place of Honeymoons
      The Scarlet Dragon
      The Sleep of Cyma Roget
      Stolen Moments
      Thoughtless Women
      What Women Want

Playgoers Film Co.
1914 The Great Diamond Robbery
      Manon Lescaut

Plaza Pictures
1918 Angel Child
      The Law That Divides
      Petticoats and Politics
      Whatever the Cost

Plimpton Epic Pictures see also **Plimpton Pictures**
1919 The Stream of Life

Plimpton Pictures see also **Plimpton Epic Pictures**
1920 Should a Wife Work?

Plunkett, Joseph L. see **Joseph L. Plunkett**

Plymouth Film Corp.
1919 The Stream of Life

Pollard Picture Plays Co.
1916 Miss Jackie of the Navy
      The Pearl of Paradise
1917 The Butterfly Girl
      The Devil's Assistant
      The Girl Who Couldn't Grow Up

Popular Film Co.
1917 Has Man the Right to Kill?*

Popular Pictures Corp.
1917 Corruption
      Uncle Sam, Awake!*

Popular Plays and Players, Inc.
1914 Michael Strogoff
      The Ragged Earl
      The Tigress
1915 Barbara Frietchie
      Greater Love Hath No Man
      The Heart of a Painted Woman
      Her Great Match
      Her Own Way
      My Madonna
      The Shadows of a Great City
      The Shooting of Dan McGrew
      The Song of the Wage Slave
      The Vampire
1916 The Black Butterfly
      The Devil at His Elbow
      The Eternal Question
      Extravagance
      The Girl with the Green Eyes
      The Iron Woman
      The Lure of Heart's Desire
      Playing with Fire
      The Scarlet Woman
      The Soul Market
      The Spell of the Yukon
      Vanity
      The Weakness of Strength
      What Will People Say?
      A Woman's Fight
1917 Bridges Burned
      The Empress
      More Truth Than Poetry*
      The Secret of Eve
      The Soul of a Magdalen
      The Waiting Soul

Powell, Frank, Producing Corp. see **Frank Powell Producing Corp.**

Powell, Frank, Productions, Inc. see **Frank Powell Productions, Inc.**

Pre-Eminent Films, Ltd.
1915 The Running Fight

Premier Pictures Corp.
1920 Love's Protegé

Premo Feature Film Corp. see also **Premo Film Co.** and **Premo Film Corp.**
1915 The Master Hand
1916 His Brother's Wife

Premo Film Co. see also **Premo Feature Film Corp.** and **Premo Film Corp.**
1915 The Greater Will

Premo Film Corp. see also **Premo Feature Film Corp.** and **Premo Film Co.**
1916 The Devil's Toy
      The Supreme Sacrifice

Price, C. B., Co. see **C. B. Price Co.**

Private Feature Film Mfg. Co.
1916 Ignorance

Prizma, Inc.
1918 Our Navy

Producers' Distributing Corp.
1918 Her Mistake
      Sins of the Kaiser

Producers' Picture Corp.
1920 The Valley of Night

Producers Security Corp.
1920 When Dawn Came
1922 The Cynic Effect

Progress Film Co.
1914 Smashing the Vice Trust

Progressive Motion Picture Co.
1914 McVeagh of the South Seas
      The Master Cracksman

Prohibition Film Corp. (William Steiner and Robert T. Kane)
1915 Prohibition

Protective Amusement Co.
1914 Liberty Belles*
      Lord Chumley*
      The Power of the Press*
      The Rejuvenation of Aunt Mary*
      Under the Gaslight*

The Protective Pictures Corp.
1918 The Sins of the Children*

Psycho-Analytic Research Association
1918 What Does a Woman Need Most

Public Rights Film Corp.
1917 The Public Be Damned

Puritan Special Features Co.
1912 Quincy Adams Sawyer

Pyramid Photo Plays, Inc. same as **Pyramid Film Corp.**
1918 Inside the Lines
      The Man of Bronze
1920 The Woman Untamed

Q

Quality Amusement Co. see also **Quality Amusement Corp.**
1920 Eyes of Youth

Quality Amusement Corp. see also **Quality Amusement Co.**
1920 Within Our Gates

Quality Pictures Corp.
1915 Pennington's Choice
      Richard Carvel
      Rosemary
      The Second in Command
      The Silent Voice
1916 The Come-Back
      A Corner in Cotton
      In the Diplomatic Service
      Man and His Soul
      The Masked Rider
      A Million a Minute
      The Red Mouse
      Romeo and Juliet
      The Wall Between

R

Radin Pictures, Inc.
1920 Man and Woman
      Through Eyes of Men
1921 Love's Plaything
      Skinning Skinners

Radio Film Co.
1916 Defense or Tribute?

Rainey, Paul J. see **Paul J. Rainey**

Ralph Ince Film Attractions
1919 Virtuous Men

Ramo Films, Inc.
1913 In the Stretch
1914 The Criminal Path
      The Governor's Ghost
      Thou Shalt Not
      Through Dante's Flames
      The War of Wars; Or, The Franco-German Invasion

Randolph Film Corp.
1918 The Million Dollar Mystery

Rapf, Harry, Productions see **Harry Rapf Productions**

Raver Film Corp. see also **Harry Raver, Inc.**
1915 Life Without Soul*
1916 Driftwood
      The Fortunate Youth
      The Other Girl

Raver, Harry, Inc. see **Harry Raver, Inc.**

Ray, Carl, Motion Picture Co. see **Carl Ray Motion Picture Co.**

Ray, Charles, Pictures Corp. see **Charles Ray Pictures Corp.**

Ray, Charles, Productions, Inc. see **Charles Ray Productions, Inc.**

Raymond L. Ditmars
1914 The Book of Nature

Read, J. Parker, Jr., Productions see **J. Parker Read, Jr. Productions**

Realart Pictures Corp. see also **Realart Pictures, Inc.**
1919 Erstwhile Susan
      The Mystery of the Yellow Room
      Soldiers of Fortune
1920 Blackbirds
      A Cumberland Romance
      A Dark Lantern
      The Deep Purple
      Eyes of the Heart
      The Fear Market
      Food for Scandal
      The Furnace
      Her Beloved Villain
      Her First Elopement
      Jenny Be Good
      Judy of Rogue's Harbor
      The Law of the Yukon
      The Luck of the Irish
      Miss Hobbs
      The New York Idea
      Nurse Marjorie
      Oh, Lady, Lady
      She Couldn't Help It
      Sinners
      Something Different
      The Soul of Youth
      The Stolen Kiss
      Sweet Lavender
      39 East
      You Never Can Tell

Realart Pictures, Inc. see also **Realart Pictures Corp.**
1919 Anne of Green Gables

Red Feather Photoplays see **Universal Film Mfg. Co.**

Red Seal Plays see **Selig Polyscope Co.**

Reelplays Corp.
1915 The Cowpuncher

Regal Photo-Play Co.
1918 What Becomes of the Children?*

Regent Feature Film Co.
1914 La Belle Russe

Reginald Barker Productions
1920 The Branding Iron
      Dangerous Days
      Godless Men

Reid-Robards Pictures Co.
1917 Mothers of Men
Reliable Feature Film Corp.
1914 Three Weeks
Reliance
1915 For the Honor of the Kingdom‡
Reliance Motion Picture Co. *see also*
Reliance Motion Picture Corp.
1914 The Dishonored Medal
The Floor Above
The Gangsters
The Great Leap; Until Death
Do Us Part
Home, Sweet Home
The Mountain Rat
Reliance Motion Picture Corp. *see also*
Reliance Motion Picture Co.
1915 Bred in the Bone
A Child of God
The Failure
A Man and His Mate
A Man's Prerogative
The Outlaw's Revenge
Strathmore
Up from the Depths
The Wolf Man
1916 Macbeth
Renowned Pictures Corp.
1917 A Soul for Sale
1918 The Kaiser, the Beast of Berlin
Naked Hands
Republic Distributing Corp. *see also*
Republic Pictures
1915 Trilby*
1920 An Adventuress
The Amazing Woman
The Blue Pearl
Children Not Wanted
Children of Destiny
Common Sense
Dad's Girl
The Gift Supreme
Girl of the Sea
The Girl Who Dared
The Great Shadow
Man's Plaything
Mothers of Men
Mountain Madness
The One Way Trail
Republic Pictures *see also* **Republic
Distributing Corp.**
1920 The Girl Who Dared
Man's Plaything
The One Way Trail
Rex Beach *see also* **A Rex Beach
Production** *and* **Rex Beach Pictures
Co.**
1919 The Brand
Rex Beach Pictures Co. *same as* **Rex
Beach Film Corp.** *see also* **Rex Beach**
and **A Rex Beach Production**
1917 The Auction Block
The Barrier
1918 Heart of the Sunset
Laughing Bill Hyde
Too Fat to Fight
1919 The Crimson Gardenia
A Rex Beach Production *see also* **Rex
Beach** *and* **Rex Beach Pictures Co.**
1919 The Girl from Outside
Reynolds, Sidney, Co. *see* **Sidney
Reynolds Co.**
Rialto De Luxe Productions
1918 The Unchastened Woman
Rialto Film Corp.
1916 The House of Mirrors
Rialto Productions
1920 The Isle of Destiny
Richard Kipling Enterprises
1920 The Lone Hand
Richard Suratt
1919 Alaska‡
Richenback
1915 A Continental Girl*
Richman, Charles, Co. *see* **Charles
Richman Co.**
Richman, Charles, Pictures Corp. *see*
Charles Richman Pictures Corp.
Rita Jolivet Film Corp.
1918 Lest We Forget

Rivoli Film Producing Co.
1919 The Greater Sinner
Robards Players *see* **Reid-Robards
Pictures Co.**
Robert Brunton Co. *see also* **Anderson-
Brunton Co.; Robert Brunton
Productions** *and* **Robert Brunton
Studios, Inc.**
1919 The Silver Girl
Todd of the Times
Robert Brunton Productions *see also*
**Anderson-Brunton Co.; Robert
Brunton Co.** *and* **Robert Brunton
Studios, Inc.**
1918 The Goddess of Lost Lake
Two-Gun Betty
1919 The Joyous Liar
The Lord Loves the Irish
A White Man's Chance
1920 The Coast of Opportunity
The Devil to Pay
The Dream Cheater
The Girl in the Web
The Green Flame
The House of Whispers
Live Sparks
Number 99
$30,000
Robert Brunton Studios, Inc. *see also*
**Anderson-Brunton Co.; Robert
Brunton Co.** *and* **Robert Brunton
Productions**
1919 The Master Man
Robert Warwick Film Corp.
1917 The Argyle Case
The Mad Lover
The Silent Master
Robertson-Cole Co. *see also* **Robertson-
Cole Distributing Corp.** *and*
Robertson-Cole Studios, Inc.
1918 And a Still Small Voice
The Girl of My Dreams
1919 All of a Sudden Norma
Bare-Fisted Gallagher
The Beloved Cheater
Better Times
The Blue Bandanna
Bonds of Honor
The Courageous Coward
Dangerous Waters
Diane of the Green Van
The Dragon Painter
For a Woman's Honor
The Gray Horizon
A Heart in Pawn
The Heart of Juanita
Hearts Asleep
Her Purchase Price
His Debt
Hoop-La
The House of Intrigue
In Search of Arcady
Josselyn's Wife
Just Squaw
Kitty Kelly, M.D.
The Lamb and the Lion
Life's a Funny Proposition
The Long Lane's Turning
The Love Call
The Man Beneath
The Man Who Turned White
A Man's Country
Man's Desire
The Mints of Hell
Modern Husbands
The Open Door
The Other Half
The Pagan God
The Prodigal Liar
A Sage Brush Hamlet
Tangled Threads
The Tong Man
A Trick of Fate
The Turn in the Road
What Every Woman Wants
Whitewashed Walls
The Woman Michael Married
1920 The Little 'Fraid Lady
The Third Woman
A Woman Who Understood
The Wonder Man

Robertson-Cole Distributing Corp. *see
also* **Robertson-Cole Co.** *and*
Robertson-Cole Studios, Inc.
1919 Beckoning Roads
The Broken Butterfly
A Fugitive from Matrimony
The Gray Wolf's Ghost
The Illustrious Prince
Poor Relations
1920 An Arabian Knight
The Beggar Prince
Big Happiness
The Brand of Lopez
Bright Skies
The Butterfly Man
The Devil's Claim
813
The Flame of Hellgate
The Fortune Teller
Haunting Shadows
The Heart of Twenty
Kismet
Li Ting Lang
Life's Twist
The Little 'Fraid Lady
The Luck of Geraldine Laird
Moon Madness
The Notorious Mrs. Sands
Occasionally Yours
Seeing It Through
A Slave of Vanity
So Long Letty
The Stealers
The Third Generation
The Third Woman
Uncharted Channels
The White Dove
Who's Your Servant?
A Woman Who Understood
The Wonder Man
Robertson-Cole Studios, Inc. *see also*
Robertson-Cole Co. *and* **Robertson-
Cole Distributing Corp.**
1920 A Slave of Vanity
The Stealers
Roland West Film Corp.
1916 Lost Souls‡
Rolands Feature Film Co.
1914 Trapped in the Great
Metropolis
Rolfe, B. A., Photoplays, Inc. *see* **B. A.
Rolfe Photoplays, Inc.**
Rolfe Photoplays, Inc. *see also* **B. A.
Rolfe Photoplays, Inc.**
1915 The Bigger Man
Black Fear
Cora
The Cowboy and the Lady
Destiny; Or, The Soul of a
Woman
Fighting Bob
The Final Judgment
The Flaming Sword
Her Reckoning
The High Road
The House of Tears
Marse Covington
My Best Girl
One Million Dollars
The Right of Way
Satan Sanderson
When a Woman Loves
1916 The Awakening of Helena
Richie
The Blindness of Love
The Brand of Cowardice
The Dawn of Love
Dorian's Divorce
God's Half Acre
Her Great Price
The Pretenders
The Price of Malice
The Purple Lady
The Quitter
Rose of the Alley
The Snowbird
The Stolen Triumph
The Sunbeam
The Upheaval
The Upstart
The Wager
The Wheel of the Law
1917 Aladdin's Other Lamp
The Barricade
The Beautiful Lie

The Duchess of Doubt
The Greatest Power
His Father's Son
A Magdalene of the Hills
The Millionaire's Double
Miss Robinson Crusoe
Peggy, the Will O' the Wisp
The Power of Decision
Somewhere in America
Sowers and Reapers
The Trail of the Shadow
The White Raven
Romayne Super-Film Co.
1918 Me und Gott
Rothacker Film Mfg. Co. *successor to*
Industrial Moving Picture Co.
1916 Cousin Jim*
1917 Heroic France
1918 The Romance of Tarzan
1920 Forty-Five Minutes from
Broadway
Good References
Harriet and the Piper
The Inferior Sex
The Jack-Knife Man
Married Life
The Master Mind
Nomads of the North
The Notorious Miss Lisle
Old Dad
The River's End
The Yellow Typhoon
Yes or No
1921 Habit
Rothapfel Pictures Corp.
1919 False Gods
Roubert, Matty, Productions, Inc. *see*
Matty Roubert Productions, Inc.
Roy Chandler South American Pictures
1915 A Trip to the Argentine
Royal Gardens Film Co. of Chicago
1920 In the Depths of Our Hearts
Rubel, Laurence, Service Co. *see*
Laurence Rubel Service Co.
Rubinstein, Leon J. *see* **Leon J. Rubinstein**
Ruby Feature Film Co.
1913 The Shame of the Empire State
Russell-Griever-Russell
1920 Lone Hand Wilson
Witch's Gold
Russell, William, Productions, Inc. *see*
William Russell Productions, Inc.

S

S & E Enterprises
1920 It Might Happen to You
S & S Photoplays
1918 Her Mistake
Just a Woman
S-L Pictures
1919 Virtuous Men
1920 Love, Honor and Obey
S. A. Lynch Enterprises
1917 The Cold Deck
1919 The Follies Girl
Sacred and Historic Film Co.
1914 His Holiness, the Late Pope
Pius X, and the Vatican
Salisbury, Edward A. *see* **Edward A.
Salisbury**
Salisbury, Monroe, Players, Inc. *see* **The
Monroe Salisbury Players, Inc.**
Samuel Cummins
1916 The Other Girl*
1919 Wild Oats
Samuelson Film Mfg. Co. *see also*
Samuelson Producing Co.
1920 Her Story
Love in the Wilderness
The Night Riders
The Price of Silence
The Ugly Duckling
Samuelson Producing Co. *see also*
Samuelson Film Mfg. Co.
1920 David and Jonathan
Sanger and Jordan
1917 When Duty Calls‡

Santa Barbara Motion Picture Co.
1914 The Envoy Extraordinary
Sapho Feature Film Co.
1913 Sapho
Sargent, P. D., Productions see **P. D. Sargent Productions**
Savage, Henry W., Inc. see **Henry W. Savage, Inc.**
Sawyer, Inc.
1914 The Detective Queen
　　Doc
　　The Envoy Extraordinary
　　A Factory Magdalen
　　The Fatal Night
　　Hearts United
　　Joseph and His Coat of Many Colors
　　The King of the Bowery
　　The Lightning Conductor
　　Nell Gwynne
　　Nell of the Circus
　　The Spirit of the Conqueror
　　Thais
　　The Virgin of the Rocks
　　The Volunteer Parson
　　Without Hope
Scenograph Feature Film Co.
1915 In the Amazon Jungles with the Captain Besley Expedition‡
Schenck, Joseph M., Productions see **Joseph M. Schenck Productions**
Schlesinger, M. B. see **M. B. Schlesinger**
Schomer Photoplay Producing Co.
1918 Ruling Passions
Schomer-Ross Productions, Inc.
1920 The Chamber Mystery
　　The Hidden Light
　　The Sacred Flame
Schwab, D. N., Productions, Inc. see **D. N. Schwab Productions, Inc.**
Screen Classics, Inc. see also **Metro Pictures Corp.**
1918 Lest We Forget
　　The Million Dollar Dollies
　　My Own United States
　　Pals First
　　Pay Day
　　Revelation
　　To Hell with the Kaiser
　　Toys of Fate
1919 The Brat
　　Fair and Warmer
　　The Great Romance
　　The Great Victory, Wilson or the Kaiser? The Fall of the Hohenzollerns
　　Lombardi, Ltd.
　　A Man of Honor
　　The Man Who Stayed at Home
　　Please Get Married
　　Shadows of Suspicion
　　Should a Woman Tell?
1920 Alias Jimmy Valentine
　　Are All Men Alike?
　　The Best of Luck
　　Blackmail
　　The Cheater
　　Dangerous to Men
　　Held in Trust
　　Old Lady 31
　　The Right of Way
　　Shore Acres
　　The Walk-Offs
　　The Willow Tree
Screencraft Pictures, Inc.
1918 The Prodigal Wife
1919 Suspense
1920 Woman's Man
Sealed Orders Motion Picture Corp.
1918 Stolen Orders*
Seattle Film Co.
1914 In the Land of the Head Hunters
Second National Pictures Corp.
1920 David and Jonathan
　　Her Story
　　The Night Riders
Seitz, George B., Productions see **George B. Seitz Productions**

Select
1918 The Whip
Select Film Booking Agency, Inc.
1915 The Alien
　　The Eternal City
Select Photo Play Producing Co.
1914 At the Cross Roads
Select Photoplay Co.
1917 Humanity
Select Pictures Corp. see also **Lewis J. Selznick Enterprises, Inc.**
1917 Her Silent Sacrifice
　　The Honeymoon
　　Magda
　　The Moth
　　Over There
　　Scandal
　　The Secret of the Storm Country
　　Shirley Kaye
　　The Wild Girl
1918 At the Mercy of Men
　　The Better Half
　　The Burden of Proof
　　By Right of Purchase
　　Cecilia of the Pink Roses
　　The Claw
　　Code of the Yukon
　　De Luxe Annie
　　The Death Dance
　　The Forbidden City
　　The Ghosts of Yesterday
　　Good Night, Paul
　　Her Great Chance
　　Her Only Way
　　The House of Glass
　　In the Hollow of Her Hand
　　The Knife
　　A Lady's Name
　　The Lesson
　　The Marionettes
　　The Midnight Patrol
　　Mrs. Leffingwell's Boots
　　The One Woman
　　The Ordeal of Rosetta
　　A Pair of Silk Stockings
　　The Reason Why
　　The Road Through the Dark
　　The Safety Curtain
　　Sauce for the Goose
　　The Savage Woman
　　The Shuttle
　　The Studio Girl
　　Up the Road with Sallie
　　The Whirlpool
　　Woman and Wife
　　The Woman the Germans Shot
1919 The Belle of New York
　　The Better Wife
　　Bolshevism on Trial
　　Break the News to Mother
　　The Broken Melody
　　Cheating Cheaters
　　Children of Banishment
　　The Country Cousin
　　Experimental Marriage
　　The Faith of the Strong
　　Getting Mary Married
　　The Glorious Lady
　　Happiness à la Mode
　　The Heart of Wetona
　　The Hidden Truth
　　His Bridal Night
　　The Imp
　　The Indestructible Wife
　　The Isle of Conquest
　　Jacques of the Silver North
　　The Last of His People
　　Marie, Ltd.
　　The New Moon
　　Out Yonder
　　The Perfect Lover
　　The Probation Wife
　　Redhead
　　A Regular Girl
　　Romance and Arabella
　　A Scream in the Night
　　Sealed Hearts
　　The Spite Bride
　　The Undercurrent
　　Upstairs and Down
　　The Veiled Adventure
　　The Way of a Woman
　　Who Cares?
　　The World to Live In

1919-20
　　Piccadilly Jim
1920 Blind Youth
　　Broadway and Home
　　The Dangerous Paradise
　　Darling Mine
　　The Daughter Pays
　　The Desperate Hero
　　Everybody's Sweetheart
　　The Figurehead
　　The Flapper
　　A Fool and His Money
　　Footlights and Shadows
　　Greater Than Fame
　　The Greatest Love
　　His Wife's Money
　　The Invisible Divorce
　　Just a Wife
　　The Man Who Lost Himself
　　Marooned Hearts
　　Out of the Snows
　　The Palace of Darkened Windows
　　Pleasure Seekers
　　The Point of View
　　The Poor Simp
　　Red Foam
　　Seeds of Vengeance
　　The Servant Question
　　The Shadow of Rosalie Byrnes
　　She Loves and Lies
　　The Sin That Was His
　　Sooner or Later
　　The Valley of Doubt
　　Whispers
　　The Woman Game
　　The Woman God Sent
　　The Wonderful Chance
　　Youthful Folly
19-- Jennie
Selexart Pictures, Inc.
1918 Blue Blood
　　Carmen of the Klondike
　　Honor's Cross
　　Social Ambition
Selig Polyscope Co. see also **Selig Studios** and **William N. Selig**
1914 In the Days of the Thundering Herd
　　The Royal Box
　　The Spoilers
　　Your Girl and Mine: A Woman Suffrage Play
1915 A Black Sheep
　　The Carpet from Bagdad
　　The Circular Staircase
　　The History of the World's Greatest War
　　The House of a Thousand Candles
　　I'm Glad My Boy Grew Up to Be a Soldier
　　The Millionaire Baby
　　The Rosary
　　Sweet Alyssum
　　A Texas Steer
1916 The Adventures of Kathlyn
　　At Piney Ridge
　　The Country That God Forgot
　　The Crisis
　　The Cycle of Fate
　　The Garden of Allah
　　Indiana
　　Into the Primitive
　　The Ne'er-Do-Well
　　The Prince Chap
　　Thou Shalt Not Covet
　　Unto Those Who Sin
　　The Valiants of Virginia
　　War-Torn Poland
　　World Series Games 1916, Boston vs. Brooklyn
1917 The Barker
　　Beware of Strangers
　　The Danger Trail
　　The Heart of Texas Ryan
　　The Lad and the Lion
　　Little Lost Sister
　　The Mystery of Number 47
　　The Princess of Patches
　　Who Shall Take My Life?
1918 The Birth of a Race*
　　Brown of Harvard
　　The City of Purple Dreams
　　A Hoosier Romance

　　The Still Alarm
1920 The Jungle Princess
Selig Studios see also **Selig Polyscope Co.** and **William N. Selig**
1919 Auction of Souls
Selig, William N. see **William N. Selig**
Selznick, Lewis J., Enterprises, Inc. see **Lewis J. Selznick Enterprises, Inc.**
Selznick Pictures see **Lewis J. Selznick Enterprises, Inc.**
Selznick Pictures Corp.
1919 The Broken Melody
　　The Country Cousin
　　The Faith of the Strong
　　The Glorious Lady
　　The Imp
　　Out Yonder
　　The Perfect Lover
　　A Regular Girl
　　Sealed Hearts
　　The Spite Bride
　　Upstairs and Down
1919-20
　　Piccadilly Jim
1920 Broadway and Home
　　The Dangerous Paradise
　　Darling Mine
　　The Daughter Pays
　　The Desperate Hero
　　Everybody's Sweetheart
　　The Figurehead
　　The Flapper
　　A Fool and His Money
　　Footlights and Shadows
　　Greater Than Fame
　　His Wife's Money
　　The Man Who Lost Himself
　　Pleasure Seekers
　　The Point of View
　　The Poor Simp
　　Red Foam
　　The Road of Ambition
　　The Servant Question
　　The Shadow of Rosalie Byrnes
　　The Sin That Was His
　　Sooner or Later
　　The Valley of Doubt
　　Whispers
　　The Woman Game
　　The Woman God Sent
　　The Wonderful Chance
　　Youthful Folly
19-- Jennie
Seng, Frank S. see **Frank S. Seng**
Sennett, Mack, Comedies see **Mack Sennett Comedies**
Sheriott Pictures Corp.
1917 The Black Stork
Sherman-Elliott, Inc.
1916 The Crisis
Sherman Feature Film Co.
1914 Pieces of Silver; A Story of Hearts and Souls
Sherman Productions Corp. could be same as **Sherman Productions, Inc.**
1920 Man and Woman
1921 Miss 139
Sherman Productions, Inc. could be same as **Sherman Productions Corp.**
1918 The Light of Western Stars
Sherrill, William L., Feature Corp. see **William L. Sherrill Feature Corp.**
Sherry, William L., Service see **William L. Sherry Service**
Shipman, Ernest see **Ernest Shipman**
Shubert Film Corp. same as **Shubert Feature Film Co.** see also **F. Ray Comstock Film Corp.; A Shubert Feature and World Film Corp.; A Shubert Feature**
1914 When Broadway Was a Trail
1915 The Arrival of Perpetua
　　Bought
　　The Butterfly
　　A Butterfly on the Wheel
　　Camille
　　The Gray Mask
　　The Little Dutch Girl
　　Old Dutch
　　The Siren's Song
1916 As in a Looking Glass
　　Human Driftwood
　　The Pawn of Fate

The Virtuous Thief
What Every Woman Learns
1920 Alarm Clock Andy
Below the Surface
Black Is White
Dangerous Hours
Hairpins
Her Husband's Friend
Homer Comes Home
Homespun Folks
The Jailbird
Let's Be Fashionable
Mary's Ankle
An Old Fashioned Boy
Paris Green
Rookie's Return
Silk Hosiery
The Village Sleuth
What's Your Husband Doing?
The Woman in the Suitcase

Thomas H. Ince Productions, Inc. *see also* **Thomas H. Ince; Thomas H. Ince Corp.; Thomas H. Ince, Inc.** *and* **Thomas H. Ince Productions**
1917 The Price Mark
Those Who Pay
The Zeppelin's Last Raid
1918 The Hired Man
Keys of the Righteous

Thomas, Lowell *see* **Lowell Thomas**

Thomashefsky, Boris, Film Co. *see* **Boris Thomashefsky Film Co.**

Thompson, Donald C., Film Co. *see* **Donald C. Thompson Film Co.**

Tiffany Film Corp.
1915 The Heart of Maryland

Timely Feature Films
1915 War World Wide

To-Day Feature Film Corp.
1917 To-Day

Totten, Edyth, Features *see* **Edyth Totten Features**

Tourneur, Maurice, Productions, Inc. *see* **Maurice Tourneur Productions, Inc.**

Tracy, Louis, Productions, Inc. *see* **Louis Tracy Productions, Inc.**

Transatlantic Film Co. of America, Inc.
1919-20
The Marriage Blunder
1920 A Common Level

Trans-Pacific Films, Ltd.
1917 A Trip Through Japan

Triangle Distributing Corp. *see also* **Triangle Film Corp.**
1917 American—That's All
The Americano
Ashes of Hope
Back of the Man
Because of a Woman
Betsy's Burglar
Blood Will Tell
The Bond of Fear
Borrowed Plumage
The Bride of Hate
Broadway Arizona
A Case at Law
Cassidy
Cheerful Givers
Chicken Casey
The Clodhopper
The Crab
The Desert Man
The Devil Dodger
Envy
An Even Break
Fanatics
Fighting Back
The Firefly of Tough Luck
The Flame of the Yukon
Flying Colors
The Food Gamblers
For Valour
Framing Framers
The Fuel of Life
The Girl Glory
Golden Rule Kate
The Gown of Destiny
Grafters
Greed
The Gun Fighter
Hands Up!
Happiness

The Hater of Men
Her Excellency, the Governor
Her Father's Keeper
Her Official Fathers
The Iced Bullet
Idolators
In Slumberland
Indiscreet Corinne
Jim Bludso
The Last of the Ingrams
The Learnin' of Jim Benton
The Little Brother
The Little Yank
Love or Justice
A Love Sublime
Madcap Madge
The Man Hater
The Man Who Made Good
Master of His Home
The Maternal Spark
The Medicine Man
Might and the Man
The Millionaire Vagrant
The Mother Instinct
Mountain Dew
Nina, the Flower Girl
An Old Fashioned Young Man
One Shot Ross
Paddy O'Hara
Passion
Paws of the Bear
A Phantom Husband
The Pinch Hitter
Polly Ann
Pride
Princess of the Dark
The Regenerates
The Sawdust Ring
The Seventh Sin
The Ship of Doom
Sloth
The Snarl
Souls Triumphant
The Square Deal Man
Stagestruck
The Stainless Barrier
A Strange Transgressor
The Sudden Gentleman
Sudden Jim
Sweetheart of the Doomed
The Tar Heel Warrior
Ten of Diamonds
They're Off
Time Locks and Diamonds
Truthful Tulliver
Until They Get Me
Unto the End
Up or Down?
Wee Lady Betty
Wild Sumac
Wild Winship's Widow
Wolf Lowry
A Woman's Awakening
Wooden Shoes
Wrath
1918 Alias Mary Brown
The Answer
The Argument
The Atom
Betty Takes a Hand
Beyond the Shadows
The Boss of the Lazy Y
By Proxy
Cactus Crandall
Captain of His Soul
Closin' In
Crown Jewels
Daughter Angele
Desert Law
Deuce Duncan
Everywoman's Husband
Faith Endurin'
False Ambition
The Flames of Chance
The Fly God
From Two to Six
The Ghost Flower
The Golden Fleece
A Good Loser
The Grey Parasol
The Gun Woman
The Hand at the Window
The Hard Rock Breed
Heiress for a Day
Hell's End

Her American Husband
Her Decision
High Stakes
High Tide
His Enemy, the Law
An Honest Man
The Hopper
I Love You
Innocent's Progress
Irish Eyes
Keith of the Border
The Last Rebel
The Law of the Great Northwest
The Law's Outlaw
Limousine Life
Little Red Decides
The Lonely Woman
The Love Brokers
Love's Pay Day
Madame Sphinx
Mlle. Paulette
The Man Above the Law
The Man Who Woke Up
Marked Cards
The Mask
Mystic Faces
Nancy Comes Home
Old Hartwell's Cub
Old Love for New
The Painted Lily
Paying His Debt
The Pretender
The Price of Applause
Real Folks
The Reckoning Day
The Red-Haired Cupid
The Sea Panther
Secret Code
Shifting Sands
The Shoes That Danced
The Silent Rider
Society for Sale
A Soul in Trust
Station Content
Tony America
Untamed
The Vortex
Who Is to Blame?
Who Killed Walton?
Wife or Country
Wild Life
Without Honor
Wolves of the Border
You Can't Believe Everything
1919 Breezy Jim
Child of M'sieu
Devil McCare
The Follies Girl
Fruits of Passion
It's a Bear
The Little Rowdy
Love's Prisoner
The Mayor of Filbert
Mistaken Identity
Muggsy
One Against Many
Prudence on Broadway
The Railroader
A Regular Fellow
Restless Souls
The Root of Evil
A Royal Democrat
Secret Marriage
Three Black Eyes
Toton
The Unbroken Promise
Upside Down
Water Lily
A Wild Goose Chase

Triangle Film Corp. *see also* **Triangle Distributing Corp.** *and* **Triangle Film Corp.; Kay-Bee**
1915 Aloha Oe
The Coward
The Despoiler
The Disciple
Double Trouble
The Edge of the Abyss
The Golden Claw
The Iron Strain
Jordan Is a Hard Road
The Lamb
The Lily and the Rose
The Martyrs of the Alamo

Matrimony
My Valet
Old Heidelberg
The Penitentes
The Sable Lorcha
A Submarine Pirate
The Winged Idol
1916 Acquitted
American Aristocracy
The Apostle of Vengeance
The Aryan
Atta Boy's Last Race
Bawbs O' Blue Ridge
The Beckoning Flame
The Beggar of Cawnpore
Betty of Graystone
Between Men
The Bugle Call
Bullets and Brown Eyes
The Captive God
Casey at the Bat
A Child of the Paris Streets
The Children in the House
Children of the Feud
The Children Pay
Civilization's Child
The Conqueror
The Corner
A Corner in Colleens
The Criminal
Cross Currents
Daphne and the Pirate
D'Artagnan
The Dawn Maker
The Deserter
The Devil's Double
The Devil's Needle
Diane of the Follies
The Dividend
Don Quixote
The Eye of the Night
The Female of the Species
Fifty-Fifty
Flirting with Fate
The Flying Torpedo
A Gamble in Souls
Going Straight
The Good Bad Man
The Green Swamp
Gretchen, the Greenhorn
The Habit of Happiness
The Half-Breed
The Heiress at Coffee Dan's
Hell-to-Pay Austin
Hell's Hinges
His Picture in the Papers
Home
Honor Thy Name
The Honorable Algy
Honor's Altar
Hoodoo Ann
A House Built upon Sand
An Innocent Magdalene
Jim Grimsby's Boy
The Jungle Child
The Last Act
Let Katie Do It
Lieutenant Danny, U.S.A.
The Little Liar
Little Meena's Romance
The Little School Ma'am
Macbeth
Manhattan Madness
The Market of Vain Desire
The Marriage of Molly-O
Martha's Vindication
The Matrimaniac
The Microscope Mystery
The Missing Links
Mr. Goode, the Samaritan
A Modern Enoch Arden
The Moral Fabric
The No-Good Guy
Not My Sister
The Old Folks at Home
The Patriot
The Payment
Peggy
The Phantom
Pillars of Society
Plain Jane
The Price of Power
The Primal Lure
The Raiders
Reggie Mixes In

The Spy
Washington at Valley Forge
1915 Business Is Business
The Campbells Are Coming
The College Orphan
Colorado
Conscience
Coral
Courtmartialed
The Earl of Pawtucket
Father and the Boys
Fatherhood
The Frame-Up
The Garden of Lies
Heritage
Jewel
Judge Not; Or, The Woman of
   Mona Diggings
Judy Forgot
Just Jim
A Little Brother of the Rich
The Long Chance
Lord John in New York
The Man of Shame
The Marble Heart
Mrs. Plum's Pudding
The Nature Man: Or, The
   Struggle for Existence
The Primrose Path
Scandal
The Scarlet Sin
The Silent Command
The Suburban
The Supreme Test
Tainted Money
Under Southern Skies
The White Scar
The White Terror
The Wolf of Debt
The Woman Who Lied
1916 Autumn
Barriers of Society
The Beckoning Trail
Black Friday
The Black Sheep of the Family
A Child of Mystery
The Devil's Bondwoman
Doctor Neighbor
Drugged Waters
The Dumb Girl of Portici
From Broadway to a Throne
Half a Rogue
Her Bitter Cup
The Heritage of Hate
A Huntress of Men
Idle Wives
If My Country Should Call
The Iron Hand
Is Any Girl Safe?
The Isle of Life
It Happened in Honolulu
Kinkaid, Gambler
A Knight of the Range
Langdon's Legacy
The Lords of High Decision
Love's Pilgrimage to America
The Madcap
The Mainspring
The Man from Nowhere
The Man Inside
The Mark of Cain
Mixed Blood
The Morals of Hilda
The Narrow Path
The Path of Happiness
The People vs. John Doe
The Place Beyond the Winds
The Pool of Flame
A Romance of Billy Goat Hill
The Seekers
A Soul Enslaved
The Sphinx
The Target
Temptation and the Man
Thrown to the Lions
20,000 Leagues Under the Sea
Two Men of Sandy Bar
The Way of the World
What Love Can Do
Where Are My Children?
The Whirlpool of Destiny
A Yoke of Gold
A Youth of Fortune
1917 Beloved Jim
The Birth of Patriotism

The Bronze Bride
Bucking Broadway
The Circus of Life
Come Through
The Cricket
Double Room Mystery
The Double Standard
The Edge of the Law
Eternal Love
Even As You and I
Fear Not
The Field of Honor
Fighting for Love
The Fighting Gringo
Fighting Mad
The Flame of Youth
The Flower of Doom
Follow the Girl
'49-'17
The Gates of Doom
The Girl and the Crisis
The Girl Who Won Out
The Hand That Rocks the
   Cradle
Heart Strings
The Hero of the Hour
The High Sign
High Speed
John Ermine of the
   Yellowstone
The Lair of the Wolf
Like Wildfire
The Little Pirate
Love Aflame
Man and Beast
The Man from Montana
A Marked Man
The Midnight Man
Mr. Dolan of New York
Money Madness
Pay Me
The Phantom's Secret
The Plow Woman
Polly Put the Kettle On
The Price of a Good Time
The Reed Case
The Scarlet Crystal
The Secret Man
The Silent Lady
Sirens of the Sea
Society's Driftwood
A Soul for Sale‡
The Spindle of Life
Straight Shooting
The Terror
The War of the Tongs
Who Was the Other Man?
A Wife on Trial
1918 After the War
Beauty in Chains
Borrowed Clothes*
Bread
The Bride's Awakening
Crashing Through to Berlin
The Craving
Danger—Go Slow
The Flash of Fate
The Girl Who Wouldn't Quit
The Grand Passion
Hell Bent
Hell's Crater
Her Body in Bond
Keep the Home Fires Burning
Kiss or Kill
Madame Spy
The Magic Eye
The Model's Confession
Modern Love
The Mortgaged Wife
New Love for Old
Nobody's Wife
Painted Lips
The Phantom Riders
The Risky Road
The Scarlet Drop
Smashing Through
The Talk of the Town
Thieves' Gold
Three Mounted Men
The Vanity Pool
Wild Women
The Wildcat of Paris
The Wolf and His Mate
A Woman's Fool
The Yanks Are Coming

The Yellow Dog
1919 The Ace of the Saddle
The Amazing Wife
Bare Fists
The Big Little Person
Blind Husbands
The Blinding Trail
Bonnie, Bonnie Lassie
The Brute Breaker
Common Property
Creaking Stairs
The Day She Paid
The Delicious Little Devil
Destiny
The Exquisite Thief
A Fight for Love
The Fire Flingers
Forbidden
The Great Air Robbery
A Gun Fightin' Gentleman
Heads Win
The Heart of Humanity
His Divorced Wife
Home
Lasca
The Light of Victory
A Little Brother of the Rich
Loot
The Man in the Moonlight
Marked Men
The Outcasts of Poker Flats
Paid in Advance
The Petal on the Current
The Pointing Finger
Pretty Smooth
The Rider of the Law
Riders of Vengeance
The Right to Happiness
Roped
The Scarlet Shadow
The Silk Lined Burglar
The Sleeping Lion
The Spitfire of Seville
The Sundown Trail
The Trap
The Trembling Hour
Under Suspicion
The Unpainted Woman
The Weaker Vessel
What Am I Bid?
When a Girl Loves
The Wicked Darling
The Woman Under Cover
1920 The Adorable Savage
Alias Miss Dodd
Beautifully Trimmed
Below the Deadline
Blue Streak McCoy
The Breath of the Gods
Bullet Proof
Burnt Wings
The Devil's Passkey
Everything but the Truth
Fixed by George
The Forged Bride
The Gilded Dream
The Girl in Number 29
The Girl in the Rain
Hearts Up
Her Five-Foot Highness
Hitchin' Posts
Honor Bound
Human Stuff
In Folly's Trail
La La Lucille
Locked Lips
The Marriage Pit
Once a Plumber
Once to Every Woman
Outside the Law
Overland Red
The Path She Chose
The Peddler of Lies
The Phantom Melody
Pink Tights
The Prince of Avenue A
The Red Lane
Risky Business
The Road to Divorce
Rouge and Riches
The Secret Gift
Shipwrecked Among Cannibals
Sundown Slim
A Tokio Siren
The Triflers

Two Kinds of Love
Under Crimson Skies
Under Northern Lights
The Virgin of Stamboul
Wanted at Headquarters
West Is West
White Youth

Universal Film Mfg. Co.; Imp *see also*
Imp (Independent Moving Picture
Co.) and Imp Film Co.
1915 Conscience
Courtmartialed
The Suburban
The White Terror
The Wolf of Debt

Universal Film Mfg. Co.; Laemmle Brand
1915 Heritage

Universal Film Mfg. Co.; 101 Bison
1914 Richelieu
1915 Coral

Utah Moving Picture Co.
1913 One Hundred Years of
   Mormonism

V

V-L-S-E, Inc. *predecessor of*
Vitagraph—V-L-S-E, Inc. *see also*
Greater Vitagraph, Inc.; Greater
Vitagraph (V-L-S-E) and Greater
Vitagraph (V-L-S-E, Inc.)
1915 The Alster Case
The Battle Cry of Peace
A Black Sheep
A Bunch of Keys
The Carpet from Bagdad
The Cave Man
The Chalice of Courage
The Circular Staircase
The Climbers
The College Widow
The Crimson Wing
Crooky
A Daughter of the City
The District Attorney
The Dust of Egypt
The Eagle's Nest
Graustark
The Great Divide
The Great Ruby
Hearts and the Highway
The Heights of Hazard
The House of a Thousand
   Candles
I'm Glad My Boy Grew Up to
   Be a Soldier
In the Palace of the King
The Island of Regeneration
The Juggernaut
The Making Over of Geoffrey
   Manning
The Man Trail
The Man Who Couldn't Beat
   God
A Man's Making
The Millionaire Baby
Mortmain
The Nation's Peril
Playing Dead
A Price for Folly
The Raven
The Rights of Man: A Story of
   War's Red Blotch
The Ringtailed Rhinoceros
The Rosary
The Sins of the Mothers
The Slim Princess
The Sporting Duchess
Sweet Alyssum
A Texas Steer
Tillie's Tomato Surprise
To Cherish and Protect
The Turn of the Road
The Valley of Lost Hope
What Happened to Father
The Wheels of Justice
The White Sister
1916 According to the Code
The Alibi
Artie, the Millionaire Kid
At Piney Ridge
Britton of the Seventh
Captain Jinks of the Horse
   Marines

1919-20
　　The Tower of Jewels
　　When a Man Loves
1920　Bab's Candidate
　　The Birth of a Soul
　　The Broadway Bubble
　　Captain Swift
　　The Courage of Marge
　　　O'Doone
　　Dead Men Tell No Tales
　　Deadline at Eleven
　　Dollars and the Woman
　　The Flaming Clue
　　The Fortune Hunter
　　The Garter Girl
　　The Gauntlet
　　Human Collateral
　　A Master Stroke
　　The Midnight Bride
　　Pegeen
　　The Prey
　　The Purple Cipher
　　The Romance Promoters
　　The Sea Rider
　　Slaves of Pride
　　The Sporting Duchess
　　Trumpet Island
　　The Vice of Fools
　　The Whisper Market

Vitagraph-Liebler Feature Film Co.
1914　The Christian

Vitagraph—V-L-S-E, Inc. *successor to*
V-L-S-E, Inc. *see* **Greater Vitagraph,**
Inc.; Greater Vitagraph (V-L-S-E);
and **Greater Vitagraph (V-L-S-E,**
Inc.)

Volunteer Organist Co.
1913　The Volunteer Organist

W

W. H. Clifford Photoplay Co.
1918　Denny from Ireland
　　The Pen Vulture
　　The Prisoner of War
　　The Ranger
　　The Snail

W. H. Productions Co.
1915　The Devil*
　　On the Night Stage*
1918　Mickey
　　Staking His Life
1919　Everybody's Business
　　The Lost Battalion

W. T. Gaskell
1919　The Shepherd of the Hills

W. W. Hodkinson
1913　The Sea Wolf
1914　John Barleycorn
　　Martin Eden
　　The Valley of the Moon

W. W. Hodkinson Corp.
1918　An Alien Enemy
　　Angel Child
　　Blindfolded
　　A Burglar for a Night
　　The Challenge Accepted
　　Cupid Angling
　　The Embarrassment of Riches
　　The Goddess of Lost Lake
　　The Heart of Rachael
　　His Robe of Honor
　　Humdrum Brown
　　The Law That Divides
　　A Law unto Herself
　　Madam Who
　　Maid O' the Storm
　　A Man's Man
　　One Dollar Bid
　　Patriotism
　　Petticoats and Politics
　　Prisoners of the Pines
　　Rose O' Paradise
　　Shackled
　　Three X Gordon
　　The Turn of a Card
　　Two-Gun Betty
　　Wedlock
　　Whatever the Cost
　　The White Lie
　　With Hoops of Steel
　　Within the Cup

1919　As a Man Thinks
　　The Bandbox
　　The Best Man
　　The Blue Bonnet
　　The Capitol
　　Come Again Smith
　　Desert Gold
　　The Drifters
　　The End of the Game
　　Fighting Through
　　The Forfeit
　　The Joyous Liar
　　The Lone Wolf's Daughter
　　The Lord Loves the Irish
　　The Love Hunger
　　Sahara
　　Thunderbolts of Fate
　　The Volcano
　　The Westerners
　　A White Man's Chance
　　You Never Know Your Luck*
1920　The Broken Gate
　　The Brute Master
　　The Coast of Opportunity
　　Cynthia-of-the-Minute
　　Down Home
　　The Dream Cheater
　　The Dwelling Place of Light
　　The Green Flame
　　The Harvest Moon
　　His Temporary Wife
　　The House of Whispers
　　The Kentucky Colonel
　　King Spruce
　　Live Sparks
　　Love Madness
　　Number 99
　　Pagan Love
　　Riders of the Dawn
　　The Sagebrusher
　　Sex
　　The Silent Barrier
　　The Spenders
　　$30,000
　　The Tiger's Coat
　　The U.P. Trail

Waldorf Film Corp. *see also* **Waldorf**
Photoplays, Inc.
1920　Kismet

Waldorf Photoplays, Inc. *see also*
Waldorf Film Corp.
1919　Where Bonds Are Loosed
1920　Dad's Girl

Walker and Duke
1915　The Folly of a Life of Crime*

Walker, Lillian, Pictures Corp. *see* **Lillian**
Walker Pictures Corp.

Walker, Lillian, Pictures, Inc. *see* **Lillian**
Walker Pictures Corp.

Walter Miller Feature Film Co.
1915　Winning the Futurity

War Film Syndicate Co.
1915　On the Firing Line with the
　　Germans

War Films Inc. of Pittsburgh
1920　Chateau-Thierry, St.-Mihiel
　　and Argonne

Wark Producing Corp.
1916　Intolerance

Warner Brothers
1916　Robinson Crusoe
1918　The Kaiser's Finish
1919　Beware
　　Open Your Eyes

Warner's Features, Inc. *see also* **United**
Film Service
1913　The Man from the Golden
　　West
1914　The Adventures of Kitty Cobb
　　Alone in New York
　　The Burglar and the Lady
　　Even unto Death
　　The Light Unseen
　　The Lust of the Red Man
　　Mother Love
　　The Temptations of Satan
1916　Inherited Passions

Warren, Edward, Productions *see* **Edward**
Warren Productions

Warwick, Robert, Film Corp. *see* **Robert**
Warwick Film Corp.

Washington Motion Picture Corp.
1919　Fool's Gold

Weber, L. Lawrence, Photo
Dramas, Inc. *see* **L. Lawrence Weber Photo**
Dramas, Inc.

Weber, Lois, Productions *see* **Lois Weber**
Productions

Weber Productions, Inc. *not the same*
as **Lois Weber Productions**
1920　Children of Destiny

Webster, Harry McRae, Productions,
Inc. *see* **Harry McRae Webster**
Productions, Inc.

Weiss, Joseph Leon *see* **Joseph Leon**
Weiss

Welfare Exhibit Co.
1915　Gambling Inside and Out

Werba-Luescher, Inc.
1915　Unto the Darkness

Werner and Abrams *see also* **Abrams &**
Werner
1917-18
　　The Devil's Playground

West, Roland, Film Corp. *see* **Roland**
West Film Corp.

Western Book Supply Co.
1919　The Homesteader

Western Import Co.
1914　The Avenging Conscience;
　　　Thou Shalt Not Kill
　　The Escape*
1918　Mickey*

Western Pictures Exploitation Co.
1920　Neptune's Bride

Wharton, Inc.
1914　The Boundary Rider
　　The Pawn of Fortune
　　A Prince of India
1916　Hazel Kirke
1917　The Black Stork
　　The Great White Trail
1918-19
　　April Fool‡
　　The Candidates‡
　　Marriage a la Mode‡
　　The Missionary‡

Whitman Bennett Productions
1920　The Devil's Garden
　　The Master Mind
　　The Truth About Husbands

Whitman Features Co.
1914　Jane Eyre
　　Lena Rivers
　　The Toll of Love

Wholesome Film Corp. *same as*
Wholesome Films Corp.
1917　Cinderella and the Magic
　　　Slipper
　　The Penny Philanthropist
1918　Little Red Riding Hood
1920　Humpty Dumpty
　　Twinkle Twinkle Little Star

Wick War Film Corp.
1918　The Accidental Honeymoon

Wilbur H. Durborough
1915　On the Firing Line with the
　　Germans

Wild West Film Co.
1917　The Buffalo Bill Show

Wilk and Wilk
1918　The Curse of Iku*

Willat Productions, Inc.
1920　Down Home

Willemsen & Co.
1920　On the Trail of the
　　Conquistadores

William A. Brady *see also* **William A.**
Brady Picture Plays, Inc.
1918　The Cross Bearer
　　Stolen Orders
1919　Little Women
1920　Life

William A. Brady Picture Plays, Inc. *see*
also **William A. Brady**
1914　As Ye Sow
　　The Dollar Mark
　　A Gentleman from Mississippi
　　The Man of the Hour
　　Mother
　　The Pit
1915　After Dark
　　The Boss

　　The Cotton King
　　The Cub
　　The Face in the Moonlight
　　The Family Cupboard
　　The Impostor
　　The Ivory Snuff Box
　　Little Miss Brown
　　The Man Who Found Himself
　　The Model
　　The Sins of Society
　　The Stolen Voice
　　What Happened to Jones
1916　The Ballet Girl
　　Bought and Paid For
　　Broken Chains
　　Fruits of Desire
　　Love's Crucible
　　The Rack
　　A Woman's Power

William Christy Cabanne Producing Co.
1919　Fighting Through

William Cooper
1918　For the Freedom of the East

William D. Taylor Productions
1920　The Furnace
　　Huckleberry Finn
　　The Soul of Youth

William Fox Vaudeville Co. *predecessor*
of **Fox Film Corp.** *see also* **Box Office**
Attraction Co.
1915　A Fool There Was
　　A Gilded Fool
　　Kreutzer Sonata

William L. Sherrill Feature Corp.
1917　The Accomplice
　　The Rainbow

William L. Sherry Service
1918　The Inn of the Blue Moon
　　Marriage
　　Out of the Night
　　A Romance of the Underworld
　　The Street of Seven Stars
　　Wild Honey
1919　Calibre 38
　　Love and the Law
　　Marriage for Convenience
　　Red Blood and Yellow
　　The Son-of-a-Gun!
　　Twilight

William N. Selig *see also* **Selig Polyscope**
Co. *and* **Selig Studios**
1918　Little Orphant Annie
1920　Vengeance and the Girl
19--　Sic-Em

William Russell Productions, Inc.
1918　All the World to Nothing
　　Hearts or Diamonds?
　　Hobbs in a Hurry
　　Up Romance Road
1919　Brass Buttons
　　A Sporting Chance
　　This Hero Stuff
　　When a Man Rides Alone
　　Where the West Begins

William S. Hart Co. *see also* **William S.**
Hart Productions, Inc.
1920　The Cradle of Courage
　　Sand!
　　The Toll Gate

William S. Hart Productions, Inc. *see*
also **William S. Hart Co.**
1917　The Narrow Trail
1918　Blue Blazes Rawden
　　The Border Wireless
　　Branding Broadway
　　Riddle Gawne
　　Selfish Yates
　　Shark Monroe
　　The Tiger Man
　　Wolves of the Rail
1919　Breed of Men
　　John Petticoats
　　The Money Corral
　　The Poppy Girl's Husband
　　Square Deal Sanderson
　　Wagon Tracks
1920　The Testing Block

William Steiner Productions *same as*
William Steiner Production Co.
1920　The Bromley Case
　　Circumstantial Evidence
　　The Sacred Ruby
　　The Scrap of Paper
　　Sky Eye

The Trail of the Cigarette
The Triple Clue
The Wall Street Mystery
1920-21
  The House of Mystery
William Stoermer Enterprises
1918 The Tidal Wave
Williamson Submarine Film Corp. *see*
  also **Submarine Film Corp.**
1916 20,000 Leagues Under the Sea
Wilson, Ben, Productions *see* **Ben Wilson**
  Productions
Winsome Stars Corp.
1919 Diane of the Green Van
  A Man's Country
Wistaria Productions, Inc.
1920 Why Women Sin
Woods, A. H. *see* **A. H. Woods**
World Film Corp. *see also* subdivisions
  World Film Corp.; A Liebler Feature;
  World Film Corp.; A Shubert Feature;
  World Film Corp.; Armstrong; World
  Film Corp.; Blaney *and* **World Film**
  Corp.; Peerless
1914 Across the Pacific
  America
  As Ye Sow
  The Chimes
  The Dancer and the King
  The Dollar Mark
  For the Honor of Old Glory;
    Or, The Stars and Stripes in
    Mexico
  A Gentleman from Mississippi
  In the Land of the Head
    Hunters
  In the Name of the Prince of
    Peace
  Jess of the Mountain Country
  The Kangaroo
  Lola
  The Man of the Hour
  The Marked Woman
  Mrs. Wiggs of the Cabbage
    Patch
  Mother
  The Mystery of Edwin Drood
  One of Millions
  The Outlaw Reforms
  The Pit
  The Price of Treachery; Or,
    The Lighthouse Keeper's
    Daughter
  The Seats of the Mighty
  Uncle Tom's Cabin
  When Broadway Was a Trail
  The Wishing Ring; An Idyll of
    Old England
  Your Girl and Mine: A
    Woman Suffrage Play
1915 The Adventures of a Boy Scout
  After Dark
  Alias Jimmy Valentine
  The Arrival of Perpetua
  The Better Woman
  The Bludgeon
  Blue Grass
  Body and Soul
  The Boss
  Bought
  The Builder of Bridges
  The Butterfly
  A Butterfly on the Wheel
  Camille
  Colonel Carter of Cartersville
  The Cotton King
  The Cowardly Way
  The Cub
  The Daughter of the People
  The Daughter of the Sea
  The Deep Purple
  Divorced
  Evidence
  The Face in the Moonlight
  The Fairy and the Waif
  The Family Cupboard
  The Fifth Commandment
  The Fight
  Fine Feathers
  The Flash of an Emerald
  The Gray Mask
  The Heart of the Blue Ridge
  Hearts in Exile
  Hearts of Men

The Impostor
The Ivory Snuff Box
The Labyrinth
The Lily of Poverty Flat
The Little Dutch Girl
The Little Mademoiselle
Little Miss Brown
The Lure of Woman
The Man Who Found Himself
Marrying Money
The Master Hand
The Master of the House
Mignon
M'liss
The Model
Money
The Moonstone
Not Guilty
Old Dutch
Over Night
A Phyllis of the Sierras
The Price
Salvation Nell
Sealed Lips
The Senator
Should a Wife Forgive?
The Sins of Society
The Siren's Song
The Stolen Voice
Sunday
Trilby
The Warning
What Happened to Jones
When It Strikes Home
Wildfire
1915-16
  The Little Church Around the
    Corner
1916 All Man
  The Almighty Dollar
  As in a Looking Glass
  The Ballet Girl
  Behind Closed Doors
  Bought and Paid For
  Broken Chains
  By Whose Hand?
  A Circus Romance
  The City
  The Clarion
  The Closed Road
  The Crucial Test
  The Dark Silence
  The Devil's Toy
  The Dragon
  Fate's Boomerang
  The Feast of Life
  Friday the Thirteenth
  Fruits of Desire
  The Gilded Cage
  The Hand of Peril
  The Heart of a Hero
  Her Great Hour
  Her Maternal Right
  The Hidden Scar
  His Brother's Wife
  Human Driftwood
  Husband and Wife
  Idols
  Life's Whirlpool
  Love's Crucible
  The Madness of Helen
  Man and His Angel
  The Man Who Stood Still
  The Men She Married
  Miss Petticoats
  Passers By
  The Pawn of Fate
  Paying the Price
  The Perils of Divorce
  The Price of Happiness
  The Question
  The Rack
  The Rail Rider
  The Ransom
  The Reapers
  The Revolt
  The Rise of Susan
  Sally in Our Alley
  The Scarlet Oath
  The Shadow of a Doubt
  The Social Highwayman
  The Struggle
  Sudden Riches
  The Summer Girl
  The Supreme Sacrifice

Tangled Fates
Then I'll Come Back to You
The Twin Triangle
The Unpardonable Sin
The Velvet Paw
La Vie de Boheme
The Weakness of Man
What Happened at 22
The Woman in 47
A Woman's Power
A Woman's Way
The World Against Him
The Yellow Passport
1917 The Adventures of Carol
  As Man Made Her
  The Awakening
  The Beloved Adventuress
  Betsy Ross
  The Bondage of Fear
  The Brand of Satan
  The Burglar
  The Corner Grocer
  The Crimson Dove
  The Dancer's Peril
  Darkest Russia
  Diamonds and Pearls
  The Divorce Game
  The Dormant Power
  Easy Money
  The False Friend
  The Family Honor
  Forget-Me-Not
  A Girl's Folly
  The Good for Nothing
  The Guardian
  Her Hour
  A Hungry Heart
  The Iron Ring
  The Little Duchess
  The Maid of Belgium
  The Man Who Forgot
  Man's Woman
  The Marriage Market
  Maternity
  Moral Courage
  On Dangerous Ground
  The Page Mystery
  The Price of Pride
  Rasputin, the Black Monk
  The Red Woman
  A Self-Made Widow
  Shall We Forgive Her?
  The Social Leper
  Souls Adrift
  A Square Deal
  The Stolen Paradise
  The Strong Way
  The Tenth Case
  The Tides of Fate
  Tillie Wakes Up
  The Volunteer
  The Web of Desire
  A Woman Alone
  The Woman Beneath
  Yankee Pluck
  Youth
1918 The Appearance of Evil
  The Beautiful Mrs. Reynolds
  The Beloved Blackmailer
  Broken Ties
  By Hook or Crook
  The Cabaret
  The Cross Bearer
  The Divine Sacrifice
  Eight Bells
  Gates of Gladness
  The Golden Wall
  The Grouch
  The Heart of a Girl
  Heredity
  His Royal Highness
  Hitting the Trail
  Inside the Lines
  The Interloper
  Joan of the Woods
  Journey's End
  Just Sylvia
  Leap to Fame
  Little Orphant Annie*
  The Love Net
  The Man Hunt
  The Man of Bronze
  Merely Players
  Neighbors
  The Oldest Law

The Power and the Glory
The Purple Lily
The Road to France
The Sea Waif
A Soul Without Windows
The Spurs of Sybil
Stolen Hours
Tinsel
To Him That Hath
T'Other Dear Charmer
The Trap
The Unchastened Woman*
Under Four Flags
Vengeance
Wanted, a Mother
The Wasp
The Way Out
Whims of Society
The Witch Woman
A Woman of Redemption
The Zero Hour
1919 An Amateur Widow
  The American Way
  The Arizona Cat Claw
  The Battler
  The Black Circle
  The Bluffer
  Bringing Up Betty
  A Broadway Saint
  The Clouded Name
  Coax Me
  Courage for Two
  The Crook of Dreams
  The Devil's Trail
  Dust of Desire
  Forest Rivals
  Ginger
  The Girl Alaska
  The Hand Invisible
  Heart of Gold
  His Father's Wife
  Hit or Miss
  Home Wanted
  The Little Intruder
  Love and the Woman
  The Love Defender
  Love in a Hurry
  Mandarin's Gold
  Me and Captain Kidd
  Miss Crusoe
  The Moral Deadline
  The Oakdale Affair
  Phil-for-Short
  The Poison Pen
  The Praise Agent
  The Quickening Flame
  The Rough Neck
  The Scar
  The Social Pirate
  The Steel King
  Three Green Eyes
  Through the Toils
  The Unveiling Hand
  The Unwritten Code
  What Love Forgives
  What Shall We Do with Him?
  When Bearcat Went Dry
  Where Bonds Are Loosed
  The Woman of Lies
  You Never Know Your Luck
1920 The Blue Pearl*
World Film Corp.; A Liebler Feature *see*
  also **Liebler Co.**
1915 The Deep Purple
World Film Corp.; A Shubert Feature *see*
  also **Shubert Film Corp.**
1914 Lola
  The Marked Woman
  The Mystery of Edwin Drood
  The Wishing Ring; An Idyll of
    Old England
1915 The Flash of an Emerald
  The Heart of the Blue Ridge
  Hearts in Exile
  The Little Mademoiselle
  Marrying Money
  M'liss
  The Moonstone
  Wildfire
1916 Life's Whirlpool
  The Yellow Passport
World Film Corp.; Armstrong
1915 The Lure of Woman

257

World Film Corp.; Blaney *see also*
Charles E. Blaney Productions
1915-16
    The Little Church Around the
      Corner
World Film Corp.; Peerless *see also*
Peerless Features Producing Co.
1915 Alias Jimmy Valentine
1916 All Man
    The Dark Silence
    Friday the Thirteenth
    The Gilded Cage
    The Heart of a Hero
    The Hidden Scar
    Husband and Wife
    The Men She Married
    Miss Petticoats
    The Perils of Divorce
    The Revolt
    The Rise of Susan
    The Scarlet Oath
    Sudden Riches
    The Summer Girl
    Tangled Fates
    The Weakness of Man
    A Woman's Way
1917 As Man Made Her
    The Beloved Adventuress
    Betsy Ross
    The Bondage of Fear
    The Brand of Satan
    The Corner Grocer
    The Crimson Dove
    Darkest Russia
    The Divorce Game
    The Dormant Power
    Easy Money
    The False Friend
    The Family Honor
    Forget-Me-Not
    The Good for Nothing
    The Guardian
    A Hungry Heart
    The Iron Ring
    The Little Duchess
    The Maid of Belgium
    The Marriage Market
    Maternity
    Moral Courage
    On Dangerous Ground
    The Page Mystery
    The Price of Pride
    Rasputin, the Black Monk
    A Self-Made Widow
    Shall We Forgive Her?
    The Social Leper
    Souls Adrift
    A Square Deal
    The Stolen Paradise
    Tillie Wakes Up
    The Web of Desire
    A Woman Alone
    The Woman Beneath
    Youth
World Producing Corp.
1914 Uncle Tom's Cabin
World Series Film Co.
1915 1915 World's Championship
    Series
Wright, Harold Bell, Story Picture Corp.
see **Harold Bell Wright Story Picture**
Corp.
Wyndham Gittens Productions
1919 Give and Take

Y

Yale Feature Film Co.
1913 The Tonopah Stampede for
    Gold
Yankee Photo Corp.
1920 Headin' Home
Yearsley, C. L., Pictures *see* **A. C. L.**
Yearsley Picture
Yellowstone Productions, Inc.
1920 Dangerous Love
Yorke Film Corp.
1916 Big Tremaine
    Mister 44
    Pidgin Island
    The River of Romance

1917 The Avenging Trail
    The Haunted Pajamas
    The Hidden Children
    The Hidden Spring
    Paradise Garden
    The Promise
    The Square Deceiver
    Under Handicap
1918 Broadway Bill
    The Landloper
    Lend Me Your Name
    Pals First
1919 The Great Romance
    A Man of Honor
    Shadows of Suspicion
Young, Clara Kimball, Film Corp. *see*
Clara Kimball Young Film Corp.
Young, Clara Kimball, Picture Co. *see*
Clara Kimball Young Picture Co.
Youth Photo Play Co.
1914 A Boy and the Law

Z

Zane Grey Pictures, Inc.
1919 Desert Gold
1920 Riders of the Dawn
    The U.P. Trail
Zion Films, Inc.
1919 Broken Barriers

SUBJECT INDEX

★ As is the case with the *Personal Name* and *Corporate Name* indexes, the *Subject Index* is arranged alphabetically by headings. Film entries are subdivided chronologically, then alphabetically, beneath the headings. Most of the entries in the *Subject Index* correspond to the 10th edition of *Library of Congress Subject Headings*. However, following the philosophy of the Library of Congress to create a dynamic rather than static thesaurus, we have added a number of terms which reflect subjects important during the teens. Thus the user will find such subject headings as **Vamps** and **Falls from heights** in our index even though they are not currently listed in the Library of Congress' list of subject headings.

In the index, the reader will notice several headings which, despite efforts at paring, are enormous. **Murder**, and its related headings of **Attempted murder, Justifiable homicide** and **Manslaughter**, for example, has over 800 entries. **Impersonation and imposture** is cited over 400 times. Yet the reason why these categories are so vast is that they were extremely popular motifs in the teens. To increase the value of this seemingly overwhelming number of films, a scheme of "major" and "minor" headings was devised to divide each category. Thus, the user will find titles in Roman type representing important themes in the film, while titles listed in italics indicate minor importance in the film.

We hope that this distinction will increase the value of the index, both as a listing of important subjects and also as a motif or "key word" index for those scholars interested in knowing all films pertinent to particular themes, locations, or persons. We have also provided cross headings for similar or related terms. Under **Accidents**, for example, a non-specific term, we have indicated as *nt*, that is, narrow terms, specific types of accidents which are included under that category.

For similar, but slightly different terms, such as **Blackmail** and **Extortion**, we have indicated *rt* or related terms. Thus, a user seeking the titles of films in which blackmail is a theme can look them up under **Blackmail** and find an *rt* reference to the closely linked term **Extortion** to broaden the field.

Related term links can also be used to narrow a search. By combining entries under two or more topics, such as **Americans in foreign countries** with **Japan**, the user can more quickly find films on more specific topics, in this instance, Americans in Japan. Additional linkage is provided with *Use* references which direct the user from an inappropriate term to the correct one. Parenthetical words, called "scope notes" give brief definitions for terms such as **Orderlies** which have more than one meaning. In the "Subject Index" the term is listed twice, as **Orderlies** (hospital) and as **Orderlies** (military).

Actual historical persons and geographic locations are listed in the *Subject Index* in addition to themes. Literary works and fictional characters are also included if they were significant to the plots of individual films.

SUBJECT INDEX

261

Americans in foreign countries
1914 *Aristocracy*
    The Battle of Gettysgoat
    Captain Alvarez
    The Christian
    The Education of Mr. Pipp
    Fire and Sword
    The Giants-White Sox Tour
    Imar the Servitor
    The Lightning Conductor
    The Man from Home
    Mr. Barnes of New York
    My Official Wife
    The Mystery of the Poison Pool
    Soldiers of Fortune
    The Spitfire
    The Tigress
    The Typhoon
    The War Extra
    The Wrath of the Gods
1915 The Apaches of Paris
    Blackbirds
    The Carpet from Bagdad
    Comrade John
    The Dictator
    The Forbidden Adventure
    The Fox Woman
    The Galley Slave
    The Galloper
    The Garden of Lies
    Graustark
    The House of the Lost Court
    The Ivory Snuff Box
    Madame Butterfly
    Mr. Grex of Monte Carlo
    The Outlaw's Revenge
    The Puppet Crown
    The Rug Maker's Daughter
    Saved from the Harem
    The Slim Princess
    The Stubbornness of Geraldine
    The Unafraid
    The Unknown
    The Voice in the Fog
    The Whirl of Life
    The White Pearl
    The Woman Next Door
    The Yankee Girl
1916 The Adventures of Kathlyn
    Black Friday
    The Chalice of Sorrow
    A Corner in Colleens
    The Crucial Test
    The Diamond Runners
    Diplomacy
    The Gilded Spider
    The Girl Philippa
    Her American Prince
    The Impersonation
    An International Marriage
    The Lotus Woman
    My Lady's Slipper
    Peggy
    The Prince Chap
    The Red Widow
    The Road to Love
    The Spider and the Fly
    The Woman in the Case
    The Woman Who Dared
1917 Aladdin from Broadway
    The American Consul
    American Maid
    American Methods
    The Americano
    Arms and the Girl
    Billy and the Big Stick
    The Call of the East
    The Courage of Silence
    The Eternal Temptress
    The Fair Barbarian
    Fighting for Love
    Filling His Own Shoes
    For France
    For Liberty
    Her Silent Sacrifice
    Intrigue
    The Jaguar's Claws
    Lady Barnacle
    The Lady of the Photograph
    The Last Sentence
    The Lifted Veil
    The Little American
    The Maid of Belgium
    The Man Who Forgot
    The Martinache Marriage

Mr. Dolan of New York
On Dangerous Ground
Paws of the Bear
The Price She Paid
Princess Virtue
The Red Woman
Rosie O'Grady
The Silent Master
The Spirit of '76
Under False Colors
*Womanhood, the Glory of the
    Nation*
Wooden Shoes
Wrath
1918 An American Live Wire
    The Bird of Prey
    Bound in Morocco
    A Burglar for a Night
    Cactus Crandall
    The Curse of Iku
    A Diplomatic Mission
    The Firebrand
    For the Freedom of the East
    The Forbidden City
    Hearts of the World
    Her American Husband
    His Royal Highness
    Hitting the High Spots
    Inside the Lines
    Lafayette, We Come!
    A Man's World
    Over the Top
    Patriotism
    Revelation
    The Road Through the Dark
    The Shuttle
    The Snail
    The Strange Woman
    The Temple of Dusk
    To Hell with the Kaiser
    The Turn of the Wheel
    Under the Yoke
    Within the Cup
    A Woman of Impulse
    The Yellow Ticket
1918-19
    The Kaiser's Bride
1919 *Almost Married*
    L'Apache
    Auction of Souls
    Blind Husbands
    Bullin' the Bullsheviki
    Daring Hearts
    The Dark Star
    Forest Rivals
    The Girl Who Stayed at Home
    The Great Romance
    *The Great Victory, Wilson or
    the Kaiser? The Fall of the
    Hohenzollerns*
    Hawthorne of the U.S.A.
    Her Code of Honor
    His Parisian Wife
    The Illustrious Prince
    Love in a Hurry
    The Miracle of Love
    A Misfit Earl
    Our Better Selves
    The Pagan God
    The Prince and Betty
    The Quickening Flame
    *Reclaimed: The Struggle for a
    Soul Between Love and
    Hate*
    The Red Lantern
    The Right to Happiness
    The Scar
    A Society Exile
    Soldiers of Fortune
    The Splendid Romance
    The Splendid Sin
    Toton
    The Unwritten Code
    The Vengeance of Durand
    When a Man Rides Alone
    When Arizona Won
    When Men Desire
    Whitewashed Walls
    The Wolf
    The World and Its Woman
    Yankee Doodle in Berlin
1919-20
    Piccadilly Jim
1920 An Adventuress
    An Arabian Knight

Blind Youth
Body and Soul
Burnt Wings
Children of Destiny
The Coast of Opportunity
Crooked Streets
The Devil's Passkey
A Double Dyed Deceiver
The Empire of Diamonds
Flames of the Flesh
A Fool and His Money
The Good-Bad Wife
Her Five-Foot Highness
The Honey Bee
Little Miss Rebellion
The Luck of the Irish
The Man Who Lost Himself
The Mollycoddle
The Palace of Darkened
    Windows
Rogues and Romance
Shipwrecked Among Cannibals
The Slim Princess
Something Different
A Tokio Siren
The Truth About Husbands
Under Crimson Skies
The Virgin of Stamboul
What Women Want
The Whisper Market

Ammunition
  rt **Explosives**
1916 *American Aristocracy*
1917 *Her Country's Call*
1918 *Private Peat*

Amnesia
1913 The Girl of the Sunny South
    Hoodman Blind
1914 Born Again
    Called Back
    The Invisible Power
    The Key to Yesterday
    A Million Bid
    *The Strange Story of Sylvia
    Gray*
    Through Dante's Flames
    When Fate Leads Trump
1915 *Aloha Oe*
    Body and Soul
    The Buzzard's Shadow
    Judy Forgot
    Out of the Darkness
    The Right of Way
    The White Pearl
1916 *Autumn*
    The Devil's Toy
    A Dream or Two Ago
    Extravagance
    The Female of the Species
    The Innocent Lie
    The Island of Surprise
    The Lost Bridegroom
    Pay Dirt
    The Price of Power
    The Sign of the Poppy
    The Straight Way
    The Struggle
    The Suspect
    Thou Shalt Not Covet
    Through the Wall
    The Woman's Law
1917 The Bride's Silence
    The Edge of the Law
    The Great White Trail
    The Lad and the Lion
    The Maid of Belgium
    Poppy
    A Sleeping Memory
1918 De Luxe Annie
    The Devil's Wheel
    The Knife
    Vive La France!
1919 The Darkest Hour
    The Drifters
    A Gentleman of Quality
    The Girl from Nowhere
    The Imp
    The Man Who Won
    The Mayor of Filbert
    Please Get Married
    The Sundown Trail
1920 Do the Dead Talk?
    Footlights and Shadows
    Love Without Question
    The Right of Way

The Sin That Was His
The Skywayman
Trumpet Island

Amphibians
1914 *The Book of Nature*

Amputees
1915 *I'm Glad My Boy Grew Up to
    Be a Soldier*
    The White Sister
1917 *For Valour*
1918 Too Fat to Fight
1919 Alias Mike Moran
    The Spirit of Lafayette
    The Volcano

Anarchists
1914 *The Envoy Extraordinary*
    Martin Eden
1915 *Money*
    The Money Master
    Poor Schmaltz
1916 *Arms and the Woman*
    The Clarion
1917 The Barker
    Fanatics
    The High Sign
    The Lash of Power
1918 The City of Purple Dreams
    The German Curse in Russia
    The Hard Rock Breed
    A Little Sister of Everybody
1919 *The Adventure Shop*
    The Great Romance
    The New Moon
    The Red Viper
    The Stronger Vow
    The World Aflame
1920 The Great Shadow

Anatomists
1915 *What Happened to Jones*

Ancestry
1916 The Dawn of Freedom
    Gold and the Woman
    Miss Petticoats
    Silks and Satins
1917 She
1918 The Curse of Iku
    Fast Company
    The Wild Strain
1919 Beware
    A Yankee Princess
1920 A Splendid Hazard
1921 Love's Plaything

Andalusia (Spain)
1915 Carmen (Fox Film Corp.)

Andes Mountains
1915 In the Amazon Jungles with
    the Captain Besley
    Expedition
    A Trip to the Argentine

Andirons
1915 *God's Witness*

Angels
1914 *Home, Sweet Home*
1918 *Little Red Riding Hood*

Animal life
  rt **Animals**
1914 The Book of Nature
    The Mysterious Man of the
    Jungle
1915 The Footsteps of Capt. Kidd
    Pirate Haunts
    Wild Life of America in Films
1916 *Race Suicide*
1920 The Gift of Life
    The Jungle Princess
    The Living World

Animal trainers
1915 Simon, the Jester
1920 Her Elephant Man

Animal traps
1916 *The Bait*
1917 *The Bronze Bride*

Animals
  rt **Animal life**
    Cruelty to animals
    Vivisection
    Wild animals
  nt Specific types of animals
1914 *Cinderella*
    The Magic Cloak of Oz

1919 *Easy to Make Money*
Fool's Gold
The Greater Victory
Square Deal Sanderson
This Hero Stuff
1920 *The Shark*

Bartenders
1918 *Amarilly of Clothes-Line
Alley*
Coals of Fire
Hit-the-Trail Holliday
1919 *Speedy Meade*
The Wicked Darling

Baseball
1914 The Giants-White Sox Tour
1915 1915 World's Championship
Series
The Grandee's Ring
Little Sunset
Right off the Bat
The Stolen Voice
1916 Casey at the Bat
Somewhere in Georgia
World Series Games 1916,
Boston vs. Brooklyn
1917 The Baseball Revue of 1917
One Touch of Nature
The Pinch Hitter
The Varmint
1919 *The Final Close-Up*
Muggsy
1920 Headin' Home

Baseball players
1915 The Grandee's Ring
Little Sunset
1916 Casey at the Bat
Somewhere in Georgia
World Series Games 1916,
Boston vs. Brooklyn
1917 The Baseball Revue of 1917
1919 Better Times
The Busher
The Greater Victory

Baseball scouts
1915 *Right off the Bat*
1916 *Somewhere in Georgia*

Basket sellers
1915 *The Great Divide*

Bath (England)
1916 Sweet Kitty Bellairs

Bathhouses
1918 *Borrowed Clothes*

Bathing suits
1918 The Venus Model

Baths
1918 Johanna Enlists
The Triumph of Venus

Battered children
1912 Oliver Twist
1914 The Criminal Code
The Crucible
1915 *Colorado*
The Fairy and the Waif
From the Valley of the Missing
The High Road
Kreutzer Sonata
Rags
Regeneration
Should a Mother Tell?
1916 *April*
A Woman's Daring
1917 The Desert Man
Her Right to Live
A Kentucky Cinderella
Kitty MacKay
The Law of the Land
A Man's Law
Poppy
1918 *Heredity*
Little Miss No-Account
The Shuttle
Stella Maris
1919 Broken Blossoms
The Brute Breaker
Ginger
The Sealed Envelope
1920 Heritage
Into the Light
Judy of Rogue's Harbor
The Scoffer

Battered men
1918 Uncle Tom's Cabin

Battered women
1913 *In the Bishop's Carriage*
1914 *The Chimes*
Ill Starred Babbie
Imar the Servitor
1915 *The Battle of Ballots*
Body and Soul
The Circular Staircase
Destruction
Dr. Rameau
*From the Valley of the
Missing*
Gretna Green
Heartaches
Heritage
The House of the Lost Court
Through Turbulent Waters
The Two Orphans
The Valley of Lost Hope
1916 *The Gringo*
Inherited Passions
The Island of Happiness
The Lash
Pasquale
Witchcraft
The World's Great Snare
1917 Corruption
The Cost of Hatred
The Courage of Silence
The Dormant Power
The End of the Tour
I Will Repay
The Lair of the Wolf
The Marriage Market
Mrs. Balfame
The Moth
Open Places
The Page Mystery
The Secret of Black Mountain
Shall We Forgive Her?
Tears and Smiles
A Woman's Awakening
1918 *The Bride's Awakening*
The Guilty Man
Her Moment
The Prussian Cur
The Reason Why
The Risky Road
The Safety Curtain
The Shuttle
The Strange Woman
Tyrant Fear
Wild Youth
The Woman Who Gave
1919 *The A.B.C. of Love*
The Battler
Calibre 38
The Faith of the Strong
The Hidden Truth
The Isle of Conquest
Jinx
A Man in the Open
Man's Desire
The Midnight Stage
The Miracle Man
The Miracle of Love
Out of the Shadow
The Painted World
Rose of the West
Silent Strength
Victory
What Every Woman Learns
When the Desert Smiles
The Witness for the Defense
The Woman on the Index
1920 The Brute
The Common Sin
A Fool and His Money
The Heart of a Woman
The Notorious Mrs. Sands
The Prey
The Rose of Nome

Battles
use Specific battles

Battleships
1913 *Mexican War Pictures
(William A. Brady)*
Victory
1915 *The Dictator*
Guarding Old Glory
*History of the Great European
War*
*In the Amazon Jungles with
the Captain Besley
Expedition*

The Nation's Peril
1916 *America Preparing*
1917 *Billy and the Big Stick*
1918 Our Navy
*Your Fighting Navy at Work
and at Play*

Bavaria (Germany)
1913 *The Lure of New York*

Bazaars
rt **Carnivals**
Fairs
1920 *A Trip Through Cairo*

Beachcombers
1915 *The Beachcomber*
The Flaming Sword
1918 *The Sea Flower*
1920 The Idol Dancer
Idols of Clay
Man and Woman (A. H.
Fischer Features, Inc.)

Beaches
1917 *Pants*
Periwinkle
1918 *The Velvet Hand*
1920 It Might Happen to You

Beans
1917 Jack and the Beanstalk
1918 *String Beans*

Bears
1915 *American Game Trails*
The Chalice of Courage
The Heart of the Blue Ridge
1916 *The Wild Girl of the Sierras*
1917 *A Roadside Impresario*
1918 *Jack Spurlock, Prodigal*
1919 *Fighting for Gold*
It's a Bear
The Oakdale Affair
Through the Wrong Door

Beauty
1917 Wooden Shoes
1918 I Love You
1920 The Perfect Woman

Beauty contests
1916 *The American Beauty*
1920 The Midlanders

Beauty shops
1919 The Veiled Adventure

Bedouins
1915 The Arab
1917 The Lad and the Lion
1918 Eye for Eye
1920 Moon Madness

Beds
1920 His Pajama Girl

Beer
1914 *John Barleycorn*

Beersheba
1919 *With Allenby in Palestine and
Lawrence in Arabia*

Beggars
1915 The Prince and the Pauper
The Two Orphans
1916 *The Beggar of Cawnpore*
1917 *Aladdin from Broadway*
Beloved Jim
Lost in Transit
1918 The Star Prince
1919 Fighting Destiny
Sahara
1920 Kismet
The Virgin of Stamboul

Belgian Americans
1918 Out of a Clear Sky

Belgian Relief Fund
1916 *Dust*

Belgians
1915 *The History of the World's
Greatest War*
1917 The Maid of Belgium
1918 The Belgian
The Cross Bearer
Daughter Angele
Patriotism
Till I Come Back to You
1920 *Flame of Youth*

Belgium
1914 On the Belgian Battlefield
1915 *Stolen Goods*
1917 *Arms and the Girl*
Paws of the Bear
Who Goes There!

1918 *The Appearance of Evil*
The Belgian
Crashing Through to Berlin
The Kaiser, the Beast of Berlin
The Man Who Wouldn't Tell
My Four Years in Germany
Over the Top
Till I Come Back to You
To Hell with the Kaiser
The Unbeliever
The Woman the Germans Shot
1919 The Unpardonable Sin
Whom the Gods Would
Destroy

Belgium. Army
1915 *History of the Great European
War*
*The History of the World's
Greatest War*
1918 The Belgian

Belgrade (Yugoslavia)
1916 *War on Three Fronts*

Bellboys
1916 *Love's Pilgrimage to America*
1920 Oil

Belleau Wood, Battle of, 1918
1918 *Under Four Flags*

Bells
1918 *The Bells*

Belmont Mine (Nevada)
1913 *The Tonopah Stampede for
Gold*

Belshazzar
1919 *The Fall of Babylon*

Beltsville (Maryland)
1919 Government Poultry Farm at
Beltsville, Md.

Bering Strait
1912 *Atop of the World in Motion*

Berlin
1915 *The German Side of the War*
1917 *For Liberty*
1918 Good-Bye, Bill
Kultur
The Spreading Evil
Wanted for Murder
1918-19
The Kaiser's Bride

Sarah Bernhardt
1920 *The Luck of Geraldine Laird*

Bethlehem
1913 *From the Manger to the Cross*
1919 *With Allenby in Palestine and
Lawrence in Arabia*

Bethulia
1914 Judith of Bethulia

Betrayal
1913 *A Sister to Carmen*
1914 *Aftermath*
Beneath the Czar
Cardinal Richelieu's Ward
The Corsair
The Eagle's Mate
The Gangsters
The Greyhound
In the Name of the Prince of
Peace
Judith of Bethulia
The Man O' Warsman
1915 *The Beloved Vagabond*
The Brink
Flame of Passion
For $5,000 a Year
The Green Cloak
Hearts of Men
Not Guilty
The Pitfall
Princess Romanoff
The Rosary
A Yankee from the West
A Yellow Streak
1915-16
The Little Church Around the
Corner
1916 *Anton the Terrible*
Black Friday
Bullets and Brown Eyes
The Heart of a Hero
Her Bleeding Heart
Joan the Woman
The Kiss of Hate
Pamela's Past
The Phantom Buccaneer

Her Hour
High Play
The Law That Failed
Light in Darkness
Love Letters
A Man's Law
The Marcellini Millions
Mary Lawson's Secret
The Outsider
Outwitted
Patsy
The Phantom's Secret
The Price Mark
Richard the Brazen
S.O.S.
A Self-Made Widow
Shackles of Truth
Shall We Forgive Her?
Should She Obey?
The Silence Sellers
The Small Town Guy
Soldiers of Chance
Somewhere in America
Thou Shalt Not Steal
Transgression
The Whip
1918 All Woman
The Bird of Prey
Blindfolded
The Blindness of Divorce
Buchanan's Wife
Cecilia of the Pink Roses
The City of Purple Dreams
The Claim
Convict 993
Danger—Go Slow
The Danger Zone
The Eleventh Commandment
Face Value
Fires of Youth
The First Law
For Freedom
For Sale
The Forbidden Path
The Girl with the Champagne
   Eyes
Her Final Reckoning
His Daughter Pays
The House of Silence
I Want to Forget
In Judgment Of
In the Hollow of Her Hand
Kiss or Kill
The Liar
Loaded Dice
Marriage
The Married Virgin
The Menace
Miss Innocence
Naughty, Naughty!
A Nine O'Clock Town
Old Hartwell's Cub
On the Quiet
The Painted Lily
The Prodigal Wife
Riders of the Night
The Road Through the Dark
The Safety Curtain
Secret Strings
The Service Star
Shifting Sands
The Snail
The Song of the Soul
The Still Alarm
Three Mounted Men
To Him That Hath
The Triumph of the Weak
The Vanity Pool
The Venus Model
The Widow's Might
1919 Adele
An Adventure in Hearts
The Adventure Shop
All of a Sudden Norma
The Amazing Wife
Are You Legally Married?
The Blue Bandanna
The Crook of Dreams
Day Dreams
The Echo of Youth
Flame of the Desert
His Wife's Friend
The Lion and the Mouse
The Lone Star Ranger
Love and the Woman

The Love Auction
Love Insurance
Mary Regan
Oh, Boy!
Out of the Shadow
Pitfalls of a Big City
The Profiteers
Prudence on Broadway
The Quickening Flame
The Right to Lie
The Sealed Envelope
Snares of Paris
The Spite Bride
A Sporting Chance (American
   Film Co.)
The Test of Honor
Thin Ice
The Thirteenth Chair
The Trap
The Trembling Hour
The Two Brides
The Virtuous Thief
What Love Forgives
The Winchester Woman
The Witness for the Defense
The Woman on the Index
The Woman Under Cover
A Woman's Experience
The Wreck
1919-20
The Tower of Jewels
1920 Blackmail
The Branded Woman
Clothes
The Deep Purple
The Devil's Passkey
The Discarded Woman
Dollar for Dollar
Don't Ever Marry
The Fatal Hour
The Fear Market
The Fighting Chance
For Love or Money
The Furnace
Harriet and the Piper
Heliotrope
Her Honor the Mayor
The Little 'Fraid Lady
The Little Outcast
Love, Honor and Behave
Madame X
The Man Who Lost Himself
Man's Plaything
A Modern Salome
Mothers of Men
Other Men's Shoes
Parted Curtains
The Plunger
Polly of the Storm Country
The Prey
The Return of Tarzan
The Riddle: Woman
The River's End
A Romantic Adventuress
Scratch My Back
Sunset Sprague
While New York Sleeps
The Whisper Market
The White Dove
Why Women Sin
Would You Forgive?
1921 Miss 139
1922 The Cynic Effect
Blacks
1914 At the Cross Roads
John Barleycorn
Mrs. Black Is Back
1915 The Birth of a Nation
The Life of Sam Davis: A
   Confederate Hero of the
   Sixties
Marse Covington
Sam Davis, the Hero of
   Tennessee
A Texas Steer
The Voice of Satan
1916 At Piney Ridge
Broken Chains
The Colored American
   Winning His Suit
The Ne'er-Do-Well
Unprotected
1917 The Bar Sinister
Billy and the Big Stick
The Bride of Hate

How Uncle Sam Prepares
I Will Repay
A Kentucky Cinderella
The Little Samaritan
Tom Sawyer
The Voice of Conscience
1918 Free and Equal
The Greatest Thing in Life
1919 Come Out of the Kitchen
The Homesteader
Injustice
The Little Diplomat
A Man's Duty
The Old Maid's Baby
Sue of the South
Toby's Bow
1920 The Brute
In the Depths of Our Hearts
Our Christianity and Nobody's
   Child
Reformation
The Symbol of the
   Unconquered
Within Our Gates
Blacksmiths
1914 In Mizzoura
St. Elmo
1915 The Danger Signal
Her Shattered Idol
A Phyllis of the Sierras
1916 The Flight of the Duchess
1917 The Eye of Envy
The Girl Without a Soul
Great Expectations
His Own People
The Man Hater
The Sudden Gentleman
1918 The Kaiser, the Beast of Berlin
The Triumph of Venus
1919 God's Outlaw
Greased Lightning
His Divorced Wife
Kathleen Mavourneen
The Sawdust Doll
1920 The Little Outcast
Once to Every Woman
Something to Think About
Blind persons
1915 In the Palace of the King
The Two Orphans
1917 The Jury of Fate
Nina, the Flower Girl
Princess of the Dark
The Stolen Paradise
The Stolen Play
The Streets of Illusion
The Tell-Tale Step
The Trouble Buster
When Love Was Blind
1918 Flower of the Dusk
The Little Runaway
The Painted Lily
The Voice of Destiny
1919 Blind Man's Eyes
Dawn
Deliverance
Eyes of the Soul
Faith
The Light
Red Blood and Yellow
1920 Democracy
Blindness
1912 Quincy Adams Sawyer
1913 Across the Continent
The Sea Wolf
1914 The Boer War
Called Back
A Good Little Devil
Jane Eyre
The Redemption of David
   Corson
Samson
Should a Woman Divorce?
The Strange Story of Sylvia
   Gray
1915 Four Feathers
Her Triumph
The Runaway Wife
Satan Sanderson
Shadows from the Past
Simon, the Jester
1916 The Dark Silence
The Feast of Life
Her Great Price
The Light of Happiness

The Light That Failed
The Path of Darkness
Playing with Fire
Whom the Gods Destroy
1917 The Auction of Virtue
Behind the Mask
Beloved Rogues
Polly Put the Kettle On
The Secret of Eve
Shall We Forgive Her?
The Snarl
The Stolen Paradise
The Unforseen
Womanhood, the Glory of the
   Nation
1918 The Better Half
Flower of the Dusk
The Ghosts of Yesterday
Marriage
My Unmarried Wife
Tangled Lives
The Voice of Destiny
1919 Anne of Green Gables
The City of Comrades
The End of the Road
1920 A Beggar in Purple
Eyes of the Heart
The Hidden Light
The Leopard Woman
The Man Who Had Everything
Molly and I
The Night Riders
Pagan Love
The Sagebrusher
The Sea Wolf
The Secret Gift
Something to Think About
The Song of the Soul
The Stealers
The Veiled Marriage
When Dawn Came
Blindness—Temporary
1914 Classmates
Michael Strogoff
1916 The Rise of Susan
1918 The Belgian
Lafayette, We Come!
1919 The Blinding Trail
The Market of Souls
Marriage for Convenience
The Other Half
Blizzards
1915 The Chalice of Courage
The Girl of the Golden West
1919 The Brand
The Homesteader
The Mints of Hell
The Way of the Strong
Blood donors
1916 Her Surrender
1918 Her Mistake
Blood transfusions
1916 Doctor Neighbor
Her Surrender
The Unattainable
1918 Her Mistake
The Honor of His House
1920 The Gift Supreme
Blowguns
1915 The Moonstone
Blue Boar Inn (London)
1915 Mistress Nell
Blue Ridge Mountains
1915 The Heart of the Blue Ridge
1916 Bawbs O' Blue Ridge
1918 The Challenge Accepted
The Power and the Glory
1919 In Old Kentucky
Louisiana
Bluebirds
1918 The Blue Bird
Boarding schools
1913 Caprice
1914 A Good Little Devil
1915 The Arrival of Perpetua
The Caprices of Kitty
The Mill on the Floss
The Puppet Crown
Seven Sisters
Vanity Fair
What Happened to Jones
1916 Artie, the Millionaire Kid
Hell-to-Pay Austin
The Mischief Maker

The Brat
Brothers Divided
The Cinema Murder
Forest Rivals
The Forfeit
Fruits of Passion
The Girl Who Stayed at Home
Happy Though Married
The Heart of Humanity
Her Game
In His Brother's Place
In Honor's Web
Lord and Lady Algy
The Market of Souls
Miss Dulcie from Dixie
Red Blood and Yellow
Satan Junior
Secret Service
Told in the Hills
The Trap
The Unbroken Promise
Victory
Widow by Proxy
1920 Big Happiness
The Confession
The Cradle of Courage
Dangerous Days
Democracy
Fickle Women
Flames of the Flesh
The Frisky Mrs. Johnson
The Good-Bad Wife
Guilty of Love
A Lady in Love
Love Without Question
The Master Mind
Other Men's Shoes
Over the Hill to the Poorhouse
Passion's Playground
The Sea Rider
The Servant in the House
Shore Acres
Sundown Slim
Wait for Me
Why Pick on Me?
19-- *Barnaby Lee*

Brothers-in-law
1914 *The Reign of Terror*
1916 *Bought and Paid For*
Driftwood
Pillars of Society
1917 *The Double Standard*
1918 *The Appearance of Evil*
The Firefly of France
Humdrum Brown
In the Hollow of Her Hand
On the Quiet
The Wolf and His Mate
1919 *Spotlight Sadie*
1920 Hitchin' Posts
In Search of a Sinner
The North Wind's Malice
The Saphead
The Servant in the House
The Victim
Wait for Me

Willis Brown
1914 A Boy and the Law

Alexei Alexeevich Brusilov
1919 *Free Russia*

Brussels
1915 *History of the Great European War*
The History of the World's Greatest War
The Ivory Snuff Box
1919 *The Great Victory, Wilson or the Kaiser? The Fall of the Hohenzollerns*

Buckingham Palace
1919 *The Lone Wolf's Daughter*

Buddha
1913 *The Lotus Dancer*
The Star of India
1914 *The Wrath of the Gods*
1916 *The Pool of Flame*

Buddhism
1915 *The White Pearl*
1917 A Trip Through Japan
1918 *The Green God*
The Soul of Buddha
Vengeance
1919 Broken Blossoms

Buenos Aires
1915 *A Trip to the Argentine*
1918 *The Moral Law*
1919 *A Regular Fellow*
1920 *Madame X*

Buffalo (New York)
1915 *The Little Mademoiselle*

Buffaloes
use Bison, American

Bugles
1916 *The Bugle Call*

Bulgaria
1915 The Chocolate Soldier

Bullfighters
1915 *Carmen* (Fox Film Corp.)
Carmen (Jesse L. Lasky Feature Play Co.)
The Pretty Sister of Jose
1916 Charlie Chaplin's Burlesque on "Carmen"
The Pearl of Paradise
1920 *The Brand of Lopez*

Bullies
1914 *The Hoosier Schoolmaster*
The Virginian
1915 *Chimmie Fadden*
1916 *The Mirror of Life*
1917 *The Golden Rosary*
The Mainspring
Their Compact
Under Handicap
1918 Jules of the Strong Heart
That Devil, Bateese
1919 The Brute Breaker
His Bridal Night
Rough Riding Romance
When a Girl Loves

Bureaucrats
1918 The Mantle of Charity

Burglars
1914 *The Voice at the Telephone*
1915 The Edge of the Abyss
The Frame-Up
A Gentleman of Leisure
His Turning Point
Keep Moving
The Kindling
Playing Dead
The Pretenders
Secretary of Frivolous Affairs
The Wheels of Justice
1916 *As a Woman Sows*
The Battle of Life
The Foolish Virgin
The Lost Bridegroom
Love's Pilgrimage to America
Mrs. Dane's Danger
Oliver Twist
The Ragamuffin
The River of Romance
1917 *Bab's Burglar*
Charity Castle
Come Through
The Ghost House
The Haunted Pajamas
The Millionaire's Double
Two Little Imps
Vengeance Is Mine
When False Tongues Speak
A Wife on Trial
1918 Ann's Finish
The Bride of Fear
Dolly Does Her Bit
Fires of Youth
The Girl Who Came Back
Social Quicksands
Under Suspicion
Wanted—A Brother
1919 Burglar by Proxy
Charge It to Me
The Cry of the Weak
The Game's Up
The Girl Dodger
The Girl with No Regrets
The Hornet's Nest
The Life Line
The Lost Battalion
Molly of the Follies
Nobody Home
Peggy Does Her Darndest
Please Get Married
The Silver King
Virtuous Sinners
The Woman of Lies

1920 The Fourteenth Man
A Full House
Leave It to Me
Luring Shadows
Nothing but the Truth
Sherry

Burglary
1914 *False Colours*
1915 *The Curious Conduct of Judge Legarde*
The Kindling
To Cherish and Protect
1916 *The Dead Alive*
The Lost Bridegroom
Mrs. Dane's Danger
Oliver Twist
The Price of Happiness
The Ragamuffin
The Shadow of a Doubt
The Victim
The Woman's Law
1917 *Cheerful Givers*
Her Life and His
The Prison Without Walls
When False Tongues Speak
A Wife on Trial
1918 The Danger Game
Dolly Does Her Bit
The Eagle
Fires of Youth
A Japanese Nightingale
Just for Tonight
Kidder and Ko
Social Quicksands
Together
Under Suspicion
Wanted—A Brother
1919 *The City of Comrades*
The Dub
The Gamblers
An Innocent Adventuress
The Lamb and the Lion
The Long Lane's Turning
The Mystery of the Yellow Room
Through the Toils
1919-20
The Tower of Jewels
1920 *Sherry*
The Ugly Duckling
While New York Sleeps

Burial
rt **Cemeteries**
Funerals
Graves
Live burial
1915 *The Battles of a Nation*
The Warring Millions
1916 *Hell's Hinges*
1918 *Among the Cannibal Isles of the South Pacific*
Out of the Night
Peg of the Pirates
1919 *When a Man Rides Alone*

Buried treasure
rt **Treasure**
1915 *An American Gentleman*
1918 *Huns Within Our Gates*
Such a Little Pirate
1919 Captain Kidd, Jr.

Burlesque
1915 *The College Orphan*
1917 The Clean-Up
1918 *One Thousand Dollars*
A Perfect Lady
1919 *A Broadway Saint*
The Painted World
The Quickening Flame

Burns
1916 *The Victim*

William J. Burns
1914 The $5,000,000 Counterfeiting Plot

Aaron Burr
1918 The Beautiful Mrs. Reynolds
My Own United States

Buru
1920 *Shipwrecked Among Cannibals*

Busboys
1920 *An Amateur Devil*

Business
1915 *York State Folks*
1916 The Little Shepherd of Bargain Row
Phantom Fortunes
1917 Back of the Man
The Customary Two Weeks
Shirley Kaye
Skinner's Dress Suit
Sudden Jim
A Trip Through China
The Yankee Way
1920 The Dancin' Fool
Dollar for Dollar
The Fortune Hunter

Business competition
1915 *The Immigrant*
Just Out of College
The Yankee Girl
1916 Father and Son
The Final Curtain
The Lords of High Decision
The Mainspring
Wild Oats
1917 *Beloved Rogues*
The Boy Girl
The Customary Two Weeks
Like Wildfire
On Record
Pardners
The Web of Desire
What Money Can't Buy
1918 Beans
Beyond the Shadows
A Burglar for a Night
The Winning of Beatrice
1919 The Lion's Den
1920 A Beggar in Purple
The Blooming Angel
A Common Level
The Dancin' Fool
The Deadlier Sex
Excuse My Dust
Sky Eye

Business ethics
1917 Her Father's Keeper
1920 The Third Generation

Business management
1918 The Venus Model
Why I Would Not Marry

Businessmen
rt **Entrepreneurs**
Industrialists
Specific types of business magnates
Tycoons
1914 *As Ye Sow*
Captain Alvarez
Facing the Gattling Guns
The Fortune Hunter
Hearts and Flowers
The Making of Bobby Burnit
The Pit
The Ring and the Man
The Taint
1915 Business Is Business
The Commuters
The Fool and the Dancer
A Fool There Was
The Little Girl That He Forgot
The Old Homestead
The Sable Lorcha
Silver Threads Among the Gold
The Soul of Broadway
1916 According to Law
Broken Fetters
The Chattel
A Circus Romance
The Devil's Bondwoman
The Dividend
Extravagance
The Gates of Eden
The Heritage of Hate
The Highest Bid
Honor's Altar
The Little Shepherd of Bargain Row
The Love Hermit
The Mainspring
Man and His Soul
The Man from Manhattan
Mrs. Dane's Danger
My Lady Incog.

Cairo
1914 The Last Egyptian
1916 *Thou Shalt Not Covet*
1919 *Sahara*
1920 A Trip Through Cairo

Calais (France)
1914 *The Spitfire*
1917 *The Scarlet Pimpernel*

Calendars
1918 The Widow's Might

California
1914 The Country Mouse
    In the Days of the Thundering Herd
    John Barleycorn
    Rose of the Rancho
    Salomy Jane
    The Valley of the Moon
1915 The Lily of Poverty Flat
    M'liss
    My Valet
    A Phyllis of the Sierras
    Stolen Goods
1916 *The Adventures of Kathlyn*
    The Beckoning Trail
    Dulcie's Adventure
    The End of the Rainbow
    The Flying Torpedo
    The Heir to the Hoorah
    The Honorable Friend
    The Mediator
    Miss Jackie of the Navy
    The Right Direction
    The Whirlpool of Destiny
    The Wood Nymph
1917 *Peggy Leads the Way*
    A School for Husbands
    The Secret of Black Mountain
1918 *Blindfolded*
    Cavanaugh of the Forest Rangers
    Cupid Angling
    Fields of Honor
    "Flare-Up" Sal
    The Man Hunt
    Mickey
    The Only Road
    Real Folks
    The Romance of Tarzan
    A Society Sensation
    Tongues of Flame
    Who Is to Blame?
    The Wine Girl
1919 As the Sun Went Down
    False Evidence
    The Gray Wolf's Ghost
    The Lincoln Highwayman
    A Man's Fight
    The Trembling Hour
    Trixie from Broadway
1920 Fighting Cressy
    For the Soul of Rafael
    The Inner Voice
    Jack Straw

California—History
1915 The Pageant of San Francisco
1916 Ramona
    A Sister of Six

California—History—To 1846
1915 Captain Courtesy
1916 A Yoke of Gold
1920 The Mark of Zorro

California—History—1846-1850
1915 The Girl of the Golden West
1916 The Argonauts of California—1849
    The Daughter of the Don
    The Love Mask
1918 Hell's Crater
    M'liss
    The Vigilantes
1919 The End of the Game
    A Man's Country
    Scarlet Days
    The Sundown Trail
1920 Days of Daring

Cameos
1914 *Cameo Kirby*

Cameras
1915 At Bay
1917 *The Flashlight*
    This Is the Life

Camorra
  rt **Black Hand**
    Mafia
1918 The Ghost Flower

Colin Campbell
1915 The Campbells Are Coming

Camping
1915 *The Adventures of a Boy Scout*
    The Chalice of Courage
    The Nature Man: Or, The Struggle for Existence
1916 *The Child of Destiny*
    The Storm
    The Twin Triangle

Camps
1918 *The Beloved Blackmailer*
1919 *The Heart of Youth*
    Men, Women and Money

Canaan
1914 *Joseph in the Land of Egypt*

Canada
1914 *The Boundary Rider*
    A Mother's Heart
    Pierre of the Plains
    The Wolf
1915 *Heléne of the North*
    Pennington's Choice
1916 Autumn
    The End of the Trail
    Nanette of the Wilds
    The Place Beyond the Winds
    The Precious Packet
    The Primal Lure
    The Snowbird
    The Target
1917 The Bronze Bride
    For Valour
    One Hour
    Open Places
    The Savage
1918 *Headin' South*
    Hugon, the Mighty
    Mrs. Dane's Defense
    The Pen Vulture
    Prisoners of the Pines
    The Purple Lily
    Tyrant Fear
1919 The Broken Butterfly
    A Fight for Love
    The Last of His People
    Paid in Advance
    The Wilderness Trail
    The Wolf
    You Never Know Your Luck
1920 *Behold My Wife*
    The Challenge of the Law
    The Red Lane
    The Right of Way
    The River's End
    The Sin That Was His
    The Stolen Kiss

Canada—History
1914 *The Seats of the Mighty*
    Wolfe; Or, The Conquest of Quebec

Canada. Army
1915 *The History of the World's Greatest War*
    The Sins of Society
1916 *At the Front with the Allies*
1918 *Crashing Through to Berlin*
    The Great Love
    The Splendid Sinner
1919 *Alias Mike Moran*
    America Was Right
    The City of Comrades

Canadian Arctic Expedition
1914 Rescue of the Stefansson Arctic Expedition

Canadian border
1916 *The Snowbird*
    The World Against Him
1917 *Until They Get Me*
1918 *Ace High*
1920 The Cyclone

Canadian Northwest
1914 The Call of the North
1915 Armstrong's Wife
    The Bulldogs of the Trail
    Jack Chanty
    The Right of Way
1916 The Dawn Maker

1917 The Jury of Fate
    The Land of Long Shadows
1918 Baree, Son of Kazan
    Beyond the Shadows
    Closin' In
    Code of the Yukon
    Heart of the Wilds
    The Law of the Great Northwest
    The Sign Invisible
    The World for Sale
1920 The Barbarian
    The Confession
    Isobel; Or, The Trail's End
    The Night Riders
    Nomads of the North
    The One Way Trail
    Out of the Snows
    Skyfire
    The Valley of Doubt

Canadians
1914 *Thou Shalt Not*
1916 The American Beauty
1917 For Valour
1919 *Beckoning Roads*
    The Heart of Humanity
    In the Land of the Setting Sun; Or, Martyrs of Yesterday
    Rose of the West

Canal Zone
  rt **Panama**
    Panama Canal
1915 Pirate Haunts

Cancer
1916 *The Closed Road*

Candy
1916 *Rolling Stones*
    The Sunbeam
1918 *Angel Child*
1919 *The Heart of Youth*
    The Little Intruder

Candy stores
  rt **Confectioners and confectionaries**
1918 *The Hope Chest*
    Innocent's Progress

Canneries
1915 Children of Eve
    Out of the Darkness
1916 *The Corner*
1918 *Beans*
    String Beans
    The Wasp

Cannery workers
1915 *Children of Eve*
    Out of the Darkness

Cannibals
1914 *The Mystery of the Poison Pool*
1915 *Pretty Mrs. Smith*
1916 Robinson Crusoe
1917 *Love Aflame*
    She
1918 *Among the Cannibal Isles of the South Pacific*
1919 The Jungle Trail
1920 Shipwrecked Among Cannibals

Canoes
1913 *The Fortune Hunters*
1914 *In the Land of the Head Hunters*
1915 *American Game Trails*
    The Footsteps of Capt. Kidd
    The Nature Man: Or, The Struggle for Existence
    The Stolen Voice
1916 *The Chaperon*
    The Pearl of Paradise
1918 *The Great Adventure*
1919 *The American Way*
    The Brute Breaker
    In Wrong
    Three Men and a Girl
    The Wolf

Cape Cod (Massachusetts)
1914 *As Ye Sow*
1918 *The Deciding Kiss*
    A Petticoat Pilot

Cape Haitien (Haiti)
1916 *United States Marines Under Fire in Haiti*

Cape Town (South Africa)
1918 The King of Diamonds

Albert Capellani
1915 The Flash of an Emerald

Capes
1918 Little Red Riding Hood

Capital punishment
  rt **Executions**
1914 *The Little Angel of Canyon Creek*
    A Woman's Triumph
1915 Conscience
    Hearts and the Highway
    Thou Shalt Not Kill
1916 And the Law Says
1917 Who Shall Take My Life?
1920 The Gray Brother
    The Victim

Capitalism
1915 The Bigger Man
1918 Keep the Home Fires Burning
1920 Democracy

Capitalists
1919 *Heart O' the Hills*

Caporetto (Italy)
1919 From the Disaster of Caporetto to Rescue of Trentino and Trieste

Capri
1917 The Pulse of Life

Caravans
1918 *The Winding Trail*
1919 *Her Purchase Price*
    The Man Who Turned White

Card games
  nt Specific types of card games
1914 *The Little Angel of Canyon Creek*
    The Mysterious Mr. Wu Chung Foo
1915 *Gambling Inside and Out*
    The Girl of the Golden West
    The Heart of a Painted Woman
    The Masqueraders
1916 *The Decoy*
    Pay Dirt
    The Thoroughbred (American Film Co.)
    Two Men of Sandy Bar
1917 *The Bride of Hate*
    The Firefly of Tough Luck
    The White Raven
    Wild Sumac
1918 *Blue Blazes Rawden*
    Faith Endurin'
    Hands Down
    The Heart of a Girl
    Social Hypocrites
    Thieves' Gold
    The Turn of a Card
    The Uphill Path
    Vengeance
    When Do We Eat?
1920 *Hearts Are Trumps*
    Hitchin' Posts

Cardinals
1914 *His Holiness, the Late Pope Pius X, and the Vatican*
    Richelieu
1918 The Cross Bearer

Cardsharps
1915 The Deathlock
    The Fatal Card
    Gambling Inside and Out
    Heléne of the North
    When a Woman Loves
1916 The Man from Nowhere
1917 *The Cold Deck*
1918 Marriage
1919 *The American Way*
    The Bluffer
    Breed of Men
    The End of the Game
    The Son-of-a-Gun!
    Venus in the East
    When Doctors Disagree
1920 *The Sporting Duchess*
1920-21
    The House of Mystery

Career women
1916 *Love's Crucible*
1917 The Weaker Sex
1920 Deadline at Eleven
Caretakers
1916 *Betty of Graystone*
1917 Troublemakers
1919 The Phantom Honeymoon
       A Stitch in Time
Carmel (California)
1914 *The Valley of the Moon*
Carnegie Museum
1912 *The Alaska-Siberian*
       Expedition
Carnivals
   rt **Bazaars**
       Circuses
       Fairs
       Sideshows
1915 *Comrade John*
1918 The Woman Between Friends
1919 The Stronger Vow
1920 *The Frisky Mrs. Johnson*
       The Woman and the Puppet
Carpenters
1918 *Hearts of the World*
Carpet makers
1915 *The Rug Maker's Daughter*
Carpetbaggers
1915 *The Birth of a Nation*
1917 *My Fighting Gentleman*
Carpets
1915 *Blackbirds*
       The Carpet from Bagdad
       The Rug Maker's Daughter
Venustiano Carranza
1916 Following the Flag in Mexico
Carriages
1913 *In the Bishop's Carriage*
1916 *Honor Thy Name*
1917 *Lost in Transit*
1920 *She Couldn't Help It*
Carthage (Missouri)
1913 *One Hundred Years of*
       Mormonism
Carthaginians
1914 *Damon and Pythias*
Cartoonists
1914 *The Adventures of Kitty Cobb*
1917 *The Little Terror*
       The Magnificent Meddler
Cashiers
1916 *Acquitted*
       The Traffic Cop
1918 *And a Still Small Voice*
       Quicksand
1919 The Bondage of Barbara
Casino employees
1916 Behind Closed Doors
       Mixed Blood
       The Parson of Panamint
1918 *The Border Raiders*
Casino owners
1915 *The Pitfall*
1916 *Behind Closed Doors*
       The Girl Who Doesn't Know
       The Other Side of the Door
1918 *The Gun Woman*
       Little Miss No-Account
1920 The Gamesters
Casinos
   rt **Gambling houses**
1916 *Behind Closed Doors*
       The Girl Who Doesn't Know
       The Parson of Panamint
       Redeeming Love
1917 *The New York Peacock*
1918 *Staking His Life*
1919 The Prince and Betty
1920 *Blind Love*
       $30,000
Castaways
1914 *Hearts Adrift*
       Hearts of Oak
       The Land of the Lost
1915 Aloha Oe
       The Beachcomber
       Coral
       Enoch Arden
       The Flaming Sword
       The Island of Regeneration
       The Quest
       The Sins of Society

The White Pearl
1916 *The Captive God*
       Cross Currents
       A Gamble in Souls
       The Girl O' Dreams
       The Grasp of Greed
       Into the Primitive
       The Island of Surprise
       The Isle of Love
       The Pearl of Paradise
       The Struggle
       Thou Shalt Not Covet
1917 *The Deemster*
       The Island of Desire
       The Lad and the Lion
       Lorelei of the Sea
       Periwinkle
       The Ship of Doom
       The Show Down
       Souls Adrift
       When a Man Sees Red
1918 Bonnie Annie Laurie
       By the World Forgot
       The Curse of Iku
       Every Mother's Son
       The Honor of His House
       Maid O' the Storm
       The Sea Flower
       Treasure Island
       Wild Women
1920 David and Jonathan
       Girl of the Sea
       Half a Chance
       The Hell Ship
       The Isle of Destiny
       Marooned Hearts
       Miss Nobody
       The Sea Wolf
       The Shark
       Shore Acres
       The Woman Untamed
1921 *Love's Plaything*
Castles
   rt **Palaces**
1913 *Ivanhoe*
1914 *The Ghost Breaker*
       The Mystery of Richmond
       Castle
       The Ragged Earl
       Richelieu
       Il Trovatore
1915 *The Captive*
       The Garden of Lies
       The Unafraid
1916 *Whom the Gods Destroy*
1917 *Borrowed Plumage*
       Intrigue
       The Little Duchess
       Wee Lady Betty
       The Woman God Forgot
1918 *A Daughter of France*
       A Diplomatic Mission
       The Firefly of France
1919 *La Belle Russe*
       Day Dreams
       Human Passions
       Lure of Ambition
       The Phantom Honeymoon
       The White Heather
1920 A Fool and His Money
       The White Circle
Catatonia
1916 The Supreme Temptation
Cathedrals
1918 *The Blue Bird*
       Sunshine Nan
Catherine de Médicis, Queen, Consort of
   Henry II, 1519-1589
1914 *The Fatal Night*
1916 *Intolerance*
Catholic Church
1914 The Fatal Night
       His Holiness, the Late Pope
       Pius X, and the Vatican
       Uriel Acosta
1915 *The Penitentes*
1920 American Catholics in War
       and Reconstruction
       The Victim
Catigny, Battle of
1918 *Crashing Through to Berlin*

Cats
1919 *The American Way*
       A Dangerous Affair
       The Heart of Youth
       Nobody Home
Catskill Mountains
1918 The Inn of the Blue Moon
Cattle
1915 *The Cowpuncher*
1917 *The Learnin' of Jim Benton*
       The Yankee Way
1918 *Two-Gun Betty*
1919 *Treat 'Em Rough*
       The Unbroken Promise
       When the Desert Smiles
Cattle Annie
1915 *Passing of the Oklahoma*
       Outlaw
Cattlemen
1914 *Forgiven; Or, The Jack of*
       Diamonds
       Should a Woman Divorce?
1915 *The Girl from His Town*
       A Texas Steer
1917 *By Right of Possession*
       The Captain of the Gray Horse
       Troop
       The Heart of Texas Ryan
       The Learnin' of Jim Benton
       The Man from Painted Post
       Men of the Desert
1918 *Cactus Crandall*
       Cavanaugh of the Forest
       Rangers
       A Desert Wooing
       Faith Endurin'
       The Phantom Riders
       Winner Takes All
       With Hoops of Steel
1919 The Ace of the Saddle
       Calibre 38
       Eastward Ho!
       The Forfeit
       Lasca
       The Road Called Straight
       The Veiled Adventure
1920 The Desert Scorpion
       The Flame of Hellgate
       The Galloping Devil
       Human Stuff
       Sink or Swim
       Sundown Slim
       Two Moons
Cavalry
   rt Cavalries of specific countries
       United States. Army. Cavalry
1915 *The Battle and Fall of*
       Przemysl
1919 *Common Property*
       His Majesty, the American
Cave dwellers
1915 *Her Shattered Idol*
       'Twas Ever Thus
Edith Cavell
1919 The Great Victory, Wilson or
       the Kaiser? The Fall of the
       Hohenzollerns
Caves
1913 *A Princess of Bagdad*
1914 *The Corsair*
       Samson
1915 *The Heart of the Blue Ridge*
       The Island of Regeneration
       Sealed Valley
1917 *Lorelei of the Sea*
1918 Ali Baba and the Forty
       Thieves
       Huck and Tom; Or, The
       Further Adventures of Tom
       Sawyer
       Peg of the Pirates
       Queen of the Sea
1919 *Forest Rivals*
       Just Squaw
       A Man of Honor
       Riders of Vengeance
       The Shepherd of the Hills
1920 *The Daredevil*
       Miss Nobody
Cawnpore (India)
1916 *The Beggar of Cawnpore*

Cayuse Indians
1919 In the Land of the Setting Sun;
       Or, Martyrs of Yesterday
Cellars
1917 *War and the Woman*
1920 *The Flaming Clue*
Cement
1915 *Fine Feathers*
       The Incorrigible Dukane
Cemeteries
   rt **Funerals**
       Graves
1916 *The Fighting Germans*
1917 *Great Expectations*
1918 *The Blue Bird*
       Huck and Tom; Or, The
       Further Adventures of Tom
       Sawyer
       The Street of Seven Stars
Central America
1915 *Captain Macklin*
       The Dictator
       Fighting Bob
       The Footsteps of Capt. Kidd
       On the Spanish Main
       Pirate Haunts
1918 A Man's Man
Chambermaids
   rt **Housemaids**
       Maids
1914 *The Ghost Breaker*
       The Pride of Jennico
       Shannon of the Sixth
1915 *Stop Thief!*
1917 *Zollenstein*
1918 Miss Ambition
1920 *Bright Skies*
       Twin Beds
Champagne
1918 *The Craving*
       Sylvia on a Spree
1919 *Her Game*
Changelings
1914 Under the Gaslight
1915 The Goose Girl
1916 April
       The Price of Silence
1918 *Blue Blood*
1920 The Brand of Lopez
Chaperons
1916 *The Lotus Woman*
1919 *The Game's Up*
1920 Black Shadows
       Harriet and the Piper
Chaplains
1919 *Daring Hearts*
Charles Chaplin
1918 *The Shoes That Danced*
Charge accounts
1919 Charge It to Me
Chariots
1914 *Damon and Pythias*
1919 *The Fall of Babylon*
Charitable organizations
1917 *The Adventurer*
       A Night in New Arabia
1918 The Mantle of Charity
       The Reckoning Day
1919 *Life's a Funny Proposition*
       Suspense
Charity
1914 The Dancer and the King
       The Gangsters
       Hearts and Flowers
       The House Next Door
       Joseph in the Land of Egypt
       A Lady of Quality
       Nell Gwynne
       The Redemption of David
       Corson
1915 *The Dawn of a Tomorrow*
       The Hungarian Nabob
       Up from the Depths
1916 The Birth of a Man
       Gloriana
       The Good Bad Man
       A Prince in a Pawnshop
       Warning! The S.O.S. Call of
       Humanity
1917 *The Lady in the Library*
       Little Shoes
       The Penny Philanthropist

Charity
- 1918 The Answer
  - *Battling Jane*
  - The Blue Bird
  - The Midnight Burglar
  - Miss Ambition
  - *The Soap Girl*
- 1919 *Hell Roarin' Reform*
  - His Debt
- 1920 *Do the Dead Talk?*
  - The Inner Voice
  - *Passers-By*

Charity workers
- 1915 *Chimmie Fadden*
- 1916 Dust
  - Gloriana
- 1917 The Money Mill
- 1919 Everywoman
- 1920 When Dawn Came
  - *Whispering Devils*
  - The White Moll

Charlatans
- 1917 Love Letters
- 1918 The Fall of the Romanoffs
  - His Majesty, Bunker Bean
  - *Life or Honor?*
  - The Scarlet Trail
  - The Zero Hour

Charles II, King of England, 1630-1685
- 1914 Nell Gwynne
- 1915 Mistress Nell

Charles II, King of Spain, 1665-1700
- 1915 Don Caesar de Bazan
- 1920 *The Adventurer*

Charles IX, King of France, 1550-1574
- 1916 Intolerance

Charleston (South Carolina)
- 1915 On the Spanish Main

Charwomen and cleaners
-   *rt* **Scrubwomen**
- 1914 Hearts and Flowers
- 1916 *The American Beauty*
  - *Inherited Passions*
  - *Madame La Presidente*
- 1920 Dinty

Chases
- 1913 Ben Bolt
  - *Traffic in Souls*
- 1914 *Detective Craig's Coup*
  - The Great Leap; Until Death
    Do Us Part
  - In the Land of the Head
    Hunters
  - *Jess of the Mountain Country*
  - *My Official Wife*
  - The Mystery of Richmond
    Castle
  - *The Price of Treachery; Or,
    The Lighthouse Keeper's
    Daughter*
  - A Prince of India
  - 'Round the World in 80 Days
  - Shannon of the Sixth
  - *Tillie's Punctured Romance*
  - The Toll of Mammon
  - Trapped in the Great
    Metropolis
  - *Uncle Tom's Cabin*
- 1915 *Betty in Search of a Thrill*
  - The Eagle's Nest
  - Flame of Passion
  - The Flying Twins
  - The Folly of a Life of Crime
  - Hearts in Exile
  - Money
  - *The Rights of Man: A Story of
    War's Red Blotch*
  - *Sam Davis, the Hero of
    Tennessee*
  - Tillie's Tomato Surprise
  - *A Trade Secret*
  - Unto the Darkness
  - *What Happened to Father*
  - *What Happened to Jones*
- 1916 *American Aristocracy*
  - Arms and the Woman
  - The Gringo
  - *Immediate Lee*
  - The Traveling Salesman
- 1917 *The Blue Streak*
  - The Frozen Warning
  - *Has Man the Right to Kill?*
  - Her Bargain
  - Her Fighting Chance
  - The Lone Wolf

- 1918 *Brave and Bold*
  - *By Proxy*
  - Cactus Crandall
  - Cupid's Roundup
  - *The Green God*
  - *The Guilt of Silence*
  - *Heart of the Wilds*
  - *The Hell Cat*
  - In Pursuit of Polly
  - Midnight Madness
  - *Mr. Logan, U.S.A.*
  - *Nobody's Wife*
  - *The Rainbow Trail*
  - *Riders of the Purple Sage*
  - *Smashing Through*
  - *Stolen Orders*
  - The Sunset Princess
  - *Swat the Spy*
  - *Thieves' Gold*
  - *The Transgressor*
  - *Unexpected Places*
  - Zongar
- 1919 *Fighting Destiny*
  - *The Island of Intrigue*
  - *Jacques of the Silver North*
  - *The Joyous Liar*
  - *The Mother and the Law*
  - *Putting One Over*
  - The Roaring Road
  - *Something to Do*
  - *The Teeth of the Tiger*
  - *The Unpardonable Sin*
  - *The Web of Chance*
  - *When Men Desire*
- 1920 *An Adventuress*
  - *Below the Deadline*
  - *Bullet Proof*
  - *Cupid, the Cowpuncher*
  - *A Fool and His Money*
  - The Furnace
  - Go and Get It
  - *Hearts Are Trumps*
  - *His Pajama Girl*
  - Married Life
  - *A Master Stroke*
  - *My Lady's Garter*
  - Number 99
  - Paris Green
  - *Prairie Trails*
  - *The Rose of Nome*
  - The Skywayman
  - Something New
  - The Toll Gate

Chastity
- 1915 The Hungarian Nabob
  - The Wonderful Adventure
- 1917 Indiscretion

Chateau Thierry (France)
- 1919 Ginger

Chateau-Thierry, Battle of, 1918
- 1918 *Crashing Through to Berlin*
  - *The Tidal Wave*
  - *Under Four Flags*
- 1920 Chateau-Thierry, St.-Mihiel
    and Argonne

Chauffeurs
- 1914 Hearts United
  - *The Lightning Conductor*
  - *The Line-Up at Police
    Headquarters*
- 1915 *The Destroying Angel*
  - My Best Girl
  - *The Waif*
- 1916 *The Heart of Nora Flynn*
  - *Lord Loveland Discovers
    America*
  - The Race
  - The Soul Market
  - *The Upstart*
  - *A Woman's Daring*
- 1917 *The Golden God*
  - Pots-and-Pans Peggy
  - The Square Deceiver
  - Sunshine and Gold
  - The Upper Crust
- 1918 *The Fall of the Romanoffs*
  - *The Firefly of France*
  - *Her Country First*
  - Nancy Comes Home
  - *The Ordeal of Rosetta*
  - Thirty a Week
  - The Turn of a Card
  - *The Unbeliever*
  - The Wasp
  - Which Woman?

-     *Wives and Other Wives*
- 1919 *The End of the Road*
  - *The Exquisite Thief*
  - The Game's Up
  - *The Invisible Bond*
  - Little Comrade
  - *Lombardi, Ltd.*
  - *Male and Female*
  - *A Man and His Money*
  - *Molly of the Follies*
  - The Moonshine Trail
  - *Never Say Quit*
  - One of the Finest
  - *One-Thing-at-a-Time O'Day*
  - *Our Better Selves*
  - *Over the Garden Wall*
  - *The Profiteer*
  - A Sporting Chance (Famous
    Players-Lasky Corp.)
  - *Under Suspicion*
  - Upstairs
- 1920 *The City of Masks*
  - Crooked Streets
  - Double Speed
  - High Speed
  - *The Very Idea*
  - *You Never Can Tell*

Cheating
- 1916 *Temptation and the Man*
- 1917 The Silent Man
  - *The War of the Tongs*
  - *Wild Sumac*
- 1918 *Social Hypocrites*
  - Vengeance
- 1919 *Courage for Two*
  - Gambling in Souls
- 1920 *The County Fair*
  - The Return of Tarzan
  - *The Tiger's Cub*
  - Twins of Suffering Creek

Checks
- 1917 *Fanatics*
  - *A Game of Wits*
  - The Girl at Home
  - *The Whip*
- 1918 Dodging a Million
  - *The Golden Fleece*
  - Keith of the Border
- 1920 *Man's Plaything*
  - *The Prey*

Chefs
-   *rt* **Cooks**
- 1916 *Love's Pilgrimage to America*

Chemical formulas
-   *rt* **Secret formulas**
- 1914 The Patchwork Girl of Oz
- 1917 The Greatest Power
- 1918 Sunshine Nan
- 1920 The Hidden Code

Chemists
- 1915 *The Bludgeon*
  - Fine Feathers
  - *My Best Girl*
  - A Trade Secret
  - *The Wolf Man*
- 1916 The Blue Envelope Mystery
  - *Bluff*
- 1917 *The Dream Doll*
  - The Hungry Heart
  - The Road Between
- 1918 *Hearts or Diamonds?*
  - Smashing Through
  - The Spreading Evil
  - Sunshine Nan
- 1919 *A Sporting Chance (American
    Film Co.)*
- 1920 *The Empire of Diamonds*
  - The Hidden Code

Cherokee Indians
- 1917 The Conqueror

Cherry Valley Massacre, 1778
- 1917 *The Spirit of '76*

Chesapeake Bay (Maryland)
- 1919 Miss Crusoe

Chess
- 1917 *Putting the Bee in Herbert*
- 1919 *The Cry of the Weak*
  - *A Dangerous Affair*
  - *His Wife's Friend*

Chewing gum factories
- 1917 *Broadway Jones*

Chewing gum magnates
- 1919 *The Amazing Impostor*

Cheyenne (Wyoming)
- 1918 *The Hell Cat*

Cheyenne Indians
- 1918 Indian Life

Chicago
- 1914 The Jungle
  - *The Pit*
- 1915 A Black Sheep
  - Jim the Penman
  - *The Luring Lights*
  - *A Mother's Confession*
- 1916 Cousin Jim
  - The Right to Live
  - Three Pals
- 1917 *Her Strange Wedding*
  - *The Penny Philanthropist*
  - The Small Town Guy
  - The Sudden Gentleman
  - Uncle Sam, Awake!
  - *A Woman Alone*
  - *The Yankee Way*
- 1918 *And the Children Pay*
  - *Kidder and Ko*
  - Limousine Life
  - *A Perfect Lady*
  - True Blue
- 1919 *Blind Man's Eyes*
  - Breed of Men
  - *Crooked Straight*
  - *The Egg Crate Wallop*
  - *The Gray Towers Mystery*
  - *A Gun Fightin' Gentleman*
  - The Money Corral
  - The Road Called Straight
  - Sue of the South
  - *That's Good*
  - *The Turn in the Road*
  - Where's Mary?

Chicago—Tenderloin District
- 1916 *The Little Girl Next Door*

Chicago White Sox
- 1914 The Giants-White Sox Tour
- 1917 The Baseball Revue of 1917

Chickens
- 1918 Little Miss Hoover
- 1919 Government Poultry Farm at
    Beltsville, Md.
- 1920 *Everything but the Truth*

Child custody
- 1914 The Monster and the Girl
  - *The Unwelcome Mrs. Hatch*
  - *Your Girl and Mine: A Woman
    Suffrage Play*
- 1915-16
  - The Little Church Around the
    Corner
- 1916 Bobbie of the Ballet
  - The Children Pay
  - *Civilization's Child*
  - *Fifty-Fifty*
  - The House of Mirrors
  - *Intolerance*
  - *That Sort*
  - A Youth of Fortune
- 1917 Polly Redhead
  - Sleeping Fires
  - *The Tenth Case*
  - Unconquered
  - When Baby Forgot
- 1918 American Buds
  - *The Appearance of Evil*
  - *Just a Woman*
  - *Kildare of Storm*
  - The Law That Divides
  - The Lost Chord
  - *Tinsel*
  - *Together*
  - Tony America
  - Woman and the Law
- 1920 Curtain
  - *A Fool and His Money*
  - *The Fortune Teller*
  - *The Harvest Moon*
  - *The Jack-Knife Man*
  - The Little Outcast
  - *The Soul of Youth*

Child labor
- 1912 Oliver Twist
- 1914 *Your Girl and Mine: A Woman
    Suffrage Play*
- 1915 *Children of Eve*
  - *Heritage*

Choirs
1915 *The Hypocrites*
Cholera
1915 *The Unfaithful Wife*
1916 *The Beggar of Cawnpore*
The Isle of Life
1918 *The Safety Curtain*
1919 *The Secret Garden*
1920 *Stronger Than Death*
Chorus girls
bt **Dancers**
rt **Showgirls**
1913 An Hour Before Dawn
1914 *Mother*
The Typhoon
What's His Name
1915 The Chorus Lady
The Country Boy
Her Triumph
A Man's Making
The Reward
Through Turbulent Waters
When It Strikes Home
1916 A Gamble in Souls
New York
Saving the Family Name
The Smugglers
1917 *Blood Will Tell*
Easy Money
God's Crucible
It Happened to Adele
1918 Broadway Love
The Family Skeleton
The Great Adventure
Irish Eyes
On the Quiet
Our Mrs. McChesney
A Perfect Lady
The Scarlet Road
Sylvia on a Spree
1919 *The Girl Dodger*
Mind the Paint Girl
Pettigrew's Girl
Taxi
Trixie from Broadway
Who Cares?
1920 *The Chorus Girl's Romance*
Conrad in Quest of His Youth
Food for Scandal
Forty-Five Minutes from Broadway
A Full House
The Golden Trail
Her Five-Foot Highness
In Folly's Trail
It Might Happen to You
Rouge and Riches
Sex
The Star Rover
The Thirteenth Commandment
39 East
Two Weeks
The Village Sleuth
Christian Science
1915 Jewel
1918 And a Still Small Voice
1919 Better Times
Christianity
nt Specific denominations
1913 The Daughter of the Hills
From the Manger to the Cross
Hiawatha
1914 St. Elmo
The Sign of the Cross
Thais
When Rome Ruled
The Wrath of the Gods
1915 *China*
1916 The Martyrdom of Philip Strong
1917 *Thais*
1918 *The City of Dim Faces*
1919 *In the Land of the Setting Sun; Or, Martyrs of Yesterday*
1920 The Great Redeemer
The Idol Dancer
Madonnas and Men
The Man Who Dared
The Servant in the House
Christians
1915 The Arab
The Beachcomber
1918 Restitution
1919 Auction of Souls
Male and Female

Christmas
1914 *Hearts and Flowers*
The Life of Big Tim Sullivan; Or, From Newsboy to Senator
The Power of the Press
1915 Silver Threads Among the Gold
1916 The Right to Be Happy
1917 A Bit O' Heaven
1918 The Blue Bird
Every Mother's Son
Ruler of the Road
The Shell Game
A Woman's Fool
1919 Gates of Brass
The Spark Divine
1920 *The Girl of My Heart*
Christopher, Saint
1916 Lieutenant Danny, U.S.A.
Church of Jesus Christ of Latter-Day Saints
1913 One Hundred Years of Mormonism
1917 A Mormon Maid
1918 The Rainbow Trail
Riders of the Purple Sage
1920 *The Fighting Shepherdess*
Churches (*Places of worship*)
nt Specific types of churches
1914 *The Criminal Path*
Hearts of Oak
The Mystery of Edwin Drood
1915 Destiny; Or, The Soul of a Woman
My Madonna
The Right of Way
The Rosary
Sin
1915-16 *The Little Church Around the Corner*
1916 *Hell's Hinges*
Immediate Lee
The Parson of Panamint
United States Marines Under Fire in Haiti
1917 *The Last of the Ingrams*
The Little American
Little Miss Optimist
The Little Samaritan
The Pride of the Clan
Tom Sawyer
The Valentine Girl
1918 *The Cross Bearer*
The Forbidden Path
Go West, Young Man
I'll Say So
Mirandy Smiles
Naughty, Naughty!
Social Briars
The Struggle Everlasting
1919 *The Best Man*
The Eternal Magdalene
The Faith of the Strong
Hell Roarin' Reform
In His Brother's Place
The Lady of Red Butte
Riders of Vengeance
The Stream of Life
Under the Top
1920 Hell's Oasis
Pink Tights
The Right of Way
The Servant in the House
The White Moll
Cigar stores
1918 *The Greatest Thing in Life*
Cigarette girls
1917 The Cigarette Girl
1918 Amarilly of Clothes-Line Alley
1919 Tin Pan Alley
Cigarette makers
1920 The Woman and the Puppet
Cigarettes
1919 *Help! Help! Police!*
1920 *The Trail of the Cigarette*
Cigars
1920 *Partners of the Night*
Cinderella
1916 *The Crippled Hand*

Circumstantial evidence
1915 *A Butterfly on the Wheel*
The Cowboy and the Lady
The Family Stain
The Green Cloak
1916 *And the Law Says*
The Closed Road
The Marriage Bond
The Wheel of the Law
1917 Feet of Clay
Her Better Self
In the Hands of the Law
The Lair of the Wolf
The Pulse of Life
The Recoil
Society's Driftwood
The Tenth Case
Troublemakers
The Voice of Conscience
1918 A Game with Fate
In Judgment Of
The Spurs of Sybil
1919 The Grim Game
The Heart of a Gypsy
Secret Marriage
1920 Circumstantial Evidence
Love, Honor and Behave
Love's Battle
Circus managers
1916 The Rainbow Princess
1917 *The Barker*
The Butterfly Girl
1920 *The Forbidden Thing*
The Fortune Teller
Circus owners
1917 The Barker
1918 *Eye for Eye*
1919 *Jinx*
1920 *Pink Tights*
Through Eyes of Men
Circus performers
rt **Trapezists**
nt **Acrobats**
Aerialists
1914 *Kate*
Mrs. Wiggs of the Cabbage Patch
Nell of the Circus
1915 *Still Waters*
1916 The Rainbow Princess
1917 The Butterfly Girl
The Little Terror
Polly of the Circus
1918 *The Wild Strain*
1919 Hoop-La
Jinx
One-Thing-at-a-Time O'Day
1920 Her Elephant Man
Through Eyes of Men
Circuses
rt **Carnivals**
Fairs
Sideshows
1914 The Circus Man
Mrs. Wiggs of the Cabbage Patch
1915 *The Flying Twins*
The Gentleman from Indiana
Still Waters
1916 A Circus Romance
The Rainbow Princess
1917 The Barker
The Butterfly Girl
Flirting with Death
The Little Terror
Polly of the Circus
The Sawdust Ring
The Woman and the Beast
1918 The Biggest Show on Earth
The Dawn of Understanding
Eye for Eye
Little Red Riding Hood
The Wild Strain
1919 Jinx
The Little White Savage
The Love Hunger
The Merry-Go-Round
The Old Maid's Baby
A Regular Girl
Under the Top
1920 The Fortune Teller
Her Elephant Man
Man and Woman (Tyrad Pictures, Inc.)
Pink Tights

Through Eyes of Men
Citizenship
1914 An American Citizen
1915 *Her Great Match*
1916 *The American Beauty*
The Crown Prince's Double
1917 Follow the Girl
1918 One More American
Ruggles of Red Gap
City life
use **Lure of the city**
Urban life
City slickers
1914 Tillie's Punctured Romance
1918 *The Beloved Blackmailer*
1919 *The Egg Crate Wallop*
Greased Lightning
Nugget Nell
Rose O' the River
The Shepherd of the Hills
City-country contrast
rt **Lure of the city**
1913 Caprice
The Daughter of the Hills
1914 The Folks from Way Down East
The Gangsters
The House of Bondage
Wildflower
1915 The Adventures of a Madcap
Are They Born or Made?
The Bridge of Sighs
The Chorus Lady
The Country Boy
The Dancing Girl
Emmy of Stork's Nest
The Governor's Lady
Jack Chanty
The Old Homestead
On Dangerous Paths
The Politicians
Saved from the Harem
A Texas Steer
Virtue
When a Woman Loves
1916 The Beast
Caprice of the Mountains
Feathertop
Fruits of Desire
Hesper of the Mountains
The Salamander
1917 An Amateur Orphan
Burning the Candle
The Checkmate
The Defeat of the City
The Golden God
In the Balance
Jack and Jill
The Maternal Spark
Miss Deception
Mother O' Mine
The Night Workers
1918 The Impostor
Little Miss Grown-Up
Naughty, Naughty!
A Nine O'Clock Town
A Nymph of the Foothills
The Other Woman
Social Briars
1919 The Bramble Bush
A Broadway Saint
The Busher
The Country Cousin
Crooked Straight
Destiny
The Egg Crate Wallop
The Greater Sinner
Heart O' the Hills
The Light
The Little Boss
The Lord Loves the Irish
The Love Defender
Luck in Pawn
The Miracle Man
The Money Corral
The Moonshine Trail
The Perfect Lover
The Poor Boob
Poor Relations
Pretty Smooth
Prudence on Broadway
Rose O' the River
Roses and Thorns
The Rough Neck
Rough Riding Romance

The Marriage Speculation
Reaching for the Moon
The Renaissance at Charleroi
A Sleeping Memory
The Soul Master
Two-Bit Seats
The War of the Tongs
1918 *Dodging a Million*
The Grain of Dust
Innocent's Progress
Kidder and Ko
Playthings
The Richest Girl
The Silent Woman
The Still Alarm
Why I Would Not Marry
1919 *The Amateur Adventuress*
The Final Close-Up
The Four-Flusher
Hearts of Men
The Love Cheat
The Loves of Letty
Sis Hopkins
1920 *Homer Comes Home*
Nineteen and Phyllis
Shore Acres

Cleveland
1920 *The Sagebrusher*

Henry Clinton
1919 *The Spirit of Lafayette*

Clocks
1917 *The Clock*

Clothes
1914 *A Prince of India*
The Spy
The Thief
The Woman of Mystery
1915 *The Cheat*
The Mating
Matrimony
1916 *The Beast*
Peggy
Phantom Fortunes
Plain Jane
The Sable Blessing
Vanity
1917 *Framing Framers*
The Gilded Youth
The Gown of Destiny
The Haunted Pajamas
Her Bargain
The Indian Summer of Dry
Valley Johnson
Melissa of the Hills
Paradise Garden
A School for Husbands
The Seven Swans
Skinner's Dress Suit
Sunny Jane
The Sunset Trail
Weavers of Life
1918 Borrowed Clothes
By Proxy
Dodging a Million
Face Value
Fair Enough
False Ambition
The Fighting Grin
Flower of the Dusk
He Comes Up Smiling
Hell Bent
Limousine Life
Little Miss Grown-Up
The Marriage Ring
The Model's Confession
Nancy Comes Home
Naughty, Naughty!
A Pair of Silk Stockings
A Perfect 36
The Vamp
The Way of a Man with a
Maid
Western Blood
Whatever the Cost
1919 *Alias Mike Moran*
The Amateur Adventuress
God's Outlaw
Heart of Gold
John Petticoats
Louisiana
Nugget Nell
Over the Garden Wall
23 1/2 Hours' Leave
Wanted—A Husband
What Every Woman Wants

1920 Blind Wives
Clothes
Help Wanted—Male
Man and Woman (A. H.
Fischer Features, Inc.)
Pink Tights
Silk Hosiery
The Stolen Kiss
The Thief
Twin Beds

Clothing business
1918 Our Mrs. McChesney
1919 That's Good
The Uplifters

Clothing industry
1914 *The Million*
1917 The Peddler

Clouds
1920 *Shipwrecked Among
Cannibals*

Clowns
1913 *Ben Bolt*
1914 *The Circus Man*
Nell of the Circus
1916 The Clown
Thrown to the Lions
1917 *Polly of the Circus*
1919 *Hoop-La*

Clubs
1914 *For the Honor of Old Glory;
Or, The Stars and Stripes in
Mexico*
The Long Arm of the Law
The Man from Mexico
*The Mysterious Mr. Wu Chung
Foo*
1915 *Are You a Mason?*
The Edge of the Abyss
The Marriage of Kitty
Who's Who in Society
1916 Between Men
The Five Faults of Flo
Home
The Moral Fabric
The Tarantula
The Valley of Decision
1917 *Please Help Emily*
Putting the Bee in Herbert
1918 *The Girl of My Dreams*
A Lady's Name
The Square Deal
Three X Gordon
The Yellow Dog
1919 *The Woman Next Door*
1920 *Bubbles*
Even As Eve
The Paliser Case

Coachmen
1915 *Lady Audley's Secret*

Coal
1914 *The Trail of the Lonesome
Pine*
1915 The Cave Man
1917 *The Road Between*
1918 *The Grey Parasol*
1919 *Heart O' the Hills*
In Old Kentucky
1920 *Dad's Girl*

Coal miners
1913 Buried Alive in a Coal Mine
1914 *Ill Starred Babbie*
1916 *The Dawn of Freedom*
A Woman's Honor
A Woman's Way
1917 Threads of Fate

Coal mines
1914 Through Fire to Fortune
1916 *The Dawn of Freedom*
1917 *Little Miss Optimist*
Mr. Opp
Threads of Fate
1920 The Key to Power

Coats
1914 Joseph and His Coat of Many
Colors
1916 Phantom Fortunes
The Sable Blessing
1918 *Under Suspicion*

Cobalt (Canada)
1914 *The Dollar Mark*

Cobblers
1913 *A Princess of Bagdad*
1916 *Little Lady Eileen*
Peck O' Pickles
The Price of Happiness
1917 *Mary Lawson's Secret*
1918 *Rose O' Paradise*
1920 *Chains of Evidence*

Cocaine
1913 *The Port of Doom*
1914 Cocaine Traffic; Or, The Drug
Terror
Dope
1915 Black Fear
June Friday
1916 *Acquitted*
Big Jim Garrity
1917 Fear Not

Cocoa
1915 *Pirate Haunts*

Codes
rt **Secret codes**
1915 The House of Fear
A Submarine Pirate
1919 *The False Code*

William F. Cody
1917 The Adventures of Buffalo Bill

Coffee
1915 *The Footsteps of Capt. Kidd*
1918 *Unexpected Places*

Coffeyville (Kansas)
1918 *Beyond the Law*

Coffins
1916 *The Heart of the Hills*
1920 *Isobel; Or, The Trail's End*

Coins
1915 *The Clue*

Coliseum (Rome)
1913 *The Daughter of the Hills*
1914 The Coliseum in Films
The Sign of the Cross
1920 Madonnas and Men

College life
1915 The College Orphan
The College Widow
The Grandee's Ring
The Juggernaut
A Little Brother of the Rich
The Mating
Old Heidelberg
Wheat and Tares; A Story of
Two Boys Who Tackle Life
on Diverging Lines
When We Were Twenty-One
1916 *Betrayed*
1917 *Happiness*
The Heart of Ezra Greer
The Lust of the Ages
The Pinch Hitter
Redemption
1918 Jack Spurlock, Prodigal
1919 Oh, Boy!
*Whom the Gods Would
Destroy*
1920 *Li Ting Lang*
Up in Mary's Attic

College students
1914 *In Mizzoura*
Liberty Belles
The Rejuvenation of Aunt
Mary
1916 *The Innocent Lie*
Langdon's Legacy
Plain Jane
Rose of the South
The Strength of the Weak
The Thousand Dollar Husband
1917 The Courage of the Common
Place
Crime and Punishment
The Curse of Eve
Each to His Kind
The Gift Girl
The Girl at Home
*The Girl Who Couldn't Grow
Up*
The Lad and the Lion
One Touch of Nature
The Silent Witness
Whither Thou Goest
1918 *The City of Dim Faces*
Joan of the Woods
The Kid Is Clever
Real Folks

The Wasp
*What Becomes of the
Children?*
1919 *Daddy-Long-Legs*
The Girl Dodger
The Golden Shower
The Great Romance
The Scarlet Shadow
The Unwritten Code
Wanted—A Husband
What Love Forgives
The Winning Stroke
1920 *The Blooming Angel*
Sweet Lavender

Colleges
1920 *The Blooming Angel*

Colombia
1915 The Footsteps of Capt. Kidd

Colonists
1914 When Broadway Was a Trail
When Rome Ruled
1915 *The Pageant of San Francisco*
1917 *The Hidden Children*

Colorado
1914 *The Brute*
The Only Son
The Three of Us
1915 Colorado
The Heights of Hazard
The Incorrigible Dukane
1916 *The Blacklist*
The Target
1917 *By Right of Possession*
Money Magic
1918 Believe Me Xantippe
The Naulahka
Virtuous Wives
1919 *Venus in the East*
1920 *Madame Peacock*

Columbia University
1919 *The Great Romance*

Christopher Columbus
1914 *America*
1916 *United States Marines Under
Fire in Haiti*

Columbus (New Mexico)
1916 *Following the Flag in Mexico*

Comanche Indians
1920 The Daughter of Dawn

Comas
1917 *Mentioned in Confidence*
1919 *The Unpardonable Sin*
1920 The Sleep of Cyma Roget

Combat
1912 *Richard III*
1913 Mexican War Pictures (Lubin
Mfg. Co.)
1915 *The Birth of a Nation*
*History of the Great European
War*
The History of the World's
Greatest War
1916 *At the Front with the Allies*
Civilization
The Daughter of the Don
The Light That Failed
A Message to Garcia
Peck O' Pickles
The Primal Lure
Race Suicide
Rose of the South
United States Marines Under
Fire in Haiti
War on Three Fronts
War-Torn Poland
Whom the Gods Destroy
The Zeppelin Raids on London
and the Siege of Verdun
1917 *Filling His Own Shoes*
For the Freedom of the World
Heroic France
Wild and Woolly
1918 *Bonnie Annie Laurie*
The German Curse in Russia
Hearts of the World
Lafayette, We Come!
The Legion of Death
Tell It to the Marines
The Tiger Man
Too Fat to Fight
Wanted for Murder
The Way Out
Why America Will Win
*Your Fighting Navy at Work
and at Play*

1920   *American Catholics in War and Reconstruction*
Combat zone life
1914   On the Belgian Battlefield
       The War of the World
1915   *The Battles of a Nation*
       On the Firing Line with the Germans
       A Soldier's Oath
1916   *Joan the Woman*
1917   *The Seventh Sin*
       Sloth
1918   *America's Answer; Following the Fleet to France*
       Missing
       The Unbeliever
1919   *The Common Cause*
       The Lost Battalion
Comedians
1915   *Her Triumph*
Charles A. Comiskey
1914   *The Giants-White Sox Tour*
Communal living
1919   *Bolshevism on Trial*
Companions
       rt **Traveling companions**
1918   *In the Hollow of Her Hand*
       Resurrection
Composers
       rt **Songwriters**
1915   *The Concealed Truth*
       The Melting Pot
       Temptation
       What Happened to Father
1917   *It Happened to Adele*
       Panthea
1918   *The Love Brokers*
       The Song of Songs
1919   *The Broken Butterfly*
       A Damsel in Distress
       A Fallen Idol
       Heartsease
       Mind the Paint Girl
       Words and Music By—
1920   *Greater Than Fame*
Concerts
1918   *The Lost Chord*
1919   *The Social Pirate*
1920   *The Hidden Light*
Coney Island (New York)
       use **New York City—Coney Island**
Confectioners and confectionaries
       rt **Candy stores**
1913   *Traffic in Souls*
1916   Bluff
1917   *The Marriage Speculation*
       The Pinch Hitter
1918   The Winning of Beatrice
Confession (Indirect)
       rt **Confession (law)**
       Confession (religion)
1914   Born Again
       Forgiven; Or, The Jack of Diamonds
       The Ghost Breaker
       Ill Starred Babbie
       A Lady of Quality
       Lena Rivers (Cosmos Feature Film Corp.)
       Lena Rivers (Whitman Features Co.)
       Marta of the Lowlands
       Pieces of Silver; A Story of Hearts and Souls
1915   *Evidence*
       The Flaming Sword
       The Frame-Up
       His Wife
       Judge Not; Or, The Woman of Mona Diggings
       The Labyrinth
       Marrying Money
       Monsieur Lecoq
       The Penitentes
       The Plunderer
       The Price of Her Silence
       Ranson's Folly
       The Rosary
       The Runaway Wife
       The Siren's Song
       Strathmore
       The Suburban
       Sunday
       To Cherish and Protect

The Unbroken Road
The Vampire
When It Strikes Home
The Woman
1916   *As in a Looking Glass*
       The Big Sister
       The Breaker
       A Circus Romance
       The City of Illusion
       The Drifter
       The Dupe
       Gloriana
       The Havoc
       Her Bleeding Heart
       The Kiss of Hate
       A Wife's Sacrifice
       A Woman's Daring
       The Woman's Law
1917   *The Angel Factory*
       Apartment 29
       The Bar Sinister
       The Beautiful Lie
       The Burglar
       Camille
       The Flaming Omen
       Her Life and His
       Kitty MacKay
       The Lifted Veil
       Lost in Transit
       Madame Sherry
       A Magdalene of the Hills
       The Man Hater
       The Man Who Forgot
       The Medicine Man
       The Phantom's Secret
       The Price Mark
       The Pride of the Clan
       The Princess of Patches
       Shall We Forgive Her?
1918   American Buds
       Buchanan's Wife
       The Business of Life
       The Impostor
       Marriage
       Merely Players
       The Model's Confession
       Nancy Comes Home
       The Reckoning Day
       A Soul in Trust
1919   *The Black Gate*
       The Gray Horizon
       Just Squaw
       Mandarin's Gold
       The Market of Souls
       Modern Husbands
       Out Yonder
       Red Blood and Yellow
       Shadows of the Past
       Should a Husband Forgive?
       Should a Woman Tell?
       The Splendid Sin
       Treat 'Em Rough
       Upstairs and Down
       The Way of the Strong
       When a Girl Loves
       Where the West Begins
       Why Smith Left Home
       Wings of the Morning
       The Woman Under Oath
       A Woman's Experience
1920   *The Frisky Mrs. Johnson*
       Mothers of Men
       Sunset Sprague
       Through Eyes of Men
       The Triple Clue
       The Web of Deceit
       Whispering Devils
1921   *Midsummer Madness*
Confession (law)
1913   *The Battle of Shiloh*
       An Hour Before Dawn
       The Third Degree
1914   Called Back
       The Criminal Path
       Escaped from Siberia
       The Gamblers
       Hook and Hand
       The Master Cracksman
       One of Our Girls
       The Squaw Man
       A Suspicious Wife
       The Thief
       The Voice at the Telephone
1915   At Bay
       Bred in the Bone

The Brink
The Butterfly
Chimmie Fadden
The Circular Staircase
The Clemenceau Case
The Clue
The Concealed Truth
Conscience
Courtmartialed
David Harum
The District Attorney
The Family Stain
The Final Judgment
The Game of Three
The Heart of a Painted Woman
The Heart of Jennifer
The House of the Lost Court
June Friday
Lord John in New York
Lydia Gilmore
The Majesty of the Law
The Man of Shame
The Master Hand
The Model
My Madonna
The Mystery of Room 13
One Million Dollars
Pearls of Temptation
The Ploughshare
Shadows from the Past
Should a Mother Tell?
The Sins of the Mothers
Thou Shalt Not Kill
Through Turbulent Waters
The Wheels of Justice
The White Scar
The Wild Olive
The Woman Next Door
The Woman Who Lied
A Woman's Past
A Yankee from the West
1916   *Acquitted*
       Big Jim Garrity
       Big Tremaine
       The Birth of Character
       The Black Sheep of the Family
       Broken Chains
       By Whose Hand?
       The Closed Road
       The Come-Back
       Common Ground
       The Conflict
       The Conscience of John David
       The Decoy
       The Destroyers
       Doctor Neighbor
       The Eye of God
       For the Defense
       The Half Million Bribe
       In the Web of the Grafters
       Intolerance
       Just a Song at Twilight
       The Lash of Destiny
       The Man Behind the Curtain
       The Man from Bitter Roots
       The Man from Nowhere
       The Missing Links
       A Night Out
       Not My Sister
       The Ocean Waif
       The Ordeal of Elizabeth
       The Other Side of the Door
       The People vs. John Doe
       The Rack
       The Torch Bearer
       The Twinkler
       The Unwritten Law
       Vanity
       Vultures of Society
       What Happened at 22
       The Wheel of the Law
       Who Killed Joe Merrion?
       Wild Oats
       The Witching Hour
       The Woman in the Case
       A Woman's Fight
       The Yellow Pawn
1917   *The Accomplice*
       Back of the Man
       Because of a Woman
       The Bond of Fear
       Clover's Rebellion
       The Darling of Paris

The Derelict
Double Crossed
Fear Not
The Golden Fetter
Her Better Self
Her Fighting Chance
Her Temptation
The Hidden Spring
High Play
His Sweetheart
The Inevitable
The Inspirations of Harry Larrabee
The Judgement House
The Last of the Carnabys
The Law of the North
Life's Whirlpool
The Man Trap
The Mark of Cain
The Marriage Market
Mary Lawson's Secret
Mothers of Men
My Fighting Gentleman
The Mystic Hour
On Trial
Peggy, the Will O' the Wisp
The Phantom Shotgun
The Price of Pride
The Price of Silence
The Pulse of Life
Richard the Brazen
The Road Between
Runaway Romany
Sister Against Sister
Sleeping Fires
The Social Leper
Society's Driftwood
Susan's Gentleman
Tangled Lives
The Tenth Case
Transgression
Triumph
Trooper 44
The Voice of Conscience
The Weaker Sex
Wild Sumac
Within the Law
A Woman's Awakening
1918   *All Woman*
       The Argument
       Broken Ties
       The Burden of Proof
       Confession
       The Danger Zone
       The Eagle
       Faith Endurin'
       Fedora
       $5,000 Reward
       For Freedom
       The Girl Who Came Back
       Green Eyes
       The Green God
       Heart of the Wilds
       Hearts or Diamonds?
       Her Boy
       His Daughter Pays
       Hitting the Trail
       In Judgment Of
       In the Hollow of Her Hand
       A Japanese Nightingale
       Just a Woman
       Kildare of Storm
       The Liar
       Life or Honor?
       The Lonely Woman
       Madame Sphinx
       The Man from Funeral Range
       The Menace
       Miss Innocence
       M'liss
       Money Mad
       No Man's Land
       One Dollar Bid
       Playthings
       The Queen of Hearts
       Quicksand
       Rosemary Climbs the Heights
       Sandy
       The Squaw Man
       Sunshine Nan
       La Tosca
       The Trail to Yesterday
       The Venus Model
       The Voice of Destiny
       The Whirlpool

Wild Life
Wild Youth
The Winning of Beatrice
A Woman of Impulse
1919 *L'Apache*
The Battler
Blind Man's Eyes
The Blue Bandanna
The Brat
Calibre 38
The Courageous Coward
The Drifters
False Gods
The Forbidden Room
The Gamblers
A Girl at Bay
The Gray Wolf's Ghost
The Law of Men
A Man's Fight
The Master Man
The Mother and the Law
Out of the Shadow
The Profiteers
Sacred Silence
The Silver King
Thin Ice
The Third Degree
Thunderbolts of Fate
The Trembling Hour
A Trick of Fate
The Unbroken Promise
The Vengeance of Durand
The Virtuous Thief
The Woman Next Door
The Woman Under Cover
1920 *Circumstantial Evidence*
The Confession
The Dangerous Talent
The False Road
The Good-Bad Wife
The Hidden Light
The House of Whispers
Love Madness
The Man Who Dared
The Paliser Case
Risky Business
The Round-Up
The Sin That Was His
The Strange Boarder
The Victim
Woman's Man

Confession (religion)
1915 *Sealed Lips*
1919 *The Faith of the Strong*
1920 *The Confession*
The Sin That Was His
The Victim

Confidence games
1914 *The Little Jewess*
1915 *The Deep Purple*
1916 *The Flirt*
1917 *The Road Between*
1918 *The Shell Game*

Confidence men
rt **Confidence women**
Swindlers
1915 *The Gentleman from Indiana*
The Vampire
1916 *The Bait*
The Dream Girl
A Stranger from Somewhere
Susan Rocks the Boat
1917 *Betty and the Buccaneers*
Builders of Castles
Flirting with Death
The Road Between
The Small Town Guy
1918 *Just Sylvia*
The Mating
The Shell Game
1919 *Crooked Straight*
Gates of Brass
1920 *Blackmail*
The Deep Purple
His Pajama Girl

Confidence women
rt **Confidence men**
Swindlers
1918 *Just Sylvia*
1920 *Blackmail*
The Cheater

Confucianism
1920 *Outside the Law*

Connecticut
1915 *The Flying Twins*
Kreutzer Sonata
The Sable Lorcha
The Woman Next Door
1917 *The Indian Summer of Dry*
Valley Johnson
1920 *A Connecticut Yankee at King*
Arthur's Court

Conscience
rt **Guilt**
1914 *Home, Sweet Home*
1915 *The Glory of Youth*
The Italian
A Yankee from the West
1916 *According to the Code*
The Black Sheep of the Family
The Chain Invisible
The Conscience of John David
Man and His Soul
1917 *Conscience*
Crime and Punishment
The Flame of the Yukon
Has Man the Right to Kill?
The Hidden Spring
A Night in New Arabia
The Power of Decision
The Price of Silence
The Recoil
Vengeance Is Mine
The Warfare of the Flesh
1918 *The Whispering Chorus*

Conscientious objectors
1917 *The Volunteer*

Conspiracy
1912 *Cleopatra*
Richard III
1913 *The Count of Monte Cristo*
From Dusk to Dawn
1914 *The Dancer and the King*
Liberty Belles
My Official Wife
Richelieu
The Three Musketeers
Three Weeks
Washington at Valley Forge
1915 *The Face in the Moonlight*
The Governor's Boss
The Master Hand
Mr. Grex of Monte Carlo
Mistress Nell
Pennington's Choice
The Puppet Crown
The Rights of Man: A Story of
War's Red Blotch
A Royal Family
Simon, the Jester
The Woman Next Door
1916 *A Daughter of the Gods*
Elusive Isabel
The Fall of a Nation
The Final Curtain
The Hero of Submarine D-2
Intolerance
Langdon's Legacy
The Wall Between
The White Rosette
The Witching Hour
The Woman in Politics
1917 *The Adventurer*
The Barricade
The Bitter Truth
The Book Agent
Bringing Home Father
The Desire of the Moth
An Even Break
Fighting Odds
His Sweetheart
Kidnapped
The Man of Mystery
The Message of the Mouse
Money Madness
A Mormon Maid
The Silent Partner
A Wife by Proxy
1918 *A Burglar for a Night*
The Caillaux Case
Danger Within
Hungry Eyes
Loaded Dice
My Own United States
Salome
The Source

Stolen Honor
Winner Takes All
The Yellow Dog
1919 *Boots*
The Burning Question
The Long Arm of Mannister
1920 *Go and Get It*
Held in Trust
If I Were King
Judy of Rogue's Harbor
Little Miss Rebellion
The Purple Cipher
The Scrap of Paper
West Is West

Constables
bt **Police**
1913 *A Sister to Carmen*
1917 *Troublemakers*
1919 *Captain Kidd, Jr.*
Love in a Hurry
Oh, Boy!

Constantinople
1915 *The Rug Maker's Daughter*
1917 *Love Aflame*
1920 *The Right to Love*
The Virgin of Stamboul

Construction
1916 *The Challenge*
1917 *Youth*
1919 *The Dub*
1920 *The Eternal Union of the Seas*
His Own Law

Construction camps
1916 *Overalls*
The Selfish Woman
1920 *Just a Wife*

Construction foremen
1914 *Facing the Gattling Guns*
1915 *The Incorrigible Dukane*
The Warning
1916 *Overalls*
1919 *The Burning Question*

Construction workers
1914 *Facing the Gattling Guns*
1915 *The Bigger Man*
The Incorrigible Dukane
The Man Who Couldn't Beat
God
1916 *Overalls*
The Selfish Woman
1918 *Cecilia of the Pink Roses*
Fast Company
The Marriage Lie

Consuls
rt **Diplomats**
1915 *The Dictator*
1918 *A Japanese Nightingale*
1919 *The Poor Boob*
1920 *A Double Dyed Deceiver*

Contests
1915 *The Bachelor's Romance*
The Man Trail
The Masqueraders
1916 *Plain Jane*
The Summer Girl
1917 *Putting the Bee in Herbert*
1918 *Neighbors*
1919 *The Busher*
Daughter of Mine
Heart of Gold
Poor Relations

Contractors
1914 *The Brute*
Facing the Gattling Guns
1915 *The Evangelist*
The Immigrant
The Incorrigible Dukane
The Man Who Couldn't Beat
God
The Wonderful Adventure
1917 *Jim Bludso*
A Kiss for Susie
Pride and the Man
1918 *Her Husband's Honor*
1919 *The Burning Question*
Day Dreams
The Dub
The Forbidden Room
A Yankee Princess
1920 *The Greatest Love*
Hidden Charms
His Own Law
The Wall Street Mystery

Contracts
1915 *The Labyrinth*
The Man Trail
1916 *The Black Crook*
The Bruiser
The Devil's Toy
A Fool's Paradise
Phantom Fortunes
1917 *All for a Husband*
Efficiency Edgar's Courtship
Loyalty
Mr. Dolan of New York
The Question
Richard the Brazen
Sudden Jim
1918 *Beans*
Brave and Bold
Her Husband's Honor
Her Price
Journey's End
The She-Devil
Untamed
1919 *Over the Garden Wall*
The Poor Boob
The Web of Chance
1920 *What's Your Hurry?*

Convalescence
rt **Nursing back to health**
1915 *In the Shadow*
1916 *Her Bitter Cup*
Hesper of the Mountains
His Brother's Wife
Whom the Gods Destroy
1917 *The Mad Lover*
The Primrose Ring
1918 *The Fly God*
Her Body in Bond
Over the Top
Patriotism
Paying His Debt
The Pretender
The Racing Strain
The Red, Red Heart
The Sea Waif
1919 *The Crook of Dreams*

Conventions (*Gatherings*)
1918 *The Heart of a Girl*
1919 *Open Your Eyes*

Convents
rt **Nuns**
1913 *The Legend of Provence*
1914 *In the Name of the Prince of*
Peace
Manon Lescaut
Thais
Threads of Destiny
Too Late
1915 *Ghosts*
His Wife
The Secret Orchard
The Sins of the Mothers
The White Sister
1916 *Bullets and Brown Eyes*
The Reapers
The Sorrows of Love
Tennessee's Pardner
1917 *The Conqueror*
The Courage of Silence
The Love Doctor
Should She Obey?
The Slave Market
Wrath
1918 *The Demon*
Let's Get a Divorce
The Lure of Luxury
The Marionettes
Miss Innocence
The Only Road
A Romance of the Underworld
Under the Yoke
1919 *The Avalanche*
The Capitol
The Chosen Path
Human Desire
The Right to Lie
Speedy Meade
1920 *For the Soul of Rafael*
The Midlanders
Passion's Playground
The Red Lane
Scratch My Back
Through Eyes of Men

1920 What's Your Hurry?
Dance hall girls
1914 Burning Daylight: The
Adventures of "Burning
Daylight" in Alaska
*Burning Daylight: The
Adventures of "Burning
Daylight" in Civilization*
The Invisible Power
The Mountain Rat
The Spoilers
1915 *The Commanding Officer*
On the Night Stage
Should a Wife Forgive?
Up from the Depths
1916 The Aryan
The Craving
Hell's Hinges
Immediate Lee
The Man from Bitter Roots
The Reapers
Reggie Mixes In
Sins of Her Parent
Three Pals
The World's Great Snare
1917 Ashes of Hope
The Cold Deck
The Desert Man
The Devil Dodger
The Firefly of Tough Luck
The Flame of the Yukon
The Golden Rosary
The Narrow Trail
On the Level
One Touch of Sin
The Silent Lie
The Siren
The White Raven
1918 Carmen of the Klondike
"Flare-Up" Sal
The Guilt of Silence
Hell Bent
Hell's Crater
The Home Trail
Nobody's Wife
The Panther Woman
Staking His Life
Three Mounted Men
Tongues of Flame
Tyrant Fear
Whatever the Cost
Wild Honey
Wild Life
1919 The Brand
The Clouded Name
The Heart of Juanita
A Man's Country
The Midnight Stage
The Rider of the Law
Scarlet Days
Shadows
The Westerners
1920 Burglar Proof
*Dr. Jekyll and Mr. Hyde
(Famous Players-Lasky
Corp.)*
The Forbidden Thing
The Law of the Yukon
The Lone Hand
*Man and Woman (Tyrad
Pictures, Inc.)*
The Man from Nowhere
Out of the Dust
The Rose of Nome
The Spirit of Good
The Terror
The U.P. Trail
The Woman in the Suitcase
Dance hall owners
1915 *The Fight*
The Plunderer
1916 *Human Driftwood*
1917 *The Devil Dodger*
Golden Rule Kate
The Magnificent Meddler
Pay Me
Trooper 44
1918 Carmen of the Klondike
The Gun Woman
Selfish Yates
1919 *The Heart of Juanita*
Scarlet Days
1920 Hell's Oasis
The Law of the Yukon
The Rose of Nome

The Spirit of Good
The U.P. Trail
Dance halls
1915 *The Call of the Dance*
The Cowboy and the Lady
Should a Wife Forgive?
1916 *The Reapers*
Rose of the Alley
1917 *Chicken Casey*
Hell Morgan's Girl
Her Secret
Magda
A Romance of the Redwoods
Should She Obey?
The Silent Lie
The Siren
Trooper 44
Wild and Woolly
1918 *The Bird of Prey*
Hell's Crater
The Home Trail
Keys of the Righteous
A Perfect Lady
Prisoners of the Pines
Revenge
Selfish Yates
Social Ambition
Wild Life
1919 *Calibre 38*
Courage for Two
The Girl from Nowhere
Paid in Advance
1920 Burglar Proof
The Forbidden Thing
The Rose of Nome
The Testing Block
The U.P. Trail
Dance schools
1917 The Dancer's Peril
Dance teachers
1915 *The Fool and the Dancer*
1916 *The Lights of New York*
1918 *The She-Devil*
1919 A Trick of Fate
1920 *A Romantic Adventuress*
Scratch My Back
Dancers
nt Specific types of dancers
1913 The Black Snake
The Lotus Dancer
1914 The Dancer and the King
The Idler
The Million
1915 *Alice in Wonderland*
The Apaches of Paris
The Butterfly
The Call of the Dance
*Carmen (Jesse L. Lasky
Feature Play Co.)*
The Dancing Girl
Don Caesar de Bazan
The Fool and the Dancer
Midnight at Maxim's
A Modern Magdalen
Nearly a Lady
The Outcast
A Price for Folly
The Spanish Jade
Strathmore
The Vow
When We Were Twenty-One
The Whirl of Life
1916 *The Ballet Girl*
The Children in the House
A Circus Romance
The Daughter of MacGregor
A Dream or Two Ago
The Girl Philippa
Jealousy
The Narrow Path
Nearly a King
A Night Out
A Parisian Romance
The Quest of Life
The Rainbow Princess
The Red Widow
Reggie Mixes In
The Scarlet Road
Susie Snowflake
The Tarantula
The Twin Triangle
The Victory of Conscience
1917 *The Accomplice*
The Butterfly Girl
The Clodhopper

The Darling of Paris
Fighting Mad
The Flower of Doom
For Valour
Giving Becky a Chance
Her Soul's Inspiration
Love's Law
The Medicine Man
The Pulse of Life
The Wax Model
The Weaker Sex
1918 A Broadway Scandal
The Cabaret
The Death Dance
Empty Pockets
Eye for Eye
The Ghost of the Rancho
The Great Love
Her Body in Bond
Her Decision
How Could You, Caroline?
Lawless Love
Little Miss Grown-Up
Maid O' the Storm
Money Isn't Everything
The Naulahka
One Thousand Dollars
A Perfect Lady
Playing the Game
The Primitive Woman
The Romance of Tarzan
The Safety Curtain
The She-Devil
The Sins of the Children
The Street of Seven Stars
The Velvet Hand
We Can't Have Everything
When a Woman Sins
1919 La Belle Russe
The Delicious Little Devil
The Devil's Trail
Eyes of the Soul
The Follies Girl
*The Girl Who Stayed at
Home*
The Golden Shower
Hay Foot, Straw Foot
Jacques of the Silver North
Keali
Molly of the Follies
The Moral Deadline
The Painted World
Redhead
The Sundown Trail
A Trick of Fate
Upside Down
The Woman Under Cover
Yankee Doodle in Berlin
Yvonne from Paris
1919-20
The Marriage Blunder
1920 *The Adventurer*
The Chorus Girl's Romance
The Dancin' Fool
The Garter Girl
The Good-Bad Wife
The Heart of a Child
Hell's Oasis
*Man and Woman (Tyrad
Pictures, Inc.)*
On with the Dance
Rogues and Romance
A Romantic Adventuress
Rouge and Riches
Scratch My Back
The Sins of St. Anthony
The Stolen Kiss
Stronger Than Death
The Tiger's Coat
The Very Idea
What Happened to Rosa
The Woman and the Puppet
Dances (Parties)
1914 *Classmates*
The Three of Us
1915 *The Cub*
The Pursuing Shadow
*Silver Threads Among the
Gold*
1916 *Sunshine Dad*
1917 *Bab's Matinee Idol*
Please Help Emily
1918 *The Floor Below*
Green Eyes
Money Isn't Everything

Naughty, Naughty!
1919 *The Brute Breaker*
False Evidence
The Girl Dodger
Some Bride
The Son-of-a-Gun!
1920 *Bullet Proof*
The Fighting Shepherdess
The Flapper
Dancing
1915 *Lady Mackenzie's Big Game
Pictures*
The Voice of Satan
The Whirl of Life
1916 *Charlie Chaplin's Burlesque on
"Carmen"*
The Dawn Maker
A Night Out
1917 *Her Soul's Inspiration*
1917-18
The Devil's Playground
1918 *Amarilly of Clothes-Line
Alley*
*Among the Cannibal Isles of
the South Pacific*
Salome
When a Woman Sins
1919 *Red Hot Dollars*
Upstairs
1920 *The Land of Jazz*
Stronger Than Death
Dandies
rt **Effeminacy**
Fops
1914 *The Floor Above*
1915 *The Iron Strain*
On the Night Stage
1916 *Silks and Satins*
1917 *The Scarlet Pimpernel*
Sirens of the Sea
The Stolen Treaty
Those Who Pay
Who Was the Other Man?
1918 Fast Company
1920 *An Amateur Devil*
The Mark of Zorro
The Prince of Avenue A
Danes
1918 *The Girl of Today*
1919 *The Poor Boob*
Josephus Daniels
1913 Victory
Georges Jacques Danton
1914 Charlotte Corday
Philippe Sudre Dartiguenave
1916 *United States Marines Under
Fire in Haiti*
Charles Darwin
1920 The Evolution of Man
Darwinism
1919 A Scream in the Night
Daughters-in-law
1916 A Prince in a Pawnshop
1917 American—That's All
Annie-for-Spite
1918 *Our Mrs. McChesney*
Jeff Davis
1915 The Bridge of Sighs
Sam Davis
1915 The Life of Sam Davis: A
Confederate Hero of the
Sixties
A. K. Dawson
1915 *System, the Secret of Success*
Dawson (Canada)
1914 The Chechako
Dayton-Wright Airplane Co
1918 The Yanks Are Coming
Deacons
1914 Mother Love
1918 *Naughty, Naughty!*
A Perfect Lady
1919 Hard Boiled
In His Brother's Place
Deaf-mutes
rt **Aphasia**
Mutes
1917 *The Dummy*
A Mute Appeal
1919 The Big Little Person
Deliverance

Deafness
  1915 *The Silent Voice*
  1918 *Rimrock Jones*
Death (*Personification*)
  1914 One of Millions
  1915 The Cowardly Way
        The Right of Way
Death and dying
  1913 *The Fortune Hunters*
        The Lotus Dancer
  1914 Lola
  1915 *Beulah*
        The Destroying Angel
  1917 The Black Stork
        Maternity
  1918 And the Children Pay
Death by animals
  1913 *A Prisoner in the Harem*
  1914 *Joseph and His Coat of Many*
        Colors
        The Wolf
  1915 *The Deathlock*
  1916 God's Country and the
        Woman
  1917 *The Land of Long Shadows*
  1918 *The Law of the North*
        Tarzan of the Apes
  1919 *The Faith of the Strong*
        Jacques of the Silver North
        The Wolf
Death by shock
    rt **Heart disease**
  1914 *A Million Bid*
        Mother Love
        The Port of Missing Men
  1915 *Dr. Rameau*
        Eugene Aram
        Trilby
  1916 *The Devil's Prize*
        Each Pearl a Tear
        The End of the Trail
        The Feast of Life
        The Gilded Spider
        The Green-Eyed Monster
        Her Great Hour
        The Lights of New York
        The Salamander
        The Stolen Triumph
        Wild Oats
  1917 *Her Strange Wedding*
        The Inevitable
        The Lady in the Library
        Magda
        A Roadside Impresario
        The Soul of a Magdalen
  1918 *Keys of the Righteous*
        The Lost Chord
        Vengeance
        The Whispering Chorus
        The Wife He Bought
  1919 *His Father's Wife*
        The Petal on the Current
        Thin Ice
Death Valley (California)
  1915 *Chimmie Fadden Out West*
  1916 *Life's Whirlpool*
  1918 *A Man's Man*
Death warrants
  1915 Hearts and the Highway
  1919 *Bare Fists*
Debt
  1913 *In the Stretch*
        The Lure of New York
  1914 *Aristocracy*
        The Boer War
        Cameo Kirby
        The Hand of Destiny
        Hearts and Flowers
        Home, Sweet Home
        The Jungle
        The Last Egyptian
        Lord Chumley
        The Master Cracksman
        Mrs. Black Is Back
        The Ragged Earl
        The Thief
        The Walls of Jericho
        A Woman Who Did
        The Yellow Traffic
  1915 Blue Grass
        Her Great Match
        Her Reckoning
        His Wife
        The Hungarian Nabob

        The Man Who Beat Dan Dolan
        The Raven
        The Second in Command
        The Sins of the Mothers
        The Soul of Broadway
        The Suburban
        What Happened to Father
        The Wild Goose Chase
        The Woman Pays
  1916 *The Abandonment*
        The Conflict
        The Craving
        The Feast of Life
        Her Debt of Honor
        His Brother's Wife
        Husband and Wife
        Hypocrisy
        Idols
        Kennedy Square
        The Lash of Destiny
        Lord Loveland Discovers
        America
        Lying Lips
        My Lady's Slipper
        Paying the Price
        The Race
        Rose of the Alley
        The Sting of Victory
        The Thousand Dollar Husband
        The Traveling Salesman
        The World's Great Snare
  1917 The Barricade
        The Cold Deck
        The Debt
        Diamonds and Pearls
        The Divorce Game
        The Duplicity of Hargraves
        The Heart of a Lion
        The Last of the Carnabys
        The Last of the Ingrams
        Pride and the Man
        The Rainbow
        The Stolen Treaty
        The Vicar of Wakefield
        Yankee Pluck
        Young Mother Hubbard
  1918 *A Bit of Jade*
        Brown of Harvard
        "Flare-Up" Sal
        The Guilty Man
        Heiress for a Day
        The Hired Man
        His Daughter Pays
        The Landloper
        The Marionettes
        The Model's Confession
        More Trouble
        The Queen of Hearts
        The Reason Why
        Tony America
        Wild Youth
  1919 *An Adventure in Hearts*
        The Avalanche
        The Beauty Market
        Bonds of Honor
        Cupid Forecloses
        The Divorcee
        Good Gracious, Annabelle
        His Debt
        Mandarin's Gold
        Men, Women and Money
        The Misleading Widow
        Other Men's Wives
        Prudence on Broadway
        A Romance of Happy Valley
        What Am I Bid?
        What Every Woman Wants
        The Winning Girl
        The Wreck
  1920 *The Bromley Case*
        The Desperate Hero
        The Devil's Passkey
        Dollars and Sense
        Everything but the Truth
        The Girl in the Web
        Hearts Are Trumps
        The Man Who Dared
        The Man Who Lost Himself
        The Notorious Mrs. Sands
        The Round-Up
        She Loves and Lies
        The Thief
        The Thirteenth Commandment
        $30,000
        Women Men Love

  1921 Habit
Debutantes
    rt **Heiresses**
        Socialites
  1915 *Infatuation*
        Snobs
        Who's Who in Society
  1917 *Her Better Self*
        The Law That Failed
  1918 The Danger Mark
        Her Country First
        In Judgment Of
        Molly, Go Get 'Em
        The Primitive Woman
        The Soap Girl
        Social Quicksands
  1919 *The Hand Invisible*
  1920 The Hope
        Jenny Be Good
        The Vice of Fools
Decapitation
  1914 *Judith of Bethulia*
  1918 *Salome*
Deception
    rt **Duplicity**
  1914 *As Ye Sow*
        The Lure
        The Man from Mexico
        The Man of the Hour
        A Million Bid
  1915 The House of a Thousand
        Candles
  1919 Dust of Desire
        Fair and Warmer
Declaration of Independence
  1915 *A Continental Girl*
  1917 *The Spirit of '76*
Deeds
    rt **Mortgages**
  1914 The Human Bloodhound
  1915 *Marse Covington*
        Mrs. Plum's Pudding
  1916 The Salamander
        The Snowbird
  1917 *The Primitive Call*
  1918 *The Last Rebel*
        Love's Pay Day
  1919 *The Price of Innocence*
  1920 Girl of the Sea
        Woman's Man
Deer
  1916 *Undine*
Defense—National
  1915 *The Battles of a Nation*
  1916 Defense or Tribute?
        The Eagle's Wing
  1917 America Is Ready
        How Uncle Sam Prepares
        In Again—Out Again
  1918 The Birth of a Race
Delaware Indians
  1920 *The Last of the Mohicans*
Delhi (India)
  1914 Shannon of the Sixth
  1915 *The Moonstone*
Delicatessens
  1918 *The City of Tears*
  1919 *Molly of the Follies*
Delilah
  1914 Samson
Delirium tremens
    rt **Alcoholics**
        Alcoholism
  1915 *The Battle of Ballots*
  1917 *The Inner Shrine*
  1919 *The Witness for the Defense*
  1920 *It Might Happen to You*
Delivery boys
    rt **Errand boys**
        Office boys
  1917 *Betsy's Burglar*
        Like Wildfire
        A Night in New Arabia
  1918 *Face Value*
        Mystic Faces
  1919 In Wrong
Democracy
  1918 The Birth of a Race
  1919 The Great Romance
        Hawthorne of the U.S.A.
        His Majesty, the American

Democratic Party
  1916 *Half a Rogue*
Denmark
  1920 *The Riddle: Woman*
Dentists
  1916 Life's Whirlpool
Denver (Colorado)
  1913 *The Inside of the White Slave*
        Traffic
  1915 *Colorado*
        A Mother's Confession
  1917 *The Easiest Way*
        Mary Moreland
        The Silent Witness
  1918 *A Man's Man*
        A Woman's Fool
  1919 The Joyous Liar
Department store owners
  1919 *The Day She Paid*
Department stores
  1914 *The $5,000,000 Counterfeiting*
        Plot
  1915 *The Cup of Life*
        Heartaches
        Pearls of Temptation
        Young Romance
  1916 *The Footlights of Fate*
        The Saleslady
        The Shop Girl
        Tangled Fates
  1917 *The Price of a Good Time*
        A Sleeping Memory
        The Soul Master
        Weavers of Life
  1918 *The Eyes of Julia Deep*
        The Fallen Angel
        Her Great Chance
        Hidden Fires
        Playthings
        The Triumph of the Weak
  1919 *Alias Mike Moran*
        Common Clay
        It Pays to Advertise
  1920 Girls Don't Gamble
        Help Yourself
        Her Story
        Mrs. Temple's Telegram
Deportation
  1916 *Elusive Isabel*
  1918 *The Snail*
Derby Day
  1914 *The Christian*
Derelicts
  1915 Aloha Oe
        The Warning
  1916 *The Habit of Happiness*
        Wall Street Tragedy
        The Wasted Years
  1917 The Awakening
        Cassidy
        The Derelict
        Mary Lawson's Secret
        Who Shall Take My Life
  1918 The City of Purple Dreams
        Huck and Tom; Or, The
        Further Adventures of Tom
        Sawyer
        Keys of the Righteous
        The Other Man
        The Savage Woman
  1919 The City of Comrades
        The Price of Innocence
        Speedy Meade
        Through the Toils
        The Turn in the Road
  1920 *The Idol Dancer*
        Polly with a Past
        When Dawn Came
Deserters—Military
  1913 *The Girl of the Sunny South*
  1914 Northern Lights
  1915 *The Coward*
        My Best Girl
        Under Southern Skies
  1916 The Deserter
        Souls in Bondage
        A Woman's Power
  1917 *The Streets of Illusion*
  1918 *The Challenge Accepted*
        A Daughter of France
Desertion (*Marital*)
  1913 *Hoodman Blind*
        Tess of the D'Urbervilles

1914 *Absinthe*
At the Cross Roads
The Banker's Daughter
Damaged Goods
Dope
Forgiven; Or, The Jack of
Diamonds
Frou Frou
The Idler
Lena Rivers (Cosmos Feature
Film Corp.)
Lena Rivers (Whitman
Features Co.)
Manon Lescaut
Mrs. Wiggs of the Cabbage
Patch
Nell of the Circus
The Red Flame of Passion
Should a Woman Divorce?
The Strange Story of Sylvia
Gray
The Woman in Black
1915 *After Dark*
Bred in the Bone
The Disciple
Divorced
The Evangelist
The Galley Slave
Gambling Inside and Out
The Green Cloak
Her Reckoning
His Wife
The House of Tears
Madame Butterfly
The Master of the House
Milestones of Life
The Money Master
The Moth and the Flame
*The Mummy and the
Humming Bird*
Pretty Mrs. Smith
The Runaway Wife
The Scarlet Sin
The Shooting of Dan McGrew
Up from the Depths
The Valley of Lost Hope
When We Were Twenty-One
1916 Ben Blair
The Bondman
Caprice of the Mountains
The Chattel
A Circus Romance
The City
Common Sense Brackett
The Country That God Forgot
The Courtesan
The Devil's Prayer-Book
Diane of the Follies
The Dragon
East Lynne
The Faded Flower
Fathers of Men
The Garden of Allah
The Girl with the Green Eyes
God's Half Acre
Her Husband's Wife
The Heritage of Hate
The Hunted Woman
Idols
Inherited Passions
The Isle of Love
The Land Just Over Yonder
Little Miss Happiness
The Man Who Stood Still
The Men She Married
The Moment Before
The Moral Fabric
A Parisian Romance
The Perils of Divorce
The Price of Power
The Ransom
The Reapers
The Reward of Patience
Sorrows of Happiness
The Spider
The Straight Way
The Target
The Unwelcome Mother
The Upstart
Vultures of Society
The Wasted Years
The Wild Girl of the Sierras
1917 The Beautiful Lie
Behind the Mask
The Bronze Bride

The Checkmate
The Devil's Assistant
The Door Between
The Easiest Way
The End of the Tour
The Eternal Mother
Fighting Mad
The Flaming Omen
Glory
The Heart of Ezra Greer
Heart Strings
Her Hour
Idolators
The Iron Ring
Jim Bludso
The Last Sentence
The Law of Compensation
The Love Doctor
Magda
A Magdalene of the Hills
The Master Passion
Mayblossom
A Mother's Ordeal
One Touch of Sin
Open Places
Outcast
Pay Me
The Price of Pride
The Price She Paid
The Pulse of Life
Rosie O'Grady
Satan's Private Door
Should She Obey?
The Soul Master
Sowers and Reapers
Stagestruck
The Sunset Trail
Threads of Fate
The Waiting Soul
Wife Number Two
The Woman Beneath
1918 *An Alien Enemy*
Battling Jane
The Beloved Impostor
The Better Half
Buchanan's Wife
*Cavanaugh of the Forest
Rangers*
The Claim
Code of the Yukon
Conquered Hearts
The Danger Zone
A Daughter of the West
De Luxe Annie
The Desired Woman
The Forbidden Path
The Girl of My Dreams
The Great Love
The Guilty Man
Her Decision
Her One Mistake
Her Price
The Home Trail
Joan of the Woods
Less Than Kin
Life or Honor?
Loaded Dice
The Model's Confession
A Mother's Sin
Naked Hands
The Prodigal Wife
Prunella
A Rich Man's Darling
Riders of the Purple Sage
Rosemary Climbs the Heights
The Seal of Silence
Secret Strings
Shackled
Station Content
Stolen Honor
That Devil, Bateese
Toys of Fate
True Blue
*What Becomes of the
Children?*
Wild Primrose
Without Honor
Woman
A Woman's Fool
1918-19
Once to Every Man
1919 A Bachelor's Wife
The Capitol
The Gray Horizon
The Hushed Hour

Sahara
The Way of the Strong
The Weaker Vessel
What Love Forgives
1920 Common Sense
Deep Waters
The Desert Scorpion
The Devil's Claim
The Discarded Woman
Fighting Cressy
Godless Men
Greater Than Love
Guilty of Love
Half an Hour
Harriet and the Piper
A Lady in Love
Locked Lips
Out of the Dust
The Sea Rider
Smoldering Embers
The Spirit of Good
The Stealers
The Testing Block
To Please One Woman
The Tree of Knowledge
The Truth About Husbands
Way Down East
The Woman and the Puppet

Deserts
1914 *Fire and Sword*
Imar the Servitor
Thais
Uriel Acosta
When Rome Ruled
1915 The Buzzard's Shadow
The Carpet from Bagdad
Environment
The Lone Star Rush
The Long Chance
The Toast of Death
The Unknown
1916 *The Aryan*
Life's Whirlpool
A Yoke of Gold
1917 Aladdin and the Wonderful
Lamp
Barbary Sheep
The Bond of Fear
The Firefly of Tough Luck
A Mormon Maid
Sands of Sacrifice
The Siren
Thais
Their Compact
The Undying Flame
Whither Thou Goest
The Yellow Bullet
1918 *Bound in Morocco*
Heart of the Sunset
Hell Bent
The Home Trail
The Law's Outlaw
The Red, Red Heart
Revenge
Salome
Selfish Yates
The Tiger Man
1919 Chasing Rainbows
Desert Gold
The Lady of Red Butte
Leave It to Susan
The Long Arm of Mannister
Lost Money
The Man Who Turned White
Marked Men
Partners Three
The Unveiling Hand
Wagon Tracks
1920 The Challenge of the Law
The Coast of Opportunity
The Leopard Woman
The Round-Up
Woman's Man

Despots
rt **Dictators**
1914 *Captain Alvarez*
Damon and Pythias
1915 The Rights of Man: A Story of
War's Red Blotch
1918 The Kaiser, the Beast of Berlin
1919 Whitewashed Walls

Detective agencies
1916 *The No-Good Guy*
1919 The Web of Chance

1920 Leave It to Me
Detectives
rt **Private detectives**
Railroad detectives
1912 The Adventures of Lieutenant
Petrosino
1913 Chelsea 7750
The Fight for Millions
*The Man from the Golden
West*
The Rogues of Paris
1914 *The Avenging Conscience;
Thou Shalt Not Kill*
The Conspiracy
The Criminal Path
Detective Craig's Coup
The Education of Mr. Pipp
The Floor Above
The Line-Up at Police
Headquarters
The Little Jewess
The Lure
The Master Cracksman
The Murders in the Rue
Morgue
The Mysterious Mr. Wu Chung
Foo
One Wonderful Night
Over Niagara Falls
The Pawn of Fortune
'round the World in 80 Days
Trapped in the Great
Metropolis
The Woman of Mystery
1915 An Affair of Three Nations
Alias Jimmy Valentine
The Alster Case
The Billionaire Lord
Blackbirds
The Bulldogs of the Trail
The Butterfly
The Chorus Lady
The Circular Staircase
The Clue
The Dictator
The Earl of Pawtucket
The Family Stain
The Fighting Hope
The Flying Twins
The Game of Three
A Gilded Fool
The Gray Mask
The Great Ruby
The House of Fear
The Ivory Snuff Box
Jim the Penman
The Last of the Mafia
Lord John in New York
The Majesty of the Law
The Menace of the Mute
Monsieur Lecoq
On Her Wedding Night
The Politicians
The Pretenders
The Running Fight
Secretary of Frivolous Affairs
Stop Thief!
The Woman
The Woman Next Door
1916 *The Alibi*
Between Men
*The Black Sheep of the
Family*
*The Colored American
Winning His Suit*
The Flying Torpedo
Her Maternal Right
Kinkaid, Gambler
The Missing Links
My Lady Incog.
The Net
The No-Good Guy
The People vs. John Doe
The Purple Lady
Shadows and Sunshine
Sherlock Holmes
The Smugglers
Through the Wall
The Twinkler
Vanity
The Victim
The Vital Question
Vultures of Society
The Wager
The Wharf Rat

A Man's Duty
The Moonshine Trail
My Little Sister
Oh, Boy!
One Week of Life
Paid in Advance
The Painted World
The Petal on the Current
Playthings of Passion
Redhead
The Scarlet Shadow
Secret Marriage
The Spite Bride
A Taste of Life
A Temperamental Wife
The Third Degree
Three Black Eyes
The Trap
The Unbroken Promise
The Unwritten Code
What Every Woman Learns
What Love Forgives
Who Will Marry Me?
The Wolf
The Wreck
1920 *Bachelor Apartments*
Blind Love
The Common Sin
The Discarded Woman
The Great Accident
Help Yourself
His Own Law
It Might Happen to You
Lifting Shadows
Love, Honor and Obey
The Man Who Lost Himself
The Midnight Bride
The Right of Way
The Tattlers
Twin Beds
The Valley of Doubt
Wings of Pride
1921 *Miss 139*

Dual personality
1914 Lola
The Woman of Mystery
1915 The Case of Becky
The Curious Conduct of Judge
  Legarde
Double Trouble
1916 The Struggle
1917 The Brand of Satan
A Sleeping Memory
1918 De Luxe Annie
The Two-Soul Woman
1919 The Darkest Hour
The Poison Pen
1920 Body and Soul
Dr. Jekyll and Mr. Hyde
  (Famous Players-Lasky
  Corp.)
Dr. Jekyll and Mr. Hyde
  (Pioneer Film Corp.)
The Valley of Night
When Quackel Did Hide

Marie Jeanne Bécu Du Barry
1915 Du Barry

Dublin
1916 *A Corner in Colleens*
Sweet Kitty Bellairs
1920 *Hidden Charms*

Ducks
1915 *American Game Trails*
1919 *Day Dreams*

Dudes
1917 Anything Once
Ashes of Hope
The Man from Painted Post
The Tenderfoot
Their Compact
1920 *The White Rider*

Duels
1914 The Banker's Daughter
Cameo Kirby
The Dancer and the King
The Envoy Extraordinary
Frou Frou
Mr. Barnes of New York
One of Our Girls
Il Trovatore
When Fate Leads Trump
The Will O' the Wisp
1915 *The Breath of Araby*
Carmen (Fox Film Corp.)

The Celebrated Scandal
The Chocolate Soldier
The Clemenceau Case
A Continental Girl
Don Caesar de Bazan
The Fixer
The Garden of Lies
The Great Divide
The Long Chance
The Man of Shame
The Ploughshare
A Price for Folly
The Secret Orchard
The Spanish Jade
Strathmore
A Trade Secret
The Unfaithful Wife
A Woman's Resurrection
1916 *According to the Code*
Fathers of Men
Her Father's Son
Kennedy Square
The Man from Nowhere
Sweet Kitty Bellairs
The Valiants of Virginia
1917 The Adopted Son
American Methods
The Awakening
Babbling Tongues
Betsy Ross
Black Orchids
The Black Wolf
The Greater Law
Her Greatest Love
A Hungry Heart
The Inner Shrine
*The Inspirations of Harry
  Larrabee*
The Little Chevalier
The Painted Lie
Princess Virtue
Reaching for the Moon
The Tenderfoot
Who Goes There!
1918 The Beautiful Mrs. Reynolds
Her Final Reckoning
The Lost Chord
Six Shooter Andy
Viviette
1919 *As the Sun Went Down*
The Feud
His Divorced Wife
The Lone Star Ranger
More Deadly Than the Male
One of the Finest
Paid in Advance
The Phantom Honeymoon
The Scar
Should a Husband Forgive?
The Silver Girl
The Sneak
The Spitfire of Seville
The Sundown Trail
The Wilderness Trail
The Wolf
1920 *The Challenge of the Law*
Children of Destiny
The Corsican Brothers
The Dangerous Paradise
The Kentucky Colonel
The Phantom Melody
The Return of Tarzan
A Splendid Hazard
Twins of Suffering Creek
White Youth
The World and His Wife

Duma
1918 *The German Curse in Russia*

Dummies
1915 *The Magic Toy Maker*
1917 *The Wax Model*
1919 *The Man Beneath*
1920 *Blind Wives*

Dungeons
1915 *The Rug Maker's Daughter*
1916 *The Black Crook*
1920 *A Fool and His Money*
Kismet

Duplicity
rt **Deception**
1914 Hearts and Flowers
Hook and Hand
The Human Bloodhound
Joseph in the Land of Egypt
Marta of the Lowlands

Pieces of Silver; A Story of
  Hearts and Souls
The Spitfire
The Walls of Jericho
1915 *All for a Girl*
The Chocolate Soldier
Esmeralda
The Flying Twins
The Galley Slave
The Girl from His Town
The Girl I Left Behind Me
A Girl of Yesterday
Her Atonement
Her Great Match
Her Own Way
Jim the Penman
Lady Audley's Secret
The Lone Star Rush
The Lonesome Heart
The Lost House
Maciste
May Blossom
The Model
My Best Girl
Pennington's Choice
Prohibition
The Runaway Wife
The Second in Command
Shadows from the Past
The Shooting of Dan McGrew
Snobs
The Song of Hate
The Soul of Broadway
The Spendthrift
The Way Back
The White Sister
The White Terror
The Wolf of Debt
The Woman Pays
1916 *As in a Looking Glass*
Barriers of Society
Between Men
Bobbie of the Ballet
The Bruiser
*Captain Jinks of the Horse
  Marines*
The Chain Invisible
The Chalice of Sorrow
The Craving
The Dark Silence
The Daughter of the Don
The Devil's Bondwoman
Each Pearl a Tear
The Enemy
Faith
The Female of the Species
A Fool's Paradise
The Gates of Eden
Gold and the Woman
Gretchen, the Greenhorn
Hazel Kirke
The Heart of Nora Flynn
His Wife's Good Name
The Honorable Friend
Honor's Altar
Love and Hate
Passers By
The Path of Happiness
The Pawn of Fate
The Perils of Divorce
Pillars of Society
The Smugglers
The Test
The White Rosette
A Wife's Sacrifice
Witchcraft
1917 *Alma, Where Do You Live?*
Baby Mine
Betrayed
Billy and the Big Stick
Builders of Castles
The Call of Her People
A Child of the Wild
The Devil's Assistant
Hashimura Togo
Her New York
Her Sister
The Hunting of the Hawk
In Slumberland
In the Balance
The Iron Ring
Madame Sherry
Persuasive Peggy
The Phantom Shotgun
The Primitive Call

The Princess of Patches
The Snarl
When False Tongues Speak
1918 The Bride's Awakening
Brown of Harvard
Buchanan's Wife
The Burden of Proof
The Business of Life
The Deciding Kiss
For Sale
A Gentleman's Agreement
A Heart's Revenge
Her Body in Bond
Hitting the High Spots
The House of Gold
The House of Mirth
Humdrum Brown
Missing
A Nine O'Clock Town
A Romance of the Air
Rough and Ready
Virtuous Wives
The Way Out
Winning Grandma
The Winning of Beatrice
Zongar
1919 *As a Man Thinks*
The Faith of the Strong
The Feud
Fool's Gold
For a Woman's Honor
Girls
The Glorious Lady
Hearts of Men
I'll Get Him Yet
The Jungle Trail
Lure of Ambition
The Market of Souls
The Open Door
Paid in Advance
Partners Three
Putting It Over
Roped
The Sundown Trail
The Trap
Who Will Marry Me?
1919-20
When a Man Loves
1920 Her Beloved Villain
Homer Comes Home
Mrs. Temple's Telegram
The Paliser Case
Passion's Playground
The Phantom Melody
Seeds of Vengeance
She Couldn't Help It
The Silver Horde
The Six Best Cellars
The Soul of Youth
The Terror
Why Leave Your Husband?

Dutch
rt **Pennsylvania Dutch**
1914 *Uriel Acosta*
When Broadway Was a Trail
1916 *Gretchen, the Greenhorn*
Hulda from Holland
The Pearl of Paradise
1917 *Sylvia of the Secret Service*
1918 *By the World Forgot*
1920 The Secret Gift
*Shipwrecked Among
  Cannibals*

Dwarfs
1914 *The Patchwork Girl of Oz*
1915 *Rumpelstiltskin*
Simon, the Jester
1916 Snow White
1917 *The Princess' Necklace*
1918 *The Star Prince*

Dynamite
1915 *The Bigger Man*
The Danger Signal
The Immigrant
The Incorrigible Dukane
1916 *Reclamation*
1917 *The Maid of Belgium*
War and the Woman
1918 *Brave and Bold*
1919 *Children of Banishment*
The Little Boss
Man's Desire
Wolves of the Night

Epidemics
   rt **Disease**
     Specific types of disease
1914 *The Red Flame of Passion*
1915 Beulah
1916 *The Making of Maddalena*
     The Primal Lure
     Saints and Sinners
     The Surprises of an Empty Hotel
1917 *The Courage of Silence*
     The Evil Eye
1918 *Danger Within*
     The Landloper
     Love's Law
     The Shuttle
1919 The Boomerang
     In the Land of the Setting Sun; Or, Martyrs of Yesterday
     The Lady of Red Butte

Errand boys
   rt **Delivery boys**
     Office boys
1917 The Wild Girl

Escapes
   rt **Rescues**
1913 *The Battle of Shiloh*
     Chelsea 7750
     The Fight for Millions
     The Lure of New York
     Robin Hood
     The Sea Wolf
1914 Beneath the Czar
     The Boundary Rider
     A Boy and the Law
     The Burglar and the Lady
     Captain Alvarez
     Charlotte Corday
     The Chechako
     The Conspiracy
     The Corsair
     The Crucible
     Hook and Hand
     The House of Bondage
     In the Days of the Thundering Herd
     Jess
     Officer 666
     The Pride of Jennico
     Salomy Jane
     The Seats of the Mighty
     The Spirit of the Poppy
     The Spy
     Thou Shalt Not
     Threads of Destiny
     Through Dante's Flames
     Il Trovatore
     Uncle Tom's Cabin
     Winning His First Case
1915 *A Black Sheep*
     Body and Soul
     The Brink
     The Campbells Are Coming
     Carmen (Fox Film Corp.)
     The Chocolate Soldier
     Courtmartialed
     Don Caesar de Bazan
     Fighting Bob
     The Fixer
     The Flash of an Emerald
     The Folly of a Life of Crime
     The Forbidden Adventure
     From the Valley of the Missing
     The Heart of Maryland
     Hearts in Exile
     In the Palace of the King
     The Lonesome Heart
     The Lost House
     Maciste
     The Patriot and the Spy
     The Puppet Crown
     What Happened to Jones
     Winning the Futurity
     A Yankee from the West
1915-16
     The Little Church Around the Corner
1916 *The Blue Envelope Mystery*
     The Catspaw
     The Crucial Test
     The Daring of Diana
     Dorian's Divorce
     The Dream Girl
     An Enemy to the King

     For the Defense
     The Gilded Cage
     Going Straight
     The Golden Chance
     Kinkaid, Gambler
     The Oval Diamond
     The Witching Hour
     The World Against Him
     The World's Great Snare
1917 *Arms and the Girl*
     The Bond of Fear
     The Danger Trail
     The Girl by the Roadside
     Heart and Soul
     Her Official Fathers
     The High Sign
     The Honor System
     Kidnapped
     The Land of Long Shadows
     The Little American
     The Little Boy Scout
     The Lone Wolf
     The Long Trail
     Love's Law
     Nan of Music Mountain
     The Princess of Park Row
     Raffles, the Amateur Cracksman
     The Range Boss
     The Scarlet Pimpernel
     The Ship of Doom
     The Sixteenth Wife
     Sunshine and Gold
     Tangled Lives
     This Is the Life
     Until They Get Me
     The Voice of Conscience
     War and the Woman
     The World Apart
     Young Mother Hubbard
1918 *Alias Mary Brown*
     Among the Cannibal Isles of the South Pacific
     Bound in Morocco
     Brave and Bold
     By Hook or Crook
     The City of Purple Dreams
     The Curse of Iku
     Danger Within
     De Luxe Annie
     The Empty Cab
     The Firefly of France
     "Flare-Up" Sal
     From Two to Six
     The Golden Wall
     Heart of the Sunset
     Hell Bent
     Her Husband's Honor
     The Home Trail
     The Hopper
     How Could You, Caroline?
     Huck and Tom; Or, The Further Adventures of Tom Sawyer
     The Lady of the Dugout
     Lawless Love
     Leap to Fame
     Lest We Forget
     Madam Who
     Madame Spy
     The Midnight Trail
     Miss Innocence
     M'liss
     The Only Road
     Over the Top
     The Price of Applause
     Riders of the Purple Sage
     The Road Through the Dark
     A Romance of the Air
     Rose O' Paradise
     The Savage Woman
     The Sea Panther
     Selfish Yates
     The She-Devil
     The Shoes That Danced
     The Triumph of Venus
     Uncle Tom's Cabin
     Up Romance Road
     Wanted—A Brother
     The Wasp
     Which Woman?
     The Wildcat of Paris
     The Woman the Germans Shot

1919 *An Amateur Widow*
     Auction of Souls
     Bare Fists
     Bonds of Honor
     Breezy Jim
     Daring Hearts
     Daughter of Mine
     The End of the Game
     The Exquisite Thief
     A Favor to a Friend
     The Grim Game
     A Heart in Pawn
     Hell Roarin' Reform
     The Island of Intrigue
     The Jungle Trail
     The Little White Savage
     The Moral Deadline
     My Little Sister
     The New Moon
     Peppy Polly
     The Pest
     The Probation Wife
     Rustling a Bride
     Sandy Burke of the U-Bar-U
     A Scream in the Night
     Secret Service
     The Sheriff's Son
     Something to Do
     A Sporting Chance (American Film Co.)
     Square Deal Sanderson
     The Teeth of the Tiger
     Turning the Tables
     The Unpardonable Sin
     When Men Desire
     A White Man's Chance
     The Wilderness Trail
     A Woman of Pleasure
     The World and Its Woman
1920 *Below the Deadline*
     The Blue Moon
     The Challenge of the Law
     The Fourteenth Man
     Half a Chance
     Held by the Enemy
     Held in Trust
     Miss Nobody
     Nomads of the North
     The Sea Wolf
     The Toll Gate
19-- *Barnaby Lee*

Eskimos
1912 The Alaska-Siberian Expedition
     Atop of the World in Motion
1914 An Odyssey of the North
1917 Alaska Wonders in Motion
1919 Alaska

Espionage
   rt **Foreign agents**
     Secret agents
     Spies
1914 The Envoy Extraordinary
     For the Honor of Old Glory; Or, The Stars and Stripes in Mexico
     In the Name of the Prince of Peace
     The Last Volunteer
     The Man on the Box
     The Taint
     The Tigress
     With Serb and Austrian
1915 An Affair of Three Nations
     The Campbells Are Coming
     The Clue
     The Gray Mask
     The Life of Sam Davis: A Confederate Hero of the Sixties
     Sam Davis, the Hero of Tennessee
     The Vampire
1916 Anton the Terrible
     Behind the Lines
     The Girl Philippa
     The Heart of a Hero
     Paying the Price
     Shell Forty-Three
     Somewhere in France
1917 *Pots-and-Pans Peggy*
     Sacrifice
     The Secret Game
     Souls in Pawn
     The Spy
     Womanhood, the Glory of the Nation

1918 An Alien Enemy
     Berlin Via America
     The Flames of Chance
     The Greatest Thing in Life
     Hearts of the World
     The Hillcrest Mystery
     Joan of Plattsburg
     Kultur
     Lafayette, We Come!
     Madame Spy
     The Man Who Wouldn't Tell
     Secret Code
     Wife or Country
1919 *Adele*
     The Best Man
     The Highest Trump
     Love in a Hurry
     Luck and Pluck
     Secret Service
1920 The Cup of Fury
     Dangerous Days
     Wanted at Headquarters
     Who's Your Servant?

Ether
1915 *Mortmain*
1920 A Sister to Salome

Ethics
1917 Her Excellency, the Governor
1918 The Mysterious Client

Etiquette
1914 *Tillie's Punctured Romance*
1915 *The Cave Man*
     The Danger Signal
     Her Shattered Idol
     Heritage
     The Iron Strain
     The Morals of Marcus
     Samson
1917 *A Bit O' Heaven*
     The Fair Barbarian
     Miss Deception
1918 *Fuss and Feathers*
     The Hope Chest
     Impossible Susan
     Oh, Johnny!
     Painted Lips
     Ruggles of Red Gap
     Twenty-One
1919 *Almost Married*
     The Crook of Dreams
     A Gun Fightin' Gentleman
     Her Purchase Price
     John Petticoats
     The Merry-Go-Round
     The Road Called Straight
     Strictly Confidential
     Where the West Begins
1920 Huckleberry Finn
     The Misfit Wife

Eugenics
1914 The Escape
1916 *Where Are My Children?*
1917 The Black Stork
     Married in Name Only
1920 Their Mutual Child
     The Very Idea

Europe
1914 The Man from Home
1915 *The Lily of Poverty Flat*
1916 *Miss Petticoats*
     The Prima Donna's Husband
1917 *The Tides of Barnegat*
1918 *Crown Jewels*
     The Divine Sacrifice
     The Fallen Angel
     The Life Mask
     A Mother's Secret
     The Way Out
1919 Injustice
     Josselyn's Wife
     Two Women

Europe—History—1920-1930
1920 Starvation

Euthanasia
   rt **Murder**
1916 *Doctor Neighbor*
1917 Has Man the Right to Kill?

Evacuation
1917 *Down to Earth*
1919 Auction of Souls
     Broken Barriers

Expeditions
- 1920 Shipwrecked Among Cannibals

Experiments
- 1916 Bluff
  - The Flight of the Duchess
  - The Return of Eve
- 1918 Amarilly of Clothes-Line Alley
  - The Knife
  - The Light Within
- 1919 The Mystery of the Yellow Room
- 1920 The Poor Simp

Explorers
- 1912 The Alaska-Siberian Expedition
  - Paul J. Rainey's African Hunt
- 1914 Florida Historic Scenes and Florida in Mid-Winter
  - John Barleycorn
  - Rescue of the Stefansson Arctic Expedition
- 1915 The Explorer
  - The Pageant of San Francisco
  - The Pearl of the Antilles
- 1916 The Jungle Child
  - The Misleading Lady
  - The Road to Love
- 1918 The Savage Woman
- 1919 The Call of the Soul
  - Dust of Desire
  - The Splendid Sin
  - A Wild Goose Chase
  - The Woman Thou Gavest Me

Explosions
- 1913 Buried Alive in a Coal Mine
  - Chelsea 7750
  - From Dusk to Dawn
- 1914 Ready Money
  - Shannon of the Sixth
  - Through Fire to Fortune
  - The Toll of Mammon
  - A Woman Who Did
- 1915 Colorado
  - The Fatal Card
  - The House of a Thousand Scandals
  - Keep Moving
  - A Trade Secret
  - The Valley of Lost Hope
  - The White Sister
  - The Wolf Man
- 1916 Bluff
  - The Clarion
  - The Dawn of Freedom
  - The Dragon
  - The Hero of Submarine D-2
  - The Lords of High Decision
  - The Surprises of an Empty Hotel
- 1917 Daughter of Destiny
  - Jim Bludso
  - The Little Patriot
  - Pardners
  - The Rose of Blood
  - The Snarl
  - Souls Adrift
  - Under Handicap
  - War and the Woman
  - The Zeppelin's Last Raid
- 1918 The Craving
  - Eight Bells
  - The Glorious Adventure
  - Huns Within Our Gates
  - The Kaiser's Finish
  - Marriages Are Made
  - Mrs. Slacker
  - My Unmarried Wife
  - The Prussian Cur
  - The Wasp
  - Whims of Society
  - The Wife He Bought
- 1919 The City of Comrades
  - Fires of Faith
- 1920 Dangerous Days
  - Dangerous Hours
  - Dead Men Tell No Tales
  - The Hidden Code
  - In the Heart of a Fool
  - The Key to Power
  - Lifting Shadows
  - Marooned Hearts
  - My Lady's Garter
  - The Price of Redemption
  - Water, Water Everywhere

Explosives
- rt **Ammunition**
  - **Bombs**
  - **Mines (war explosives)**
- 1913 An Hour Before Dawn
- 1914 The Better Man
  - Without Hope
- 1915 The Clue
  - The Gray Mask
  - My Best Girl
- 1916 My Country First
  - Paying the Price
- 1917 The Greatest Power
  - His Sweetheart
  - The Hungry Heart
  - One Touch of Sin
- 1918 The Claws of the Hun
  - The Craving
  - Swat the Spy
  - Till I Come Back to You
  - Treason
- 1919 America Was Right
  - Fool's Gold
  - Miss Crusoe
  - Whom the Gods Would Destroy
- 1920 The Hidden Code
  - The Sea Rider

Expulsion from school
- 1914 Over Niagara Falls
  - The Wishing Ring; An Idyll of Old England
- 1915 Captain Macklin
  - The College Orphan
- 1916 The Measure of a Man
- 1917 The Antics of Ann
  - The Bad Boy
  - Blood Will Tell
  - God's Man
  - Madcap Madge
  - Some Boy!
  - The Varmint
- 1918 Ann's Finish
  - Jack Spurlock, Prodigal
  - Joan of the Woods
  - On the Quiet
  - What Becomes of the Children?
- 1919 The Little Rowdy
- 1920 Old Dad

Extortion
- rt **Blackmail**
- 1914 Captain Alvarez
- 1915 The Despoiler
  - The End of the Road
  - Forbidden Fruit
  - The Galley Slave
  - Her Triumph
  - Time Lock Number 776
  - Young Romance
- 1916 The Bait
  - Between Men
  - The Conqueror
  - The Dupe
  - Honor Thy Name
  - The Kiss of Hate
  - The Lash of Destiny
  - Love and Hate
  - A Woman's Fight
- 1917 The Burglar
  - Cy Whittaker's Ward
  - The Final Payment
  - The Little Chevalier
  - The Maelstrom
  - The Man from Montana
  - The Millionaire's Double
- 1918 The Bird of Prey
  - The Bride of Fear
  - The Mysterious Client
  - Smashing Through
  - A Son of Strife
  - The Splendid Sinner
  - String Beans
  - Wild Primrose
  - The Wine Girl
- 1919 Shadows of the Past
- 1920 Dangerous Hours
  - The Fighting Chance
  - The Purple Cipher
  - The Tiger's Cub
  - The Way Women Love
  - The White Rider
  - The Woman Above Reproach

Extrasensory perception
- 1918 In Judgment Of
- 1919 Faith
- 1920 The Dark Mirror

Extravagance (Financial)
- 1914 Brewster's Millions
  - A Million Bid
  - Paid in Full
- 1915 The Absentee
  - The Cheat
  - The Climbers
  - Destruction
  - Du Barry
  - Fine Feathers
  - A Gilded Fool
  - Sweet Alyssum
- 1916 Bought and Paid For
  - The Evil Women Do
  - The Five Faults of Flo
  - A Fool's Paradise
- 1917 The Heir of the Ages
  - The Price of a Good Time
- 1918 The Heart of Romance
  - Heiress for a Day
  - Old Love for New
- 1919 Extravagance
  - False Gods
  - The Love That Dares
  - A Man and His Money
  - The Misleading Widow
  - A Taste of Life
  - Tin Pan Alley
- 1920 Blind Wives
- 1921 Habit

Eye surgery
- 1915 Satan Sanderson
- 1916 The Dark Silence
  - The Feast of Life
  - Her Great Price
- 1917 Princess of the Dark
- 1918 Marriage
  - My Unmarried Wife
- 1919 Dawn
  - Marriage for Convenience
- 1920 Eyes of the Heart
  - Molly and I

Eyes
- 1913 The Man from the Golden West
- 1914 The Win(k)some Widow

F

Factories
- rt **Mills**
- 1914 What Is to Be Done?
- 1915 Friends and Foes
  - Hearts of Men
  - Heritage
  - The Mystery of Room 13
- 1916 Dust
  - Her Bitter Cup
  - Mister 44
  - Rolling Stones
  - Saint, Devil and Woman
- 1917 Fires of Rebellion
  - House of Cards
  - The Marriage Speculation
  - Reaching for the Moon
  - A Son of the Hills
- 1918 Good-Bye, Bill
  - The Hillcrest Mystery
  - Sunshine Nan
  - The Thing We Love
  - Up Romance Road
  - Whims of Society
- 1919 The Poor Boob
  - The Third Kiss
- 1920 The Face at Your Window
  - Homer Comes Home
  - The Strongest

Factory foremen
- 1915 The Evangelist
  - The Mystery of Room 13
- 1916 The Undertow
- 1917 Fires of Rebellion
- 1918 Cheating the Public
- 1919 The Right to Happiness
- 1920 The Path She Chose

Factory management
- 1915 The White Terror
- 1916 The City of Failing Light
  - The Price of Power

Factory owners
- 1915 The Absentee
- 1916 Dust
  - Her Bitter Cup
  - A Soul Enslaved
- 1917 Moral Courage
- 1918 Hitting the Trail
- 1920 The Face at Your Window

Factory workers
- 1915 The Mystery of Room 13
  - The Spender
- 1916 The City of Failing Light
  - Dust
  - Her Bitter Cup
  - Is Any Girl Safe?
  - The Price of Power
  - The Redemption of Dave Darcey
  - The Sunbeam
  - The Three Godfathers
  - The Undertow
  - A Woman's Fight
- 1917 Moral Courage
  - Sowers and Reapers
- 1918 All Woman
  - Doing Their Bit
  - Hitting the Trail
  - A Little Sister of Everybody
  - The Thing We Love
  - The Winning of Beatrice
- 1919 Redhead
  - Tin Pan Alley
  - The Virtuous Model
  - The Winning Girl
- 1920 The Heart of Twenty
  - The Path She Chose
  - Uncharted Channels
  - The Woman God Sent

Fairies
- 1914 Cinderella
  - Fantasma
  - A Good Little Devil
  - The Magic Cloak of Oz
- 1915 Keep Moving
  - Rumpelstiltskin
- 1916 Little Lady Eileen
- 1917 The Babes in the Woods
  - Castles for Two
  - Cinderella and the Magic Slipper
  - Jack and the Beanstalk
  - Modern Mother Goose
  - The Seven Swans
- 1918 The Blue Bird
  - The Star Prince
  - Wanted, a Mother

Fairs
- rt **Bazaars**
  - **Carnivals**
  - **Circuses**
- 1916 The Daughter of MacGregor
- 1918 Dolly Does Her Bit
  - Indian Life
  - T'Other Dear Charmer
- 1919 Greased Lightning
  - Kathleen Mavourneen
- 1920 The County Fair
  - The Desperate Hero

Faith
- 1914 The Lust of the Red Man
- 1915 The Dawn of a Tomorrow
  - Dr. Rameau
  - Jewel
- 1917 God's Crucible
  - God's Man
  - The Greater Woman
  - The Pride of the Clan
- 1918 The Sign Invisible
  - A Soul Without Windows
- 1919 The Girl with No Regrets
  - The Turn in the Road
- 1920 The Girl of My Heart
  - The Idol Dancer
  - Into the Light
  - The Spirit of Good

Faith cures
- rt **Cures**
  - **Miraculous cures**
- 1915 Jewel
- 1916 The Reapers
  - The World and the Woman

The Undertow
- 1919 The Greater Victory
  - The Spender

1917 *Rasputin, the Black Monk*
1920 The Cheater
Faith healers
1916 *The Reapers*
       The World and the Woman
1919 The Miracle Man
1920 The Cheater
       Faith
Falls
   rt **Falls from heights**
1915 *The Final Judgment*
       Lady Audley's Secret
1916 *A Dream or Two Ago*
       The Victim
       The World and the Woman
1917 *The Lady of the Photograph*
       The Woman and the Beast
1918 *Shackled*
       The Turn of a Card
1919 The Big Little Person
       The Mayor of Filbert
1921 Habit
Falls from heights
   rt **Falls**
       Jumps from heights
1913 Traffic in Souls
1914 The Great Leap; Until Death
          Do Us Part
       The Greyhound
       The Land of the Lost
       The Million Dollar Robbery
       The Monster and the Girl
       Over Niagara Falls
       The Spirit of the Poppy
       A Suspicious Wife
1915 *An American Gentleman*
       The Birth of a Nation
       The Bludgeon
       The Brink
       The Butterfly
       Carmen (Fox Film Corp.)
       The Circular Staircase
       A Continental Girl
       Cora
       The Dancing Girl
       The Eagle's Nest
       The Forbidden Adventure
       The Fox Woman
       The Great Divide
       The Great Ruby
       The Heart of Jennifer
       The Heart of the Blue Ridge
       The Price of Her Silence
       Salvation Nell
       Sunshine Molly
1916 *The Dawn of Love*
       The End of the Rainbow
       The Girl of the Lost Lake
       He Fell in Love with His Wife
       Honor Thy Name
       Judith of the Cumberlands
       The Snowbird
       Unto Those Who Sin
       The Velvet Paw
       The Whirlpool of Destiny
1917 *The Adopted Son*
       Ashes of Hope
       Dead Shot Baker
       The Deemster
       The Devil's Bait
       The Eyes of the World
       The Ghost of Old Morro
       Her Bargain
       It Happened to Adele
       The Little Terror
       The Regenerates
       The Reward of the Faithless
       Sirens of the Sea
       A Sleeping Memory
       Sunlight's Last Raid
       The Warfare of the Flesh
       The Web of Life
1918 *The House of Gold*
       In Judgment Of
       The Marriage Ring
       Milady O' the Beanstalk
       Other Men's Daughters
       Riddle Gawne
       The Savage Woman
       The Scarlet Road
       The Silent Woman
       Stolen Orders
       La Tosca
       The Transgressor
       Wanted, a Mother

Without Honor
Zongar
1919 *The Arizona Cat Claw*
       The Avalanche
       Blind Husbands
       Desert Gold
       Destiny
       Dust of Desire
       The End of the Game
       A Fight for Love
       Fighting Destiny
       Forest Rivals
       Getting Mary Married
       The Gray Horizon
       The Gray Towers Mystery
       His Divorced Wife
       His Wife's Friend
       Human Passions
       In Old Kentucky
       The Invisible Bond
       The Last of His People
       The Man Hunter
       The Man Who Won
       Marriage for Convenience
       The Quickening Flame
       The Rider of the Law
       Should a Woman Tell?
       Snares of Paris
       Twilight
       The Two Brides
       Under the Top
       The Westerners
       The Winchester Woman
       A Woman of Pleasure
       The Wreck
1920 *The Broadway Bubble*
       Clothes
       Dad's Girl
       The Fatal Hour
       Felix O'Day
       The Golden Trail
       The Mollycoddle
       The Night Riders
       Seeds of Vengeance
       The Silent Barrier
       The Toll Gate
       Trumpet Island
False accusations
   rt **False arrests**
       Frame-ups
1913 The Black Snake
       Checkers
       Eighty Million Women Want-?
       From Dusk to Dawn
       The Girl of the Sunny South
       Ivanhoe
       Leah Kleschna
       Shadows of the Moulin Rouge
1914 *Beating Back*
       The Boundary Rider
       The Call of the North
       The Christian
       The Circus Man
       The Crucible
       The Eagle's Mate
       A Factory Magdalen
       The Governor's Ghost
       The Greyhound
       The Hoosier Schoolmaster
       Imar the Servitor
       *The Little Angel of Canyon
          Creek*
       The Million Dollar Robbery
       A Mother's Heart
       *The Mystery of the Poison
          Pool*
       The Royal Box
       A Suspicious Wife
       The Three of Us
       Through Fire to Fortune
       The Walls of Jericho
       A Woman's Triumph
1915 The Blindness of Virtue
       Bondwomen
       The Broken Law
       The Butterfly
       Colorado
       The Concealed Truth
       Coral
       Destruction
       The Eagle's Nest
       The End of the Road
       The Explorer
       The Fatal Card
       Father and the Boys

The Final Judgment
Gambier's Advocate
The Heart of Jennifer
Heartaches
The High Hand
In the Shadow
Jack Chanty
The Pitfall
Scandal
The Secret Sin
Secretary of Frivolous Affairs
The Silent Voice
Sold
The Stubbornness of Geraldine
Sunday
Sweet Alyssum
The Unknown
The Voice in the Fog
When It Strikes Home
Who's Who in Society
The Wolf of Debt
A Woman's Past
1916 *The Bait*
       Big Tremaine
       Black Friday
       Broken Chains
       The Chaperon
       The City of Illusion
       The Code of Marcia Gray
       The Dawn of Love
       Diplomacy
       The Dollar and the Law
       Dollars and the Woman
       Dorian's Divorce
       East Lynne
       The Eternal Sapho
       The Five Faults of Flo
       The Flower of Faith
       The Girl of the Lost Lake
       The Girl with the Green Eyes
       Gloriana
       The Green Swamp
       Half a Rogue
       The Half-Breed
       The Haunted Manor
       The Heart of the Hills
       Her Great Hour
       His Brother's Wife
       Hypocrisy
       The Idol of the Stage
       It Happened in Honolulu
       The Kiss
       Love and Hate
       The Man Behind the Curtain
       The Ocean Waif
       The Other Side of the Door
       *The Redemption of Dave
          Darcey*
       A Romance of Billy Goat Hill
       Silas Marner
       Spellbound
       The Torch Bearer
       The Unwritten Law
       Vanity
       Wild Oats
       Witchcraft
       The World's Great Snare
1917 *Alias Mrs. Jessop*
       The Angel Factory
       At First Sight
       Babbling Tongues
       Back of the Man
       Because of a Woman
       The Birth of Patriotism
       The Blood of His Fathers
       Blood Will Tell
       The Bond of Fear
       The Bride's Silence
       The Burglar
       The Cold Deck
       Crime and Punishment
       The Crimson Dove
       The Darling of Paris
       Durand of the Bad Lands
       Every Girl's Dream
       The Eyes of the World
       The Final Payment
       The Flashlight
       The Girl Without a Soul
       The Golden Fetter
       The Great White Trail
       Happiness
       The Happiness of Three
          Women
       Her Fighting Chance

Her Good Name
His Mother's Boy
The Hungry Heart
Indiscretion
The Inevitable
Infidelity
The Law of the Land
Little Miss Fortune
The Little Samaritan
Love or Justice
A Magdalene of the Hills
A Man's Law
The Mark of Cain
Melissa of the Hills
Mentioned in Confidence
The Midnight Man
Mrs. Balfame
A Modern Monte Cristo
Mother Love and the Law
Mountain Dew
The Mystery of Number 47
On Record
On Trial
The Painted Lie
Pride and the Devil
Richard the Brazen
The Saintly Sinner
The Scarlet Car
The Secret of Eve
Susan's Gentleman
Sylvia of the Secret Service
Who Shall Take My Life?
1918 *Annexing Bill*
       Baree, Son of Kazan
       Blue-Eyed Mary
       Borrowed Clothes
       The Brazen Beauty
       Brown of Harvard
       Captain of His Soul
       Cupid's Roundup
       The Debt of Honor
       Eye for Eye
       The Face in the Dark
       Faith Endurin'
       The Girl of Today
       The Girl Who Came Back
       The Guilt of Silence
       I Want to Forget
       In the Hollow of Her Hand
       The Inn of the Blue Moon
       Inside the Lines
       Irish Eyes
       Just a Woman
       The Love Swindle
       The Man Who Wouldn't Tell
       Marked Cards
       The Midnight Trail
       Old Hartwell's Cub
       On the Quiet
       The Only Road
       Patriotism
       The Ranger
       Revenge
       Riders of the Night
       The Road to France
       A Romance of the Air
       Rose O' Paradise
       Sandy
       Social Hypocrites
       Suspicion
       Together
       The Trail to Yesterday
       Wild Life
       Wild Youth
       Winning Grandma
1919 Anne of Green Gables
       Bill Apperson's Boy
       Blind Man's Eyes
       The Brat
       Break the News to Mother
       Burglar by Proxy
       Calibre 38
       Come Again Smith
       The Dark Star
       The End of the Game
       A Fight for Love
       Fighting for Gold
       Fool's Gold
       Fortune's Child
       The Girl from Nowhere
       A Girl in Bohemia
       The Girl-Woman
       God's Outlaw
       The Gray Wolf's Ghost
       Heart O' the Hills

The Making of Maddalena
The Man from Manhattan
The Manager of the B. and A.
The Narrow Path
The Ne'er-Do-Well
The Old Folks at Home
The Overcoat
The Patriot
The Saleslady
The Serpent
Shadows and Sunshine
The Sphinx
The Turmoil
Two Men of Sandy Bar
The Upheaval
Vanity
The Weakness of Man
What the World Should Know
The Whirlpool of Destiny
Who Killed Joe Merrion?
Wild Oats
The Writing on the Wall
1917 *The Accomplice*
American—That's All
The Argyle Case
The Bad Boy
Blind Man's Luck
Blood Will Tell
The Blue Streak
The Bond Between
The Boy Girl
The Call of Her People
The Candy Girl
Charity Castle
The Chosen Prince, or the
  Friendship of David and
  Jonathan
The Clodhopper
The Corner Grocer
The Courage of the Common
  Place
The Frame Up
The Gift Girl
God's Law and Man's
Hell Morgan's Girl
The Hero of the Hour
High Finance
The Highway of Hope
His Father's Son
His Old-Fashioned Dad
The Image Maker
In the Hands of the Law
The Inevitable
The Iron Heart
The Jury of Fate
Lady Barnacle
The Law of the Land
Like Wildfire
The Lincoln Cycle
Little Lost Sister
The Little Terror
Moral Courage
The New York Peacock
One of Many
The Peddler
Peggy Leads the Way
The Pinch Hitter
Polly Ann
The Promise
The Red Woman
The Rose of Blood
Some Boy!
The Son of His Father
A Stormy Knight
The Submarine Eye
Sudden Jim
This Is the Life
Under Handicap
Until They Get Me
Vengeance Is Mine
The Weaker Sex
Weavers of Life
What Money Can't Buy
When You and I Were Young
Within the Law
Youth
1918 Betty Takes a Hand
Brace Up
By Hook or Crook
Cavanaugh of the Forest
  Rangers
The Fighting Grin
Gates of Gladness
Go West, Young Man
The Hard Rock Breed

Her Great Chance
His Birthright
His Enemy, the Law
His Own Home Town
The Hun Within
In Judgment Of
Jack Spurlock, Prodigal
Just for Tonight
Keys of the Righteous
Kidder and Ko
Leap to Fame
Life or Honor?
Madame Spy
Mlle. Paulette
More Trouble
A Mother's Sin
A Nine O'Clock Town
The Poor Rich Man
Real Folks
A Rich Man's Darling
The Scarlet Trail
A Son of Strife
The Song of Songs
The Spreading Evil
Such a Little Pirate
True Blue
The Venus Model
Wanted—A Brother
Without Honor
Wives of Men
Woman and the Law
A Woman of Redemption
1919 *Almost Married*
Beckoning Roads
The Belle of the Season
Bill Apperson's Boy
Bonnie, Bonnie Lassie
Brothers Divided
Calibre 38
Come Again Smith
The Dragon Painter
Easy to Make Money
Full of Pep
Gambling in Souls
The Gray Wolf's Ghost
The Hand Invisible
The Heart of Juanita
Hearts of Men
The Homebreaker
The Illustrious Prince
It Pays to Advertise
It's a Bear
Johnny-on-the-Spot
Josselyn's Wife
The Lion and the Mouse
The Midnight Stage
The Moral Deadline
The Other Half
The Poppy Girl's Husband
Roses and Thorns
The Rough Neck
The Shepherd of the Hills
The Speed Maniac
A Stitch in Time
Toton
The Valley of the Giants
The Way of the Strong
The World to Live In
The Wreck
1920 Below the Surface
The Gift Supreme
Godless Men
Homespun Folks
Huckleberry Finn
Human Stuff
The Iron Rider
It Might Happen to You
A Light Woman
The Little Wanderer
The Man Who Had Everything
Over the Hill to the Poorhouse
Pleasure Seekers
Roman Candles
The Saphead
Seeds of Vengeance
Sink or Swim
Smoldering Embers
That Something
The Ugly Duckling
Uncharted Channels
The Valley of Doubt
Vengeance and the Girl
The White Dove
19-- *Barnaby Lee*

Fatherhood
  rt **Father-daughter relationship**
     Father-son relationship
     Parentage
1916 What the World Should Know
1917 Skinner's Baby
1918 *Prisoners of the Pines*
     The Sins of the Children
1919 *The Burning Question*
     Heads Win
Fathers-in-law
1915 The Fifth Commandment
     The Spender
     Thou Shalt Not Kill
     Was She to Blame? Or, Souls
       That Meet in the Dark
1916 The Saleslady
1917 American—That's All
     Brand's Daughter
     The Candy Girl
     Moral Courage
     Putting the Bee in Herbert
     The Web of Life
1919 Beckoning Roads
     The Homesteader
1919-20
     When a Man Loves
1920 Excuse My Dust
     The Price of Redemption
Faust
1914 *The Pit*
1916 *The Woman Who Dared*
1918 *Find the Woman*
1919 The Price Woman Pays
Feats of strength
1914 Samson
1919 Twilight
Female impersonation
  rt **Disguise**
     Impersonation
     Impersonation and imposture
     Male impersonation
     Mistaken identity
1914 *The Million*
     Mrs. Black Is Back
1915 *The Billionaire Lord*
     C.O.D.
1916 *Artie, the Millionaire Kid*
1917 The Clever Mrs. Carfax
     The Countess Charming
     The Haunted Pajamas
     Some Boy!
1918 Alias Mary Brown
     Bound in Morocco
     Madame Spy
     The Widow's Might
1919 Yankee Doodle in Berlin
1920 An Adventuress
     Old Lady 31
1920-21
     The House of Mystery
Feminism
1918 *A Man's World*
1919 Experimental Marriage
     Oh, You Women
1920 Miss Hobbs
Fences
1917 *The Lady in the Library*
1918 Midnight Madness
1919 *Hearts Asleep*
     Love's Prisoner
Fencing
1916 *The Vagabond Prince*
Ferryboats
1916 The River of Romance
Fertility
1919 The Splendid Sin
1920 A City Sparrow
Festivals
1915 *Du Barry*
     Sin
Feuds
1914 The Great Leap; Until Death
       Do Us Part
     The Trail of the Lonesome Pine
1915 The Cub
     The Love Route
1916 The Apostle of Vengeance
     The Call of the Cumberlands
     Children of the Feud
     Fathers of Men
     The Feud Girl
     The Iron Hand
     Judith of the Cumberlands

Romeo and Juliet (Fox Film
  Corp.)
Romeo and Juliet (Quality
  Pictures Corp.)
The Stronger Love
The Valiants of Virginia
1917 The Adopted Son
     The Little Chevalier
     Man and Beast
     Melissa of the Hills
     Men of the Desert
1918 Her Man
1919 Cowardice Court
     The Feud
     The Heart of Youth
     Red Hot Dollars
     The Stronger Vow
     Sue of the South
     The Thunderbolt
     The Unbroken Promise
1920 The Birth of a Soul
     The Dead Line
     The Desert Scorpion
     Fighting Cressy
     Forbidden Valley
     Honeymoon Ranch
     Sundown Slim
     Two Moons
Fez (Morocco)
1914 *Fire and Sword*
Fidelity
1913 The Fight for Millions
     A Prisoner in the Harem
     The Prisoner of Zenda
1914 Aristocracy
1915 The Avalanche
     A Butterfly on the Wheel
     The Celebrated Scandal
     The Fox Woman
     Heartaches
     Judge Not; Or, The Woman of
       Mona Diggings
     Madame Butterfly
     The Man Who Found Himself
     A Man's Prerogative
     Matrimony
     The Model
     Nedra
     On Dangerous Paths
     Peer Gynt
     The Shadows of a Great City
     Silver Threads Among the Gold
     Sin
     The Wolf of Debt
1916 Alien Souls
     Betty of Graystone
     Captain Jinks of the Horse
       Marines
     The Country That God Forgot
     The Devil's Needle
     Dollars and the Woman
     Dulcie's Adventure
     The Female of the Species
     The Fighting Chance
     For a Woman's Fair Name
     Fruits of Desire
     God's Half Acre
     Honor's Altar
     The Idol of the Stage
     The Lash
     Mixed Blood
     The White Rosette
1917 *The Babes in the Woods*
     Even As You and I
     Heart's Desire
     The Hungry Heart
     In Slumberland
     The Iron Ring
     It Happened to Adele
     The Lonesome Chap
     Money Magic
     Open Places
     The Power of Decision
     Pride
     The Rainbow Girl
     The Road Between
     Under Handicap
1918 The Beloved Traitor
     Beyond the Shadows
     The Clutch of Circumstance
     Her Mistake
     The Honor of His House
     The House of Mirth
     Missing
     Pay Day

Sauce for the Goose
Suspicion
1919 As a Man Thinks
Blackie's Redemption
Blind Husbands
Children of Banishment
The Climbers
Creaking Stairs
The Divorce Trap
Evangeline
Fit to Win
The Girl Who Stayed at Home
Lasca
Paid in Full
The Spirit of Lafayette
The Virtuous Model
The Winchester Woman
1920 Fickle Women
For the Soul of Rafael
The Gift Supreme
Silk Husbands and Calico
    Wives
A Splendid Hazard
The Way Women Love
The Willow Tree
Women Men Forget
Yes or No

Fights
rt Specific types of fights
1914 *The Floor Above*
The Mountain Rat
*A Romance of the Mexican
    Revolution*
The Straight Road
The Voice at the Telephone
1915 *The Adventures of a Boy
    Scout*
Aloha Oe
The Buzzard's Shadow
Captain Courtesy
Children of the Ghetto
Chimmie Fadden
The College Orphan
Colorado
The Concealed Truth
Conscience
The Cub
The Danger Signal
The Deep Purple
The Devil's Daughter
The Dictator
Don Caesar de Bazan
The Eagle's Nest
For $5,000 a Year
The Gambler of the West
The Game of Three
Her Atonement
The Juggernaut
A Man's Making
Prohibition
The Right of Way
Rule G
Salvation Nell
Shadows from the Past
The Shadows of a Great City
The Siren's Song
A Submarine Pirate
The Truth About Helen
Vengeance of the Wilds
Wildfire
The Winged Idol
Winning the Futurity
1916 *All Man*
The Almighty Dollar
Between Men
The Conscience of John David
The Country That God Forgot
The Crippled Hand
Cross Currents
The Dawn of Love
Fathers of Men
The Feud Girl
The Girl of the Lost Lake
*God's Country and the
    Woman*
Going Straight
The Golden Chance
A Gutter Magdalene
The Habit of Happiness
Half a Rogue
He Fell in Love with His Wife
Her Bleeding Heart
The Honor of Mary Blake
Life's Whirlpool
Love's Toll

Manhattan Madness
The Market of Vain Desire
The Mirror of Life
The Misleading Lady
The Moment Before
New York
Not My Sister
The Path of Darkness
The Pawn of Fate
The Pillory
Playing with Fire
Sins of Her Parent
The Snowbird
The Sphinx
The Stain in the Blood
A Stranger from Somewhere
The Suspect
Then I'll Come Back to You
Three Pals
To Have and to Hold
A Tortured Heart
The Traveling Salesman
The Unattainable
The Unpardonable Sin
Vengeance Is Mine
The Victim
The Victory of Conscience
The Voice of Love
The Wharf Rat
What Happened at 22
What Will People Say?
When Love Is King
Where Is My Father?
The Woman in Politics
A Woman's Daring
The Wrong Door
The Years of the Locust
Youth's Endearing Charm
1917 *Alma, Where Do You Live?*
The Debt
Hell Morgan's Girl
Her Secret
In Slumberland
The Innocent Sinner
The Island of Desire
The Jaguar's Claws
Knights of the Square Table
The Lad and the Lion
The Land of Long Shadows
The Learnin' of Jim Benton
Little Miss Optimist
A Love Sublime
The Love That Lives
Paradise Garden
The Range Boss
The Recoil
The Regenerates
Reputation
A Rich Man's Plaything
Rosie O'Grady
The Scarlet Car
A School for Husbands
The Secret of Black Mountain
The Secret of Eve
Souls Adrift
The Sudden Gentleman
The Tenderfoot
Thou Shalt Not Steal
The Trail of the Shadow
Transgression
The Web of Life
Who Shall Take My Life
Who Was the Other Man
Whose Wife?
The Wild Girl
Wild Sumac
The Winged Mystery
1918 *Bound in Morocco*
Brace Up
The Bride of Fear
Broadway Bill
Broadway Love
A Burglar for a Night
Cactus Crandall
The Craving
The Crucible of Life
The Dawn of Understanding
Faith Endurin'
Fame and Fortune
The Family Skeleton
"Flare-Up" Sal
The Ghost Flower
The Girl in the Dark
A Good Loser
The Gun Woman

Hands Down
The Hard Rock Breed
A Heart's Revenge
Hell's End
Her Body in Bond
Her Mistake
The Hired Man
Hitting the High Spots
Hugon, the Mighty
The Hun Within
In Bad
In Judgment Of
Innocent's Progress
Irish Eyes
Kidder and Ko
Kildare of Storm
The Law of the North
The Law's Outlaw
The Liar
Madame Jealousy
The Marriage Ring
Naked Hands
Nine-Tenths of the Law
Old Hartwell's Cub
Old Love for New
Other Men's Daughters
Painted Lips
Pals First
Playing the Game
Playthings
The Purple Lily
Real Folks
The Red, Red Heart
Riddle Gawne
Rough and Ready
Shark Monroe
The Sign Invisible
The Sins of the Children
Social Ambition
A Society Sensation
The Source
Stolen Orders
String Beans
The Sunset Princess
Sunshine Nan
Swat the Spy
Tongues of Flame
Treason
Treasure Island
The Turn of the Wheel
The Two-Soul Woman
Under the Greenwood Tree
The Vanity Pool
The Velvet Hand
The Voice of Destiny
When Men Betray
The White Man's Law
The Winning of Beatrice
The Wolf and His Mate
The Woman Who Gave
The Yellow Dog
1919 *An Adventure in Hearts*
The Amazing Wife
Are You Legally Married?
The Bandbox
La Belle Russe
Bill Henry
The Blinding Trail
The Bluffer
The Bondage of Barbara
The Brand of Judas
The Cinema Murder
Courage for Two
Crimson Shoals
Dangerous Waters
A Daughter of the Wolf
The Day She Paid
Devil McCare
The Drifters
Easy to Make Money
The End of the Game
Eve in Exile
The Exquisite Thief
A Fallen Idol
The False Code
The False Faces
The Fear Woman
A Fight for Love
Fighting for Gold
Fighting Through
The Fire Flingers
Fool's Gold
Forest Rivals
Ginger
The Girl Dodger

The Girl from Nowhere
Go Get 'Em Garringer
God's Outlaw
The Gray Horizon
Happy Though Married
Hay Foot, Straw Foot
Heartsease
Help! Help! Police!
In for Thirty Days
Jacques of the Silver North
The Joyous Liar
Jubilo
Kitty Kelly, M.D.
The Light
The Little Rowdy
The Littlest Scout
Lost Money
The Love Burglar
The Love Call
Love, Honor and—?
The Love That Dares
A Man and His Money
The Man Hunter
A Man in the Open
The Man Who Won
A Man's Duty
The Market of Souls
Marriage for Convenience
Mary Regan
The Mayor of Filbert
The Mints of Hell
Miss Arizona
Mistaken Identity
Modern Husbands
Molly of the Follies
The Mother and the Law
Muggsy
Never Say Quit
One-Thing-at-a-Time O'Day
Out Yonder
Putting One Over
Sacred Silence
Satan Junior
The Sheriff's Son
Should a Woman Tell?
Snares of Paris
The Spitfire of Seville
The Steel King
The Test of Honor
This Hero Stuff
The Tiger Lily
Trixie from Broadway
Two Women
The Unbroken Promise
The Unpainted Woman
The Unwritten Code
Upstairs
The Valley of the Giants
Virtuous Men
The Weaker Vessel
What Am I Bid?
When a Girl Loves
When Doctors Disagree
When Fate Decides
Where Bonds Are Loosed
The White Heather
A White Man's Chance
The Wilderness Trail
The Winning Stroke
The Wolf
The Wreck
1920 *The Fighting Chance*
Fighting Cressy
The Gamesters
The Gauntlet
Godless Men
The Golden Trail
Hitchin' Posts
Honor Bound
Human Stuff
The Idol Dancer
The Isle of Destiny
Locked Lips
A Manhattan Knight
Married Life
Miss Nobody
The Mollycoddle
Moon Madness
The Mother of His Children
Nomads of the North
On with the Dance
Once a Plumber
Outside the Law
Prairie Trails
The Price of Redemption

The Grand Passion
The Gun Woman
The Hired Man
Lawless Love
Less Than Kin
Madam Who
The Man of Bronze
Riddle Gawne
The Safety Curtain
Sunshine Nan
Too Many Millions
The Transgressor
Under the Yoke
Why America Will Win
1919 *An Amateur Widow*
The Blinding Trail
Brothers Divided
The Brute Breaker
Checkers
The Fall of Babylon
Help! Help! Police!
Hit or Miss
Hoop-La
Human Passions
The Lady of Red Butte
The Life Line
The Outcasts of Poker Flats
The Petal on the Current
Please Get Married
The Third Kiss
Trixie from Broadway
Why Smith Left Home
1920 *The Butterfly Man*
Circumstantial Evidence
The Devil's Garden
Footlights and Shadows
Hearts Up
Hell's Oasis
Man and Woman (Tyrad
  Pictures, Inc.)
The North Wind's Malice
Pegeen
Pink Tights
The Song of the Soul
The Stealers
A Woman Who Understood
1922 The Cynic Effect

Fireworks
1920 Roman Candles

Firing squads
1915 *Courtmartialed*
Don Caesar de Bazan
1916 *Following the Flag in Mexico*
1917 *Betrayed*
Betsy Ross
The Little American
1918 *After the War*
1919 *The Great Romance*
The New Moon

Fish
1915 *On the Spanish Main*

Fish packing
1918 *Kidder and Ko*
Love's Pay Day

Fisheries
1915 *Wild Life of America in Films*
1917 *The Devil-Stone*

Fishermaids
1917 *The Devil-Stone*

Fishermen
1913 *Jack London's Adventures in*
  the South Sea Islands
1914 *John Barleycorn*
The Monster and the Girl
The Mystery of Edwin Drood
1915 *Coral*
The Daughter of the Sea
Enoch Arden
In the Shadow
A Man's Making
1916 *The American Beauty*
The Battle of Hearts
The Dawn of Love
The Feast of Life
Maria Rosa
The Net
Undine
1917 *The Awakening of Ruth*
The Best Man
The Bottle Imp
The Deemster
The Final Payment
Forget-Me-Not
The Last Sentence

The Mother Instinct
The Pride of the Clan
The Pulse of Life
The Ship of Doom
The Spindle of Life
1918 The Belgian
The Beloved Traitor
Love's Pay Day
A Society Sensation
The Triumph of Venus
1920 *The Beggar Prince*
The Forbidden Thing
The Sea Rider
The Silver Horde

Fishing
1914 *Neptune's Daughter*
1915 *The Adventures of a Boy*
  Scout
American Game Trails
Pirate Haunts
1917 *The Mad Lover*
Paradise Garden
1918 *The Interloper*
1919 *The Forbidden Room*
A Fugitive from Matrimony
1920 *Honest Hutch*
The Silver Horde
A Trip Through Cairo

Fishing boats
1915 *The Siren's Song*
1916 *The Battle of Hearts*
The Dawn of Love
1917 *Souls Adrift*

Fishing rights
1914 Neptune's Daughter
1920 *The Silver Horde*

Fishing villages
1915 Enoch Arden
His Wife
A Man's Making
May Blossom
The Siren's Song
1916 The Eye of the Night
1917 *The Best Man*
Lorelei of the Sea
1918 *Irish Eyes*
Love's Pay Day
Peg O' the Sea
The Sea Waif
The Trap
1919 The Captain's Captain
Miss Adventure
The Price of Innocence
Should a Woman Tell?
1920 *Broadway and Home*
The Forbidden Thing

Fishmongers
1916 *It Happened in Honolulu*
1920 *Nurse Marjorie*

Fistfights
1914 *As Ye Sow*
Classmates
1915 *The Heart of the Blue Ridge*
My Best Girl
Pennington's Choice
Rags
A Trade Secret
What Happened to Father
The Woman Next Door
A Yankee from the West
The Yankee Girl
1916 *Blue Blood and Red*
Charlie Chaplin's Burlesque on
  "Carmen"
The Come-Back
Reggie Mixes In
1917 *Framing Framers*
The Inevitable
Jack and Jill
The Silent Witness
The Small Town Guy
Tom Sawyer
When Men Are Tempted
1918 *Cyclone Higgins, D.D.*
A Diplomatic Mission
The Golden Fleece
Green Eyes
Untamed
What Becomes of the
  Children?
The Wild Strain
1919 Brass Buttons
The Brute Breaker
The Challenge of Chance

Children of Banishment
The Coming of the Law
The Microbe
1920 *Blind Love*
The Chorus Girl's Romance
The Confession
Firebrand Trevison
A Fool and His Money
The Heart of a Woman
Hearts Up
Man and His Woman
The Man from Nowhere
Our Christianity and Nobody's
  Child
Out of the Dust
The Path She Chose
Peaceful Valley
The Poor Simp
The Right of Way
The Road of Ambition
Should a Wife Work?
The Stranger

Fixed automobile races
  rt **Automobile racing**
1920 High Speed

Fixed elections
1913 Eighty Million Women Want-?

Fixed fights
1917 *Jack and Jill*
1920 *The Brute*

Fixed football games
  rt **Football**
1916 *The Craving*

Fixed horseraces
  rt **Horseracing**
1913 In the Stretch
1915 *The Suburban*
Wildfire
1916 *Atta Boy's Last Race*
Sporting Blood
1918 *Sandy*
1919 Should a Husband Forgive?
1920 *The Sport of Kings*

Flagellation
1915 *The Winged Idol*
1916 *The Cossack Whip*
1917 *The Law of the Land*

James Montgomery Flagg
1914 *The Adventures of Kitty Cobb*

Flags
1915 Barbara Frietchie
A Continental Girl
1916 *Whom the Gods Destroy*
1917 *Betsy Ross*
The Slacker (Metro Pictures
  Corp.)
The Slacker's Heart
1918 *Tony America*
1919 Fighting Through
The Girl Who Stayed at
  Home
The Volcano

Flanders (Belgium)
1915 *Somewhere in France*
1919 *Fit to Win*
The Heart of Humanity

Flappers
1918 *His Majesty, Bunker Bean*
1919 *The Girl Problem*
1920 *Flying Pat*

Flattery
1919 *Everywoman*

Flirtation
1914 *The Envoy Extraordinary*
A Florida Enchantment
The Path Forbidden
1915 The Avalanche
Bought
The Builder of Bridges
A Butterfly on the Wheel
The Buzzard's Shadow
The Chocolate Soldier
Crooky
Divorçons
Inspiration
The Little Gypsy
Matrimony
Midnight at Maxim's
The Voice of Satan
1916 The Five Faults of Flo
A Huntress of Men
The Island of Surprise
Mrs. Dane's Danger
The Price of Happiness

1917 *Alimony*
His Own People
Indiscretion
The Little Yank
A Woman Alone
1918 *By Right of Purchase*
A Desert Wooing
For Husbands Only
Her Husband's Honor
Journey's End
The Marionettes
Old Love for New
A Pair of Sixes
The Rough Lover
The Silent Woman
Wives of Men
1919 The Amateur Adventuress
The Arizona Cat Claw
As a Man Thinks
Be a Little Sport
The Devil's Trail
Fair and Warmer
The Fear Woman
From Headquarters
The Gay Lord Quex
Josselyn's Wife
Lasca
The Last of the Duanes
The Light
The Little Intruder
Lure of Ambition
Mandarin's Gold
Man's Desire
The Misleading Widow
More Deadly Than the Male
The Scarlet Shadow
A Sporting Chance (Famous
  Players-Lasky Corp.)
Stepping Out
The Stronger Vow
A Temperamental Wife
True Heart Susie
Twilight
The Vengeance of Durand
A Very Good Young Man
A Virtuous Vamp
Who Cares?
Yankee Doodle in Berlin
1920 *Hairpins*
The New York Idea
The Week-End

Flirts
  rt **Teases**
Temptresses
Vamps
1914 *The Country Mouse*
1915 *Double Trouble*
Little Miss Brown
The Turn of the Road
1916 Charlie Chaplin's Burlesque on
  "Carmen"
The Flirt
Seventeen
Sweet Kitty Bellairs
The Two Edged Sword
1917 Each to His Kind
Flying Colors
Her Official Fathers
The Masked Heart
A Modern Cinderella
Princess Virtue
The Silence Sellers
1918 The Beloved Impostor
The Seal of Silence
The Soul of Buddha
The Unchastened Woman
Virtuous Wives
Viviette
1919 *False Evidence*
His Bridal Night
Some Bride
Two Women
1920 The Dangerous Paradise
Husband Hunter
In Search of a Sinner
In the Heart of a Fool
The Inferior Sex
A Modern Salome
Reformation
Remodelling Her Husband
Respectable by Proxy
The Vice of Fools

Little Lady Eileen
Lord Loveland Discovers
   America
Man and His Soul
The Men She Married
A Modern Enoch Arden
The Plow Girl
The Return of Eve
The Reward of Patience
The Selfish Woman
The Social Secretary
*The Thousand Dollar
   Husband*
The Turmoil
Unto Those Who Sin
1917 Annie-for-Spite
   The Antics of Ann
   Anything Once
   The Apple-Tree Girl
   At First Sight
   The Auction of Virtue
   The Beautiful Adventure
   Broadway Jones
   The Car of Chance
   Castles for Two
   The Clean Gun
   The Clever Mrs. Carfax
   Come Through
   The Debt
   Diamonds and Pearls
   Forbidden Paths
   Forget-Me-Not
   Her Official Fathers
   Her Temptation
   High Play
   The Inner Shrine
   Madame Bo-Peep
   The Man Who Took a Chance
   The Marriage Speculation
   Mayblossom
   Miss Deception
   The Moth
   Outcast
   The Question
   Red, White and Blue Blood
   The Silent Partner
   A Song of Sixpence
   A Square Deal
   The Square Deceiver
   Wooden Shoes
1918 *Arizona*
   The Bride's Awakening
   Her Aviator
   How Could You, Caroline?
   The Man Hunt
   The Mask
   Men
   Mile-a-Minute Kendall
   Molly, Go Get 'Em
   Shackled
   The Shuttle
   The Two-Soul Woman
   Under the Greenwood Tree
   The Vortex
1919 Alias Mike Moran
   Bringing Up Betty
   Checkers
   The Gay Lord Quex
   The Homebreaker
   In Search of Arcady
   Johnny-on-the-Spot
   The Little Intruder
   Nobody Home
   The Old Maid's Baby
   Through the Wrong Door
   Turning the Tables
1920 *Blind Youth*
   Bonnie May
   The Butterfly Man
   Cupid, the Cowpuncher
   Dangerous to Men
   The Dream Cheater
   Faith
   The Fighting Chance
   Footlights and Shadows
   The Fortune Hunter
   *Forty-Five Minutes from
      Broadway*
   The Gilded Dream
   Help Wanted—Male
   Her Elephant Man
   Her First Elopement
   His Temporary Wife
   The Hope
   Just a Wife

The Ladder of Lies
Life
Life's Twist
Live Sparks
The Midnight Bride
A Modern Salome
Passion's Playground
Pinto
The Road of Ambition
The Romance Promoters
Rouge and Riches
Stronger Than Death
Thoughtless Women
A Thousand to One
The Tree of Knowledge
The Veiled Marriage
The Walk-Offs
The Week-End
Why Leave Your Husband?
A Woman's Business
You Never Can Tell

Fortune-tellers
1915 The Winged Idol
1916 *A Circus Romance*
   In the Web of the Grafters
1917 *Her Sister*
   The Mysterious Mrs. M.
   A Phantom Husband
1918 The Dream Lady
   False Ambition
   The Knife
   Why I Would Not Marry
   Within the Cup
1919 *The Heart of a Gypsy*
   Me and Captain Kidd
1920 The Fortune Teller
   A Manhattan Knight
   *Sophy of Kravonia; Or, The
      Virgin of Paris*
   The Thirtieth Piece of Silver
   What Happened to Rosa

Foster brothers
1914 *Captain Swift*
1919 Twilight
1920 The Restless Sex

Foster children
1913 *The Volunteer Organist*
1919 *A Rogue's Romance*

Foster daughters
1915 *M'liss*
   The Model
1916 Gloriana
   The Gods of Fate
   The Wrong Door
1917 Heart Strings
   The Peddler
1918 The Gulf Between
   Social Ambition
1919 The Little Diplomat
   Someone Must Pay
1920 *The County Fair*

Foster fathers
1914 The Criminal Code
   The Dishonored Medal
   Hearts of Oak
   Jess
   Mr. Barnes of New York
   *The Mysterious Mr. Wu Chung
      Foo*
1915 *The Adventures of a Madcap
      Coral*
   An Enemy to Society
   The Eternal City
   The Fool and the Dancer
   The Little Dutch Girl
   M'liss
   The Model
   The Raven
   Strathmore
1916 *Autumn*
   A Bird of Prey
   The Flower of No Man's Land
   The Hidden Law
   The Ocean Waif
   The Sex Lure
   The Shrine of Happiness
   Silas Marner
1917 *The Cricket*
   A Crooked Romance
   A Jewel in Pawn
   Little Miss Nobody
   A Man's Law
   The Princess of Patches
   Shame
   The Silent Lie

   The Spotted Lily
1918 *Ace High*
   An Alien Enemy
   Breakers Ahead
   Broken Ties
   The Girl Who Wouldn't Quit
   The Temple of Dusk
1919 Sealed Hearts
1919-20
   When a Man Loves
1920 Eyes of the Heart
   The Harvest Moon
   Heritage
   The Jack-Knife Man
   Lahoma
   The Little Outcast
   The Midlanders
   The Restless Sex
   The Tiger's Cub
   The U.P. Trail
   The Untamed

Foster mothers
1914 *False Colours*
1915 *Jordan Is a Hard Road*
   June Friday
1916 *A Dream or Two Ago*
   Nancy's Birthright
1917 A Kentucky Cinderella
   Periwinkle
   Zollenstein
1918 *After the War*
   The Guilty Wife
   The Law That Divides
   The Seal of Silence
   Social Briars
   A Soul in Trust
   Tarzan of the Apes
   The Venus Model
1919 A Girl Named Mary
1920 *Huckleberry Finn*

Foster parents
1915 *Greater Love Hath No Man*
   Heritage
   Should a Mother Tell?
   Sunday
1916 *The American Beauty*
   April
   Audrey
   Broken Fetters
   Destiny's Toy
   The Devil's Prayer-Book
   The Dream Girl
   The Flames of Johannis
   Little Mary Sunshine
   Merely Mary Ann
   Should a Baby Die?
   The Stain in the Blood
   Youth's Endearing Charm
1917 Kitty MacKay
   Pay Me
   The Secret of Eve
   Sirens of the Sea
   Threads of Fate
   Young Mother Hubbard
1918 *The Girl of My Dreams*
1919 Anne of Green Gables
   The Firing Line
1920 *The Cup of Fury*
   The Unfortunate Sex

Foster sisters
1914 *A Celebrated Case*
1916 Cross Currents

Foster sons
1918 *A Successful Adventure*
1919 The Outcasts of Poker Flats
   Toton
1920 Rio Grande

Foundlings
1912 Quincy Adams Sawyer
1913 *The Legend of Provence*
1914 The Pawn of Fortune
   A Woman's Triumph
1915 *Bred in the Bone*
   *Destiny; Or, The Soul of a
      Woman*
   Environment
   *From the Valley of the
      Missing*
   June Friday
   The Little Dutch Girl
   The Little Gypsy
   The Reform Candidate
1916 *The American Beauty*
   The Criminal
   The Foundling

1917 *A Crooked Romance*
   Every Girl's Dream
   The Great White Trail
   The Heart of Ezra Greer
   Her New York
   The Hidden Children
   Lost in Transit
1918 Miss Innocence
   A Pair of Cupids
1919 *Twilight*
1920 *The Untamed*

Foundry foremen
1916 *The Eagle's Wing*
1918 *All Man*

Foundry workers
1914 *The Lost Paradise*
1915 *Temptation*
1918 *The Goat*
1919 *The Master Man*
   Red Hot Dollars
1920 The Heart of a Woman

Fountains
1916 *Undine*

Fourth of July
1919 *Whitewashed Walls*

Fox hunts
1915 *Mistress Nell*

Fox ranches
1914 *Prince Edward Island in
      Motion; Home of the Silver
      Black Fox Industry*

Frame-ups
  rt **False accusations**
     False arrests
1913 Across the Continent
   Ben Bolt
   The Count of Monte Cristo
1914 Cameo Kirby
   The Coming Power
   Detective Craig's Coup
   Escaped from Siberia
   Fighting Death
   The Gamblers
   The Great Diamond Robbery
   The Hand of Destiny
   Hook and Hand
   In Mizzoura
   Joseph in the Land of Egypt
   The Littlest Rebel
   The Man of the Hour
   The Mystery of Edwin Drood
   The Power of the Press
   The Scales of Justice
   The Seats of the Mighty
   The Trail of the Lonesome Pine
   Winning His First Case
1915 Alias Jimmy Valentine
   The Alien
   The Beachcomber
   The Bridge of Sighs
   The College Orphan
   Courtmartialed
   David Harum
   The District Attorney
   Double Trouble
   Eugene Aram
   Excuse Me
   The Failure
   The Governor's Boss
   The House of the Lost Court
   The Man from Oregon
   The Man of Shame
   Pearls of Temptation
   Silver Threads Among the Gold
   Stolen Goods
   Stop Thief!
   Tillie's Tomato Surprise
   To Cherish and Protect
   The Unbroken Road
   The Wheels of Justice
   The White Scar
   The Wild Olive
   Winning the Futurity
   The Woman Next Door
   The Woman Who Lied
1916 The Alibi
   Anton the Terrible
   Big Jim Garrity
   The Big Sister
   The Catspaw
   The Chalice of Sorrow
   The Colored American
      Winning His Suit
   Common Ground

The Seal of Silence	
The Splendid Sinner	
Staking His Life	
Stolen Orders	
The Turn of a Card	
The Turn of the Wheel	
Tyrant Fear	
1919 *An Adventure in Hearts*	
The Avalanche	
Better Times	
Bonds of Honor	
The Brand	
False Gods	
Hawthorne of the U.S.A.	
The Home Town Girl	
Lord and Lady Algy	
Love, Honor and—?	
Mandarin's Gold	
Men, Women and Money	
The Midnight Stage	
Prudence on Broadway	
The Son-of-a-Gun!	
Todd of the Times	
Vagabond Luck	
A Very Good Young Man	
The Virtuous Thief	
1920 Lone Hand Wilson	
Man's Plaything	
Passion's Playground	
Reformation	
The Sport of Kings	
The Strange Boarder	
$30,000	
Twins of Suffering Creek	
The Valley of Doubt	
Women Men Love	

Gambling houses
  rt **Casinos**
1913 *Checkers*
      In the Stretch
1914 *The Bargain*
      Over Niagara Falls
1915 *Betty in Search of a Thrill*
      The Brink
      Her Atonement
      Judge Not; Or, The Woman of Mona Diggings
      The Sins of the Mothers
1916 The House of Mirrors
      Vanity
1917 *Forget-Me-Not*
      High Play
      The New York Peacock
      The Price of Pride
      The Soul of Satan
      The War of the Tongs
1918 The Blindness of Divorce
      By Proxy
      The Embarrassment of Riches
      Go West, Young Man
      Her Moment
      Innocent
      Little Miss No-Account
      Mystic Faces
      The Painted Lily
      The Queen of Hearts
      The Song of the Soul
      The Splendid Sinner
      The Spurs of Sybil
      Stolen Hours
      The Whirlpool
1919 *The Adventure Shop*
      Fortune's Child
      Gambling in Souls
      His Debt
      The Lady of Red Butte
      The Scar
1920 The Branded Woman
      The Gamesters
      The Man from Nowhere
      The Saphead
      The Strange Boarder

Gamekeepers
1917 *His Own People*
1919 *The Mystery of the Yellow Room*
1920 Hearts Are Trumps
Games
1917 *Greed*
Gang wars
1914 The Gangsters
1915 *Are They Born or Made?*
1917 The War of the Tongs

Gangrene
1916 *Behind the Lines*
Gangs
1913 *In the Stretch*
1914 *The Mysterious Mr. Wu Chung Foo*
      The Yellow Traffic
1915 The Brink
      The Carpet from Bagdad
      The Closing Net
      The Curious Conduct of Judge Legarde
      The Gray Mask
      The Green Cloak
      His Turning Point
      The Lily of Poverty Flat
      Regeneration
      The Way Back
1916 The Decoy
      The Dividend
      Hop, the Devil's Brew
      Immediate Lee
      A Law unto Himself
      Lieutenant Danny, U.S.A.
      The Little Girl Next Door
      The Lost Bridegroom
      Madame X
      The Mediator
      Medicine Bend
      My Lady Incog.
      Nanette of the Wilds
      The No-Good Guy
      Oliver Twist
      The Patriot
      The Phantom Buccaneer
      The Ragamuffin
      Reggie Mixes In
      The Shadow of a Doubt
      The Sign of the Poppy
      The Sign of the Spade
      The Sunbeam
      The Torch Bearer
1917 *The Climber*
      Dead Shot Baker
      The Lone Wolf
      The Maelstrom
      One Shot Ross
      The Silent Master
      The Small Town Girl
      Straight Shooting
      Sylvia of the Secret Service
      The War of the Tongs
      The Wildcat
1918 *Blindfolded*
      The Border Legion
      The Border Raiders
      Cactus Crandall
      Chase Me Charlie
      Code of the Yukon
      Convict 993
      Crown Jewels
      The Crucible of Life
      Cupid's Roundup
      A Daughter of the West
      The Empty Cab
      The Eyes of Mystery
      Face Value
      Fame and Fortune
      The Girl in the Dark
      In Bad
      Keith of the Border
      Lawless Love
      Midnight Madness
      Rimrock Jones
      The Shoes That Danced
      The Tiger Man
      Unclaimed Goods
      The White Lie
1919 *The Amazing Impostor*
      The Best Man
      The Black Circle
      Cheating Cheaters
      Courage for Two
      The End of the Game
      The Forfeit
      Go Get 'Em Garringer
      The Great Air Robbery
      Hell Roarin' Reform
      The Joyous Liar
      The Lamb and the Lion
      The Lone Wolf's Daughter
      Loot
      The Love Burglar
      Mary Regan
      The Miracle Man

Miss Crusoe	
The Mother and the Law	
Red Blood and Yellow	
A Regular Fellow	
Thieves	
When a Girl Loves	
When Bearcat Went Dry	
The Wilderness Trail	
The Woman on the Index	

1919-20
      The Tower of Jewels
1920 Below the Deadline
      Blackbirds
      The Border Raiders
      Bullet Proof
      Chains of Evidence
      The Cheater
      Cinderella's Twin
      The Coast of Opportunity
      The Cradle of Courage
      Dangerous Trails
      The Discarded Woman
      Drag Harlan
      From Now On
      The Girl in Number 29
      The Gray Brother
      The Green Flame
      Hell's Oasis
      His Pajama Girl
      Lahoma
      The Last Straw
      A Manhattan Knight
      Miss Nobody
      The Night Riders
      The One Way Trail
      Outside the Law
      Over the Hill to the Poorhouse
      Overland Red
      The Penalty
      The Poor Simp
      The Red Lane
      The Romance Promoters
      Sand!

Gangsters
  rt **Criminals**
        Hoodlums
1913 The Fight for Millions
      The Stranglers of Paris
1914 *Dope*
      The Kangaroo
      The Mystery of Richmond Castle
      The Pawn of Fortune
1915 *Are They Born or Made?*
      The Gentleman from Indiana
1916 The Cycle of Fate
      Her Father's Gold
      His Great Triumph
      The Mirror of Life
      The No-Good Guy
      The Redemption of Dave Darcey
      Reggie Mixes In
      Salvation Joan
      The Sign of the Spade
      Temptation and the Man
      Thrown to the Lions
      The Twinkler
      Warning! The S.O.S. Call of Humanity
      The Wrong Door
1917 *The Angel Factory*
      The Blue Streak
      The Bondage of Fear
      Kick In
      A Love Sublime
      The Narrow Trail
      The Terror
1918 Convict 993
      Danger—Go Slow
      The Devil's Wheel
      The Flash of Fate
      Hell's End
      His Royal Highness
      Hitting the Trail
      The Mysterious Mr. Browning
1919 *Eastward Ho!*
1920 *Away Goes Prudence*
      Blackbirds
      The Brute
      The Dark Mirror
      Love Madness
      A Manhattan Knight
      Outside the Law
      The Penalty

The Valley of Night	
Wanted at Headquarters	
While New York Sleeps	
The White Moll	

1921 *Miss 139*
Garages
1915 *The Little Mademoiselle*
1916 *The Race*
Garbage trucks
1914 *Charlotte Corday*
1917 *The Secret Man*
Gardeners
1914 *His Majesty, the Scarecrow of Oz*
      The Wishing Ring; An Idyll of Old England
1915 *The Circular Staircase*
      The Little Dutch Girl
1916 *Just a Song at Twilight*
      The Thoroughbred (American Film Co.)
1917 *The Ghost House*
      The Lair of the Wolf
      A Self-Made Widow
1918 *Beauty and the Rogue*
      The Bravest Way
      Wanted, a Mother
1919 *A Man's Fight*
      Over the Garden Wall
1920 *Everybody's Sweetheart*
Gardens
1918 Prunella
1919 *Cupid Forecloses*
      The Secret Garden
Garment unions
1915 *Cohen's Luck*
Garment workers
1915 The High Road
1916 Mister 44
1919 The End of the Road
David Garrick
1916 *David Garrick*
Garters
1916 Sunshine Dad
1920 *The Garter Girl*
Gas warfare
1918 *The German Curse in Russia*
      The Service Star
Gaya (India)
1920 *Stronger Than Death*
Gaza
1919 *With Allenby in Palestine and Lawrence in Arabia*
Geese
1919 *Day Dreams*
Geishas
1915 *The White Pearl*
1917 *The Door Between*
1918 A Japanese Nightingale
1919 A Heart in Pawn
      The Unwritten Code
Gem dealers
1914 The Master Cracksman
1917 *His Father's Son*
1920 *Children Not Wanted*
Gems
  rt **Diamonds**
        Jewelry
1913 The Lotus Dancer
1914 The Mystery of Richmond Castle
      Shannon of the Sixth
      The Spitfire
1916 *The Foolish Virgin*
      Spellbound
1917 *Betsy's Burglar*
      The Devil-Stone
      The Devil's Bait
      Double Room Mystery
1918 *High Stakes*
      Midnight Madness
      The Midnight Trail
      The Mystery Girl
      The Naulahka
      Vengeance
1919 *The Girl with No Regrets*
      The Trembling Hour
1920 A Full House
Genealogy
1920 Milestones

1916 Bluff
Her Father's Gold
Land O' Lizards
The Man from Bitter Roots
Silas Marner
The Spell of the Yukon
1917 *The Firefly of Tough Luck*
'49-'17
A Kentucky Cinderella
The Silent Man
1918 *Find the Woman*
Go West, Young Man
The Goddess of Lost Lake
Hoarded Assets
In Bad
Laughing Bill Hyde
1919 *The Great Air Robbery*
When a Girl Loves
When a Man Rides Alone
1920 Dead Men Tell No Tales
Fighting Cressy
The Sin That Was His
Two Kinds of Love
Wanted at Headquarters

Gold diggers
  rt **Adventuresses**
    Fortune hunters
    Vamps
1915 Bella Donna
The Cup of Life
The Girl from His Town
The Golden Claw
Jewel
When We Were Twenty-One
The Wolf of Debt
1916 *The Combat*
Diplomacy
The Drifter
The Fighting Chance
A Fool's Paradise
The Heir to the Hoorah
Her Maternal Right
The Highest Bid
The Scarlet Road
1917 *Peggy Leads the Way*
The Red Woman
1918 By Right of Purchase
The Guilt of Silence
Her Mistake
Limousine Life
One Thousand Dollars
The Wine Girl
1919 *The Echo of Youth*
The End of the Road
The Homebreaker
The Hushed Hour
Jane Goes A-Wooing
A Midnight Romance
Over the Garden Wall
Sealed Hearts
A Stitch in Time
Through the Wrong Door
Venus in the East
The World to Live In
1920 *A Beggar in Purple*
The Furnace

Gold miners
1914 Burning Daylight: The
Adventures of "Burning
Daylight" in Alaska
The Idler
1915 The Valley of Lost Hope
1916 The Argonauts of
California—1849
The Aryan
The Beckoning Trail
A Bird of Prey
1917 *The Easiest Way*
The Flame of the Yukon
The Golden Rosary
Master of His Home
Shall We Forgive Her?
1918 Naked Hands
1919 The Brand
Breezy Jim
The Girl from Outside

Gold mines
1914 Ready Money
The Three of Us
1915 *Chimmie Fadden Out West*
Colorado
1916 The Beckoning Trail
The Girl of the Lost Lake
The Highest Bid
Philip Holden—Waster

1917 Betty to the Rescue
The Highway of Hope
The Man from Montana
The Money Mill
Salt of the Earth
The Yellow Bullet
1918 *Code of the Yukon*
Laughing Bill Hyde
A Man's Man
Mickey
Social Ambition
1919 Desert Gold
Fighting for Gold
Fool's Gold
The Girl Alaska
The Mints of Hell
The Rider of the Law
When the Desert Smiles
1920 Blue Streak McCoy
The Discarded Woman
Drag Harlan
Girl of the Sea
The Inner Voice
Overland Red
Something New
The Terror

Gold mining
1912 *Atop of the World in Motion*
1913 The Tonopah Stampede for
Gold
1915 Little Pal
The Lone Star Rush

Gold rushes
1913 The Tonopah Stampede for
Gold
1914 Burning Daylight: The
Adventures of "Burning
Daylight" in Alaska
The Chechako
In the Days of the Thundering
Herd
1915 *The Girl of the Golden West*
The Lily of Poverty Flat
The Lone Star Rush
The Pageant of San Francisco
The Shooting of Dan McGrew
1916 The Argonauts of
California—1849
1918 Carmen of the Klondike
Closin' In
"Flare-Up" Sal
The Guilt of Silence
Hell's Crater
The Vigilantes
1919 The End of the Game
1920 *Burning Daylight*
Days of Daring

Goldsmiths
1918 Find the Woman

Golf
1915 *A Girl of Yesterday*
1917 *The Apple-Tree Girl*
His Sweetheart
1918 *Uneasy Money*
1919 *The Imp*

Gondolas and gondoliers
1915 *The House of the Lost Court*
The Italian

Good Friday
1915 *The Penitentes*

Good Samaritans
1913 Across the Continent
1914 *The House of Bondage*
1915 The Dawn of a Tomorrow
Father and the Boys
Hearts in Exile
1916 The Habit of Happiness
Mr. Goode, the Samaritan
The Sunbeam
1917 *Her New York*
1918 *The Fly God*
Wild Women
1919 The Challenge of Chance
A Dangerous Affair
Deliverance
The Hornet's Nest
The Lady of Red Butte
The Love Hunger
Marked Men
The Son-of-a-Gun!
The Speed Maniac
Square Deal Sanderson
Virtuous Sinners

1920 *Alias Miss Dodd*
*The Courage of Marge
O'Doone*
The Inner Voice
Pollyanna

Gorillas
1920 Go and Get It

Gossip
1914 *The Country Mouse*
Even unto Death
The School for Scandal
1915 *The Devil*
Gladiola
Scandal
1916 *Betty of Graystone*
A Circus Romance
The Daughter of MacGregor
The Girl with the Green Eyes
The Madcap
The Ninety and Nine
A Woman's Way
1917 Babbling Tongues
The Crab
Polly of the Circus
1918 Find the Woman
The Lonely Woman
A Man's World
The Silent Woman
The Strange Woman
Suspicion
1919 *Anne of Green Gables*
A Broadway Saint
Dawn
Dawn
The Misleading Widow
One of the Finest
Sue of the South
The Third Kiss
Thou Shalt Not
Trixie from Broadway
The Veiled Adventure
1920 *The Inferior Sex*
39 East
Whispers
The World and His Wife

Gossip columnists
1920 *Parlor, Bedroom and Bath*

Governesses
  rt **Nursemaids**
1914 Jane Eyre
1915 *The Lonesome Heart*
The Master of the House
1916 *East Lynne*
Gloriana
That Sort
What Happened at 22
1917 *An Amateur Orphan*
The Rose of Blood
Tears and Smiles
The Test of Womanhood
1918 A Daughter of the West
The Firebrand
The Man of Bronze
Out of the Night
Wanted, a Mother
*What Becomes of the
Children?*
Woman and Wife
1919 Bonds of Love
1920 *The City of Masks*
Guilty of Love
Her Story
His House in Order
Passers-By

Government agencies
1917 The Mysterious Mr. Tiller

Government agents
1913 *The Black Snake*
1914 America
The Boundary Rider
The $5,000,000 Counterfeiting
Plot
For the Honor of Old Glory;
Or, The Stars and Stripes in
Mexico
1915 *Chimmie Fadden Out West*
The End of the Road
The Folly of a Life of Crime
1916 The Beckoning Flame
Broken Chains
My Country First
The Patriot
1917 *The Girl Angle*
The Girl of the Timber Claims

In Again—Out Again
Richard the Brazen
The Silent Man
The Small Town Guy
The Tides of Fate
1918 *The Border Raiders*
The Burden of Proof
The Grey Parasol
Mr. Logan, U.S.A.
Swat the Spy
Western Blood
1919 Breezy Jim
The Heart of Wetona
The Pagan God
The Red Viper

Governors
  rt **State governors**
    Territorial governors
1916 *The Beckoning Flame*
The Man from Nowhere
1918 *Inside the Lines*
The One Woman
1919 *Erstwhile Susan*
The Last of the Duanes
The Lincoln Highwayman
Love and the Law
The Master Man
The Mother and the Law
Peppy Polly
The Praise Agent
Thunderbolts of Fate
Virtuous Sinners
Whitewashed Walls
1920 *The Mark of Zorro*
Rogues and Romance
19-- *Barnaby Lee*

Governors general
1918 *The Cross Bearer*
1920 Man and Woman (A. H.
Fischer Features, Inc.)
The Slim Princess

Graft
1915 The Fighting Hope
Fine Feathers
A Gentleman of Leisure
The High Hand
Up from the Depths
1916 *The City*
A Law unto Himself
The Rummy
A Son of Erin
1917 *The Barker*
The Downfall of a Mayor
The Prison Without Walls
1918 *The Midnight Patrol*
One More American
1919 Beating the Odds
A Fighting Colleen
The Mayor of Filbert

Edith Graham
1919 Auction of Souls

Grand Canyon
1914 *America*
1917 *God's Crucible*
A Modern Musketeer

Grand viziers
1914 *Fire and Sword*

Grandchildren
1915 God's Witness
The Wild Goose Chase
1916 *A Prince in a Pawnshop*
1917 Man and Beast
1918 Daughter Angele

Granddaughters
1913 *The Fortune Hunters*
1915 Still Waters
1916 A Child of Mystery
Nancy's Birthright
The Plow Girl
The Wharf Rat
1917 *The Book Agent*
The Little Terror
The Mate of the Sally Ann
The Night Workers
1918 Blue-Eyed Mary
The Last Rebel
Such a Little Pirate
Winning Grandma
1920 *Milestones*

Grandfathers
1914 *The Scales of Justice*
*Your Girl and Mine: A Woman
Suffrage Play*

Grocers
1919 The Lion's Den

Grocery stores
1915 *The Man Who Found Himself*
1916 *Pasquale*
1917 The Corner Grocer
Peggy Leads the Way
1919 Oh, You Women

Groves
1919 *The Valley of the Giants*

Guards
1914 *Ill Starred Babbie*
1915 *Du Barry*
The Eternal City
The Forbidden Adventure
Midnight at Maxim's
1916 *The Diamond Runners*
Don Quixote
Her American Prince
1917 *Intrigue*
1919 One of the Finest
The World Aflame
1920 *Little Miss Rebellion*

Guests
1918 *All Night*
1920 *The Thief*

Guides
1915 *Wild Life of America in Films*
1917 *The Bond of Fear*
High Finance
1919 *Blind Husbands*
The Jungle Trail
Told in the Hills
The Unveiling Hand
Wagon Tracks
1920 *The Purple Cipher*
The Silent Barrier

Guillotine
1914 *Charlotte Corday*
The Typhoon
1915 *Du Barry*
1919 The Brand of Judas

Guilt
rt **Conscience**
1912 Richard III
1913 *The Black Snake*
The Prisoner of Zenda
1914 The Avenging Conscience;
Thou Shalt Not Kill
A Lady of Quality
1915 *Eugene Aram*
Jim the Penman
Lady Audley's Secret
The Man Who Couldn't Beat
God
Sealed Lips
Should a Mother Tell?
Sin
The Sins of the Mothers
The Victory of Virtue
Wormwood
1916 East Lynne
The Eternal Sapho
The Eye of God
The Gods of Fate
The Green-Eyed Monster
Her Debt of Honor
The Heritage of Hate
Macbeth
Man and His Angel
The Marble Heart
The Silent Battle
Soul Mates
The Stolen Triumph
Tempest and Sunshine
Thou Art the Man
20,000 Leagues Under the Sea
Warning! The S.O.S. Call of
Humanity
Who Killed Joe Merrion?
1917 *The Bond of Fear*
Crime and Punishment
Heart Strings
The Iron Ring
The Kill-Joy
The Lifted Veil
A Night in New Arabia
Polly Put the Kettle On
The Price of Her Soul
Pride and the Devil
Tangled Lives
1918 The Argument
At the Mercy of Men
The Bells
The Better Half

Beyond the Shadows
The Claw
A Daughter of France
Fedora
*The Girl with the Champagne
Eyes*
The Guilty Man
Her Boy
Her Decision
Hidden Pearls
His Daughter Pays
In Judgment Of
*The Kaiser, the Beast of
Berlin*
A Man's World
Mrs. Slacker
Out of the Night
The Scarlet Road
A Son of Strife
1919 Mandarin's Gold
What Love Forgives
1920 The Devil's Garden
Love Without Question
Mothers of Men
The Sins of Rosanne

Gun accidents
rt **Firearms**
1913 *Caprice*
1915 *The Breath of Araby*
In the Shadow
The Labyrinth
The Man of Shame
The Quest
Should a Wife Forgive?
Sold
The Soul of Broadway
The Vow
1916 *Ambition*
The Country That God Forgot
The Heart of New York
Hoodoo Ann
Love's Toll
Playing with Fire
Slander
Vengeance Is Mine
A Woman's Daring
1917 *Back of the Man*
The Learnin' of Jim Benton
Pay Me
Reputation
A School for Husbands
Sleeping Fires
1918 *Gates of Gladness*
Thieves' Gold
The Two-Soul Woman
The Wolf and His Mate
1919 *The Scar*
1920 *Man's Plaything*

Gunfighters
1916 Hell's Hinges
Immediate Lee
The Mediator
1917 *The Blue Streak*
The Gun Fighter

Gunfights
1915 *Buckshot John*
The Folly of a Life of Crime
Little Pal
The Man Trail
On the Night Stage
The Shooting of Dan McGrew
1916 *Arms and the Woman*
Blue Blood and Red
Going Straight
Hell's Hinges
Immediate Lee
A Knight of the Range
The Mediator
A Romance of Billy Goat Hill
Rose of the Alley
The Three Godfathers
1917 *The Adopted Son*
Dead Shot Baker
The Gun Fighter
Her Fighting Chance
One Shot Ross
Pay Me
Seven Keys to Baldpate
The Square Deal Man
Straight Shooting
Sunlight's Last Raid
The Tides of Fate
1918 Blue Blazes Rawden
The Boss of the Lazy Y
Desert Law

The Home Trail
Hungry Eyes
The Phantom Riders
Staking His Life
Unclaimed Goods
Wolves of the Border
1919 *Bare Fists*
The Challenge of Chance
The Coming of the Law
A Man's Country
The She Wolf
Speedy Meade
Square Deal Sanderson
1920 *The Coast of Opportunity*
The Dead Line
The Deep Purple
Drag Harlan
Honeymoon Ranch
Lahoma
The Last Straw
The Orphan
Sand!
Sherry

Gunrunners
1916 A Million a Minute
1918 No Children Wanted

Guns
use **Firearms**

Gunshot wounds
1913 *Eighty Million Women Want-?*
1914 *Captain Swift*
Doc
The Invisible Power
The Voice at the Telephone
1915 *The Cheat*
The Closing Net
Colorado
Fighting Bob
The Fighting Hope
The Game of Three
The Girl of the Golden West
The Heart of the Blue Ridge
Her Triumph
His Turning Point
The House of Tears
The Outcast
When a Woman Loves
1916 *As in a Looking Glass*
The Beckoning Trail
Between Men
Children of the Feud
The Crippled Hand
Destiny's Toy
The Dividend
Don Quixote
For a Woman's Fair Name
The Great Problem
The Gringo
A Gutter Magdalene
The Habit of Happiness
The Heart of Nora Flynn
The Man Who Would Not Die
The Marriage Bond
Oliver Twist
The Path of Happiness
The Pillory
*The Redemption of Dave
Darcey*
A Romance of Billy Goat Hill
Rose of the Alley
The Sign of the Spade
Sins of Her Parent
*The Strength of Donald
McKenzie*
Tangled Hearts
Then I'll Come Back to You
*The Trail of the Lonesome
Pine*
The Velvet Paw
What Love Can Do
The Wild Girl of the Sierras
1917 *Heart's Desire*
Hell Morgan's Girl
Her Country's Call
Her Strange Wedding
The Iced Bullet
Kick in
Sands of Sacrifice
Shame
Sunlight's Last Raid
Wild Sumac
1918 *Back to the Woods*
Blue Blazes Rawden
A Broadway Scandal
Daybreak

A Desert Wooing
The Doctor and the Woman
Faith Endurin'
The Firebrand
The First Law
The Guilt of Silence
The Gun Woman
The Hand at the Window
Heart of the Wilds
Her Man
His Bonded Wife
Hungry Eyes
Lawless Love
The Law's Outlaw
The Man from Funeral Range
Paying His Debt
The Red-Haired Cupid
Riddle Gawne
The Scarlet Drop
The Sea Waif
Secret Strings
The Service Star
The Struggle Everlasting
Suspicion
The Temple of Dusk
Thieves' Gold
Tyrant Fear
Wild Honey
Wild Youth
The Woman Between Friends
1919 *The Black Gate*
Break the News to Mother
Breed of Men
Cowardice Court
Crooked Straight
The Cry of the Weak
Dangerous Waters
Eve in Exile
Forbidden
The Gray Towers Mystery
His Debt
Louisiana
The Peace of Roaring River
The Red Viper
The Sleeping Lion
The Splendid Sin
The Steel King
The Wicked Darling
You Never Know Your Luck
1920 *Black Is White*
The Blood Barrier
The Brand of Lopez
The Branding Iron
Children of Destiny
The Cradle of Courage
A Cumberland Romance
The Dwelling Place of Light
The Fighting Chance
Fighting Cressy
The Fighting Kentuckians
The Fighting Shepherdess
Forbidden Valley
The Gamesters
The Girl in Number 29
The Golden Trail
The Hidden Light
Huckleberry Finn
Love in the Wilderness
The Man from Nowhere
The Misfit Wife
Once to Every Woman

Nell Gwynne
1914 Nell Gwynne
1915 Mistress Nell

Gymnasiums
1918-19
Once to Every Man
1919 *Put Up Your Hands*

Gypsies
1913 Hoodman Blind
1914 The Redemption of David
Corson
Il Trovatore
The Woman in Black
1915 The Adventures of a Madcap
An American Gentleman
The Broken Law
Carmen (Fox Film Corp.)
*Carmen (Jesse L. Lasky
Feature Play Co.)*
The Goose Girl
Hearts of Men
Kilmeny
The Little Gypsy
Mignon

His Bonded Wife
Little Miss No-Account
The Man Hunt
T'Other Dear Charmer
The Two-Soul Woman
Under the Greenwood Tree
Uneasy Money
Up the Road with Sallie
Woman and the Law
1919 *An Amateur Widow*
The Belle of the Season
The Brand of Judas
Dawn
Diane of the Green Van
Her Purchase Price
The House of Intrigue
The Miracle of Love
A Society Exile
The Third Kiss
Turning the Tables
Upstairs
1920 *Black Shadows*
Blind Love
The Butterfly Man
The Fortune Hunter
Forty-Five Minutes from
Broadway
The Fourteenth Man
His Wife's Money
Husbands and Wives
Merely Mary Ann
Passion's Playground
The Romance Promoters
She Loves and Lies
Something Different

Heirs
  rt **Disinheritance**
       Heiresses
       Inheritance
       Wills
1914 The Kangaroo
The Making of Bobby Burnit
The Port of Missing Men
1915 *The Daughter of the Sea*
Dora Thorne
The Girl from His Town
The Grandee's Ring
The Hungarian Nabob
Jack Chanty
The Morals of Marcus
The Unknown
1916 The Heir to the Hoorah
John Needham's Double
Lonesome Town
Love's Lariat
Love's Pilgrimage to America
The Net
Pudd'nhead Wilson
The River of Romance
The Shop Girl
The Suspect
The Turmoil
1917 Annie-for-Spite
The Argyle Case
Easy Money
Every Girl's Dream
Kidnapped
Lost in Transit
The Marriage Speculation
The Medicine Man
Miss U.S.A.
One Hour
Paradise Garden
S.O.S.
The Siren
Wee Lady Betty
1918 The Demon
The Eyes of Julia Deep
The Family Skeleton
The Greatest Thing in Life
A Mother's Sin
The Naulahka
Society for Sale
A Soul in Trust
Uneasy Money
1919 *La Belle Russe*
Fighting for Gold
The Glorious Lady
The Hand Invisible
Her Game
Love Insurance
Me and Captain Kidd
Silent Strength
The Teeth of the Tiger
The Unknown Quantity

A Yankee Princess
1920 *Democracy*
From Now On
The House of the Tolling Bell
Rookie's Return
Sherry

Karl Helffrich
1915 *System, the Secret of Success*
Hell
1915 *Black Fear*
The Devil
The Magic Skin
The Warning
1916 *The Black Crook*
The Devil's Bondwoman
1918 To Hell with the Kaiser
Arthur Henderson
1919 *Free Russia*
Henry IV, King of France, 1553-1610
1914 *The Fatal Night*
Henry VIII, King of England, 1491-1547
1912 *Richard III*
1915 *Queen and Adventurer*
Herbs
1916 *The Witch*
Hereditary tendencies
1915 Heritage
The Sins of the Mothers
1916 *The Ballet Girl*
Inherited Passions
The Silent Battle
The Social Highwayman
1917 The Black Stork
The Brand of Satan
Fear Not
A Game of Wits
The Girl in the Checkered Coat
Hate
Married in Name Only
1918 Blue Blood
The Danger Mark
High Tide
In Judgment Of
The Menace
1918-19
Once to Every Man
1919 The Avalanche
A Dangerous Affair
The Fear Woman
The Greater Sinner
A Heart in Pawn
The Love Auction
The Moonshine Trail
The Scarlet Shadow
Hereditary traits
1918 The Face in the Dark
The Family Skeleton
Heredity
1913 The Seed of the Fathers
Tess of the D'Urbervilles
1914 Northern Lights
1915 Prohibition
The Secret Orchard
1916 *The Fighting Chance*
The Hand of Peril
1918 The Scarlet Trail
1920 The Harvest Moon
Heresy
1916 *The Birth of Character*
1920 *A Sister to Salome*
Hermits
1914 The Land of the Lost
1915 The Disciple
1916 The Destroyers
1917 *Barbary Sheep*
Daughter of Maryland
*John Ermine of the
Yellowstone*
1918 *A Nymph of the Foothills*
One Dollar Bid
1919 Good Gracious, Annabelle
The Heart of Juanita
1920 *The Girl of My Heart*
Two Kinds of Love
Heroes
  rt **War heroes**
1919 The Man Who Stayed at Home
Heroin
1914 The Spirit of the Poppy

Heroism
  rt **Courage**
1914 *The Ordeal*
1915 Four Feathers
The Girl I Left Behind Me
The Lamb
The Man Behind the Door
*The Man Who Couldn't Beat
God*
My Valet
The Puppet Crown
Right off the Bat
The Rights of Man: A Story of
War's Red Blotch
Rosemary
The Scarlet Sin
The Sentimental Lady
A Soldier's Oath
The Spender
A Yellow Streak
1916 *Behind the Lines*
The Brand of Cowardice
The Deserter
Don Quixote
The Hero of Submarine D-2
The Highest Bid
His Great Triumph
His Picture in the Papers
Joan the Woman
The Parson of Panamint
Prudence the Pirate
The Red Widow
The Wall Between
1917 The Courage of the Common
Place
The Darling of Paris
For the Freedom of the World
Her Country's Call
In Again—Out Again
Jack and Jill
The Little American
The Little Patriot
Might and the Man
Over There
Pots-and-Pans Peggy
The Princess' Necklace
Redemption
The Scarlet Pimpernel
The Slacker (Peter P. Jones
Film Co.)
Up or Down?
The Woman and the Beast
1918 The Beloved Blackmailer
The Border Wireless
Empty Pockets
Fast Company
Her Country First
The Hired Man
Hitting the High Spots
Humdrum Brown
I'll Say So
Kidder and Ko
Marriages Are Made
On the Jump
Peg of the Pirates
The Price of Applause
The Source
The Spirit of '17
1919 Adele
Boots
The Common Cause
The Fall of Babylon
Ginger
In Wrong
Life's Greatest Problem
Male and Female
Never Say Quit
The New Moon
Nugget Nell
Out Yonder
The Petal on the Current
The Sawdust Doll
The Sheriff's Son
Treat 'Em Rough
Twilight
A Wild Goose Chase
1920 *The Butterfly Man*
Circumstantial Evidence
The Daredevil
The Devil's Garden
Girls Don't Gamble
Just Pals
The Mark of Zorro
Pink Tights
The Price of Redemption

Sherry
The Song of the Soul
Herring
1919 *Married in Haste*
Herzegovina
1914 Such a Little Queen
Hessians
1914 *Washington at Valley Forge*
Highwaymen
1916 Society Wolves
Tennessee's Pardner
1917 Peggy, the Will O' the Wisp
1918 The Fly God
Thieves' Gold
1919 In Mizzoura
The Lincoln Highwayman
Himalayas
1919 *The Man Who Won*
Paul von Hindenburg
1915 *On the Firing Line with the
Germans*
1916 *War on Three Fronts*
1918 *Crashing Through to Berlin*
1919 Yankee Doodle in Berlin
Hindus
  rt **East Indians**
1913 The Lotus Dancer
The Star of India
1914 The Quest of the Sacred Jewel
Shannon of the Sixth
The Woman of Mystery
1915 *The Bulldogs of the Trail*
1916 The Beckoning Flame
The Dawn of Freedom
The Leopard's Bride
Less Than the Dust
Spellbound
Sunshine Dad
1917 Each to His Kind
Infidelity
Lady Barnacle
1918 *A Bit of Jade*
Vengeance
1919 *For a Woman's Honor*
The Man Beneath
The Phantom Honeymoon
1920 *Children Not Wanted*
The Devil's Claim
The Sacred Ruby
The Sleep of Cyma Roget
Twisted Souls
Hippodrome Theater (New York City)
1914 America
Hired hands
1915 *The Pretenders*
1916 *The Microscope Mystery*
The Ragged Princess
1918 The Hired Man
A Hoosier Romance
How Could You, Jean?
1920 The County Fair
The Desperate Hero
The Village Sleuth
Hired killers
1913 *A Sister to Carmen*
1914 *Neptune's Daughter*
1915 *Princess Romanoff*
1916 Flirting with Fate
The Heart of New York
The Man Who Would Not Die
*The Strength of Donald
McKenzie*
1917 *The Barker*
The Terror
1918 *Kultur*
M'liss
Rose O' Paradise
The Trail to Yesterday
Untamed
1919 Some Liar
The Tong Man
1920 *The Girl of My Heart*
Hoarding
1915 The Daughter of the People
Hoaxes
1915 Blackbirds
Buckshot John
A Bunch of Keys
Chimmie Fadden Out West
The Earl of Pawtucket
The Fixer
Jane
The Mating
One Million Dollars

1916 *Arms and the Woman*
Civilization's Child
The Criminal
The Fall of a Nation
The Gilded Spider
Gretchen, the Greenhorn
Hulda from Holland
Light at Dusk
Love's Pilgrimage to America
Man and His Angel
The Morals of Hilda
Pasquale
Sold for Marriage
A Son of Erin
The Woman in 47
A Woman's Honor
1917 *Hashimura Togo*
His Sweetheart
A Roadside Impresario
The Tell-Tale Step
The Trouble Buster
Unknown 274
The Woman and the Beast
1918 *The Bravest Way*
Denny from Ireland
Fields of Honor
The Golden Wall
Her Moment
His Royal Highness
The Million Dollar Mystery
One More American
The Ordeal of Rosetta
Out of a Clear Sky
Sandy
Tony America
1919 *Deliverance*
The Lord Loves the Irish
Who's Your Brother?
A Yankee Princess
Yvonne from Paris
1920 Behold My Wife
The Cup of Fury
Darling Mine
Dinty
The Face at Your Window
The Greatest Love
Hidden Charms
Lifting Shadows
The Riddle: Woman
The Secret Gift
19-- The Slave Market

Immortality
1917 She
1918 The Triumph of Venus

Impeachment
1913 The Shame of the Empire State
1914 The Lion and the Mouse
1915 The Governor's Boss
1919 The Lion and the Mouse

Imperialism
1915 *The Campbells Are Coming*

Impersonation and imposture
  rt **Deception**
    Disguise
    Doubles
    Female impersonation
    Male impersonation
    Mistaken identity
1913 *Caprice*
The Fight for Millions
The Fortune Hunters
An Hour Before Dawn
The Prisoner of Zenda
Shadows of the Moulin Rouge
The Stranglers of Paris
1914 Across the Pacific
La Belle Russe
The Burglar and the Lady
Called Back
Captain Swift
The Circus Man
The Education of Mr. Pipp
False Colours
Hearts United
In the Name of the Prince of Peace
The Kangaroo
The Lightning Conductor
The Little Jewess
The Littlest Rebel
Lord Chumley
The Man from Home
The Man from Mexico
The Man on the Box
The Master Cracksman

Michael Strogoff
The Million
A Mother's Heart
My Official Wife
The Mystery of Richmond Castle
Officer 666
The Port of Missing Men
The Pride of Jennico
The Reign of Terror
The Rejuvenation of Aunt Mary
The School for Scandal
The Spy
Three Weeks
Trapped in the Great Metropolis
The Unwelcome Mrs. Hatch
Uriel Acosta
Without Hope
Wolfe; Or, The Conquest of Quebec
The Woman in Black
1915 Alias Jimmy Valentine
An American Gentleman
The Apaches of Paris
Are You a Mason?
The Billionaire Lord
Blackbirds
A Bunch of Keys
The Caprices of Kitty
The Cave Man
The Dawn of a Tomorrow
The Dictator
The Earl of Pawtucket
The End of the Road
The Fighting Hope
The Fixer
The Flash of an Emerald
Four Feathers
The Galloper
The Game of Three
The Garden of Lies
The Girl of the Golden West
The Goose Girl
The Gray Mask
The Great Ruby
Gretna Green
Heartaches
Hearts in Exile
Heléne of the North
The House of Tears
The Impostor
In the Palace of the King
The Iron Strain
Jane
The Labyrinth
The Life of Sam Davis: A Confederate Hero of the Sixties
Little Miss Brown
The Lost House
Maciste
The Making Over of Geoffrey Manning
The Man Trail
The Man Who Found Himself
The Man Who Vanished
Marrying Money
Mary's Lamb
The Master Hand
Mr. Grex of Monte Carlo
My Best Girl
My Valet
The Nation's Peril
Nedra
Old Dutch
Over Night
Pennington's Choice
The Politicians
Poor Schmaltz
The Price of Her Silence
The Prince and the Pauper
The Pursuing Shadow
A Royal Family
Sam Davis, the Hero of Tennessee
Secretary of Frivolous Affairs
Seven Sisters
Should a Wife Forgive?
The Slim Princess
A Soldier's Oath
The Soul of Broadway
The Spender
Stolen Goods

Stop Thief!
Strathmore
A Submarine Pirate
The Tale of the Night Before
To Cherish and Protect
A Trade Secret
The Unfaithful Wife
The Unknown
The Voice in the Fog
What Happened to Jones
The Wheels of Justice
Who's Who in Society
The Wild Goose Chase
The Wild Olive
The Wonderful Adventure
A Yellow Streak
Young Romance
1916 *According to the Code*
The Adventures of Kathlyn
American Aristocracy
And the Law Says
Ashes of Embers
Bobbie of the Ballet
The Catspaw
A Circus Romance
The City of Failing Light
The Daring of Diana
The Dawn of Love
The Dead Alive
The Devil's Bondwoman
The Devil's Prayer-Book
The Dream Girl
The Drifter
The Dumb Girl of Portici
The Eternal Question
The Evil Women Do
The Feast of Life
The Female of the Species
For the Defense
The Fortunate Youth
The Foundling
The Gates of Eden
The Gilded Cage
The Golden Chance
The Heart of a Hero
Her Double Life
In the Diplomatic Service
An Innocent Magdalene
Into the Primitive
The Intrigue
The Island of Surprise
John Needham's Double
The Lash of Destiny
The Light of Happiness
Little Lady Eileen
The Love Mask
Madame La Presidente
The Mainspring
A Man of Sorrow
The Man Who Would Not Die
The Masked Rider
The Matrimonial Martyr
A Million a Minute
Miss Jackie of the Navy
My Lady Incog.
The Other Girl
Other People's Money
The Phantom Buccaneer
Phantom Fortunes
The Plow Girl
The Pretenders
The Price of Fame
The Red Widow
Reggie Mixes In
The Rise of Susan
Rolling Stones
The Scarlet Oath
The Sign of the Poppy
Somewhere in France
The Soul Market
A Stranger from Somewhere
Sunshine Dad
The Suspect
Through the Wall
The Truant Soul
Vultures of Society
The Wager
Wanted—A Home
The Weakness of Man
What Happened at 22
When Love Is King
A Wife's Sacrifice
The Woman in the Case
The Woman's Law
The Yaqui

The Yellow Passport
Youth's Endearing Charm
1917 The Adventurer
An Alabaster Box
Aladdin from Broadway
Alias Mrs. Jessop
All for a Husband
An Amateur Orphan
The Antics of Ann
Arsene Lupin
Bab's Diary
The Barker
Behind the Mask
Betty Be Good
Beware of Strangers
Blind Man's Luck
Borrowed Plumage
The Bottom of the Well
Brand's Daughter
The Bride of Hate
Bringing Home Father
The Broadway Sport
Castles for Two
The Checkmate
Cheerful Givers
Chicken Casey
Chris and His Wonderful Lamp
The Cinderella Man
The Clever Mrs. Carfax
The Clock
The Co-Respondent
The Countess Charming
The Deemster
The Divorcee
The Duchess of Doubt
The Dummy
Fighting Odds
The Fires of Youth
For the Freedom of the World
A Game of Wits
The Girl Angle
The Girl from Rector's
The Girl Who Couldn't Grow Up
The Girl Without a Soul
The Greatest Power
Her Father's Keeper
Her Fighting Chance
The Hero of the Hour
High Finance
The High Sign
Hinton's Double
His Father's Son
His Mother's Boy
His Old-Fashioned Dad
The Hunting of the Hawk
In Again—Out Again
Indiscreet Corinne
Infidelity
A Kiss for Susie
The Little Duchess
The Lone Wolf
Madame Sherry
The Man from Painted Post
The Man Who Took a Chance
The Marriage Speculation
The Message of the Mouse
Might and the Man
The Millionaire's Double
Miss Deception
Miss Nobody
Mr. Dolan of New York
Molly Entangled
The Mysterious Miss Terry
The Mysterious Mr. Tiller
The Mystery of Number 47
The Narrow Trail
New York Luck
A Night in New Arabia
The Page Mystery
Pants
The Phantom's Secret
Polly Put the Kettle On
Polly Redhead
Pride
The Prison Without Walls
Rasputin, the Black Monk
The Reward of the Faithless
A Rich Man's Plaything
Richard the Brazen
A Romance of the Redwoods
Royal Romance
Runaway Romany
Sally in a Hurry

The Scarlet Pimpernel
A Self-Made Widow
The Siren
A Square Deal
The Square Deceiver
Susan's Gentleman
Sweetheart of the Doomed
Sylvia of the Secret Service
Thou Shalt Not Steal
Threads of Fate
Under False Colors
The Understudy
The Upper Crust
The Voice of Conscience
Who Was the Other Man?
The Winning of Sally Temple
Womanhood, the Glory of the
  Nation
Wooden Shoes
1918 All Night
Annexing Bill
Back to the Woods
The Beloved Impostor
Berlin Via America
The Better Half
Betty Takes a Hand
Beyond the Shadows
Boston Blackie's Little Pal
The Brass Check
The Brazen Beauty
The Cabaret Girl
The Cast-Off
Crown Jewels
The Danger Game
Daughter Angele
The Divine Sacrifice
The Embarrassment of Riches
The Eyes of Mystery
The Fair Pretender
False Ambition
$5,000 Reward
The Flames of Chance
"Flare-Up" Sal
Free and Equal
Gates of Gladness
The Girl from Beyond
The Girl of Today
The Goddess of Lost Lake
Good Night, Paul
The Grey Parasol
The Guilty Wife
The Gun Woman
He Comes Up Smiling
Headin' South
Hell Bent
Her Aviator
Her Boy
Her Country First
Her Inspiration
Hidden Fires
His Bonded Wife
His Own Home Town
His Royal Highness
Hobbs in a Hurry
How Could You, Jean?
Humility
The Impostor
In Pursuit of Polly
Inside the Lines
Jilted Janet
Just for Tonight
Just Sylvia
Kidder and Ko
The King of Diamonds
Lafayette, We Come!
Lawless Love
Lend Me Your Name
Little Miss Hoover
A Little Sister of Everybody
The Love Net
The Love Swindle
The Man Hunt
The Marriage Lie
The Mating of Marcella
Midnight Madness
The Midnight Trail
Miss Mischief Maker
Mr. Fix-It
Mrs. Dane's Defense
M'liss
Molly, Go Get 'Em
Money Mad
The Moral Law
A Mother's Sin
My Unmarried Wife

The Mysterious Mr. Browning
Nobody's Wife
The Painted Lily
Pals First
The Pretender
The Primitive Woman
The Prodigal Wife
The Ranger
A Rich Man's Darling
A Romance of the Air
The Rose of the World
The Sea Flower
Secret Strings
The Service Star
Set Free
She Hired a Husband
The Shell Game
Shifting Sands
Social Quicksands
The Song of Songs
A Successful Adventure
The Thing We Love
Till I Come Back to You
To Hell with the Kaiser
T'Other Dear Charmer
Twenty-One
Unexpected Places
When Do We Eat?
Who Is to Blame?
Wild Primrose
The Winding Trail
With Neatness and Dispatch
Wolves of the Rail
The Yellow Ticket
You Can't Believe Everything
1919 An Adventure in Hearts
The Adventure Shop
Alias Mike Moran
All of a Sudden Norma
Almost Married
An Amateur Widow
The Amazing Impostor
The Amazing Wife
The American Way
L'Apache
A Bachelor's Wife
La Belle Russe
The Best Man
Bonds of Honor
Boots
Brass Buttons
Breezy Jim
The Burning Question
The Captain's Captain
Cheating Cheaters
The Cinema Murder
Come Out of the Kitchen
Courage for Two
The Crook of Dreams
Cupid Forecloses
The Delicious Little Devil
The Exquisite Thief
The False Code
The False Faces
Fighting Destiny
Fighting for Gold
The Fire Flingers
Flame of the Desert
The Follies Girl
Fools and Their Money
A Fugitive from Matrimony
The Game's Up
Getting Mary Married
The Girl Dodger
The Haunted Bedroom
Hell Roarin' Reform
The Hellion
Her Game
Her Purchase Price
The Hidden Truth
The Highest Trump
His Bridal Night
His Official Fiancée
The Homebreaker
The Hornet's Nest
The House of Intrigue
Human Passions
The Imp
In His Brother's Place
In Old Kentucky
In Search of Arcady
The Island of Intrigue
Johnny Get Your Gun
Johnny-on-the-Spot
The Joyous Liar

The Jungle Trail
Keali
The Knickerbocker Buckaroo
Leave It to Susan
The Lincoln Highwayman
The Little Intruder
The Lone Wolf's Daughter
The Lost Princess
Louisiana
The Love Burglar
The Love Cheat
The Love Hunger
Love Insurance
Luck in Pawn
The Man Who Turned White
Man's Desire
The Mayor of Filbert
A Midnight Romance
The Miracle Man
The Misleading Widow
Molly of the Follies
The Moral Deadline
More Deadly Than the Male
My Little Sister
The New Moon
One Against Many
One Week of Life
Our Better Selves
The Pagan God
The Parisian Tigress
Peggy Does Her Darndest
The Poor Boob
The Prince and Betty
The Prodigal Liar
Putting One Over
Red Blood and Yellow
A Rogue's Romance
Sadie Love
Sandy Burke of the U-Bar-U
Secret Service
Some Bride
Something to Do
Speedy Meade
Square Deal Sanderson
Suspense
The Third Kiss
Toby's Bow
Too Many Crooks
A Trick of Fate
Turning the Tables
The Twin Pawns
Under Suspicion
The Uplifters
The Veiled Adventure
Wanted—A Husband
When a Girl Loves
When Doctors Disagree
When Men Desire
A White Man's Chance
Widow by Proxy
Wild Oats
The Winchester Woman
The Woman Next Door
The Woman of Lies
A Yankee Princess
You're Fired
Yvonne from Paris
1920 Alarm Clock Andy
Alias Miss Dodd
Always Audacious
April Folly
The Beggar Prince
Big Happiness
Billions
Black Is White
The Broadway Bubble
Captain Swift
The Dangerous Paradise
The Dangerous Talent
A Daughter of Two Worlds
The Desperate Hero
A Double Dyed Deceiver
Double Speed
Duds
Easy to Get
813
Faith
Flying Pat
The Girl with the Jazz Heart
Go and Get It
Going Some
Good References
Hearts Up
Help Wanted—Male
Her Five-Foot Highness

Her Unwilling Husband
Homer Comes Home
Huckleberry Finn
In Search of a Sinner
Jack Straw
Love Madness
The Man Who Lost Himself
A Manhattan Knight
The Mark of Zorro
Mary's Ankle
The Master Mind
Miss Hobbs
Mrs. Temple's Telegram
Molly and I
Number 99
Nurse Marjorie
Officer 666
Other Men's Shoes
The Phantom Melody
Polly with a Past
Respectable by Proxy
Riders of the Dawn
The River's End
The Servant in the House
The Servant Question
She Loves and Lies
Silk Hosiery
The Sin That Was His
The Sins of St. Anthony
The Square Shooter
Stop Thief
The Third Generation
The Toll Gate
Too Much Johnson
The Triflers
The Unknown Ranger
The Village Sleuth
Voices
The Walk-Offs
Wanted at Headquarters
What Happened to Jones
While New York Sleeps
Why Women Sin
Wits vs. Wits
The Woman Game
The Wonderful Chance

Importers
1915 Help Wanted
1916 *Alien Souls*
     The Social Buccaneer
1918 *Her American Husband*
     The Song of Songs
1919 The Four-Flusher

Impresari
1915 *The Girl from His Town*
     Temptation
1916 *The Price of Happiness*
     The Yellow Passport
1917 *The Dancer's Peril*
1918 *Maid O' the Storm*
1920 Greater Than Fame

Imprisonment
1913 The Count of Monte Cristo
     A Princess of Bagdad
1914 *Beating Back*
     The Chechako
     The Criminal Path
     Damon and Pythias
     Detective Craig's Coup
     Dope
     The $5,000,000 Counterfeiting
       Plot
     The Gangsters
     The Hand of Destiny
     Jane Eyre
     Joseph and His Coat of Many
       Colors
     The Mysterious Mr. Wu Chung
       Foo
     Neptune's Daughter
     An Odyssey of the North
     The Pride of Jennico
     The Reign of Terror
     The Seats of the Mighty
     Shorty Escapes Marriage
     The Taint
     The Tigress
     The Valley of the Moon
     The Woman of Mystery
1915 *The Boss*
     Buckshot John
     Carmen (Fox Film Corp.)
     Du Barry
     The Face in the Moonlight

The Failure
The Fighting Hope
The Forbidden Adventure
Forbidden Fruit
The Girl of the Golden West
The Glory of Youth
Greater Love Hath No Man
The House of the Lost Court
In the Palace of the King
The Italian
Keep Moving
The Man of Shame
The Man Who Found Himself
May Blossom
The Melting Pot
Mignon
The Morals of Marcus
My Madonna
Not Guilty
The Rug Maker's Daughter
Rumpelstiltskin
The Sable Lorcha
Saved from the Harem
Sealed Lips
The Siren's Song
A Soldier's Oath
The Soul of Broadway
Stolen Goods
What Happened to Father
The Wheels of Justice
The White Scar
The Wild Goose Chase
The Woman Who Lied
1916 *Anton the Terrible*
Ashes of Embers
Big Jim Garrity
The Birth of Character
The Black Crook
The Bondman
The Captive God
The Challenge
A Child of the Paris Streets
The Code of Marcia Gray
The Daring of Diana
The Deserter
The End of the Trail
Extravagance
The Eye of God
Fighting Blood
The Fourth Estate
The Gilded Cage
The Great Problem
The Gringo
The Half Million Bribe
Her American Prince
Her Husband's Wife
His Great Triumph
The Honorable Friend
The Idol of the Stage
An Innocent Magdalene
Love Never Dies
Lovely Mary
Love's Pilgrimage to America
The Man Inside
Maria Rosa
The Mark of Cain
The Matrimaniac
The Mirror of Life
My Lady's Slipper
The Ne'er-Do-Well
The Prima Donna's Husband
The Primal Lure
The Seekers
The Shadow of a Doubt
The Stain in the Blood
The Sunbeam
The Supreme Sacrifice
Temptation and the Man
The Test
To Have and to Hold
The Victim
Vultures of Society
War Brides
The Wheel of the Law
The Woman in the Case
A Woman's Daring
A Woman's Fight
The World Against Him
The Wrong Door
1917 *The Bitter Truth*
Fighting Odds
The Gates of Doom
The Hand That Rocks the Cradle
Heart Strings

Her Country's Call
Her Life and His
Her Official Fathers
Hinton's Double
The Honor System
In Again—Out Again
In the Hands of the Law
Infidelity
Jack and the Beanstalk
Light in Darkness
Like Wildfire
Love's Law
A Phantom Husband
The Price of Silence
A Roadside Impresario
The Saintly Sinner
Sapho
The Silent Master
The Sixteenth Wife
Snap Judgement
Society's Driftwood
The Spindle of Life
A Tale of Two Cities
Think It Over
The Tides of Fate
Trooper 44
The Vicar of Wakefield
War and the Woman
What Money Can't Buy
The Wild Girl
Within the Law
Wrath
1917-18
The Devil's Playground
1918 *All Man*
Among the Cannibal Isles of the South Pacific
Beyond the Law
The Bird of Prey
Blindfolded
Blue Blood
The Border Raiders
Bound in Morocco
The Bride of Fear
By Hook or Crook
The Caillaux Case
Crown Jewels
Desert Law
Deuce Duncan
Eight Bells
The Eleventh Commandment
The Firebrand
For Freedom
The Girl from Beyond
The Girl Who Wouldn't Quit
Good-Bye, Bill
The Grouch
Her Country First
Her One Mistake
The Hun Within
Just a Woman
The Kid Is Clever
Little Miss No-Account
The Midnight Trail
Miss Innocence
Money Mad
The Mysterious Client
Salome
The Sea Panther
The She-Devil
Shifting Sands
Stella Maris
Tangled Lives
The Testing of Mildred Vane
To Him That Hath
Treasure of the Sea
The Triumph of Venus
Under the Greenwood Tree
Wedlock
The Wife He Bought
The Wild Strain
Woman and Wife
1920 *Dad's Girl*
Excuse My Dust
Eyes of the Heart
Good References
Polly of the Storm Country
The Price of Silence
The Scoffer
She Couldn't Help It
Thou Art the Man
What's Your Husband Doing?

In-laws
rt Specific types of relationships by marriage
1917 The Tar Heel Warrior
1919 Bonds of Love
1920 The Misfit Wife
Thoughtless Women
Inca Indians
1914 *The Captain Besley Expedition*
1915 In the Amazon Jungles with the Captain Besley Expedition
1917 *The Flaming Omen*
Thomas H. Ince Studios
1917 *The Iced Bullet*
Incense
1920 Locked Lips
Incest
1915 Her Mother's Secret
A Mother's Confession
1916 *The City*
1917 *Hands up!*
Kitty MacKay
The Spirit of '76
1918 *The Law That Divides*
1920 Do the Dead Talk?
Income tax
rt Taxes
1919 *I'll Get Him Yet*
Incurable illness
1915 *Milestones of Life*
Simon, the Jester
1916 The Closed Road
The Fugitive
Her Debt of Honor
1917 *Has Man the Right to Kill?*
1918 The Scarlet Trail
Indentured servants
1914 The Hoosier Schoolmaster
1918 One Dollar Bid
India
1913 The Lotus Dancer
The Star of India
1914 *The Quest of the Sacred Jewel*
The School for Scandal
1915 *One Million Dollars*
The Sporting Duchess
The Toast of Death
1916 *The Adventures of Kathlyn*
The Beckoning Flame
The Beggar of Cawnpore
The Heart of Tara
The Heart of the Hills
The Leopard's Bride
Less Than the Dust
The Light
The Ruling Passion
Thou Art the Man
20,000 Leagues Under the Sea
1917 Each to His Kind
God's Law and Man's
Lady Barnacle
1918 The Naulahka
The Rose of the World
The Safety Curtain
Vengeance
1919 For a Woman's Honor
A Gentleman of Quality
The Man Beneath
The Secret Garden
The Witness for the Defense
The Woman Thou Gavest Me
1920 *Conrad in Quest of His Youth*
The Palace of Darkened Windows
The Price of Redemption
Stronger Than Death
India—History—Sepoy Rebellion, 1857-1858
1915 *The Campbells Are Coming*
1916 *The Beggar of Cawnpore*
The Victoria Cross
Indian agents
1917 *The Squaw Man's Son*
Wild and Woolly
Indian reservations
1916 *Her Debt of Honor*
1917 The Squaw Man's Son
1918 Indian Life

Indian Territory
1917 *The Hidden Children*
Indiana
1914 *The Hoosier Schoolmaster*
1915 The Gentleman from Indiana
1916 *A Son of the Immortals*
1918 *A Hoosier Romance*
1919 *A Little Brother of the Rich*
Indiana—History
1916 Indiana
Indians (persons from India)
use East Indians
Indians—Mixed blood
1915 *The Buzzard's Shadow*
A Child of God
Heléne of the North
Jack Chanty
1916 The Dawn Maker
The Half-Breed
Nanette of the Wilds
Ramona
1917 The Barrier
The Danger Trail
The Gun Fighter
Her Own People
The Jury of Fate
The Law of the North
The Plow Woman
The Savage
The Spirit of '76
The Squaw Man's Son
Wild Sumac
1918 *Baree, Son of Kazan*
Broken Ties
Laughing Bill Hyde
The Squaw Man
Tongues of Flame
1919 *The Gray Towers Mystery*
The Heart of Wetona
In the Land of the Setting Sun; Or, Martyrs of Yesterday
Jacques of the Silver North
Just Squaw
The Light of Victory
Rose of the West
The Westerners
The Wilderness Trail
The Wolf
1920 Behold My Wife
Out of the Snows
The Stranger
The Third Woman
Indians of Central America
nt Specific tribes
1915 The Footsteps of Capt. Kidd
The Penitentes
1920 On the Trail of the Conquistadores
Indians of North America
nt Specific tribes
1913 *The Call of the Blood*
Hiawatha
1914 Across the Pacific
The Call of the North
The Chechako
Fighting Death
The Good-for-Nothing
Hearts United
In the Days of the Thundering Herd
In the Land of the Head Hunters
The Indian Wars
Life's Shop Window
The Little Angel of Canyon Creek
The Lust of the Red Man
The Man on the Box
Northern Lights
The Outlaw Reforms
Pierre of the Plains
Sitting Bull—The Hostile Sioux Indian Chief
The Squaw Man
Where the Trail Divides
The Wolf
1915 *A Continental Girl*
The Cowpuncher
The Eagle's Nest
Environment
The Gambler of the West
Life of American Indian sic
The Lure of Woman
Sealed Valley

The Woman Gives
The Woman in Room 13
The Woman in the Suitcase
A Woman Who Understood
A Woman's Business
Women Men Forget
Women Men Love
The World and His Wife
A World of Folly
Would You Forgive?
The Wrong Woman
You Never Can Tell
Young Mrs. Winthrop
Youthful Folly
1921 *Midsummer Madness*

Infirmaries
1917 *The Innocent Sinner*

Informers
1914 *The Circus Man*
The Greyhound
The Three of Us
1915 *The Curious Conduct of Judge Legarde*
1916 *The Catspaw*
The Dawn of Love
1917 *Trooper 44*
Within the Law
1918 *The Moral Law*
The Ranger
1919 *Eastward Ho!*
The Forfeit
Red Blood and Yellow
The Stronger Vow
Virtuous Sinners
1920 The Gray Brother

Ingenues
1914 Wildflower
1915 The Deep Purple
The Failure
For $5,000 a Year
The Little Dutch Girl
The Secret Orchard
Still Waters
The Victory of Virtue
1916 Destiny's Toy
1917 Her Greatest Love
Indiscretion
Lorelei of the Sea
The Rescue
Rosie O'Grady
1918 For Husbands Only
How Could You, Caroline?
Miss Innocence
Social Briars
1919 *Nugget Nell*
1920 A Lady in Love
Mary Ellen Comes to Town

Ingratitude
rt **Gratitude**
1916 King Lear
1917 Mother O' Mine
1919 *The Gay Old Dog*

Inheritance
rt **Disinheritance**
Heiresses
Heirs
Wills
1913 *Hoodman Blind*
The Rogues of Paris
1914 An American Citizen
Behind the Scenes
Brewster's Millions
The Brute
Called Back
Clothes
The Floor Above
The Good-for-Nothing
The Idler
The Making of Bobby Burnit
The Money Lender
The Monster and the Girl
The Mystery of Richmond Castle
Nell of the Circus
One Wonderful Night
Pieces of Silver; A Story of Hearts and Souls
'Round the World in 80 Days
Shorty Escapes Marriage
The Thief
Tillie's Punctured Romance
Under the Gaslight
1915 *The Alien*
Always in the Way
The Arrival of Perpetua

A Black Sheep
A Bunch of Keys
The Clemenceau Case
The Concealed Truth
Emmy of Stork's Nest
The Family Stain
Flame of Passion
The Galley Slave
The Gambler of the West
A Gilded Fool
A Girl of Yesterday
Gretna Green
Heléne of the North
The House of a Thousand Candles
The House of a Thousand Scandals
Little Miss Brown
The Lonesome Heart
The Man Who Beat Dan Dolan
The Marriage of Kitty
Marrying Money
M'liss
The Model
The Moonstone
One Million Dollars
The Ploughshare
Snobs
Strathmore
The Supreme Test
Tillie's Tomato Surprise
The Vanderhoff Affair
The Voice in the Fog
The Way Back
The White Sister
Young Romance
1915-16
The Little Church Around the Corner
1916 Bawbs O' Blue Ridge
A Corner in Colleens
The Craving
The Devil's Toy
Dimples
Diplomacy
Divorce and the Daughter
The Dollar and the Law
Feathertop
The Gay Lord Waring
The Gods of Fate
Gold and the Woman
The Grasp of Greed
The Heiress at Coffee Dan's
Her Father's Son
A House Built upon Sand
The Jungle Child
Langdon's Legacy
Less Than the Dust
Little Meena's Romance
Lovely Mary
Love's Lariat
Merely Mary Ann
A Modern Enoch Arden
Oliver Twist
The Other Side of the Door
Overalls
The Phantom Buccaneer
The Return of Eve
Rolling Stones
Saint, Devil and Woman
The Scarlet Road
Sorrows of Happiness
Sudden Riches
The Surprises of an Empty Hotel
The Thousand Dollar Husband
Three Pals
True Nobility
The Unpardonable Sin
Unto Those Who Sin
The Wasted Years
A Woman's Daring
A Youth of Fortune
1917 *Alma, Where Do You Live?*
American Methods
An American Widow
Annie-for-Spite
Anything Once
The Argyle Case
Beloved Rogues
Betty to the Rescue
The Black Wolf
The Blood of His Fathers
The Book Agent
The Boy Girl

Broadway Jones
The Broadway Sport
By Right of Possession
The Car of Chance
The Climber
The Clock
The Cloud
The Customary Two Weeks
The Divorce Game
The Duchess of Doubt
Easy Money
Eternal Love
Filling His Own Shoes
Flying Colors
Freckles
The Gentle Intruder
The Golden Idiot
Grafters
Great Expectations
Hell Morgan's Girl
Her Soul's Inspiration
Her Temptation
The Inner Shrine
The Iron Heart
The Land of Promise
The Little Boy Scout
Madame Bo-Peep
The Magnificent Meddler
The Marcellini Millions
The Mark of Cain
Mayblossom
The Medicine Man
Melting Millions
The Millionaire's Double
Miss U.S.A.
Mr. Opp
Mother Love and the Law
The Night Workers
The Peddler
Pride
The Princess of Patches
The Range Boss
A School for Husbands
The Slave
The Small Town Guy
The Spirit of Romance
The Square Deceiver
Stranded in Arcady
The Sudden Gentleman
Threads of Fate
The Web of Desire
A Wife by Proxy
The Wild Girl
1918 *Alias Mary Brown*
All the World to Nothing
All Woman
Annexing Bill
The Answer
A Bachelor's Children
Daddy's Girl
Dodging a Million
The Dream Lady
Eve's Daughter
The Fallen Angel
False Ambition
Five Thousand an Hour
Friend Husband
The Girl from Bohemia
The Girl of My Dreams
The Goddess of Lost Lake
The Great Love
The Grouch
He Comes Up Smiling
Heiress for a Day
His Majesty, Bunker Bean
His Own Home Town
Humdrum Brown
The Kid Is Clever
The King of Diamonds
Little Miss No-Account
Mirandy Smiles
Mrs. Dane's Defense
M'liss
The Model's Confession
Money Mad
My Unmarried Wife
My Wife
On the Quiet
One Thousand Dollars
The Romance of Tarzan
Society for Sale
Too Many Millions
Twenty-One
Uneasy Money
Up the Road with Sallie

Wedlock
Whims of Society
The Wine Girl
1919 A Bachelor's Wife
Bare-Fisted Gallagher
Bill Henry
A Broadway Saint
The Country Cousin
A Dangerous Affair
The Follies Girl
Getting Mary Married
The Girl with No Regrets
The Gray Towers Mystery
Her Code of Honor
His Father's Wife
The Hornet's Nest
The House Without Children
Human Passions
Johnny Get Your Gun
Johnny-on-the-Spot
The Life Line
Love's Prisoner
A Man and His Money
Married in Haste
A Misfit Earl
Miss Adventure
Miss Dulcie from Dixie
The Secret Garden
Taxi
Under Suspicion
Venus in the East
Widow by Proxy
The Woman Next Door
You Never Saw Such a Girl
1920 The Barbarian
Billions
Clothes
Down Home
Down on the Farm
Forty-Five Minutes from Broadway
The Fourteenth Man
From Now On
The Gilded Dream
Haunting Shadows
Held in Trust
Help Wanted—Male
Her Five-Foot Highness
His Temporary Wife
Honeymoon Ranch
The Jailbird
La La Lucille
The Last Straw
Love Without Question
The Luck of the Irish
Mary's Ankle
Merely Mary Ann
The Miracle of Money
Overland Red
Respectable by Proxy
The Rich Slave
Rookie's Return
The Sagebrusher
She Loves and Lies
Smoldering Embers
The Spenders
The Symbol of the Unconquered
Thoughtless Women
Trumpet Island
Up in Mary's Attic

Injustice
1916 The Eye of God
Intolerance
The Patriot
1917 The Hidden Spring
The Law That Failed

Innkeepers
1914 *Escaped from Siberia*
1915 *Mignon*
1916 *La Vie de Boheme*
1917 *The Ghost of Old Morro*
The Girl Glory
Seven Keys to Baldpate
The Sudden Gentleman
1918 The Bells
Find the Woman
1919 *The A.B.C. of Love*
1920 *The Fighting Shepherdess*
Unseen Forces

Innocence (*Personification*)
1915 *The Absentee*

Jails
- 1914 The Man from Mexico
  - *The Toll of Love*
- 1915 *The Little Gypsy*
- 1917 In Again—Out Again
- 1918 *Old Hartwell's Cub*
  - Petticoats and Politics
  - The Prussian Cur
  - *The Ranger*
- 1919 *Breezy Jim*
  - Charge It to Me
  - Common Clay
  - Easy to Make Money
  - The Gray Towers Mystery
  - Hawthorne of the U.S.A.
  - *Heart of Gold*
  - In for Thirty Days
  - Johnny Get Your Gun
  - The Petal on the Current
- 1920 *The Broken Gate*

Jamaica and Jamaicans
- 1915 Flame of Passion
  - The Pearl of the Antilles
- 1916 *The Ne'er-Do-Well*

James I, King of England, 1566-1625
- 1916 To Have and to Hold

Janitors
- 1915 *A Texas Steer*
- 1916 Bluff
- 1917 *A Daughter of the Poor*
- 1920 *$30,000*

Japan
- 1914 The Wrath of the Gods
- 1915 The Fox Woman
  - Japan
  - Madame Butterfly
  - *The White Pearl*
- 1916 The Soul of Kura-San
- 1917 *The Call of the East*
  - The Door Between
  - Hashimura Togo
  - A Trip Through Japan
- 1918 The Curse of Iku
  - Fan Fan
  - Her American Husband
  - His Birthright
  - A Japanese Nightingale
  - *The Temple of Dusk*
- 1919 Woman, Woman!
- 1920 The Breath of the Gods
  - *A Tokio Siren*
  - The Willow Tree

Japanese
- 1914 The Typhoon
- 1915 An Affair of Three Nations
  - *After Five*
  - The Cheat
  - The Clue
  - Japan
  - *A Trade Secret*
  - The White Pearl
- 1916 Alien Souls
  - The Soul of Kura-San
- 1917 *The Call of the East*
  - Forbidden Paths
  - Hashimura Togo
  - The Secret Game
  - *Yankee Pluck*
- 1918 The Bravest Way
  - The Curse of Iku
  - Fan Fan
  - Her American Husband
  - *Her Husband's Honor*
  - His Birthright
  - A Japanese Nightingale
  - The Temple of Dusk
  - Who Is to Blame?
- 1919 Bonds of Honor
  - The Courageous Coward
  - *A Dangerous Affair*
  - The Dragon Painter
  - A Heart in Pawn
  - The Illustrious Prince
  - The Unwritten Code
- 1920 The Breath of the Gods
  - *Locked Lips*
  - A Tokio Siren
  - *The Wall Street Mystery*
  - Who's Your Servant?

Japanese Americans
- 1916 The Honorable Friend
- 1918 The Bravest Way
  - *The Honor of His House*

- 1919 The Courageous Coward
  - The Gray Horizon
  - His Debt
  - Keali
  - *The Woman on the Index*

Java
- 1913 *Jack London's Adventures in the South Sea Islands*
- 1918 *The Soul of Buddha*
- 1920 *Shipwrecked Among Cannibals*

Jazz
- 1919 *In His Brother's Place*
  - Upstairs

Jealousy
- *rt* Envy
- 1913 The Black Snake
  - Hoodman Blind
  - The Prisoner of Zenda
  - Sapho
- 1914 After the Ball
  - The Avenging Conscience;
    - Thou Shalt Not Kill
  - *The Call of the North*
  - The Circus Man
  - Classmates
  - *Clothes*
  - The Corsair
  - *The Country Mouse*
  - The Daughters of Men
  - Fighting Death
  - A Florida Enchantment
  - The Gamblers
  - Joseph in the Land of Egypt
  - Lena Rivers (Cosmos Feature Film Corp.)
  - Lena Rivers (Whitman Features Co.)
  - Paid in Full
  - The Royal Box
  - Shannon of the Sixth
  - *The Strange Story of Sylvia Gray*
  - The Tangle
- 1915 The Caprices of Kitty
  - Carmen (Fox Film Corp.)
  - Carmen (Jesse L. Lasky Feature Play Co.)
  - Coral
  - The Daughter of the Sea
  - *The Devil*
  - Divorçons
  - *Du Barry*
  - *The Dust of Egypt*
  - *Flame of Passion*
  - The Flaming Sword
  - *The Forbidden Adventure*
  - *The Girl of the Golden West*
  - A Girl of Yesterday
  - The Glory of Youth
  - *The Green Cloak*
  - Hearts Aflame
  - Her Triumph
  - His Wife
  - The Iron Strain
  - *Jane*
  - *John Glayde's Honor*
  - *Judy Forgot*
  - *Kilmeny*
  - The Last Concert
  - *The Little Dutch Girl*
  - The Lure of Woman
  - The Man Who Vanished
  - A Man's Prerogative
  - Matrimony
  - *M'liss*
  - *The Model*
  - *Niobe*
  - Not Guilty
  - *On Dangerous Paths*
  - The Patriot and the Spy
  - The Pitfall
  - *The Politicians*
  - *Pretty Mrs. Smith*
  - *The Pretty Sister of Jose*
  - The Price
  - Prohibition
  - *The Ring of the Borgias*
  - The Rosary
  - *A Royal Family*
  - Saved from the Harem
  - Scandal
  - The Secret Sin
  - The Song of Hate
  - The Stolen Voice

- Sunday
  - The Unknown
  - Via Wireless
  - When a Woman Loves
  - Wormwood
- 1916 *According to Law*
  - *All Man*
  - *Autumn*
  - *The Ballet Girl*
  - *Blue Blood and Red*
  - *Bobbie of the Ballet*
  - Captain Jinks of the Horse Marines
  - *The Catspaw*
  - The Chain Invisible
  - The Chalice of Sorrow
  - Children of the Feud
  - The Combat
  - *The Come-Back*
  - A Coney Island Princess
  - The Conflict
  - *The Conscience of John David*
  - *The Dragon*
  - *The Enemy*
  - *The Essanay-Chaplin Revue of 1916*
  - The Faded Flower
  - The Five Faults of Flo
  - *A Gamble in Souls*
  - The Girl with the Green Eyes
  - The Green Swamp
  - The Green-Eyed Monster
  - *The Heart of Nora Flynn*
  - *The Heart of Tara*
  - *Honor's Altar*
  - *A Huntress of Men*
  - *The Light That Failed*
  - The Love Thief
  - *Lovely Mary*
  - Master Shakespeare, Strolling Player
  - *Miss Petticoats*
  - *A Modern Thelma*
  - The Moral Fabric
  - *The Narrow Path*
  - The Price of Happiness
  - *Sally in Our Alley*
  - Snow White
  - *The Strength of Donald McKenzie*
  - *Sweet Kitty Bellairs*
  - Tangled Hearts
  - Tempest and Sunshine
  - Those Who Toil
  - The Twin Triangle
  - *La Vie de Boheme*
  - *The Voice of Love*
  - *Wanted—A Home*
  - The Wharf Rat
  - What Will People Say?
  - The Woman's Law
  - The Yellow Pawn
- 1917 Alma, Where Do You Live?
  - The Angel Factory
  - The Apple-Tree Girl
  - As Men Love
  - Big Timber
  - A Child of the Wild
  - *The Chosen Prince, or the Friendship of David and Jonathan*
  - The Clean Gun
  - Clover's Rebellion
  - *The Debt*
  - The Eyes of the World
  - *The Fibbers*
  - *Filling His Own Shoes*
  - *The Happiness of Three Women*
  - Hedda Gabler
  - *Hell Morgan's Girl*
  - Her Bargain
  - *Her Life and His*
  - Her Strange Wedding
  - *His Own People*
  - The Honeymoon
  - *The Land of Promise*
  - *Life's Whirlpool*
  - *The Little Chevalier*
  - Love's Law
  - The Mad Lover
  - The Man Hater
  - The Masked Heart
  - The Master Passion
  - Miss Robinson Crusoe

- Mountain Dew
  - Nina, the Flower Girl
  - *The Phantom Shotgun*
  - *The Rainbow Girl*
  - Reputation
  - *The Runaway*
  - *Sally in a Hurry*
  - *The Scarlet Crystal*
  - *A School for Husbands*
  - *A Self-Made Widow*
  - Sirens of the Sea
  - *The Slave Market*
  - *The Social Leper*
  - *A Son of the Hills*
  - *The Soul Master*
  - *The Spreading Dawn*
  - *The Tides of Fate*
  - *Transgression*
  - *The Trufflers*
  - *Two-Bit Seats*
  - *The Weaker Sex*
  - What Money Can't Buy
  - *The Wild Girl*
  - *The Woman and the Beast*
  - Wrath of Love
- 1918 *Borrowed Clothes*
  - The Business of Life
  - *The Cabaret*
  - Captain of His Soul
  - *Chase Me Charlie*
  - Convict 993
  - *The Cruise of the Make-Believes*
  - *The Doctor and the Woman*
  - "Flare-Up" Sal
  - The Floor Below
  - A Gentleman's Agreement
  - *The Grain of Dust*
  - Green Eyes
  - A Heart's Revenge
  - *Hell's End*
  - *Her Inspiration*
  - *Her Mistake*
  - Hitting the Trail
  - *Humility*
  - Hungry Eyes
  - *In Judgment Of*
  - Innocent
  - *Journey's End*
  - *Jules of the Strong Heart*
  - *The Lady of the Dugout*
  - *The Little Runaway*
  - Madame Jealousy
  - The Mating of Marcella
  - *Merely Players*
  - *Midnight Madness*
  - Mrs. Leffingwell's Boots
  - *The Model's Confession*
  - Old Wives for New
  - *The Oldest Law*
  - On the Quiet
  - *A Pair of Sixes*
  - Pals First
  - *Patriotism*
  - *The Pretender*
  - *Revenge*
  - *Rosemary Climbs the Heights*
  - *Social Hypocrites*
  - Suspicion
  - *Tempered Steel*
  - *Tongues of Flame*
  - *The Trap*
  - *Wanted for Murder*
  - Who Killed Walton?
  - The Wife He Bought
  - Wild Honey
  - Wives and Other Wives
  - Wives of Men
  - Wolves of the Border
  - A Woman of Impulse
- 1919 *The A.B.C. of Love*
  - *Bare-Fisted Gallagher*
  - *The Big Little Person*
  - *The Black Gate*
  - *The Blue Bonnet*
  - *Boots*
  - *Break the News to Mother*
  - *Castles in the Air*
  - *The Clouded Name*
  - *Coax Me*
  - *Daddy-Long-Legs*
  - *A Daughter of the Wolf*
  - *Dust of Desire*
  - *Erstwhile Susan*

Martin E. Johnson
1913   Jack London's Adventures in the South Sea Islands
1918   Among the Cannibal Isles of the South Pacific

Osa Johnson
1918   Among the Cannibal Isles of the South Pacific

Joliet State Penitentiary
1914   Joliet Prison, Joliet, Ill.

Joseph, Saint
1913   *From the Manger to the Cross*
1919   The Eternal Light

Joseph of Canaan
1914   Joseph and His Coat of Many Colors
       Joseph in the Land of Egypt

Journalists
   rt   **Reporters**
1914   The Chechako
1915   The Galloper
1916   *Her Double Life*
1918   Caught in the Act
       The Way Out
       The Yellow Ticket

Juarez (Mexico)
1913   *Barbarous Mexico*
1916   *Following the Flag in Mexico*
1919   *The Challenge of Chance*

Judas Iscariot
1915   *Business Is Business*

Judea
1914   *Judith of Bethulia*
1916   *Intolerance*
1918   *Salome*

Judges
   rt   **Courts**
       Juries
       Trials
1913   *Eighty Million Women Want-?*
1914   A Boy and the Law
       The Lion and the Mouse
       A Mother's Heart
       The Scales of Justice
       The Spoilers
1915   The Curious Conduct of Judge Legarde
       Double Trouble
       Judge Not; Or, The Woman of Mona Diggings
       Lydia Gilmore
       The Majesty of the Law
       The Outcast
       The Running Fight
       Thou Shalt Not Kill
       The Woman Next Door
1916   *According to Law*
       According to the Code
       And the Law Says
       April
       The Child of Destiny
       A Child of Mystery
       A Child of the Paris Streets
       Children of the Feud
       Civilization's Child
       Common Ground
       The Devil's Prayer-Book
       Fifty-Fifty
       The Fires of Conscience
       The Fourth Estate
       Friday the Thirteenth
       The Girl of the Lost Lake
       His Great Triumph
       I Accuse
       The Little Liar
       Madame La Presidente
       The Mirror of Life
       Miss George Washington
       The Pillory
       The Rainbow Princess
       The Seekers
       The Shine Girl
       The Upstart
       Who Killed Joe Merrion?
1917   *The Bitter Truth*
       The Bond of Fear
       The Chosen Prince, or the Friendship of David and Jonathan
       The Cost of Hatred
       The Double Standard
       Fear Not
       '49-'17
       The Girl Who Won Out

Glory
I Will Repay
The Last Sentence
The Law That Failed
The Mark of Cain
The Mate of the Sally Ann
Mothers of Men
The Price of Pride
The Price of Silence
Society's Driftwood
Southern Justice
The Whip
1918   Danger—Go Slow
Fields of Honor
Free and Equal
Friend Husband
The Girl and the Judge
The Heart of Romance
His Robe of Honor
In Judgment Of
Joan of the Woods
Keys of the Righteous
Leap to Fame
Nine-Tenths of the Law
One Dollar Bid
Sandy
Up the Road with Sallie
The Whirlpool
With Hoops of Steel
Wives and Other Wives
1919   Common Clay
The Cry of the Weak
Easy to Make Money
Extravagance
Eyes of the Soul
Ginger
A Girl at Bay
The Girl-Woman
The Hushed Hour
In for Thirty Days
John Petticoats
Jubilo
The Lion and the Mouse
The Long Lane's Turning
Oh, Boy!
Peppy Polly
The Pest
The Red Viper
Stripped for a Million
The Test of Honor
1920   *The Branded Woman*
The Broken Gate
Chains of Evidence
Dinty
Firebrand Trevison
Forbidden Trails
The Forged Bride
Half a Chance
The Life of the Party
The Little 'Fraid Lady
Love, Honor and Behave
The New York Idea
Nineteen and Phyllis
The River's End
The Soul of Youth
Tarnished Reputations
The Valley of Night

Judith
1914   Judith of Bethulia

Jug manufacturers
1920   The Dancin' Fool

Jujitsu
1919   *A Dangerous Affair*
       Peggy Does Her Darndest

Jumps from heights
   rt   **Falls from heights**
1914   *The Avenging Conscience; Thou Shalt Not Kill*
       Fighting Death
1915   *The Apaches of Paris*
       The College Widow
       Jack Chanty
       Sweet Alyssum
       Unto the Darkness
1916   The Years of the Locust
1918   *The Ghosts of Yesterday*
1919   *Out of the Fog*
       The Tong Man
1920   *The Unseen Witness*

Jungle fever
1917   *Poppy*

Jungles
1914   *The Captain Besley Expedition*
       The Mysterious Man of the Jungle
1915   *The Campbells Are Coming*
       The Footsteps of Capt. Kidd
       On the Spanish Main
       Unto the Darkness
1916   The Jungle Child
       The Leopard's Bride
       Thou Shalt Not Covet
1917   Man and Beast
       Poppy
1918   *The Romance of Tarzan*
       Tarzan of the Apes
1919   A Scream in the Night
       Where Bonds Are Loosed
1920   *Her Elephant Man*
       The Return of Tarzan

Junk dealers
1917   Lost in Transit

Junks
1915   *The Sable Lorcha*

Juries
   rt   **Courts**
       Trials
1916   The Old Folks at Home
       Public Opinion
       Pudd'nhead Wilson
1917   On Trial
1918   *Resurrection*
1919   The Master Man
       The Woman Under Oath

Justices of the peace
1916   *Judith of the Cumberlands*
       The Missing Links
1917   *Stagestruck*
1919   *Puppy Love*
1920   *The Jack-Knife Man*

Justifiable homicide
   rt   **Manslaughter**
       Murder
1915   *A Man and His Mate*
       The Man Trail
       Monsieur Lecoq
       The Pearl of the Antilles
       Regeneration
       The Suburban
1916   *The Abandonment*
       Broken Fetters
       The End of the Trail
       The Hand of Peril
1917   Hate
       The Yellow Bullet
1919   *The Parisian Tigress*
       Victory
       What Every Woman Learns
       The Witness for the Defense

Juvenile delinquents
1914   A Boy and the Law
1917   *A Bit of Kindling*
       Knights of the Square Table
       The Rise of Jennie Cushing
1919   *The Lion's Den*

K

Kaffirs
1919   *Lost Money*
1920   *The Sins of Rosanne*

Kali
1920   *The Sacred Ruby*

Kankakee (Illinois)
1915   *Saved from the Harem*

Kanpur (India)
1916   *The Victoria Cross*

Kansas
1918   Naughty, Naughty!
       A Perfect Lady
1919   Bare Fists

Kansas City (Kansas or Missouri)
1920   Forbidden Trails
       Lahoma

Kansas City (Missouri)
1919   *Chasing Rainbows*

Stephen Watts Kearny
1915   *Captain Courtesy*

Helen Keller
1919   Deliverance

Kenai Indians
1917   Alaska Wonders in Motion

Kentucky
1914   *His Last Dollar*
       Lena Rivers (Cosmos Feature Film Corp.)
1915   Blue Grass
       Thou Shalt Not Kill
       The Vow
1916   The Apostle of Vengeance
       April
       The Trail of the Lonesome Pine
       A Woman's Power
1917   A Kentucky Cinderella
       The Little Yank
       Miss Deception
       They're Off
1918   Her Inspiration
       One Dollar Bid
       The Racing Strain
       Riders of the Night
       Sandy
       Uncle Tom's Cabin
1919   The Feud
       Heart O' the Hills
       His Divorced Wife
       In Old Kentucky
       The Moonshine Trail
       A Romance of Happy Valley
       The Thunderbolt
       Told in the Hills
       When Bearcat Went Dry
1920   *The Birth of a Soul*
       A Cumberland Romance
       Fighting Cressy
       The Fighting Kentuckians
       Forbidden Valley

Kentucky Derby
1918   Sandy

Alexander Kerensky
1917   *Rasputin, the Black Monk*
1918   *The Fall of the Romanoffs*
       The German Curse in Russia
1919   Free Russia

Keyport (Washington)
1920   Deep Waters

Keys
1914   *The Key to Yesterday*

William Kidd
1919   *Me and Captain Kidd*

Kidnapping
   rt   **Abduction**
1913   Chelsea 7750
       The Fight for Millions
       Ivanhoe
       Shadows of the Moulin Rouge
1914   As Ye Sow
       Brewster's Millions
       The Day of Days
       Doc
       The Governor's Ghost
       The Great Diamond Robbery
       The Last Egyptian
       Over Niagara Falls
       The Tigress
       Il Trovatore
1915   The Alien
       The Barnstormers
       A Black Sheep
       Captivating Mary Carstairs
       The Cotton King
       An Enemy to Society
       Fighting Bob
       Flame of Passion
       From the Valley of the Missing
       The Galley Slave
       The Gambler of the West
       The Garden of Lies
       The Goose Girl
       The Grandee's Ring
       The Heart of the Blue Ridge
       Hearts of Men
       Her Triumph
       His Turning Point
       The Ivory Snuff Box
       Just Jim
       Keep Moving
       Kilmeny
       The Last of the Mafia
       The Lily of Poverty Flat
       Maciste
       Mignon

Money
Right off the Bat
The Ringtailed Rhinoceros
Rumpelstiltskin
The Sable Lorcha
Secretary of Frivolous Affairs
Tillie's Tomato Surprise
Time Lock Number 776
The Two Orphans
The Waif
The Whirl of Life
The White Pearl
Winning the Futurity
Young Romance
1916 The Adventures of Kathlyn
American Aristocracy
April
As a Woman Sows
As in a Looking Glass
The Blue Envelope Mystery
The Brand of Cowardice
A Child of Mystery
A Child of the Paris Streets
Daphne and the Pirate
The Daughter of the Don
The Devil at His Elbow
Dorian's Divorce
The End of the Trail
The Eternal Question
The Folly of Revenge
The Fool's Revenge
For the Defense
The Gilded Spider
God's Country and the Woman
The Good Bad Man
Gretchen, the Greenhorn
The Habit of Happiness
The Heart of Paula
The Heart of Tara
The Heart of the Hills
The Hunted Woman
The Idol of the Stage
The Isle of Life
Langdon's Legacy
Love and Hate
The Love Girl
The Mainspring
A Modern Enoch Arden
My Country First
My Lady's Slipper
Nancy's Birthright
Poor Little Peppina
The Precious Packet
Prudence the Pirate
The Sex Lure
The Sign of the Poppy
The Sign of the Spade
The Torch Bearer
The Twin Triangle
The Victoria Cross
Vultures of Society
*Warning! The S.O.S. Call of
   Humanity*
The World Against Him
1917 *Aladdin's Other Lamp*
The Bar Sinister
Betsy's Burglar
Cassidy
The Darling of Paris
The Dummy
The Heart of Texas Ryan
The Hero of the Hour
The Honor System
The Innocent Sinner
Intrigue
Kidnapped
The Kill-Joy
The Lady in the Library
The Magnificent Meddler
The Man Who Took a Chance
Melting Millions
A Modern Musketeer
The Pride of New York
The Princess of Park Row
The Recoil
Sleeping Fires
The Son of His Father
Sowers and Reapers
The Stolen Play
Sunshine and Gold
Tangled Lives
Unknown 274
What Money Can't Buy
The Winged Mystery

1918 Back to the Woods
Beauty and the Rogue
The Beloved Blackmailer
Brave and Bold
The Eyes of Mystery
The Ghost of the Rancho
The Girl from Beyond
The Girl in the Dark
Heart of the Sunset
His Daughter Pays
The Kaiser's Shadow, or the
   Triple Cross
Leap to Fame
The Light of Western Stars
Little Red Decides
Love's Conquest
The Menace
The Million Dollar Mystery
The Mystery Girl
Nine-Tenths of the Law
A Pair of Cupids
The Return of Mary
The Sea Flower
Six Shooter Andy
Sporting Life
The Triumph of the Weak
Unexpected Places
Up Romance Road
The Vigilantes
We Should Worry
Wild Women
Winner Takes All
The Wolf and His Mate
Wolves of the Border
1919 *The Adventure Shop*
Coax Me
The Enchanted Barn
Fortune's Child
The Great Air Robbery
The Hellion
The Island of Intrigue
The Littlest Scout
Luck and Pluck
Nugget Nell
The Oakdale Affair
The Poison Pen
The Prodigal Liar
A Scream in the Night
The Sealed Envelope
The Sheriff's Son
The Spark Divine
The Stronger Vow
This Hero Stuff
The Westerners
The World Aflame
1920 Away Goes Prudence
The City of Masks
The Coast of Opportunity
Crooked Streets
Easy to Get
The Girl in the Web
Heritage
The Hidden Code
Leave It to Me
Li Ting Lang
Love's Protegé
The Luck of the Irish
A Manhattan Knight
Officer 666
*Our Christianity and Nobody's
   Child*
Paris Green
Parted Curtains
Polly of the Storm Country
The Purple Cipher
Rogues and Romance
Rookie's Return
The Rose of Nome
Sooner or Later
The Strongest
Terror Island
Their Mutual Child
Vengeance and the Girl
The Wonderful Chance

Kiev (Russia)
1914 Escaped from Siberia
1916 *Civilization's Child*
The King's Game

Kings
   rt Specific kings
1914 Neptune's Daughter
1915 *Queen and Adventurer*
1916 Macbeth
Undine

1917 *The Chosen Prince, or the
      Friendship of David and
      Jonathan*
Fighting for Love
The Slave
The Undying Flame
What Money Can't Buy
1918 *Crown Jewels*
Kiowa Indians
1920 The Daughter of Dawn
Kishinev (Russia)
1915 *The Melting Pot*
Kisses
1915 *The Commanding Officer*
The Cub
1916 The Kiss
1917 *Paradise Garden*
1918 A Camouflage Kiss
I Love You
Love Watches
Pay Day
1919 The Beloved Cheater
Dangerous Waters
The End of the Road
Everywoman
False Evidence
His Bridal Night
In His Brother's Place
The Love Call
The Market of Souls
Out of the Fog
The Third Kiss
Upstairs and Down
The Virtuous Model
Why Smith Left Home
1920 *The Land of Jazz*
The Stolen Kiss
Frank E. Kleinschmidt
1912 The Alaska-Siberian Expedition
1914 Captain F. E. Kleinschmidt's
      Arctic Hunt
Kleptomania
1915 Stolen Goods
Stop Thief!
1917 *The Dazzling Miss Davison*
1918 The Girl and the Judge
1920 *Stop Thief*
Klondike
1917 *The Great White Trail*
The Greater Law
1918 Carmen of the Klondike
Knife fights
1915 *Carmen* (Fox Film Corp.)
Carmen (Jesse L. Lasky
      Feature Play Co.)
1919 *The Heart of Juanita*
The Last of His People
The Wilderness Trail
1920 *The Law of the Yukon*
Knife wounds
1915 *Body and Soul*
A Continental Girl
Courtmartialed
In the Palace of the King
The Spanish Jade
Sunday
1916 *The Crippled Hand*
Cross Currents
The Feast of Life
The Foolish Virgin
Her Surrender
Pamela's Past
The Twin Triangle
What Will People Say?
1917 *A Love Sublime*
The Price Mark
To the Death
Triumph
1918 *A Daughter of France*
The Devil's Wheel
The Ghosts of Yesterday
1919 *The Bishop's Emeralds*
False Evidence
From Headquarters
Lasca
The Painted World
The Sneak
The Two Brides
1920 *The Dangerous Talent*
The Face at Your Window
The Gift Supreme
Rogues and Romance

Knights
1913 Ivanhoe
1916 Don Quixote
The Foolish Virgin
Undine
The White Rosette
1919 Day Dreams
You're Fired
1920 A Connecticut Yankee at King
      Arthur's Court
Knights of Columbus
1919 *The Burning Question*
1920 American Catholics in War
      and Reconstruction
Knitting
1919 *Sing-Sing and Great Meadows
      Prison*
John Knowles
1915 The Nature Man: Or, The
      Struggle for Existence
Kodiak Island (Alaska)
1917 Alaska Wonders in Motion
Ku Klux Klan
1915 The Birth of a Nation
1920 The Symbol of the
      Unconquered
Kurds
1919 Auction of Souls
Alexei Nikolaievich Kuropatkin
1919 *Free Russia*

L

Labor activists
   rt Strikes
1915 The High Road
The Incorrigible Dukane
1916 Her Bitter Cup
The Quality of Faith
Those Who Toil
1917 The Bottom of the Well
The Spindle of Life
Threads of Fate
1918 The Glorious Adventure
1919 The Uplifters
Labor agitators
   rt Strikes
1913 From Dusk to Dawn
1914 *Facing the Gattling Guns*
1915 *The Bigger Man*
The Boss
The Plunderer
1916 *The Thoroughbred (American
      Film Co.)*
1917 *By Right of Possession*
The Courage of the Common
      Place
Fanatics
The Raggedy Queen
1918 The Hard Rock Breed
Mr. Logan, U.S.A.
The Spirit of '17
The Transgressor
The Vamp
The Winning of Beatrice
1919 *The Belle of the Season*
A Man's Fight
The Undercurrent
Virtuous Men
The World Aflame
1920 *A Beggar in Purple*
Dangerous Hours
The Face at Your Window
Riders of the Dawn
Uncharted Channels
Labor leaders
1914 *The Daughters of Men*
The Spirit of the Conqueror
1915 *The Making Over of Geoffrey
      Manning*
A Man's Making
A Modern Magdalen
The Song of the Wage Slave
1916 The Bruiser
The Dumb Girl of Portici
The Fourth Estate
1917 *The Public Be Damned*
The Royal Pauper
1918 *The Golden Goal*
1920 *The Face at Your Window*
The Great Shadow
Nurse Marjorie

Labor unions
   rt **Strikes**
1913 From Dusk to Dawn
1914 What Is to Be Done?
1916 *The Bruiser*
1917 The Car of Chance
       The Spindle of Life
1918 Jack Spurlock, Prodigal
1920 The Great Shadow
       Uncharted Channels

Labor violence
1914 The Better Man
1915 The Absentee
       The Bigger Man
       A Modern Magdalen
       Money
       The Spender
1916 *The Blacklist*
       Hesper of the Mountains
       The Lords of High Decision
       The Manager of the B. and A.
       The Right Direction
       The Selfish Woman
       The Thoroughbred (American
          Film Co.)
       Those Who Toil
       What Love Can Do
1917 *The Girl and the Crisis*
1918 Love's Pay Day
1919 The Right to Happiness
       The Undercurrent
       The Wilderness Trail
1920 The Strongest

Laboratories
1915 *Divorçons*
1917 *The Little Patriot*
       Redemption
1918 *The Craving*
       The Grain of Dust
       Hearts or Diamonds?
       Huns Within Our Gates
       Sunshine Nan
       Swat the Spy
1919 *Hit or Miss*
       *The Mystery of the Yellow
          Room*
1920 *Dr. Jekyll and Mr. Hyde
          (Famous Players-Lasky
          Corp.)*

Laboratory technicians
1918 *The Seal of Silence*

Laborers
1916 *The Dumb Girl of Portici*
       The Weakness of Man
       The Whirlpool of Destiny
1917 *His Mother's Boy*
       A Rich Man's Plaything
1918 More Trouble
       Wanted, a Mother
       The Wine Girl

Lace makers
1917 *To the Death*

John Lackland
1913 *Ivanhoe*

Marquis de Lafayette
1919 The Spirit of Lafayette

Jean Lafitte
1919 The Millionaire Pirate

Laguna Beach (California)
1914 The Pursuit of the Phantom

Lakes
1915 *Betty in Search of a Thrill*
1916 The Chaperon
       The Girl of the Lost Lake
1918 *Jilted Janet*
       Wanted, a Mother
1919 Three Men and a Girl
       Why Smith Left Home
1920 *The Dark Mirror*

Land claims
1916 Land O' Lizards

Land developers
1916 Land O' Lizards
1919 *Go Get 'Em Garringer*

Land promoters
1915 *The Valley of Lost Hope*
1919 Breed of Men
       Gates of Brass

Land rights
1914 *The Country Mouse*
       Rip Van Winkle
       Rose of the Rancho

1915 *The Man from Oregon*
       The Man Trail
       The Mill on the Floss
1916 The End of the Rainbow
       The Feud Girl
       Gold and the Woman
       Lonesome Town
       Lovely Mary
       The Secret of the Swamp
       The Snowbird
1917 Anything Once
       The Avenging Trail
       *The Captain of the Gray Horse
          Troop*
       The Fettered Woman
       The Girl of the Timber Claims
       Glory
       Heart's Desire
       The Medicine Man
       The Planter
       The Primitive Call
1918 *The Beautiful Mrs. Reynolds*
       Hugon, the Mighty
       The Phantom Riders
       The Trail to Yesterday
       The Widow's Might
       Winner Takes All
       The Wolf and His Mate
1919 Breed of Men
       The Cambric Mask
       Children of Banishment
       Cowardice Court
       The Gray Towers Mystery
       The Gray Wolf's Ghost
       A Gun Fightin' Gentleman
       Heart O' the Hills
       The Heart of Youth
       Her Kingdom of Dreams
       In Old Kentucky
       The Price of Innocence
       Sis Hopkins
       The Valley of the Giants
       When the Desert Smiles
       You Never Know Your Luck
1920 The Coast of Opportunity
       Even As Eve
       Fighting Cressy
       Firebrand Trevison
       The Flame of Hellgate
       Forbidden Trails
       Hitchin' Posts
       The Joyous Troublemaker
       King Spruce
       Peaceful Valley
       Seeing It Through
       Two Moons
       Vengeance and the Girl

Land rushes
1920 Hitchin' Posts

Land sales
1916 *All Man*
       Artie, the Millionaire Kid
       The Challenge
       Hulda from Holland
1917 *The Road Between*
1919 Hearts of Men

Land speculation
1914 *A Gentleman from Mississippi*
       Shore Acres

Landladies
1914 *Martin Eden*
1915 *The Magic Skin*
1916 *The Hidden Law*
1918 *Betty Takes a Hand*
       The Doctor and the Woman
       The Girl and the Judge
       Miss Mischief Maker
       Say, Young Fellow!
       Tony America
1919 *An Innocent Adventuress*
       Putting It Over
       The Sealed Envelope
       The Wicked Darling
1920 *Way Down East*

Landlords
1916 The Clarion
       The Dividend
       Lone Star
       The Man from Manhattan
       The Writing on the Wall
1917 Heart's Desire
       In Slumberland
       The War of the Tongs
       The Winning of Sally Temple
       Young Mother Hubbard

1918 *Denny from Ireland*
       Everybody's Girl
       The Little Runaway
       The Midnight Burglar
1920 A Child for Sale

Landowners
1914 *Marta of the Lowlands*
1915 *The Adventures of a Boy
          Scout*
1916 The End of the Rainbow
       The Marriage of Molly-O
       To Have and to Hold
1918 Out of a Clear Sky
       Under the Greenwood Tree
1920 Polly of the Storm Country

Landslides
1915 *The Great Divide*
       The Silent Voice
1920 *Bullet Proof*
       The Mollycoddle

Larceny
1917 *The Bad Boy*
1919 Heart of Gold
       Lost Money
       Something to Do

Larchmont (New York)
1915 *A Fool There Was*

Las Vegas (Nevada)
1916 Boots and Saddles

Latin America
1913 *Victory*
1915 *The Yankee Girl*
1916 Elusive Isabel
1917 *The American Consul*
1919 Full of Pep
       Whitewashed Walls
1920 On the Trail of the
          Conquistadores

Laudanum
1914 *The Dream Woman*
       Pierre of the Plains

Launderers
1917 *Happiness*

Laundresses
   rt **Washerwomen**
1914 *The Valley of the Moon*
1915 *The Blindness of Virtue*
1916 *The Invisible Enemy*
       Shoes
1918 *Amarilly of Clothes-Line
          Alley*
1919 *All Wrong*
1920 Suds

Laundries
1918 *Face Value*

Lava
1914 *Hearts Adrift*
1917 *The Man of Mystery*

Law (Concept)
1917 *The Bond of Fear*
       The Double Standard
       Mothers of Men
1918 *Her Man*
       His Enemy, the Law
1920 Half a Chance

Law and order
1914 *The Eagle's Mate*
1916 The Argonauts of
          California—1849
1917 Men of the Desert
       One Shot Ross
1918 *Branding Broadway*
1919 The Coming of the Law
       The Devil's Trail
1920 The Iron Rider

Law clerks
1915 *The Alster Case*
       Mortmain
1919 *Hawthorne of the U.S.A.*

Law students
1915 *The Blindness of Virtue*
       Her Reckoning
1916 *And the Law Says*
1919 *Almost a Husband*
       The Courageous Coward
       The Fighting Roosevelts
1920 *The Corsican Brothers*
       The Sacred Flame

Thomas Edward Lawrence
1919 With Allenby in Palestine and
          Lawrence in Arabia

Laws
1915 Gretna Green
       The Woman
       York State Folks
1916 *Dust*
       The Eagle's Wing
       The Upheaval
       The Valley of Decision
       The Velvet Paw
       War Brides
1917 *The Food Gamblers*
       The Hand That Rocks the
          Cradle
       The Hawk
       Her Excellency, the Governor
       The Honor System
       The Kill-Joy
       The Law That Failed
       Light in Darkness
       The Public Be Damned
       Who's Your Neighbor?
1918 *Rimrock Jones*
1919 In for Thirty Days
1920 *The Woman God Sent*

Lawsuits
1915 Forbidden Fruit
1917 *The Calendar Girl*
       The Co-Respondent
       A Game of Wits
       The Squaw Man's Son
1919 Her Game
       The Road Called Straight
1920 Are All Men Alike?
       The Great Accident
       Jes' Call Me Jim

Lawyers
   rt **Attorneys-general**
      District attorneys
      Public defenders
1913 Eighty Million Women Want-?
       From Dusk to Dawn
       The Third Degree
1914 *After the Ball*
       Beating Back
       The County Chairman
       The Criminal Code
       Damaged Goods
       The Gamblers
       The Human Bloodhound
       The Man from Home
       The Monster and the Girl
       A Mother's Heart
       *The Mystery of Richmond
          Castle*
       The Opened Shutters
       The Path Forbidden
       The Spoilers
       Winning His First Case
       A Woman Who Did
       *Your Girl and Mine: A Woman
          Suffrage Play*
1915 *Aloha Oe*
       Always in the Way
       At Bay
       The Avalanche
       The Bludgeon
       Blue Grass
       A Bunch of Keys
       Camille
       The Concealed Truth
       The Earl of Pawtucket
       The Edge of the Abyss
       The Fairy and the Waif
       Gambier's Advocate
       God's Witness
       Hearts Aflame
       June Friday
       Lydia Gilmore
       A Man's Prerogative
       The Marriage of Kitty
       Marrying Money
       Marse Covington
       The Mill on the Floss
       The Model
       The Outcast
       Prohibition
       The Right of Way
       The Sentimental Lady
       The Seventh Noon
       Shadows from the Past
       The Silent Command
       Snobs
       Through Turbulent Waters
       The Unwelcome Wife
       The Way Back

The Bitter Truth
The Blue Streak
The Bond of Fear
Bridges Burned
Broadway Arizona
Bucking Broadway
The Butterfly Girl
The Cigarette Girl
The Crimson Dove
Envy
Even As You and I
An Even Break
Love's Law
Mothers of Men
A Mute Appeal
1918 The Make-Believe Wife
Prunella
1919 Everywoman
Eyes of Youth
The Millionaire Pirate
Restless Souls
The Spark Divine
The Turn in the Road
1920 The Devil's Riddle
The Dream Cheater
Sweet Lavender

Love tests
1914 The Ring and the Man
The Three of Us
1915 *Heartaches*
Her Shattered Idol
1916 The Summer Girl
1917 Her Own People
A Modern Cinderella
The Mysterious Miss Terry
The Natural Law
Royal Romance
1918 *On the Quiet*
1919 The Moral Deadline
Trixie from Broadway
1920 Nurse Marjorie
The Woman and the Puppet

Lovelorn
1914 Hearts Adrift
Jess of the Mountain Country
1918 The Man of Bronze

Lowell (Massachusetts)
1917 *The Little Boy Scout*

Lower classes
1914 The House of Bondage
The Straight Road
1916 *Don Quixote*
The Dumb Girl of Portici
Hazel Kirke
1917 *The Angel Factory*
Annie-for-Spite
A Daughter of the Poor
The Rise of Jennie Cushing
Royal Romance
1918 His Bonded Wife
1920 Suds

Lower Klamath Lake (California)
1915 *Wild Life of America in Films*

Loyalty
1914 Damon and Pythias
Dan
The Daughters of Men
Judith of Bethulia
1915 The Fighting Hope
Gladiola
In the Palace of the King
Infatuation
1916 The Alibi
The Black Sheep of the Family
The Blacklist
Casey at the Bat
The Crisis
D'Artagnan
The Daughter of the Don
Elusive Isabel
Her Maternal Right
1917 Her Beloved Enemy
Loyalty
The Rose of Blood
Unto the End
1918 The Birth of a Race
Good-Bye, Bill
Hands Down
The Heart of Romance
Her Husband's Honor
The Hun Within
More Trouble
1919 Fighting Through

1920 Lady Rose's Daughter
1921 The Jucklins
Lübeck (Germany)
1915 *The History of the World's Greatest War*
Lucerne (Switzerland)
1914 *Three Weeks*
Lucknow (India)
1915 The Campbells Are Coming
Raoul Lufberry
1917 *Heroic France*
Lumber camp foremen
1915 The Heart of Jennifer
The Man Trail
1916 *The Come-Back*
The Daughter of MacGregor
Fighting Blood
1917 *The Avenging Trail*
The False Friend
Little Miss Nobody
The Promise
1918 Broadway Bill
Jules of the Strong Heart
The Source
A Woman of Redemption
1919 *Children of Banishment*
1920 *King Spruce*
Lumber camps
1915 *Heléne of the North*
The Man Trail
Sunday
The Wild Olive
1916 The Come-Back
The Daughter of MacGregor
Hell-to-Pay Austin
The Measure of a Man
1917 *Big Timber*
The Cook of Canyon Camp
The Crimson Dove
Freckles
The Heart of a Lion
Little Miss Nobody
The Promise
The Silent Lie
1918 *Broadway Bill*
Jules of the Strong Heart
Prisoners of the Pines
The Silent Woman
The Source
1919 The American Way
The Blinding Trail
The Brute Breaker
The Clouded Name
The Darkest Hour
The Faith of the Strong
Impossible Catherine
The Little Boss
Man's Desire
Virtuous Men
1920 King Spruce
Smiling All the Way
The Valley of Doubt
Lumber foremen
1919 *The Valley of the Giants*
Virtuous Men
Lumber industry
1916 *The Strength of Donald McKenzie*
1917 The Avenging Trail
The Girl of the Timber Claims
Sudden Jim
1918 Back to the Woods
A Woman of Redemption
1919 The Bondage of Barbara
Twilight
The Valley of the Giants
1920 King Spruce
Lumber magnates
1916 The End of the Rainbow
1917 *A Magdalene of the Hills*
The Promise
1918 The Silent Woman
Lumber yards
1917 *A Crooked Romance*
Lumbering
1918 *The Vigilantes*
Lumberjacks
1914 *The Redemption of David Corson*
1915 *The Man Trail*
A Phyllis of the Sierras
Sunday
1916 The Chain Invisible
The Come-Back

Fighting Blood
Hell-to-Pay Austin
1917 Big Timber
Pay Me
The Promise
The Silent Lie
1918 Blue Blazes Rawden
Jules of the Strong Heart
The Man Hunt
Prisoners of the Pines
She Hired a Husband
The Source
That Devil, Bateese
1919 *John Petticoats*
The Little Boss
Rose O' the River
The Rough Neck
Twilight
1920 The Lumber Jack
Smiling All the Way
Lunatics
1917 All for a Husband
1920 Everything but the Truth
The Misleading Lady
Lure of the city
rt **City-country contrast**
Lure of the country
Urban life
1914 The Adventures of Kitty Cobb
Burning Daylight: The Adventures of "Burning Daylight" in Civilization
Hearts and Flowers
1915 *Through Turbulent Waters*
1916 *The Lash of Destiny*
The Soul of a Child
The Wasted Years
1917 Broadway Jones
Bucking Broadway
The Co-Respondent
The Defeat of the City
Fires of Rebellion
A Girl's Folly
The Lash of Power
A Mute Appeal
On Record
Paradise Garden
The Road Between
The Small Town Guy
A Song of Sixpence
The Understudy
When You and I Were Young
A Woman Alone
1918 Innocent's Progress
The Lesson
Limousine Life
Love's Pay Day
A Nine O'Clock Town
Rosemary Climbs the Heights
The Square Deal
1919 The Bondage of Barbara
The Chosen Path
Forbidden
Heart of Gold
The Lost Princess
My Little Sister
Open Your Eyes
Putting It Over
A Romance of Happy Valley
The Silver Girl
The Social Pirate
The Stream of Life
Under Suspicion
Venus in the East
The Wishing Ring Man
A Woman's Experience
1920 Broadway and Home
Cupid, the Cowpuncher
Dad's Girl
The Gilded Dream
Homer Comes Home
Mary Ellen Comes to Town
Silk Husbands and Calico Wives
The Spenders
39 East
Youth's Desire
Lure of the country
rt **City-country contrast**
Lure of the city
1919 Extravagance
Forbidden
In Search of Arcady
Poor Relations

S.S. *Lusitania*
1916 Her Redemption
1918 *Crashing Through to Berlin*
The Kaiser, the Beast of Berlin
Lest We Forget,
Over the Top
The Price of Applause
Lust
1914 *Charlotte Corday*
A Florida Enchantment
Home, Sweet Home
1915 *Black Fear*
Body and Soul
Evidence
The Little Dutch Girl
Mary's Lamb
1916 The Garden of Allah
1917 *A Branded Soul*
Builders of Castles
Conscience
Even As You and I
The Love Doctor
The Sea Master
The Ship of Doom
The Test of Womanhood
1918 *I Want to Forget*
1919 *Castles in the Air*
It Happened in Paris
The Man Who Turned White
When Men Desire
1920 *Godless Men*
Into the Light
Whispering Devils
Luxor (Egypt)
1920 An Arabian Knight
Lynching
rt **Executions**
1914 *The Good-for-Nothing*
1915 The Birth of a Nation
The Commanding Officer
The Cotton King
The Cowboy and the Lady
A Man and His Mate
The Patriot and the Spy
1916 *The Flower of Faith*
The Haunted Manor
Judith of the Cumberlands
A Law unto Himself
The Man from Manhattan
The Other Side of the Door
Tennessee's Pardner
1917 *Ashes of Hope*
The Captain of the Gray Horse Troop
Exile
The Girl Angle
My Fighting Gentleman
A Romance of the Redwoods
The Wildcat
1918 *Blue Blazes Rawden*
Her Inspiration
M'liss
Paying His Debt
Selfish Yates
Winner Takes All
A Woman of Redemption
1919 *Breed of Men*
Breezy Jim
False Evidence
The Gray Wolf's Ghost
Just Squaw
The Knickerbocker Buckaroo
The Midnight Stage
The Oakdale Affair
The Unpainted Woman
1920 The Birth of a Soul
The Blue Moon
A Broadway Cowboy
The Broken Gate
The Gauntlet
The Lone Hand
Red Foam
Within Our Gates

M

John J. McGraw
1914 *The Giants-White Sox Tour*
Machine shops
1919 *The Profiteer*
The Undercurrent

The Hungry Heart
Idolators
The Inner Shrine
The Innocent Sinner
The Iron Heart
The Iron Ring
The Lair of the Wolf
The Land of Long Shadows
The Last Sentence
The Law of Compensation
Life's Whirlpool
The Lifted Veil
Light in Darkness
The Little Boy Scout
Little Miss Nobody
The Little Pirate
The Long Trail
Love Letters
Loyalty
The Mad Lover
The Maid of Belgium
Man and Beast
Man's Woman
The Marcellini Millions
Married in Name Only
Mary Moreland
Master of His Home
The Master Passion
The Maternal Spark
The Mirror
Mrs. Balfame
The Moral Code
Moral Courage
The Moth
Mother Love and the Law
Mothers of Men
Mountain Dew
My Little Boy
One Law for Both
One of Many
One Touch of Nature
Open Places
Panthea
Pardners
Persuasive Peggy
The Piper's Price
The Power of Decision
The Price Mark
Pride and the Devil
The Rainbow
Redemption
Scandal
The Scarlet Crystal
The Seventh Sin
Shall We Forgive Her?
The Silent Partner
The Single Code
Skinner's Bubble
Skinner's Dress Suit
The Social Leper
The Spreading Dawn
A Square Deal
A Stormy Knight
The Tenth Case
Tillie Wakes Up
Unconquered
The Unforseen
Vera, the Medium
The Waiting Soul
The Weaker Sex
When Duty Calls
When False Tongues Speak
Whose Wife?
Wife Number Two
The Wife Who Wouldn't Tell
Wild and Woolly
The Winning of Sally Temple
A Woman Alone
The Woman and the Beast
The Woman in White
A Woman's Awakening
Wrath of Love

1918 An Alien Enemy
All Man
The Answer
Blindfolded
Blue Blood
The Business of Life
By Right of Purchase
The Cast-Off
The City of Dim Faces
The Clutch of Circumstance
Daddy's Girl
The Desired Woman
The Divine Sacrifice

Does Your Wife Obey?
A Doll's House
Everywoman's Husband
Fires of Youth
The First Law
Five Nights
For Husbands Only
For Sale
The Girl from Beyond
A Good Loser
Good Night, Paul
The Grouch
The Guilty Wife
The Heart of Rachael
Her Decision
Her Husband's Honor
Her Mistake
High Stakes
His Bonded Wife
His Daughter Pays
His Enemy, the Law
Hoarded Assets
The Home Trail
The House of Glass
The House of Gold
Humility
I Love You
The Interloper
Joan of the Woods
Journey's End
Just a Woman
The King of Diamonds
A Lady's Name
A Law unto Herself
Lend Me Your Name
The Lesson
Let's Get a Divorce
The Lie
Limousine Life
The Love Brokers
Love Watches
Madame Jealousy
Marriage
The Marriage Lie
The Marriage Ring
Men
Men Who Have Made Love to Me
Miss Ambition
Mrs. Leffingwell's Boots
The Moral Law
The Mortgaged Wife
Nine-Tenths of the Law
No Man's Land
A Nymph of the Foothills
Old Wives for New
The Other Woman
Our Little Wife
Our Mrs. McChesney
The Painted Lily
A Pair of Silk Stockings
Pay Day
The Phantom Riders
Prisoners of the Pines
Prunella
The Prussian Cur
The Purple Lily
Revelation
The Rose of the World
Ruling Passions
Salome
The Scarlet Trail
Secret Code
The Song of Songs
The Song of the Soul
The Splendid Sinner
The Square Deal
Station Content
Stella Maris
Stolen Hours
The Strange Woman
Thirty a Week
Too Many Millions
The Whirlpool
Why I Would Not Marry
Wife or Country
Wives and Other Wives
Wives of Men
Woman
A Woman's Fool
Women's Weapons

1918-19
Marriage a la Mode
1919 The A.B.C. of Love
An Adventure in Hearts

All Wrong
The Amazing Wife
Are You Legally Married?
Atonement
A Bachelor's Wife
Be a Little Sport
The Beauty Market
Blind Husbands
The Blinding Trail
The Bramble Bush
Carolyn of the Corners
The Climbers
The Common Cause
Common Property
Creaking Stairs
The Darkest Hour
The Day She Paid
The Dragon Painter
Dust of Desire
Experimental Marriage
Extravagance
Eyes of the Soul
Fair and Warmer
Faith
False Gods
The Fire Flingers
Forbidden
The Forfeit
The Glorious Lady
Good Gracious, Annabelle
Happiness à la Mode
Happy Though Married
Her Game
Her Purchase Price
The Highest Trump
His Divorced Wife
His Father's Wife
His Parisian Wife
His Wife's Friend
The Homesteader
A House Divided
The House Without Children
The Hushed Hour
I'll Get Him Yet
Impossible Catherine
The Indestructible Wife
The Invisible Bond
Josselyn's Wife
The Law of Nature
Let's Elope
The Little Intruder
The Long Arm of Mannister
Lord and Lady Algy
The Lottery Man
The Love Auction
The Love Defender
Love, Honor and—?
The Love That Dares
Mandarin's Gold
Mary Regan
The Mother and the Law
One Week of Life
Our Better Selves
Paid in Full
The Painted World
Partners Three
Playthings of Passion
Poor Relations
The Profiteers
Redhead
The Rescuing Angel
Restless Souls
The Right to Lie
The Root of Evil
Roped
Roses and Thorns
The Scar
Shadows
Should a Woman Tell?
Silent Strength
The Silver Girl
Sis Hopkins
Snares of Paris
The Sneak
A Society Exile
Someone Must Pay
The Splendid Sin
Stepping Out
The Stronger Vow
A Taste of Life
A Temperamental Wife
The Third Degree
Thunderbolts of Fate
Todd of the Times
The Trap

Trixie from Broadway
The Two Brides
The Unpainted Woman
The Unwritten Code
Upside Down
The Virtuous Model
What Every Woman Learns
What Love Forgives
When Fate Decides
Wolves of the Night
The Woman Next Door
The Woman on the Index
The Woman Under Cover
Woman, Woman!
A Woman's Experience
The Wreck

1919-20
The Marriage Blunder
When a Man Loves
1920 Black Is White
Blind Wives
The Broadway Bubble
Burnt Wings
Children of Destiny
Common Sense
The Cost
Curtain
The Daughter Pays
Deep Waters
The Devil's Passkey
Dollars and the Woman
Earthbound
Easy to Get
Empty Arms
The Eternal Mother
Fixed by George
Flying Pat
The Frisky Mrs. Johnson
The Furnace
The Girl with the Jazz Heart
Greater Than Love
Hairpins
The Heart of a Woman
Her Beloved Villain
His House in Order
His Wife's Money
The House of Toys
Husbands and Wives
In Folly's Trail
The Inferior Sex
The Invisible Divorce
The Ladder of Lies
A Lady in Love
Let's Be Fashionable
The Little Grey Mouse
Love Madness
The Luck of Geraldine Laird
Madame Peacock
Madame X
Married Life
Mary's Ankle
The Master Mind
Mid-Channel
The Misfit Wife
Mrs. Temple's Telegram
Molly and I
My Husband's Other Wife
The Mysteries of Paris
The New York Idea
The North Wind's Malice
Nothing but the Truth
The Notorious Miss Lisle
An Old Fashioned Boy
Old Lady 31
On with the Dance
Parlor, Bedroom and Bath
Pegeen
Pleasure Seekers
The Price of Redemption
Red Foam
Remodelling Her Husband
Respectable by Proxy
The Riddle: Woman
The Right to Love
Seeds of Vengeance
Sex
Shod with Fire
Should a Wife Work?
Silk Husbands and Calico Wives
So Long Letty
Something to Think About
The Song of the Soul
The Strongest
The Tattlers

The Firing Line
Go Get 'Em Garringer
The Isle of Conquest
Jacques of the Silver North
Marriage for Convenience
The Marriage Price
Paid in Advance
Phil-for-Short
The Road Called Straight
The Rough Neck
Sealed Hearts
The Spark Divine
The Spite Bride
The Steel King
Three Green Eyes
Told in the Hills
The Unveiling Hand
The Weaker Vessel
What Every Woman Wants
Who Will Marry Me?
The Witness for the Defense
Wolves of the Night
The Woman Michael Married
A Woman of Pleasure
1920 Thoughtless Women
The Virgin of Stamboul
What Women Want
The White Dove
White Lies

Marriage—Mixed
1914 *Escaped from Siberia*
Where the Trail Divides
1915 *Kreutzer Sonata*
Madame Butterfly
1916 *Gold and the Woman*
1917 *Her Own People*
1918 The Forbidden City
Free and Equal
The Soul of Buddha
The Squaw Man
1919 Broken Barriers
Daughter of Mine
The Other Man's Wife

Marriage—Proxy
1914 Shorty Escapes Marriage
1917 A Wife by Proxy

Marriage—Secret
1914 *Lena Rivers (Whitman Features Co.)*
Life's Shop Window
The Mountain Rat
1915 Colonel Carter of Cartersville
The End of the Road
The Goose Girl
Jane
The Price of Her Silence
1916 The Combat
Idols
The Island of Surprise
The Ne'er-Do-Well
The Ordeal of Elizabeth
A Tortured Heart
The War Bride's Secret
Warning! The S.O.S. Call of Humanity
1917 Blue Jeans
Daughter of Destiny
A Magdalene of the Hills
The Mate of the Sally Ann
Mayblossom
Mutiny
The Plow Woman
The Recoil
The Regenerates
The Secret Man
The Secret of the Storm Country
Zollenstein
1918 *American Buds*
The Appearance of Evil
The Beautiful Mrs. Reynolds
The Bride's Awakening
Brown of Harvard
The Forbidden City
Heart of the Sunset
The Hope Chest
Joan of the Woods
A Law unto Herself
On the Quiet
The Sins of the Children
Social Hypocrites
A Soul in Trust
Wild Primrose
With Hoops of Steel

1919 *Behind the Door*
The Bishop's Emeralds
The Clouded Name
Crimson Shoals
The Eternal Magdalene
The Firing Line
The Follies Girl
Gambling in Souls
Girls
Hoop-La
Oh, Boy!
The Parisian Tigress
The White Heather
1920 Up in Mary's Attic
White Lies
The Wrong Woman
1921 *Habit*

Marriage—Trial
1920 So Long Letty

Marriage brokers
1918 *The City of Dim Faces*
A Japanese Nightingale

Marriage licenses
1914 *Shorty Escapes Marriage*
1915 *The Siren's Song*
1919 *A Bachelor's Wife*
Desert Gold
The Intrusion of Isabel
The Life Line
Under the Top
The White Heather
1920 The Midnight Bride

Marriage of convenience
1912 Cleopatra
1914 An American Citizen
The Eagle's Mate
The Fatal Night
The Light Unseen
The Ragged Earl
1915 *The Blindness of Devotion*
The Climbers
The Marriage of Kitty
The Ploughshare
The Right of Way
1916 God's Country and the Woman
He Fell in Love with His Wife
The Immortal Flame
An International Marriage
The Jungle Child
Whoso Findeth a Wife
1917 American Methods
An American Widow
Anything Once
Back of the Man
The Boy Girl
The Cigarette Girl
The Conqueror
Easy Money
The Land of Promise
Molly Entangled
Money Magic
A Wife on Trial
The Woman Beneath
1918 All the World to Nothing
Friend Husband
The Life Mask
The Light Within
Mrs. Slacker
My Unmarried Wife
My Wife
The Talk of the Town
Tony America
1919 The Better Wife
The Bluffer
Break the News to Mother
The Love Burglar
The Probation Wife
The Sundown Trail
The Third Kiss
Who Cares?
1920 Just a Wife
She Loves and Lies
Stronger Than Death
A Thousand to One
Trumpet Island
The Truth About Husbands
A Woman's Business

Marseilles (France)
1913 The Count of Monte Cristo
1916 *War As It Really Is*

Marshall Field (Chicago)
1919 *It Pays to Advertise*

Martha's Vineyard (Massachusetts)
1919 *The False Faces*

Martyrs
1919 *Male and Female*

Mary, Blessed Virgin, Saint
1913 *From the Manger to the Cross*
1919 The Eternal Light

Mary I, Queen of England, 1516-1558
1915 Queen and Adventurer

Mary Louise (Spain)
1915 Don Caesar de Bazan

Mary MacLane
1918 Men Who Have Made Love to Me

Mary Magdalene, Saint
1919 *The Eternal Magdalene*
Thou Shalt Not
The Woman of Lies

Maryland
1915 The Heart of Maryland
1917 Daughter of Maryland
1918 Little Miss Hoover
1919 The Brand of Judas
19-- Barnaby Lee

Mascots
1915 *Little Sunset*

Masks
1916 The Love Mask
1917 The Masked Heart
1919 *The Blue Bandanna*
The Cambric Mask
Six Feet Four

Masons (bricklayers)
1917 A Kiss for Susie

Masons (fraternal order)
1915 Are You a Mason?

Masquerades
1916 The Kiss
Vultures of Society
1917 *Aladdin's Other Lamp*
The Spirit of Romance
Weavers of Life
1918 *Prunella*
1919 *Lord and Lady Algy*
1920 Beware of the Bride
Harriet and the Piper
Risky Business
What Happened to Rosa

Massachusetts
1915 *The Daughter of the People*
1919 Widow by Proxy
1920 Pink Tights

Massacres
1914 *Across the Pacific*
The Envoy Extraordinary
In the Days of the Thundering Herd
The Next in Command
Sitting Bull—The Hostile Sioux Indian Chief
1915 The Arab
The Battle Cry of Peace
The Campbells Are Coming
The Eagle's Nest
The Folly of a Life of Crime
The Gambler of the West
The Martyrs of the Alamo
The Melting Pot
The Penitentes
1916 *Britton of the Seventh*
Civilization's Child
The Cossack Whip
The Wild Girl of the Sierras
1917 Durand of the Bad Lands
The Yellow Bullet
1919 The Feud
In the Land of the Setting Sun; Or, Martyrs of Yesterday
Who's Your Brother?
1920 The Last of the Mohicans
The U.P. Trail

Masturbation
1919 The Solitary Sin

Matchmakers
1917 The Girl Who Couldn't Grow Up
A Man and the Woman
1918 *Just Sylvia*
The Mysterious Client
1919 Castles in the Air
Coax Me
1920 Cupid, the Cowpuncher
The Love Expert

Rookie's Return
The Truth

Mate swapping
1920 So Long Letty

Materialism
1919 Cheating Herself

Mates
1916 The Dumb Girl of Portici

Mathematics
1919 *The Old Maid's Baby*

Matricide
1919 *The Wilderness Trail*

Matrimonial agencies
1920 The Girl with the Jazz Heart

Mary Maurice
1915 *How Cissy Made Good*

Hudson Maxim
1915 *The Battle Cry of Peace*

Maxim's (New York City)
1915 Midnight at Maxim's

May Day
1915 *Fanchon the Cricket*
1919 *When Doctors Disagree*

Mayan Indians
1914 *The Pawn of Fortune*

Mayors
1914 The Man of the Hour
The Ring and the Man
1915 *Double Trouble*
The Fight
The High Road
The Politicians
The White Terror
1916 *In the Web of the Grafters*
Life's Shadows
The Man from Manhattan
The Parson of Panamint
The Woman in Politics
1917 *Betty Be Good*
The Gown of Destiny
Her Right to Live
Mr. Opp
Seven Keys to Baldpate
Transgression
1918 *Les Miserables*
String Beans
1919 *Brass Buttons*
A Fighting Colleen
The Mayor of Filbert
The World Aflame
1920 *The Amazing Woman*
The Family Honor
The Great Accident
Her Honor the Mayor
The Scarlet Dragon
Smoldering Embers

Measles
1917 Bab's Matinee Idol
1919 *In the Land of the Setting Sun; Or, Martyrs of Yesterday*

Meatpackers and meatpacking
1914 The Jungle
Such a Little Queen
1917 One Touch of Nature
Some Boy!
1919 The Boomerang
The Road Called Straight

Mecca
1920 *Kismet*

Mechanics
1915 *The Cup of Life*
Right off the Bat
1916 The Race
1919 *The Greater Victory*

Medical students
1914 *Kate*
Over Niagara Falls
1916 Lone Star
The Supreme Temptation
1917 *His Old-Fashioned Dad*
On Dangerous Ground
1918 *The Street of Seven Stars*

Medicine
1916 *Behind the Lines*
Lone Star
1917 *The Deemster*
The Question
1918 *A Pair of Sixes*
The Spreading Evil
1919 *In the Land of the Setting Sun; Or, Martyrs of Yesterday*
Miss Crusoe
The Test of Honor

Milliners
1915 *Du Barry*
1916 *The Wasted Years*
1917 *The Gun Fighter*
    Infidelity
1919 *Modern Husbands*
    True Heart Susie
1920 *The Broken Gate*
    The Gilded Dream
    Jes' Call Me Jim
    The Miracle of Money
    A Woman's Business

Millinery factories
1920 The Path She Chose

Millinery stores
1919 Marie, Ltd.

Millionaires
1913 *The Fight for Millions*
    Leah Kleschna
1914 *Born Again*
    Brewster's Millions
    The Brute
    Clothes
    The Folks from Way Down
      East
    His Last Dollar
    The Line-Up at Police
      Headquarters
    The Long Arm of the Law
    The Man from Home
    The Million Dollar Robbery
    The Pursuit of the Phantom
    What's His Name
1915 All for a Girl
    The Avalanche
    The Brink
    C.O.D.
    The Dawn of a Tomorrow
    The Final Judgment
    The Galloper
    The Glory of Youth
    The Heart of a Painted Woman
    The House of a Thousand
      Candles
    The Iron Strain
    Lord John in New York
    The Lure of the Mask
    A Man's Making
    The Pearl of the Antilles
    The Puppet Crown
    The Quest
    The Rug Maker's Daughter
    The Slim Princess
    The Spendthrift
    Stop Thief!
    When It Strikes Home
    The Winged Idol
1916 *All Man*
    Artie, the Millionaire Kid
    Ashes of Embers
    The Birth of a Man
    Blue Blood and Red
    Bought and Paid For
    The Corner
    Cross Currents
    The Dead Alive
    The Devil's Bondwoman
    The Fall of a Nation
    The Girl O' Dreams
    The Golden Chance
    The Habit of Happiness
    Hazel Kirke
    The Heir to the Hoorah
    His Wife's Good Name
    A House Built upon Sand
    Hypocrisy
    The Innocence of Ruth
    The Island of Happiness
    Jealousy
    Just a Song at Twilight
    The Land Just Over Yonder
    Man and His Soul
    The Martyrdom of Philip
      Strong
    Mister 44
    Molly Make-Believe
    Other People's Money
    The Overcoat
    The Power of Evil
    The Price of Happiness
    The Quitter
    The Raiders
    The Return of Eve
    The Salamander
    The Scarlet Road

The Shadow of a Doubt
The Soul Market
Souls in Bondage
The Storm
The Torch Bearer
The Traffic Cop
Unto Those Who Sin
The Unwritten Law
Whoso Findeth a Wife
The Woman's Law
A Youth of Fortune
Youth's Endearing Charm
1917 *The Adventurer*
    Aladdin from Broadway
    Alimony
    Annie-for-Spite
    The Apple-Tree Girl
    The Argyle Case
    The Auction of Virtue
    The Babes in the Woods
    The Beautiful Adventure
    Betty Be Good
    The Blue Streak
    The Bondage of Fear
    A Branded Soul
    Brand's Daughter
    Broadway Arizona
    The Car of Chance
    Charity Castle
    The Checkmate
    The Cigarette Girl
    The Cinderella Man
    The Clean Gun
    The Co-Respondent
    The Edge of the Law
    Envy
    The Fires of Youth
    The Golden God
    The Golden Idiot
    Hell Morgan's Girl
    High Finance
    Indiscreet Corinne
    The Last of the Carnabys
    The Little Terror
    The Millionaire Vagrant
    The Millionaire's Double
    A Modern Musketeer
    A Night in New Arabia
    One Touch of Nature
    The Page Mystery
    Peggy Leads the Way
    The Penny Philanthropist
    The Red Woman
    A Rich Man's Plaything
    The Show Down
    The Snarl
    A Soul for Sale
    Souls Adrift
    Sowers and Reapers
    The Spirit of Romance
    A Square Deal
    The Square Deceiver
    The Submarine Eye
    Sunny Jane
    Sunshine Alley
    They're Off
    Under Handicap
    Unknown 274
    The Waiting Soul
    The Web of Desire
    When a Man Sees Red
    When Men Are Tempted
    Yankee Pluck
1918 All Night
    And a Still Small Voice
    Annexing Bill
    Branding Broadway
    Broadway Love
    Empty Pockets
    Everybody's Girl
    Eve's Daughter
    Fair Enough
    The Floor Below
    The Girl from Beyond
    The Girl of My Dreams
    The Golden Wall
    The Hard Rock Breed
    Hell's End
    Her Body in Bond
    Her Great Chance
    Her Price
    His Majesty, Bunker Bean
    Hobbs in a Hurry
    How Could You, Jean?
    I Love You

Innocent's Progress
Lest We Forget
The Life Mask
The Light Within
Love Me
The Love Net
Love's Law
The Mantle of Charity
The Mating of Marcella
The Midnight Trail
The Million Dollar Dollies
Miss Ambition
Money Isn't Everything
Rich Man, Poor Man
A Rich Man's Darling
The Risky Road
Rose O' Paradise
Ruling Passions
Say, Young Fellow!
The Shell Game
The Shuttle
Tangled Lives
Too Many Millions
Under Suspicion
Uneasy Money
The Vortex
Which Woman?
The Widow's Might
1919 *The Belle of New York*
    The Bluffer
    The Boomerang
    Brass Buttons
    Cheating Herself
    The Climbers
    Come Again Smith
    The Crimson Gardenia
    Daddy-Long-Legs
    A Damsel in Distress
    Everywoman
    Eyes of Youth
    The Four-Flusher
    His Majesty, the American
    Jane Goes A-Wooing
    The Love That Dares
    Luck in Pawn
    The Marriage Price
    Married in Haste
    Men, Women and Money
    The Miracle Man
    Never Say Quit
    Peggy Does Her Darndest
    Pettigrew's Girl
    The Price of Innocence
    Red Hot Dollars
    The Rescuing Angel
    Sealed Hearts
    The Spite Bride
    A Sporting Chance (American
      Film Co.)
    Spotlight Sadie
    Too Many Crooks
    Trixie from Broadway
    Where the West Begins
    The Woman Next Door
1920 *The Dangerous Talent*
    Dollar for Dollar
    Double Speed
    Flames of the Flesh
    Footlights and Shadows
    For Love or Money
    The Furnace
    His Pajama Girl
    In Folly's Trail
    The Jungle Princess
    A Modern Salome
    Officer 666
    Old Dad
    Once a Plumber
    The Point of View
    The Saphead
    Sex
    A Slave of Vanity
    Their Mutual Child
    The Thief
    You Never Can Tell
1921 Habit

Mills
  rt **Factories**
    Mill foremen
    Mill owners
    Mill towns
    Mill workers
  nt Specific types of mills
1913 *Ben Bolt*

1915 *The End of the Road*
    The Mill on the Floss
    The White Terror
1916 *The Argonauts of*
      California—1849
1917 *The Eternal Mother*
    The Fires of Youth
1918 *The Glorious Adventure*
    Out of the Night
    The Power and the Glory
    Whims of Society
1919 *The Belle of the Season*
    The Boomerang
1920 The Dwelling Place of Light

Milos (Greece)
1918 *The Triumph of Venus*

John Milton
1917 *Conscience*

Mine claims
1914 *The Chechako*
    The Mountain Rat
    The Spoilers
    The Three of Us
1915 *The Lily of Poverty Flat*
    Little Pal
    The Lone Star Rush
    The Long Chance
1916 *A Bird of Prey*
    Langdon's Legacy
    The Love Mask
    Pay Dirt
    The Quitter
    A Sister of Six
1917 *The Mainspring*
    The Silent Man
    Their Compact
1918 *Carmen of the Klondike*
    Code of the Yukon
    Hell's Crater
    The Power and the Glory
    Rimrock Jones
1919 *The End of the Game*
    The Mints of Hell
    The Silver Girl
    This Hero Stuff
    Through the Wrong Door
1920 The Coast of Opportunity
    Dangerous Love
    Girl of the Sea
    The Golden Trail
    The Inner Voice
    The Symbol of the
      Unconquered
    Vengeance and the Girl

Mine disasters
1917 *The Courage of the Common*
      Place

Mine foremen
1914 Through Fire to Fortune
1916 Langdon's Legacy
    The Thoroughbred (American
      Film Co.)
1917 *The Americano*
    The Courage of the Common
      Place
    The Flame of Youth
    Twin Kiddies
    The World Apart
1918 *A Diplomatic Mission*
    The Girl Who Wouldn't Quit
    Laughing Bill Hyde
    The Man Hunt
1919 A Woman of Pleasure
1920 *In the Heart of a Fool*
    West Is West

Mine owners
1915 The Impostor
    The Plunderer
1916 Between Men
    Big Jim Garrity
    The Dawn of Freedom
    The Quitter
    The Ragged Princess
    The Right Direction
    Secret Love
    The Surprises of an Empty
      Hotel
    Wall Street Tragedy
    A Woman's Way
1917 *Come Through*
    The Evil Eye
    The Heir of the Ages
    Princess of the Dark
    The Raggedy Queen

Just a Song at Twilight
The Lash of Destiny
A Modern Enoch Arden
Naked Hearts
The Sex Lure
The Straight Way
The War Bride's Secret
1917 Betsy Ross
Daughter of Destiny
The Eternal Mother
The Field of Honor
*The Girl of the Timber
  Claims*
The Great Bradley Mystery
The Greater Law
The Last Sentence
The Man of Mystery
The Man Without a Country
Mayblossom
The Recoil
A Roadside Impresario
The Scarlet Car
The Silent Witness
Troublemakers
Whose Wife?
1918 The Claw
The Divine Sacrifice
The Eyes of Mystery
A Game with Fate
Hitting the High Spots
A Mother's Secret
Painted Lips
Pals First
Pay Day
The Poor Rich Man
The Price of Applause
The Rose of the World
The Safety Curtain
The Whispering Chorus
1919 An Amateur Widow
The Amazing Wife
Atonement
La Belle Russe
The Bishop's Emeralds
Blind Man's Eyes
The Broken Butterfly
Brothers Divided
Carolyn of the Corners
The Cinema Murder
The Dragon Painter
For Better, for Worse
The Heart of a Gypsy
Man's Desire
The Master Man
The Other Man's Wife
The Quickening Flame
Rose of the West
The Unveiling Hand
What Every Woman Wants
Where Bonds Are Loosed
Widow by Proxy
Wolves of the Night
The Woman Thou Gavest Me
1920 The Phantom Melody
Pink Tights
The Purple Cipher
Respectable by Proxy
The Round-Up
A Thousand to One
What Happened to Rosa
While New York Sleeps
19-- *Barnaby Lee*
Mission, Battle of the, 1890
1914 *The Indian Wars*
Missionaries
1914 The Mystery of the Poison Pool
1915 Always in the Way
The Arab
China
The Dictator
The Fox Woman
Pretty Mrs. Smith
The White Scar
1917 *The Fighting Gringo*
1918 *The Temple of Dusk*
1919 *The Dark Star*
In the Land of the Setting Sun;
  Or, Martyrs of Yesterday
When Bearcat Went Dry
A Woman There Was
1920 *Godless Men*
The Idol Dancer

Missions
1914 *The Gangsters*
The Wrath of the Gods
1916 *A Gamble in Souls*
Susan Rocks the Boat
Temptation and the Man
The Waifs
1917 *The Single Code*
1918 *The Floor Below*
The Golden Goal
Hitting the Trail
To Him That Hath
1919 *Auction of Souls*
The Girl with No Regrets
The Gray Horizon
In the Land of the Setting Sun;
  Or, Martyrs of Yesterday
A Man's Fight
Playthings of Passion
The Red Lantern
Virtuous Sinners
Who Will Marry Me?
1920 The Gift Supreme
Mississippi
1914 A Gentleman from Mississippi
Mississippi River
1917 Tom Sawyer
1918 Uncle Tom's Cabin
1920 *Hitchin' Posts*
Huckleberry Finn
The Jack-Knife Man
The Midlanders
Missouri
1918 *Why America Will Win*
1919 In Mizzoura
1920 *Red Foam*
Missouri Pacific Railroad
1914 *In Mizzoura*
Mistaken identity
rt **Disguise**
  Doubles
  Impersonation and imposture
1913 *A Sister to Carmen*
1914 Captain Swift
The Key to Yesterday
The Last Egyptian
Mr. Barnes of New York
Officer 666
A Suspicious Wife
The Tangle
Thou Shalt Not
1915 All for a Girl
Aloha Oe
Betty in Search of a Thrill
C.O.D.
The Commuters
The Coward
Crooky
The Face in the Moonlight
The Fairy and the Waif
The Galloper
The Gray Mask
Hearts Aflame
His Wife
The Impostor
Judy Forgot
Little Miss Brown
The Man Behind the Door
The Man Who Vanished
Marrying Money
Money
Nearly a Lady
Nedra
The Old Homestead
The Patriot and the Spy
The Pretenders
*The Rights of Man: A Story of
  War's Red Blotch*
The Sable Lorcha
The Stubbornness of Geraldine
What Happened to Jones
The Woman Who Lied
1916 *Ashes of Embers*
The Crown Prince's Double
The Folly of Revenge
From Broadway to a Throne
Her American Prince
Human Driftwood
The Innocent Lie
The King's Game
A Knight of the Range
The Mainspring
The Man Who Would Not Die
The Prince of Graustark
A Stranger from Somewhere

A Tortured Heart
The Wild Girl of the Sierras
1917 Aladdin from Broadway
Alias Mrs. Jessop
American Maid
Bab's Burglar
Bab's Matinee Idol
The Barrier
The Beautiful Adventure
Betrayed
Betsy Ross
Betty Be Good
Borrowed Plumage
The Bottom of the Well
The Calendar Girl
Castles for Two
A Child of the Wild
The Crimson Dove
The Danger Trail
A Daughter of the Poor
The Divorcee
The Eternal Sin
The Flame of the Yukon
The Ghost House
The Girl of the Timber Claims
The Grell Mystery
The Haunted Pajamas
Man's Woman
The Millionaire's Double
Miss Jackie of the Army
The Mother Instinct
Next Door to Nancy
One Hour
The Outsider
The Price of Pride
The Princess of Park Row
Sacrifice
Sister Against Sister
Snap Judgement
The Stolen Paradise
The Upper Crust
The Voice of Conscience
Who Shall Take My Life?
1918 The Accidental Honeymoon
All the World to Nothing
An American Live Wire
The Floor Below
The Girl in His House
The Inn of the Blue Moon
Mrs. Leffingwell's Boots
Nobody's Wife
Opportunity
A Pair of Silk Stockings
Paying His Debt
Playing the Game
The Return of Mary
A Rich Man's Darling
The Risky Road
The Rough Lover
Ruggles of Red Gap
The Savage Woman
Set Free
The Spurs of Sybil
The Turn of a Card
The Whispering Chorus
The Witch Woman
Wives and Other Wives
1919 Alias Mike Moran
All Wrong
An Amateur Widow
L'Apache
La Belle Russe
The Beloved Cheater
The Blue Bandanna
Brass Buttons
The Crimson Gardenia
Everywoman
A Favor to a Friend
The Fire Flingers
A Fugitive from Matrimony
A Gentleman of Quality
The Girl Dodger
Good Gracious, Annabelle
The Hellion
In Search of Arcady
It Happened in Paris
Leave It to Susan
The Love Burglar
Love in a Hurry
Mistaken Identity
Over the Garden Wall
Put Up Your Hands
A Regular Girl
Rustling a Bride
Sandy Burke of the U-Bar-U

Silent Strength
A Sporting Chance (Famous
  Players-Lasky Corp.)
A Taste of Life
Turning the Tables
Under Suspicion
The Unpardonable Sin
Upstairs
Wanted—A Husband
When Doctors Disagree
Widow by Proxy
Yvonne from Paris
1920 Bachelor Apartments
The Chamber Mystery
The Fourteenth Man
Hearts Up
Her First Elopement
Human Stuff
The Ladder of Lies
The Shadow of Rosalie Byrnes
Silk Hosiery
Sooner or Later
Three Gold Coins
Too Much Johnson
Twin Beds
Two Kinds of Love
The Veiled Marriage
What Happened to Jones
Why Pick on Me?
Wolves of the Street
The Wonderful Chance
The Wrong Woman
You Never Can Tell

Mistresses
1913 *Sapho*
The Seed of the Fathers
1914 *Absinthe*
At the Cross Roads
The Battle of the Sexes
The Escape
Manon Lescaut
The Marked Woman
The Master Mind
Nell Gwynne
Threads of Destiny
1915 *The Absentee*
Anna Karenina
The Cup of Life
The Devil
Divorced
Du Barry
The Eternal City
The Family Stain
The Fighting Hope
The Frame-Up
Her Mother's Secret
The Immigrant
A Modern Magdalen
My Best Girl
Pearls of Temptation
Salvation Nell
Shadows from the Past
Strathmore
Temptation
The Warning
Zaza
1916 *The Daring of Diana*
Driftwood
The Eternal Grind
The Evil Thereof
The Footlights of Fate
The Haunted Manor
Her Bleeding Heart
The Immortal Flame
Inherited Passions
The Libertine
The Old Folks at Home
The Ordeal of Elizabeth
The Other Side of the Door
The Payment
The Price of Happiness
The Ransom
The Scarlet Woman
Sins of Men
A Soul Enslaved
The Stain in the Blood
The Strength of the Weak
Unprotected
Vultures of Society
What Will People Say?
The Wild Girl of the Sierras
Wild Oats
1917 As Man Made Her
The Auction of Virtue
The Birth of Patriotism

Marquis de Montcalm
1914 Wolfe; Or, The Conquest of
Quebec
Monte Carlo
1914 *The Man on the Box*
1915 *The House of the Lost Court*
The Lure of the Mask
Mr. Grex of Monte Carlo
1916 *The Way of the World*
1917 *The Tiger Woman*
1918 The Turn of the Wheel
1919 The Divorcee
Hawthorne of the U.S.A.
1920 *Children of Destiny*
The Mollycoddle
Passion's Playground
A Romantic Adventuress
Montenegro
1915 The Captive
The Unafraid
**Montezuma II, Aztec Emperor,
1480-1520**
1916 *The Captive God*
1917 The Woman God Forgot
Montreal
1917 *The Jury of Fate*
1918 *The Purple Lily*
That Devil, Bateese
1919 *Paid in Advance*
1920 *Isobel; Or, The Trail's End*
Moonshiners
1914 *The Eagle's Mate*
Fighting Death
1915 The Heart of the Blue Ridge
1916 *Broken Chains*
Judith of the Cumberlands
The Masked Rider
The Stronger Love
The Trail of the Lonesome Pine
1917 Her Country's Call
Mountain Dew
1918 *The Challenge Accepted*
Her Inspiration
One Dollar Bid
The Scarlet Drop
1919 *In Old Kentucky*
The Shepherd of the Hills
When Bearcat Went Dry
1920 The Dead Line
The Gauntlet
1922 The Cynic Effect
Moors
1915 *In the Palace of the King*
1916 *Robinson Crusoe*
Moose
1915 *American Game Trails*
Moral corruption
1913 The Inside of the White Slave
Traffic
Traffic in Souls
1914 Absinthe
The Battle of the Sexes
A Gentleman from Mississippi
The Invisible Power
Kate
Protect Us
The Temptations of Satan
1915 The Apaches of Paris
The Blindness of Devotion
The Cup of Life
Eugene Aram
The Failure
The Fight
Flame of Passion
A Fool There Was
The Fox Woman
The Gambler of the West
The Game of Three
Ghosts
The Heart of a Painted Woman
The Hungarian Nabob
The Voice of Satan
A Woman's Resurrection
1916 The Black Crook
The Blindness of Love
Hell-to-Pay Austin
Idle Wives
The Libertine
Macbeth
Out of the Drifts
Warning! The S.O.S. Call of
Humanity
Wild Oats

1917 The Devil Dodger
The Devil's Pay Day
The Dormant Power
The Heart of a Lion
The Inevitable
The Last of the Carnabys
1918 All Man
And the Children Pay
The Fall of the Romanoffs
Just a Woman
Parentage
A Perfect Lady
Restitution
The Struggle Everlasting
1919 A Very Good Young Man
1920 Dad's Girl
The Deceiver
Democracy
Dr. Jekyll and Mr. Hyde
(Pioneer Film Corp.)
Eyes of the Heart
The Forbidden Thing
Idols of Clay
Love Madness
Sinners
Twisted Souls
Voices
Moral reformation
1913 Ten Nights in a Barroom
1914 The Battle of the Sexes
The Good-for-Nothing
The Little Gray Lady
Mother
The Only Son
St. Elmo
The Straight Road
The Walls of Jericho
A Woman Who Did
1915 *The Builder of Bridges*
Children of Eve
The Cowardly Way
The Dancing Girl
The Explorer
The Face in the Moonlight
The Frame-Up
The Galley Slave
Gambling Inside and Out
A Gentleman of Leisure
The Great Divide
Help Wanted
Her Atonement
Jordan Is a Hard Road
A Little Brother of the Rich
The Magic Toy Maker
A Modern Magdalen
The Money Master
The Old Homestead
On the Night Stage
A Price for Folly
The Right of Way
The Unknown
The Victory of Virtue
When a Woman Loves
The Woman Who Lied
A Woman's Resurrection
1916 The Blindness of Love
The Chattel
The City
The Clarion
The Conqueror
The Conscience of John David
Divorce and the Daughter
The Eternal Grind
Fighting Blood
The Half Million Bribe
Hell's Hinges
Humanizing Mr. Winsby
Husband and Wife
Idle Wives
Is Any Girl Safe?
The Isle of Life
It May Be Your Daughter
Light at Dusk
Love's Lariat
The Other Side of the Door
Out of the Drifts
The Overcoat
Pay Dirt
The Power of Evil
Prudence the Pirate
The Quality of Faith
The Reapers
Redeeming Love
The Right to Be Happy
Rose of the Alley

The Sin Ye Do
The Social Secretary
The Soul of a Child
The Spider and the Fly
Warning! The S.O.S. Call of
Humanity
Who Killed Joe Merrion?
Wild Oats
1917 *The Auction Block*
Babette
The Bad Boy
A Branded Soul
The Circus of Life
Come Through
Conscience
A Crooked Romance
Even As You and I
The Food Gamblers
The Fuel of Life
The Gentle Intruder
The Gift Girl
The Girl by the Roadside
The Heart of Ezra Greer
Heart Strings
The Judgement House
The Man Who Forgot
A Marked Man
The Night Workers
Outcast
The Painted Madonna
The Peddler
Periwinkle
The Price of Her Soul
Sapho
The Scarlet Car
The Secret Game
The Slacker (Metro Pictures
Corp.)
The Slacker's Heart
Somewhere in America
Souls Triumphant
The Square Deal Man
Stagestruck
Thais
Weavers of Life
The Web of Life
Youth
1918 *All Woman*
Blue Blazes Rawden
Cecilia of the Pink Roses
Denny from Ireland
The Eyes of Julia Deep
False Ambition
The Grand Passion
No Children Wanted
Out of the Night
A Petticoat Pilot
The Price of Applause
The Prodigal Wife
The Purple Lily
Restitution
Revelation
The Road to France
Ruling Passions
The Struggle Everlasting
Three X Gordon
The Venus Model
*What Becomes of the
Children?*
When a Woman Sins
Wild Primrose
1919 Alias Mike Moran
All of a Sudden Norma
As the Sun Went Down
Beating the Odds
The Bluffer
The Bramble Bush
The Capitol
The Career of Katherine Bush
Children of Banishment
The Common Cause
Deliverance
Gates of Brass
Ginger
The Greater Victory
The Hushed Hour
The Knickerbocker Buckaroo
The Law of Nature
The Light of Victory
The Long Lane's Turning
The Love Hunger
A Man's Duty
The Market of Souls
The Master Man
The Mayor of Filbert

Men, Women and Money
The Miracle Man
The Moonshine Trail
The Perfect Lover
The Price of Innocence
The Quickening Flame
Redhead
The Shepherd of the Hills
The Stream of Life
That's Good
The Unbroken Promise
When a Girl Loves
1919-20
Piccadilly Jim
1920 The Brute Master
Captain Swift
The Cheater
A Common Level
The Cradle of Courage
The Deceiver
Earthbound
The Family Honor
The Great Accident
The Great Redeemer
The Heart of a Woman
Heart Strings
The Jack-Knife Man
Remodelling Her Husband
The Spirit of Good
The Third Generation
A Thousand to One
The Truth
Uncharted Channels
Unseen Forces
Voices
When Dawn Came
The Woman Gives
Women Men Love
19-- The Slave Market
Frank Moran
1916 Willard-Moran Fight
Henry Morganthau
1919 *Auction of Souls*
Moroccans
1918 Bound in Morocco
Morocco
1914 Fire and Sword
1916 Robinson Crusoe
1918 Bound in Morocco
Moroni
1913 *One Hundred Years of
Mormonism*
Moros
1918 *Why America Will Win*
Morphine
1914 *Dope*
The Span of Life
1916 *The Beggar of Cawnpore*
Doctor Neighbor
The Truant Soul
1917 *The Serpent's Tooth*
The Squaw Man's Son
Morse code
1913 *Chelsea 7750*
1918 The Flash of Fate
1920 *Cynthia-of-the-Minute*
Mortgages
rt **Deeds**
1913 *Ten Nights in a Barroom*
1914 *Rip Van Winkle*
Shore Acres
1915 *A Child of God*
The End of the Road
It's No Laughing Matter
*The Man Who Beat Dan
Dolan*
Marse Covington
1916 Humanizing Mr. Winsby
My Lady Incog.
Susie Snowflake
1917 *Every Girl's Dream*
Grafters
The Little Samaritan
Rebecca of Sunnybrook Farm
Sowers and Reapers
1918 *Danger—Go Slow*
The Last Rebel
The Love Net
To the Highest Bidder
1919 *Caleb Piper's Girl*
Cupid Forecloses
Sandy Burke of the U-Bar-U
Toby's Bow
Vagabond Luck

Motion picture scriptwriters
1915 How Cissy Made Good
1916 Extravagance
    Nearly a King
1917 The Iced Bullet
    New York Luck

Motion picture studios
1915 How Cissy Made Good
    The Stolen Voice
1916 *The Essanay-Chaplin Revue of 1916*
1917 All for a Husband
    A Girl's Folly
    The Volunteer

Motion picture stuntmen
1918 The Goat

Motion picture theaters
1915 *The Battle of Ballots*
    Maciste
1916 *Extravagance*

Motion pictures
1914 *Facing the Gattling Guns*
    Fighting Death
1915 *The Governor's Boss*
    The Stolen Voice
1916 The Essanay-Chaplin Revue of 1916
    Extravagance
    Hoodoo Ann
    Idle Wives
1917 A Girl's Folly
    Sowers and Reapers
    This Is the Life
    The Volunteer
    The Warfare of the Flesh
1918 The Goat
    The Kid Is Clever
    Pay Day
    Tell It to the Marines
1919 Ginger
    The Scarlet Shadow
    Stepping Out
1920 Shipwrecked Among Cannibals

Motorboats
1914 *The Price of Treachery; Or, The Lighthouse Keeper's Daughter*
1915 *A Trade Secret*
1916 *The Wharf Rat*

Motorcycle accidents
1917 *Has Man the Right to Kill?*

Motorcycles
1915 *His Turning Point*
1918 *Beans*
    Smashing Through

Mount Fuji
1917 *A Trip Through Japan*

Mount Vesuvius
1917 *The Man of Mystery*

Mountain climbing
1915 In the Amazon Jungles with the Captain Besley Expedition
1916 A Modern Thelma
1918 *The Make-Believe Wife*
1919 Blind Husbands
1920 The Silent Barrier

Mountain life
1913 Caprice
1914 *The Eagle's Mate*
    Jess of the Mountain Country
1915 The Governor's Lady
    The Heart of the Blue Ridge
    The Silent Voice
    Thou Shalt Not Kill
    The Vow
1916 *The Apostle of Vengeance*
    The Call of the Cumberlands
    Caprice of the Mountains
    Children of the Feud
    Fate's Boomerang
    The Highest Bid
    Judith of the Cumberlands
    The Salamander
    The Wild Girl of the Sierras
1917 *Her Country's Call*
    The Long Trail
    Loyalty
    Mountain Dew
    The Price of Her Soul
1918 The Goddess of Lost Lake
    Her Inspiration
    A Nymph of the Foothills
    One Dollar Bid

Riders of the Night
1919 Heart O' the Hills
    His Divorced Wife
    In Old Kentucky
    Louisiana
    A Man in the Open
    Mary Regan
    The Rebellious Bride
    The Shepherd of the Hills
    Silent Strength
    Twilight
    Two Women
    When Bearcat Went Dry
1920 A Cumberland Romance
    The Dead Line
    Forbidden Valley

Mountaineers
1914 *The Great Leap; Until Death Do Us Part*
1916 The Call of the Cumberlands
    Caprice of the Mountains
    Children of the Feud
    The Feud Girl
    Jim Grimsby's Boy
    Judith of the Cumberlands
    The Path of Darkness
    The Stronger Love
    Then I'll Come Back to You
    A Woman's Power
1917 The Adopted Son
    A Magdalene of the Hills
    A Man's Law
    Mountain Dew
1918 Her Inspiration
    Her Man
    A Nymph of the Foothills
1919 Bill Apperson's Boy
    What Am I Bid?
1920 A Cumberland Romance
    The Dead Line
    Forbidden Valley
    The Little Shepherd of Kingdom Come
    Love's Protegé
    The Valley of Tomorrow

Mountains
1916 *The Place Beyond the Winds*
    Thou Art the Man
1917 *The Flashlight*
    The Savage
    The Sin Woman
    Snap Judgement
    A Son of the Hills
    The Wildcat
1918 The Changing Woman
    The Girl of My Dreams
    New Love for Old
    The Primitive Woman
    The Purple Lily
    The Tiger Man
    A Woman of Redemption
1919 *Other Men's Wives*
    The Outcasts of Poker Flats
    The Poppy Girl's Husband
    The Road Called Straight
    Roses and Thorns
    The Spitfire of Seville
    Whitewashed Walls
1920 Mountain Madness

Mukden (China)
1918 Innocent

Mulattoes
  rt **Blacks**
    Octoroons and Quadroons
1914 *A Florida Enchantment*
1915 The Birth of a Nation
    The Nigger
1916 *At Piney Ridge*
    Pudd'nhead Wilson
1917 The Bar Sinister
    Sold at Auction
1918 *Free and Equal*

Mules
1914 *The Magic Cloak of Oz*

Mummies
1915 The Dust of Egypt
    Lord John in New York
1918 *His Majesty, Bunker Bean*

Munitions factories
1915 *The Battles of a Nation*
1916 Arms and the Woman
    The Redemption of Dave Darcey

1917 *Bab's Matinee Idol*
    Wrath
1918 Doing Their Bit
    The Girl of Today
    The Grand Passion
    The Great Love
    Her Country First
    On the Jump
    The Sea Flower
    The Thing We Love
    Till I Come Back to You
    The Wasp
1919 *The Petal on the Current*

Munitions manufacturers
1916 Daredevil Kate
    Powder
1917 *This Is the Life*
1918 The Claws of the Hun

Murder
  rt **Attempted murder**
    Justifiable homicide
    Manslaughter
  nt Specific types of murder
1912 The Adventures of Lieutenant Petrosino
1913 *Checkers*
    An Hour Before Dawn
    In the Stretch
    The Man from the Golden West
    One Hundred Years of Mormonism
    The Prisoner of Zenda
    The Seed of the Fathers
    A Sister to Carmen
    The Stranglers of Paris
    Tess of the D'Urbervilles
    The Third Degree
1914 *Absinthe*
    At the Cross Roads
    The Avenging Conscience; Thou Shalt Not Kill
    Beating Back
    The Boundary Rider
    Called Back
    A Celebrated Case
    Cocaine Traffic; Or, The Drug Terror
    The Coming Power
    The Conspiracy
    The Criminal Path
    Dope
    The Dream Woman
    Facing the Gattling Guns
    A Factory Magdalen
    The Floor Above
    The Ghost Breaker
    The Governor's Ghost
    The Great Diamond Robbery
    The Idler
    The Invisible Power
    Jess
    Judith of Bethulia
    The Jungle
    The Kangaroo
    The Last Egyptian
    Lena Rivers (Cosmos Feature Film Corp.)
    The Little Angel of Canyon Creek
    The Marked Woman
    Marta of the Lowlands
    The Master Mind
    Michael Strogoff
    Mrs. Wiggs of the Cabbage Patch
    The Murders in the Rue Morgue
    The Mystery of Edwin Drood
    The Mystery of the Poison Pool
    The Next in Command
    The Nightingale
    The Outlaw Reforms
    Over Niagara Falls
    The Phantom Violin
    Pierre of the Plains
    The Pride of Jennico
    The Quest of the Sacred Jewel
    Salomy Jane
    Samson
    The Scales of Justice
    Shannon of the Sixth
    The Squaw Man
    The Strange Story of Sylvia Gray

A Suspicious Wife
The Taint
Tess of the Storm Country
Thou Shalt Not
Threads of Destiny
Three Weeks
The Tigress
The Toll of Mammon
The Trail of the Lonesome Pine
The Walls of Jericho
The War of Wars; Or, The Franco-German Invasion
Winning His First Case
The Wolf
Your Girl and Mine: A Woman Suffrage Play
1915 An Affair of Three Nations
    After Dark
    The Alster Case
    An American Gentleman
    Armstrong's Wife
    The Battle Cry of Peace
    Bella Donna
    The Bludgeon
    The Breath of Araby
    Bred in the Bone
    The Broken Law
    The Bulldogs of the Trail
    The Butterfly
    The Call of the Dance
    Carmen (Fox Film Corp.)
    Carmen (Jesse L. Lasky Feature Play Co.)
    The Chalice of Courage
    The Circular Staircase
    The Clemenceau Case
    The Closing Net
    The Clue
    The Commanding Officer
    The Concealed Truth
    The Cowboy and the Lady
    The Darkening Trail
    The Destroying Angel
    Divorced
    The Eternal City
    The Explorer
    The Face in the Moonlight
    The Family Stain
    The Final Judgment
    Flame of Passion
    The Folly of a Life of Crime
    The Frame-Up
    Gambier's Advocate
    The Garden of Lies
    The Gray Mask
    The Great Ruby
    Greater Love Hath No Man
    The Green Cloak
    The Heart of a Painted Woman
    The Heart of Jennifer
    Hearts Aflame
    The Ivory Snuff Box
    Kreutzer Sonata
    The Last of the Mafia
    Life Without Soul
    The Long Chance
    Lord John in New York
    The Lure of the Mask
    A Man and His Mate
    The Man of Shame
    A Man's Prerogative
    Marse Covington
    The Masqueraders
    The Menace of the Mute
    The Model
    Mortmain
    A Mother's Confession
    The Mummy and the Humming Bird
    My Madonna
    The Mystery of Room 13
    On Her Wedding Night
    One Million Dollars
    The Pitfall
    The Ploughshare
    A Price for Folly
    Princess Romanoff
    The Pursuing Shadow
    Queen and Adventurer
    Ranson's Folly
    Regeneration
    The Right of Way
    The Ring of the Borgias

The Panther Woman
Pay Day
Playthings
The Prussian Cur
The Queen of Hearts
The Reckoning Day
Resurrection
Revenge
Riddle Gawne
Riders of the Night
The Road to France
Rose O' Paradise
Rosemary Climbs the Heights
The Shoes That Danced
Six Shooter Andy
The Soul of Buddha
Stella Maris
The Still Alarm
The Temple of Dusk
Tongues of Flame
The Transgressor
The Triumph of Venus
The Turn of the Wheel
Under the Yoke
Unexpected Places
Untamed
The Vanity Pool
The Velvet Hand
The Voice of Destiny
Whatever the Cost
Whims of Society
The Whirlpool
The White Lie
Wild Life
Wild Youth
Winner Takes All
The Winning of Beatrice
The Witch Woman
A Woman of Impulse
A Woman of Redemption
The Yellow Ticket
Zongar
1919 *The Amazing Wife*
L'Apache
As the Sun Went Down
Bare Fists
The Battler
Behind the Door
The Bishop's Emeralds
The Black Gate
Broken Blossoms
Calibre 38
The Clouded Name
The Devil's Trail
Dust of Desire
The End of the Game
The Eternal Magdalene
Extravagance
False Gods
The Feud
A Fight for Love
Fool's Gold
For a Woman's Honor
Forest Rivals
A Girl at Bay
The Girl from Outside
The Gray Horizon
The Gray Towers Mystery
The Gray Wolf's Ghost
The Great Victory, Wilson or
   the Fall of the Kaiser? The Fall of the
   Hohenzollerns
The Greater Victory
The Greatest Question
The Grim Game
A Heart in Pawn
The Heart of a Gypsy
The Hellion
The Hidden Truth
High Pockets
His Divorced Wife
His Wife's Friend
The Illustrious Prince
In Honor's Web
In Mizzoura
Just Squaw
Keali
Kitty Kelly, M.D.
The Law of Men
The Love Auction
The Love Call
The Love That Dares
The Man Beneath
Mandarin's Gold
A Man's Fight

The Master Man
The Midnight Stage
The Mints of Hell
The Mother and the Law
*The Mystery of the Yellow
   Room*
The New Moon
The Oakdale Affair
The Open Door
Out of the Shadow
The Quickening Flame
Reclaimed: The Struggle for a
   Soul Between Love and Hate
Riders of Vengeance
Rose of the West
Sacred Silence
Should a Husband Forgive?
A Society Exile
The Spitfire of Seville
The Stronger Vow
Suspense
Tangled Threads
The Teeth of the Tiger
Thin Ice
The Thirteenth Chair
Thunderbolts of Fate
The Trembling Hour
A Trick of Fate
The Unbroken Promise
The Undercurrent
The Unveiling Hand
The Virtuous Thief
Wagon Tracks
The Westerners
When Fate Decides
Where's Mary?
A White Man's Chance
Who Will Marry Me?
Wings of the Morning
The Woman Next Door
A Woman of Pleasure
The Woman Under Cover
The Woman Under Oath
The Wreck
You Never Know Your Luck
1920 *The Amateur Wife*
Below the Deadline
Blind Wives
The Blue Moon
Body and Soul
Broadway and Home
The Broken Gate
The Bromley Case
Bullet Proof
Chains of Evidence
Children Not Wanted
Circumstantial Evidence
The Common Sin
The Confession
The Cradle of Courage
The Dangerous Talent
The Dark Mirror
A Daughter of Two Worlds
Deadline at Eleven
Desert Love
The Devil's Garden
Dice of Destiny
Dr. Jekyll and Mr. Hyde
   (Famous Players-Lasky
   Corp.)
*Dr. Jekyll and Mr. Hyde
   (Pioneer Film Corp.)*
Dollar for Dollar
A Double Dyed Deceiver
Drag Harlan
Earthbound
813
The Fighting Chance
The Fighting Shepherdess
The Flame of Hellgate
The Forbidden Thing
The Fourth Face
The Gauntlet
Go and Get It
The Good-Bad Wife
Greater Than Love
The Greatest Love
Held in Trust
Heliotrope
Hell's Oasis
The Hidden Code
The Hidden Light
The House of Whispers
The Law of the Yukon
Life

Live Sparks
The Lone Hand
Lone Hand Wilson
The Love Flower
Love Madness
Love Without Question
Love's Battle
Luring Shadows
Madame X
The Mutiny of the Elsinore
On with the Dance
One Hour Before Dawn
The One Way Trail
Other Men's Shoes
Out of the Snows
The Paliser Case
The Penalty
The Plunger
The Price of Redemption
The Price of Silence
Red Foam
The Riddle: Woman
Riders of the Dawn
The Rose of Nome
Rouge and Riches
The Scrap of Paper
The Shadow of Rosalie Byrnes
Skyfire
The Star Rover
Stolen Moments
The Strange Boarder
Sunset Sprague
The Tiger's Cub
The Trail of the Cigarette
The Triple Clue
Twisted Souls
Two Kinds of Love
Two Moons
The U.P. Trail
Under Northern Lights
The Unseen Witness
The Victim
The Village Sleuth
The Virgin of Stamboul
The Wall Street Mystery
The Way Women Love
While New York Sleeps
Within Our Gates
Wolves of the Street
The Woman in Room 13
The Wrong Woman
The Yellow Typhoon
1920-21
   The House of Mystery
1921 *Miss 139*

Museums
1914 *Through Dante's Flames*
1917 *The Bond Between*
1918 *Midnight Madness*
Music
1915 The Melting Pot
   The Shooting of Dan McGrew
1917 *The Door Between*
1918 *Among the Cannibal Isles of
   the South Pacific*
The Lost Chord
Music halls
   rt **Vaudeville**
1918 *The Safety Curtain*
1919 *Sahara*
1920 *Scratch My Back*
Music students
1916 *Love's Toll*
   The Ordeal of Elizabeth
   Revelations
   The Yellow Passport
1917 *Darkest Russia*
   Magda
   The Price She Paid
   The White Raven
1918 *The Cabaret Girl*
   Her Price
   The Street of Seven Stars
1919 The Splendid Romance
   The Test of Honor
1920 Once to Every Woman
   Out of the Storm
   Voices
Music teachers
1915 *The Making Over of Geoffrey
   Manning*
1917 *The Price She Paid*
   Unknown 274
1920 Should a Wife Work?

Musical instruments
1917 *Efficiency Edgar's Courtship*
Musical reviews
1915 *The Fairy and the Waif*
1919 A Favor to a Friend
   Hard Boiled
   Lombardi, Ltd.
   Spotlight Sadie
   Strictly Confidential
   Trixie from Broadway
   What Love Forgives
   Words and Music By –
Musicians
1914 Mother Love
1915 *The Beloved Vagabond*
   The Fifth Commandment
   The Last Concert
   The Magic Skin
   Mortmain
   The Silent Voice
   Trilby
1916 Civilization's Child
   The Crippled Hand
   The Daughter of MacGregor
   Love Never Dies
   Merely Mary Ann
   The Waifs
1917 *The Girl Without a Soul*
   Little Miss Optimist
   The Rainbow Girl
   The Woman and the Beast
1918 The Lost Chord
   Love's Law
   Mirandy Smiles
   The Song of Songs
   The Struggle Everlasting
   Wild Life
1919 *Child of M'sieu*
   A Royal Democrat
   You're Fired
1920 The Hidden Light
   Love's Harvest
   The Point of View
Muslims
1917 The Gift Girl
1919 Auction of Souls
1920 Kismet
Mutes
   rt **Aphasia**
   Deaf-mutes
1915 *The Menace of the Mute*
   The Stolen Voice
1916 A Romance of Billy Goat Hill
1918 *The Guilt of Silence*
1920 *While New York Sleeps*
Mutiny
1913 The Sea Wolf
1915 *The Unknown*
1916 Robinson Crusoe
   To Have and to Hold
   Unprotected
1917 Mutiny
   The Phantom Shotgun
   The Sea Master
   The Ship of Doom
   The Sixteenth Wife
1918 *The Sea Panther*
   Tarzan of the Apes
   Treasure Island
   Wild Women
1919 *Loot*
   Miss Adventure
   The Profiteer
1920 The Brute Master
   Cynthia-of-the-Minute
   The Hell Ship
   The Mutiny of the Elsinore
   Something Different
   Treasure Island
   Under Crimson Skies
   The Woman Untamed
Mystics
1915 *The Wonderful Adventure*
1916 *Sunshine Dad*
1919 The Jungle Trail
   Upside Down
Mythical characters
1915 The Absentee
   Alice in Wonderland
1916 *The Soul's Cycle*
1917 The Bottle Imp
1918 Queen of the Sea
1919 Dangerous Waters
   The Dragon Painter

All of a Sudden Norma
The Amazing Impostor
The American Way
Bonds of Honor
The Brand of Judas
The Career of Katherine Bush
Cowardice Court
The Delicious Little Devil
Diane of the Green Van
The Divorcee
Fighting for Gold
The Gay Lord Quex
A Gentleman of Quality
The Glorious Lady
Her Purchase Price
His Wife's Friend
The Illustrious Prince
In Search of Arcady
Injustice
Johnny Get Your Gun
Lord and Lady Algy
Love in a Hurry
Love Insurance
Love's Prisoner
Lure of Ambition
Male and Female
Mind the Paint Girl
The Miracle of Love
A Misfit Earl
Our Better Selves
The Parisian Tigress
Peg O' My Heart
A Royal Democrat
Sadie Love
Sahara
A Society Exile
Strictly Confidential
A Temperamental Wife
The Two Brides
The Usurper
The Vengeance of Durand
The White Heather
The Woman Thou Gavest Me
A Woman's Experience
The World and Its Woman
A Yankee Princess
You Never Know Your Luck
1920 The Adventurer
All-of-a-Sudden-Peggy
April Folly
The Best of Luck
Billions
The Cheater
Children of Destiny
The City of Masks
Conrad in Quest of His Youth
The Devil's Garden
Faith
The Fatal Hour
A Fool and His Money
The Fourteenth Man
The Frisky Mrs. Johnson
The Furnace
Half an Hour
The Heart of a Child
Hearts Are Trumps
Her Five-Foot Highness
The Hope
If I Were King
Lady Rose's Daughter
The Man Who Lost Himself
Merely Mary Ann
Milestones
The Mother of His Children
The Mysteries of Paris
Nurse Marjorie
On with the Dance
Out of the Storm
Passers-By
The Peddler of Lies
The Phantom Melody
The Return of Tarzan
The Right to Love
The Romance Promoters
The Servant Question
Silk Hosiery
Simple Souls
A Slave of Vanity
The Spenders
The Street Called Straight
The Strongest
Suds
White Lies
The Woman and the Puppet
The Wonderful Chance

The World and His Wife
1921 *Love's Plaything*
Nome (Alaska)
1912 *Atop of the World in Motion*
1914 The Spoilers
1919 The Girl from Outside
1920 The Rose of Nome
Nonconformists
1916 The Isle of Life
1919 *The Siren's Song*
Nonviolence
1919 The Ace of the Saddle
Bare Fists
The Unbroken Promise
Normandy (France)
1914 *Charlotte Corday*
1916 The Pawn of Fate
North Africa
   rt **Africa**
      South Africa
1914 When Rome Ruled
1916 *The Bugler of Algiers*
The Light That Failed
1919 The Unveiling Hand
North Carolina
1915 *On the Spanish Main*
1916 The Colored American
     Winning His Suit
The Foolish Virgin
The Masked Rider
1917 A Son of the Hills
1919 Twilight
1921 *The Jucklins*
North West Mounted Police
1914 *Pierre of the Plains*
Thou Shalt Not
1915 *Armstrong's Wife*
The Bulldogs of the Trail
Heléne of the North
1916 Autumn
The Destroyers
Nanette of the Wilds
1917 Her Fighting Chance
The Land of Long Shadows
The Law of the North
The Savage
The Tides of Fate
Until They Get Me
Wild Sumac
1918 Ace High
Closin' In
Headin' South
Heart of the Wilds
The Law of the Great
     Northwest
Nobody's Wife
1919 Beauty-Proof
The Devil's Trail
A Fight for Love
The Man in the Moonlight
1920 The Challenge of the Law
The Cyclone
Isobel; Or, The Trail's End
The Night Riders
Nomads of the North
The One Way Trail
Out of the Snows
The River's End
The Rose of Nome
Skyfire
Under Northern Lights
Northerners
1915 The End of the Road
Marse Covington
1916 *The Crisis*
Her Father's Son
1918 *Green Eyes*
Wild Primrose
Norway
1915 *Peer Gynt*
1916 A Modern Thelma
Norwegians
1915 Peer Gynt
A Yankee from the West
1916 Pillars of Society
Nostalgia
1914 A Good Little Devil
1918 *The Man Hunt*
The Man of Bronze
1920 Conrad in Quest of His Youth

Nottingham (England)
1913 *Robin Hood*
Nouveaux riches
1914 Burning Daylight: The
     Adventures of "Burning
     Daylight" in Civilization
1915 *Blackbirds*
The Bludgeon
Business Is Business
Esmeralda
The Family Cupboard
A Girl of Yesterday
The Governor's Lady
Mrs. Plum's Pudding
The Spender
Who's Who in Society
1916 Home
1917 A Kiss for Susie
The Lady of the Photograph
Pride
The Road Between
1918 Cupid by Proxy
Fair Enough
Just Sylvia
Oh, Johnny!
Real Folks
1919 Cowardice Court
The Fear Woman
Fools and Their Money
A Fugitive from Matrimony
The Gay Old Dog
Rough Riding Romance
The Silver King
The Usurper
Venus in the East
A Yankee Princess
1920 *Cinderella's Twin*
Jack Straw
Nova Scotia (Canada)
1917 The Best Man
Novelists
   rt **Authors**
1915 *The Broken Law*
Lord John in New York
'Twas Ever Thus
1916 *The Flying Torpedo*
God's Half Acre
The Grasp of Greed
The Hunted Woman
The Ocean Waif
The Strength of the Weak
1917 Chicken Casey
More Truth Than Poetry
The Mortal Sin
Poppy
The Power of Decision
Seven Keys to Baldpate
Stranded in Arcady
Up or Down?
1918 *Ann's Finish*
Back to the Woods
The Danger Game
A Daughter of the Old South
A Lady's Name
Marriage
The Mating
My Unmarried Wife
Within the Cup
Women's Weapons
1919 *Almost a Husband*
The Avalanche
The Brat
Broken Commandments
Captain Kidd, Jr.
Daughter of Mine
A Girl in Bohemia
Let's Elope
The Little Rowdy
The Microbe
The Probation Wife
A Society Exile
Through the Toils
Toby's Bow
Treat 'Em Rough
The Woman Under Oath
1920 April Folly
The Devil's Claim
The Little Grey Mouse
Molly and I
Stolen Moments
Novels
1916 Jaffery
1918 The Danger Game
How Could You, Caroline?

Novices (religious)
   rt **Convents**
      Nuns
1915 *His Wife*
1916 For the Defense
Novogeorgievsk (Russia)
1915 *On the Firing Line with the*
     Germans
Nudity
1915 *Sold*
1916 *The Mischief Maker*
Purity
1918 *The Craving*
The Girl of My Dreams
The Wildcat of Paris
1919 *The Virtuous Model*
1920 *Hearts Are Trumps*
Nuns
   rt **Convents**
      Novices (religious)
1913 The Legend of Provence
1914 Pieces of Silver; A Story of
     Hearts and Souls
The Red Flame of Passion
Thais
1915 *The Hypocrites*
The Sins of the Mothers
The White Sister
1916 *Naked Hearts*
The Sorrows of Love
The Victory of Conscience
1917 The Golden Rosary
The Slave
Thais
1919 *Our Better Selves*
Nursemaids
   rt **Governesses**
1914 *John Barleycorn*
The Ragged Earl
1916 *April*
The Battle of Life
A Child of the Paris Streets
The Heart of Nora Flynn
The Mark of Cain
The Price of Silence
Tangled Hearts
1917 *The Hand That Rocks the*
     Cradle
A Kentucky Cinderella
The Poor Little Rich Girl
1918 *Boston Blackie's Little Pal*
Mrs. Dane's Defense
The Seal of Silence
What Becomes of the
     Children?
1919 *The Crook of Dreams*
1920 *The Brand of Lopez*
Bubbles
1921 *Midsummer Madness*
Nursery rhymes
1917 Modern Mother Goose
Nurses
1915 Beulah
The Birth of a Nation
The Crimson Wing
The Galloper
I'm Glad My Boy Grew Up to
     Be a Soldier
The Impostor
A Modern Magdalen
The Money Master
On Dangerous Paths
The Sporting Duchess
Stolen Goods
When It Strikes Home
1916 Behind the Lines
The Black Butterfly
The Dark Silence
Her Double Life
The Last Man
Lone Star
Love's Toll
The Making of Maddalena
Martha's Vindication
The Path of Darkness
The Place Beyond the Winds
Public Opinion
The Rise of Susan
The Serpent
Souls in Bondage
Sudden Riches
Those Who Toil
Three of Many
The Truant Soul

United States Marines Under
   Fire in Haiti
Wanted—A Home
The Whirlpool of Destiny
The Witch
1917 American Maid
   The Beloved Adventuress
   The Book Agent
   The Courage of Silence
   The Dummy
   The Great White Trail
   Has Man the Right to Kill?
   The Heart of a Lion
   The Judgement House
   The Lady in the Library
   The Man Without a Country
   Mentioned in Confidence
   Over There
   The Pride of New York
   The Primrose Ring
   The Silent Lady
   The Slacker (Peter P. Jones
      Film Co.)
   Tangled Lives
   The Waiting Soul
1918 *The Birth of a Race*
   Bonnie Annie Laurie
   By Right of Purchase
   The Crucible of Life
   The Doctor and the Woman
   The Forbidden City
   Good Night, Paul
   The Great Love
   Lafayette, We Come!
   The Life Mask
   My Unmarried Wife
   My Wife
   The Prodigal Wife
   Revelation
   Ruling Passions
   A Son of Strife
   The Splendid Sinner
   The Spurs of Sybil
   When a Woman Sins
   The Woman the Germans Shot
1919 Adele
   Alias Mike Moran
   America Was Right
   Beware
   The Call of the Soul
   The Common Cause
   Dawn
   The End of the Road
   Evangeline
   The Great Victory, Wilson or
      the Kaiser? The Fall of the
      Hohenzollerns
   The Highest Trump
   His Debt
   The Market of Souls
   The Moonshine Trail
   A Regular Girl
   Rose O' the River
   Some Bride
   Tangled Threads
   Three Men and a Girl
   Turning the Tables
   Where Bonds Are Loosed
   Wild Oats
1920 *The Gift Supreme*
   His Temporary Wife
   Man and His Woman
   Nurse Marjorie
   The Rich Slave
   Sick Abed

Nursing back to health
   rt **Convalescence**
1913 *Sapho*
1914 The Bargain
   The Nightingale
   The Outlaw Reforms
   Thou Shalt Not
   The Virginian
   The War of Wars; Or, The
      Franco-German Invasion
1915 The Beachcomber
   The Closing Net
   The Devil's Daughter
   A Phyllis of the Sierras
1916 *The Destroyers*
   The Feast of Life
   For a Woman's Fair Name
   Her Debt of Honor
   Immediate Lee
   The Light That Failed

The Net
Oliver Twist
The Power of Evil
The Strength of Donald
   McKenzie
Susan Rocks the Boat
The Suspect
The Whirlpool of Destiny
The Wild Girl of the Sierras
A Yoke of Gold
1917 *The Bronze Bride*
   Dead Shot Baker
   Heart's Desire
   The Raggedy Queen
   The Savage
   Wolf Lowry
   The World Apart
1918 All Man
   Amarilly of Clothes-Line
      Alley
   Back to the Woods
   The Belgian
   Berlin Via America
   The Border Legion
   The Firefly of France
   Fuss and Feathers
   A Gentleman's Agreement
   The Girl of My Dreams
   A Good Loser
   Humility
   The Inn of the Blue Moon
   Maid O' the Storm
   A Man's Man
   The Mating of Marcella
   Missing
   Paying His Debt
   The Red, Red Heart
   Riddle Gawne
   Social Ambition
   Staking His Life
   The Two-Soul Woman
   Under the Greenwood Tree
   Wanted for Murder
1919 *A Bachelor's Wife*
   The Belle of New York
   The Better Wife
   Broken Blossoms
   The City of Comrades
   The Coming of the Law
   Fires of Faith
   The Firing Line
   The Follies Girl
   The Girl Alaska
   Go Get 'Em Garringer
   His Debt
   The Lady of Red Butte
   The Last of the Duanes
   The Light
   Louisiana
   The Love Call
   Maggie Pepper
   A Man's Country
   Man's Desire
   The Market of Souls
   The Mints of Hell
   Mrs. Wiggs of the Cabbage
      Patch
   The Peace of Roaring River
   The Red Viper
   The She Wolf
   Should a Woman Tell?
   Tangled Threads
   Three Green Eyes
   Treat 'Em Rough
   The Unknown Love
   What Am I Bid?
1920 *The Dark Mirror*
   Footlights and Shadows

Nymphs
1916 *Undine*
1920 *Neptune's Bride*

O

Oakland (California)
1914 *Martin Eden*
Oarsmen
1915 The Man Behind the Door
1918 Brown of Harvard
1919 The Winning Stroke

Obesity
1914 *The Battle of Gettysgoat*
1915 The Slim Princess
1916 *Charlie Chaplin's Burlesque on*
      "Carmen"
   The Traveling Salesman
1918 Too Fat to Fight
   The Way of a Man with a
      Maid
1919 *Life's a Funny Proposition*
   Nobody Home
   The Poor Boob
   Puppy Love
   The Rebellious Bride
1920 The Slim Princess
Obsession
1913 The Star of India
1917 Maternity
   The Mystic Hour
1919 *The Dragon Painter*
1920 *A Splendid Hazard*
Ocean liners
   rt **Steamships**
   bt **Ships**
1915 *A Fool There Was*
   A Gentleman of Leisure
   Lord John in New York
   Nedra
   The Price of Her Silence
   The Stubbornness of
      Geraldine
   The Voice in the Fog
   The White Pearl
1916 *The American Beauty*
   As in a Looking Glass
   The Girl O' Dreams
   The Shop Girl
   Through the Wall
1917 *The Hunting of the Hawk*
   Pride
   The Show Down
   The Sixteenth Wife
   The Snarl
   This Is the Life
1918 *The Savage Woman*
1919 The Bandbox
1920 *The Branded Woman*
   Cynthia-of-the-Minute
   David and Jonathan
   Half a Chance
   Mary's Ankle
   The Return of Tarzan
   The Sport of Kings
William Henry O'Connell
1920 *American Catholics in War*
      and Reconstruction
Octavia
1912 *Cleopatra*
Octopi
1915 *The Price of Her Silence*
1920 *Girl of the Sea*
Octoroons and Quadroons
   rt **Blacks**
      Mulattoes
1916 Pudd'nhead Wilson
1917 *The Renaissance at Charleroi*
1920 *Broken Hearts*
Office boys
   rt **Delivery boys**
      Errand boys
1917 Back of the Man
   The Night Workers
1919 *The Poor Boob*
1920 *The Plunger*
Office clerks
1917 *The Innocent Sinner*
1919 You're Fired
Ohio
1919 *The Country Cousin*
   The Mayor of Filbert
1920 *Polly with a Past*
Ohio River
1918 *Uncle Tom's Cabin*
Oil
1914 *Through Fire to Fortune*
1915 *Mrs. Plum's Pudding*
1916 *The Lords of High Decision*
   The Pretenders
1917 *Bab the Fixer*
   The Peddler
1918 *Hitting the High Spots*
1919 *Gates of Brass*
   The Greatest Question
   Hearts of Men

   Rough Riding Romance
   Sis Hopkins
1920 *The Invisible Divorce*
   Jack Straw
   Shore Acres
   The Symbol of the
      Unconquered
   Three Gold Coins
   Too Much Johnson
Oil companies
1916 Those Who Toil
1917 *The Jaguar's Claws*
1920 *Beautifully Trimmed*
   Everything but the Truth
   Live Sparks
   Sky Eye
Oil fields
1915 *Sunshine Molly*
1917 *His Mother's Boy*
1920 *The Notorious Mrs. Sands*
   Oil
   Witch's Gold
Oil lands
1914 *Where the Trail Divides*
1915 *M'liss*
1917 *Glory*
   Southern Justice
   Sunny Jane
1918 *Desert Law*
   Real Folks
1919 *Bill Henry*
   When the Clouds Roll By
1920 *Hitchin' Posts*
   The Jailbird
Oil magnates
1916 Those Who Toil
1917 *A Branded Soul*
   The Girl Who Couldn't Grow
      Up
   Glory
1918 *The Man of Bronze*
1919 *In His Brother's Place*
   The Island of Intrigue
1920 *Everything but the Truth*
   Live Sparks
   Sky Eye
Oil wells
1915 *M'liss*
   Sunshine Molly
1916 *Those Who Toil*
1917 His Mother's Boy
1920 *The Jailbird*
   Oil
   Witch's Gold
Oilmen
1915 *Double Trouble*
   The Secret Sin
   Sweet Alyssum
1918 *The Girl from Beyond*
   The Turn of a Card
Okefenokee Swamp (Florida)
1918 *The Grouch*
Oklahoma
1914 *Beating Back*
1915 Passing of the Oklahoma
      Outlaw
1918 *The Red-Haired Cupid*
   The Turn of a Card
1920 *Lahoma*
Old men
   rt **Aged persons**
1914 *The Chechako*
1917 *Babbling Tongues*
   The Crab
   The Fortunes of Fifi
   A Girl Like That
   God's Crucible
   The Hater of Men
   The Man of Mystery
   Melissa of the Hills
   Miss Robinson Crusoe
   Money Magic
   My Little Boy
   The Natural Law
   Pots-and-Pans Peggy
   The Price She Paid
1918 *A Hoosier Romance*
1920 *Her Beloved Villain*
Old women
   rt **Aged persons**
1916 Pay Dirt
1917 Polly Put the Kettle On
1918 *The Flames of Chance*
   Winning Grandma

Omaha (Nebraska)
1914 Clothes
Onions
1918 Jack Spurlock, Prodigal
Opera
　rt **Opera singers**
1915 *Du Barry*
　　　The Lure of the Mask
　　　Temptation
　　　Trilby
　　　What Happened to Father
1916 *The Black Butterfly*
　　　Captain Jinks of the Horse
　　　　Marines
　　　The Chalice of Sorrow
　　　Love Never Dies
1917 *The Cinderella Man*
　　　Her Beloved Enemy
　　　It Happened to Adele
　　　More Truth Than Poetry
　　　Panthea
　　　The Snarl
1918 *Sauce for the Goose*
　　　Social Briars
1919 Heartsease
　　　Words and Music By—
1920 The Great Lover
　　　Greater Than Fame
　　　Once to Every Woman
　　　Out of the Storm
　　　The Paliser Case
　　　The Place of Honeymoons
　　　Scratch My Back
　　　Whispers
Opera singers
　rt **Opera**
1914 *The House Next Door*
　　　The Million
　　　The Nightingale
1915 *Cora*
　　　The Girl from His Town
　　　How Molly Malone Made
　　　　Good
　　　The Song of Hate
　　　Trilby
1916 *The Flower of No Man's Land*
　　　A Parisian Romance
　　　The Price of Happiness
　　　The Prima Donna's Husband
　　　Revelations
　　　Tongues of Men
　　　The Woman Who Dared
　　　The Yellow Passport
1917 *Her Greatest Love*
　　　The Master Passion
　　　Mayblossom
　　　The Snarl
　　　The White Raven
1918 After the War
　　　An American Live Wire
　　　The Changing Woman
　　　The City of Tears
　　　The Danger Zone
　　　Find the Woman
　　　Her Price
　　　Lest We Forget
　　　My Cousin
　　　Rosemary Climbs the Heights
　　　La Tosca
　　　A Woman of Impulse
1919 *Eyes of Youth*
　　　A Man in the Open
　　　The Right to Lie
　　　The Splendid Romance
　　　The World and Its Woman
1920 *The Fear Market*
　　　Old Dad
　　　Once to Every Woman
　　　Out of the Storm
　　　The Place of Honeymoons
　　　Polly with a Past
　　　Romance
　　　A Sister to Salome
Opium
1914 The Boundary Rider
　　　The Mystery of Edwin Drood
1915 *The Seventh Noon*
　　　The Wonderful Adventure
1916 Hop, the Devil's Brew
1917 *Captain Kiddo*
　　　God's Man
　　　Loyalty
　　　The Man Who Forgot
　　　Queen X

1918 The Border Raiders
　　　The Midnight Patrol
　　　The Whispering Chorus
1919 *The Tong Man*
1920 *Crooked Streets*
　　　Dinty
　　　Man and His Woman
　　　The Scarlet Dragon
　　　The Scrap of Paper
　　　The Unknown Ranger
　　　The Whisper Market
　　　The Woman Gives
Opium dens
1915 *The Secret Sin*
1917 The Flower of Doom
1919 *Fighting Destiny*
　　　Forbidden
1920 *Idols of Clay*
　　　The Woman Gives
Opportunists
1915 The Billionaire Lord
1917 Forget-Me-Not
　　　The Girl Without a Soul
Optimism
1916 The Habit of Happiness
Oranges
1914 *Nell Gwynne*
1917 *Betty to the Rescue*
Orators
1916 *The Measure of a Man*
　　　The Velvet Paw
1918 *The Fall of the Romanoffs*
1920 The Blooming Angel
Orchestras
1919 *Victory*
Orderlies (hospital)
1917 *A Love Sublime*
Orderlies (military)
1914 *The Boer War*
1919 *Wings of the Morning*
Ordination
1914 *His Holiness, the Late Pope*
　　　　Pius X, and the Vatican
　　　Manon Lescaut
1916 *The Waifs*
Ordnance
1915 *The Battles of a Nation*
　　　The German Side of the War
　　　Guarding Old Glory
　　　The Lamb
　　　Russian Battlefields
　　　Somewhere in France
　　　Via Wireless
1916 *At the Front with the Allies*
　　　The Fighting Germans
　　　The Love Thief
　　　Powder
　　　The Zeppelin Raids on London
　　　　and the Siege of Verdun
1918 *The Firebrand*
1920 Dangerous Days
　　　The Scuttlers
　　　Under Crimson Skies
Oregon
1915 *The Man from Oregon*
1919 In the Land of the Setting Sun;
　　　　Or, Martyrs of Yesterday
Organ grinders
1914 *The Nightingale*
1916 *The Eternal Question*
1917 *The Adventures of Carol*
1920 *Bright Skies*
Organ makers
1915 York State Folks
Organists
1913 *The Volunteer Organist*
1914 The Mystery of Edwin Drood
1917 *Little Miss Optimist*
Organized crime
　rt **Black Hand**
　　　Crime
　　　Mafia
1914 Smashing the Vice Trust
1916 The Little Girl Next Door
1917 Beware of Strangers
　　　The Terror
1918 *Baree, Son of Kazan*
1920 The Scarlet Dragon
Orphanage mistresses
1915 *The Lonesome Heart*
1920 The Rich Slave

Orphanages
1913 *In the Bishop's Carriage*
1914 *The Conspiracy*
　　　The Criminal Code
1915 *Beulah*
　　　The Lonesome Heart
1916 *Charity*
　　　Faith
　　　The Foundling
　　　God's Half Acre
　　　Hoodoo Ann
　　　Joy and the Dragon
　　　Little Miss Nobody
　　　The Ragged Princess
1917 *An Amateur Orphan*
　　　Cheerful Givers
　　　The Girl Who Won Out
　　　The Night Workers
　　　Shame
　　　A Strange Transgressor
　　　Unknown 274
　　　Wrath
1918 *The Answer*
　　　Joan of Plattsburg
　　　Little Orphant Annie
　　　The Triumph of the Weak
1919 Daddy-Long-Legs
　　　The Heart of Humanity
　　　Home Wanted
　　　Mrs. Wiggs of the Cabbage
　　　　Patch
　　　The Pointing Finger
1920 *The Devil's Garden*
　　　Polly of the Storm Country
　　　The Rich Slave
　　　She Couldn't Help It
　　　The Soul of Youth
Orphans
1912 Oliver Twist
1914 Across the Pacific
　　　Aftermath
　　　The Day of Days
　　　Hearts of Oak
　　　Jess of the Mountain Country
　　　The Little Angel of Canyon
　　　　Creek
　　　Marta of the Lowlands
　　　The Opened Shutters
　　　The Outlaw Reforms
　　　Where the Trail Divides
1915 *The Caprices of Kitty*
　　　Captain Courtesy
　　　The College Orphan
　　　The Deathlock
　　　The Eagle's Nest
　　　Enoch Arden
　　　Father and the Boys
　　　The Little Girl That He
　　　　Forgot
　　　The Lonesome Heart
　　　The Morals of Marcus
　　　Stolen Goods
　　　Sunday
　　　The Two Orphans
　　　Vanity Fair
1916 *Audrey*
　　　The Ballet Girl
　　　Bobbie of the Ballet
　　　Broken Fetters
　　　Charity
　　　Common Sense Brackett
　　　Daredevil Kate
　　　God's Half Acre
　　　Hell-to-Pay Austin
　　　Her Debt of Honor
　　　The Hidden Law
　　　Hoodoo Ann
　　　The Innocence of Lizette
　　　The Innocence of Ruth
　　　Joy and the Dragon
　　　The Jungle Child
　　　Let Katie Do It
　　　Lonesome Town
　　　Merely Mary Ann
　　　Mice and Men
　　　The Narrow Path
　　　Oliver Twist
　　　The Patriot
　　　The Ragged Princess
　　　The Return of Eve
　　　The Sex Lure
　　　The Stain in the Blood
　　　The Unborn
　　　La Vie de Boheme
　　　Youth's Endearing Charm

1917 *Alias Mrs. Jessop*
　　　Annie-for-Spite
　　　The Apple-Tree Girl
　　　Blue Jeans
　　　Charity Castle
　　　The Charmer
　　　Cheerful Givers
　　　The Cricket
　　　The Crystal Gazer
　　　A Daughter of the Poor
　　　Eternal Love
　　　Follow the Girl
　　　The Gift Girl
　　　The Girl at Home
　　　The Girl Who Won Out
　　　Heart and Soul
　　　Her Right to Live
　　　Her Sister
　　　A Jewel in Pawn
　　　A Kentucky Cinderella
　　　The Kill-Joy
　　　The Lady in the Library
　　　The Little Boy Scout
　　　The Little Duchess
　　　Little Miss Fortune
　　　Little Miss Nobody
　　　The Little Orphan
　　　The Little Princess
　　　The Little Samaritan
　　　The Man Without a Country
　　　A Man's Law
　　　My Little Boy
　　　Pay Me
　　　Polly Ann
　　　Polly Redhead
　　　Poppy
　　　The Royal Pauper
　　　The Runaway
　　　Satan's Private Door
　　　Shame
　　　The Silent Lady
　　　Stagestruck
　　　The Trouble Buster
　　　A Wife by Proxy
　　　Young Mother Hubbard
1918 Ace High
　　　After the War
　　　An Alien Enemy
　　　American Buds
　　　A Bachelor's Children
　　　Breakers Ahead
　　　Captain of His Soul
　　　The Cast-Off
　　　Chase Me Charlie
　　　The Daredevil
　　　The Debt of Honor
　　　The Deciding Kiss
　　　The Dream Lady
　　　The Girl with the Champagne
　　　　Eyes
　　　Humility
　　　Joan of Plattsburg
　　　Little Orphant Annie
　　　Little Red Decides
　　　The Marionettes
　　　Miss Mischief Maker
　　　The Rainbow Trail
　　　Riddle Gawne
　　　Riders of the Purple Sage
　　　Selfish Yates
　　　Six Shooter Andy
　　　A Soul Without Windows
　　　Stella Maris
　　　The Unbeliever
　　　Wild Life
　　　Woman and Wife
1919 *The A.B.C. of Love*
　　　Child of M'sieu
　　　Daddy-Long-Legs
　　　The Faith of the Strong
　　　The Gray Towers Mystery
　　　Home Wanted
　　　A House Divided
　　　Jinx
　　　The Lady of Red Butte
　　　The Little Diplomat
　　　The Old Maid's Baby
　　　Pettigrew's Girl
　　　The Pointing Finger
　　　Reclaimed: The Struggle for a
　　　　Soul Between Love and Hate
　　　The Rider of the Law
　　　Roses and Thorns
　　　A Royal Democrat
　　　Sandy Burke of the U-Bar-U

Panama-Pacific International Exposition
- 1915 *Chimmie Fadden Out West*
  - The Exposition's First Romance
  - *The Pageant of San Francisco*
- 19-- Official Motion Pictures of the Panama Pacific Exposition Held at San Francisco, Calif.

Paper mills
- 1915 The Song of the Wage Slave
- 1920 A Beggar in Purple

Parachutists
- 1917 Flirting with Death
- 1919 The Old Maid's Baby
- 1920 Pink Tights

Parades
- 1917 *The Girl Glory*
- 1919 *The Gay Old Dog*
  - *The Lost Battalion*
  - *The Red Lantern*
  - *The Spirit of Lafayette*
- 19-- *Official Motion Pictures of the Panama Pacific Exposition Held at San Francisco, Calif.*

Paradise Lost
- 1917 *Conscience*

Paralysis
- 1914 *One of Millions*
  - *Three Weeks*
- 1916 *The Marble Heart*
  - The Reapers
- 1917 A Wife on Trial
- 1918 A Soul Without Windows
  - *Stella Maris*
- 1919 The Hand Invisible
- 1920 Children of Destiny
  - Pollyanna
  - What Would You Do?
  - The Woman in His House

Paralytics
- 1913 Chelsea 7750
  - *An Hour Before Dawn*
- 1916 *The Marble Heart*
  - The Reapers
- 1917 A Wife on Trial
- 1919 Brothers Divided
- 1920 Pollyanna
  - *While New York Sleeps*

Parasites
- 1917 The Auction Block
  - *The Marcellini Millions*

Pardons
- 1915 *The Birth of a Nation*
  - The Shadows of a Great City
- 1916 *I Accuse*
  - *Just a Song at Twilight*
  - The Land Just Over Yonder
  - *Unprotected*
- 1917 *Beloved Rogues*
  - *Betsy Ross*
  - The Curse of Eve
  - *Darkest Russia*
  - The Desire of the Moth
  - Durand of the Bad Lands
  - *The Guardian*
  - *The Gun Fighter*
  - Mothers of Men
  - *Panthea*
- 1918 *Cheating the Public*
  - *Kildare of Storm*
  - *Thieves' Gold*
  - Three Mounted Men
  - *The Triumph of the Weak*
  - *Wedlock*
- 1920 *The Triple Clue*
  - *Two Kinds of Love*

Pardons (legal)
- 1913 *Robin Hood*
- 1914 *Beating Back*
  - A Celebrated Case
  - *The Last Volunteer*
  - *The Littlest Rebel*
  - A Woman's Triumph
- 1915 *Alias Jimmy Valentine*
  - *Buckshot John*
  - *The Concealed Truth*
  - *The Eternal City*
  - *Gambling Inside and Out*
  - The Heart of Maryland
  - The Little Girl That He Forgot
  - *Not Guilty*
  - The Running Fight

The Unbroken Road
- 1916 *The Bondman*
  - *The Challenge*
  - *The Combat*
  - *The Crisis*
  - *The Devil's Prayer-Book*
  - *Warning! The S.O.S. Call of Humanity*
  - *Whom the Gods Destroy*
- 1917 *The Hand That Rocks the Cradle*
  - *The Honor System*
  - *In Again—Out Again*
  - *Kick in*
  - *The Learnin' of Jim Benton*
  - *Light in Darkness*
  - *The Recoil*
- 1918 The House of Glass
  - The One Woman
- 1919 *Brothers Divided*
  - *The Last of the Duanes*
  - *Love and the Law*
  - *Marked Men*
  - The Mother and the Law
  - *Virtuous Sinners*

Parentage
- rt **Fatherhood**
- **Motherhood**
- 1912 Quincy Adams Sawyer
- 1914 At the Cross Roads
  - A Celebrated Case
  - The Pawn of Fortune
  - Sins of the Parents
  - *The Taint*
  - Il Trovatore
- 1915 *Children of Eve*
  - The Daughter of the Sea
  - *An Enemy to Society*
  - The Eternal City
  - The Family Stain
  - The Fifth Commandment
  - Forbidden Fruit
  - From the Valley of the Missing
  - Ghosts
  - *The Goose Girl*
  - June Friday
  - Just Jim
  - Kilmeny
  - *The Little Gypsy*
  - The Lonesome Heart
  - The Millionaire Baby
  - *The Nigger*
  - The Outcast
  - The Penitentes
  - The Supreme Test
  - *Under Southern Skies*
  - When It Strikes Home
  - A Woman's Past
- 1916 The American Beauty
  - *And the Law Says*
  - April
  - *At Piney Ridge*
  - *The Child of Destiny*
  - The Children Pay
  - *A Circus Romance*
  - The City
  - Common Sense Brackett
  - The Courtesan
  - Destiny's Toy
  - The Devil's Prayer-Book
  - The Devil's Prize
  - The Discard
  - Faith
  - *The Flames of Johannis*
  - The Fortunate Youth
  - The Foundling
  - The Gates of Eden
  - *The Girl Philippa*
  - *The Gods of Fate*
  - *The Good Bad Man*
  - The Grip of Jealousy
  - The Half-Breed
  - The Hand of Peril
  - Her Husband's Wife
  - Joy and the Dragon
  - Less Than the Dust
  - Nancy's Birthright
  - New York
  - Oliver Twist
  - Pay Dirt
  - The Pillory
  - The Plow Girl
  - The Price of Silence
  - The Question
  - The Shadow of a Doubt

Should a Baby Die?
Silas Marner
The Sin Ye Do
Sins of Her Parent
A Son of the Immortals
The Spell of the Yukon
The Spider
The Straight Way
Tennessee's Pardner
That Sort
A Tortured Heart
The Unborn
The Voice of Love
Where Are My Children?
The Wild Girl of the Sierras
- 1917 The Adventures of Carol
  - The Barker
  - Blue Jeans
  - The Book Agent
  - The Bottom of the Well
  - The Brand of Satan
  - The Bride of Hate
  - The Call of Her People
  - The Call of the East
  - The Circus of Life
  - Corruption
  - The Dancer's Peril
  - The End of the Tour
  - The Eternal Sin
  - Every Girl's Dream
  - Fighting Mad
  - The Flaming Omen
  - Giving Becky a Chance
  - God's Law and Man's
  - Hands Up!
  - Hate
  - *The Heart of Ezra Greer*
  - Heart Strings
  - *Her Country's Call*
  - *Her Hour*
  - Her Secret
  - House of Cards
  - Infidelity
  - John Ermine of the Yellowstone
  - Kitty MacKay
  - The Last Sentence
  - *The Little Patriot*
  - *The Little Samaritan*
  - *Lorelei of the Sea*
  - *Lost in Transit*
  - The Maid of Belgium
  - A Man and the Woman
  - Married in Name Only
  - The Mate of the Sally Ann
  - Miss Nobody
  - A Mother's Ordeal
  - An Old Fashioned Young Man
  - Pay Me
  - The Piper's Price
  - *The Planter*
  - The Poor Little Rich Girl
  - The Pride of the Clan
  - *The Princess of Patches*
  - *The Raggedy Queen*
  - *Runaway Romany*
  - The Scarlet Letter
  - The Sea Master
  - The Seventh Sin
  - *The Silent Witness*
  - Sins of Ambition
  - *Sold at Auction*
  - The Soul Master
  - Sunshine and Gold
  - Susan's Gentleman
  - Threads of Fate
  - Wild Sumac
- 1918 American Buds
  - Breakers Ahead
  - *Crown Jewels*
  - *The Divine Sacrifice*
  - The Forbidden City
  - The Girl in His House
  - The Girl of My Dreams
  - *The Guilty Man*
  - Joan of the Woods
  - *Just a Woman*
  - The Kaiser's Finish
  - *A Law unto Herself*
  - Madame Jealousy
  - One Dollar Bid
  - The Only Road
  - *A Petticoat Pilot*
  - The Ranger
  - The Sea Waif

The Seal of Silence
The Snail
A Society Sensation
A Soul in Trust
A Soul Without Windows
The Testing of Mildred Vane
Tongues of Flame
Tony America
- 1919 Broken Commandments
  - Desert Gold
  - The Echo of Youth
  - A Girl Named Mary
  - The Hand Invisible
  - A Heart in Pawn
  - The Heart of a Gypsy
  - Her Code of Honor
  - Home Wanted
  - The House Without Children
  - Injustice
  - Just Squaw
  - The Lamb and the Lion
  - The Last of His People
  - The Lone Wolf's Daughter
  - Love and the Woman
  - The Love Hunger
  - *A Man's Duty*
  - The Merry-Go-Round
  - The Mints of Hell
  - Out Yonder
  - The Right to Lie
  - Wolves of the Night
  - You Never Saw Such a Girl
- 1919-20
  - When a Man Loves
- 1920 Birthright
  - The Blue Moon
  - The Brand of Lopez
  - Bright Skies
  - *The Broken Gate*
  - Broken Hearts
  - *Captain Swift*
  - A Child for Sale
  - Children of Destiny
  - The Dark Mirror
  - Everybody's Sweetheart
  - The Fatal Hour
  - Forbidden Valley
  - The Forged Bride
  - The Forgotten Woman
  - The Gamesters
  - Godless Men
  - The Great Lover
  - *Greater Than Love*
  - *The Harvest Moon*
  - Heliotrope
  - *Hell's Oasis*
  - Heritage
  - The Jack-Knife Man
  - Judy of Rogue's Harbor
  - The Kentucky Colonel
  - King Spruce
  - *The Last of the Mohicans*
  - The Little Outcast
  - Love's Protegé
  - Madame X
  - A Manhattan Knight
  - *The Riddle: Woman*
  - *Rio Grande*
  - *The Strongest*
  - Sweet Lavender
  - The Third Woman
  - Under Northern Lights
  - The Web of Deceit
  - The White Dove
  - White Lies
  - Wings of Pride

Paris
- 1913 *Leah Kleschna*
  - The Rogues of Paris
  - Sapho
  - The Stranglers of Paris
- 1914 *Absinthe*
  - *The Banker's Daughter*
  - Charlotte Corday
  - *The Education of Mr. Pipp*
  - *The Key to Yesterday*
  - *The Lightning Conductor*
  - Manon Lescaut
  - The Murders in the Rue Morgue
  - *The Nightingale*
  - *The Phantom Violin*
  - *The Three Musketeers*
  - *The Typhoon*

1918 *A Bachelor's Children*
Betty Takes a Hand
A Camouflage Kiss
The Death Dance
The Desired Woman
Five Thousand an Hour
Good Night, Paul
He Comes Up Smiling
The Hillcrest Mystery
The Home Trail
Lawless Love
A Man's Man
Money Isn't Everything
More Trouble
Oh, Johnny!
A Pair of Sixes
Parentage
Ruling Passions
Suspicion
Untamed
Waifs
The Wasp
The White Man's Law
The Winning of Beatrice
1919 The Dub
The False Code
Fighting for Gold
Fool's Gold
The Lion's Den
A Man of Honor
Man's Desire
Partners Three
The Root of Evil
1920 The Dancin' Fool
Dollar for Dollar
Forbidden Trails
The Gamesters
The Inner Voice
King Spruce
The Ladder of Lies
The Little Wanderer
The Man from Nowhere
Nothing but Lies
Once a Plumber
Out of the Snows
Partners of the Night
She Couldn't Help It
Smiling All the Way
The Square Shooter
Stop Thief!
The Tiger's Cub
What Would You Do?
What's Your Husband Doing?

Passover
1915 Children of the Ghetto
Passports
1917 *Arms and the Girl*
Sacrifice
The Winged Mystery
1918 *The Kaiser's Finish*
1919 *The Unpardonable Sin*
1920 *The Whisper Market*
Patagonia
1916 *The Misleading Lady*
Patent medicines
1915 The White Terror
1916 *The Clarion*
1918 *The Scarlet Trail*
1919 *Beating the Odds*
Full of Pep
Patent rights
1916 The Race
1920 Jes' Call Me Jim
Paternity
1916 Human Driftwood
The Idol of the Stage
The Kid
The Way of the World
1917 The Bottom of the Well
A Case at Law
The Circus of Life
The End of the Tour
God's Law and Man's
The Mate of the Sally Ann
An Old Fashioned Young Man
The On-the-Square-Girl
Outwitted
1918 *The Guilt of Silence*
1919 As a Man Thinks
1920 *The Great Accident*
Paterson (New Jersey)
1920 *Dangerous Hours*

Patricide
1914 The Circus Man
The Dishonored Medal
Dope
The Master Cracksman
1915 *From the Valley of the Missing*
1916 *What the World Should Know*
1917 Hate
1919 The Homesteader
Patriotism
1914 The Ordeal
The Typhoon
Washington at Valley Forge
1915 The Battle Cry of Peace
Guarding Old Glory
I'm Glad My Boy Grew Up to Be a Soldier
1916 Bullets and Brown Eyes
A Corner in Colleens
Defense or Tribute?
My Country First
Shell Forty-Three
1917 Draft 258
For Liberty
For Valour
The Gown of Destiny
The Little American
The Little Patriot
The Man Without a Country
Miss U.S.A.
The Slacker (Metro Pictures Corp.)
Sloth
The Spy
1918 *An Alien Enemy*
The Challenge Accepted
Come On In
A Daughter of France
For the Freedom of the East
The Girl from Bohemia
Her Boy
Her Country First
The Kaiser's Finish
Little Miss Hoover
Me und Gott
My Own United States
On the Jump
The Spirit of '17
The Thing We Love
Treason
Why America Will Win
Wife or Country
The Wildcat of Paris
The Yellow Dog
1919 Everybody's Business
Fighting Through
Little Comrade
The Red Viper
The Undercurrent
The Woman on the Index
1920 The Cup of Fury
The Face at Your Window
Uncle Sam of Freedom Ridge
Patrons
1914 *The Price He Paid*
Through Dante's Flames
1916 The Payment
1917 *Babette*
The Fibbers
The Glory of Yolanda
The Martinache Marriage
Mother Love and the Law
Panthea
1918 *Toys of Fate*
The Unchastened Woman
1920 *Greater Than Fame*
Hidden Charms
Once to Every Woman
Out of the Storm
Two Weeks
Paul, the Apostle, Saint
1913 *The Daughter of the Hills*
Pawnbrokers
1914 The Light Unseen
1915 *The Sins of Society*
Time Lock Number 776
1916 *The Smugglers*
1917 *Crime and Punishment*
A Jewel in Pawn
Miss Nobody
1918 *The Beautiful Mrs. Reynolds*
Joan of the Woods
1919 *The Blue Bonnet*
False Gods

Luck in Pawn
The Wicked Darling
Paymasters
1914 Paid in Full
When Fate Leads Trump
John Howard Payne
1914 Home, Sweet Home
Peace
1917 National Red Cross Pageant
Peace activists
1915 The Battle Cry of Peace
1916 Civilization
1917 *The Zeppelin's Last Raid*
Peace conferences
1919 Whom the Gods Would Destroy
Peacemakers
1917 The Captain of the Gray Horse Troop
Peacocks
1916 *Snow White*
Pearl diving
1915 *Japan*
1919 *The Millionaire Pirate*
A Woman There Was
1920 The Blue Moon
Pearls
1914 The Long Arm of the Law
1915 Pearls of Temptation
The White Pearl
1916 Each Pearl a Tear
Pidgin Island
1917 The Island of Desire
The Midnight Man
1918 *The Girl Who Came Back*
Hidden Pearls
Money Mad
1919 The Wicked Darling
A Woman There Was
1920 *The Blue Moon*
The Blue Pearl
It's a Great Life
Risky Business
Terror Island
Peasants
1913 *The Stranglers of Paris*
Tess of the D'Urbervilles
1914 *The Envoy Extraordinary*
1915 *The Beloved Vagabond*
The Face in the Moonlight
The Goose Girl
The Hungarian Nabob
A Woman's Resurrection
1916 *The Black Butterfly*
The Eternal Question
The Gilded Cage
Light at Dusk
Poor Little Peppina
The Serpent
The Social Highwayman
Sold for Marriage
War on Three Fronts
1917 *A Branded Soul*
The Glory of Yolanda
His Own People
Rasputin, the Black Monk
1918 *Her Moment*
I Love You
The Legion of Death
Resurrection
The She-Devil
Wanted for Murder
1919 Kathleen Mavourneen
A Royal Democrat
The Siren's Song
1920 The Mysteries of Paris
On with the Dance
Peddlers
1916 *The People vs. John Doe*
A Woman's Daring
1917 *The Book Agent*
The Peddler
The Upper Crust
1918 Tony America
1919 In Search of Arcady
1920 *The Peddler of Lies*
Peking
1915 China
1917 *The Door Between*
1919 The Red Lantern

Penal colonies
1916 Unprotected
1917 *Great Expectations*
Pendleton (Oregon)
1913 The Pendleton, Oregon, Round-Up
1915 Where Cowboy Is King
Pennsylvania
1914 *The House of Bondage*
1916 *The Flames of Johannis*
Little Meena's Romance
The Reward of Patience
Those Who Toil
A Woman's Honor
1917 *Trooper 44*
1918 *A Soul Without Windows*
The Vamp
1919 *The Best Man*
Prudence on Broadway
1920 *Dad's Girl*
Pennsylvania Dutch
rt **Dutch**
1916 *Little Meena's Romance*
1918 Johanna Enlists
1919 *Erstwhile Susan*
Penology
1920 The Gray Brother
Pensions
1914 Shore Acres
1917 *The Rainbow Girl*
Perfume
1915 *Hearts of Men*
1916 *Diplomacy*
1917 *The Hero of the Hour*
1920 Heliotrope
Perjury
1914 *The Million Dollar Robbery*
The Power of the Press
1915 *Lydia Gilmore*
Not Guilty
1916 *By Whose Hand?*
Fifty-Fifty
The Ordeal of Elizabeth
Slander
1917 *The Last of the Carnabys*
1918 *Wedlock*
1919 *The Right to Lie*
1920 *Forbidden Trails*
Homespun Folks
John J. Pershing
1916 *Following the Flag in Mexico*
1918 *Crashing Through to Berlin*
Pershing's Crusaders
Under Four Flags
Why America Will Win
1919 *The Fighting Roosevelts*
The Spirit of Lafayette
1920 *American Catholics in War and Reconstruction*
Persia. Army
1919 *The Fall of Babylon*
Persians
1915 *The Breath of Araby*
1918 *The Demon*
1920 *The Devil's Claim*
Personal finance
1917 *The Divorce Game*
1920 The Walk-Offs
Personality changes
1914 The Escape
1915 *The Danger Signal*
1917 Charity Castle
The Crab
The Girl Angle
The Love Doctor
1918 Mile-a-Minute Kendall
1919 The Busher
Courage for Two
Don't Change Your Husband
Impossible Catherine
Love Is Love
A Man and His Money
Our Better Selves
1920 Why Change Your Wife?
Peru
1914 *The Captain Besley Expedition*
1915 In the Amazon Jungles with the Captain Besley Expedition
1916 *Langdon's Legacy*
1917 *The Flaming Omen*

Planters
1916 *The City of Illusion*
Tempest and Sunshine
1917 *Heart and Soul*
The Planter
1918 Kildare of Storm
1920 *The Isle of Destiny*
Something Different
Within Our Gates
1921 The Jucklins

Platinum
1918 *A Diplomatic Mission*
1919 *The Man Who Won*

Platonic love
rt **Love**
1915 *The Chalice of Courage*
Evidence

Plattsburgh (New York)
1916 *America Preparing*
1917 *America Is Ready*
1918 *Joan of Plattsburg*

Playboys
rt **Heirs**
Millionaires
1914 *Wildflower*
1915 The Man Behind the Door
1916 The Beckoning Trail
The Brand of Cowardice
Caprice of the Mountains
The Conscience of John David
The Eternal Grind
The Fear of Poverty
Feathertop
The Half Million Bribe
Honor's Altar
The Lost Bridegroom
A Parisian Romance
The Power of Evil
1917 *Bringing Home Father*
Enlighten Thy Daughter
The Girl from Rector's
The Girl Who Didn't Think
The Master Passion
The Mirror
Miss Robinson Crusoe
A Modern Musketeer
The Painted Madonna
The Scarlet Crystal
To Honor and Obey
Whose Wife?
1918 The Brazen Beauty
Broadway Bill
Fair Enough
For Husbands Only
Her American Husband
Limousine Life
Love Me
The Talk of the Town
1919 The Beloved Cheater
The Bramble Bush
Upstairs and Down
1920 Flame of Youth
Hairpins
The Inferior Sex
It Might Happen to You
The Luck of the Irish
The Truth About Husbands
The Vice of Fools
Wait for Me
Way Down East
A World of Folly
You Never Can Tell

Playing cards
1915 *Alice in Wonderland*
The Fatal Card
1916 *The Devil's Double*
The Sign of the Spade
1918 *Social Hypocrites*

Plays
1916 The Last Act
1917 Apartment 29
Babbling Tongues
Chicken Casey
The Cricket
The Duplicity of Hargraves
The Fibbers
1918 The Fair Pretender

Playwrights
1914 Home, Sweet Home
The Strange Story of Sylvia Gray
1915 *The Failure*
Pearls of Temptation

1916 The Faded Flower
The Footlights of Fate
Half a Rogue
Lord Loveland Discovers America
The Madcap
The Stolen Triumph
1917 *An American Widow*
Apartment 29
Babbling Tongues
The Fibbers
Idolators
The Inspirations of Harry Larrabee
Little Miss Nobody
The Stolen Play
Triumph
The Trufflers
1918 *Bread*
The Fair Pretender
Her Inspiration
His Own Home Town
Social Ambition
1919 *The A.B.C. of Love*
The Bandbox
The Cinema Murder
Experimental Marriage
Jane Goes A-Wooing
Louisiana
Satan Junior
A Society Exile
Too Many Crooks
When My Ship Comes In
Yvonne from Paris
1920 Bonnie May
The Branding Iron
Darling Mine
The Devil's Passkey
The Girl in Number 29
The Harvest Moon
The Luck of Geraldine Laird
Married Life
The Misleading Lady
My Husband's Other Wife
Tarnished Reputations

Pledges
1913 The Legend of Provence
The Volunteer Organist
1914 The Banker's Daughter
The Bargain
The Pride of Jennico
The Tangle
Uncle Tom's Cabin
Winning His First Case
The Wishing Ring; An Idyll of Old England
The Wolf
1915 The Fatal Card
The Juggernaut
The White Sister
1916 The Almighty Dollar
Between Men
The Bugler of Algiers
The Child of Destiny
The Dividend
The Eye of God
The White Rosette
Who Killed Joe Merrion?
1917 *Her Father's Keeper*
Her New York
The Hostage
The Image Maker
The Jury of Fate
Little Shoes
Paws of the Bear
Pride and the Man
The Promise
Queen X
1918 *The Biggest Show on Earth*
The Golden Wall
The Hand at the Window
An Honest Man
Huck and Tom; Or, The Further Adventures of Tom Sawyer
Love's Conquest
Marriage
The Midnight Burglar
Milady O' the Beanstalk
The Ordeal of Rosetta
The Seal of Silence
Uncle Tom's Cabin
Wolves of the Rail
1919 Girls
God's Outlaw

The Lone Star Ranger
Lord and Lady Algy
Love, Honor and—?
Some Liar
The Unbroken Promise
The Woman Michael Married
The Woman Under Oath
1920 For the Soul of Rafael
His Own Law
Seeds of Vengeance

Plumbers
1917 One Touch of Nature
1920 The Luck of the Irish
Once a Plumber

Pneumonia
1915 The Darkening Trail
1917 *Next Door to Nancy*
1918 *Ashes of Love*
A Good Loser
The Light Within
Little Red Decides
The Mating
1919 *Break the News to Mother*
Someone Must Pay

Poachers
1915 *Wild Life of America in Films*
1916 *The Strength of Donald McKenzie*
1917 His Own People
1918 *Denny from Ireland*

Edgar Allan Poe
1915 The Raven

Poetry
1918 *String Beans*
1919 Evangeline
The Wishing Ring Man

Poets
1914 *Martin Eden*
1915 *Children of the Ghetto*
It's No Laughing Matter
Pretty Mrs. Smith
1916 *The House of Lies*
The Man from Manhattan
Philip Holden—Waster
Purity
The Strength of Donald McKenzie
1917 The Cinderella Man
Her New York
Sapho
1918 *The Ghost Flower*
New Love for Old
Peg of the Pirates
The Price of Applause
The Temple of Dusk
1919 *The Fall of Babylon*
A Girl in Bohemia
1920 Billions
If I Were King
My Lady's Garter
The Point of View
Sundown Slim
The World and His Wife

Pogroms
1914 Threads of Destiny
1919 *The Right to Happiness*

Poison
1915 The Final Judgment
1916 The Heart of the Hills
1917 *Corruption*
The Eternal Sin
The Highway of Hope
Mrs. Balfame
1920 *Flames of the Flesh*
Locked Lips
The Poor Simp
A Sister to Salome
The Tattlers

Poisoning
1914 *The Great Diamond Robbery*
The Mystery of the Poison Pool
The Span of Life
Il Trovatore
1915 *Bella Donna*
The Blindness of Devotion
The Buzzard's Shadow
The Crimson Wing
Destruction
The Failure
The Moonstone
The Ring of the Borgias
The Seventh Noon
The Spanish Jade
The Toast of Death

The Wolf Man
A Woman's Resurrection
1916 *The Folly of Revenge*
The Green-Eyed Monster
Public Opinion
The Pursuing Vengeance
Snow White
Unto Those Who Sin
Wanted—A Home
1917 Black Orchids
The Bride of Hate
Her Temptation
The Judgement House
The Tiger Woman
1918 *The Honor of His House*
The King of Diamonds
The Life Mask
A Man's Man
Over the Top
The Panther Woman
The Ranger
Revenge
The Still Alarm
Stolen Orders
Toys of Fate
Unexpected Places
Wife or Country
A Woman's Fool
1919 *The Ace of the Saddle*
The Avalanche
A Dangerous Affair
Human Passions
Keali
The Law of Men
The Master Man
The Red Lantern
The Secret Garden
A Sporting Chance (American Film Co.)
Square Deal Sanderson
Thin Ice
A Woman's Experience
1920 *Dr. Jekyll and Mr. Hyde (Famous Players-Lasky Corp.)*
The Purple Cipher

Poker
1915 *A Black Sheep*
The Voice in the Fog
When a Woman Loves
1916 *A Gutter Magdalene*
Temptation and the Man
The Thousand Dollar Husband
The Traveling Salesman
1917 *Anything Once*
The Bride of Hate
Fools for Luck
1918 *All the World to Nothing*
Carmen of the Klondike
Faith Endurin'
Little Red Decides
A Pair of Sixes
Ruggles of Red Gap
Two-Gun Betty
When Do We Eat?
1919 *Bill Henry*
A Dangerous Affair
Fair and Warmer
Hit or Miss
Keali
A Man's Country
Sandy Burke of the U-Bar-U
The She Wolf
1920 *The Gamesters*
The Tiger's Cub

Poland
1915 The Battles of a Nation
Russian Battlefields
1916 *The Fighting Germans*
War-Torn Poland
1920 Starvation

Poles
1918 *The Bells*

Police
rt **Policemen**
Specific types of police
1912 *The Adventures of Lieutenant Petrosino*
1913 *The Fight for Millions*
The Fortune Hunters
The Third Degree
Traffic in Souls
1914 *The Burglar and the Lady*
The Line-Up at Police Headquarters

The Long Arm of the Law
The Million
The Million Dollar Robbery
My Official Wife
The Mystery of Richmond
   Castle
The Mystery of the Poison
   Pool
Protect Us
Smashing the Vice Trust
The Spirit of the Poppy
Tillie's Punctured Romance
The Toll of Love
Trapped in the Great
   Metropolis
The Voice at the Telephone
1915 The Brink
C.O.D.
Crooky
The Edge of the Abyss
An Eye for an Eye
The Failure
The Fighting Hope
The Glory of Youth
The Gray Mask
The Ivory Snuff Box
The Lost House
Maciste
The Man from Oregon
The Menace of the Mute
The Morals of Marcus
The Old Homestead
Poor Schmaltz
Regeneration
The Running Fight
The Sable Lorcha
Stop Thief!
A Texas Steer
Tillie's Tomato Surprise
Via Wireless
The Wheels of Justice
A Yankee from the West
1916 Acquitted
The Black Sheep of the
   Family
The Breaker
The Children in the House
The Criminal
The Crown Prince's Double
The Daring of Diana
The Devil's Prize
The Discard
Dulcie's Adventure
The Fugitive
The Gods of Fate
The Golden Chance
Gretchen, the Greenhorn
The Hand of Peril
The Heiress at Coffee Dan's
Her Bleeding Heart
The Innocence of Ruth
The King's Game
The Kiss
The Marriage Bond
The Matrimaniac
Oliver Twist
The Pawn of Fate
The Phantom
The Price of Happiness
The Prima Donna's Husband
The Pursuing Vengeance
The Social Highwayman
Society Wolves
The Soul Market
Where D'Ye Get That Stuff?
The Wrong Door
1917 Apartment 29
Arsene Lupin
Betty Be Good
The Burglar
The Frame Up
Her Better Self
High Play
Idolators
Kick in
The Lady in the Library
Little Lost Sister
The Lone Wolf
Lost in Transit
Love Letters
A Love Sublime
The Maelstrom
The Mysterious Mr. Tiller
The Penny Philanthropist
The Princess of Park Row

The Small Town Girl
The Strong Way
The Tides of Fate
The Voice of Conscience
Who Was the Other Man
The Winged Mystery
Within the Law
1918 Blindfolded
Bound in Morocco
Brave and Bold
The Floor Below
The Girl of Today
The Golden Fleece
The Hand at the Window
Hearts or Diamonds?
Her Body in Bond
His Birthright
His Daughter Pays
Honor's Cross
The House of Glass
Humdrum Brown
Kiss or Kill
The Love Swindle
Madame Sphinx
The Menace
The Midnight Patrol
No Children Wanted
A Perfect 36
Prisoners of the Pines
The Shoes That Danced
The Studio Girl
Sylvia on a Spree
Unexpected Places
We Should Worry
Which Woman?
The Wildcat of Paris
The Wine Girl
The Yellow Ticket
1919 The False Code
His Majesty, the American
A Rogue's Romance
The Third Degree
The Tiger Lily
Under Suspicion
The Woman on the Index
1920 The Fourteenth Man
A Full House
Married Life
Mary Ellen Comes to Town
Number 99
Partners of the Night
The Right to Love
Someone in the House
Wanted at Headquarters
Wits vs. Wits
19-- The Policewoman
Police chiefs
1914 The Ring and the Man
1915 The Song of Hate
1916 The Cossack Whip
1917 The Hand That Rocks the
   Cradle
1918 The Girl in the Dark
La Tosca
1919 The Forbidden Room
Love Is Love
Police commissioners
1915 A Gentleman of Leisure
1916 The Kiss of Hate
The Wager
1917 Darkest Russia
Kick in
1918 Fair Enough
With Neatness and Dispatch
1919 The Fighting Roosevelts
1920 The Blue Pearl
Partners of the Night
Police inspectors
1918 Les Miserables
1919 Thieves
The Thirteenth Chair
Police raids
   rt Raids
      Vice raids
1914 The Criminal Path
The Greyhound
The Kangaroo
The Toll of Mammon
1915 At Bay
What Happened to Jones
1917 The Barker
The Hand That Rocks the
   Cradle
Trooper 44

1918 The Face in the Dark
The Midnight Patrol
Mystic Faces
The Painted Lily
The Sea Waif
1919 The Chosen Path
Common Clay
Crooked Straight
The Exquisite Thief
Fortune's Child
The Light
The Probation Wife
Spotlight Sadie
A Very Good Young Man
Water Lily
1920 Love Madness
Once a Plumber
Policemen
   rt Police
   nt Specific types of policemen
1914 Alone in New York
Officer 666
1915 The Fairy and the Waif
The Seventh Noon
1916 The Dragon
Fathers of Men
In the Web of the Grafters
Other People's Money
Rose of the Alley
A Son of Erin
The Traffic Cop
1917 The Adventures of Carol
Please Help Emily
Trooper 44
1918 All Man
A Broadway Scandal
The Danger Game
The Eleventh Commandment
Fair Enough
Fedora
The Little Runaway
The Road to France
1919 Brass Buttons
Extravagance
The House of Intrigue
The Joyous Liar
The Lincoln Highwayman
The Lord Loves the Irish
Love and the Law
One of the Finest
Pitfalls of a Big City
Secret Marriage
Shadows
1919-20
   The Marriage Blunder
1920 Below the Deadline
The Cradle of Courage
The Deep Purple
813
Life
Officer 666
The One Way Trail
The Star Rover
Poliomyelitis
1917 As Men Love
1920 The Woman in His House
Polish Americans
1918 Love's Law
Political alliances
1912 Richard III
1915 The Goose Girl
Graustark
Old Heidelberg
On the Russian Frontier
A Royal Family
1916 The Crown Prince's Double
Whom the Gods Destroy
1917 Cleopatra
The Fighting Gringo
The Little Yank
The Magnificent Meddler
My Fighting Gentleman
Royal Romance
1918 His Royal Highness
The Wooing of Princess Pat
Political bosses
   rt Politicians
1913 Eighty Million Women Want-?
1914 The County Chairman
The Man of the Hour
1915 Are They Born or Made?
The Danger Signal
The Frame-Up
The Governor's Boss
The Immigrant

The Italian
The Nigger
The Reform Candidate
Tainted Money
A Texas Steer
The Unbroken Road
1916 According to the Code
Ambition
The Courtesan
The Heart of New York
The Hero of Submarine D-2
The Immortal Flame
The Iron Hand
A Law unto Himself
The Mirror of Life
The No-Good Guy
The Unwritten Law
The Upheaval
The Vagabond Prince
The Wheel of the Law
1917 Come Through
Cy Whittaker's Ward
The Devil Dodger
Double Crossed
Hate
Her Excellency, the Governor
Her Life and His
Her Right to Live
The Magnificent Meddler
The Public Be Damned
Those Who Pay
1918 Baree, Son of Kazan
Conquered Hearts
Desert Law
The Embarrassment of Riches
The Finger of Justice
Go West, Young Man
The Grand Passion
His Robe of Honor
Honor's Cross
One More American
Petticoats and Politics
Quicksand
A Romance of the Underworld
The Vanity Pool
1919 The Railroader
The Rough Neck
The Sealed Envelope
1920 The Figurehead
The Great Accident
Her Honor the Mayor
Homespun Folks
The Prince of Avenue A
The Star Rover
Why Women Sin
Wings of Pride
Political campaigns
   rt Elections
1913 From Dusk to Dawn
1914 Beating Back
The Coming Power
The County Chairman
The Governor's Ghost
The Truth Wagon
1915 At Bay
The Battle of Ballots
The Fight
The Gentleman from Indiana
The High Hand
The Politicians
The Reform Candidate
The Truth About Helen
The Unbroken Road
York State Folks
1916 The City
The City of Illusion
The Courtesan
The Fortunate Youth
Half a Rogue
The Iron Hand
Life's Shadows
The Price of Fame
1917 All for a Husband
The Bitter Truth
Framing Framers
Hate
Her Hour
Her Right to Live
Mary Jane's Pa
An Old Fashioned Young Man
Out of the Wreck
1918 The Heart of a Girl
The Landloper
Petticoats and Politics

A Very Good Young Man
When Bearcat Went Dry
The Woman of Lies
The Woman on the Index
1919-20
   The Tower of Jewels
1920 An Amateur Devil
The Amazing Woman
Blind Wives
The Broken Gate
The Copperhead
Dangerous Business
Down Home
Everything but the Truth
Fickle Women
The Fighting Shepherdess
The Figurehead
The Forbidden Woman
Hearts Are Trumps
Her Story
High Speed
The Inferior Sex
The Key to Power
The Law of the Yukon
The Life of the Party
Love's Flame
The Midnight Bride
Mothers of Men
The Notorious Miss Lisle
The Notorious Mrs. Sands
Old Dad
Pink Tights
Polly of the Storm Country
The Prey
The Restless Sex
Riders of the Dawn
Rouge and Riches
The Spenders
The Tattlers
The Turning Point
Under Northern Lights
Way Down East
The Week-End
What Women Love
The Whisper Market
Whispers
The Woman Above Reproach

Rescues
  rt **Escapes**
1913 Buried Alive in a Coal Mine
A Prisoner in the Harem
The Prisoner of Zenda
Shadows of the Moulin Rouge
Traffic in Souls
1914 Across the Pacific
The Adventures of Kitty Cobb
The Better Man
Brewster's Millions
Dan
The Day of Days
Doc
Escaped from Siberia
A Factory Magdalen
Fantasma
Fire and Sword
The Great Diamond Robbery
Hearts Adrift
Hearts United
Hook and Hand
The Human Bloodhound
Imar the Servitor
In the Days of the Thundering
   Herd
In the Land of the Head
   Hunters
Jess of the Mountain Country
The Land of the Lost
The Last Egyptian
The Lure
The Lust of the Red Man
The Magic Cloak of Oz
Martin Eden
Mrs. Wiggs of the Cabbage
   Patch
Over Niagara Falls
The Path Forbidden
The Ragged Earl
The Reign of Terror
Rescue of the Stefansson Arctic
   Expedition
Richelieu
Shannon of the Sixth
Sitting Bull—The Hostile
   Sioux Indian Chief
The Span of Life

The Spitfire
Tillie's Punctured Romance
Il Trovatore
Uncle Tom's Cabin
The War of Wars; Or, The
   Franco-German Invasion
When Rome Ruled
The Will O' the Wisp
The Wrath of the Gods
1915 The Adventures of a Boy
   Scout
After Dark
All for a Girl
Aloha Oe
Are They Born or Made?
The Barnstormers
The Billionaire Lord
The Birth of a Nation
The Broken Law
The Bulldogs of the Trail
The Buzzard's Shadow
The Call of the Dance
The Campbells Are Coming
Captain Macklin
The Captive
Chimmie Fadden
The College Widow
Comrade John
The Cotton King
The Daughter of the Sea
The Deathlock
Don Caesar de Bazan
The Eagle's Nest
Emmy of Stork's Nest
The End of the Road
Enoch Arden
Fanchon the Cricket
Fatherhood
Fighting Bob
Flame of Passion
Four Feathers
The Gambler of the West
The Garden of Lies
The Grandee's Ring
Graustark
Greater Love Hath No Man
The Heart of Maryland
Hearts of Men
Her Shattered Idol
Her Triumph
His Turning Point
The Immigrant
The Last of the Mafia
The Lily of Poverty Flat
Maciste
The Man Who Couldn't Beat
   God
Mignon
Milestones of Life
Money
My Valet
Nearly a Lady
Nedra
Out of the Darkness
The Outlaw's Revenge
The Pearl of the Antilles
The Price of Her Silence
Ranson's Folly
The Right of Way
The Rug Maker's Daughter
Rumpelstiltskin
Saved from the Harem
Sealed Valley
Secretary of Frivolous Affairs
Snobs
The Stolen Voice
The Turn of the Road
The Two Orphans
Unto the Darkness
The Vanderhoff Affair
Via Wireless
When a Woman Loves
The Whirl of Life
The White Pearl
The Wolf Man
The Yankee Girl
Young Romance
1916 The Adventures of Kathlyn
Barriers of Society
The Battle of Hearts
The Beast
The Beckoning Flame
The Beggar of Cawnpore
Bobbie of the Ballet
Bullets and Brown Eyes

The Captive God
The Chain Invisible
A Child of Mystery
Cross Currents
The Daughter of the Don
The Foolish Virgin
The Gay Lord Waring
The Half-Breed
The Heart of Paula
The Heart of Tara
Her American Prince
Her Bitter Cup
The Hero of Submarine D-2
Hidden Valley
Hoodoo Ann
Is Any Girl Safe?
The Jungle Child
The Kiss
Miss Jackie of the Navy
A Modern Enoch Arden
The Net
The Ninety and Nine
Pamela's Past
Prudence the Pirate
The Raiders
The Road to Love
The Scarlet Road
Silks and Satins
Sunshine Dad
The Surprises of an Empty
   Hotel
Susan Rocks the Boat
The Target
That Sort
The Victory of Conscience
The Wharf Rat
When Love Is King
Where Love Leads
The Woman in Politics
The Wood Nymph
The Writing on the Wall
1917 The Adopted Son
Aladdin and the Wonderful
   Lamp
The Americano
The Avenging Trail
Betty and the Buccaneers
The Bronze Bride
Cassidy
The Conqueror
The Crimson Dove
Daughter of Maryland
Dead Shot Baker
Durand of the Bad Lands
The Fibbers
The Firefly of Tough Luck
For France
'49-'17
The Gates of Doom
The Girl Angle
The Golden Rosary
The Gun Fighter
Has Man the Right to Kill?
The Heart of Texas Ryan
The Heir of the Ages
Her Beloved Enemy
The Hidden Children
The Hidden Spring
Hinton's Double
The Innocent Sinner
The Inspirations of Harry
   Larrabee
Intrigue
It Happened to Adele
The Jaguar's Claws
The Jury of Fate
Knights of the Square Table
The Lad and the Lion
Lady Barnacle
The Lady of the Photograph
The Love That Lives
Man and Beast
The Man from Painted Post
Maternity
Melting Millions
Men of the Desert
Miss Jackie of the Army
A Modern Musketeer
Mutiny
Nan of Music Mountain
Next Door to Nancy
One Shot Ross
One Touch of Sin
Paws of the Bear
Periwinkle

The Planter
The Plow Woman
Polly of the Circus
Polly Put the Kettle On
Poppy
Pride and the Man
The Pride of New York
The Pride of the Clan
The Princess of Park Row
The Range Boss
Red, White and Blue Blood
Redemption
The Reed Case
A Roadside Impresario
Royal Romance
Runaway Romany
The Savage
The Sea Master
Shall We Forgive Her?
Snap Judgement
A Soul for Sale
The Stolen Paradise
The Streets of Illusion
The Submarine Eye
Sunlight's Last Raid
The Tides of Barnegat
The Tides of Fate
Trooper 44
Unconquered
When a Man Sees Red
The Wild Girl
A Woman Alone
Wooden Shoes
The Yellow Bullet
1918 Ace High
Ann's Finish
Beauty and the Rogue
The Boss of the Lazy Y
Bound in Morocco
Brace Up
The Brass Check
Brave and Bold
The Bravest Way
Breakers Ahead
Broadway Bill
By the World Forgot
Cactus Crandall
The Changing Woman
The Claws of the Hun
Come on In
The Curse of Iku
The Devil's Wheel
The Eyes of Mystery
The Finger of Justice
The Flash of Fate
Friend Husband
Fuss and Feathers
The Ghost of the Rancho
The Girl from Beyond
The Girl from Bohemia
The Girl in the Dark
The Girl Who Came Back
The Girl with the Champagne
   Eyes
The Goddess of Lost Lake
The Grain of Dust
The Grand Passion
The Grey Parasol
Heart of the Sunset
Hearts of Love
Hearts of the World
A Heart's Revenge
Hell Bent
Her Aviator
Her Country First
High Stakes
The Hired Man
His Birthright
His Daughter Pays
His Royal Highness
Hitting the Trail
An Honest Man
The Honor of His House
How Could You, Jean?
Huck and Tom; Or, The
   Further Adventures of Tom
   Sawyer
The Hun Within
In Judgment Of
In the Hollow of Her Hand
Innocent's Progress
Jules of the Strong Heart
The Kid Is Clever
The Kingdom of Youth
The Last Rebel

Leap to Fame
The Light of Western Stars
The Love Net
The Love Swindle
Love's Conquest
Madam Who
Mlle. Paulette
The Magic Eye
The Man Above the Law
The Man Hunt
A Man's Man
Marriages Are Made
The Mating
Midnight Madness
The Million Dollar Mystery
Les Miserables
Mrs. Slacker
Morgan's Raiders
Mystic Faces
The Naulahka
Neighbors
New Love for Old
No Man's Land
Old Hartwell's Cub
On the Jump
The Only Road
The Only Road
Peg O' the Sea
Peg of the Pirates
Petticoats and Politics
Queen of the Sea
The Rainbow Trail
The Red-Haired Cupid
Revenge
Riddle Gawne
Rimrock Jones
The Romance of Tarzan
Ruling Passions
The Safety Curtain
The Scarlet Drop
The Sea Flower
The Service Star
She Hired a Husband
The Shuttle
The Sign Invisible
The Silent Rider
Six Shooter Andy
Smashing Through
A Society Sensation
A Soul Without Windows
Sporting Life
The Spurs of Sybil
The Squaw Man
The Star Prince
The Still Alarm
String Beans
The Struggle Everlasting
The Sunset Princess
Sunshine Nan
Tarzan of the Apes
The Testing of Mildred Vane
Three Mounted Men
Too Fat to Fight
The Trail to Yesterday
Uncle Tom's Cabin
Unexpected Places
Waifs
Wanted for Murder
We Should Worry
Western Blood
The Wife He Bought
The Wild Strain
Winner Takes All
The Wolf and His Mate
Wolves of the Border
The World for Sale
You Can't Believe Everything
1919 *The Ace of the Saddle*
Adele
Alias Mike Moran
An Amateur Widow
The American Way
Auction of Souls
The Bandbox
Bare-Fisted Gallagher
Beauty-Proof
Behind the Door
The Belle of the Season
Blind Husbands
The Bluffer
Bolshevism on Trial
Bonds of Love
Breed of Men
Breezy Jim
Bringing Up Betty

Broken Blossoms
The Brute Breaker
The Burning Question
The Call of the Soul
The Cambric Mask
The Captain's Captain
Chasing Rainbows
Checkers
Children of Banishment
The Clouded Name
Coax Me
The Common Cause
The Crimson Gardenia
Daring Hearts
The Dark Star
A Daughter of the Wolf
Desert Gold
The Devil's Trail
Dust of Desire
Eastward Ho!
The Enchanted Barn
The End of the Game
The Faith of the Strong
A Fallen Idol
The False Faces
A Favor to a Friend
Fighting for Gold
Fighting Through
Fires of Faith
Flame of the Desert
Fool's Gold
For a Woman's Honor
*The Girl Who Stayed at
  Home*
Girls
The Glorious Lady
The Great Romance
The Greatest Question
The Heart of Youth
Hell Roarin' Reform
Help! Help! Police!
Her Game
Hit or Miss
Human Passions
Impossible Catherine
In Old Kentucky
In Wrong
The Isle of Conquest
Jinx
John Petticoats
Just Squaw
Kathleen Mavourneen
Kitty Kelly, M.D.
The Knickerbocker Buckaroo
The Last of the Duanes
Life's Greatest Problem
The Lion's Den
The Little Boss
The Lone Star Ranger
Lost Money
The Lost Princess
Louisiana
Luck and Pluck
Male and Female
A Man and His Money
The Man Who Turned White
The Man Who Won
A Man's Country
Man's Desire
The Mints of Hell
Miss Adventure
Mistaken Identity
The Money Corral
The Nature Girl
The New Moon
Nugget Nell
Out of the Fog
Out Yonder
The Pagan God
Partners Three
The Railroader
Red Hot Dollars
The Rider of the Law
Riders of Vengeance
The Road Called Straight
The Root of Evil
Rough Riding Romance
Sandy Burke of the U-Bar-U
The Scarlet Shadow
Secret Service
The She Wolf
The Sheriff's Son
The Sleeping Lion
Soldiers of Fortune
Something to Do

Speedy Meade
The Spirit of Lafayette
*A Sporting Chance (Famous
  Players-Lasky Corp.)*
Sue of the South
The Sundown Trail
Taxi
The Third Kiss
This Hero Stuff
Through the Wrong Door
Told in the Hills
The Tong Man
Treat 'Em Rough
Trixie from Broadway
The Twin Pawns
Two Women
Under the Top
The Undercurrent
The Unpainted Woman
The Unpardonable Sin
The Unwritten Code
The Uplifters
The Usurper
The Valley of the Giants
Victory
Virtuous Sinners
Water Lily
The Weaker Vessel
What Am I Bid?
When Arizona Won
When Bearcat Went Dry
When My Ship Comes In
Who Cares?
*Whom the Gods Would
  Destroy*
The Wicked Darling
A Wild Goose Chase
Wings of the Morning
The Woman Michael Married
A Woman There Was
1919-20
When a Man Loves
1920 Alias Jimmy Valentine
Before the White Man Came
A Broadway Cowboy
Cynthia-of-the-Minute
The Daredevil
Desert Love
Dinty
Duds
Empty Arms
The Fighting Kentuckians
The Flaming Clue
Footlights and Shadows
The Heart of Twenty
The Hidden Code
Jes' Call Me Jim
The Joyous Troublemaker
Just Pals
The Key to Power
Lahoma
Love's Protegé
The Luck of the Irish
My Lady's Garter
Out of the Dust
The Palace of Darkened
  Windows
Paris Green
Pegeen
Prairie Trails
The Purple Cipher
The Return of Tarzan
Risky Business
The Sea Rider
Smiling All the Way
Something New
The Stranger
*The Symbol of the
  Unconquered*
Terror Island
The Toll Gate
The Valley of Tomorrow
Water, Water Everywhere
Way Down East
What's Your Hurry?
Witch's Gold
19-- *The Slave Market*
Resorts
1914 *A Florida Enchantment*
Without Hope
1915 Destiny; Or, The Soul of a
  Woman
Marrying Money
The Sentimental Lady
Young Romance

1916 *American Aristocracy*
The Surprises of an Empty
  Hotel
1917 *The Duchess of Doubt*
Fools for Luck
Her Bargain
The Marriage Speculation
Two Little Imps
1918 *The Girl of My Dreams*
Mlle. Paulette
New Love for Old
Our Little Wife
The Poor Rich Man
The Widow's Might
Women's Weapons
You Can't Believe Everything
1919 *The Fear Woman*
The Final Close-Up
Hit or Miss
The Little Intruder
Louisiana
Luck in Pawn
The Man Who Stayed at Home
A Midnight Romance
One Week of Life
Some Bride
1920 *Alarm Clock Andy*
Billions
Blind Love
Dad's Girl
A Dark Lantern
Don't Ever Marry
The Forged Bride
The Gamesters
Help Wanted—Male
Jenny Be Good
The Joyous Troublemaker
Neptune's Bride
Peaceful Valley
The Peddler of Lies
Why Change Your Wife?
Restauranteurs
1915 Cohen's Luck
1920 *In the Depths of Our Hearts*
Restaurants
  rt **Cafes**
      Inns
      Night clubs
      Taverns
1913 *In the Stretch*
1914 *Kate*
1915 *Fatherhood*
A Submarine Pirate
Temptation
1916 *The Dupe*
The Lure of Heart's Desire
Three Pals
The Unpardonable Sin
1917 The Cook of Canyon Camp
The Gilded Youth
High Play
Please Help Emily
Princess Virtue
Sally in a Hurry
The Yankee Way
1918 *At the Mercy of Men*
The Blind Adventure
A Broadway Scandal
Ruggles of Red Gap
Together
Who Killed Walton?
1919 *A Fighting Colleen*
Hit or Miss
The Loves of Letty
The Weaker Vessel
Where the West Begins
You're Fired
1920 *The Gift Supreme*
Smiling All the Way
Retirement homes
1916 *God's Half Acre*
1918 *The Spirit of '17*
1920 Old Lady 31
Reunions
1914 *La Belle Russe*
Forgiven; Or, The Jack of
  Diamonds
Hearts Adrift
*In the Days of the Thundering
  Herd*
The Little Jewess
The Pawn of Fortune
The Price of Treachery; Or,
  The Lighthouse Keeper's
  Daughter

Sins of the Parents
The Taint
The Unwelcome Mrs. Hatch
1915 *Always in the Way*
An American Gentleman
Bondwomen
Bought
Children of the Ghetto
1916 *His Brother's Wife*
1917 Aladdin's Other Lamp
Big Timber
A Bit of Kindling
The Charmer
The Cook of Canyon Camp
The Courage of Silence
The Cricket
The End of the Tour
God's Crucible
Great Expectations
The Master Passion
Mutiny
The Renaissance at Charleroi
Wrath
1918 Ace High
Madame Jealousy
The Man of Bronze
Milady O' the Beanstalk
Miss Innocence
Moral Suicide
Morgan's Raiders
A Mother's Secret
1919 Break the News to Mother
The Capitol
The Devil's Trail
Evangeline
Heart O' the Hills
1920 The Devil's Riddle
The Testing Block
That Something
The Third Generation
The Unfortunate Sex
What Would You Do?

Revenge
1913 The Black Snake
The Count of Monte Cristo
Hoodman Blind
Shadows of the Moulin Rouge
A Sister to Carmen
1914 *At the Cross Roads*
The Battle of the Sexes
The Call of the North
Cameo Kirby
The County Chairman
Damaged Goods
Doc
The Dream Woman
Facing the Gattling Guns
A Factory Magdalen
Forgiven; Or, The Jack of
Diamonds
The Greyhound
The Idler
In the Land of the Head
Hunters
The Kangaroo
The Last Egyptian
The Littlest Rebel
The Man of the Hour
The Marked Woman
The Master Mind
Mr. Barnes of New York
Neptune's Daughter
An Odyssey of the North
One of Millions
The Red Flame of Passion
Salomy Jane
Samson
Thou Shalt Not
Three Weeks
The Tigress
Il Trovatore
Under the Gaslight
The War of Wars; Or, The
Franco-German Invasion
The Wolf
The Woman in Black
A Woman Who Did
1915 An American Gentleman
The Butterfly
Captain Courtesy
The Closing Net
A Continental Girl
The Darkening Trail
The Despoiler
An Enemy to Society

Evidence
The Explorer
The Failure
The Fool and the Dancer
Forbidden Fruit
The Frame-Up
From the Valley of the Missing
The Gray Mask
The Greater Will
*The Heart of a Painted
Woman*
The Heart of Jennifer
The Heart of Maryland
The Heart of the Blue Ridge
The Italian
Life Without Soul
The Little Girl That He Forgot
The Lure of the Mask
The Man of Shame
The Man Trail
Mignon
The Money Master
A Mother's Confession
Mother's Roses
The Mummy and the
Humming Bird
The Outlaw's Revenge
The Ploughshare
The Pretty Sister of Jose
The Price
Princess Romanoff
The Ring of the Borgias
Rule G
Rumpelstiltskin
The Sable Lorcha
Samson
Saved from the Harem
The Shooting of Dan McGrew
The Slim Princess
The Soul of Broadway
The Spanish Jade
The Sporting Duchess
Strathmore
Temptation
Through Turbulent Waters
The Toast of Death
The Unfaithful Wife
The Vampire
The Vow
The Way Back
The Wolf of Debt
A Yankee from the West
Zaza
1915-16
The Little Church Around the
Corner
1916 *The Alibi*
Anton the Terrible
The Apostle of Vengeance
April
At Piney Ridge
Ben Blair
A Bird of Prey
The Bondman
A Child of the Paris Streets
Children of the Feud
The City
Civilization's Child
The Come-Back
The Conflict
The Corner
A Corner in Cotton
The Cossack Whip
The Crippled Hand
Daredevil Kate
The Dawn of Love
Destiny's Toy
The Devil's Bondwoman
The Dream Girl
Extravagance
Fathers of Men
The Feast of Life
The Flower of No Man's Land
The Folly of Revenge
The Fool's Revenge
The Fourth Estate
Friday the Thirteenth
The Gates of Eden
The Girl of the Lost Lake
The Girl with the Green Eyes
The Good Bad Man
The Great Problem
The Gringo
The Heart of Tara
Hell's Hinges

The Heritage of Hate
The Hero of Submarine D-2
The Honorable Friend
I Accuse
It May Be Your Daughter
Jealousy
The Kiss of Hate
The Land Just Over Yonder
A Law unto Himself
Life's Whirlpool
The Love Hermit
The Love Thief
Madame La Presidente
The Madcap
The Man from Manhattan
The Masked Rider
The Missing Links
The Moral Fabric
The Ne'er-Do-Well
Pamela's Past
The Path of Darkness
The Patriot
The Pawn of Fate
Pay Dirt
The Perils of Divorce
Poor Little Peppina
The Price of Happiness
Rose of the Alley
The Serpent
The Sex Lure
Sherlock Holmes
Slander
Somewhere in France
Sorrows of Happiness
Soul Mates
The Soul of Kura-San
The Stepping Stone
The Straight Way
Sudden Riches
The Suspect
The Tarantula
Temptation and the Man
20,000 Leagues Under the Sea
The Twin Triangle
The Two Edged Sword
Two Men of Sandy Bar
Wall Street Tragedy
Who Killed Joe Merrion?
A Woman's Honor
A Woman's Power
The World Against Him
The Yellow Passport
1917 As Man Made Her
The Auction Block
The Bar Sinister
Barbary Sheep
The Barker
The Barricade
Behind the Mask
Beware of Strangers
The Bitter Truth
The Bride of Hate
The Bride's Silence
The Call of the East
Conscience
The Cost of Hatred
The Customary Two Weeks
The Danger Trail
The Devil's Assistant
The Devil's Bait
The Devil's Pay Day
The Door Between
The Dormant Power
Double Room Mystery
Each to His Kind
The Eternal Sin
The False Friend
Fanatics
Feet of Clay
Forbidden Paths
Forget-Me-Not
The Fuel of Life
The Ghost of Old Morro
Great Expectations
The Greater Law
The Greater Woman
The Heart of a Lion
Her Beloved Enemy
Her Hour
His Own People
His Sweetheart
The Inevitable
The Jaguar's Claws
The Lair of the Wolf
The Law of Compensation

Life's Whirlpool
The Long Trail
Love Letters
A Magdalene of the Hills
The Man Trap
Mary Jane's Pa
The Mate of the Sally Ann
A Modern Monte Cristo
The Mother Instinct
A Mother's Ordeal
Mountain Dew
The Mystic Hour
Nan of Music Mountain
North of Fifty-Three
Outwitted
The Painted Lie
The Phantom Shotgun
The Price Mark
The Reward of the Faithless
A Rich Man's Plaything
Rosie O'Grady
The Saintly Sinner
Sands of Sacrifice
The Sea Master
She
The Slave Market
Society's Driftwood
The Soul of a Magdalen
The Soul of Satan
Souls in Pawn
A Strange Transgressor
Ten of Diamonds
The Tiger Woman
To the Death
Vengeance Is Mine
Vengeance of the Dead
When a Man Sees Red
When Men Are Tempted
The White Raven
Whose Wife?
Within the Law
1918 Alias Mary Brown
An Alien Enemy
Baree, Son of Kazan
Beyond the Law
The Border Wireless
The Brazen Beauty
The Bride's Awakening
The Cast-Off
Cheating the Public
Code of the Yukon
The Curse of Iku
A Daughter of the Old South
The Eagle
Eye for Eye
Fedora
The Firebrand
The Flash of Fate
Flower of the Dusk
The Fly God
For Husbands Only
For the Freedom of the East
A Game with Fate
The Girl from Beyond
Green Eyes
The Grouch
The Hand at the Window
Hell's Crater
Her Man
Her Price
The Home Trail
In the Hollow of Her Hand
A Japanese Nightingale
The King of Diamonds
Life or Honor?
Madam Who
Naked Hands
The Ordeal of Rosetta
Other Men's Daughters
Painted Lips
A Pair of Sixes
The Prussian Cur
Queen of the Sea
Revenge
Riddle Gawne
Riders of the Purple Sage
A Romance of the Underworld
Ruling Passions
Salome
The Scarlet Drop
Six Shooter Andy
A Son of Strife
The Soul of Buddha
The Testing of Mildred Vane
To Hell with the Kaiser

The Trail to Yesterday
Treasure of the Sea
The Velvet Hand
Vengeance
Whims of Society
Who Killed Walton?
The Wife He Bought
The Winding Trail
The Witch Woman
1919 *America Was Right*
The Battler
Beckoning Roads
Behind the Door
The False Code
The Feud
The Forfeit
Gambling in Souls
A Girl at Bay
The Girl-Woman
Heart O' the Hills
Hearts Asleep
His Debt
His Wife's Friend
The Illustrious Prince
In Old Kentucky
Keali
The Lamb and the Lion
Lasca
The Long Arm of Mannister
Loot
Lost Money
Lure of Ambition
The Man Hunter
A Man's Country
Marriage for Convenience
Miss Arizona
The New Moon
One of the Finest
The Poppy Girl's Husband
Riders of Vengeance
A Sage Brush Hamlet
The Scar
The Sleeping Lion
A Society Exile
The Spitfire of Seville
The Steel King
The Test of Honor
The Thunderbolt
The Tiger Lily
Toton
Victory
Virtuous Men
The Westerners
The Witness for the Defense
The Wolf
The Woman of Lies
A Woman of Pleasure
The Woman Thou Gavest Me
The Woman Under Oath
1920 A Beggar in Purple
Below the Deadline
Blackmail
The Brand of Lopez
The Breath of the Gods
The Brute
Bullet Proof
The City of Masks
The Corsican Brothers
The Cost
Dangerous Days
The Daughter Pays
Desert Love
The Desert Scorpion
Dinty
Drag Harlan
The Dream Cheater
Felix O'Day
The Flame of Hellgate
Flames of the Flesh
Hearts Are Trumps
Heritage
His Wife's Money
Homespun Folks
The Inner Voice
King Spruce
Lahoma
Love's Protégé
The Master Mind
Mothers of Men
The North Wind's Malice
The Notorious Mrs. Sands
The Orphan
The Penalty
The Plunger
Polly of the Storm Country

The Price of Redemption
Seeds of Vengeance
Shod with Fire
Slaves of Pride
The Stranger
Sundown Slim
Too Much Johnson
The Triple Clue
The Unseen Witness
The Untamed
The Valley of Tomorrow
Vengeance and the Girl
The Victim
Voices
The Walk-Offs
What Women Want
Wits vs. Wits
The Woman Above Reproach
The Woman in Room 13
Young Mrs. Winthrop

Revenue agents
1915 *The Heart of the Blue Ridge*
1916 *The Stronger Love*
     The Trail of the Lonesome Pine
1917 *Her Country's Call*
1918 *Her Inspiration*
     One Dollar Bid
1919 *A Daughter of the Wolf*
     Forest Rivals
     In Old Kentucky
     The Moonshine Trail
     What Am I Bid?

Reverends
1915 *The Labyrinth*
1918 *The Midnight Trail*
1919 *The Lion's Den*

Reviviscence
1916 *Civilization*
1920 The Devil to Pay

Revolts
1914 *The Dishonored Medal*
     Neptune's Daughter
     Il Trovatore
1916 *A Daughter of the Gods*
     The Dumb Girl of Portici
     From Broadway to a Throne
     The Victoria Cross
1917 *Exile*
     Heart and Soul
     The Planter
1918 *The Claw*
     The Source
     Under the Yoke
1919 Flame of the Desert

Revolutionaries
1913 Barbarous Mexico
     The Black Snake
1914 Beneath the Czar
     Captain Alvarez
     A Fight for Freedom; Or,
       Exiled to Siberia
     The Key to Yesterday
     The Man from Home
     The Man O' Warsman
     A Romance of the Mexican
      Revolution
     The War Extra
1915 *The Dictator*
     Du Barry
     Fighting Bob
     The Outlaw's Revenge
     The Rights of Man: A Story of
      War's Red Blotch
1916 Behind the Lines
     The Cossack Whip
     The Crucial Test
     Following the Flag in Mexico
     The Gilded Cage
     The Heart of a Hero
     The Heart of Paula
     The Heart of the Hills
     Her American Prince
     The Lotus Woman
     The Love Thief
     A Message to Garcia
     One Day
     The Sorrows of Love
     United States Marines Under
      Fire in Haiti
     The Victoria Cross
     Whom the Gods Destroy
     The Witch
1917 The American Consul
     Crime and Punishment
     The Fighting Gringo

     Heart and Soul
     Rasputin, the Black Monk
     The Rose of Blood
     This Is the Life
     Under False Colors
     The Zeppelin's Last Raid
1918 At the Mercy of Men
     The Firebrand
     The German Curse in Russia
     Hitting the High Spots
     The Kid Is Clever
     A Son of Strife
     Under the Yoke
1919 The Betrayal
     Full of Pep
     The Great Romance
     The Right to Happiness
     The Undercurrent
1920 *An Adventuress*
     Lifting Shadows
     The Perfect Woman
     Rio Grande
     Rogues and Romance
     Something Different
     Sophy of Kravonia; Or, The
      Virgin of Paris
     Under Crimson Skies
19-- *Barnaby Lee*

Revolutions
1913 Victory
1914 Soldiers of Fortune
1915 Captain Macklin
1916 *The Last Man*
     The Lotus Woman
     The Ruling Passion
     The Sorrows of Love
1917 The Fighting Gringo
     Soldiers of Chance
     This Is the Life
     The Yankee Way
1918 *Crown Jewels*
1919 Hawthorne of the U.S.A.
     The Pagan God
     The Prince and Betty
1920 An Adventuress
     Li Ting Lang
     Little Miss Rebellion
     Roman Candles
     Sink or Swim
     Something Different
     Under Crimson Skies

Rewards
1914 *The Yellow Traffic*
1915 *The Fairy and the Waif*
     Fatherhood
1916 *The Breaker*
     Daphne and the Pirate
     The Flying Torpedo
     The Heiress at Coffee Dan's
     Her Surrender
     The Island of Happiness
     The Pool of Flame
     Sunshine Dad
     The Three Godfathers
1917 *An Amateur Orphan*
     Betrayed
     Lost in Transit
     Mr. Opp
     Next Door to Nancy
     The Princess' Necklace
     The Princess of Park Row
     The Silent Man
1918 He Comes Up Smiling
     Headin' South
     Lawless Love
     Mystic Faces
     A Pair of Cupids
     The Ranger
     Salome
     Wolves of the Rail
1919 Counterfeit
     The Dub
     A Fighting Colleen
     Red Blood and Yellow
     Upstairs
     The Winning Girl
1920 *Duds*
     Eyes of the Heart
     Girls Don't Gamble
     Jes' Call Me Jim
     Just Pals
     The Toll Gate

Rheims (France)
1915 *The History of the World's
     Greatest War*

Rheumatism
1919 *Fit to Win*

Rhinoceroses
1915 *The Ringtailed Rhinoceros*

Rhode Island
1916 American Aristocracy

Rhodesia
1920 Love in the Wilderness

Richard I, King of England, 1157-1199
1913 *Ivanhoe*
     Robin Hood

Richard III, King of England, 1452-1485
1912 Richard III

Richard, Duke of Clarence
1912 *Richard III*

Richelieu, Armand Jein du Plessis, Cardinal, duc de, 1582-1642
1914 Cardinal Richelieu's Ward
     Richelieu
     The Three Musketeers
1916 D'Artagnan

Richmond (Virginia)
1917 *Those Without Sin*
1918 *Madam Who*
1919 *Secret Service*

Rickshaw drivers
1915 *The Fox Woman*
1918 Who Is to Blame?

Riddles
1914 *Samson*

Riding
  rt Horsemen
1914 *The Three of Us*
1915 *Where Cowboy Is King*
1916 *A Stranger from Somewhere*
     The Traffic Cop
1917 *The Lad and the Lion*
     Where Love Is
1918 *Morgan's Raiders*
1920 *The Girl in the Rain*

Riding accidents
1915 *The Runaway Wife*
     Still Waters
1916 *The Gay Lord Waring*
     Little Lady Eileen
1917 *Polly of the Circus*
1918 *Wild Youth*
1919 *The Little Rowdy*
     Three Green Eyes
1920 *The Girl in the Rain*
     The Lone Hand
     Occasionally Yours
     What Would You Do?

Riding instructors
1914 *The Education of Mr. Pipp*
1915 *Gretna Green*

Rifles
1918 *The Kaiser's Shadow, or the
     Triple Cross*

Ringmasters
1917 The Barker
     The Sawdust Ring

Rio de Janeiro
1915 *The Fifth Commandment*
     A Trip to the Argentine

Rio Grande River
1915 *The Grandee's Ring*
1916 *Following the Flag in Mexico*
1918 *Heart of the Sunset*
     Western Blood

Riots
1913 *From Dusk to Dawn*
1914 The Christian
     The Crucible
     Facing the Gattling Guns
     The Valley of the Moon
1915 The Absentee
     Destruction
     The Little Gypsy
     A Modern Magdalen
1916 *Black Friday*
     A Corner in Colleens
     The Ne'er-Do-Well
     Those Who Toil
1917 *The Food Gamblers*
1918 *The Girl from Bohemia*
     The Scarlet Drop
     The Transgressor

1915　*The Adventures of a Boy*
　　　　Scout
　　　The Alien
　　　An American Gentleman
　　　The Brink
　　　The Closing Net
　　　The Diamond Robbery
　　　The Valley of Lost Hope
　　　The Wheels of Justice
　　　A Yankee from the West
1916　*The Birth of a Man*
　　　The Catspaw
　　　Destiny's Toy
　　　The Devil's Prayer-Book
　　　The Dollar and the Law
　　　A Dream or Two Ago
　　　The Flower of Faith
　　　Going Straight
　　　Humanizing Mr. Winsby
　　　Jim Grimsby's Boy
　　　The Lights of New York
　　　The Lost Bridegroom
　　　The Mark of Cain
　　　The Phantom
　　　The Rainbow Princess
　　　Redeeming Love
　　　The Social Buccaneer
　　　The Sultana
　　　The Sunbeam
　　　Tennessee's Pardner
　　　The Wasted Years
　　　The Wild Girl of the Sierras
　　　A Yoke of Gold
1917　*Ashes of Hope*
　　　The Avenging Trail
　　　The Bad Boy
　　　Betsy's Burglar
　　　Builders of Castles
　　　The Burglar
　　　Cassidy
　　　Come Through
　　　The Countess Charming
　　　Crime and Punishment
　　　A Crooked Romance
　　　Daughter of Maryland
　　　Envy
　　　The Family Honor
　　　'49-'17
　　　The Mysterious Miss Terry
　　　The Secret of Black Mountain
　　　Snap Judgement
　　　Sunshine Alley
　　　The Tiger Woman
　　　Time Locks and Diamonds
　　　Told at Twilight
　　　Trooper 44
　　　Within the Law
　　　The World Apart
1918　Alias Mary Brown
　　　The Bells
　　　Blue-Eyed Mary
　　　The Border Wireless
　　　Boston Blackie's Little Pal
　　　A Burglar for a Night
　　　By Hook or Crook
　　　Confession
　　　Convict 993
　　　Denny from Ireland
　　　Face Value
　　　Find the Woman
　　　The Floor Below
　　　Fuss and Feathers
　　　Gates of Gladness
　　　The Golden Fleece
　　　Hearts or Diamonds?
　　　The Law's Outlaw
　　　The Love Swindle
　　　The Menace
　　　Midnight Madness
　　　The Midnight Trail
　　　Les Miserables
　　　Old Hartwell's Cub
　　　A Perfect 36
　　　Petticoats and Politics
　　　Playing the Game
　　　The Poor Rich Man
　　　The Pretender
　　　Prisoners of the Pines
　　　The Sea Waif
　　　Secret Strings
　　　Three Mounted Men
　　　To Him That Hath
　　　Under the Greenwood Tree
　　　Up the Road with Sallie
　　　Which Woman?

　　　The Whirlpool
　　　Wives and Other Wives
1919　*L'Apache*
　　　The Blue Bonnet
　　　The Bondage of Barbara
　　　Cheating Herself
　　　Fighting for Gold
　　　Gambling in Souls
　　　Ginger
　　　Greased Lightning
　　　A Gun Fightin' Gentleman
　　　Hell Roarin' Reform
　　　Help! Help! Police!
　　　The House of Intrigue
　　　Loot
　　　The Love Burglar
　　　Love's Prisoner
　　　Mistaken Identity
　　　The Money Corral
　　　The Parisian Tigress
　　　A Regular Fellow
　　　A Rogue's Romance
　　　Three Black Eyes
　　　Toton
　　　The Trembling Hour
　　　Twilight
　　　When a Girl Loves
1920　*Away Goes Prudence*
　　　The Cradle of Courage
　　　Dad's Girl
　　　The Dangerous Talent
　　　The Desert Scorpion
　　　Dollars and the Woman
　　　Double Speed
　　　Felix O'Day
　　　Forty-Five Minutes from
　　　　Broadway
　　　Girls Don't Gamble
　　　The Iron Rider
　　　Just Pals
　　　The Law of the Yukon
　　　Love's Battle
　　　Luring Shadows
　　　The Man Who Dared
　　　Mary Ellen Comes to Town
　　　Outside the Law
　　　Parted Curtains
　　　The Skywayman
　　　The Valley of Night
　　　The Wall Street Mystery
　　　Wanted at Headquarters
Robin Hood
1913　*Ivanhoe*
　　　Robin Hood
1916　Kinkaid, Gambler
1917　The Black Wolf
Rocky Mountains
1917　The Adventures of Buffalo Bill
1919　*The Heart of Humanity*
Rodeos
　　rt　**Roundups**
　　　　Wild west shows
1913　The Pendleton, Oregon,
　　　　Round-Up
1915　Where Cowboy Is King
1918　*Wild Women*
1919　*The Money Corral*
1920　Frontier Days
　　　The Texan
Roller skating
1918　*Neighbors*
Romanoff Diamonds
1914　*The Great Diamond Robbery*
Romans
1914　Thais
　　　When Rome Ruled
Rome (Ancient)
1914　Pagan Rome
　　　The Sign of the Cross
1917　*A Branded Soul*
1918　*Woman*
1920　A Sister to Salome
Rome (Italy)
1914　The Coliseum in Films
　　　His Holiness, the Late Pope
　　　　Pius X, and the Vatican
1915　*The Song of Hate*
1916　The Making of Maddalena
1918　*La Tosca*
1919　*An Adventure in Hearts*
　　　The Splendid Romance
　　　The Two Brides
　　　The Woman Michael Married

Rome—History—Empire
1912　Cleopatra
1913　The Daughter of the Hills
1914　Pagan Rome
1916　Race Suicide
1917　Cleopatra
1920　Madonnas and Men
Rooftops
1914　*Trapped in the Great*
　　　　Metropolis
1919　*Fighting Destiny*
　　　When the Clouds Roll By
Roommates
1915　*The Grandee's Ring*
　　　The Wild Goose Chase
1918　Good Night, Paul
　　　A Lady's Name
　　　Mr. Fix-It
　　　More Trouble
　　　The Sins of the Children
　　　A Weaver of Dreams
1919　Girls
　　　Wanted—A Husband
　　　Widow by Proxy
Theodore Roosevelt
1918　Why America Will Win
1919　The Fighting Roosevelts
Roosevelt (Alaska)
1917　Alaska Wonders in Motion
Elihu Root
1918　*The German Curse in Russia*
1919　*Free Russia*
Betsy Ross
1917　Betsy Ross
Rough Riders
1919　The Fighting Roosevelts
Roulette
1915　*The Country Boy*
1916　*The Parson of Panamint*
1917　*The New York Peacock*
　　　The Tiger Woman
1918　The Devil's Wheel
　　　The Turn of the Wheel
1919　*Chasing Rainbows*
　　　Gambling in Souls
Roundups
　　rt　**Rodeos**
　　　　Wild west shows
1915　The Sioux City Round-Up
1919　*Miss Arizona*
1920　Frontier Days
Rowboats
1918　*The Kingdom of Youth*
Rowing
1918　*Brown of Harvard*
Royalty
　　nt　Specific types of royalty
1913　*Ivanhoe*
　　　A Princess of Bagdad
　　　The Prisoner of Zenda
1914　The Dancer and the King
　　　Fantasma
　　　The Ghost Breaker
　　　His Majesty, the Scarecrow of
　　　　Oz
　　　Joseph in the Land of Egypt
　　　The Last Egyptian
　　　The Last Volunteer
　　　The Magic Cloak of Oz
　　　Michael Strogoff
　　　My Official Wife
　　　The Port of Missing Men
　　　The Pride of Jennico
　　　Such a Little Queen
　　　The Three Musketeers
　　　Three Weeks
　　　Too Late
　　　With Serb and Austrian
　　　A Woman's Triumph
1915　*The Battles of a Nation*
　　　The Dust of Egypt
　　　The Garden of Lies
　　　The Girl from His Town
　　　The Goose Girl
　　　The Great Ruby
　　　Her Great Match
　　　History of the Great European
　　　　War
　　　Keep Moving
　　　The Lure of the Mask
　　　Mistress Nell
　　　Old Heidelberg
　　　The Prince and the Pauper
　　　Princess Romanoff

　　　The Puppet Crown
　　　Queen and Adventurer
　　　The Rights of Man: A Story of
　　　　War's Red Blotch
　　　The Ringtailed Rhinoceros
　　　A Royal Family
　　　Rumpelstiltskin
　　　The Slim Princess
　　　The Spender
　　　The White Sister
　　　A Woman's Resurrection
1916　The Adventures of Kathlyn
　　　Bullets and Brown Eyes
　　　Civilization
　　　The Crown Prince's Double
　　　Elusive Isabel
　　　An Enemy to the King
　　　The Fortunate Youth
　　　From Broadway to a Throne
　　　The Gilded Cage
　　　The Girl Philippa
　　　Her American Prince
　　　Intolerance
　　　King Lear
　　　Macbeth
　　　The Sowers
　　　War Brides
　　　When Love Is King
1917　*The Bottle Imp*
　　　Every Girl's Dream
　　　Fighting for Love
　　　Her Greatest Love
　　　Her Silent Sacrifice
　　　The High Sign
　　　The Image Maker
　　　In the Balance
　　　Intrigue
　　　Jack and the Beanstalk
　　　Lady Barnacle
　　　One Hour
　　　The Pride of New York
　　　The Princess' Necklace
　　　The Princess of Park Row
　　　Rasputin, the Black Monk
　　　Reaching for the Moon
　　　The Reward of the Faithless
　　　The Rose of Blood
　　　Royal Romance
　　　Zollenstein
1918　*At the Mercy of Men*
　　　The Fall of the Romanoffs
　　　For the Freedom of the East
　　　The Grain of Dust
　　　Her Final Reckoning
　　　Hidden Pearls
　　　His Royal Highness
　　　The Million Dollar Dollies
　　　The Mystery Girl
　　　The Naulahka
　　　Queen of the Sea
　　　The Savage Woman
　　　The Star Prince
　　　Who Is to Blame?
　　　Wild Women
　　　The Wooing of Princess Pat
1919　The Great Romance
　　　His Majesty, the American
　　　The Lone Wolf's Daughter
　　　The New Moon
　　　The Sneak
1920　*The Adventurer*
　　　The Breath of the Gods
　　　A Dark Lantern
　　　If I Were King
　　　Kismet
　　　The Last of the Mohicans
　　　Little Miss Rebellion
　　　Sophy of Kravonia; Or, The
　　　　Virgin of Paris
　　　Through Eyes of Men
Rubber
1915　*In the Amazon Jungles with*
　　　　the Captain Besley
　　　　Expedition
1916　*Bluff*
1917　The Planter
1919　*Dust of Desire*
Rubber magnates
1918　*The Brass Check*
1920　*Honor Bound*
Rubies
1915　The Great Ruby
　　　Stop Thief!
1916　The Heart of the Hills
　　　The Pool of Flame

1920 *Body and Soul*
Greater Than Fame
The Greatest Love
The Hope
In Search of a Sinner
In Walked Mary
The Misleading Lady
The Perfect Woman
Silk Husbands and Calico Wives
The Very Idea

Seers
  rt **Clairvoyants**
     Mediums
     Spiritualists
1914 *Joseph in the Land of Egypt*
1916 Macbeth
1917 *The Hidden Children*
1918 The Fall of the Romanoffs
      Money Mad
      Why I Would Not Marry
1920 Madonnas and Men

Seine River
1914 *The Phantom Violin*
1915 *Wormwood*

Self-confidence
1915 The Danger Signal
1916 *The Wolf Woman*
1917 The Man Who Made Good
      The Pinch Hitter
1918 His Majesty, Bunker Bean
      The Sign Invisible
1919 The Poor Boob

Self-defense
1915 *The Heart of Maryland*
      Judge Not; Or, The Woman of Mona Diggings
      June Friday
      The Nation's Peril
      The Outcast
      The Valley of Lost Hope
1916 *The Common Law*
      The Hunted Woman
      Love and Hate
      Not My Sister
      The Sin Ye Do
      The Twin Triangle
      Vanity
1917 *The Beloved Adventuress*
      The Deemster
      The Devil-Stone
      The Flashlight
      The Great Bradley Mystery
      The Honor System
      A Magdalene of the Hills
      The Marriage Market
      Out of the Wreck
      Sins of Ambition
      The Test of Womanhood
      Thais
      Triumph
      Until They Get Me
1918 *The Bird of Prey*
      The Border Legion
      The Bride of Fear
      The Danger Zone
      The Fly God
      The Hell Cat
      Her One Mistake
      The House of Silence
      In Judgment Of
      The Law That Divides
      Tempered Steel
      Wild Life
      The Yellow Ticket
1919 The Last of the Duanes
      Shadows
      The Witness for the Defense
1920 Lifting Shadows
      Man and Woman (Tyrad Pictures, Inc.)
      Mothers of Men
      Who's Your Servant?

Self-reliance
1915 The College Orphan
      The Making Over of Geoffrey Manning
      A Man's Making
      The Money Master
      The Moth and the Flame
1916 Artie, the Millionaire Kid
      The Blindness of Love
1917 Bridges Burned
      High Finance
      His Father's Son

The Little Terror
      Magda
1918 Go West, Young Man
      Humility
1919 The Beauty Market
      Come Again Smith
      Easy to Make Money
1920 The Thirteenth Commandment

Self-sacrifice
1913 Arizona
      Sapho
1914 *After the Ball*
      The Banker's Daughter
      The Boer War
      Damon and Pythias
      Dan
      Escaped from Siberia
      The Fatal Night
      The Governor's Ghost
      Hearts of Oak
      Ill Starred Babbie
      The Jungle
      The Little Angel of Canyon Creek
      The Path Forbidden
      The Price of Treachery; Or, The Lighthouse Keeper's Daughter
      Shore Acres
      The Sign of the Cross
      The Spirit of the Poppy
      The Squaw Man
      Tess of the Storm Country
      The Thief
      The Tigress
      The Toll of Love
      Il Trovatore
      Washington at Valley Forge
      When Fate Leads Trump
      A Woman's Triumph
1915 *The Bachelor's Romance*
      The Barnstormers
      The Beloved Vagabond
      The Bludgeon
      Camille
      The Cheat
      Chimmie Fadden
      The Chorus Lady
      The Clue
      The College Widow
      The Cowardly Way
      The Crimson Wing
      The Daughter of the Sea
      Du Barry
      Enoch Arden
      The Eternal City
      The Explorer
      The Fatal Card
      Four Feathers
      The Goose Girl
      Graustark
      Greater Love Hath No Man
      The Heart of Jennifer
      Hearts in Exile
      Her Own Way
      In the Palace of the King
      Jordan Is a Hard Road
      June Friday
      The Kindling
      The Little Dutch Girl
      Little Pal
      The Majesty of the Law
      The Man of Shame
      The Man Who Found Himself
      May Blossom
      The Melting Pot
      The Mill on the Floss
      Money
      The Money Master
      Monsieur Lecoq
      The Nigger
      Old Heidelberg
      The Painted Soul
      Playing Dead
      The Ploughshare
      The Price of Her Silence
      The Primrose Path
      Princess Romanoff
      The Reform Candidate
      Rosemary
      The Running Fight
      Sealed Valley
      The Second in Command
      The Seventh Noon
      The Song of the Wage Slave

The Spanish Jade
The Unwelcome Wife
The White Scar
The Wild Olive
The Woman
The Woman Pays
A Woman's Resurrection
1916 The Abandonment
      Acquitted
      The Almighty Dollar
      Ambition
      Anton the Terrible
      As in a Looking Glass
      The Awakening of Helena Richie
      The Beckoning Flame
      Behind Closed Doors
      The Bishop's Secret
      The Black Butterfly
      The Black Sheep of the Family
      The Blacklist
      Blazing Love
      The Bondman
      Bought and Paid For
      By Whose Hand?
      The Child of Destiny
      Civilization
      The Closed Road
      The Clown
      The Common Law
      A Coney Island Princess
      The Conflict
      The Criminal
      The Crippled Hand
      Cross Currents
      The Crucial Test
      The Dark Silence
      The Dawn Maker
      The Discard
      Doctor Neighbor
      Dorian's Divorce
      Dulcie's Adventure
      The Dumb Girl of Portici
      Embers
      An Enemy to the King
      The Eye of the Night
      Faith
      The Flames of Johannis
      The Fugitive
      God's Country and the Woman
      The Great Problem
      A Gutter Magdalene
      The Heart of Nora Flynn
      Her Great Price
      Her Husband's Wife
      Her Surrender
      His Brother's Wife
      His Great Triumph
      Honor Thy Name
      The Honorable Friend
      Husband and Wife
      Idols
      The Inner Struggle
      Intolerance
      Jaffery
      Joan the Woman
      The Kiss of Hate
      A Knight of the Range
      The Leopard's Bride
      Little Eve Edgarton
      Little Miss Happiness
      Little Miss Nobody
      Love's Sacrifice
      The Mark of Cain
      Martha's Vindication
      Medicine Bend
      Mister 44
      The Morals of Hilda
      My Country First
      The Overcoat
      The Parson of Panamint
      Passers By
      The Path of Happiness
      The Primal Lure
      Purity
      The Race
      The Ragamuffin
      The Ransom
      The Scarlet Woman
      The Secret of the Swamp
      Shell Forty-Three
      Sherlock Holmes
      The Shrine of Happiness
      The Sowers

The Spider
The Supreme Sacrifice
Sweet Kitty Bellairs
Tangled Hearts
The Three Godfathers
The Truant Soul
The Unattainable
Under Two Flags
Unprotected
Vengeance Is Mine
The Waifs
War Brides
The War Bride's Secret
The Way of the World
What Love Can Do
When Love Is King
The Whirlpool of Destiny
Whispering Smith
Whoso Findeth a Wife
The Woman Who Dared
The World's Great Snare
The Years of the Locust
The Yellow Pawn
1917 The Accomplice
      The Antics of Ann
      Arms and the Girl
      As Men Love
      Ashes of Hope
      The Auction of Virtue
      The Awakening of Ruth
      The Barker
      The Barrier
      The Beloved Adventuress
      Beloved Rogues
      Betty to the Rescue
      The Birth of Patriotism
      The Bitter Truth
      Blind Man's Holiday
      The Bottle Imp
      A Branded Soul
      Camille
      The Candy Girl
      Cassidy
      The Cloud
      The Cold Deck
      The Co-Respondent
      The Corner Grocer
      The Crimson Dove
      The Crystal Gazer
      The Dancer's Peril
      The Deemster
      The Derelict
      The Desire of the Moth
      The Devil Dodger
      The Door Between
      The Dormant Power
      The Edge of the Law
      Environment
      Exile
      The Family Honor
      For Liberty
      For Valour
      Forbidden Paths
      The Fortunes of Fifi
      Freckles
      The Ghost of Old Morro
      A Girl Like That
      Giving Becky a Chance
      God's Law and Man's
      The Gun Fighter
      Hashimura Togo
      Heart and Soul
      The Heart of a Lion
      The Heir of the Ages
      Hell Morgan's Girl
      Her Good Name
      Her Right to Live
      Her Sister
      Her Strange Wedding
      High Play
      Hinton's Double
      His Old-Fashioned Dad
      A Hungry Heart
      The Inner Shrine
      The Jaguar's Claws
      John Ermine of the Yellowstone
      The Jury of Fate
      The Lady of the Photograph
      The Last of the Carnabys
      The Law of the Land
      Life's Whirlpool
      The Little American
      The Little Samaritan
      The Long Trail

Modern Husbands
The Moral Deadline
Other Men's Wives
Paid in Advance
Should a Woman Tell?
The Silver King
A Society Exile
Someone Must Pay
The Thunderbolt
Toton
The Trap
Two Women
The Unwritten Code
The Woman Michael Married
You Never Know Your Luck
1920 *Black Is White*
The Common Sin
The Cost
The Girl in the Web
Greater Than Love
The House of Toys
Husbands and Wives
In Folly's Trail
Life's Twist
Love in the Wilderness
Mid-Channel
The North Wind's Malice
An Old Fashioned Boy
A Romantic Adventuress
Their Mutual Child
Young Mrs. Winthrop

Serbia
1914 With Serb and Austrian
1915 The Chocolate Soldier

Serbians
1918 The Fall of the Romanoffs
Kultur

Serbo-Bulgarian War, 1885
1915 The Chocolate Soldier

Sermons
1915 The Hypocrites
1916 *Fighting Blood*
The Hidden Scar
The Market of Vain Desire
A Woman's Fight
1917 *The Little Samaritan*
1918 *The One Woman*
Wild Honey
1919 *In His Brother's Place*
When a Girl Loves
A Woman There Was

Serums
1918 The Light Within
1920 *Man and His Woman*

Servants
nt Specific types of servants
1913 *The Lure of New York*
The Star of India
1914 *Beneath the Czar*
A Florida Enchantment
Life's Shop Window
The Man on the Box
The Master Mind
Mrs. Wiggs of the Cabbage
Patch
Under the Gaslight
1915 *The Adventures of a Boy
Scout*
All for a Girl
Beulah
The Birth of a Nation
Chimmie Fadden
The Dancing Girl
The Fox Woman
The Game of Three
Little Pal
The Lure of the Mask
Lydia Gilmore
Maciste
The Magic Skin
Marse Covington
The Moonstone
One Million Dollars
The Outlaw's Revenge
The Price
Princess Romanoff
Secretary of Frivolous Affairs
The Silent Voice
The Sins of the Mothers
A Trade Secret
The Vanderhoff Affair
A Woman's Resurrection
1916 *The Beckoning Flame*
The Birth of a Man

The Conscience of John David
D'Artagnan
Dorian's Divorce
An Enemy to the King
Faith
Hazel Kirke
The Heart of the Hills
My Partner
Sins of Men
The Thousand Dollar Husband
Three of Many
Two Men of Sandy Bar
When Love Is King
The Yellow Pawn
Youth's Endearing Charm
1917 *Charity Castle*
Cheerful Givers
The Flame of Youth
The Gentle Intruder
Her Silent Sacrifice
House of Cards
Idolators
The Little Duchess
The Little Princess
The Message of the Mouse
Mrs. Balfame
The Page Mystery
The Poor Little Rich Girl
The Price Mark
The Rise of Jennie Cushing
Sadie Goes to Heaven
Until They Get Me
War and the Woman
1918 All Night
Cyclone Higgins, D.D.
The Girl in the Dark
Green Eyes
The Green God
Inside the Lines
Kildare of Storm
Kultur
Little Miss Grown-Up
Mickey
M'liss
Money Mad
My Unmarried Wife
No Man's Land
Over the Top
Pals First
A Perfect 36
The Queen of Hearts
The Rose of the World
Swat the Spy
Wild Youth
With Neatness and Dispatch
1919 Come Out of the Kitchen
Common Property
Cowardice Court
The End of the Road
His Wife's Friend
The Illustrious Prince
Keali
A Misfit Earl
*Reclaimed: The Struggle for a
Soul Between Love and
Hate*
Rose of the West
The Silver King
Strictly Confidential
Stripped for a Million
Sue of the South
Toby's Bow
The Unveiling Hand
Upstairs and Down
When a Man Rides Alone
Wings of the Morning
The Witness for the Defense
1920 *Children Not Wanted*
The Devil's Garden
The Girl in the Web
The Leopard Woman
The Mark of Zorro
The Mother of His Children
Mothers of Men
Rookie's Return
The Servant in the House
The Sins of Rosanne
Who's Your Servant?

Settlement workers
1914 The Christian
The Straight Road
1915 *The Kindling*
On Her Wedding Night
Regeneration
Up from the Depths

1916 *The Eternal Grind*
The Lights of New York
The Pillory
The Sign of the Spade
The Spider and the Fly
1917 The Angel Factory
The Lifted Veil
When False Tongues Speak
1918 The Answer
Humility
The Man Above the Law
The Midnight Patrol
The Vamp
1919 The Belle of the Season
The Gay Old Dog
Home Wanted
Mandarin's Gold
The Third Kiss
Virtuous Sinners
The World to Live In
1920 *The Figurehead*
The Money-Changers

Settlers
1914 The Lust of the Red Man
Sitting Bull—The Hostile
Sioux Indian Chief
1915 *The Pageant of San Francisco*
1916 The Argonauts of
California—1849
The Aryan
Gold and the Woman
1917 *Durand of the Bad Lands*
John Ermine of the
Yellowstone
Wolf Lowry
1918 The Lady of the Dugout
1919 Breed of Men
When the Desert Smiles
1920 The Courage of Marge
O'Doone

Seville (Spain)
1915 Carmen (Fox Film Corp.)
Carmen (Jesse L. Lasky
Feature Play Co.)
1919 The Spitfire of Seville
1920 *The Woman and the Puppet*

Sex change
1914 A Florida Enchantment

Sex education
1919 The End of the Road
Open Your Eyes
The Solitary Sin

Sex theories
1916 The Moral Fabric
1920 The Love Expert
Love, Honor and Obey

Sextons
1917 *The Little Samaritan*

Sexual discrimination
rt **Double standard**
Male chauvinism
Sexual harassment
1916 *The Ragged Princess*
1917 The Amazons
1920 The Unfortunate Sex

Sexual harassment
rt **Double standard**
Male chauvinism
Sexual discrimination
1914 Behind the Scenes
1915 Betty in Search of a Thrill
The Call of the Dance
Help Wanted
Temptation
1916 *Civilization's Child*
The Corner
A Corner in Cotton
The Social Secretary
The Test
1917 Fires of Rebellion
Her Second Husband
1918 Honor's Cross
Whims of Society
1919 *The Forbidden Room*
The Turn in the Road
The Virtuous Thief
1920 The Dwelling Place of Light

Shakers
1916 The Gates of Eden
1918 *A Soul Without Windows*

William Shakespeare
1916 Master Shakespeare, Strolling
Player

Shanghai (China)
1920 Crooked Streets

Shanghaiing
1917 *The Man from Montana*
1919 An Amateur Widow
The Moral Deadline
1920 *The Scuttlers*

Sharecroppers
rt **Farmers**
1920 Within Our Gates

Sharks
1920 *Girl of the Sea*

Sheep
1916 *The Unattainable*
1917 *Barbary Sheep*
1919 *The Unbroken Promise*
What Am I Bid?

Sheepherders
rt **Sheepmen**
Shepherdesses
Shepherds
1917 *Great Expectations*
Men of the Desert
1918 *Cavanaugh of the Forest
Rangers*
1919 The Love Call
1920 The Desert Scorpion
The Stranger
Two Moons

Sheepmen
1917 The Learnin' of Jim Benton
On the Level
1919 It's a Bear
Wolves of the Night
1920 The Galloping Devil
Human Stuff
Prairie Trails
Sundown Slim

Sheiks
1914 *Brewster's Millions*
The Dishonored Medal
1915 *The Arab*
1916 *A Daughter of the Gods*
1918 *Eye for Eye*
1919 Flame of the Desert
1920 *The Virgin of Stamboul*

Shell shock
1918 Missing
Vive La France!
1919 The Trembling Hour

Shells (artillery)
1918 *Wanted for Murder*

Shells (sea)
1914 Neptune's Daughter

Shepherdesses
1916 *Don Quixote*
Out of the Drifts
Race Suicide
1918 Lend Me Your Name
The Witch Woman
1920 The Fighting Shepherdess

Shepherds
1913 *The Daughter of the Hills*
1914 Marta of the Lowlands
1916 *The House with the Golden
Windows*
The Unattainable
1917 *The Chosen Prince, or the
Friendship of David and
Jonathan*
The Undying Flame
1919 *Auction of Souls*
The Shepherd of the Hills
Wolves of the Night
1920 *Faith*
The Fighting Shepherdess
The Red Lane

Sheriffs
1913 *Robin Hood*
1914 The Bargain
In Mizzoura
The Walls of Jericho
1915 *The Disciple*
The Folly of a Life of Crime
The Girl of the Golden West
The Wild Goose Chase
Wildfire
A Yellow Streak
1916 *The Abandonment*
Children of the Feud
The Conscience of John David
The Fires of Conscience
A Gutter Magdalene

1919 The Brat
Lombardi, Ltd.
Marie, Ltd.
Spotlight Sadie
Tin Pan Alley
1920 A City Sparrow
Footlights and Shadows
The Spirit of Good

Shrews
1917 *Every Girl's Dream*
The Eyes of the World

Shrines
1916 *Sunshine Dad*
1917 *The Call of the East*
A Trip Through Japan
1919 *Lasca*

Shushana Mine (Alaska)
1915 *The Lure of Alaska*

Shyness
1916 Davy Crockett
1918 *A Camouflage Kiss*
His Majesty, Bunker Bean
String Beans
The Two-Soul Woman
1919 Life's a Funny Proposition
Mistaken Identity
A Temperamental Wife
1920 Alarm Clock Andy
The Heart of Twenty
The Poor Simp
She Loves and Lies

Siam
1920 *Shipwrecked Among Cannibals*

Siamese twins
1920 The Corsican Brothers

Siberia
1912 The Alaska-Siberian Expedition
Atop of the World in Motion
1914 *Called Back*
Escaped from Siberia
A Fight for Freedom; Or,
Exiled to Siberia
The Man from Home
The Marked Woman
Michael Strogoff
An Odyssey of the North
Threads of Destiny
1915 *Hearts in Exile*
A Woman's Resurrection
1916 War on Three Fronts
1917 Darkest Russia
Panthea
The Tiger Woman
1918 *The Fall of the Romanoffs*
Resurrection
1919 *The Man Who Won*

Sicilians
1919 *A Gentleman of Quality*

Sicily
1912 The Adventures of Lieutenant
Petrosino
1918 *The Ordeal of Rosetta*

Sideshows
rt Carnivals
Circuses
1919 The Little White Savage
Molly of the Follies

Sieges
1914 *Judith of Bethulia*
1915 *The Explorer*
1916 *The Bugle Call*
The Deserter
An Enemy to the King
The Last Man
1917 *Heart and Soul*
His Own People
The Hostage
*John Ermine of the
Yellowstone*
The Plow Woman
Straight Shooting
1918 *Beyond the Shadows*
Good-Bye, Bill
1919 The Fall of Babylon
Her Purchase Price
The Man Who Turned White
1920 The Last of the Mohicans

Sierra Leone
1918 The White Man's Law

Sierra Nevada Mountains
1915 *A Phyllis of the Sierras*
1916 *The Unattainable*
The Wild Girl of the Sierras

Silk
1917 *Exile*
1918 *A Pair of Silk Stockings*

Silver mines
1913 The Tonopah Stampede for
Gold
1914 *The Outlaw Reforms*
1918 The Power and the Glory

William Sowden Sims
1919 *The Fighting Roosevelts*

Sin
1915 Black Fear

Upton Sinclair
1914 The Jungle

Sing Sing Prison
1913 *In the Bishop's Carriage*
*The Man from the Golden
West*
1915 *Alias Jimmy Valentine*
The Man Who Found Himself
1916 *The Supreme Sacrifice*
1918 *The Lonely Woman*
1919 *A Fugitive from Matrimony*
Sing-Sing and Great Meadows
Prison
1920 *Her Story*

Singapore
1919 Wings of the Morning

Singers
nt Specific types of singers
1914 The Temptations of Satan
1915 *An Eye for an Eye*
Her Atonement
The Labyrinth
The Lure of the Mask
The Stolen Voice
Temptation
What Happened to Father
Zaza
1916 *Arms and the Woman*
The Black Butterfly
Captain Jinks of the Horse
Marines
The Chalice of Sorrow
Shoes
The Stain in the Blood
The Unattainable
The Vagabond Prince
1917 *Big Timber*
The Door Between
The Girl at Home
Little Lost Sister
Magda
The Price She Paid
Putting the Bee in Herbert
The Spotted Lily
The White Raven
1918 The Bravest Way
The Cabaret Girl
The Claim
Honor's Cross
The Impostor
Painted Lips
The Sea Waif
The Shoes That Danced
Social Briars
1919 *Almost Married*
The Broken Melody
The Courageous Coward
The Echo of Youth
Hard Boiled
The Hidden Truth
The Love Burglar
Mind the Paint Girl
The Siren's Song
Virtuous Sinners
What Love Forgives
The Woman Michael Married
Words and Music By—
1920 *The Amazing Woman*
The Brand of Lopez
Cupid, the Cowpuncher
The Great Lover
Greater Than Fame
Out of the Dust
The Paliser Case
Reformation
Should a Wife Work?

Sioux City (Iowa)
1915 The Sioux City Round-Up

Sioux Indians
1914 The Indian Wars
1915 *The Folly of a Life of Crime*

Sisters
1913 Hoodman Blind
Traffic in Souls
1914 La Belle Russe
The Floor Above
Frou Frou
Ill Starred Babbie
Jess
A Lady of Quality
The Marked Woman
The Money Lender
Mother
Neptune's Daughter
Without Hope
A Woman's Triumph
1915 *Alice in Wonderland*
The Apaches of Paris
Beulah
Black Fear
The Chorus Lady
The Cup of Life
An Eye for an Eye
Gretna Green
The Hungarian Nabob
In the Palace of the King
Kreutzer Sonata
A Modern Magdalen
The Price of Her Silence
The Rosary
Scandal
The Secret Sin
Seven Sisters
When a Woman Loves
1916 *The Adventures of Kathlyn*
All Man
The Almighty Dollar
Ashes of Embers
Bobbie of the Ballet
The Children Pay
A Corner in Colleens
The Cossack Whip
Daredevil Kate
The Dead Alive
Driftwood
The Essanay-Chaplin Revue of
1916
The Eternal Grind
The Feast of Life
The Fugitive
The Girl Who Doesn't Know
Green Stockings
King Lear
A Man of Sorrow
Not My Sister
The Scarlet Oath
Sorrows of Happiness
Souls in Bondage
Tangled Fates
Tempest and Sunshine
The Vixen
Wanted—A Home
The Yellow Pawn
1917 The Antics of Ann
Bab's Burglar
Bab's Diary
Betsy Ross
The Butterfly Girl
The Checkmate
The Crystal Gazer
The Ghost House
The Girl in the Checkered Coat
The Girl Who Won Out
The Girl Without a Soul
Golden Rule Kate
The Grell Mystery
Heart and Soul
Her Sister
Her Temptation
A Hungry Heart
Little Lost Sister
Little Miss Nobody
The Man Hater
A Modern Cinderella
The Mother Instinct
The Plow Woman
Polly Put the Kettle On
Sister Against Sister
The Snarl
A Song of Sixpence
Those Who Pay

The Tides of Barnegat
To the Death
Troublemakers
Truthful Tulliver
Two Little Imps
Who Shall Take My Life?
1918 *American Buds*
A Bachelor's Children
The Better Half
Borrowed Clothes
Doing Their Bit
The Fallen Angel
False Ambition
Fields of Honor
The Guilty Wife
Her Decision
His Daughter Pays
How Could You, Caroline?
Journey's End
Keith of the Border
The Knife
The Lie
The Love Swindle
The Mask
Men
The Million Dollar Dollies
Missing
Neighbors
New Love for Old
The Ordeal of Rosetta
Out of the Night
Selfish Yates
Shifting Sands
The Shuttle
Swat the Spy
Tell It to the Marines
We Should Worry
Whims of Society
The Winding Trail
With Neatness and Dispatch
The Wolf and His Mate
A Woman of Impulse
The Zero Hour
1919 The Broken Butterfly
The Divorcee
The Gay Old Dog
The Girl with No Regrets
His Bridal Night
Marriage for Convenience
My Little Sister
One Against Many
Peggy Does Her Darndest
Pitfalls of a Big City
Pretty Smooth
Smiles
Spotlight Sadie
The Trap
The Turn in the Road
Upstairs and Down
The Woman Under Oath
1920 Bitter Fruit
Black Is White
Blind Wives
The Brand of Lopez
The Broadway Bubble
The Dark Mirror
Desert Love
The Frisky Mrs. Johnson
The Gift Supreme
The Hell Ship
Judy of Rogue's Harbor
The Last of the Mohicans
Love
Love in the Wilderness
Love's Flame
The Path She Chose
Riders of the Dawn
Risky Business
The Scarlet Dragon
The Shadow of Rosalie Byrnes
Sooner or Later
The Web of Deceit
White Lies
Women Men Love

Sisters-in-law
1915 *The Closing Net*
The Cowardly Way
The Runaway Wife
What Happened to Jones
1916 *Lying Lips*
The Ruling Passion
The Turmoil
1917 The Land of Promise
Life's Whirlpool

1918 *The Impostor*
      The Turn of the Wheel
      Woman and Wife
1919 *The House Without Children*
      The Woman Next Door
1920 *The Inferior Sex*
      The Little Outcast
      Women Men Love

Sitting Bull
1914 *Sitting Bull—The Hostile*
      Sioux Indian Chief

Skagway (Alaska)
1918 *Shark Monroe*

Skeletons
1914 *The Pursuit of the Phantom*
1917 *The Little Duchess*
1918 *Life or Honor?*

Skin grafts
1920 *A Woman Who Understood*

Skyscrapers
1914 *The Million Dollar Robbery*

Slackers
      rt **Draft dodgers**
1914 *The Ordeal*
1917 *The Pride of New York*
      The Slacker (Metro Pictures
         Corp.)
      The Slacker (Peter P. Jones
         Film Co.)
      The Slacker's Heart
1918 *Berlin Via America*
      The Claws of the Hun
      Every Mother's Son
      Little Miss Hoover
      Mrs. Slacker
      The Wildcat of Paris

Slander
1916 *The Law Decides*
      The Martyrdom of Philip
         Strong
      Slander
      The Stain in the Blood
      Thrown to the Lions
      The Traveling Salesman
      The Yellow Passport
1917 *Beloved Jim*
      The Deemster
      The Eyes of the World
      Over the Hill
      Reputation
      Sirens of the Sea
      Their Compact
1918 *The Boss of the Lazy Y*
      The Brazen Beauty
      Breakers Ahead
      Brown of Harvard
      Carmen of the Klondike
      Fields of Honor
      The Heart of a Girl
      A Japanese Nightingale
      The Lie
      The Test of Loyalty
1919 *Almost a Husband*
      Caleb Piper's Girl
      The Divorcee
      Eve in Exile
      Ginger
      His Father's Wife
1920 *Fickle Women*
      The Figurehead
      Love, Honor and Obey

Slang
1915 *The Earl of Pawtucket*
1918 *Fair Enough*
1920 *The Chorus Girl's Romance*
      A Connecticut Yankee at King
         Arthur's Court

Slave markets
1917 *The Slave Market*
1918 *The Demon*
1919 *Auction of Souls*
      Her Purchase Price

Slave traders
1916 *The Road to Love*
1917 *The Ship of Doom*
1918 *Uncle Tom's Cabin*
1920 *The Idol Dancer*

Slavery
1914 *Joseph in the Land of Egypt*
      Uncle Tom's Cabin
1915 *The Birth of a Nation*
      Marse Covington
1916 *Robinson Crusoe*
      The Sting of Victory

      The Yaqui
1917 *The Planter*
      When a Man Sees Red
1918 *Eye for Eye*
      Uncle Tom's Cabin
1920 *Huckleberry Finn*

Slavery of women
1914 *The Will O' the Wisp*
1918 *The Rainbow Trail*
1919 *Common Property*
      The Great Victory, Wilson or
         the Kaiser? The Fall of the
         Hohenzollerns
      The New Moon
      The World and Its Woman

Slaves
1914 *Cameo Kirby*
      Dan
      Imar the Servitor
      The Littlest Rebel
      The Mysterious Mr. Wu Chung
         Foo
1916 *The Grip of Jealousy*
      Robinson Crusoe
1917 *The Bride of Hate*
      The Duplicity of Hargraves
1918 *Ali Baba and the Forty*
         Thieves
      Hearts of Love
      Uncle Tom's Cabin
1919 *The Brand of Judas*
      Male and Female
1920 *Huckleberry Finn*

Sleds
1920 *Isobel; Or, The Trail's End*

Sleeping potions
1914 *One of Millions*
      Rip Van Winkle
1919 *A Woman's Experience*

Sleighs
1917 *The Sin Woman*
1918 *The Bells*
      The Fall of the Romanoffs
1920 *A Fool and His Money*

Slums
1914 *The Christian*
      The Straight Road
1915 *Are They Born or Made?*
      The Beloved Vagabond
      The Dawn of a Tomorrow
      The Kindling
      The Money Master
      Regeneration
      The Supreme Test
1916 *The Clarion*
      The Dividend
      The Girl Who Doesn't Know
      The Half Million Bribe
      His Great Triumph
      Intolerance
      The Little Liar
      Lone Star
      The Martyrdom of Philip
         Strong
      The Narrow Path
      The Pillory
      A Prince in a Pawnshop
      The Quest of Life
      The Right Direction
      Sally in Our Alley
      Salvation Joan
      The Sunbeam
      Susan Rocks the Boat
      The Upheaval
      The Waifs
      The Writing on the Wall
1917 *The Angel Factory*
      Bondage
      The Climber
      The Food Gamblers
      A Jewel in Pawn
      The Lady in the Library
      The Little Duchess
      The Love Doctor
      Love or Justice
      The Love That Lives
      The Millionaire Vagrant
      Sadie Goes to Heaven
      The Saint's Adventure
      Susan's Gentleman
      When False Tongues Speak
1918 *The Cruise of the*
         Make-Believes
      The Devil's Wheel

      The Golden Goal
      Hell's End
      Honor's Cross
      The Midnight Burglar
      The Other Man
      The Vanity Pool
1919 *The Hoodlum*
      Mind the Paint Girl
      The Twin Pawns
      The Virtuous Model
1920 *The Dark Mirror*
      The Eternal Mother
      The Gift Supreme
      The Gray Brother
      The Little Wanderer
      The Prince Chap
      When Dawn Came

Small town life
1914 *The Criminal Code*
      The Fortune Hunter
      The Hoosier Schoolmaster
      Mother Love
1915 *The Country Boy*
      The Deep Purple
      The Old Homestead
1916 *Bluff*
      Common Sense Brackett
      The Conquest of Canaan
      The Conscience of John David
      Humanizing Mr. Winsby
      The Little School Ma'am
      The Man from Manhattan
      Susie Snowflake
      Tongues of Men
      The Wasted Years
      Where D'Ye Get That Stuff?
1917 *The Clean-Up*
      The Lash of Power
      The Marcellini Millions
      Peggy Leads the Way
      The Runaway
      A Woman Alone
1918 *The Girl and the Judge*
      His Own Home Town
      Hit-the-Trail Holliday
      Humdrum Brown
      The Impostor
      Innocent's Progress
      The Lesson
      The Lonely Woman
      The Man Who Woke Up
      Naughty, Naughty!
      A Nine O'Clock Town
      Old Hartwell's Cub
      The Only Road
      Parentage
      A Perfect Lady
      Social Briars
      The Strange Woman
      The Uphill Path
      The World for Sale
1918-19
      Once to Every Man
1919 *The Busher*
      Easy to Make Money
      The Egg Crate Wallop
      The Eternal Magdalene
      The Gold Cure
      Hard Boiled
      In for Thirty Days
      In His Brother's Place
      In Wrong
      The Lion's Den
      Oh, You Women
      Puppy Love
      That's Good
      True Heart Susie
      Under the Top
      The Weaker Vessel
      The Winchester Woman
      Woman, Woman!
1920 *The Broken Gate*
      The Fortune Hunter
      Homer Comes Home
      Once to Every Woman
      Other Men's Shoes
      The Parish Priest
      Pegeen
      Pink Tights
      Pollyanna
      The Road to Divorce
      The Scoffer
      Silk Husbands and Calico
         Wives
      Sweet Lavender

Smallpox
1914 *The Good-for-Nothing*
      Hearts of Oak
1916 *The Woman in Politics*
1918 *Danger Within*

Joseph Smith
1913 *One Hundred Years of*
      Mormonism

Alfred E. Smith
1919 *The Volcano*

Smithsonian Institution
1912 *Paul J. Rainey's African Hunt*

Smoking
1915 *The Cup of Life*
1919 *The Love Defender*

Smugglers
1913 *A Sister to Carmen*
1914 *The Spitfire*
1915 *Blackbirds*
      Carmen (Jesse L. Lasky
         Feature Play Co.)
      Heléne of the North
      His Wife
      Just Jim
1916 *The Battle of Hearts*
      Charlie Chaplin's Burlesque on
         "Carmen"
      The Dawn of Love
      The Diamond Runners
      Dorian's Divorce
      Hop, the Devil's Brew
      Nanette of the Wilds
      Pidgin Island
      Under Cover
1917 *Blind Man's Luck*
      The Bond Between
      The Bottom of the Well
      Captain Kiddo
      The Ghost of Old Morro
      On the Level
      Queen X
1918 *Brace Up*
      The Sea Flower
1919 *The Black Circle*
      The Devil's Trail
      A Fallen Idol
      Forest Rivals
      Miss Adventure
      Shadows of the Past
1920 *The Challenge of the Law*
      Crooked Streets
      The Cyclone
      Dinty
      Duds
      Idols of Clay
      Miss Nobody
      The Mollycoddle
      The Red Lane
      The Sins of Rosanne
      Thou Art the Man
      The Unknown Ranger

Smuggling
1914 *The Boundary Rider*
      The Yellow Traffic
1915 *The Sable Lorcha*
1916 *Hop, the Devil's Brew*
      Pamela's Past
      The Smugglers
1917 *God's Man*
1918 *The Border Raiders*
      The Midnight Patrol
      Whatever the Cost
1919 *A Daughter of the Wolf*
1920 *The Border Raiders*
      Out of the Snows
      Under Crimson Skies

Snakes
      rt **Reptiles**
1912 *Cleopatra*
1914 *The Mystery of the Poison*
         Pool
      The Woman of Mystery
1915 *The Bulldogs of the Trail*
      In the Shadow
1916 *Race Suicide*
1917 *The Firefly of Tough Luck*
1919 *The Phantom Honeymoon*
      Treat 'Em Rough

Snobbery
1914 *The Folks from Way Down*
         East
      Hearts and Flowers
      Jess of the Mountain Country
      The Mountain Rat

1915 The Footsteps of Capt. Kidd
1916 *Kennedy Square*
　　The Lotus Woman
　　Madame X
　　The Man Inside
　　The Phantom Buccaneer
1917 The Americano
　　The Inner Shrine
　　Soldiers of Chance
　　This Is the Life
1918 An American Live Wire
　　The Changing Woman
　　The Kid Is Clever
　　Less Than Kin
　　The Marriage Lie
1919 Dust of Desire
　　Happy Though Married
　　The Scar
　　The Social Pirate
　　Soldiers of Fortune
　　A Trick of Fate
1920 A Double Dyed Deceiver
　　Honor Bound
　　Love
　　Roman Candles
　　Their Mutual Child
　　What Would You Do?

South Americans
1914 *The Great Diamond Robbery*
　　The Key to Yesterday
　　Trapped in the Great
　　　Metropolis
1917 *Indiscreet Corinne*
1918 *Woman and the Law*
1919 *The Four-Flusher*
　　Here Comes the Bride
　　Married in Haste
　　The Woman of Lies
1920 *Honor Bound*
　　Risky Business
　　Stolen Moments

South Dakota
1918 *Indian Life*
1919 The Homesteader

South Pacific
1915 The Island of Regeneration

South Sea Islands
1913 Jack London's Adventures in
　　　the South Sea Islands
1914 *Hearts Adrift*
　　Martin Eden
　　McVeagh of the South Seas
1915 The Quest
1916 *Where Is My Father?*
1917 The Island of Desire
　　Lorelei of the Sea
　　Love Aflame
　　When a Man Sees Red
1918 By the World Forgot
　　A Diplomatic Mission
　　The Sea Flower
　　Such a Little Pirate
1919 Male and Female
　　Victory
　　A Woman There Was
1920 Girl of the Sea
　　Godless Men
　　Idols of Clay
　　The Love Flower
　　Marooned Hearts
　　Terror Island
　　The Woman Untamed

South Seas
1914 The Capture of a Sea Elephant
　　　and Hunting Wild Game in
　　　the South Pacific Islands
1920 *The Hell Ship*

Southampton (New York)
1919 *The Life Line*

Southern belles
　　rt **Southerners**
　　　United States—South
1913 The Girl of the Sunny South
1915 *May Blossom*
　　Under Southern Skies
1916 *Molly Make-Believe*
　　The Valiants of Virginia
1917 Southern Justice
　　Those Without Sin
1918 Cyclone Higgins, D.D.
1920 *The Little Shepherd of*
　　　Kingdom Come

Southerners
　　rt **Southern belles**
　　　United States—South
1914 Cameo Kirby
　　Dan
　　Lena Rivers (Cosmos Feature
　　　Film Corp.)
　　Lena Rivers (Whitman
　　　Features Co.)
　　The Littlest Rebel
1915 Barbara Frietchie
　　The Birth of a Nation
　　Marse Covington
　　May Blossom
　　'Twas Ever Thus
1916 The City of Illusion
　　The Crisis
　　Dulcie's Adventure
　　Friday the Thirteenth
　　Her Father's Son
　　An Innocent Magdalene
　　Kennedy Square
　　Sins of Her Parent
　　The Sting of Victory
　　Tempest and Sunshine
1917 The Bride of Hate
　　Daughter of Maryland
　　The Duplicity of Hargraves
　　How Uncle Sam Prepares
　　My Fighting Gentleman
　　Southern Justice
　　The Stainless Barrier
　　The Tar Heel Warrior
　　Those Without Sin
1918 The Glorious Adventure
　　Huns Within Our Gates
　　The Interloper
　　Kildare of Storm
　　The Knife
　　The Last Rebel
　　Madam Who
　　The Man Who Woke Up
　　Morgan's Raiders
　　Peg of the Pirates
　　The Racing Strain
　　The Scarlet Drop
　　A Soul in Trust
　　A Successful Adventure
　　Tempered Steel
　　Uncle Tom's Cabin
　　Wild Primrose
1919 Checkers
　　Come Out of the Kitchen
　　The Greater Sinner
　　Her Kingdom of Dreams
　　The Intrusion of Isabel
　　Marriage for Convenience
　　Mistaken Identity
　　The Test of Honor
　　A Trick of Fate
　　The Virtuous Thief
　　The Way of a Woman
1920 The Family Honor
　　The Forgotten Woman
　　The Good-Bad Wife
　　Hitchin' Posts
　　Husbands and Wives
　　In Walked Mary
　　The Kentucky Colonel
　　The Little Shepherd of
　　　Kingdom Come
　　On with the Dance
　　Respectable by Proxy
　　The Symbol of the
　　　Unconquered
　　White Youth
　　A Woman's Business
1921 Love's Plaything

Spain
1913 *A Sister to Carmen*
1914 The Ghost Breaker
　　Il Trovatore
　　Uriel Acosta
1915 Carmen (Jesse L. Lasky
　　　Feature Play Co.)
　　The Celebrated Scandal
1916 Maria Rosa
1917 *Transgression*
1918 Beauty in Chains
　　The She-Devil
1920 Rogues and Romance

Spain—History—16th century
1915 In the Palace of the King

Spain—History—17th century
1915 *Don Caesar de Bazan*
1916 Don Quixote
1920 The Adventurer

Spain—History—19th century
1915 The Spanish Jade

Spaniards
1914 *The Red Flame of Passion*
　　Richelieu
　　Rose of the Rancho
　　Shorty Escapes Marriage
1915 *The Grandee's Ring*
　　On Her Wedding Night
　　The Pageant of San Francisco
　　The Pretty Sister of Jose
　　Strathmore
1916 The Captive God
　　The Daughter of the Don
　　A Message to Garcia
　　Mixed Blood
　　The Ne'er-Do-Well
1917 The Black Wolf
　　The Bride of Hate
　　The Woman God Forgot
1918 *A Daughter of the Old South*
　　Dodging a Million
　　The She-Devil
　　Under the Yoke
1919 The Gray Wolf's Ghost
　　Lure of Ambition
　　The Scar
　　The Stronger Vow
1920 *The Best of Luck*
　　The Jungle Princess
　　Rogues and Romance
　　The Woman and the Puppet
　　The World and His Wife

Spanish Armada
1920 *The Best of Luck*

Speculation
1914 The Pit
　　Through Fire to Fortune
1915 *The Builder of Bridges*
　　The Cheat
　　The Climbers
　　The Fairy and the Waif
　　Fine Feathers
　　A Gilded Fool
　　Her Own Way
1916 Between Men
　　Boots and Saddles
　　The Conqueror
　　The Dollar and the Law
　　Each Pearl a Tear
　　Husband and Wife
　　Sudden Riches
1917 *The Barricade*
　　Brand's Daughter
　　The Food Gamblers
　　Greed
　　The Son of His Father
　　The Tar Heel Warrior
　　To Honor and Obey
1918 *The Eleventh Commandment*
　　The Scarlet Road
　　Social Ambition
1919 *Beating the Odds*
　　Bill Henry
　　The Climbers
　　The Lottery Man
　　The Root of Evil
　　Someone Must Pay
　　The Stream of Life
　　The Unknown Quantity
　　A Woman's Experience
1920 *Shore Acres*
　　The Spenders

Speculators
1919 The Gray Wolf's Ghost
　　The Greater Sinner

Speech impediments
1920 Alarm Clock Andy

Speeches
1917 *The Public Be Damned*
1918 *The Heart of a Girl*
　　Hit-the-Trail Holliday
　　The Wildcat of Paris

Speechwriters
1916 *The Price of Fame*

Spells
1914 His Majesty, the Scarecrow of
　　　Oz
1916 The Ruling Passion
　　Saint, Devil and Woman

Spellbound
1918 *The Million Dollar Dollies*
　　The Two-Soul Woman
1920 The Sins of Rosanne
　　The Sleep of Cyma Roget

Spendthrifts
1913 Ten Nights in a Barroom
　　The Third Degree
1914 Clothes
　　Rip Van Winkle
　　The Thief
1915 *The Marriage of Kitty*
　　A Price for Folly
　　The Spender
　　The Spendthrift
1916 All Man
　　The Fear of Poverty
　　Husband and Wife
　　The Man Who Would Not Die
　　The No-Good Guy
　　The Scarlet Road
　　Sudden Riches
1917 Bab's Burglar
　　Betty to the Rescue
　　Broadway Jones
　　The Heart of a Lion
　　The Red Woman
　　A Square Deal
　　Tangled Lives
1918 The Eyes of Julia Deep
　　Moral Suicide
　　More Trouble
　　The Shuttle
　　Vengeance
　　The Way of a Man with a
　　　Maid
1919 Married in Haste
　　The Spender
　　Stripped for a Million
　　The Wreck
1920 *Burglar Proof*
　　Clothes
　　The Devil's Passkey
　　A Modern Salome
　　On with the Dance
　　Pleasure Seekers
　　Sherry
　　The Thirteenth Commandment
　　Uncharted Channels

Sphinxes
1918 *Madame Sphinx*

Spiders
1916 The Tarantula

Spies
　　rt **Espionage**
　　　Foreign agents
　　　Secret agents
1913 *The Battle of Shiloh*
1914 *Across the Pacific*
　　The Adventures of Kitty Cobb
　　The Battle of Gettysgoat
　　Beneath the Czar
　　Captain Alvarez
　　A Romance of the Mexican
　　　Revolution
　　The Seats of the Mighty
　　The Spy
　　The Taint
　　The Tigress
　　The War Extra
　　Washington at Valley Forge
　　Without Hope
1915 *The Crimson Wing*
　　The Heart of Maryland
　　The Ivory Snuff Box
　　May Blossom
　　Mr. Grex of Monte Carlo
　　The Nation's Peril
　　The Patriot and the Spy
　　Sam Davis, the Hero of
　　　Tennessee
　　The Song of Hate
　　The Warrens of Virginia
1916 *Arms and the Woman*
　　As in a Looking Glass
　　The Blue Envelope Mystery
　　Diplomacy
　　The Eagle's Wing
　　The Flying Torpedo
　　The Girl Philippa
　　In the Diplomatic Service
　　The Intrigue
　　Reclamation
　　Salvation Joan
　　The Scarlet Oath

Suburban life
1915 The Commuters
1917 Putting the Bee in Herbert
1919 I'll Get Him Yet
1920 Let's Be Fashionable
The Six Best Cellars

Subway accidents
1916 *The Almighty Dollar*

Subways
1915 *After Dark*
The Danger Signal
1917 *The Adventures of Carol*

Sudan
1914 The Next in Command
1917 The Undying Flame

Sudanese
1919 *With Allenby in Palestine and Lawrence in Arabia*

Suffocation
1915 *Time Lock Number 776*

Suffragettes
rt **Women's suffrage**
1913 Eighty Million Women Want-?
1915 *The Commuters*
1916 *The Fall of a Nation*
1917 *By Right of Possession*
Mothers of Men
1918 *The German Curse in Russia*
The Heart of a Girl
1919 The Praise Agent

Sugar
1915 *Pirate Haunts*

Sugar mills
1915 *The Footsteps of Capt. Kidd*

Leonard Sugden
1915 *The Lure of Alaska*

Suicide
rt **Attempted suicide**
Hara-kiri
Suicide notes
Suicide pacts
1912 *Cleopatra*
1913 The Third Degree
1914 The Avenging Conscience;
Thou Shalt Not Kill
Burning Daylight: The
Adventures of "Burning
Daylight" in Alaska
*Burning Daylight: The
Adventures of "Burning
Daylight" in Civilization*
Cameo Kirby
The Crucible
Damaged Goods
Even unto Death
The Great Diamond Robbery
Hearts Adrift
Kate
The Man of the Hour
Martin Eden
The Master Cracksman
One of Our Girls
The Phantom Violin
Sins of the Parents
The Span of Life
The Squaw Man
Through Fire to Fortune
The Toll of Love
Il Trovatore
Uriel Acosta
The Woman of Mystery
1915 After Five
Anna Karenina
The Apaches of Paris
Armstrong's Wife
The Birth of a Nation
Black Fear
The Blindness of Devotion
The Breath of Araby
The Broken Law
Carmen (Fox Film Corp.)
The Chalice of Courage
The Climbers
Colonel Carter of Cartersville
The Cowardly Way
The Crimson Wing
The Dancing Girl
Dora Thorne
The Failure
The Family Stain
Fine Feathers
The Flash of an Emerald
Ghosts
The Glory of Youth

Greater Love Hath No Man
The Greater Will
Her Mother's Secret
Her Reckoning
Jordan Is a Hard Road
June Friday
Kreutzer Sonata
Life Without Soul
The Lily and the Rose
The Little Dutch Girl
Lord John in New York
Lydia Gilmore
Madame Butterfly
The Magic Skin
Mignon
M'liss
The Moonstone
Niobe
On Her Wedding Night
The Outlaw's Revenge
Playing Dead
The Pretty Sister of Jose
Princess Romanoff
Ranson's Folly
The Ring of the Borgias
Should a Mother Tell?
Sin
The Sins of the Mothers
The Song of the Wage Slave
Strathmore
Sweet Alyssum
Through Turbulent Waters
To Cherish and Protect
Wormwood
1916 *The Alibi*
Anton the Terrible
The Beckoning Flame
Behind Closed Doors
Betrayed
Blazing Love
The Chain Invisible
*Charlie Chaplin's Burlesque on
"Carmen"*
The Child of Destiny
The City
Civilization
Cross Currents
The Discard
Dorian's Divorce
The Dumb Girl of Portici
The Enemy
The Eternal Sapho
The Evil Women Do
The Fear of Poverty
The Folly of Revenge
For a Woman's Fair Name
The Gilded Spider
The Heart of Paula
Her Great Price
Her Husband's Wife
Hop, the Devil's Brew
Jealousy
John Needham's Double
The Law Decides
The Leopard's Bride
The Libertine
The Light
The Little Liar
The Lotus Woman
The Love Liar
Lying Lips
Macbeth
The Mainspring
The Man Inside
The Marble Heart
The Mark of Cain
The Narrow Path
The Ne'er-Do-Well
The Ocean Waif
The Other Side of the Door
A Parisian Romance
The Price of Happiness
The Rise of Susan
Romeo and Juliet (Fox Film
Corp.)
Romeo and Juliet (Quality
Pictures Corp.)
Saint, Devil and Woman
Saving the Family Name
The Serpent
Seventeen
The Sign of the Poppy
Slander
Somewhere in France
Soul Mates

The Soul of Kura-San
The Stepping Stone
The Stolen Triumph
The Struggle
The Supreme Temptation
Thou Shalt Not Covet
To Have and to Hold
A Tortured Heart
20,000 Leagues Under the Sea
The Two Edged Sword
The Valiants of Virginia
The Vital Question
War Brides
A Wife's Sacrifice
The Wolf Woman
The Woman in 47
The Woman in the Case
The Yaqui
1917 *The Adventurer*
Alimony
Behind the Mask
The Bride of Hate
The Bride's Silence
*The Chosen Prince, or the
Friendship of David and
Jonathan*
Cleopatra
Conscience
Corruption
The Crystal Gazer
The Debt
The Derelict
Diamonds and Pearls
The Door Between
The Dormant Power
The Easiest Way
The Eternal Temptress
The Family Honor
The Fettered Woman
The Flaming Omen
Forget-Me-Not
Hedda Gabler
Her Better Self
The Inner Shrine
The Lad and the Lion
The Last of the Carnabys
The Law That Failed
The Mainspring
The Marriage Market
Mentioned in Confidence
A Mormon Maid
The Moth
The Painted Lie
The Piper's Price
The Price of a Good Time
Princess of the Dark
The Rainbow
S.O.S.
The Saintly Sinner
The Scarlet Crystal
The Secret Game
A Sleeping Memory
The Squaw Man's Son
The Stolen Play
To Honor and Obey
Triumph
The Trufflers
The Understudy
The Unforseen
Vengeance Is Mine
The Web of Desire
When Men Are Tempted
Whose Wife?
Wife Number Two
1918 *An American Live Wire*
The Answer
The Beautiful Mrs. Reynolds
The Better Half
The Bird of Prey
Broken Ties
The Death Dance
Dodging a Million
The Eagle
Fields of Honor
The Flash of Fate
Flower of the Dusk
A Gentleman's Agreement
The Great Love
The Heart of Rachael
Her American Husband
Her Husband's Honor
His Birthright
Honor's Cross
The King of Diamonds
The Mating of Marcella

Mrs. Dane's Defense
Naked Hands
The Ordeal of Rosetta
The Ranger
The Scarlet Trail
The Soul of Buddha
The Spreading Evil
The Squaw Man
Stella Maris
Tangled Lives
To Hell with the Kaiser
To Him That Hath
La Tosca
Toys of Fate
The Turn of a Card
*What Becomes of the
Children?*
When a Woman Sins
The White Man's Law
Wife or Country
The Witch Woman
Woman and Wife
A Woman's Fool
1919 *All of a Sudden Norma*
L'Apache
The Avalanche
Beckoning Roads
Better Times
Beware
The Bluffer
Broken Blossoms
The Clouded Name
The End of the Road
Eve in Exile
The Fall of Babylon
The False Code
The Firing Line
Gambling in Souls
A Heart in Pawn
The Highest Trump
The Homesteader
John Petticoats
Keali
The Law of Men
The Love Auction
The Love That Dares
Marriage for Convenience
The Marriage Price
Out of the Fog
The Outcasts of Poker Flats
The Pagan God
Paid in Full
The Painted World
The Parisian Tigress
The Red Lantern
The Rider of the Law
A Society Exile
Tangled Threads
Thin Ice
The Third Degree
The Thirteenth Chair
Thunderbolts of Fate
The Undercurrent
The Vengeance of Durand
Wolves of the Night
The Woman on the Index
The Woman Thou Gavest Me
1920 *The Amateur Wife*
The Amazing Woman
Blind Youth
The Blood Barrier
The Breath of the Gods
A City Sparrow
The Confession
The Cup of Fury
The Dark Mirror
The Daughter of Dawn
The Devil to Pay
Dr. Jekyll and Mr. Hyde
(Famous Players-Lasky
Corp.)
Dollar for Dollar
The Fear Market
Flames of the Flesh
The Forbidden Woman
Hitchin' Posts
Homespun Folks
Idols of Clay
The Little 'Fraid Lady
Love in the Wilderness
Love Without Question
The Man Who Dared
The Man Who Lost Himself
A Manhattan Knight
A Master Stroke

Taxes
1916 *The Dumb Girl of Portici*
    The Traveling Salesman
1920 *The Beggar Prince*
Taxi drivers
1915 *The Closing Net*
    The Dictator
1916 The Pretenders
1917 *Bab's Burglar*
    The Frame Up
1919 Charge It to Me
    Married in Haste
    My Little Sister
    Taxi
1920 Oil
    Passers-By
Taxidermists
1912 *Paul J. Rainey's African Hunt*
1914 *The Red Flame of Passion*
Taxis
1917 *The Frame Up*
1918 *Broadway Love*
    The Empty Cab
    Leap to Fame
    The Spurs of Sybil
1919 *The Adventure Shop*
    The Best Man
    A Damsel in Distress
    The Illustrious Prince
    The Law of Nature
    Married in Haste
1920 *Half an Hour*
Tea houses
1919 *The Game's Up*
Tea shops
1917 *The War of the Tongs*
Teachers
1916 *Common Sense Brackett*
    The Cycle of Fate
    The Mischief Maker
1917 *A Child of the Wild*
    Cy Whittaker's Ward
    The Golden Fetter
    The Hater of Men
    Mountain Dew
    North of Fifty-Three
    Open Places
    Pardners
1918 *Her Man*
1919 Deliverance
Teamsters
1914 *The Valley of the Moon*
Teases
  rt **Flirts**
    Temptresses
    Vamps
1915 *The Country Boy*
1919 *The Invisible Bond*
    The Last of His People
    Mind the Paint Girl
Telegrams
1914 *Imar the Servitor*
    The Rejuvenation of Aunt Mary
    The Yellow Traffic
1915 *Hearts Aflame*
1916 *The Aryan*
    It Happened in Honolulu
    Love's Lariat
1917 *An American Widow*
    The Bride's Silence
    The Great Bradley Mystery
1918 *Boston Blackie's Little Pal*
    Closin' in
    Hidden Fires
    The Magic Eye
    The Man Who Wouldn't Tell
    Missing
    The Moral Law
    Playing the Game
1919 *Her Kingdom of Dreams*
    The Misleading Widow
1919-20
    When a Man Loves
1920 *The Strange Boarder*
Telegraph
1915 *Fighting Bob*
1916 *Humanizing Mr. Winsby*
    The Matrimaniac
1918 *The Border Wireless*
    Desert Law
    A Diplomatic Mission
    The Hillcrest Mystery
    The Locked Heart

    Unclaimed Goods
Telegraph operators
1914 *The War Extra*
1916 The Traveling Salesman
1917 *Because of a Woman*
    Treason
1918 The Border Wireless
    The Girl Who Wouldn't Quit
    Lest We Forget
    Station Content
1919 Secret Service
Telephone operators
1914 The Voice at the Telephone
1915 The Woman
1916 *The Final Curtain*
1918 *Wedlock*
1919 *The Divorce Trap*
1920 *The Girl with the Jazz Heart*
    The Ugly Duckling
Telephones
1913 *Chelsea 7750*
1915 *Old Dutch*
    A Submarine Pirate
1916 The Matrimaniac
1917 *The Little American*
1918 *The Greatest Thing in Life*
    Who Killed Walton?
1919 *The Crimson Gardenia*
1920 *The Devil to Pay*
Temperance
  rt **Liquor**
    Prohibition
1913 Ten Nights in a Barroom
1915 *Jordan Is a Hard Road*
1916 *Peck O' Pickles*
    The Unwritten Law
1917 *Bringing Home Father*
    A Case at Law
    The Circus of Life
    The Girl Glory
1918 *Coals of Fire*
    Hit-the-Trail Holliday
1918-19
    Once to Every Man
1920 The Great Accident
    It Might Happen to You
    The Six Best Cellars
    Water, Water Everywhere
Temples
1913 *The Lotus Dancer*
    The Star of India
1914 *The Quest of the Sacred Jewel*
    Samson
1915 *The Forbidden Adventure*
    The Moonstone
1917 *A Trip Through Japan*
1918 *The Green God*
    The One Woman
    Vengeance
Temporary insanity
  rt **Insanity**
1917 *The Lair of the Wolf*
1919 *Out of the Shadow*
Temptresses
  rt **Flirts**
    Teases
    Vamps
1915 Carmen (Fox Film Corp.)
    Carmen (Jesse L. Lasky
      Feature Play Co.)
    Destiny; Or, The Soul of a Woman
    Destruction
    Flame of Passion
    Her Atonement
    Peer Gynt
    The Wonderful Adventure
1916 As in a Looking Glass
    A Huntress of Men
    The Velvet Paw
1917 Black Orchids
    The Eternal Temptress
    The Greater Woman
    The New York Peacock
    Paradise Garden
1918 Prisoners of the Pines
    The Purple Lily
    When a Woman Sins
1919 *Devil McCare*
    For a Woman's Honor
    The Pagan God

Tenant farmers
  rt **Farmers**
    Sharecroppers
1917 *Peggy, the Will O' the Wisp*
Tenements
1914 *The Folks from Way Down East*
    The Gangsters
1915 *The Call of the Dance*
    The Cup of Life
    Heritage
    The House of a Thousand Scandals
    The Kindling
    On Her Wedding Night
    Salvation Nell
1916 *The Criminal*
    Gretchen, the Greenhorn
    His Great Triumph
    The Invisible Enemy
    The Martyrdom of Philip Strong
    The Path of Darkness
    The Place Beyond the Winds
    Reggie Mixes In
    The Wasted Years
    The Woman in Politics
1917 *The Adventures of Carol*
    The Angel Factory
    Annie-for-Spite
    The Crystal Gazer
    Pants
    A Rich Man's Plaything
    The Small Town Girl
1918 Amarilly of Clothes-Line Alley
    Conquered Hearts
    Empty Pockets
    Hell's End
    A Little Sister of Everybody
    The Midnight Burglar
    Wives of Men
1919 *A Fighting Colleen*
    Ginger
1920 *Darling Mine*
    The Dream Cheater
Tennessee
1915 The Cotton King
    The Life of Sam Davis: A Confederate Hero of the Sixties
    Sam Davis, the Hero of Tennessee
1917 *The Adopted Son*
    The Conqueror
    Melissa of the Hills
    Youth
1918 The Desired Woman
    Out of a Clear Sky
    Pals First
1919 Sue of the South
1920 The Gauntlet
Tennis
1915 *A Girl of Yesterday*
1917 *A Wife on Trial*
1919 *The Fear Woman*
Territorial governors
  rt **Governors**
    State governors
1915 *Jack Chanty*
1916 Langdon's Legacy
    The Ruling Passion
    The Sting of Victory
    To Have and to Hold
    The Witch
    Witchcraft
1917 *Exile*
    The Little Chevalier
Tests of character
1915 Just Jim
    Just Out of College
1916 The Half Million Bribe
    His Picture in the Papers
    Jim Grimsby's Boy
    A Knight of the Range
1917 The Courage of the Common Place
    The Hero of the Hour
    The Man Who Took a Chance
    The Man Who Was Afraid
    Melting Millions
    A Rich Man's Plaything
1918 Dodging a Million
    The Heart of Romance
    The Poor Rich Man

1919 Captain Kidd, Jr.
    Faith
    The Fear Woman
    The House of Intrigue
    The Marriage Price
    Stripped for a Million
    Thin Ice
1920 The Romance Promoters
Tetanus
1916 *The Green Swamp*
Texans
1915 A Texas Steer
1917 Richard the Brazen
1919 *Human Passions*
Texas
1914 *Forgiven; Or, The Jack of Diamonds*
    The Tangle
1915 The Martyrs of the Alamo
    Ranson's Folly
1917 *The Adopted Son*
    The Conqueror
    The Dormant Power
    His Mother's Boy
    Madame Bo-Peep
    Some Boy!
1918 *The Girl from Beyond*
    Heart of the Sunset
1919 The Forfeit
    The Last of the Duanes
    A Man in the Open
    The Unbroken Promise
1920 *A Double Dyed Deceiver*
    Her Five-Foot Highness
    Live Sparks
    Prairie Trails
    Sink or Swim
    The Texan
Texas Rangers
1918 Heart of the Sunset
    Keith of the Border
    The Rainbow Trail
    The Ranger
    Riders of the Purple Sage
    The Silent Rider
1919 *The Last of the Duanes*
    The Lone Star Ranger
    The Rider of the Law
    Speedy Meade
    When a Man Rides Alone
1920 The Border Raiders
    Rio Grande
    The Unknown Ranger
Textile mills
1919 *The Winning Girl*
1920 *Dangerous Hours*
Thanksgiving Day
1915 *The College Widow*
    The Mating
The Taming of the Shrew
1919 The Indestructible Wife
Theater
1914 Nell Gwynne
    The Royal Box
1915 *Her Triumph*
    A Little Brother of the Rich
1916 *David Garrick*
    The Final Curtain
    His Brother's Wife
    The Madcap
    The Twin Triangle
    The Wasted Years
1917 Idolators
    Two-Bit Seats
1918 A Pair of Silk Stockings
    The Vamp
1919 Castles in the Air
    A Sporting Chance (American Film Co.)
    Too Many Crooks
1920 Bonnie May
    The Branding Iron
    The Broadway Bubble
    A Broadway Cowboy
    The Devil's Passkey
    The Girl in Number 29
    The Heart of a Child
    Heritage
    The Luck of Geraldine Laird
    Madame Peacock
    Man and Woman (Tyrad Pictures, Inc.)
    Married Life
    The Misleading Lady

One-Thing-at-a-Time O'Day
The Pest
The Pointing Finger
The Sneak
The Social Pirate
The Speed Maniac
Thin Ice
Too Many Crooks
Under Suspicion
The Virtuous Thief
The Web of Chance
The Wilderness Trail
1920　*Black Shadows*
Blackbirds
The Blue Pearl
The Bromley Case
Chains of Evidence
Cinderella's Twin
The County Fair
Cynthia-of-the-Minute
The Empire of Diamonds
Even As Eve
From Now On
The Girl in the Rain
The Girl in the Web
The Heart of Twenty
Heart Strings
Jes' Call Me Jim
Leave It to Me
The Little Outcast
Live Sparks
A Manhattan Knight
My Lady's Garter
The North Wind's Malice
Over the Hill to the Poorhouse
The Peddler of Lies
The Rose of Nome
The Round-Up
The Sacred Ruby
She Couldn't Help It
A Slave of Vanity
Someone in the House
The Soul of Youth
A Splendid Hazard
Stop Thief!
Sunset Sprague
The Terror
The Thief
$30,000
The Tiger's Cub
The Trail of the Cigarette
The Web of Deceit
What Happened to Jones
The White Moll
Who's Your Servant?

Theosophy
1918　His Majesty, Bunker Bean
Thieves
　　rt　**Robbers**
　　　　Theft
　　nt　Specific types of thieves
1913　Leah Kleschna
1914　*After the Ball*
　　　　The Long Arm of the Law
　　　　The Master Cracksman
　　　　The Master Mind
　　　　The Million
　　　　Officer 666
　　　　A Prince of India
　　　　Under the Gaslight
1915　Blackbirds
　　　　The Bridge of Sighs
　　　　An Enemy to Society
　　　　The Eternal City
　　　　The Fatal Card
　　　　The Game of Three
　　　　The Gray Mask
　　　　The Great Ruby
　　　　The Prince and the Pauper
　　　　The Rug Maker's Daughter
　　　　Salvation Nell
　　　　Stop Thief!
　　　　The Two Orphans
　　　　The Way Back
　　　　Who's Who in Society
1916　The Black Crook
　　　　The Country That God Forgot
　　　　The Daughter of MacGregor
　　　　A Dream or Two Ago
　　　　Dulcie's Adventure
　　　　The Little Liar
　　　　Oliver Twist
　　　　The Phantom
　　　　The Pretenders
　　　　The Purple Lady

The Pursuing Vengeance
The Social Buccaneer
The Social Highwayman
A Stranger from Somewhere
The Sultana
Sunshine Dad
Those Who Toil
Three Pals
Vultures of Society
The Wager
1917　American Maid
　　　　Arsene Lupin
　　　　Babette
　　　　The Bad Boy
　　　　Betsy's Burglar
　　　　The Bond Between
　　　　The Broadway Sport
　　　　The Dazzling Miss Davison
　　　　Feet of Clay
　　　　Flying Colors
　　　　The Ghost House
　　　　The Girl in the Checkered Coat
　　　　The Guardian
　　　　Her Strange Wedding
　　　　The Inspirations of Harry
　　　　　　Larrabee
　　　　The Lady in the Library
　　　　Miss Nobody
　　　　On Trial
　　　　Raffles, the Amateur
　　　　　　Cracksman
　　　　Sally in a Hurry
　　　　Satan's Private Door
　　　　The Small Town Girl
　　　　Sylvia of the Secret Service
　　　　Thou Shalt Not Steal
　　　　Time Locks and Diamonds
　　　　The Trouble Buster
　　　　The Valentine Girl
　　　　Within the Law
1918　Ali Baba and the Forty Thieves
　　　　Battling Jane
　　　　Blindfolded
　　　　Code of the Yukon
　　　　Crown Jewels
　　　　The Crucible of Life
　　　　The Danger Game
　　　　De Luxe Annie
　　　　The Eagle
　　　　The Face in the Dark
　　　　Friend Husband
　　　　Just for Tonight
　　　　Laughing Bill Hyde
　　　　The Law That Divides
　　　　Less Than Kin
　　　　The Mystery Girl
　　　　Parentage
　　　　The Spurs of Sybil
　　　　A Successful Adventure
　　　　To Him That Hath
　　　　Together
　　　　The Triumph of the Weak
　　　　The Turn of a Card
　　　　Which Woman?
　　　　The White Lie
1919　The Amazing Impostor
　　　　The Bandbox
　　　　Bill Apperson's Boy
　　　　The Bishop's Emeralds
　　　　Blackie's Redemption
　　　　The Capitol
　　　　The Darkest Hour
　　　　The Egg Crate Wallop
　　　　The Exquisite Thief
　　　　The Final Close-Up
　　　　Fortune's Child
　　　　A Fugitive from Matrimony
　　　　Give and Take
　　　　Hearts Asleep
　　　　The Lone Wolf's Daughter
　　　　Love's Prisoner
　　　　Luck and Pluck
　　　　Maggie Pepper
　　　　Married in Haste
　　　　The Merry-Go-Round
　　　　Mistaken Identity
　　　　Pretty Smooth
　　　　The Probation Wife
　　　　A Rogue's Romance
　　　　A Romance of Happy Valley
　　　　Six Feet Four
　　　　Thieves
　　　　A Very Good Young Man
1920　April Folly
　　　　The Blue Pearl

813
The Green Flame
Miss Nobody
My Lady's Garter
Officer 666
The Path She Chose
The Peddler of Lies
The Right of Way
Risky Business
The Sagebrusher
The Servant Question
She Couldn't Help It
The Sins of Rosanne
The Skywayman
Someone in the House
The Soul of Youth
Stop Thief!
The Village Sleuth
Wits vs. Wits
The Wonder Man
Thirst
1915　The Buzzard's Shadow
1918　*Hell Bent*
　　　　The Home Trail
　　　　The Winding Trail
1919　*The Lady of Red Butte*
　　　　The Long Arm of Mannister
　　　　Wagon Tracks
1920　*The Leopard Woman*
Albert Thomas
1919　*Free Russia*
Thought control
1915　Trilby
1916　The Light
　　　　Saint, Devil and Woman
1917　*Rasputin, the Black Monk*
1920　Something to Think About
Thousand Islands
1916　The River of Romance
Threats
1915　*The Crimson Wing*
Thrill-seeking
1919　The Adventure Shop
　　　　The Amateur Adventuress
　　　　A Broadway Saint
　　　　Desert Gold
　　　　Diane of the Green Van
　　　　His Majesty, the American
　　　　Miss Adventure
　　　　Miss Crusoe
　　　　More Deadly Than the Male
　　　　The Prodigal Liar
Tidal waves
1920　*Do the Dead Talk?*
Tigers
1913　A Prisoner in the Harem
1918　*Vengeance*
1920　*Shipwrecked Among
　　　　　Cannibals*
Tightrope walkers
1919　Under the Top
William Tilghman
1915　*Passing of the Oklahoma
　　　　　Outlaw*
Timidity
1915　The Danger Signal
　　　　Double Trouble
1918　The Gypsy Trail
　　　　The Rough Lover
Tin can industry
1918　Kidder and Ko
S.S. Titanic
1915　*Bought*
Tobacco
1914　*The Master Cracksman*
1917　*They're Off*
1918　*One Dollar Bid*
1919　*When Doctors Disagree*
Tobacco factories
1915　*Carmen* (Fox Film Corp.)
　　　　Carmen (Jesse L. Lasky
　　　　　Feature Play Co.)
Tobaggon accidents
1919　*The Blinding Trail*
Tokyo
1919-20
　　　　When a Man Loves
Tolerance
1916　The Gates of Eden
　　　　The Hidden Scar
　　　　The Madness of Helen
　　　　A Soul Enslaved

1917　The Single Code
1919　The Eternal Magdalene
　　　　Thou Shalt Not
1920　Lady Rose's Daughter
　　　　Whispering Devils
Tomboys
1914　The Crucible
　　　　A Lady of Quality
1915　*A Bunch of Keys*
　　　　A Phyllis of the Sierras
1917　The Amazons
　　　　The Boy Girl
　　　　A Child of the Wild
　　　　The Fair Barbarian
　　　　Patsy
　　　　Sunny Jane
　　　　The Sunset Trail
1918　Mickey
　　　　M'liss
　　　　The Only Road
　　　　Opportunity
　　　　Peck's Bad Girl
　　　　Sunshine Nan
　　　　Whatever the Cost
1919　Miss Adventure
　　　　Miss Arizona
　　　　Muggsy
　　　　Nugget Nell
　　　　Peggy Does Her Darndest
1920　Are All Men Alike?
　　　　Bubbles
Tombs
　　rt　**Graves**
1914　*The Last Egyptian*
　　　　The Phantom Violin
1915　China
　　　　The Unfaithful Wife
1917　*The Image Maker*
　　　　The Reward of the Faithless
1918　*In Bad*
1919　*The Haunted Bedroom*
1920　*A Trip Through Cairo*
Tombs Prison (New York)
1918　*The House of Glass*
Tombstone (Arizona)
1915　A Black Sheep
Tongs
1917　The Flower of Doom
　　　　The War of the Tongs
1919　*The Lost Battalion*
　　　　The Tong Man
Tonics
1918　Jack Spurlock, Prodigal
Toothaches
1919　*Burglar by Proxy*
　　　　When Doctors Disagree
Tories
1914　The Spy
1916　The Heart of a Hero
Tornadoes
1919　*A Man's Fight*
Torpedoes
1914　*My Official Wife*
1915　*The Nation's Peril*
1916　The Flying Torpedo
　　　　Through the Wall
　　　　20,000 Leagues Under the Sea
1917　The Frozen Warning
　　　　The Little American
　　　　The Little Patriot
　　　　The Slacker's Heart
　　　　Under False Colors
1918　*A Game with Fate*
　　　　Hidden Fires
　　　　Lest We Forget
　　　　The Magic Eye
　　　　Our Navy
　　　　The Spreading Evil
　　　　*Your Fighting Navy at Work
　　　　　and at Play*
1919　*The False Faces*
　　　　The Isle of Conquest
　　　　The Light of Victory
　　　　A Midnight Romance
Torreón (Mexico)
1914　The Life of General Villa
1916　*Following the Flag in Mexico*
Torture
1913　Tortures Within Prison Walls
1914　*Beneath the Czar*
　　　　Fire and Sword
　　　　Mcveagh of the South Seas
　　　　Michael Strogoff

1918 The Tiger Man
1919 Wagon Tracks
    The Westerners
1920 *Out of the Dust*

Waifs
1913 In the Bishop's Carriage
1914 *The Little Angel of Canyon Creek*
    The Pursuit of the Phantom
1915 The Adventures of a Madcap
    The Fairy and the Waif
    Fanchon the Cricket
    The Waif
1916 *The Twin Triangle*
1917 Aladdin's Other Lamp
    Chicken Casey
    The Corner Grocer
    Cy Whittaker's Ward
    The Desert Man
    Freckles
    Glory
    Little Miss Optimist
    Little Shoes
    The Lone Wolf
    The Raggedy Queen
1918 Battling Jane
    Danger—Go Slow
    The Dream Lady
    Face Value
    Heredity
1919 The Microbe
    The Sleeping Lion
    Under Suspicion
1920 Bright Skies
    The Forgotten Woman
    Judy of Rogue's Harbor
    The Little Shepherd of Kingdom Come
    The Little Wanderer
    The Woman God Sent

Waiters
1914 *The Man Who Could Not Lose*
    The Million
    Without Hope
1915 *The Outcast*
    A Submarine Pirate
1916 *Lord Loveland Discovers America*
1917 *The Highway of Hope*
    Please Help Emily
1918 *The Guilty Man*
    Jack Spurlock, Prodigal
1919 *Under Suspicion*
1920 Jack Straw
    Sink or Swim
19-- Sic-Em

Waitresses
1913 *The Third Degree*
1915 Fatherhood
    When a Woman Loves
1916 The Heiress at Coffee Dan's
    The Mediator
    Shadows and Sunshine
1917 Sally in a Hurry
1918 *Battling Jane*
    Branding Broadway
    The Hope Chest
    To the Highest Bidder
    A Woman's Fool
1919 Chasing Rainbows
    Partners Three
    The Weaker Vessel
    The Wicked Darling
1920 *In the Depths of Our Hearts*
    The Little Wanderer

Waldorf-Astoria Hotel (New York)
1915 *The Earl of Pawtucket*
1920 *Sooner or Later*

Walla Walla River
1919 *In the Land of the Setting Sun; Or, Martyrs of Yesterday*

Wallpaper
1918 *Find the Woman*

Walruses
1912 *Atop of the World in Motion*

Wanderers
1914 *The Idler*
1915 Peer Gynt
1916 *The Eye of God*
1917 *The Bond of Fear*
    Mary Jane's Pa
    Men of the Desert
    Threads of Fate

1918 Fame and Fortune
    New Love for Old
1919 A Royal Democrat

War
1914 A Romance of the Mexican Revolution
    Too Late
1915 I'm Glad My Boy Grew Up to Be a Soldier
    Old Heidelberg
    The Rights of Man: A Story of War's Red Blotch
    A Royal Family
    Via Wireless
1916 Civilization
    Defense or Tribute?
    Race Suicide
    Three of Many
    War Brides
    What the World Should Know
1917 The Hostage
    The Lust of the Ages
    National Red Cross Pageant
    The Test of Womanhood
    Treason
    War and the Woman
    Womanhood, the Glory of the Nation
1918 *The Woman Who Gave*
1919 *Bullin' the Bullsheviki*
1920 *Before the White Man Came*

War atrocities
1914 *The Ordeal*
1918 *Hearts of the World*
    My Four Years in Germany
1919 *The Heart of Humanity*
    The Spirit of Lafayette
    The Unpardonable Sin

War correspondents
  rt **Reporters**
1914 *Across the Pacific*

War crimes
1917 Motherhood (Frank Powell Producing Corp.)
1918 The Cross Bearer
    Tell It to the Marines
1919 Beware
    What Shall We Do with Him?

War debt
1915 *Graustark*

War games
1918 *Vive La France!*

War heroes
  rt **Heroes**
1913 *The Battle of Shiloh*
1914 The Boer War
    The Last Volunteer
1915 I'm Glad My Boy Grew Up to Be a Soldier
    In the Palace of the King
    The Life of Sam Davis: A Confederate Hero of the Sixties
    The Patriot and the Spy
    Sam Davis, the Hero of Tennessee
    The Second in Command
1916 The Bugler of Algiers
    The Dawn of Freedom
    The Kiss
    Mice and Men
    The Victoria Cross
1917 For Valour
    The Gown of Destiny
    The Hostage
    The Judgement House
    The Pride of New York
    Treason
1918 For Freedom
    Over the Top
    Private Peat
    The Service Star
    Too Fat to Fight
    The Wildcat of Paris
1919 Alias Mike Moran
    Break the News to Mother
    Fit to Win
    The Girl Who Stayed at Home
    The Heart of Humanity
    The Light of Victory
    The Lost Battalion
    Our Better Selves
    A Rogue's Romance
    This Hero Stuff

    The Volcano
    When Arizona Won
1920 Dangerous Business
    The Sins of St. Anthony
    The Skywayman
    The Wonder Man

War injuries
1913 Mexican War Pictures (Lubin Mfg. Co.)
1915 *The Birth of a Nation*
    Friends and Foes
    The History of the World's Greatest War
1916 *The Fighting Germans*
    Pasquale
    War As It Really Is
    The War Bride's Secret
    Whom the Gods Destroy
1917 *The Pride of New York*
    Sweetheart of the Doomed
    The Tides of Fate
    Treason
1918 *The Belgian*
    Berlin Via America
    Bonnie Annie Laurie
    Every Mother's Son
    The German Curse in Russia
    Hearts of the World
    How France Cares for Wounded Soldiers
    Over the Top
    Private Peat
    Revelation
    A Son of Strife
    Too Fat to Fight
    T'Other Dear Charmer
    The Unbeliever
1919 Alias Mike Moran
    The Amazing Wife
    La Belle Russe
    Dawn
    Eyes of the Soul
    Ginger
    The Greater Victory
    A Society Exile
    The Spirit of Lafayette
    The Unknown Love
1920 Humoresque
    The Phantom Melody
    The Skywayman

War materials
1917 *Richard the Brazen*
1918 *Mr. Logan, U.S.A.*
    Pershing's Crusaders
1919 *Fools and Their Money*
    Full of Pep
    Three Black Eyes

War refugees
1915 The History of the World's Greatest War

War victims
1914 *In the Name of the Prince of Peace*
    One of Millions
    Too Late
1917 *The Little Orphan*
1918 *Hearts of the World*
    Private Peat
    The Road Through the Dark
1919 *America Was Right*
    Beware
    The Burning Question
    Deliverance
    The Great Victory, Wilson or the Kaiser? The Fall of the Hohenzollerns
    The Greatest Question
    The Heart of Humanity
    The Lost Battalion
    The Market of Souls
    Who's Your Brother?

Warbonnet
1917 The Adventures of Buffalo Bill

Warbonnet Creek, Battle of, 1876
1914 *The Indian Wars*

Wardrobe mistresses
1914 *False Colours*
1915 *Bred in the Bone*
1917 *Her Soul's Inspiration*
1918 *The Vamp*

Wards and guardians
1913 The Rogues of Paris
1914 Cardinal Richelieu's Ward
    Classmates

    The Magic Cloak of Oz
    The Man from Home
    Richelieu
    The Royal Box
    The Span of Life
    Threads of Destiny
1915 *After Five*
    The Alster Case
    The Arrival of Perpetua
    The Bachelor's Romance
    The Caprices of Kitty
    Captain Courtesy
    An Enemy to Society
    Gretna Green
    Her Mother's Secret
    Her Shattered Idol
    The Lonesome Heart
    The Lost House
    Lydia Gilmore
    The Man of Shame
    Rags
    The Ring of the Borgias
    The Rosary
    Satan Sanderson
    The Second in Command
1916 *Audrey*
    The Child of Destiny
    The Decoy
    Doctor Neighbor
    Dorian's Divorce
    The Girl Philippa
    Gold and the Woman
    The Great Problem
    Hell-to-Pay Austin
    The Human Orchid
    The Innocence of Lizette
    The Innocence of Ruth
    It May Be Your Daughter
    The Kid
    The Light of Happiness
    Little Miss Nobody
    Manhattan Madness
    A Million a Minute
    A Million for Mary
    The No-Good Guy
    The Plow Girl
    The Prince Chap
    The Ruling Passion
    The Soul of a Child
    Susie Snowflake
    Tennessee's Pardner
    To Have and to Hold
    The Traffic Cop
    The Undertow
    Witchcraft
1917 *The Adventurer*
    The Beautiful Adventure
    Beloved Jim
    Beloved Rogues
    Betty to the Rescue
    Blind Man's Luck
    The Bottom of the Well
    The Boy Girl
    The Butterfly Girl
    Charity Castle
    The Charmer
    Conscience
    The Crab
    The Cricket
    A Crooked Romance
    The Desert Man
    Eternal Love
    Every Girl's Dream
    Filling His Own Shoes
    The Flaming Omen
    Forbidden Paths
    The Gates of Doom
    The Girl at Home
    The Girl in the Checkered Coat
    Great Expectations
    The Guardian
    The Heart of Ezra Greer
    Her Official Fathers
    Her Soul's Inspiration
    The Inner Shrine
    Kitty MacKay
    The Lonesome Chap
    Lorelei of the Sea
    Love Letters
    Melting Millions
    Miss Nobody
    Mr. Dolan of New York
    The More Excellent Way
    Mother Love and the Law

Z

GENRE INDEX

★ Each film whose genre has been determined is listed on the following pages under the appropriate heading. When a film reflects more than one genre or subgenre it is listed under each of the appropriate headings. The following is a complete alphabetical list of genres used within the *Catalog*.

Adventure	Instructional
Allegory	Melodrama
Biographical	Mystery
Comedy	Northwest drama
Comedy-drama	Rural
Compilation	Science Fiction
Crime	Social
Detective	Society drama
Documentary	War drama
Drama	War preparedness
Espionage	Western
Fantasy	Wild animals
Historical	World War I
Horror	

GENRE INDEX

Gift O' Gab
The Gilded Youth
The Girl Who Couldn't Grow Up
Hashimura Togo
Her Official Fathers
High Speed
The Honeymoon
The Iced Bullet
In Again—Out Again
The Indian Summer of Dry Valley Johnson
The Kill-Joy
Lady Barnacle
Madame Sherry
Madcap Madge
The Magnificent Meddler
The Man Who Made Good
Melting Millions
Miss Deception
Mr. Dolan of New York
Nearly Married
The Pinch Hitter
Putting the Bee in Herbert
Red, White and Blue Blood
The Runaway
A School for Husbands
Seven Keys to Baldpate
Skinner's Dress Suit
Snap Judgement
The Son of His Father
The Square Deceiver
A Stormy Knight
Tillie Wakes Up
Two-Bit Seats
Two Little Imps
The Upper Crust
The Varmint
Wild and Woolly
Wild Winship's Widow

1918 Amarilly of Clothes-Line Alley
Believe Me Xantippe
The Beloved Blackmailer
A Bit of Jade
The Brazen Beauty
By Hook or Crook
By Proxy
Caught in the Act
Chase Me Charlie
The Danger Game
The Demon
Dodging a Million
Dolly's Vacation
Eight Bells
The Fighting Grin
The Goat
Good-Bye, Bill
The Gypsy Trail
He Comes Up Smiling
His Majesty, Bunker Bean
I'll Say So
Jack Spurlock, Prodigal
Jilted Janet
The Kid Is Clever
Kidder and Ko
A Lady's Name
Lend Me Your Name
Less Than Kin
Let's Get a Divorce
Limousine Life
Little Miss Grown-Up
Mlle. Paulette
The Make-Believe Wife
The Marionettes
The Million Dollar Dollies
Miss Mischief Maker
Mr. Fix-It
Mrs. Leffingwell's Boots
Molly, Go Get 'Em
Naughty, Naughty!
On the Quiet
A Pair of Silk Stockings
A Pair of Sixes
A Perfect 36
The Red-Haired Cupid
The Rough Lover
Ruggles of Red Gap
Sauce for the Goose
The Studio Girl
Sylvia on a Spree
Too Many Millions
Twenty-One
Two-Gun Betty
Under the Greenwood Tree
Uneasy Money

Up the Road with Sallie
The Way of a Man with a Maid
Wild Women
With Neatness and Dispatch
1919 All Wrong
Almost a Husband
Almost Married
The Amateur Adventuress
An Amateur Widow
The Amazing Impostor
A Bachelor's Wife
Be a Little Sport
The Beloved Cheater
The Best Man
Bill Henry
Bonnie, Bonnie Lassie
Boots
Brass Buttons
A Broadway Saint
Bullin' the Bullsheviki
Burglar by Proxy
Captain Kidd, Jr.
Castles in the Air
Charge It to Me
Cheating Herself
Coax Me
Come Again Smith
Come Out of the Kitchen
Daddy-Long-Legs
A Damsel in Distress
The Delicious Little Devil
Don't Change Your Husband
Easy to Make Money
The Egg Crate Wallop
Experimental Marriage
Fair and Warmer
A Favor to a Friend
The Follies Girl
Fools and Their Money
The Four-Flusher
A Fugitive from Matrimony
Full of Pep
The Game's Up
Getting Mary Married
The Girl Dodger
Girls
The Gold Cure
Good Gracious, Annabelle
Greased Lightning
Happiness à la Mode
Hawthorne of the U.S.A.
Hay Foot, Straw Foot
Help! Help! Police!
Here Comes the Bride
His Bridal Night
His Official Fiancée
Hit or Miss
Home Wanted
The Homebreaker
Hoop-La
I'll Get Him Yet
In for Thirty Days
In Wrong
The Indestructible Wife
An Innocent Adventuress
It Pays to Advertise
It's a Bear
Jinx
Johnny Get Your Gun
Johnny-on-the-Spot
The Joyous Liar
Leave It to Susan
Let's Elope
Life's a Funny Proposition
Little Comrade
The Little Rowdy
Lombardi, Ltd.
Lord and Lady Algy
The Lost Princess
The Lottery Man
The Love Hunger
Love Insurance
Luck in Pawn
A Man and His Money
Marie, Ltd.
Married in Haste
A Misfit Earl
The Misleading Widow
Mrs. Wiggs of the Cabbage Patch
Molly of the Follies
Never Say Quit
Nobody Home
Nugget Nell

Oh, Boy!
Oh, You Women
One-Thing-at-a-Time O'Day
Over the Garden Wall
Peggy Does Her Darndest
Phil-for-Short
Please Get Married
The Poor Boob
The Praise Agent
Pretty Smooth
The Prince and Betty
The Prodigal Liar
Prudence on Broadway
Puppy Love
Putting It Over
The Rebellious Bride
Red Hot Dollars
A Regular Fellow
A Regular Girl
The Rescuing Angel
The Roaring Road
Romance and Arabella
Rustling a Bride
Sadie Love
Satan Junior
The Scarlet Shadow
Sis Hopkins
Smiles
Some Bride
Some Liar
Something to Do
The Spender
A Sporting Chance (Famous Players-Lasky Corp.)
Spotlight Sadie
Stepping Out
Strictly Confidential
Stripped for a Million
A Taste of Life
Taxi
A Temperamental Wife
That's Good
This Hero Stuff
Three Black Eyes
Three Men and a Girl
Through the Wrong Door
Toby's Bow
Todd of the Times
Too Many Crooks
Turning the Tables
23 1/2 Hours' Leave
Under Suspicion
Under the Top
The Uplifters
Upside Down
Upstairs
Upstairs and Down
The Veiled Adventure
A Very Good Young Man
A Virtuous Vamp
Wanted—A Husband
The Web of Chance
When Doctors Disagree
When the Clouds Roll By
Where the West Begins
Whitewashed Walls
Why Smith Left Home
Widow by Proxy
Yankee Doodle in Berlin
You're Fired
1919-20
Piccadilly Jim
1920 Alarm Clock Andy
Alias Miss Dodd
All-of-a-Sudden-Peggy
An Amateur Devil
Away Goes Prudence
Bab's Candidate
Bachelor Apartments
The Beggar Prince
Beware of the Bride
Billions
The Blooming Angel
A Broadway Cowboy
Bubbles
Burglar Proof
The Chamber Mystery
The Chorus Girl's Romance
Cinderella's Twin
Civilian Clothes
Cupid, the Cowpuncher
The Dancin' Fool
Dangerous Business
Dangerous to Men
The Daredevil

Don't Ever Marry
Double Speed
Down on the Farm
Easy to Get
Excuse My Dust
Fixed by George
The Flapper
Flying Pat
The Fortune Hunter
Forty-Five Minutes from Broadway
The Fourteenth Man
The Frisky Mrs. Johnson
A Full House
Girls Don't Gamble
Going Some
Help Wanted—Male
Help Yourself
Her Beloved Villain
Her Unwilling Husband
His Pajama Girl
His Temporary Wife
Honest Hutch
In Search of a Sinner
It Might Happen to You
It's a Great Life
Jack Straw
Just Out of College
La La Lucille
The Land of Jazz
Leave It to Me
Let's Be Fashionable
The Love Expert
Love, Honor and Behave
Married Life
Mary Ellen Comes to Town
Mary's Ankle
The Misleading Lady
Miss Hobbs
Mrs. Temple's Telegram
The New York Idea
Nineteen and Phyllis
Nothing but Lies
Nothing but the Truth
Officer 666
Oh, Lady, Lady
An Old Fashioned Boy
Once a Plumber
Parlor, Bedroom and Bath
The Perfect Woman
The Poor Simp
Prairie Trails
Remodelling Her Husband
Rookie's Return
Scratch My Back
Sick Abed
Silk Hosiery
The Sins of St. Anthony
The Six Best Cellars
So Long Letty
Sooner or Later
The Texan
39 East
Too Much Johnson
The Trail of the Arrow
Twin Beds
Up in Mary's Attic
The Very Idea
The Walk-Offs
The Week-End
What Happened to Jones
What Happened to Rosa
What's Your Husband Doing?
When Quackel Did Hide
Why Change Your Wife?
Why Pick on Me?
Youth's Desire
1921 Skinning Skinners
1922 The Cynic Effect
19-- Sic-Em

Comedy-drama
1913 Caprice
Checkers
1914 An American Citizen
The Good-for-Nothing
His Last Dollar
The Man on the Box
The Million
The Ragged Earl
Ready Money
The Rejuvenation of Aunt Mary
The Spitfire
What's His Name

How Life Begins
Seeing America
United States Marines Under
　Fire in Haiti
War As It Really Is
War on Three Fronts
War-Torn Poland
The Whaling Industry
Willard-Johnson Boxing Match
Willard-Moran Fight
World Series Games 1916,
　Boston vs. Brooklyn
The Zeppelin Raids on London
　and the Siege of Verdun
1917 The Adventures of Buffalo Bill
Alaska Wonders in Motion
America Is Ready
The Baseball Revue of 1917
Birth
Birth Control
The Buffalo Bill Show
Heroic France
How Uncle Sam Prepares
Motherhood (Minerva Motion
　Picture Co.)
A Trip Through China
A Trip Through Japan
Uncle Sam, Awake!
1918 America's Answer; Following
　the Fleet to France
Among the Cannibal Isles of
　the South Pacific
Crashing Through to Berlin
The German Curse in Russia
How France Cares for
　Wounded Soldiers
Indian Life
Keep the Home Fires Burning
The Men of the Hour
On the Isonzo
Our Bridge of Ships
Our Navy
Pershing's Crusaders
Under Four Flags
The Yanks Are Coming
Your Fighting Navy at Work
　and at Play
1919 Alaska
Deliverance
Free Russia
From the Disaster of Caporetto
　to Rescue of Trentino and
　Trieste
Government Poultry Farm at
　Beltsville, Md.
Sing-Sing and Great Meadows
　Prison
Through Hell and Back with
　the Men of Illinois
With Allenby in Palestine and
　Lawrence in Arabia
1920 American Catholics in War
　and Reconstruction
Chateau-Thierry, St.-Mihiel
　and Argonne
The Eternal Union of the Seas
Frontier Days
The Gift of Life
The Living World
Pictorial History of the War
Shipwrecked Among Cannibals
Starvation
A Trip Through Cairo
19-- The Making of a Sailor
Official Motion Pictures of the
　Panama Pacific Exposition
　Held at San Francisco, Calif.
Drama *see also* **Adventure; Allegory;
Comedy-drama; Fantasy;
Melodrama; Mystery; Northwest
drama; Science Fiction; War drama;
Western**
1912 The Adventures of Lieutenant
　Petrosino
Cleopatra
Oliver Twist
Richard III
1913 Across the Continent
The Black Snake
Buried Alive in a Coal Mine
Chelsea 7750
The Count of Monte Cristo
The Daughter of the Hills
Eighty Million Women Want-?
The Fight for Millions

The Fortune Hunters
From Dusk to Dawn
From the Manger to the Cross
The Girl of the Sunny South
Hiawatha
Hoodman Blind
An Hour Before Dawn
In the Bishop's Carriage
In the Stretch
The Inside of the White Slave
　Traffic
Ivanhoe
Leah Kleschna
The Legend of Provence
The Lotus Dancer
The Lure of New York
Moths
One Hundred Years of
　Mormonism
The Port of Doom
A Prisoner in the Harem
The Rogues of Paris
Sapho
The Sea Wolf
The Seed of the Fathers
Shadows of the Moulin Rouge
The Shame of the Empire State
A Sister to Carmen
The Star of India
The Stranglers of Paris
Ten Nights in a Barroom
Tess of the D'Urbervilles
The Third Degree
Tortures Within Prison Walls
Traffic in Souls
The Volunteer Organist
1914 Absinthe
Across the Pacific
After the Ball
Aftermath
Alone in New York
Aristocracy
As Ye Sow
At the Cross Roads
The Avenging Conscience;
　Thou Shalt Not Kill
Bandits of the Border Mine
The Banker's Daughter
The Battle of the Sexes
Behind the Scenes
La Belle Russe
Beneath the Czar
The Better Man
The Boer War
Born Again
A Boy and the Law
The Brute
The Burglar and the Lady
Burning Daylight: The
　Adventures of "Burning
　Daylight" in Civilization
The Call of the North
Called Back
Cameo Kirby
Captain Alvarez
Captain Swift
Cardinal Richelieu's Ward
A Celebrated Case
Charlotte Corday
The Chimes
The Christian
The Circus Man
Classmates
Clothes
Cocaine Traffic; Or, The Drug
　Terror
The Coming Power
The Criminal Code
The Criminal Path
The Crucible
Damaged Goods
Damon and Pythias
The Dancer and the King
The Daughters of Men
The Day of Days
Detective Craig's Coup
The Detective Queen
The Dollar Mark
Dope
The Dream Woman
The Eagle's Mate
The Envoy Extraordinary
The Escape
Escaped from Siberia
Even unto Death

Facing the Gattling Guns
False Colours
The Fatal Night
A Fight for Freedom; Or,
　Exiled to Siberia
The $5,000,000 Counterfeiting
　Plot
The Folks from Way Down
　East
For the Honor of Old Glory;
　Or, The Stars and Stripes in
　Mexico
Forgiven; Or, The Jack of
　Diamonds
The Gamblers
The Gangsters
A Gentleman from Mississippi
The Ghost Breaker
The Governor's Ghost
The Great Diamond Robbery
The Great Leap; Until Death
　Do Us Part
The Greyhound
The Hand of Destiny
Hearts Adrift
Hearts and Flowers
Hearts of Oak
Hearts United
Home, Sweet Home
Hook and Hand
The Hoosier Schoolmaster
The House Next Door
The House of Bondage
The Human Bloodhound
The Idler
Ill Starred Babbie
Imar the Servitor
In Mizzoura
In the Land of the Head
　Hunters
The Invisible Power
Jane Eyre
Jess
Jess of the Mountain Country
John Barleycorn
Joseph and His Coat of Many
　Colors
Joseph in the Land of Egypt
Judith of Bethulia
The Jungle
The Kangaroo
Kate
The Key to Yesterday
A Lady of Quality
The Land of the Lost
The Last Egyptian
Lena Rivers (Cosmos Feature
　Film Corp.)
Lena Rivers (Whitman
　Features Co.)
The Life of Big Tim Sullivan;
　Or, From Newsboy to
　Senator
Life's Shop Window
The Light Unseen
The Line-Up at Police
　Headquarters
The Lion and the Mouse
The Little Gray Lady
The Little Jewess
The Littlest Rebel
Lola
Lord Chumley
The Lost Paradise
The Lure
The Lust of the Red Man
McVeagh of the South Seas
The Making of Bobby Burnit
The Man from Home
The Man O' Warsman
The Man of the Hour
The Man Who Could Not Lose
Manon Lescaut
The Marked Woman
Marta of the Lowlands
Martin Eden
The Master Cracksman
The Master Mind
The Merchant of Venice
Michael Strogoff
A Million Bid
The Million Dollar Robbery
Mr. Barnes of New York
Mrs. Wiggs of the Cabbage
　Patch

The Money Lender
The Monster and the Girl
Mother
Mother Love
A Mother's Heart
My Official Wife
The Mysterious Mr. Wu Chung
　Foo
Nell Gwynne
Nell of the Circus
The Nightingale
Northern Lights
One of Our Girls
One Wonderful Night
The Only Son
The Opened Shutters
Over Niagara Falls
Paid in Full
The Path Forbidden
The Pawn of Fortune
The Phantom Violin
Pieces of Silver; A Story of
　Hearts and Souls
The Pit
The Poison Needle
The Port of Missing Men
The Power of the Press
The Price of Treachery; Or,
　The Lighthouse Keeper's
　Daughter
The Pride of Jennico
A Prince of India
Protect Us
The Pursuit of the Phantom
The Quest of the Sacred Jewel
The Red Flame of Passion
The Redemption of David
　Corson
The Reign of Terror
Richelieu
The Ring and the Man
Rip Van Winkle
A Romance of the Mexican
　Revolution
The Royal Box
St. Elmo
Samson
The Scales of Justice
The Seats of the Mighty
Shore Acres
Should a Woman Divorce?
The Sign of the Cross
Sitting Bull—The Hostile
　Sioux Indian Chief
Smashing the Vice Trust
Soldiers of Fortune
The Span of Life
The Spirit of the Conqueror
The Spirit of the Poppy
The Spoilers
Springtime
The Spy
The Squaw Man
The Straight Road
The Strange Story of Sylvia
　Gray
Such a Little Queen
A Suspicious Wife
Tess of the Storm Country
Thais
The Thief
Threads of Destiny
The Three Musketeers
The Three of Us
Three Weeks
Through Dante's Flames
Through Fire to Fortune
The Tigress
The Toll of Love
The Toll of Mammon
Too Late
The Trail of the Lonesome Pine
The Traitor
Trapped in the Great
　Metropolis
Il Trovatore
The Truth Wagon
The Typhoon
Uncle Tom's Cabin
The Unwelcome Mrs. Hatch
Uriel Acosta
The Valley of the Moon
The Virgin of the Rocks
The Voice at the Telephone
The Volunteer Parson

The Walls of Jericho
Washington at Valley Forge
What Is to Be Done?
When Broadway Was a Trail
When Fate Leads Trump
When Rome Ruled
Wildflower
The Will O' the Wisp
Winning His First Case
The Wishing Ring; An Idyll of
    Old England
With Serb and Austrian
The Wolf
Wolfe; Or, The Conquest of
    Quebec
A Woman's Triumph
The Wrath of the Gods
The Yellow Traffic
Your Girl and Mine: A
    Woman Suffrage Play
1915 The Adventures of a Boy Scout
Alias Jimmy Valentine
Aloha Oe
Always in the Way
Anna Karenina
The Apaches of Paris
Are They Born or Made?
At Bay
The Avalanche
The Battle Cry of Peace
The Battle of Ballots
The Beachcomber
Bella Donna
The Beloved Vagabond
The Better Woman
Beulah
The Bigger Man
The Birthmark
Black Fear
The Black Heart
Blackbirds
The Blindness of Devotion
The Blindness of Virtue
The Bludgeon
Blue Grass
Body and Soul
Bondwomen
The Boss
Bought
The Breath of Araby
Bred in the Bone
The Bridge of Sighs
The Brink
The Broken Law
The Builder of Bridges
Business Is Business
The Butterfly
A Butterfly on the Wheel
The Buzzard's Shadow
The Call of the Dance
Camille
Cap'n Eri
Captain Courtesy
Carmen (Fox Film Corp.)
Carmen (Jesse L. Lasky
    Feature Play Co.)
The Case of Becky
The Celebrated Scandal
The Chalice of Courage
The Cheat
A Child of God
Children of Eve
Children of the Ghetto
The Clemenceau Case
The Climbers
The Closing Net
The Clue
Colonel Carter of Cartersville
The Commanding Officer
Comrade John
The Concealed Truth
Conscience
The Coquette
Cora
Coral
Courtmartialed
The Cowardly Way
The Cup of Life
The Curious Conduct of Judge
    Legarde
The Dancing Girl
The Danger Signal
A Daughter of the City
The Daughter of the People
The Daughter of the Sea

The Dawn of a Tomorrow
The Deep Purple
Destiny; Or, The Soul of a
    Woman
The Destroying Angel
Destruction
The Devil
The Devil's Daughter
The Diamond Robbery
Divorced
Dr. Rameau
Dora Thorne
Du Barry
The Edge of the Abyss
Emmy of Stork's Nest
An Enemy to Society
Enoch Arden
Esmeralda
The Eternal City
Eugene Aram
The Evangelist
Evidence
The Exposition's First
    Romance
An Eye for an Eye
The Face in the Moonlight
The Failure
The Fairy and the Waif
The Family Cupboard
Fanchon the Cricket
The Fatal Card
The Fifth Commandment
The Fight
Fighting Bob
The Fighting Hope
The Final Judgment
Fine Feathers
The Flaming Sword
The Flash of an Emerald
The Flying Twins
The Fool and the Dancer
A Fool There Was
Forbidden Fruit
Four Feathers
The Fox Woman
The Frame-Up
From the Valley of the Missing
Gambier's Advocate
Gambling Inside and Out
The Game of Three
The Garden of Lies
The Gentleman from Indiana
Ghosts
The Girl from His Town
Gladiola
The Glory of Youth
God's Witness
The Golden Claw
The Goose Girl
The Governor's Boss
The Governor's Lady
The Grandee's Ring
The Gray Mask
The Great Ruby
Greater Love Hath No Man
The Greater Will
Hear Ye, Israel
The Heart of a Painted Woman
Heartaches
Hearts Aflame
Hearts and the Highway
Hearts in Exile
Hearts of Men
The Heights of Hazard
Help Wanted
Her Great Match
Her Mother's Secret
Her Reckoning
Her Triumph
Heritage
The High Hand
The High Road
His Turning Point
His Wife
The House of a Thousand
    Candles
The House of a Thousand
    Scandals
The House of Tears
The House of the Lost Court
The Hungarian Nabob
The Hypocrites
The Immigrant
The Impostor
In the Palace of the King

In the Shadow
Infatuation
Inspiration
The Island of Regeneration
The Italian
Jewel
The Jewish Crown
Jim the Penman
John Glayde's Honor
Judge Not; Or, The Woman of
    Mona Diggings
The Juggernaut
June Friday
Just Jim
The Kindling
Kreutzer Sonata
The Labyrinth
Lady Audley's Secret
The Last Concert
The Last of the Mafia
The Life of Sam Davis: A
    Confederate Hero of the
    Sixties
Life Without Soul
The Lily and the Rose
A Little Brother of the Rich
The Little Dutch Girl
The Little Girl That He Forgot
The Little Gypsy
The Little Mademoiselle
The Lone Star Rush
The Lonesome Heart
The Lure of the Mask
The Luring Lights
Lydia Gilmore
Maciste
Madame Butterfly
The Magic Skin
The Magic Toy Maker
The Majesty of the Law
The Making Over of Geoffrey
    Manning
The Man from Oregon
The Man of Shame
The Man Who Beat Dan Dolan
The Man Who Couldn't Beat
    God
The Man Who Found Himself
The Man Who Vanished
A Man's Making
A Man's Prerogative
The Marble Heart
Marse Covington
The Martyrs of the Alamo
The Masqueraders
The Master of the House
The Mating
Matrimony
May Blossom
Mignon
The Melting Pot
Milestones of Life
The Mill on the Floss
The Millionaire Baby
The Miracle of Life
Mr. Grex of Monte Carlo
Mistress Nell
The Model
A Modern Magdalen
The Money Master
Mortmain
The Moth and the Flame
A Mother's Confession
Mother's Roses
The Mummy and the
    Humming Bird
My Madonna
The Nation's Peril
Nedra
The Nigger
Not Guilty
Old Heidelberg
The Old Homestead
On Dangerous Paths
Out of the Darkness
The Outcast
The Outlaw's Revenge
The Pageant of San Francisco
The Painted Soul
The Pearl of the Antilles
Pearls of Temptation
The Penitentes
The Period of the Jew
A Phyllis of the Sierras
The Pitfall

Playing Dead
The Ploughshare
The Pretty Sister of Jose
The Price
A Price for Folly
The Price of Her Silence
The Primrose Path
Princess Romanoff
The Puppet Crown
The Pursuing Shadow
Queen and Adventurer
The Quest
Rags
The Raven
The Reform Candidate
Regeneration
The Reward
Richard Carvel
The Right of Way
Right off the Bat
The Ring of the Borgias
The Rosary
Rosemary
A Royal Family
The Running Fight
Salvation Nell
Sam Davis, the Hero of
    Tennessee
Samson
Satan Sanderson
Scandal
The Scarlet Sin
Sealed Lips
The Second in Command
The Secret Orchard
The Secret Sin
Secretary of Frivolous Affairs
The Senator
The Sentimental Lady
The Seventh Noon
The Shadows of a Great City
The Shame of a Nation
Should a Mother Tell?
Should a Wife Forgive?
The Silent Voice
Simon, the Jester
Sin
The Sins of Society
The Sins of the Mothers
The Siren's Song
Sold
A Soldier's Oath
The Song of Hate
The Soul of Broadway
The Spanish Jade
The Spendthrift
Stolen Goods
The Stolen Voice
Strathmore
The Stubbornness of Geraldine
The Suburban
Sunday
The Supreme Test
Sweet Alyssum
Tainted Money
Temptation
Thou Shalt Not Kill
Through Turbulent Waters
Time Lock Number 776
To Cherish and Protect
The Toast of Death
A Trade Secret
Trilby
The Truth About Helen
The Turn of the Road
The Two Orphans
The Unafraid
The Unbroken Road
Under Southern Skies
The Unfaithful Wife
Up from the Depths
The Vampire
Vanity Fair
Vengeance of the Wilds
Via Wireless
The Victory of Virtue
Virtue
The Voice of Satan
The Vow
The Waif
The Warning
Was She to Blame? Or, Souls
    That Meet in the Dark
The Way Back
What Should a Woman Do to
    Promote Youth and
    Happiness?

Wheat and Tares; A Story of
    Two Boys Who Tackle Life
    on Diverging Lines
The Wheels of Justice
When a Woman Loves
When It Strikes Home
The White Pearl
The White Sister
The White Terror
The Wild Olive
Wildfire
The Winged Idol
Winning the Futurity
The Wolf Man
The Wolf of Debt
The Woman
The Woman Next Door
The Woman Pays
The Woman Who Lied
A Woman's Past
A Woman's Resurrection
The Wonderful Adventure
Wormwood
A Yankee from the West
A Yellow Streak
York State Folks
Zaza

1915-16
    The Little Church Around the
      Corner
    The Sins That Ye Sin

1916 The Abandonment
According to Law
According to the Code
Acquitted
The Alibi
Alien Souls
The Almighty Dollar
Ambition
The American Beauty
And the Law Says
Anton the Terrible
The Apostle of Vengeance
April
The Argonauts of
    California—1849
As a Woman Sows
As in a Looking Glass
Ashes of Embers
At Piney Ridge
Atta Boy's Last Race
Audrey
The Awakening of Bess Morton
The Awakening of Helena
    Richie
The Ballet Girl
Barriers of Society
The Battle of Hearts
The Battle of Life
Bawbs O' Blue Ridge
The Beckoning Flame
The Beckoning Trail
The Beggar of Cawnpore
Behind Closed Doors
Behind the Lines
Ben Blair
Betrayed
Bettina Loved a Soldier
Betty of Graystone
Between Men
Big Jim Garrity
The Big Sister
Big Tremaine
A Bird of Prey
The Birth of a Man
The Birth of Character
The Bishop's Secret
The Black Butterfly
Black Friday
The Black Sheep of the Family
The Blacklist
Blazing Love
The Blindness of Love
The Blue Envelope Mystery
Bobbie of the Ballet
The Bondman
Boots and Saddles
Bought and Paid For
The Brand of Cowardice
The Breaker
Britton of the Seventh
Broken Chains
Broken Fetters
The Bruiser
The Bugle Call

The Bugler of Algiers
Bullets and Brown Eyes
The Call of the Cumberlands
Caprice of the Mountains
Casey at the Bat
The Catspaw
The Chain Invisible
The Chalice of Sorrow
The Challenge
The Chattel
The Child of Destiny
A Child of Mystery
A Child of the Paris Streets
The Children in the House
Children of the Feud
The Children Pay
A Circus Romance
The City
The City of Failing Light
The City of Illusion
Civilization
Civilization's Child
The Clarion
The Closed Road
The Clown
The Code of Marcia Gray
The Colored American
    Winning His Suit
The Combat
The Come-Back
Common Ground
The Common Law
Common Sense Brackett
The Conflict
The Conqueror
The Conquest of Canaan
The Conscience of John David
The Corner
A Corner in Cotton
The Cossack Whip
The Country That God Forgot
The Courtesan
The Craving
The Criminal
The Crippled Hand
The Crisis
Cross Currents
The Crown Prince's Double
The Crucial Test
The Cycle of Fate
Daredevil Kate
The Daring of Diana
The Dark Silence
The Daughter of the Don
Davy Crockett
The Dawn of Freedom
The Dawn of Love
The Dead Alive
The Decoy
Defense or Tribute?
Destiny's Toy
The Destroyers
The Devil at His Elbow
The Devil's Bondwoman
The Devil's Needle
The Devil's Prayer-Book
The Devil's Prize
The Devil's Toy
The Diamond Runners
Dimples
The Discard
The Dividend
Divorce and the Daughter
Doctor Neighbor
The Dollar and the Law
Dollars and the Woman
Don Quixote
Dorian's Divorce
The Dragon
The Dream Girl
A Dream or Two Ago
The Drifter
Driftwood
Dulcie's Adventure
The Dumb Girl of Portici
The Dupe
Dust
Each Pearl a Tear
The Eagle's Wing
East Lynne
Elusive Isabel
Embers
The End of the Rainbow
The Enemy
An Enemy to the King

The Eternal Grind
The Eternal Question
The Eternal Sapho
The Evil Thereof
The Evil Women Do
Extravagance
The Eye of God
The Eye of the Night
The Faded Flower
Faith
The Fall of a Nation
Fate's Boomerang
Fate's Chessboard
Fathers of Men
The Fear of Poverty
The Feast of Life
Feathertop
The Female of the Species
The Feud Girl
Fifty-Fifty
Fighting Blood
The Fighting Chance
The Final Curtain
The Fires of Conscience
The Five Faults of Flo
The Flames of Johannis
The Flirt
The Flower of Faith
The Flower of No Man's Land
The Flying Torpedo
The Folly of Revenge
The Foolish Virgin
A Fool's Paradise
The Fool's Revenge
The Footlights of Fate
For a Woman's Fair Name
For the Defense
The Fortunate Youth
The Foundling
The Fourth Estate
Friday the Thirteenth
Fruits of Desire
The Fugitive
A Gamble in Souls
The Garden of Allah
The Gates of Eden
The Gay Lord Waring
The Gilded Cage
The Gilded Spider
The Girl O' Dreams
The Girl of the Lost Lake
The Girl Philippa
The Girl Who Doesn't Know
The Girl with the Green Eyes
Gloriana
God's Half Acre
The Gods of Fate
Going Straight
Gold and the Woman
The Golden Chance
The Grasp of Greed
The Great Problem
The Green Swamp
The Green-Eyed Monster
Gretchen, the Greenhorn
The Grip of Jealousy
A Gutter Magdalene
Half a Rogue
The Half Million Bribe
The Half-Breed
The Hand of Peril
The Haunted Manor
The Havoc
Hazel Kirke
He Fell in Love with His Wife
The Heart of New York
The Heart of Nora Flynn
The Heart of Paula
The Heart of Tara
The Heart of the Hills
Her American Prince
Her Bitter Cup
Her Bleeding Heart
Her Debt of Honor
Her Double Life
Her Father's Gold
Her Great Hour
Her Great Price
Her Husband's Wife
Her Maternal Right
Her Redemption
Her Surrender
The Heritage of Hate
The Hero of Submarine D-2
Hesper of the Mountains

The Hidden Law
The Hidden Scar
Hidden Valley
The Highest Bid
His Brother's Wife
His Great Triumph
His Wife's Good Name
The Honor of Mary Blake
Honor Thy Name
The Honorable Friend
Honor's Altar
Hop, the Devil's Brew
The House of Lies
The House of Mirrors
The House with the Golden
    Windows
Hulda from Holland
Human Driftwood
The Human Orchid
The Hunted Woman
A Huntress of Men
Husband and Wife
Hypocrisy
I Accuse
Idle Wives
The Idol of the Stage
Idols
Ignorance
The Immortal Flame
In the Web of the Grafters
Indiana
Inherited Passions
The Inner Struggle
The Innocence of Ruth
The Innocent Lie
An Innocent Magdalene
Into the Primitive
Intolerance
The Intrigue
The Invisible Enemy
The Iron Hand
The Iron Woman
Is Any Girl Safe?
The Island of Happiness
The Island of Surprise
The Isle of Life
The Isle of Love
It May Be Your Daughter
Jaffery
Jealousy
Joan the Woman
John Needham's Double
Joy and the Dragon
Judith of the Cumberlands
The Jungle Child
Just a Song at Twilight
Kennedy Square
The Kid
King Lear
Kinkaid, Gambler
The Kiss of Hate
The Land Just Over Yonder
Langdon's Legacy
The Lash
The Lash of Destiny
The Last Act
The Last Man
The Law Decides
The Leopard's Bride
Less Than the Dust
Let Katie Do It
The Libertine
Life's Blind Alley
Life's Whirlpool
The Light
Light at Dusk
The Light of Happiness
The Light That Failed
The Lights of New York
The Little Girl Next Door
Little Lady Eileen
The Little Liar
Little Mary Sunshine
Little Miss Happiness
Little Miss Nobody
The Little School Ma'am
The Little Shepherd of Bargain
    Row
Lone Star
The Lords of High Decision
Lost Souls
The Lotus Woman
Love and Hate
The Love Girl
The Love Hermit

A Branded Soul
Brand's Daughter
The Bride of Hate
Bridges Burned
Builders of Castles
The Burglar
Burning the Candle
The Butterfly Girl
The Call of Her People
The Call of the East
Camille
The Candy Girl
A Case at Law
Cassidy
Castles for Two
The Charmer
The Checkmate
A Child of the Wild
The Chosen Prince, or the
  Friendship of David and
  Jonathan
The Cigarette Girl
Cinderella and the Magic
  Slipper
The Circus of Life
The Clean Gun
Cleopatra
The Climber
The Cloud
Come Through
The Conqueror
The Cook of Canyon Camp
The Co-Respondent
The Corner Grocer
Corruption
The Cost of Hatred
The Courage of Silence
The Courage of the Common
  Place
The Crab
The Cricket
Crime and Punishment
The Crimson Dove
A Crooked Romance
The Crystal Gazer
The Curse of Eve
Cy Whittaker's Ward
The Dancer's Peril
Darkest Russia
The Darling of Paris
Daughter of Maryland
The Debt
The Deemster
The Defeat of the City
The Derelict
The Devil's Assistant
The Devil's Bait
The Devil's Pay Day
Diamonds and Pearls
A Doll's House
The Door Between
The Dormant Power
Double Crossed
The Double Standard
The Downfall of a Mayor
Draft 258
Du Barry
The Dummy
Each to His Kind
The Easiest Way
Easy Money
The Edge of the Law
The Empress
The End of the Tour
Enlighten Thy Daughter
Environment
Envy
Eternal Love
The Eternal Mother
The Eternal Sin
The Eternal Temptress
Every Girl's Dream
The Evil Eye
Exile
The False Friend
The Family Honor
Fanatics
Fear Not
The Fettered Woman
The Field of Honor
The Fighting Gringo
Fighting Odds
The Final Payment
Fires of Rebellion
The Fires of Youth

The Flame of Youth
The Flaming Omen
The Flower of Doom
Flying Colors
The Food Gamblers
Forbidden Paths
Forget-Me-Not
The Fortunes of Fifi
Freckles
The Fringe of Society
The Frozen Warning
The Fuel of Life
The Gates of Doom
The Gentle Intruder
The Ghost of Old Morro
The Gift Girl
The Girl and the Crisis
The Girl at Home
The Girl by the Roadside
The Girl from Rector's
The Girl in the Checkered Coat
A Girl Like That
The Girl Who Didn't Think
The Girl Who Won Out
The Girl Without a Soul
Giving Becky a Chance
The Glory of Yolanda
God of Little Children
God's Crucible
God's Law and Man's
God's Man
The Golden God
The Good for Nothing
Grafters
Great Expectations
The Great White Trail
The Greater Woman
The Greatest Power
Greed
The Guardian
The Hand That Rocks the
  Cradle
The Happiness of Three
  Women
Has Man the Right to Kill?
Hate
The Hawk
Heart and Soul
The Heart of a Lion
The Heart of Ezra Greer
Heart Strings
Heart's Desire
Hedda Gabler
The Heir of the Ages
Hell Hath No Fury
Hell Morgan's Girl
Her Bargain
Her Better Self
Her Country's Call
Her Excellency, the Governor
Her Father's Keeper
Her Good Name
Her Greatest Love
Her Hour
Her Life and His
Her New York
Her Own People
Her Right to Live
Her Second Husband
Her Secret
Her Silent Sacrifice
Her Sister
Her Soul's Inspiration
Her Strange Wedding
Her Temptation
The Hidden Children
The Hidden Spring
High Finance
High Play
The High Sign
Hinton's Double
His Mother's Boy
His Old-Fashioned Dad
His Own People
His Sweetheart
The Honor System
The Hostage
House of Cards
A Hungry Heart
The Hungry Heart
I Will Repay
Idolators
The Image Maker
In Slumberland
In the Balance

In the Hands of the Law
Indiscretion
The Inevitable
Infidelity
The Inner Shrine
Innocence
The Innocent Sinner
Intrigue
The Iron Heart
The Iron Ring
It Happened to Adele
A Jewel in Pawn
Jim Bludso
The Judgement House
The Jury of Fate
A Kentucky Cinderella
Kick In
Knights of the Square Table
The Lady in the Library
The Lair of the Wolf
The Land of Promise
The Lash of Power
The Last of the Carnabys
The Last of the Ingrams
The Last Sentence
The Law of Compensation
The Law of the Land
The Law That Failed
Life's Whirlpool
The Lifted Veil
Light in Darkness
The Lincoln Cycle
The Little Boy Scout
The Little Brother
The Little Chevalier
The Little Duchess
Little Lost Sister
Little Miss Fortune
Little Miss Optimist
The Little Orphan
The Little Patriot
The Little Pirate
The Little Princess
The Little Samaritan
Little Shoes
The Lone Wolf
The Lonesome Chap
Lorelei of the Sea
Lost and Won
Lost in Transit
The Love Doctor
Love Letters
Love or Justice
A Love Sublime
The Love That Lives
Love's Law
Loyalty
The Lust of the Ages
The Mad Lover
Magda
A Magdalene of the Hills
The Maid of Belgium
Man and Beast
A Man and the Woman
The Man of Mystery
The Man Trap
The Man Who Forgot
The Man Who Made Good
The Man Without a Country
Man's Woman
The Marcellini Millions
The Marriage Market
Married in Name Only
The Martinache Marriage
Mary Jane's Pa
Mary Lawson's Secret
Mary Moreland
The Masked Heart
Master of His Home
The Master Passion
The Maternal Spark
Maternity
Mayblossom
Melissa of the Hills
Mentioned in Confidence
The Message of the Mouse
The Midnight Man
Might and the Man
The Millionaire Vagrant
The Millionaire's Double
The Mirror
Miss Jackie of the Army
Miss Nobody
Miss U.S.A.
Mr. Opp

A Modern Cinderella
A Modern Monte Cristo
Molly Entangled
Money Madness
Money Magic
The Money Mill
The Moral Code
Moral Courage
The More Excellent Way
More Truth Than Poetry
A Mormon Maid
The Mortal Sin
The Moth
The Mother Instinct
Mother Love and the Law
Mother O' Mine
Motherhood (Minerva Motion
  Picture Co.)
Mothers of Men
A Mother's Ordeal
A Mute Appeal
Mutiny
My Fighting Gentleman
My Little Boy
The Mysterious Mrs. M.
The Natural Law
New York Luck
The New York Peacock
Next Door to Nancy
A Night in New Arabia
The Night Workers
Nina, the Flower Girl
An Old Fashioned Young Man
On Record
The On-the-Square-Girl
On Trial
One Hour
One Law for Both
One of Many
Out of the Wreck
Outcast
The Outsider
Outwitted
Over the Hill
The Painted Lie
The Painted Madonna
Panthea
Paradise Garden
Passion
The Peddler
Peggy Leads the Way
Peggy, the Will O' the Wisp
The Penny Philanthropist
Periwinkle
Persuasive Peggy
The Phantom's Secret
The Piper's Price
The Planter
Polly of the Circus
Polly Put the Kettle On
Poppy
The Power of Decision
The Price Mark
The Price of a Good Time
The Price of Her Soul
The Price of Silence
The Price She Paid
Pride
Pride and the Devil
Pride and the Man
The Pride of the Clan
The Primrose Ring
The Princess of Patches
Princess of the Dark
Princess Virtue
The Prison Without Walls
The Promise
The Public Be Damned
The Public Defender
The Pulse of Life
Queen X
The Question
Raffles, the Amateur
  Cracksman
The Raggedy Queen
The Rainbow
The Rainbow Girl
Rasputin, the Black Monk
Rebecca of Sunnybrook Farm
The Recoil
Redemption
The Regenerates
The Renaissance at Charleroi
Reputation
The Rescue

The Reward of the Faithless
A Rich Man's Plaything
The Rise of Jennie Cushing
The Road Between
A Roadside Impresario
The Rose of Blood
Rosie O'Grady
The Royal Pauper
Runaway Romany
S. O. S.
The Saintly Sinner
The Saint's Adventure
Sands of Sacrifice
Sapho
Satan's Private Door
The Sawdust Ring
The Scarlet Car
The Scarlet Crystal
The Scarlet Letter
The Scarlet Pimpernel
The Secret Game
The Secret of Eve
The Secret of the Storm
　　Country
The Serpent's Tooth
The Seventh Sin
Shackles of Truth
Shall We Forgive Her?
Shame
She
The Ship of Doom
Shirley Kaye
Should She Obey?
The Show Down
The Silence Sellers
The Silent Lady
The Silent Master
The Silent Partner
The Sin Woman
The Single Code
Sins of Ambition
Sirens of the Sea
Sister Against Sister
The Skylight Room
The Slacker (Metro Pictures
　　Corp.)
The Slacker (Peter P. Jones
　　Film Co.)
The Slacker's Heart
The Slave
The Slave Mart
Sleeping Fires
A Sleeping Memory
Sloth
The Small Town Girl
The Snarl
The Social Leper
Society's Driftwood
Sold at Auction
Somewhere in America
A Son of the Hills
A Song of Sixpence
A Soul for Sale
The Soul Master
The Soul of a Magdalen
The Soul of Satan
Souls Adrift
Souls in Pawn
Souls Triumphant
Southern Justice
Southern Pride
Sowers and Reapers
The Spindle of Life
The Spirit of Romance
The Spirit of '76
The Spotted Lily
The Spreading Dawn
A Square Deal
Stagestruck
The Stainless Barrier
The Stolen Paradise
The Stolen Play
The Stolen Treaty
A Strange Transgressor
The Streets of Illusion
Strife
The Strong Way
Sudden Jim
The Sunset Trail
Sunshine Alley
Susan's Gentleman
Sylvia of the Secret Service
A Tale of Two Cities
The Tar Heel Warrior
Tears and Smiles

The Tell-Tale Step
Ten of Diamonds
The Tenth Case
The Terror
Thais
They're Off
Think It Over
Those Who Pay
Those Without Sin
Threads of Fate
The Tides of Barnegat
The Tides of Fate
The Tiger Woman
Time Locks and Diamonds
To Honor and Obey
To the Death
To-Day
Told at Twilight
Transgression
Triumph
Trooper 44
The Trouble Buster
Troublemakers
The Trufflers
Twin Kiddies
Two Men and a Woman
Unconquered
Under False Colors
The Understudy
The Undying Flame
The Unforeseen
Unknown 274
Unto the End
The Valentine Girl
Vengeance Is Mine
Vengeance of the Dead
Vera, the Medium
The Vicar of Wakefield
The Voice of Conscience
The Volunteer
The Waiting Soul
The War of the Tongs
The Wax Model
The Way to Happiness
The Weaker Sex
Weavers of Life
The Web of Desire
The Web of Life
Wee Lady Betty
What Money Can't Buy
When a Man Sees Red
When Baby Forgot
When Duty Calls
When False Tongues Speak
When Love Was Blind
When Men Are Tempted
When You and I Were Young
Where Love Is
The White Raven
Whither Thou Goest
Who Shall Take My Life?
Who Was the Other Man?
Who's Your Neighbor?
Whose Wife?
A Wife by Proxy
Wife Number Two
A Wife on Trial
The Wife Who Wouldn't Tell
The Wild Girl
The Winning of Sally Temple
Within the Law
A Woman Alone
The Woman and the Beast
The Woman Beneath
The Woman God Forgot
A Woman's Awakening
Wooden Shoes
Wrath
Wrath of Love
Yankee Pluck
Young Mother Hubbard
Youth
Zollenstein
1917-18
　　The Devil's Playground
　　Will You Marry Me?
1918　Alias Mary Brown
　　All Man
　　All Woman
　　And a Still Small Voice
　　And the Children Pay
　　The Answer
　　The Appearance of Evil
　　Arizona
　　An Armenian Crucifixion

Arms in France
Ashes of Love
At the Mercy of Men
The Atom
A Bachelor's Children
The Beautiful Mrs. Reynolds
Beauty in Chains
The Bells
The Beloved Impostor
The Beloved Traitor
Berlin Via America
The Better Half
Betty Takes a Hand
Beyond the Law
The Biggest Show on Earth
The Bird of Prey
The Birth of a Race
Blindfolded
The Blindness of Divorce
The Blot
Blue Blood
Blue-Eyed Mary
Bonnie Annie Laurie
Borrowed Clothes
Boston Blackie's Little Pal
Brace Up
The Bravest Way
Bread
Breakers Ahead
The Bride of Fear
The Bride's Awakening
Broadway Bill
Broadway Love
Broken Ties
Brown of Harvard
Buchanan's Wife
The Burden of Proof
The Business of Life
By Right of Purchase
By the World Forgot
The Cabaret
The Cabaret Girl
The Caillaux Case
The Cast-Off
Cecilia of the Pink Roses
The Challenge Accepted
Cheating the Public
The City of Dim Faces
The City of Purple Dreams
The Claw
The Claws of the Hun
The Clutch of Circumstance
Coals of Fire
Confession
Conquered Hearts
Convict 993
The Craving
The Crime of the Hour
Crown Jewels
The Crucible of Life
The Cruise of the
　　Make-Believes
Cupid Angling
The Curse of Iku
Daddy's Girl
The Danger Mark
Danger Within
The Danger Zone
A Daughter of the Old South
Daybreak
De Luxe Annie
The Death Dance
The Debt of Honor
The Deciding Kiss
A Desert Wooing
The Desired Woman
The Devil's Wheel
The Divine Sacrifice
The Doctor and the Woman
Does Your Wife Obey?
A Doll's House
The Eleventh Commandment
The Empty Cab
Everywoman's Husband
Eye for Eye
Face Value
The Fall of the Romanoffs
The Fallen Angel
False Ambition
The Family Skeleton
Fedora
Find the Woman
The Finger of Justice
Fires of Youth
Five Nights

The Flash of Fate
Flower of the Dusk
For Freedom
For Sale
For the Freedom of the East
The Forbidden City
The Forbidden Path
Gates of Gladness
Gay and Festive Claverhouse
A Gentleman's Agreement
The Ghost Flower
The Ghost of Rosy Taylor
The Ghosts of Yesterday
The Girl and the Judge
The Girl from Beyond
The Girl in His House
The Girl of My Dreams
The Girl Who Came Back
The Girl with the Champagne
　　Eyes
The Glorious Adventure
The Goddess of Lost Lake
The Golden Goal
The Grain of Dust
Green Eyes
The Grouch
The Guilty Man
The Guilty Wife
The Hard Rock Breed
The Heart of a Girl
The Heart of Rachael
A Heart's Revenge
Hell's End
Her American Husband
Her Body in Bond
Her Boy
Her Decision
Her Final Reckoning
Her Great Chance
Her Husband's Honor
Her Inspiration
Her Man
Her Mistake
Her Moment
Her One Mistake
Her Only Way
Her Price
Heredity
Hidden Pearls
High Tide
His Birthright
His Daughter Pays
His Enemy, the Law
His Own Home Town
His Robe of Honor
Hitting the Trail
Hoarded Assets
The Honor of His House
Honor's Cross
The House of Glass
The House of Gold
The House of Mirth
Human Clay
Humility
The Hun Within
Huns Within Our Gates
I Love You
I Want to Forget
In Judgment Of
The Inn of the Blue Moon
Innocent
Innocent's Progress
The Interloper
Irish Eyes
A Japanese Nightingale
Joan of the Woods
Just a Woman
Keys of the Righteous
Kildare of Storm
The King of Diamonds
Kiss or Kill
The Knife
The Landloper
The Last Rebel
The Law That Divides
The Legion of Death
The Liar
The Lie
The Light Within
A Lion of the Hills
Little Orphant Annie
Loaded Dice
The Locked Heart
The Lone Avenger
The Lonely Woman

The Lost Chord
The Love Brokers
Love Me
Love's Conquest
Love's Law
Love's Pay Day
The Lure of Luxury
The Magic Eye
Maid O' the Storm
The Man of Bronze
The Man Who Woke Up
The Man Who Wouldn't Tell
A Man's World
Marked Cards
Marriage
The Marriage Lie
The Marriage Ring
The Married Virgin
The Mating of Marcella
Men
Men Who Have Made Love to
  Me
The Menace
Merely Players
The Midnight Patrol
Les Miserables
Miss Ambition
Miss Innocence
Missing
Mrs. Dane's Defense
The Model's Confession
Modern Love
The Moral Law
Moral Suicide
The Mortgaged Wife
A Mother's Secret
A Mother's Sin
My Own United States
My Unmarried Wife
The Narrow Path
New Love for Old
No Children Wanted
A Nymph of the Foothills
Old Hartwell's Cub
Old Love for New
Old Wives for New
The Oldest Law
One Dollar Bid
One More American
The One Woman
The Ordeal of Rosetta
The Other Man
Other Men's Daughters
The Other Woman
Out of a Clear Sky
Out of the Night
The Painted Lily
Painted Lips
Pals First
The Panther Woman
Parentage
Peg O' the Sea
Playthings
The Power and the Glory
The Prisoner of War
The Prodigal Wife
The Queen of Hearts
Quicksand
The Racing Strain
The Reason Why
Resurrection
The Return of Mary
Revelation
Rich Man, Poor Man
Riders of the Night
The Risky Road
A Romance of the Underworld
The Rose of the World
Rosemary Climbs the Heights
Ruler of the Road
Ruling Passions
The Safety Curtain
Salome
The Sand Rat
Sandy
The Scarlet Road
The Scarlet Trail
The Sea Waif
The Seal of Silence
Secret Code
Secret Strings
The Secret Trap
The Service Star
The Seventy-Five Mile Gun
Shackled

She Hired a Husband
The She-Devil
The Shell Game
Shifting Sands
The Shoes That Danced
The Shuttle
The Sins of the Children
Sins of the Kaiser
Social Hypocrites
Society for Sale
The Song of Songs
The Song of the Soul
A Soul in Trust
The Soul of Buddha
A Soul Without Windows
The Source
The Spirit of '17
Sporting Life
The Spreading Evil
The Spurs of Sybil
The Square Deal
Station Content
Stella Maris
The Still Alarm
Stolen Honor
Stolen Hours
Stolen Orders
The Strange Woman
The Street of Seven Stars
Suspicion
The Talk of the Town
Tangled Lives
Tempered Steel
The Temple of Dusk
That Devil, Bateese
The Thing We Love
Tinsel
To Him That Hath
To the Highest Bidder
Tony America
La Tosca
Toys of Fate
The Transgressor
The Trap
Treason
Treasure of the Sea
The Triumph of the Weak
The Two-Soul Woman
The Unchastened Woman
Uncle Tom's Cabin
Under the Yoke
The Uphill Path
The Vanity Pool
The Velvet Hand
Vengeance
The Vigilantes
Virtuous Wives
Viviette
The Vortex
Wanted—A Brother
Wanted, a Mother
The Way Out
A Weaver of Dreams
Wedlock
What Becomes of the
  Children?
What Does a Woman Need
  Most
When a Woman Sins
When Men Betray
Whims of Society
The Whip
The Whirlpool
The Whispered Word
The Whispering Chorus
The White Man's Law
Who Is to Blame?
Who Loved Him Best?
Why America Will Win
The Wife He Bought
Wife or Country
Wild Primrose
Wild Youth
The Wine Girl
The Witch Woman
Within the Cup
Without Honor
Wives of Men
Woman
Woman and the Law
Woman and Wife
The Woman Between Friends
A Woman of Impulse
A Woman of Redemption
The Woman Who Gave

The Yellow Dog
The Yellow Ticket
You Can't Believe Everything
The Zero Hour
Zongar

1918-19
April Fool
The Candidates
The Kaiser's Bride
Marriage a la Mode
The Missionary
Once to Every Man

1919 The A.B.C. of Love
The Amazing Wife
L'Apache
Are You Legally Married?
As a Man Thinks
Atonement
Auction of Souls
The Avalanche
The Battler
Beating the Odds
The Beauty Market
Beckoning Roads
Behind the Door
The Belle of New York
The Belle of the Season
The Betrayal
Better Times
The Better Wife
The Big Little Person
Bill Apperson's Boy
The Bishop's Emeralds
The Black Circle
Blackie's Redemption
Blind Husbands
Blind Man's Eyes
The Blinding Trail
The Blue Bonnet
The Bluffer
Bolshevism on Trial
The Bondage of Barbara
Bonds of Honor
Bonds of Love
The Boomerang
The Bramble Bush
The Brand
The Brand of Judas
The Brat
Break the News to Mother
Broken Barriers
Broken Blossoms
The Broken Butterfly
Broken Commandments
The Broken Melody
Brothers Divided
The Brute Breaker
The Burning Question
The Call of the Soul
The Cambric Mask
The Capitol
The Career of Katherine Bush
Carolyn of the Corners
Child of M'sieu
The Chosen Path
The Cinema Murder
The City of Comrades
The Clouded Name
Common Clay
Common Property
Counterfeit
The Country Cousin
The Courageous Coward
Creaking Stairs
The Crimson Gardenia
Crimson Shoals
The Crook of Dreams
Crooked Straight
The Cry of the Weak
Cupid Forecloses
A Dangerous Affair
Dangerous Waters
The Darkest Hour
Daughter of Mine
Dawn
Day Dreams
The Day She Paid
Deliverance
Destiny
Diane of the Green Van
The Divorce Trap
The Divorcee
The Dragon Painter
The Drifters
Dust of Desire

Eastward Ho!
The Echo of Youth
The Enchanted Barn
The End of the Road
Erstwhile Susan
The Eternal Light
The Eternal Magdalene
Evangeline
Eve in Exile
Everybody's Business
The Exquisite Thief
Extravagance
Eyes of the Soul
Eyes of Youth
Faith
The Faith of the Strong
The Fall of Babylon
A Fallen Idol
The False Code
False Gods
The Fear Woman
The Feud
A Fighting Colleen
Fighting Destiny
The Fighting Roosevelts
Fighting Through
The Final Close-Up
The Fire Flingers
Fires of Faith
The Firing Line
Flame of the Desert
Fool's Gold
For a Woman's Honor
For Better, for Worse
Forbidden
The Forbidden Room
Forced to Wed
Fortune's Child
From Headquarters
Fruits of Passion
The Gamblers
Gambling in Souls
Gates of Brass
The Gay Lord Quex
The Gay Old Dog
A Gentleman of Quality
Ginger
The Girl Alaska
A Girl in Bohemia
A Girl Named Mary
The Girl Problem
The Girl with No Regrets
The Girl-Woman
Give and Take
The Glorious Lady
The Golden Shower
The Gray Horizon
The Greater Sinner
The Greater Victory
The Greatest Question
The Grim Game
The Hand Invisible
The Haunted Bedroom
Heads Win
A Heart in Pawn
The Heart of a Gypsy
Hearts Asleep
Hearts of Men
Heartsease
The Hellion
Her Code of Honor
Her Game
Her Kingdom of Dreams
Her Purchase Price
The Hidden Truth
His Debt
His Divorced Wife
His Father's Wife
His Parisian Wife
Home
The Homesteader
The Hornet's Nest
A House Divided
The House of Intrigue
The House Without Children
Human Desire
The Hushed Hour
The Illustrious Prince
The Imp
In Honor's Web
In the Land of the Setting Sun;
  Or, Martyrs of Yesterday
Injustice
The Invisible Bond
The Island of Intrigue

The Isle of Conquest
It Happened in Paris
Jane Goes A-Wooing
Josselyn's Wife
Kathleen Mavourneen
Keali
The Law of Men
The Law of Nature
The Life Line
The Light
The Lion and the Mouse
The Lion's Den
A Little Brother of the Rich
Little Women
The Long Arm of Mannister
The Long Lane's Turning
Loot
Lost Money
Louisiana
Love and the Woman
The Love Auction
The Love Burglar
The Love Defender
Love, Honor and—?
Love in a Hurry
Love Is Love
The Love That Dares
The Loves of Letty
Love's Prisoner
Luck and Pluck
Lure of Ambition
Male and Female
The Man Beneath
The Man Hunter
The Man Who Won
Mandarin's Gold
A Man's Duty
A Man's Fight
The Market of Souls
Marriage for Convenience
The Marriage Price
Mary Regan
The Master Man
The Mayor of Filbert
Men, Women and Money
A Midnight Romance
The Millionaire Pirate
Mind the Paint Girl
The Miracle Man
The Miracle of Love
Miss Dulcie from Dixie
Mistaken Identity
Modern Husbands
The Money Corral
The Moonshine Trail
The Moral Deadline
Mother of Shadows
My Little Sister
The Nature Girl
The Old Maid's Baby
One Against Many
One Week of Life
Open Your Eyes
The Other Half
The Other Man's Wife
Other Men's Wives
Out of the Fog
Out of the Shadow
Out Yonder
The Pagan God
Paid in Full
The Painted World
The Parisian Tigress
The Pawn of Fortune
The Peace of Roaring River
The Perfect Lover
The Petal on the Current
Pettigrew's Girl
The Phantom Honeymoon
Pitfalls of a Big City
Playthings of Passion
The Pointing Finger
Poor Relations
The Poppy Girl's Husband
The Price of Innocence
The Price Woman Pays
The Profiteers
Putting One Over
The Quickening Flame
The Railroader
Reclaimed: The Struggle for a
　Soul Between Love and Hate
The Red Lantern
The Red Peril
The Red Viper

Redhead
Restless Souls
The Right to Happiness
The Right to Lie
A Rogue's Romance
A Romance of Happy Valley
A Romance of Seattle
Rose O' the River
Roses and Thorns
The Rough Neck
A Royal Democrat
Sacred Silence
Sahara
The Sawdust Doll
The Scar
A Scream in the Night
The Sealed Envelope
Sealed Hearts
The Secret Garden
Secret Marriage
Shadows of the Past
The Shepherd of the Hills
Should a Husband Forgive?
Should a Woman Tell?
The Silk Lined Burglar
The Silver Girl
The Silver King
The Siren's Song
Snares of Paris
The Sneak
The Social Pirate
A Society Exile
Soldiers of Fortune
The Solitary Sin
Someone Must Pay
The Spark Divine
The Speed Maniac
The Spirit of Lafayette
The Spite Bride
The Spitfire of Seville
The Splendid Romance
The Splendid Sin
The Steel King
The Stream of Life
Sue of the South
Tangled Threads
The Test of Honor
Thieves
Thin Ice
The Third Degree
Thou Shalt Not
Through the Toils
The Thunderbolt
Thunderbolts of Fate
The Tiger Lily
Tiger of the Sea
The Tong Man
Toton
A Trick of Fate
Trixie from Broadway
True Heart Susie
The Turn in the Road
Twilight
The Twin Pawns
The Two Brides
Two Women
The Undercurrent
The Unknown Quantity
The Unpainted Woman
The Unpardonable Sin
The Unveiling Hand
The Unwritten Code
The Usurper
The Vengeance of Durand
Victory
Virtuous Men
The Virtuous Model
Virtuous Sinners
The Virtuous Thief
The Volcano
Water Lily
The Way of a Woman
What Am I Bid?
What Every Woman Learns
What Every Woman Wants
What Love Forgives
When Arizona Won
When Bearcat Went Dry
When Fate Decides
When Men Desire
When My Ship Comes In
Where Bonds Are Loosed
Where's Mary?
The White Heather
Who Will Marry Me?

Whom the Gods Would
　Destroy
Who's Your Brother?
The Wicked Darling
Wild Oats
The Winchester Woman
Wings of the Morning
The Winning Stroke
The Wishing Ring Man
The Witness for the Defense
The Woman Michael Married
The Woman Next Door
The Woman of Lies
The Woman on the Index
A Woman There Was
The Woman Thou Gavest Me
The Woman Under Cover
Woman, Woman!
A Woman's Experience
Words and Music By—
The World Aflame
The World and Its Woman
The World to Live In
The Wreck
You Never Know Your Luck
You Never Saw Such a Girl
1919-20
　The Tower of Jewels
　When a Man Loves
1920　The Adorable Savage
　The Adventurer
　Alias Jimmy Valentine
　Always Audacious
　The Amateur Wife
　The Amazing Woman
　April Folly
　Beautifully Trimmed
　Behold My Wife
　Below the Deadline
　Below the Surface
　The Best of Luck
　Beyond the Great Wall
　Big Happiness
　The Birth of a Soul
　Birthright
　Bitter Fruit
　Black Is White
　Black Shadows
　Blackbirds
　Blackmail
　Blind Love
　Blind Wives
　Blind Youth
　The Blood Barrier
　The Blue Moon
　Body and Soul
　Bonnie May
　Brain Cinema
　The Brand of Lopez
　The Branded Woman
　The Branding Iron
　The Breath of the Gods
　Bright Skies
　Broadway and Home
　The Broadway Bubble
　The Broken Gate
　Broken Hearts
　The Brute
　The Brute Master
　Burning Daylight
　Burnt Wings
　The Butterfly Man
　Captain Swift
　The Cheater
　Children Not Wanted
　The City of Masks
　A City Sparrow
　Clothes
　A Common Level
　Common Sense
　The Common Sin
　The Confession
　The Copperhead
　The Corsican Brothers
　The Cost
　The County Fair
　The Cradle of Courage
　Crooked Streets
　A Cumberland Romance
　The Cup of Fury
　Curtain
　Dad's Girl
　Dangerous Days
　Dangerous Hours
　The Dangerous Paradise

The Dangerous Talent
A Dark Lantern
The Dark Mirror
Darling Mine
A Daughter of Two Worlds
The Daughter Pays
David and Jonathan
The Dead Line
Deadline at Eleven
The Deceiver
The Deep Purple
Deep Waters
Democracy
The Devil's Claim
The Devil's Garden
The Devil's Passkey
The Devil's Riddle
Dice of Destiny
Dinty
The Discarded Woman
Do the Dead Talk?
Dr. Jekyll and Mr. Hyde
　(Famous Players-Lasky
　Corp.)
Dr. Jekyll and Mr. Hyde
　(Pioneer Film Corp.)
Dollar for Dollar
Dollars and Sense
Dollars and the Woman
A Double Dyed Deceiver
Down Home
The Dream Cheater
The Dwelling Place of Light
Earthbound
The Empire of Diamonds
Empty Arms
The Eternal Mother
Even As Eve
Everybody's Sweetheart
Eyes of the Heart
Eyes of Youth
The Face at Your Window
Faith
The False Road
The Family Honor
The Fatal Hour
The Fear Market
Felix O'Day
Fickle Women
The Fighting Chance
The Fighting Kentuckians
The Figurehead
Flame of Youth
Flames of the Flesh
The Flaming Clue
A Fool and His Money
Footlights and Shadows
For Love or Money
For the Soul of Rafael
The Forbidden Thing
Forbidden Valley
The Forbidden Woman
The Forged Bride
The Forgotten Woman
The Fortune Teller
From Now On
The Furnace
The Gamesters
The Garter Girl
The Gauntlet
The Gift Supreme
The Gilded Dream
The Girl in Number 29
The Girl in the Rain
Girl of the Sea
Godless Men
The Good-Bad Wife
The Gray Brother
The Great Accident
The Great Lover
The Great Redeemer
The Great Shadow
Greater Than Fame
The Greatest Love
The Green Flame
Guilty of Love
Half a Chance
Half an Hour
Harriet and the Piper
The Harvest Moon
The Heart of a Child
The Heart of a Woman
Hearts Are Trumps
Held in Trust
Heliotrope

A Florida Enchantment
A Good Little Devil
His Majesty, the Scarecrow of
 Oz
The Magic Cloak of Oz
Neptune's Daughter
The Patchwork Girl of Oz
The Spirit of the Conqueror
1915 Alice in Wonderland
 The Miracle of Life
 Peer Gynt
 Rumpelstiltskin
1916 The Black Crook
 The Call of the Soul
 A Daughter of the Gods
 The Dawn of Freedom
 Little Lady Eileen
 Snow White
 Undine
1917 Aladdin and the Wonderful
 Lamp
 Aladdin's Other Lamp
 The Babes in the Woods
 The Bottle Imp
 Cinderella and the Magic
 Slipper
 The Dream Doll
 Jack and the Beanstalk
 Modern Mother Goose
 The Princess' Necklace
 The Seven Swans
 She
1918 Ali Baba and the Forty Thieves
 The Blue Bird
 Little Red Riding Hood
 Movie Marionettes
 Prunella
 Queen of the Sea
 The Star Prince
 The Triumph of Venus
 The Wooing of Princess Pat
1919 Eyes of Youth
 What Shall We Do with Him?
1920 Cinderella's Twin
 Humpty Dumpty
 Twinkle Twinkle Little Star

Historical
1912 Cleopatra
 Oliver Twist
 Richard III
1913 The Battle of Gettysburg
 The Battle of Shiloh
 The Count of Monte Cristo
 The Daughter of the Hills
 From the Manger to the Cross
 Ivanhoe
 One Hundred Years of
 Mormonism
 The Volunteer Organist
1914 The Boer War
 Cameo Kirby
 Cardinal Richelieu's Ward
 Charlotte Corday
 Damon and Pythias
 Dan
 The Fatal Night
 The Hoosier Schoolmaster
 Joseph and His Coat of Many
 Colors
 Joseph in the Land of Egypt
 Judith of Bethulia
 The Littlest Rebel
 Manon Lescaut
 Nell Gwynne
 The Ordeal
 Pagan Rome
 The Reign of Terror
 Richelieu
 Samson
 The Seats of the Mighty
 Shannon of the Sixth
 The Sign of the Cross
 Springtime
 The Spy
 Thais
 The Three Musketeers
 Il Trovatore
 Uriel Acosta
 Washington at Valley Forge
 When Broadway Was a Trail
 When Rome Ruled
 Wolfe; Or, The Conquest of
 Quebec
1915 Barbara Frietchie
 The Birth of a Nation

The Campbells Are Coming
Captain Courtesy
Colonel Carter of Cartersville
A Continental Girl
The Coward
Don Caesar de Bazan
Du Barry
Eugene Aram
Evidence
The Face in the Moonlight
Gretna Green
The Heart of Maryland
Hearts and the Highway
In the Palace of the King
The Life of Sam Davis: A
 Confederate Hero of the
 Sixties
The Magic Skin
The Man of Shame
The Martyrs of the Alamo
May Blossom
The Mill on the Floss
Mistress Nell
The Pageant of San Francisco
The Penitentes
The Ploughshare
The Prince and the Pauper
Queen and Adventurer
Sam Davis, the Hero of
 Tennessee
Under Southern Skies
Vanity Fair
The Warrens of Virginia
York State Folks
1916 The Argonauts of
 California—1849
 Black Friday
 Britton of the Seventh
 The Captive God
 The Crisis
 D'Artagnan
 The Daughter of the Don
 Davy Crockett
 Don Quixote
 The Dumb Girl of Portici
 An Enemy to the King
 The Grip of Jealousy
 The Heart of a Hero
 Her Father's Son
 Indiana
 Intolerance
 Joan the Woman
 Kennedy Square
 Macbeth
 My Lady's Slipper
 Naked Hearts
 Ramona
 Rose of the South
 Silks and Satins
 The Sting of Victory
 To Have and to Hold
 The Victoria Cross
 Witchcraft
 A Yoke of Gold
1917 Betsy Ross
 The Bride of Hate
 Camille
 The Conqueror
 Darkest Russia
 The Darling of Paris
 Du Barry
 The Eternal Sin
 The Field of Honor
 The Hidden Children
 The Lincoln Cycle
 The Little Chevalier
 The Little Yank
 A Mormon Maid
 My Fighting Gentleman
 The Princess of Patches
 Rasputin, the Black Monk
 The Scarlet Letter
 The Scarlet Pimpernel
 The Spirit of '76
 Thais
 Those Without Sin
 The Winning of Sally Temple
 The Woman God Forgot
1918 The Beautiful Mrs. Reynolds
 The Fall of the Romanoffs
 Hearts of Love
 Love's Conquest
 Madam Who
 Les Miserables
 Morgan's Raiders

My Own United States
Restitution
Salome
The Sea Panther
The Vigilantes
1919 The Betrayal
 The Brand of Judas
 The Eternal Light
 Evangeline
 The Fall of Babylon
 In the Land of the Setting Sun;
 Or, Martyrs of Yesterday
 The Red Lantern
 A Royal Democrat
 Secret Service
 The Spirit of Lafayette
1920 The Adventurer
 The Copperhead
 Held by the Enemy
 If I Were King
 The Last of the Mohicans
 The Little Shepherd of
 Kingdom Come
 Madonnas and Men
 The Mark of Zorro
 Milestones
 The Mysteries of Paris
19-- Barnaby Lee

Horror
1915 Life Without Soul
 Mortmain
1919 Creaking Stairs
 The Haunted Bedroom
1920 Dr. Jekyll and Mr. Hyde
 (Famous Players-Lasky
 Corp.)
 Dr. Jekyll and Mr. Hyde
 (Pioneer Film Corp.)

Instructional
1915 The Adventures of a Boy Scout
1916 How Life Begins
1917 Motherhood (Minerva Motion
 Picture Co.)
1918 The Yanks Are Coming
1919 The End of the Road
 Fit to Win
 Open Your Eyes
1920 The Living World

Melodrama
1914 A Factory Magdalen
 Fighting Death
 Frou Frou
 The Price He Paid
 Sins of the Parents
 The Taint
 The Temptations of Satan
 Under the Gaslight
 The Woman in Black
 A Woman Who Did
1915 After Dark
 The Alien
 The Cotton King
 The District Attorney
 The Eagle's Nest
 The End of the Road
 Flame of Passion
 For $5,000 a Year
 The Galley Slave
 The Heart of the Blue Ridge
 Her Own Way
 How Molly Malone Made
 Good
 The Lost House
 The Master Hand
 Money
 Prohibition
 Rule G
 The Runaway Wife
 Shadows from the Past
 Silver Threads Among the Gold
 The Sporting Duchess
 The Unwelcome Wife
1916 Charity
 The Supreme Sacrifice
 Temptation and the Man
 The Vital Question
 Wanted—A Home
 Warning! The S.O.S. Call of
 Humanity
1917 The Auction Block
 The Plow Woman
 Tangled Lives
 The Whip
 The Woman in White

1918 Free and Equal
 Rose O' Paradise
 The Testing of Mildred Vane
1919 La Belle Russe
 Checkers
 Human Passions
 In Old Kentucky
 The Lone Wolf's Daughter
 The Midnight Stage
 The Mother and the Law
 The New Moon
 The Profiteer
 The Stronger Vow
 A Woman of Pleasure
1920 A Beggar in Purple
 A Child for Sale
 Children of Destiny
 Heart Strings
 Parted Curtains
 The Rich Slave
 The Scoffer
 Should a Wife Work?
 The Sleep of Cyma Roget
 The Sporting Duchess
 Way Down East
 The Way Women Love
 The Woman Above Reproach
1921 Love's Plaything

Mystery
1914 The Conspiracy
 The Floor Above
 The Murders in the Rue
 Morgue
 The Mystery of Edwin Drood
 The Mystery of Richmond
 Castle
 The Woman of Mystery
1915 An Affair of Three Nations
 The Alster Case
 The Circular Staircase
 The Family Stain
 The Green Cloak
 The House of a Thousand
 Candles
 The House of Fear
 The Ivory Snuff Box
 Lord John in New York
 The Menace of the Mute
 Monsieur Lecoq
 The Moonstone
 The Mystery of Room 13
 On Her Wedding Night
 One Million Dollars
 The Silent Command
 The Vanderhoff Affair
 The Voice in the Fog
1916 By Whose Hand?
 The Missing Links
 The Red Mouse
1917 Apartment 29
 The Argyle Case
 The Blackmailers
 The Bride's Silence
 The Dazzling Miss Davison
 The Devil-Stone
 Feet of Clay
 The Flashlight
 The Great Bradley Mystery
 The Grell Mystery
 Her Beloved Enemy
 The Hunting of the Hawk
 The Iced Bullet
 The Inspirations of Harry
 Larrabee
 Love Letters
 The Maelstrom
 The Mark of Cain
 Mrs. Balfame
 The Mysterious Miss Terry
 The Mysterious Mr. Tiller
 The Mystic Hour
 The Page Mystery
 The Phantom Shotgun
 The Reed Case
 Seven Keys to Baldpate
 The Silent Witness
 A Stormy Knight
 Thou Shalt Not Steal
 The Winged Mystery
1918 The Argument
 The Blind Adventure
 Captain of His Soul
 The Empty Cab
 Empty Pockets
 The Eyes of Mystery

The Face in the Dark
The First Law
$5,000 Reward
A Game with Fate
The Girl in the Dark
The Green God
The Hand at the Window
Hearts or Diamonds?
High Stakes
The Hillcrest Mystery
The House of Silence
In the Hollow of Her Hand
Just for Tonight
The Life Mask
Life or Honor?
Madame Sphinx
Midnight Madness
The Midnight Trail
The Million Dollar Mystery
Money Mad
The Mysterious Client
The Mysterious Mr. Browning
The Queen of Hearts
The Turn of the Wheel
The Voice of Destiny
The White Lie
Who Killed Walton?
1919 The Bandbox
The Black Gate
Cheating Cheaters
A Girl at Bay
His Wife's Friend
The Lincoln Highwayman
The Mystery of the Yellow
    Room
The Open Door
The Poison Pen
A Sporting Chance (American
    Film Co.)
Suspense
The Teeth of the Tiger
The Thirteenth Chair
The Trembling Hour
The Woman Under Oath
1919-20
The Marriage Blunder
1920 The Blue Pearl
The Bromley Case
Chains of Evidence
Circumstantial Evidence
The Devil to Pay
Duds
813
The Evolution of Man
The Fourth Face
The Girl in the Web
Greater Than Love
The House of the Tolling Bell
The House of Whispers
Love Without Question
Luring Shadows
A Manhattan Knight
My Lady's Garter
One Hour Before Dawn
The Paliser Case
The Peddler of Lies
The Price of Silence
The Purple Cipher
The Sacred Ruby
The Scrap of Paper
Terror Island
$30,000
The Trail of the Cigarette
The Triple Clue
The Unseen Witness
The Wall Street Mystery
The Way Women Love
The Woman in Room 13
1920-21
The House of Mystery
Northwest drama
1914 Burning Daylight: The
    Adventures of "Burning
    Daylight" in Alaska
The Call of the North
The Chechako
Pierre of the Plains
Thou Shalt Not
1915 Armstrong's Wife
The Bulldogs of the Trail
The Darkening Trail
The Deathlock
The Heart of Jennifer
Heléne of the North
The Iron Strain

Jack Chanty
Jordan Is a Hard Road
Little Pal
The Man Trail
Pennington's Choice
The Shooting of Dan McGrew
The Song of the Wage Slave
The White Scar
1916 Autumn
The Bait
The Dawn Maker
The End of the Trail
God's Country and the Woman
Nanette of the Wilds
The Primal Lure
1917 The Avenging Trail
The Bronze Bride
The Danger Trail
The Flame of the Yukon
The Girl of the Timber Claims
The Golden Rosary
The Greater Law
Her Fighting Chance
The Land of Long Shadows
The Law of the North
Little Miss Nobody
The Long Trail
A Man's Law
North of Fifty-Three
The Savage
The Silent Lie
Until They Get Me
Wild Sumac
1918 Ace High
Baree, Son of Kazan
Beyond the Shadows
Carmen of the Klondike
Cavanaugh of the Forest
    Rangers
Closin' In
Code of the Yukon
The Guilt of Silence
Heart of the Wilds
Hugon, the Mighty
Jules of the Strong Heart
Laughing Bill Hyde
The Law of the Great
    Northwest
The Law of the North
Nine-Tenths of the Law
Nobody's Wife
The Pen Vulture
Prisoners of the Pines
The Purple Lily
Rough and Ready
Shark Monroe
The Sign Invisible
The Silent Woman
Social Ambition
Tyrant Fear
The Wolf and His Mate
The World for Sale
1919 Beauty-Proof
Children of Banishment
A Daughter of the Wolf
The Devil's Trail
False Evidence
A Fight for Love
Forest Rivals
The Girl from Nowhere
The Girl from Outside
Jacques of the Silver North
The Last of His People
The Little Boss
The Man in the Moonlight
Man's Desire
The Mints of Hell
Paid in Advance
Rose of the West
Shadows
Silent Strength
The Trap
The Valley of the Giants
The Way of the Strong
The Wilderness Trail
The Wolf
Wolves of the Night
1920 The Barbarian
The Challenge of the Law
The Courage of Marge
    O'Doone
The Cyclone
The Golden Trail
Isobel; Or, The Trail's End
King Spruce

The Night Riders
Nomads of the North
The One Way Trail
Out of the Snows
The River's End
The Rose of Nome
Skyfire
The Tiger's Cub
Under Northern Lights
The Valley of Doubt
Rural
1912 Quincy Adams Sawyer
1915 A Bunch of Keys
C.O.D.
The Cub
David Harum
Emmy of Stork's Nest
The End of the Road
Gladiola
The Heart of the Blue Ridge
It's No Laughing Matter
The Little Dutch Girl
The Majesty of the Law
The Old Homestead
The Pretenders
Silver Threads Among the Gold
Still Waters
Sunshine Molly
The Wild Goose Chase
York State Folks
1916 The Apostle of Vengeance
April
The Missing Links
The Trail of the Lonesome Pine
The Wood Nymph
1917 The Adopted Son
The Charmer
A Child of the Wild
The Clean-Up
Flirting with Death
The Girl Without a Soul
Her Good Name
A Magdalene of the Hills
Melissa of the Hills
Peggy, the Will O' the Wisp
A Son of the Hills
Southern Justice
1918 Her Inspiration
The Mating
Naughty, Naughty!
A Nine O'Clock Town
Riders of the Night
The Sea Waif
String Beans
A Woman of Redemption
1919 Almost a Husband
Cowardice Court
Erstwhile Susan
The Feud
Hay Foot, Straw Foot
Heart O' the Hills
The Heart of Youth
His Divorced Wife
Home
The Home Town Girl
In for Thirty Days
In Old Kentucky
In Wrong
Jinx
The Lion's Den
Louisiana
A Romance of Happy Valley
The Shepherd of the Hills
Sue of the South
Twilight
The Unpainted Woman
When Bearcat Went Dry
1920 The Birth of a Soul
The County Fair
A Cumberland Romance
The Dead Line
The Fighting Kentuckians
Forbidden Valley
Huckleberry Finn
Peaceful Valley
Science Fiction
1919 The Great Air Robbery
Social
1913 Eighty Million Women Want-?
From Dusk to Dawn
The Inside of the White Slave
    Traffic
The Lure of New York
The Shame of the Empire State
Ten Nights in a Barroom

Traffic in Souls
1914 A Boy and the Law
Damaged Goods
Protect Us
Trapped in the Great
    Metropolis
Your Girl and Mine: A
    Woman Suffrage Play
1915 The Absentee
Are They Born or Made?
The Battle of Ballots
The Bigger Man
Black Fear
The Blindness of Virtue
Bondwomen
The Boss
The Bridge of Sighs
Children of Eve
Conscience
The Daughter of the People
The Dawn of a Tomorrow
Destruction
The Fight
Gambling Inside and Out
Ghosts
Her Great Match
Heritage
The High Road
The Italian
The Kindling
A Man's Prerogative
The Melting Pot
A Modern Magdalen
Money
The Money Master
The Outcast
Prohibition
Regeneration
Rule G
Salvation Nell
The Voice of Satan
The Warning
The White Terror
The Wolf of Debt
The Woman
1916 And the Law Says
The Corner
Dust
The Heart of New York
Her Bitter Cup
Ignorance
Inherited Passions
Is Any Girl Safe?
The Little Girl Next Door
The Right to Live
The Undertow
Unprotected
The Valley of Decision
The Waifs
War Brides
What the World Should Know
Where Are My Children?
The Woman in Politics
The Writing on the Wall
1917 The Angel Factory
The Bar Sinister
The Best Man
Birth Control
The Black Stork
The Bottom of the Well
Burning the Candle
A Case at Law
Corruption
The Double Standard
Enlighten Thy Daughter
The Eternal Mother
The Fires of Youth
The Food Gamblers
The Girl and the Crisis
The Girl Who Didn't Think
The Girl Who Won Out
Has Man the Right to Kill?
Hate
Her Life and His
The Honor System
In the Hands of the Law
The Man Who Forgot
Master of His Home
The Millionaire Vagrant
The Natural Law
One Law for Both
One of Many
The Price of Her Soul
The Prison Without Walls
The Public Be Damned

The Public Defender
Queen X
The Royal Pauper
S.O.S.
The Saint's Adventure
Should She Obey?
The Single Code
The Social Leper
Who Shall Take My Life?
Who's Your Neighbor?
1918 The Craving
Free and Equal
Honor's Cross
A Little Sister of Everybody
A Man's World
The Mantle of Charity
The Midnight Burglar
Out of the Night
Parentage
Resurrection
A Romance of the Underworld
The Scarlet Trail
The Shoes That Danced
The Sins of the Children
The Spreading Evil
To Him That Hath
Tony America
The Transgressor
Uncle Tom's Cabin
What Becomes of the
    Children?
Whims of Society
1918-19
Once to Every Man
1919 The Amateur Adventuress
Are You Legally Married?
As a Man Thinks
The Boomerang
The Burning Question
The End of the Road
Everybody's Business
The Greater Victory
Heads Win
The House Without Children
Little Comrade
The Long Lane's Turning
The Love Auction
The Man Beneath
The Master Man
Mrs. Wiggs of the Cabbage
    Patch
The Moonshine Trail
The Mother and the Law
My Little Sister
Open Your Eyes
The Other Half
The Praise Agent
The Profiteers
The Red Lantern
The Red Peril
The Red Viper
The Solitary Sin
Thou Shalt Not
The Undercurrent
The Unknown Quantity
The Unwritten Code
The Uplifters
Virtuous Men
The Volcano
Where's Mary?
Wild Oats
The World Aflame
1920 Children Not Wanted
The Face at Your Window
The Gift Supreme
The Gray Brother
The Soul of Youth
The Woman God Sent
Society
1915 Anna Karenina
The Arrival of Perpetua
The Blindness of Devotion
Bought
The Breath of Araby
A Butterfly on the Wheel
The Cave Man
The Cheat
The Climbers
The Dancing Girl
A Daughter of the City
The Edge of the Abyss
The Golden Claw
Her Own Way
Heritage
A Little Brother of the Rich

A Price for Folly
Scandal
Snobs
The Spendthrift
The Sporting Duchess
Who's Who in Society
1916 American Aristocracy
Cousin Jim
A Fool's Paradise
Home
Mrs. Dane's Danger
Vultures of Society
What Will People Say?
A Wife's Sacrifice
1917 Her Sister
The Martinache Marriage
The Masked Heart
Moral Courage
Outcast
Red, White and Blue Blood
The Rescue
The Road Between
The Silence Sellers
A Soul for Sale
1918 The Mask
Men
A Rich Man's Darling
The Shuttle
Social Hypocrites
Society for Sale
The Song of Songs
Sylvia on a Spree
Tinsel
The Unchastened Woman
The Vanity Pool
Virtuous Wives
The Vortex
We Can't Have Everything
The Wild Strain
You Can't Believe Everything
1918-19
The Kaiser's Bride
1919 The Career of Katherine Bush
The Climbers
Common Clay
Dangerous Waters
False Gods
The Gay Lord Quex
Hearts Asleep
Heartsease
The Hellion
His Father's Wife
His Parisian Wife
The Homebreaker
I'll Get Him Yet
The Illustrious Prince
The Intrusion of Isabel
Jane Goes A-Wooing
Josselyn's Wife
A Little Brother of the Rich
Lord and Lady Algy
Love and the Woman
The Love Auction
The Love Cheat
Love, Honor and—?
Love Insurance
The Love That Dares
The Loves of Letty
Lure of Ambition
Male and Female
A Man and His Money
Marie, Ltd.
The Marriage Price
Men, Women and Money
A Midnight Romance
The Miracle of Love
A Misfit Earl
The Moral Deadline
The Other Man's Wife
Other Men's Wives
Prudence on Broadway
Redhead
Restless Souls
A Society Exile
The Steel King
Strictly Confidential
The Third Kiss
Upstairs and Down
The Veiled Adventure
Venus in the East
A Virtuous Vamp
A Woman's Experience
1920 An Amateur Devil
Children of Destiny

The Common Sin
The Dangerous Paradise
For Love or Money
The Furnace
Help Yourself
Her Story
The Hope
A Lady in Love
Oh, Lady, Lady
Risky Business
Silk Hosiery
A Slave of Vanity
Thoughtless Women
Wait for Me
Wings of Pride
The Woman Above Reproach
The Woman Game
Women Men Love
The Wrong Woman
1921 Habit
War drama
1913 The Battle of Gettysburg
The Battle of Shiloh
Victory
1914 Dan
In the Name of the Prince of
    Peace
The Last Volunteer
One of Millions
The Ordeal
Shannon of the Sixth
The Tangle
The War Extra
The War of Wars; Or, The
    Franco-German Invasion
1915 Barbara Frietchie
The Birth of a Nation
The Campbells Are Coming
Captain Macklin
The Captive
A Continental Girl
The Coward
The Crimson Wing
The Despoiler
The Heart of Maryland
I'm Glad My Boy Grew Up to
    Be a Soldier
On the Russian Frontier
The Patriot and the Spy
The Rights of Man: A Story of
    War's Red Blotch
The Warrens of Virginia
1916 Arms and the Woman
The Gringo
The Heart of a Hero
If My Country Should Call
The Impersonation
A Message to Garcia
Powder
Shell Forty-Three
Somewhere in France
1917 Arms and the Girl
The Dark Road
Daughter of Destiny
For France
For Liberty
For the Freedom of the World
For Valour
The Gown of Destiny
The Little American
The Little Yank
The Man Who Was Afraid
Motherhood (Frank Powell
    Producing Corp.)
On Dangerous Ground
Over There
Paws of the Bear
The Pride of New York
Sacrifice
The Spy
Sweetheart of the Doomed
The Test of Womanhood
Treason
War and the Woman
Who Goes There!
Womanhood, the Glory of the
    Nation
The Zeppelin's Last Raid
1918 After the War
An Alien Enemy
The Belgian
The Cross Bearer
The Daredevil
Daughter Angele
A Daughter of France

Every Mother's Son
Fields of Honor
The Firebrand
The Firefly of France
The Girl of Today
The Great Love
The Greatest Thing in Life
The Grey Parasol
Hearts of Love
Hearts of the World
Inside the Lines
The Kaiser, the Beast of Berlin
The Kaiser's Finish
The Kaiser's Shadow, or the
    Triple Cross
Kultur
Lafayette, We Come!
A Law unto Herself
Lest We Forget
Madam Who
Me und Gott
Morgan's Raiders
My Four Years in Germany
The Mystery Girl
No Man's Land
Over the Top
Patriotism
The Price of Applause
Private Peat
The Prussian Cur
The Reckoning Day
The Road Through the Dark
The Road to France
A Romance of the Air
The Sea Flower
A Son of Strife
The Splendid Sinner
The Test of Loyalty
The Tidal Wave
Till I Come Back to You
To Hell with the Kaiser
The Unbeliever
Vive La France!
Wanted for Murder
The Wildcat of Paris
The Woman the Germans Shot
1919 Adele
Alias Mike Moran
America Was Right
Beware
Daring Hearts
The False Faces
The Girl Who Stayed at Home
The Great Victory, Wilson or
    the Kaiser? The Fall of the
    Hohenzollerns
The Heart of Humanity
The Highest Trump
Life's Greatest Problem
The Light of Victory
The Littlest Scout
The Lost Battalion
Love and the Law
The Man Who Stayed at Home
Our Better Selves
Secret Service
Shadows of Suspicion
The Unknown Love
1920 Held by the Enemy
The Little Shepherd of
    Kingdom Come
War preparedness
1915 Guarding Old Glory
The Nation's Peril
Via Wireless
1916 America Preparing
Defense or Tribute?
The Eagle's Wing
The Hero of Submarine D-2
My Country First
Paying the Price
1917 America Is Ready
Draft 258
The Greatest Power
How Uncle Sam Prepares
The Little Patriot
The Man Without a Country
The Message of the Mouse
Miss Jackie of the Army
Miss U.S.A.
The Slacker (Metro Pictures
    Corp.)
The Slacker's Heart
Uncle Sam, Awake!
Who Was the Other Man?

GEOGRAPHIC INDEX

★ The following is a list of those films included in the *Catalog* that were filmed either wholly or partially on location, that is, outside the confines of a traditional motion picture studio. Locations within the United States are listed first, subdivided alphabetically by state, then by city or area. Foreign locations follow, in alphabetical order by country, and subdivided by city or region. We have included only those films for which location shooting has been verified in contemporary sources. Although we have included only dramatic films in this list, researchers interested in geographic locations used in the production of documentaries can compare those films listed in the *Genre Index* under "Documentary" with specific locations cited within the *Subject Index*.

GEOGRAPHIC INDEX

Pasadena
1915 Mr. Grex of Monte Carlo
     The Yankee Girl
1917 Hell Hath No Fury
1918 The Vortex
1919 Better Times
     The Girl Alaska
     The Pointing Finger
     The Woman Michael Married
1920 The Best of Luck

Pine Crest
1918 Revenge

Pleasanton
1918 Revenge
1920 Dangerous to Men

Rio Vista
1917 Jim Bludso

Sacramento
1915 The High Hand
1916 Atta Boy's Last Race
1920 The Girl in the Rain

Sacramento River
1915 Jack Chanty

San Bernardino
1916 The Corner

San Bernardino Mountains
1916 Davy Crockett
     Fighting Blood
1919 Heart O' the Hills
     When Doctors Disagree

San Diego
1915 Pretty Mrs. Smith
     A Submarine Pirate
1917 The Butterfly Girl
1918 Her American Husband
1919 The Highest Trump
     Pettigrew's Girl
1920 Captain Swift
     The Purple Cipher

San Diego—Exposition Park
1919 Toton
1920 Roman Candles

San Diego Military Reservation
1915 The Buzzard's Shadow

San Fernando Valley
1915 The Explorer
1918 The Legion of Death
1919 Sis Hopkins
1920 The Mark of Zorro
     Old Lady 31

San Francisco
1914 Burning Daylight: The
     Adventures of "Burning
     Daylight" in Civilization
     Damaged Goods
     John Barleycorn
     The Valley of the Moon
1915 The Marriage of Kitty
     Mignon
1916 Atta Boy's Last Race
     The Grip of Jealousy
     Hop, the Devil's Brew
1917 Jim Bludso
1919 Eyes of Youth
     A Heart in Pawn
     The Petal on the Current
1920 The Brute Master
     The Cradle of Courage
     Dinty
     Excuse My Dust
     The Fighting Chance
     The Forbidden Woman
     The Inferior Sex
     Outside the Law
     The Prince of Avenue A
     The Purple Cipher
     The Skywayman
     The Unfortunate Sex

San Francisco—Chinatown
1915 Just Jim
1920 Outside the Law

San Francisco—Golden Gate Park
1919 One of the Finest

San Francisco—Nob Hill
1920 Outside the Law

San Francisco Bay Area
1919 The Spite Bride

San Gabriel Canyon
1917 The Eyes of the World

San Jacinto Mountains
1918 Under the Yoke

San Juan Capistrano—San Juan Mission
1920 Hearts Are Trumps

San Pedro
1916 The Daughter of the Don
1918 The Legion of Death
1919 Pettigrew's Girl
     The White Heather
1920 The Best of Luck

San Quentin Prison
1919 Pitfalls of a Big City
     The Trembling Hour

San Rafael
1920 Hearts Are Trumps

Santa Ana
1915 Double Trouble

Santa Barbara
1920 The Blue Moon
     The Gilded Dream
     A Master Stroke

Santa Barbara—Mission
1916 The Garden of Allah

Santa Barbara Islands
1917 Lorelei of the Sea

Santa Catalina Island
1914 The Valley of the Moon
1915 The Woman
     The Yankee Girl
1916 Undine
1917 Sirens of the Sea
1918 No Man's Land
     Treasure of the Sea
1919 Loot
     Miss Adventure
1920 The Corsican Brothers
     A Tokio Siren
     Trumpet Island

Santa Cruz
1917 Hell Hath No Fury
1919 The Island of Intrigue
1920 Jes' Call Me Jim

Santa Cruz Islands
1915 The Quest
1917 The Curse of Eve
1919 Male and Female
1920 The Brute Master

Santa Cruz Mountains
1917 The Girl of the Timber Claims
1920 The Flame of Hellgate

Santa Monica
1914 The Wrath of the Gods
1915 Mr. Grex of Monte Carlo
1918 Without Honor
1919 The Speed Maniac

Santa Ynez Mountains
1916 Judith of the Cumberlands
     Youth's Endearing Charm
1917 Hands Up!

Seven Oaks
1917 The Savage

Sierra Madre Mountains
1918 He Comes Up Smiling
1919 Nugget Nell

Sierra Nevada Mountains
1916 The Unattainable
1919 Children of Banishment
     The Gray Horizon
     The Mints of Hell
1920 The Round-Up

Sonoma County
1920 The Toll Gate

Stockton
1920 The Jack-Knife Man

Sunland
1916 A Sister of Six
1920 The Family Honor
     The Kentucky Colonel

Truckee
1914 Burning Daylight: The
     Adventures of "Burning
     Daylight" in Alaska
     Burning Daylight: The
     Adventures of "Burning
     Daylight" in Civilization
     The Chechako
     An Odyssey of the North
1917 The Greater Law
1918 Baree, Son of Kazan
1919 The Brand
     A Daughter of the Wolf
     Man's Desire
     The Mints of Hell
     The Outcasts of Poker Flats
     The Way of the Strong
1920 Burning Daylight
     The Courage of Marge
     O'Doone
     The Deadlier Sex
     Unseen Forces

Tuolomne County
1920 The Toll Gate

Venice
1915 The Italian

Ventura
1918 Say, Young Fellow!

Whittier
1919 When Doctors Disagree

Yosemite National Park
1915 Just Jim
1917 The Spirit of '76
     The Woman God Forgot
1919 The Dragon Painter
     The Faith of the Strong

Colorado

Colorado Springs
1915 The Eagle's Nest

Denver
1913 The Inside of the White Slave
     Traffic
1920 Dangerous Love

Connecticut
1915 What Should a Woman Do to
     Promote Youth and
     Happiness?
1916 Betty of Graystone
1917 The Apple-Tree Girl

Bridgeport—Fayerweather's Island
1916 The Light That Failed

Greenwich
1915 Via Wireless

Lake Waramang
1916 War Brides

New Haven
1919 The Winning Stroke

New Haven—Yale University
1917 The Courage of the Common
     Place

New London
1913 Ben Bolt
1919 The Winning Stroke

Stamford
1915 How Molly Malone Made
     Good
1920 The Fatal Hour
     The Misleading Lady
     The Sporting Duchess

Wilton
1915 How Molly Malone Made
     Good

Winsted
1915 Right off the Bat

District of Columbia
1914 The Man O' Warsman
1915 Graustark
     The Senator
     The Slim Princess
     The Victory of Virtue
1916 The Colored American
     Winning His Suit
     The Dollar and the Law
     Paying the Price

1917 The Velvet Paw
     The Beloved Adventuress
     The Man Who Forgot
     Yankee Pluck
1918 Little Miss Hoover
     The Service Star
1919 The Capitol
     The Girl Who Stayed at Home
     A Temperamental Wife
1920 In the Shadow of the Dome
     The Key to Power
     Whispers

Florida
1915 Bella Donna
1916 Her Father's Gold
     Hidden Valley
     Lovely Mary
     The Moment Before
1917 Exile
     Heart's Desire
     The Image Maker
     Lady Barnacle
     The Law of the Land
     Strife
     The Undying Flame
     The Warfare of the Flesh
1918 Journey's End
     Queen of the Sea
     The Triumph of Venus
1919 The Isle of Conquest
     Johnny Get Your Gun
     Three Green Eyes
1920 The Flapper
     The Return of Tarzan

Anastasia Island
1917 Thais

Anna Maria Key
1920 The Isle of Destiny

Dry Tortugas
1919 Where Bonds Are Loosed

Everglades
1919 Diane of the Green Van
     The Jungle Trail
1920 Bitter Fruit

Fort Lauderdale
1920 The Idol Dancer

Fort Marion
1918 La Tosca

Jacksonville
1914 Classmates
1915 The Garden of Lies
     Life Without Soul
     Satan Sanderson
     The Stubbornness of Geraldine
1916 Audrey
     Dimples
     The Haunted Manor
     I Accuse
     The Idol of the Stage
     The Lotus Woman
     Man and His Soul
     Tempest and Sunshine
1917 Broadway Jones
     One Hour
1918 The Danger Mark
     Her Boy
     The Knife
     Our Little Wife
     La Tosca
1920 Blackbirds
     Cynthia-of-the-Minute

Mayport
1918 The Danger Mark

Miami
1916 The Struggle
1918 The Life Mask
1919 A Fallen Idol
     The Firing Line
     The Jungle Trail
     Never Say Quit
     A Woman There Was
1920 Cynthia-of-the-Minute
     Marooned Hearts
     The Very Idea
     Why Women Sin
     The Woman Game

Oriental Island
1920 The Isle of Destiny

Pittsburgh
1915 Via Wireless
1916 The Lords of High Decision
1918 Just a Woman
1920 The North Wind's Malice

Shohola
1917 A Mute Appeal

South Bethlehem
1915 The Cave Man

West Chester
1920 The Flaming Clue

Wilkes-Barre
1914 The Three of Us

Rhode Island
1913 Ben Bolt

Block Island
1915 The Daughter of the Sea
      A Man's Making
1917 The Deemster

Conimicut
1915 Cap'n Eri

Newport
1915 The Nation's Peril
1916 The Hero of Submarine D-2
      Paying the Price

North Scituate
1914 The Christian

South Carolina

Charleston
1918 Peg of the Pirates

South Dakota

Bad Lands
1917 The Adventures of Buffalo Bill

Tennessee
1920 The Gauntlet

Chattanooga
1915 The Man Trail

Texas
1914 The Tangle
1915 The Cowpuncher
      The Shooting of Dan McGrew
1919 The Unbroken Promise
1920 Sky Eye

Burkburnett
1920 Witch's Gold

Corpus Christi
1918 Heart of the Sunset

Eagle Pass
1918 Heart of the Sunset

Ellington Aviation Field
1920 Sky Eye

Kingville
1919 The Forfeit

Rio Grande
1919 The Ace of the Saddle

San Antonio
1919 The Forfeit
      You Never Know Your Luck

Vermont

White River Junction
1920 Way Down East

Virginia
1913 The Daughter of the Hills
1916 The Colored American
      Winning His Suit
1918 The Street of Seven Stars

Quantico
1918 The Unbeliever

Richmond
1915 Blue Grass
1917 The Mad Lover

Washington

Bellingham—Lummi Island
1920 The Silver Horde

Cascade Mountains
1919 Fool's Gold

Columbia River
1919 The Faith of the Strong

Seattle
1914 An Odyssey of the North
1919 A Romance of Seattle
1920 The Silver Horde

Spokane
1919 Fool's Gold

West Virginia

Allegheny Mountains
1920 The Key to Power

Charleston
1920 The Key to Power

Logan
1920 The Key to Power

Wisconsin
1920 In the Depths of Our Hearts

Kilbourn
1916 The Return of Eve

Milwaukee
1916 The Misleading Lady

Richland Center
1916 The Truant Soul

Wyoming
1915 The Cowpuncher

Big Horn Mountains
1920 Before the White Man Came

Black Hills
1917 The Adventures of Buffalo Bill

Cody
1918 Heart of the Wilds
      The Hell Cat

Laramie
1917 The Man from Painted Post

Yellowstone National Park
1918 Heart of the Wilds

LOCATIONS IN OTHER COUNTRIES

Austria

Vienna
1918 The Tidal Wave

Azores

Ponta Delgada
1920 Rogues and Romance

Bahamas
1916 20,000 Leagues Under the Sea
1917 Souls Adrift
1920 The Love Flower

Nassau
1915 Nedra
1917 The Submarine Eye
1920 Girl of the Sea
      Marooned Hearts

New Providence
1920 The Idol Dancer

Belgium
1918 The Cross Bearer
      Hearts of the World
1920 Flame of Youth

Bermuda
1915 Always in the Way
1916 The Innocent Lie
1918 Queen of the Sea

Brazil
1918 Tarzan of the Apes

Manaca
1916 The Struggle

Canada
1915 The Shooting of Dan McGrew
1916 The Precious Packet
1917 For the Freedom of the World

Hudson Bay
1914 The Wolf

Labrador
1916 The Price of Malice

Ontario

Cobalt
1914 The Dollar Mark

Moose Factory
1914 The Call of the North

Niagara Falls
1914 Over Niagara Falls

Quebec
1915 The Man of Shame

Cuba
1913 Victory
1914 Marta of the Lowlands
      A Woman's Triumph
1915 The Dictator
1916 The Feast of Life
      A Message to Garcia
1917 The Ghost of Old Morro
      The Slave Market
      The Tides of Fate

Havana
1916 The Chain Invisible
1920 Civilian Clothes

Santiago
1914 Soldiers of Fortune

Egypt
1913 From the Manger to the Cross

France
1914 Absinthe
1915 The Crimson Wing
1918 Hearts of the World

Chateau Thierry
1918 The Greatest Thing in Life

Le Havre
1914 Manon Lescaut

Marne River
1918 The Greatest Thing in Life

Nice
1920 The Empire of Diamonds

Paris
1914 The Lightning Conductor
1916 That Sort
1918 The Tidal Wave
1919 The Virtuous Model
1920 The Empire of Diamonds

Paris—Amiens
1914 Manon Lescaut

Germany

Berlin
1918 The Tidal Wave

Great Britain
1914 Absinthe
1915 The Eternal City
1918 The Great Love
      Hearts of the World
1920 The Fatal Hour

Dover
1916 That Sort

London
1914 The Lightning Conductor
1916 That Sort
1918 Hearts of the World
1919 You Never Know Your Luck

1920 The Empire of Diamonds

Guatemala
1917 The Planter

Indonesia
1920 Shipwrecked Among Cannibals

Italy
1915 The Eternal City
1918 Stolen Orders

Rome
1914 The Coliseum in Films
1915 The Eternal City
1918 The Tidal Wave

Jamaica
1915 Flame of Passion
      The Pearl of the Antilles
1916 A Woman's Honor
1918 Queen of the Sea

Kingston
1916 A Daughter of the Gods
      The Ruling Passion
      A Wife's Sacrifice

Mexico
1914 The Man O' Warsman
1915 The Outlaw's Revenge
      The Shame of a Nation
1916 The Yaqui
1918 The Light of Western Stars
      Queen of the Sea

Juarez
1915 Fighting Bob

Tijuana
1916 The Heart of Paula

Monaco

Monte Carlo
1916 That Sort
1920 The Empire of Diamonds

New Guinea
1920 Shipwrecked Among Cannibals

Palestine
1913 From the Manger to the Cross

Panama
1916 The Ne'er-Do-Well

Panama Canal Zone
1916 The Ne'er-Do-Well

Scotland

Edinburgh
1920 Brain Cinema

Scottish Highlands
1920 Brain Cinema

Spain
1920 Rogues and Romance

Thailand
1920 Shipwrecked Among Cannibals

Union of Soviet Socialist Republics

Moscow
1918 The Tidal Wave

West Indies
1920 Girl of the Sea

LITERARY AND DRAMATIC CREDIT INDEX

★ The following is a list of authors on whose works films included in the *Catalog* are based. Please note that the title of the film and the year of production, not the title of the original literary work, is provided under the author's name. In cases where a film was based on the works of more than one author, the film's title is entered under all of the appropriate names. Following the current practice of *Anglo-American Cataloging Rules II*, names are entered here under their predominant form, whereby pseudonyms are preferred over the author's full name. The reader will thus find entries under the name Mark Twain rather than Samuel Langhorne Clemens.

For complete bibliographic information on literary and dramatic sources, please consult the individual entries in Volume I of the *Catalog*.

LITERARY AND DRAMATIC SOURCE INDEX

Abbott, Eleanor Hallowell
1916 Little Eve Edgarton
        Molly Make-Believe
1920 Old Dad
Abdullah, Achmed
1920 Pagan Love
Adams, Frank Ramsay
1918 My Unmarried Wife
        Unexpected Places
1919 The Pointing Finger
1920 Molly and I
Adams, Frederick Upham
1917 The Bottom of the Well
        When Men Are Tempted
Adams, H. Austin
1919 Out of the Fog
Adams, Justin
1912 Quincy Adams Sawyer
Adams, Samuel Hopkins
1916 The Clarion
1917 A Love Sublime
        Triumph
1919 Wanted—A Husband
Addison, Thomas
1918 The Grand Passion
Ade, George
1914 The County Chairman
1915 The College Widow
        Father and the Boys
        Just Out of College
        Marse Covington
        The Slim Princess
1916 Artie, the Millionaire Kid
1920 Just Out of College
        The Slim Princess
Aiken, George L.
1914 Uncle Tom's Cabin
1918 Uncle Tom's Cabin
Aitken, Robert
1916 A Million a Minute
Albion, Louis
1915 The Running Fight
Alcott, Louisa May
1919 Little Women
Aldrich, Thomas Bailey
1914 Judith of Bethulia
Aleichem, Shalom
1919 Broken Barriers
Alfriend, Edward M.
1914 The Great Diamond Robbery
Allen, Irving Ross
1919 Beating the Odds
Altimus, Henry
1919 The Microbe
Andersen, Hans Christian
1917 The Seven Swans
Anderson, David Wolf
1920 The Blue Moon
Anderson, Frederick Irving
1918 The Golden Fleece
Andrews, Mary Raymond Shipman
1917 The Courage of the Common
        Place
1918 The Unbeliever
Angellotti, Marion Polk
1918 The Firefly of France
Anson, Harris
1917 Her Soul's Inspiration
Anspacher, Louis K.
1918 The Embarrassment of Riches
        The Unchastened Woman
        A Woman of Impulse
Anstey, Frederick
1920 The Fourteenth Man

Arden, Edwin
1915 The Eagle's Nest
Armstrong, Paul
1914 The Escape
        The Greyhound
        Salomy Jane
1915 Alias Jimmy Valentine
        The Bludgeon
        Blue Grass
        The Deep Purple
        The Lure of Woman
        Via Wireless
1916 The Heir to the Hoorah
1918 A Romance of the Underworld
1920 Alias Jimmy Valentine
        The Deep Purple
        Going Some
Arthur, Joseph
1917 Blue Jeans
1918 The Still Alarm
Arthur, Lee
1915 Cohen's Luck
Arthur, Mack
1920 The Isle of Destiny
Arthur, Timothy Shay
1913 Ten Nights in a Barroom
Atherton, Gertrude
1917 Mrs. Balfame
1918 The Panther Woman
1919 The Avalanche
1920 Out of the Storm
Auber, Daniel François Esprit
1916 The Dumb Girl of Portici
Ayres, Ruby Mildred
1918 The Model's Confession
Bacon, Josephine Daskam
1918 The Ghost of Rosy Taylor
Bailey, Oliver D.
1918 Pay Day
1919 A Stitch in Time
1920 The Branded Woman
        In Walked Mary
Baily, Waldron
1915 The Heart of the Blue Ridge
Baird, Edwin
1918 The City of Purple Dreams
Baker, George D.
1919 As the Sun Went Down
Baker, Robert
1914 The Conspiracy
1917 Arms and the Girl
Balestier, Charles Wolcott
1918 The Naulahka
Ballard, Frederick
1918 Believe Me Xantippe
Balmer, Edwin
1915 Via Wireless
1919 Blind Man's Eyes
Balzac, Honore de
1915 The Magic Skin
1920 The Dream Cheater
Barbier, Jules
1915 Mignon
Barbour, Edwin
1914 Northern Lights
Barcus, James S.
1915 The Governor's Boss
Barnard, Charles
1920 The County Fair
Barnes, Howard McKent
1916 The Little Shepherd of Bargain
        Row
Barratt, Augustus
1915 My Best Girl

Barrett, Wilson
1913 Hoodman Blind
1914 The Sign of the Cross
1916 A Man of Sorrow
Barrie, James M.
1915 The Little Gypsy
1919 Male and Female
1920 Half an Hour
Barron, Elwyn Alfred
1918 The House of Silence
Barry, Thomas
1916 The Upstart
Barrymore, Jean
1917 The Black Wolf
Barstow, Montagu
1917 The Scarlet Pimpernel
Bartholomae, Philip
1915 Little Miss Brown
        Over Night
1916 Daredevil Kate
Bartlett, Frederick Orin
1915 The Seventh Noon
1917 The Lady in the Library
1919 Alias Mike Moran
        The Lion's Den
        The Spender
Bartley, Nalbro
1918 The Lure of Luxury
        The Vanity Pool
1919 The Bramble Bush
1920 The Amateur Wife
1922 The Cynic Effect
Bartram, Clara *see* **Miller, Alice Duer**
Baum, L. Frank
1914 His Majesty, the Scarecrow of
        Oz
        The Last Egyptian
        The Patchwork Girl of Oz
Beach, Rex
1914 The Spoilers
1916 The Ne'er-Do-Well
1917 The Auction Block
        The Barrier
        Pardners
1918 Heart of the Sunset
        Laughing Bill Hyde
        Too Fat to Fight
1919 The Brand
        The Crimson Gardenia
        The Girl from Outside
        The Vengeance of Durand
1920 Going Some
        The North Wind's Malice
        The Silver Horde
Beban, George
1915 The Alien
Bechdolt, Frederic R.
1918 The Hard Rock Breed
        Thieves' Gold
Belasco, David
1914 La Belle Russe
        Lord Chumley
        Rose of the Rancho
1915 Du Barry
        The Girl I Left Behind Me
        The Girl of the Golden West
        The Heart of Maryland
        May Blossom
        Zaza
1916 Sweet Kitty Bellairs
1919 La Belle Russe
Bell, C. W.
1920 Parlor, Bedroom and Bath
Bell, Pearl Doles
1920 Her Elephant Man
        Love's Harvest

Belot, Adolphe
1913 The Stranglers of Paris
Bennet, Robert Ames
1916 Into the Primitive
1920 His Temporary Wife
Bennett, Arnold
1920 Milestones
Bennett, John
19-- Barnaby Lee
Bennett-Thompson, Lillian
1920 The Gauntlet
Benrimo, J. H.
1920 The Willow Tree
Beresford, Leslie *see* **Pan**
Bernard, Tristan
1919 The Love Cheat
Bernauer, Rudolph
1915 The Chocolate Soldier
Bernstein, Henri
1914 The Thief
1915 Samson
1920 The Thief
Berr, Georges
1914 The Million
Berton, Pierre François Samuel
1915 Zaza
Biggers, Earl Derr
1917 The Gown of Destiny
        Seven Keys to Baldpate
1918 The Blind Adventure
        Inside the Lines
1919 Love Insurance
Bishop, Henry Rowley
1914 Home, Sweet Home
Bisson, Alexandre
1916 Madame X
1920 Her Beloved Villain
        Madame X
Bizet, Georges
1916 Charlie Chaplin's Burlesque on
        "Carmen"
Blackwood, John H.
1919 Come Again Smith
Blair, Nan
1919 Whom the Gods Would
        Destroy
Blaney, Charles E.
1914 Across the Pacific
        The Dancer and the King
Bleneau, Adele
1919 Adele
Blossom, Henry Martyn
1913 Checkers
1915 The Slim Princess
1919 Checkers
1920 The Slim Princess
Boggs, Russell A.
1920 Sand!
Bolton, Guy
1919 Oh, Boy!
1920 Oh, Lady, Lady
        Polly with a Past
Bonelli, William
1915 An American Gentleman
Bonner, Geraldine
1918 Sauce for the Goose
1920 The Girl in the Web
Booth, Hilliard
1919 The Black Gate
Borrow, George
1915 The Broken Law
Boucicault, Dion
1913 Across the Continent
1914 Rip Van Winkle
1915 After Dark

Eddy, Mary Baker
1918 And a Still Small Voice
Edgelow, Thomas
1919 The Amateur Adventuress
1920 Life's Twist
Edwards, I. W.
1915 Via Wireless
Eggleston, Edward
1914 The Hoosier Schoolmaster
Eliot, George
1915 The Mill on the Floss
1916 Silas Marner
1920 The Little Outcast
Elliott, Francis Perry
1917 The Haunted Pajamas
The Square Deceiver
1918 Lend Me Your Name
Pals First
Ellis, Edith
1917 Mary Jane's Pa
1918 The Triumph of the Weak
1920 The Point of View
Ellis, John Breckenridge
1915 Emmy of Stork's Nest
1919 The Love Hunger
1920 Lahoma
Ellis, Sidney R.
1917 Darkest Russia
Emerson, John
1914 The Conspiracy
Empey, Arthur Guy
1918 Over the Top
Endicott, Ruth Belmore
1919 Carolyn of the Corners
England, George Allan
1916 The Alibi
1918 The Brass Check
1920 The Gift Supreme
English, Thomas Dunn
1913 Ben Bolt
Enthoven, Gabriel
1916 The Quest of Life
Erastov, George
1915 Sold
Erckmann, Emile
1918 The Bells
Esmond, Henry V.
1915 When We Were Twenty-One
1918 Under the Greenwood Tree
1920 Dangerous to Men
Evans, August J.
1914 St. Elmo
1915 Beulah
God's Witness
1920 The Price of Silence
Evans, Ida M.
1918 Limousine Life
The Way of a Man with a
Maid
1920 The Path She Chose
Evans, Larry
1916 Then I'll Come Back to You
1917 Cassidy
The Silent Lie
When a Man Sees Red
1918 The Wife He Bought
1918-19
Once to Every Man
1920 Someone in the House
Fagan, James B.
1915 Bella Donna
1919 Hawthorne of the U.S.A.
Fairfax, Marion
1916 The Chaperon
Fargus, Frederick John see **Conway,
Hugh**
Farrere, Claude
1920 The Right to Love
Fauley, Wilbur Finley
1920 Jenny Be Good
Faust, Frederick see **Brand, Max**
Fechter, Charles
1913 The Count of Monte Cristo
Fenn, Frederick
1920 Suds
Fenollosa, Mary McNeil
1917 The Eternal Mother
1918 Such a Little Pirate
1919 The Dragon Painter
1920 The Breath of the Gods

Ferber, Edna
1918 Our Mrs. McChesney
1919 The Gay Old Dog
Ferguson, William Blair Morton
1917 Zollenstein
Ferike, Boris
1915 Seven Sisters
Feuillet, Octave
1916 A Parisian Romance
Field, Salisbury
1920 Twin Beds
Fielding, Howard
1917 The Inspirations of Harry
Larrabee
Mentioned in Confidence
Fischer, Parker
1919 Stripped for a Million
Fisher, Harry Conway (Bud)
1919 The Adventure Shop
Fiske, Harrison Grey
1915 The District Attorney
Fitch, Clyde
1914 The Straight Road
1915 Barbara Frietchie
The Climbers
The Cowboy and the Lady
Her Great Match
Her Own Way
The Moth and the Flame
The Stubbornness of Geraldine
1916 Captain Jinks of the Horse
Marines
The City
The Girl with the Green Eyes
The Heart of a Hero
The Way of the World
The Woman in the Case
1917 Her Sister
1918 The Girl and the Judge
1919 The Climbers
Girls
A Virtuous Vamp
1920 The Frisky Mrs. Johnson
The Truth
Fitzball, Edward
1915 Don Caesar de Bazan
Fitzgerald, F. Scott
1920 The Chorus Girl's Romance
Husband Hunter
Flagg, James Montgomery
1914 The Adventures of Kitty Cobb
Flaubert, Gustav
1917 Wife Number Two
Fleming, Carroll
1915 The Master Hand
Flers, Robert de
1917 The Beautiful Adventure
1918 Love Watches
Flexner, Anne Crawford
1914 Mrs. Wiggs of the Cabbage
Patch
1919 Mrs. Wiggs of the Cabbage
Patch
1920 The Blue Pearl
Fontaine, Lorne H.
1919 The Scarlet Shadow
Foote, John Tainter
1919 Toby's Bow
Footner, Hulbert
1915 Jack Chanty
Sealed Valley
1917 Shirley Kaye
Forbes, James
1915 The Chorus Lady
The Commuters
1916 The Traveling Salesman
Ford, Harriet
1916 The Fourth Estate
1917 The Argyle Case
The Dummy
1920 A Lady in Love
Forest, Louis
1915 The Curious Conduct of Judge
Legarde
Forman, Justus Miles
1915 The Garden of Lies
1918 Buchanan's Wife
Forst, E.
1919 Fools and Their Money

Foster, David S.
1916 The Oval Diamond
Foster, Mary Louise
1920 Old Lady 31
Foster, Maximilian
1918 Rich Man, Poor Man
Fox, John, Jr.
1914 The Trail of the Lonesome Pine
1916 The Trail of the Lonesome Pine
1919 Heart O' the Hills
1920 A Cumberland Romance
The Little Shepherd of
Kingdom Come
France, Anatole
1914 Thais
1917 Thais
Frankau, Mrs. Julia Davis see **Danby,
Frank**
Franklin, Edgar
1916 The Rail Rider
1917 Lady Barnacle
1918 All Night
Annexing Bill
Opportunity
1919 The Dub
The Web of Chance
1920 Beware of the Bride
Don't Ever Marry
Everything but the Truth
Fixed by George
Frappa, Jean Jose
1920 Billions
Fredericks, Arnold see **Kummer,
Frederick Arnold**
Freeman, Mary Eleanor (Wilkins)
1917 An Alabaster Box
1919 False Evidence
French, Anne Warner
1918 Gay and Festive Claverhouse
Freud, Sigmund
1917 The Mystic Hour
Froest, Frank
1917 The Grell Mystery
The Maelstrom
Frondaie, Pierre
1920 The Right to Love
The Woman and the Puppet
Fulda, Ludwig
1914 The Lost Paradise
Fulton, Maude
1919 The Brat
Furness, Edith Ellis
1915 Seven Sisters
Furniss, Grace Livingston
1914 The Pride of Jennico
1915 Gretna Green
Furthmann, Julius Grinnell
1918 A Camouflage Kiss
Futrelle, Jacques
1915 The High Hand
1916 Elusive Isabel
1919 The Painted World
1920 My Lady's Garter
Futrelle, May Peel
1915 Secretary of Frivolous Affairs
Fyles, Franklyn
1915 The Girl I Left Behind Me
Gabault, Paul
1918 The Richest Girl
Gaboriau, Emile
1915 The Family Stain
Monsieur Lecoq
1916 The Evil Women Do
1917 Thou Shalt Not Steal
Galdós, Benito Pérez
1918 Beauty in Chains
Gallet, Louis
1917 Thais
Gallon, Tom
1918 The Cruise of the
Make-Believes
Gambier, Kenyon
1919 Love in a Hurry
Gannet, Lotta
1918 Her Decision
Garcia Gutierrez, Antonio
1914 Il Trovatore
Garland, Hamlin
1916 Hesper of the Mountains
1917 The Captain of the Gray Horse
Troop
Money Magic

1918 Cavanaugh of the Forest
Rangers
Gates, Eleanor
1914 Doc
1917 The Plow Woman
The Poor Little Rich Girl
1920 Cupid, the Cowpuncher
Gates, H. L.
1919 Auction of Souls
Gavault, Paul
1918 My Wife
Gebest, Charles J.
1916 The Red Widow
Geoffreys, Oliver W.
1916 The Ransom
Gerald, Florence
1915 The Woman Pays
Gerard, James W.
1918 My Four Years in Germany
Gérard, Rosemond
1914 A Good Little Devil
Gershwin, George
1920 La La Lucille
Gibbs, George
1915 The Flaming Sword
1916 The Silent Battle
1917 Paradise Garden
1919 Shadows of Suspicion
Gibson, Charles Dana
1914 The Education of Mr. Pipp
Giesy, John U.
1918 The Eyes of Mystery
The Kaiser's Shadow, or the
Triple Cross
Gilbert, Sir William Schwenck
1918 Fan Fan
Gillette, William
1915 Esmeralda
1916 Sherlock Holmes
1919 Secret Service
1920 Held by the Enemy
Too Much Johnson
Gillmore, Rufus
1915 The Alster Case
Gilmore, Paul
1914 Captain Alvarez
Giltner, Leigh Gordon
1917 The Understudy
1920 The Broadway Bubble
Glyn, Elinor
1914 Three Weeks
1916 One Day
1917 One Hour
1918 The Reason Why
1919 The Career of Katherine Bush
Goddard, Charles W.
1914 The Ghost Breaker
1916 The Misleading Lady
1920 The Misleading Lady
Goethe, Johann Wolfgang von
1915 Mignon
Goldman, Mayer C.
1917 The Public Defender
Goldsmith, Oliver
1917 The Vicar of Wakefield
Gollomb, Joseph
1919 A Girl at Bay
More Deadly Than the Male
Goodchild, George
1920 The Tiger's Cub
Goodhue, Willis M.
1915 The Fixer
Goodman, Jules Eckert
1914 Mother
1915 The Silent Voice
1916 Love's Crucible
The Man Who Stood Still
1919 The Trap
Goodrich, Arthur
1920 Yes or No
Goose, Elizabeth Foster
1917 Polly Put the Kettle On
Gordin, Jacob
1915 Kreutzer Sonata
Gordon, Charles William see **Connor,
Ralph**
Gordon-Lennox, Cosmo
1917 Her Sister

Gorman, Jack
1917 Corruption
Gorsse, Henri de
1918 The Studio Girl
Goss, Charles Frederick
1914 The Redemption of David
         Corson
Goulding, Edmund
1916 The Quest of Life
Graeve, Oscar
1919 The Home Town Girl
Granville-Barker, Harley
1918 Prunella
Gray, Maxwell
1915 Sealed Lips
1917 The Last Sentence
Gray, Thomas
1915 The Labyrinth
Gray, William B.
1913 The Volunteer Organist
Greene, Clay M.
1914 Forgiven; Or, The Jack of
         Diamonds
Greene, Frances Nimmo
1920 The Devil to Pay
Gregory, Jackson
1917 The Man from Painted Post
         The Secret of Black Mountain
         Under Handicap
1919 Six Feet Four
1920 The Joyous Troublemaker
Gresac, Fred de
1915 Cora
         The Marriage of Kitty
Grey, Zane
1917 The Heart of Texas Ryan
1918 The Border Legion
         The Light of Western Stars
         The Rainbow Trail
         Riders of the Purple Sage
1919 Desert Gold
         The Last of the Duanes
         The Lone Star Ranger
1920 Riders of the Dawn
         The U.P. Trail
Grimm, Jakob Ludwig Karl
1915 Rumpelstiltskin
1916 Snow White
1917 The Babes in the Woods
Grimm, Wilhelm
1915 Rumpelstiltskin
1916 Snow White
1917 The Babes in the Woods
Grismer, Joseph R.
1920 Way Down East
Grove, F. C.
1917 Forget-Me-Not
Guernon, Charles
1919 Eyes of Youth
1920 Eyes of Youth
Guillemaud, Marcel
1914 The Million
Guimerá, Ángel
1914 Marta of the Lowlands
1916 Maria Rosa
Gunter, Archibald Clavering
1914 A Florida Enchantment
         Mr. Barnes of New York
1915 The Man Behind the Door
1916 The Surprises of an Empty
         Hotel
1917 The Man of Mystery
Guthrie, Thomas Anstey see Anstey,
   Frederick
Hackett, Walter
1915 Regeneration
1919 It Pays to Advertise
Haggard, H. Rider
1914 Jess
1916 The Grasp of Greed
1917 Heart and Soul
         She
Hale, Charles H.
1915 A Black Sheep
Hale, Edward Everett
1917 The Man Without a Country
1918 My Own United States
Halévy, Ludovic
1914 Frou Frou
1916 Bettina Loved a Soldier
         Charlie Chaplin's Burlesque on
         "Carmen"

1917 A Hungry Heart
Hall, Bert
1918 A Romance of the Air
Hall, Blair
1917 Alias Mrs. Jessop
         The Silence Sellers
1918 The Marriage Lie
Hall, Franklyn
1920 Parted Curtains
Hall, Holworthy
1920 The Six Best Cellars
Hall, Howard
1917 The Natural Law
Hallowell, James Mott
1919 The Spirit of Lafayette
Halsey, Forrest
1918 The Triumph of the Weak
Hamilton, Cosmo
1915 The Blindness of Virtue
1917 Scandal
1918 The Sins of the Children
1919 Eve in Exile
         Men, Women and Money
         The Miracle of Love
         Restless Souls
         Who Cares?
1921 Midsummer Madness
Hamilton, Hale
1918 The Return of Mary
Hamilton, Henry
1915 The Great Ruby
         The Sins of Society
         The Sporting Duchess
1917 The Whip
1918 Stolen Orders
1919 The White Heather
1920 The Best of Luck
         The Hope
         The Sporting Duchess
The Hanlon brothers
1914 Fantasma
Harben, Will N.
1918 The Desired Woman
Harcourt, Cyril
1918 A Lady's Name
         A Pair of Silk Stockings
Hardy, Thomas
1913 Tess of the D'Urbervilles
Harkins, James W., Jr.
1914 Northern Lights
Harriman, Karl
1919 Chasing Rainbows
Harris, Augustus
1915 The Sporting Duchess
1920 The Sporting Duchess
Harris, Charles K.
1914 After the Ball
1915 Always in the Way
         Hearts of Men
1919 Break the News to Mother
Harris, Corra
1920 Husbands and Wives
Harris, Credo Fitch
1918 One Dollar Bid
Harris, Elmer
1915 Pretty Mrs. Smith
1920 So Long Letty
Harris, Kennett
1917 Fools for Luck
Harris, Theodosia
1915 The Martyrs of the Alamo
Harris-Burland, John Burland
1919 His Wife's Friend
Harrison, Mrs. Burton
1914 The Unwelcome Mrs. Hatch
Harrison, Henry Sydnor
1915 Captivating Mary Carstairs
Hart, Daniel L.
1920 The Parish Priest
Harte, Bret
1914 Salomy Jane
1915 The Lily of Poverty Flat
         M'liss
         A Phyllis of the Sierras
1916 The Half-Breed
         Tennessee's Pardner
         Two Men of Sandy Bar
1918 The Dawn of Understanding
         M'liss
         Tongues of Flame
1919 The Gray Wolf's Ghost
         The Outcasts of Poker Flats

1920 Fighting Cressy
Hartman, Roger
1919 A Sporting Chance (Famous
         Players-Lasky Corp.)
Harve, Paul
1917 Alma, Where Do You Live?
Harvey, Frank
1917 Shall We Forgive Her?
Harwood, H. M.
1917 Please Help Emily
1919 The Misleading Widow
Hastings, Basil McDonald
1916 That Sort
Hatton, Fanny
1919 The Indestructible Wife
         Lombardi, Ltd.
         Upstairs and Down
1920 The Great Lover
         The Walk-Offs
Hatton, Frederic
1919 The Indestructible Wife
         Lombardi, Ltd.
         Upstairs and Down
1920 The Great Lover
         The Walk-Offs
Hatton, Joseph
1916 John Needham's Double
Hauerbach, Otto
1917 Madame Sherry
         The Silent Witness
1918 The Girl of My Dreams
1920 Youth's Desire
Hawkins, Anthony Hope see Hope,
   Anthony
Hawthorne, Nathaniel
1916 Feathertop
1917 The Scarlet Letter
Hay, Ian
1919 The Common Cause
Hay, James, Jr.
1917 The Man Who Forgot
Hay, John
1917 Jim Bludso
Hayakawa, Sessue
1919 A Heart in Pawn
Hazeltine, Horace
1915 The Sable Lorcha
1918 The Appearance of Evil
1920 The Midnight Bride
Hazelton, George Cochrane
1915 Mistress Nell
         The Raven
Heath, Evelyn
1916 Saving the Family Name
Hemmerde, Edward
1915 A Butterfly on the Wheel
Henderson, Isaac
1915 The Mummy and the
         Humming Bird
Henderson, Jessie E.
1920 An Amateur Devil
Hendryx, James B.
1917 The Promise
1919 The Mints of Hell
1920 The Texan
Hennequin, Maurice
1916 Madame La Presidente
Henry, O.
1915 Alias Jimmy Valentine
1917 Blind Man's Holiday
         The Defeat of the City
         The Duplicity of Hargraves
         I Will Repay
         The Indian Summer of Dry
         Valley Johnson
         Madame Bo-Peep
         A Night in New Arabia
         The Renaissance at Charleroi
         The Skylight Room
1918 An American Live Wire
         The Changing Woman
         Everybody's Girl
         Find the Woman
         One Thousand Dollars
1919 The Unknown Quantity
         You're Fired
1920 A Double Dyed Deceiver
         The Garter Girl
Herbert, Carl
1916 Her American Prince

Herbert, Victor
1915 Old Dutch
Herczeg, Ferencz
1915 Seven Sisters
Herman, Henry
1919 The Silver King
Herne, James A.
1914 Hearts of Oak
         Shore Acres
1920 Shore Acres
Herne, Julie
1920 The Misfit Wife
Herron, Stella Wynne
1916 Shoes
Hervey, William Addison
1914 Aftermath
Hewlett, Maurice
1915 The Spanish Jade
Heyland, Alexine
1919 The Gold Cure
Hichens, Robert Smythe
1915 Bella Donna
1916 The Garden of Allah
1917 Barbary Sheep
Hicks, Seymour
1918 Sporting Life
Higgins, David K.
1914 His Last Dollar
1916 At Piney Ridge
Hill, Ethel
1918 The Guilt of Silence
Hilliard, Robert
1915 The Avalanche
Hines, Arlin Van Ness
1920 Her Honor the Mayor
Hirsch, Louis A.
1919 Strictly Confidential
1920 Youth's Desire
Hobart, George V.
1914 Mrs. Black Is Back
1915 Old Dutch
         Wildfire
         The Yankee Girl
1917 Alma, Where Do You Live?
1918 Our Mrs. McChesney
1920 What's Your Husband Doing?
Hoffe, Monckton
1917 Panthea
Hoffman, Aaron
1920 Nothing but Lies
Holland, James G.
1920 Jes' Call Me Jim
Holland, Rupert Sargent
1917 The Winning of Sally Temple
Holmes, Mary Jane
1914 Lena Rivers (Cosmos Feature
         Film Corp.)
         Lena Rivers (Whitman
         Features Co.)
1916 Tempest and Sunshine
Hooke, Charles Witherle see Fielding,
   Howard
Hope, Anthony
1913 The Prisoner of Zenda
1919 An Adventure in Hearts
1920 Sophy of Kravonia; Or, The
         Virgin of Paris
Hope, Lawrence
1916 Less Than the Dust
Hopkins, Neje
1919 A Woman There Was
Hopkins, Seward W.
1919 The Gray Towers Mystery
Hopwood, Avery
1914 Clothes
1915 Judy Forgot
1918 Our Little Wife
1919 Fair and Warmer
         Sadie Love
1920 Clothes
         Guilty of Love
Hornblow, Arthur
1919 The Isle of Conquest
Hornung, E. W.
1917 Raffles, the Amateur
         Cracksman
1919 Out of the Shadow
1920 Dead Men Tell No Tales

Hoschna, Karl L.
1918 The Girl of My Dreams
Hough, Emerson
1915 The Campbells Are Coming
1920 The Broken Gate
        The Sagebrusher
Housman, Laurence
1918 Prunella
Housum, Robert
1918 The Gypsy Trail
1919 A Very Good Young Man
Howard, Bronson
1914 Aristocracy
        The Banker's Daughter
        One of Our Girls
1920 The Saphead
        Young Mrs. Winthrop
Howard, Clifford
1920 Locked Lips
Howard, George Fitzalan Bronson
1915 An Enemy to Society
        Snobs
1917 God's Man
Hoyt, Charles Hale
1915 A Bunch of Keys
        A Texas Steer
Hubbard, Elbert
1916 A Message to Garcia
Hubbard, George
1920 The Gauntlet
Hughes, Rupert
1915 All for a Girl
        The Bigger Man
        The Danger Signal
        Excuse Me
1916 What Will People Say?
1917 His Mother's Boy
1918 Empty Pockets
        The Ghosts of Yesterday
        Johanna Enlists
        We Can't Have Everything
1919 The Unpardonable Sin
1920 The Cup of Fury
        The Thirteenth Commandment
Hugo, Victor
1915 Don Caesar de Bazan
1917 The Darling of Paris
        The Eternal Sin
1918 Les Miserables
Hull, George Charles
1918 The Sea Flower
1919 The Light of Victory
Humphries, Joseph
1914 The Ragged Earl
Hurlbut, William J.
1915 The Fighting Hope
1916 New York
        The Writing on the Wall
1918 The Strange Woman
1919 Experimental Marriage
        Romance and Arabella
Hurst, Fannie
1918 Her Great Chance
1919 The Day She Paid
        The Petal on the Current
1920 Humoresque
Hurst, William O. H.
1917 In the Hands of the Law
Hymer, John B.
1914 The Path Forbidden
        When Fate Leads Trump
1915 In the Shadow
Ibsen, Henrik
1915 Ghosts
        Peer Gynt
1916 Pillars of Society
1917 A Doll's House
        Hedda Gabler
1918 A Doll's House
Illes, Eugene
1915 Was She to Blame? Or, Souls
        That Meet in the Dark
Ingleton, E. M.
1915 The Flash of an Emerald
Ingram, Eleanor M.
1915 The Unafraid
1917 Little Shoes
Irwin, Violet
1919 Human Desire

Irwin, Wallace
1917 Hashimura Togo
1918 A Gentleman's Agreement
1919 The Uplifters
        Venus in the East
1920 The Blooming Angel
        Help Yourself
Irwin, Will
1914 Beating Back
1918 The Lady of the Dugout
Isham, Frederic Stewart
1916 Black Friday
        The Social Buccaneer
1917 Aladdin from Broadway
1919 A Man and His Money
1920 Half a Chance
        Nothing but the Truth
Jackson, Arthur J.
1920 La La Lucille
Jackson, Charles Tenney
1917 The Golden Fetter
1920 The Midlanders
Jackson, Fred
1916 The Precious Packet
1917 Annie-for-Spite
1918 The Grey Parasol
        Money Isn't Everything
1919 Let's Elope
1920 A Full House
        La La Lucille
Jackson, Helen Hunt
1916 Ramona
Jacobi, Carl
1920 The Riddle: Woman
Jacobsen, Norman
1918 The Price of Applause
Jacobson, Leopold
1915 The Chocolate Soldier
James, Edgar
1915 The Master of the House
        Not Guilty
Jefferson, Joseph
1914 Rip Van Winkle
1915 The Shadows of a Great City
Jefferson, L. V.
1915 The Supreme Test
Jenkins, Will F.
1920 The Purple Cipher
Jennings, Al
1914 Beating Back
Jepson, Edgar
1917 Polly Redhead
Jerome, Jerome K.
1919 Strictly Confidential
1920 Miss Hobbs
Jesse, F. Tennyson
1919 The Misleading Widow
Johnson, Gladys E.
1917 Two-Bit Seats
Johnson, Julian
1920 Who's Your Servant?
Johnson, Owen
1916 The Salamander
1917 The Varmint
1918 Virtuous Wives
1920 The Woman Gives
Johnston, Mary
1916 Audrey
        To Have and to Hold
Johnston, William Andrew
1920 The House of Whispers
Jókai, Mór
1915 The Hungarian Nabob
Jones, Henry Arthur
1913 Hoodman Blind
1915 The Dancing Girl
        The Evangelist
        Lydia Gilmore
        The Masqueraders
1916 A Man of Sorrow
        Saints and Sinners
1918 The Lie
        Mrs. Dane's Defense
1919 The Silver King
        A Society Exile
1920 The Cheater
        Whispering Devils
Jordan, Elizabeth
1920 The Girl in Number 29

Jordan, Kate
1917 The Tides of Fate
1918 Secret Strings
1919 Castles in the Air
1920 A City Sparrow
Josephus, Flavius
1918 Salome
Judson, Jeanne
1919 Beckoning Roads
Kahler, Hugh M.
1920 The Six Best Cellars
Kaplan, De Witte
1920 Mothers of Men
Kaufman, Edward A.
1916 Soul Mates
Kaufman, George S.
1920 Someone in the House
Kaufmann, Reginald Wright
1914 The House of Bondage
Kelland, Clarence Budington
1917 Efficiency Edgar's Courtship
        The Hidden Spring
        Sudden Jim
1918 The Source
Kelley, Ethel May
1918 The Deciding Kiss
Kelly, Eleanor Mercein
1918 Kildare of Storm
Kelly, Florence Finch
1918 With Hoops of Steel
Kennedy, Charles Ryan
1920 The Servant in the House
Kenyon, Charles
1915 The Kindling
1916 Husband and Wife
1918 The Claim
Kern, Jerome
1919 Oh, Boy!
1920 Oh, Lady, Lady
Kerr, Sophie
1916 The Blue Envelope Mystery
1919 The Invisible Bond
1920 Fickle Women
Kester, Paul
1920 Food for Scandal
Kester, Vaughan
1916 The Manager of the B. and A.
Khayyám, Omar
1915 Flame of Passion
Kidder, Edward E.
1914 Shannon of the Sixth
1920 Peaceful Valley
Kildare, Owen
1915 Regeneration
King, Basil
1915 The Wild Olive
1917 The Inner Shrine
        The Lifted Veil
        The Spreading Dawn
1919 The City of Comrades
1920 The Street Called Straight
King, Captain John
1915 A Woman's Past
Kingsley, Florence Morse
1917 An Alabaster Box
        Sloth
1918 To the Highest Bidder
1919 Cupid Forecloses
Kinkead, Cleves
1919 Common Clay
Kipling, Rudyard
1915 A Fool There Was
1916 The Light That Failed
1918 The Naulahka
Kistemaeckers, Henry
1918 Eye for Eye
Klein, Charles
1913 The Third Degree
1914 The Daughters of Men
        The Gamblers
        The Lion and the Mouse
1915 The District Attorney
1918 The Guilty Man
1919 The Gamblers
        Heartsease
        The Lion and the Mouse
        Maggie Pepper
        The Third Degree
Klein, Manuel
1914 America

Knapp, George L.
1916 Lost Souls
        A Woman's Honor
Knapp, Penelope
1919 The Broken Butterfly
Knibbs, Henry Herbert
1919 The Unbroken Promise
1920 Overland Red
        Sundown Slim
Knight, Percival
1919 The Common Cause
Knoblock, Edward
1920 Blind Wives
        Kismet
        Milestones
Kreider, J. Basil
1920 Bubbles
Kummer, Clare
1919 Good Gracious, Annabelle
        The Rescuing Angel
Kummer, Frederick Arnold
1914 The Brute
1915 The Ivory Snuff Box
        One Million Dollars
1916 The Yellow Pawn
1917 The Slave Market
        A Song of Sixpence
1918 The Green God
        The Other Woman
Kyne, Peter B.
1915 The Long Chance
1916 Humanizing Mr. Winsby
        The Land Just Over Yonder
        The Parson of Panamint
        The Three Godfathers
1917 Light in Darkness
        One Touch of Nature
        Salt of the Earth
1918 A Man's Man
1919 Marked Men
Lacy, Ernest
1914 The Ragged Earl
Lait, Jack
1915 Help Wanted
1919 The Love Burglar
La Motte Fouqué, Friedrich de
1916 Undine
Landeck, Benjamin
1915 The Model
Landis, Frederick
1920 The Copperhead
Landon, Herman
1920 The Way Women Love
Lathrop, Lorin Andrews see **Gambier, Kenyon**
Lathrop, Lottie Blair
1915 Under Southern Skies
Laughlin, Clara E.
1917 The Penny Philanthropist
Lawson, Thomas William
1916 Friday the Thirteenth
Lawson, Captain Wilbur
1915 The Wonderful Adventure
Le Baron, William
1920 The Very Idea
Leblanc, Maurice
1917 Arsene Lupin
1919 The Teeth of the Tiger
1920 813
Lee, Jennette Barbour Perry
1918 Ruler of the Road
Le Gallienne, Richard
1916 The Chain Invisible
Lengel, William Charles
1919 Tin Pan Alley
        Words and Music By—
Lengyel, Menyhert
1914 The Typhoon
Lennox, Cosmo Gordon
1915 The Marriage of Kitty
Leroux, Gaston
1919 The Mystery of the Yellow
        Room
Lestocq, W. H.
1915 Jane
Leverage, Henry
1916 The Twinkler
Levin, Edwina
1919 Happiness à la Mode
1920 The Devil's Riddle

Montgomery, James
1914 Ready Money
1920 Nothing but the Truth
      Youth's Desire

Montgomery, Lucy Maud
1919 Anne of Green Gables

Moody, William Vaughn
1915 The Great Divide

Moore, Carlyle
1915 Stop Thief!
1920 Stop Thief

Moore, Thomas
1920 Hidden Charms

Moreau, Émile
1912 Cleopatra
1917 Cleopatra
1919 The Midnight Stage

Morgan, Byron
1919 The Roaring Road
1920 A Broadway Cowboy
      Excuse My Dust
      What's Your Hurry?

Morosco, Oliver
1915 Pretty Mrs. Smith
1920 So Long Letty

Moroso, John A.
1917 Vengeance Is Mine
1918 The Hand at the Window
      The Shoes That Danced
1920 Dice of Destiny

Morris, Gouverneur
1918 The Fallen Angel
1919 Behind the Door
      When My Ship Comes In
1920 The Penalty

Morris, I. N.
1917 Jim Bludso
1919 The Usurper

Morris, Ramsay
1916 The Ninety and Nine

Morris, William
1920 Mrs. Temple's Telegram

Morrow, Honore McCue Willsie
1918 The Red, Red Heart

Morton, Martha
1915 The Bachelor's Romance

Morton, Michael
1917 The Runaway
1918 The Impostor
      My Wife
      The Richest Girl
      The Yellow Ticket
1920 Deep Waters
      On with the Dance

Morton, Victoria
1918 The Whirlpool

Morton, William
1917 Feet of Clay

Moses, Barr
1917 The Clean Gun

Mulford, Clarence E.
1920 The Orphan

Mumford, Ethel Watts
1920 Dollar for Dollar
      Sick Abed

Murdock, Frank
1916 Davy Crockett

Murfin, Jane
1918 Daybreak
1919 A Temperamental Wife

Murger, Henri
1916 La Vie de Boheme

Murphy, Will C.
1920 Why Women Sin

Murray, Douglas
1915 The Impostor

Najac, Émile de
1915 Divorçons
1918 Let's Get a Divorce

Neidig, William J.
1919 The Fire Flingers

Neilson, Francis
1915 A Butterfly on the Wheel

Nethersole, Olga
1916 The Writing on the Wall

Nicholls, Harry
1915 Jane

Nicholson, Meredith
1914 The Port of Missing Men
1915 The House of a Thousand
      Candles

1916 The Lords of High Decision
1918 The Hopper
1920 Haunting Shadows

Norris, Frank
1914 The Pit
1916 Life's Whirlpool

Norris, Kathleen
1918 The Heart of Rachael
1919 Josselyn's Wife
1920 Harriet and the Piper
      The Luck of Geraldine Laird

Norton, Roy
1915 The Plunderer
1916 The Mediator

Nyitray, Emil
1918 He Comes Up Smiling
1919 The Millionaire Pirate

O'Connor, Mary H.
1917 Souls Triumphant

Ogden, George Washington
1918 Winner Takes All

O'Higgins, Harvey J.
1917 The Argyle Case
      The Dummy

Ohnet, Georges
1915 Dr. Rameau
1917 American Methods

Olsen, Harry B.
1918 Good Night, Paul

Ongley, Byron
1914 Brewster's Millions
1918 He Comes Up Smiling

Oppenheim, E. Phillips
1914 The Floor Above
1915 Mr. Grex of Monte Carlo
1916 The World's Great Snare
1917 In the Balance
      The Silent Master
      A Sleeping Memory
1919 The Cinema Murder
      The Illustrious Prince
      The Long Arm of Mannister
      The Test of Honor

Oppenheim, James
1916 Idle Wives

Orcutt, William Dana
1917 The Moth

Orczy, Emmuska, Baroness
1917 The Scarlet Pimpernel

Ordonneau, Maurice
1917 Madame Sherry

Orlob, Harold
1915 The Labyrinth

Orth, Marion
1919 A Midnight Romance
1920 To Please One Woman

Osborne, Charles
1915 The Face in the Moonlight

Osborne, William Hamilton
1915 The Running Fight
1916 The Catspaw
      The Half Million Bribe
1918 Hearts or Diamonds?
1919 The Boomerang
      Love and the Law

Osbourne, Lloyd
1915 Infatuation

Osmun, Leighton Graves
1918 The Clutch of Circumstance
1920 The Fortune Teller

Ostrander, Isabel
1919 The Island of Intrigue
      Suspense

Ouida
1913 Moths
1915 The Little Dutch Girl
      Strathmore
1916 Under Two Flags
1917 Her Greatest Love

Oxenham, John
1915 Hearts in Exile

Oyen, Henry
1915 The Man Trail
1917 The Avenging Trail

Packard, Frank L.
1915 Greater Love Hath No Man
1918 The Beloved Traitor
1919 The Miracle Man
1920 The Sin That Was His
      The White Moll

Page, Gertrude
1920 Love in the Wilderness

Page, Thomas Nelson
1915 The Outcast

Paine, Ralph D.
1916 The Wall Between

Pan
1920 Big Happiness
      The Furnace

Parker, Gilbert
1914 Pierre of the Plains
      The Seats of the Mighty
1915 Jordan Is a Hard Road
      The Right of Way
1917 The Judgement House
1918 Heart of the Wilds
      Wild Youth
      The World for Sale
1919 You Never Know Your Luck
1920 Behold My Wife
      The Right of Way
19-- Sic-Em

Parker, Lottie Blair
1920 Way Down East

Parker, Louis N.
1914 Joseph and His Coat of Many
      Colors
1915 Rosemary

Parrish, Randall
1918 Keith of the Border

Patterson, Joseph Medill
1914 Dope
1915 A Little Brother of the Rich
1916 The Fourth Estate
1919 A Little Brother of the Rich

Paulton, Edward A.
1915 Niobe

Paulton, Harry
1915 Niobe

Payne, John Howard
1914 Home, Sweet Home

Peacocke, Capt. Leslie T.
1916 Love's Pilgrimage to America
1920 Neptune's Bride

Peake, Elmore Elliott
1919 His Divorced Wife

Peat, Harold Reginald
1918 Private Peat

Peck, George Wilbur
1918 Peck's Bad Girl

Pelley, William Dudley
1919 One-Thing-at-a-Time O'Day

Pendexter, Hugh
1919 A Daughter of the Wolf

Peple, Edward
1914 The Littlest Rebel
      The Spitfire
1915 The Love Route
1916 The Prince Chap
1917 Richard the Brazen
1918 A Pair of Sixes
1919 The Silver Girl
1920 The Prince Chap

Percival, Walter
1920 Someone in the House

Perkin, David
1915 The Running Fight

Perrault, Charles
1914 Cinderella
1918 Little Red Riding Hood
1920 Cinderella's Twin

Pettus, Maude
1917 The Edge of the Law

Pezet, Washington
1915 Marrying Money

Phelps, Pauline
1919 Out Yonder

Philipp, Adolph
1917 Alma, Where Do You Live?
      The Corner Grocer

Philips, Francis Charles
1916 As in a Looking Glass

Phillips, David Graham
1917 The Hungry Heart
      The Price She Paid
1918 The Grain of Dust
      Old Wives for New
1919 Don't Change Your Husband
1920 The Cost

Phillips, Henry Albert
1917 The Royal Pauper

Phillips, Henry Wallace
1918 By Proxy
      The Red-Haired Cupid

Piantadosi, Al
1915 I'm Glad My Boy Grew Up to
      Be a Soldier

Pidgin, Charles Felton
1912 Quincy Adams Sawyer

Pinero, Arthur Wing
1917 The Amazons
1919 The Gay Lord Quex
      The Loves of Letty
      Mind the Paint Girl
1920 His House in Order
      Mid-Channel
      A Slave of Vanity
      Sweet Lavender
      The Truth About Husbands

Poate, Ernest M.
1915 A Trade Secret

Pocock, Roger S.
1919 A Man in the Open

Poe, Edgar Allan
1914 The Avenging Conscience;
      Thou Shalt Not Kill
      The Murders in the Rue
      Morgue

Pollock, Alice Leal
1917 The Co-Respondent

Pollock, Channing
1914 Clothes
      The Little Gray Lady
      Such a Little Queen
1915 My Best Girl
      The Secret Orchard
1916 The Red Widow
1918 A Perfect Lady
1920 Clothes
      She Couldn't Help It

Porter, Eleanor H.
1919 Dawn
1920 Pollyanna

Porter, Gene Stratton
1917 Freckles

Porter, Harold Everett *see* **Hall, Holworthy**

Porter, William Sydney *see* **Henry, O.**

Post, Van Zo
1919 Satan Junior

Potter, George
1920 The Tiger's Cub

Potter, Paul M.
1914 The War of Wars; Or, The
      Franco-German Invasion
1915 Trilby
1917 Arsene Lupin
      The Girl from Rector's
      The Test of Womanhood
1919 A Woman's Experience

Poynter, Beulah
1915 The Little Girl That He Forgot
1920 The Miracle of Money

Presbrey, Eugene W.
1915 The Right of Way
1917 Raffles, the Amateur
      Cracksman

Prévost, Abbé
1914 Manon Lescaut

Procter, Adelaide Anne
1913 The Legend of Provence

Provost, Agnes Louise
1919 Her Kingdom of Dreams

Pryce, Richard
1920 Suds

Pulver, Mary Brecht
1917 The Man Hater

Putnam, John Wesley
1916 Whoso Findeth a Wife

Putnam, Nina Wilcox
1918 The Price of Applause
1919 In Search of Arcady

Quick, Herbert
1915 Double Trouble

Quinlan, J.
1916 The Test

Rabell, Du Vernet
1919 The Woman Michael Married

Rabinowitz, Solomon *see* Aleichem, Shalom
Raceward, Thomas
1915 Sunday
Ragsdale, Lulah
1919 Miss Dulcie from Dixie
Raine, William MacLeod
1919 Eastward Ho!
Fighting for Gold
The Sheriff's Son
Raleigh, Cecil
1915 The Great Ruby
The Sins of Society
The Sporting Duchess
1917 The Whip
1918 Sporting Life
Stolen Orders
1919 The White Heather
1920 The Best of Luck
The Fatal Hour
Hearts Are Trumps
The Hope
The Sporting Duchess
Ramée, Louise de la *see* Ouida
Ramsey, Alicia
1918 Eve's Daughter
Social Hypocrites
Rankin, Mckee
1915 The Runaway Wife
Rath, E. J.
1916 Mister 44
The River of Romance
1919 Too Many Crooks
1920 Good References
Read, Opie
1915 A Yankee from the West
1919 Almost a Husband
1920 The Kentucky Colonel
1921 The Jucklins
Reade, Charles
1919 The Midnight Stage
1920 White Lies
Redmond, Fergus
1914 A Florida Enchantment
Reed, Myrtle
1918 Flower of the Dusk
A Weaver of Dreams
Reid, Hal
1914 At the Cross Roads
1915 The Cowpuncher
1917 The Peddler
1920 The Confession
Reizenstein, Elmer L. *see* Rice, Elmer L.
Remington, Frederic
1917 John Ermine of the Yellowstone
Reynolds, Mrs. Baillie
1920 The Daughter Pays
The Notorious Miss Lisle
Reynolds, Gertrude M. Robins *see* Reynolds, Mrs. Baillie
Rhodes, Harrison
1914 A Gentleman from Mississippi
1919 An Adventure in Hearts
1920 The Willow Tree
Rice, Alice Hegan
1914 Mrs. Wiggs of the Cabbage Patch
1916 A Romance of Billy Goat Hill
1917 Mr. Opp
1918 Sandy
Sunshine Nan
1919 Mrs. Wiggs of the Cabbage Patch
Rice, Edward E.
1913 The Prisoner of Zenda
Rice, Elmer L.
1917 On Trial
Rice, Gitz
1919 The Common Cause
Rice, Louise
1917 The Alien Blood
Richardson, Abby Sage
1914 The Pride of Jennico
Riley, James Whitcomb
1918 A Hoosier Romance
Little Orphant Annie
Rinehardt, John
1914 The Scales of Justice

Rinehart, Mary Roberts
1915 The Circular Staircase
What Happened to Father
1916 Acquitted
1917 Bab's Burglar
Bab's Diary
Bab's Matinee Idol
1918 The Doctor and the Woman
Her Country First
The Street of Seven Stars
1919 23 1/2 Hours' Leave
1920 Dangerous Days
It's a Great Life
Rising, Lawrence Irving
1919 His Bridal Night
Ritchie, Robert Welles
1920 Two Moons
Ritter, John P.
1917 Poppy
Rives, Amélie (Princess Troubetzkoy)
1920 The Fear Market
Rives, Hallie Erminie
1915 Satan Sanderson
1916 The Valiants of Virginia
1919 The Long Lane's Turning
Robbins, Katherine Leiser
1918 The Risky Road
1919 The Scarlet Shadow
1920 The Gilded Dream
In Folly's Trail
Roberts, Alice M.
1914 When Fate Leads Trump
Roberts, Kenneth L.
1918 The Shell Game
With Neatness and Dispatch
Roberts, William L.
1920 Hell's Oasis
Robertson, T. W.
1916 David Garrick
Robins, Elizabeth
1919 My Little Sister
1920 A Dark Lantern
Robinson, Charles Larned
1918 The Scarlet Trail
Robinson, Sidney
1917 The Spindle of Life
Robson, May
1916 A Night Out
Roche, Arthur Somers
1919 Loot
1920 The Sport of Kings
Rockey, Howard P.
1920 Li Ting Lang
Roe, E. P.
1916 He Fell in Love with His Wife
Roe, Vingie E.
1916 The Primal Lure
1918 Wild Honey
1919 Twilight
Rohlfs, Anna Katharine Green
1915 The Millionaire Baby
Rose, Edward
1915 Fighting Bob
Rose, Edward E.
1915 The Rosary
Rosenfeld, Sydney
1916 The Purple Lady
1920 Children of Destiny
Rostand, Maurice
1914 A Good Little Devil
Rouse, William Merriam
1918 Jules of the Strong Heart
Rowland, Henry C.
1915 The Closing Net
1916 The Sultana
1917 Filling His Own Shoes
1919 Bonnie, Bonnie Lassie
1920 Duds
The Peddler of Lies
Royle, Edwin Milton
1914 The Squaw Man
1916 The Unwritten Law
1917 The Squaw Man's Son
1918 The Squaw Man
The Struggle Everlasting
Ruck, Berta
1919 His Official Fiancée
Ryan, Marah Ellis
1919 Told in the Hills
1920 For the Soul of Rafael

Ryley, Madeleine Lucette
1914 An American Citizen
1916 Mice and Men
Sand, George
1915 Fanchon the Cricket
Sanders, Charles Wesley
1918 $5,000 Reward
Sardou, Victorien
1912 Cleopatra
1915 Divorçons
Princess Romanoff
The Pursuing Shadow
The Song of Hate
1916 Diplomacy
The Witch
1917 Cleopatra
1918 The Burden of Proof
Fedora
Let's Get a Divorce
Love's Conquest
La Tosca
1919 Three Green Eyes
Savage, Richard Henry
1914 My Official Wife
Savery, James
19-- Sic-Em
Sawyer, Ruth
1917 The Primrose Ring
Sayre, Theodore Burt
1915 The Commanding Officer
Scarborough, George
1914 The Lure
1915 At Bay
Schomer, Abraham S.
1917 To-Day
Scott, Hugh S. *see* Merriman, Henry Seton
Scott, Lady John
1918 Bonnie Annie Laurie
Scott, Leroy
1916 The Supreme Sacrifice
1918 To Him That Hath
1919 Mary Regan
1920 A Daughter of Two Worlds
Partners of the Night
Scott, Mansfield
1920 One Hour Before Dawn
Scott, Sir Walter
1913 Ivanhoe
1914 A Woman's Triumph
Scribe, Eugène
1916 The Dumb Girl of Portici
Seawell, Molly Elliot
1917 The Fortunes of Fifi
The Sixteenth Wife
Seitz, George B.
1916 The King's Game
1920 Rogues and Romance
Selby, Charles
1915 The Marble Heart
Seltzer, Charles Alden
1917 The Range Boss
1918 The Boss of the Lazy Y
Fame and Fortune
Riddle Gawne
The Trail to Yesterday
1919 The Coming of the Law
Square Deal Sanderson
Treat 'Em Rough
1920 Firebrand Trevison
Forbidden Trails
Selwyn, Edgar
1914 Pierre of the Plains
1915 The Arab
The Country Boy
1916 Rolling Stones
1917 Nearly Married
1919 Let's Elope
Service, Robert W.
1915 My Madonna
The Shooting of Dan McGrew
The Song of the Wage Slave
1916 The Lure of Heart's Desire
The Spell of the Yukon
1920 The Law of the Yukon
Shakespeare, William
1912 Cleopatra
Richard III
1914 The Merchant of Venice
1916 King Lear
Macbeth
Romeo and Juliet (Fox Film Corp.)
Romeo and Juliet (Quality Pictures Corp.)

1917 Cleopatra
Shannon, Robert Terry
1920 The Girl with the Jazz Heart
Sharp, Hilda Mary
1918 A Mother's Sin
Shaw, George Bernard
1915 The Chocolate Soldier
Shaw, Stanley
1919 Fighting Destiny
Sheehan, Perley Poore
1916 The Bugler of Algiers
1918 Brave and Bold
A Society Sensation
The Whispering Chorus
1919 Upstairs
Sheldon, Charles Monroe
1916 The Martyrdom of Philip Strong
Sheldon, E. Lloyd
1918 Out of the Night
1919 False Gods
Sheldon, Edward
1915 The Boss
The High Road
The Nigger
Salvation Nell
1916 A Coney Island Princess
1917 The Call of Her People
1918 The Song of Songs
1920 Romance
Sheldon, H. S.
1915 A Daughter of the City
1916 The Havoc
He Fell in Love with His Wife
1918 Men
Shelley, Mary Wollstonecraft
1915 Life Without Soul
Sherbrooke, Norman
1918 Who Killed Walton?
You Can't Believe Everything
Sheridan, Richard B.
1914 The School for Scandal
Sherman, Charles
1917 The Upper Crust
1918 He Comes Up Smiling
Shewell, L. R.
1915 The Shadows of a Great City
Shields, James K.
1919 The Stream of Life
Shipman, Louis Evan
1917 John Ermine of the Yellowstone
1918 The Grain of Dust
Shipman, Samuel
1920 The Woman in Room 13
Shirley, Arthur
1915 The Model
Short, Marion
1917 The Waiting Soul
1919 Out Yonder
Simon, Charles
1915 Zaza
Sims, George R.
1919 The Life Line
Sinclair, Arthur Stuart
1920 Children Not Wanted
Sinclair, Bertha Muzzy *see* Bower, B. M.
Sinclair, Bertrand W.
1917 Big Timber
Sinclair, Upton
1914 The Jungle
1917 The Adventurer
1920 The Money-Changers
Slayton, Frank
1920 The Inferior Sex
Sloane, A. Baldwin
1914 Tillie's Punctured Romance
Sloane, Edgar
1914 Tillie's Punctured Romance
Smith, Alice M.
1916 The Strength of the Weak
Smith, Edgar
1915 Old Dutch
Smith, F. Hopkinson
1915 Colonel Carter of Cartersville
1916 Kennedy Square
1917 A Kentucky Cinderella
The Tides of Barnegat
1920 Deep Waters
Felix O'Day

Smith, Frank Berkeley
1917 Babette
Smith, Garret
1920 Honest Hutch
Smith, Harry B.
1915 The Labyrinth
Smith, Harry James
1915 Blackbirds
1920 Blackbirds
Smith, Winchell
1914 Brewster's Millions
    The Fortune Hunter
    The Making of Bobby Burnit
    The Only Son
1915 Via Wireless
1920 The Fortune Hunter
    The Saphead
Snyder, Rev. John M.
1914 As Ye Sow
Solomons, Theodore Seixas
1920 The Barbarian
Soutar, Andrew
1918 High Stakes
1919 His Parisian Wife
1920 A Beggar in Purple
    Other Men's Shoes
Spearman, Frank H.
1916 Medicine Bend
    Whispering Smith
1917 Money Madness
    Nan of Music Mountain
Spears, Raymond Smiley
1918 Hoarded Assets
Spillman, Rev. Joseph
1920 The Victim
Spooner, Cecil
1914 Nell of the Circus
Stacpoole, Henry de Vere
1920 The Man Who Lost Himself
Stagg, Clinton H.
1920 High Speed
Stapleton, John
1915 A Gentleman of Leisure
Stearns, Edgar Franklin see **Franklin, Edgar**
Steck, H. Tipton
1917 Gift O' Gab
Steele, Rufus
1915 Rule G
1916 Hop, the Devil's Brew
Steger, Julius
1915 The Fifth Commandment
Stephens, Robert N.
1916 An Enemy to the King
Stephenson, B. C.
1915 The Fatal Card
Sterrett, Frances Roberta
1918 Up the Road with Sallie
Stevenson, Burton Egbert
1916 The Pursuing Vengeance
1917 On Dangerous Ground
Stevenson, John
1920 Hidden Charms
Stevenson, Robert Louis
1917 The Bottle Imp
    Kidnapped
1918 Treasure Island
1920 Dr. Jekyll and Mr. Hyde
    (Famous Players-Lasky
    Corp.)
    Dr. Jekyll and Mr. Hyde
    (Pioneer Film Corp.)
    Treasure Island
    The White Circle
Stewart, Grant
1917 Arms and the Girl
Stock, Ralph
1920 The Adorable Savage
    The Love Flower
Stocking, Charles Francis
1919 The Mayor of Filbert
Stockley, Cynthia
1917 Poppy
1918 The Claw
1920 April Folly
    The Sins of Rosanne
Stodard, Robert
1915 Up from the Depths

Stone, Mary
1916 The Social Highwayman
Stowe, Harriet Beecher
1914 Uncle Tom's Cabin
1918 Uncle Tom's Cabin
Straus, Oscar
1915 The Chocolate Soldier
Street, Julian
1919 The Country Cousin
Stringer, Arthur
1916 The Breaker
    The Hand of Peril
1918 From Two to Six
1919 The House of Intrigue
1920 Are All Men Alike?
Stroheim, Erich von
1919 Blind Husbands
Strong, Austin
1914 A Good Little Devil
Stuart, Leslie
1915 The Slim Princess
1920 The Slim Princess
Sudermann, Hermann
1916 The Flames of Johannis
    Revelations
1917 Magda
Sue, Eugène
1920 The Mysteries of Paris
Sullivan, Arthur
1918 Fan Fan
    The Lost Chord
Sullivan, Francis William
1918 The Flames of Chance
1919 Children of Banishment
    The Wilderness Trail
Sutro, Alfred
1914 The Walls of Jericho
1915 The Builder of Bridges
    John Glayde's Honor
Swan, Mark
1917 The Princess of Patches
1920 Parlor, Bedroom and Bath
Swerling, Joseph
1919 The Love Burglar
Talbot, Haydon
1914 The Truth Wagon
Tarkington, Booth
1914 Cameo Kirby
    The Man from Home
    Springtime
1915 The Gentleman from Indiana
1916 The Conquest of Canaan
    The Flirt
    Seventeen
    The Turmoil
1919 The Country Cousin
Taylor, Charles
19-- The Girl from Alaska
Taylor, Howard P.
1913 Caprice
Taylor, Katharine Haviland
1918 Cecilia of the Pink Roses
Taylor, Marvin
1919 Luck in Pawn
Taylor, Mary Imlay
1919 Putting One Over
1920 The Good-Bad Wife
Taylor, Tom
1916 The Fool's Revenge
Teal, Ben
1917 Poppy
Tellegen, Lou
1920 Blind Youth
Tenno, Heliodore
1919 The Third Kiss
Tennyson, Alfred Tennyson, Baron
1915 Enoch Arden
1916 A Modern Enoch Arden
    Naked Hearts
Terhune, Albert Payson
1916 Dollars and the Woman
    The Years of the Locust
1917 The Happiness of Three
    Women
1918 The Square Deal
1919 The Railroader
1920 Dollars and the Woman
    The Thirtieth Piece of Silver
Terriss, William
1915 The Pursuing Shadow

Terry, J. E. Harold
1919 The Man Who Stayed at Home
Thackeray, William Makepeace
1915 Vanity Fair
Thayer, E. L.
1916 Casey at the Bat
Thew, Harvey F.
1919 The Delicious Little Devil
Thomas, A. E.
1917 The Rainbow
1919 Come Out of the Kitchen
Thomas, Ambroise
1915 Mignon
Thomas, Augustus
1913 Arizona
1914 The Education of Mr. Pipp
    In Mizzoura
    Soldiers of Fortune
1915 Colorado
    The Earl of Pawtucket
1916 The Other Girl
    The Witching Hour
1917 The Burglar
1918 Arizona
    Her Man
    Mrs. Leffingwell's Boots
    On the Quiet
1919 As a Man Thinks
    The Capitol
    In Mizzoura
    Soldiers of Fortune
1920 The Copperhead
    The Harvest Moon
    Rio Grande
Thomas, Eugene
1914 The Man O' Warsman
Thompson, Charlotte
1916 The Strength of the Weak
1917 Rebecca of Sunnybrook Farm
1920 In Search of a Sinner
Thompson, Denman
1915 The Old Homestead
Thompson, Maravene
1916 The Woman's Law
1917 Persuasive Peggy
Thurston, E. Temple
1920 David and Jonathan
Tilden, Freeman
1917 The Customary Two Weeks
    The Small Town Guy
Tillinghast, A. W.
1920 The Discarded Woman
Tilton, Dwight
1916 Miss Petticoats
Titus, Harold
1920 The Last Straw
    Shod with Fire
Toler, Sidney
1918 Playthings
Tolstoy, Leo
1915 Anna Karenina
    Kreutzer Sonata
    A Woman's Resurrection
1916 The Weakness of Man
1918 Resurrection
1919 Atonement
Tompkins, Juliet Wilbor
1919 A Girl Named Mary
    Little Comrade
Townley, Houghton
1916 The Gay Lord Waring
1919 The Bishop's Emeralds
Townsend, Edward Waterman
1915 Chimmie Fadden
    Chimmie Fadden Out West
Tracy, Louis
1914 One Wonderful Night
1919 Wings of the Morning
1920 The Silent Barrier
Train, Arthur
1915 Mortmain
1916 Rose of the South
Trant, Joseph H.
1915 The Devil's Daughter
    Princess Romanoff
Tremayne, W. A.
1915 The Avalanche
Trent, Paul
1917 God's Law and Man's

Treynore, Albert M.
1917 The Flashlight
Troubetzkoy, Princess see **Rives, Amélie (Princess Troubetzkoy)**
Tully, May
1920 Mary's Ankle
Tully, Richard Walton
1914 Rose of the Rancho
Tupper, Edith Sessions
1920 The House of the Tolling Bell
Turnbull, Margaret
1914 Classmates
Turner, George Kibbe
1920 Held in Trust
Turner, John Hastings
1920 Simple Souls
Tuttiett, Mary Gleed see **Gray, Maxwell**
Twain, Mark
1915 The Prince and the Pauper
1916 Pudd'nhead Wilson
1917 Tom Sawyer
1918 Huck and Tom; Or, The
    Further Adventures of Tom
    Sawyer
1920 A Connecticut Yankee at King
    Arthur's Court
    Huckleberry Finn
Tyler, Charles W.
1919 The Exquisite Thief
Tyler, Georgie Vere
1917 The Wax Model
Unger, Gladys
1918 The Marionettes
Uzzell, Thomas H.
1916 Anton the Terrible
Van Campen, Helen
1915 The Man Who Beat Dan Dolan
Van de Water, Virginia Terhune
1916 If My Country Should Call
Van Loan, Charles E.
1915 Buckshot John
    Little Sunset
Van Slyke, Lucille
1920 The Stolen Kiss
Van Vorst, Marie
1915 The Girl from His Town
1916 Big Tremaine
1917 Mary Moreland
Vanardy, Varick see **Dey, Frederic Van Rensselaer**
Vance, Louis Joseph
1914 The Day of Days
1915 The Destroying Angel
1916 The Footlights of Fate
    The Pool of Flame
1917 The Lone Wolf
    The Mainspring
    The Outsider
1918 No Man's Land
1919 The Bandbox
    The False Faces
1920 Cynthia-of-the-Minute
    The Dark Mirror
Vane, Sutton
1914 The Span of Life
1915 The Cotton King
Veber, Pierre
1916 Madame La Presidente
1918 The Studio Girl
Veiller, Bayard
1915 The Fight
    The Primrose Path
1917 Within the Law
1919 The Thirteenth Chair
1920 Burnt Wings
Verdi, Giuseppe
1914 Il Trovatore
Vermilye, Mrs. F. M. see **Jordan, Kate**
Verne, Jules
1914 Michael Strogoff
    'Round the World in 80 Days
1916 20,000 Leagues Under the Sea
Vickers, Harold
1916 The Men She Married
1918 The Talk of the Town
1920 The Ladder of Lies
Voegtlin, Arthur
1914 America
Vollmöller, Karl Gustav
1913 The Legend of Provence

SELECTED BIBLIOGRAPHY

★ The following is a list of books the Catalog staff found valuable for background and note material during the compilation of the Teens volume.

Ackerman, Forrest J. *Lon of a 1000 Faces.* Beverly Hills: Morrison, Raven-Hill Co., 1983.

Aitken, Roy E. and Al P. Nelson. *The Birth of a Nation Story.* Middleburg, Va.: Denlinger, 1965.

Allen, Robert C. and Douglas Gomery. *Film History: Theory and Practice.* New York: Alfred A. Knopf, 1985.

Allgood, Jill. *Bebe and Ben.* London: Robert Hale and Company, 1975.

Allvine, Glendon. *The Greatest Fox of Them All.* New York: Lyle Stuart, Inc., 1969.

Altomara, Rita Ecke. *Hollywood on the Palisades: A Filmography of Silent Features Made in Fort Lee, New Jersey, 1903-1927.* New York: Garland Publishing, Inc., 1983.

American Film Institute Catalog of Feature Films, 1921-1930. Edited by Kenneth Munden. New York: R. R. Bowker, 1971.

Anderson, Gillian B., comp. *Music for Silent Films (1894-1929): An Index.* Washington, D.C.: Library of Congress, nd.

Anderson, Robert G. *Faces, Forms, Films: The Artistry of Lon Chaney.* South Brunswick & New York: A. S. Barnes, 1971.

Asplund, Uno. *Chaplin's Films.* Translated from the Swedish by Paul Britton Austen. South Brunswick and New York: A. S. Barnes, 1976.

Balio, Tino. *United Artists: The Company Built by the Stars.* Madison: The University of Wisconsin Press, 1976.

Ball, Eustace Hale. *Photoplay Scenarios: How to Write and Sell Them.* New York: Hearst's International Library Co., 1917.

Barrow, Kenneth. *Helen Hayes: First Lady of the American Theater.* Garden City, N.Y.: Doubleday and Company, Inc. 1985.

Barry, Iris. *D. W. Griffith: American Film Master.* New York: The Museum of Modern Art, 1940.

Barrymore, John. *Confessions of an Actor.* Indianapolis: The Bobbs-Merrill Co., 1926.

Barrymore, Lionel with Cameron Shipp. *We Barrymores.* New York: Appleton-Century-Crofts, Inc., 1951.

Baxter, John. *King Vidor.* New York: Monarch Press, 1976.

Bertsch, Marguerite. *How to Write for Moving Pictures: A Manual of Instruction and Information.* New York: George H. Doran Co., 1917.

Birchard, Robert S. "Jack London and His Movies." *Film History* 1 (1987): 15-38.

Bitzer, G. W. *Billy Bitzer: His Story.* New York: Farrar, Straus and Giroux, 1973.

Blesh, Rudi. *Keaton.* New York: Macmillan, 1966.

Blum, Daniel. *A Pictorial History of the Silent Screen.* New York: G. P. Putnam's Sons, 1953.

Bodeen, DeWitt. *From Hollywood: The Careers of 15 Great American Stars.* South Brunswick and New York: A. S. Barnes and Company, 1976.

Bodeen, DeWitt. *More From Hollywood: The Careers of 15 Great American Stars.* South Brunswick and New York: A. S. Barnes and Company, 1977.

Bogdanovich, Peter. *Allan Dwan: The Last Pioneer.* New York: Praeger Publishers, Inc. 1971.

Bogdanovich, Peter. *John Ford.* Berkeley: University of California Press, 1968.

Bogle, Donald. *Toms, Coons, Mulattoes, Mammies, and Bucks: An Interpretive History of Blacks in American Films.* New York: The Viking Press, 1973.

Bojarski, Richard and Kenneth Beale. *The Films of Boris Karloff.* Secaucus, N.J.: The Citadel Press, 1974.

Bordwell, David, Janet Staiger and Kristen Thompson. *The Classical Hollywood Cinema: Film Style and Mode of Production to 1960.* New York: Columbia University Press, 1985.

Bordwell, David and Kristin Thompson. *Film Art: An Introduction.* Reading, Mass.: Addison-Wesley, 1979.

Bronner, Edwin J. *The Encyclopedia of the American Theater, 1900–1975*. San Diego and New York: A. S. Barnes and Company, 1980.

Brown, Karl. *Adventures with D. W. Griffith*. New York: Farrar, Straus and Giroux, 1973.

Brownlow, Kevin. *Hollywood: The Pioneers*. Photographs selected by John Kobal. New York: Alfred A. Knopf, 1979.

Brownlow, Kevin. *The Parade's Gone By*. New York: Alfred A. Knopf, 1968.

Brownlow, Kevin. *The War the West and the Wilderness*. New York: Alfred A. Knopf, 1978.

Burke, Billie with Cameron Shipp. *With a Feather on My Nose*. New York: Appleton-Century-Crofts, Inc., 1949.

Campbell, Craig W. *Reel American and World War I: A Comprehensive Filmography and History of Motion Pictures in the United States, 1914-1920*. Jefferson, N.C.: McFarland & Company, Inc., 1985.

Carey, Gary. *Doug & Mary: A Biography of Douglas Fairbanks & Mary Pickford*. New York: E. P. Dutton, 1977.

Carr, Catherine. *The Art of Photoplay Writing*. New York: The Hannis Jordan Co., 1914.

Castle, Irene. *Castles in the Air*. New York: Da Capo Press, Inc., 1980.

Chaplin, Charles. *My Autobiography*. New York: Simon and Schuster, 1964.

Christopher, Milbourne. *Houdini: The Untold Story*. New York: Thomas Y. Crowell Co., 1965.

Coffee, Lenore. *Storyline: Recollections of a Hollywood Screenwriter*. London: Cassell & Company Ltd., 1973.

Cook, David. *A History of Narrative Film*. New York: W. W. Norton & Company, 1981.

Cooper, Miriam with Bonnie Herndon. *Dark Lady of the Silents: My Life in Early Hollywood*. Indianapolis: The Bobbs-Merrill Co., 1973.

Coppedge, Walter. *Henry King's America*. Metuchen, N.J.: The Scarecrow Press, Inc., 1986.

Cripps, Thomas. *Slow Fade to Black: The Negro in American Film, 1900-1942*. London: Oxford University Press, 1977.

Crowther, Bosley. *Hollywood Rajah: The Life and Times of Louis B. Mayer*. New York: Holt, Rinehart and Winston, 1960.

Croy, Homer. *Star Maker: The Story of D. W. Griffith*. New York: Duell, Sloan and Pearce, 1959.

Curtiss, Thomas Quinn. *Von Stroheim*. New York: Farrar, Straus and Giroux, 1971.

Dardis, Tom. *Keaton: The Man Who Wouldn't Lie Down*. New York: Charles Scribner's Sons, 1979.

DeMille, Cecil B. *The Autobiography of Cecil B. DeMille*. Edited by Donald Hayne. Englewood Cliffs, N.J.: Prentice-Hall, Inc., 1959.

Drew, William M. *D. W. Griffith's Intolerance: Its Genesis and Its Vision*. Jefferson, N.C.: McFarland & Company, Inc., 1986.

Drinkwater, John. *The Life and Adventures of Carl Laemmle*. London: William Heinemann Ltd., 1931.

Durxman, Michael B. *Make It Again, Sam: A Survey of Movie Remakes*. South Brunswick, N.J.: A. S. Barnes, 1975.

Easton, Carol. *The Search for Sam Goldwyn: A Biography*. New York: William Morrow and Company, Inc., 1976.

Emerson, John and Anita Loos. *How to Write Photoplays*. New York: The James A. McCann Co., 1920.

Epstein, Lawrence J. *Samuel Goldwyn*. Boston: Twayne Publishers, 1981.

Erens, Patricia. *The Jew in American Cinema*. Bloomington: Indiana University Press, 1984.

Essoe, Gabe. *Tarzan of the Movies: A Pictorial History of More Than Fifty Years of Edgar Rice Burroughs' Legendary Hero*. New York: The Citadel Press, 1968.

Everson, William K. *American Silent Film*. New York: Oxford University Press, 1978.

Everson, William K. *A Pictorial History of the Western Film*. Secaucus, N.J.: The Citadel Press, 1969.

Fell, John L. *A History of Films*. New York: Holt, Rinehart and Winston, 1979.

The Film Index: A Bibliography. Compiled by Workers of the Writers' Program of the Work Projects Administration in the City of New York. 3 vols. New York: The Museum of Modern Art, rpr 1966–85.

Finler, Joel W. *Stroheim*. Berkeley: University of California Press, 1967.

Ford, Dan. *Pappy: The Life of John Ford*. Englewood Cliffs, N.J.: Prentice-Hall, Inc., 1979.

Fowler, Gene. *Father Goose: The Story of Mack Sennett*. New York: Covici-Friede, 1934.

Fox, Stuart, comp. *Jewish Films in the United States: A Comprehensive Survey and Descriptive Filmography*. Boston: G. K. Hall & Co., 1976.

Franklin, Joe. *Classics of the Silent Screen*. New York: The Citadel Press, 1959.

Friedman, Lester D. *Hollywood's Image of the Jew*. New York: Frederick Ungar Publishing Co., 1982.

Gallagher, Tag. *John Ford: The Man and His Films*. Berkeley and Los Angeles: University of California Press, 1986.

Garbicz, Adam and Jacek Klinowski. *Cinema, the Magic Vehicle: A Guide to its Achievement. Journey One: The Cinema Through 1949*. New York: Schocken Books, 1983.

Gardner, A. G. *Certain People of Importance*. London: Jonathan Cape, 1926.

Geduld, Harry M., ed. *Focus on D. W. Griffith*. Englewood Cliffs, N.J.: Prentice-Hall, Inc., 1971.

Gelman, Barbara, ed. *Photoplay Treasury*. New York: Crown Publishers, Inc., 1972.

George Kleine Collection of Early Motion Pictures in the Library of Congress. Prepared by Rita Horwitz and Harriet Harrison with the assistance of Wendy White. Washington, D.C.: Library of Congress, 1980.

Gifford, Denis. *The British Film Catalogue 1895-1970: A Guide to Entertainment Films*. Newton Abbot, Devon: David & Charles, 1973.

Gish, Lillian. *Dorothy and Lillian Gish*. Edited by James E. Frasher. New York: Macmillan, 1973.

Gish, Lillian with Ann Pinchot. *Lillian Gish: The Movies, Mr. Griffith, and Me*. Englewood Cliffs, N.J.: Prentice-Hall Inc., 1969.

Graham, Cooper, Steven Higgins, Elaine Mancini and Joao Luiz Vieira. *D. W. Griffith and the Biograph Company*. Metuchen, N.J.: The Scarecrow Press, Inc., 1985.

Grau, Robert. *The Theatre of Silence: A Volume of Progress and Achievement in the Motion Picture Industry*. New York: Benjamin Blom, 1914; reissued 1969.

Guiles, Fred Lawrence. *Marion Davies: A Biography*. New York: McGraw-Hill Book Company, 1972.

Hampton, Benjamin B. *History of the American Film Industry from its Beginnings to 1931*. New York: Dover, 1970. (Originally titled: *A History of the Movies*.)

Hanson, Patricia King and Stephen L. Hanson, eds. *The Film Review Index. Volume I, 1882–1949*. Phoenix: Oryx Press, 1986.

Hart, James, ed. *The Man Who Invented Hollywood: The Autobiography of D. W. Griffith, a Memoir and Some Notes*. Louisville, Ky.: Touchstone Publishing Company, 1972.

Hart, William S. *My Life East & West*. New York: Benjamin Blom, 1929; reissued 1968.

Hayakawa, Sessue. *Zen Showed Me the Way*. Indianapolis: Bobbs-Merrill, 1961.

Henderson, Robert M. *D. W. Griffith: His Life and Work*. New York: Oxford University Press, 1972.

Henderson, Robert M. *D. W. Griffith: The Years at Biograph*. New York: Farrar, Straus and Giroux, 1970.

Herndon, Booton. *Mary Pickford and Douglas Fairbanks: The Most Popular Couple the World Has Ever Known*. New York: W. W. Norton and Company, Inc., 1977.

Higashi, Sumiko. *Cecil B. Demille: A Guide to References and Resources*. Boston: G. K. Hall & Co., 1985.

Higham, Charles. *Cecil B. DeMille*. New York: Charles Scribner's Sons, 1973.

Higham, Charles. *Warner Brothers*. New York: Charles Scribner's Sons, 1975.

Holm, Bill and George Irving Quimby. *Edward S. Curtis in the Land of the War Canoes: A Pioneer Cinematographer in the Pacific Northwest*. Seattle: University of Washington Press, 1980.

Hopper, DeWolf with Wesley Winans Scott. *Once a Clown, Always a Clown: Reminiscences of DeWolf Hopper*. Boston: Little, Brown, and Company, 1927.

Hudson, Richard M. and Raymond Lee. *Gloria Swanson*. South Brunswick and New York: A. S. Barnes and Company, 1970.

Huff, Theodore. *Intolerance: The Film by David Wark Griffith. Shot-By-Shot Analysis*. New York: The Museum of Modern Art, 1966.

Irwin, Will. *The Home That Shadows Built*. Garden City, N.Y.: Doubleday, Doran and Company, Inc., 1928.

Jacobs, Lewis. *The Emergence of Film Art*. New York: Hopkinson and Blake, 1982.

Jacobs, Lewis. *Introduction to the Art of the Movies*. New York: Noonday Press, 1960.

Jacobs, Lewis. *The Rise of the American Film*. New York: Harcourt, Brace and Company, 1939.

Janis, Elsie. *So Far, So Good! An Autobiography*. New York: E. P. Dutton and Company, Inc., 1932.

Jobes, Gertrude. *The Motion Picture Empire*. Hamden, Conn.: Archon Books, 1966.

Johnson, Osa. *I Married Adventure: The Lives and Adventures of Martin and Osa Johnson*. Philadelphia: J. B. Lippincott, 1940.

Jorgens, Jack. *Shakespeare on Film*. Bloomington: University of Indiana Press, 1977.

Katz, Ephraim. *The Film Encyclopedia*. New York: Thomas Y. Crowell, 1979.

Kauffmann, Stanley, ed. *American Film Criticism: From the Beginnings to Citizen Kane*. New York: Liveright, 1972.

Kerr, Walter. *The Silent Clowns*. New York: Alfred A. Knopf, 1979.

Ketchum, Richard M. *Will Rogers: His Life and Times*. New York: American Heritage Publishing Company, Inc., 1973.

Klotman, Phyllis Rauch. *Frame by Frame: A Black Filmography*. Bloomington, Ind. and London: Indiana University Press, 1979.

Kobler, John. *Damned in Paradise: The Life of John Barrymore*. New York: Atheneum, 1977.

Koszarski, Diane Kaiser. *The Complete Films of William S. Hart: A Pictorial Record*. New York: Dover Publications, Inc., 1983.

Koszarski, Richard, ed. *Hollywood Directors: 1914-1940*. New York: Oxford University Press, 1976.

Koszarski, Richard. *The Man You Loved to Hate: Erich von Stroheim and Hollywood*. Oxford: Oxford University Press, 1983.

Koszarski, Richard, ed. *The Rivals of D. W. Griffith*. Minneapolis, Minn.: Walker Art Center, 1976.

Kotsilibas-Davis, James. *The Barrymores: The Royal Family in Hollywood*. New York: Crown Publishers, Inc. 1981.

Lahue, Kalton C. *Dreams for Sale: The Rise and Fall of the Triangle Film Corporation*. South Brunswick and New York: A. S. Barnes and Company, 1971.

Lahue, Kalton C. *Mack Sennett's Keystone: The Man, the Myth and the Comedies*. South Brunswick and New York: A. S. Barnes and Company, 1971.

Lahue, Kalton C. *Motion Picture Pioneer: The Selig Polyscope Company*. South Brunswick and New York: A. S. Barnes and Company, 1973.

Lamster, Frederick. *Souls Made Great Through Love and Adversity: The Film Work of Frank Borzage*. Metuchen, N.J.: The Scarecrow Press, Inc., 1981.

Lasky, Jesse L. with Don Weldon. *I Blow My Own Horn*. Garden City, N.Y.: Doubleday & Company, Inc., 1957.

Lauritzen, Einer and Gunnar Lundquist. *American Film Index, 1908-1915*. Stockholm: Film-Index, 1976.

Lauritzen, Einer and Gunnar Lundquist. *American Film Index, 1916-1920*. Stockholm: Film-Index, 1984.

Lazarou, George A. *Images in Low Key: Cinematographer Sol Polito, A.S.C.* Athens, Greece: George A. Lazarou, 1985.

Leab, Daniel J. *From Sambo to Superspade: The Black Experience in Motion Pictures*. Boston: Houghton Mifflin Company, 1975.

Lennig, Arthur. *The Silent Voice: A Text*. Albany, N.Y.: Lane Press of Albany, Inc., 1969.

Library of Congress. *Wonderful Inventions: Motion Pictures, Broadcasting, and Recorded Sound at the*

Library of Congress. Washington, D.C.: Library of Congress, 1985.

Limbacher, James L. *Haven't I Seen You Somewhere Before? Remakes, Sequels and Series in Motion Pictures and Television, 1896–1978*. Ann Arbor, Mich.: The Pierian Press. 1979.

Lindsay, Nicholas Vachel. *The Art of the Moving Picture*. New York: Liveright, 1915.

Loos, Anita. *Cast of Thousands*. New York: Grosset & Dunlap, 1927.

Loos, Anita. *A Girl Like I*. New York: The Viking Press, 1974.

Loos, Anita. *Kiss Hollywood Goodbye*. New York: The Viking Press, 1974.

Loos, Anita. *The Talmadge Girls: A Memoir*. New York: The Viking Press, 1978.

Lounsbury, Myron Osborn. *The Origins of American Film Criticism, 1909-1939*. New York: Arno Press, 1973.

Love, Bessie. *From Hollywood with Love*. London: Elm Trees Books, Ltd., 1977.

Low, Rachel. *The History of the British Film, 1906–1914*. London: George Allen & Unwin Ltd, 1948.

Low, Rachel. *The History of the British Film, 1914–1918*. London: George Allen & Unwin Ltd, 1950.

Low, Rachel. *The History of the British Film, 1918–1929*. London: George Allen & Unwin Ltd, 1971.

Lyon, Christopher, ed. *The International Dictionary of Films and Filmmakers*. Chicago: St. James Press, 1984.

Lyons, Timothy. *Charles Chaplin: A Guide to References and Resources*. Boston: G. K. Hall & Co., 1979.

Lyons, Timothy. *The Silent Partner: The History of the American Film Manufacturing Company, 1910–1921*. New York: Arno Press, 1974.

McCaffrey, Donald W. *Focus on Chaplin*. Englewood Cliffs, N.J.: Prentice-Hall, Inc. 1971.

MacCann, Richard Dyer and Jack C. Ellis, ed. *Cinema Examined: Selections from Cinema Journal*. New York: E. P. Dutton, Inc., 1982.

McDonald, Gerald D., Michael Conway and Mark Ricci. *The Films of Charlie Chaplin*. New York: Bonanza Books, 1977.

Magill, Frank N., ed. *Magill's Survey of Cinema. Silent Films*. Englewood Cliffs, N.J.: Salem Press, 1982.

Manvell, Roger. *The Film and the Public*. Baltimore: Penguin Books, 1955.

Manvell, Roger. *Shakespeare and the Film*. South Brunswick, N.J.: A. S. Barnes and Company, 1979.

Manvell, Roger. *Theater and Film*. Rutherford, N.J.: Fairleigh Dickinson University Press, 1979.

Marcosson, Issac F. and Daniel Frohman. *Charles Frohman: Manager and Man*. New York: Harper & Brothers, 1916.

Marill, Alvin H. *Samuel Goldwyn Presents*. South Brunswick and New York: A. S. Barnes and Company, 1976.

Marion, Frances. *Off with Their Heads!: A Serio-Comic Tale of Hollywood*. New York: The Macmillan Company, 1972.

Marx, Arthur. *Goldwyn: A Biography of the Man Behind the Myth*. New York: W. W. Norton & Company, Inc., 1976.

Marx, Samuel. *Mayer and Thalberg: The Make-Believe Saints*. New York: Random House, 1975.

Mast, Gerald. *The Comic Mind: Comedy and the Movies*. 2nd ed. Chicago: University of Chicago Press, 1979.

Mock, James R. and Cedric Larson. *Words That Won the War: The Story of the Committee on Public Information 1917–1919*. Princeton, N.J.: Princeton University Press, 1939.

Motion Pictures 1912–1939. Washington, D.C.: Copyright Office, The Library of Congress, 1951.

Mould, David H. *American Newsfilm 1914–1919: The Underground War*. New York: Garland Publishing, Inc. 1983.

Munsterberg, Hugo. *The Photoplay: A Psychological Study*. New York: D. Appleton and Company, 1916.

Nelson, Richard Alan. *Florida and the American Motion Picture Industry 1898–1980*. New York: Garland Publishing, Inc., 1983.

Niver, Kemp R. *D. W. Griffith: His Biograph Films in Perspective*. Los Angeles: np, 1974.

Niver, Kemp R. *The First Twenty Years: A Segment of Film History*. Los Angeles: Locare Research Group, 1968.

Niver, Kemp R. *Klaw and Ehrlanger Present Famous Plays in Pictures*. Los Angeles: Locare Research Group, 1976.

Noble, Peter. *Hollywood Scapegoat: The Biography of Erich von Stroheim*. London: The Fortune Press, 1950.

Nunn, Curtis. *Marguerite Clark: America's Darling of Broadway and the Silent Screen*. Fort Worth: The Texas Christian University Press, 1981.

O'Dell, Scott. *Representative Photoplays Analyzed*. Hollywood: Palmer Institute of Authorship, 1924.

O'Leary, Liam. *Rex Ingram: Master of the Silent Cinema*. Dublin, Ireland: The Academy Press, 1980.

Palmer, Frederick. *Photoplay Writing Simplified and Explained*. Los Angeles, Palmer Photoplay Corporation, 1918.

Parsons, Louella. *How to Write for the "Movies"*. Chicago: A. C. McClurg and Company, 1915.

Peacocke, Captain Leslie T. *Hints on Photoplay Writing*. Chicago: Photoplay Publishing Co., 1916.

Petrova, Olga. *Butter with My Bread: The Memoirs of Olga Petrova*. Indianapolis: The Bobbs-Merrill Co., 1942.

Pickford, Mary. *Sunshine and Shadow*. London: William Heinemann Ltd, 1956.

Place, J. A. *The Western Films of John Ford*. Secaucus, N.J.: The Citadel Press, 1974.

Pohle, Robert W., Jr. and Douglas C. Hart. *Sherlock Holmes on the Screen: The Motion Picture Adventures of the World's Most Popular Detective*. South Brunswick and New York: A. S. Barnes and Company, 1977.

Powell, A. Van Buren. *The Photoplay Synopsis*. Springfield, Mass.: The Home Correspondence School, 1919.

Pratt, George. *Spellbound in Darkness: A History of the Silent Film*. Greenwich, Conn.: New York Graphic Society, Ltd., 1966.

Prendergast, Roy M. *A Neglected Art: A Critical Study of Music in Films*. New York: New York University Press, 1977.

Quirk, Lawrence J. *The Films of Gloria Swanson*. Secaucus, N.J.: The Citadel Press, 1984.

Ragan, David. *Who's Who in Hollywood 1900-1976*. New Rochelle, N.Y.: Arlington House Publishers, 1976.

Rainey, Buck. *The Fabulous Holts: A Tribute to a Favorite Movie Family*. Nashville: Western Film Collector Press, 1976.

Rainsberger, Todd. *James Wong Howe: Cinematographer*. San Diego and New York: A. S. Barnes & Company, Inc., 1981.

Ramsaye, Terry. *A Million and One Nights: A History of the Motion Picture*. New York: Simon & Schuster, 1926.

Reade, Eric. *Australian Silent Films: A Pictorial History, 1896-1929*. Melbourne: Lansdowne Press, 1970.

Rehrauer, George. *The Macmillan Film Bibliography*. New York: Macmillan, 1982.

Rigdon, Walter. *The Biographical Encyclopedia & Who's Who of the American Theater*. New York: James H. Heineman, Inc., 1965.

Ringgold, Gene and DeWitt Bodeen. *The Films of Cecil B. DeMille*. Secaucus, N.J.: The Citadel Press, 1974.

Robinson, David. *Buster Keaton*. Bloomington: Indiana University Press, 1969.

Robinson, David. *The History of World Cinema*. New York: Stein and Day, 1973.

Rollins, Peter C. *Will Rogers: A Bio-Bibliography*. Westport, Conn.: Greenwood Press, 1984.

Rotha, Paul. *The Film Till Now: A Survey of the Cinema*. New York: Jonathan Cape and Harrison Smith, 1930.

Sadoul, Georges. *Dictionary of Films*. Translated, edited, and updated by Peter Morris. Berkeley: University of California Press, 1972.

Sadoul, Georges. *Histoire générale du cinéma, Tome III: Le Cinéma deviant un art 1909-1920*. Paris: Denoel, 1951.

Sampson, Henry T. *Blacks in Black and White*. Metuchen, N.J.: The Scarecrow Press, 1977.

Schickel, Richard. *D. W. Griffith: An American Life*. New York: Simon and Schuster, 1984.

Schickel, Richard. *His Picture in the Papers: A Speculation on Celebrity in America Based on the Life of Douglas Fairbanks, Sr*. New York: Charterhouse, 1973.

Schulberg, Budd. *Moving Pictures: Memories of a Hollywood Pioneer*. New York: Stein and Day, 1981.

Scott, Evelyn F. *Hollywood: When Silents Were Golden*. New York: McGraw-Hill Book Co., 1972.

Selznick, Irene Mayer. *A Private View*. New York: Alfred A. Knopf, 1983.

Sennett, Mack with Cameron Shipp. *King of Comedy*. Garden City, N.Y.: Doubleday and Company, Inc., 1954.

Shipman, Nell. *The Silent Screen and My Talking Heart: An Autobiography*. Boise, Idaho: Boise State University, 1987.

Silva, Fred, ed. *Focus on The Birth of a Nation*. Englewood Cliffs, N.J.: Prentice-Hall, Inc., 1971.

Slide, Anthony, ed. *The American Film Industry*. Westport, Conn.: Greenwood Press, 1986.

Slide, Anthony. *Aspects of American Film History Prior to 1920*. Metuchen, N.J.: The Scarecrow Press, 1978.

Slide, Anthony with Alan Gevinson. *The Big V: A History of the Vitagraph Company*. Rev. ed. Metuchen, N.J.: The Scarecrow Press, 1987.

Slide, Anthony. *Early American Cinema*. New York: A. S. Barnes, 1970.

Slide, Anthony. *Early American Women Directors*. New York: Da Capo, 1984.

Slide, Anthony and Edward Wagenknecht. *Fifty Great American Silent Films, 1912-1920: A Pictorial Survey*. New York: Dover Publications, Inc., 1980.

Slide, Anthony. *The Griffith Actresses*. South Brunswick and New York: A. S. Barnes and Company, 1975.

Slide, Anthony. *The Idols of Silence*. New York: A. S. Barnes, 1976.

Slide, Anthony. *The Kindergarten of the Movies: A History of the Fine Arts Company*. Metuchen, N.J.: The Scarecrow Press, Inc., 1980.

Slide, Anthony, ed. *Selected Film Criticism, 1912-1920*. Metuchen, N.J.: The Scarecrow Press, Inc., 1982.

Smith, Albert E. with Phil A. Koury. *Two Reels and a Crank*. Garden City, N.Y.: Doubleday & Company, Inc., 1952.

Spehr, Paul. *The Movies Begin: Making Movies in New Jersey, 1887-1920*. Newark: The Newark Museum in cooperation with Morgan and Morgan, Inc., 1977.

Sterling, Bryan B. and Frances N. Sterling. *Will Rogers in Hollywood*. New York: Crown Publishers, Inc., 1984.

Stern, Seymour. *Cinemages Special Issue No. 1: Published on the Occasion of the Screening of The Birth of a Nation*. New York: The Group for Film Study, Inc. 1955.

Stern, Seymour. "Griffith: I. The Birth of a Nation, Part I." *Film Culture* (Spring–Summer, 1965).

Sternberg, Josef von. *Fun in a Chinese Laundry*. New York: The Macmillan Company, 1965.

Steward, John. *Filmarama, Volume I, The Formidable Years, 1893-1919*. Metuchen, N.J.: The Scarecrow Press, 1975.

Stone, Fred. *Rolling Stone*. New York: McGraw-Hill Book Company, 1945.

Stott, Kenhelm W., Jr. *Exploring with Martin and Osa Johnson*. Chanute, Kans.: Martin and Osa Johnson Safari Museum Press, 1978.

Swanson, Gloria. *Swanson on Swanson*. New York: Random House, 1980.

Talmadge, Margaret. *The Talmadge Sisters: Norma, Constance, Natalie*. Philadelphia: J. B. Lippincott Company, 1924.

Thames Television's The Art of Hollywood: Fifty Years of Art Direction. Devised and produced by John Hambley and Patrick Downing. Catalogue designed by Kathryn Jenkins. London: Thames Television Ltd, 1919.

Thomas, Bob. *King Cohn: The Life and Times of Harry Cohn*. New York: G. P. Putnam's Sons, 1967.

Tibbetts, John C. and James M. Welsh. *His Majesty the American*. South Brunswick and New York: A. S. Barnes Company, 1977.

Trimble, Marian Blackton. *J. Stuart Blackton: A Personal Biography by His Daughter*. Metuchen, N.J.: The Scarecrow Press, Inc., 1985.

Truitt, Evelyn Mack. *Who Was Who on Screen*. New York and London: R. R. Bowker and Company, 1983.

Tuska, Jon. *The Filming of the West*. Garden City, N.Y.: Doubleday, 1976.

Van Loan, H. H. *"How I Did It"*. Los Angeles: The Whittingham Press, 1922.

Vidor, King. *A Tree Is a Tree*. New York: Garland Publishing Company, Inc., 1977.

Wagenknecht, Edward and Anthony Slide. *The Films of D. W. Griffith*. New York: Crown Publishers, Inc., 1975.

Wagenknecht, Edward. *The Movies in the Age of Innocence*. Norman: University of Oklahoma Press, 1962.

Wagenknecht, Edward. *Stars of the Silents*. Metuchen, N.J.: The Scarecrow Press, Inc., 1987.

Walker, Alexander. *Rudolph Valentino*. New York: Stein and Day, 1976.

Walsh, Raoul. *Each Man in His Own Time*. New York: Farrar, Straus & Giroux, 1974.

Ward, Larry Wayne. *The Motion Picture Goes to War: The U.S. Government Film Effort During World War I*. Ann Arbor: UMI Research Press, 1985.

Warner, Jack L. with Dean Jennings. *My First Hundred Years in Hollywood*. New York: Random House, 1964.

Weaver, John T., comp. *Twenty Years of Silents, 1908–1928*. Metuchen, N.J.: The Scarecrow Press, Inc., 1971.

Weinberg, Herman G. *Stroheim: A Pictorial Record of His Nine Films*. New York: Dover Publications, Inc., 1975.

Weitzel, Edward. *Intimate Talks with Movie Stars*. New York: Dale Publishing Co., 1921.

Welch, Jeffry Egan. *Literature and Film: An Annotated Bibliography, 1909–1977*. New York: Garland Publishing, Inc., 1981.

Wenden, D. J. *The Birth of the Movies*. New York: E. P. Dutton, 1974.

White-Hensen, Wendy, comp. *Archival Moving Image Materials: A Cataloging Manual*. Washington, D.C.: Library of Congress, Motion Picture, Broadcasting and Recorded Sound Division, 1984.

Who Was Who in the Theatre: 1912-1976. Detroit: Gale Research Company, 1978.

Windeler, Robert. *Sweetheart: The Story of Mary Pickford*. New York: Praeger Publishers, 1974.

Wood, Leslie. *The Romance of the Movies*. London: William Heinemann Ltd, 1937.

Wright, William Lord. *The Motion Picture Story: A Textbook of Photoplay Writing*. Chicago: Cloud Publishing Co., 1914.

Yallop, David A. *The Day the Laughter Stopped: The True Story of Fatty Arbuckle*. New York: St. Martin's Press, 1976.

Zambrano, A. L. *Dickens and Film*. New York: Gordon Press, 1977.

Zukor, Adolph with Dale Kramer. *The Public Is Never Wrong: The Autobiography of Adolph Zukor*. New York: G. P. Putnam's Sons, 1953.